P9-DCF-092
SOUTH PACIFIC
HAWAIIAN ISLANDS
Pearl Harbor
CHRISTMAS ISLANDS
Seattle
San Francisco
LINES
FLEET AXIS
CL
DD
CV
CVL
BB
CLAA
TYPICAL TASK FORCE FORMATION
AIR DEFENSE DISPOSITION WITH CARRIERS
BEACHES
LCI ROCKETS
AMPHIBS
CLOSE-IN FIRE SUPPORT DESTROYERS
INNER LINE OF DEPARTURE
BOAT LANES
OUTER LINE OF DEPARTURE
BOATS ON CALL
TRACTOR GROUP LST'S
DEEP FIRE SUPPORT
TRANSPORTS
1000
2000
3000
4000
5000
6000
YDS
DESTROYER FIRE SUPPORT FOR LANDINGS
ABDA-ANZAC DEFENSIVE AREAS
ABDA
ANZAC

UNITED STATES

DESTROYER OPERATIONS

IN

WORLD WAR II

U N C O N Q U E R A B L E

UNITED STATES

DESTROYER OPERATIONS

IN

WORLD WAR II

By Theodore Roscoe

RESEARCH AND TECHNICAL EDITING BY
REAR ADMIRAL THOMAS L. WATTLES
U. S. NAVY (RETIRED)

DESIGNED AND ILLUSTRATED BY
LIEUT. COMDR. FRED FREEMAN, U.S.N.R.

Published by

Naval Institute Press

Annapolis, Maryland

Fifth printing 1972

Library of Congress Catalog Card Number 53-4273

ISBN 0-87021-726-7

PRINTED IN THE UNITED STATES OF AMERICA

None of them knew the colour of the sky. Their eyes glanced level, and were fastened upon the waves that swept toward them. These waves were of the hue of slate, save for the tops, which were of foaming white, and all of the men knew the colours of the sea. The horizon narrowed and widened, and dipped and rose, and at all times its edge was jagged with waves that seemed thrust up in points like rocks.

Many a man ought to have a bathtub larger than the boat which here rode upon the sea. These waves were most wrongfully and barbarously abrupt and tall, and each froth-top was a problem in small-boat navigation . . . .

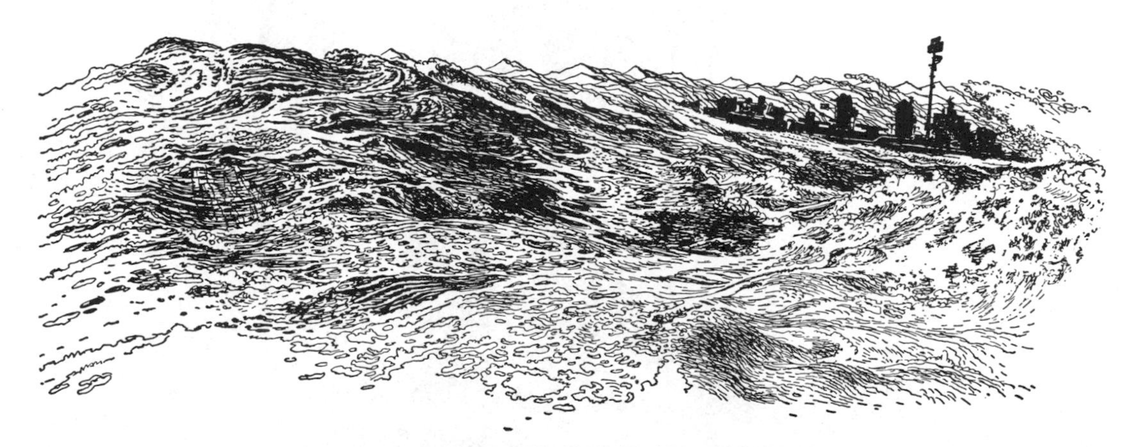

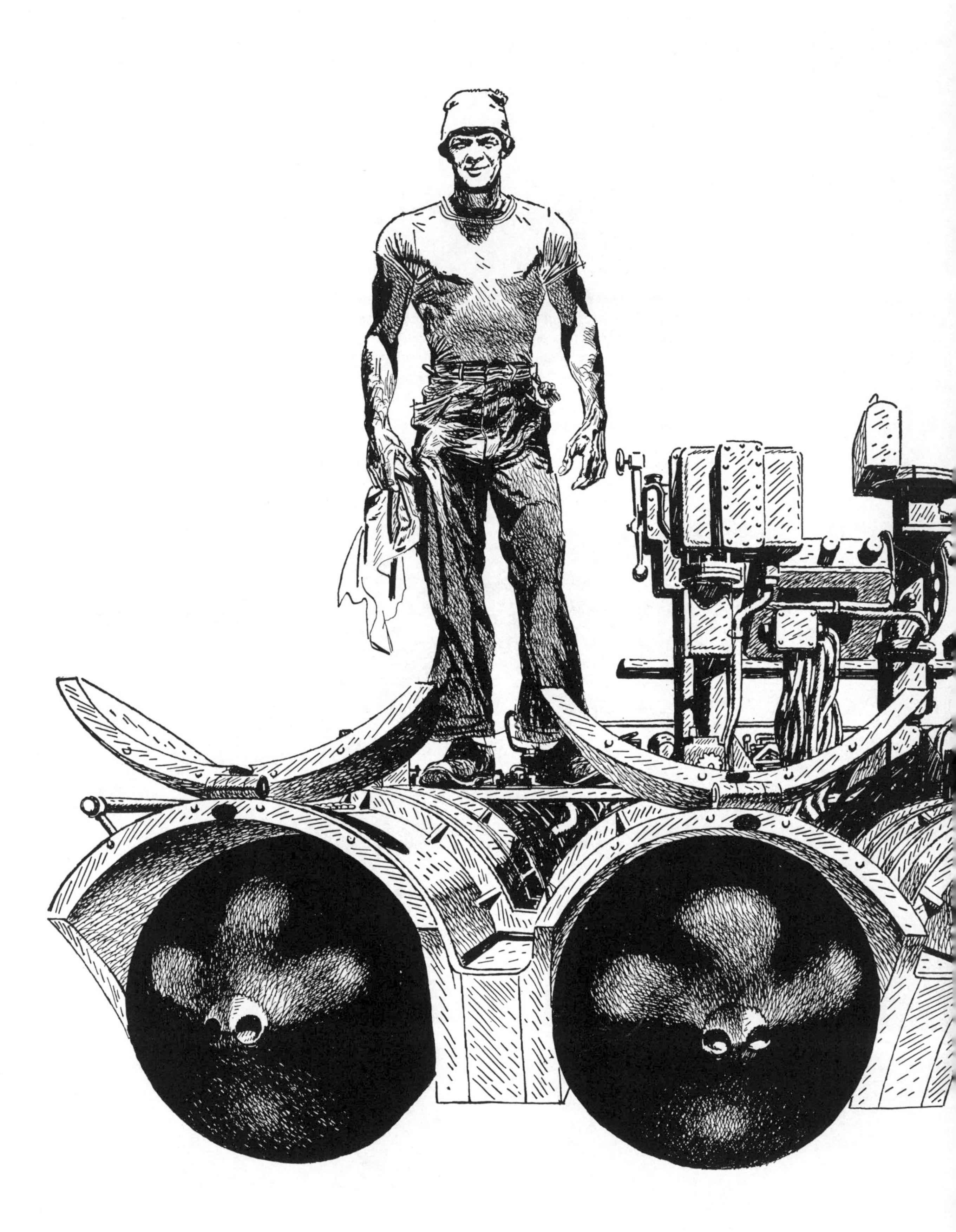

. . . To the Destroyermen

of the United States Navy,

Past, Present, and Future . . .

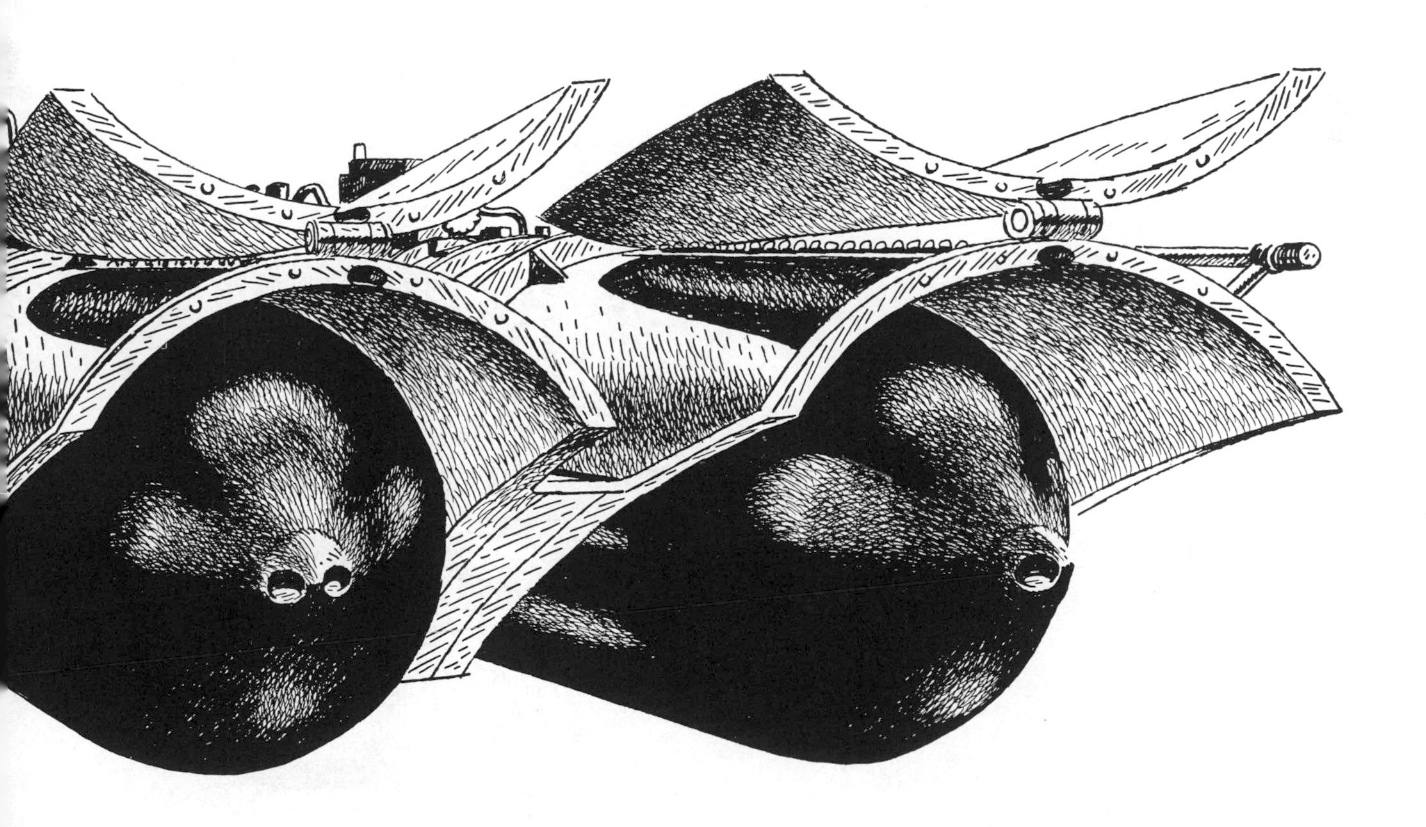

C O N T E N T S

PART V

DESTROYERS TO EUROPE

PART VI

DESTROYERS TO ASIA

PART VII

SMALL BOYS FINISH BIG JOB

CHARTS AND PICTURES

DIAGRAMS

AREA CHARTS

BATTLE CHARTS

A note about the Battle Charts:—for purposes of clarity these charts have been divided arbitrarily into time sequences, avoiding where possible the crossing and re-crossing of ships' tracks. Time, speed and distance given are as accurate as space requirements and available information will permit but the emphasis in these charts has been placed on TACTICS. The effort has been to show graphically the movement of units with relation to corresponding movements of opposing units during the same time interval. The first section of each chart is labelled "Approach." After that, the sequence of sections is indicated by the time-interval strip in each section of the chart. Enemy as well as American sources have been utilized freely.

ILLUSTRATIONS

PHOTOGRAPHS

Most of the more than 300 photographs are official U. S. Navy and U. S. Coast Guard releases; a very few are from private sources. Space limitations do not permit individual credits.

UNMOORING

P R E F A C E

U. S. DESTROYER OPERATIONS IN WORLD WAR II presents the dramatic story of the United States Navy's Destroyer Service—the story of the DD's and DE's and the destroyermen that waged and won the greatest sea, anti-submarine, and surface-air battles in naval history.

This volume is not the official operational history, nor is it a formal history in the academic sense. Many aspects of destroyer warfare which would normally go unrecorded in a purely historical account are discussed in this text. Technical features of destroyer work are herein detailed to explain the technological "how" which is linked with the "who, when, where, what, and why" of destroyer missions and combat actions. The historical record is thus paralleled by a review of methods and techniques, which supports the volume's primary purpose—to serve as an informative, instructive, and inspirational text for those in Naval Service who are interested, directly or indirectly, in destroyer warfare. Members of the United States Naval Academy, of the Navy's various training schools and NROTC units, officers and men of the Naval Reserve, and officers and men on active duty afloat and ashore will find this volume on destroyer warfare a work that teaches for the present and future while telling of the past. But the history story is in no way abridged or neglected. Featured in the following chapters are every major and a multitude of minor destroyer battles, missions, and undertakings—the actions and activities which engaged the destroyers and destroyer-escorts of DesLant and DesPac during World War II. Told in dramatic narrative are exploits of seamanship, marksmanship, and leadership that highlight a record in which every Navy man may share the pride of partnership—a record well contrived to evoke the interest and admiration of every layman reader. The veteran destroyerman and the destroyermen of tomorrow will cherish the achievements of the Destroyer Service recounted in this volume.

This history serves, too, as a companion volume for *U. S. Submarine Operations in World War II*—a popular text by the author of the present work. Received by professional Navy critic and professional literary critic alike, the submarine history prompted the publication of a similar volume on destroyers—a volume containing the anti-submarine view of the undersea warfare picture. But the versatile destroyer was neither wholly nor largely engaged as an anti-submarine vessel; the story of destroyer operations encompasses a range wider than that of any other warship type.

Beginning with a brief account of the destroyer's inception as a warship and its World War I development, the book details Destroyer Force activities in the "short of war" operations which came as an Atlantic overture to World War II. Recounted is the Pearl Harbor assault which plunged the destroyers of DesPac into the desperate struggle against the rampaging forces of Imperial Japan. The life-and-death Battle of the Atlantic which featured the little DD as a convoy escort and coast-defense bulwark against the predatory Nazi U-boat—the homeric Battle for the Pacific, wherein the old "four-pipers" made a last-ditch stand at the Malay Barrier while Pacific Destroyers raced to hold the Australia-Midway-Aleutians line—these great stories are chaptered in chronological sequence. The coming of search radar and improved guns, the building of the destroyer-escort, the development of "hunter-killer" groups, and the subsequent downing of Doenitz's wolf-packs are headline episodes told in detail. Also detailed are the parts played by destroyers in the Midway drama and the Aleutian struggle, the Coral Sea, the savage engagements of the Solomons Campaign, the bitter fight for the South Pacific. There follow in turn the destroyer missions of "Operation Torch" and the great troop lifts to England and North Africa; the Battle for the Mediterranean, and destroyer work in the drives on Sicily, Salerno, and Anzio; the Normandy landings, and the landings in Southern France. With Fortress Europe unlocked by "Overlord," the story returns to the DesPac effort in the Navy's vast trans-Pacific drives—destroyer operations in the patterns of "Galvanic," "Flintlock," "Cherry Tree," and in the Third Fleet's drive through the Bismarck Barrier to the doorstep of the Philippines. Surigao Strait, Leyte Gulf, and Ormoc Bay—battles which put destroyers and destroyermen to the ultimate test—are recounted in detail, as are the actions which squelched the Japanese submarine effort. With relentless pace the DesPac story leads to Saipan and to the epic struggle at Okinawa where the "small boys" fought the greatest destroyer battle of all history in their stand as picket boats against the ravening *Kamikazes*.

The historical narrative serves as a background against which destroyers and destroyer escorts are silhouetted in many roles—the DE as convoy escort and sub-hunter extraordinary; the DD as jack-of-all-trades and master of all: scout, A/S vessel, screen for larger warship, bombardment ship, rescue vessel, blockade runner, transport, supply ship, radar picket, and all-around fighting ship capable of trading blows with everything from enemy submarine to battleship, enemy coastal battery to dive bomber. Threaded through the narrative are discussions of destroyer tactics, with special emphasis on A/S tactics and anti-aircraft tactics—subjects of particular interest to all destroyermen.

Destroyer losses and failures are recounted in this volume as well as destroyer gains and successes. Unless one bows to Napoleon's definition of history as "a fiction agreed upon," mistakes must be recorded, if only in the interest of veracity. Aside from the manifest virtue of a truthful record, an honest accounting of mistakes contains instruction value—if man learns through trial, he may also learn through error. The leaders of the Navy's Destroyer Service, acknowledging this forthright doctrine, subscribe to the standard set by the ancient Lucian of Samosata: "The historian's one task is to tell the thing as it happened." As it happened, the Navy's destroyermen committed their share of errors, and the share included tactical flounders, collisions, clashes with friendly ships or aircraft through recognition or communication failures, and other mistakes of commission and omission. Altogether serious errors were remarkably few—amazingly few when one considers the global scope of the destroyer effort, the number of ships involved, and the hazardous circumstances of their involvement—but those few major errors are herein reported for their instructive worth. So is the story of the wretched torpedo performance caused by a defective torpedo—a weapon's failure which hampered the Navy's destroyer effort, even as it hamstrung the Navy's submarine effort, from the start of World War II until the torpedo's belated correction in 1943. From such mistakes lessons were learned which may serve to guide the destroyerman of tomorrow.

This volume, however, is not to be considered a textbook on any aspect of destroyer warfare. A type history, it presents a comprehensive picture of destroyer operations—the record of a service, and a summary of its achievements—the story of a war effort composed of, by, and for the destroyermen of the United States Navy.

The book is based on material drawn from action reports, ship diaries, and war records on file in the Office of Naval History. Made available by the courtesy of Rear Admiral John B. Heffernan, U.S.N., said material was researched by Rear Admiral Thomas L. Wattles, U.S.N. (Ret.), a veteran destroyer officer who saw action in Atlantic, Mediterranean, and Pacific theaters, and whose experience with Navy Training Activities admirably qualified him for the research task—a labor involving the study, selection, and meticulous checking of hundreds of documentary items and thousands of reports. Additional material was drawn by author and researcher from contemporary news and periodical accounts, from authoritative reference works, from the notes of individual officers and men, and from the works of contemporary historians, with particular acknowledgement due the writings of Rear Admiral Samuel Eliot Morison, U.S.N.R. (Ret.), eminent historian, and Captain Walter Karig, U.S.N.R., author of *Battle Report*. Current volumes by the forementioned authors were studied for views of the general war panorama. Statistical data and ship- and submarine-sinking assessments offered in the present volume are drawn from the compilations of the United States Strategic Bombing Survey, the Joint Army-Navy Assessment Committee, and *The U. S. Navy at War, Official Reports*, by Fleet Admiral Ernest J. King, U.S.N. The text as presented was organized and written by Theodore Roscoe, former specialist in the employ of the Training Publications Section, Training Division, Bureau of Naval Personnel.

The book was designed and illustrated by Lieutenant Commander Fred Freeman, U.S.N.R., whose work distinguished *U. S. Submarine Operations in World War II.* The photographs were selected by Freeman from thousands sighted in the photograph libraries at Anacostia, the Public Information Division of the U. S. Coast Guard, various destroyer bases, Navy archives, and Bureau of Naval Personnel, and private collections. Miss Mary A. Baer and Mrs. Velma L. Mitchell of the Naval Still Picture Library were of material assistance in locating photographs, and Daniel Payne, AOC, U.S.N. and James E. Crickey, RDI, U.S.N. pulled over 17,000 prints from library files. Freeman's drawings were reconstructed from action reports, war diaries, and from sketches made by the artist while serving on tour of duty in destroyers.

All technical aspects of naval and destroyer operations, herein presented, were subject in manuscript form to the editing of Rear Admiral Thomas L. Wattles. Additional technical assistance was furnished by officers on duty with the Training Division, Bureau of Naval Personnel. The manuscript's preparation was generously aided by critical comment from a number of destroyer officers, especially valuable being that of Vice Admiral Walden L. Ainsworth, U.S.N. (Ret.); Rear Admiral E. T. Woolridge, U.S.N. (ComDesLant, 1949); Rear Admiral Arleigh A. Burke, U.S.N.; Rear Admiral Ralph Earle, Jr., U.S.N.; and Captain J. W. Boulware, U.S.N.

First draft of the manuscript was edited by Lieutenant Commander John J. Hession, U.S.N.R., who freely contributed spare hours to this effort, and to whom the author is indebted for literary counsel. Miss Loretta McCrindle, and Miss Barbara Gilmore, of the Office of Naval History, appreciably aided the research effort. Publication of the work was suggested and sponsored by Captain J. B. Rooney, U.S.N., Captain H. P. Rice, U.S.N., Captain A. L. Renken, U.S.N., and Captain G. W. Pressey, U.S.N., all of the Training Division, Bureau of Naval Personnel, and ardent advocates of Destroyer Service. While the Bureau of Naval Personnel is not the publisher of this history, the writing and publication of the work were made possible by the enthusiastic interest and initiative of the forenamed officers.

INTRODUCTION

Nearly one hundred and fifty years ago, Lord Nelson, chasing a phantom Villeneuve across countless leagues of the Atlantic, fiercely complained, "When I die, you will find this want of frigates graven upon my heart." By World War II the lifting sail of these fast, light ships had given way to the airplane for the primary service of reconnaissance, but the complaints of the Admirals were much the same. When at grips with the enemy on the sea, under the sea, or in the air, no Task Force Commander ever had enough destroyers.

For these swift, small ships, grown to light cruiser stature from the torpedo boats of former wars, were indispensable in every operation—the advance guard of the strong, the protector of the weak; the lance to thrust, and the shield to parry. They were the eyes and ears of the Fleet, the radar screen to detect attack by air, and the sub-surface sound screen to ward off attack from beneath the sea. Mounting multiple weapons for every type of offense, these ships had the power of sixty thousand horses to carry this armament swiftly to the attack. The enemy in every fiber of his being was to suffer from the rapier-like thrusts of the destroyer—the torpedo for the battleship, the depth charge for the submarine, the gun for the airplane or the pillbox on the beach—the greatest concentration of power in a lightweight fighter the seas have ever seen.

In war, the strength of the offensive is as the strength of the line of communications—the service of supply. In the pages to follow will be found the saga of the small ships whose unwearied watch brought thousands of our youth safely to distant shores to form for the assault; whose guns blazed the way across the beach for them; and whose youth then returned to the weary watch to escort yet more ships to distant shores with those thousands of tons of supplies required to make the assault successful.

And these small ships with the lethal punch were versatile; no job was too small, no task too great. The older ships became fast minelayers and minesweepers; some were converted into destroyer-transports; some even became patrol plane tenders, to bring the service of information ever closer to the enemy. Many types were evolved for special duties, principal among these being destroyer escorts, designed to meet and defeat the submarine menace. And defeat it they did. And, with the changes war itself must bring, the character of the first-line destroyer itself was changed.

Thus the Carrier Task Force became our greatest offensive weapon, and its screening a major destroyer mission; thus the enemy threat from the air overshadowed all else, and the destroyer bristled with anti-aircraft guns.

Finally, as the war in the Pacific entered its latter stages, the once proud Japanese Navy had disappeared from the surface of the sea; there were no targets left for torpedoes, so for us the torpedo boat as such ceased to exist. In her place was still the destroyer, now to fight its greatest battle as the radar picket in the battle for Okinawa. Torpedoes had been replaced by new detection devices to find and plot the "bogey," and fighter-director teams were placed on board to bring our own planes into action. In addition each ship could now put up a veritable curtain of anti-aircraft fire—the knockout punch for the *Kamikaze.*

The ring-down of the curtain at Okinawa—the end of the show—brought the most bitter naval battle of the war to the destroyer, and ended in victory for the radar picket. Day after day, week after week, the suicide assault from the air took its toll of the small ships; day after day other pickets took their place—to hold the screen and to shoot the enemy down. The Jap had to destroy the screen before any attack on the transports could meet with success. For us, there could be no driving in of pickets. The line *must* hold.

Our soldiers and marines went ashore standing up; the bitter battle for them lay ahead, but an unbroken line of supply was to insure their victory. The real victory came first to the small ships who held the line—but at what cost! At the end of six weeks our losses in ships sunk and severely damaged on the picket line were greater than the total number of United States destroyers in commission at the beginning of the war. Our naval casualties in killed and missing—the men who would never come home—were greater than those of the combined Army and Marine forces on shore. But—the last despairing effort of the *Kamikaze* was defeated—the line held—the work horse of the Fleet had proved once more a thoroughbred.

Many of the readers of the following pages will be those who served in Industry on the home front—the source of supply which made possible the winning of the War. They will take pride in reading of the men who went down to the sea in small ships to help keep the supply lines open. And then there will be the soldiers—who varied the monotony of their progress overseas by watching the destroyers knife their zigzag course in search of the preying submarine. They may well take pride in reading about what the sailors went through to get the Army over there.

And, lastly, there will be those of that half million officers and men, Regular and Reserve, who joined the war to live and sweat, fight and die, in these small ships. They held their heads high, with fierce pride. They became the soul and spirit of the Destroyer Navy. Of them we may all be very, very proud.

WALDEN L. AINSWORTH
Vice Admiral, U. S. Navy (Retired)
COMMANDER DESTROYERS
PACIFIC FLEET
July 1942 to January 1943
October 1944 to July 1945

PART I

LITTLE SHIPS INTO ACTION

Give me a fast ship
for I intend to go in harm's way.

JOHN PAUL JONES

CHAPTER 1

DESTROYERS AND DESTROYERMEN

Here Come The Small Boys!

Night, and a sea lathered with storm. A small gray ship, her bows streaming spume, fights her way across the heaving slopes and sinking valleys of water. Off in the blowing murk another vessel rides the sea—a low-lying craft that slides through the waves like a gliding shark. Suddenly the little gray ship spears the blackness with a shaft of light that reveals the second craft in dim silhouette. At once the little gray ship charges, rolling her beam ends under. There is a crash, the shock of collision. Pinned together, the two vessels wrestle in the storm; then the shark, wounded, burrows into the sea. In her wake, the small gray ship releases a tumble of iron cylinders. Lightning flashes beneath the waves, and there is thunder down under. Some time later a deep-sea blast is heard. The little ship steams away. She is U.S.S. BORIE, and she has just killed a German submarine. . . .

On the other side of the world, equatorial ocean. And three little ships advancing across blue water. Abruptly they pause, circle about, spatter the surface with darts that dig into the water like needles. And presently the surface is rumpled by explosions—up comes a dark blot of oil, scraps of rubbish, a bit of flotsam. The three little ships sail on. They are U.S.S. ENGLAND, U.S.S. GEORGE, and U.S.S. RABY, conducting one of the greatest submarine hunts in naval history. By the time it is over, little ENGLAND, single-handed, will have demolished five Japanese undersea boats, and dealt the *coup-de-grace* to a sixth. Thereby upsetting a Japanese defense plan and undermining a stand by the Japanese Imperial Navy. . . .

And here is a dark foreshore under a ridge of frowning mountains. Inland the guns are thundering, and the foothills are splashed with bursts of fire and smoke. Littered with crates, bales, boxes, gear, tarpaulins, the beaches are alive with crawling machinery—jeeps, bulldozers, tractors, trucks, tanks. Streaming shoreward are herds of snubnosed iron scows, parades of troop-carrying barges, ugly little ferries that swim in like armored beetles. Offshore are the transports, farther out the men-of-war: battleships, cruisers, perhaps a carrier on the horizon. And with them those little gray ships—always those little gray ships.

Someone signals for a shore bombardment. The little gray ships open fire in company with the big, steaming close inshore with batteries booming. Down the sky comes a flock of enemy planes. The little gray ships raise a savage anti-aircraft barrage. The scene can be Sicily, or it can be Saipan. It can be Normandy or Okinawa. Saipan or Sicily, Normandy or Okinawa—wherever American invasion forces go ashore, one sees U.S.S. NEWCOMB . . . LONGSHAW . . . HAZELWOOD . . . F. C. DAVIS . . . MONSSEN . . . CORRY . . . HAMBLETON . . . DALLAS . . . COLHOUN . . . OBERRENDER—divisions and squadrons of these little gray ships. . . .

Another scene: a group of American escort-carriers steaming along in the early morning of a dangerous day. Salt wind, and a pastel twilight; then sunrise painting the open sea. And now on the horizon appear enemy masts: four battleships, eight cruisers, eleven destroyers—dragons wanting nothing better than to get their teeth into baby flat-tops. Planes take to the sky like angered bees. Guns rumble, and the ocean's surface is splashed by shells. And as the carrier group wheels to escape, a little gray ship—the U.S.S. JOHNSTON—swerves about and makes a dash straight for the oncoming leviathans.

The little ship's guns are blazing, her torpedoes streak the water like an opening fan. Behind her, other little gray ships are coming—HOEL and HEERMANN, JOHN C. BUTLER, DENNIS, RAYMOND, and SAMUEL B. ROBERTS.

SMALL BOYS *comes a crackling order by voice radio.* SMALL BOYS ON MY STARBOARD QUARTER INTERPOSE WITH SMOKE BETWEEN MEN AND ENEMY CRUISERS

The "men" are the United States carriers of Admiral C. A. F. Sprague. The "small boys" are the little gray ships which are rushing into battle like terriers attacking Great Danes. In the coiling drifts of smoke they disappear, reappear, dart in and out, firing as they dodge. Explosions flash around them. Thunderous blasts hurl up foaming stacks of water. Now little JOHNSTON is hit, reeling about; her companions slashed and scorched in the tempest of shellfire.

Again the voice radio crackles.

SMALL BOYS FORM FOR OUR SECOND ATTACK

The little gray ships form up and carry on, fighting one of the decisive battles of the Pacific War.

"Small boys," Admiral Sprague called them. But those litttle gray ships did a man-size job. They, and scores like them. They were the destroyers and the destroyer-escorts of the United States Navy.

Some called them "cans." They meant the word for a noun. But the destroyers changed it to a verb. "Can" meaning "Wilco," and "able to do."

And they did. . . .

On escort-of-convoy duty United States destroyers, destroyer-escorts, and destroyer-men waged relentless undersea warfare against German U-boats and Japanese submarines. Or screening the fleet, they traded blows with enemy light cruisers, heavy cruisers, battleships. They held their own against the *Luftwaffe* and shot it out with the *kamikazes.* They scouted and reconnoitered, penetrated enemy minefields, entered enemy harbors, delivered devastating shore bombardments. They served as life-savers and vedettes, as weather-reporters, as minelayers, as frontier guards, as radar pickets. They operated as blockaders and troop carriers, and surface raiders. And they worked with everything from amphibious teams landing a party of Army scouts on a fly-speck atoll, to invasion armadas landing armies on a continental coast.

Fighting the Battle of the Atlantic, the Atlantic Destroyer Force (DesLant) patrolled America's coastline from Labrador to Brazil, guarded the Gulf of Mexico, the Caribbean, and the approaches to the Panama Canal. DesLant destroyers escorted convoy after convoy to Britain. They guarded the great troop-lifts to North Africa and the United Kingdom; carried the "Torch" to the beachheads of Morocco; screened the invasion forces in the Mediterranean; stormed the beaches of Italy, Southern France, and Normandy. Operating with baby flat-tops in "hunter-killer" groups, these stalwart DD's and doughty DE's scourged Hitler's wolfpacks from the mid-Atlantic. Significantly enough, a DesLant destroyer fired the first American shot of World War II, and in Long Island Sound a few hours before Germany's surrender, DesLant depth charges destroyed the last Nazi U-boat raider downed in American waters.

Fighting the Battle of the Pacific, a DD of the Pacific Destroyer Force (DesPac) fired the opening shot at Pearl Harbor. Veteran Asiatic Fleet destroyers bore the brunt of the Japanese naval onslaught on the Philippines, and Pacific destroyers held the battle-line in the Aleutians and contested the enemy's advance on Australia. In the Coral Sea and at Midway they screened the Navy's embattled task groups. They hammered the invader in the Solomons, spearheaded the New Guinea counter-offensive, battered the enemy's Bismarck citadel. From the Gilberts to the Marianas, from Palau to Leyte Gulf, and from the Philippines to the Bonins and the Nansei Shoto, Pacific destroyers and destroyer-escorts were in the vortex of combat. Heroically enduring the fiery ordeal of Okinawa, these dauntless warships were more than entitled to lead the victorious United States Fleet to Japan.

In four years of two-ocean conflict there was scarely a naval operation, battle, or campaign wherein these big little-ships were not in action.

The destroyers took punishment—no other type of United States warship suffered as many combat casualties. From all causes, 71 American DD's and 11 DE's —a total of 82 "small boys"—were lost during the war. But the percentage of the number that saw war duty (some 514 destroyers and 414 destroyer-escorts) ameliorates the casualty figure. So does comparison with enemy destroyer losses (the Japanese, for instance, lost some 126 of a destroyer fleet of 177). And if American DD's and DE's took punishment, they dealt it out in overwhelming reprisal. In battle areas that ranged from North Atlantic to South Pacific, from Mediterranean to Bering Sea, they sank over 100 Axis submarines, destroyed at least as many of the enemy's surface warships, demolished thousands of tons of enemy supply vessels, transports, and auxiliary craft, and shot down scores of enemy planes. The wholesale damage inflicted by their innumerable shore bombardments defies accurate statistical assessment. Nor could adding machines total the value of anti-submarine sweeps that cleared the way for Allied merchant shipping and troop transports—or the value of destroyer screens which time and again successfully thwarted enemy attack on the aircraft carriers, battleships, and cruisers of the United States Atlantic and Pacific Fleets.

Steel ships and steel men, the Navy's Destroyer Forces made valiant history in World War II. In so doing they fulfilled the promise of a service which had developed as a powerful fleet arm in the previous half century.

This is their story.

Destroyer Ancestry (DD Origin)

Cinnamon-bearded David Dixon Porter was an Admiral who got things done.

In the autumn of 1864 the Civil War circumstances called for decisive action on the part of the Federal Navy. Up the Roanoke River (in a cornfield, no less) the Confederates had constructed a powerful ironclad ram, the C. S. S. ALBEMARLE. Launched in the spring of 1864, this behemoth had waddled downstream and shot to kindling a task group of wooden blockaders in the estuary. Lurking up the Roanoke, she became a menace to Federal plans for a drive against Fort Fisher down the Carolina coast.

The drive had to go. Fort Fisher guarded Wilmington, the sole remaining Confederate outlet on the Atlantic seaboard. Its capture would deprive the South of vital sustenance by cutting Lee's last major supply line from overseas. But there was ALBEMARLE, up the Roanoke, waiting to rush from her lair to intercept any southbound invasion fleet.

Admiral Porter found the antidote for this poison. In New York Navy Yard two astute engineers, Messrs. Wood and Lay, had designed a new type of picket boat—a 30-foot launch, shallow draught, powered by steam, carrying a "spar torpedo" in the bow. A special rigging permitted the spar to be raised, lowered, and otherwise manipulated. Thus the operator could detach the torpedo and leave it planted under the target ship's keel. A lanyard could be yanked to pull the bomb-trigger when the launch had retired to safe distance.

Porter heard about this torpedo-armed launch from a 21-year-old naval officer, Lieutenant W. B. Cushing, a combat veteran whose war record was an anthology of exploits. With ALBEMARLE in mind, Cushing had fitted out three spar-torpedo launches in the New York yard and set out with the little craft for Hampton Roads. One launch foundered at sea, another went aground on the Virginia capes. Battered by high seas which swept clothing and instruments overboard, Cushing's sole surviving launch made it, the eight-man crew half starved from a week on hardtack, the young lieutenant as gaunt as the spar on the bow—and as volatile as the terminal torpedo.

Reporting personally to Porter on the Admiral's flagship, Cushing begged permission to make a single-handed attack on the ALBEMARLE. Go up the Roanoke, beard the iron rhinoceros in her lair!

David Dixon Porter, who had participated in similarly hazardous ventures, gave this venture his permission. He also gave Cushing reinforcements—extra hands for his crew, and instructions to the squadron blockading the Roanoke to go to the rescue if the ram pursued the raider down river.

Date: October 27, 1864. Scene: channel of the Roanoke River, black under misty night rain. Cushing's boat chugged quietly up the waterway, towing a cutter from the U.S.S. SHAMROCK. In the launch with Cushing were six officers and eight bluejackets. The cutter was crowded with armed seamen.

On the thwarts the men crouched with guns cocked. Only a cat-eyed helmsman could see in this murk, but the launch seemed to find her own way. In the bow stood Lieutenant Cushing, grasping the rigging lines and the lanyard of the spar torpedo.

Deep in Confederate territory they passed enemy sentinels. No challenge. They swung across the channel; there was the great ram snugged against a wharf. In the dimness she resembled an enormous iron Ark surrounded by a boom of floating logs—an Ark that could blow Cushing's party out of existence with a single broadside of its 100-pounders.

Cushing gave the word, and the launch bore in. ALBEMARLE heard something and hailed; then a sentry's shot stabbed the gloom. On the river bank a signal fire blazed (conveniently illuminating the ram); up went the shrill Rebel yell. Too late the raider launch was sighted; Cushing was already on target. Glimpsing the log barrier, he had circled off to come back in a headlong charge. Driving in through a storm of rifle fire, he sent the launch skidding over the slippery logs in a rush that carried her right under ALBEMARLE's casemates. The ironclad fired a broadside. Cushing lowered the boom.

Cannon roar and torpedo blast shook the night. The launch was swamped by the explosion. Through a tempest of gunfire Cushing and his men swam downstream. Only the young lieutenant and one seaman escaped; the others were riddled, drowned, or made prisoner. But the coastal way was cleared for the Federal invasion fleet. Downed at her berth up the Roanoke, the ironclad ALBEMARLE lay in ruin, torpedoed.

Thus naval traditions (and ships) are born. The Cushing spirit—a synonym for intrepidity—was to become a tradition cherished by the U.S. Navy's destroyermen. And Cushing's torpedo boat influenced naval warfare to the point of affecting tactics and ship construction. For Naval authorities at once saw the value of a small warcraft, fast and agile, which could race in to strike under a larger warship's guard. Manifest were the possibilities of the torpedo punch below the waterline.

A direct descendant of Cushing's launch, then, was the torpedo boat, progenitor of the torpedo-boat destroyer. From it was derived the World War I "four-piper," the immediate predecessor of the modern fleet destroyer and the sub-hunting destroyer-escort. From the acorn of Cushing's little boat grew the oak of the Destroyer Force—a force of little ships designed to take on large assignments. More than a few DD's and DE's in World War II raced into action against ALBEMARLE odds. Among the Navy's modern destroyermen there were many Cushings.

How appropriate, too, that the naval leader who sponsored Cushing's launch was an Admiral whose initials were D. D.

The Torpedo Boat (1870-1898)

Six months after the Cushing exploit the Navy acquired its first torpedo boat, the SPUYTEN DUYVIL (Dutch for "spit on the Devil"). She was armed, weighed 206 tons, and carried a heavy spar torpedo.

Five years later Congress authorized the building of two torpedo-boat rams, the 800-ton ALARM and the 1150-ton INTREPID. These were a backward step—wooden ships burdened with bulky underwater beaks that slowed their speed, hampered maneuverability, and thereby impeded the employment of their spar torpedo weapons.

The true torpedo boat did not appear until the advent of the self-guiding mobile torpedo, invented in the early 1870's by an Austrian naval officer, Commander Lupius, and the British engineer Whitehead. Given a torpedo that could run on its own power and explode upon striking the target, and provided with tubes for the launching of such thunderbolts, naval architects lost no time in designing appropriate vessels to carry the weapon into battle. Congress, however, was dilatory in regard to appropriations. The first American torpedo boat equipped with automobile torpedoes and launching tubes was not commissioned until 1890. But her name was CUSHING.

Torpedo boat CUSHING was a wooden 150-footer, powered with 1720-horsepower engines that gave her a top speed of 22.5 knots. She carried three torpedo tubes. Her torpedoes had a maximum effective range of a scant 550 yards, but they were steered by a marvelous gyroscopic device which controlled the vertical rudder—invention of an American naval officer, Lieutenant Howell. Thirty-five torpedo boats were commissioned in the United States between 1890 and 1898. The largest of these—PORTER, DUPONT, and ROWAN—were three-tube 185-tonners capable of well over 27 knots.

The Torpedo-Boat Destroyer (Spanish-American War Threat)

Production of the torpedo boat, and development of the torpedo attack, gave rise to defensive invention. Defense called for an armed vessel possessed of a speed which enabled it to overtake the torpedo boat, plus fire-power for the demolishment of the latter. Born was the torpedo-boat destroyer, itself a small but powerful warcraft armed with torpedoes, and carrying sizable batteries for gun attack. Its name was soon shortened to "destroyer," and its mission was enlarged to include such surface actions as had previously been delegated to gunboats, small monitors, and naval vessels of that caliber.

The sinking of an iron warship by torpedo boats in the Chilean Civil War of 1891 gave impetus to the building of torpedo-boat destroyers. In the Battle of Yalu (1894), Japanese destroyers completely thwarted a squadron of Chinese torpedo boats. And a few months later, in a dramatic turnabout at Wei-Hai-Wei, Jap torpedomen disabled 14,000 tons of Chinese naval vessels. By 1898, when the United States went to war with Spain, torpedo warfare was an established naval threat, and destroyers were universally on, and in, order.

So far as the United States Navy was concerned, they were only on order—the U.S. Fleet did not at that date possess any destroyers. The Spaniards, on the other hand, were possessed of a destroyer flotilla. American intelligence placed several Spanish destroyers (apparently erroneously) in Manila Bay. It was rumored that one or two were in Cuban waters. And a destroyer division crossed the Atlantic with Admiral Cervera's ill-fated fleet.

But Cervera's destroyers barely made the Atlantic crossing. In common with the other Spanish warships, they were barnacle-heavy and in slovenly condition. Defective boilers plagued the engineers, and the three had to be towed most of the way. TERROR's boilers gave out at Martinique, where the fleet put in for coal, and only PLUTÓN and FUROR managed to reach the fatal harbor of Santiago, Cuba.

At Santiago the Spanish destroyers might have accomplished something, but for the over-cautiousness of Cervera. Inactive, they lay at anchor in the harbor while United States warships set up an iron blockade. At the end (July 3, 1898) they sailed out and were sacrificed with Cervera's fleet when it made its suicidal sortie. Target for American cruiser guns, the two destroyers never had a chance. PLUTÓN was promptly driven off course, and FUROR was soon staggered by a shell-hit. They were finished off by the American armed yacht GLOUCESTER which had been stationed inshore to deal with the pair. The yacht poured rapid pompom fire into the PLUTÓN, which blew up. And the FUROR, riddled, went down flying a pathetic white flag.

The few American torpedo craft had no opportunities except in shore bombardments and cable-cutting expeditions, and the war ended without a successful torpedo attack by either side.

But the threat had been obvious and the lesson was learned. American destroyers, then building, were hurried down the ways. U.S.S. BAINBRIDGE, the Navy's first destroyer, was launched in the summer of 1901. By 1906 the American destroyer flotilla numbered 16 ships. Thereafter it was steadily enlarged to meet the threat of German sabre-rattling. As the force grew, so did the size, armament, and over-all mission of the destroyer.

Early Destroyer To "Four-Piper" (1898-1917)

BAINBRIDGE, completed in 1902, was a 420-tonner, carrying two torpedo tubes, armed with two 3-inch 50's and five 6-pounders. Top speed was about 28 knots. BARRY, CHAUNCEY, DALE, DECATUR, HOPKINS, HULL, LAWRENCE, and MACDONOUGH soon followed.

In 1901 destroyers TRUXTUN, WHIPPLE, and WORDEN came down the ways—435-tonners carrying two tubes each; armed with 3-inch 50's and 6-pounders. During the ensuing decade (under the influence of Theodore Roosevelt) some 26 destroyers were commissioned for duty in the U.S. Fleet.

Steaming in 1915, destroyers CUSHING, ERICSSON, and MCDOUGAL were 1,050-tonners, carrying eight torpedo tubes and armed with four 4-inch guns. The ships were prototypes for 17 more American destroyers commissioned by 1916.

With World War I raging in Europe, the Kaiser's U-boats on the rampage, and German aggression menacing the United States, Congress voted a hasty naval-building program, and a large number of new destroyers were authorized in 1916. The DD of this period averaged 1,150 tons, carried twelve torpedo tubes, and 4-inch guns.

The destroyer's mission now included scouting and screening for the fleet. Destroyer tactics were designed to suit fast torpedo attacks and hot gun actions. Smoke screens were on the duty list. Following a British cue, American destroyer experts were experimenting with anti-submarine devices. The DD was becoming versatile.

Destroyers, World War I

The new American destroyer that steamed into battle in World War I was the famous "four-piper" —so-called because of its four smoke stacks. A flush-decker, and rakish, the "four-piper" averaged 1,150 to 1,215 tons, and had a maximum speed of about 32 knots. It carried twelve torpedo tubes, and was armed with four 4-inch guns and one 3-inch gun. Anti-aircraft (AA) guns were a 1917 innovation. Another innovation was anti-submarine (A/S) equipment—detection gear and weapons. Armed to fight a three-dimensional war, the "four-piper" was the Buck Rogers ship of its day. After America's entry into the war, Congress authorized the building of 242 of these destroyers.

This huge building program was prompted by a German submarine drive which had taken the European Allies by surprise and was threatening to sink Great Britain.

The Germans began the undersea war in the summer of 1914 with 28 submarines, only ten of which were Diesel-powered. But by January 1916 there were 41 Imperial German submarines at sea, and exactly one year later there were 103. These new U-boats were long-range Diesel jobs—the largest had a surface displacement of 1,930 tons—and as their number increased, they played havoc on the sea lanes to Britain. Britain was in a fair way to being starved into defeat.

Desperate cases require desperate remedies. Against the U-boats they had tried everything from nets to Q-boat decoy ships. Among the best of the anti-submarine (A/S) devices produced were the hydrophone (a listening instrument) and depth charges. The standard depth charge was the "ashcan" type—a cylindrical container packed with TNT. Rolled overside, this weapon was deadly if it exploded close aboard a submerged submarine. Ships were needed to carry the "ashcans" into action. By and large the task was shouldered by destroyers.

But the Royal Navy lacked a large destroyer force. Some 200 British destroyers were available at the start of 1917, most of them war-worn and weary, and at least half of them needed with the fleet. And merchant sinkings were increasing at an alarming rate. When the United States entered the war on April 6, 1917, the British Empire was on the verge of defeat.

"We must stop these losses and stop them soon,"

First Sea Lord Admiral Jellicoe informed visiting American Admiral W. S. Sims. "It is impossible for us to go on if such losses continue."

After a look at the British figures—military, naval, and economic—Sims cabled Washington that England had less than a month's food supply, and that only the immediate dispatch of American warships, especially destroyers, to British waters could save the Allied situation.

To U.S. destroyers, then, fell the first play. And from Boston Navy Yard they were under way at once—six of them under the leadership of Commander J. K. Taussig. So it was that on May 4, 1917, Queenstown, Ireland, was the scene of a historic drama. Into the harbor on that date steamed United States destroyers WADSWORTH (flagship), CONYNGHAM, PORTER, McDOUGAL, DAVIS, and WAINWRIGHT.

Vice Admiral Sir Lewis Bayly, R.N., himself a veteran destroyer officer, assumed that the American ships would need time for some overhaul. "How soon," he inquired of Commander Taussig, "will you be ready to go out on patrol?" Taussig's reply was to become a Destroyer Force slogan. *"We are ready now, sir, that is, as soon as we finish refuelling."*

By July there were 34 American destroyers in Britain's home waters. They arrived just in time. In April of that year the Germans had sunk a stupendous 900,000 tons of Allied shipping; London, cowering in blackout under Zeppelin raids, was going hungry; the British Empire was practically on the rocks. The American destroyers brought moral as well as physical support that helped to turn the war-tide.

American destroyer O'BRIEN severely damaged a U-boat with depth charges on June 16, Taussig's flagship WADSWORTH disabled a German sub a few days later, and destroyer BENHAM dealt injuries to a third before the month was out.

But it was not as offensive anti-submarine (A/S) vessels that American destroyers starred in World War I. Sub-hunting and killing techniques were still in the trial-and-error stage of development. During the war, American A/S forces demolished no more than three or four German U-boats, and U.S. destroyers downed only one of these.

The destroyer's big role was as a convoy escort. The British had tried and abandoned convoying as a futile effort. They asserted it was over-costly in warships, in port facilities, in time; altogether convoying was not feasible.

American Admiral Sims thought otherwise. When a trial convoy, early in May 1917, steamed from Gibraltar to London without loss of a ship, the "nays" were silenced. They became enthusiastic "yeas" when a sizable trans-Atlantic convoy, which left Hampton Roads on May 24, made the crossing without mishap.

Convoying was under way. Allied cruisers escorted the big ship-trains on the mid-ocean laps where shipping had previously been threatened by German surface raiders. Destroyers took over at rendezvous points (usually within 200 miles of the British Isles) to conduct the convoys into port.

Adoption of the convoy system spelled *"kaput"* for the Imperial German submarine effort. Allied sinkings steadily declined from the 900,000-ton high of April 1917 to less than 300,000 tons the following November. Some 140 U-boats were in active service that autumn, but they were losing the Atlantic battle.

As numerous other types of craft were fighting the anti-submarine war, it would be an exaggeration to state that destroyers were the backbone of the Allied A/S effort of World War I. But the World War I destroyer was more than worth its weight in "ashcans" as a protector of shipping. As of November 1917, some 227 British destroyers were giving their full time to A/S warfare. Eventually about 80 American destroyers were similarly engaged in European waters. Altogether, Allied destroyers sank 34 of the Kaiser's U-boats—a little better than half the number sunk by surface vessels of other types.

The World War I U-boat was a tough customer. Case in point, and typical: on August 3, 1917, the American destroyer PARKER sighted the U-103 on the surface, and went after the sub at top speed. The U-boat immediately dived. She was trailing oil, however, and the destroyermen were able to trace her by the oil slick. They overhauled the submerged submarine; the U-boat's blurred silhouette could be seen deep under. PARKER dumped one "ashcan" after another down on the submersible. The water boiled and boomed; oil rose to the surface; PARKER retired, all hands confident they had wrecked the U-boat. U-103 was severely damaged, but she survived.

The U-boat crews, however, were not quite so durable as their boats. Depth-charging was always hard on crew morale. The submariners, who had enjoyed a Roman holiday early in the war, were now suffering chronic battle fatigue.

On November 17, 1917, American destroyers FANNING and NICHOLSON teamed up to finish a German submarine, the U-58. The two DD's were serving as convoy escorts at the time. FANNING's lookouts spotted an approaching periscope, and the destroyer's skipper, Lieutenant A. S. Carpender, drove the stalking sub under with a fast depth-charge assault that prevented torpedo attack. Dashing through the convoy's disordered columns, destroyer NICHOLSON (Commander F. D. Berrien) steamed to the spot to drop "ashcans" on the submerged target. FANNING's depth-charge salvo disabled the U-boat's motors, burst some oil pipes, and jammed the diving gear. The sub went down 278 feet before her crew could regain control. The dive was too much for the U-boat skipper. Ordering his boys to blow all ballast, he brought the sub popping to the surface, and the crew scrambled out of the conning tower with shouts of *"Kamerad!"*

As the men lined up on deck to surrender, their captain ordered the seacocks opened, and the scuttled U-boat went down with a plunge, taking some of the crew with her. Four officers, among them Herr Kapitan Amberger, and 36 men were hauled from the water and made prisoner by the American destroyermen. The exploit evoked a cheerful message from Admiral Sims:

GO OUT AND DO IT AGAIN

The FANNING-NICHOLSON victory—a "first" in American naval history—suggested the destroyer team and the coordinated A/S attack of the future. However, historically speaking, destroyers were still in their infancy; undersea warfare was a pioneer enterprise; A/S methods had yet to be developed, practiced, and perfected. Throughout that conflict the U-boat operated pretty much as a lone wolf. And the destroyer fought the A/S war in the main as a convoy escort or as a patrol vessel beating an assigned area on the lookout for the undersea foe.

It was while she was engaged in patrol duty that the U.S.S. JACOB JONES (Lieutenant Commander D. W. Bagley) was torpedoed. Steaming alone in the English Channel on December 6, 1917, the destroyer was struck by a torpedo fired by the U-53. The destroyer went down in eight minutes, taking 64 of her crew down with her. Exhibiting a chivalry by no means the rule in the Imperial German U-boat Force, the submarine commander, Kapitan Hans Rose, brought his sub to the surface, aided in the rescue of some of the survivors, and went so far as to dispatch a radio message detailing their position.

JACOB JONES was the first United States warship to fall victim to a long-range torpedo. And she was the only American warship torpedoed during World War I (although the enemy torpedoed an American revenue cutter, an empty transport, and an armed yacht).

A second destroyer, the U.S.S. CHAUNCEY, was lost through collision. The wonder was that, operating blindly with unlighted convoys, and working in all sorts of Atlantic weather, more of these fast-moving American "four-pipers" were not sunk by fatal collisions.

Heavy casualties were suffered by the U.S.S. MANLEY in March 1918 when she was jostled against a British cruiser while coming alongside in rough seas. Eighteen of the destroyer's depth charges exploded, wrecking her stern and killing or wounding 56 of her crew. In October 1918 the destroyer SHAW (Commander W. A. Glassford), her steering gear jammed, had her bow sheared off by the liner AQUITANIA. The liner sliced into the destroyer just forward of the bridge; twelve bluejackets were killed.

There were other destroyers damaged by storm and accident. For in addition to trans-Atlantic convoying and operations in British waters, American destroyers conducted patrols in the Bay of Biscay (some 43 were eventually stationed at Brest), and a division of small old-timers operated out of Gibraltar in the Mediterranean. A considerable number patrolled the American East Coast in the summer and autumn of 1918 when five or six U-boats crossed the ocean to invade American coastal waters. Altogether, American destroyers fought about 250 A/S actions during World War I.

While the destroyer of that day operated primarily as an anti-submarine vessel, its activities were by no means confined to A/S warfare. Operating with the fleets, they scouted, screened, and laid smoke. American destroyers screened the five coal-burning American dreadnaughts that crossed the Atlantic in December 1917 to reinforce the British Grand Fleet.

They were also armed against enemy air attack. Aerial warfare had burst like a tornado over Europe in the autumn of 1914. Almost overnight the awkward flying-machine—a rickety "box-kite" flown by a daredevil—had developed into a speedy battle plane piloted by a sharpshooting ace. Simultaneously, naval aviation was taking wing.

The early hydroplane, slow and cumbersome, with inaccurate bombsights and relatively small bombs, was no match for the anti-aircraft guns hastily manufactured by both sides and mounted on naval vessels to meet the threat. The seaplanes of World War I were best used against submarines and such targets as the U-boat pens on the Belgian coast. But German hydroplanes attacked a British destroyer force off Heligoland on Christmas Day, 1914, and the sea-air war was on. American destroyermen took note!

The first anti-aircraft (AA) guns placed on United States warships were 3-inchers. The gun crews had little chance to practice with these new weapons, and enemy planes proved rarer than pheasants in hunting season. But anti-aircraft gunners on American destroyers were ready to take a crack at aerial warfare by the time the A.E.F. needed escort overseas.

As participants in the great convoy effort which transported Pershing's army to France, the Navy's destroyermen chalked up a perfect record. Of all the U.S. Army forces which crossed to Europe under American escortage—nearly two million men!—not a single soldier was lost through enemy action en route. The U-boats were active enough. A number of empty westbound transports were torpedoed while in convoy, but no troopships escorted to Europe by the U.S. Navy were sunk.

By war's end the Destroyer Force was established as the good right arm of the U.S. Navy.

In the autumn of 1918 the Yanks cracked the Hindenburg Line. There was a mutiny in the U-boat Force at Wilhelmshaven which spread through the German dreadnaught fleet at Kiel. The Kaiser fled to Holland. Ludendorf surrendered. It was over.

In retrospect, Navy men would see World War I as a preview of World War II. Much of the pattern was there: the struggle to maintain overseas shipping —Britain slowly succumbing to submarine blockade—London under aerial bombardment—United States forces to the rescue—a U-boat counter-invasion of American waters—American destroyers in the thick of the A/S battle—in the Atlantic, at least, history was to repeat.

Even as history repeated, some of the World War I "four-pipers" would once more steam into action. And some of the graduates of that World War I Destroyer Force would be leaders in World War II. Lieutenant A. S. ("Chips") Carpender of FANNING would become ComDesLant (Commander Destroyers Atlantic) and Lieutenant J. L. Kauffman of CALDWELL would become ComDesPac (Commander Destroyers Pacific). Commander H. R. ("Betty") Stark, who brought a division of little old destroyers from the Philippines to Gibraltar, was Chief of Naval Operations at the time of Pearl Harbor; eventually he was Commander of U.S. Naval Forces in Europe. The Lieutenant (jg) A. S. Merrill in destroyer CONYNGHAM, 1917-18, was Rear Admiral "Tip" Merrill in the Solomons. On board the "four-piper" ALLEN was Lieutenant (jg) M. L. Deyo; Rear Admiral Deyo (ComDesLant in 1943) was a destroyerman's destroyerman. Lieutenant O. C. Badger of ALLEN's crew was Rear Admiral (later Vice Admiral) O. C. Badger, Deyo's predecessor as ComDesLant.

Four stars were in the future for Lieutenant R. L. Conolly in the crew of "four-piper" SMITH. Lieutenant Commander R. C. Giffen, skipper of TRIPPE; Lieutenant C. H. ("Sock") McMorris, in the crew of SHAW; Lieutenant L. E. Denfeld, who served in AMMEN—these and other destroyer officers were destined to wear stars. Not to mention the constellation in store for the World War I skipper of BENHAM and SHAW, Lieutenant Commander W. F. Halsey, Jr.

And there was a destroyer named CASSIN. And a Gunner's Mate named Ingram. In October 1917 the U.S.S. CASSIN was patrolling off the Irish coast when Gunner's Mate Ingram, on watch, suddenly spied the wake of a torpedo heading straight for the CASSIN's stern and the rack of depth charges there. Shouting a warning, he rushed aft to release the charges from the racks, to get as many overside as soon as possible. Before he could jettison all the charges, the "tin fish" struck home. The destroyer's stern was shattered; Gunner's Mate Ingram was killed. But the destroyer remained afloat.

In World War II there was a destroyer CASSIN.

And a Nazi U-boat was sunk by a "killer" group containing a destroyer named INGRAM.

The Passing of the "Four-Piper"

After Armistice Day, November 11, 1918, American destroyers—most of them—turned their bows for America, and the Destroyer Force settled down for a period of peace-time routine. War-time construction had expanded the force into the Navy's largest. From destroyers ABBOT, ALDEN, AULICK, and CHARLES AUSBURNE to YARBOROUGH, YARNALL, ZANE, and ZEILIN, the roster of DD's newly commissioned and building numbered 242 at war's end. These, added to the prewar flotilla, gave the U.S. Navy the world's largest destroyer fleet.

As was to be expected, many of these ships were demobilized. In 1919 a United States Pacific Fleet was organized, and a number of destroyer squadrons were dispatched to join this fleet. Some of the "four-pipers" were slated to go to the Philippines. Others were sent to naval bases on the East and West Coasts. By 1922 the Navy's personnel was reduced from a war-time total of 497,000 to a peace-time complement of 86,000. The Destroyer Force was reduced proportionately.

With the great Naval Disarmament Treaty of 1922, most of the U.S. destroyers went into "mothballs." Some 200 DD's were laid up. About 40 of the older ships were sold out or broken up.

Between 1919 and 1930 no American destroyers were built. As the calendar leafed toward 1931, veteran destroyermen shook their heads. The World War I destroyers were great ships, but they weren't growing any younger. Some of the eldest were already obsolete. New designs called for DD's with increased fire power and bigger and better engines. The old "four-pipers" were relics of another day and time.

Still, they were serviceable, and it was good to have that "mothball fleet" in reserve. In the event of emergency, it might prove an ace in the hole.

It did.

CHAPTER 2

THE MODERN DD

Thunder Before Storm (1930-1938)

"There won't be another war," optimists said. "No nation can afford one." But—

In 1931 a Japanese army swept into Manchuria. In 1934 Adolph Hitler became full-fledged dictator of Germany. In 1935 the Italians invaded Ethiopia. In 1937 Japan's legions invaded free China. And in 1938 Nazi Germany seized Austria. On the horizon loomed the Rome-Berlin-Tokyo Axis. The Far East was in flames; Europe was a vast powder mine; the League of Nations was tottering; the democratic world was facing a deadly crisis.

How did U.S. destroyers fare during this time? Between 1930 and 1935 some 45 new DD's were authorized for the American Destroyer Force. Smallest of these were eight 1,395-tonners (FARRAGUT, DEWEY, HULL, MACDONOUGH, WORDEN, AYLWYN, DALE, MONAGHAN). They were armed with four 5-inch guns, four 40 mm. automatic guns, and eight torpedo tubes, and were capable of about 36 knots. Largest were eight 1,805-ton flotilla leaders (PORTER, SELFRIDGE, MCDOUGAL, WINSLOW, PHELPS, MOFFETT, CLARK, BALCH). These were armed with eight 5-inch guns, eight 1.1-inch anti-aircraft guns, and eight torpedo tubes, and had a top speed of around 37 knots. Of intermediate tonnage, the other new destroyers were given 5-inch and 40 mm. batteries, but were equipped with more torpedo tubes than the large and small types, one class carrying 12 tubes, and another carrying 16. Destroyer tacticians were still looking forward to surface actions and torpedo attacks.

But during this same period 40 pre-World War destroyers were sold as scrap, and 66 "four-pipers" of World War construction sold out of the service. Replacements far from balanced reductions.

But the destroyer-building pace was quickened in the critical period between 1935 and 1940. Either launched, under construction, or contracted for during this time were 24 DD's. Many were not completed and commissioned until long after Pearl Harbor, but at least they were coming up.

The World War II DD

At time of the war's outbreak, the U.S. Navy's modern destroyer fleet was largely composed of the BENSON and BRISTOL (or LIVERMORE) classes, such destroyers as those of the PORTER and CRAVEN classes, and the husky FLETCHER class. The latter remained the fleet-destroyer heavyweight until 1944 when new destroyers of the ALLEN M. SUMNER class were commissioned. Biggest of American DD's to steam into action were the GEARING class destroyers which appeared in 1945.

The table on page 20 gives the principal characteristics of the various classes of destroyers.

The gun armament of these destroyers was subject to change during the war. All the modern DD's were equipped with depth-charge launching and throwing apparatus (racks and K-guns), anti-submarine detection devices, and improved electronics devices.

A warship has been defined as a "floating platform designed to carry weapons into battle." A glance at the plan drawing of a typical World War II destroyer (page 21) will point up the obvious over-simplification of this definition.

This warship is something more than a "floating platform." Its turbine-engined power plant is a marvel of marine engineering, capable of 40,000 to 60,000 horsepower. Compressed in the steel hull are 82 compartments, storerooms, lockers, and cubicles. Through this vessel runs a maze of air, oil, and water lines. Another maze of electrical lines and cables carries light and motor-power and the sensory means of communication to the various nerve centers of the ship—to the navigational instruments, fire-control instruments, electronic gear for the operation of radio and radar and sonar.

Providing accommodations for anywhere from 200 to 350 officers and men, the ship contains living quarters, mess rooms, galley, refrigerators, laundry, showers, post office, and store. Its hospital (sick bay) is equipped to handle any case requiring emergency medicine or surgery. Space is found and apparatus is made available for classroom instruction (the ship maintains various schools), for recreation (boxing matches, movies), for chapel.

Smaller than some private yachts, the destroyer bristles with armament. Every superfluous item of gear is eliminated; every available foot of deck space that can be so devoted is utilized for gun mounts, fire-control apparatus, depth-charge gear, torpedo tubes, and munitions storage.

The vessel's hull is streamlined to the *nth* practical degree. Armor is sacrificed for speed, the cruising range is sacrificed for speed. Fastest ship afloat, the destroyer depends for protection chiefly on speed, maneuverability, the use of smoke screens, and, of course, fire-power.

Destroyer Organization during World War II

In common with all warships, a destroyer's organization is designed to meet the man-of-war's primary imperative—battle efficiency.

There are no supernumeraries in a destroyer's company. The average U.S. destroyer's complement in World War II contained the following officers:

Commanding Officer—the ship's captain. Regardless of rank (he may be a Commander, Lieutenant Commander, even a Lieutenant) he is always addressed as "Captain," and he has full authority over all hands serving in his vessel. He is also fully responsible for the safety and operation of the ship, and the performance and welfare of the crew. Informally referred to as "Skipper"—"Old Man" to junior officers and bluejackets—his average age was thirty to forty.

Executive Officer—the Captain's chief assistant. He might be called "ship's general manager." He is charged with the maintenance of upkeep, good order, and efficiency of both vessel and crew. He is broadly responsible for execution of the Captain's orders, and he stands ready to step into the Captain's shoes and serve as relief Commanding Officer. Among other duties he is in charge of the C.I.C. It takes a good officer to qualify as "Exec."

(For the purposes of administration and operation, men-of-war are departmentally organized. The destroyer organization of World War II contained a Gunnery Department, Navigation Department, Engineering Department, Construction and Repair [C. and R.] Department, and Supply Department. Reporting to the Commanding Officer are the officers assigned to head these departments. They are listed below.)

Gunnery Officer—responsible for the maintenance and employment of the ship's guns, fire-control gear, A/S weapons, torpedoes, munitions. His subordinate assistants are the Assistant Gunnery Officer, Assistant Fire-control Officer, Torpedo Officer (in charge of torpedoes, A/S weapons, and smoke generators), and other officers detailed to gunnery and fire-control.

Navigating Officer, or Navigator—responsible for all navigating gear (except electrical) and for fixing the position of the ship at all times. Usually acts as the ship's tactical officer. Among other duties, he keeps the ship's log and war diary.

Engineer Officer (commonly known as the "Chief Engineer")—charged with the maintenance and operation of the power plant, all of the ship's machinery, and all electrical apparatus with the exception of radio, radar, and sonar gear. He is assisted by the Assistant Engineer Officer and other subordinates.

Damage-Control Officer and First Lieutenant—in charge of the Construction and Repair Department. He is responsible for placing the ship in material readiness for battle, for all damage-control equipment and work, and for emergency repairs. As "First Lieutenant" he assists the Executive Officer in arranging the ship's work and drills. His immediate subordinate is the Assistant Damage-Control Officer.

Supply Officer—charged with the maintenance and distribution of the ship's supplies. Commissary provisions, stores, bunker fuel, material equipment are his responsibility. He is also in charge of accounts and disbursement of ship's funds.

Communication Officer—not a department head, but with comparably important duties. He is responsible for all radio and sound equipment, all visual signalling apparatus, and for the recording and appropriate relay of routine dispatches. In his custody are the code books, all secret and confidential documents, and related material.

Medical Officer—the ship's doctor. Not a depart-

Airplane view of the U.S.S. Rhind, showing deck arrangement. On the fantail are the depth-charge roller rails; beyond are two 5-inch gun mounts, two 40 mm mounts (covered), two life rafts, two quadruple torpedo tube mounts, and two 20 mm gun tubs just abaft the stack. K-guns were usually along rails, hedgehogs outboard of bridge superstructure, smoke generators on fantail.

A destroyer's bridge arrangement seen from aft. From the stack, reading from left to right, are the searchlight (on the stack platform), flag bag and signal hoists, captain's sea cabin (open door) with wheelhouse beyond, torpedo director (covered), and bridge wing. Above is the flying bridge and main battery director, and radar, the biggest secret of early war days, above that.

Engine-room scene on the destroyer Nicholas. One man tends throttle; the second man is messenger, and the third is the machinist's mate on watch.

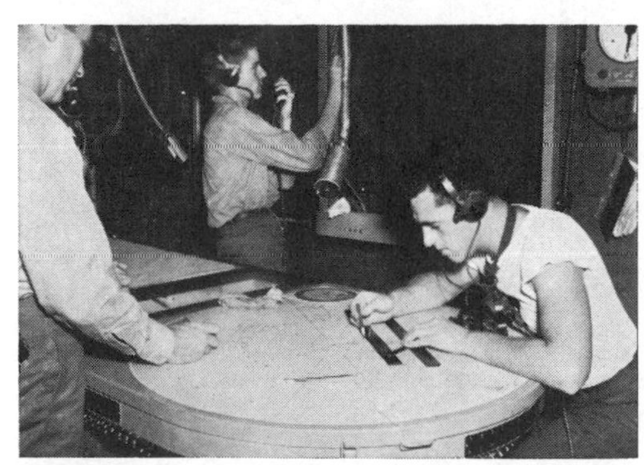

"Battle Brains." A corner of Combat Information Center (CIC), showing tactical plot in foreground, dead reckoning tracer (DRT), and status board.

Fire-room of the U.S.S. Jouett. Firemen man their stations under the watchful eye of the chief. Water gauges, steam gauges, pipes, valves—and the boilers ready to give that flank speed the ship may need at any moment.

ment head on a destroyer, but with a full share of responsibilities. He is in charge of health and sanitation, and the treatment of battle casualties.

To each department are assigned divisions of the ship's company. Under charge of a division officer, each division is composed of the petty officers and non-rated men who are trained for the work of that particular department.

A World War II destroyer's Ordnance Division, for example, contained Gunner's Mates, Torpedomen, Fire-Controlmen, Radarmen, and Ordnance strikers—the men who manned the guns, director gear, depth-charge projectors, and related ordnance equipment.

In the Communication Division of the Navigation Department were Radiomen and Radio Technicians, Sonarmen, Quartermasters, Signalmen, Yeomen, Pharmacist's Mates, and strikers.

The Engineer Division contained Machinist's Mates, Motor-Machinist's Mates, Electrician's Mates, Firemen, Water Tenders, and Metalsmiths.

In the First and Second Deck Divisions of the Construction and Repair (C and R) Department served Boatswain's Mates, Coxswains, Carpenter's Mates, Shipfitters, Seamen, and apprentices.

The Supply Division was manned by Commissary Stewards, Ship's Cooks, Bakers, Storekeepers, Officer's Steward, Officer's Cook, Mess Attendants, Supply strikers.

In war-time the crew members of a naval vessel are always "on call," like fire-fighters ready to answer an alarm. But for the performance of routine duty, and to suit messing and sleeping arrangements, the crew works in shifts. Or, to put it nautically, it is divided into sections for watch-standing.

On a modern United States destroyer there are three watch sections; the normal duty watch is of four hours duration, and the crew stands watch "four hours on and eight off." With the exception of Commanding Officer and Executive Officer, everyone in the ship is placed in a watch section.

When the destroyer goes into action, all hands go into action with it. Such routine duties as swabbing down, inspecting the "head," tinkering with a faulty gun-mechanism, and trying to degarble the latest "ALNAV," are instantly abandoned. When the alarm, "General Quarters" (Battle Condition I), is sounded, the crew gets set to fight. On or off watch, all hands report at once to their battle stations.

Every officer and man in the ship has his particular battle station. And in so far as it can be arranged, all hands work at posts and occupy quarters in the vicinity of those stations.

As the primary ship-control station is on the destroyer's bridge—there the ship is steered, or "conned," to use the Navy term—the bridge is the Commanding Officer's battle station. And during World War II the battle station of the Executive Officer was the Combat Information Center; Gunnery Officer's battle station, the main battery director; Navigation Officer's battle station, the bridge, where he relieved the Officer of the Deck. Engineer Officer's battle station was the forward engine-room; Damage Control officer's battle station, No. 1 repair station; Supply Officer's battle station, Coding Board. The Communication Officer's battle station was the communication office, C.I.C., or signal bridge; the Medical Officer's battle station was the primary dressing station (usually the wardroom).

All division officers and men report to their various posts—gunners to their mounts, fire-controlmen to their instruments, torpedomen to torpedo and depth-charge stations, and so on. Every man fits into the ship's fighting team somewhere. Mess attendants may take station as ammunition passers, and the ship's storekeeper may man a searchlight.

"General Quarters" (with the exception of drills) is only sounded when the ship makes contact with the enemy, or is approached by an unidentified vessel or planes. Or at dawn or dusk when twilight is dangerous.

Under Battle Condition II or III (for war cruising) ship-control and lookout stations are fully manned; all detection apparatus is manned; the watertight integrity watch is posted; half of the armament is manned.

Destroyer Group Organization

During World War II the Navy's destroyers were under the over-all command of Admiral E. J. King,

---

For the uninitiated, a word on naval time-keeping and watch periods. Naval time is recorded by the European system which counts the hours consecutively from 0000 (midnight) through to 2400 (the following midnight). For instance, 0700 is 7:00 A.M., and 1400 is 2:00 P.M.

A nautical day is divided into six 4-hour watch periods.

THE MID-WATCH
(midnight to 4:00 A.M.—Navy time, 0000 to 0400).

THE MORNING WATCH
(4:00 A.M. to 8:00 A.M.—Navy time, 0400 to 0800).

THE FORENOON WATCH
(8:00 A.M. to noon—Navy time, 0800 to 1200).

THE AFTERNOON WATCH
(noon to 4:00 P.M.—Navy time, 1200 to 1600).

THE DOG WATCH
(4:00 P.M. to 8:00 P.M.—Navy time, 1600 to 2000).

THE FIRST WATCH
(8:00 P.M. to midnight—Navy time, 2000 to 2400).

who as Commander in Chief of the United States Fleet (Cominch) headed the Navy. Destroyers attached to the Navy's fleets—Atlantic, Pacific, Asiatic—came directly under the control of the various Fleet commanders, namely Admirals Ingersoll, Nimitz, and Hart. When attached to Spruance's Fifth Fleet, or Halsey's Third Fleet, or Kinkaid's Seventh (Southwest Pacific) Fleet, or Ingram's South Atlantic Fleet, they would be operationally controlled by those subordinate Fleet commanders.

For administrative purposes, two main destroyer-force commands were organized. (The term "force" was not officially applied to United States battleship, cruiser, and destroyer groups during World War II.) Destroyers assigned to the Atlantic Fleet were designated "Destroyers, Atlantic Fleet" (DesLant). Those assigned to the Pacific Fleet were designated "Destroyers, Pacific Fleet" (DesPac).

The administrative heads of these two destroyer "forces" were known as Type Commanders. They were designated "Commander Destroyers, Atlantic Fleet" (ComDesLant), and "Commander Destroyers, Pacific Fleet" (ComDesPac). ComDesLant and ComDesPac were responsible for maintenance, basing facilities, and the dispatch of DD's. They kept track of the destroyers attached to the various Fleets. And from the "ship pool" they furnished destroyers when wanted for such operations as convoy escort duty, a "hunter-killer" campaign, or service with the local defense forces of a sea frontier.

The Type Commanders were something more than "desk admirals" behind the line. An intimate knowledge of destroyers and a great deal of know-how were demanded of the Type Commanders. They were in over-all charge of all DD personnel. They advised on strategy and tactics. They recommended new battle gear and improvements of old. They requisitioned facilities, matériel, and equipment. They sponsored new training activities, and were in charge of training new DD's and of "refresher training" for veteran ships. They pushed ship construction. They broke bottlenecks. Many of the destroyer successes recounted in this history were spark-plugged by the officers who served as ComDesLant and ComDesPac. This is the roster:

COMDESLANT	*Date In Command*
Rear Admiral F. L. Reichmuth	*As of Oct. 1941*
Rear Admiral A. S. Carpender	*Dec. 22, 1941*
Rear Admiral O. C. Badger	*June 3, 1942*
Rear Admiral M. L. Deyo	*Dec. 15, 1942*
Rear Admiral J. Cary Jones	*Jan. 1, 1944*
Rear Admiral O. M. Read	*Sept. 20, 1944*
Rear Admiral F. E. Beatty	*Oct. 6, 1945*

COMDESPAC	
Rear Admiral M. F. Draemel	*As of Sept. 1940*
Rear Admiral R. A. Theobald	*Dec. 31, 1941*
Rear Admiral W. L. Ainsworth	*July 4, 1942*
Rear Admiral M. S. Tisdale	*Jan. 8, 1943*
Rear Admiral J. L. Kauffman	*Jan. 2, 1944*
Rear Admiral W. L. Ainsworth	*Oct. 31, 1944*
Rear Admiral W. H. P. Blandy	*July 13, 1945*

The largest destroyer group within the Fleet set-up is the flotilla. The word, defined as "A fleet of small ships, or a small fleet," applies destroyer-wise, either way.

At the beginning of the war there were two Destroyer Flotillas in the Pacific. They were commanded by Rear Admiral R. A. Theobald (ComDesFlot One), and Rear Admiral M. F. Draemel (ComDesFlot Two).

Destroyers were also grouped in Task Flotillas. There were six of these Task Flotillas in operation during the war. Like the larger flotillas, their make-up was flexible. A Fleet Commander might borrow ships from one Task Flotilla to support another, or to carry out some special assignment. Effort was made, however, to keep these groups semi-permanent, and employ them as a body. The Commander of a Destroyer Flotilla (ComTaskFlot) was a Commodore. The officers who served in this capacity are listed for reference in the Addenda.

The Destroyer Task Flotilla is composed of two or more destroyer squadrons. Destroyer squadrons are composed of two (occasionally three) destroyer divisions. There is no standard size for the squadron; no set number of ships in the division. The average squadron contained nine destroyers—a division composed of five, and a division of four. However, the destroyer squadron (DesRon) may contain two full divisions and two units of a third division. A destroyer division (DesDiv) may contain four, five, or six DD's.

A World War II newcomer was the Escort Division (CortDiv), which was composed of destroyer-escorts.

The commander of a destroyer squadron (ComDesRon) was usually a Captain. He would fly his "broad command pennant" in the designated flagship of his squadron, and he was in charge of all ships in the squadron.

The commander of a destroyer division (ComDesDiv) was usually a Commander, although he might be a Captain. He flew his pennant in the ship that was division leader.

The commander of an escort division (ComCortDiv) was usually a Commander, although occasionally a Lieutenant Commander. He flew his pennant in the lead-ship of his division.

Comparable to military field commanders, destroyer squadron and division commanders were combat leaders who fought the war on the front line—often enough, behind the enemy's lines. Tactical officers, they led their ships into action and quarterbacked the destroyer team-play.

The names of these All-American destroyer leaders are listed in the Addenda.

Destroyer Guns

Unlike warships of larger type, the World War II destroyer did not carry turret guns. Largest caliber on the American DD was the 5-inch 38 which was housed in a movable mount. The average destroyer (medium size) carried four such guns, the FLETCHER class carried five, and the larger SUMNER and GEARING classes, which came later, carried six of them in three twin mounts.

Hydraulic machinery moved the mount in train (to left or right), and it also elevated or depressed the gun. This gun housing is neither shell- nor bombproof, but serves as a splinter shield.

Such lighter guns as the 20-mm. and the 40 mm. stood in open "gun tubs." These "tubs" were stationary and served as shields only.

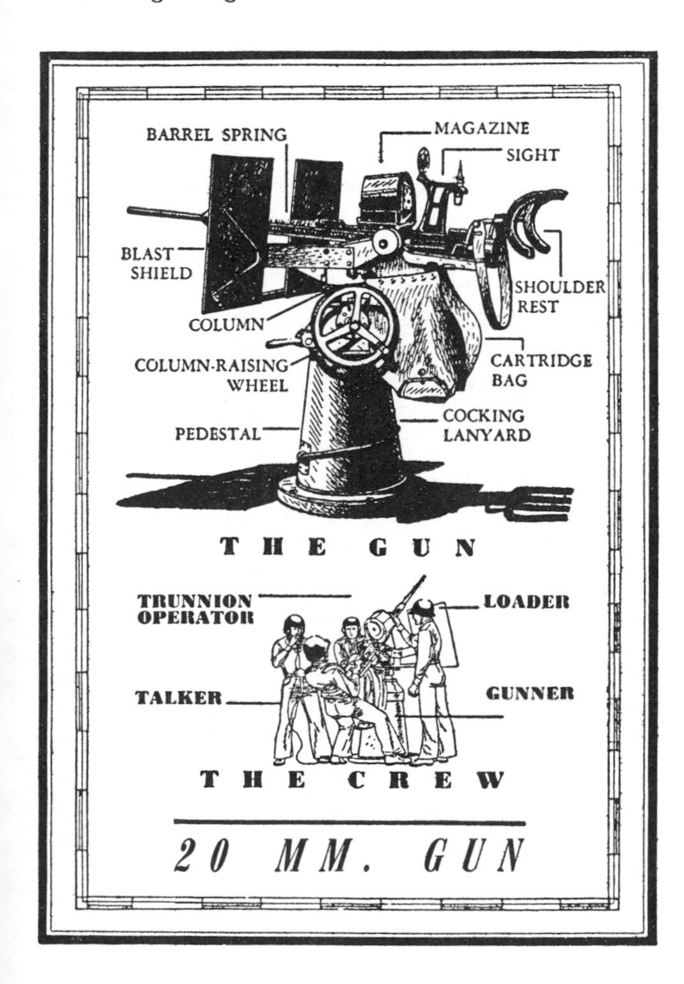

20 MM. GUN

The 5-inch 38's composed the destroyer's main battery. The lighter automatic guns composed the secondary battery. The ship's arsenal also included such machine-guns as the Browning .50 caliber, "Tommy guns," rifles, and weapons of similar caliber.

For a close-up of the guns, the 20 mm. (or Oerlikon) is a close-range, air cooled, automatic anti-aircraft gun firing an explosive projectile with a maximum range of something over 4,000 yards. Mounted on a pedestal, it is trained, elevated, loaded, and fired by manual operation.

The gun fires automatically as long as the trigger is depressed and there is ammunition in the drum-shaped magazine. It may be aimed by means of ring sight with the more or less conventional "peep sight," or the target may be tracked by means of a complicated sight which gives a mirror view and contains a gyroscopic device that compensates for the roll, pitch, yaw, or speed-change of the ship.

The rate of fire is about 450 rounds per minute. Ammunition includes tracer—the glowing projectile which goes through the air like a ball of phosphorescent light, and which indicates to the gunner the direction of fire.

The gun crew consists of the gunner (who aims and fires the weapon), trunnion operator (who adjusts the trunnion height to correspond with the gunner's position), range setter (who sets the range data into the gyroscopic sight), and two loaders.

The 40 mm., designed after the Swedish Bofors gun, is a rapid-fire, automatic, anti-aircraft gun possessed of the qualities of both a cannon and a machine-gun. It is capable of firing approximately 160 rounds per minute. Effective range varies with the type of ammunition used, but most useful range is somewhere around 2,800 yards.

The 40 mm. "single" is air cooled, manually controlled, and fired by the crew at the gun. The twins and quads (double-barreled and quadruple-barreled, respectively) are water cooled, and can be operated by remote director control, as well as local control. The local control of these mounts can be accomplished by hand-wheel operation of the gear train, or by a "joystick" control of the hydraulic system. Two types of power drives are used to position the 40 mm. mounts in train and elevation—in all-electric, found in most twin mounts, and the electric-hydraulic in nearly all the quads. The remote or director control of these mounts is accomplished by means of a fire-control director.

Ammunition is fed into the gun's loader by hand, in clips of four rounds. The gun machinism is fully

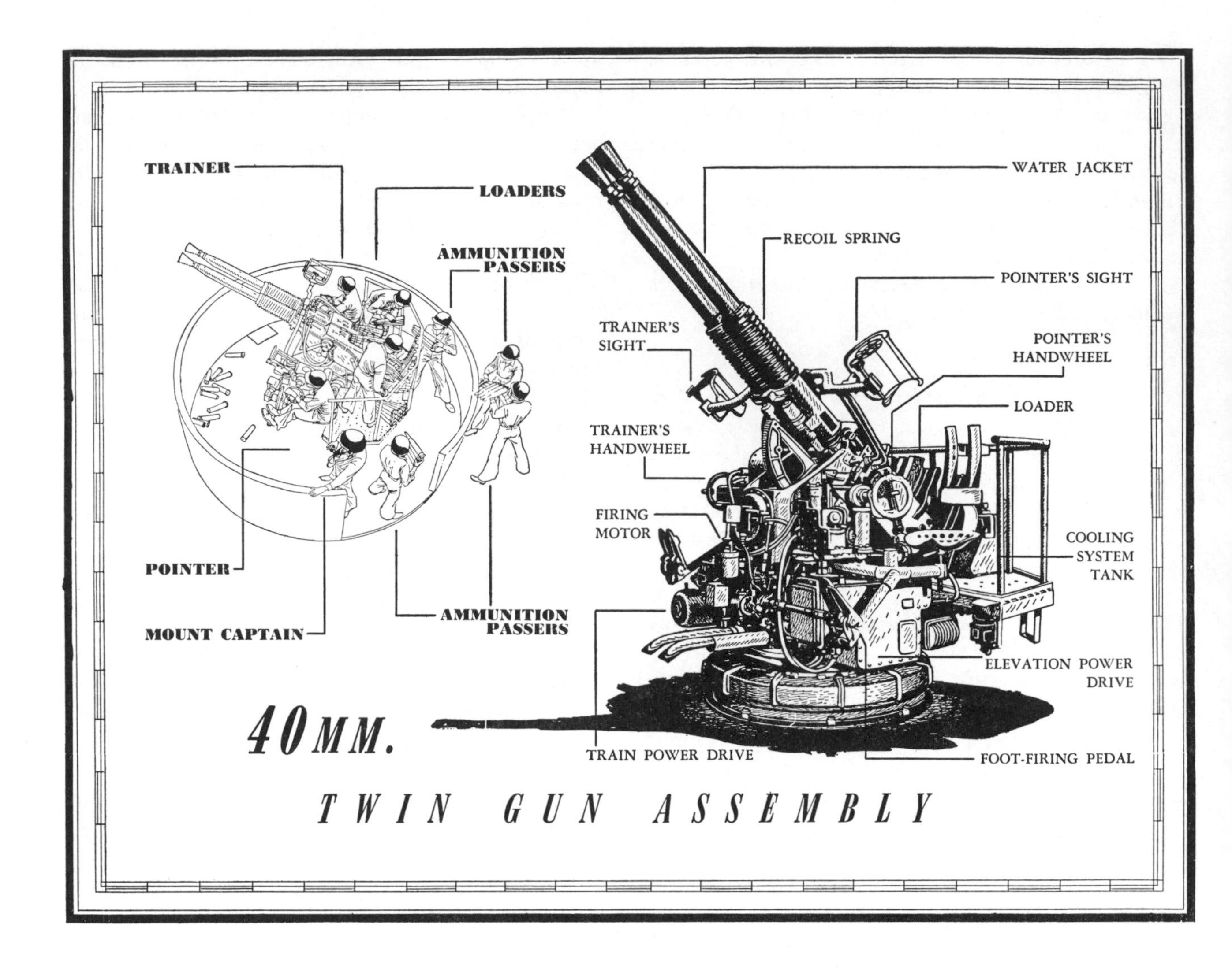

automatic in that it operates through recoil. There are three methods of firing: manual fire, local-power fire, and director-power fire. Under local control, the gun may be fired by means of a foot treadle, or by a firing motor operated by a clutch. Under director (remote) control, the gunners at the mount stand by and the gun is power-fired by the director.

The local sight assembly consists of a pointer's sight and a trainer's sight, and is similar to the ring-type sight of the 20 mm. When the gun is director controlled, these sights are not used; the target is tracked by the director.

The size of the 40 mm. gun crew depends on the mount. The crew of a single consists of four men: pointer, trainer, and two loaders. In the crew of a twin there are seven men: pointer, trainer, gun captain, and four loaders. The quad crew contains eleven men: pointer, trainer, gun captain, and eight loaders. When the mount is under local control, the pointer moves the gun in train and elevation, and fires the gun by foot pedal. In all-electric power drive mounts, the trainer moves the mount in train. The gun captain oversees the gun's operation, coaches the team work of the crew, and steps in as a replacement in the event of a crew casualty.

The 40-mm. is the Navy's largest machine-gun.

For a while U.S. destroyers carried 1.1-inch anti-aircraft guns, but owing to problems of operation and maintenance these were eventually discarded.

The 5-inch 38-caliber, the destroyer's main-battery weapon, is a dual-purpose, semi-automatic, rapid-fire gun good for an anti-aircraft barrage, for salvos at surface targets, and for shore bombardment. In its movable, enclosed mount, it possesses such features as high-speed power drives for train and elevation, a hydraulic rammer which loads the gun, local handwheel control and remote director control, a firing key for electrical firing, a foot mechanism for percussion firing, a sight mechanism which contains three telescopes, and a set of instruments which receive fire-control directions transmitted from a remote gun-director.

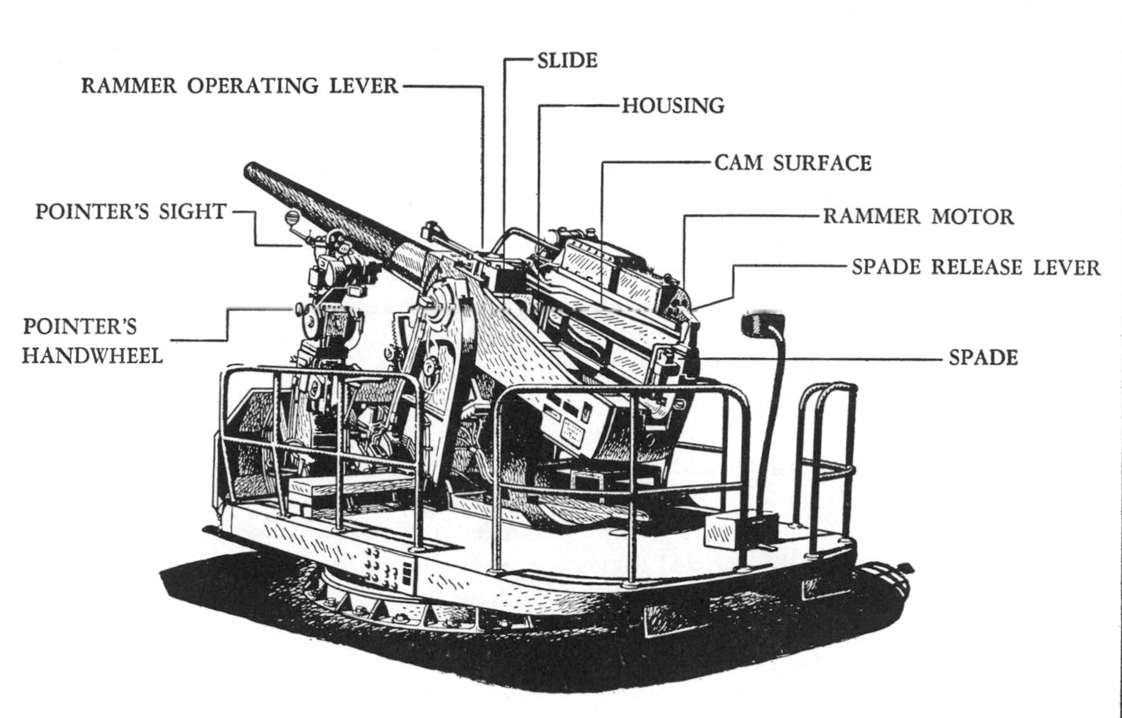

THE GUN

SINGLE MOUNT, REAR VIEW

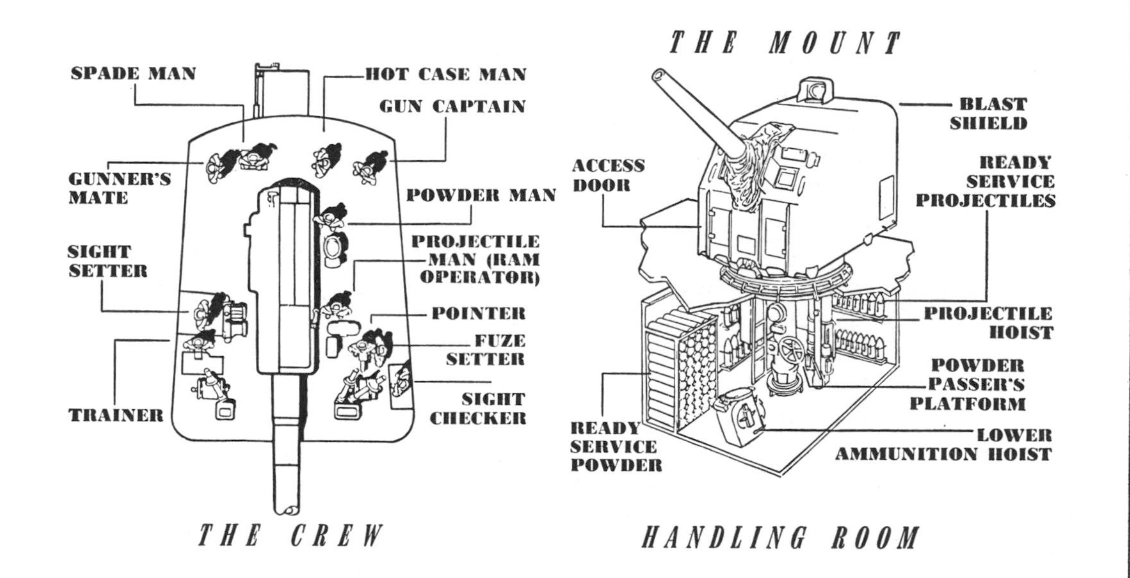

THE CREW *HANDLING ROOM*

5-INCH 38-CALIBER GUN

TYPICAL DESTROYER GUN OF WORLD WAR II

Shooting at a surface target, this big gun can throw a 54-pound projectile a good 18,000 yards. Its maximum aerial range is over six miles! The gun fires an average of 15 rounds per minute, and crack destroyer gun crews obtained a rate of fire as high as 22 rounds per minute.

The single-mount 5-inch 38 and the twin-mount 5-inch 38 are both moved in train and elevation by hydraulic power drives. The gun crew is composed of pointer, trainer, sight-setter, gun captain, fuse-setter, hot shellman, loaders, and handling-room crew. When the gun is under local control, the pointer and trainer operate handwheels and speed selectors which control the power drives. Automatic (remote) control from a director system is accomplished by means of electric signals transmitted to mechanisms which control the mount's hydraulic machinery. The sight mechanism of this big gun is too complicated for brief discussion.

The 5-inch 38 mount is usually installed over an ammunition handling room, and the gun is serviced by means of power-driven powder and projectile hoists equipped with automatic fuse-setting devices for adjusting the fuse on a projectile according to order.

Torpedoes and Tube Mounts

The torpedoes carried into World War II by American destroyers were complicated weapons. Various models were used, but the best in service at war's beginning were 21-inchers (21 inches in diameter) propelled by the air-alcohol-water, superheated gas-turbine system. This torpedo weighed 2,215 pounds when readied for a warshot, and cost about $10,000.

By a complex set of mechanisms the torpedo, once launched, maneuvered itself to run at a pre-selected depth and steered itself to the target. The 21-incher could maintain a speed of 46 knots for a run of 4,500 yards. In effect, it operated as a miniature self-guiding submarine carrying an explosive charge of about 500 pounds of T.N.T. to the bull's-eye. (In later models the charge was increased to 1,100 pounds of torpex.) There was only one trouble with this remarkable engine of destruction. Too often it missed the mark.

Early in the war American submariners and destroyermen discovered that the weapon's depth-setting mechanism contained "bugs" which caused the torpedo to run deeper than set. When this flaw was corrected by various adjustments, the problem of duds plagued the Navy's torpedomen. The fault lay in a defective exploder device attached to the warhead. Adopted by the Navy and issued to the Destroyer Service late in 1941, this exploder mechanism was a "Buck Rogers" affair which was supposed to detonate the warhead when the torpedo came within the target ship's field of magnetic influence. Desired result was an explosion which would occur just under an enemy vessel's keel or immediately beneath the protective bulges of an enemy capital ship. Such an explosion was calculated to do more damage than the blast of a contact hit.

Unfortunately the magnetic exploder proved a "bust." Highly sensitized, it frequently "prematured"—blew up at a point near the target, but too far from the hull to wreak damage. Flooding was another common fault of this exploder. And its tricky firing system was subject to maladjustment when the launched torpedo struck water in a plunge and went racing through the sea at high speed. Ironically enough, the Nazis, who invented this mechanism, had discarded it as unreliable in 1939, preferring the tried and true certainty of the conventional contact exploder. After months of painful error, the U.S. Navy abandoned the device. (On July 24, 1943, Admiral Nimitz, Commander-in-Chief Pacific Fleet, ordered ComDesPac to inactivate magnetic exploders on all torpedoes.)

In other respects the American torpedo was below par. The Japanese had the jump on this deadly weapon. By 1933 their ordnance experts had produced a torpedo which ran on fuel enriched with oxygen. Next Japanese development was a torpedo entirely oxygen-fueled. During the war, they showed up with a 24-inch torpedo which had a speed of 49.2 knots and a range of almost 6,000 yards, and was armed with a warhead containing 1,210 pounds of explosive—over twice the charge of the American 21-incher. Before war's end the Japanese produced a torpedo with a range of 22,000 yards. These oxygen-driven monsters were practically "wakeless."

By comparison, the American torpedo was a poor "fish." But the torpedomen in the U.S. Destroyer Service made the best and the most of it. And before the war was over the Bureau of Ordnance was issuing electrical (battery-driven) torpedoes and was working on a "homing" torpedo possessed of an accoustic device which would lead it to the target. These late-war torpedo developments were of great value to the American Submarine Force, but destroyer warfare had by then passed the torpedo stage. After the Battle for Leyte, U.S. destroyers had little opportunity to make torpedo attacks. Perhaps the chief reason was dearth of enemy targets—the Pacific was all but "fished out" by that date. But the DD itself had changed character. Originally designed as a torpedo vessel, the destroyer had assumed new and more important roles as a sub-hunter, gunfighter, and AA vessel.

Standard torpedo launching-gear on American destroyers consisted of tube mounts located on deck amidships. On old destroyers the mounts were placed on the port and the starboard side of the ship. New destroyers usually carried the tube mounts on the center line. The modern mount was quintuple—a battery of five individual tubes. The mounts revolved automatically, were trained by director-control, and were fired by remote control. Torpedoes could be fired individually or in salvo. Carrying two mounts, a destroyer could thus launch a full salvo of ten torpedoes at a time.

Destroyer Fire-Control System (Featuring the Director)

As the foregoing sketch concerning destroyer armament would indicate, the automatic guns carried by the DD's of World War II were mechanical marvels: the gunners become stand-by auxiliaries; only the loaders are needed to feed the weapon. Because it is one of the principal elements in the modern destroyer's fire-control system (the others are the computer or range-keeper, and the gyroscopic stable element or stable vertical), the director merits brief discussion.

The director is an instrument that locates the target. The computer, linked to the director, automatically solves the fire-control problem and transmits electrical gun signals to position (aim) the gun. The gyroscopic stable element provides corrections for pitch and roll of the ship.

The director station is located above the ship's bridge. The director gear includes telescopes, which operate like the pointer's and trainer's of an individual gun, an optical range finder, and radar.

The controlmen get on the target and keep it

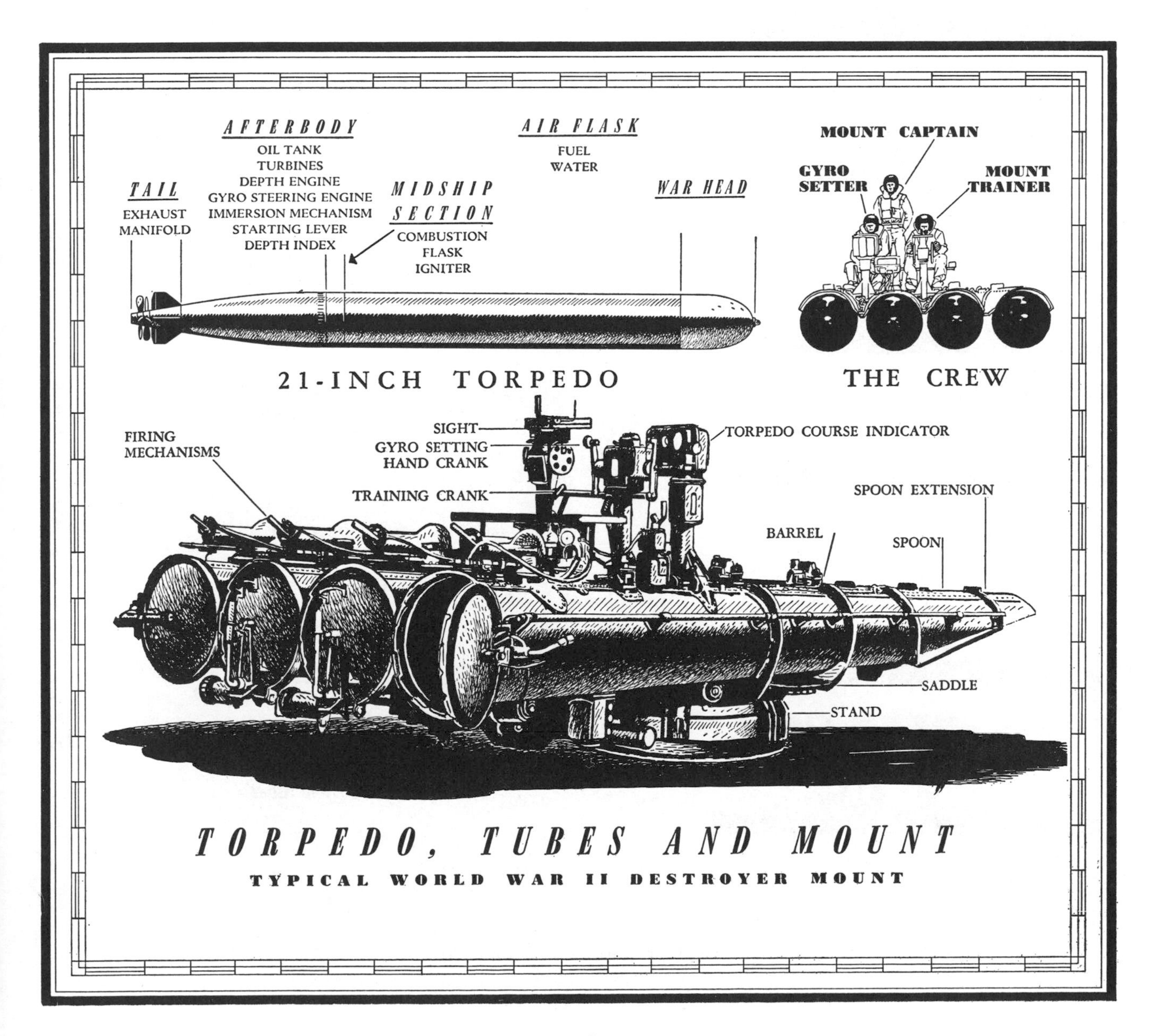

TORPEDO, TUBES AND MOUNT

TYPICAL WORLD WAR II DESTROYER MOUNT

CHARACTERISTICS OF THE WORLD WAR II DESTROYER

Destroyer Class	*Displacement (Tons)*	*Length (Feet)*	*Speed (Knots) (Approximately)*	*Complement (Approximately)*	*Original Armament*	*Year Commissioned*
CLEMSON 	*1,200*	*314*	*35*	200	*four 4-inch 50's* *six 21-inch tubes*	*1916* *1920*
CRAVEN 	*1,500*	*341*	*35*	*250*	*four 5-inch 38's* *sixteen 21-inch tubes*	*1934*
MAHAN 	*1,450*	*341*	*35*	*250*	*five 5-inch 38's* *twelve 21-inch tubes*	*1936*
SIMS 	*1,570*	*347*	*37*	*250*	*five 5-inch 38's* *twelve 21-inch tubes*	*1939* *1940*
BRISTOL 	*1,630*	*348*	*37*	*275*	*four 5-inch 38's* *two 40-mm twins* *ten 21-inch tubes*	*1940* *1943*
FLETCHER	*2,050*	*376½*	*35*	*345*	*five 5-inch 38's* *five 40-mm twins* *ten 21-inch tubes*	*1942* *1944*
RUDDEROW *(Destroyer Escort)* 	*1,450*	*306*	*24*	220	*two 5-inch 38's* *two 40-mm twins* *three 21-inch tubes*	*1943* *1945*
SUMNER 	*2,200*	*376½*	*34*	*345*	*six 5-inch 38's* *two 40-mm quads* *two 40-mm twins* *ten 21-inch tubes*	*1944* *1945*

(All ships armed with 20 mm. A.A.)

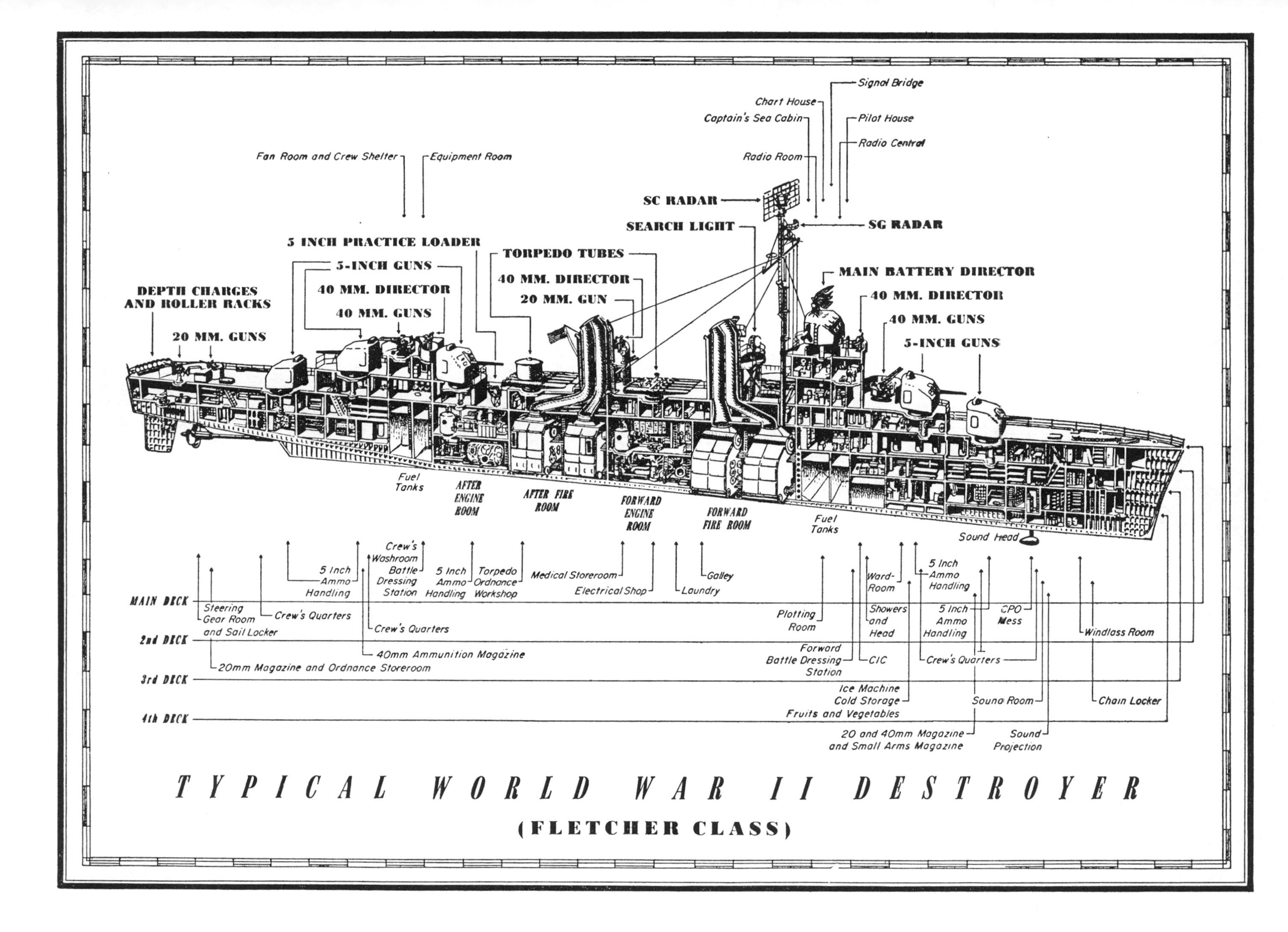

TYPICAL WORLD WAR II DESTROYER
(FLETCHER CLASS)

lined up on the crosshairs of their telescopes. Range and line-of-sight data are then transmitted electrically to a plotting room below decks where other factors such as speed and direction of the ship, probable speed of target, target angle, ballistics, and weather factors are calculated. These computations are made by means of the computer, a mechanism of intricate gears, shafting, and dials which may be called the "brains" of the system which has the director as its "eyes."

Through electrical lines and synchro-electric motors, gun orders are transmitted from the computer to indicators at the different gun mounts. By this means the electro-hydraulically driven mounts are automatically positioned in train and elevation. Fuze settings are similarly relayed; types of ammunition to be fired may be signalled to the mounts; the guns are fired electrically. Under this type of director control (known as automatic control) the gun crew at the mount has no duties to perform other than load the gun.

If the fully automatic mechanism should fail, the pointer and trainer at the mount can turn their handwheels to match the dials with the incoming signals. The mount is still under director control since the gun orders are still coming from the director and computer, and registering on the indicator on the mount. The training and elevation of the gun are handled by "matching pointers."

The fire-control system described above applies to the destroyer's 5-inch 38 batteries. The 40 mm. batteries may operate under a less complicated system, although on some installations they can be hooked up to the 5-inch director system.

The director used for the 40 mm. anti-aircraft gun is somewhat similar to the plane-tracking device familiar to patrons of the Penny Arcade where the customer looks through a telescope at a miniature target plane travelling across a screen, and tracks the plane by moving a handle. The operator of the 40 mm. director tracks his target in much the same manner, training and elevating by means of handle grips to follow the plane across the sky. The movements of the director are transmitted through synchro-electric motors to the gun mount which automatically "goes through the motions" in train and elevation.

Guns lifting their muzzles to the sky, swinging this way and that, firing rapid salvos—and the crew never moving a hand except to load? Mechanical marvels, yes. But modern destroyers were supplied with even more wonderful devices. The new word in 1940 was "electronics." Short wave radio—sonar—radar!

Radio, of course, is essentially a communication instrument. As such, it serves as a fire-control aid much as would a speaking trumpet, semaphore signals, or any other device for conveying information and orders. Reference in point is to the radiotelephone which was installed in modern destroyers.

Radio was indispensable as the Navy's long-range messenger. For the handling of radio traffic, the Navy had long used the "Fox System." In this system a small number of powerful shore-side radio stations collected the messages intended for ships at sea, and these were broadcast in code on long-range, very-low frequency broadcasts known as "Fox" schedules. Each ship had an individual call sign and could receive messages, but it would not answer them. For the "Fox" symbol meant "Do not answer—or the enemy's direction-finders might locate you by your signals."

But communications between the ships of a task group or convoy, and between surface vessels and aircraft, were another problem. Visual signals and even steam whistles might be employed, but fog or wild weather could prevent the use of these signals, and blinker lights at night would, of course, breach the blackout. The best method of intra-group communication was the high-frequency voice radio or radiotelephone, which normally had a range of something less than 30 miles.

By 1941 many ships of the Navy, destroyers included, were equipped with the TBS—a low-powered, short-range voice radio dubbed "Talk Between Ships." Other types of radiotelephones were currently in use. A portable set (the TBY) was eventually supplied to many merchantmen. Aircraft also were provided with special radiotelephones.

The TBS instrument was extremely handy for destroyer work. It enabled destroyers on escort duty to talk with vessels in convoy. Destroyer squadron or division commanders could bark rapid-fire orders to their units. The group leader of a "hunter-killer" destroyer team could call the moves like a quarterback on the gridiron. Born with voice radio was the fighter-director system by means of which a DD carrying a trained fighter-director officer could summon friendly aircraft and coach the fighters into position to intercept attacking enemy bombers. By TBS, too, a destroyer could exchange words with a shore party equipped with "walky-talky."

The radio-telephone system was an open "party line," and the enemy might listen in. Voice radio was short-range, but, owing to what is known as "skip zone" phenomena, voice messages were occasionally heard 600, 700, and even 900 miles away.

Radio and radiotelephony, then, were not unmixed blessings. And since the enemy possessed such

Heavyweight champion of U.S. destroyer forces during the toughest war years was the Fletcher-class. In their 2,050 tons and 376½ foot length they carried complements of 330 at 35 knots speed. Their lethal punch of five 5-inch and five 40 mm guns and eight torpedo tubes was abetted by depth charges, sonar, and electronics. Shown here is U.S.S. Terry, off Saipan in early 1944.

Early victim of a German submarine torpedo. The U.S.S. Jacob Jones, torpedoed by the U-53 during World War I, was the first and only American man-o'-war sunk by torpedo during that war.

The second Jacob Jones was likewise unlucky. One of the older "four-pipers," patrolling alone, she was sunk by a German submarine off Cape May, just before dawn on February 28, 1942.

A real nest of trouble! In this picture four different types of the mighty "cans" are shown tied up alongside the destroyer tender Dobbin. From left to right are the Dobbin, the Lovering (a destroyer escort), the Welles (a Bristol-class DD), the Mustin (of the Sims class), and the Fletcher (of the "Fighting Fletcher" class). This picture was taken in Seeadler Harbor, Admiralty Islands.

Old Ocean comes aboard. It was up to the destroyers to keep the sea and they refueled underway in all sorts of weather. Here the U.S.S. Zellars is shown refueling from the carrier Kearsarge. A Sumner-class destroyer, the Zellars was 2,200 tons displacement, with a complement of 345, and carried six 5-inch guns, twelve 40 mm guns in four mounts, torpedo tubes, and depth charges.

equipment, these instruments gave the Navy's warships no singular advantage. It was in the field of electronic detection gear—radar and sonar—that the advantage was all on the American (and Allied) side. Radar, in particular. The Germans were never able to cope with it, and the Japanese never caught up with it.

Radar: a long-range detection device for locating objects on the sea or in the air—icebergs, surface ships, surfaced submarines, aircraft. In effect, a superhuman lookout, an "all-seeing eye."

Sonar: a detection device for locating objects under the sea—submerged obstacles, submarines. In effect, an acute underwater perception-instrument nerved to communicate sound to a sensitive "ear."

Emitting impulses similar to radio waves, both radar and sonar "bounced a beam" off the intercepted target—a beam which came back to the sender, and was registered as a flicker of light or "pip" on the radar screen, or an audible crackle, an echoing "ping," in the sonarman's listening gear.

An indirect descendant of the early hydrophone, and cousin of the British "Asdic," sonar was common in the U.S. Navy before the outbreak of World War II. An instrument for submarine detection, it was a natural for destroyers, and all American DD's were equipped with the apparatus. A brief account of its workings follows in Chapter 5.

Radio phenomena noted by two American scientists working at the Naval Aircraft Radio Laboratory in Anacostia, D.C., in 1922 led to the discovery of radar. Informed of the American experiments, British scientists followed the lead, and American and British radar devices were developed simultaneously. The first radar sets widely in action were the aircraft-detectors that went a long way toward winning the Battle of Britain. Surface radar (the Navy's "search radar") was just emerging from the experimental chrysalis at that time.

The first American search radar set went to sea in April 1937 on the United States destroyer LEARY. Installed by the Naval Research Laboratory, the set was a "hush-hush" item if there ever was one.

In December 1938 the U.S.S. NEW YORK was equipped with radar gear designed by the Naval Research Laboratory. Battleship TEXAS was given an RCA-built radar in January 1939. Six American naval vessels received radar installations before the end of 1940—CALIFORNIA, CHESTER, CHICAGO, PENSACOLA, NORTHAMPTON, YORKTOWN. By the autumn of 1941, the weird "bedsprings" were a familiar sight topside; installations were spreading through the Fleet, and American destroyers were slated to receive their share. Pioneering, destroyer LEARY could take a bow for making the first radar contact on a U-boat in American naval history. The date was November 19, 1941. But it was not until the summer of 1942 that most of the Navy's warships were furnished with radar of one kind or another. The improved, long-range SG ("Sugar George") model, designed for use against ships only, was not distributed until the autumn of that year. The destroyer that carried search radar in 1941 considered itself lucky.

Radar's radical influence on naval warfare was comparable to that of the Crecy cannon on medieval military tactics. No longer could an enemy ship or squadron or plane make an undetected approach in black night or blinding fog. No longer could a submarine lie low on the surface, confident it could not be seen in darkness, "sun slick," or surface haze.

Operating with radar, scouting destroyers could cover an area many leagues larger than those covered by scouts dependent on 20-20 vision and binoculars. As pickets on the lookout for enemy aircraft, radar-carrying DD's could penetrate an overcast and spot enemy planes miles beyond the range of binocular vision. With the "pip" on the luminous screen recording the target's range and bearing, radar became the key element in the warship's fire-control system. And radar was equally invaluable in navigation.

With the single exception of the atom bomb, radar was the most amazing development of World War II.

Combat Information Center (The C.I.C.)

Invention of the radiotelephone and the advent of radar and other detection devices introduced a new problem into the operational picture. With all kinds of information coming in on all sorts of instruments from all points of the compass, the warship on the receiving end was swamped with vital intelligence. The need for a coordinating center, a sort of information clearing-house on board ship, became imperative. In order to assemble, evaluate and disseminate all this data continually arriving via radio, visual means, radar, and sonar, a central "brain" was needed. In consequence, the Combat Information Center (C.I.C.) was organized early in the war.

The C.I.C. was not a mechanical brain, although switchboards, computers, and other contrivances were in the set-up. It was simply an agency for collecting and evaluating incoming information, fitting the various items into their respective places in the tactical scheme of things, and relaying same to appropriate control stations on the ship, or to neighboring vessels.

Here is a flash from the radar watch: "Target 10,000 yards ahead!" A moment later, word over

TBS from a near-by DD: "Enemy submarine to starboard!" Simultaneously, a signal from a distant squadron leader ordering a course change—say, a turn to the right. And then the aircraft radar picks up enemy planes approaching astern. To complicate the problem, assume the destroyer receiving these flashes is operating with a task group steaming into battle against an enemy force. A dozen near-by ships, American or Allied, are in sight. Another group is on the radar screen. How to keep track of the friendly ships, to handle the target ahead, to cope with the submarine situation, to evade the detected aircraft—it was up to the ship's C.I.C. to make order out of this chaos, and to inform the conning officer and gunnery officer accordingly.

The Combat Information Center, then, was comparable to a military field headquarters, which received and digested dozens of reports, maintained an over-all picture of the constantly shifting battle scene, and sent various forces into action.

In destroyers the charthouse originally served as the information collection center. As the C.I.C. organization developed, so did the need for space, and the center was soon provided with its own room. The C.I.C. was manned by a team of officers and men trained for this complex activity. Size and composition of the team varied according to the ship and the information-gathering equipment available. In charge of the C.I.C. was the ship's Executive Officer.

Second World War

When the Chief of Naval Operations, Admiral W. D. Leahy, announced the formation of the Navy's Atlantic Squadron in September 1938, the American destroyer fleet had yet to be modernized. About 40 of the BENHAM, SIMS, BENSON, BRISTOL, PORTER, CRAVEN, and MAHAN class DD's were on the ocean. The old flush-deck four-stackers were still the mainstay of the destroyer arm. By the summer of 1939 destroyer strength of the Atlantic Squadron consisted of Destroyer Divisions 10, 21, 25, 30, 31, 32—about 30 DD's. About 50 destroyers were on duty with the Pacific forces based at Pearl Harbor. A squadron of old-timers was serving with the Asiatic Fleet in the Philippines area. At Norfolk, Newport, and other bases a few new destroyers were readying for "shakedown" cruises.

Then, on September 1, 1939, Hitler touched off the Armageddon that was to kill 20,000,000 people. World War II was begun.

On September 3, 1939, England and France, honoring treaty commitments, declared war on Nazi Germany. Twelve hours later the British passenger liner ATHENIA with many Americans aboard was torpedoed and sunk by a U-boat off northwest Ireland with the loss of 112 passengers, including many women and children. The Battle of the Atlantic was on.

On September 8, 1939, President Roosevelt issued a proclamation of limited national emergency to *"safeguard and enforce"* the neutrality of the United States, and to *"strengthen our national defenses."* Empowered to do so by the Neutrality Act, the President forbade American shipping to enter the war zones, which included the North Sea, the Bay of Biscay, and the waters around the British Isles to a line some 350 miles west of Ireland.

On September 14, 1939, the Navy Department announced that 40 of the 110 destroyers in "mothballs" would be recommissioned for neutrality-patrol duty. That same day the U.S.S. MUSTIN—60th destroyer built since 1934—was commissioned.

History Repeats

Aside from such spectacular exploits as the sinking of the aircraft carrier H.M.S. COURAGEOUS (September 17, 1939) and the torpedoing of the battleship ROYAL OAK in Scapa Flow (October 14, 1939), the Nazi U-boat Force enjoyed no such early success as its World War I predecessor. During the winter of the "phony war" British naval and merchant shipping losses were relatively light. Prompt institution of a British Anti-Submarine Warfare Command softened the enemy's undersea punch. Land-based aircraft prevented a tight U-boat blockade of the United Kingdom.

Then the tide abruptly turned against the Allies. Numerous factors caused the turn. To begin with, the German Navy entered the war with only 76 U-boats in commission, and but 43 ready for combat duty. This number was quickly raised by a building program geared for rapid expansion. By the summer of 1940 German submarine construction had jumped from a monthly output of two or three to something like 25.

The German submariners entered the war with a torpedo equipped with a defective "influence exploder" mechanism. After U-47 (*Kapitan-Leutnant* Gunther Prien) fired a brace of duds during the Scapa Flow raid, this faulty magnetic exploder was promptly discarded in favor of the old, reliable contact exploder.

Then the German seizure of Norway in the spring of 1940 put U-boat bases on Britain's northern flank. Seizure of Holland and Belgium installed them on the Channel. When France collapsed in June 1940, Germany became an Atlantic power. Italy's "backstab" entry into the war at that time placed the Axis athwart the Mediterranean. And British shipping losses promptly mounted to an alarming figure.

But it was the *Rudeltaktik,* or wolfpack, that sank Britain's hopes of holding the Atlantic line. The wolfpack was the creation of Admiral Karl Doenitz, keen and ruthless commander of the German U-boat Force. Instead of trying to clamp a blockade on the British Isles, the new idea was to cut Britain's shipping lanes in the open Atlantic. Simply move the U-boats to mid-ocean where they would be beyond range of Allied land-based aircraft. Work the subs in teams—packs of eight or nine. Mass attack, always stronger than individual, could scatter the convoy's defenses, force the escorts to disperse. Then the stalking subs could strike in through the tattered screen.

The *Rudeltaktik* called for surface attacks at night. Convoys spotted in daytime were reported by the sub which made contact. Doenitz's headquarters would then order the nearest pack to converge on the convoy and lie in ambush. After dark the pack would strike. Thus the U-boat could take advantage of night's cover and of the high speed of a surface run under Diesel-engine power.

Deprived of air cover, the convoy in mid-ocean was bereft of one of its strongest defenses. Protection was entirely up to the escort vessels guarding the ship-train. "Asdic," the British submarine-detection device, was not enough. Deck guns and depth charges were not enough. And at the outset the British were caught short of escort vessels.

All types of escort vessels were in demand—corvettes, cutters, any ship that could be rigged to carry A/S gear. But the big need, the crying need was destroyers. Great Britain did not have them. The Royal Navy, at the start of the war, possessed only 185 DD's. And at Dunkerque in May 1940 the British suffered staggering destroyer casualties—ten destroyers sunk and 75 disabled.

In May 1940 Winston Churchill sent a cable to Franklin D. Roosevelt.

WE URGENTLY NEED DESTROYERS

The Great Swap (Fifty Over-Age DD's for Bases)

At the date of Churchill's cable, the United States Navy had in service 171 destroyers, counting the 40 old-timers recommissioned in the autumn of 1939. There remained 70 of the old-fashioned World War I four-pipers in "mothballs."

Roosevelt turned down Churchill's proposition—a trade of bases for 50 of the over-age destroyers.

There was a fortnight in the following July when the Royal Navy lost 11 more DD's. Britain's situation was desperate. Alone, her people faced the Nazi conquerors of Western Europe. Backs to the wall, they prepared to meet invasion. The Prime Minister sent Roosevelt another urgent appeal.

MR PRESIDENT WITH GREAT RESPECT I MUST TELL YOU THAT IN THE LONG HISTORY OF THE WORLD THIS IS A THING TO DO NOW

Convinced of Britain's jeopardy, Roosevelt agreed to the destroyer trade. Existing law had tied his hands; he could not dispose of military supplies unless they were condemned as useless. Admiral Stark, however, found a legal loophole in the exchange for Atlantic bases. As Thomas Jefferson had acted without the consent of Congress to purchase Louisiana, so Roosevelt now acted to trade the 50 over-age U.S. destroyers for 99-year rights to establish United States bases in the Bahamas, Jamaica, Antigua, St. Lucia, Trinidad, and British Guiana. The old DD's were worth millions of dollars—but the naval bases were worth many aircraft carriers. Both sides were agreed it was a fair deal.

The destroyer-naval base agreement was reached on September 2, 1940. On September 4th the old U.S.S. AARON WARD steamed out of Boston Harbor, bound for Halifax, to be turned over to the British there. She was followed by destroyers HALE and ABEL P. UPSHUR, with 47 more to follow.

They were old-timers, all right, these 1,190-ton, over-age destroyers, with their four 4-inch guns and single 3-inch anti-aircraft gun. But they could make 35 knots, and they could drop depth charges with the best of them.

The exchange sent reverberations through Fascist Rome and Nazi Berlin. Hitler raged. Mussolini threatened. Doenitz was ordered to throw unrestricted submarine warfare into high gear. The tide which had turned so heavily against Britain was temporarily stemmed.

Entering the Royal Navy, the old "four-pipers" were given new names. The British, always appreciative of symbolism, decided to rechristen the DD's with names common to towns in both England and the United States. Hence U.S.S. AARON WARD was rechristened H.M.S. CASTLETON. U.S.S. PHILIP became H.M.S. LANCASTER. U.S.S. MACKENZIE became H.M.S. ANNAPOLIS. And so on.

Seven of these old-timers went down in action with the enemy—H.M.S. BEVERLEY (formerly U.S.S. BRANCH); H.M.S. STANLEY (formerly U.S.S. MCCALLA); H.M.S. BELMONT (formerly U.S.S. SATTERLEE); H.M.S. BATH (formerly U.S.S. HOPEWELL); H.M.S. BROADWATER (formerly U.S.S. MASON); H.M.S. ROCKINGHAM (formerly U.S.S. SWASEY); H.M.S. CAMPBELTOWN (formerly U.S.S. BUCHANAN).

The old greyhounds did not go under without

a fight. They, and all 50, struck punishing blows in the Battle of the Atlantic. H.M.S. Beverly killed a U-boat. H.M.S. Stanley killed three. H.M.S. Broadway (formerly U.S.S. Hunt) killed two U-boats. H.M.S. Leamington (formerly U.S.S. Twiggs) killed one. And H.M.S. Campbeltown, sacrificed in the exploit, blew up the entry to the harbor of St. Nazaire.

After Pearl Harbor there were officials who criticized the handing over of the 50 destroyers to Britain. To one outspoken critic Admiral Stark replied that the transferred DD's, instead of sitting immobile, had been fighting the Atlantic Battle for nearly a year.

The 50 over-age destroyers with their American and British names are listed below.

U.S. NAME	BRITISH NAME	U.S. NAME	BRITISH NAME	U.S. NAME	BRITISH NAME
Herndon	Churchill	Hunt	Broadway	Meade	Ramsey
Aaron Ward	Castleton	Satterlee	Belmont	Shubrick	Ripley
W. C. Wood	Chesterfield	Laub	Burwell	Swasey	Rockingham
Hale	Caldwell	McLanahan	Bradford	Claxton	Salisbury
A. P. Upshur	Clare	Aulick	Burnham	Robinson	Newmarket
Crowninshield	Chelsea	Thatcher	Niagara	Fairfax	Richmond
Welles	Cameron	MacKenzie	Annapolis	Ringgold	Newark
Buchanan	Campbeltown	Wickes	Montgomery	Tillman	Wells
Hopewell	Bath	Conner	Leeds	Sigourney	Newport
Doran	St. Mary's	McCalla	Stanley	Mason	Broadwater
Foote	Roxborough	Conway	Lewes	Williams	St. Clair
Cowell	Brighton	Twiggs	Leamington	Kalk	Hamilton
Thomas	St. Albans	Yarnall	Lincoln	Haraden	Columbia
Maddox	Georgetown	Philip	Lancaster	Bancroft	St. Francis
Abbot	Charleston	Rodgers	Sherwood	McCook	St. Croix
Branch	Beverely	Evans	Mansfield	Stockton	Ludlow
Edwards	Buxton	Bailey	Reading		

TORPEDOING OF THE KEARNY

CHAPTER 3

DESTROYERS "SHORT OF WAR"

(OPENING GUN, 1941)

Storm Approaches America

Late in January, 1941, U. S. Army and Navy leaders met with British military and naval representatives in Washington to discuss plans for collaboration and to decide over-all strategy to be employed in the event of American involvement in a global war. Both the British and the United States Governments hoped at that time to prevent the Japanese from unleashing a Pacific conflict. But the "Little Prussians of the East," proclaimed Allies of Germany and Italy, were striking attitudes that grew more menacing with every mile of their advance in China.

By the end of March a number of British-American agreements had been reached. With regard to the European aggressors, it was decided that the United States would pursue a policy of "belligerent neutrality" and conduct various "short of war" operations which included Atlantic Safety Belt patrols, the defense of Greenland, and joint protection of shipping to or from the waters of the Eastern Atlantic war zone. It was also decided that if worldwide war exploded, the Allies would hold the line in the Pacific and concentrate on first defeating Nazi Germany as Global Enemy No. 1.

The strategic decision concerning Germany was based on the fact that the Nazis constituted the major enemy. Given time, they might build impregnable defenses for their Fortress Europa and redouble the blitz that was slowly crushing England. It was known that German scientists, more to be feared than the Japanese variety, were working overtime on nuclear fission and guided missiles. And it was reasonable to assume that defeat of Germany and Italy would assure the ultimate defeat of isolated Japan, whereas defeat of Japan would not guarantee victory over the European Axis partners.

Germany, then, was to be the priority target—a decision that manifestly influenced United States naval, hence destroyer, operations.

By the spring of 1941 the DD's of DesLant were engaged in "short-of-war" activities just a chalkline this side of open conflict. Readying for escort-of-convoy operations, the Navy in March organized a support force for Atlantic duty to be commanded by Rear Admiral A. L. Bristol, Jr. (flagship PRAIRIE), composed of destroyers, Navy aircraft, and accompanying tenders. The Support Force destroyer roster was as follows:

DESTROYER SQUADRON 7
Capt. J. L. Kauffman

PLUNKETT (*Flagship DesRon 7.*)	*Lt. Comdr. P. G. Hale*
NIBLACK	*Lt. Comdr. E. R. Durgin*
BENSON	*Lt. Comdr. A. L. Pleasants, Jr.*
GLEAVES	*Lt. Comdr. E. H. Pierce*
MAYO	*Lt. Comdr. C. D. Emory*
MADISON	*Lt. Comdr. T. E. Boyce*
LANSDALE	*Lt. Comdr. John Connor*
HILARY P. JONES	*Lt. Comdr. S. R. Clark*
CHARLES F. HUGHES	*Lt. Comdr. G. L. Menocal*

DESTROYER SQUADRON 30
Capt. M. Y. Cohen

DALLAS (*Flagship DesRon 30.*)	*Lt. Comdr. H. B. Bell*

ELLIS	*Lt. Comdr. J. M. Kennaday*
BERNADOU	*Lt. Comdr. G. C. Wright*
COLE	*Lt. Comdr. W. L. Dyer*
DUPONT	*Lt. Comdr. E. M. Waldron*
GREER	*Lt. Comdr. Forrest Close*
TARBELL	*Lt. Comdr. S. D. Willingham*
UPSHUR	*Lt. Comdr. W. K. Romoser*
LEA	*Lt. Comdr. C. Broussard*

DESTROYER SQUADRON 31
Capt. Wilder D. Baker

MACLEISH *(Flagship DesRon 31.)*	*Lt. Comdr. A. C. Wood*
BAINBRIDGE	*Lt. Comdr. E. P. Creehan*
OVERTON	*Lt. Comdr. J. B. Stefanac*
STURTEVANT	*Lt. Comdr. W. S. Howard, Jr.*
REUBEN JAMES	*Lt. Comdr. H. L. Edwards*
MCCORMICK	*Lt. Comdr. J. H. Lewis*
BROOME	*Lt. Comdr. T. E. Fraser*
SIMPSON	*Lt. Comdr. F. D. McCorkle*
TRUXTUN	*Lt. Comdr. H. B. Heneberger*

Originally designated the Northeastern Escort Force—a title descriptive of its general mission—the Support Force was formally constituted on March 1. Meantime the Patrol Force had been renamed "Atlantic Fleet," and Rear Admiral E. J. King, promoted to Admiral, assumed command as CinCLant (Commander in Chief Atlantic).

In March Hitler had extended U-boat activities by proclaiming that Iceland and its surrounding waters were now in the war zone. The U-boats' successes in the North Atlantic impelled Admiral Stark to warn on April 4, *"The situation is obviously critical. . . . In my opinion, it is hopeless except as we take strong measures to save it."*

One measure taken was the transfer of three battleships, an aircraft carrier, four light cruisers, and Destroyer Squadrons 8 and 9 from the Pacific to the Atlantic.

In his ultimatum regarding Iceland, Hitler had stretched the war zone across Denmark Strait to the three-mile limit of Greenland. On April 9, 1941, the United States, at Denmark's behest, agreed to assume responsibility for the protection of Greenland until Denmark was free of the Nazi yoke. The Navy projected a Greenland Patrol (and laid plans for Iceland). But while these plans and projects were on paper, the U-boats were at sea. That April nearly 600,000 tons of British-controlled shipping went down to submarine fire.

On May 19 the Egyptian steamer ZAMZAM, carrying about 150 American passengers, was shelled by a German raider and sunk in the South Atlantic. Two days later the American freighter ROBIN MOOR, bound for South Africa with general cargo, was torpedoed and sunk in the South Atlantic. American tempers went up at these sinkings. But an event occurred on May 24 which caused in Washington a reaction more on the order of a chill. This was the sinking of the British battle cruiser HOOD by the new German battleship BISMARCK. Although British warships and aircraft trapped and sank the BISMARCK three days later, the destruction of HOOD in the waters between Iceland and Greenland left an icy pall over the North Atlantic.

On May 27, the day BISMARCK was blasted under, President Roosevelt declared an "Unlimited National Emergency." Broadcasting to the nation, he warned: *"The war is approaching the brink of the Western Hemisphere itself. It is coming very close to home. . . . It would be suicide to wait until they* (the aggressors) *are in our front yard. . . . We have, accordingly, extended our patrol in North and South Atlantic waters."*

The Navy was bending every effort to build a protective fence along the eastern border of that Atlantic front yard—a fence whose pickets would be mostly destroyers—extending from Greenland's frosty waters to the tropic seas of Brazil.

"Short-of-War" Bases

Newfoundland, a huge land mass with ragged coasts separated from the Canadian mainland by the Gulf of St. Lawrence and the Strait of Belle Isle, is North America's nearest approach to Europe. As such, it was the "jumping-off place" for Allied convoys bound for Britain. In 1940 the Navy selected the harbor of Argentia, deeply recessed in the Avalon Peninsula, as an advanced base for convoy escorts.

Construction units found Argentia a ghost town near the site of long-extinct silver mines. But when the Marines moved in on February 13, 1941, barracks and repair facilities were going up, and Argentia was looking alive.

On July 15, 1941, the United States Naval Air Station and Naval Operating Base were formally commissioned. Rear Admiral Bristol arrived in flagship PRAIRIE on September 19, and thereafter the base was "headquarters" for the destroyers of the Support Force.

The destroyermen found Argentia anything but Snug Harbor. Flailed by winter storms, the bay was a rough anchorage; the frost-bitten village provided little for the entertainment of weary blue-jackets. But Navy tenders were there to rejuvenate tired

DD's. And Argentia would look like Paradise to destroyers after North Atlantic convoy hauls to such ocean rendezvous areas as "Eastomp" (long. 22 E), "Westomp" (long. 52 W) and "Momp" (an oceanic area about midway between the British Isles and Canada, where convoy escorts peeled off for the run to Iceland or made rendezvous with eastbound or westbound ship trains).

Even so, Argentia remained a cheerless Paradise. Casco Bay in Maine was a pleasure resort by comparison. Selected for a destroyer base in the summer of 1941, Casco Bay ("Base Sail" to destroyermen) soon boomed with DD business. As the escort program developed, Casco became a regular stop on the itinerary. Upon concluding a convoy run at Argentia or Halifax, the DD would steam to Boston. After a seven-day overhaul at Boston Navy Yard, the destroyer would proceed to "Base Sail" for a training refresher and gunnery practice. Next stop, Argentia, for another convoy job. That was the ideal. As it eventuated, the duty-worn destroyer was unusually lucky if she had five days for grooming at Boston.

So Bermuda seemed like a holiday for the DD's that made this balmy landfall in the Gulf Stream. There, the Navy located its largest base installations on a site opposite Hamilton Island. The Bermuda Naval Operating Base was commissioned on April 7, 1941. The following day Task Group 7.2 under Rear Admiral A. B. Cook arrived. The group included the aircraft carrier RANGER (flagship), heavy cruisers WICHITA and TUSCALOOSA, and destroyers KEARNY (Lieutenant Commander A. L. Danis) and LIVERMORE (Lieutenant Commander V. Huber).

Working out of the Bermuda base, a powerful task group under Admiral Cook's command was presently engaged in conducting the Central Atlantic Neutrality Patrol. For a time this patrol force consisted of the carriers RANGER, WASP, YORKTOWN, and LONG ISLAND; cruisers QUINCY and VINCENNES, and Destroyer Squadron 11 under Captain M. L. Deyo in SAMPSON.

The force patrolled the Central Atlantic as far east as long. 30 W—practically within gunshot of the Azores. Extension of the "Western Hemisphere" to this mid-ocean parallel was a move to counter Nazi contemplation of the Azores Islands as target for a German grab.

Though they were a threat that served to make the Nazis think twice about an Azores invasion, "short-of-war" patrols in the Bermuda Area were not so rigorous as some. But the destroyermen in Deyo's squadron did not loll in any doldrum. Spare time went into training and gunnery practice.

Neutrality patrols in the Caribbean Area also kept the destroyermen alert, if not on tenterhooks. By Lend-Lease arrangement the Navy had acquired such West Indies bases as Kingston, Jamaica, and Port-of-Spain, Trinidad. Demerara, British Guiana, gave the Navy a southern anchorage on the north coast of South America. Patrols from these and other Caribbean bases covered the approaches to the Gulf of Mexico and the Panama Canal, and guarded such valuable islands as the oil-rich Curaçao Group. In addition, San Juan, Puerto Rico, and Guantanamo, Cuba, were key bastions of the Caribbean defense.

The U-boats had already invaded the Caribbean to rake Dutch Curaçao with shellfire and commit other depredations. And a nasty situation had developed in the French West Indies where the collapse of France had left "Vichy" Admiral Georges Robert in control of Martinique and Guadeloupe. Under Robert's command was a French West Indies Fleet which included the aircraft carrier BÉARN, the training cruiser JEANNE D'ARC, light cruiser EMILE BERTIN, and some smaller warships.

To keep an eye on this doubtful "Vichy" squadron, the U.S. Navy in 1940 established a special patrol which operated out of San Juan, Puerto Rico. The patrol was originally conducted by Destroyer Squadron 2 and 12 VP planes, under command of Captain W. L. Ainsworth in MOFFETT.

On April 18, 1941, the Navy organized the Caribbean Patrol. When eventually built up to strength, this patrol consisted of destroyers BLAKELEY (Lieutenant Commander E. S. Von Kleeck, Jr.), and BARNEY (Lieutenant Commander J. H. Long), a pair of ancient Eagle boats, and 12 Catalina flying boats. These forces were under command of Rear Admiral R. A. Spruance, then of Rear Admiral J. H. Hoover, Commandant Tenth Naval District and Commander Caribbean Sea Frontier at San Juan.

Destroyers to Iceland (NIBLACK and CHARLES F. HUGHES *in Action*)

President Roosevelt's answer to Hitler's Icelandic war zone ultimatum was a quiet directive to Admiral Stark ordering the Navy to reconnoiter the approaches to Iceland.

The strategic value of that island, where British troops had been stationed since the spring of 1940, was not lost on America's leaders. Iceland lay just 450 miles from the Scottish coast and only 530 nautical miles from the coast of Nazi-occupied Norway. Invading Denmark in April 1940, the Germans had captured Iceland's mother country. The United States had no intention of allowing Hitler to extend his dominion to an island so threateningly placed across the northern trans-Atlantic routes.

Hence the President's reconnaissance directive, and an order that sent an American destroyer steaming northward to conduct the special mission. The destroyer chosen for this sensitive task was the U.S.S. NIBLACK (Lieutenant Commander E. R. Durgin), flying the pennant of Commander D. L. Ryan, ComDesDiv 13.

NIBLACK was on her way early in April, 1941. The North Atlantic run proved uneventful until the 10th, and on that date things happened. Nearing Iceland, the destroyer sighted three lifeboats in the surface haze—survivors of a torpedoed Dutch merchantman! Durgin and company promptly went into action as lifesavers. They accomplished the rescue nimbly, the destroyer maneuvering with expert precision to pick up each boatload of exhausted seamen.

As the last of the bedraggled survivors were coming up the ship's side, NIBLACK's sonar instruments registered a submarine contact. The range was closing; apparently the U-boat was boring in to launch an attack. Durgin rushed NIBLACK's crew to General Quarters, and Division Commander Ryan ordered a depth-charge salvo.

Over went the ashcans, a booming "embarrassing pattern" that evidently embarrassed the sub to the point of a hasty retirement. These seem to have been the first depth charges fired in anger by American destroyermen in World War II.

NIBLACK's reconnaissance mission, and observation flights by Navy planes, pioneered the way for the American occupation of Iceland, a move to forestall possible German occupation. On June 15 Admiral King issued a new Operation Plan which named Iceland an outpost of the Western Hemisphere. The following day Admiral Stark advised Admiral King that President Roosevelt had issued orders that United States troops were to relieve the British garrison on Iceland. On July 1 U.S. Marines steamed from Argentia. Destination: Reykjavik.

For this major operation the Navy had assembled the first American Naval Task Force organized for foreign service. Designated TF 19, under command of Rear Admiral D. McD. LeBreton, the force consisted of 25 American ships. The Marines were carried by four naval transports. The escort included two battleships, two cruisers, and nine destroyers.

As indicated in the roster, the formation included an "Inner" and "Outer" destroyer screen. The DD's in the Outer Screen were positioned some 10,000 yards ahead of the main body. Patrolling out in front, the four old "four-pipers" and BUCK led the parade. No one knew what sort of reception committee might be waiting at the gates of Denmark Strait.

TASK FORCE 19

Rear Admiral D. McD. LeBreton, Commander, in NEW YORK

NEW YORK	*Capt. J. G. Ware*
ARKANSAS	*Capt. C. F. Bryant*
BROOKLYN	*Capt. E. S. Stone*
NASHVILLE	*Capt. F. S. Craven*

INNER SCREEN

Capt. J. L. Kauffman

DESTROYER SQUADRON 7, *Capt. Kauffman*

PLUNKETT	*Lt. Comdr. W. A. Graham*

DESTROYER DIVISION 13, *Comdr. D. L. Ryan*

NIBLACK	*Lt. Comdr. E. R. Durgin*
BENSON	*Lt. Comdr. A. L. Pleasants*
GLEAVES	*Lt. Comdr. E. H. Pierce*
MAYO	*Lt. Comdr. C. D. Emory*

DESTROYER DIVISION 14, *Comdr. F. D. Kirtland*

CHARLES F. HUGHES	*Lt. Comdr. G. L. Menocal*
LANSDALE	*Lt. Comdr. John Connor*
HILARY P. JONES	*Lt. Comdr. S. R. Clark*

OUTER SCREEN

Comdr. J. B. Heffernan

DESTROYER DIVISION 60, *Comdr. Heffernan*

ELLIS	*Lt. Comdr. L. R. Lampman*
BERNADOU	*Lt. Comdr. G. C. Wright*
UPSHUR	*Lt. Comdr. W. K. Romoser*
LEA	*Lt. Comdr. Clarence Broussard*
BUCK	*Lt. Comdr. H. C. Robison*

TRANSPORT BASE FORCE

Capt. F. A. Braisted

WILLIAM P. BIDDLE (ex-SAN FRANCISCO)	*Capt. C. D. Edgar*
FULLER (ex-NEWPORT NEWS)	*Capt. P. S. Theiss*
HEYWOOD (ex-BALTIMORE)	*Capt. R. J. Carstarphen*
ORIZABA	*Capt. C. Gulbranson*
ARCTURUS (ex-MORMACHAWK)	*Comdr. Henry Hartley*
HAMUL (ex-DOCTOR LYKES)	*Comdr. E. M. Tillson*
SALAMONIE (ex-ESSO COLUMBIA)	*Comdr. T. M. Waldschmidt*
CHEROKEE	*Lt. Comdr. P. L. F. Weaver*

However, on July 7 the task force reached Reykjavik in one piece—with the exception of a destroyer which had left the formation to perform a rescue feat that was as thrilling as any Hollywood drama. The destroyer was the CHARLES F. HUGHES with Lieutenant Commander Menocal, commanding officer, and Commander Kirtland, ComDesDiv 14, on her bridge.

The drama began on June 5 when ten American women, members of the Harvard Unit of Red Cross nurses, set sail from New Orleans for England on the Norwegian motor-ship VIGRID.

On the 23rd the VIGRID, slowed by engine trouble, dropped out of the convoy. That night a roaming wolfpack scented the disabled ship, and at 0735 the following morning the helpless vessel was torpedoed.

Crowded into four lifeboats, 37 seamen and the ten American nurses were adrift on the lonely ocean.

The next day the survivors glimpsed a convoy . . . and suffered the harrowing disappointment of seeing the ships steam on over the horizon.

The survivors decided to proceed in independent groups. Two of the lifeboats set a course for Ireland, and one of this pair was finally rescued by a British naval vessel. The other two lifeboats set a northwesterly course for Greenland. They chose a gruelling alternative. The little boats were overtaken by a storm that turned the voyage into a nightmare. The hardtack supply petered out. The water ration dwindled. One night one of the boats disappeared. The remaining lifeboat clung stubbornly to existence.

In this last boat there were 14 survivors, including VIGRID's captain and four of the Red Cross nurses. "We thought help would never come." That was the outlook by July 5 when the water ration was reduced to two swallows a day, the food ration to half a biscuit. But that evening the help was there—destroyer CHARLES F. HUGHES coming out of the dusk, big as an express train, big as a hospital, big as the United States Navy.

When the survivors were safe on board, the destroyermen conducted a search for the other lifeboat, but the North Atlantic vastness refused to relinquish the missing.

When the HUGHES arrived at Reykjavik on July 8, she found Task Force 19 crowding the harbor, the Marines going ashore, and the situation better than well in hand. If the Icelanders were not exactly cordial, neither were they truculent; and a few days of occupation served to melt some of the Viking reserve. And Reykjavik acquired an American name—"Rinky Dink."

Located about 25 miles from Reykjavik, the protected anchorage of Hvalfjordur ("Valley Forge" to the Marines) served to accommodate large warships and a Navy tank farm. On July 15 the Navy organized Task Force 1 for the support of Icelandic defenses and to escort American and Icelandic shipping "including shipping of any nationality which may join such . . . convoys between United States ports . . . and Iceland." The quoted stipulation was, in effect, a permit which allowed American escorts to conduct British convoys to the eastern margin of the "Western Hemisphere," at which point British escortage could take over, while the American escorts proceeded northward with vessels Iceland-bound.

Early in September 1941, Army troops under Major General C. H. Bonesteel were en route to Iceland to relieve the Marines. The convoy sailed from a point off Boston. It contained a train of Navy transports under escort of battleships IDAHO (flagship) and NEW MEXICO, heavy cruiser VINCENNES, and 14 destroyers. Convoy was under command of Rear Admiral W. R. Munroe. Destroyer screen was commanded by Captain W. L. Ainsworth.

In the DD complement were nine modern 1,630-tonners and five elderly "four-pipers," the oldsters composing an advance screen under command of Captain Wilder D. Baker. Altogether it was a sizable convoy that headed east-by-north across the troubled September seas. Destination: Reykjavik.

Convoy proceeded without incident—so much routine—until September 12. Then, at a point southeast of Greenland (lat. 58-30 N, long. 25 W) the destroyermen had a glimpse of the Atlantic Battle in prospect.

Evening of the 12th brought fog. Steaming on northerly course across calm water, the convoy tightened up defensively, the usual twilight procedure. Plodding in the outer screen, destroyers MACLEISH, TRUXTUN, REUBEN JAMES, OVERTON, and BAINBRIDGE sharpened the lookout as they sliced into blowing banks of vapor.

At 1844, while hundreds of Army men sat at chow in the crowded transports, "G.Q." sent the destroyermen to battle stations—the customary dusk alert. The fog was nasty—cotton-thick in patches, but thinning here and there into open spaces ("fog-dogs" in the vernacular) which appeared unexpectedly, like clearings in a misty forest. One minute a ship was plowing blindly through an opalescent cloud. Next minute she was in the clear, exposed.

Destroyer TRUXTUN, for example. In right-hand position of in-line advance screen, well ahead of the convoy, she trudged out of one fogbank about 1904 and found herself heading across open water for another. At her secondary conning station her "Exec," Lieutenant Commander G. W. Pressey, was occupied with routine detail (perhaps winding his wristwatch). Lookouts at their stations were scanning the fog-bank ahead. TRUXTUN was keeping her station steady as she goes. Then, at 1905—

"Mr. Pressey," said a young Quartermaster striker at the Executive Officer's elbow, "what's that over there?"

Mr. Pressey looked. "That over there" was a Nazi U-boat which had just emerged from the fog-bank and was approaching TRUXTUN on opposite course. If TRUXTUN was startled by this encounter, the U-boat was no less so. Things happened on both vessels. Just as Sound reported the stunning contact to TRUXTUN's bridge, someone in the Nazi's conning tower must have shouted, *"Himmelherrgott!"* As TRUXTUN's gunners made a grab for weapons, the U-boat started deep with a plunge.

Destroyer and submarine passed at a distance of about 50 yards. Commander Pressey wrote later, *"The mutual sighting must have been as great a surprise to the Germans as to the personnel of the* TRUXTUN, *and it was probably this surprise, with buck fever, which prevented either ship from taking any offensive action in the few seconds before the submarine crash-dived."*

Trailing the sub with sonar, TRUXTUN and her companion "four-pipers" hammered the water with depth-charge salvos that stirred up a tremendous rumpus in the fog. The alarmed convoy promptly executed evasive maneuvers, and for the rest of the evening nobody thought much of chow. Probably the U-boaters had their share of indigestion. Evidently they got away, but Doenitz may have "chewed them out" for missing a crack at the American convoy. Which subsequently reached Iceland without mishap.

Apparently TRUXTUN scored the first sighting of an enemy sub in the short-of-war period which overtured America's entry into World War II. That she failed to score the first kill was a matter which could be laid to inexperience and to the difficulties of A/S work in night and fog without benefit of radar. The Germans would soon take advantage of this situation, and one of TRUXTUN's companion "four-pipers," REUBEN JAMES, would be the victim.

On September 1, 1941, Admiral King organized a task group for Denmark Strait Patrol. This group was composed of the heavy cruisers WICHITA and TUSCALOOSA, two of the three battleships IDAHO, MISSISSIPPI, and NEW MEXICO, according to availability, and Destroyer Squadron 2 (Captain W. L. Ainsworth in MORRIS) plus Destroyer Division 22 (Commander J. S. Roberts in GWIN). Based at Hvalfjordur, this task group—the "White Patrol" to the Navy—was under command of Rear Admiral R. C. ("Ike") Giffen, with flag in WICHITA. Express mission of Giffen's group was to keep German raiders out of Denmark Strait—in particular such a raider as the big battleship TIRPITZ, presumably lurking in the fiords of Norway.

The northern trans-Atlantic routes had become particularly important because on June 22 Hitler had stunned the world by his sudden all-out attack on Russia.

Launching the war's biggest military campaign, he had hurled 121 divisions across the 2,000-mile Russian border. With the huge Soviet Union plunged into the conflict, the British and United States governments immediately offered assistance to Stalin in an effort to support the Red Army. Lend-Lease was extended to Russia, and North-Russian (code designator PQ) convoys were started in August 1941. The Royal Navy accepted responsibility for these convoys to Murmansk and to ports in the White Sea. And United States escorts participated in this convoy effort, one of the toughest of the war.

Flanking the North Russian route, Greenland and Iceland assumed a new strategic importance, and the TIRPITZ threat became more menacing as Lend-Lease cargoes were forwarded to Murmansk.

Destroyers Escort President to Atlantic Conference

DesLant destroyermen had scant time for "spit and polish" during short-of-war operations. Nevertheless, in the summer of 1941 there was one DD whose "bright work" shone with a dazzle seldom beheld on brass. The destroyer McDOUGAL was all dressed up, and she had a place to go.

The story begins, however, with the presidential yacht POTOMAC sailing from New London on the morning of August 3. Two days later American newspapers had the word—F.D.R. was on a holiday cruise. What the Press did not learn was that President Roosevelt's yacht met the U.S.S. AUGUSTA off Martha's Vineyard. There the President boarded Admiral King's flagship. After which AUGUSTA, escorted by U.S.S. TUSCALOOSA and several destroyers, headed northward for Argentia, Newfoundland.

Simultaneously heading for Argentia was H.M.S. PRINCE OF WALES carrying Prime Minister Churchill, his Chiefs of Staff, and Mr. Harry Hopkins, who had just completed an important mission to Moscow. In the making was the first meeting of Roosevelt and Churchill—the historic "Atlantic Conference" that was to set Allied objectives in the global war to come, and to furnish Allied people with the inspiring goals embodied in the Atlantic Charter.

The rendezvous was Placentia Bay, at 0900, morning of August 9. On hand ahead of time were AUGUSTA with her escorts. The battleship ARKANSAS and the destroyers of DesDiv 17—McDOUGAL (flagship), WINSLOW, MOFFETT, and SAMPSON—were also standing by in the bay.

PRINCE OF WALES entered the scene escorted by Canadian destroyers RIPLEY, RESTIGOUCHE, and ASSINIBOINE. Churchill boarded the AUGUSTA for a conference at 1100, and dined with the President that evening.

The following day, Sunday, President Roosevelt was to visit the PRINCE OF WALES. This was destroyer MCDOUGAL's big moment. Captained by Commander William W. Warlick, she was tied up alongside AUGUSTA, waiting. She had been selected to transport the President to the PRINCE OF WALES meeting, and a destroyer with the Commander in Chief of the United States Navy on board is one proud DD.

If pride goeth before a fall, MCDOUGAL's case was the exception to the rule. Stepping smartly across the bay, she approached the PRINCE OF WALES with the President's flag flying. As the destroyer's bow was level with the British battleship's fantail, she was called upon to execute a fancy maneuver—bring her bow alongside the PRINCE's stern in what sailors call a "Chinese landing." But MCDOUGAL's destroyermen accomplished the maneuver as though they had spent a lifetime in practicing it.

There stood F.D.R. on the destroyer's foc'sle.

There stood Churchill, sea cap aslant, on the great battleship's stern.

There stood a Chief Boatswain's Mate on MCDOUGAL's bow. "Hey!" he shouted to the solitary figure on the PRINCE's fantail. "Will you take a line?"

The Former Naval Person answered, "Certainly!" And before the British tars could recover from shock, he had caught the line and was deftly hauling it in.

With that sort of spirit among the participants, the Atlantic Conference was bound to succeed. And so was the Navy's Destroyer Force.

Could anyone imagine Hitler hauling in a line—or a Nazi Boatswain's Mate daring to throw him one?

Attack on U.S.S. Greer

In March 1941 Hitler had proclaimed the seas off Iceland a danger zone for Allied and neutral shipping. And in the ocean southeast of Cape Farewell one merchantman after another had since been blown to the bottom by sharpshooting U-boats. "Torpedo Junction" the seamen called it—an apt name for North Atlantic waters where the wolfpacks waited to meet the east-bound Allied convoys.

The United States destroyer GREER was not steaming with a convoy when she neared "Torpedo Junction" on the morning of September 4, 1941. Flying the pennant of Commander G. W. Johnson, ComDesDiv 61, the GREER was proceeding independently, Argentia to Reykjavik, with mail and supplies for the American Icelandic base.

The DD was an old "four-piper," one of the 1200-ton flush-deckers recommissioned for Atlantic patrol in September 1939. Her captain, Lieutenant Commander L. H. Frost, had been in command just one month.

Heading for Iceland, GREER was deep in the submarine danger zone at daybreak, September 4. She was about 175 miles from Reykjavik, with the clock at 0840, when she was approached by a British patrol plane which flashed a U-boat warning. A German sub had been spotted about ten miles distant, directly in GREER's path. The destroyer acknowledged the warning, and the plane winged back to the spot where the enemy had been sighted.

Frost stepped up speed to 20 knots, sounded General Quarters, and sent the DD ahead on a fast zigzag. When the destroyer reached the submarine's reported position, the Commanding Officer slowed speed to 10 knots (to accommodate sonar work), and the destroyer's "pinging" gear went into action. The submerged U-boat was presently detected—at a point about 150 miles southwest of Reykjavik—and GREER had a submarine on her hands. Or, to sharpen the metaphor, she had a tiger by the tail.

For the destroyermen, the situation was peculiar, to say the least. On the one hand, the United States was not at war with Nazi Germany; on the other, "belligerent neutrality" wasn't peace. Concerning a meeting between a U.S. naval vessel and a German U-boat, the Navy's operational plan was ambiguous. Could the destroyer fire upon the sub, or must she wait for the sub to open fire? Without express authority to shoot, the destroyermen could only hold on, and keep their fingers crossed. Which is what GREER's destroyermen did.

They held on. For the next two hours GREER maintained sonar contact with the U-boat, and reported the submarine's position, course, and speed to all ships and planes within radio range. Frost kept the destroyer's bow pointed at the undersea menace, moving his ship this way and that as the sub maneuvered to evade. At 1000 the British patrol plane inquired if GREER was going to attack. The Commanding Officer was compelled to signal negative. At 1032 the British plane swooped down and dropped four random depth charges. Then the pilot signaled he was returning to base to refuel.

"There she goes," one of the destroyermen said. "Now what!"

From the bridge came an order that held GREER hard on the submarine's tail. The destroyer would continue to hold on.

She was holding on at 1100. Still holding at 1130. The tension was as nerve-wracking as a hang-fire—suspense that became intolerable. How long before the British aircraft would reappear? How long would the U-boat commander withhold an itching finger from the firing key? Sooner or later an annoyed tiger was bound to turn. When?

The U-boat turned at 1240, and headed straight for the American destroyer. GREER's sonar instruments registered the closing range. Then the destroyer's lookouts sighted a discoloration and disturbance of the water a few hundred yards off to starboard. They did not see a periscope, but at 1248 they sighted the impulse bubble of a fired torpedo. The U-boat had let fly!

The destroyer seemed to leap at the warning cry, "*Torpedo*!" Frost sent his ship in a swing to evade, and a moment later the foaming wake was sighted sizzling through the water about 100 yards astern.

Exactly two minutes after the shot was fired, Commander Johnson, acting with the authority of Division Commander, ordered GREER to counterattack. Counterattack she did, steaming forward on the warpath to try for the submerged foe with a pattern of eight depth charges that boomed overside at 1256.

At 1258 another torpedo was sighted racing for the destroyer on collision course. Frost called for a hard turn to port; the destroyer swung to the left; the lethal "fish" missed the mark by a good 300 yards.

Contact was lost in the turmoil of exploding depth charges and evasion maneuvers, but GREER's sonar crew regained it at 1312, a few minutes after Division Commander Johnson ordered the search resumed. At 1315 a British plane skimmed across the seascape, and dropped two smoke pots on the spot where GREER had dumped her depth charges. Probing for the target with sonar fingers, the destroyer continued the sub-hunt, and the U-boat apparently went deep to evade. GREER was still searching when the British destroyer I-26 arrived on the scene at 1415.

The British destroyermen asked the Americans if they desired to conduct a coordinated search. Division Commander Johnson replied in the negative, and the British DD departed after dropping a random depth charge.

At 1512 GREER made sonar contact which was evaluated as "submarine," and the destroyermen delivered another attack. Eleven depth charges thundered down into the sea, but results were evidently zero. No oil slick, no debris, no sign of a shattered U-boat. GREER went on with the search until 1840 when she received orders from Iceland to proceed to her destination.

Throughout, the GREER had handled the U-boat meeting with complete propriety, following the rules of International Law as scrupulously as possible. For almost three hours and thirty minutes the destroyer was in contact with the submarine. Although exposed to attack, she was careful not to take the first hostile action. Remarking on her conduct, Admiral King commented, "*The action taken by the* GREER *was correct in every particular in accordance with then existing orders.*"

In a memo to Admiral Stark, Chief of Naval Operations, President Roosevelt advised, "*I think it is essential that . . . two facts be made to stand out so clearly that they cannot be separated by any hostile press—first, that two hours elapsed between the bombing of the submarine by the British plane and the firing of the first torpedo by the submarine; and second, that no weapon was fired by the* GREER *until after the torpedo attack began.*"

Three days after the GREER episode, the American merchantman STEEL SEAFARER was bombed and sunk in the Red Sea by Nazi aircraft. On September 11, President Roosevelt made an historic radio address. Broadcasting to the world from the White House, he declared:

"*Upon our naval and air patrol—now operating in large numbers over a vast expanse of the Atlantic Ocean—falls the duty of maintaining the American policy of Freedom of the Seas. That means . . . our patrolling vessels and planes will protect all merchant ships, not only American ships, but ships of any flag, engaged in commerce in our defense waters.*

"*From now on, if German or Italian vessels enter the waters, the protection of which is necessary for American defense, they do so at their own peril.*

"*The orders which I have given as Commander-in-Chief of the United States Army and Navy are to carry out that policy at once.*"

Spoken one week after GREER's brush with the U-boat, this was the famous "shoot on sight" order which untied the hands of United States forces defending Western Hemisphere waters. From that hour on the United States was involved in a *de facto* naval war with Nazi Germany. The war was undeclared, but the term "*de facto*" means actual, or patently existing.

Translation by U.S.S. GREER.

Convoy To "Momp" (Eberle Rescues Crew of Nigaristan)

Convoy HX-150 was the first to employ United States escorts for part of the trans-Atlantic voyage. The undertaking was in accordance with the operational plan issued by Admiral King on September 1, 1941. Chosen for this pioneer duty was Captain

Morton L. Deyo's escort group, Task Unit 4.1.1.

The group consisted of the following destroyers:

ERICSSON *Lt. Comdr. G. E. Sage, Flying pennant of Capt. Deyo, Escort Commander and* COMDESRON 11
EBERLE *Lt. Comdr. E. R. Gardner, Jr.*
DALLAS *Lt. Comdr H. B. Bell, Jr. Flying pennant of Capt. M. Y. Cohen,* COMDESRON 30
UPSHUR *Lt. Comdr. W. K. Romoser*
ELLIS *Lt. Comdr. L. R. Lampman Flying pennant of Comdr. J. B. Heffernan,* COMDESDIV 60

ERICSSON and EBERLE were the only modern destroyers in the group. The others were over-age "four-pipers," equipped with outmoded gear, and of low fuel capacity.

Under Canadian escortage, the eastbound convoy sailed from Halifax on September 16. The American escort group took over the following day at a point some 350 miles east of Halifax. Deyo's Task Unit was to escort the convoy to "Momp," at which point the British would assume responsibility for escortage to the United Kingdom while the American escorts proceeded to Reykjavik with the three American merchantmen and one Icelandic vessel bound for that port.

There were 44 merchant ships in convoy at the time Captain Deyo's group relieved the Canadian escorts. The assemblage composed a heterogeneous melange which included the stately luxury liner EMPRESS OF ASIA and the rusty S.S. NIGARISTAN with crew from the Levant. Convoy Commander, Rear Admiral E. Manners, R.N. (Retired), signalled Deyo,

DELIGHTED TO HAVE ALL OF YOU TO GUARD THIS CONVOY FOR THE NEXT FEW DAYS

Under conduct of Captain Deyo, the convoy paraded in nine columns with the escorts disposed to form a cordon. Distance between the columns was set at three cables (600 yards). Flag destroyer ERICSSON was stationed some 2,000 yards ahead of the convoy's front. ELLIS was positioned on the convoy's starboard bow; UPSHUR was positioned on the port. Abreast of the last ships in column, EBERLE paced to starboard and DALLAS to port. During daytime the destroyers patrolled at a distance anywhere from 500 to 2,000 yards from the convoy.

At night the convoy's columns drew closer together, and the escorts patrolled no more than 1,000 yards from the convoy. Whereas the destroyers maintained continuous patrolling by day, after-dark patrolling was restricted to clear nights; on dark or foggy nights the DD's were to keep station. Time was soon coming when escorts would patrol as far out as 5,000 yards from a convoy, night patrols would be conducted—whatever the condition of visibility—and the DD which abandoned a U-boat search at the expiration of an hour would be censured.

Fortunately Convoy HX-150 did not encounter any U-boats during the run from Canadian waters to "Momp." Combat would certainly have proved an ordeal for the escorts, hampered as they were by inexperience.

But although Convoy HX-150 was not ambushed, it experienced some misadventures which kept the escorts busy. Stragglers were a source of constant trouble. Breakdowns and laggards created a ragged formation, and the convoy made numerous course changes to give stragglers a chance to overhaul. All of which meant extra work for the escorts riding herd.

"Ship afire!"

The alarm was flashed to flag destroyer ERICSSON on the night of September 24-25, when the convoy was nearing "Torpedo Junction." A night as black as India ink, with the barometer reading 28.60, a gale blowing, and the ships flogged by violent rain squalls as they struggled to keep pace in tumbling seas.

Fire! The baleful tocsin had sounded aboard the S.S NIGARISTAN. An ugly smolder had gotten out of hand in the freighter's bunkers. The vessel was in distress, her decks going hot underfoot, when Captain Deyo received the word and dispatched destroyer EBERLE to the rescue.

Fighting high winds and rolling seas, Commander Gardner's destroyer galloped through the night with all her knots tied on. The destroyer made the run in record time, and picked up NIGARISTAN's company in masterful fashion. The freighter's crew abandoned in lifeboats that were kicked about like corks in the broiling sea. Maneuvering with precision, EBERLE got out her lines and took aboard the freightermen. Despite furious wind and leaping wave, the 63 members of NIGARISTAN's crew were rescued without loss of a man.

This perfect score was achieved through the valiance of one of EBERLE's young officers. Alongside the destroyer a lifeboat was dipping and rising on the heaving water while bluejackets and merchant seamen struggled to control the lines. A sudden shout, a wail, and one of the NIGARISTAN's black gang, Hassan Amirkhan by name, was floundering in the foam between boat and ship, in imminent danger of being crushed against the destroyer's side. Ensign L. C. Savage went overside with a bowline and seized the dangling sailor about the waist. Some desperate acrobatics were required to fend off the lifeboat, hold the frantic seaman, and hang on while the destroyermen hauled in. But adept work by all hands got Ensign Savage and the seaman safe on board.

Extract from EBERLE'S report: *IT IS CONSIDERED THAT THE ACTION OF ENSIGN SAVAGE WAS BEYOND THE NORMAL CALL OF DUTY.*

On September 25 the convoy reached the "Momp" rendezvous point where the British escorts were to relieve the American. Not far over the horizon another ship-train had passed in the night, on opposite course. This was Convoy ON-18, the first westbound, trans-Atlantic convoy under American escortage. Destroyers MADISON, GLEAVES, HUGHES, SIMPSON, and LANSDALE, under group command of Captain F. D. Kirtland, had assumed the guardianship of ON-18 at a "Momp" point south of Iceland on September 24.

In spite of the shipping activity in the "Momp" area, the U-boats failed to ambush either of these convoys under pioneer American escortage. Thus the Navy's first World War II convoys effort was concluded with a cordial exchange by the Allied participants. But, although the enterprise was eminently successful, its conduct was not quite so smooth as the concluding amenities. By no means satisfied with the operation, Captain Deyo made a number of adversely critical comments in his report, and urged a stiff training program for destroyermen facing the titanic job of anti-submarine (A/S) work.

That the job was going to demand an amalgam of crack leadership, seamanship, and marksmanship was a fact punched home to the Navy's Destroyer Forces by the torpedoing of the U.S.S. KEARNY.

Torpedoing of U.S.S. Kearny

As was to be expected, even a limited naval war with Nazi Germany could not be waged without casualties. And American destroyermen escorting convoys to and from "Momp" were aware that a showdown was in the making. The mid-Atlantic was boiling. American merchant ships and escorting destroyers were bound to bear the brunt when the explosion came.

For the U.S.S. KEARNY it came early in the morning of October 17, 1941.

KEARNY was one of the new 1630-ton destroyers launched in 1940—a five-million-dollar warship, powered by engines that could drive her at close to 40 knots. Her fire-control apparatus, sonar devices, and weapons were the latest thing on the sea. Her crew was a smartly-trained team. Her captain, Lieutenant Commander A. L. Danis, ran a taut ship. Yet expert crew and the best detection gear and weapons proved unavailing when death stalked.

Destiny beckoned to KEARNY while she was at Reykjavik in company with an American destroyer division which had made the Iceland run. Her sortie was in response to a distress call from a convoy which had floundered into a wolfpack ambush about 400 miles south of Iceland. This convoy, SC-48, sailed from Canada on October 10. Plagued by bad weather and breakdowns, the train of 50 merchantmen had advanced along a *Via Dolorosa*. By October 15, eleven stragglers, among them the Convoy Commodore's flagship, had dropped out. The convoy could do no better than 7½ knots. The escort, consisting of four Canadian corvettes and the Canadian destroyer COLUMBIA, was unable to cope with the wolfpack that struck during the night. Three ships had gone down, torpedoed, when the call for help reached Reykjavik.

The Navy answered by dispatching four destroyers to the scene of action. Under group command of Captain L. H. Thebaud, ComDesRon 27, the DD quartet included PLUNKETT (Lieutenant Commander W. A. Graham) flying Captain Thebaud's pennant; LIVERMORE (Lieutenant Commander V. Huber) flying the pennant of Commander H. B. Broadfoot, ComDesDiv 21; DECATUR (Lieutenant Commander J. C. Sowell); and KEARNY.

The old "four-piper" GREER, the British warship BROADWATER, and the Free French corvette LOBELIA were also dispatched from various nearby areas to the battle scene. Convoy SC-48 was in dire need of all the aid that could be rushed. When Captain Thebaud's destroyer group arrived shortly before sundown of the 16th, the Canadian escorts were literally staggering with exhaustion, the merchantmen were panicky, and the U-boats were in the offing biding their time for another strike.

PLUNKETT, LIVERMORE, DECATUR, and KEARNY took station to shield the nine-column formation, and the convoy crawled forward through a dusk as gray as apprehension. In conformance with prevailing doctrine, the American destroyers were positioned 1,000 to 1,500 yards from the convoy. As DesLant leaders were to learn, such a screen was too tight. Obviously if escorts hugged a convoy, stalking submarines were permitted to come within close range of the ships. While attaining short torpedo-range, the U-boats could fire from positions beyond range of the destroyers' sound gear. Thus a tight screen gave submarines a decided edge. The mauling dealt Convoy SC-48 was a case in point.

As night spread its black wing over the seascape, the wolfpack closed in. About two hours before midnight, a merchantman was torpedoed. A burst of orange flame, thudding explosions, and frantic signals sent the convoy milling. Dropping helter-skelter depth charges and firing starshells, the escorts broke up the attack, but they failed to discourage, much less demolish, the assailant.

With the clock nearing 2315 the U-boats struck again. This time torpedoes, ploughing into the center of the convoy, blasted two more merchantmen to the bottom.

About three hours later (around 0200 in the morning of October 17) the wolfpackers struck a third time. Unleashing a series of three swift attacks, they sent torpedoes ripping through the convoy like chain-lightning. Four merchant vessels were fatally hit. And it was during this tumult of fire, water, and explosion that KEARNY was struck by an undersea thunderbolt.

Her crew at General Quarters, the destroyer was advancing into the fray at 15 knots, lookouts straining for a glimpse of U-boats running with decks awash. Pyrotechnics arched and flared in the night, illumining the seascape with frenzied fireworks. Tinted smoke bulged over the carcasses of sinking ships. Some 1,200 yards from the KEARNY a torpedoed tanker was burning. A belch of flame from the tanker shed a sudden gush of light across the scene. The glare silhouetted a British corvette maneuvering in to pick up survivors, and it also silhouetted KEARNY as she commenced a port swing and dropped "embarrassing charges."

The destroyermen were rolling ashcans from the racks to drive off subs which might be astern. Sighting the corvette which was cutting across her bow, KEARNY slowed to avoid collision. And at that moment a U-boat lurking somewhere ahead drew a bead on the destroyer. Three torpedoes were aimed at the DD—murderous fingers reaching for KEARNY's bow. Stretching across fire-lit water, the rushing wakes were unseen.

Executing the turn to port, the destroyer swung, heeling. A torpedo whipped through the water just ahead. As the lookouts stared in shock, another hissed by astern. Then, as men braced themselves on the canted deck, the ship was rocked by a stunning explosion.

Struck on the starboard side by a torpedo, KEARNY was hard hit. The war head caught her at the turn of the bilge, smashing into the No. 1 fireroom. Vented forward and upward, the explosion wrecked the fireroom, ruptured the forward bulkhead of the boiler-room, burst the deck overhead, ripped off the starboard bridge-wing, knocked the forward funnel acockbill, and damaged the deckhouse. Four men were flung overside by the blast. Seven were scalded in the flooded boiler-room. Others, bleeding, scorched, wounded by flying debris, were felled on deck or snared in the mangle below. Drowning the dead, the sea plunged in through the rent in KEARNY's side. Jammed open, the steam siren poured raw sound from its throat.

The ship came out of a stagger, steadied on, and slowly regained headway.

Lieutenant R. J. Esslinger was engineering and damage-control officer, Chief Motor Machinist's Mate Aucie McDaniel was a veteran "motormac." Immediately after the explosion, they found the forward bulkhead of the forward engine-room buckling. With all hell loose around them, and iron plates threatening to give way to crushing tons of water, they managed to shore up the bulkhead and save the engine-room.

Similar courage was displayed on the destroyer's damaged bridge. Third Class Shipfitter Samuel Kurtz was at the depth-charge release station when the torpedo struck. Thrown from his feet by the blast which demolished the starboard bridge wing, Kurtz was hurled to the edge of the smashed wing where he clung in jagged wreckage with both legs broken. Every lurch of the ship threatened to pitch him overside. Despite terrible peril and agonizing fractures, Kurtz hung on with gritted teeth, silently enduring a wait for help.

Grit inspires grit. Chief Yeoman Henry Leenknecht inched his way out on the tattered bridge-wing to rescue his shipmate. Clinging in a dangle of broken framework, Leenknecht got an arm around Kurtz and brought him in to solid deck.

While all hands topside fought battle damage, First Class Seaman H. C. Barnard stumbled through darkness below to check watertight fittings. Alone in a locked compartment, Quartermaster John Booth stood at his post, manning the steering engine. Aware that power was lost and the ship must be steered by hand, he contrived to make the necessary shift to permit manual operation of the helm. Realizing that Booth might be trapped at his solitary station, Muscoe Holland, another quartermaster, raced to open the bolted escape hatch of the steering-engine room and give Booth a hand.

Noteworthy as were the performances in mention, they were typical of the conduct of KEARNY's crew. Under baptismal fire, they exhibited the steady courage of veterans. But the ship's salvation did not come through courage alone. These destroyermen were trained for emergency action. They knew their jobs—what to do, and how to do it.

As was usually the case with battle damage, initial injuries developed a host of successive complications. KEARNY suffered her share of these. But expert damage control and ship-handling held her on an even keel, and about ten minutes after the torpedo smash she was able to steam at 10 knots.

A Very flare brought an American destroyer to KEARNY's aid—the old "four-stacker" GREER (Lieutenant Commander L. H. Frost). It was a dramatic coincidence: the first American DD to be shot at by a Nazi U-boat, running to assist the first American destroyer to be struck by a Nazi torpedo.

Lieutenant Commander Danis informed GREER that the injured destroyer could make Iceland. GREER was directed to search for the four men hurled into the sea by the torpedo explosion. The old flush-decker combed the area, but the missing men were not to be recovered. Later that morning an urgent call for blood plasma brought a Catalina winging down from Iceland with plasma from the cruiser WICHITA.

So the *de facto* Battle of the Atlantic collected its death toll. Casualty cost to the U.S.S. KEARNY—11 killed, 24 wounded. The losses had been held to a minimum by the stamina of such durable men and hard-to-sink warships.

KEARNY was a destroyer of the BENSON class—a new class which had been adversely criticized by "experts" who considered these DD's top-heavy. The naval architects who fashioned the destroyers thought differently. Gave them double bottoms to protect them from underwater weapons. Special reinforcement to absorb the shock of hits. Numerous compartments which could be closed off to prevent the spread of fire or flooding. Powerful engines capable of tremendous workloads. Destroyers of this class would go down in World War II. So would some of the heavier PORTERS and CRAVENS, some of the big FLETCHERS. But few of these modern DD's would succumb to a single torpedo. In the main, those sunk were battered under by shellfire, pounded by bombs, blasted by aerial onslaught—and they took a tremendous punishing before they went down.

With a yawning hole in her side, KEARNY steamed to Iceland under her own power. There she was turned over to the Navy repair ship VULCAN (Captain L. S. Fiske). A few months later she was off the "binnacle list" and once more ready for active duty.

In passing, it may be noted that the repair job was something of a masterwork. Iceland furnished few facilities for a major operation on a seriously injured man-of-war, but VULCAN's forges worked overtime, and her technicians labored like giants with the delicate craft of surgeons to put KEARNY back into shape.

KEARNY's destroyermen also won well deserved citations. For Lieutenant Commander Danis, Chief Motor Machinist's Mate McDaniel, and Engineering Officer Esslinger, the Navy Cross. Letters of Commendation to a dozen other members of the crew, including Shipfitter Kurtz and Yeoman Leenknecht. Promotions for men who merited immediate advancement. And for all hands a "Well Done!"

DD's In The South Atlantic

On April 24, 1941, Rear Admiral Jonas H. Ingram, Commander Cruiser Division 2, was ordered to proceed with his group from Newport, Rhode Island, to the South Atlantic. Mission: to patrol the Brazil area. The waters to be covered by this "neutrality patrol" were embraced by a triangle roughly delineated by a line drawn from the West Indies to the "hump" of Brazil, from there to the Cape Verdes, from the Cape Verdes to the West Indies. A large area, and its patrol was a large order.

To handle this order Admiral Ingram's forces were augmented, and the groups under his command were designated Task Force 3.

Task Force 3 was composed of the four elderly light cruisers MEMPHIS (flagship), CINCINNATI, MILWAUKEE, OMAHA. The cruisers were accompanied by Destroyer Squadron 9: SOMERS (Commander J. C. Metzel), flying the pennant of Captain T. A. Symington, ComDesRon 9; JOUETT (Commander G. W. Clark); DAVIS (Commander C. C. Hartman), flagship of Commander T. G. Peyton, ComDesDiv 18; WINSLOW (Commander P. R. Heineman); and MOFFETT (Commander G. W. Johnson).

Axis pressure at that date was heavy on South America where Nazi and Fascist agents were working like termites to undermine the Monroe Doctrine. Brazil, territorially larger than the United States, was an important key to Hemispheric defense. In Rio de Janeiro, Axis propaganda was stoked white-hot in an effort to melt that key. Would the Brazilians side with the Allies? They gave their answer in September by opening the ports of Bahia and Recife to Admiral Ingram's naval vessels.

In October, several units of Task Force 3 undertook a South Atlantic convoy mission. At Trinidad on the 15th, cruiser MILWAUKEE (Captain A. McGlasson) and destroyer WARRINGTON (Commander F. G. Fahrion) were assigned to escort the S.S. ACADIA to Recife. In the service of the Maritime Commission, the ACADIA was carrying Pan-American Air Technicians and equipment for the construction of air bases in Africa. Under guard of MILWAUKEE and WARRINGTON the ship arrived at Recife on the 21st. There Admiral Ingram took over the convoy.

ACADIA steamed from Recife that evening under guard of flag cruiser MEMPHIS and destroyers DAVIS and JOUETT (the latter now captained by Commander

Curtain raiser to the war. The U.S.S. Kearny, guarding a convoy against a Nazi wolfpack, was torpedoed off Iceland by a German U-boat a month before Pearl Harbor. Smashed from fireroom to bridge, with 11 men killed and 24 wounded, she made Iceland under her own power, to rejoin the Fleet eventually. She was the first U.S. destroyer torpedoed in what was to be World War II.

Rocky shores and wintry seas. This view of a U.S. destroyer at Hvalfjordur, Iceland, in early 1942 reveals the conditions faced by the wartime patrols in the far north. A ship on the rocks might last perhaps an hour; a swimmer froze in minutes.

Not an icebreaker, but a destroyer. Nevertheless the U.S.S. Gleaves, on her way to Argentia, in 1942 had to make her own passageway.

Veteran ship and veteran men. On the slippery deck of the U.S.S. Greer these officers are fighting to keep their footing against rolling seas and North Atlantic gale. This is the same Greer that dodged the first German torpedo in September, 1941.

Trouble ahead! The U.S.S. Bulmer here makes her bow to Argentia, jumping-off place on the stormy, U-boat infested route to Europe.

Death dogs a convoy. This is convoy SC-48, which U.S.S. Kearny was escorting when she was torpedoed on October 17, 1941. Ambushed by a wolfpack, the convoy lost almost a dozen ships in frightful days and nights of harassing wolfpack onslaughts. This picture was taken only ten hours after the Kearny's torpedoing from an airplane flying blood plasma for the ship's wounded.

J. C. Pollock). Daylight air cover was furnished for the entire voyage, a plane hovering over the convoy from dawn to dark of each passing day.

No U-boats were encountered during the 2600-mile run across the Atlantic. When the convoy arrived at Lagos, West Africa, Admiral Ingram asked the British naval authorities to provide ACADIA with adequate protection. After fueling, his task group set out on patrol for San Juan, Puerto Rico.

Destroyerwise, this successful convoy mission was without notable incident. But the curtain was up in the South Atlantic theater, and the American players were on stage. Meantime, in the North Atlantic a second United States destroyer had fallen prey to the Nazi enemy.

Loss of U.S.S. Reuben James

They called her *"The Rube"*—a nickname that expressed the affection of American destroyermen for a DD which bore one of the proudest names in the U.S. Navy—a name that harked back to the Tripolitan Wars and a battle with the Barbary pirates.

She was far from modern as ships go; some of her gear verged on the obsolete, but she got around with an agility that won her the favor of the task force commander. Her captain, Lieutenant Commander H. L. ("Tex") Edwards, had been a champion matman at the Naval Academy and a wrestler on the Olympic team. The crew were worthy of both her name and her captain.

From Iceland she was dispatched to the States to engage in escort-of-convoy duty. And so came a day in the latter part of October when REUBEN JAMES headed out into the North Atlantic as one of a group of five destroyers (under Commander R. E. Webb in BENSON) screening eastbound convoy HX-156—a ship-train freighting Lend-Lease goods to the British Isles.

The convoy of 44 merchantmen made a slow 8.8 knots through the late October seas. REUBEN JAMES steamed on the port beam of the formation, abreast of the last ship in column. Destroyers HILARY P. JONES (Lieutenant Commander S. R. Clark) and BENSON (Lieutenant Commander A. L. Pleasants) were positioned on the port bow and starboard bow, respectively. Destroyer TARBELL (Lieutenant Commander S. D. Willingham) was positioned off the starboard beam, abreast of the last ship in column. These escorts were stationed some 3,000 yards from the convoy's body. Destroyer NIBLACK (Lieutenant Commander E. R. Durgin) covered the convoy's rear, and patrolled about 1,000 yards astern. NIBLACK was the only one of the group equipped with radar.

There was tension in the ocean air. The escorts had heard of the KEARNY incident; all hands were aware the convoy was in wolfpack water. But the voyage during that last week of October was proving uneventful. Routine steaming. Nothing to report. Nothing—until the morning of the 31st.

On that date the convoy was in the "Momp" area, about 600 miles west of Ireland. Night was dissolving into a faint suggestion of day, and the convoy was marching steadily eastward in good formation, not zigzagging, while the escorts rode herd in their assigned positions, dipping along in the swinging seas. The hazy dark-before-dawn revealed no hint of impending disaster. The hint came on a gust of ocean wind, invisible, about 0525, when a guardship picked up a "foreign" radio transmission close aboard.

Afterward there was a question concerning REUBEN JAMES' exact position at this crucial moment—whether she was maintaining station or had begun daylight patrol. Whatever the circumstance, she was about 2,000 yards on the convoy's flank, and on the point of turning to investigate the direction-finder bearing when (time: 0539) she was struck by an unseen torpedo.

The war head hit her on the port side near No. 1 stack. A sheet of fire flagged skyward. Blending with the torpedo explosion, a stupendous blast almost lifted the destroyer from the water. Evidently the torpedo-burst exploded the forward magazine, for the ensuing blast amputated the destroyer's entire forward section, which carried away aft of the No. 3 stack.

Crew members were hurled overside like straws in a gust of scrap iron. Seamen who had been asleep in their bunks found themselves swimming in a nightmare of flotsam and black oil. Clinging to life jackets and balsa floats, the survivors stared aghast at the hulk which was all that remained of the REUBEN JAMES. For about five minutes the stern section remained afloat, a jagged segment in the debris-littered sea. Then this section sank, rumbling and roaring as it went down. The thunder came from exploding depth charges—blasts that killed some of the swimmers who had survived the torpedoing.

The men clung to the slippery rafts, dazed, sick with shock, trying to shout encouragement to one another. Some, like Seaman D. J. Del Grosso, thought the oil warmed the water. Actually they were numbed by the icy brine, slowly freezing. Some of them lost their grips on rafts and debris, and were drowned before their comrades could aid them. Others went down attempting to help injured shipmates. A pillar of flame towered from the sea where the destroyer went under. Its glare illumined the scene with an unearthly light—the bobbing rafts, the slicked water, the oil-smeared faces of the men.

Help comes slowly in the hour of disaster—yet the rescuers were on the way at top speed. Destroyers NIBLACK and HILARY P. JONES were dispatched to the scene to search for survivors. Blazing oil and pitiless sea almost frustrated the rescue ships. Only 45 REUBEN JAMES men, including one chief petty officer, were recovered. About 115 of the destroyer's complement had perished in the torpedoing or drowned in the icy water. Lieutenant Commander Edwards went down with his ship. So did every other officer of the ship's company.

The killer submarine was neither sighted nor detected by any of the escorts or ships in the convoy before the strike. But as the convoy drew away from the scene of the torpedoing, BENSON made three possible sonar contacts, and launched urgent attacks on the target. TARBELL also delivered several attacks. However, one murderous shot had been enough, and after that one shot, the submarine bent its efforts on a getaway. Its hit-and-run tactics were only too successful.

The following day a British escort group, nearing the "Momp" junction where the American escorts were to be relieved, sighted a pair of stalking U-boats. These wolves were chased off with hot gunnery. Whether the sub responsible for the destruction of REUBEN JAMES was one of this pair or not remained an unanswered question.

One question, however, was definitely answered. The attacks on GREER and KEARNY might conceivably have been the work of hotheaded submarine commanders. But the attack on REUBEN JAMES was obviously deliberate. Manifestly the Nazis were dedicated to an all-out war with the United States; the U-boats had been passed the word.

On November 1, 1941—within 36 hours of the REUBEN JAMES sinking—President Roosevelt, as authorized by act of Congress, transferred the Coast Guard to the Navy. Thereafter the U.S.C.G. was to operate as part of the U.S.N. until returned to the Treasury Department by Executive Order.

Aroused by the thunder of torpedo-fire, Congress voted the following week to amend the Neutrality Act. Two amendments were passed. The first permitted the arming of American merchantmen so that they might defend themselves against attack. The second abolished the restriction which denied European waters to American shipping. The Navy could now convoy Lend-Lease goods to ports in the United Kingdom; the unrealistic postures of "isolationism" and "belligerent neutrality" were virtually ended.

Many Americans continued to believe that the nation was at peace. Neither wishing nor words made it so. In the autumn of 1941, weeks before Pearl Harbor, American Navy men were fighting the Battle of the Atlantic.

The destroyer REUBEN JAMES was the first United States warship lost in World War II.

What Ship Is That? (Destroyermen Aid Capture of Suspected "Slaver")

Early in 1820 the United States sloop-of-war CYANE, under a Captain Trenchard, arrived in the waters off darkest West Africa to inaugurate a new American naval patrol. The previous year Congress had passed a law forbidding the importation of Negro slaves. Whereas most American skippers were ready to abandon the nefarious traffic, there were criminal elements equally ready to indulge in slave smuggling. It was to stop this felonious game at the outset that the Navy established the African Patrol.

That a suspected slaver would turn up in the South Atlantic in November 1941 was a phenomenon expected by no modern naval authority. But "short-of-war" operations led to all manner of surprises.

The surprise was in the making on November 6, when three ships approached a point about 657 miles from Recife, Brazil. Steaming in company as Task Group 3.6, on patrol, the United States light cruiser OMAHA (Captain T. E. Chandler) and destroyer SOMERS (Commander J. C. Metzel) were heading in for Recife. Steaming independently, the third vessel, a motorship whose stern bore the name S.S. WILLMOTO of Philadelphia, was heading northward.

OMAHA and SOMERS were surprised to sight WILLMOTO—a darkened ship with American flags painted large on her sides—and they changed course to intercept and investigate. For her part WILLMOTO was apparently surprised to encounter the American cruiser and destroyer. She ran up code flags spelling out her name. But when hailed, she did not answer.

OMAHA and SOMERS closed in for a sharper scrutiny. Stars and Stripes flew above the freighter's taffrail—why her silence?

A destroyer lookout eyed a shipmate on SOMERS' bridge. "There's something queer about that bucket!"

OMAHA's captain thought so too. The steamer was signalled to lie to and await a boarding party. Then, as the cruiser's launch set out for the enigmatic vessel, a confetti of flags appeared on the freighter's halyards. The message constituted another surprise.

AM SINKING SEND BOATS

Captain Chandler had already sent a boat. As OMAHA's launch drew alongside, the boarding party saw WILLMOTO's crew abandoning. The shouting merchant seamen did not sound like Philadelphians, although they might have been Pennsylvania Dutch.

"They were Dutch, all right," a Navy man described afterwards. "But they weren't from Pennsylvania, and they weren't from Holland."

While the boarders were clambering up to the WILLMOTO's deck, two muffled explosions sounded in the vessel's hold. Demolition charges! Tendrils of smoke reeled from the hatches. Lieutenant G. K. Carmichael and visiting bluejackets made a dash for ladders going below. Quick work took care of the damage, and instead of settling to the bottom, the motor-ship remained stolidly on the surface. Another surprise, and an unpleasant one for Captain Gerhart Loers, the vessel's skipper.

It now appeared that Loers was a German. Equally Teutonic were the mates, and other crew members. The WILLMOTO was the ODENWALD sailing under false colors—a blockade-runner. En route to Germany from Japan, she was laden with general cargo, the bulk of which consisted of some 3,800 tons of rubber.

German ship, cargo, captain, and crew were escorted to Port of Spain, Trinidad, by cruiser OMAHA and destroyer SOMERS. Since the United States was not officially at war with Nazi Germany there was some doubt as to the legality of the prize capture.

However, one good euphemism deserves another. And the "short-of-war" technicality invited a very fine bit of counter casuistry. Harking back to the old days of "blackbirding," Commander Task Group 3.6 reported that ODENWALD had been captured as a "suspected slaver"!

Escorts to Asia (Convoy "William Sail")

In November 1941 United States destroyers participated in a large-scale convoy operation that was planned with such secrecy that even the enemy failed to hear about it.

That was the autumn when Britain was fighting back-to-the-wall. Rommel's panzers were pounding on the gates of Suez. And the desperate British, called upon to reinforce their crumbling front in the Near East, were denied the Mediterranean by the Italian Navy and the German Air Force on Crete.

A British division, 22,000 strong, was waiting at home. The long way around—South Atlantic, Cape of Good Hope, Indian Ocean—was the only way it could reach the Persian Gulf. But the Admiralty lacked the shipping to transport these troops, and the Royal Navy could not muster the escortage. Could Uncle Sam furnish transports and escorts?

The answer was affirmative, and the result was Convoy WS-124—the Allies' first America-to-Orient troop convoy under escort of the U.S. Navy.

For the Americans involved, the convoy-duty began at "Momp." There the British transports were taken from their Royal Navy escorts by Rear Admiral H. K. Hewitt's task force. The destroyers in the force which escorted this big convoy on the "Momp"-to-Canada run were: MORRIS (flying the broad command pennant of Captain W. L. Ainsworth), SIMS, HUGHES, MUSTIN, HAMMANN, RUSSELL, WALKE, O'BRIEN, and ANDERSON.

At Halifax the Tommies were unloaded for transshipment; the British transports retired; destroyers HAMMANN and ANDERSON returned to Iceland; Ainsworth led the rest of DesRon 2 to Casco Bay for a breather. And fresh troopships and escort force stepped in. Convoy WS-124 was readied for the long voyage *via* the South Atlantic and Cape of Good Hope.

Dubbed "William Sail" (from the code letters "WS"), the convoy steamed from Halifax on November 10. In command was Rear Admiral A. B. Cook, Commander Air Force Atlantic Fleet, in the United States aircraft carrier RANGER. Convoy Commodore was Captain D. B. BEARY in U.S.S. MOUNT VERNON.

American transports were provided. The biggest of these ships were the U.S.S. MOUNT VERNON (ex-liner WASHINGTON), U.S.S. WAKEFIELD (ex-MANHATTAN), and U.S.S. WEST POINT (ex-AMERICA). Also in the ship-train were the transports LEONARD WOOD, JOSEPH T. DICKMAN, and ORIZABA.

For escort duty the Navy provided a powerful warship force. The armada was designated Task Group 14.4. The "big guns" were carried by the aircraft carrier RANGER and the heavy cruisers QUINCY and VINCENNES. Eight destroyers composed the convoy's screen, as follows:

WAINWRIGHT — *Lt. Comdr. T. L. Lewis*
Flying pennant of Screen Commander, Capt. T. C. Kinkaid, COMDESRON 8
MOFFETT — *Comdr. P. R. Heineman*
MCDOUGAL — *Comdr. D. L. Madeira*
Flying pennant of Comdr. L. K. Swenson, COMDESDIV 17
WINSLOW — *Comdr. H. R. Holcomb*
MAYRANT — *Lt. Comdr. E. A. Taylor*
Flying pennant of Comdr. T. V. Cooper, COMDESDIV 16
RHIND — *Comdr. H. T. Read*
ROWAN — *Lt. Comdr. B. R. Harrison*
TRIPPE — *Lt. Comdr. R. L. Campbell, Jr.*

The task group steamed for Trinidad. There the Navy tanker CIMARRON was attached to the convoy.

At Trinidad Captain Kinkaid was detached for transfer to the Pacific as Rear Admiral in charge of a cruiser division. He was replaced as Screen Commander by Commander Swenson, who transferred his pennant from McDougal to Wainwright.

About midway between Brazil and the Islands of St. Helena, the Ranger left the formation. With her went destroyers Trippe and Rhind. Captain C. E. Battle in Quincy assumed command of the convoy.

December 6 found the convoy bucking its way for the Cape in the teeth of a caterwauling gale. Shouldered roughly by the tempest, the convoy slowed and changed course. And then came word of another storm—a Pacific storm. Word that stunned every man and jack in the convoy and changed the troopships' destinations from Basra to India and Singapore. *"Japanese have attacked Pearl Harbor. United States Pacific Fleet immobilized!"*

War Declared!

On December 8, 1941, the United States Government declared war on Japan. On December 11, Germany and Italy declared war on the United States, and Congress promptly returned the compliment. This was *it!*

But to the forces of DesLant, "it" was only so much anti-climax. The official declaration of war found the U.S. Navy's destroyermen already fighting the Atlantic Battle with their gloves off. In the war from that hour when a Nazi U-boat took a shot at Greer, they had long since dispensed with formalities. And after the Kearny and Reuben James torpedoings, the only gloves in evidence in the DesLant Force had been those on the hands of the "hot shell" men.

DESTROYERS OF THE UNITED STATES ATLANTIC FLEET

(December 7, 1941)

Plunkett	Jacob Jones	Mustin	Meredith
Gleaves	Ellis	Walke	Buck
Lansdale	Dupont	Stark	Edison
McDougal	Upshur	Mayrant	Nicholson
Sampson	Bainbridge	Rowan	Morris
Somers	McCormick	Babbitt	Hughes
Livermore	Truxtun	Roper	Russell
Ericsson	Niblack	Herbert	Wainwright
Grayson	Mayo	Bernadou	Sterett
Woolsey	Hilary P. Jones	Greer	Trippe
Bristol	Winslow	Lea	Decatur
Swanson	Davis	Overton	Leary
Anderson	Warrington	Broome	Dickerson
Sims	Eberle	Benson	Dallas
O'Brien	Gwin	Charles F. Hughes	Cole
Lang	Monssen	Madison	Tarbell
Wilson	Ludlow	Moffett	MacLeish
Rhind	Wilkes	Jouett	Sturtevant
Badger	Ingraham	Roe	Simpson
	Hammann	Kearny	

Schenck

★

DESTROYER TENDERS

Denebola	Altair	Melville	Prairie

DesDiv 66

Breckinridge	Barney	Biddle	Blakeley

Assigned temporarily to the Atlantic Fleet from 15th Naval District (Canal Zone)

CHAPTER 4

PACIFIC EXPLOSION

DesPac, December 7

The Samauri sword of Damocles that fell on December 7, 1941, plunging the United States into a two-ocean war, was aimed at decapitating the U.S. Pacific Fleet at Pearl Harbor and leaving the United States Navy impotent, if not dead, in the Pacific. It would be an exaggeration to say that the destroyers of the Destroyer Pacific (DesPac) Force based at Pearl served as a shield which fended off the blow on that fatal Sunday, or even nicked the edge of that swinging Japanese blade. Pearl Harbor was caught with its neck bared, and the Pacific Fleet lay prostrate after the slashing onslaught.

But destroyers fought the enemy from the first alarm. In fact, a DesPac destroyer transmitted the first alarm a few minutes after the approaching Executioner was detected—almost four hours before the deadly blow was delivered.

Throughout the autumn of 1941 the DesPac Force had been holding realistic exercises and battle drills, and had been patrolling various areas of the Pacific on the alert. On several occasions, during October and November, they had reported enemy submarines off Hawaii and Wake. The DD's at Pearl were not asleep when the vanguard of Admiral C. Nagumo's Striking Force arrived.

On December 7, 1941, there were 54 destroyers on duty with the Pacific Fleet. The roster is listed on page 44. About half of these destroyers were at sea when the Japanese raiders struck at Oahu. A considerable number were in Pearl Harbor. And the wonder is that nearly all of the DD's at Pearl escaped the blizzard of bombs which fell on the shipping off Pearl City, Ford Island, Kuahua, and the Navy Yard at Keanapuaa. Only three of the destroyers in the Harbor were blasted out of action; one of these, badly damaged, returned to action after overhaul; the two hardest hit were eventually rebuilt, and their names were never stricken from the Navy's active list.

At anchor or docked in Pearl Harbor on December 7 were eight battleships, nine cruisers, some twenty-nine destroyers, five submarines, a hospital ship, and the usual complement of tenders, tugs, fleet oilers, repair ships, and auxiliaries.

Many sailors were ashore on week-end liberty and leave, and most of the ships were manned by skeleton forces. The usual routine. Honolulu drifted off to sleep Saturday night with no thought of the nightmare to come. The clock ticked somnolently into Sunday—a day that began as any other day. That is to say, it began peacefully for the Americans. Japan had already gone to war.

Closing in on Hawaii like an assassin in the night was a Japanese Carrier Force. The ships were fully armed and manned; the aircraft were ready to go. For weeks the pilots had trained for this strike. They had studied charts of Oahu and worked with exact-replica models of Pearl Harbor. At a top-secret Japanese island they had rehearsed every move of the assassination. Fighters, bombers, and torpedo-planes had drilled as teams for the onslaught. Every bomb and torpedo was counted, timed, and ticketed for a marked target. The Japanese did not know the exact location of the ships in the harbor, but cunning Intelligence work had provided them with a fair idea of what they would find in East Loch and anchored off Ford Island. Marked for special attention was "Battleship Row." Also marked for attention were the Oahu airfields.

Ahead of Admiral Nagumo's carriers prowled an Advance Expeditionary Force of I-boats, to lie off the harbor entrance and ambush any warships which attempted to escape the December 7 slaughter. For a minor mission, several of these large subs were to release midget submarines which had been trained for special work in the target area. The midgets were to reconnoiter the entrance channel, and if possible enter the harbor. In one of the more amazing feats of modern submarining, a Jap midget did succeed in entering the harbor and circuiting Ford Island in the very heart of the great naval base—a daredevil exploit comparable to the undetected prowl of a Bengal tiger around Times Square. The "baby sub" apparently got in at 0430, circled the island counter-clock-

---

DESTROYERS IN THE U.S. PACIFIC FLEET

(December 7, 1941)

Phelps	Benham	Bagley	Tucker
Macdonough	Rathburne	Jarvis	Flusser
Dale	Waters	Gridley	Cushing
Clark	Chew*	McCall	Smith
Downes	Dewey	Fanning	Helm
Shaw	Worden	Dent	Mugford
Porter	Farragut	Litchfield	Patterson
Lamson	Cassin	Allen*	Craven
Perkins	Reid	Hull	Dunlap
Selfridge	Cummings	Aylwin	Ellet
Blue	Drayton	Monaghan	Talbot
Ralph Talbot	Mahan	Conyngham	*Schley
Balch	Preston	Case	*Ward
	Maury	Henley	

* *Attached to 14th Naval District (Pearl Harbor)*

DESTROYER TENDERS

Dixie	Dobbin	Whitney

DESTROYERS ASSIGNED TO NAVAL DISTRICTS

(December 7, 1941)

11TH NAVAL DISTRICT (SAN DIEGO)

Crane	Crosby	Kennison	Kilty

12TH NAVAL DISTRICT (SAN FRANCISCO)

Lawrence	Humphreys	King	Sands

13TH NAVAL DISTRICT (SEATTLE)

Gilmer	Hatfield	Brooks	Fox	Kane

15TH NAVAL DISTRICT (CANAL ZONE)

Borie	Breckinridge*	Barney*	*Blakeley
Biddle*	Barry	Goff	Tattnall
	J. Fred Talbott		

* *Temporarily assigned to Atlantic Fleet; also listed under Atlantic Fleet.*
(Not included in the above table are certain destroyers converted into minecraft, such as Tracy, Preble, Trever, *and* Breese.)

---

wise, and got out an hour later. It was eventually captured, complete with chart showing the route of its incredible junket. Not the least incredible feature of this nocturnal invasion was the fact that it occurred *after* another midget had been spotted and sunk off the harbor entrance.

The opening shot at Pearl Harbor was fired by the destroyer WARD. Here is the story—

Ward and Condor Kill Midget

On December 5, 1941, destroyer WARD steamed out of Pearl Harbor to patrol the waters outside the harbor entrance.

WARD was an old "four-piper" of World War I vintage. Her guns were old-fashioned 4-inch 50's; she had to strain to make 30 knots. But she could still roll "ashcans" and get out the shells.

At 0300 in the morning of December 7, WARD was heading into Pearl Harbor on the homestretch of her patrol. The patrol had been singularly uneventful—a fact which pleased Lieutenant W. W. Outerbridge, her skipper, as this was his first command. It also pleased the officers of WARD's crew, who were Naval Reservists and eager to show their skills. As for the men in WARD, the ship's company was typical of that blend of professional Navy man and civilian-in-uniform which was to man the United States Fleet's destroyers and destroyer-escorts during World War II.

About 0357 Ensign L. F. Platt, U.S.N.R., reported to Lieutenant Outerbridge that WARD had just received a blinker message from the minesweeper CONDOR. CONDOR had sighted something which resembled the periscope of a submarine.

The minesweeper had spotted this suspicious "stick" skulking through the dark water at 0350. At that time the CONDOR was conducting sweeping operations approximately one and three-quarter miles southwest of the Pearl Harbor entrance buoys.

Outerbridge sent the WARD to General Quarters. For about an hour WARD searched the area. Her lookouts saw nothing; her sonar detected nothing. Circling across the seascape, she approached CONDOR and Outerbridge spoke the minesweeper over TBS (radiotelephone).

The talk between the two ships was intercepted by a naval radio station on Oahu. The radio mentor copied the dialogue, which went somewhat as follows:

WHAT WAS THE APPROXIMATE DISTANCE AND COURSE OF THE SUBMARINE SIGHTED? Answer: THE COURSE WAS ABOUT 020 MAGNETIC AND SOME 1,000 YARDS FROM THE HARBOR ENTRANCE. Question: DO YOU HAVE ANY ADDITIONAL INFORMATION? Answer: NO ADDITIONAL INFORMATION. Question: WHEN WAS THE LAST TIME YOU SAW THE SUBMARINE? Answer: APPROXIMATELY 0350, AND IT WAS APPARENTLY HEADING FOR THE ENTRANCE.

WARD's skipper was about convinced that the little minesweeper had sighted a "phantom." He gave the word to secure, and returned to his bunk. At 0637 he was awakened by Lieutenant (jg) O. W. Goepner, U.S.N.R., Officer of the Deck. *"Captain! Quick! Come out on the bridge!"*

Outerbridge hit the deck with both feet. On the bridge he found excited men pointing at a vessel which was towing a lighter into the entrance channel. The vessel was the target ship ANTARES. Not an unusual sight. But the spectacle of *a small submarine* trailing the ANTARES was *most* unusual.

Outerbridge immediately sent WARD steaming toward the queer little sub. In the dim morning light the submarine's silhouette was positively identified as "stranger." These were restricted waters for foreign submarining, and as soon as the destroyer's guns could be brought to bear, Outerbridge ordered the crews to open fire. The range was about 100 yards when the bow gun flashed and roared. The first United States shot in the Pacific War was fired at 0645.

That No. 1 shot from WARD's No. 1 gun missed the undersized conning tower. But her second shot, fired from her No. 3 gun at a range of 75 yards, slammed into the base of the conning tower with a dazzling flash. The little sub heeled over, slowed, and began to sink. The destroyer passed ahead, and Outerbridge shouted an order which started the "ashcans" rolling. Chief Torpedoman W. C. Maskzawitz adjusted the depth settings with deft precision and released the first charge directly under the midget's nose. In all, four charges were dropped. The sub swam squarely into the explosions, and went down in 1,200 feet of water. American destroyermen had killed their first Jap submersible.

The kill was timed at 0645. Outerbridge immediately notified "Com14" at Pearl Harbor.

WE HAVE ATTACKED, FIRED UPON, AND DROPPED DEPTH CHARGES UPON SUBMARINE OPERATING IN DEFENSIVE SEA AREA!

After waiting several minutes, he spoke the Naval Radio Station at Bishop's Point to check the communication. About 0712 the Bishop's Point operator acknowledged the dispatch.

But somehow the message evaporated in the misty dawnlight over Pearl. As old Navy men phrase it, "Someone always fails to get the word." This time the commanders at Pearl Harbor failed to get it. Neither Com14 nor Commander-in-Chief Pacific received the word in time. Apparently no one took it seriously. As CinCPac later stated,

During the previous year there had been several reports of submarine contacts, all of which turned out to be false.

It was the old story of "Wolf! Wolf!" A series of false alarms had dulled the guard at Pearl Harbor, and the impact of WARD's communique hardly dented the local intelligence.

Back on board the WARD the lookouts saw oil swilling to the surface where the invader sub had gone down. The destroyermen searched the area. Someone spotted a fishing craft sailing out in the sunrise across restricted water. WARD steamed over to investigate this trespasser. The craft proved to be a motor-driven sampan from Honolulu, with a Jap crew. The vessel hove to as WARD came up, and the destroyermen turned her over to a Coast Guard cutter which took the suspicious sampan into custody. With every nerve quivering, the WARD continued to search the harbor entrance, and while she was so doing her lookouts sighted a large number of aircraft over Pearl. Some columns of black smoke climbed into the morning sky over the Harbor. Heavy-footed explosions echoed across the water. If these were war games, they were unusually realistic. Suddenly a plane raced across the seascape and dropped a bomb near the Coast Guardsman towing the sampan. WARD's sailors stared in astonishment at the plane. Its wings were marked with a red fireball. Someone shouted, *"That's Japanese!"*

The United States was in the throes of World War II.

The Onslaught

The morning was fair; visibility good. In Honolulu church bells were clanging. On board the ships in Pearl Harbor sailors were shining their shoes and sprucing up for morning service. At 0755 all thought of Sabbath observances came to a rude end. Over Hickam Field roared a squadron of some 18 Japanese dive-bombers. In a moment the Army aircraft parked in neat rows on the field went skyhigh in bursts of debris. About half of the Japanese bombers roared on past to blast the American battlewagons conveniently tied up two by two at Ford Island. Torpedo-planes followed the bombers. What happened to the tethered battleships is a story too well-known for recapitulation in this text on destroyer warfare.

At 0825 the first wave receded.

At 0840 the enemy came over in a high-level bombing attack that lasted until 0915.

At 0915 Jap dive-bombers plummeted on the Harbor.

At 0945 the dive-bombing wave receded, and the roar of battle gradually ebbed away. A few Jap planes reappeared. But the raid was concluded by 1000. By that time the Pacific Fleet was "immobilized."

And Pearl Harbor was a charnel of wreckage, agony, and death. Out of this wreckage some 17 American destroyers emerged with heads bloody but unbowed. In the midst of unparalleled carnage they had acquitted themselves well. Only three of the DD's in the Harbor had been battered out of action. And these three victims of Japan's surprise onslaught had been trapped in drydock.

Damaging of Shaw

On that morning of December 7, destroyer SHAW (Lieutenant Commander W. Glenn Jones) was in the old NEW ORLEANS floating drydock at the Navy Yard. With her in the dock was the tug SOTOYOMO. The crews of both DD and tug were ashore, as was customary for vessels undergoing overhaul in drydock, and only a few men were on hand when the bombs started to fall.

Between 0755 and 0915 SHAW was hit by three bombs which were released by steep-diving planes at about 1,000-foot altitude. Apparently all three hits were made simultaneously. The ship may have been struck by two 250-kilo general purpose bombs and a 16-inch armor-piercing specimen. The first two bombs exploded in the crew's mess. The third smashed through the bridge. Fire spurted from ruptured oil tanks. About 20 minutes later the forward magazines blew up, evidently exploded by the heat of burning oil and wooden blocking in the dock. The drydock was purposely flooded to extinguish the conflagration, and as it sank SHAW's bow toppled to starboard and went under with the dock. The yard tug also sank. As the dock submerged, flaming oil swirled around SHAW.

Eventually SHAW's stern section was docked on the marine railway. A temporary bow was built on the ship, and under her own power she voyaged to the West Coast for permanent repairs. She was a tough little destroyer to thus survive an assassination carnival which sent a number of battleships to the bottom.

Damaging of Cassin and Downes

When the Japs came over, the destroyers CASSIN (Lieutenant Commander D. F. J. Shea), flagship of Commander L. P. Lovette, Commander Destroyer Division 5 (ComDesDiv 5), and DOWNES (Lieutenant Commander W. R. Thayer), were in Drydock No.1. With them in the dock was battleship PENNSYLVANIA.

War without warning. Out of the peaceful skies bombs suddenly dropped on the U.S.S. Shaw in floating drydock at Pearl Harbor, December 7, 1941. Hit almost simultaneously by three bombs, the destroyer erupted in flames and explosions. The Shaw's stern section was eventually salvaged, a temporary bow patched on, and she steamed to the West Coast to obtain complete repairs.

Wreckage of the Cassin and Downes. Both these destroyers were in drydock when the Japanese struck Pearl Harbor. Fighting back, Downes was bombed into a wreck whose exploding ammunition and blazing oil set the Cassin ablaze too. Flooding the dock extinguished the fires, and much of the machinery and plates of both destroyers was salvaged for repairing other ships.

She lived to fight again—stages in the life of U.S.S. Shaw. In the upper left she appears in the peaceful days before her immolation at Pearl Harbor, pictured elsewhere. Lower left, she steams for the mainland with a patchwork temporary bow. Upper right, she awaits her new bow in drydock at Mare Island. Lower right, she steams back to the battle zone, all set to fight again.

The two destroyers occupied the southern end of the dock. Both ships were undergoing overhaul. Their 5-inch guns were inoperative, with parts missing, and DOWNES' .50-caliber machine-guns were dismantled.

For about an hour the ships were protected by a huge curtain of AA fire which was raised by battleship PENNSYLVANIA, flagship of the Pacific Fleet. CASSIN's .50 calibers were furiously chattering in chorus with PENNSYLVANIA's. But DOWNES' machine-gunners had to break out ammunition and assemble the guns before they could shoot. About 15 minutes after the start of the attack, they too opened fire. But the destroyermen were hampered by gear on deck, and by the fact that key men were ashore. CASSIN's skipper was on board, but Lieutenant Commander Thayer of DOWNES was ashore, and when the holocaust exploded in the Harbor, Lieutenant (jg) J. D. Parker assumed command of the ship.

DOWNES was the first destroyer in Drydock No. 1 to be struck. Her gunners were firing at three dive-bombers when a bomb struck in the dock between the two DD's and hurled a sheet of fire over DOWNES' stern. The ship's side was riddled; a fuel oil tank was ruptured and set aflame; and the incendiary bomb drenched the vessel's fantail with a yellow-green liquid that burned like gasoline jelly. By 0920 the flames were out of control, and Lieutenant Parker ordered the survivors (some five officers and 140 men) to leave the ship. After all hands went overside the destroyer became molten. The oil in her bunkers exploded. Some of the torpedoes on her deck blasted off. In a short time the vessel was a mass of twisted steel and scrap. But her men stubbornly remained at dockside, fighting the fire with feeble hoses and dodging showers of debris hurled skyward by explosions. Lieutenant Parker's neck was gashed by a flying jag of metal, but he directed the fire-fighting to the last ditch. The drydock was flooded, and the DOWNES was deliberately swamped. No one would have believed that any part of the vessel was salvageable. But so much of her was salvaged by expert Navy technicians that the ship was never considered lost.

Destroyer CASSIN was similarly incinerated. Senior destroyer officer present in the drydock, her skipper, Lieutenant Commander Shea, ordered both DD's "closed up" as soon as the fireball planes struck the Harbor. When DOWNES was hit, CASSIN was showered with liquid fire. In a few minutes she was blazing from stern to stem, and Shea ordered all hands to quit the vessel.

Hose lines were rushed from the Yard, and CASSIN's crew valiantly fought the conflagration, playing water on depth charges and torpedoes to prevent explosions. So intense was the heat that war heads melted, and the fire-fighters were forced back from the dock. CASSIN slipped her blocks and rolled over on the burning DOWNES. Then explosion followed explosion, hurling debris at the destroyermen. As described in CASSIN's Action Report:

"About 0915 there was a terrific explosion on the DOWNES, *and flames shot about 60 feet in the air, which was filled with (flying) fragments. Hoses were practically torn away from fire-fighting parties consisting of men from* CASSIN, DOWNES, *and yard employees. All hands retreated from the dock and sprawled on the road."*

The flames which ravaged CASSIN were eventually subdued at 1045. Like DOWNES, the ship was a crushed, ruptured, tangled mass of calcined metal, her hull wrinkled by crucible heat and ripped by internal and external blasting. Yet this destroyer, too, was not entirely destroyed; much of her machinery, deck gear, and hull were ultimately salvaged. Like DOWNES, she would compose another fighting ship. And her crew steamed out of Pearl Harbor to fight the Pacific war.

Destroyers Versus Pearl Raiders

One of the first destroyers to open fire on the Japs at Pearl Harbor was the BAGLEY (Lieutenant Commander G. A. Sinclair). She was moored in Berth B-22 at the Navy Yard for repairs to her starboard bilge keel. Her crew raced to General Quarters at the time a torpedo-bomber flung a "fish" into the battleship OKLAHOMA.

BAGLEY's AA gunners broomed the sky with flak. Other ships in the harbor were doing the same. A number of Jap planes stunted away trailing smoke, and others crashed in the water.

At 0940 the ship got under way and stood seaward, pausing only to pick up the skipper of destroyer PATTERSON, who was subsequently transferred to his own ship at sea. She also picked up the Commanding Officer and "Exec" of destroyer BLUE, who were sent to Pearl Harbor the following evening in a ship's boat. BAGLEY was taken to sea by Lieutenant P. W. Cann, whose quick-thinking sortie doubtless saved the ship from severe punishment. She operated in the off-shore patrol area until she returned to the Harbor on December 9.

In Berth X-9, East Loch, on the morning of December 7 were destroyers SELFRIDGE, CASE, TUCKER, REID, and CONYNGHAM. About four minutes before morning colors, the Officer of the Deck on board SELFRIDGE saw a Jap plane launch a torpedo at cruiser RALEIGH. He sounded General Quarters, and at about 0758 SELFRIDGE's machine-gunners opened .50 caliber fire on Jap planes. At 1000 she pulled out of the nest, and headed seaward. She was presently followed by

CASE, TUCKER, and REID. CONYNGHAM, undergoing tender overhaul, did not get out of the berth until that evening. All four ships in SELFRIDGE's wake opened fire on the attacking aircraft.

At Berth No. 6 destroyers JARVIS and MUGFORD were moored side by side. MUGFORD opened fire about 0804. By 0815 JARVIS was shooting at the Japs. JARVIS' skipper arrived on board during a lull at 0915, and the ship cast off and stood out of the Harbor about an hour later. She had opened up on the enemy with 5-inch fire, perhaps the first destroyer at Pearl Harbor to shoot at the foe with her main batteries. MUGFORD had to take on fuel before she could move, and she did not get out of her berth until noon.

Destroyers CUMMINGS, TRACY, and PREBLE were nesting at Berth B-15. At 0803 CUMMINGS opened fire with her .50's, shooting at Jap torpedo-planes. Her main batteries boomed at dive-bombers attacking Battleship Row at 0811. At 1040 she moved out of the Harbor and joined the A/S patrol off the entrance. She made several depth-charge attacks on what may have been a submarine, but results were inconclusive. TRACY, PREBLE, and destroyer SCHLEY (at Berth No. 20) also shot at the Jap raiders, and escaped death in the Harbor frying pan.

When the storm broke over Pearl, the destroyers of DesDiv 1 (of Captain A. R. Early's Squadron 1) were nested alongside the tender DOBBIN. DesDiv 1 included PHELPS, MACDONOUGH, WORDEN, DEWEY, and HULL.

Destroyer PHELPS was standing a "cold iron" watch in the Engineering Department, as she was receiving steam, electricity, and fresh and flushing water from the tender. At 0758 the gangway watch saw the fire-ball planes roar in over Kuahua to dive-bomb the BB's moored in Battleship Row. PHELPS' crew was immediately rushed to General Quarters. The electrical load was shifted from the tender to the ship's emergency Diesel generators. She opened fire with her forward 1.1-inch gun at 0802, and with the after mount about 13 minutes later. By 0825 two boilers were lighted off, and an hour later the destroyer got under way and stood out to sea through North Channel. She cleared the entrance buoys at 0950, and for the next five hours she operated with cruiser ST. LOUIS on anti-submarine patrol. Senior officer on board, the ship's Engineer Officer, Lieutenant B. E. S. Trippensee, assumed command, took the ship out of the Harbor, and conned her almost continuously for some 33 hours.

Flying his pennant in destroyer WORDEN was Commander Walfrid Nyquist, ComDesDiv 1. He had assumed command of the division only the previous day. The war began in earnest for WORDEN when a Jap bomb hit the water about 50 yards astern and showered her fantail with a mixture of scrap iron and brine. WORDEN's machine-gun crews whipped shots at the attacking planes. The destroyer slipped out from under tender DOBBIN's mothering wing at 1040, and stood seaward through South Channel.

DEWEY sounded General Quarters at 0757. Five minutes later her machine-guns were blazing at the raiders. At 0810 her 5-inchers roared at the assassins. Excerpt from DEWEY's Action Report:

"0900: Second wave of attack started by light bombers which lasted ten minutes. Under fire by DEWEY *throughout attack. 0945: Third wave of attack started by dive-bombers. In this attack the* DOBBIN *and Destroyer Division 1 became a target, three or four planes attacking the nest. One bomb hit close aboard starboard quarter of the* DOBBIN *and one hit water between the* HULL *and* DEWEY *about 75 feet astern. No damage sustained by these close hits.... All of the action was astern. However, Guns No. 1 and No. 2 and forward machine-guns fired when not blanked off by* DOBBIN *or upper works in the nest. The bridge force fired automatic-rifles and rifles."*

DEWEY got under way and stood out of the Harbor at 1505. She was the last unit of DesDiv 1 to escape the crucible.

MACDONOUGH's men raced to battle stations at 0758, and her gunners opened fire with 5-inch batteries and machine-guns at 0804. For more than an hour and a half they banged away at Jap aircraft. At 1220 the ship had steam up, and she pulled out of the Harbor at 1235. By mid-afternoon she was busily engaged in screening cruiser DETROIT in company with WORDEN and PHELPS.

Destroyer HULL sounded General Quarters at 0757. The crews were racing to battle stations when the gangway watch opened fire on the Japs—with a .45 service automatic. Within a few minutes the ship's batteries were roaring and chattering at the Jap planes. About 0910 three enemy aircraft with yellow disks on their wings attacked DOBBIN and her brood. As the planes swooped in on the tender's starboard quarter, DOBBIN and the destroyers lashed the yellow disks with fire. If the Japs had a glimpse of the sailor at HULL's gangway shooting at them with a .45 pistol, they saw a typical American destroyerman doing his best with the equipment available.

When all hell exploded in the Harbor, destroyers HENLEY, PATTERSON, and RALPH TALBOT were moored to Buoy X-11 in East Loch. Through a freakish error HENLEY's crew was at battle stations when the first Jap planes appeared in the sky—someone had sounded General Quarters instead of Quarters for

Muster. The green hand who made this mistake inadvertently gave his ship a chance to fire the first destroyer shot at the rampaging Japanese.

At 0830 HENLEY shoved off from the buoy. While she was slipping her chain, a heavy bomb struck the water about 150 yards on the port bow. Just as she cleared the nest she received a signal, "Submarine in harbor!" Directly ahead of her the MACDONOUGH dropped depth charges. Swerving to side-step this action, HENLEY raced on out of the entrance channel, the third ship to sortie. After she rounded Hospital Point she was strafed by a light bomber. Her machine-gunners lashed at the plane with .50 calibers. Outside the Harbor she made sonar contact with what may have been a midget submarine. Two depth charges were dropped, but results could not be determined. During the raid and sortie the ship was under command of Lieutenant F. E. Fleck, Jr. The ship's captain, Lieutenant Commander Robert Hall Smith, and her Executive Officer, Lieutenant H. G. Corey, were ashore when the raid began. They put to sea on the destroyer TREVER. Because of the submarine alarms off the harbor entrance, the ships could not halt for a passenger transfer. So HENLEY was jockeyed into position ahead of TREVER; a life raft was streamed on a long lead of manila line from Henley's fantail; the two officers sprang from TREVER to the raft, and were thus hauled in by HENLEY.

Destroyer PATTERSON opened fire on the Jap planes shortly after HENLEY started the barrage. Lieutenant A. F. White conned the ship away from the nest at 0900 to take her out of the shell-shocked harbor. PATTERSON's regular Commanding Officer, Lieutenant Commander F. R. Walker, chased the sortiing DD in a small boat, and finally boarded her about two miles south of the harbor entrance at 0930.

Destroyer RALPH TALBOT joined PATTERSON in the getaway. By 0934 she was out at sea, her engines going full speed, the smoke of battle trickling from her guns. She was taken out of the Harbor by her Commanding Officer, Lieutenant Commander Ralph Earle, Jr.

As exciting a sortie as any at Pearl was made by destroyer BLUE. About 85 per cent of her regular crew were on board when the Jap raiders struck. Seated in the wardroom at that fatal hour were Ensigns N. F. Asher, M. J. Moldafsky, U.S.N.R., J. P. Wolfe, U.S.N.R., and R. S. Scott, U.S.N.R. These four were the only officers on board. Assuming temporary command, Ensign Asher rushed the crew to battle stations. BLUE's gunners opened fire with main batteries and machine-guns as the Japs roared over. At 0847 she got under way. She maintained a furious fire while negotiating the difficult channel. By 0910 the ship had passed the entrance buoys and was proceeding to her patrol station.

At 0950 her sonar registered a contact. BLUE made two depth-charge attacks. On her first run she dropped four charges; on the second she dropped two. A large oil slick and a thick cluster of bubbles appeared on the surface. It seems probable that BLUE abolished one of the five midget submarines spawned by the Jap I-boat Expeditionary Force operating off Pearl Harbor.

Not long after this A/S action, BLUE dropped two depth charges on another detected sub. When this scrimmage was over she screened the cruiser ST. LOUIS. All of which constituted a busy morning for a short-handed destroyer officered by four Ensigns. When BLUE returned to Pearl Harbor on the evening of the 8th, Ensign Asher and the ship's company were lauded for better-than-good work.

Another midget submarine was probably sunk off the harbor entrance by destroyer HELM (Lieutenant Commander C. E. Carroll). HELM was under way when the attack exploded the Sunday quiet. She was steaming in West Loch when Jap torpedo-planes raced in over Barber's Point. Flying low, the planes skimmed over the Loch, and HELM was strafed but not hit. She could not shoot at the enemy because the only guns that could be brought immediately to bear were coated with preservative grease. But by 0805 her machine-guns were cleaned and firing, and two minutes later her 5-inchers flamed at the raiders. At 0813 the ship galloped past the gate vessel and on out to sea.

At 0817 HELM's lookouts sighted the conning tower of a sub not far from the No. 1 entrance buoy. The sub submerged before the destroyermen could shoot. At 0819 the conning tower reappeared HELM fired at the sub at 0820. Probably damaged, the sub again submerged. At 0821 a torpedo passed close under HELM's stern. This was probably a parting shot from a midget submerging for the last time.

HELM continued a search for the little undersea boat, but the vessel had apparently gone for good. Jap aircraft attacked the hunting destroyer. At 0915 she battled a Jap fighter which tried to get her with two bombs. One burst in the water 50 yards off the HELM's port bow, and one exploded 20 yards off her starboard bow. The ship's forecastle was deluged; her seams were sprung; she shook as though her hull were seized with ague. Power steering went out; her gyro was injured; her sonar went out of commission. It was 15 minutes before the bridge could regain steering control. Shaken up though she was, HELM went on with her patrol until 1215, at which time she received orders to join cruiser DETROIT.

In Middle Loch there were four destroyer-minelayers, old "four-stackers" which had been turned into mine vessels back in 1921. One of these, the U.S.S. BREESE, made sound contact with a submerged target as she was steaming down channel during the air raid. Her "ashcans" brought up a swirl of oil and debris which indicated an injured midget if not a dead one. If this pygmy pig-boat managed to escape BREESE, it probably did not get very far. The Middle Loch waters off Pearl City were by that time boiling with destroyer activity, and the exit was barred by a number of heavy-hitting new DD's.

Among the new DD's off Pearl City were the destroyers of DesDiv 2 (Commander R. S. Riggs). These were AYLWIN, DALE, FARRAGUT, and MONAGHAN. When Jap torpedo-planes attacked the old UTAH lying off the western side of Ford Island, they were flogged by AA fire from the four DesDiv 2 destroyers which were berthed at Buoy X-18 in East Loch. At 0828 the division received orders to leave the nest and clear the Harbor.

MONAGHAN left the nest immediately. Having had the ready duty that morning, she was better prepared for action than the other destroyers within the Harbor, and she had already been ordered out to assist the WARD.

DALE followed MONAGHAN at 0840. Senior officer on board, Ensign F. M. Radel assumed command. As DALE was backing clear, a torpedo, apparently aimed at cruiser RALEIGH, passed under her bow and exploded on the foreshore of Ford Island. DALE pulled up short while MONAGHAN charged the sub, which had been detected near the seaplane tender CURTISS. Then DALE tied on 25 knots and loped out of the Harbor, dodging dive-bomber attacks as she neared the channel entrance. Evidently the Japs were bent on sinking a ship to block the channel, and DALE was the selected target. She was shaken by several close-misses as she raced on out past the entrance buoys. Good work by Ensign Radel and company.

FARRAGUT hauled out of the nest at 0852. Maneuvering to clear the Harbor, she maintained a steady fire; was attacked by a strafing plane; had a number of close shaves, but got to sea with slight damage topside and no casualties to crew. The ship was conned on the sortie by Lieutenant E. K. Jones, her Engineer Officer.

Destroyer AYLWIN, rocked by a bomb which fell about 75 yards off her starboard bow, got under way at 0858. In precipitous departure she left her anchor chain and stern wire at the buoys. With guns blazing she stood out of the channel. Senior officer on board AYLWIN was Ensign Stanley Caplan, U.S.N.R., who was ably seconded by Ensign H. C. Anderson, U.S.N.R. AYLWIN's regular Commanding Officer, Lieutenant Commander R. H. Rodgers, was at home in Honolulu when the fireworks began. Racing to Pearl Harbor, he secured a motor launch and with other AYLWIN officers chased the destroyer to sea. ComDesRon 1 would not permit a transfer at sea, so Rodgers and the others boarded the destroyer CHEW and remained with that ship until the following day. Commending the handling of AYLWIN during and after the sortie, Lieutenant Commander Rodgers wrote: *"THE CONDUCT OF ENSIGN S. CAPLAN, U.S.N.R. . . . IN TAKING COMMAND FOR 33 HOURS DURING WAR OPERATIONS OF THE SEVEREST KIND, IS CONSIDERED OUTSTANDING."*

Meantime, MONAGHAN was having it out with the midget submarine that attacked the CURTISS. Ordered out at 0753 to join WARD in an A/S hunt off the harbor entrance, she had been getting up steam when her lookouts sighted a mountain of black smoke rearing a dark head over Schofield Barracks. Then a Jap torpedo-plane attacked the UTAH. MONAGHAN's skipper, Lieutenant Commander W. P. Burford, knew the war was on! A moment later MONAGHAN was in the thick of it, firing at high-altitude bombers with her machine-guns and 5-inch batteries. At 0827 she was ordered by cruiser DETROIT to sortie, and about the same time she was directed over the TBS to establish offshore patrol with DesDiv 2. As she was maneuvering away from the nest she noticed that CURTISS was flying a submarine-alarm signal. This was hardly reported before MONAGHAN's lookouts sighted a midget conning tower about 250 yards from CURTISS.

The midget was under fire from the seaplane tender and the minesweeper TANGIER. Lieutenant Commander Burford squared away to ram, and at 0837 MONAGHAN rushed at the sub. The midget fired a torpedo which missed. MONAGHAN did not miss. A slight shock shivered the ship as she passed over the sub. She dropped two depth charges which raised a haystack of water and brought the midget thrashing to the surface. As the sub rolled over and sank, MONAGHAN backed emergency to avoid collision with a derrick moored off Beckoning Point. It took some jockeying, but at 0847 she swung out into the channel to steam out of the Harbor astern of destroyer DALE. By 0908 she was at sea and proceeding to her assigned station in the offshore patrol.

So, singly and severally, the DesPac DD's sortied from the furnace of Pearl Harbor and fought their way out to sea. Just which ship or which guns or gunners shot down what is something that can never be definitely established. Planes were shot down and everybody had a hand in it. From Pearl Harbor sailed men-of-war which were to write indelible names on the oceanic seascapes of the war-tossed Pacific—PHELPS, RALPH TALBOT, BAGLEY, PATTERSON, HENLEY, AYLWIN, MONAGHAN, BLUE, JARVIS, MUGFORD, WORDEN, CONYNGHAM, MACDONOUGH, SELFRIDGE, CUMMINGS, DEWEY, REID, and others. From Pearl Harbor sailed destroyer officers who were to make records equally indelible—Outerbridge, Early, Austin, Riggs, Rodgers, Nyquist, Rorschach, Walker, Robert Hall Smith, Burford, Earle, and others. Sailing with these officers were crews second to none in the United States or any naval service.

Behind them the sortiing DesPac destroyers left a fleet which had been blasted to ruin. Battleships ARIZONA, OKLAHOMA, CALIFORNIA, and WEST VIRGINIA were on the bottom. The old UTAH was sunk. Battleships PENNSYLVANIA, MARYLAND, TENNESSEE, and NEVADA were damaged. Cruisers HELENA, HONOLULU, and RALEIGH were badly battered. Three heavy cruisers and three light cruisers had gotten out; these and the destroyers which escaped the cauldron were about all that was left of the surface force which had been trapped in the Harbor. They, and the carriers at sea, and the Pacific Submarine Force, would be compelled to hold the line from the Aleutians to Australia.

Manila Strike (Destroyers Asiatic)

Like a delayed-action bomb, the Japanese strike at Manila exploded on December 10.

Compared with the Juggernaut forces of the Japanese Imperial Navy bearing down on the Philippines, the defending American Asiastic Fleet was little more than a squadron.

As of December, 1941, the Asiatic Fleet consisted of the heavy cruiser HOUSTON (flagship of Admiral Thomas C. Hart, Commander in Chief), light cruisers MARBLEHEAD and BOISE, 13 venerable destroyers of the 1917-18 class, and 29 submarines. There were also 30 elderly PBY's, six PT-boats, several aircraft tenders, three submarine tenders, a destroyer tender, a few small mine vessels, and a miscellany of little gunboats, oilers, and auxiliaries. Ordered to defend the hundreds of miles of coastline and the myriad miles of sea from northern Luzon to southern Mindanao, Admiral Hart's naval forces were presented with an impossible mission. Then the Japanese strike at Manila and the blasting of the Asiatic Fleet base at Cavite put an end to the possibility of even a delaying-action fight for the Philippines capital. Beaten at the start, the Asiatic Fleet could only retreat.

Composing DesRon 29, under leadership of Captain H. V. Wiley, whose broad command pennant was in destroyer PAUL JONES (Lieutenant Commander J. J. Hourihan), were DesDivs 50, 57, and 58. The ships and commanders are listed below. The destroyers were serviced by the tender BLACK HAWK.

DESDIV 50
Comdr. P. H. Talbot

PEARY	*Comdr. H. H. Keith*
POPE	*Lt. Comdr. W. C. Blinn*
FORD	*Lt. Comdr. J. E. Cooper*
PILLSBURY	*Lt. Comdr. H. C. Pound*

DESDIV 57
Comdr. E. M. Crouch

WHIPPLE	*Lt. Comdr. E. S. Karpe*
ALDEN	*Lt. Comdr. L. E. Coley*
JOHN D. EDWARDS	*Comdr. H. E. Eccles*
EDSALL	*Lt. J. J. Nix*

DESDIV 58
Comdr. T. H. Binford

STEWART	*Lt. Comdr. H. P. Smith*
PARROTT	*Lt. Comdr. E. N. Parker*
BULMER	*Comdr. L. J. Manees*
BARKER	*Comdr. L. J. McGlone*

At the beginning of December Admiral Hart's ships were disposed in various areas of the Philippine Archipelago. Flying the flag of Vice Admiral W. A. Glassford, cruiser HOUSTON was at Iloilo in the central Philippines. BOISE was at Cebu. MARBLEHEAD and destroyers PAUL JONES, STEWART, BARKER, BULMER, and PARROTT had been ordered to Tarakan, Borneo, to loiter off that possible target island. Tender BLACK HAWK and destroyers WHIPPLE, ALDEN, J. D. EDWARDS, and EDSALL had steamed to Balikpapan, Borneo, another potential target for the Japanese.

In drydock at Cavite were destroyers PEARY and PILLSBURY, undergoing overhaul after a collision some weeks before. Repairs were almost concluded by December 10: a few more hours and the ships would have been ready to go. The other two destroyers of DesRon 29—POPE and JOHN D. FORD—were patrolling in the Manila area when the first air raid struck Manila Bay.

The Cavite raid was not a carbon copy of the Pearl Harbor massacre; there were fewer ships corraled for the slaughter. But the Japs smashed the Cavite docks and Navy Yard into junk, and pulverized the junk into rubble. The air strikes began early in the afternoon, after the Army Air defenses at Clark and Iba fields near Manila had been taken by surprise and battered to rubbish—a repetition of the Hickam Field disaster. Cavite's 3-inch AA batteries barked in frenzy, but they failed to bite the high-level bombers. The defenders could only sit and take it while the ships tried to get out. Among others, destroyer PILLSBURY made a fast getaway. But the submarine SEALION was sunk at her berth. And destroyer PEARY, badly mauled, escaped only by the grace of Providence and a brave little minesweeper named WHIPPOORWILL. The latter's skipper, Lieutenant Commander C. A. Ferriter, subsequently told the following story (*U. S. Naval Institute Proceedings*, November, 1942):

Saving of U.S.S. Peary

"Cavite Navy Yard was a mass of flame. . . . The PIGEON *was playing her hoses on some barges that were burning at the end of Guadeloupe Pier. I made out a destroyer at the small pier between Machina Wharf and Guadeloupe Pier.*

"I sent the PIGEON *a signal: 'The* WHIP *is going in and take out that destroyer.' We went in between Guadeloupe Pier and Machina Wharf. It was a mess. It was the* PEARY. *The ship had many little fires all over her. She had been strafed and had been struck by bomb fragments and debris. The war heads and torpedo air flasks in the torpedo overhaul shop on Machina Wharf next to her were exploding. The air was filled with clouds of debris. A small motorboat under the command of an Ensign, a young Reserve officer attached to Inshore Patrol, assisted in the efforts to take out the* PEARY. *The heat and explosions made ship-handling difficult. The pressure would be on one side and then on the other. The Ensign tried to take lines from the* WHIP *to the* PEARY *without success as we made our approach. We put our bow against her stern. We made fast with a 6-inch line. We backed and parted the line. The heat of a falling fragment might have caused the line to part. We tried it again. Again the line parted. It became more difficult to keep in position for backing out. The wind and the current kept working to put the* WHIP *broadside to the end of the pier. This was bad. Guadeloupe Pier and Machina Wharf each extended a good distance beyond this little pier. We went quite far up on her port quarter. This was the side away from the pier. I sent a man over to the* PEARY *to make sure that she had no mooring lines to the pier. The* WHIP'S *man reported when the lines were clear. We backed and she came away.*

"We backed clear of the dock. There was shoal water not far from the piers. We went alongside the PEARY. *This was more easily done than jackknifing her. The* WHIP *went between the* PEARY *and the burning barges off Guadeloupe Pier. We had all of our hoses going all of the time. . . .*

"We put our Damage Control party aboard the PEARY *as soon as she came clear to the pier. She had no power and was helpless. The Damage Control party with the aid of the* PEARY'S *crew put out the fires and cleared away the wreckage. The Pharmacist's Mate and a working party tended the wounded and removed the bodies of the casualties to the* WHIP: *Our boat took the wounded to the hospital in Canacao. . . ."*

During the bombing which lacerated PEARY, her captain, Commander Harry H. Keith, was severely wounded. Lieutenant Commander J. M. Bermingham subsequently took over the command.

Retreat to the Malay Barrier

After the shattering of Cavite the naval forces in the Manila area had to draw what sustenance they could from the city's waterfront. In an effort to save the defenseless capital from useless carnage, General MacArthur declared it an open city, and the Asiastic Fleet became an orphan in a storm. The uncompleted base at Mariveles Bay was useless, and Admiral Hart ordered a general retirement to Soerabaja, Java. Among the last ships to leave Manila Bay were destroyers PEARY and PILLSBURY, steaming down the Bay on the 27th of December.

PILLSBURY made the voyage to Soerabaja without incident. PEARY'S road was thorny. The day before she sortied, Jap aircraft almost got her again off Cavite. They tagged her a second time when she ran into Campomanes Bay on the island of Negros. The next day they trailed her down into the Celebes Sea. As she ran on south she was harried by enemy torpedo-planes. Then, as she raced into Molucca Passage, she was attacked through error by Lockheed Hudsons of the Royal Australian Air Force. On the last day of 1941 the destroyer staggered into Ambon, her decks fire-scarred, her crew exhausted.

So the Asiatic Fleet and its destroyer complement pulled out of the Philippines. On January 1, 1942, the Japanese conquerors paraded into Manila. The Asiatic Fleet, retiring to the Netherlands East Indies, prepared to make a stand at the Malay Barrier. In that first month of the New Year Admiral Hart's forces became part of the ABDA (American-British-Dutch-Australian) Fleet committed to the defense of Indonesia. Little help could be expected from the United States Pacific Fleet for months to come. And when Jap aircraft sank H.M.S. REPULSE and PRINCE OF WALES off Singapore on December 10, 1941, the Royal Navy lost its Asiatic punch. The ABDA Fleet was left a skeleton force. But the American destroyers in that force fought as though they were the spearheads of an armada.

TORPEDO-TUBE MOUNT SIGHT (LOCAL CONTROL)

PART II

SHIELD AND SPEARHEAD

Who's there, besides foul weather?
KING LEAR

CHAPTER 5

DESTROYING THE SUBMARINE

(DESTROYER A/S WEAPONS, METHODS, AND TACTICS)

U-Boat Killer

As was stated in Chapter I, the destroyer, originally designed as a torpedo-boat, was soon employed as a patrol craft, a vedette, a scout, a fleet "errand boy." And it emerged in the First World War as the archenemy of the submarine.

Fighting in the forefront of the World War I U-boat battle, the DD showed its mettle offensively as a sub-hunter, and defensively as a convoy protector. By the end of that war its reputation as an A/S vessel was fully established.

As is so often the case with generalities, the broad statement (and it was made) that the submarine had met its match in the modern destroyer was subject to a great deal of qualification. Naval engineers and designers had worked overtime to improve the undersea boat. For at least a decade the major Powers, abiding by surface-warship building restrictions, concentrated on the production and development of submersibles. In consequence, the U-boat (true also of Allied submarines) entered World War II as a highly modernized war vessel, a submarine as far ahead of the World War I variety as the modern Ford was ahead of the Model T.

The Diesel-electric powered U-boat of 1939 was rugged, deepgoing, fast. It packed a stunning punch. Its torpedoes were deadlier than the "tin fish" of World War I. Its cruising range was far more extensive. And that was at the very beginning of hostilities. With the prolongation of the war, the U-boat became even faster, tougher, deeper-going. The typical 1943 model was hard to hit and harder to sink. In the summer of that year one of these specimens was caught by an A/S force off Trinidad. Six U. S. Navy planes, a Navy blimp, and an Army bomber worked on the submarine for 17 hours before it was rendered *hors de combat.* Obviously the modern U-boat was possessed of extraordinary stamina.

On the other hand, the DD steamed into the Battle of the Atlantic equipped with marvelous new detection devices. And it was in this field of detection that the destroyer achieved an immediate superiority in the game of hide-and-seek with the undersea foe. But it was not enough to tag the enemy. He then had to be downed.

New A/S ammunition was demanded: explosives with sufficient destructive power to crush the submarine's reinforced pressure hull; bombs and depth charges with accelerated sinking speeds that would improve their accuracy; launchers and projectors that would get off fast salvos and heavier barrages. Improved fire control was also a requisite.

British destroyers entered the Battle of the Atlantic with A/S ammunition similar to the type employed in World War I. On neutrality patrol American DD's carried the same type. But the old reliable "ashcan" did not prove reliable enough to meet the Atlantic Battle emergency. American science and invention were immediately called upon to increase the "ashcan's" punch and to better its design. The U. S. Navy's Bureau of Ordnance was not long in developing the streamlined model known as the "teardrop."

Then in 1942 came a new A/S weapon known as "hedgehog." Thrown ahead of the destroyer, hedgehog ammunition had the virtue of buckshot in that the discharge covered a relatively large area. "Mouse-

Hatching of a sea dragon. Here a German U-boat begins to take final form on the building ways of the Dachsmag Submarine Factory at Bremen, Germany. From this ugly bow the Nazi submariners could fire a spread of six torpedoes at hostile man-o'-war or hapless merchantman. The destroyers and destroyer escorts were the U-boat's most deadly and worst feared enemies.

Listening for a "ping." With his small hand wheel the sonar operator turns the echo ranging gear to search the sea from aft forward at 5 degree intervals. An echoing "ping" presaged action.

Silent Witness. The lifeboat of a torpedoed merchantman whose survivors were machine-gunned by the German submarine which sank their ship. Circles outline the bullet holes.

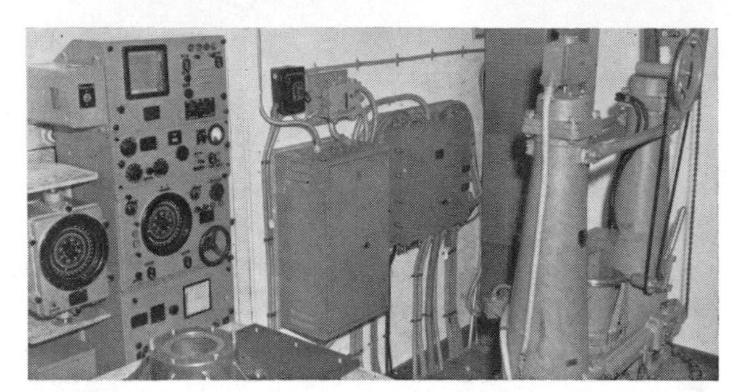

Mock-up of a sonar set-up. Hoist for raising and lowering the sound head is at right, the operator's panel for echo ranging and listening at left. Skillful operators were a first essential.

One of the biggest takes white water aboard. Here one of the Allen M. Sumner class of 2,200-ton destroyers heaves herself up out of a heavy sea. Taken from the quarter, this picture gives a good view of the depth charges racked up on each side of the fantail, with the after twin 5-inch gun mount beyond. In line with the after stack is a 40 mm gun mount, with K-guns beneath.

trap," a variation of hedgehog, was subsequently developed for use on small A/S vessels. At the close of the war the British produced another ahead-thrown weapon known as the "squid." These Necessity-mothered inventions (presently to be discussed) went a long way toward cracking the U-boat's steel.

But the veteran ashcan (discussed below) was not discarded.

Cumbersome though it was, this depth charge had desirable qualities—virtues inherent in its very bulk. When it connected with the target, its explosion was massive and devastating. And a barrage of ashcans could, and frequently did, raise the dead.

The Depth Charge

The depth charges commonly used by American destroyermen in World War II resembled 25 and 50 gallon oil drums in size and shape and contained explosive charges of 300 or 600 pounds of TNT. On the deck of a ship these depth charges were harmless enough, but when the firing mechanism was activated by hydrostatic pressure they became deadly weapons. The ashcan firing mechanism was located in a central tube and was, in essence, a bellows which was operated by water pressure. By the adjustment of an external pointer mechanism the ashcan could be set to fire at various depths below the surface.

In the early part of the war it was customary for a ship in possible submarine waters to keep her depth charges set for a mean average depth in order that time might be saved in a sudden attack. Later this strike advantage was sacrificed for safety when experience taught expensive lessons in the danger to men in the water from the explosions of ashcans carried down to their set depth by sinking ships. It, therefore, became the practice to keep all charges set on safe until immediately before a drop.

It was not necessary to hit the submarine with an ashcan (or with a teardrop) depth charge. As liquid cannot be compressed, a large pressure may be developed by a relatively small force applied to a small area of confined water.

The ocean, of course, is not "confined water." But the force of an undersea explosion is readily transmitted, and develops tremendous pressure in the immediate area. If a submarine is in the immediate area, this pressure puts a "squeeze" on the hull—a squeeze which is almost equally powerful on all areas of that hull. A direct hit, then, is desirable enough, but unnecessary. The blast of an ashcan close aboard may crush the submarine's hull or deal the submersible a jolt that starts fatal leakage or wrecks the interior machinery.

Of course, the submarine does not play willing

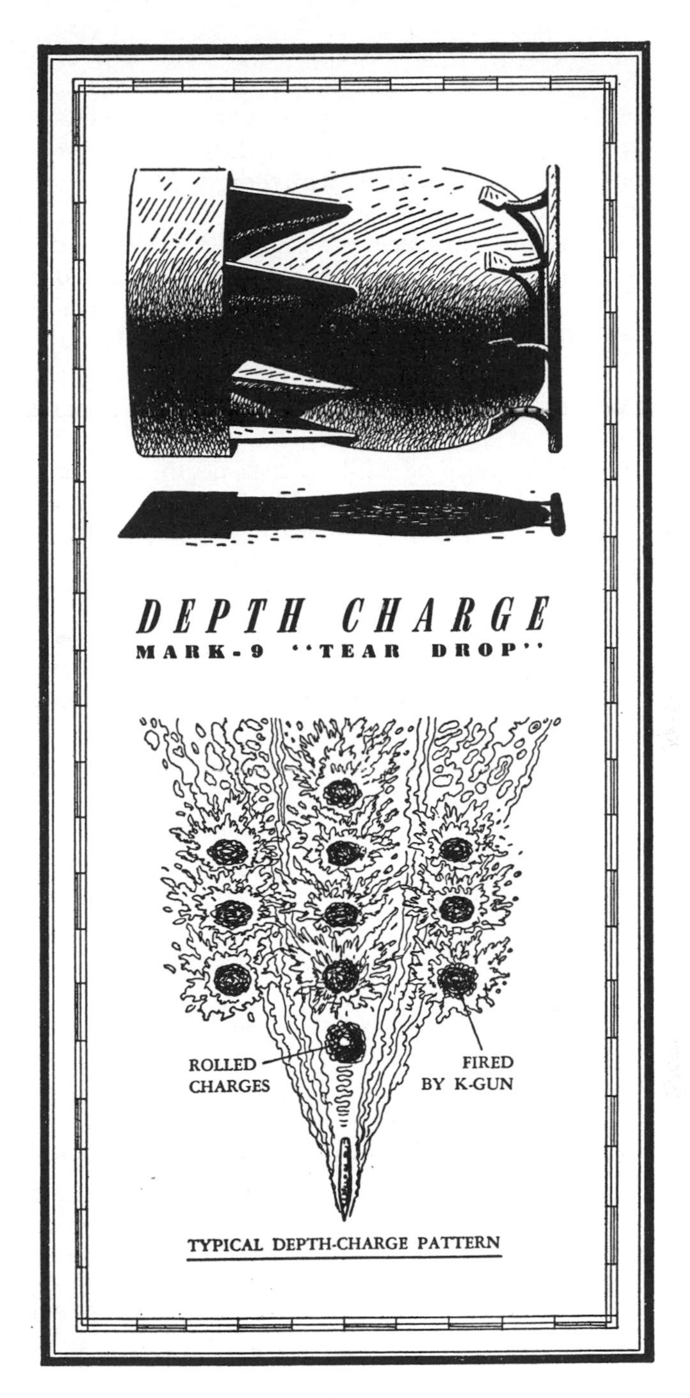

target for a barrage of depth charges. It hears the hunter overhead, and before the TNT starts coming down, it does its best (in submarine vernacular) to "get the hell out of there."

The technical term for these escape maneuvers is "evasion tactics." The submarine may begin these maneuvers as soon as it suspects it has been detected by the enemy. Or it may employ them as a last-minute dodge to side-step an attack. To elude a depth charging, the sub changes course, goes deep and levels off, lies low, idles and coasts and drifts. It may find a sea-bottom foxhole and lie motionless, with machinery shut off, playing 'possum. It may go "fishtailing" ahead of the hunters, weaving this way and that. Operating in a three-dimensional sphere, the submerged submarine has as many choices of direction as an aircraft.

The sub-hunter, then, was usually shooting blindly at a moving target—a target he tracked by sound. But sound contact was sporadic, and at close range it was lost. Moreover, the evading submarine could escape in "depth" as well as "plane." Sonar contact could not give the hunter a submersible's exact depth. During World War I, no instrument was devised for accurately determining a submarine's depth, and many an attack failed because the depth charges were set too shallow or too deep. In early World War II subhunters were similarly frustrated.

Of course, the speed at which the attack could be delivered, once the target was within range, was a most important factor. Primarily this depended on the launching or projecting gear. But much depended on the sinking speed of the depth charge.

Obviously, too, the directional accuracy of the sinking depth charge was important. The old-type ashcan was not a high-speed weapon. Rolled off the destroyer's stern, it was tumbled by the vessel's wake. Sinking, it tended to wobble, or go down tail-over-teacup. These underwater acrobatics reduced the sinking speed, and they might send the ashcan off on a tangent.

To correct these and other depth-charge shortcomings, Ordance men produced the depth charge known as the "teardrop."

This depth charge was developed to provide an antisubmarine weapon that would have a higher sinking velocity, more stable underwater flight, and hence greater accuracy than the older type ashcan.

Drop a can of beans into a pond, and the chances are it will sink at an erratic tangent and hit bottom some distance from the point where you dropped it, especially if there's any current in the pond. Now drop a pear-shaped sinker of the same weight, and you will see the sinker go down much more rapidly, heavy-end first, and on a fairly straight line from your hand.

Obviously a streamlined depth charge shaped like a pear or a teardrop would have several advantages over one with ordinary cylindrical shape.

So destroyermen were presented with the "teardrop."

No submarine lingers long in the vicinity when a destroyer is weeping these teardrops. Let one of them explode close aboard, and the effect is positively lethal.

Depth-Charge Launching Gear

Three types of depth-charge launching gear were used by destroyers during World War II.

The old-type ashcan was originally sent on its way by the simple principle of "roll out the barrel." A track of flanged rails was set on an incline at the ship's stern. Hoist the ashcan on to the rails, and let 'er go.

Improvements created the "depth-charge release gear" in use by 1918 and employed by United States destroyers in World War II. The gear consisted of a

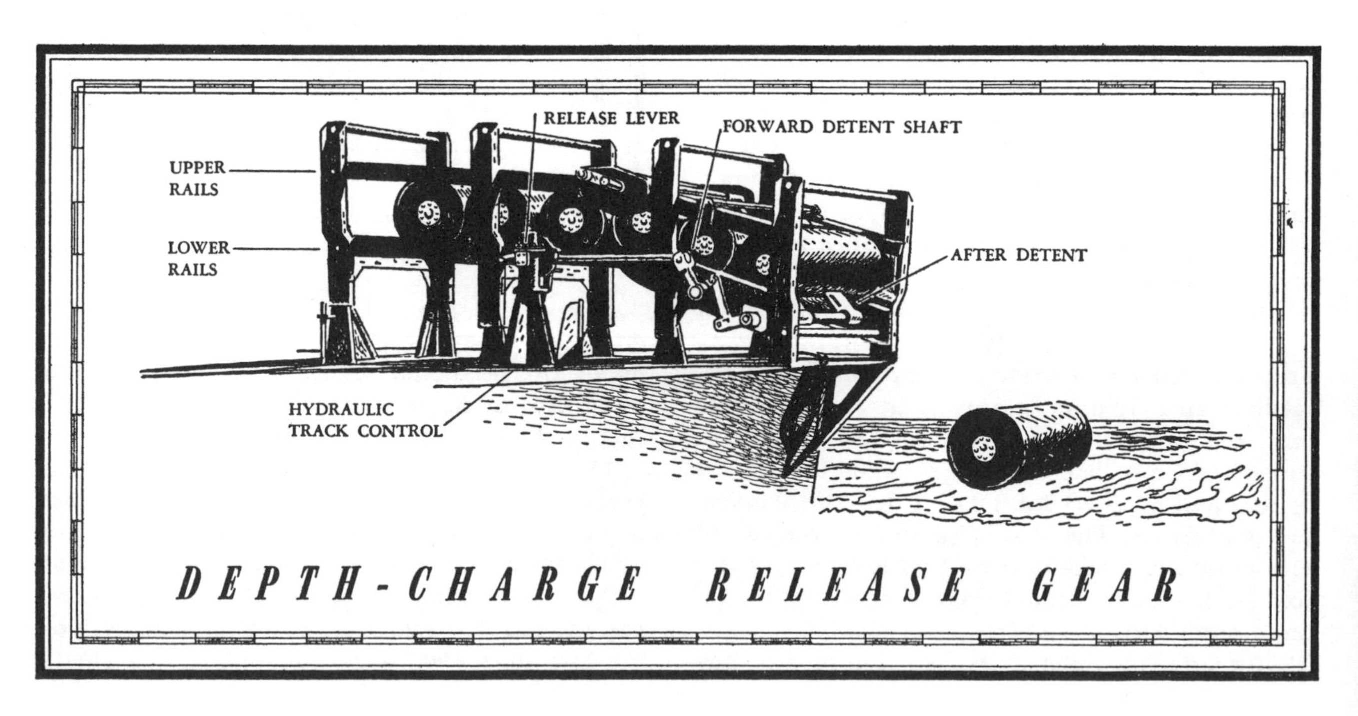

DEPTH-CHARGE RELEASE GEAR

track (called a "rack") down which the depth charge rolled on an incline, a framework in which the ready ashcans were all set to roll, and a hydraulic control which unleashed the depth charge at a release trap, permitting the ashcan to drop astern. The hydraulic release mechanism could be operated by local control at the track or by remote control from the vessel's bridge. The release mechanism was also arranged to permit manual operation of the controls, independent of the hydraulic system. A crew at the rack—controls on the bridge—the original "roll out the barrel" operation developed complexities by the time of World War II.

Normally such ashcan racks were installed in pairs at the vessel's stern. Each rack had its individual controls. The crew at the rack included a Gunner's Mate or Chief who supervised the loading of the apparatus and who worked with an agile wrench to adjust the depth settings on the depth charge. Usually these settings were ordered by the ASW (Anti-Submarine Warfare) Officer who determined them as the ship raced in on the attack.

The depth-charge rack was designated a "secondary release station." Ordinarily the charges were released by remote control from the release station on the bridge (a station designated "depth charge") on orders from "conn" (the primary ship-control station). The order from conn-to-depth-charge-to-rack might be as follows: "Fire Medium Pattern," meaning "Use six charges from racks, five-second interval, set to 150 feet, and stand by to start pattern. . . . Mark!" The ensuing "Fire one! Fire two—!" would be acknowledged by a terse repetition or a brisk "Aye, aye!" from the men at the controls.

The various patterns to be employed were specified by the depth setting on the charges. From conn-to-depth-charge-to-rack might come the order, "Stand by for Shallow Pattern." Later, in some ships, number or letter designations were used for various patterns.

The term "thrower" was applied to the device which projected or lobbed a depth charge overside. The term was also used to indicate the station where the throwing device was loaded and fired. Such stations were commonly designated "starboard throwers," or "port throwers," or, more specifically, "No. 3 thrower," and so on.

Because charges which were stern-dropped could be spaced along only one axis of a pattern, some sort of projector was called for to widen the pattern's area. So the "Y" gun was invented. Produced in 1918, this apparatus tossed or lobbed two depth charges out over the water. Shaped like a "Y," it was a bulky affair with somewhat the appearance of a giant slingshot. However, it worked as a gun, not a sling. The depth charge was placed in a saddle or "arbor," atop this gear, and was fired overside by an explosive charge.

The Y-gun permitted an advantageous distribution of depth charges lobbed to port or starboard of the vessel's beam, and it tossed the lethal charge a good distance from the ship. It was made obsolescent, however, by the K-gun.

Installed in most American destroyers by 1942, the K-gun was a much-used projector during the battle against Hitler's U-boats. Weighing about one-fourth as much as the Y-gun, this depth-charge thrower had a single, stubby barrel with a fast-operating breech mechanism and a comparatively simple firing system.

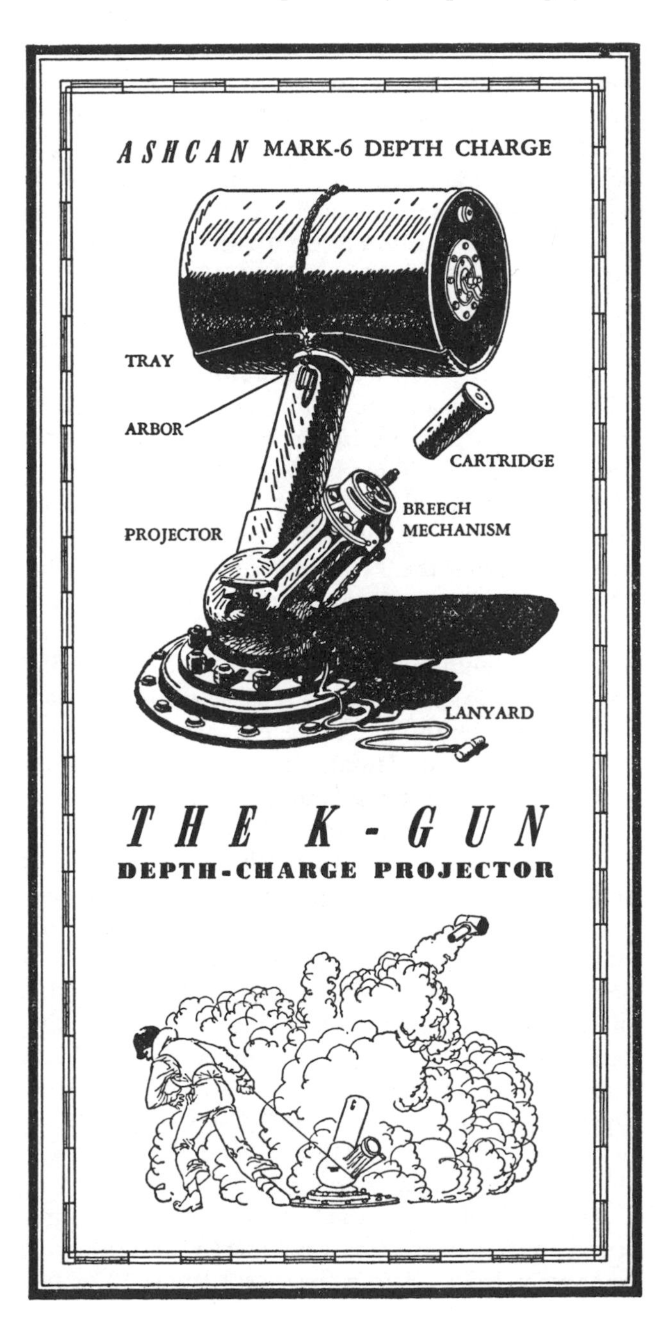

The depth charge was placed in a tray-like arbor which sat in the K-gun's mortar-type barrel. When the gun was fired, the ashcan went flying.

The firing mechanism, mounted in the K-gun's breech, could fire the propelling charge either by percussion or by electricity. In percussion fire, the mechanism was worked by a lanyard. Where operated by electricity the gun was fired by means of a firing key on the bridge.

K-guns were mounted in pairs, one on either side of the ship. As many could be installed topside as seemed feasible, and additional projectors expanded the area under fire and bettered the depth-charge pattern.

Although projecting gear (Y- and K-guns) were generally considered an important supplement to the old-type release gear on the stern, their employment involved operational service that took time. A string of depth charges could be adjusted and rolled off the stern tracks in a matter of seconds. The K-gun had to be reloaded for each salvo, and a depth charge had to be hoisted into place each time the projector was fired. So, in the forepart of 1942, the "roller loader" made its appearance. This device greatly facilitated the reloading of K-guns and proved a boon to hard-working depth-charge crews.

Rough seas made the handling of heavy ashcans and teardrops difficult in any case. The 720-pound Mark 7's and the 340-pound Mark 9's were not easily hustled and hoisted on a heaving deck, and if one broke away from its handlers, results could be disastrous. Not that the TNT was liable to explode. But a heavy cylinder rampaging around on a ship's deck can endanger life, limb, and deck-gear. And if the charge accidentally rolled overside, and the setting was not on "safe," the depth charge might detonate at a shallow depth, and damage the ship.

To prevent accidental depth-charge explosions most destroyer captains kept the depth charges on "safe" until the moment the DD started a run on the attack. Appropriate depth settings could then be made in a few seconds by the crew at K-gun or rack. There was always a chance that a destroyer might be fatally hit during battle, and the depth charges, if not on "safe," would explode as the ship went under. In a number of instances during the war, sinking destroyers were blasted and escaping crews slain by their own depth charges—charges which were either defective, or not set on "safe." Cases in point: the destroyer HAMMAN at Midway, and the STRONG in the Solomon Islands.

Ashcans and streamlined depth charges, then, possessed some adverse features. They were bulky and sometimes balky. Before they were launched or projected, their settings had to be adjusted. And they could not be "aimed" with anything like exactitude and precision. A nimbler charge—a projector that was easy to handle—these were desirables sought after by Ordnance inventors working on devices for undersea warfare.

British designers and Captain Paul Hammond, U.S.N.R., found an answer in "hedgehog."

Hedgehog

Early in 1942, Captain Hammond, serving on the U.S. Naval Attaché's staff in London, had an opportunity to inspect the designs for a new A/S weapon. The weapon operated on an entirely novel charge-projecting principle. It consisted of a steel cradle in which were planted four rows of spike-like spigots. (Hence the name "Hedgehog.") In effect, this projector worked as a rocket-firer. However, it did not fire conventional rockets.

The apparatus fired 24 projectiles, lobbing them a considerable distance. The projectiles, made to fit over the spigots in the projector, could be easily positioned for firing. In turn, they exploded upon contact with the target, much like the ordinary artillery shell. Lobbed into the sea, they sank swiftly, shooting down through the water like a school of barracuda—steel barracuda with deadly snouts.

The hedgehog projectile, however, had to make a direct hit to explode. It did not carry the colossal charge of a big ashcan. But it went off with the damaging blast of a shell-hit. And, in one respect, contact explosion was a virtue rather than a limitation. Heretofore the destroyermen had never been certain of a hit. The conventional depth charge exploded when it reached the pre-set depth, and the hunters on the surface did not know at the time whether the blast was a bull's-eye or a miss that was as good as a mile. But a hedgehog explosion could be taken to mean a sure-thing hit—except that in shallow water the projectiles would explode when they hit bottom, and under those circumstances the situation could remain ambiguous. But an explosion in deep water told the destroyermen they were on target, and it also assured them the target had suffered damage.

Captain Hammond became enthusiastic. From England the hedgehog was sent to the United States. The strange projector, with its firing "spigots," and the rocket-like projectiles were developed as "top secrets," and were smuggled aboard anti-submarine vessels like so much contraband. After the first trials American destroyermen were all for hedgehog. Eventually the new A/S weapon was widely installed on frigates (PF's) and destroyer-escorts.

The direct-hit feature was not the weapon's only

virtue. It possessed a more valuable feature. Because hedgehog projectiles were thrown ahead of the ship, the weapon could frequently be fired before sound contact with the submarine was broken. In other words, the A/S craft could be "on the beam" when it opened fire with hedgehog—the destroyermen were not shooting more or less blindly, as in the case with ashcans and teardrops. And the projector could be tilted to some extent to take care of last-minute errors in attack maneuver, and to compensate somewhat for roll.

The weighty hedgehog projector had a mule-kick recoil, and it was unsuitable for small anti-submarine vessels. So a smaller launcher capable of firing six rocket projectiles was designed. This weapon was called "mousetrap."

A few mousetrap launchers were installed in destroyers for experimental purposes. After meeting test requirements, the weapon was employed by a variety of anti-sub vessels, including patrol craft and smaller types. Mousetrap packed a potent punch—its 65-pound rocket loaded with torpex was the same size and had the same explosive content as the hedgehog projectile. But, although employed with success by the British, mousetrap did not feature in many American A/S actions during World War II, and, so far as is known, American mousetrap did not single-handedly "catch" an enemy submarine.

Hedgehog, however, was frequently employed by Atlantic hunter-killer ships. And it enjoyed even greater popularity with the destroyermen of the Pacific. It was favored in the Pacific, perhaps, by sea and weather conditions.

The ahead-thrown projectile did not make obsolete the veteran depth charge, however. Throughout the war, teardrops and ashcans continued to lob and roll from the decks of DD's. Destroyers did not carry hedgehog; it was installed, in the main, in the DE's and PF's which made their appearance in mid-war. Diving in to hit sharp, savage blows, ahead-thrown projectiles were deadly. But it was necessary for these projectiles to strike. Whereas a depth-charge explosion anywhere in the close vicinity of a submarine might do it mortal damage.

Depth-charge barrages were often used to supplement hedgehog attacks—to deliver the knockout on a groggy submarine, or nail a sub which had gone deep. The ponderous depth charge was good for deep-sea blasting, and for situations which prevented or did not favor an ahead-thrown attack.

Sonar

With A/S depth-charge or hedgehog fire, as with surface gunnery, the No. 1 problem concerned aim—the business of locating and getting on target. In gunnery, aim depends chiefly on sighting. In A/S warfare, the submerged target is located by "ear"—electronic detection devices which come under the general heading of "Sonar."

After the smashing U-boat surprise of 1914, the British bent every effort to the creation of instruments which could detect the submerged submarine. Eventually they produced the hydrophone—a sensitive listening device which could pick up the sound of a moving submarine. Installed on the bottom of a ship, the instrument conveyed to the operator's earphones the whisper of the U-boat's propellers and the general location of the sub. Apparently the first instance of submarine detection by hydrophone occurred on April 23, 1916, when the UC-3, caught in the meshes of a mine net, was traced by sound and destroyed by the listening surface craft.

In 1916 the U.S. Navy developed and installed SC "listening gear" similar to the British hydrophone. By the end of World War I the gear was widely employed by Allied A/S vessels, and improvements had made the device amazingly acute. A U-boat fearing detection might coast for a brief time with motors cut off, or might lie motionless on the sea floor. But the hydrophone could pick up the slightest sound—even the thin whine made by the motor of a gyroscopic compass.

However, the hydrophone had serious limitations. To begin with, it picked up *all* propeller sounds in the area—not just the submarine's. And the sharper its acoustic properties, the more sounds it picked up. The SC operator could not tune out interfering noises. All kinds of static crackled in his earphones, and the problem became one of acute hearing and accurate sound-identification on his part.

And although the hydrophone gave some indication of direction, it did not indicate range. At the end of World War I the submarine-hunters were still baffled by the problem of range—a matter most intimately associated with the business of getting on target. The hydrophone, therefore, fell far short of the aim imperative. If skillfully operated, it detected the submerged submarine and pointed to the general direction of the target. But it did not measure the range to the submarine. In effect, the operator (the "Sound man" in Navy parlance) could only point over the side and declare, "down there in that direction."

Between wars, electronic scientists labored to overcome some of the hydrophone's shortcomings. Both the British and the American Navies produced sound gear capable of indicating the submerged submarine's range. This supersonic electronic gear functioned in a performance known as "echo-ranging." The British named the device "Asdic." The Americans had a word for it—"Sonar"—from "Sound-Navigation-Ranging."

The electronic workings of sonar are too complex for brief discussion, and the scientific "how" must be hastily by-passed in this narrative for a descriptive "what." The sonar gear is housed in a "dome" or container on the ship's bottom. The operator may employ the gear in two ways: as "listening gear" to pick up the sound of a submarine's propellers or internal machinery, or as "echo-ranging gear" to locate the submarine and give an accurate indication of its range. Both functions are based on acoustics. "Listening," of course, means just that; like the hydrophone operator, the sonar operator listens to underwater noises and keeps a sharp ear cocked for submarine sounds. Sonar's "echo-ranging" performance is somewhat more complicated.

Echo-ranging is defined as the process of determining the bearing and distance of a submerged object by sending out a directional sound signal and receiving the echo on a directional sound device. When echo-ranging, the sonar operator sends out an underwater beam—a sharp "ping." Similar to a radio wave, this electronic impulse travels miles from the sender, and may strike any intervening object. Imbued with peculiar properties of its own, the sonar beam echoes, boomerang-fashion, from anything it strikes. In effect, the "ping" works like a miraculous rubber bullet that hits and bounces back on a beeline to the sender. The time it takes for the "ping" to return (echo) gives the target range, and the "ping's" line of travel gives the bearing on the target.

Sonar "echoes" also come back with varying degrees of pitch (frequency) which are caused by reflection of the sound wave from a moving object, and may thereby inform the operator as to the nature and

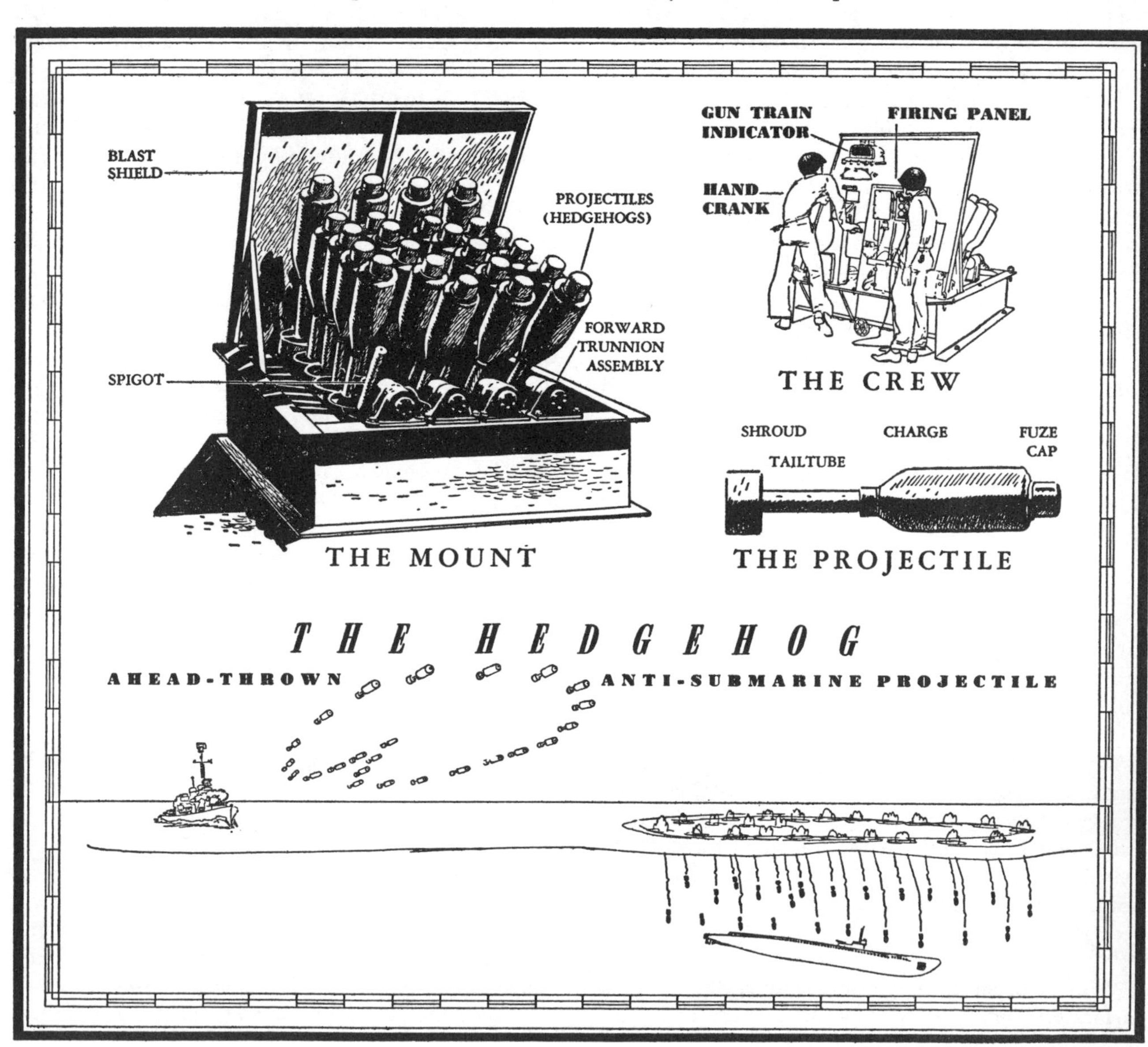

movements of the target. By this pitch variation (known as the "doppler effect"), and by other sonic effects a skilled sonar operator can often tell whether the "ping" is echoing back from a moving ship, a stationary submerged hulk, a submarine, or a whale.

With the advent of sonar, many naval leaders believed the submarine's invisible cloak was undone. Any sonar-equipped A/S vessel could now "put the finger" on the undersea boat. All that would be necessary then would be to dump an ashcan of TNT down on the cowering submersible.

Again, the optimists were overly hopeful. Doenitz's submariners tried to thwart sonar with *Pillenwerfer* —chemical pellets that created gas bubbles which deflected echo-ranging "pings." But a *Pillenwerfer* "ping" contact produced no doppler effect, and a sharp-eared operator soon learned to recognize the variety. So the gas bubbles were unavailing. By and large, the Sound man's difficulties were inherent in echo-ranging rather than created by deliberate opposition.

For sonar's success required operators skilled enough to make order out of the chaotic cacaphony picked up by the listening gear, and able to identify the echoes obtained by the "pinging gear." Only highly trained men could operate and service the gear, and only trained officers could use its information to best advantage.

Then, as has been mentioned, sonar contact could not be continuously maintained even when once established. For example, a destroyer might make sonar contact at 1015—lose it at 1016—regain it at 1030—hold it until 1045—then lose it again at 100-yard range in the last lap of an attack. Further, the crashing disturbance of a depth charge exploding served to deafen the echo-ranging gear temporarily, and water where depth charges exploded provided a mask behind which the submarine could hide. Under certain circumstances contact might be permanently lost.

Sea water lies in varying layers of density. These "density layers" are mostly caused by temperature (surface water is usually warmer than deep water) and by the chemical content of the water (some areas of the sea are saltier than others). It is possible for a submarine to evade sonar detection by gliding from one level to another, and taking refuge, so to speak, under a density layer which will "bend" or "reflect" the sonar beam or send it off on a tangent. Also, sonar could be used by the submarine itself to detect and locate the hunter on the surface.

So the game of hide-and-seek was not all in the hunter's favor. And the submarine was far from obsolete as it torpedoed its deadly way through the two-ocean war.

American destroyers were experimenting with echo-ranging devices as early as 1934. The gear was first installed in the ships of DesDiv 20 (Commander J. C. Jones, Jr.). The destroyers—RATHBURN, WATERS, TALBOT, and DENT—and two submarines were the first United States naval vessels to carry echo-ranging equipment. When the European situation grew threatening, Navy heads decided to recommission the old four-pipers and fit them out with sonar gear for service as A/S vessels. By September 1939, some 60 DD's in the United States Fleet were sonar-equipped. And at this time the Navy was opening the first of its Sound Schools.

Sound Schools

During 1939 the West Coast Sound School was established at San Diego. The school's beginnings were modest—a couple of the DD's from DesDiv 20 tied up at the San Diego Destroyer Base to demonstrate and teach the arts of sonar listening and echo-ranging. But eventually the San Diego Sound School was equipped and staffed with material and faculty for the teaching of 1200 students.

The East Coast (Atlantic Fleet) Sound School came into being at about the same time. It was opened at the Submarine Base, New London, Connecticut, on November 15, 1939. In charge of the school was Captain Richard S. Edwards. Chief Radioman W. A. Braswell served as instructor. The first sonar class contained 16 students, men slated for duty on a quartet of DesLant four-pipers. These veteran World War I destroyers—the BERNADOU, COLE, DUPONT, and ELLIS—were the first DD's to carry sonar gear in the Atlantic.

An experienced submarine officer, Captain Edwards brought to the training course much inside knowledge on the tricks of submarining. He also knew the tricks of training. When the Edwards-trained operators went aboard BERNADOU, COLE, DUPONT, and ELLIS, they knew their sonar gear.

In the autumn of 1940 the Atlantic Fleet Sound School was moved to Key West, Florida, where weather and sea conditions were better for sonar practice. Captain Edwards, presently to become Commander of the Atlantic Submarine Force, returned to the Submarine Force, and the Key West Sound School opened in December 1940 under Commander E. H. Jones, leader of DesDiv 54. The division—destroyers ROPER, JACOB JONES, HERBERT, and DICKERSON—participated in the Key West training activity.

The Key West Sound School and the San Diego Sound School were in full operation by the time the United States entered the war. By that date 170 American destroyers were equipped with sonar gear.

Then additional training facilities were made available at Quonset, R.I., at Bermuda, at Guantanamo, at Coco Solo, at Trinidad, and at Recife, Brazil, where exercises were conducted with American destroyers and other A/S forces playing hunter and with American submarines playing target. Similar sonar training exercises were conducted at Pearl Harbor and at other bases in the Pacific.

Miami Subchaser School

At the beginning they dubbed it the "Donald Duck Navy"—the heterogeneous force composed of PC's, SC's, armed yachts and whatnot that sailed out to chase enemy submarines early in the war. Presently the 180-foot PCE contributed its services to the effort, and in 1943 the destroyer-escort (DE) was on the scene. "Donald Duck" was gaining weight.

Meantime, a subchaser school was organized at Miami. Officially titled the Submarine Chaser Training Center, its express mission was the schooling of officers and men for "Donald Duck" service. As the subchasers were to be officered by Reservists, many of them with little or no sea experience, a strenuous curriculum was in order.

The school was commissioned at Miami on March 26, 1942. On April 8 Commander E. F. McDaniel, veteran destroyerman just in from rough North Atlantic duty in U.S.S. LIVERMORE, took over as schoolmaster. He was a flinty teacher, but an expert on the subject from "ashcan" to "pigboat," and the student body appreciated an educator who knew his stuff.

By the end of 1943 over 10,000 officers and 37,000 enlisted men had learned the ins and outs of submarine-chasing at Miami's famous SCTC. These graduates composed the crews for about 400 SC's, 213 PC's, about 200 A/S craft of other types, and 285 destroyer-escorts. Little subchasers and DE's were already hitting the U-boats hard. As the year turned on 1944 there was nothing quack about the "Donald Duck Navy."

Small, lightly-armed, the SC's were bantams in the A/S ring, and could do little more than badger a submarine in combat. But they performed Homeric feats as harbor guards, coastal patrolmen, and convoy escorts. The not-much-bigger PC's managed to kill a few ocean-going submarines—something any destroyer would be proud of. As for the destroyer-escorts! Steaming from Miami into action, the DE's were the drive-wheels of a "hunter-killer" machine that went far to eradicate the Axis submarine threat in the Atlantic, Mediterranean, and Pacific.

The crews of these A/S vessels, looking back, would revere the Miami Subchaser School with the affection of "old grads" for Alma Mater. To scores and hundreds of destroyermen the Training Center on Biscayne Bay was "McDaniel's Academy"—an expression of regard for the officer who had turned a "Donald Duck" kindergarten into an A/S university. More than a few of the DE crews which trained at Miami painted the flag of dead U-boat or I-boat on their ship's war-weathered bridge. One of the skippers who graduated from the Miami Subchaser School was captain of a DE named ENGLAND. That alone (as will be seen) would have justified the existence of "McDaniel's Academy."

The Sound-Range Recorder

Early in the war a new sonar instrument was produced by the British—the "sound-range recorder." The recorder is not a detection device; it serves, rather, to record detection. Housed in a metal box with a glass top, the recorder contains a roll of graph-like paper and a small stylus (automatic pen) which travels across the unrolling paper and leaves a trace. This trace records the echo received by the sonar gear when the operator is echo-ranging.

From the angle of these traces the operator may plot the rate at which the range is closing—whereby the sub-hunters are informed on the correct time to open fire on the submerged target. Thus the importance of the recorder, a device which greatly facilitated anti-sub fire-control.

The U.S. Navy received this valuable fire-control instrument from the British in the autumn of 1941, and a number were installed on American destroyers operating out of Argentia on convoy duty. Sonar men and A/S/W officers were so enthusiastic over the device that its adoption was immediate. Contracts for the production of recorders were let, and the first American-made recorders were delivered on February 1, 1942. Thereafter it was regularly installed with echo-ranging gear.

Radar Versus Submarines

As noted in a previous chapter, American-built radar sets were installed by the Naval Research Laboratory in several United States warships before 1939. Six U.S. warships received permanent radar installations in 1940. But radar was still something of a novelty at the time of Pearl Harbor. Installations were difficult. Antennae were cumbersome, and the gear below decks occupied considerable space. Operators were at a premium, and the electronics gear was scarce. When the war broke out only a few A/S vessels had radar. It was customary at that time to assign one radar-carrying escort to a convoy.

The manifest value of radar as a submarine-detector gave it a high priority on the "must" list for

A/S warfare. Every DD, every cutter, every escort craft begged for this "all-seeing eye" which could penetrate fog, dusk, or Stygian dark and put an electronic finger on the U-boat lying on the surface. Even if the submarine were awash, it could be detected by a radar sweep, and the "pip" would show up on the screen.

As far as is known, the first radar contact made on an enemy submarine by an American warship was dated November 19, 1941. The warship which distinguished itself in this historic fashion was the pioneer radar-carrying destroyer LEARY. She was at that time engaged in escorting Convoy HX-160.

By August 1942 most of the combat ships in the Atlantic Fleet were equipped with radar sets, and the gear had been distributed to the naval forces in the Pacific. The SG (Sugar George) microwave radar—an improved "surface radar" that presented a brighter and more easily identified "pip"—was issued to the Navy's fighting forces in the autumn of 1942. In 1943 came microwave radar for aircraft. But as aircraft were teaming up with destroyers on the submarine hunt, anything which aided the aviator in turn aided the destroyerman. And microwave radar was the bane of the U-boat. The Germans tried all manner of tricks in their effort to frustrate search radar. They sent up decoy balloons which trailed tinfoil streamers which created a "false target." They attempted to develop a "black U-boat" which would absorb radar beams. They tried to "jam" the airwaves. *Nicht gut!* Nor could German search receivers detect this new S-brand radar. Even the hard-to-catch *Schnorkel* stack (more of which in a later chapter) was vulnerable. After the war German Submarine Admiral Doenitz blamed two things for the U-boat's defeat. One: short-sightedness on the part of Hitler, who failed to provide the German Navy with a sufficient number of submarines. Two: long-sightedness on the part of search radar.

So radar was the "eye" of the submarine-hunter, while sonar served as an "ear." One for surface action, the other for use in detecting submerged subs, both gave the hunter information on the furtive enemy's location and provided range and bearing information for fire-control.

"Huff-Duff"

Early in the war the Royal Navy developed a method for determining the general location of U-boats at long range. The principle was fairly obvious—just intercept the submarine's radio transmissions and then obtain cross-bearings by means of high-frequency direction-finders stationed along the coast.

Every amateur radio fan is acquainted with the loop-finder which small ships and yachts employ to obtain cross-bearings on radio beams from stations along the coast. The British merely reversed the play by placing the "finders" ashore to pick up the radio beams from submarines at sea. The U-boats were continually transmitting messages of one kind or another, and high-frequency finders could intercept these transmissions.

High-frequency direction-finders (HF/DF, or "Huff-Duff") did not translate intercepted messages. Huff-Duff merely established the whereabouts of the transmitting submarine, and temporarily fixed its position. The sender might be in the middle of the Atlantic, or cruising around in the Caribbean. Ten minutes after getting off a radio transmission it might submerge and head for another area. But as the submarine moved from here to there, surfacing on occasion to transmit radio messages, the Huff-Duff system could determine the sub's course, and could follow it from day to day.

A sub in mid-ocean does not generally cruise around in aimless circles. A careful Huff-Duff watch might discern, for example, that a U-boat heading westward from Denmark Strait was bound toward Halifax or veering southward toward Bermuda. A lot of radio conversation by German subs in any particular area would inform Huff-Duff's operators that a wolfpack was gathering in those waters, probably intent on picking up fuel. Such information would be relayed by Huff-Duff stations to a central station where specially trained personnel would keep track of the subs in a given area or plot the course of a lone-wolf coming across the ocean. In turn this information would be relayed to A/S forces at sea to send them speeding to intercept the wolfpack or lone-wolf.

But if Huff-Duff could give A/S forces a "fix" at long range, why not improve the system by shortening the range? Why not install high-frequency direction-finders on escort ships *at sea,* thereby permitting them to intercept U-boat transmissions on locale and thus determine the position of near-by subs? This would eliminate the lengthy relay from shore stations.

After observing HF/DF on Canadian escort vessels, Captain P. R. Heineman, who had just been at sea as an escort commander, promptly recommended its installation in American ships.

Early in the autumn of 1942, HF/DF gear was installed in the Coast Guard cutters SPENCER and CAMPBELL. Shortly thereafter the equipment was installed in the American destroyer ENDICOTT. It subsequently became the practice to equip two or three DD's of each squadron with Huff-Duff gear.

So the HF/DF system provided sub-hunters with another means for detecting the enemy. The detection gave convoys a chance for evasive routing, and it informed escorts on the location of "submarine water." Later in the war, Huff-Duff information obtained by shore stations put many a hunter-killer group on the track of a U-boat or a submarine concentration.

When Huff-Duff began to point them out as though they were magnetized, the U-boats did strive to maintain radio silence. But fairly frequent transmissions were necessary for wolfpack operation. They were also necessary for the relay of sub-to-shore information—reports to Headquarters, acknowledgement of orders received, positional information. The U-boat could not play dumb for days on end, or Doenitz would believe it was sunk.

Often enough it was. By American destroyermen acting on information from Huff-Duff.

The A/S Warfare Unit

In the first week of February 1942 a group of destroyer officers and others concerned with A/S warfare sat in conference at the Boston Navy Yard. From this conference emerged the Atlantic Fleet Anti-Submarine Warfare Unit—a body to study the ways and means of A/S warfare, devise methods for combatting the U-boat, and train instructors for the Atlantic Fleet Sound School.

Set up in Boston, the A/S Warfare Unit went into action on March 2, 1942, under the leadership of Captain W. D. Baker. Allied with Captain Baker's unit was ASWORG—the Anti-Submarine Warfare Operations Research Group composed of distinguished civilian scientists and educators whose mission was to collate and analyze all information appertaining to submarine warfare, and to create new devices or methods for tracking, attacking, and destroying submarines.

Heretofore, A/S warfare had been conducted in a somewhat hit-or-miss fashion. The A/S vessels at sea lacked specific methods; no new doctrines had been formulated for A/S operations; the results obtained by current A/S measures had not been carefully assembled and scientifically studied since the Battle of the Atlantic began.

Captain Baker's unit and the ASWORG scientists pitched in to remedy the situation. The Group studied the action reports of A/S/W units direct from the Atlantic firing line. Statistics were gathered and analyzed. For example, hits and misses were tabulated. Depth-charge performance was studied: How many Mark 6 ashcans had it taken to do the job? What patterns had proved most effective? The workings of sonar and radar were re-examined. Destroyer tactics were put "under the microscope": Which ones were proving most effective? What were the mathematical chances of Destroyer DD demolishing Submarine SS under circumstances from A to Z?

Always in anti-submarine warfare there was the "Unknown X" factor imposed by the loss of contact with the submerged target at the 200- to 600-yard point, and the fact that the submarine's depth could not be determined with sharp accuracy. Captain Baker's Navy-and-Scientist group worked night and day to minimize that "X" factor and take the guesswork out of the attack formula. Or, at least, to alter guesses to good estimates.

So the scientist working with the A/S Warfare Unit did more than analyze reams of data. They improved the techniques of sub-fighting. ASWORG analysts and mathematicians developed search patterns for regaining contact with submarines. They produced highly efficient patterns for the laying of depth-charge barrages—neat designs which told destroyermen where, how many, how deep. They worked out scientifically planned escort-screens for warships and convoys—so many van DD's for a convoy with a front of so many yards; DD's on the flanks at such and such a position.

ASWORG's scientists also developed new instruments for the detection, frustration, and destruction of submarines. But they first came to the fore with improved ways and means for the employment of the weapons at hand.

Destroyer A/S Tactics (The Attack)

Given the anti-submarine tools, American destroyermen sailed out on the embattled seas of World War II to do the job.

As has previously been described, DD's and DE's (and kindred A/S vessels) played a dual role in the drama of A/S warfare.

Defensively, destroyers and companion A/S craft were employed as patrol vessels to guard harbor entrances, coastal waters, and other sub-menaced areas. Or as guardians to protect major warships and other vessels from submarine onslaught—an activity which came under the general terms of "escorting" and "screening."

On the A/S offensive, destroyers and companion anti-sub vessels went all out to track down, attack, and destroy the undersea enemy. Destroyers and DE's with escort-carriers (CVE's), designated as hunter-killer groups, were in this category.

The foregoing is a generality, but it roughly describes the tactical employment of destroyers in A/S warfare, and the terms "offensive" and "defensive" apply only broadly to the over-all operation. The destroyer serving as an escort in a screen was frequently called upon to take the offensive and "go get" the detected enemy. The DD or DE serving in a hunter-killer group might be ordered to assume a guard position while companion vessels took the field against the foe. But whether operating as escorts or hunter-killers, DD's and DE's were at all times prepared to attack the undersea antagonist.

Obviously a destroyer's A/S tactics were to a large extent dictated by the tactical employment of the vessel itself. Upon contacting an enemy submarine, a destroyer member of a hunter-killer team might pursue a course of action radically different from that followed by a lone DD escorting a damaged cruiser back to base.

The Navy's Destroyer Forces, however, had devised a number of doctrines to meet most given situations of A/S warfare. Plans were designed and combat maneuvers devised—maneuvers which were more or less standardized, like the opening gambits of chess. For example:

An A/S vessel (call it a destroyer) is serving as a convoy escort in the screen in front of a convoy. Suddenly the DD picks up a sound contact, or sights a periscope "feather" immediately ahead. Obviously the enemy is a dangerous threat to the convoy (presumably some thousands of yards astern). Immediate action is required to prevent the sub from getting off an accurate torpedo salvo. So the destroyer flashes a warning over the TBS (voice radio) and launches an attack to force the enemy to break off his approach and "go deep."

The sub thus driven down cannot fix a periscopic eye on the advancing convoy to draw a bead for a torpedo shot. Nor can it follow the maneuvers of the warned convoy, which may swiftly execute a radical course-change to side-step the line of fire. If the sub has already opened fire before submerging, such an emergency turn by the convoy may cause the torpedoes to miss, since the torpedo fire-control was based on the convoy's previous course and speed.

Meantime, the defending escort stays between the sub and the convoy until the convoy is well clear. To force the enemy to stay under or go deeper, the DD may deliver some random depth-charge salvos to worry the sub. The point is, so long as the submarine is deep under it cannot watch the convoy and it may lose the track entirely. Moreover, the submerged sub must run at slow speeds. If driven under and held down long enough, it will be unable to overhaul the surface ships.

When the convoy is out of danger, the defending escort (assisted by another escort, if one can be spared from the screen) may take the offensive in an effort to develop the contact and launch attacks to kill the sub. Otherwise, and according to the dictates of circumstance, the escort will rejoin the convoy screen and resume normal patrolling.

A submarine detected at the convoy's rear might invite a similar gambit—an attack to drive the enemy under, and some depth-charging to make him keep his periscope-head down, thereby frustrating torpedo fire and subsequent tracking of the convoy.

The sub at the rear does not endanger the convoy as does the one ahead, for the simple reason that the convoy is running away (instead of into) a possible torpedo salvo. A stern chase is always a long one, and if the sub is held under for a sufficient length of time, its chance of overhauling the convoy is practically nil. In either case, the attack delivered ahead or at the convoy's rear is calculated to fluster the enemy, frustrate his periscopic sight, and fend off a torpedo strike.

The advent of search radar introduced long-range surface detection, and echo-ranging facilitated careful tracking of the submerged submarines. As the war progressed and Allied A/S forces were enlarged, anti-submarine screens around convoys or combat forces were improved. Relatively few subs were able to penetrate an alerted screen and deliver a surprise torpedo attack. Deliberately the sub-hunters went into action to down the foe. And many a U-boat and Jap submarine was killed by an attack which culminated a prolonged and relentless search.

Aware of playing "it" in this deadly game of tag, the submerged enemy employed strenuous and crafty evasive measures to escape the hunters. Trapping a sub which had "gone deep" to elude pursuit was never an easy task.

Destroyer A/S Tactics (The Hold-Down)

Obviously a submarine's oxygen supply is limited, and submariners have to breathe. In a manner of speaking, the submersible itself must "breathe." Diesel-driven on the surface, a submarine employs electric motors when running under the sea; the batteries are exhaustible, and the sub must gain the surface to charge them by Diesel operation. Expand the oxygen supply or let the batteries give out, and the submerged submarine is *in extremis.* Moreover, prolonged submergence can erode the nerve of the hardiest undersea crew. Hence the necessity for a periodic rise by the submarine—a rise which can be untimely if enemies are waiting with cocked guns.

Frequently employed by DD's, DE's, and other sub-hunters (including aircraft), the *hold-down tactic* was designed to keep a submarine submerged to the point of suffocation, desperation, or exhaustion. At which extremity the submariners would be literally forced to come up and fight it out on the surface—a climax which usually spelled disaster for the embattled submarine.

The tactic might be essayed by a single A/S vessel, by subchaser and aircraft, or by a large group of hunter-killers acting cooperatively. Naturally, the more numerous the A/S craft, the better the odds on their side. But there were instances in World War II wherein a single A/S vessel successfully "held down" an enemy submarine to the point of its forced exposure and destruction.

A typical hold-down might begin with the radar detection of a surfaced submarine on the flank of a convoy. Contact! Several escorting destroyers peel off and go after the sub. Down goes the undersea boat to lie low. The DD's gain sonar contact, and the hunt is on.

The gambit may develop into an endurance contest between the submerged sub and the hunters "upstairs." The submariners know the destroyermen are up there, and they use every dodge to make a getaway. Echo-ranging, the hunters follow the submarine's trail; they have only to maintain contact and wait for the inevitable rise. Time is on their side in this cat-and-mouse play. Time, and the fact that men and engines need air.

Maintaining contact is, of course, the key to a successful hold-down; the hunters must stay on the trail. Above all they must prevent the submarine from surfacing undetected—an upshot which would give the sub a chance to cut and run for it on high-speed Diesels. Consequently, the hunters in the submarine's vicinity keep under constant observation all positions that the sub could possibly occupy. Radar sweeps are made continuously.

If the sub has been held down all day, vigilance must be tightened at nightfall, for the obvious reasons that the quarry may try to take advantage of night's cover, and that sub and submariners will be nearer the end of their undersea rope. Coming late in World War II, *Schnorkel* gear and ingenious new air-conditioning devices considerably altered the time-element, but for the greater part of the war submarine endurance was limited to about 50 hours' submergence. Hold-down tactics could be timed accordingly.

For a typical culmination: the hounded submersible rises to engage in combat with the A/S craft. As the submarine broaches, the hunters pick up the "pip," and close in. Worn out from hours of fouling air and nerve strain, the desperate submariners rush topside to man the deck guns. The advantage is all on the A/S vessel's side, particularly if the ship is a heavily-armed DD, DE, or Coast Guardsman which can out-run and out-shoot the submersible.

Seldom were submarines able to fight their way out when trapped by a persistent hold-down. On record is the exploit of a severely damaged sub which gained the surface after long submergence and then gun-battled its way to freedom through a quartet of hounding A/S vessels. But the submarine in this instance was American—the SALMON (Commander H. K. Nauman)—and the hold-downers were Japanese.

That American destroyermen executed the hold-down tactic most effectively is a fact which will be evidenced by a number of A/S actions detailed in subsequent chapters.

Convoy Escort Duty

The typical ocean convoy, consisting of 40 to 70 merchant ships, steamed in a rectangular formation of nine to fourteen columns. The columns were spaced 1,000 yards apart, and the ships in column were spaced at 600-yard intervals. An eleven-column convoy, therefore, presented a frontage of five nautical miles and had a depth of one and a half miles or more, depending upon the number of ships placed in column.

A ship was assigned a number in accordance with its position in the formation.

Responsible for the internal discipline of the convoy proper, the Convoy Commodore usually flew his pennant in a column leader near the center of the convoy. The Vice-Commodore rode another column leader. In over-all command was the Escort Commander, generally a destroyer squadron commander or an officer of comparable rank and experience. He usually flew his pennant in one of the van escorts stationed within easy visual signalling distance of the Convoy Commodore's ship.

The escorts formed a screen on the periphery of the convoy. They were, of course, stationed in positions carefully calculated to provide the best protection for the convoy.

To strike at the convoy, a submarine had to pass through the screen undetected and attack at a range short enough to ensure a hit, or else fire a torpedo from a position outside the screen—a so-called "browning shot." If the escort vessels were drawn in to form a tight screen, the sub had a better chance of hitting with a browning shot (for the obvious reason that if the escorts closely hugged the convoy, the attacking sub could make a nearer approach). On the other hand, if the escorts were stationed far out, the sub was more likely to penetrate the screen undetected. To reduce the sub's chances to a minimum, screening diagrams were scientifically designed to place the escorts at such distances that a sub's chance of penetrating the screen was on a par with its chance of making a hit with a browning shot.

Escorts used their sonar gear continuously, "pinging" as they went. Radar kept the surface lookout, on the watch for enemy submarines and other vessels, and it was employed to maintain proper station, especially during periods of low visibility.

The parading of a large ship-train through fog, rough water, or night's blackout demanded expert navigation by all parties concerned. Each merchantman had its own capacities, cranks, and quirks. A fast ship might range ahead. A slow ship might straggle. Engine breakdown might send a vessel staggering out of line. Collisions could occur in a flash, especially if the convoy were making an abrupt course-change, or zigzagging.

Large, slow convoys—they were given the code designation "S" (for slow)—generally steamed on steady courses. Zigzagging cut down the distance made good, and in a slow convoy it tended to create confusion and cause straggling. Moreover, its tactical value was doubtful—"many a ship saved by a fortuitous zig was lost through an unlucky zag." Accordingly, slow convoys zigzagged or made emergency turns only if suddenly attacked or menaced. However, evasive course changes of 20 to 40 degrees on each side of the base course and lasting for a couple of hours or more were commonly made by slow convoys to avoid wolfpack ambush or otherwise elude the enemy.

Each convoy was given a route through designated ocean positions before it sailed—a route always subject to change by radio dispatch. And the Escort Commander had authority to steer evasive courses if he believed such action was called for.

Upon the Escort Commander, then, rested much of the responsibility for the convoy's passage. His escort group was charged with its defense. He, himself, was responsible for screening operations. And within limits he had the authority to regulate the convoy formation and direct the convoy's run. The destroyer officer who served in that capacity had a full load on his shoulder-boards.

Troop convoys were in a different category from the slow merchant convoys just discussed. Consisting of transports and auxiliaries, they were usually Navy manned. Fast convoys (designated "F"), they steamed at a higher speed than slow convoys, and they were furnished heavier escort.

One or more battleships or cruisers guarded the troop convoy against surface raiders. The Escort Commander was customarily a Rear Admiral commanding a battleship or cruiser division, or a senior, capital-ship Captain. The DD screen was heavily augmented to provide the utmost protection.

The senior destroyer officer was designated Screen Commander. Answering to the Escort Commander, he was specifically in charge of the destroyer group.

Escort carriers were sometimes attached to convoys. But as a rule these "baby flat-tops" and their screening DD's and DE's were organized as hunter-killer groups to conduct anti-wolfpack campaigns. However, these task groups frequently acted as a covering force for convoys passing through their operating areas.

Escort carriers were not available early in the war, and air-cover by land-based planes did not get very far to sea. When finally contrived, extended air coverage turned the Atlantic Battle's tide. But for the greater part of the war the bulk of the convoy escort burden was carried by the destroyermen. And many hundreds of ships and many thousands of tons of war material went safely overseas, thanks to the effective anti-submarine tactics of the tactlessly-named "tin cans."

ROPER VS U-85

CHAPTER 6

DESLANT INTO BATTLE (Part 1)

Dual Mission, Atlantic

After formal declaration of war, the United States Navy was confronted in the Atlantic with a dual problem.

Mission No. 1: the Navy must maintain the transportation lines to Europe—clear the way for, and otherwise protect, the shipping which carried Lend-Lease goods and American troops overseas.

Mission No. 2: the Navy must keep open the coastal shipping lanes off America's Eastern Seaboard—protect the coastwise trunk lines all the way from South America to Canada, and through the Gulf of Mexico and the Caribbean.

Trans-Atlantic convoying and defense of home-coast shipping were the priority tasks at once assigned to the Navy's Atlantic forces; tasks which principally featured escort-of-convoy duty and offensive anti-submarine warfare.

Destroyers, therefore, were what was called for. Escorts by profession, and submarine-hunters by design. Already the Navy's DD's were swinging along on North Atlantic convoy runs. Already they had traded blows with Hitler's wolfpacks. To DesLant, then, fell much of the Atlantic Battle burden.

The Iceland run had been only a sample of convoy duty. Now destroyers were to escort North Atlantic convoys all the way to Londonderry, Northern Ireland. The Atlantic Battle was to be all-out.

Many of the available destroyers lacked radar gear. Many were employing sonar for the first time. Most of the crews had never conducted a cooperative submarine search. Very few had ever seen a shot or a depth charge fired in anger.

Appointed Commander in Chief United States Fleet (Cominch) on December 20, 1941, Admiral Ernest J. King, with headquarters in Washington, assumed over-all command of the Navy's Atlantic and Pacific Fleets, and hence of its Destroyer Forces. On December 30, 1941, Admiral Royal E. Ingersoll became Commander in Chief Atlantic Fleet (CinCLant). On December 22, Rear Admiral A. S. Carpender replaced Rear Admiral F. L. Reichmuth as ComDesLant. Destroyer operations in the Atlantic were directed by CinCLant and ComDesLant. Commander Task Force 24 (Rear Admiral A. L. Bristol), at Argentia, retained the responsibility for the operation and escortage of merchant convoys in the North Atlantic.

American troop convoys (designated NA and AT) began to cross the North Atlantic in February 1942. Such convoys ordinarily contained more escorts than transports. Sailing from New York on February 19, Convoy AT-12 was composed of 15 transports and 18 escorts. At a later date, a combined 17-ship convoy (AT-15 and NA-8) was escorted by the battleship New York, the light cruiser Brooklyn, and 12 American destroyers. These were typical of the "troopers" that carried U.S. Army forces across the North Atlantic to the British Isles.

Under heavy escort, too, went the tanks, trucks and munitions, the food, clothing, gasoline, the locomotives and lubricants, the vast quantities of Lend Lease staples and war materials needed to supply the United Kingdom and the overseas American forces.

At Londonderry in January 1942 the destroyers began to put in. The port's repair facilities offered the DD's opportunity for upkeep; the hospitable Scotch-Irish offered the destroyermen recreation. A local "dome teacher" for anti-aircraft training, and several training submarines for A/S schooling, gave the destroyermen a chance to sharpen their combat techniques. Usually the last two days of the stay at Londonderry were devoted to A/S refresher training.

Not many U-boats were contacted in the North Atlantic during the weeks immediately following the war declaration. In January 1942 the wolfpacks were walking softly. Ships continued to go down to torpedo-fire—14 in American waters, 12 off the Canadian coast, 9 in the Bermuda area. But no more than 10 were downed in North Atlantic Convoy areas that month—a slump of certain significance.

The slack-off suggested a realignment of wolfpack forces, a revision of U-boat strategy, rather than defeat and retreat. The U-boat Force was gathering muscle for an offensive.

The tempo quickened in February when 12 ships were torpedo-sunk in North Atlantic convoy areas. The long, hard battle to get the goods across was only beginning.

Onslaught on ON-67 (DD's versus Wolfpack)

One of the tough convoy-wolfpack battles fought in the first quarter of 1942 involved the American destroyers EDISON, NICHOLSON, LEA, and BERNADOU. The quartet comprised the ocean escort for Convoy ON-67, west-bound for Halifax from the United Kingdom. In charge of the escort was EDISON's skipper, Commander A. C. Murdaugh.

If flaws showed up in the performance of the escorts, the cause was deficient equipment and unfamiliarity with modern A/S techniques; NICHOLSON's was the only radar which worked consistently, and BERNADOU was just out of "mothballs."

Leaving Hvalfjordur, Iceland, on February 16, Murdaugh's destroyer group picked up the convoy three days later at "Momp."

The convoy consisted of 35 ships steaming in 8-column formation. Falling in, the American destroyers relieved the British escorts, with the exception of H.M.C.S. ALGOMA, the latter being directed to stay with the convoy as long as her fuel permitted. Among the 35 merchantmen was the British rescue ship S. S. TOWARD, equipped with special life-saving gear and carrying "Huff-Duff."

Under Escort Commander Murdaugh's direction, the convoy proceeded in its 8-column formation, steaming at 8½ knots. Stationed about 4,000 yards from the convoy's rectangle, the screening destroyers patrolled at 12½ knots. Murdaugh positioned them in day formation as follows:

EDISON (flagship)	*Off convoy's starboard bow.*
NICHOLSON	*Comdr. J. S. Keating. Off convoy's port bow.*
LEA	*Lt. Comdr. C. Broussard. Off convoy's starboard flank, abreast of last ship in column.*
BERNADOU	*Lt. Comdr. R. E. Braddy, Jr. Off convoy's port flank, abreast of last ship in column.*
H.M.C.S. ALGOMA	*Directly astern of convoy.*

In night formation the screen retained its circular coverage, but defense weight was shifted to the convoy's front.

The hours of February 19 and 20 were uneventful. Morning of the 21st the convoy, on course 204°, was smoking badly. With visibility about 10 miles, the billowing smudge was as obvious as an Indian signal. Fog set in around noon—perfect cover for stalking enemies. And as the convoy advanced through thickening vapor, EDISON's sonar picked up a contact.

The echo was indistinct, a "doubtful." Taking no chances, Commander Murdaugh ran it down. EDISON dropped a pattern of five depth charges. Thereafter, Sound was unable to regain the contact. EDISON returned to her patrol station.

Visibility improved during the afternoon. And at 1730 the rescue ship TOWARD picked up a submarine's signal on her "Huff-Duff" gear. Bearing 107°. But after searching for about an hour, LEA reported "no contact," and resumed her station.

Evidently LEA's search should have been more persistent. For an enemy was in the vicinity. At 0305 the following morning a U-boat attacked the left rear flank of the convoy.

At this hour the escorts were patrolling in night formation, with LEA and BERNADOU shifted to the convoy's forward flanks. Striking at the exposed rear flank, the submarine was undetected. Apparently it fired from outside the screen. The long-range "browning shots" struck home. Thunder boomed in the night. Mushrooming smoke and orange fire, two ships staggered to a halt, hard hit.

NICHOLSON fell back to join TOWARD and ALGOMA in picking up survivors. The rescue vessel's big dip net featured in this life-saving detail, as did her special hospital facilities. The destroyermen, grim and determined, hauled their own share of shivering merchant seamen from the brine.

Daylight of February 22 revealed a seascape devoid of submarines. But they might be down under the seascape. At any rate, none appeared during the day. At 1730 the convoy's course was changed to 240°; at 2130 to 200°. These evasion tactics were at least temporarily effective. There were no attacks that night.

Nevertheless, the enemy kept the convoy under surveillance. At 1210 next day EDISON once more picked up sound contact, a sharp one that definitely spelled "submarine." Murdaugh ordered attack on the sub, which was directly ahead of column 8. A pattern of five depth charges rumbled under the sea. Due to interference from the convoy, the DD was unable to regain contact. But EDISON searched the vicinity until the convoy was over the horizon, then rejoined at 25 knots.

During the afternoon, BERNADOU and LEA repeated their offensive sweeps of the previous day. LEA's radar was now operating, but she made no surface contacts. BERNADOU, however, picked up a sound contact at 1615, twelve miles on the convoy's port beam. Lieutenant Commander Braddy tried for the target with two depth-charge patterns. The contact evaporated.

These sporadic contacts suggested a wolfpack in the convoy area, and Murdaugh bent every effort to avoid ambush. Commander Murdaugh ordered several course changes to throw the enemy off the track. But in spite of utmost vigilance and precaution, the U-boats got in.

The first strike came at 0030 in the morning of February 24th. Thereafter successive attacks were made until 0645. The convoy was beset from both quarters by five or six sharpshooting submarines. Four merchantmen were torpedoed. Two of the damaged vessels kept on going. Two went to the bottom.

During this onslaught, "snowflake" illumination was used by the convoy to give the Armed Guard on the merchant vessels a chance to spot surfaced U-boats. But the brilliant light failed to silhouette any targets for the deck-gunners.

While the battle was at its climax, Commander Murdaugh sent a radio dispatch to the Chief of Naval Operations, recommending that the convoy disperse or make a drastic, evasive course-change. When permission was granted, the convoy's course was radically shifted to 285°. Meantime, offensive screening operations were extended and intensified.

Early that afternoon the rescue ship TOWARD picked up foreign signals on her "Huff-Duff." Running 15 miles ahead to investigate the direction-finder bearing, NICHOLSON sighted two surfaced submarines. The destroyer staged a single-handed double play, forcing the two U-boats to dive, and keeping them down under until after dark.

Simultaneously LEA dropped astern to run down a direction-finder bearing. Returning to her original station after a fruitless search, she was sent out 20 miles on the convoy's starboard flank. There she encountered a U-boat on the surface. When the sub submerged, LEA went after the target with depth charges. Lieutenant Commander Broussard reported that the barrage laid by his destroyer probably did some damage.

The wolfpack closed in hungrily at dusk. Following their favorite *Rudeltaktik,* the U-boats surfaced after dark to run ahead for high-speed lunges at the advancing convoy. Not long after nightfall EDISON picked up a sound contact on the convoy's starboard bow. Then the lookouts sighted a U-boat silhouette slinking through the moonlight. The silhouette slid out of sight before the deck-gunners could get in a shot, but EDISON's depth charges went overside in the water where the U-boat submerged.

After six depth-charge attacks the destroyermen were unable to regain contact. Murdaugh held the DD in the vicinity for a thorough search before ordering her to resume her station in the screen. Then, while rejoining the convoy at 0205 in the morning of the 25th, EDISON spotted another submarine.

This U-boat was close aboard—200 yards!—and nearly abeam. A barely glimpsed spectre in the gloom, it faded into the water before EDISON could turn to ram, and before the destroyer's main battery could be brought to bear. So spectral was this submarine that EDISON's sonar gear was unable to pick it up. The destroyermen dropped one depth charge on the vanished target, after which EDISON patrolled between the convoy and the point of submergence until dawn.

As a result of these A/S efforts, no attacks were made on the convoy during the night of February 24-25. But daylight did not dispel the submarine peril. Fog surged across the seascape at 1410, and with its onset the ranging escorts were recalled. The screen was reforming when TOWARD's "Huff-Duff" picked up another suspicious signal. BERNADOU, running down the direction-finder bearing, established sound contact at 1459. She dropped a pattern of seven depth charges on this unseen target, and searched the vicinity until dark.

Fog wallowed around the ships throughout that night (February 25-26), and morning brought rough seas. Daylight also brought the Coast Guard cutter SPENCER (Commander E. H. FRITZSCHE, U.S.C.G.) toiling up through the heavy weather to join the convoy as a welcome reinforcement. Convoy ON-67 was now well along on the home stretch, and the last lap of the westward voyage proved uneventful.

For the destroyermen in Commander Murdaugh's unit, however, the voyage had been sufficiently trying. The convoy's merchant crews had also endured

Ally of the German raiders was this type of weather encountered in the North Atlantic during several months of each year. January, 1942, when this photograph was made, proved to be the lull before the wolfpack storm. With the beginning of American troop convoys in February, escorting became Navy's first duty. Typical "troopers" often contained more escorts than transports.

Coast Guard Cutter Icarus encountered U-352 on a maiden cruise off Cape Lookout in May, 1942. American sonar, combined with effective depth charges, terminated the U-boat's career and transferred 33 German submariners into prisoners of war. Here American orders are being transmitted by a German officer to his compatriots under supervision of the conquerors.

Early in 1942 Edison was flagship of a west-bound convoy which sustained gruelling losses to a hounding wolfpack. These losses, however, drove home specific needs for better search equipment, better tactics, better training.

Truxtun was lost through grounding on the rocky southeastern Newfoundland coast early in 1942. High seas and arctic weather caused considerable loss of life, but risky rescue work by Newfoundlanders saved many lives.

Operation Paukenschlag's effect. Such merchantmen losses as these—Bensen, Dixie Arrow, and Tiger—proved escorting better tactics than roving patrols.

their portion of ordeal. Four ships sunk and two damaged by torpedo fire were eventful enough for any convoy's log. Although two U-boats may have been damaged in reprisal, the damage was no more than "probable." The four ship fatalities were decidedly "on the bottom." ON-67 made port as the first convoy under U. S. command which sustained gruelling losses.

An important lesson brought home to the Navy's Destroyer Forces was the urgent need for search radar in A/S work. Another lesson: destroyermen were short of training in sonar applications. Depth-charging methods needed sharpening.

Admiral Bristol's comment on the Escort Commander was as follows:

... THE PERFORMANCE OF DUTY BY COMMANDER A. C. MURDAUGH, AS COMMANDING OFFICER OF THE EDISON AND AS COMMANDER ESCORT UNIT, WAS PARTICULARLY OUTSTANDING. IN THE FACE OF DETERMINED ENEMY CONCENTRATION AND PRESSURE HE HANDLED HIS FORCES SKILLFULLY AND AGGRESSIVELY, COMPLETELY DISRUPTED THE ENEMY PLAN OF CONCENTRATED ATTACK, AND DELIVERED HEAVY AND EFFECTIVE ATTACKS ON THE ENEMY. REGARDLESS OF THE FATE OF THE SUBMARINES ATTACKED, COMMANDER MURDAUGH OUTMANEUVERED AND OUTFOUGHT A CONCENTRATION OF ENEMY SHIPS AND EFFECTIVELY BROKE UP THE ENEMY'S EFFORTS.

Loss of U.S.S. Truxtun

On May 28, 1940, the British Army evacuated Dunquerque. On that same day, the United States heavy cruiser VINCENNES received orders to proceed with escorting destroyers SIMPSON and TRUXTUN to Lisbon, Portugal, on diplomatic business.

There is a destiny that shapes the ends of ships as well as of mortals. Two of the warships which shared this mission to Portugal were fated to follow courses that led to ports of no return. VINCENNES' final course would lead her to the bourne of Savo Sound in the South Pacific. TRUXTUN's was to take her into fatal seas off the coast of Newfoundland.

The third week of February 1942. Captained by Lieutenant Commander Ralph Hickox, TRUXTUN, in company with the destroyer WILKES (Commander J. D. Kelsey) flying the pennant of Commander W. W. Webb, ComDesDiv 26, was escorting the Navy cargo vessel POLLUX from Portland, Maine, to Argentia. The night of February 17-18 brought a tumultuous winter gale—foaming waters and a snowstorm that reduced visibility to zero. Blindfolded, the little convoy bucked its way through white midnight, the ships rolling their beam ends under.

But wicked February seas off Newfoundland were the rule rather than the exception. And the convoy, heading for Placentia Bay early in the morning of the 18th, was given no intimation of impending disaster. TRUXTUN apparently had no warning. Steaming on the southwest side of Ferryland Point, she was unable to determine that in the blizzarding gale the convoy had gone off course. If booming surf were heard by the lookouts, or churning breakers were glimpsed, the menace was detected too late.

At 0410 TRUXTUN struck with a crash. Hard aground, she was immediately assailed by furious seas that pounded her with catapult force. Waves plunged across her listing decks, swept her superstructure, and shouldered her across jagged rocks. Wrenched beyond endurance, her frames buckled; her plates caved, letting in the icy flood.

Then, before TRUXTUN could warn them, both the POLLUX and WILKES ran aground. At once the freighter's plight was as desperate as the destroyers'; however, WILKES backed clear with comparatively light damage.

Blizzard and wild seas prevented WILKES from aiding the grounded ships or their men. TRUXTUN broke up soon after she went aground, and valiant destroyermen went down with the wreckage to succumb to freezing wind and wave. Some of her crew were rescued from the waters by the courageous work of Newfoundland natives who risked their lives in small boats and on the icy cliffs ashore. Only a few of TRUXTUN's crew survived; among those lost was the destroyer's captain, Lieutenant Commander Hickox, who stayed with his ship and led his men until washed into the sea. POLLUX's crew was able to reach the shore over booms and lines carried through raging seas by brave men, but the ship herself did not long survive.

The tragedy tells a story well known to veteran Navy men—the story of the age-old conflict between mariner and storm. In this battle for mastery, the sea asks no quarter, and it gives none. Neither do the men who go down to the sea in warships.

Send More Destroyers

A convoy escort-group which lacked a swift destroyer or two was at a decided disadvantage in an A/S surface action. The average Coast Guard cutter made 19 knots; corvettes made around 14. The 500-ton U-boat could attain a surface speed of 17.6 knots —fast enough to outrun a corvette or dodge a distant cutter. Consequently Admiral Bristol strove to obtain a pair of DD's for each escort unit, and the standard for that spring was a group composed of two American destroyers and four Canadian corvettes. But some merchant convoys, such as HX-196 (containing 22 freighters and 21 oil tankers), made the trans-Atlantic run without benefit of destroyer escortage. Convoy HX-196 was escorted by two American Coast Guard cutters and the usual quartet of Canadian corvettes.

Although Convoy HX-196 crossed the ocean without misadventure, Commander H. C. Fitz, in charge of the escort, reported:

> *Even if a submarine is sighted shadowing on the surface, there is no ship of this unit that can make any appreciable gain on a submarine if it takes its maximum surface speed.*

Other Escort Commanders who took convoys safely across in the opening months of 1942 were Captain J. B. Heffernan (flagship GLEAVES); Commander R. W. Hungerford (BRISTOL); Commander W. K. Phillips (MAYO); Commander P. R. Heineman (BENSON). Convoy ON-68 lost two ships in a wolfpack scrimmage during March; but aside from that, the worst enemies encountered were the fogs, ice, blizzards, and storms of the North Atlantic itself.

A DesLant Force destroyer suffered a serious collision off the Delaware Capes that month, but the DD was not on escort-of-convoy duty. The injured ship was the destroyer STACK (Commander Isaiah Olch). In the morning of March 17, 1942, she collided with the aircraft carrier WASP, while acting as the carrier's escort. Both ships were smothered by fog when the crash came at about 0550, the big carrier striking STACK on the starboard side. The impact ruptured the destroyer's hull. Her No. 1 fireroom flooded; the lighting circuits blacked out; she was heeled over at a steep angle while being raked by the carrier's bow.

In this precarious situation there was imminent danger of the destroyer's depth charges becoming dislodged—a climax that would result in a fatal blast if the injured charges exploded. First Class Torpedoman Frank L. Knight saw the peril. Wading waist deep, he made his way aft in the darkened vessel, and set all the depth charges on safe. Navy Cross for Torpedoman Knight.

So March came in like a lion and went out like a lion while DD's on the North Atlantic saw little wolfpack activity. April 1942 proved equally devoid of A/S action. But American destroyermen knew that with the coming of mild weather and long evenings, the U-boats were bound to renew the attack in North Atlantic convoy areas. And escort groups would have their hands full.

"Come and get it!" a trailing U-boat, blinking international code, had taunted an escort group led by Coast Guard cutters. Unable to desert the screen on this occasion, the Coast Guardsmen had been forced to swallow this gall. To meet the U-boat challenge, more fast destroyers were needed for North Atlantic escort-of-convoy duty. But American DD's in that first half of 1942 were at a premium—for Fleet operations, for escort of troop convoys, for service with the British Home Fleet, for training schools, for special missions. And for A/S duty in American coastal waters where the enemy was applying the heavy pressure.

U-Boats Off Atlantic Coast (DD's On Roving Patrol)

The day after Nazi Germany declared war on the United States, German Admiral Raeder conferred with Adolph Hitler. The outcome of this meeting of master minds was a decision to open a U-boat campaign against American coastwise shipping.

Prior to that date (December 12, 1941) Hitler had prohibited the extension of U-boat operations into the western Atlantic, although Admiral Raeder had urged a campaign in Canadian waters. Now that the lid was off in the Pacific a U-boat squadron was readied for Operations *Paukenschlag.*

Paukenschlag means "Roll on the Drums." Very military. Fortunately for the United States, the U-boat Force could not begin this drumming immediately. Only six U-boats were available for the trans-Atlantic invasion.

The U-boats, 500-tonners, were not ready until January 1942. By February, several more were added to the drum-squad.

The din began on January 12, 1942—a torpedo blast that sent a British merchantman sloughing to the bottom some 300 miles off Cape Cod. Two days later, the Panamanian tanker NORNESS was downed off Cape Hatteras. On the 15th, the British oiler COIMBRA went down with a boom. On the 18th, the American tanker ALLAN JACKSON. On the 19th, a Latvian merchantman and the American freighter CITY OF ATLANTA. Then six more tankers went down, one after the other, in the coastal waters between New York and Cape Hatteras. Before the year's first month was out, 14 ships were blown to the bottom off America's Eastern Seaboard.

In February 1942 the drumming loudened. Fourteen ships were sunk off the Eastern Seaboard that month. March was worse; the U-boats took a toll of 28. Almost at leisure the invaders roamed the coastal sea lanes between Wilmington, North Carolina, and Norfolk. They lay in ambush off Diamond Shoals buoy; they patrolled the entrance waters of Chesapeake Bay.

Tankers were their favorite targets, but they beat their death-march drumroll for any likely victim. For example, the collier DAVID H. ATWATER, ambushed between Cape Charles and Cape Henlopen around 2100 in the evening of April 2. The collier was unarmed. So the U-boat closed in on the surface to a range of 600 yards. Then, giving the ATWATER crew no chance to abandon, the Nazi submariners opened fire. The collier was blown to pieces. Swimming seamen were riddled by the U-boat machine-gunners. At 2400 two American destroyers arrived on the scene. Three survivors were fished from the sea—all that remained of a crew of 27.

The destroyers which visited the scene of the ATWATER massacre were on roving A/S patrol—an operation established at the request of Vice Admiral Adolphus Andrews. As Commander of the Eastern Sea Frontier, Admiral Andrews was in charge of forces responsible for the defense of coastal shipping. In the first quarter of 1942 those forces were pathetically meager. By the end of that period some 23 large and 42 small Coast Guard cutters, three PC's, 12 old-time wooden-hulled Eagle boats and converted yachts, and an odd assortment of armed trawlers—these comprised the naval vessels available for regular duty on the Eastern Sea Frontier. Some 170 planes, Army and Navy, and several blimps were flying offshore A/S patrols. Not much for the picketing of a coastal front that extended all the way from the Canadian border to Florida.

To stiffen these defenses, Admiral Andrews asked for 15 destroyers to undertake roving anti-submarine patrols, and in February 1942 he was allocated seven destroyers on temporary detail.

Among the destroyers which engaged in these A/S patrols were JACOB JONES, ROPER, HAMBLETON, and EMMONS. A good example of a roving patrol may be found in the reports of the HAMBLETON-EMMONS team.

Shortly after the attack on Pearl Harbor, the forenamed sister ships (HAMBLETON just commissioned) conducted a combination shakedown cruise and good-will tour of South America's Pacific ports. While en route from South America to New York in March, the HAMBLETON (Lieutenant Commander Forrest Close) and EMMONS (Lieutenant Commander T. C. Ragan) were diverted to assist in a U-boat hunt in Windward Passage. Wreckage and several life rafts were sighted, but the DD's were unable to flush a submarine.

The following day they put in at Guantanamo, Cuba, to refuel. The pumping was hardly begun before a submarine report sent both destroyers racing seaward on another fruitless hunt. That night a distress call from the S.S. TEXAN sent HAMBLETON racing at high speed around to the north coast of Cuba. No TEXAN survivors or wreckage were found. But search planes directed the DD to a point about 15 miles west of the TEXAN's reported position, and there HAMBLETON came upon the sinking collier S.S. OLGA. Torpedoed at 0300 that morning, OLGA had been unable to call for assistance; the explosion had destroyed her radio. HAMBLETON picked up the survivors of this chance-found vessel, continued a search for the missing TEXAN (which remained missing), then dashed back to Guantanamo at 35 knots. Operation *Paukenschlag* could keep a destroyer busy.

On March 13 HAMBLETON made rendezvous with the U.S.S. AUGUSTA to escort her to New York. Dusk, evening of the 15th, a lookout sighted a weak red light abeam to starboard. Investigating, HAMBLETON discovered six men huddled on a life raft—survivors of the S.S. CEIBRA, another U-boat casualty. "There is another raft," the survivors declared. "On it are ten persons, including a woman and a child. But we lost sight of it." HAMBLETON searched the vicinity. Like the S.S. TEXAN, this raft was nowhere to be found.

So *Paukenschlag* was going full blast when HAMBLETON and EMMONS (after a run to Casco Bay, Maine) were ordered to report to Commander Eastern Sea Frontier for an anti-submarine patrol between Wimble Shoals and Cape Lookout, N.C.

No sooner did HAMBLETON and EMMONS reach the Wimble Shoals vicinity than they were fired upon by the American freighter DELSUD. About 12,000 yards south of the DD's, the merchantman uncorked a shot (which fell wide of the mark), and began to broadcast frantic submarine warnings. By advancing at high speed and signalling friendly intentions, HAMBLETON finally convinced the nervous freighter that all was well; that the destroyers were not U-boats.

The U-boats were not far distant, however. At 0208 in the morning of April 6 the destroyers sighted the flare of an explosion. A 12-mile, 40-minute sprint brought EMMONS and HAMBLETON to a familiar scene. In the foreground the Sun Oil tanker S.S. BIDWELL lay dead in the water with a torpedo hole in her side. Somewhere in the background, invisible, was a retiring U-boat.

BIDWELL was seaworthy despite her raw wound, and the crew, which had abandoned, were boarding the vessel to take her into port. The two DD's started an immediate search for the submarine. Pinging and probing with detection gear, they hunted until well after sunrise. About 0920 HAMBLETON's sonar crew reported a deep-sea contact. The target was stationary. After a depth-charge salvo, the destroyermen realized they were attacking a sunken wreck.

The following day the patrolling destroyers sighted a capsized merchant vessel off Cape Hatteras. A Coast Guard craft stood by, lending assistance. HAMBLETON and EMMONS soon concluded their patrol and steamed into Norfolk to engage in escort duty.

The BIDWELL torpedoing, the capsized vessel, glimpses of derelict life rafts and wreckage: these were typical incidents indicating the futility of roving A/S patrols by an individual destroyer or a pair of DD's.

Protection was the need, rather than detective work after the horse was stolen. And escortage was the best protective measure. Roving destroyer patrols along the eastern seaboard were merely a measure of desperation—one that cost the DesLant Force its first destroyer loss through enemy action after America's all-out entry into World War II.

The torpedoing occurred late in February, antedating the HAMBLETON-EMMONS patrol. Ironic coincidence that the destroyer which went down commemoratively bore the name of the only American DD downed by a U-boat in World War I—the JACOB JONES.

Loss of U.S.S. Jacob Jones

The disaster which befell the second JACOB JONES clearly pointed to the fatal futility of employing lone destroyers on roving anti-submarine patrols.

JACOB JONES had been with Squadron 40-T in the Mediterranean on the day the Nazis invaded Poland. The following year, a member of Destroyer Division 54, she had participated in the opening of the Key West Sound School. But, like the majority of her companion American destroyers, she had not yet graduated from that hardest of all schools, the school of showdown performance wherein techniques are fully tested and practice proves theory. And into the hottest of American coastal waters steamed the JACOB JONES.

The Delaware Capes. U-boats had become so bold in this area that ships had been torpedoed within sight of watchers on the beach. A sludge of oily flotsam scummed the Jersey shore. At Cape May the bodies of drowned merchant seamen came in with the dark tide. In those waters, patrolling alone, JACOB JONES was in dire peril. Her captain, Lieutenant Commander H. D. Black, Jr., had been instructed to hunt Nazi submarines.

It was a case of the hunter becoming the hunted. The U-boats were there. They saw her first.

Early in the morning of February 28, 1942, JACOB JONES was steaming on a southerly course, speed 15 knots, her wake a broad, bright avenue trailing astern on the calm, moonlit sea. Scanning the seascape with binoculars, the lookouts saw no ominous sign.

At some moment between 0400 and the ensuing hour, a U-boat began its stealthy approach. Perhaps it had been stalking for some time. Perhaps luck had placed it directly in the destroyer's track. Whatever the circumstance, the enemy readied the torpedoes and crouched in ambush. Then, at 0500—

Two (perhaps three) shattering explosions sent the destroyer reeling. The blasts hurled sleeping men from their bunks, and others, not asleep, were killed instantly.

General Alarm! Bluejackets racing topside to man battle stations. Flame leaping through passageways and water plunging into compartments. Surging smoke; spurting steam; a smell of scorched metal, burning oil, and fuming chemicals.

The men in JACOB JONES fought a losing fight to save their ship.

Mortally stricken, the torpedoed destroyer listed over on her side. She remained afloat for about an hour while the flood poured in and fire ravaged her internally. Some 35 men got clear of the sinking vessel. She went down at 0600.

As she sank, her depth charges exploded, hurling debris high in the air. All except 11 men were killed by this final blasting. Few destroyers suffered heavier casualties in the war. Not a single officer survived the JACOB JONES disaster.

Rescue ships were rushed from near-by shore stations, and the 11 survivors were recovered the following day. The sinking constituted an almost singular triumph for the undersea enemy.

Singular in the literal sense of the word. For, excluding the REUBEN JAMES (lost on "short-of-war" duty), only one other United States destroyer would go down to U-boat torpedo fire in the Battle of the Atlantic. And but two destroyer escorts (DE's) were torpedoed and sunk. In turn, by way of reprisal, American destroyers in the Atlantic accounted for at least a dozen U-boats, and American DE's sank 36 more!

Loss of JACOB JONES pointed to the danger as well as the futility of A/S patrols conducted by lone DD's.

Roper Kills U-85 (First Blood)

Companion of JACOB JONES in Destroyer Division 54 was the destroyer ROPER, flagship of Division Commander S. C. Norton, and captained by Lieutenant Commander H. W. Howe. Like JACOB JONES, she was an old four-stacker with the salt of years of sea duty on her record. In company with JACOB JONES she had served at the Key West Sound School as a schoolship to provide novice Sound crews with sea-going sonar training. She was among the first American destroyers to carry radar.

The sinking of JACOB JONES had come as a shock to the other DD's of DesDiv 54, and the destroyermen in ROPER had hungered for a crack at the undersea enemy. Their chance came sooner than expected.

On the night of April 13-14, ROPER was steaming south from Norfolk. She was moving at 18 knots, and she had just put Wimble Shoal Light astern when (time: 0006) a "pip" flickered across her radar screen. With the range at 2,700 yards, ROPER's skipper stepped up speed to 20 knots to close in.

The target vessel appeared to be zigzagging. ROPER's Sound operator heard rapidly turning propellers, and obtained range and bearings which coincided with those obtained by radar. At 2,100 yards the wake of a small vessel was discerned. ROPER's skipper was cautious; in coastal waters there was always a chance of contacting a friendly vessel, perhaps a convoy "stray." Then, with the range closed to 700 yards, the wake of a torpedo was sighted. The lethal ribbon streaked through the water, and passed close aboard the destroyer's port side.

Lieutenant Commander Howe seemed determined not to fire until he saw the whites of this enemy's eyes. At 300 yards he shot the ray of a 24-inch searchlight pointblank at the stranger—a German submarine.

With the gray silhouette positively identified, Howe ordered ROPER's gunners to open fire. A 3-incher blazed. Machine-guns lashed at the target. A shell smote the U-boat at the waterline under the conning tower. Smoke and debris spurted skyward. A whip of bullets cut down the Germans huddled at a gun mount. The sea surged over the submarine's settling stern.

Evidently smashed, the U-boat went soddenly under as though sinking in quicksand. Attacking on sonar contact, ROPER hammered down the submarine with a barrage of 11 depth charges.

Twenty-nine bodies were recovered the following morning. They were identified as crewmen of the U-85. A 500-tonner launched the previous June, this U-boat had stabbed two ships with her torpedoes before U.S.S. ROPER stepped in as executioner.

ROPER's kill won for her a singular distinction. Awarded the Navy Cross, Commander S. C. Norton, ComDesDiv 54, was cited for *"SUCCESSFUL ATTACK UPON THE SUBMARINE . . . CAUSING COMPLETE DESTRUCTION OF THAT ENEMY VESSEL WITHOUT INJURY TO HIS FLAGSHIP OR ITS PERSONNEL."*

The Navy Cross was also awarded to the destroyer's captain, Lieutenant Commander Howe, who *"WITH AN OFFENSIVE SINGLENESS OF PURPOSE TRACKED, ATTACKED, AND DESTROYED THE U-85."*

The U-85 was the first German submarine sunk in World War II by a United States man-of-war.

Icarus Kills U-352

This is Coast Guard history.

The story is included in the present text (as are some others featuring the U.S.C.G.) because the Coast Guardsmen were a bulwark of the American home-sea defense, and their A/S operations were geared to those of the DesLant Force. Early in the war they were frequently called upon to pinch-hit for the destroyermen. They were stalwart pinch-hitters. Case in point, the U-boat killing by the cutter ICARUS.

Subject for execution was the new 500-ton U-352 on a maiden cruise that sent her trespassing in the shallow waters off Cape Lookout. The submarine commander was another Doenitz-picked expert, Herr Kapitan Leutnant Hellmut Rathke. Lieutenant Commander Maurice Jester, U.S.C.G., was the Coast Guard skipper who trumped this Nazi ace.

Patrolling off Cape Lookout, ICARUS picked up the submarine contact on her sonar gear at 1625 in the afternoon of May 9, 1942. When the cutter maneuvered for an attack position, brash Kapitan Rathke fired a torpedo. The torpedo missed, and the U-boat found itself with too few fathoms for deep evasion.

Down came the Coast Guard's depth charges—explosions hammering the U-boat's pressure hull like pile drivers pounding on a boiler. After a number of close blasts the U-boat was in trouble. When the blasts came even closer, the submarine captain's nerves frazzled out, and he decided to abandon. The U-boat broached on the rise; the crew fought its way out of the conning tower; the submarine, scuttled, went down for the last time.

Running in to capture survivors, ICARUS fished 33 submariners from the water, among them Kapitan Leutnant Rathke. The cutter took this haul to Charleston, S.C., where the Navy was able to report the destruction of the fourth U-boat downed on the Eastern Sea Frontier since the war's outbreak. (The score: U-656 and U-503 sunk by Navy aircraft in March; U-85 by destroyer ROPER in April; U-352 by ICARUS).

Four U-boats. Slim recompense for the 87 merchant ships already torpedoed and sunk off America's Atlantic Coast by the undersea raiders. But the U-boats downed by destroyer ROPER and Coast Guard cutter ICARUS were merely the leaders of a long hit parade.

CHAPTER 7

DESLANT INTO BATTLE (Part 2)

DD'S Escort Relief To Malta (Mediterranean Sideline)

In the spring of 1942 American destroyers participated in two missions which meant much to British forces defending the Mediterranean. The missions—"Operation Calendar" and "Operation Bowery"—sent the United States aircraft carrier *Wasp* through the Straits of Gibraltar with reinforcements for the hard-pressed island of Malta.

Situated directly south of Sicily, Malta guards the British Gibraltar-to-Suez lifeline. Since the outbreak of the war the island had served as a titanic aircraft carrier anchored in the path of Axis communication lines to North Africa. But if Malta was a figurative "carrier," it also had the fixed position of a "sitting duck." No sooner did Mussolini enter the conflict than Italian planes began to bomb the island. German aircraft swept over from Greece, and came storming up from Tripoli. Malta's air defenses melted under the blasting. Axis submarines applied an undersea tourniquet to tighten a blockade and cut off supplies by sea. As of April 1942 the besieged Maltese were facing starvation, and only a handful of pilots and planes remained to fend off the blitz.

Hence "Operation Calendar," a move to rush British fighter planes to Malta, with U.S.S. WASP (Captain J. W. Reeves, Jr.), doing the rushing. The race began at Glasgow, Scotland, where WASP picked up 47 Spitfires with pilots and crews, and sailed out of the Clyde escorted by "Force W."

A unit of the British Home Fleet, "Force W" was commanded by Commodore C. S. Daniel, R.N., in H.M. battle cruiser RENOWN. The screen included four British destroyers and the American destroyers LANG (Lieutenant Commander E. A. Seay) and MADISON (Commander W. B. Ammon). Captain W. W. Warlick, ComDesDiv 15, was screen commander with his pennant in LANG.

Departure date was April 14. On the 19th the WASP group was through the Straits, steaming in waters described by Mussolini as a Fascist lake. The description was apt enough with Rommel's Army dominating North Africa, Italian naval forces roaming the seascape, the dubious Vichy French in neutralized Morocco and Algeria, and enemy eyes watching near the Pillars of Hercules. The WASP group was entering enemy territory, and the van destroyers probed ahead like tight-nerved advance guards prodding for Teller mines.

They reached water some 50 miles off Algiers—a point within flying range of Malta. Moving at high speed, WASP launched the British planes at daybreak, April 20. All 47 Spitfires took off without mishap. All landed safely at Malta.

The WASP group headed westward for the home run to England, and made it safely on the 26th. Mission accomplished. This in flat contradiction to a broadcast by "Axis Sally" announcing that WASP's presence in the Mediterranean was known, and that the carrier would be on the bottom of that sea directly.

Instead, the WASP was on the surface of the Mediterranean just three weeks later. "Operation Bowery," another run with 47 Spitfires to reinforce Malta.

Undertaking this mission, the WASP group left the United Kingdom on May 3. WASP was accompanied by H.M.S. ECHO and INTREPID, and subsequently joined by British carrier EAGLE from Gibraltar. In the "Force W" escort screen were American destroyers LANG (making her second run) and STERETT (Commander J. G. Coward). Screen Commander Warlick rode in STERETT.

Again the ships ran the Gibraltar bottle-neck safely. And again flat-top WASP successfully launched the British planes, sending them off in the early morning of May 9.

On May 11 WASP received a message from Winston Churchill. *"Many thanks to you all for the timely help. Who said a wasp couldn't sting twice?"*

The destroyermen had done more than a little to bolster the island's defense. The planes ferried on the WASP enabled the Maltese to hold out that critical summer against the Luftwaffe.

American destroyers, then, were in part responsible for the warning often heard by Nazi bombers over Malta that summer—*"Achtung! Spitfeuer!"*

Loss of U.S.S. Sturtevant

About one o'clock in the afternoon of April 26, 1942, the destroyer STURTEVANT (Lieutenant Commander C. L. Weigle) stood out of Key West. Her orders: to rendezvous with a convoy off Southwest Pass in the Gulf waters at the mouth of the Mississippi River.

At 1515, STURTEVANT was about eight miles north of the Marquesas Keys. She was drumming along at good speed, her bow knifing through warm seas, when a sudden, shattering explosion heaved her up by the stern. The ship shuddered, wallowed in a billow of smoke, and was rocked by a second shattering blast.

Stunned officers and men thought the destroyer had been torpedoed. Below decks they fought flood and flame while lookouts and gun crews topside strained their eyes for a glimpse of periscopes or torpedo wakes.

The damage was not to be controlled, for ruptured plates buckled, the sea rushed in, and vital machinery was deluged. Nor were the gun crews given a shot at a stalking U-boat. STURTEVANT had not been torpedoed. She had run headlong into a newly planted minefield—American mines!

Mortally stricken, the destroyer went down—the third destroyer of Captain W. D. Baker's original Squadron 31 to be lost through unexpected disaster, the first two being REUBEN JAMES and TRUXTUN. One hundred and thirty-seven STURTEVANT survivors were taken to Key West by small craft. Casualty list: *"Three dead, 12 missing."*

Always in mined water there was this risk. For the mine, an impartial weapon, may strike friend or foe, alike. The field in question had been planted only the day before STURTEVANT sailed. It was part of an extensive barrier of 3,460 mines which guarded the anchorage on the Gulf side of Key West. Within a nine-week period following the STURTEVANT catastrophe, three merchantmen fouled friendly mines in this field, and were sunk in consequence.

STURTEVANT'S Commanding Officer said he had not been given advance information about this new minefield. Someone had blundered. Somewhere there was negligence—on the part of either the responsible informant, or the bridge which should have taken steps to become informed.

Navy men had a maxim for such cases. "Somebody always fails to get the word."

Blitz Below New Orleans (DD's versus U-boats in the Gulf)

In May, June, and July 1942 the U-boats rampaged in the Gulf of Mexico. Forty-one ships went down to their torpedoes in the opening month of this blitzkrieg, the biggest harvest reaped by the enemy in any American coastal area during any one month of the war.

Probably no more than six U-boats were simultaneously operating in the Gulf during this period. And most of the time the number was two. But they caught the American defenders by surprise.

The majority of the victims of this ship-massacre had been steaming without escort, for the Navy's warships and planes could not be everywhere. The Gulf Sea Frontier, established the first week in February 1942, extended from Jacksonville, Florida, to the southeast coast of Yucatan. Its seaward boundaries embraced most of the Bahama Group, the north- and south-western coasts of Cuba, the waters off the Yucatan Peninsula, and the enclosed reaches of the Gulf. Jacksonville, Miami, Key West, Havana, Mobile, New Orleans, the Texas oil ports, Tampico, and Vera Cruz—these were possible focal points for torpedoes thirsting for American oil shipping. And for defense of this extensive area, Captain R. S. Crenshaw, Commander Gulf Sea Frontier and Commandant Seventh Naval District, with headquarters in Key West, had less than little to go on.

Available at the beginning were two medium-sized Coast Guard cutters, one small Coast Guard cutter, a converted yacht, and whatever naval vessels might be borrowed from the Key West Sound School for emergency use. Nineteen Coast Guard planes stationed here and there, plus a squadron of Army observation planes and two medium bombers based at Miami, were on hand for air operations. A Fleet Air Detachment based at Miami and a few more

Army aircraft (West Palm Beach) were presently inserted into the Florida coastal defense. By April six small cutters, two more armed yachts, and the venerable destroyers SEMMES and DAHLGREN had been added to the surface force. But there still remained an impossible surface to cover.

In the latter part of February the U-boats got in, downing the tanker PAN MASSACHUSETTS and two merchantmen. March and April were relatively quiet. Then, on May 6, the freighter ALCOA PURITAN went down 100 miles from Mobile. On the 13th the tankers GULF PENN and DAVID MCKELVEY were sunk off the Mississippi Passes, while a Mexican oiler went down a few miles from Miami. On the 19th another American tanker was sunk near Cuba. Then tanker after tanker and freighter after freighter played target for Nazi torpedoes. Especially vulnerable (and valuable) were the highly volatile tankers with their priority cargoes of oil and high octane gas.

Raced into action were the American destroyers NOA (replacement for SEMMES) and DAHLGREN. The Sound School also contributed DALLAS to the defense effort, and the seasoned veteran GREER. Only four destroyers to patrol a whole wilderness of water. Often they arrived at the scene of a torpedoing long after the *fait accompli,* to find a burning ship and a cold trail. Again, they might be diverted from a hot one before they had a chance to score.

DALLAS had this experience. On May 7 the destroyer, captained by Lieutenant Commander B. Katz, spotted a U-boat in the approaches to Miami. The sub went under as the DD steamed into gun range. DALLAS obtained sound contact, and delivered a depth-charge salvo. Then, while trying to regain contact, she was summoned to a nearby area by a plane engaged in holding down a U-boat presumably damaged and bottomed the previous day. After making a fast run to this spot, the destroyermen discovered the target was a sunken wreck. (A common sonar-deceiver early in the war, wrecks were eventually charted for the benefit of submarine hunters.)

But in June NOA, DAHLGREN, and GREER participated in a cooperative search that resulted in the bagging of big game.

On June 3, 1942, Rear Admiral J. L. ("Reggie") Kauffman, veteran from the Iceland front, was appointed Commander Gulf Sea Frontier. About the same time the defense forces were strengthened by the addition of 16 small Coast Guard cutters, five PC's (Patrol Craft) and SC's (Subchasers) and miscellaneous small craft. The surface reinforcements might have gone for little had not Admiral Kauffman, abandoning the futile system of roving patrols, sponsored "killer groups" of aircraft and naval vessels to team up on a detected U-boat and stay on the hunt until the foe was finished.

Thetis Kills U-157

On June 10 the U-157 attacked a merchantman in the Old Bahama Channel off the north coast of Cuba. The following morning the submarine was detected and bombed by an Army observation plane, and sighted by a Pan-American plane. Meanwhile Admiral Kauffman had rushed his killer groups into action. From Key West a group of PC's raced to patrol Nicholas Channel. From Miami another PC group sped to Santarem Channel. The NOA (Lieutenant Commander B. N. Wev) was sent to Old Bahama Channel; GREER (Lieutenant Commander L. H. Frost) to that channel's eastern entrance; DAHLGREN (Lieutenant Commander R. W. Cavenagh) to a point about midway between Matanzas, Cuba, and Andros Island.

On June 12 the U-boat was radar-detected by an Army observation plane off the Florida Keys. The plane missed with an attack, and a defective radio prevented prompt report of the contact. However, early in the morning of the 13th an observation plane was dispatched to the submarine's predicted position. So were DAHLGREN, NOA, and a bevy of PC's. The plane sighted the U-boat, which immediately submerged. Ensued a game of hide-and-seek, with four more Army planes and the Coast Guard cutter THETIS (Lieutenant [jg] N. C. McCormick, U.S.C.G.) arriving to participate.

THETIS and her Coast Guardsmen led the attack. At 1550 of that afternoon they obtained sound contact on the submarine, and dropped seven depth charges on the target. A spew of oil rose to the surface. The five PC's in the vicinity followed through with depth-charge salvos. There was thunder down under, and within the next twelve hours the depths gave up a mass of splintered deck gratings and two pair of trousers labeled *"Fabrikken am Deutsch."* U-157 had gone beyond the reach of mortal contacting.

The sinking of U-157 was not without significance. A demonstration of coordinated A/S effort by air and surface craft, it certified the value of such teamwork, and emphasized the urgent need. It showed the shape of things to come—the "hunter-killer" groups of the future.

DD's in the Caribbean

Extending from the Gulf Sea Frontier to the waters off the Guianas and westward to the eastern boundaries of the Panama Sea Frontier, the Caribbean Sea Frontier embraced most of the islands of the

Navy Yard Wedding. This method of repair, using part of one ship to repair another, thus speeding one ship back to battle, was a common practice during World War II. This picture of the torpedoed destroyer Blakeley acquiring a new bow from the Taylor, shows the complicated melding of plates and beams necessary to fit the parts together. Note the halved port hole.

Spring of 1942 saw the whole Caribbean flaming with torpedo explosions and burning ships. Patrolling destroyers fell victim, too—like the U.S.S. Blakeley, shown here with her bow blown off.

But her damage control men plugged up holes, shored up bulkheads, and built some sort of temporary bow across. Then she steamed 1,000 miles to the States for her new permanent bow.

Something out of nothing! The Blakeley lost anchors as well as bow. So her crew made a new anchor out of an old truck axle, with two leaf springs welded on.

The Coast Guard in action. The U.S. Coast Guard cutter Northland, above, captured the German armed trawler, Exsterstiene, below, which had established weather stations in Greenland, and forced abandonment of another.

Dressed for heavy weather. Watch standers on a destroyer on convoy escort on the North Atlantic run found submarines hard to detect in cresting seas.

Part of the catch. With hands in air, German prisoners cornered by the Northland surrender to Coast Guard guns. In addition to the trawlers and prisoners, the Northland captured two well equipped weather stations.

Spanish Main—Haiti and Santo Domingo, Puerto Rico, eastern Cuba, Jamaica, the Leewards and Windwards (including Trinidad), and the Curaçao Group—these and that intricate web of ship lanes linking the Atlantic to the Panama Canal.

Thirty-one ships went down to Nazi torpedoes in the Caribbean area in February 1942; 19 were torpedo-sunk in March; in May, 38; in June, 35—random scores indicative of crimson havoc. In the waters off Trinidad (bauxite shipping) and Curaçao (oil) the U-boats had a high old time. On February 16, for example, a surfaced U-boat bombarded an oil refinery at Aruba. Two nights later, a U-boat punched torpedoes into two American steamships at anchor off Port of Spain. On March 15 the Coast Guard cutter ACACIA (tender class) was shelled and sunk by a U-boat. That set the pace for another *Paukenschlag* festival.

With headquarters at San Juan, Puerto Rico, Rear Admiral J. H. Hoover, Commander Caribbean Sea Frontier, had a tremendous job guarding against U-boats and at the same time keeping a watchful eye on Vichy Admiral Robert and the French forces at Martinique. For this Herculean duty (A/S warfare and watch on the French) Admiral Hoover had available the destroyers BLAKELEY and BARNEY, two wooden-hulled Eagle boats, three elderly S-boats, 12 PBY's (flying boats) and the tender LAPWING.

Small patrol craft, Catalinas, and land-based Army planes eventually augmented the Caribbean defense forces. But it was still the story of a big job and a little shovel.

Destroyers BARNEY and BLAKELEY ran the usual footless races in answer to submarine alarms and distress calls. U-boats were sighted, but the destroyermen were unable to score.

In the Caribbean that July, the destroyer CORRY (Lieutenant Commander E. C. Burchett) staged an interesting rescue. She was not operating under Commander Caribbean Sea Frontier, and the rescue was by happenstance rather than mission.

A member of Task Force 22, CORRY was steaming with her group en route from Newport, Rhode Island, to Trinidad, B.W.I. On July 4 the destroyer's lookouts sighted four men on a life raft, and she immediately stood by to pick up these derelicts. They were found to be American citizens, sole survivors of the S.S. RUTY, a freighter which had been hauling magnesium ore from Rio de Janeiro to Baltimore.

CORRY's ship-history recounts the incident as follows:

> The survivors said that immediately after sinking the ship the enemy submarine surfaced nearby. The submarine Captain hailed the raft upon which three of the survivors had climbed and told them that another survivor was nearby in the water. When the raft could make no headway due to the wind and sea, the submarine made a lee for them and held the man up by a boat hook until the raft could come alongside. The personnel of the U-boat then questioned the survivors regarding the tonnage of the sunken ship, nature of the cargo, whether any of the survivors were officers, etc. After about 15 minutes alongside, the submarine submerged, leaving word with the raft's crew that nearest land was 270 miles away and that they should keep calm as they were in a frequented steamer lane and would be picked up. The survivors said the submarine was definitely German, of a large type, and the crew spoke good English, though with an accent. The officers and crew all appeared to be extremely young, no small arms were in evidence, and the survivors were treated kindly and courteously. The four rescued men were in good physical condition despite having been afloat for six days, as the raft was large and seaworthy, and had been well stocked with water, chocolate, and hardtack.

The U-boaters in the foregoing episode displayed a humane, if not fraternal, attitude. "Attitude" is probably the term for it, although the solicitude of the young submariners may have been sincere. The *Herrenvolk* character (as would perhaps that of any people) reflected a schizoid personality. There was the U-boat captain who gunned down the swimming survivors of the ATWATER. Then there was the undersea skipper who called, "Sorry I had to do it! Hope you make it in!" to the survivors of the ALCOA PURITAN. And the RUTY incident, just related. But perhaps this was all a part of German military *schrechlikeit*—good "strategy of terror"—the benign smile followed by the murderous slap.

That the Nazi enemy could be a peculiarly vicious foe was a fact evidenced by a ship-shooting which occurred in the waters off Panama.

Destroyer Patrols Off Panama

The Panama Sea Frontier was a two-ocean front defended jointly by Army forces under Lieutenant General Frank Andrews and naval forces commanded by Rear Admiral C. E. Van Hook. The Pacific side was menaced by Japanese I-boats. The Caribbean approaches were threatened by German submarines which came prowling down the Mosquito Coast and presumably received stores and information from Nazi agents and other undercover men secreted in isolated Central American ports.

It was reasonable to assume that German periscopes would be eyeing the approaches to the Canal. A parade of United States warships was scheduled to pass through to the Pacific. Already this naval traffic was heavy, and Cristobal was the focal point for a vast tonnage of military shipping. To protect this focal point Admiral Van Hook had available one division of venerable destroyers—BORIE, BARRY, TATTNALL, and GOFF. Another four-piper, the J. FRED TALBOTT, was being overhauled.

Supporting these elderly DD's were the gunboats NIAGARA and ERIE, a pair of PC's, a tugboat, and a couple of armed yachts. Air support was provided by the 24 Catalinas of Patrol Wing Three (PatWing 3), but the planes did double duty on both sides of the Isthmus. The four old destroyers patrolled without benefit of radar. The gunboats lacked modern detection gear. And on June 5, gunboat NIAGARA was detached. Admiral Van Hook's command was not burdened with an embarrassment of riches.

On June 9 the Nazi invader struck. Laden with Army stores for the Canal Zone, the cargo vessel MERRIMACK was ambushed and torpedoed near Cozumel Island off Yucatan. BORIE (Lieutenant Commander P. R. Osborn) was not far from the area. She had been escorting two British ships to Key West, and now she was ordered to hunt for the sub and the MERRIMACK's survivors. A week later she found the survivors—eight emaciated figures on a raft—but the sub got away.

Meantime, two cargo ships were torpedo-sunk off Swan Island; three vessels were downed in the waters off Old Providence and St. Andrews; and a merchantman under escort of gunboat ERIE was torpedoed within 85 miles of the Canal entrance. All this in two days' time (June 9-10) while BORIE was busy in the Yucatan area, and BARRY, GOFF, and TATTNALL were on off-shore patrol. Then on the 13th two cargo ships were torpedoed and sunk at the very entrance of the Canal.

The raid put the Canal Zone in an uproar. Cristobal was closed to Caribbean-bound traffic while Admiral Van Hook assembled a task group to hunt down the invader.

The submarine responsible for this five-day blitz was the U-159. An Army plane spotted her in the sea 80 miles north of Colon, and the hunters were rushed to that vicinity. The Task Group included the destroyers EDISON (Lieutenant Commander W. R. Headden) and BARRY (Lieutenant Commander L. K. Reynolds), the former having just arrived at Cristobal with a Navy tanker. Several Navy aircraft and an Army plane joined the hunt.

EDISON and BARRY made a coordinated search for the U-boat, but except for bringing in survivors the search was without success. The U-159 went on her merry way.

Then on June 17 a British tanker was sunk by the shellfire of two U-boats that ambushed her within 75 miles of Cristobal. Not long after that two merchantmen were downed off Santa Marta, Venezuela. And on June 24 a surfaced U-boat waylaid the schooner RESOLUTE between St. Andrews and Old Providence.

The RESOLUTE was crowded with island passengers. Without ado the U-boat closed to machine-gun range and opened fire, slaughtering the women and children who stood screaming on the schooner's deck.

By any definition, this was murder. Only the appearance of a patrol plane interrupted the massacre, but the submerging U-boat left in her wake a sufficient flotsam of bloody work. The Caribbean had not seen anything like this since the days of Blackbeard and his bloodthirsty pirates.

The U.S. Navy was determined to end this murderous onslaught. It mustered at Cristobal every A/S vessel available. Canal Zone convoys were strengthened. PatWing 3 was reinforced by radar-carrying planes. Army Air contributed patrols to cover the waters of the South American coast. Central American coast patrols were tightened, and a seaplane base was established at Puerto Castilla, Honduras.

Before these A/S forces could be organized, a U-boat glided into the Costa Rican harbor of Puerto Limon, and fired a deadly spread of torpedoes at a freighter alongside the wharf. Something had to be done quickly. And it was. By Army and Navy aircraft, and the destroyer LANSDOWNE.

Lansdowne and Aircraft Kill U-153

The submarine raider at Puerto Limon was the U-153. Not as smart as the skipper of U-159, her captain allowed her to suffer a bombing by Army patrol planes which sighted her on June 6. Apparently the damage was not extensive, but it must have been hampering. On July 11 the U-153 attacked the net-tender MIMOSA off Almirante. She missed with a spread of five torpedoes, three of which passed under the net-tender. Then she was slow on the getaway.

At 0355 in the following morning, a PBY picked up the sub by radar. The plane dropped flares and straddled the U-boat with four depth charges. Undoubtedly hurt, the submarine went deep.

PC-458 (the EVELYN R.) was ordered to the scene. So was another Navy plane. The patrol craft reached the spot in the morning of July 13, and sighted an oil slick. Assisted by the PBY, she dropped four depth charges just ahead of the oil bubbles. Making another careful run, she dropped two more charges.

With 1050 on the clock, the patrol craft stepped aside to let the PBY and several Army planes attack. During the ensuing 10 hours, the aircraft dropped 24 depth bombs and eight depth charges, while trailing the sub some 25 miles.

Enter the destroyer LANSDOWNE (Lieutenant Commander W. R. Smedberg III), dispatched from Cristobal, where she had arrived as a convoy escort. Ordered to join the sub-hunt at top speed, she reached the scene at 1830 in the evening of the 13th.

LANSDOWNE relieved little PC-458, and set to work to get a bead on the target. Within a quarter of an hour after taking over, the DD picked up a sharp sound contact. The destroyermen raced to battle stations. Smedberg maneuvered his ship into attack position. A brisk run. A pattern of 11 depth charges appropriately laid. Thunder under the sea. Then up came a great spreading swell of oil that carpeted the near-by seascape.

LANSDOWNE probed the area with detection gear. Sound instruments could obtain no answering echo from water 1500 fathoms deep. A night of radar searching found nothing on the surface. But next day oil was still rising from the depths.

U-153 was 1500 fathoms down. The Nazi blitz on Panama Canal traffic was over.

Murder On The Murmansk Run (DD's versus Luftwaffe)

This has been called the "grimmest convoy battle of the entire war." Certainly few convoys were given such punishment as was dealt Convoy PQ-17—Iceland-Archangel. None suffered a worse ordeal.

The men who manned this Iceland-to-Archangel convoy did not anticipate a delightful excursion. The Murmansk Run had already acquired an evil reputation for bad weather, angry seas, and angrier Nazi attacks. The flanking Norwegian coast was a littoral of U-boat lairs, and alive with Luftwaffe hives. And the run to Archangel was even more perilous, in that it extended the Murmansk journey by a long haul down the White Sea.

The men of Convoy PQ-17 were fully aware of the hazards. Confidence was encouraged, however, by the fact that the ships sailed from Iceland under guard of one of the largest escort forces yet assembled in those waters. And powerful support and covering forces supplemented the escort. Convoy PQ-17 was a big ship-train. It was carrying some seven hundred million dollars' worth of munitions for besieged Russia.

The convoy of 33 merchant vessels (22 of them American) sailed from Reykjavik on June 27, 1942. Responsible for the escortage, the Royal Navy provided six destroyers, two flak ships, two submarines, and eleven smaller craft.

The Allied Support Force under Rear Admiral L. H. K. Hamilton, R.N., sailed from Seidisfjord, Iceland, on July 1 to join the convoy in Denmark Strait. The Support Force consisted of British cruisers LONDON and NORFOLK, American cruisers WICHITA and TUSCALOOSA, and a screen which contained three destroyers. Two of the destroyers were American—the WAINWRIGHT (Lieutenant Commander R. H. Gibbs) and ROWAN (Lieutenant Commander B. R. Harrison). The former was flagship of Captain D. P. Moon, ComDesRon 8. The third destroyer was H.M.S. SOMALI.

The Allied Covering Force, under Admiral Sir John Tovey, had sailed from Scapa Flow the previous day. This task force was to operate in the waters between Iceland and Spitzbergen, where it would shield Convoy PQ-17 from a possible thrust by the German warships based at Alten Fjord. It was also responsible for the safe return of a westbound convoy. The force included a British battleship, an American battleship, a British aircraft carrier, three British cruisers, a squadron of British DD's and corvettes, and American destroyers MAYRANT (Commander E. A. Taylor), flagship of Commander C. C. Hartman, ComDesDiv 16, and RHIND (Lieutenant Commander H. T. Read). As it eventuated, this powerful task group was diverted to an area far distant from the convoy, hence was unable to lend PQ-17 any direct assistance.

The Nazis knew about the big munitions convoy, its make-up, even its sailing date. Thus informed, the German Admiralty set in motion an operation they called "Knight's Gambit." Plan was to send a battle force led by TIRPITZ out of Alten Fjord to menace the convoy as it simultaneously came under the fire of U-boats and land-based bombers. But as soon as German air scouts reported the presence of the Allied Covering Force off Spitzbergen, TIRPITZ was ordered back into her lair. To that extent Admiral Tovey's Covering Force aided the convoy.

The bulk of the convoy's surface defense was up to Admiral Hamilton's Support Force. Then there were the convoy's escort screen and the Naval Armed Guard. But, as will be seen, the escort screen dissolved. As for the Armed Guard, the gunners were stouter than their weapons. But one ship (Panama registry) carried a 4-inch 50-caliber gun. Only three of the American merchantmen were armed with 3-inch AA's. The rest carried .50-caliber and .30-caliber machine guns. Naturally these merchantmen depended on the accompanying warships for security.

The convoy's route skirted northern Iceland, took a north-by-east tack, went past Jan Mayen Island, continued northward toward Spitzbergen and Bear Island, then swung southeast through the Barents Sea to skirt the Kola Peninsula and enter the White Sea. On July 1 a Nazi reconnaissance plane approached the convoy and was shot down. The Germans made their first attack on July 2, U-boats and long-range torpedo-bombers striking at the convoy near Jan Mayen Island. Operating with Support Force, American destroyermen were promptly engaged in countering these opening moves of "Knight's Gambit."

The battle exploded just as the destroyer ROWAN, only recently dispatched to join the convoy for fueling, reached the area. The six attacking U-boats were driven off by the convoy's escorts. An umbrella of anti-aircraft fire frustrated the four attacking planes. Scorching the sky with their A/A batteries, ROWAN's destroyermen helped to raise the umbrella. Then one of her sharpshooting gun crews got a Swastika in the sights, and down came a Luftwaffe specimen. Score one for the U.S.S. ROWAN.

Later that day, ROWAN came under fire. Another quartet of German planes. Another torpedo attack. And one of the torpedo-planes struck at ROWAN. Sighting two oncoming wakes, the destroyer's lookouts cried the warning in time. Commander Harrison maneuvered to avoid, and the vengeful "fish" failed to find the mark.

So far so good—but for Convoy PQ-17 that was only a beginning. The following afternoon 26 German planes attacked the ship-train. Low clouds screened the convoy, and the bombing went amiss. But the next day, July 4, brought more fireworks.

It was a Fourth of July that American merchant seamen in the convoy would never forget. Neither would the Britishers who manned the six DD's in the convoy's escort—destroyers KEPPEL, OFFA, LEDBURY, WILTON, FURY, and LEAMINGTON (ex-U.S.S. EVANS).

It started early in the morning when a Heinkel roared out of a fog bank to stab a torpedo into a Liberty ship. Fatally hit, the S. S. CHRISTOPHER NEWPORT had to be abandoned and sunk.

Then came a group of attacking Heinkels. Bombs and torpedoes—zigzagging ships—three Heinkels shot down. Sweating destroyermen and Armed Guard gunners breathed a sigh of relief when that assault was broken up. But it was only the second round.

Round Three began about 1647—a slam-bang attack that knocked two merchantmen out of the convoy. In the vortex of this action was the American destroyer WAINWRIGHT, flagship of Captain Moon, the Support Force screen commander.

Earlier that afternoon the WAINWRIGHT had been directed to leave the Support Force formation and join the convoy train to take on fuel from the British tanker ALDERSDALE. The destroyer was approaching the convoy when six torpedo-planes raced in to strike at the merchantmen. WAINWRIGHT's anti-aircraft guns added weight to an aerial barrage that dispersed the enemy. At 1700, shooting at long range, her marksmen drove off still another torpedo-plane.

Determined to dig this thorn out of their side, the Germans now concentrated on the American DD. Down through the overcast roared a flock of dive-bombers. By ordering hard right rudder and top speed, the destroyer's skipper, Lieutenant Commander Gibbs, got her out from under the blasting.

At 1820 the Germans resumed the attack, some 25 Heinkels coming over the horizon. Sweeping in from the southward, the German planes formed two attack groups—one aimed to strike the convoy's starboard quarter, the other circling to strike the starboard bow. Captain Moon immediately sent WAINWRIGHT to an ahead position to meet the bow attack. Steaming out through the escort screen, the DD opened long-range fire on the planes closing the starboard quarter, then raked the Heinkels coming in on the convoy's bow. WAINWRIGHT's gunners put up a shield that compelled the bow attackers to let fly at long range. When the bombers dropped their torpedoes WAINWRIGHT went hard right to parallel and comb the tracks.

Thanks to WAINWRIGHT, then, the torpedoes dropped by the bow group missed the convoy. On the convoy's starboard quarter, where there was no destroyer defense, some of the Heinkels got in. Liberty ship WILLIAM HOOPER was torpedoed. The crew abandoned without orders, and the derelict, left to burn, had to be sunk by an escort. A torpedo struck the Russian tanker AZERBAIDJAN, but her damage-controlmen kept her going.

Not a devastating score for the Luftwaffe. Although destroyer WAINWRIGHT was severely strafed, the enemy's aim was poor. No man had been injured on the American DD, and she had damaged several Heinkels in return. So Convoy PQ-17 was holding her own on that Fourth of July.

However, at that stage of the run the convoy had reached that point on the route to Russia just south of Spitzbergen. There were many miles of the Murmansk highway remaining. And at that critical point the British Admiralty sent to the convoy Support Force a fatal dispatch ordering Admiral Hamilton's warships to quit the convoy area.

Hamilton transmitted the crucial message:

CRUISER FORCE WITHDRAW TO WESTWARD AT HIGH SPEED OWING TO THREAT FROM SURFACE SHIPS CONVOY IS TO DISPERSE AND PROCEED TO RUSSIAN PORTS X CONVOY IS TO SCATTER

American officers in the Support Force stared at the signals in unbelief. Their departure would leave the convoy defenseless. Left to fend for themselves, the merchantmen would be set-ups for air and submarine attack. "I know you will be as distressed as I am," Admiral Hamilton informed the American cruiser TUSCALOOSA, "at having to leave that fine collection of ships to find their own way to harbor."

The order was, in effect, a death warrant for Convoy PQ-17. Tragically enough, it was based on misinformation which led the British Admiralty to believe that the battleship TIRPITZ, the pocket battleship SCHEER, and eight German destroyers had sortied to intercept the convoy.

Actually on that evening of July 4 the German warships were in Alten Fjord. They did not move until July 5. Then, with TIRPITZ, SCHEER, the heavy cruiser HIPPER, and seven destroyers, German Admiral Carls made a brief run up the Norwegian coast, dodging back to base on the 6th.

A flounder by the German Admiral; a blunder by the British—two overly wary antagonists. It can be said for the latter that they hoped to lure the German warships westward, and thus decoy them away from Convoy PQ-17. However, the withdrawal of the Support Force left the Allied convoy hopelessly exposed. So urgent was the word from London that the convoy's screen commander, although not directed to do so, ordered the six British DD's of the screen to cover the Support Force as it headed westward. The deserted merchantmen were left to play a desperate game of run-sheep-run.

Because destroyers WAINWRIGHT and ROWAN, operating with the Support Force, were withdrawn from the area, the convoy's death-battle with German submarines and aircraft has no direct relation to destroyer history. Yet the battle merits a brief account in this text as an unforgettable illustration of what could happen to a convoy bereft of the DD's defensive arm.

In compliance with orders, the merchantmen scattered and set out singly and in little groups, heading in the general direction of North Russia. They ran into arctic snowstorms. They encountered ice floes. They lost their way in dense fog. And in this limbo they were caught by U-boats and Junker bombers.

On July 5 the tanker CARLTON, steaming independently, was torpedoed and sunk by a U-boat. That same afternoon a flight of Junkers bombed and sank the cargo ship WASHINGTON, two accompanying British freighters, and the Dutch freighter PAULUS POTTER.

On July 6 the S.S. OLOPANA, answering the WASHINGTON's S-O-S, was torpedoed and sunk. A few hours later three Junker dive-bombers found and downed the freighter FAIRFIELD CITY off Nova Zembla.

With FAIRFIELD CITY was the Liberty ship DANIEL MORGAN. The German bombers pounded the MORGAN from pillar to post. Late that night the mangled vessel was sunk by a U-boat. Morgan's valiant Navy gun crew was rescued by the Soviet tanker DONBASS. In turn they saved the tanker by manning her forward gun and fighting off another Junker attack.

On July 9 the Liberty ship SAMUEL CHASE was leading a remnant group of merchantmen along the coast of Nova Zembla. Junkers struck at the ships, and down went the S.S. HOOSIER and the S.S. EL CAPITAN. The SAMUEL CHASE received a savage flogging. Her courageous gun crew managed to shoot down two Junkers, but the ship was nearly wrecked.

The sea between Murmansk and Nova Zembla became an inferno. The ships ran this way and that, seeking cover in fog, haven in unknown coastal waters. Several of the merchantmen went aground. And fog offered little protection from stalking submarines.

The U-boats torpedoed and sank the ALCOA RANGER, the HONOMU, the JOHN WITHERSPOON. Merchantmen PAN ATLANTIC, PAN-KRAFT, and PETER KERR were sunk by dive-bombers. The British fleet oiler ALDERSDALE was bombed and sunk. So were British merchantmen EARLSTON, EMPIRE BYRON, BOLTON CASTLE, HARTLEBURY. Finally the rescue ship ZAAFARAN, severely damaged by dive-bombers, was scuttled by her crew.

The last battered remnants of the convoy staggered into Archangel on July 25. When the final count was in, 11 of the convoy's 33 ships were on hand. The other 22 had been sunk. Of the 22 American merchantmen that started with the convoy, only eight survived. The tonnage loss was stupendous—millions of dollars' worth of cargo. Loss of life was proportionately high—the icy waters and lonely reaches of the Barents Sea did not abet rescue. Not only did this massacre deprive the Russians of urgently needed war supplies, but it left a costly hole in Allied shipping and severely strained the morale of the merchant service.

Here, at the price of many ships and lives, was a costly example of the slow merchantman's abject vulnerability when it traveled independently without escort. Only convoys with sufficient escortage could "carry the goods" to Europe—sufficient escortage meaning a strong destroyer screen and adequate air cover to cope with enemy aircraft and submarine wolfpacks.

The U.S. Navy was already working on a program to meet these imperatives. Coming off the line were new escort vessels—destroyer-escorts and baby flat-tops readying to fight the Battle of the Atlantic. Never again would a group of American merchantmen be left on their own to run a gantlet through submarine-infested seas under skies controlled by dive-bombers.

The Germans were jubilant over the success of "Knight's Gambit." But they might have noted their win was by way of a fool's-mate—the result of blunders an opponent is unlikely to repeat.

Atlantic Summary, January-July '42

"It was rugged going," a destroyerman said. The official consensus, reduced to the vernacular.

All things considered, DesLant losses for the first six-and-a-half months of the Atlantic Battle had not been heavy. One destroyer sunk in U-boat combat. One lost through storm. One sunk by a "friendly" mine.

On the other hand few U-boats had been downed by American A/S forces. Eight kills between January 1 and July 14—only four of these by surface vessels.

And in this period some 350 merchantmen had been torpedoed and sunk by Nazi submarines for a total loss to the Allies of close to 2¼ million tons.

General Marshall to Admiral King (June 19, 1942):

The losses by submarines off our Atlantic seaboard and in the Caribbean now threaten our entire war effort. The following statistics bearing on the subject have been brought to my attention.

Of the 74 ships allocated to the Army for July by the War Shipping Administration, 17 have already been sunk. Twenty-two per cent of the Bauxite fleet has already been destroyed. Twenty per cent of the Puerto Rican fleet has been lost. Tanker sinkings have been 3.5 per cent per month of tonnage in use.

We are all aware of the limited number of escort craft available, but has every conceivable improvised means been brought to bear on this situation? I am fearful that another month or two of this will so cripple our means of transport that we will be unable to bring sufficient men and planes to bear against the enemy in critical theatres to exercise a determining influence on the war.

Admiral King to General Marshall (June 21, 1942):

I have long been aware, of course, of the implications of the submarine situation as pointed out in your memorandum of 19 June. I have employed—and will continue to employ—not only regular forces but also such improvised means as give any promise of usefulness. However, it is obvious that the German effort is expanding more rapidly than our defense, and if we are to avoid disaster not only the Navy itself but all other agencies concerned must continue to intensify the anti-submarine effort. . . .

Though we are still suffering heavy losses outside the east coast convoy zone the situation is not hopeless. We know that a reasonable degree of security can be obtained by suitable escort and air coverage. . . .

I might say in this connection that escort is not just one way of handling the submarine menace; it is the only way that gives any promise of success. . . .

There simply were not enough destroyers and long-range aircraft to go around. Coast Guard cutters, corvettes, PC's, SC's, and other craft had put up a valiant effort, but, as Admiral King stated in a report to Navy Secretary Knox, *"Stout hearts in little boats cannot handle an opponent as tough as the submarine."*

Naturally there was elation in the Nazi camp, especially with German yards turning out anywhere from 20 to 25 new submarines a month.

Submarine Admiral Doenitz to Adolph Hitler (June 15, 1942): *"I foresee vast possibilities through a rapid increase in the number of U-boats and the use of supply submarines."* And to a German war correspondent (summer of 1942): *"Our submarines are operating close inshore along the coast of the United States of America, so that bathers and sometimes entire coastal cities are witnesses to that drama of war, whose visual climaxes are constituted by the red glorioles of blazing tankers."*

The only possible reply to this bombastic (but unfortunately truthful) rhetoric was the one made by the U.S. Navy. More radar; improved search techniques; bigger and better weapons. And teams of small aircraft carriers, destroyers, and destroyer escorts—"baby flat-tops and tin cans"—to hunt down the mid-ocean wolfpacks.

CHAPTER 8

ORDEAL OF DESRON 29

(THE BATTLE FOR THE MALAY BARRIER)

Edsall and Corvettes Kill I-124 (First Blood)

A good many depth charges had been dropped in the Pacific by the third week in January 1942. They jolted Japanese nerves, but so far as is known they did little damage to the Emperor's submarines. Aside from the midgets demolished at Pearl, the Japanese Submarine Force, during the first six weeks of the Pacific War, suffered only one loss at American hands—an I-boat sunk by carrier aircraft. United States destroyers had yet to score against a full-sized Jap submersible. On the DD agenda the reckoning was overdue.

First honors fell to the U.S.S. EDSALL. One of the Asiatic Fleet veterans of DesRon 29, she was one of that valiant squadron of oldsters bearing the brunt of the Japanese onslaught on Indonesia. It was fair reward that one of these old grayhounds should participate in the first major submarine kill for American destroyers in the Pacific.

The scene: off Port Darwin, the "ghost town" emergency naval base on the north coast of Australia. There the few Allied reinforcements dribbling in were meeting the first of the refugees driven down from the Philippines and the Netherlands East Indies—battered Asiatic Fleet submarines, the tender HOLLAND, tramp freighters and schooners scorched by the hot glare of the Rising Sun over Borneo, Celebes, and the Bismarck Archipelago. There, on the morning of January 20, 1942, the destroyer EDSALL, captained by Lieutenant Joshua J. Nix, member of an escort group conducting a convoy into Darwin, picked up sound contact with an enemy sub.

The destroyer could not abandon the convoy to race off on a submarine hunt. But as she steamed into Darwin with the ship-train, her call brought a group of Australian corvettes to the scene. The invading sub was promptly made "it" in a deadly game of tag.

That afternoon the EDSALL was dispatched from Port Darwin to join the game. She was off at 1633. That evening, at 1900, she formed a scouting line just northwest of Melville Island with her companion "four-piper" ALDEN (Lieutenant Commander L. E. Coley).

Three Australian corvettes—His Majesty's Australian ships DELORAINE, LITHGOW, and KATOOMBA—were at that time maneuvering around the spot where the sub had been first contacted by EDSALL. And the Jap submarine was on the spot! One of the corvettes had just completed an attack when EDSALL exchanged signals with the A/S craft. The flash from the "Aussies" was all the American destroyermen needed.

Heading for the scene of action, EDSALL's sonar "put the finger" on the sub at 1929. The destroyermen endured a four-minute wait while H.M.A.S. DELORAINE made a depth-charge run over the target. Then EDSALL laid a thunderous pattern in DELORAINE's wake.

The sea boomed and boiled and bubbled. Up came a flood of oil and an effervescent, murky swirl which bore evidence that a large Jap submarine had been erased from the Imperial Navy's roster. And destroyer EDSALL and corvette DELORAINE could each paint a Rising Sun naval flag on the ship's "scoreboard."

Final inquest (autopsy might be a better term) was made by divers of the U.S.S. HOLLAND. Going down at lat. 12-05 S., long. 130-06 E., they boarded the remains of the Japanese submarine I-124. For American destroyers in the Pacific she was No. 1 on the "Hit Parade."

Abdafloat Versus Japanese Juggernaut

As has been related, the Allies in the Asiatics organized the ABDA Command on January 15, 1942. This American-British-Dutch-Australian military and naval combine was under the supreme command of Field Marshall Sir Archibald Wavell. Its military elements included ABDAAIR (a few RAF and Dutch planes) and ABDAARM (British Army forces in Indonesia, and the Netherlands East Indies Army).

But the big stick of the ABDA organization was its naval element, the sea forces designated ABDAFLOAT. (Note chart of ABDA area on inside front cover of book.)

ABDAFLOAT was composed of Admiral T. C. Hart's U.S. Asiatic Fleet, British (including Australian) naval forces under Admiral Sir Geoffrey Layton, R.N., and Dutch naval forces under Vice Admiral Conrad Helfrich. Table 1 in the adjacent column details the composition of these Allied naval forces which were originally placed under Admiral Hart's over-all command.

Lumped together, the ABDA naval forces look fairly formidable: 2 heavy cruisers, 7 light cruisers, 23 destroyers, 46 submarines, several tenders, a couple of oilers, and a few auxiliaries. But Admiral Hart was compelled to divide the ABDA sea forces into several groups to cover even as much as a corner of the vast Southwest Pacific area, which included the Philippines, Borneo, Celebes, the western half of New Guinea, all of Malaya, Sumatra, Java, the rest of the Netherlands East Indies, and the northwest coast of Australia. The Malayan coastline alone is as long as the United States' Eastern Seaboard. And if placed in the Atlantic Ocean, the Netherlands East Indies would reach from America to Europe.

Also, the ABDA ships were practically without air cover. United States Army Air had been all but annihilated in the Philippines. Allied land-based air forces were decidedly sketchy, and the few British planes were needed for the defense of Singapore. Valiant little Pat Wing 10 was soon reduced to three planes. ABDAFLOAT did not possess a single carrier. This, in a day when such men-of-war as REPULSE and PRINCE OF WALES could be swiftly slaughtered by enemy bombers.

The Allied submarine situation was as bad—or worse. Cause: the previously mentioned matter of defective American torpedoes. Expected to hold the Navy's front line in the Philippines, the 27 sub-

Table 1

ABDAFLOAT

ADMIRAL THOMAS C. HART
Relieved February 12, 1942
BY ADMIRAL CONRAD HELFRICH, R.N.N.

UNITED STATES ASIATIC FLEET

ADMIRAL THOMAS C. HART
Relieved February 4, 1942
BY VICE ADMIRAL W. A. GLASSFORD

TASK FORCE 5 (*Striking Force*)
REAR ADMIRAL W. A. GLASSFORD

HOUSTON	*Heavy cruiser*
BOISE	*Light cruiser*
MARBLEHEAD	*Light cruiser*

DESTROYER SQUADRON 29
PAUL JONES *Flagship*

DESDIV 57	DESDIV 58	DESDIV 59
WHIPPLE	BULMER	POPE
ALDEN	BARKER	PEARY
JOHN D. EDWARDS	PARROTT	PILLSBURY
EDSALL	STEWART	JOHN D. FORD

TASK FORCE 4 (*PatWing 10*)
28 Catalinas, and
Tenders CHILDS, HERON, and WILLIAM B. PRESTON

TASK FORCE 3 (*Submarine Force*)
27 Submarines

TASK FORCE 2 (*Service Force*)

LANGLEY	*Seaplane tender*
PECOS and TRINITY	*Oilers*
GOLD STAR	*Auxiliary*
BLACK HAWK	*Destroyer tender*
ASHEVILLE	*Gunboat*
ISABEL	*Converted yacht*

BRITISH NAVAL FORCES
ADMIRAL SIR GEOFFREY LAYTON, R.N.

EXETER	*Heavy cruiser*
HOBART and PERTH	*Light cruisers*
ELECTRA, ENCOUNTER, and JUPITER	*Destroyers*

SUBMARINE SQUADRON
3 Submarines

NETHERLANDS NAVAL FORCES
VICE ADMIRAL C. E. L. HELFRICH, R.N.N.

JAVA, DE RUYTER, and TROMP	*Light cruisers*

DESTROYER SQUADRON

VAN NES	WITTE DE WITH
EVERTSEN	VAN GHENT
KORTENAER	PIET HEIN

BANCKERT

SUBMARINE SQUADRON
12 ocean-going submarines — *4 coastal subs*

Vice Admiral Kondo's Southwestern Pacific Naval Force rolled south of the Philippines, deep into the Java Sea. Despite insurmountable handicaps of an untried international military organization, acute lack of supplies and repair facilities, and overwhelming enemy forces, ABDA units performed outstandingly before the rich southern islands fell to the conquerors.

This deck view of the Overton shows the four-piper conversion features embodied in World War II destroyers. At the time of Pearl Harbor several units of DesRon 29 of the U.S. Asiatic Fleet were members of this class. Their stubborn resistance as participants in the four nation ABDAFLOAT did not upset the conquest time tables greatly, but did cause the Japanese trouble.

Ghost ship. The U.S.S. Stewart was one of the little destroyer force that attempted to stem the onslaught of the whole Japanese Navy in the early months of the war—without air cover, without supplies, without facilities. But the Stewart, after battling in the night action at Badoeng Strait, risked drydocking at Soerabaja—and so began her weird, almost incredible career.

Paul Jones gave no one cause to doubt her willingness to fight at the Battle of Balikpapan, during the Japanese drive into Borneo's rich oil region. With a display of dash and courage befitting a destroyer of that name, the Paul Jones pressed home an attack which spoiled Japanese self-confidence during the first surface action fought by U.S. Naval Forces in the Pacific War.

The ship that vanished—U.S.S. Edsall, which fought to the bitter end against superior Japanese naval forces deep in the Java Sea. Her fate was a mystery for a full decade until 1952 when captured enemy films revealed an American destroyer of Edsall's characteristics being sunk by a Japanese heavy cruiser. The few men who survived died of wounds or privation before war's end.

Table 2

JAPANESE NAVAL FORCES SOUTHWEST PACIFIC

VICE ADMIRAL NOBUTAKE KONDO

WESTERN FORCE

VICE ADMIRAL J. OZAWA

COVERING GROUP

ADMIRAL OZAWA

HEAVY CRUISER SQUADRON

CHOKAI, SUZUYA, MOGAMI, MIKUMA, KUMANO

DESTROYER SQUADRON

MURAKUMO, SHIRAYUKI, HATSUYUKI
URANAMI, SHIRAKUMO, AYANAMI
ISONAMI

ATTACK GROUP

Nine transports *Two minesweepers*

BALI FORCE

REAR ADMIRAL K. KUBO

NAGARA — *Light cruiser*

DESTROYER SQUADRON

HATSUSHIMO, WAKABA, ARASHIO
OSHIO, NENOHI, MICHISHIO
ASASHIO

Two transports

SOUTHERN FORCE

VICE ADMIRAL KONDO

KONGO and HARUNA — *Battleships*
TAKAO, ATAGO, and MAYA — *Heavy cruisers*
Two destroyer divisions

CARRIER STRIKING FORCE

VICE ADMIRAL C. NAGUMO

AKAGI, KAGA, HIRYU, and SORYU — *Aircraft carriers*
TONE and CHIKUMA — *Heavy cruisers*
Eight destroyers *Eight tankers and auxiliaries*

CENTRAL FORCE

VICE ADMIRAL HIROSE

DESTROYER SQUADRON 4

REAR ADMIRAL NISHIMURA

NAKA — *Light cruiser*

DESTROYERS

ASAGUMO, HARUSAME, SAMIDARE
YUDACHI, NATSUGUMO, MURASAME
MINEGUMO

ADVANCE ECHELON

ADMIRAL HIROSE

ITSUKUSHIMA, WAKATAKA, IMIZU MARU — *Mine layers*
SANYO MARU and SANUKI MARU — *Seaplane tenders*
Four minesweepers *Fifteen transports*
One special transport

ESCORT GROUP

REAR ADMIRAL S. HASHIMOTO

YURA and KASHI — *Light cruisers*

DESTROYER SQUADRON

FUBUKI, KAWAUCHI, YUGIRI
SHIRAYUKI, AMAGIRI, ASAGIRI
HATSUYUKI

AIR GROUP

REAR ADMIRAL K. KAKUTA

RYUJO — *Aircraft carrier*
SHIKINAMI — *Destroyer*

EASTERN FORCE

VICE ADMIRAL I. TAKAHASHI

COVERING GROUP

REAR ADMIRAL T. TAKAGI

NACHI, HAGURO, and MYOKO — *Heavy cruisers*
IKAZUCHI and INAZUMA — *Destroyers*

ESCORT GROUP

REAR ADMIRAL R. TANAKA

JINTSU — *Light cruiser*

DESTROYER SQUADRON

YUKIKAZE, KURASHIO, OSHIO
AMATZUKAZE, OYASHIO, ARASHIO
TOKITSUKAZE, NATSUSHIO, HATSUKAZE
HAYASHIO

ATTACK GROUP

Ten transports carrying Special Naval Landing Force

BASE GROUP AND ESCORT COVERING GROUP

Rear Admiral Kubo's Bali Force

CLOSE COVER GROUP

DESTROYER SQUADRON

UMIKAZE, KAWAKAZE, ASAGUMO
MINEGUMO, NATSUGUMO

Four minesweepers

AIR GROUP

REAR ADMIRAL FUJITA

ZUIHO — *Light cruiser*
CHITOSE — *Seaplane tender*
Three patrol boats and subchaser

COVERING GROUP

REAR ADMIRAL TAKAGI

Takagi's heavy cruiser squadron, less HAGURO
INAZUMA, AKEBONO, and YAMAKAZE — *Destroyers*
Plus one from Close Cover Group

marines of the Asiatic Fleet failed to sink a single enemy warship during December 1941 and January 1942. One old S-boat sank a Jap destroyer off Makassar City in February. That was the sum total scored by the 27 American submarines in the Battle for the Malay Barrier.

Lacking air cover, and with the American submarines practically disarmed, the ABDA naval forces were hopelessly handicapped. A comparison of the ABDA sea forces with the huge Japanese armada reduces the size of ABDAFLOAT to something miniscule.

Figures best summarize the ABDAFLOAT-Japanese armada disparity. In fact, the story of the Allied naval defeat in the Philippines, Malaya, and the Netherlands East Indies is contained in the following statistical table:

	ABDAFLOAT	*JAPANESE SOUTHWEST PACIFIC FORCE*
Battleships	*0*	*2*
Aircraft carriers	*0*	*5*
Light carriers	*0*	*1*
Heavy cruisers	*2*	*14*
Light cruisers	*7*	*5*
Destroyers	*23*	*43*
*Submarines**	*46*	*(Unknown)†*

** (Effort cancelled by faulty torpedo)* *† (But operating with the best torpedo in the Pacific)*

The odds were so overwhelming as to be impossible. The best of strategy could hardly have compensated for the disparity in numbers and weight, the lack of air cover, and the submarine-torpedo failure which handicapped ABDAFLOAT. And the ABDA sea forces were burdened by other handicaps. Asiatic Fleet, Dutch, and British squadrons could not count on reinforcements for months to come, if at all.

Neither could ABDAFLOAT count on overhaul or refits. This meant that a badly crippled ship must either retire in disablement, or fight on as best she could, although seriously lamed.

Finally there was the language handicap. Most of the American naval officers could not speak three words of Dutch; nor were they able to read the Dutch charts and sailing instructions, which were far superior to the American charts for the Netherlands East Indies Area. The ABDA forces employed four different sets of signals, and the coding officers were compelled to grapple with an interchange of American, British, and Dutch code. Communication errors and misunderstandings plagued the ABDA forces from the first.

Yet in spite of the odds and handicaps, ABDAFLOAT fought several of the great battles of the Pacific War. In those desperate battles for the Malay Barrier, American destroyers—the old "four-pipers" of Captain Wiley's DesRon 29—participated in a manner that assumes heroic proportions.

The Battle of Balikpapan

Aside from their strategic value, the Dutch islands of Indonesia were rich with economic treasure, not the least of which was "liquid gold." The wells of Tarakan Island, off the northeast coast of Borneo, gushed oil of unusual purity. To capture these liquid gold mines, the Japanese Central Force stormed down through the Celebes Sea. Tarakan was handily taken on January 11. On the 21st the invaders headed down Makassar Strait to seize Balikpapan.

The Balikpapan invasion force was commanded by Rear Admiral S. Nishimura in the light cruiser NAKA. The force consisted of one Japanese destroyer squadron (12 destroyers led by Nishimura's flagship) and 16 transports. An advance echelon composed of two transports under escort of two DD's steamed in the van of the main body.

As it moved southward down the Strait of Makassar, this Japanese force was sighted and reported by the Catalinas of PatWing 10. Then it was pecked at by Dutch aircraft and American submarines. Dutch planes destroyed one of the 16 transports.

At the time the Japanese launched this invasion of eastern Borneo the skimpy forces of ABDAFLOAT were divided three ways. The British were holding the Singapore-Palembang area, the western flank of the Malay Barrier. The Dutch naval forces were committed to the "center," the Java Sea. The Americans were disposed to hold the eastern flank—area which extended, roughly, from Bali to Australia.

As Balikpapan on Makassar Strait lay to the north and east of Bali, the Japanese advance was in "American territory." In consequence Admiral Hart, in operational command of ABDAFLOAT, ordered Admiral Glassford's Striking Force to intercept the Japs in Makassar Strait.

When the order to move arrived (on the morning of January 20), Admiral Glassford's force was fueling in Koepang Bay, Timor, at the eastern end of the Netherlands Indies Archipelago. As originally organized, Glassford's Striking Force contained the light cruisers BOISE and MARBLEHEAD, and eight destroyers of DesRon 29. But the entire force was not on hand. In company with HOUSTON, destroyers WHIPPLE and JOHN D. EDWARDS were escorting a convoy to Torres Straits. Destroyers ALDEN and EDSALL were also on convoy duty. And several DD's were undergoing repair. So only the two light cruisers and no more than six destroyers were available to Glassford. And as it turned out, only four of the destroyers—JOHN D.

Ford, Pope, Parrott, and Paul Jones—led by Commander P. H. Talbot, ComDesDiv 59, with his pennant in the Ford, would be available for the crack at Balikpapan.

The destroyers were fed fuel by the Marblehead. And then, with his abbreviated force, Admiral Glassford set out for the Strait of Makassar. The ships steamed westward across the Savu Sea, then swung northward to slip through Sape Strait between Komodo and Soembawa Islands.

Here Glassford's force received its first setback at the hands of Chance and Blunder, those capricious war-gods given to upsetting the best laid plans of mice and men-of-war. In Sape Strait there was (by Chance) a pinnacle rock which reared from the water like an upthrust dagger. It caught the light cruiser Boise as she steamed through the strait, and gave her a wicked slash along the keel. With her bottom laid open, Boise had to head for the nearest port. The little force was minus one light cruiser, plus the destroyer required to escort her to port.

Meantime, Marblehead had been slowed by a turbine casualty which cut her speed to 15 knots. Admiral Glassford in Boise ordered both cruisers into Warorada Bay, Soembawa. And so another DD was detached to screen this cruiser. That reduced the Striking Force group to four destroyers—the four old "four-pipers" under Commander Talbot. Doggedly this little quartet steamed on through Sape Strait, then headed across the Flores Sea for Cape Mandar, Celebes, at the southern end of Makassar Strait.

The situation had now drastically changed. Instead of an attack group of six DD's with a couple of cruisers to cover their retirement, the strike was up to a quartet which would have to go it alone. Four tired old "cans" of World War I manufacture advancing to hit a Jap invasion force which contained some 12 destroyers and several armed auxiliaries. Not to mention Admiral Nishimura's light cruiser Naka.

Odds notwithstanding, Talbot led his four destroyers northward up Makassar Strait during the afternoon of January 23. Making 25 knots, the old grayhounds bucked through walloping swells that slopped over their bows and showered their bridgewings with brine. To confuse possible aerial observation, Talbot then ordered a deceptive course-change to the east—the enemy might take it that they were bound for Mandar Bay, Celebes. However, Jap reconnaissance planes were not in evidence; the only aircraft sighted was a patrolling PBY.

About an hour after sunset, with the ships' clocks at 1930, Talbot swung the column on an abrupt left turn that headed the ships for Balikpapan, Borneo.

Commander Talbot passed the word over the TBS. TORPEDO ATTACK. USE OWN DISCRETION IN ATTACKING INDEPENDENTLY WHEN TARGETS ARE LOCATED. . . . WHEN ALL TORPS FIRED, CLOSE WITH ALL GUNS. . . . USE INITIATIVE AND DETERMINATION.

As the little column started an oblique run across the Strait, speed was stepped up to 27 knots. Through the darkness the four old-timers galloped—flagship John D. Ford (Lieutenant Commander J. E. Cooper); Pope (Lieutenant Commander W. C. Blinn); Parrott (Lieutenant Commander E. N. Parker); Paul Jones (Lieutenant Commander J. J. Hourihan).

At midnight the ships were still racing through the blackout; the sea had calmed, and the destroyers were moving on a beeline.

Presently Ford's lookouts sighted the firelight of a couple of burning Jap transports, handiwork of Dutch airmen who had attacked the invader the previous afternoon. Then Balikpapan came to view under a sky flushed crimson. The whole shoreline was an angry smolder. The Dutch had blown up the local refineries. Against this netherworldish glow, Japanese transports were intermittently silhouetted; for a moment, a ship would be seen, then it would be screened by a surge of smoke. But the smoke which screened the herd of transports also served to screen the approaching American destroyers. And the old "four-pipers" were not detected.

So Chance, capricious as always, provided DesDiv 59 with a break at Balikpapan. It was a destroyerman's set-up—the anchored transports; the smoke-smudge which screened the attacking DD's; the fiery shoreline which just silhouetted the targets.

Suddenly a searchlight stabbed from the darkness on Ford's starboard bow. A Jap destroyer, one of four crossing the American column from starboard to port, blinked a challenge at the American DD's. Talbot ordered a swift course-change, and the column kept on going. Another course change put it back on the "main line" for Balikpapan.

Talbot led his ships in on the attack with a high-speed dash. Their opening strike was aimed at a line of transports anchored about five miles off the entrance of Balikpapan Harbor. Parrott was the first to loose her torpedoes. She launched at close range—a spread of three. The three missed.

Lieutenant Commander Parker ordered a slight turn to port. About two minutes after the first torpedo salvo, Parrott fired a brace of five torpedoes at a target some 1,000 yards to starboard. She was shooting, so to speak, at the broadside of a barn. All five torpedoes missed.

Simultaneously Ford let fly at an anchored transport. In an article subsequently published by the *Naval Institute Proceedings* (May 1943) Lieutenant

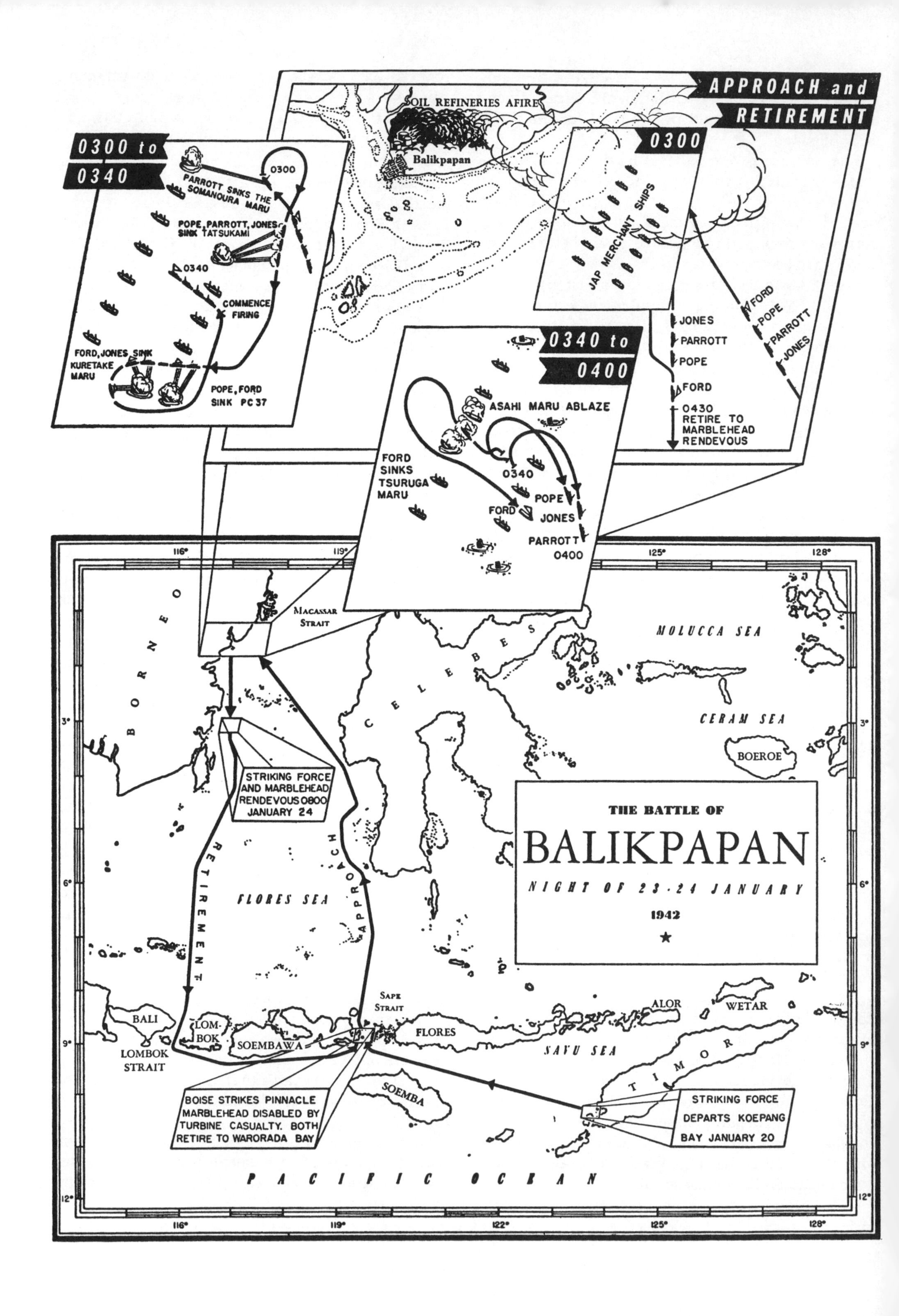
APPROACH and RETIREMENT
OIL REFINERIES AFIRE
Balikpapan
0300
JAP MERCHANT SHIPS
JONES
PARROTT
POPE
FORD
0430
RETIRE TO
MARBLEHEAD
RENDEVOUS
FORD
POPE
PARROTT
JONES
0300 to 0340
PARROTT SINKS THE SOMANOURA MARU
POPE, PARROTT, JONES SINK TATSUKAMI
0340
COMMENCE FIRING
FORD, JONES SINK KURETAKE MARU
POPE, FORD SINK PC 37
0340 to 0400
ASAHI MARU ABLAZE
FORD SINKS TSURUGA MARU
0340
POPE
FORD
JONES
PARROTT
0400
BORNEO
MACASSAR STRAIT
CELEBES
MOLUCCA SEA
CERAM SEA
BOEROE
STRIKING FORCE AND MARBLEHEAD RENDEVOUS 0800 JANUARY 24
RETIREMENT
APPROACH
FLORES SEA
THE BATTLE OF
BALIKPAPAN
NIGHT OF 23-24 JANUARY
1942
SAPE STRAIT
ALOR
WETAR
BALI
LOMBOK
SOEMBAWA
FLORES
LOMBOK STRAIT
SAVU SEA
TIMOR
SOEMBA
BOISE STRIKES PINNACLE MARBLEHEAD DISABLED BY TURBINE CASUALTY. BOTH RETIRE TO WARORADA BAY
STRIKING FORCE DEPARTS KOEPANG BAY JANUARY 20
PACIFIC OCEAN
116°
119°
122°
125°
128°
3°
6°
9°
12°

William P. Mack, FORD's Gunnery Officer, vividly describes that dramatic torpedo shot.

"Suddenly we found ourselves right in the midst of the Jap transports. Down on the bridge I could hear Captain Cooper saying 'Action port! Action port!' and Lieutenant Slaughter readying the torpedo battery. Back aft the tube mounts swung to follow his director. 'Fire one,' he said. 'Fire one,' repeated his telephone talker. Then came the peculiar combination of a muffled explosion, a whine, a swish, and a splash, that follows the firing of a torpedo. I watched the torpedo come to the surface once and then dive again as it steadied on its run. Astern, the POPE, PAUL JONES, *and* PARROTT *were carefully picking targets and firing. . . . My talker was calmly counting off seconds as our first torpedo ran toward its target. 'Mark!' he shouted, as the time came for it to hit. Seconds passed. Nothing happened. We knew our first had missed."*

End-ship in the column, PAUL JONES fired a torpedo at 0257, shooting at a vague silhouette which loomed up in the smoke as a destroyer or a cruiser. As it eventuated, the vessel was a small minesweeper. And that torpedo also missed!

So Blunder once more reared its ugly head to bedevil this force. Ten torpedo shots at "sitting duck" targets, and not a single hit! Critics there were who later suggested that the old "four-pipers" were moving too fast for accurate marksmanship. But evidence indicates that it was the torpedoes that failed, and not the destroyermen.

And now the chance for surprise was lost; the punch was "telegraphed"; the enemy was sounding the alarm. Among the Japanese ships all was hue, cry, and confusion. In the oily smoke-fog, Jap patrol craft began to dash this way and that. Signals twinkled, and there was some aimless shooting. Meanwhile (time: 0300) Commander Talbot brought his column circling about for another run past the line of transports. As the DD's started the loop, PARROTT fired three torpedoes at a ship dimly glimpsed on her port bow. This time the torpedoes found the mark. The transport, SOMANOURA MARU, blew up with a night-shaking blast. Out of Balikpapan Bay, pell-mell, came Japanese Admiral Nishimura's destroyer squadron. This pack of modern DD's should have dealt Talbot's old quartet a homicidal thrashing. They did nothing of the kind. Somehow convinced that his transports were under submarine attack, Nishimura led his destroyer squadron steaming out into Makassar Strait to conduct a vigorous sub-hunt.

While the befuddled Admiral's destroyers searched for a sub that wasn't there, Talbot's "four-pipers" ran riot through the Jap transport fleet.

Highballing on the back track, destroyer POPE at 0306 launched a spread of five torpedoes at a silhouetted target. Two minutes later PARROTT fired a torpedo salvo at the same ship, and PAUL JONES unleashed a salvo two minutes after that. Another dazzling eruption illumined the night, and down went the 7,000-ton transport TATSUKAMI MARU.

The column raced southward, then swung hard right to clip through the southern end of the anchorage. At 0319 POPE and PARROTT loosed simultaneous torpedo salvos at what looked like a Jap destroyer off to port. The shots demolished a small patrol boat.

At 0322 FORD and PAUL JONES launched single torpedoes at the dim silhouette of a good-sized transport. A ruffle of froth at her stern, the vessel was under way, and she managed to dodge the "fish." Talbot brought the column circling around this target, and PAUL JONES fired a killing torpedo at 0325. Victim was the 5,000-ton KURETAKE MARU.

Once more the column headed northward on a dash paralleling the transport line. Then Talbot ordered an abrupt turn to westward to begin a long run that would take the speeding DD's through an inner line of transports.

As the column began the long westward loop, all four DD's opened fire with their deck guns. POPE and PARROTT and PAUL JONES were out of torpedoes. FORD was retaining her final salvos for fat targets.

By now POPE, PARROTT, and PAUL JONES reported "all torpedoes expended." Giving the other three destroyers orders to proceed independently with gunfire, Talbot directed the FORD to attack again with her remaining torpedoes.

The following excerpt from the account by FORD's Gunnery Officer describes this final round.

". . . We reversed course and ran through the convoy again, firing torpedoes on both sides as transports loomed out of the dark. By now there were only three of us, the PAUL JONES *having lost us as we came around the last turn. At one time I could count five sinking ships. A third time we reversed course and ran through the demoralized convoy. Once we had to veer to port to avoid a sinking transport. The water was covered with swimming Japs. Our wash overturned several lifeboats loaded with Japs. Other ships looked as if they were covered with flies. Jap soldiers were clambering down their sides in panic. It was becoming difficult to keep from firing at transports that had already been torpedoed. . . . So far I believed the Japs had not discovered that we were in their midst, attributing the torpedoes to submarines and believing we were their own destroyers.*

"Down on the bridge I heard 'Fire ten!' Just two

torpedoes left. Now only the POPE *was left astern of us. We fired our last two torpedoes at a group of three transports. Now I knew the stage was mine. Many a time I had fired at target rafts, but this was the real thing. 'Commence firing!' rang in my earphones. I was ready, but how different this was from peacetime firings! I could still remember the sonorous arguments of the publications I had studied at the Naval Academy over the relation effectiveness of searchlights and starshells. I didn't use either, nor did we use any of the complicated fire-control apparatus installed. This was draw-shooting at its best. As targets loomed out of the dark at ranges of 500 to 1,500 yards, we trained on and let go a salvo or two, sights set at their lower limits, using the illumination furnished by burning ships. Finally we sighted a transport far enough away to let us get in three salvos before we had passed it. The projectile explosions were tremendous. Deck-plates and debris flew in all directions. When we last saw her she was on end, slipping slowing under. . . . A transport began firing at us. I turned my guns on her, but before we could silence her a shell had hit us aft. Flames grew and spread around the area. Over the telephone I could hear a torpedoman describing the damage — 'four men wounded, the after deckhouse wrecked, ammunition burning.' Thirty seconds later the burning ammunition had been thrown over the side, the wounded men cared for, and the gun crew was firing again.*

"By now the POPE *had also lost us, and we were fighting alone. One more transport we mauled badly, then there was nothing left to shoot at. On the bridge I heard our Division Commander give the order to withdraw. Back aft the blowers began to whine even louder as the Chief Engineer squeezed the last ounce of speed out of the old boat. Later I learned we were making almost 32 knots, faster than the* FORD *had gone since her trials. In the east the sky was growing uncomfortably bright. Astern of us the sky was also bright, but from the fires of burning ships. . . ."*

Apparently one of those ships was the transport ASAHI MARU, damaged and set ablaze by FORD's gunnery. Another seems to have been the TSURUGA MARU, a 7,000-tonner torpedoed and sunk in the last-round foray. Lieutenant Mack's account concludes:

"For almost 30 minutes we ran south before dawn came. All hands strained their eyes astern for signs of pursuit that we thought inevitable. We could see none. The only ships in sight were three familiar shapes on the port bow that we knew to be the PARROTT, PAUL JONES, *and* POPE. *Proudly they fell in astern of us, and sped south together. Down on the bridge a flag hoist whipped out smartly. 'Well done!' it said."*

So ended the Battle of Balikpapan. Steaming in inky darkness down the unlighted channel through the reefs on the east coast of Borneo—an endeavor as harrowing and dangerous in some respects as the battle itself—the destroyers made rendezvous shortly after 0800 with the light cruiser MARBLEHEAD which had come up to cover their retirement.

The four old "four-pipers," which had ridden roughshod over the Japanese transport-herd, got back to base without a single fatality. Only casualties: the four men wounded in FORD. Sole battle damage: FORD's superficial injury, a smashed torpedo-workshop aft.

Behind them Talbot's destroyers left wreckage and total destruction. On the bottom off Balikpapan Bay lay four Japanese transports: The cargoman KURETAKE MARU, 5,175 tons; and passenger-cargomen TSURUGA MARU, 6,988 tons; TATSUKAMI MARU, 7,064 tons; SOMANOURA MARU, 3,519 tons. With them lay Japanese patrol craft PC-37, 750 tons. Altogether 23,496 tons of enemy shipping.

In the flame light of later torpedoings, this tonnage might appear insignificant. But in January 1942 the torpedoings by Talbot's destroyers created the one bright spot in the Southwest Pacific War picture. They had won the first surface action fought by United States naval forces in the Pacific War—the first surface action fought by United States naval forces since the Spanish-American War!

ABDA Setbacks

But undeterred by four little destroyers, the Japanese Juggernaut continued its drive southward, implacably bent on overrunning the Netherlands East Indies.

Down through the South China Sea came Admiral Ozawa's Western Force, on western Borneo, Malaya, and Sumatra. Down through Molucca Passage came the Eastern Force of Admiral Takahashi to make a three-pronged thrust at the southeast coast of Celebes, the island of Ambon in the Banda Sea, and the Bismarck Archipelago above New Guinea. Down through the Strait of Makassar came the Central Force of Admiral Hirose, scorching the eastern coast of Borneo.

By the end of January 1942, Singapore was under siege in the west, and the Japs had thrust as far east as Rabaul in the Bismarcks. The Allied flanks of the Southwest Pacific front were crumbling, and the Americans striving to hold the line felt as though they were struggling in quicksand.

The destroyermen in Captain Wiley's DesRon 29 were delighted by the Balikpapan victory, but they knew what they were up against. The 13 Asiatic Fleet "four-pipers" serving with ABDAFLOAT were orphans of the storm. Already Soerabaja, provisional headquarters of the Asiatic Fleet on the north coast of Java, was menaced by the Jap advance on Borneo. On the south coast of Java the port of Tjilatjap (pronounced Chillachap) offered a few basing facilities but scarcely enough. The Jap thrust into the Bismarck Archipelago directly threatened the security of Darwin, Australia. About the only front-line base the destroyers could count on was the tender BLACK HAWK. And that overworked ship would soon be as bare of supplies as Mother Hubbard's cupboard.

"We scraped barrel-bottom for food stores," a DesRon 29 bluejacket recalled later. "As for repairs, some of those shabby old cans got along with practically nothing but bailing wire and chewing gum. Everybody improvised. But it was hard to improvise rest and recuperation. We could hardly find sack-time. Relaxation? A cup of Java."

It was a bitter cup of Java, off the Malay Barrier in February 1942. With the enemy in Kendari, Celebes, and pushing down Makassar Strait toward Bandjermasin on the south coast of Borneo, the ABDA naval commanders knew the time had come to fight a decisive delaying action. On February 2 Admiral Hart, in over-all command of ABDAFLOAT, placed Dutch Admiral Doorman in charge of a Combined Allied Striking Force, with directions to hit the invaders then advancing on either Makassar City or Bandjermasin.

The ABDA Combined Striking Force consisted of Doorman's flagship, the light cruiser DE RUYTER, the American heavy cruiser HOUSTON, American light cruiser MARBLEHEAD, Dutch light cruiser TROMP, an American division of four destroyers (DesDiv 58), and a Dutch division of three destroyers.

Led by Commander T. H. Binford, the American destroyers were flagship STEWART (Lieutenant Commander Harold P. Smith); JOHN D. EDWARDS (Commander H. E. Eccles); BARKER (Commander L. J. Mc Glone), and BULMER (Lieutenant David A. Harris). The Dutch destroyers were VAN GHENT, PIET HIEN, and BANCKERT.

Against the enemy surface forces which had been detected on the move, Doorman's task force stood a better than even chance. But Japanese aircraft, already striking at Java, constituted a deadly danger. Admiral Doorman hoped to counter this peril by fighting a night action. His directive to Combined Striking Force read: *"Enemy transports will be attacked and destroyed in night attack."*

Such an attack, however, demanded daylight running across the Java Sea. At 0000 February 4, Doorman led his striking force out from Madoera Strait off Soerabaja on an eastward course.

Flagship DE RUYTER, in the lead, was followed by cruisers HOUSTON, MARBLEHEAD, and TROMP. The American destroyers steamed in guard positions on either flank of the cruiser column. The three Dutch DD's brought up the rear.

Morning brought a sky partly overcast and a moderate following sea. Then disaster. At 0949 when the ships were well on their way, DE RUYTER's lookouts spotted an approaching flight of Jap aircraft.

The planes were "Nells"—naval bombers from Takahashi's Eastern Force. Some 37 in number, they had taken off from Kendari that morning for a strike at Soerabaja. Now they found a likelier target.

Doorman radioed the warning to his captains, and the American and Dutch ships scattered, every man-of-war for herself. The "Nells" came swarming over, and down came the bombs.

Four courageous U.S. Navy Catalinas tried to disrupt the attack. They were promptly shot down. The destroyermen manned their anti-aircraft guns, but the Jap bombers scorned the DD's. Beginning an onslaught that was to last throughout the morning, they devoted their attention to the cruisers. So the action off Madoera Strait featured the fighting of the American cruisers MARBLEHEAD and HOUSTON, and Dutch DE RUYTER. The destroyers were pretty much out of it.

As they dodged and twisted at top speed, hurling up anti-aircraft fire, both United States cruisers received terrible punishment. HOUSTON was severely damaged by a bomb which set off a blast in her after turret, slaying some 50 officers and men, and wounding 20 more. Fire-blackened and mutilated, she retired through Bali Strait and set a course for Tjilatjap.

MARBLEHEAD received a worse blasting. Landing on her fantail, one bomb smashed through the deck, wrecked her steering gear, and ruptured the fuel tanks. Another bomb shattered her wardroom and sick bay. A near miss stove in several plates on the ship's bow. A mass of flames, the vessel went logy by the head, assumed a starboard list, and began to reel in aimless circles.

The Japs continued the attack until shortly after noon. Desperate damage-control measures kept MARBLEHEAD afloat, subdued the raging fires, and reduced the angle of her jammed rudder. Steering her by her engines, the cruisermen headed her for Lombok Strait. As any further attempt to carry out the Makassar Strait mission would have been suicidal,

Doorman ordered the rest of the Striking Force to retire. The American destroyers and the Dutch cruiser DE RUYTER formed a cordon around MARBLEHEAD as she staggered southward, and eventually they got her into Tjilatjap.

For the forces of ABDAFLOAT the Madoera Strait repulse was an ominous forecast of what was to come. With U.S.S. HOUSTON badly damaged, and U.S.S. MARBLEHEAD out of the campaign, the battle for the Malay Barrier was going to be a back-to-the-wall fight.

Meantime the enemy occupied Makassar City, Celebes, and moved into southern Borneo. Now they were within easy bombing distance of Soerabaja, and that ABDA base was growing warm. Tjilatjap on the south coast of Java offered the Allied naval forces in the area a not-too-secure haven. From there Admiral Hart dispatched Doorman with an enlarged Striking Force to Sumatran waters to intercept Jap invasion convoys bearing down on Palembang, the capital of Sumatra.

Assembled for this mission, the Allied Striking Force consisted of the Dutch light cruisers DE RUYTER, JAVA, and TROMP, British heavy cruiser EXETER, Australian light cruiser HOBART, four Dutch destroyers, and six of the DesRon 29 DD's. The six American destroyers were STEWART, BARKER, BULMER, J. D. EDWARDS, PILLSBURY, and PARROTT.

The ships fueled in Pigi Bay on the south coast of Java, and stood westward for Sumatra on February 13. It was not a lucky day.

The run to Sumatra proved costly. En route, the Dutch destroyer VAN GHENT piled up on a reef in Stoltze Strait during the night of February 14. Dutch destroyer BANCKERT was left behind to take off the stranded VAN GHENT's crew. One destroyer lost, and another out of the running.

The rest of the task force pushed on to the waters northeast of Bangka. There Doorman discovered that the enemy was already in Bangka Strait, off Palembang's foreshore.

In the morning of February 15 the Japs launched a series of bomber strikes at the ABDA force. Without air cover, the milling Allied ships were once more hopelessly exposed. For six hours the Jap bombers kept it up. They failed to sink any of the ABDA vessels, but near misses gave the old "four-pipers" BARKER and BULMER a severe jolting. Both destroyers were damaged to an extent that required emergency repair. Early that afternoon Doorman signalled for a retirement eastward.

As the ABDA Striking Force withdrew into the Java Sea, the whole Allied world was shaken by the fall of Singapore. Loss of this "impregnable" British base, the Gibraltar of the East, was a crushing defeat for Britain. And Singapore's capture by the Japanese collapsed the western flank of the Malay Barrier.

Meantime, the Americans on the Southwest Pacific front heard another stunner—Admiral Hart had been recalled to the United States. Dutch Admiral Conrad Helfrich replaced him as over-all commander of ABDAFLOAT.

On February 18 the Japs swept down from Celebes and took Bali airfield by storm. With the entire front crumbling, and the Japs closing in from east and west, the Allied commanders hardly knew where to turn. A few P-40's had been shipped to Java; they had melted away like confetti in a furnace. And ABDAFLOAT at this critical climax had lost the services of light cruiser MARBLEHEAD, a Dutch destroyer, and destroyers BARKER and BULMER. In company with the destroyer tender BLACK HAWK, the two bomb-shaken American DD's were slated to go to Exmouth Gulf, Australia, for an overhaul.

The two lamed old-timers and the tender left Tjilatjap for Exmouth Gulf on February 19. And on that dismal day, the destroyermen with ABDAFLOAT heard more bad news. The word came from Port Darwin—loss of the American destroyer PEARY.

Loss of U.S.S. Peary

Early in the morning of February 15, 1942, the U.S.S. HOUSTON and destroyer PEARY escorted a convoy out of Port Darwin, Australia. Destination: Timor, at the eastern end of the Netherlands East Indies.

The Japs at that date were advancing on this tropical island, occupation of which would put them less than 500 miles from Darwin. A Dutch-Portuguese possession, Timor was practically undefended by its colonial holders. To stiffen such defenses as there were, the Allied Command was sending two American field artillery regiments and several thousand Australian troops as reinforcement. U. S. Army transports MEIGS and MAUNA LOA carried the artillerymen. Two small transports, TULAGI and PORTMAR, shipped the "Aussies." Destroyer PEARY screened ahead of cruiser HOUSTON (Captain Rooks) as the convoy moved westward across the Timor Sea. Australian corvettes SWAN and WARREGO covered the convoy's flanks.

The ships were not long at sea before they were sighted by an enemy flying boat. As the convoy approached Timor the next morning, it was subjected to an all-out air attack.

The aircraft, some 36 land-based bombers and 10 seaplanes, came over in a roaring series of waves.

Putting up a monumental defense, HOUSTON raised an AA fire that swept the sky like a tornado. The Japs loosed cascades of bombs on the maneuvering ships. But none of the warships was hit. At least 23 bombs exploded in the water close aboard PORTMAR, but the little trooper got clear. Sole casualties: two men in transport MAUNA LOA, wounded by flying shrapnel.

Meanwhile ABDA Headquarters had received word that a strong Japanese Carrier Force was at that time somewhere in the Banda Sea or the Flores Sea. The onslaught on the Allied convoy verified this information. With Jap carrier aircraft in striking range, the convoy's situation was extremely hazardous, and the effort to reinforce Timor was too little and too late. Captain Rooks was ordered to return the convoy to Port Darwin.

The ships entered Darwin Harbor in the morning of February 18. The crews heaved sighs of relief. But as it eventuated, the convoy had retired into a trap.

Transports MEIGS and MAUNA LOA put their troops ashore at the dock. The TULAGI and the PORTMAR dropped anchor. The harbor was crowded; it was occupied by an Australian hospital ship, an "Aussie" trooper, a Norwegian tanker, an American freighter, a Brazilian merchantman, and several corvettes. In an elbow of the harbor the American seaplane tender WILLIAM B. PRESTON, a converted "four-piper," lay at anchor. HOUSTON and PEARY refuelled at once, and that same evening were away, ordered to join Admiral Doorman's ABDA Force in the Java Sea.

Outside Darwin that night destroyer PEARY picked up a submarine contact. Lieutenant Commander J. M. Bermingham and company conducted the usual vigorous search. The Jap submarine escaped. The long game of hide-and-seek diminished PEARY's fuel supply. She was ordered back to Darwin to "top off" (refuel), while cruiser HOUSTON was to proceed westward independently.

For HOUSTON it was a reprieve; for PEARY, an unpurposed death sentence. About 0930 in the morning of February 19, a great flock of Japanese bombers came droning over the horizon. Darwin had no radar warning. Warehouses, docks, the local airport—the town itself was practically blown to rubble. Nearly every ship in the harbor was destroyed. And sunk in the midst of the shambles was the U.S.S. PEARY.

The first attack wave—18 heavy bombers—concentrated on the docks. MEIGS and MAUNA LOA had moved out into the harbor, giving place to British ships NEPTUNA and ZEALANDIA, which were unloading ammunition. Struck by bombs, the two British vessels disintegrated in an earthquaking blast.

The Norwegian tanker was downed by a hit. A near-by vessel went under. A flight of ten American P-40's, returning from a mission, tried to disrupt the attack. One of the silver-skinned Jap bombers was shot down. A P-40 plunged down, flaming.

To knock out the air defenses, a second wave of 18 Jap bombers flew over the airport and gave it a blasting. Then they dropped incendiary bombs on the town.

After this overture a flight of dive-bombers arrived to assail the harbor shipping. By that time most of the vessels which could move were steaming for the harbor entrance in an effort to escape.

Army transport MAUNA LOA took two bombs down an open hatch, and sank with a rush. Struck by about 20 bombs and blasted by an aerial torpedo, Army transport MEIGS went down in 18 fathoms. The troopship TULAGI was severely damaged. Punctured by a near miss, the PORTMAR was beached. Hard hit, the Brazilian DON ISIDORO was gutted by fire after escaping from the harbor mouth. Answering the Brazilian's distress call, a coastal steamer was bombed and sunk. S.S. ADMIRAL HALSTEAD, American freighter loaded with high-octane gasoline, was sunk. Two Australian corvettes were blown to the bottom.

In the vortex of this cataclysm the ex-destroyer PRESTON and the destroyer PEARY fought their hearts out to beat back the enemy. At the start of the raid the two old "four-stackers" had headed for the harbor mouth, PRESTON in the lead.

The seaplane tender's skipper, Lieutenant Commander Etheridge Grant, had kept steam up for just such an emergency. With equal foresight he had obtained a number of .50- and .30-caliber machine-guns —relics from Patrol Wing Ten—and emplaced them on PRESTON's afterdeck. Precautionary steam and extra armament paid off. At 1010 four dive-bombers came hurtling down from the blue to attack PRESTON and PEARY. When two of the bombers struck at PRESTON they were raked by a sheet of AA fire that sent them kiting.

But the other two broke through the barrage. Three bombs hit the seaplane tender. Another burst close aboard. The ship was thrashed by flying iron; Lieutenant Commander Grant was blown overboard. The PRESTON, however, was not downed. She remained afloat and firing to the last—one of the few vessels to survive the blasting of Darwin.

Less fortunate was the U.S.S. PEARY. She was zigzagging as best she could in the cluttered harbor, and holding up her end of the anti-aircraft barrage, when the bombers dived. She was staggered by two savage hits. One blast wrecked her fantail, demolishing the depth charge racks, shearing off the propeller guards, and flooding the steering-engine room. The other bomb, an incendiary, crashed into the galley and left the ship in flames.

Lieutenant Commander Bermingham and his men fought battle damage and dive-bombers for the next three hours. The planes kept coming. Again and again the destroyer's AA gunners drove them off. She took another bomb hit, a blast that left her maimed and bleeding. A fourth bomb exploded the forward ammunition magazine. Mutilated and fire-blackened, dragging her wrecked fantail, she kept on going. Kept on until a fifth bomb, another incendiary, smashed through to the after engine room.

Even then she continued to fight. She was fighting at the last when, at 1300, she broke up and sank in a pall of smoke and fire. A witness reported that a .30-caliber and a .50-caliber machine-gun were blazing away as PEARY's shattered remains went under.

About 80 of the crew, and PEARY's captain, Lieutenant Commander Bermingham, went down with the ship. Only one officer, Lieutenant W. J. Catlett, Jr., survived. Lieutenant Catlett was the Engineer Officer.

The U.S.S. PEARY was the first Asiatic Fleet destroyer fatality of the war. She was the first United States destroyer in the Pacific to be lost after Pearl Harbor.

BATTLE OF THE JAVA SEA—US DESTROYER TORPEDO ATTACK

CHAPTER 9

ORDEAL OF DESRON 29

(RETREAT TO AUSTRALIA)

The Battle of Badoeng Strait

While Barker and Bulmer in company with Black Hawk limped for Exmouth Gulf, while Peary fought a battle to the death in Port Darwin, while the Japs marched into southern Sumatra and waded ashore at Bali, destroyers John D. Ford and Pope, heroic veterans of Balikpapan, steamed into action.

Available for duty with Admiral Doorman's Combined Striking Force, Ford and Pope were at Tjilatjap when word of the enemy's advance on Bali was first received. That was on February 17, 1942.

Unfortunately, Doorman's striking force was divided. He himself was at Tjilatjap on the south coast of Java with his flagship De Ruyter, Dutch cruiser Java, several Dutch DD's and Ford and Pope. The Dutch cruiser Tromp was at Soerabaja on the north coast of Java. Commander Binford's DesDiv 58—Stewart, Parrott, John D. Edwards, and Pillsbury— were at Ratai Bay, Sumatra. The British cruisers, like damaged Houston, were on convoy duty. The rest of the ABDA warships were widely scattered, some operating hither, others yon.

Doorman was unable to collect a force strong enough to prevent the Japs from landing on Bali. However, he determined to strike at the invasion shipping in the roadstead off the Bali beachheads. His plan called for a three-wave attack. In De Ruyter he would lead the ABDA warships out of Tjilatjap for a gunfire and torpedo attack on the enemy ships off Bali. De Ruyter and her group would then retire through Lombok Strait. That would be the first wave.

The second wave would come from Soerabaja—the light cruiser Tromp (Commander J. B. de Meester, R.N.N.) and American destroyers Stewart, Parrott, Edwards, and Pillsbury. This group would attack the Bali invasion ships about three hours after the initial strike.

As a mop-up wave, a small group of Dutch PT boats would then slough into the Japanese force, to finish off the residue. On paper, at least, this made a nice finale to a feasible-looking plan.

But American Admiral Glassford, serving as Commander U.S. Naval Forces Southwest Pacific, had his doubts. So did a number of American destroyer officers. An attack by successive echelons would be one of decreasing surprise. Also Doorman was counting heavily on gunfire. The old "four-pipers" were not too strong in that department, and night gun-actions were likely to be haphazard for ships without surface radar.

However, at 2200 in the evening of February 18 the De Ruyter group got under way. And at the very take-off, in the narrow harbor mouth of Tjilatjap, the Dutch destroyer Kortenaer ran aground. This left only the Dutch destroyer Piet Hien, and the Americans Ford and Pope, to screen the two Dutch cruisers.

The two old "four-pipers," under leadership of Lieutenant Commander E. N. Parker in Ford, were in turn led by the modern Piet Hien. As the ships headed eastward in the night, Ford and Pope moved out in front to form a Sound screen ahead of the cruisers.

The group approached the southeast coast of Bali at 2100 in the evening of February 19. In attack formation DE RUYTER led, with JAVA astern. Far astern of the cruisers PIET HIEN led the destroyer column.

About 2200 the group steamed northward into Badoeng Strait, the narrow waterway between Bali and Nusa Besar, a fragment of island lying in Lombok Strait. The enemy ships were in Badoeng Strait, hugging the Bali shore—one transport, the SASAGO MARU, and Japanese destroyers ASASHIO and OSHIO. The bulk of the Jap invasion convoy had already left Bali.

Not much of a catch, one MARU and two DD's. But snaring even the prizes proved unexpectedly difficult.

JAVA opened fire at 2225. The Japs answered with a searchlight sweep, star shell, and gunnery. In the first exchange of shots, JAVA was hit on the stern, but only slightly damaged.

Next, destroyer PIET HIEN, coming within range, opened fire with her guns and unleashed a torpedo. Then, swerving on a sudden zigzag to starboard, she laid down a screen of smoke. This move baffled the American destroyers, trying to follow PIET HIEN's maneuvers. Upping their speed to 28 knots, FORD and POPE ploughed through the smoke and fell in 1,000 yards astern of the Dutch DD. She then led the column on a sharp veer to port. As FORD executed this tight turn, her lookouts spotted the Jap transport steaming northwestward and a Jap warship heading northeast.

The warship was I.J.N.S. OSHIO, her guns smoking from the exchange of shots with Dutch cruiser JAVA. As PIET HIEN and the two Americans raced on a westward loop, they opened fire on the Jap silhouettes. Shells struck the Jap transport. The Jap DD evaded. Both FORD and POPE flung torpedoes at the transport, and a burst of orange fire suggested a hit.

But the transport was not fatally hurt. And a moment later PIET HIEN was engulfed in a volcanic burst of flames. Either struck by a deadly gun-salvo or a torpedo from the Jap destroyer ASASHIO, the Dutch destroyer was left dead in the water, sinking.

FORD and POPE now were plunged into a raging gun battle with ASASHIO and OSHIO. The Dutch cruisers, according to plan, had steamed on northward out of Badoeng Strait, but the American destroyers found it impossible to follow. Trading hammer-and-tongs gunnery with ASASHIO, hard-pressed FORD (Lieutenant Commander J. E. Cooper), was driven southward. POPE (Lieutenant Commander W. C. Blinn) trailed FORD. The OSHIO bore down with blazing guns, and for about six minutes the seascape was livid with shellfire.

Division Commander Parker headed the two old "four-stackers" over toward Nusa Besar island. The American DD's were out of portside torpedoes, and Parker wanted to bring the starboard torpedoes into action. As FORD and POPE swung across Badoeng Strait, they crossed OSHIO's bow, and the Jap destroyer hurled a stream of shells at the American ships. While FORD laid a wall of smoke to cover her, POPE replied to OSHIO's fire with five starboard torpedoes. The entire spread missed. Were they "deep-runners," or dumb-headed duds?

It was time to disengage, and at 2310 the American destroyers were hightailing southward in column, POPE in the lead—as Navy men phrase it, "getting the hell out of there." Behind them, the Japs were still firing furiously. As it happened, ASASHIO had come up unexpectedly—perhaps through a drift of FORD's smoke—and OSHIO took her for another enemy. The two Jap DD's were shooting savagely at each other as the two American hauled south out of Badoeng Strait and struck westward for Tjilatjap.

That ended the first wave of the ABDA Striking Force attack at Bali. Not at all a successful venture. The three Jap ships had suffered some damage, but the damage was insignificant compared to the cost of delivery—the sinking of Dutch destroyer PIET HIEN.

Lack of communication between PIET HIEN and the American destroyers she was leading probably contributed to her destruction. And it would seem that the Dutch light cruisers were too far afield. DE RUYTER, for instance, did not fire a single shot during the engagement. The destroyers bore the brunt of the foray, and probably FORD and POPE were fortunate to get off as they did, without casualties. FORD's battle damage was negligible. POPE was unscathed.

And now the hour had arrived for the second Striking Force wave to wash through Badoeng Strait. Light cruiser TROMP and American destroyers STEWART (Lieutenant Commander H. P. Smith) flagship of Commander T. H. Binford, ComDesDiv 58, PARROTT (Lieutenant J. N. Hughes), EDWARDS (Commander H. E. Eccles), and PILLSBURY (Lieutenant Commander H. C. Pound) were on the way.

Binford's four destroyers had made a fast run along the coast of southern Java to join TROMP at the appointed rendezvous. Dutch Commander de Meester in TROMP headed the group for Bali on schedule. Binford attempted to communicate with FORD and POPE by radio. But STEWART's operator was unable to obtain an answer, and Binford could not find out how the first wave fared.

About midnight off Bali, the Dutch group commander in TROMP formed the attack column. STEW-

ART was placed in the lead. The other "four-pipers" trailed Binford's flagship, and TROMP brought up the rear. The DD's were to open with a torpedo attack; the Dutch cruiser was to follow through with heavy gunfire.

Steaming at 25 knots, the column entered Badoeng Strait at 0135 in the morning of February 20. The Bali shoreline was misty, and the Jap ships, twinkling signals at each other, appeared as wraithlike silhouettes in the haze. Out in the clear, under radiant stars, the little ABDA force was exposed. To hit fast and first, Binford ordered an immediate torpedo barrage.

Time: 0136. Both STEWART and PARROTT let go with spreads of six torpedoes. PILLSBURY fired three. Launched from portside tubes, the torpedoes streaked across the water. The destroyermen ticked off the seconds, listening for detonations. Nothing. All fifteen missed.

The enemy, warned, wheeled to do battle.

Charging to meet the oncoming Americans, the two Jap destroyers, ASASHIO and OSHIO, rushed at STEWART's port beam. Glimpsing enemy bows, STEWART flashed on a searchlight, fired torpedoes, and hurled shellfire at 0143. Behind her, EDWARDS tried a torpedo salvo. Two torpedoes leapt away, and missed. Two others jammed in the tubes.

The Japs replied with furious gunnery, promptly straddling Binford's old "four-pipers." At 0146 STEWART got it from a ricochetting projectile—one man killed; Executive Officer Lieutenant C. B. Smiley agonizingly wounded. Then a shell smashed into her steering-engine room, flooding the steering machinery.

STEWART kept on shooting, and kept on going. Afterwards her skipper reported,

I WISH TO COMMEND LIEUTENANT C. B. SMILEY WHO KEPT THE CONN THOUGH PAINFULLY WOUNDED AND BLEEDING BADLY, AND DENIED INJURY. . . . WHEN I DISCOVERED HIS CONDITION AND HAD HIM TAKEN BELOW HE REQUESTED TO REMAIN ON THE BRIDGE. LATER HE SENT MESSAGES . . . REQUESTING TO RETURN TO THE BRIDGE TO HELP, SINCE HIS LEG HAD BEEN BANDAGED.

After she was hit, Binford swung STEWART to starboard, leading the column northeastward. On the turn PARROTT and PILLSBURY came within paint-width of colliding. The close shave threw PILLSBURY out of the column. But all four "four-pipers" continued to race northeastward up Badoeng Strait. And now TROMP joined the gun battle. The Jap destroyers had rounded on de Meester's cruiser, and the Dutchman answered their fire by hitting OSHIO with a shell that killed about seven of her bridge personnel. TROMP sustained some ten hits in return, and was sorely hurt.

After the exchange with the Dutch light cruiser, OSHIO and ASASHIO lost contact. But the battle was not yet over. As the ABDA group steamed northward toward the Lombok Strait exit, two more Jap destroyers were heard from.

The newcomers were units of Admiral Kubo's Bali Force which had previously entered the area to support the Bali invasion. Dispatched to Badoeng Strait by Kubo when he received word of Doorman's attack, these DD's—I.J.N. ARASHIO and I.J.N. MICHISHIO—made a fast dash southward to the scene of action. Wherewith they came butting into Badoeng Strait just as Binford's destroyers and TROMP were retiring.

At the northern entrance of Badoeng Strait the opposing ships practically met head-on. Time: 0219. ARASHIO and MICHISHIO fired pointblank at STEWART and EDWARDS. Ensued a lightning exchange of shells, oaths, more shells, torpedoes. Then PILLSBURY, out of column and racing up on the enemy's port hand, struck MICHISHIO with a staggering main-battery salvo. As the Jap destroyer veered from the shock, EDWARDS caught her from starboard with a solid shell-hit. Finally TROMP struck her in passing. MICHISHIO sloughed to a halt, 96 of her crew dead, dying, or wounded.

The four American destroyers and TROMP sprinted on out into Lombok Strait. PARROTT's sprint was rudely interrupted when her steering control jammed with her rudder swinging her left. The ship was steaming at 28 knots toward a nest of rocks, and Lieutenant Hughes and crew did some sweating as the engines were ordered full speed astern.

Luckily Kubo was too far distant to intercept. And Chance again took an amazing hand in the proceedings. Earlier that evening FORD had jettisoned a motor-whaleboat, and into that castaway craft crawled 33 survivors of the Dutch destroyer PIET HIEN. Then PARROTT jettisoned a drum of gasoline. The Dutch survivors picked that up, too, and motor-boated safely back to Java!

But those incidents were not all. Overboard from U.S.S. PARROTT fell Raymond E. Padgett, Chief Water Tender. Having fallen overside and been swept beyond help's reach, he proceeded to swim for shore. Perhaps inspired by the propeller insignia on his sleeve, he made it. And on Bali beach he encountered a party of Dutch soldiers. In their good company, the C.P.O. made his way to Java in time to rejoin his ship at Soerabaja.

"Chief Padgett reporting on board, sir."

"Man, are *you* lucky!"

Perhaps all survivors of Doorman's Badoeng Strait raiding force were blessed with luck. The three-wave strike plan had been a shaky one to begin with. Following through at the end, the third wave (five Dutch PT-boats) claimed they saw no sign of the enemy.

But although the ABDA ships had dealt damage to destroyers OSHIO and ASASHIO, and had given MICHISHIO a fiery thrashing, they made no dent in the Bali invasion. And the raid was a costly one for ABDAFLOAT—PIET HIEN sunk, TROMP badly damaged, and the old "four-piper" STEWART disabled. And after Badoeng Strait the ABDA naval forces sailed into desperate seas of misfortune.

Loss of U.S.S. Stewart (and a Remarkable Resurrection)

This is the story of a warship's loss, and her aparitional reappearance—a story with a singular denouement.

It happened in waters accustomed to the fabulous and the phenomenal. Although the Cape of Good Hope is usually considered the cruising ground of the "Flying Dutchman," in the waters below Borneo and Celebes mariners may see weird things on nights when the moon is shining, or in twilights cobwebbed with fog. But even in that area no one expected to see the apparition of a United States destroyer, her silhouette ghostly but unmistakable. Such phantasmal sailings by a DD were entirely unlikely, though the vessel were an ancient "four-piper."

However—

With her steering gear disabled by a 5-inch shell-hit, the U.S.S. STEWART steamed out of the Battle of Badoeng Strait, and headed for Soerabaja. The veteran "four-stacker," flagship of Destroyer Division 58 was not in bad shape. There was damage topside, but nothing serious. She was, however, badly in need of routine repairs. This meant drydock in Soerabaja—if she could make Soerabaja, and if a drydock was still in existence when she got there.

STEWART's captain, Lieutenant Commander Harold P. Smith, and every member of her crew worked beyond the limit of exhaustion to take the ship safely into port. With her were destroyers EDWARDS, PILLSBURY, and PARROTT, and the battered Dutch light cruiser TROMP. And the little ABDA force made Soerabaja. And a drydock was to be had. Only the one made available—a 15,000-ton-lift floating drydock owned by a private shipyard—seemed luck too good to be true.

It was. Everything in Soerabaja was at sixes and sevens at the time. At the shipyards, both Dutch and native workmen refused to work on Sunday. Moreover, spare parts, tools, all sorts of necessary equipment, could not be begged or borrowed. And finally the dockers and yardhands were panicked by the constant enemy air-raids.

Under such conditions workmanship was sloppy and slipshod. When placed in drydock STEWART was not properly positioned on the keel blocks. Nor was she correctly shored up. As the dock began to lift, the destroyer keeled over on her port side, like a beached whale.

Before the destroyer could be righted and floated, Japanese aircraft struck Soerabaja a devastating smash, and the prostrate STEWART was hit by a bomb. That settled it. There was no chance of repairing the thrice-damaged ship. Soerabaja was fast becoming untenable. On February 24 the air raiders sank the Dutch destroyer BANCKERT in the harbor. A Dutch submarine was sunk at her Soerabaja moorings. Docks, shipyards, repair shops, and warehouses were crumbling. One after another the ABDA ships were ordered to leave. By March 1, 1942, the evacuation was almost complete. Of the American warships which had been at Soerabaja, only helpless STEWART remained.

To prevent her capture by the invading Japanese, demolition crews rigged their high explosives in the vessel. These were set off on March 2. So it was reported that the U.S.S. STEWART met her end at Soerabaja on March 2, 1942. The Navy was satisfied that STEWART would never be seen at sea again.

The enemy swarmed over the Malay Barrier and stormed down into the Solomons. The war swirled around Midway, and spread to the Aleutians. Guadalcanal, Tarawa, New Guinea, Eniwetok—the United States and Allied forces started the long, hard drive for Manila and Tokyo. And then one fine day some American airmen were surprised to see an American warship steaming deep within the heart of the Greater East Asia Co-Prosperity Sphere.

The aviators had only a glimpse. The ship was a "three-stacker" with a tripod foremast—Japanese features. Especially the tripod, and the forward stack of the "raked" type, shaped like a shoe. But that plumb bow, flush deck, and those two after stacks—

"Look again, fly boy! That ship was made in America!"

The first aviators to see her looked again. And other aviators saw her, and looked twice. She was an American by all that was holy in the silhouette book!

She was seen here. And she was seen there. She

was seen hull down, and she was seen coming over the horizon. And always she was seen behind the Japanese lines, cruising inside their territory.

And so the legend grew. A spectral yet corporeal American destroyer, a sort of living apparition, was operating behind the enemy's lines. No one knew her name and number; no one could say how she came where she was.

"But she's there," the airmen would swear. "I tell you, we've seen her."

Somehow she was never torpedoed. Not even when United States submarines were downing everything from aircraft carriers to sampans. Somehow she was never blasted and sunk. Not even at the last when United States and Allied forces were closing in on Japan, and crushing Japanese harbors and naval shipping under avalanches of shells and bombs.

So there was something uncanny about this man-of-war. She was found on October 15, 1945, by the American occupation forces in Japan. She was located in a residual huddle of Japanese shipping in the Kure-Hiroshima Area, the very heart of the enemy homeland. Then it was that she was identified as the former U.S.S. STEWART, the old "four-piper" lost in March, 1942, at Soerabaja.

It would seem the demolition party detailed to destroy the STEWART on that date had failed in the mission. Or perhaps the old destroyer was just plain indestructible. At any rate she had been salvaged and resuscitated by the invading Japanese, who gave her a "raked" stack and tripod mast, and sent her to sea as PATROL VESSEL 102.

On October 28, 1945, the ex-STEWART was taken over by a United States Navy prize crew at Hiro Wan. The following day she was placed in commission by Vice Admiral J. B. Oldendorf, the Commander of the Southwestern Japan Force. Her "Enoch Arden" return—one of the few in United States naval history—had left her without a name. As the U.S.S. STEWART (DD 224) she had been stricken from the Navy Register on March 25, 1942. Her name had been assigned to a destroyer-escort (DE 238). So the original STEWART was left with only her official number. She was thus officially designated at Hiro Wan—as (DD 224). On November 3, 1945, she was ordered to the United States.

But the destroyermen had a name for the vessel. They called her "RAMP," for "Recovered Allied Military Personnel."

Jacks Versus Juggernaut

February 20, 1942. In the west the Japs held Malaya and Sumatra. In the center they clutched Borneo. In the east they were in possession of Celebes and Bali, and their vanguards were in the distant Bismarck Archipelago. It was on this February 20 that British Field Marshall Wavell, in over-all command of the ABDA forces, decided that the Netherlands East Indies could not be held.

The Dutch violently protested; they were determined on a last-ditch stand. Admiral Glassford, in charge of American naval forces, took his orders from the United States. He was directed to stand with the Dutch.

Thus far the Japanese naval forces storming the Malay Barrier had lost no more than a couple of destroyers and some expendable transports. The Allies had lost the great naval base of Singapore and the port of Palembang. They had lost oil bases in Borneo and Celebes. Port Darwin, Australia, was wiped out. As for ships, they had lost the services of American light cruisers BOISE and MARBLEHEAD; four Dutch destroyers had been lost, and the American destroyer PEARY was sunk. Also out of the campaign were American destroyers BARKER, BULMER, STEWART, PILLSBURY, and PARROTT—the last two sorely in need of overhaul after the Badoeng Strait raid. And POPE, having sprung feed-water leaks in the Badoeng foray, was now tied up in Soerabaja, awaiting repairs.

Two other DesRon 29 "four-pipers" were hurt at this critical time. EDSALL, making a submarine attack, was damaged by one of her own depth charges which exploded close aboard her stern. WHIPPLE was lamed by a collision with Dutch cruiser DE RUYTER. Both injured destroyers continued to operate off the south coast of Java, but neither was in condition to enter action with the ABDA Striking Force.

Heavy cruisers U.S.S. HOUSTON and H.M.S. EXETER (HOUSTON with a dead after turret), two Dutch and an Australian light cruiser, three British destroyers, three Dutch destroyers, and American destroyers EDWARDS, PAUL JONES, ALDEN, and FORD—these were the only ABDA combat ships available for battle against the Japanese Juggernaut that was approaching Java.

That Juggernaut, now designated the Japanese Southern Striking Force, contained battleships KONGO, HIEI, HARUNA, and KIRISHIMA. It contained aircraft carriers AKAGI, KAGA, SORYU, HIRYU, and RYUJO. It contained eight heavy cruisers, five light cruisers, some 42 destroyers, a seaplane carrier, and a seaplane tender.

On February 25 Dutch Admiral Helfrich assumed over-all command of ABDA's embattled forces. And on February 26 some of the American destroyermen heard that help was coming. Coming were the American aircraft tender LANGLEY, carrying 32 fighter planes with American Air Force crews, and the British freighter SEAWITCH with 27 fighter planes and crews.

Destroyers EDSALL and WHIPPLE steamed out of Tjilatjap on the morning of February 27 to escort "Old Covered Wagon" LANGLEY in. They picked her up some 100 miles offshore at about 0730.

At 0900 the aircraft tender was spotted by a Jap scouting plane. About noon a flight of nine Jap dive-bombers struck at the ship. EDSALL and WHIPPLE could not fend off the attack. LANGLEY turned, twisted, and raised a tempestuous AA fire. But she could not evade five bombs which smashed into her deck, shattered a number of the P-40's she was carrying, and left her listing and afire.

A stiff breeze whipped the flags of flame into roaring billows. By 1300 the ship was an inferno. An order to lower boats was misunderstood, and many of the crew prematurely abandoned, leaping into the sea. At 1332 LANGLEY's captain, Commander R. P. McConnell, gave the order to abandon.

Destroyers WHIPPLE and EDSALL closed in on the rescue. Together they picked up all but 16 of LANGLEY's crew and Air Force passengers. The destroyers then sank the burning hull with gunnery and torpedo-fire.

As the "Old Covered Wagon" went down, so did the last hope of providing the ABDA ships with even a little air cover. The SEAWITCH, far astern of LANGLEY, escaped attack, and made Tjilatjap in the morning of February 28. But her help was too little and too late. By that hour the ABDA Striking Force was fighting the fatal Battle of the Java Sea.

The Battle of the Java Sea

Admiral Kondo's Southern Striking Force closed in on Java for the kill.

"Poor American boys," commiserated Tokyo Rose. "Your ships are swiftly being sunk. You haven't a chance. Why die to defend foreign soil which never belonged to the Dutch or British in the first place? Go home, before the slackers steal your wives and girls."

The propaganda broadcasts by the siren in Tokyo were about the one source of amusement left to the destroyermen of DesRon 29. The outlook on February 27, 1942, was dead black. The men who manned the old "four-pipers" were dog-tired, and their ships were tired. Where were those air reinforcements? Where were the reserves? The strain of weeks of campaigning without a letup was beginning to tell in haggard features and tight nerves.

For the past two days Doorman's ABDA Striking Force had been making sweeps in the Java Sea in the vicinity of Bawean Island, scouting in search of the enemy's vanguard.

Doorman's force at this date consisted of flagship DE RUYTER, heavy cruisers HOUSTON and EXETER, light cruisers JAVA and PERTH, Dutch destroyers WITTE DE WITH and KORTENAER, British destroyers JUPITER, ELECTRA, and ENCOUNTER, and the American "four-pipers" EDWARDS, ALDEN, FORD, and PAUL JONES. To refuel the destroyers and give the exhausted officers and men a few hours in port, Admiral Doorman led his ABDA ships into Soerabaja on the afternoon of February 27.

But there was to be no rest for the weary. The ships were hardly through the minefield in the outer entrance to the harbor before Doorman received from Admiral Helfrich orders to attack a large Japanese naval force detected off Bawean Island about 100 miles north of Soerabaja. With no time to devise an attack plan, Doorman turned his ships "about face" with the message, *"Am proceeding to intercept enemy unit. Follow me."*

Thanks to differences in code, Doorman's tactical signals had to be translated into American and British before U.S.S. HOUSTON, H.M.S. EXETER, H.M.A.S. PERTH, and the American and British destroyers knew the score. American translating was done by a liaison officer in DE RUYTER. The messages were then relayed to HOUSTON, and HOUSTON passed them on over TBS. This awkward relay fouled, with the result that Commander Binford, ComDesDiv 58, was unsure of orders, and the American destroyers finally operated in a fog of confusion.

For another hitch in the operation, the quick turnabout in Soerabaja channel cost the Striking Force a destroyer reinforcement. Her leaky feed-water system repaired, the U.S.S. POPE had been waiting to join up in the harbor. But she was unable to overtake Doorman's column as it sortied, and so she was left behind.

Almost as soon as Doorman's force was away from Soerabaja, the Allied ships came under air attack. At 1600 Doorman radioed an urgent appeal for fighter cover. He was crying into an empty barrel. At Soerabaja there were no more than eight land-based fighter planes, and the Dutch Air Commander was holding them for shore defense.

Running northwestward in the Java Sea, Doorman's column shook off the first aerial onslaught. Then it encountered the large Japanese naval force which was covering an invasion convoy. The show-down battle was on.

The Jap warships sighted were those of Rear Admiral Takagi's Eastern Covering Group: heavy cruisers NACHI and HAGURO, light cruiser JINTSU

Stewart rose from her own "ashes." This destroyer survived the Badoeng Strait action and was placed in Soerabaja drydock. After she rolled off her blocks and was bombed by the enemy, her crew attempted demolition. Our Navy considered her lost. Repaired and activated by the Japanese, the Stewart became a ghost off the enemy coast until redeemed by our forces in 1945.

Japanese air power smashed Soerabaja installations and warships. Initial enemy strategy in the East Indies integrated air, sea, and land strength. Here the Japanese did not repeat their Pearl Harbor failure to strike at naval shore facilities. Japanese pressure against Java combined superior surface fleets, amphibious forces, and air groups against the Allies, wherever found.

Burning dockside wreckage. Here at Soerabaja two Allied destroyers were blown up, and one was captured. Fighting every inch of the way in early 1942, the ABDA fleet eventually was knocked out. Isolated in an advanced area of enemy encirclement, the Allied Far Eastern forces either were sunk or forced to retreat. Four years later the tables were turned by our sea power.

The Parrott's time had not yet come. This destroyer, shown here fueling from the fast fleet oiler Merrimac, was one of the few Allied warships to return home after the fighting retreat from the Far East in 1942. A superior Japanese fleet hadn't been able to destroy this vessel; yet, rammed by a merchant ship off Norfolk in 1944, the Parrott was sunk. Collisions increase war's costs.

(Rear Admiral Tanaka), and seven destroyers. This group, glimpsed to the northwest, was supported by a second which came over the horizon due north—Rear Admiral Nishimura's Eastern Attack Group, containing light cruiser NAKA and seven destroyers.

Totaling two heavy cruisers, two light cruisers, and 14 DD's, the enemy force was almost matched in size and weight by Doorman's Striking Force. But the ABDA ships lacked air cover. Moreover, they were without spotting planes; contemplating a night action on the 26th, Doorman had unshipped the several cruiser-carried planes, and left them ashore. NACHI and HAGURO used seaplane spotters during the ensuing action.

Steaming northwestward, the Jap ships were crossing the ABDA formation's bows when contact was made. Doorman had his cruisers in column, flagship DE RUYTER followed by EXETER, HOUSTON, PERTH, and JAVA. Ahead of the column screened the three British destroyers. Destroyers JUPITER and ENCOUNTER were on either side of ELECTRA. The two Dutch destroyers and four American were on the port side and to the rear of the cruiser column—a disposition which was to prove highly disadvantageous. For Doorman swung the formation to westward soon after the enemy was sighted. The Japs also bore to the west, roughly paralleling the Allied course. The Dutch DD's and the American destroyers were thus left on the disengaged side of the ABDA formation, a decidedly unfavorable position from which to launch a torpedo attack.

Moreover, Doorman had ordered a flank speed of 26 knots, as he was striving to close the range to bring his cruisers' 6-inch batteries into action. Dutch destroyer KORTENAER, panting with boiler trouble, could make no better than 24 knots. The American destroyers had been instructed not to pass the Dutch DD's in their lead, and so the whole destroyer column was slowed.

At 1616 Takagi's heavy cruisers opened fire at extreme range (about 28,000 yards), hurling salvos at U.S.S. HOUSTON and H.M.S. EXETER. The Allied heavies replied a moment later.

Then light cruiser JINTSU joined the fray, closing to 18,000 yards to fire at the British van destroyers. With three spotting planes in the air, the Jap fire was hot and accurate. Six- and eight-inch splashes doused the ABDA cruisers. At 1631 Doorman's flagship was pierced by an 8-inch dud which smashed into her auxiliary engine-room.

The Japs had been racing at top speed, evidently bent on crossing Doorman's T. In an effort to avoid that tactical trump, Doorman swung his formation more to the west. For a few minutes the opposing forces steamed on courses almost parallel, firing as they ran.

By this time the American destroyers, baffled by confused orders, had put on enough speed to bring them abreast of flagship DE RUYTER. They were still on the disengaged side of the ABDA formation, too far away to launch torpedoes or fire at the Jap ships. And as the old "four-pipers" pulled like Roman chariots to maintain this assigned position, they raced in column in the following order: JOHN D. EDWARDS (Commander H. E. Eccles) flying the pennant of Commander T. H. Binford, ComDesDiv 58; ALDEN (Lieutenant Commander L. E. Coley); JOHN D. FORD (Lieutenant Commander J. E. Cooper) flying the pennant of Lieutenant Commander E. N. Parker, ComDesDiv 59; and PAUL JONES (Lieutenant Commander J. J. Hourihan).

At 1632 the Japs unleashed a torpedo attack on the ABDA cruisers. The first salvo was fired by light cruiser NAKA which had rushed down from the north to join the battle; NACHI, JINTSU, and HAGURO also fired torpedo spreads—all at extreme range, and all without effect.

Completing their torpedo attacks, the Jap destroyers laid dense smoke screens to shield the Jap heavy cruisers. They closed the range, and launched more torpedoes. No hits. But at 1708 an 8-inch shell struck British heavy cruiser EXETER, and burst in a powder chamber. The savage explosion staggered the ship, and as she slowed abruptly, the cruisers behind her swerved off course in confusion. A few minutes later the Dutch destroyer KORTENAER, not far from the EDWARDS, was torpedoed.

"There was a heavy whitish explosion flinging debris 100 feet in the air," the captain of EDWARDS noted in this action report. "KORTENAER *heeled away over and yawed. . . . She poised momentarily and then turned turtle and folded up like a jackknife. . . . Men were blown high in the air. . . . No survivors could be seen in the water."*

With Japanese armor-piercing shells and super-powerful torpedoes on target, and the Allied formation broken, the ABDA force was in desperate trouble. Doorman swung his flagship in a wide arc, striving to realign his disordered formation. An order was transmitted to the British DD's, directing them to cover injured EXETER, and counterattack. Leading an attack on Jap cruiser JINTSU, the British destroyer ELECTRA was fatally struck by a blizzard of shells. Battered and burning, ELECTRA settled in a shroud of steam and smoke.

Now, at twilight, the whole seascape was fogged with the smoke of explosions, shellfire, and conflagration. The surface was littered with debris and

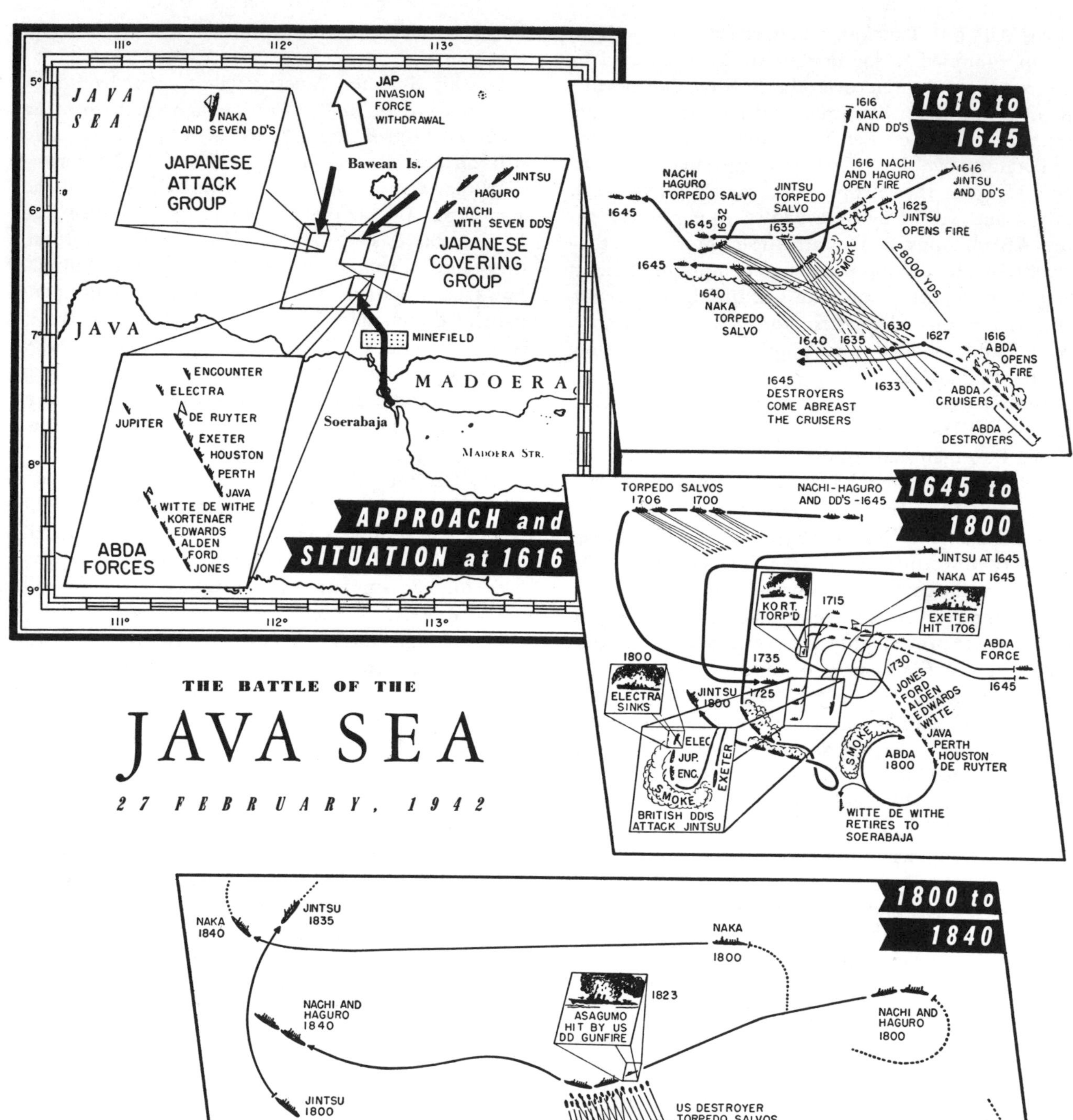

THE BATTLE OF THE

JAVA SEA

27 FEBRUARY, 1942

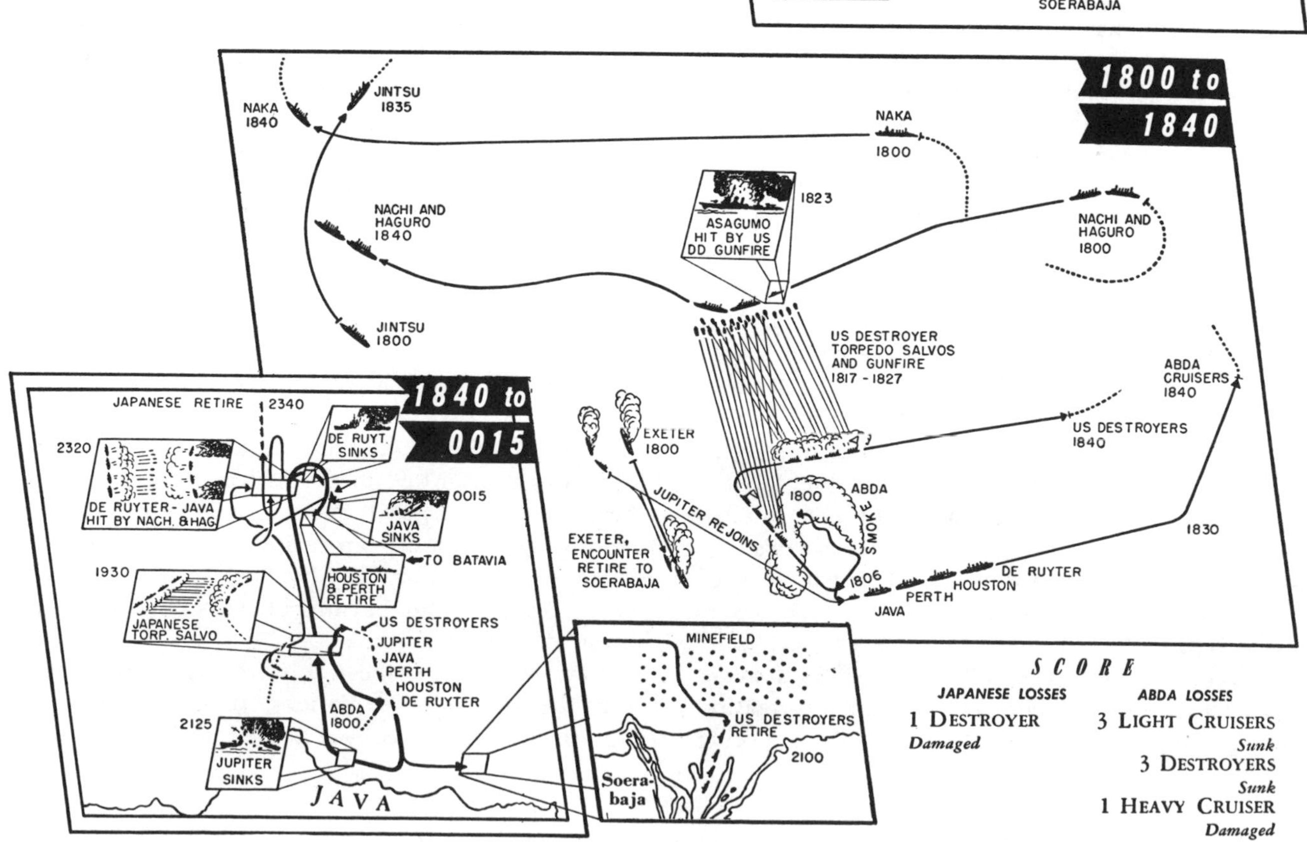

SCORE

JAPANESE LOSSES	ABDA LOSSES
1 Destroyer *Damaged*	3 Light Cruisers *Sunk*
	3 Destroyers *Sunk*
	1 Heavy Cruiser *Damaged*

streaked with oil. Intermittently the wakes of torpedo spreads came tracking through the water. The Allied destroyermen thought Jap submarines had entered the battle—another antagonist to worry about.

Two ships down, and as yet no visible damage to the enemy. Doorman finally jockeyed his cruisers into ragged formation, and swung them southward to escape torpedo broadsides and sharpshooting gunnery. Then, at 1806, he ordered the American destroyers to counterattack. DE RUYTER's radio had gone bad, and HOUSTON's TBS was out of kilter, so the order was flashed by blinker.

At once Division Commander Binford turned EDWARDS, ALDEN, FORD, and PAUL JONES northward to carry out the attack. As the destroyers were wheeling to face the foe, Doorman flashed a countermanding order:

CANCEL COUNTERATTACK

The American destroyers were now (at last) positioned between the ABDA cruisers and the enemy. Commander Binford wondered if he were reading Doorman's signals aright. Came a third message:

COVER MY RETIREMENT

One American method for covering a retirement was a sharp counterattack. With no time for crossword puzzles, Commander Binford ordered a strike at the oncoming enemy. Plunging northward through the smoke they had been laying, the American destroyers sighted Jap ships about 22,000 yards off to starboard.

Binford called for torpedoes—starboard salvos to be fired at 10,000-yard range. This was a long-range fire, but if he sent the old "four-pipers" any closer to the Jap cruisers, the Japs would massacre them.

Excerpt from Action Report of U.S.S. ALDEN:

Although it was the first time under fire for all but five men in the crew, the morale was excellent. At the time of receiving the signal to attack with torpedoes, although every one on board knew we were straining every rivet to maintain our position with the cruisers at 28 knots, one man on the bridge was heard to remark, "I always knew these old four-pipers would have to go in and save the day!" This remark called forth a laugh from all hands.

After the firing of starboard salvos, Binford ordered reverse course, and EDWARDS, ALDEN, FORD, and PAUL JONES fired portside torpedoes. All torpedoes missed, and the brave attack was a total fizzle.

But the destroyers did something with their old 4-inch guns. The Jap destroyer ASAGUMO got a shell through her hull above the water line, and stopped dead with paralyzed engines. ALDEN's captain, Lieutenant Commander Coley, thought he saw a hit on one Jap warship's superstructure.

With torpedoes expended, Binford turned the American destroyers southward. At 1831 he caught a blinker message from Admiral Doorman:

FOLLOW ME

Binford stepped up speed to keep on the trail of the ABDA cruisers. The dusk was blackening, and the big guns had gone silent.

Excerpt from U.S.S. EDWARDS' Action Report:

Darkness set in and we followed the main body, endeavoring to regain station, and having not the slightest idea as to Admiral Doorman's plans and still only a vague idea of what the enemy was doing.

Doorman was trying to locate and intercept the convoy. Without scouting planes (and, of course, without radar) he was groping blindfolded, and his movements baffled the Japs as well as Commander Binford.

The Japanese bafflement was to the good, but the American destroyers were hard put to follow the leader. Slowed by leaky condensers, fouled bottoms, and general disrepair, the war-weary "four-stackers" had to work like Trojans to make 29 knots and keep pace. The best the American DD's could do was hang on to the rear of the cruiser column.

For about an hour the ABDA force ran northward through the night. At 1930 enemy aircraft swooped overhead to drop parachute flares over the Allied cruisers. DE RUYTER's lookouts sighted Jap ships to port. Cruisers HOUSTON and PERTH opened fire, and the Japs answered with torpedo salvos.

Doorman swung his ships eastward and doubled back on a run south. The ABDA formation was trailed by enemy float planes which dropped more flares. By 2100 the Allied cruiser column was nearing shoal water just off the Java coast at a point about 50 miles west of Soerabaja. At this point Doorman made a sharp turn to the west. Out of torpedoes, low on fuel, and on the verge of engine breakdown, the American destroyer division dropped out of the race, and headed eastward for Soerabaja. As Binford reported it:

"Realizing that I had no more torpedoes and that further contact with the enemy would be useless, since my speed and gunpower were less than anything I would encounter. . . . I retired to Soerabaja."

A Jap plane trailed the exhausted "four-pipers," and dropped a flare on them as they maneuvered through the Soerabaja minefield. Silhouetted by this fiery chrysanthemum, the old grayhounds panted into the harbor.

Before the ABDA Striking Force went into action, Binford had been instructed to retire when all torpedoes were expended. Now, in Soerabaja channel, he received orders to proceed to Batavia, Java, for fresh torpedoes. He replied that it was necessary to replenish fuel at Soerabaja. But he was never to receive another directive from Admiral Doorman.

Steaming on westward, Doorman led the diminished ABDA force into wholesale disaster. At 2125 the British destroyer JUPITER was ripped apart by a tremendous blast. Apparently she was sunk by a friendly mine.

Then, heading northward, the ABDA cruisers ran headlong into Jap cruisers NACHI and HAGURO. In bright moonlight both sides opened fire. Then the Japs launched torpedoes. Both DE RUYTER and JAVA were fatally blasted. By midnight it was all over. Doorman ordered cruisers HOUSTON and PERTH to retire to Batavia. Battered cruiser EXETER and destroyer ENCOUNTER made their way to Soerabaja. The Battle of the Java Sea was finished. And so was the Allied effort to hold the Netherlands East Indies.

Aside from opening the path for a Japanese invasion of Java, the Battle of the Java Sea was a ghastly defeat for the Allies. The ABDA force had lost light cruiser DE RUYTER, light cruiser JAVA, Dutch destroyer KORTENAER, and British destroyers ELECTRA and JUPITER. British heavy cruiser EXETER had been disabled. In counter for this mayhem, the Allied ships had scored only one solid hit on the enemy—a hole punctured in the Japanese destroyer ASAGUMO.

If any morsel of satisfaction could be dredged from the battle's Slough of Despond, it was the fact that one of Binford's old "four-pipers" fired the only damaging shot.

In retiring to Soerabaja, EDWARDS, ALDEN, FORD, and PAUL JONES escaped a gruesome aftermath. Able to fuel, they were promptly dispatched by Admiral Glassford to Australia. As will be seen, they were more fortunate than their squadron mate POPE, ordered to proceed at a later date. By the time she left Soerabaja (evening of February 28) the Java Sea had become a molten crucible.

Cruisers U.S.S. HOUSTON and H.M.A.S. PERTH were caught by the enemy on the last night of February while attempting to escape the crucible through Soenda Strait between Java and Sumatra. Fighting to the last gun, both cruisers were hammered to the bottom.

HOUSTON's destruction was not the only heartbreaking sequel to the Java Sea defeat. Elsewhere the battered old-timers of DesRon 29 were overwhelmed by the conquering enemy.

Loss of U.S.S. Edsall

As has been related, the aircraft tender LANGLEY was sunk during the afternoon of February 27, 1942, and her survivors picked up by escorting destroyers WHIPPLE (Lieutenant Commander E. S. Karpe) and EDSALL (Lieutenant J. J. Nix).

To relieve the two old "four-pipers" of LANGLEY's men, the Navy oiler PECOS, Ceylon-bound from Tjilatjap, was directed to make rendezvous with EDSALL and WHIPPLE at a point off Christmas Island.

The destroyers met the tanker at the appointed spot on the morning of the 28th. The LANGLEY survivors were about to be transferred to PECOS when a flight of Jap land-based bombers came winging down from Java. Riding in WHIPPLE, Commander E. M. Crouch, ComDesDiv 57, ordered the ships on a southward run that took them out of range. The following day (March 1) the LANGLEY men were put on board PECOS, and the tanker parted company with the destroyers.

But about two hours after she separated from the destroyers, PECOS sighted (and was sighted by) a Jap aircraft-carrier plane. The tankermen knew they were in for it.

Two hours later (time: 1145) the enemy struck. Over the horizon came the bombers, three of them, to blast the tanker with a Japanese *blitz*. Then three more bombers roared over. Then came three waves of Jap dive-bombers. The aircraft (planes from the carrier SORYU) intermittently pounded, pelted, and lambasted the lone American vessel. Near misses jarred her with tumultuous explosions. Hits smashed out sections of her deck, her bridge, and her forecastle. An explosion close aboard on the port side, forward, finished the battered ship. Her skipper, Commander E. P. Abernethy, had just given the order to abandon.

"The ship slowly settled forward," he reported later, *"and finally plunged bow first into the sea, leaving the stern poised in the air for an instant before finally sinking."*

The PECOS went under at 1548. Tankermen and LANGLEY survivors had jumped overside in a welter of oil and debris. Now several more Jap planes arrived. Flying low over the water, these late-comers strafed swimmers and survivors huddled on rafts and on mats of flotsam. Before the Jap planes departed, the sea was blood-streaked and strewn with dead.

It was only by merest chance that any of the PECOS-LANGLEY survivors were rescued. A few minutes before the tanker was abandoned, Commander Abernethy had ordered a distress call put on the air in the hope that EDSALL, WHIPPLE, or some other Allied ship in the area would respond. But the tanker's radio had been set off frequency by the bombing, and just by luck WHIPPLE's radio operator picked up the call. Miles distant from the disaster scene, WHIPPLE reversed course, and raced to PECOS' rescue.

Still lame from her collision with DE RUYTER, the destroyer made the gruelling run with every ounce of speed she could manage. But it was 2000 in the evening before WHIPPLE reached the drifting huddle of survivors.

It was heart-rending work, hauling out these oil-smeared and half-drowned Americans—men who were bleeding, men who were dumb from shock, men who were dying. And before all survivors could be recovered, WHIPPLE's lifesaving operations were interrupted by a submarine alarm. Nothing for it, but she had to go after the undersea enemy, detected on the fringe of the rescue scene.

The anti-submarine action proved cruelly futile. WHIPPLE punished the sea with depth charges; then the contact faded, and the ocean's surface revealed no evidence of a submarine's destruction. After this time-consuming effort, the lifesaving task was hopeless. There were no more survivors to be found.

Casualties in the PECOS-LANGLEY disaster were heavy. The combined losses of both ships numbered about 50 men, and some 150 wounded. WHIPPLE rescued, and safely delivered in Freemantle, some 220.

Perhaps fatalities would have been fewer had the destroyer EDSALL too been able to answer PECOS' distress call. Where at that time was the EDSALL? Did she intercept the Navy tanker's distress signal?

No one knows.

After parting company with PECOS and WHIPPLE on the morning of March 1, EDSALL headed in a northeasterly direction. Lieutenant Joshua J. Nix and his brave company went over the horizon—and into oblivion.

Was this lonely "four-piper" attacked and sunk by Jap carrier planes off the coast of Java—the same SORYU aircraft that bombed PECOS? That was the original supposition.

But after war's end, Navy investigators uncovered conflicting information. Interrogated by officers of the United States Naval Technical Mission to Japan, a number of Japanese naval officers stated that the EDSALL was overhauled and attacked by two battleships of Kondo's division and two cruisers of the Japanese Light Cruiser Squadron. A pair of SORYU bombers joined the onslaught. The American destroyer fought a hopeless action against this overwhelming force—an action that ended on the afternoon of March 1, 1942. According to this testimony (and reports in the War Diary of Japanese Battleship Division 3) EDSALL was finally sunk by gunfire from the battleships HIEI and KIRISHIMA.

A somber cloud of mystery veiled the destroyer's final hour. Of her crew of some 150 officers and men, there were no survivors. Not one of her company was mentioned in Japanese records, or located in a Japanese prison camp. It is seldom that a surface ship's entire complement is lost without trace. Such a casualty toll is usually associated with the loss of a submarine. Or it may be attributed to ruthless massacre.

It was not until the spring of 1952 that details of EDSALL's end came to light. On a dim strip of film taken by Japanese cruiser ASHIGARA—the cruiser firing pointblank at the trapped little ship. In grim shadow-drama she went down before the eyes of shocked investigators, who were subsequently led by the ASHIGARA clue to a forgotten South Pacific cemetery. There they found the graves of five unidentifiable destroyermen who had been prisoners of war—the sole survivors of the ESDALL.

And in that excruciating climax of the Malay Barrier campaign, the EDSALL tragedy was to have a counterpart in the loss of the destroyer PILLSBURY.

Loss of U.S.S. Pillsbury

Out of torpedoes and in need of repair, destroyers PILLSBURY and PARROTT, withdrawn from the ABDA Striking Force, were still at Tjilatjap on that fatal morning of March 1 when Admiral Helfrich ordered the evacuation. At once Admiral Glassford directed all American naval vessels to leave the threatened harbor and clear for Exmouth Gulf, Australia.

PILLSBURY (Lieutenant Commander H. C. Pound) and PARROTT (Lieutenant J. N. Hughes) moved out with a nondescript little flotilla which included American gunboats ASHEVILLE and TULSA, schooner LANIKAI, minesweepers LARK and WHIPPOORWILL, the converted yacht ISABEL, and the Australian gunboat YARRA.

At best speed the ships headed southeastward into the morning light—a thousand miles to go to Australia and "down under." Only the two little minesweepers, the converted yacht, schooner LANIKAI, gunboat TULSA, and the destroyer PARROTT made it.

Somewhere off the Java Coast the U.S.S. PILLSBURY, U.S. gunboat ASHEVILLE, and Australian gunboat YARRA were overtaken by the warships of Admiral Kondo. Somewhere in that area of the Indian Ocean the American destroyer and the two gunboats fought their last battle against the mighty enemy which had driven the United States Asiatic Fleet out of the Philippines, and had shattered the ABDA fleet.

It is believed that PILLSBURY and ASHEVILLE, in a desperate night action, were sunk by three cruisers of the Japanese Fourth Cruiser Squadron and two destroyers of the Japanese Fourth Destroyer Division.

Details of this battle are entirely lacking. After leaving Tjilatjap, PILLSBURY and ASHEVILLE steamed into an oblivion deeper than that which enfolded EDSALL. And scraps of information concerning them uncovered by the U.S. Naval Technical Mission after the war were vague and discrepant.

Both American ships were battered under by Japanese gunfire in what must have been a running battle of some hours' duration. Time of the sinkings, and even the date, could not be determined from Japanese post-war testimony. There was no Japanese record of survivors. The gunboat and the old "four-piper" were blotted out. All hands were lost with ASHEVILLE. All hands were lost with PILLSBURY.

It is possible that in each case they went down in a ship smothered under a tempest of 8-inch shellfire. More probable that some of the crew members got overside, and were left adrift on life rafts and debris—overlooked (or ignored) by the rampaging enemy. No man was recovered.

Sinking of U.S.S. PILLSBURY raised American destroyer fatalities to three DD's lost in that disastrous Java evacuation. And still another DesRon 29 destroyer was to go down in the maelstrom. The old "four-piper" POPE.

Loss of U.S.S. Pope

POPE got away from Soerabaja in the evening of February 28, 1942. She slipped out through the minefields with H.M. cruiser EXETER and the British destroyer ENCOUNTER, and with them headed northward toward Borneo. The Dutch destroyer WITTE DE WITH was ordered to accompany this group. Her captain had granted shore leave; the crew could not be rounded up in time to sail. (For this DD the delay amounted to a reprieve. But its duration was brief. She was bombed and sunk in Soerabaja drydock on March 2.)

Rear Admiral A. F. E. Palliser, R.N., had chosen the route for EXETER and her escorts. The crippled cruiser and the two DD's were ordered to pass to the east of Bawean Island, then head westward for a daylight run down the Java Sea to Sunda Strait. It was hoped the group could make an after-dark transit of this strait between Java and Sumatra, and thus escape into the Indian Ocean for a dash to Ceylon. It was a slim chance.

At 0750 the lookouts spotted two large warships bearing down on them from south-southwest. Japanese cruisers! EXETER (Captain O. L. Gordon, R.N.) signalled for a turn to the southwestward. The evasive course-change proved futile. The Jap cruisers turned to pursue, and launched planes. EXETER, POPE, and ENCOUNTER were spotted.

In dazzling tropical daylight the fugitive Allied ships, in the middle of the Java Sea, were as exposed as a caravan in mid-desert. The enemy showed up as two heavy cruisers (CA's) accompanied by a destroyer. The CA's were the Imperial Navy's NACHI and HAGURO, under command of Rear Admiral T. Takagi—part of the force commanded by Vice Admiral Takahashi. Veering northward, the three Jap warships headed for EXETER, POPE, and ENCOUNTER.

About 0935 EXETER's lookouts spotted the pagoda masts on the horizon. Captain Gordon ordered a northwesterly course-change, but escape in that direction was blocked. Northwest of the Allied ships, and racing to cut them off, was Admiral Takahashi's flagship group—heavy cruisers ASHIGARA and MYOKO, and three destroyers.

At 1020 the Allied ships opened fire on NACHI and HAGURO. I.J.N. NACHI replied with her 8-inchers. With four heavy cruisers bearing down, a getaway to the westward was impossible. Captain Gordon swung his little group hard right on a radical course change, and they raced eastward along the Borneo coast.

There was no haven for the three Allied ships. No refuge. No place for them to go. The Japs were swarming down through Makassar Strait, and roaming the sea between Celebes and Bali. And Takahashi's four cruisers barred the West. More—down through Karimata Strait that morning steamed the Japanese aircraft carrier RYUJO, ready to unleash in the western sky a flock of dive-bombers and "Kates." EXETER, POPE, and ENCOUNTER were trapped.

Unable to make better than 26 knots, they were soon overhauled by Takahashi's cruisers. As POPE and ENCOUNTER spread a screen of smoke in her wake, H.M.S. EXETER exchanged shots with the enemy CA's. Thunder rolled across the brilliant sea, followed by the smash of bursting shells. The Jap closed the range to 18,000 yards—14,000 yards—near and nearer. EXETER's salvos were not hitting; her fire-control was out of kilter. Directed by a Jap spotter plane, Takahashi's gunners began to straddle, then to hit the British cruiser.

About 1100 of that morning some puffy clouds to eastward released rainsqualls. Praying for a chance to escape behind a squall, Captain Gordon ordered his engineers to "pour on the coal." It was a life-and-death race, and EXETER lost. Her engines were already giving their last ounce, and the enemy was closing in.

With the clocks approaching 1110, EXETER loosed a torpedo spread at ASHIGARA and MYOKO. About five minutes later POPE fired four torpedoes at these Japs. The long-range torpedo shots missed. Their guns blazing, a couple of Jap destroyers came racing in on EXETER's starboard. Covering the cruiser, U.S.S. POPE and H.M.S. ENCOUNTER exchanged a blistering fire with these DD's. But the gun duel was hopelessly one-sided. About 1120 a shell smashed into one of EXETER's boiler-rooms. As she staggered in a haze of smoke and steam, all power lost, her main-battery and secondary-battery gun controls gave out. With her big guns silenced, she slowed to four knots.

Captain Gordon ordered ENCOUNTER and POPE to run for it. The British and the American destroyer kept on going. As Jap shells pounded the stricken EXETER and Jap torpedoes reached for her in a murderous fan, Captain Gordon ordered his cruisermen to abandon. They had just gone overside when a torpedo—one of the 18 fired by the Jap destroyers—struck EXETER a mortal smash. The British cruiser capsized and went down.

A few minutes later H.M.S. ENCOUNTER received a fatal hit. She, too, was abandoned to sink under a tempest of smoke and fire. That left U.S.S. POPE, alone, in a sea of enemies.

No ship in World War II or any war was in a situation worse than that of this old "four-piper" cornered in the Java Sea below Borneo, with cannon to the right of her, cannon to the left of her; her crew ready to drop from exhaustion; her torpedoes expended; her nearest haven, Australia, a thousand miles to the east. But surrender was not in the book of this shabby old grayhound. Evidently her skipper, Lieutenant Commander W. C. Blinn, believed the old axiom "No ship is lost until her captain thinks it so." Evidently her crew had faith in the leadership of her captain. All hands were prepared to sweat it out and slug it out—to hell with the odds!

And for a moment it looked as though Fate might deal valor the fair rewards. About 1145 an opaque rainsquall swept across the seascape ahead. Commander Blinn called upon his engineers to force the last possible turn out of the turbines. Unreeling a wall of smoke behind her, the old DD dashed for the cloudburst. Enemy shells sent up geysers around her, and explosions thundered in her wake. Somehow she made it.

The rainsquall blotted her from sight; gave her a breathing spell. As she panted along through the squall, her crew had time to rush ammunition to depleted handling rooms and ready boxes; her Damage Control Officer, Lieutenant R. H. Antrim, was able to manage a few emergency repairs. He could do nothing for the brick walls of No. 3 boiler, which had collapsed from concussion; otherwise he found the battle damage fairly light.

On the bridge, Commander Blinn was heartened to see the enemy had faded out astern. POPE emerged from the rainsquall, raced across a patch of open sea, and plunged into a second downpour. Maybe they could elude pursuit; keep going east along the coast of Borneo, then, after nightfall, race south, and sprint through Lombok Strait.

But luck was not in the cards for POPE. When the second rainsquall dissolved, POPE was once more exposed under a noonday sky of tropic blue. The Borneo sun glared mercilessly down—and so did the pilot of a cruiser-carried Japanese plane.

The Jap spotter sent out a call. The call was answered by six dive-bombers from the carrier RYUJO, at that time about 100 miles due west. At 1230 the dive-bombers had the target in their sights. The hour had struck for U.S.S. POPE.

She squared away to fight with her single 3-inch anti-aircraft gun. The rackety old weapon held the Japs off for 75 rounds. Then its recoil system jammed; it would not return to battery.

POPE's gunners kept going with machine-guns. The .50 caliber volleys had little chance against the high-speed "Vals." As the old destroyer swerved and zigzagged, the planes plummeted down from the sky, leveled off, and roared over on bombing runs.

An explosion close aboard bashed a hole in her side and injured her port propeller shaft. Below decks, the crew retreated from flooded compartments. They had to secure the port engine which was vibrating violently, and the resulting loss of power left the ship a helpless set-up.

Even so, the Jap dive-bombers did not have her number. The thirteenth attack was delivered by high-level bombers, summoned from RYUJO to lend a hand. Making their runs at 3,000 feet, the "Kates" showered POPE with bombs. But the "Kates" did not have POPE's number, either.

The "Kates" were coming in on their second bombing run when Commander Blinn felt his ship going logy. She was slowly settling by the stern. When the Damage Control Officer reported the flooding could not be stemmed, Commander Blinn ordered the crew to stand by to abandon ship.

While responsible hands hurriedly destroyed the code books and similar material, others prepared to scuttle the vessel. Demolition charges were set by a crew under command of the Gunnery Officer, and vital instruments were rigged for destruction.

At 1250 Commander Blinn ordered the crew overside. Officers and bluejackets quit the ship in good order, taking their assigned places in the destroyer's motor whaleboat and on life rafts. Finally the demolition crew abandoned.

Just as all hands stood clear, a pattern of shells

splashed around the doomed vessel. The Jap cruisers had overhauled her again. So it was a cruiser salvo which sent the old "four-piper" under. An 8-inch shell found the mark, delivered the killing blow. In a shroud of smoke and steam the U.S.S. POPE went down by the stern.

Winging low across the water, a Jap seaplane skimmed over the motor whaleboat. Enraged, several of the survivors opened fire on the plane with a Browning automatic. The shooting gave the Japs an excuse to strafe the survivors, and they made the most of it. For about 30 minutes the angered seaplane and companion aircraft stunted over the whaleboat and the rafts, lashing at them with machine-gun fire. By some miracle, no one was killed.

And miraculously enough, no one of POPE's crew had been killed in the murderous battle with Takahashi's cruiser force and the RYUJO's bombers. The assailed destroyer did not suffer a single fatality through enemy action. Only one member of the crew was lost—a man killed by a demolition charge.

The miracle was to persist. Throughout the afternoon of March 1—and the following day, and the day after that—for nearly three days, the little clutter of rafts and the whaleboat carrying the POPE survivors were adrift on the Java Sea. Not an officer or man succumbed to this ordeal. On the third night of it, a Japanese destroyer hove over the horizon. All hands were picked up—151, including Commander Blinn.

Made prisoners of war, the POPE survivors were treated with fair consideration by the Jap destroyer's crew. They were fed corn beef, chipped biscuits, and sweet tea, and after two days they were landed at Makassar City, Celebes. There they spent nine days in a wretched native jail; then they were transferred to a former Dutch concentration camp where conditions were somewhat improved. Commander Blinn, along with a number of officers from POPE, EXETER, ENCOUNTER, and PERTH, was eventually shipped to Japan. Of the 151 POPE survivors, 27 men died in Java or Celebes during the war. Malnutrition.

For his stellar leadership in this destroyer drama, Lieutenant Commander Welford C. Blinn was awarded the Navy Cross. Others of POPE's crew were decorated and commended. All hands were in line for a laudatory "Well Done." But accolades cannot measure the valor of such a captain and crew.

The battle fought by the old "four-piper" brought the curtain down on the ABDAFLOAT effort. When Takahashi's cruisers opened fire on her at the last, the U.S.S. POPE was the last Allied man-of-war on the Java Sea.

SURVIVORS OF THE POPE

CHAPTER 10

PACIFIC STAND

Holding the Pacific Line

Japanese chauvanists had a term for it—*"Hakko Ichiu,"* which means "bringing the eight corners of the world under one roof." General Tojo, Admiral Yamamoto, and other architects of Japanese Imperial strategy were willing to settle for the Oriental corners of the world, however, and let the Americas and Europe go, for the next few centuries at least.

And erecting a Japanese pagoda-roof over the Orient was going to be a job. One corner of the imperial edifice could be anchored in Manchuria, perhaps, and another might be anchored in Burma or Malaya. But Japan's grand strategists were baffled by the oceanic side of the structure. How far eastward should it extend? Could Australia be appropriated for a bastion? Could Hawaii be taken for a mid-ocean cornerstone?

Some of the master minds in Tokyo were all for Australia's appropriation. The General Staff, more practical, pointed to the enormous logistics problem involved, and the demi-continent was ruled out. Rabaul in the Bismarcks could be the South Pacific bastion, or New Guinea, buttressed perhaps by the outlying Solomons.

As for Hawaii, Admiral Isoroku Yamamoto advocated an interesting plan. It was aggressive, colorful, complex enough to be impressive, and just plausible enough to make it seem feasible and worthwhile. The Admiral stuck a thumbtack in Midway Island. He stuck another far to the north in the Aleutians. On a blueprint it was all so easy.

Historians are uncertain as to the exact date of the Midway-Aleutians and Rabaul-New Guinea-Solomons decisions, but that was the Japanese grand strategy after the Pearl Harbor strike. As has been noted, Japanese forces promptly occupied the Bismarck Archipelago while driving for the Malay Barrier in the Southwest Pacific. Just why Yamamoto deferred the Midway operation and its Aleutian sideline at a time when those beachheads were wide open for exploitation still remains a mystery.

The American and Allied strategists on their part produced some down-to-earth plans designed to frustrate Japanese ambitions for Pacific conquest.

The United States Pacific Fleet was to carry out two primary missions. First, it was to hold the line of an Allied defense frontier which extended from Dutch Harbor in the Aleutians to Midway in the Central Pacific, from Midway to Samoa in the South Pacific, and from Samoa through the Fijis to the New Hebrides lying east of the Solomons. Second, the Pacific Fleet was to maintain a United States-Australia supply line which extended from the American west coast to Hawaii, from Hawaii to the Samoan group, and from Samoa to Australia, with a branch-off to New Zealand. (See chart on inside front cover.)

This side of the world is nearly all sea. So the defense and maintenance of those long, thin lines across miles of open ocean was up to the U.S. Navy —a dual mission to stagger the imagination of any navy.

And the United States Pacific Fleet—or what was left of it after the debacle of Pearl Harbor—could not undertake a stationary defense of that oceanic frontier. Enjoying the initiative, the Japanese conquerors were on the move, probing for weak spots all along the line. The defenders could not remain idle. To the Allies, uninformed on the intentions of Hideki Tojo and Yamamoto, the Japanese thrust into the Bismarcks and New Guinea looked like a drive for Australia. On January 11, 1942, a Japanese submarine bombarded the American naval station at Pago Pago, Samoa. Were the Japs also planning a drive in that direction? Their seizure of Makin Island in the Gilberts indicated as much. To check these menacing enemy moves, Admiral Nimitz, Commander in Chief Pacific, ordered Rear Admiral Raymond A. Spruance, Vice Admiral Wilson Brown, Rear Admiral Frank J. Fletcher, and Vice Admiral William F. Halsey to conduct a series of hit-and-run strikes at enemy bases and nests in the island-specked Central and South Pacific.

Highly dangerous, these strikes—for no American knew the extent or composition of the illegally constructed fortifications in the Japanese Mandate islands. No American knew the air power secreted by those bases. No American knew the inside of Truk, Japan's mid-Pacific Gibraltar. Concerning the Marshalls and Marianas, the Navy was as much in the dark as it was concerning Yamamoto's war plans.

Moreover, these newly organized task forces, and most of the ships therein, were going into action for the first time. Most of the gunners had never fired a shot in anger. And these task groups were going to steam through submarine water. Jap subs were here, there, everywhere. On the day one of them shelled Pago Pago, another intercepted the aircraft carrier SARATOGA.

Torpedoed some 500 miles southwest of Oahu, the old "SARA" remained afloat, and staggered back to Hawaii with three firerooms flooded. This disablement of a United States carrier left a serious hole in the abbreviated Pacific Fleet; the damaging or destruction of any Pacific Fleet ship at that time was extremely serious. On January 23 the LEXINGTON carrier group of Vice Admiral Wilson Brown, steaming westward to deliver the first of the Pacific strikes, was attacked by a submarine about 135 miles west of Oahu. The fleet oiler NECHES was torpedoed and sunk, and the strike at Wake had to be canceled because the group could not make the long run without fueling at sea, and there was no replacement tanker immediately available at Pearl.

Destroyers were demanded, and at once. Destroyers to guard the convoys; destroyers to screen the task groups; destroyers to patrol the waters off Dutch Harbor and Midway, off Oahu and Samoa, off the Fijis and New Hebrides—the bases in the American-Allied Pacific front line. Destroyers to guard the waters off eastern Australia, and the sea lanes down under. And destroyers to fight an all-out anti-submarine war--this last a primary mission of DesPac (Destroyers Pacific).

The South, Central, and North Pacific—that was a large order. But the destroyermen notched in their belts, spat on their hands, and pitched in.

Jarvis and Long Down I-23

On January 28, 1942, an enemy submarine was detected in the waters off Pearl Harbor. The destroyer JARVIS (Commander W. R. Thayer) and destroyer-minesweepers LONG, TREVER, and ELLIOT were soon hot on the undersea marauder's trail.

At 1447 JARVIS picked up sound contact. She presently lost it—regained it—lost it—picked it up once more—lost it again. But at 1710 the ex-destroyer LONG (Lieutenant Commander W. S. Veeder) tagged the sub with an echo-ranging "ping." Five minutes later JARVIS reestablished contact. JARVIS and LONG then teamed up to deliver a joint attack. At 1721 the destroyer dropped a booming depth-charge pattern. The old destroyer-sweeper followed through with a pattern at 1724.

An hour later both ships were once more on target, maneuvering in for a second go. Over went the successive patterns; the sea absorbed the charges; then, at 1839, two delayed explosions rumbled up from down under.

That evening the destroyermen, combing the surface for evidence, sighted dark patches of oil. JARVIS and LONG had disposed of the Japanese submarine I-23. As one of Captain K. Imaizumi's group, she had been with Admiral Nagumo's fleet in the great raid on Pearl Harbor. Her January visit was by way of a return to the scene of the crime. Only this time crime did not pay.

Destroyers with Enterprise (Pioneer Raid on Marshalls and Gilberts)

On January 9, 1942, Admiral Nimitz conferred with Vice Admiral W. F. ("Bull") Halsey on the matter of raiding the Marshall and Gilbert Islands. In command of the ENTERPRISE task force (TF 8), Admiral Halsey had been doing convoy drudgery and was looking for action.

At that date Task Force 17, commanded by Rear Admiral F. J. Fletcher, was convoying troops from San Diego to Samoa. This force contained the carrier YORKTOWN, heavy cruiser LOUISVILLE, light cruiser ST. LOUIS, and destroyers HUGHES, SIMS, RUSSELL, and WALKE. Nimitz instructed Halsey to sail for Samoa with Task Force 8. There he would join up with TF 17 and lead both forces in a strike at the Gilberts and Marshalls.

Halsey's force was composed of the aircraft carrier

ENTERPRISE, cruisers NORTHAMPTON and SALT LAKE CITY, and destroyers BALCH, MAURY, FANNING, RALPH TALBOT, GRIDLEY, MCCALL, DUNLAP, and BLUE. But the take-off on January 11 was not auspicious.

On that very day a Jap sub bombarded Pago Pago. On that day, too, the SARATOGA was torpedoed and disabled—a disaster that reduced American carrier strength in the Pacific to ENTERPRISE, YORKTOWN, and LEXINGTON. Ominous news.

Misfortune plagued TF 8 as it ran for Samoa. On the 14th, destroyer BLUE lost a man overboard. On the 16th a man was accidentally killed on SALT LAKE CITY; also an ENTERPRISE plane made a crash landing, killing a man, and a torpedo-plane failed to return from a flight. On the 17th an ENTERPRISE scout plane crashed, killing a man. And early in the morning of January 22 destroyers GRIDLEY and FANNING collided in a blinding rainstorm. Both suffered bow damage that forced them to return to Pearl Harbor for repairs.

These accidents were typical of high-speed operating by crews under tremendous pressure rushing into the unfamiliar face of the "real thing." It would take time for these pioneering task forces to iron out wrinkles and steady into smooth-running teamwork.

Admiral Halsey divided his Task Force 8 into three groups. The first (Task Group 8.1), under Rear Admiral Spruance, consisted of cruisers NORTHAMPTON and SALT LAKE CITY, and the destroyer DUNLAP (Lieutenant Commander V. R. Roane) flying the pennant of Captain E. P. Sauer, ComDesDiv 12. This group was to bombard Wotje Atoll, centrally located in the Marshall Islands.

The second group (Task Group 8.3) was composed of the cruiser CHESTER (Captain T. M. Shock) and destroyers BALCH (Commander C. J. Rend), flagship of Captain R. L. Conolly, ComDesRon 6, and MAURY (Lieutenant Commander E. D. Snare). They were slated to hit Taroa and Maloelap Atoll in the Marshalls.

The third group (Task Group 8.5), directly under Admiral Halsey, consisted of the aircraft carrier ENTERPRISE (Captain D. G. Murray), and destroyers RALPH TALBOT (Commander R. Earle, Jr.), BLUE (Commander H. N. Williams), and MCCALL (Commander Frederick Moosbrugger). For this group Halsey selected Wotje, Maloelap, and Kwajalein as Marshall Island targets. ENTERPRISE planes, incidentally, were to furnish fighter cover for TG 8.1 and TG 8.3.

While Task Force 8 was striking at the Marshalls, Task Force 17 was ordered by Halsey to hit the Gilbert Islands. Led by Rear Admiral Fletcher, this force, as noted, consisted of aircraft carrier YORKTOWN, cruisers LOUISVILLE and ST. LOUIS, and four destroyers. Under command of Captain F. G. Fahrion, ComDesDiv 3, the destroyers were: flagship HUGHES (Lieutenant Commander D. J. Ramsey); SIMS (Lieutenant Commander W. M. Hyman); WALKE (Lieutenant Commander T. E. Fraser); and RUSSELL (Lieutenant Commander G. R. Hartwig). Targets to be struck were Jaluit, Makin, and Mili.

The ENTERPRISE groups left Samoa on schedule, and steamed in company until 1830 in the evening of January 31. Then they separated to strike the Marshalls from the eastward.

Admiral Spruance's Task Group 8.1 opened fire on Wotje at 0715. They found the place dozing in the morning light. No enemy aircraft were sighted. So cruisers NORTHAMPTON and SALT LAKE CITY and destroyer DUNLAP got in some hot gunnery, shooting at what looked like Jap cruisers in Wotje lagoon.

Destroyer DUNLAP was particularly busy that morning. Her fire sank a Jap gunboat, damaged another which ran aground, and lambasted various shore installations. A shore battery took her under fire, in turn. After the withdrawal of NORTHAMPTON and SALT LAKE CITY, she continued the bombardment on her own. Meanwhile, she found time to rescue the crew of a SALT LAKE CITY plane which had crashed. After the foray, Admiral Spruance lauded DUNLAP's skipper, Lieutenant Commander V. R. Roane, for "initiative and zeal."

The destroyers with Captain Shock's Task Group 8.3 had a livelier time of it at Taroa and Maloelap Atoll. Japanese aircraft hit back fiercely, and cruiser CHESTER and her DD consorts, BALCH and MAURY, experienced some savage fighting.

Destroyer BALCH got in some fast shooting at shore installations as well as aircraft, but MAURY was fully occupied by anti-aircraft fire. Jap shore batteries joined the gunnery, but their fire was erratic. The eight twin-engined bombers that zoomed up from Taroa airfield were more accurate. Concentrating on CHESTER, they showered the dodging cruiser with iron eggs. A light bomb penetrated her main deck, killing eight of her crew and wounding 40. Without AA support from the two destroyers, the flagship of TG 8.3 might have been downed.

Six times the two DD's were subjected to dive-bomb attacks and strafing by enemy fighters. BALCH's anti-aircraft fire broke up several of these onslaughts. And MAURY raised an aerial tornado that turned the enemy back time and again. Two or three Jap planes were blown out of the air. The shore batteries were finally silenced. When TG 8.3 retired, they left fires and destruction in their wake.

"I desire," Captain Shock concluded his subsequent

action report, *"to express my appreciation of the excellent support afforded by the* BALCH *and the* MAURY. . . ."

At Wotje, Maloelap, and Kwajalein, the ENTERPRISE group (TF 8.3) had begun its striking at 0443, launching planes across a calm silver sea under a full moon. Kwajalein in the western Marshalls was the principal target. There was no interception by Jap aircraft, and the ENTERPRISE planes found some submarines, destroyers, and merchant vessels in the peaceful lagoon. After that, the lagoon was not peaceful.

Three times the ENTERPRISE launched aircraft strikes at Kwajalein, while other of her planes made sweeps over Maloelap and Wotje. Destroyers BLUE, RALPH TALBOT, and MCCALL were merely by-standers at these air proceedings. The surprised Japs could not muster aircraft for an immediate counterstrike at ENTERPRISE.

About 1300 in the afternoon of February 1 the ENTERPRISE group called it a day. The retirement inspired the word "Haul out with Halsey," which later became the slogan of the Admiral's famous task force.

However, before the original "haul out" could be accomplished, the Japs got in a few jabs at ENTERPRISE. About 1330, after TG 8.3 had been rejoined by TG 8.1, the flat-top was attacked by five twin-engined Jap "Bettys." One "Betty," attempting a suicide crash, just nicked the ship. This was the war's first *kamikaze* effort.

Again, at 1550, two "Bettys" attacked. For all their accomplishment, they might as well have been "Zeros." The pioneer raid on the Marshalls was over, and Halsey's task force was in the clear.

Meantime, Rear Admiral Fletcher's TF 17 was hitting at the Gilberts. The weather was against YORKTOWN and her consorts. Striking at Jaluit, the YORKTOWN planes ran into thunderstorms. They damaged several enemy ships, but six of the planes failed to return. Attacking Makin before sunrise, the YORKTOWN bombers could find no target better than a minelayer. The vessel was hit, but not sunk. At Mili no military objectives were found. The TF 17 destroyers fired a few rounds of AA ammunition at a single four-engined bomber which attacked YORKTOWN. This patrol plane was shot down by two American fighters. The raid on the Gilberts was over—an effort hardly worth the cost.

Altogether these pioneer strikes in the Central Pacific produced negligible results. No enemy ships had been sunk by the raiders, and the Japs were not particularly disturbed by these strikes. They boosted American morale, however, and they gave the task groups involved the sort of practice necessary for the big showdown matches of the future. And the pioneering Pacific Fleet DD's had displayed some of their wares.

First Strike at Rabaul

The Japanese advance into the Bismarck Archipelago and the landing of Jap expeditionary forces on the north coast of New Guinea worried the Australian Government. The Japs might be planning to seize the New Hebrides or New Caledonia, squarely athwart the southern end of the Allied Pacific defense line.

American troops were already on the way to New Caledonia, strategically located below the New Hebrides. This island with its capacious seaport of Nouméa was under the French flag, but the local government was apathetic, and the white populace was largely composed of transported French felons.

New Caledonia lay within the newly organized ANZAC Area, which included northern New Zealand, the Fijis, the New Hebrides, the Solomons and Bismarcks, eastern New Guinea and the entire east coast of Australia. This Command Area (which existed from late January to April 1942) was under strategic command of Admiral King and local command of Vice Admiral H. F. Leary. The Anzac Force, composed of three Australian cruisers, several Australian destroyers and corvettes, and the American cruiser CHICAGO and two American destroyers, was scarcely strong enough to contest a Japanese thrust east of Rabaul. But a reinforcement was coming. Steaming on the Central Pacific run with the New Caledonia troop convoy was Admiral Wilson Brown's LEXINGTON force. A carrier strike at the enemy on the ANZAC front was contemplated. To relieve the pressure in the South Pacific, Nimitz was to launch a simultaneous strike at Wake Island.

At Wilson Brown's suggestion, Admiral Leary planned a thunderbolt carrier strike on Rabaul. This would be another pioneering foray for American warships. The Navy's charts of the Bismarck-Solomons seas were ancient, based on Eighteenth Century exploration. The Bismarck Archipelago was a mystery, and the Solomons Islands were even darker. Aircraft forced down on those sombre coasts might expect anything, and a run through those waters by American ships was an adventure in hazard. But the target date was set—February 21.

The strike was to be made by Admiral Wilson Brown's Task Force 11—aircraft carrier LEXINGTON, cruisers INDIANAPOLIS, SAN FRANCISCO, PENSACOLA, MINNEAPOLIS, and nine destroyers. Led by Captain A. R. Early, ComDesRon 1, the destroyers were:

PHELPS	*Lt. Comdr. E. L. Beck* *Flagship of* *Capt. Early*
AYLWIN	*Comdr. R. H. Rodgers* *Flying pennant of* *Comdr. R. S. Riggs,* COMDESDIV 2
DEWEY	*Lt. Comdr. C. F. Chillingworth, Jr.* *Flying pennant of* *Comdr. W. Nyquist,* COMDESDIV 1
BAGLEY	*Lt. Comdr. G. A. Sinclair*
PATTERSON	*Comdr. F. R. Walker*
DALE	*Lt. Comdr. A. L. Rorschach*
HULL	*Lt. Comdr. R. F. Stout*
CLARK	*Comdr. M. T. Richardson*
MACDONOUGH	*Lt. Comdr. J. M. McIsaac*

The LEXINGTON's planes were to hit the target with an air attack, and if the bombing proved successful, the cruiser PENSACOLA, supported by destroyers CLARK and BAGLEY, was to follow through with a bombardment of the Rabaul anchorage.

Because a fast, direct punch was the best strategy against the Rabaul air patrols, Admiral Brown approached the island from the eastward, with the intention of launching planes 125 miles from target.

But at 1015 in the morning of February 20 the LEXINGTON force was detected off the Solomons, some 350 miles east of the objective. Two of a trio of Jap air scouts were shot down by Wildcats from the "LEX," but the third got away. That did it. At 1542 in the afternoon, the Japs struck in full fury, and the first major battle between Jap and American carrier aircraft was on.

Wildcats versus enemy "Kates," the engagement raged across the tropic sky. The American destroyers joined the fray, screening the big flat-top and the cruisers with their curtain of AA fire.

The battle ended about 1815 when the Japs retired to Rabaul. Two LEXINGTON planes were lost; enemy casualties were considerably heavier. The destroyermen saw one of the war's great aces in action —Lieutenant E. H. ("Butch") O'Hare, who won immediate headlines by shooting down five "Kates." But the Rabaul strike itself had been called off by Admiral Brown, as with the force's detection all chance for surprise had been exploded.

Raid on Wake Island

On February 24, the day after the pulverizing Japanese strike on Port Darwin, Australia, Admiral Halsey's task force struck a sharp blow at Wake. With ENTERPRISE in this exploit were cruisers NORTHAMPTON and SALT LAKE CITY, and destroyers BALCH, MAURY, DUNLAP, BLUE, RALPH TALBOT, and CRAVEN. The last named, skippered by Lieutenant Commander A. P. Calvert, was facing her baptism of fire. The others were veterans of the Marshall Islands strike. All DD's were under command of Captain R. L. Conolly, ComDesRon 6.

The two heavy cruisers and destroyers BALCH and MAURY steamed in for a shore bombardment of Peale and the northern end of Wake Island. Their shells crashed on enemy shore batteries, military buildings, and other installations. BALCH smashed a small patrol boat, and dashed in to snatch four survivors from the water. If not the first, these were among the first Jap prisoners-of-war captured by the Pacific Fleet.

While the bombardment was under way, enemy seaplanes attacked the two cruisers and the two DD's. The destroyermen and the cruisermen raised an anti-aircraft umbrella which the Jap planes found too steely to penetrate. That night ENTERPRISE, guarded by the other destroyers, closed in on the island and launched planes. Wake was subjected to another blasting. Halsey went on from there to make a fast side-swipe at Marcus Island, northwest of Wake.

The raids on Wake and Marcus demanded mountainous effort, and produced mousy results. A strike was coming up, however, which would produce monumental results both in enemy damage and morale. Destroyers would participate in this major exploit which was scheduled to strike the Japanese homeland. Enter the aircraft carrier HORNET, and Lieutenant Colonel James H. Doolittle—

Raid on Tokyo (Destroyers From Shangri-La)

On April 9, 1942, the American flag fluttered down on Bataan, and a stunned citizenry of the United States mourned the loss of a heroic army in the Philippines. Nine days later the nation was electrified by the word that the enemy Empire had been struck squarely in the heart.

As far back as January, Admiral King and his Operations Officer, Captain Francis S. ("Froggy") Low, had been considering the possibilities of landing a blow on Tokyo. Submarines had reported that the Japanese homeland was guarded by a patrol of off-shore picket boats; no American knew the strength of Japan's home defenses. But indications were that a carrier strike might succeed.

On April 2, 1942, HORNET (Captain Marc Mitscher) sailed from San Francisco on a highly secret mission. She was carrying 16 of the Army Air Force's medium bombers (Mitchells) and flight crews trained and led by Lieutenant Colonel "Jimmy" Doolittle. HORNET was escorted into the Central Pacific by the cruisers VINCENNES and NASHVILLE and destroyers

Gwin (Commander J. M. Higgins), flying the pennant of Commander H. R. Holcomb, ComDesDiv 22; Grayson (Commander T. M. Stokes); Meredith (Lieutenant Commander H. E. Hubbard); and Monssen (Commander R. N. Smoot). The group also contained the fleet oiler Cimarron.

Eleven days later the Hornet group was met by the Enterprise group at a point about midway between Kamchatka and Pearl Harbor. The combined force, designated Task Force 16, was under command of Admiral Halsey. The Enterprise group included cruisers Northampton and Salt Lake City and DesDiv 12 led by Captain R. L. Conolly, ComDesRon 6. The destroyers were: flagship Balch (Lieutenant Commander H. H. Tiemroth); Benham (Lieutenant Commander J. M. Worthington); Fanning (Commander W. R. Cooke, Jr.); and Ellet (Lieutenant Commander F. H. Gardner). Captain E. P. Sauer, ComDesDiv 12, rode in Fanning.

Halsey led this fast-moving force to a launching point within 700 miles of Tokyo. Plans called for a night attack on April 18. Everything went smoothly until the morning of that day, then the seas stood up on their hind legs and showered the ships with green water. Worse still, the force encountered a Japanese picket boat, and although this was promptly sunk by Nashville, it had to be assumed that it or its partners had sounded the alarm. So, although Halsey had hoped to launch within 400 miles of Tokyo Bay, he decided to send the flyers in for a 600-mile run.

At 0800 the planes were away. They hit the Imperial capital at 1215, dropping their bombs on gun factories, gas works, power stations, and similar targets. Nagoya and Kobe were also branded by iron and fire.

The question had been—where were these raiders to land? The answer was China, preferably Chuchow airfield.

Not one of the Doolittle planes was lost on Japanese soil. But a number, out of fuel, crashed in China, and one plane flew to Vladivostok where the Russians promptly interned the crew. One plane was ditched off the China coast, and the crew of another landed by parachute near Nanchang. The Japs pounced on the survivors. But 71 of the 80 airmen lived to tell about the raid. The Japs executed three of the prisoners, and a fourth died in prison camp. Five airmen were killed in crash landings.

Heading back for Pearl Harbor the Hornet-Enterprise team paused to shoot a large hole in the Japanese picket line. The carriers steamed into Pearl Harbor on the morning of April 25. Japanese planes had pursued, but failed to catch them.

The raid was a stunner for the war leaders in Tokyo, who had apparently believed the home islands immune. For the American public it was a great bracer. Japanese and Americans alike were mystified by the source of the lightning bolt—Where had the planes come from? President Roosevelt supplied the answer, borrowing the locale from James Hilton's best-seller *Lost Horizon*. *"The planes,"* said F. D. R., *"flew from Shangri-La."*

The Battle of the Coral Sea

Although the hit-and-run strikes at Tokyo, the Marshalls, Wake and elsewhere were a boost to American morale, they failed to slow the Japanese juggernaut in the Southwest Pacific.

By May 1942 the forces of Vice Admiral Inoue were solidly established in the Bismarck Archipelago, with headquarters at Rabaul on New Britain and a lovely anchorage at Kavieng, New Ireland. To the south the conquerors had a foothold on the north coast of New Guinea, and to the east they had a toehold on Bougainville and near-by islands in the Upper Solomons. They already had gobbled up the Philippines, Malaya, and the Netherlands East Indies. When completed, the Bismarck-New Guinea-Solomons triangle would guard the South Pacific gateway to these fabulously rich Indies.

As of that date the conquerors were only setting to work on the Solomons bastion of that strategic triangle. And their logistics problem—the problem of moving ships, troops, munitions, and supplies to their new but faraway possessions—was becoming a major headache to the Jap militarists. And they were finding that to protect each new territory, they had to conquer and hold the territory just beyond.

Thus, to hold Bougainville in the Upper Solomons, the Japs found it necessary to control Choiseul, New Georgia, and Santa Isabel in the center of the Solomons Archipelago. And to secure the Central Solomons, they were compelled to seize Guadalcanal, lower down. Toward this end, they landed on Florida Island, north of Guadalcanal, and moved into the harbor of Tulagi.

A convoy loaded with Imperial Marines steamed into Tulagi Harbor on the 4th of May. The invaders were unaware of the fact, but they were touching off the showdown sea-air engagement which was to halt the Japanese juggernaut in the South Pacific. Entering Tulagi, the Jap Marines lit the fuse to the Battle of the Coral Sea.

Equally unaware of the drama impending were the American destroyermen serving in Morris, Perkins, Hammann, Anderson, Walke, and Sims, at that date operating with Admiral Fletcher's Task Force 17. The destroyers, under Captain G. C. Hoover, ComDesRon 2, in Morris, and Commander F. X. McInerney, ComDesDiv 9, in Perkins, were operating in a Yorktown screen which included cruisers Astoria, Chester, Portland, and Chicago.

Also in the Coral Sea was Task Force 11 (Rear Admiral Aubrey W. Fitch), containing the aircraft carrier Lexington, cruisers Minneapolis and New Orleans, and destroyers Phelps, Dewey, Aylwin, Farragut, and Monaghan, under Squadron Commander Captain A. R. Early, in Phelps.

The Yorktown and Lexington forces were fueling when word had come on May 2 that the Japs on New Guinea were mustering strength for a drive on Port Moresby. Fitch informed Fletcher he could not finish fueling before the 4th. Admiral Fletcher thereupon directed Admiral Fitch to complete the job while he headed out into the Middle of the Coral Sea to conduct air search. Task Force 11 was to rendezvous with Fletcher's force on the 4th, as were Australian cruisers Hobart and Australia. But this rendezvous was never made.

On the evening of May 3 came the report that enemy vanguards were landing on Florida Island. At once Admiral Fletcher decided to jolt the Japanese advance. Detaching the fleet oiler Neosho, he sent her under escort of destroyer Russell to a rendezvous point over the westward horizon. With the rest of the Yorktown force he made a top-speed run toward Tulagi.

By 0700 in the morning of May 4, Yorktown was about 100 miles off the southwest coast of Guadalcanal. When she maneuvered into launching position, an attack group of scout planes, torpedo-planes, and bombers—40 aircraft in all—took off for the target.

The planes hit Florida Island about 0815, and plastered Japanese invasion shipping in Tulagi Harbor and near-by Gavutu. Three times the striking air groups flew across Guadalcanal, bombed the enemy at Tulagi and Gavutu, and returned to Yorktown's flight deck. As was to be the case in many similar carrier strikes later in the war, the destroyers in Yorktown's screen saw nothing of the action at the bull's-eye objective, nothing of the work done on the target by the planes. Their main job was to screen against the enemy and to act as lifeguards for friendly planes that might crash in the water.

Returning to Yorktown, three of her aircraft failed to reach the carrier. Two pilots, losing their way, were forced down on Guadalcanal. A third pilot ditched at sea. Destroyer Perkins (Lieutenant Commander W. C. Ford) conducted a needle-in-haystack hunt for the plane downed at sea, but was unable to find the aircraft. Destroyer Hammann (Commander A. E. True), dispatched to rescue the airmen on Guadalcanal, had better luck.

Two aviators were located on the beach near Cape Henslow. Shoreward in Hammann's motor whaleboat went Ensign R. P. F. Enright, U.S.N.R., and bluejackets to pick up the stranded flyers. Darkness and squally weather impeded the destroyermen, and their effort to gain the beach was hampered by dangerous shoals and acrobatic surf. Through heroic life-saving efforts, especially by Boatswain's Mate, Second, A. S. Jason and Coxswain G. W. Knapp, Jr., both aviators were rescued.

The strike at Tulagi cost the Japs the destroyer Kikuzuki (demolished), several small landing craft (sunk), five seaplanes riddled, and a destroyer and a minelayer severly damaged. This gratuitous blasting may have hurried the Japanese advance on the Bismarck-Solomons-New Guinea front. In any event, on May 5 Admiral Fletcher received word that the enemy was rushing preparations to drive on Port Moresby *via* the Louisiade Archipelago off the eastern end of New Guinea. On that same day a Japanese carrier group, which included carriers Shokaku and Zuikaku, was located near Bougainville.

Admiral Fletcher gathered his forces in the Coral Sea to combat the enemy drive. At this juncture Task Force 11 combined with Task Force 17. Fletcher organized the force in three combatant groups:—an Attack Group of cruisers and destroyers to engage the enemy's surface forces; a Support Group of cruisers and destroyers to cover the carriers; and an Air Group composed of Yorktown, Lexington, and destroyer screen. A fueling and a search group complemented the combatant groups. The Task Force 17 organization is listed on the following page.

Had Vice Admiral Inoue at Rabaul obtained full information on the Allied naval force steaming to intercept his invasion ships, he might have hesitated over the Port Moresby thrust. But the news of Corregidor's surrender, broadcast on May 6, doubtless stimulated the Commander of the Imperial Navy's Southeast Area Fleet. Inoue ordered his invasion fleet to proceed. The fleet was composed of a Striking Force and an Occupation Force. The Striking Force contained aircraft carriers Shokaku and Zuikaku, three heavy cruisers, a light cruiser, six destroyers, a minelayer, and a fleet oiler. The Occupation Force consisted of the light aircraft carrier Shoho, four heavy cruisers, three light cruisers, seven destroyers, five transports, a minelayer, and a seaplane carrier. Operating with this force was a scouting group of six submarines.

TASK FORCE 17

Rear Admiral F. J. Fletcher

ATTACK GROUP

Rear Admiral T. C. Kinkaid

HEAVY CRUISERS

MINNEAPOLIS — NEW ORLEANS
CHESTER — PORTLAND
ASTORIA

DESTROYERS

Under Capt. A. R. Early

PHELPS *Flagship*	*Lt. Comdr. E. L. Beck*
DEWEY	*Lt. Comdr. C. F. Chillingworth*
AYLWIN	*Lt. Comdr. G. R. Phelan*
FARRAGUT	*Comdr. G. P. Hunter*
MONAGHAN	*Lt. Comdr. W. P. Burford*

FUELING GROUP

Capt. J. S. Phillips

FLEET OILERS

NEOSHO — TIPPECANOE

DESTROYERS

SIMS	*Lt. Comdr. W. M. Hyman*
WORDEN	*Lt. Comdr. W. G. Pogue*

AIR GROUP

Rear Admiral A. W. Fitch

AIRCRAFT CARRIERS

YORKTOWN — LEXINGTON

DESTROYERS

Capt. G. C. Hoover

MORRIS *Flagship*	*Comdr. H. B. Jarrett*
ANDERSON	*Lt. Comdr. J. K. B. Ginder*
HAMMANN	*Comdr. A. E. True*
RUSSELL	*Lt. Comdr. G. R. Hartwig*

SUPPORT GROUP

Rear Admiral J. G. Crace, R.N.

HEAVY CRUISERS

AUSTRALIA — CHICAGO

LIGHT CRUISER

HOBART

DESTROYERS

Comdr. F. X. McInerney

PERKINS *Flagship*	*Lt. Comdr. W. C. Ford*
WALKE	*Lt. Comdr. T. E. Fraser*

SEARCH GROUP

Comdr. G. H. DeBaun

Seaplane Tender TANGIER

Informed on some of the movements of Inoue's ships, and deducing others, Admiral Fletcher headed the Allied task force in a northwesterly direction. On the evening of the 6th he detached the tanker NEOSHO and her escorting destroyer SIMS, ordering them over the southward horizon. The following morning he dispatched Admiral Crace's Support Group, plus destroyer FARRAGUT, to Jomard Passage in the Louisiades to block the Jap vanguard there. With the rest of his force, he continued northward.

He was hunting big game, and he found it. About 0845 that morning of May 7 American scouting planes spotted a portion of the Jap Occupation Force north of Misima Island in the Louisiades. And the portion spotted was a sizable one. It included several transports and the light carrier SHOHO.

Mistakenly the SHOHO was identified as a large carrier, and the scouts thought they saw a second carrier in this vanguard. Hoping for a crack at SHOKAKU and ZUIKAKU, the "YORK" and "LEX" airmen took off at rocket speed. Because of an incorrectly coded contact report, some 92 American planes were sent winging northwestward. A report from Australian land-based aircraft eventually steered them to the waters off Misima Island where they located the targets at about 1130.

The few Zero fighters that rose to intercept were brushed aside as though they were flies. While SHOHO reeled in frantic circles, trying to escape destruction, the "YORK" and "LEX" dive-bombers plastered the flat-top with an explosive rain that left the ship a listing, burning Ark. Then torpedo-planes, flying in under the smoke, pumped one "fish" after another into the flaming vessel. Not long after the tenth torpedo smashed through her hull, the SHOHO went down in a cerement of steam. Buried with her in

"That others might live." Lexington's survivors go over the side as this carrier is abandoned after damage in the Coral Sea action. Dimly seen in the drifting smoke from the burning carrier is the destroyer Morris, braving smoke, flame, and the imminent danger of exploding gasoline and ammunition in order to rescue the carrier's crew. Note the men sliding down into the water.

The price of strategic victory. The Japanese tried to extend their defensive perimeter by seizing the Aleutians and Midway. A stout American naval defense smashed the Midway invasion thrust and sank four carriers. The Yorktown, after wonderful hull resistance to the combined effects of four torpedoes and three bombs, finally sank. Above, destroyers take off her crew.

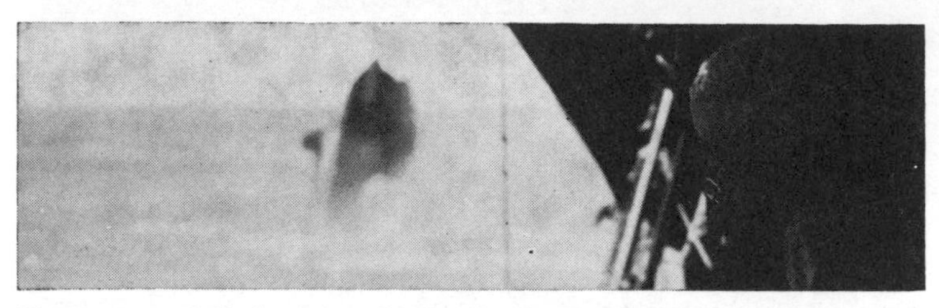

Hammann and Yorktown sunk. Late in the Battle of Midway a Japanese submarine fired a deadly torpedo spread and sent these warships to the bottom. The Hammann, shown plunging, was aiding Yorktown when hit.

Ubiquitous American greyhounds. Balch, Benham, and Fanning (foreground) helped Doolittle bomb Japan in the daring carrier raid of April, 1942.

Is a destroyer a carrier's best friend? This picture of the Battle of Midway shows the Yorktown and a scrappy "can" firing on two enemy planes. Our destroyers became increasingly able in air defense as the war progressed.

Ships fight on fuel. In the Midway action the Phelps' tanks were perilously low. Fuel is as necessary as ammunition. Oil gauges can also be victory's gauges.

Snatched from the cradle of the deep. Midway survivors from the destroyer Hammann return to Pearl Harbor aboard the Benham. Fleet destroyers perform almost countless maritime services in war and peace. The Hammann was one of many DD's which acted as good Samaritans. Damage control for the benefit of others was a particular function of our destroyers.

the sea were some 200 of her crew. Nine of her fighter planes had been shot out of the air. Total American loss: three bombers.

The demolishment of SHOHO and the appearance of Allied warships near Jomard Passage induced Admiral Inoue to call off the Port Moresby expedition. The remnant Occupation Force was already retiring northward. The SHOKAKU-ZUIKAKU Striking Force was farther from home, however. Having rounded the eastern end of the Solomons chain, it was by this time well south of Guadalcanal. And while aircraft from YORKTOWN and LEXINGTON had been flying destruction to the Japanese carrier SHOHO, planes from SHOKAKU and ZUIKAKU had been dealing death to the destroyer SIMS.

Loss of U.S.S. Sims

During the night of May 6-7 the Japanese Striking Force with SHOKAKU and ZUIKAKU had run steadily southward in the Coral Sea to a point about 250 miles due south of Guadalcanal. And as misty daylight sifted through the overcast, the Jap carriers launched scouting planes to search for the Allied force reported in the area.

At about this time American air scouts took off from carriers YORKTOWN and LEXINGTON, some 200 miles to the west, on a hunt for the big Jap carriers. The lowering overcast concealed the opposing forces, and the scouts failed to detect each other. But the Jap planes, winging southward, spotted SIMS and NEOSHO, which Admiral Fletcher had detached and sent southward, presumably out of reach of the enemy.

After the war it was learned that the Jap scouts identified NEOSHO as a carrier—all that was needed to bring from SHOKAKU and ZUIKAKU a flock of fighters and bombers 70 strong. When the first wave roared over the horizon the American destroyermen and tankermen knew they were in for it.

In the opening attack, Jap marksmanship was lacklustre. About 0910 a bomb intended for SIMS landed in the water a goodly yardage to port, and showered her with nothing but brine. The destroyer and the tanker dodged and dashed out from under the assault.

Twenty minutes later 16 high-level bombers attacked in two waves. Again, no hits. But at 1130 a flight of 24 dive-bombers came hurtling down from the ceiling, and SIMS was plunged into what was to be her final battle.

Her anti-aircraft guns rattled, slammed, and crashed. Flame splattered the sky, and into the sea fell a tattered plane. Then the dive-bombers were on top of the destroyer. Several of them were gunned out of the air; two or three, unable to pull out of screaming power dives, were blasted into extinction by their own bombs. But SIMS took three back-breaking hits. Not long after the third direct hit, she broke in two and sank in a pall of smoke and steam. Only 14 of her crew survived the sinking. Lost with the rest was SIMS' Commanding Officer, Lieutenant Commander W. M. Hyman.

The Battle of the Coral Sea (Continued)

Destroyer SIMS was not alone in her agony. Struck by a spate of bombs and a burning plane, the tanker NEOSHO was reduced to a floating wreck. A helpless derelict, she drifted for four days before she was located by the destroyer HENLEY (Commander Robert Hall Smith), dispatched on the 8th to the rescue. After the tankermen and SIMS survivors were taken off, HENLEY sank NEOSHO's charred hulk with a pair of torpedoes. All told, she rescued 14 destroyermen and 109 tanker sailors.

Some 176 of NEOSHO's crew were fatalities. Sixty-eight had recklessly abandoned ship on a float fashioned of four life rafts fastened together. For ten days this wretched party was adrift. When destroyer HELM (Lieutenant Commander C. E. Carroll) finally located the float, only four men were found alive.

In the meantime the Battle of the Coral Sea thundered on to its climax. On the afternoon of May 7 Admiral Crace's Support Group, which included destroyers PERKINS, WALKE, and FARRAGUT, was attacked south of the Louisiades where it had been sent to block Jomard Passage. The Allied ships were assailed by 12 Jap torpedo-planes with fighter escort from the 25th Air Flotilla at Rabaul. The three destroyers under Commander McInerney elevated a solid curtain of AA fire to protect cruisers H.M.A.S. AUSTRALIA and HOBART and U.S.S. CHICAGO. The cruisers also did some hot sky-shooting. In consequence, the little group escaped battle damage, and ten of the dozen attacking bombers were wiped out of the air.

While the Support Group battled the enemy off the Louisiades, Admiral Fletcher's Air Group conducted an intensive search for the Japanese carrier force in the Coral Sea. Distress calls from SIMS and NEOSHO had failed to specify the type of attacking aircraft, and Fletcher was at first unable to determine whether they were carrier planes or land-based.

By late afternoon of the 7th it became apparent that the numerous aerial "pips" showing up on the radar screens must be planes from an enemy carrier force near at hand. American Wildcats, boring through the cloudy ceiling, intercepted some Zeros and carrier-type dive-bombers. Five Zeros and two

Wildcats were shot down in savage dog-fighting. Then, as twilight gloomed the seascape, several Jap planes hovered over LEXINGTON and YORKTOWN, evidently mistaking the Americans for their own flat-tops. Driven off by ack-ack, the addled Japs flew eastward. LEXINGTON tracked them with her far-vision radar, and the enemy carrier force was located. The SHOKAKU-ZUIKAKU force was at that hour no more than 30 miles distant!

Admiral Fitch urged a night attack by cruisers and destroyers—strike in the dark. His proposal was vetoed by Admiral Fletcher, who directed that an all-out air assault be made the following morning. To this end Fletcher ordered the American Air Group southward to widen the range. Simultaneously the Jap carrier force made a northward run. However, the Jap force reversed course early in the morning of May 8. By daybreak the Jap carriers had reached a point about 250 miles southwest of Guadalcanal. Farther to the southwest, the American Air Group was some 170 miles distant from the Jap.

The enemy, under a front of clouds, had the better position; YORKTOWN and LEXINGTON were steaming beneath sunny skies. Both forces sent out scout planes at dawn. Japanese and American carriers were soon detected by the competing scouts, and at 0900 the opposing carriers launched attack squadrons. From the "YORK" and the "LEX" a total of 82 planes took off; some 70 soared away from SHOKAKU and ZUIKAKU. These enemy squadrons passed each other without making contact, and both were on target at about 1100 of that morning.

First to strike the Japanese foe, aircraft from YORKTOWN pounced on the SHOKAKU. The "YORK" torpedo-planes missed the mark, but the bombers scored two 1,000-pound hits that wrecked the carrier's flight deck and ruptured her gasoline tanks. A brilliant flag of flame unfurled at the carrier's prow; smoke surged across her shattered deck; when the YORKTOWN planes departed, the SHOKAKU, afire, was wandering in an aimless circle.

The LEXINGTON attack group had trouble in locating the ZUIKAKU. None of the bombers found the target. A swarm of Zeros put up furious opposition, and the "LEX" scouts and torpedo-planes, low on gas, were unable to score a direct hit on the carrier. But near misses raked the vessel, killed many of the deck crew, and sent her limping back to Truk with damage that would lay her up for a month.

While the planes from YORKTOWN and LEXINGTON were hammering at the Jap flat-tops, aircraft from SHOKAKU and ZUIKAKU were returning the compliment. They returned it with interest, concentrating their heaviest onslaught on LEXINGTON, the larger of the two American carriers. Maneuvering to evade the attacks, YORKTOWN and LEXINGTON took divergent courses which led them three or four miles apart. Bulk of the cruiser escort (ASTORIA, PORTLAND, and CHESTER) went with YORKTOWN, drawing with it destroyers RUSSELL, PHELPS, HAMMANN, and AYLWIN. This left LEXINGTON to bear the battle's brunt with cruisers MINNEAPOLIS and NEW ORLEANS, and destroyers MORRIS, ANDERSON, and DEWEY.

Skillful ship-handling by Captain Elliot Buckmaster brought YORKTOWN unscathed through three torpedo attacks, while her escorts saturated the air with an AA fire that forced the planes to launch their "fish" at long-range. A dive-bomber, however, managed to hit the carrier with a heavy bomb that penetrated three decks and burst in the aviation storeroom, killing 37 men. Near misses peppered the ship, and her crew was fighting painful battle damage when the final attack was over.

Less fortunate was the LEXINGTON. In spite of masterful maneuvering by Captain F. C. ("Ted") Sherman, the great carrier, assailed by torpedo-planes from port and starboard, took two blasting portside hits. Then dive-bombers whistled down to puncture the ship with near misses and stagger her with two direct hits. A 1,000-pound bomb smashed the port forward battery, and another bomb exploded inside the carrier's funnel. Severely wounded, the "LEX" carried on.

During the afternoon, LEXINGTON's damage-controlmen doused fires and corrected the vessel's list. For a time the crew was convinced the ship could be saved. But the blasting had ruptured her gasoline pipes; a steady leakage of fumes choked the vessel's compartments with combustible vapor. A sudden series of explosions shook the damaged carrier and touched off internal fires. About 1500 in the afternoon, LEXINGTON came to a dead-stop under a mountainous cauliflower of smoke. All pressure had died in her hose lines. But determined to make a last-ditch effort, LEXINGTON's captain appealed to Admiral Fitch for fire-fighting destroyers.

"The Admiral directed destroyers to come alongside, and told me to disembark my excess personnel to them," Captain Sherman recounted. *"The* MORRIS *passed over two hoses, while all of our crew who could be spared started down the lines to her deck. However, the fire was already beyond control. Explosions were occurring all the time. There was danger of the ship blowing up at any minute."*

That danger was more than apparent to the captain and crew of MORRIS. Alongside the huge, smoke-hazed carrier, the little DD was nuzzling a rumbling volcano. Nevertheless Commander Jarrett and his destroyermen coolly went about their business, passing lines through the billowing smudge, and taking aboard the carriermen who came down the ship's side.

At 1707 Admiral Fitch ordered Captain Sherman to abandon. Admiral Kinkaid, placed in charge of rescue operations, sent destroyers ANDERSON (Lieutenant Commander Ginder) and HAMMANN (Commander True) to join MORRIS alongside the carrier and take off survivors. Cruisers MINNEAPOLIS and NEW ORLEANS also moved in to stand by.

It took adroit conning to maneuver alongside this floating Vesuvius. The water around was crowded with rafts and swimmers. On a thread-like maze of lines men were sliding down the ship's side. Jockeying this way and that, destroyers MORRIS, ANDERSON, and HAMMANN had to move with the precision of figure skaters to avoid colliding with rafts, the burning carrier, and each other.

At 1720 Admiral Kinkaid ordered destroyer HAMMANN around to the carrier's starboard side to rescue swimmers and men on rafts. By expert conning, Commander True worked his destroyer through the clotted sea without upsetting rafts or running down swimmers, and Ensigns T. E. Krepski and R. L. Holton shoved off in HAMMANN's boats to snatch drowning officers and bluejackets from the seething water.

Having picked up nearly 100 men, HAMMANN was just backing clear, her deck crowded with survivors, when a tremendous explosion in LEXINGTON showered the destroyer with firebrands. The debris fouled HAMMANN's circulating pumps, slowing her back-up. But no one was injured.

About 1800 Captain Sherman with a few last-standers quit the ship. They were the last to leave. Of the LEXINGTON's complement of nearly 3,000, all but 26 officers and 190 men survived the gruelling ordeal of battle, inferno, and abandonment. So far as could be determined, not a carrierman was drowned in the maelstrom overside.

At 1853 the destroyer PHELPS (Lieutenant Commander Beck) was directed to sink the LEXINGTON with torpedo fire. Five torpedoes were shot at the abandoned carrier; four exploded against her smoldering hull. About an hour later the great ship listed over and went down to the accompaniment of last tremendous explosions.

The Battle of the Coral Sea signaled a tidal turn in the South Pacific. The Japanese drive below the equator had been stopped.

Battle-cost to the Allies was heavy—carrier LEXINGTON, destroyer SIMS, fleet oiler NEOSHO; YORKTOWN badly damaged; 66 aircraft lost; death toll of 543 officers and men.

But the Japanese paid for their eastward trespassing with the light carrier SHOHO, destroyer KIKUZUKI, and four landing barges; SHOKAKU crippled; ZUIKAKU's wings plucked; OKINASHIMA disabled; 80 aircraft lost; death toll of some 900 officers and men.

The Coral Sea Battle had another important consequence: it sent SHOKAKU limping to the repair yards and left ZUIKAKU temporarily bereft of planes. Thereby depriving the Imperial Navy of two first-line carriers which had been slated for the drive on Midway.

The deprivation may have meant all the difference between victory and defeat in the Central Pacific, where one of the decisive battles of the war was soon to be fought. And the DD's of DesPac were to fight in that battle, although they first were to participate in an incident that was more amusing than deadly.

The "Battle of Sydney Bay"

This was not a major engagement of the Pacific War. But its minor features were interesting.

A submarine raid on Sydney, Australia, might have worried the Allies considerably on that last night in May, 1942. A pair of I-boats firing torpedoes and shells into Sydney Bay would have been cause for genuine alarm. But a raid by two pint-size midget submarines—that was something else again.

However, the Japanese had an egotistical talent for underestimating the opposition. So two baby subs were piggy-backed within range of Sydney Harbor, and cut loose from their mother-subs' apron strings on the evening of May 31.

In Sydney Harbor that evening were American heavy cruiser CHICAGO and destroyer PERKINS, veterans of the Battle of the Coral Sea. Also the American destroyer tender DOBBIN.

CHICAGO, there for repair and overhaul, was moored at Buoy 2 near the Australian naval station on Garden Island. PERKINS was moored at near-by Buoy 4. Most of the harbor was under blackout, dark and silent, lulled by the nocturnal whisper and slip-slap of restless water.

At 2230 the harbor watch relayed a sudden submarine alarm. Alerted, the lookouts on the American and Allied ships strained their eyes to detect any sign of the enemy in the channel. And presently a sharp-eyed lookout on CHICAGO sighted a ruffle of foam on the water 300 yards distant.

Thunder clattered in the night as the heavy cruiser opened fire with 5-inch and 1.1-inch guns. PERKINS (Lieutenant Commander W. C. Ford) promptly got under way to screen CHICAGO. The periscope-feather disappeared.

At 0030 a torpedo came ripping across the channel, a watery lightning-streak. The luminous wake passed close aboard PERKINS, whisked on past CHICAGO, and struck a concrete wharf of Garden Island, demolishing a ferryboat with the blast. A second midget-fired torpedo sped through the water and struck the shore, but this one failed to explode.

At 0217 the American destroyer escorted the heavy cruiser down the dangerous bay, and the two ships headed seaward. Periscope sighted! The serpent-headed neck was so close aboard that CHICAGO could not depress her guns to fire at the sub. Then CHICAGO seemed to run right over the thing. It was gone in the cruiser's wake, perhaps rammed to the bottom. The midget-sub raid on Sydney was over.

By daybreak, June 1, PERKINS and CHICAGO were offshore, steaming in open water.

At that hour the drive on Midway was under way, and Japanese diversionary forces were moving across the North Pacific.

The Battle of Midway

There was nothing midget about the Japanese effort to seize Midway Island, though. Yamamoto's men-of-war included 10 battleships, 5 carriers, some 18 cruisers, 57 destroyers, 3 seaplane tenders, and various auxiliaries. A number of submarines operated with this immense fleet, and it was supported by aircraft from the Marshall Islands and the Marianas. The invasion convoy carried all the necessary military paraphernalia and some 3,500 case-hardened troops.

The Admiral had reason to believe that he could capture Midway almost without a fight. He knew that LEXINGTON and YORKTOWN had been plastered with bombs; heavy damage was certain, and it was possible that both carriers had been sunk. The Admiral was also informed that carriers HORNET and ENTERPRISE were in the South Pacific, and that SARATOGA in Puget Sound was still undergoing repair. With all American aircraft carriers in the Pacific thus accounted for, it should be easy for KAGA, AKAGI, HIRYU and SORYU, plus light carrier ZUIHO and the battleships and cruisers, to wipe out anything that stood between them and Midway.

Yamamoto's information was far from accurate. YORKTOWN was neither sunk nor damaged beyond the possibility of high-speed repairs. ENTERPRISE and HORNET were not so far afield in the South Pacific that they could not steam to the Midway area by the third day in June. These three flat-tops made it (and SARATOGA came within an ace of making it). Still, three carriers, one of them shaky from an emergency repair job, were heavily outnumbered by five.

And Admiral Nimitz was unable to scrape up any battleships for Midway's defense. In addition to the three carriers, just eight cruisers, 16 destroyers, and a couple of fleet oilers completed the American surface force at Midway. A total of some 33 United States ships facing the Japanese armada of 100!

A few Marine, Army, and Navy aircraft—Brewsters, Flying Forts, and elderly Catalinas—could be put in the balance against the Jap squadrons from the Marshalls and the Marianas. Pillar of the American defense was supposedly composed of 25 fleet submarines dispatched to the waters of Midway. Most of these subs were stationed to the west of the island as vedettes to guard the approaches and intercept the oncoming enemy. As it eventuated, this submarine effort was by and large a washout. A big V-boat sank a disabled Jap carrier, and another sub scared two Jap cruisers into a collision. Otherwise, no score.

Two big advantages the Americans had. Nimitz knew that Yamamoto was coming. Knew it from carefully assembled fragments of information, reports from here and there. So the Japanese lunge at Midway was robbed of surprise.

The other American advantage was radar. Not all of the ships had it, but enough of them, including the carriers, were so equipped. Whereas the Japs did not begin to install radar in any of their ships until the following August.

Exploding on June 3, 1942, and ending on June 6, the Battle of Midway was a long-range air engagement, similar to the Battle of the Coral Sea. In extent, fury, and consequence, it was the Coral Sea doubled and redoubled. A detailed account of this stupendous carrier duel—one of the crucial naval battles of all time, and perhaps the decisive battle of the Pacific War—cannot be included in this destroyer history. Its major moves and moments are sketched herein only to furnish the general background of the on-the-spot destroyer activity.

The American naval forces at Midway were composed of Task Force 16 (the HORNET-ENTERPRISE group) and Task Force 17 (the YORKTOWN group). At Pearl Harbor Rear Admiral Raymond A. Spruance assumed command of the HORNET-ENTERPRISE group, replacing Admiral Halsey, who was hospitalized with severe dermatitis. Rear Admiral F. J. Fletcher was in command of the YORKTOWN group.

Spruance headed his ships for Midway on May 28. Fletcher's force was en route for Midway two days later. On June 2 the two forces met, and from this rendezvous point they were ordered by Admiral Nimitz (who retained over-all tactical command of the forces) to steam into waters to the north of Midway. Under local command of Admiral Fletcher, the carrier forces proceeded to the designated area.

With HORNET and ENTERPRISE (TF 16) were cruisers MINNEAPOLIS, NORTHAMPTON, PENSACOLA, NEW

Orleans, Vincennes, and Atlanta, and fleet oilers Cimarron and Platte. And the following destroyers:

Phelps *Lt. Comdr. E. L. Beck*
Flagship of
Capt. A. R. Early, comdesron 1
Dewey *Lt. Comdr. C. F. Chillingworth, Jr.*
Worden *Lt. Comdr. W. G. Pogue*
Balch *Lt. Comdr. H. H. Tiemroth*
Flagship of
Capt. E. P. Sauer, comdesron 6
Benham *Lt. Comdr. J. M. Worthington*
Ellet *Lt. Comdr. F. H. Gardner*
Maury *Lt. Comdr. G. L. Sims*
Monssen *Comdr. R. N. Smoot*
Conyngham *Lt. Comdr. H. C. Daniel*
Monaghan *Lt. Comdr. W. P. Burford*
Aylwin *Lt. Comdr. G. R. Phelan*
Flying pennant of
Comdr. R. S. Riggs, comdesdiv 2

With Yorktown (TF 17) were cruisers Portland and Astoria. And the following destroyers.

Morris *Comdr. H. B. Jarret*
Flagship of
Capt. G. C. Hoover, comdesron 2
Anderson *Lt. Comdr. J. K. B. Ginder*
Hughes *Lt. Comdr. D. J. Ramsey*
Russell *Lt. Comdr. G. R. Hartwig*
Flying pennant of
Capt. R. G. Tobin, comdesdiv 4
Hammann *Comdr. A. E. True*
Gwin *Comdr. J. M. Higgins*
Flying pennant of
Comdr. H. R. Holcomb, comdesdiv 22

Yamamoto had his forces divided into three groups: a Main Body containing six battleships, three cruisers, a destroyer squadron, and Yamamoto in person; a Striking Force composed of the aircraft carriers Kaga, Akagi, Hiryu, and Soryu (all veterans of the Pearl Harbor raid) with screen; and an Occupation Force of transports escorted by two battleships, eight cruisers, and destroyers. The Striking Force, coming down from the northwest, spearheaded the attack. The Occupation Force, coming up from the Marianas, simultaneously approached Midway from the southwest. The Main Body, built around super battleship Yamato, followed. Japanese submarines scouted ahead of the armada with orders to take a line west of Pearl Harbor and intercept any American forces rushed to Midway's defense.

To deceive and confuse the Americans, Jap naval forces made a simultaneous thrust at the Aleutian Islands west of Alaska, hoping to divert attention from the real target of Midway.

But things did not go according to Yamamoto's plans. Nimitz was not deceived by the Aleutian strike made on the morning of June 3. That same morning the Jap armada was spotted 700 miles off Midway by an air scout. Then, an American submarine sighted the Japanese Occupation Force. On the night of the 3rd, the armada was hit by planes from Midway. Next morning the island's PBY search patrol spotted the Striking Force 200 miles to the northwest. Jap aircraft were already buzzing in to strike. Flashed to Midway, the alarm sent every plane on the island into the air. A flight of Flying Forts, already aloft, was directed to bomb the Jap flat-tops.

Totaling some 100 bombers and torpedo-planes, escorted by Zero fighters, the first waves of Jap aircraft swept in to blast the island. About 30 miles off shore they were met by a handful of Marine pilots who staged a tooth-and-nail dogfight to break up the attack. The Marine planes were no match for the faster Zeros. Fifteen Marines were shot down; and Midway's hour had come.

Other Midway aircraft—B-26's, Navy torpedo planes, Flying Forts, Marine dive-bombers—were swept from the sky as they strove to attack the Jap carriers. Where were the American carrier forces? Tying on every knot they could make to reach the scene. But they were unable to reach the battle area until dawn of June 4.

Then Jap air scouts sighted the Enterprise-Hornet-Yorktown threat on the horizon. The word was flashed to the Japanese Striking Force, and Kaga, Akagi, Hiryu, and Soryu were promptly headed northeastward to intercept the American carriers. The Jap carrier planes, which had been loading bombs for a delivery upon Midway, were ordered to shift from bombs to torpedoes. This switch in Striking Force procedure entailed a delay which proved of benefit to the Americans.

When the Jap carrier group made its abrupt course-change, planes from Enterprise and Hornet were aloft. The bombers from Enterprise flew in a westward direction, but those from Hornet made a beeline for the enemy's previously reported position —and found vacant waters. Ensued a frantic search across miles of open ocean, some of the Hornet fighters going down at sea, out of fuel, and others making forced landings at Midway. The Enterprise squadrons were also counting every drop of gasoline in swiftly draining tanks.

Then came the break. Yorktown's planes, climbing high, sighted the elusive enemy and coached the Hornet and Enterprise pilots in on the target. Providentially they hit the Jap Striking Force just as its bombers were reloading.

In the wild air battle that exploded over the Japanese Striking Force at 0920, all 15 of the planes of HORNET Torpedo Squadron 8, winging in on the attack, were shot down by Zero fighters or anti-aircraft fire. But planes from ENTERPRISE and YORKTOWN slashed their way through the Jap carrier screen.

Four bombs struck the KAGA, tore her island to pieces, wrecked her deck, and left her dead in the water, a floating blast-furnace. And then AKAGI was afire from bomb hits, and left wallowing. Then SORYU. Far over the horizon, carrier HIRYU turned tail and fled.

Twenty YORKTOWN and ENTERPRISE planes were lost in the aerial battle, but United States Navy aircraft had turned the tide at Midway. They had dealt the Jap armada a paralyzing smash, wrecking three carriers in record time.

However, while KAGA, AKAGI, and SORYU were transformed from carriers into catafalques, YORKTOWN, some 200 miles away, was attacked by 18 Jap dive-bombers accompanied by 18 Zero fighters. YORKTOWN spotted the attackers on her radar screen, and a dozen of her fighters soared to meet the foe. As the enemy came over, destroyers MORRIS, ANDERSON, HUGHES, RUSSELL, and HAMMANN, maneuvering around the big flat-top, swept the sky with fire. Cruisers ASTORIA and PORTLAND also scorched the sky, as did YORKTOWN's AA batteries. Only eight of the Jap bombers—single-engined Bakugekis from HIRYU—managed to dodge YORKTOWN's fighters and break through the anti-aircraft screen. One of these was gunned down as it roared in on the attack. A second caught a load of ack-ack, but before it died in the air, the damaged plane landed a bomb on YORKTOWN's deck. A third plane was blown to fragments by sharpshooting AA gunners as it made its bombing run. Then YORKTOWN took two bombs in quick succession. One smashed into her starboard side. The other blasted her No. 1 elevator. But all eight attacking bombers were wiped out in payment.

YORKTOWN was hurt, but her damage-controlmen soon had fires and wreckage in hand. Within two hours the carrier was capable of 20 knots, and her planes were returning to her flight deck.

Then the radar screen picked up another flock of enemy "bogies." Up went six YORKTOWN fighters to intercept, but before they could do so, the Japs were within striking range of the flat-top.

These were torpedo-planes from HIRYU—some 16 or so—escorted by the usual cordon of vicious Zeros. They ran into a curtain of fire from the AA guns of the carrier and of destroyers HAMMANN, RUSSELL, MORRIS, ANDERSON, and HUGHES. In less than six minutes all 16 torpedo-planes were consumed as so much confetti tossed into a furnace.

But before they died, four of them slipped torpedoes into the water within range of YORKTOWN. Striking her on her port side amidships, two of the torpedoes blew huge holes in the carrier's hull, jolting her with immense explosions that left her listing and reeling. With white smoke gushing from her stacks, the great flat-top swung in a helpless circle, her lights blown out, her flight deck canted, the ocean pouring in below decks.

The guardian destroyers closed in around her. YORKTOWN's damage-controlmen could do nothing to stem the inrushing flood. The port list increased to an angle that threatened an imminent overturn. Fearing his ship would capsize at any moment, Captain Elliott Buckmaster gave the order to abandon. The destroyers moved forward to pick up the men who came sliding down the carrier's tilted deck. The time was 1455.

Strangely coincident, about the time wounded YORKTOWN was torpedoed by Jap aircraft, the disabled SORYU in a distant quarter of the battle area was fatally torpedoed by the American submarine NAUTILUS. The SORYU sank at dusk. She was presently joined on the bottom by the gutted KAGA. Later that night the derelict AKAGI took the plunge. And by that hour the carrier HIRYU was on her way to the Hereafter.

Last of the Striking Force carriers, HIRYU had been located by scouts sent out from YORKTOWN to track down the American carrier's tormentors. The scouts brought bombers from ENTERPRISE racing to the target. With them were bombers from YORKTOWN, planes now orphaned and bent on retribution. Pouncing on HIRYU at about 1700, they dealt this enemy flat-top a fearful flogging. When a squadron from HORNET arrived some time later, they found HIRYU a burning hulk. The "Hornets" thereupon bombed the battleship KIRISHIMA and other HIRYU escorts. Throughout the night the battered Jap carrier drifted aimlessly, a floating funeral pyre. Obsequies were concluded the following morning by torpedoes from a Jap destroyer.

As for YORKTOWN, she remained stubbornly afloat. Presently she was on a tow line tethered to the American minesweeper VIREO, dispatched to haul her home to Pearl Harbor. Two destroyers arrived on the scene that afternoon to assist the smoldering carrier—U.S.S. GWIN (Commander Higgins) and U.S.S. MONAGHAN (Lieutenant Commander Burford).

GWIN placed a salvage party on the flat-top, as did HUGHES. It took nerve to board this smoke-choked, fire-blackened carrier which might suddenly keel up or trap all hands in the wreckage of a belated explosion. But Commander Holcomb, the Division Commander in Gwin, correctly judged the vessel safe enough for the venture, and the destroyermen who boarded her knew their business. They were able to accomplish little, however, and at nightfall they were taken off.

Yamamoto still had at hand his Main Body—six battleships, light carrier Zuiho, a cruiser division, and a squadron of destroyers. Led by mighty super-battleship Yamato, this force would have been facing two weary American carrier groups whose air complements were sorely depleted and whose surface crews were ready to drop from exhaustion. But Yamamoto was unwilling to risk his Main Body, and at 2200 on June 4 he ordered his forces to retire.

As for the face-saving cruiser bombardment, it ended in fiasco after cruisers Mogami and Mikuma collided. Next, these two warships were caught and dealt a ferocious thrashing by planes from Midway. Then they were caught by planes from Enterprise and Hornet. The Mikuma was summarily sunk. The Mogami was mangled beyond all recognition, but somehow she managed to crawl away to Truk.

By the time Gwin's salvage party boarded Yorktown the residue of Yamamoto's armada was retiring westward, pursued by American planes. The withdrawal permitted the dispatch of more destroyers to the aid of Yorktown. That night Captain Buckmaster arrived on the scene with Balch (Lieutenant Commander Tiemroth), Benham (Lieutenant Commander Worthington), and Hammann (Commander True), the DD's under command of Captain Sauer in Balch. With the coming of daylight (June 6) a salvage crew of the Captain, 29 officers, and 141 men boarded the smoldering Yorktown.

Captain Buckmaster believed his ship could be saved, and he sent Hammann in on the starboard side of the drifting vessel to assist the fire-fighters and to furnish power for fire-fighting apparatus. One gang went to work pumping out some flooded compartments and flooding others to shift the water below decks and bring the ship on even keel. Another gang fought the fires. Others labored at repairs.

By early afternoon the salvage work was showing results. Yorktown's list had been reduced. Hammann, secured alongside, was steadily pumping, and the carrier's internal fires were being smothered. At 1530 they were winning the fight. At 1535 all was lost.

"Torpedo!"

Four watery lightning-streaks sped into view on Yorktown's starboard side. Two torpedoes hit her directly below her island, smashing through the hull as though it were eggshell. And one torpedo struck the Hammann. An enormous cloud of smoke billowed skyward, and the two ships, side by side, were mortally stricken.

The time was 1536.

The Battle of Midway had exploded its aftermath.

Loss of U.S.S. Hammann

The submarine that torpedoed Yorktown and Hammann at 1536 in the afternoon of June 6 was the I-168. Executing an unquestionably daring attack, she struck the one killing blow the Japs were able to deal to the United States surface forces at Midway.

Hammann's destroyermen saw it coming. General Quarters sent them leaping to their stations at the instant the torpedo wakes were sighted. On the bridge Commander True ordered full speed astern on the inboard engine, attempting to sheer away and avoid the deadly "fish." Below decks, the engineers raced the turbine. Topside, the Gunnery Officer, Lieutenant (jg) C. C. Hartigan, ordered machine-gunners to fire on the torpedoes, praying that a fusillade might explode them.

"The first torpedo appeared to pass under the Hammann *in the vicinity of No. 2 gun."* So Commander True subsequently recalled. This first torpedo struck Yorktown. There was a deafening thunderclap, followed by a deep-bellying roar. And then True was flung from his feet, stunned by a shocking blast. Hammann had been hit.

Bursting into the destroyer's No. 2 fireroom, the torpedo exploded with a violence that broke the ship's back. Spouts of oil and water and a cloud of debris were flung skyward by the upvented explosion. Hammann lowered her head in the water, and began to settle. True, thrown across the pilot-house, had suffered a broken rib. The "Exec" on the bridge gave the order, "Abandon ship!"

Within four minutes of the torpedo blast, the destroyer was under the sea.

While Hammann was sinking, First Class Torpedoman Berlyn Kimbrel made a top-speed recheck of the depth-charges to be sure they were set on "Safe." He spent a final moment passing lifejackets to his shipmates. Last man to leave the ship's fantail, Kimbrel was lost. A minute after the destroyer went down, the sea was tossed by a tremendous underwater detonation. It may have been a defective depth charge, or one of Hammann's torpedoes. Torpedoman Kimbrel was killed by the blast he had tried so heroically to avert.

Hammann sunk! Yorktown at death's door! Destroyers Gwin, Hughes, Benham, Monaghan, and Balch conducted a high-pressure hunt for the killer responsible for this slaughter. They ran down contacts and bombed the sea with depth-charge patterns in a hunt that lasted until after midnight. I-168 escaped by the skin of her chattering teeth.

Meantime HAMMANN's survivors were rescued and cared for. As acting Executive Officer, Lieutenant (jg) Hartigan reported the valiant efforts of the lifesavers. Among them: *"Alonza Crawford, Jr., Mess Attendant, 1/c, did wonderful work on board the* U.S.S. BENHAM *in taking care of wounded. He stayed up all the first night and worked almost continuously the first day."*

HAMMANN did not go down alone. At 0701 the following morning, YORKTOWN capsized and sank. These were the only United States men-of-war lost in the Battle of Midway—one aircraft carrier, and one destroyer.

The battle cost the Imperial Japanese Navy four aircraft carriers and a heavy cruiser.

Midway—Stand Tide

Midway was where the war-tide stood still. The point where the Japanese onrush was halted. The beginning of its ebb. And the place where the Imperial Japanese Navy suffered its first defeat since 1592.

The victory was costly enough for the United States. Total American losses included 150 aircraft, and 307 officers and men, as well as carrier YORKTOWN and destroyer HAMMANN. But these losses were light compared with those suffered by the enemy.

In addition to four aircraft carriers and a cruiser, the Japs lost at Midway some 253 planes and about 3,500 officers and men, the cream of the Imperial Navy. The cruiser MOGAMI, a half-sunk wreck, was out of the war for many months, and a Jap destroyer was similarly disabled.

The American destroyers which participated in the battle had been unable to strike the foe with a torpedo or gun attack, but they had put up a four-star anti-air defense; had screened the carriers in masterful fashion; had worked with unsurpassed valor and skill as salvage ships and rescue vessels.

Observed Captain G. C. Hoover, ComDesRon 2: *"THE MARKED IMPROVEMENT IN . . . ANTI-AIRCRAFT FIRE WAS PARTICULARLY GRATIFYING IN VIEW OF THE RELATIVELY POOR SHOWING MADE BY THESE WEAPONS IN THE ENGAGEMENT OF THIS TASK FORCE IN THE CORAL SEA. THIS CAN BE ATTRIBUTED PERHAPS TO ADDITIONAL TRAINING AND TO THE STEADYING EFFECT OF BATTLE EXPERIENCE."*

As for rescue work, two of BALCH's destroyermen, recovering YORKTOWN survivors, had put on a performance long to be remembered by all who witnessed it. Commending A. E. Lewis, Seaman First, and H. E. Prideaux, Fireman Second, BALCH's Commanding Officer noted:

"THESE TWO MEN WERE VERY ACTIVE AND TIRELESS IN CARRYING BUOYED LINES FROM 300 TO 400 YARDS OUT TO EXHAUSTED SWIMMERS TIME AFTER TIME. EACH OF THESE VOLUNTARILY, AND WITH DISREGARD FOR HIS OWN SAFETY, ENTERED THE OILY WATERS TO RENDER PROMPT PERSONAL ASSISTANCE TO WOUNDED, EXHAUSTED, OIL-SOAKED MEN WHO WERE IN DANGER OF BEING LOST IF IMMEDIATE ASSISTANCE WERE NOT FORTHCOMING. DURING THIS TIME FREQUENT REPORTS ON THE WARNING NET INDICATED EVERY POSSIBILITY OF THE RETURN OF ENEMY AIRCRAFT FOR FURTHER ATTACKS. ALL DESTROYERS WERE ORDERED TO MAKE FULL SPEED IN THE EVENT OF ANOTHER AIR ATTACK. PERSONNEL WHO PARTICIPATED IN THE PROMPT RESCUE WORK DESCRIBED ABOVE, DID SO WITH KNOWLEDGE THAT THEIR OWN CHANCES OF SAFETY WERE VERY SLIGHT IF A SECOND AIR ATTACK MATERIALIZED DURING RESCUE OPERATIONS."

It was that sort of effort that defeated the Japanese armada at Midway.

LOSS OF THE HAMMANN

PART III

HOLDING THE OCEANIC FRONT

But here are men who fought in gallant actions
As gallantly as ever heroes fought. . . .

BYRON

CHAPTER 11

CONVOY ESCORTS VERSUS WOLFPACKS

(July-December 1942)

All-Out U-Boat Drive

In the summer of 1942 the U-boats renewed the offensive against Atlantic shipping. It was typical Doenitz strategy—hammer at a soft spot, then, when the defense is strengthened, shift the attack to another weak sector.

Thus, when American A/S defenses were tightened on the Eastern Sea Frontier the U-boats struck in the Gulf of Mexico. With the strengthening of Gulf defenses the raiders attacked coastal shipping off Panama. The *Paukenschlag* operation was then diverted to a Caribbean Campaign while the mid-ocean wolfpacks resumed their drive, slashing at trans-Atlantic traffic.

Westbound Convoy ON-115—a train of 41 ships under Canadian escortage—was ambushed in the North Atlantic on July 31. For five days the escorts fought off the pack which grew to eight or nine U-boats as the scrimmage progressed. Excellent screening and counterattacking held the foe at bay; not a ship was torpedoed, and U-588 was sunk by Canadian escorts WETASKIWIN and SKEENA.

On August 6 the same wolfpack attacked eastbound Convoy SC-94, also under Canadian escortage. Again aggressive counter-attacks drove off the wolves, and the Canadian DD ASSINIBOINE sank the U-210. Two days later the convoy was ambushed by another wolfpack; three ships were sunk by torpedo fire. Retaliating with a vengeance, H.M. corvette DIANTHUS hunted down and forced to the surface the U-379, which she immediately rammed to the bottom.

Although the score was auspicious—three merchantmen to three U-boats—the onslaught was ominous. It presaged a wolfpack rampage that was to go full blast in the Atlantic for the rest of the year.

The U-boats struck at every trans-ocean merchant convoy which crossed in August 1942. Twenty-four ships were sunk in North Atlantic Convoy Areas that month. In September the North Atlantic sinkings mounted to 28. In October they totaled 25. In November, 29. And in Central and South Atlantic Areas, the U-boats were equally destructive. A wolfpack prowled right into the Gulf of St. Lawrence and sank seven ships in the approaches to Quebec.

Brazil entered the war against the Axis on August 22, 1942, after the U-boats attacked shipping off the Brazilian hump. Simultaneously campaigns raged in the waters off West Africa and the approaches to Capetown. And the Murmansk Run was still murderous for Allied convoys.

Too, the Germans were trying out several innovations. *Pillenwerfer*. Acoustic torpedoes. Schemes for making submarines radar-proof. For the most part, these novelties would prove ineffective (*Pillenwerfer* and acoustic torpedoes were easily countered by the Allies, and the Germans could do little to counter radar). However, one Doenitz-sponsored innovation did much to empower and accelerate the U-boat offensive. The innovation: supply submarines, big 1600-tonners, to fuel and provision the wolfpacks at sea, thereby obviating the necessity for frequent returns to base.

These supply submarines (or "milk cows," as Americans dubbed them) were stationed in various open-sea areas suitable for safe rendezvous. The Azores area, for example. Relatively secure from air attack, the "milk cow" would meet up with her brood to feed the hungry U-boats fresh supplies of oil, water, groceries, spare parts, and torpedoes. Analyzing the "milk cow" effort, the ASW Research Operations Group found that the average U-boat cruise of 4½ weeks was extended to 9 weeks by the supply-sub program. Postwar inquiry disclosed that some of the 500-ton U-boats were continuously at sea for 16 weeks.

Late in July 1942 one of the first supply submarines, the U-460, took station off the Brazilian coast and made rendezvous with a wolfpack of ten U-boats. Shortly after this clandestine meeting, five Brazilian merchantmen went to the bottom, torpedoed. Brazil's response was a prompt declaration of war on the Nazi-Fascist powers. Thereafter Vice Admiral Jonas H. Ingram's Task Force had its hands full with A/S warfare. The lid was off in the South Atlantic Ocean.

So DesLant destroyers were urgently needed that autumn—for operations in the South Atlantic; for A/S duty in the West Indies; for convoy escortage in the North Atlantic. Most urgently they were needed for the escort of United States troop convoys which were carrying Army forces to Britain in preparation for the invasions of Continental Europe and North Africa.

Atlantic Command Areas (July-December 1942)

As in the war's beginning, the Royal Navy was responsible for most of the convoying in the eastern reaches of the North and South Atlantic. To relieve United States destroyers for duty with the "troop lift," the Royal Navy and the Canadian Navy late in the spring of 1942 assumed responsibility for the bulk of all trans-Atlantic merchant convoying.

The chart inside the back cover shows the various sea frontiers and command areas which the Allies had established by the summer of 1942. Note the four North Atlantic Convoy Areas designated "Western Local," "Mid-Ocean," "Eastern Local," and "Iceland Shuttle."

As shown, the Western Local Area lay between Cape Cod and "Westomp" at long. 52 W. Eastbound convoys were escorted to the "Westomp" junction by Canadian and British warships under Canadian Command. Eight escort units based at Boston served the Western Local Area.

The Mid-Ocean Area, lying between "Westomp" (long. 52 W) and "Eastomp" (long. 22 W), was jointly covered by British and American forces under command of Rear Admiral R. M. Brainard. Fourteen units were available for escortage. Composed of American destroyers and British or Canadian corvettes, three of the units were under American tactical command. Under British tactical command were seven units composed of Royal Navy and Canadian destroyers and corvettes. A pair of Polish destroyers, the BLYSKAWICA and the BURZA, and several Free French corvettes operated with these Mid-Ocean groups. Eastbound convoys were met by these units at "Westomp" and escorted as far as "Eastomp." There the Mid-Ocean escorts were relieved by British escorts assigned to the Eastern Local Area. The Britishers conducted the convoy to its destination while the relieved escorts steamed to Londonderry to refuel. Westbound convoys were escorted by Mid-Ocean groups from "Eastomp" to "Westomp" where they were turned over to Western Local escortage, the relieved groups proceeding to Argentia to refuel.

Lying between long. 22 W and the British Isles, the Eastern Local Area was the Royal Navy's responsibility. The Iceland Shuttle was covered by United States naval units under American command; one or two U.S. destroyers based at Hvalfjordur did the escorting to or from a "Momp" rendezvous point.

These arrangements generally held good until the summer of 1943.

North Atlantic Torpedo Tempest

Attacking Atlantic shipping on all fronts, the wolfpacks sank some 88 Allied vessels in September 1942. Much of this tonnage went down in areas under American control. But American escorts were still short of A/S equipment, training, and experience.

One of the heavy losers that autumn was North Atlantic Convoy SC-100. Ambushed during a three-day storm, and attacked by a pack that numbered at least seven U-boats, the 24-ship convoy had to fight tempest as well as torpedoes. The running battle began on September 20, and ended two nights later. The escorts, among them United States Coast Guard cutters SPENCER and CAMPBELL, under command of Captain P. R. Heineman, put up a vigorous defense. But the convoy was unable to keep formation in the storm. Four ships, two of them stragglers, were struck and downed by torpedo salvos.

The cutters sighted the U-boats, but were unable to overhaul, and the enemy escaped in high seas. Apparently the U-boats employed *Pillenwerfer* to thwart sonar contact.

Not long after the attack on Convoy SC-100, westbound Convoy ON-127 was ambushed. Seven ships were torpedoed and sunk in the battle that ensued.

As ship sinkings once more climbed, the Allies strove to extend air cover in Western Local and Eastern Local areas. And on October 10, eastbound convoys were put on an eight-day cycle to make the most of available escortage. The measure did little to relieve the situation. Eastbound Convoy SC-104 was ambushed that month in the misty ocean due south of Cape Farewell. Eight merchantmen went plunging to the bottom. Convoy HX-212 was similarly assailed on this northerly route. The escort unit, which included the destroyer BADGER (Lieutenant Commander R. A. Wolverton) and Coast Guard cutter CAMPBELL, was unable to prevent the torpedoing of five more ships. Before the month was out, the wolfpacks had cost Allied shipping in the North Atlantic an October toll of some 189,000 tons.

But these wolfpack attacks were confined mostly to merchant convoys, and American destroyers on convoy duty in the North Atlantic were almost wholly engaged in screening trans-ocean (AT-TA) troop convoys.

Although troop convoys were priority targets for U-boat torpedoes, they escaped submarine attack because of two factors: speed and strong escortage. Deprived of these, the troopers were as vulnerable to wolfpack assault as any other type of shipping. As witness the onslaught on Convoy SG-6.

Attack on SG-6 (Sinking of Army Transport Chatham)

On August 25, 1942, Convoy SG-6 left Sydney, Cape Breton, and headed northward for the Gulf of St. Lawrence. The convoy was formed in two groups, one fast, the other slow. The slow group contained three merchantmen, the Navy tanker LARAMIE, and the Navy salvage vessel HARJURAND (a converted tug), under escort of medium-sized Coast Guard cutters ALGONQUIN and MOHAWK. The fast group was composed of the Army transport CHATHAM (ex-MARITIME COMMISSION) under escort of the 1,780-ton Coast Guard cutter MOJAVE. The convoy was to take the inside route through the Strait of Belle Isle between Newfoundland and Labrador. Destination: Greenland.

The fast group of Convoy SG-6 was struck by a torpedo salvo almost as soon as it emerged from the Strait of Belle Isle. Morning clear—sea calm—time: 0915. A thundering crash, and Army transport CHATHAM heeled over on her side, vomiting smoke.

The attack had come without warning; screening no more than 1,000 yards ahead, the cutter MOJAVE failed to detect the enemy, nor was she able to contact the U-boat afterward. MOJAVE's skipper, Lieutenant Commander J. A. Kerrins, U.S.C.G., directed life-saving operations with professional Coast Guard efficiency. Some 25 men lost their lives in the sinking; 139 of the ship's crew and 430 American and Canadian soldiers were saved.

As a result of MOJAVE's failure to report the attack, the slow SG-6 group transited the Strait of Belle Isle that evening and advanced blindly into the trap which had snared CHATHAM. Moonlight—placid sea—time: 2132. Torpedo-thunder smashed the stillness. Navy oiler LARAMIE and the freighter S. S. ARLYN staggered to a halt under shrouds of smoke. Escorts MOHAWK and ALGONQUIN dashed this way and that, hunting the author of this surprise attack. Again the U-boat escaped detection.

ARLYN was loaded with explosives, and the crew abandoned in wild disorder. Discipline and competent damage-control kept the Navy tanker LARAMIE afloat, and eventually she was taken into port.

Low speed and insufficient escortage conspired to bring on disaster to this convoy. CHATHAM's top speed was about 12 knots, and she was making only 9 when torpedoed. She was the first American troopship lost in the war.

In February 1943 troop transports DORCHESTER and HENRY R. MALLORY would go down under similar handicap—slow convoys and inadequate protection. But the fast trans-Atlantic (AT-NA) troop convoys, under heavy escort and screened by United States destroyers, ran the wolfpack gantlet without casualties.

Concerning the disastrous voyage of Convoy SG-6, Rear Admiral Brainard offered some instructive criticisms. Among other things, he pointed to the following imperatives:

"(a) Necessity for retaining all escorts and ships of the convoy together in order to provide maximum protection. . . .

"(b) The importance of zigzagging in the case of fast ships and steering evasive courses in the case of slower ships. . . .

"(c) The absolute necessity for immediately reporting contact with the enemy, including the position thereof. . . .

"(d) The relative unimportance of radio silence when in contact with the enemy, and the necessity of keeping appropriate authorities informed by high frequency radio even when not in contact with the enemy, in order to permit necessary coordinating action on the part of operational authorities."

He also remarked on *"the inadequate protection provided by escorts maintaining stations 500-1,000 yards from the convoy."*

From the first week in July until the last of December 1942, troop convoys crossed to Britain in a steady procession. They were escorted by Task Force 37 (Rear Admiral L. C. Davidson) composed of cruiser PHILADELPHIA, battleship NEW YORK, and six to twelve destroyers, and Task Force 38 (Captain C. F. Bryant, Jr.) consisting of battleship ARKANSAS, cruiser BROOKLYN, and seven to eleven DD's. Anywhere from eight to fifteen transports were in convoy. Not a soldier was lost through enemy action in the six-month period in mention, and not a ship suffered torpedo attack.

Two serious voyage disasters marred the record, however. The first was visited upon Task Force 37, and resulted in calamitous destroyer casualties. The second ruined a large transport in a convoy escorted by Task Force 38.

Loss of U.S.S. Ingraham

The disaster which overtook the destroyer INGRAHAM furnishes a striking example of the fatal chain-of-events sometimes unleashed by a trivial happenstance or minor incident.

At 0623 in the morning of August 22, 1942, eastbound convoy AT-20, under escort of Task Force 37, was standing seaward from Halifax Harbor. There were ten ships in the troop convoy. Accompanying PHILADELPHIA and NEW YORK, nine destroyers made up the escort group. Screen Commander was Captain J. B. Heffernan with his pennant in the destroyer BUCK.

Both the forenoon watch and the afternoon watch were uneventful. Then (time: 1730) the fateful incident. The ships were making routine radar sweeps, and the radar of troopship LETITIA registered a contact on a "stranger." The report was duly made, and the Screen Commander ordered destroyer SWANSON to investigate.

SWANSON searched for well over an hour, assisted by INGRAHAM. Then at 1920 it appeared that the sonar target had been a large school of frightened porpoises. The radar "pip" may have been a U-boat —or a phantom.

The diversion created the usual realignment in the escort screen and consequent jockeying for position when the involved destroyers resumed their patrol stations. On this occasion, at 2200 fog added to the trouble.

At 2205 the flag destroyer BUCK received orders over TBS (voice radio) from Commander Task Force 37 to go close aboard the LETITIA and escort her to her proper station 1000 yards on cruiser PHILADELPHIA's starboard beam. The smother was so opaque that BUCK, running on radar ranges and bearings, was ordered to use her bull horn to direct LETITIA to her proper station as she shifted position in the shuffled screen.

At 2225, as BUCK was crossing through the column, a ship loomed out of the fog only 30 yards from the destroyer's beam. The lookout's shout was drowned by a grinding crash as the transport AWATEA rammed BUCK in the starboard quarter. The transport's steep bow almost sheared off the destroyer's fantail. Dislodged from its arbor, a 300-pound depth charge hurtled from a K-gun and exploded near BUCK's churning propellers. The blast mangled the destroyer's gashed fantail and damaged the port propeller. BUCK reeled away, dragging a wrecked stern.

A moment later the damaged destroyer heard a thunderous explosion—a tremendous blast that tinted the fog off to starboard where the fleet oiler CHEMUNG (Commander J. J. Twomey) had been steaming. BUCK's bridge personnel and Screen Commander Heffernan thought the CHEMUNG had been torpedoed.

The eruption, however, was that of a destroyer blowing up. Disaster had ricochetted to strike the U.S.S. INGRAHAM as her captain, Commander W. M. Haynsworth, maneuvered her through the blinding mist. Ordered to investigate the BUCK-AWATEA collision, INGRAHAM had steamed directly across the bow of the CHEMUNG, and the fleet oiler had run into the destroyer headlong.

Cutting in like a plow blade, the tanker's prow slashed through steel plates and framework as though they were cardboard. As INGRAHAM listed over, her depth charges exploded. CHEMUNG backed away with a crushed forepeak scorched by the blasting. Nothing could be done for INGRAHAM. Lying on her side, the destroyer seemed to burst asunder internally. Apparently all of her depth charges let go. Rescuers were unable to approach the roaring inferno.

The destroyer's entire crew was nearly immolated, only ten men and one officer escaped the bursting warship. Commander Haynsworth was lost with the others.

At 0510 of that black morning BUCK's crew cut away her demolished fantail, and CHEMUNG moved in to take disabled BUCK in tow. Seven destroyermen had been killed in the BUCK-AWATEA collision. Several of CHEMUNG's crew had been seriously injured in the collision with INGRAHAM. While the tanker passed BUCK a tow line, the destroyer was able to exchange assistance by sending blood plasma to CHEMUNG.

The destroyer BRISTOL was directed to escort the injured ships back to port. Convoy AT-20 continued eastward. Altogether, it had been ravaged as though by a wolfpack battle. Destroyer INGRAHAM sunk with heavy casualties. Destroyer BUCK severely damaged. Tanker CHEMUNG badly damaged. Transport AWATEA crippled and forced to turn back. Four ships, plus destroyer BRISTOL (necessarily detached), deleted from the convoy at one stroke. And perhaps none of it would have occurred if an inexperienced sonar man had not mistaken a school of porpoises for an enemy submarine.

Fire At Sea! (Escorts To The Rescue of Transport Wakefield)

Naturally, the best accident "insurance" is the prevention that stops trouble before it starts. Next best is the prompt alarm and immediate response by well-trained trouble shooters and rescue crews. Catastrophes result when accidents are allowed to get out of hand through blunder.

Fire, for example.

Aboard United States warships, accidental fires were relatively rare during the war. Of course, the fireproofed naval vessel is not so vulnerable as the average merchantman. Acute fire hazard always hovered over the loaded oil tanker, the freighter carrying inflammable cargo, and the crowded passenger transport.

Bearing evidence to the Navy's efficient fire-prevention program is the fact that but one or two large merchantmen under Navy control were gutted by accidental fire at sea during World War II. One of these was the transport WAKEFIELD, the ex-luxury liner MANHATTAN. Under captaincy of Commander H. G. Bradbury, U.S.C.G., she was making the westward passage, United Kingdom to New York, as a member of Convoy TA-18, escorted by Task Force 38 (Captain C. F. Bryant, Jr.).

WAKEFIELD was crowded to capacity with some 1,000 civilian construction workers from camps in the British Isles. Fire broke out late in the afternoon of September 3, 1942, when the convoy was little more than a day's run out of New York.

At 1830 lookouts on the escorting cruiser BROOKLYN saw a cloud of gray smoke surge from WAKEFIELD's superstructure, directly below the bridge. WAKEFIELD hoisted the signal, "I am on fire!" and turned to port to clear the formation and put the fire to leeward. Task Force Commander Bryant ordered destroyers MAYO and NIBLACK to screen the burning ship. He then slowed the convoy to maneuver in WAKEFIELD's vicinity.

As soon as the alarm was reported, the cruiser BROOKLYN cleaned for emergency action. Her Commanding Officer, Captain F. C. Denebrink, had schooled the cruiser for precisely this detail. All hands had been rigorously trained; rescue operations had been carefully planned; provisions and accommodations had been reserved for survivors.

When WAKEFIELD called for help, BROOKLYN obtained permission to assist, and made a top-speed run to the transport's aid. Leaving formation, she was screened by the destroyer HILARY P. JONES (Lieutenant Commander R. B. Ellis) who fell in as A/S bodyguard.

Meantime, the destroyer MAYO (Lieutenant Commander F. S. Habecker) obtained permission to leave her patrol station on WAKEFIELD's flank and also go to the transport's assistance. Clouds of hot smoke and steam gushed from the liner's leeward side, and the flames amidships had driven several hundred passengers to the ship's bow. Some twice that number were congregated on her after decks. Fortunately the sea was calm; the liner lolled on easy ground swells, and MAYO, closing in at 1900, was able to come alongside.

First to reach the WAKEFIELD, the destroyer sidled under the liner's port bow and grappled for rope ladders which had been lowered to serve as gangways from ship to ship. WAKEFIELD's passengers swayed nimbly across to the destroyer's deck. In 17 minutes MAYO took off 247 men.

Cruiser BROOKLYN reached the burning ship at 1907, maneuvering to bring her starboard bow alongside WAKEFIELD's port quarter. Three lines were tossed from BROOKLYN's forward deck to the transport's after deck, and WAKEFIELD's abandon-ship nets were hauled over by the cruisermen. At 1927 the cruiser cast off with some 800 of WAKEFIELD's passengers. About 300 men remained on board the liner, whose captain believed the fire could be brought under control.

But as MAYO and BROOKLYN headed away, stack-high towers of flame swirled up from the liner's superstructure. The Task Force Commander ordered BROOKLYN to stand by as MAYO, crowded to capacity, rejoined the convoy and the destroyer MADISON (Commander W. B. Ammon) left formation to cover the cruiser.

With the fire now going like a volcano, WAKEFIELD's captain gave the order to abandon, and signalled BROOKLYN to come alongside her stern.

MADISON moved in on the liner's port bow. In a few minutes the destroyer picked up 80 men from the drifting lifeboats. The rest of WAKEFIELD's crew scrambled across the nets to BROOKLYN's forward deck.

After cutting the line and standing clear, BROOKLYN hunted WAKEFIELD's decks with searchlights and combed the littered water for survivors. One crowded lifeboat was picked up by destroyer NIBLACK (Lieutenant Commander W. L. Dyer). MADISON was directed to remain with the burning ship, as screen, and BROOKLYN headed away. When the cruiser, screened by NIBLACK, set a course for New York, all hands had been removed from the burning liner.

As a fire-rescue feat this cooperative performance by cruiser and destroyers was tops. Operations had gone without a hitch. That over 1,400 men had been snatched from the inferno without a single fatality speaks well for the Navy's training and discipline.

And by way of an epilogue, WAKEFIELD herself was subsequently saved. Destroyer MADISON stood by the abandoned liner until noon of September 5. Early in the morning of the 5th, destroyers RADFORD and MURPHY arrived from Halifax. A few hours later two tugs arrived from Portland, escorted by Coast Guard cutter CAMPBELL. By the 7th several more vessels were on the job, and WAKEFIELD was towed into Halifax on the 8th. Then the fire was finally overcome, and by spring of 1944 the transport was back in service again.

Operation Easy-Unit (DD's Make The Run To Russia)

After the wholesale massacre of Convoy PQ-17, the British Admiralty abruptly discontinued convoying to North Russia, and His Majesty's Government informed the Soviet Union that future convoys to Russia would have to be routed through the Persian Gulf. Stalin bitterly denounced the decision and appealed to Washington for urgently needed aircraft munitions and electronic gear. To show good faith, the U.S. Navy was ordered to carry a token shipment of these items to Russia, special delivery.

Hence "Operation Easy-Unit"—the task force composed of heavy cruiser TUSCALOOSA (Captain N. C. Gillette) and escorting destroyers EMMONS (Lieutenant Commander T. C. Ragan) and RODMAN (Lieutenant Commander W. G. Michelet). Mission: deliver the goods to Russia.

Cargo was loaded at Greenock on the Clyde, August 12, 1942. TUSCALOOSA took aboard 300 tons of war supplies. Destroyers RODMAN and EMMONS each loaded 39 tons of R.A.F. provisions and war material. Four R.A.F. officers, seven R.N. officers, and 167 men embarked as passengers. The task group sailed on August 13.

TUSCALOOSA and the two destroyers reached Seidisfjordur, Iceland, on the 19th. British destroyer ONSLAUGHT joining the screen, the group stood seaward that evening. Destination: Kola Inlet.

The run across the Barents Sea was not uneventful. A gracious fog fortuitously curtained the task group and grounded most of the Luftwaffe. No submarine attacks. No TIRPITZ. The task group was off Kola Inlet, North Russia, on August 22. It was met by British destroyers MARTIN and MARNE. The following day the group was joined by Russian destroyer GREMIASTCHI, and quietly escorted into Vaenga Bay.

By 0700 in the morning of August 24 the cargo was discharged, and about 240 British and American Navy men and Merchant Marine personnel boarded the TUSCALOOSA. Destroyers EMMONS and RODMAN and the three British DD's took on board some 300 passengers. Four Russian diplomats embarked on the destroyers. At 0749 that same morning the American warships were on their homeward way. On August 28 the group made safe arrival at Seidisfjordur. Mission accomplished.

The American destroyermen who participated in this mission did more than escort a cruiser bearing a few hundred tons of war cargo to Soviet Russia. They escorted a cruiser bearing a cargo of diplomatic good will that went far to mend a dangerous breach in Allied relations.

The Interlocking Convoy System (Coastal convoys)

Early in the spring of 1942 a naval board, established by Admiral King, convened to study the problem of coastal convoys and their defense. Represented on the board were Cominch, CinCLant, and the Eastern, Gulf, and Caribbean Sea Frontier commands. The board devised tentative plans for New York-Key West convoys, and for ocean convoys running between Guantanamo, Cuba, and Halifax. A pattern of convoy routes was designed, and the program proposed eventual extension and link-up with West Indies, Gulf, and Canal Zone convoys. Shortage of destroyers temporarily postponed the program, but eventually 42 A/S vessels were assigned for the coastal program. (See chart inside back cover).

The coastal convoy program immediately paid dividends. Sinkings on the Eastern Sea Frontier dropped precipitately. Only three ships were sunk in that area in July 1942. In August not a single ship was lost. And the U-boats failed to score during the remainder of the year.

Of course, this score applied only to the Eastern Sea Frontier, and the U-boat offensive that summer was concentrating on the Caribbean and the Gulf. They downed over a million tons of merchant shipping in those warm waters before autumn's end, and they might have forced the American shipping effort into bankruptcy but for such counter measures as the Interlocking Convoy System.

Evolving from the coastal convoy program set up the previous May, the Interlocking System served to link together the Eastern Sea, Gulf, Panama, and Caribbean convoy operations much as a giant merger might combine a number of railroads. Schedules were established to accommodate priority shipments, "timetables" were devised for regular convoy runs, and ship-trains, like their railroad counterparts, were highballed through or sidetracked according to contingency. By means of this system a "branch line" convoy (Aruba-to-Guantanamo, for example) could be scheduled to hitch on to a main-line express (Guantanamo-to-New York). In turn, the latter could be scheduled to steam into the New York terminal in time to join a trans-Atlantic convoy bound for Britain. Regular escort groups were assigned to the various runs, and all convoys were furnished with at least a modicum of protection.

The Interlocking Convoy System was built around two major "trunk lines"—Key West-New York and return (KN-NK), and Guantanamo-New York and return (GN-NG). Subsidiary runs operated between Key West and Galveston (Houston), Texas (KH-HK), Key West and Pilottown (New Orleans) (KP-PK), and Guantanamo-Aruba-Trinidad (GAT-TAG). Smaller runs operated between Guantanamo and the Canal Zone, Trinidad and Dutch Guiana or Brazil, the Canal Zone and Curaçao, and other Caribbean ports.

The northbound convoy runs in the main led to the New York terminus where the heavy-laden oil or cargo vessels joined the big trains to Europe.

Destroyers on escort duty were presently plying these main and branch lines with the regularity of steam locomotives. The escort shortage persisted, but the lack was largely compensated by efficient organization, concentration of effort, and improved air cover. As a result, torpedoings in the Gulf, Panama, and Caribbean Areas promptly declined.

During the last quarter of 1942 the U-boats failed to score a sinking in the Gulf of Mexico or in the waters off Panama. However, they managed to continue a stubborn offensive in the Caribbean. In the western Caribbean area 25 ships had gone down to torpedo fire in September. The number dwindled to 15 for the entire Caribbean in October, then climbed to another 25 in November. Shipping in the Trinidad sector was particularly marked for U-boat attack. And where the enemy got in, some of the escorts, inexperienced or insufficiently armed, found themselves in hot water.

Case in point: Convoy TAG-18.

Ambush off Trinidad (Lea and Escorts Versus Wolf-pack)

A focal point for oil and bauxite shipping, the Trinidad sector was a natural bull's-eye for enemy torpedoes. The U-boats found the mark in August, and 35 merchantmen were blown to the bottom on the Trinidad-West Africa run that month. In September the wolfpacks closed in, and 24 ships went down in the island's vicinity.

On September 3 three British destroyers downed the U-162 about 50 miles south of Barbados. Indications suggested that some eight or nine submarines were roaming the waters off Trinidad, but the next kill did not occur until October 2. On that date a Douglas B-18A of the 99th U. S. Army Bombing Squadron, based at Trinidad, caught and sank a U-boat not far from French Devil's Island. The plane dropped a rubber raft for possible survivors. Ten days later the destroyer ELLIS sighted the raft and picked up a lonely submariner. Sole survivor of the U-512, he was a unique specimen in more ways than one. For the U-512 was the only Nazi submarine downed by U. S. forces in the Caribbean that autumn.

Lack of A/S success could not always be blamed on mischance. For example, the experience of the destroyer LEA.

Late in the summer she had been serving in the screen of tanker Convoy TAW-15 (Trinidad to Key West). In the escort group with her were a Dutch minelayer, three Canadian corvettes, a PC, and three SC's. The evening of August 27 found the convoy approaching Windward Passage off Haiti. About 2300, a U-boat crept in on the convoy's flank.

Before LEA could go into action a Catalina on night patrol from Guantanamo spotted the sub (the U-94) and stunned it with a depth-charge blasting. Then the near-by Canadian corvette OAKVILLE rushed in to attack the damaged submersible. By the time LEA reached the scene, OAKVILLE had rammed the U-boat three times running. The Canadians requested a chance to finish the job, but informed LEA that their corvette, damaged by the ramming, was leaking badly. OAKVILLE's lusty tars boarded the sub as the Germans abandoned. The boarding party searched the U-boat, scrambled to safety just as it sank, and concluded the exploit by capturing five submariners, including the U-boat's captain. LEA picked up 21 of the U-boaters, but aside from this capture, it was an all-Canadian show, and LEA's destroyermen were figurative bystanders.

Innocent bystanders, it would seem. For the U-94 was not the only Nazi sub in the convoy's immediate vicinity. And while the OAKVILLE was trampling on this enemy, another U-boat approached the convoy, undetected, and torpedoed three ships in a row, sinking two on the spot. A demonstration, perhaps, of the old American aphorism, "Luck is where you find it."

Again, in November, the destroyer LEA arrived late (no fault of hers) on a scene of action. On this occasion she was attached to Convoy TAG-18. A slow Trinidad-Guantanamo convoy, TAG-18 headed northward from Trinidad on November 2. The con-

Not all fires at sea end as well! Clouds of smoke pour out of the burning American transport Wakefield. Fire discipline aboard ship was good. In a calm sea efficient cruisers and destroyers safely removed all personnel. Fires eventually were extinguished and she was towed to Halifax. Some eighteen months later the Wakefield again was back in service—because of Navy discipline.

A typical, bone-chilling wintry seascape in Northern zones. Here an Allied convoy escort group is forming up for the trip in the swirling morning mists.

The Wakefield prepares to abandon ship. Hundreds of civilian construction workers crowd decks aft as cargo nets have been placed over the side. Orderly disembarkation is particularly necessary in case of sudden ship disaster.

1942 German air proximity to Murmansk route jeopardized Allied convoys. Here an aerial torpedo brings destruction to an Allied ship beset by air and sea.

Geography also aided the Nazis underseas. Their capture of Norway enabled them to construct strategic submarine bases close to vital northern sea lanes. In this picture an enemy torpedo is sinking the merchant vessel to port.

"Admiral Winter." Northern convoy stability and efficiency were reduced by freezing weather. Here, aboard the Spencer, the K-guns are being steamed.

Convoy-men off watch on an American destroyer. This picture shows clearly the typical living conditions on an escort. Card games helped while away dull routine—but dull routine might become mortal action at any moment.

voy was composed of 22 merchantmen under escort of the converted yacht SIREN (Lieutenant Commander H.G. White, U.S.N.R.) and four PC's of the "Donald Duck" fleet.

Steaming along through a tranquil evening, the convoy was making 8 knots. The screening escorts were positioned some 3,000 yards from the formation. SIREN was ahead, patrolling at 10 knots. On the convoy's flanks the PC's were scooting back and forth at 15. All escorts were equipped with sound gear, but none carried radar. The sonar crews were listening, yet the first intimation of submarine activity was the crash of a torpedo blast shattering the evening's peace. A wolfpack, unseen, unheard, had struck from the dusk and stabbed two TAG-18 merchantmen with murderous torpedoes.

In the early hours of the following morning (November 3) the undetected foe struck again. Two more merchantmen went stumbling out of the convoy, and SIREN's call resulted in the dispatch of LEA to reinforce the screen.

Captained by Lieutenant Commander J. F. Walsh, the destroyer raced to join the assailed convoy. After picking up the survivors of the two torpedo-sunk merchantmen, LEA joined the screen at 2207 in the evening of November 3. Walsh took over as Escort Commander at 0600 in the morning of the 4th.

That afternoon a subsidiary convoy of 15 merchantmen joined TAG-18—an additional burden for the little escort group. The enemy laid low until after midnight. Then, between 0310 and 0315 in the morning of November 5, the wolfpack struck a third time. Again the U-boats were undetected; the torpedoes smashed home without warning. Again two merchantmen went sloughing to the bottom.

So Convoy TAG-18 crawled into Guantanamo minus six ships—the escorts reporting no hits, but a number of errors.

Captain T. L. Lewis, Atlantic Fleet ASW Officer, had several comments to offer concerning this convoy misadventure. Extracts from his commentary are quoted below:

> *During the entire period of these attacks no contact with a submarine was made through any medium. . . .*
>
> *It is noted that the convoy course was not changed at any time after the attacks began. Furthermore, the convoy was not zigzagging. Apparently there was no plan for escorts to counter the attacks of the submarine. No rockets or signalling of any sort was used by merchant vessels to indicate that torpedoing had occurred. A general lack of vigorous counter effort seems to have prevailed. . . .*
>
> *Between 0310 and 0315 on 5 November, two more ships of the convoy were torpedoed and sunk. Escorts maintained their stations but searched assigned sectors as in previous attacks. An emergency turn to port was executed 15 minutes after the first of these two attacks at the instigation of the escort commander. Fifteen minutes later the convoy returned to the base course. This evasive change of course had no value since no ship of the convoy would have been moved from the track of the base course more than about 3,000 yards. . . .*

So the TAG-18 experience contributed to the Navy's education in escort-of-convoy duty and A/S warfare. Those in group command and tactical command had yet to learn A/S techniques and acquire the knack of sub-hunting. Nor was Convoy TAG-18 the first to suffer because it was slow and under-escorted.

Battle Off Brazil

On September 16, 1942, Vice Admiral Ingram's Task Force 3 was designated South Atlantic Force. As originally composed, this force consisted of the venerable light cruisers MEMPHIS, CINCINNATI, OMAHA, and MILWAUKEE, plus destroyers DAVIS, JOUETT, SOMERS, WINSLOW, and MOFFETT (DesRon 9, under Captain T. G. Peyton, with pennant in DAVIS). Some PC's, PG's, miscellaneous small craft, and auxiliaries were added to the force from time to time, and eventually it was augmented by four gunboats, four minesweepers, and the old destroyers BARRY, GOFF, and BORIE.

The U-boat onslaught that sank seven Brazilian merchantmen in August had brought the South American Republic into the war as a most enthusiastic ally. The Brazilians contributed a well-trained air force to the war effort, and Brazilian naval vessels linked into the patrol with Admiral Ingram's warships. But the job of patrolling the whole South Atlantic was beyond the capacities of even the combined Brazilians and "Yanquis."

The eight 500-tonners and two 700-tonners of the wolfpack that opened the Brazilian campaign with their "milk cow" sank only seven ships in August. Two in September and one in October were hardly worth the effort. Italian submarines were also operating on the fringe of the Brazilian Area (near Ascension) at this time, but with little success.

But in November, the U-boats downed nine ships in the Brazilian Area, and sank an even dozen in December. Altogether they accounted for a total of some 31 merchantmen in South Atlantic waters before the year was out. And the South Atlantic Force failed to kill one U-boat. Another demonstration of the futility of A/S patrols.

But Admiral Ingram's warships did not come off empty-handed that autumn. The Germans had been making a desperate effort to maintain overseas communications with the "Little Prussians of the East." Nazi blockade-runners, racing to and from Japanese and Indonesian ports, were occasionally slipping through the Atlantic Narrows—the waters between British West Africa and the Brazilian hump.

Informed that a pair of Nazi blockade-runners were due to enter the Narrows on or about November 20, Admiral Ingram dispatched his forces to intercept. The interception was accomplished in the morning of the 21st by Rear Admiral Read's flag cruiser MILWAUKEE (Captain F. B. Royal), cruiser CINCINNATI (Captain E. M. Senn) and destroyer SOMERS (Commander A. C. Wood).

CINCINNATI picked up the radar "pip" at 17,000 yards. Dawn was coloring the sky when the three American warships overhauled the stranger, a raffish freighter with the rusty mien of a tramp. The vessel was flying a Norwegian flag. When challenged, the ship replied with a Norwegian merchantman's call letters. Admiral Read smiled to himself, and ordered SOMERS to send a boarding party to investigate.

While the destroyer's boat was approaching the tramp, three thudding explosions echoed across the seascape. Debris flew skyward from the freighter's deck, and she settled in the water, belching smoke. Down came the Norwegian ensign. Up went the Swastika. Overside came the lifeboats, the crew abandoning.

The scuttled vessel was sinking by the stern when the SOMERS party arrived alongside. Nimble destroyermen swung up the ship's side, and they stayed on board long enough to learn the vessel's mission and identity. She was the ANNELIESE ESSBERGER, 5,000 tons, Japan-bound for a load of rubber.

The SOMERS party made prisoners of the 62 members of the blockade-runner's crew. Although the ESSBERGER's companion, the KOTA NOPAN, managed to escape interception on this occasion, she was trapped on the return voyage.

Ingham Kills U-626 (One Depth Charge, One Sub!)

The last U-boat destroyed by American agency in 1942 fell prey to a United States Coast Guard cutter on December 15. And the manner of that destruction was exemplary.

Killer was the cutter INGHAM (Commander G. E. McCabe, U.S.C.G.). The episode can only be told as a short story, for brevity was its very essence.

INGHAM was one of three escorts screening the Iceland section of North Atlantic Convoy ONS-152. In company with destroyers BABBITT and LEARY, the cutter was herding the ships from Iceland toward a rendezvous with the main convoy. At 1045 in the morning of the 15th INGHAM scouted ahead in search of the big ship-train. At 1235 she made a sonar contact which could only be classified as "doubtful." McCabe directed a run over the spot; the cutter dropped one 600-pound depth charge. At 1247 INGHAM "secured" and returned to her patrol station with the Iceland group. Later that afternoon the rendezvous with the main convoy was achieved without incident.

INGHAM's Coast Guardsmen were not given to boastful announcements. Nobody believed a kill had been made, but postwar examination of German records divulged the fact. INGHAM had dropped her 600-pounder at lat. 56-46 N, long. 27-12 W. And in that position, on that specific date, the U-626 had gone out of existence.

That a cutter could sink a submarine with a single depth charge seemed fantastic. But in this case the phantasy proved real. As a DesLant sailor described it afterwards in short-short story form, "INGHAM made a hole in one."

Apotheosis Of Admiral Doenitz

As 1942 drew to a close the Battle of the Atlantic took a turn in favor of the Allies. In North and South Atlantic Areas a total of 54 merchantmen went down to U-boat torpedoes that December—a loss to the Allies of some 287,000 tons. Merchant ship construction replacements were well ahead of this figure, and the month's sinking toll was less than half the November total of over 600,000 tons sunk.

But if Allied merchantmen were coming out of the building yards at an accelerated rate, so were German submarines. As of late 1942 Admiral Doenitz was maintaining an average of about 95 U-boats in the Atlantic—plus the undersea squadrons he had rushed to the Mediterranean in an effort to intercept British and American invasion convoys steaming for Algeria and Morocco. But when the U-boats tried to tackle Allied invasion shipping—fast convoys heavily screened—they failed to get in. They were unable to lay a finger on one of the 101 ships of American Task Force 34 that transported the U.S. Army to the beachheads of Morocco in the first week of November.

The protection of North African invasion shipping was a notable feather in the hat of American A/S forces. And the December slump reflected a marked improvement in A/S measures and techniques. But that month's decline in sinkings, and wolfpack frustration by high-speed convoys, were hardly indicative of a drastic U-boat defeat. The wolfpacks were by no means conquered. One North Atlantic merchant convoy—the SC-107—had been practically torn to pieces in a November battle with the U-boats. Fifteen ships had been sunk out of this assailed convoy. And in December, North Atlantic Convoy ON-154 had lost 14 of its 44 ships.

During the 12 months of 1942 almost 1,000 ships had gone down to torpedo fire in Atlantic and Arctic Areas for a grand total of almost 6,000,000 tons. By way of reprisal, Allied A/S forces destroyed 82 U-boats. (Of these, United States A/S forces accounted for only 18.) The year's summary, then, was not so bright as December's.

Hitler was hugely pleased with the U-boat accomplishment. On January 30, 1943, he promoted Doenitz to Grand Admiral, and made him Commander in Chief of the German Navy.

CONVOY HX 212 CAMPBELL RESCUES SURVIVORS

CHAPTER 12

DESTROYERS TO NORTH AFRICA

(DD's In Operation Torch)

Play Ball!

When France collapsed under the mighty treads of the Nazi *Wehrmacht,* Hitler gloated, and French Marshal Henri Pétain came into power as head of the Vichy Government. That was in 1940. And even as Hitler exulted, British war leaders determined to prevent Algeria and French Morocco from falling into the conqueror's clutch.

Possession of Morocco and Algeria would place the Swastika on the southern flank of the western Mediterranean, an eventuality fatal to Britain's Gibraltar-to-Suez lifeline. Although Pétain promised strict adherence to the neutralizing armistice, there was always the possibility that the Germans might violate its terms at their own convenience, and seize Vichy France, Morocco, and Algeria whole hog. Foreseeing the day, the London War Office in 1941 completed a plan for the invasion of French Morocco.

When the United States entered the war, this plan was presented to the American leaders in Washington. Also, an Allied invasion of Morocco and Algeria would place British and American armies at Rommel's rear, and force the German Afrika Korps to pull back from Suez. Finally, the seizure of Morocco and Algeria would start a new "front" and relieve some of the Nazi pressure on Russia.

As ultimately designed in the summer of 1942, the invasion of North Africa entailed simultaneous operations by British and American forces—an Anglo-American force to invade Algeria on the Mediterranean front, with the Royal Navy transporting and landing the troops, while United States forces invaded Morocco through Casablanca on the Atlantic coast. Lieutenant General Dwight D. Eisenhower, appointed Commander in Chief of the Allied Forces, was in over-all command of the joint operation. British Admiral Sir Andrew B. Cunningham became Naval Commander Expeditionary Force, Eisenhower's principal naval subordinate. The United States naval forces involved in the Moroccan expedition—elements designated as the Western Naval Task Force—were led by Rear Admiral H. K. Hewitt. The American Army forces (Western Task Force U.S. Army) were under command of Major General George S. Patton. The North African invasion was titled "Operation Torch," a name appropriately associated with Liberty.

"Operation Torch" presented the Western Naval Task Force with a three-element job. It was to transport Patton's army, some 37,000 strong, across the Atlantic to French Morocco. It was to land these troops on beachheads on Morocco's Atlantic seaboard, and support a campaign to capture Casablanca—a port which would give the American forces a base for a steamroller drive across North Africa to Tunis. And it was to aid in the establishment in French Morocco of a striking force which could assure Allied control of the Straits of Gibraltar.

The transport task, a matter of convoying, was well within the Navy's experience. But the landing of a large army called for use of the Navy's new amphibious technique in an outsize effort.

For if the Vichy French chose to resist the landings, they could put up some fierce opposition. Powerful land batteries guarded the harbor of Casablanca and smaller ports along the Moroccan coast. French Army units, native infantry, and companies of the famous *Legion Étrangère* could be thrown into the battle. Mainstay of the Casablanca defense was the French fleet stationed in the harbor—the unfinished battleship JEAN BART, light cruiser PRIMAUGUET, three flotilla leaders, six destroyers, a dozen submarines, and a number of auxiliaries. JEAN BART could not move from her berth, but her big guns could throw a lot of metal seaward.

Further, even in fair weather the Moroccan seaboard was beaten by towering swells and giant surf. Known to mariners as the "Iron Coast," it was a littoral of craggy beaches and rock-studded shallows swept by wicked tides and currents.

Something could be done about the weather; American and Allied meteorologists studied it with utmost concentration, and just before D-Day five American submarines were stationed off the North African coast to observe sea conditions and serve as weather reporters. Something, too, could be done about the Vichy French; three weeks before D-Day, Major General Mark Clark and party secretly visited Algiers to sound out the political situation and pave the way for a possible truce. But the Vichy commanders in Algeria and Morocco were notoriously reactionary.

On the Algerian-Mediterranean coast the Allied forces were to land at Oran and the city of Algiers. On the Moroccan-Atlantic coast the Western Task Force was to put Patton's army ashore on three beaches flanking Casablanca. The troops were to land at Safi, 125 miles south of Casablanca; at Mehdia, 65 miles north of Casablanca; and at Fedala, 14 miles northwest of Casablanca. Once landed, the Army forces were to converge on the target seaport while the warships of the Western Task Force supported the military operation. D-Day was set for November 8, 1942—weather permitting.

Under the invasion plan for Morocco, destroyers of the DesLant Force were to screen the troop convoys of the Western Task Force on the Atlantic crossing; they were to add their guns to the fire-support effort during and after the seizure of the Moroccan beachheads; and they were to feature as special-missioners in the amphibious program. Shore bombardments, anti-aircraft gunnery, A/S work, and special missions—DesLant DD's were to serve as the right hand holding high the "Torch."

DesLant destroyers—among them BERNADOU, COLE, and DALLAS—entered the amphibious program as specialists in their own right. In addition to DALLAS' special assignment, "four-pipers" COLE and BERNADOU drew missions of a type described by the French as *extraordinaire*. In fact, these missions were so extraordinary that the two DD's were transformed into assault ships by the removal of stacks, masts, and large portions of superstructure to reduce weight and silhouette. And all hands on board these streamlined oldtimers were handpicked.

Admiral Hewitt's Western Naval Task Force contained some 102 vessels. Designated as Task Force 34, it was composed of three general groups: transports and landing craft to go in to the beaches; a covering group of warships to support the landings; and a carrier-air group to dominate the sky over the Moroccan-Atlantic seaboard.

The air group included the aircraft carrier RANGER and escort-carriers SUWANNEE, SANGAMON, SANTEE, and CHENANGO, and they with their screening destroyers assembled at Bermuda.

The heavy fire-support warships were assembled at Casco Bay, Maine. The first contingent of transports—ships bound for Safi and Mehdia—sailed from Hampton Roads at 1000 in the morning of October 23. The second contingent—ships bound for Fedala—sailed on the morning of the 24th. That same day the warship group stood out from Casco Bay. Rendezvous by the first groups was made on the 26th. The air group joined up on the 28th, as scheduled, and the united task force pointed its bows for North Africa.

For landing operations Task Force 34 was organized in four task groups: the Southern Attack Group, assigned to the Safi area; the Northern Attack Group, assigned to the Mehdia area; the Center Attack Group, assigned to the Fedala-Casablanca area; and the Covering Group to support the Center Attack Group in the Casablanca area.

Battleships MASSACHUSETTS, NEW YORK, and TEXAS, the five carriers, seven cruisers, numerous destroyers, mine vessels, and auxiliaries were variously attached to these groups. The destroyer composition of the four task groups is shown on the following page.

Traveling by deceptive routes, Task Force 34 made the Atlantic crossing on schedule. Admiral Hewitt and his task group commanders were more than meticulous about the timing. For one thing, the Moroccan landings were to coincide with those on the coast of Algiers, and the American ships had to keep pace with the invasion fleet of the Royal Navy bound for the Mediterranean from Britain.

By the evening of November 6 the Western Task Force was in African coastal waters. Favorable weather and sea reports were received on November 7, and the attack groups squared away for the

DESTROYERS OF TASK FORCE 34

SOUTHERN ATTACK GROUP
(TASK GROUP 34.10)

CONTROL AND FIRE-SUPPORT DD'S

MERVINE	*Lt. Comdr. S. D. Willingham*
	Flying the pennant of *Capt. C. C. Hartman,* COMDESRON 15
KNIGHT	*Lt. Comdr. R. B. Levin*
BEATTY	*Lt. Comdr. F. C. Stelter, Jr.*

TRANSPORT SCREEN

COWIE	*Lt. Comdr. C. J. Whiting*
	Flying the pennant of *Comdr. H. C. Robison,* COMDESDIV 30
QUICK	*Lt. Comdr. R. B. Nickerson*
DORAN	*Lt. Comdr. H. W. Gordon*

ASSAULT DD'S

COLE	*Lt. Comdr. G. G. Palmer*
BERNADOU	*Lt. Comdr. R. E. Braddy, Jr.*

AIR GROUP SCREEN

RODMAN	*Comdr. W. G. Michelet*
EMMONS	*Lt. Comdr. H. M. Heming*

NORTHERN ATTACK GROUP
(TASK GROUP 34.8)

TRANSPORT SCREEN
(Also Control and Fire-Support DD's)

ROE	*Lt. Comdr. R. L. Nolan*
	Flying the pennant of *Comdr. D. L. Madeira,* COMDESRON 11
LIVERMORE	*Comdr. V. Huber*
KEARNY	*Comdr. A. H. Oswald*
ERICSSON	*Lt. Comdr. C. M. Jensen*
PARKER	*Lt. Comdr. J. W. Bays*

AIR GROUP SCREEN

HAMBLETON	*Comdr. F. Close*
	Flying the pennant of *Capt. C. Wellborn, Jr.* COMDESDIV 19
MACOMB	*Comdr. W. H. Duvall*
EBERLE	*Lt. Comdr. K. F. Poehlmann*

ASSAULT DESTROYER

DALLAS	*Lt. Comdr. R. Brodie, Jr.*

CENTER ATTACK GROUP
(TASK GROUP 34.9)

CONTROL AND FIRE-SUPPORT DD'S

WILKES	*Lt. Comdr. J. B. McLean*
	Flying the pennant of *Comdr. E. R. Durgin,* COMDESDIV 26
SWANSON	*Lt. Comdr. L. M. Markham, Jr.*
LUDLOW	*Lt. Comdr. L. W. Creighton*
MURPHY	*Lt. Comdr. L. W. Bailey*

AIR GROUP SCREEN

ELLYSON	*Comdr. J. B. Rooney*
	Flying the pennant of *Capt. J. L. Holloway, Jr.,* COMDESRON 10
FORREST	*Lt. Comdr. M. VanMetre*
	Flying the pennant of *Capt. T. L. Wattles,* COMDESDIV 20
FITCH	*Lt. Comdr. H. Crommelin*
CORRY	*Comdr. E. C. Burchett*
HOBSON	*Lt. Comdr. R. N. McFarlane*

TRANSPORT SCREEN

BRISTOL	*Lt. Comdr. J. A. Glick*
	Flying the pennant of *Capt. J. B. Heffernan,* COMDESRON 13
WOOLSEY	*Comdr. B. L. Austin*
EDISON	*Lt. Comdr. W. R. Headden*
TILLMAN	*Lt. Comdr. F. D. McCorkle*
BOYLE	*Lt. Comdr. E. S. Karpe*
ROWAN	*Lt. Comdr. R. S. Ford*

COVERING GROUP SCREEN
(TASK GROUP 34.1)

WAINRIGHT	*Lt. Comdr. R. H. Gibbs*
	Flying the pennant of *Capt. D. P. Moon,* COMDESRON 8
MAYRANT	*Lt. Comdr. E. K. Walker*
RHIND	*Comdr. H. T. Read*
JENKINS	*Lt. Comdr. H. F. Miller*

November 8 deadline. Approaching Morocco, the DD's had their decks cleared for action. But they and all warships of the invasion fleet had been ordered to wait for the Moroccan defense forces to fire the first shot. There would be no shooting unless the Vichy French began it.

Stealthily the three Attack Groups and the Covering Group closed in on the objective beaches of Safi, Mehdia, and Fedala. If the Vichy French opened fire, the Americans were to answer with every weapon available. The signal for action was the code phrase "Play ball!"

At 0600 in the morning of November 7 the Southern Attack Group, detached from the main body of the Western Task Force, headed southward on a course for Safi, French Morocco. Task Group Commander was Rear Admiral L. A. Davidson with his flag in the cruiser PHILADELPHIA.

Destroyers MERVINE, KNIGHT, and BEATTY were units of the fire-support group which included the flag cruiser PHILADELPHIA and the battleship NEW YORK. Destroyers RODMAN and EMMONS were employed as screens for the escort-carrier SANTEE. Destroyers COWIE, QUICK, and DORAN screened the six transports of this Safi expeditionary force. COLE and BERNADOU moved in the van, bent on carrying out their extraordinary special missions.

The Southern Attack Group had not been long on its Safi course when a strange ship was sighted. The vessel turned out to be the S.S. CONTESSA, a transport of the Northern Attack Group. She had followed TG 34.10 in error. At 0905 destroyer COWIE was directed to escort the wanderer back to her distant north-bound convoy. As a result of this guide-and-guard duty, COWIE missed the D-Day doings at Safi.

The Attack on Safi (Task Group 34.10 Takes the Field)

By nightfall of November 7 all other ships of the Southern Attack Group were in waters a few miles out from Safi, whose twinkling lights seemed strangely unsuspecting and peaceful.

But Admiral Davidson was taking no chances. Two coastal batteries of naval guns guarded Safi to the north, and an army battery of 155 mm. guns was located south of the port. A local garrison of Foreign Legionnaires and Moroccan Tirailleurs could be quickly reinforced by troops from Marrakech in the interior. Safi could explode in the face of the American amphibs, and Davidson disposed his forces to counter such an explosion.

While the transports quietly approached a predetermined transport area off Safi breakwater, PHILADELPHIA and NEW YORK steamed to stations where their guns could trade shells with the coastal batteries. Destroyers MERVINE, BEATTY, and KNIGHT moved to positions where they could cover the landings with close-in fire-support.

The MERVINE was feeling her way through the dark when her lookouts spotted a foreign craft slinking across the black water. The craft proved to be a Spanish fishing vessel, presumably friendly. But instead of giving the destroyer a wide berth, she suddenly cut into her. The crash left MERVINE with a 6-foot horizontal gash in her hull, port side.

MERVINE'S misadventure occurred at 2146. It did not disrupt the invasion program. By 2345 the transports were all in the transport area, and the fire-support ships, MERVINE included, were on station. Ashore, Safi seemed sound asleep.

So clock and calendar moved silently into November 8, D-Day. H-Hour was set for 0400. Thirty minutes before H-Hour two odd-looking ships peeled away from the transport group and headed in to Safi harbor. They were the transformed "four-pipers" BERNADOU and COLE. The game was about to begin.

Bernadou and Cole Play Ball

On board the two assault destroyers the volunteer crews stood at battle stations, the lookouts straining their eyes to see ahead, the gunners in hair-trigger readiness at their mounts.

Both BERNADOU and COLE were carrying assault troops trained for special shore jobs. The troops included K and L Companies of the 47th Infantry. Mission: to land these troops inside Safi harbor where they were to seize harbor installations and shipping and prevent the destruction or damaging of local port facilities. BERNADOU'S shock troops were to go in to the beach. COLE'S were to capture the mole with its loading cranes and marine machinery —an objective of vital importance, as the transport LAKEHURST was laden with tanks which were too heavy to send ashore through the shallows, and COLE'S crews were to ready the mole for the unloading of these big tanks.

Behind the two assault destroyers chugged a procession of troop-crowded landing craft. Ahead was a little scout boat.

Then at 0410 the invaders were sighted, and a flickering light challenged BERNADOU as she approached the long breakwater. Her skipper, Lieutenant Commander R. E. Braddy, Jr., answered with a reply which seemed to satisfy the harbor watch, and the DD continued her quiet advance toward the land end of the breakwater.

Then at 0428, just as BERNADOU rounded the bell buoy off the north end of the dim mole, a shore battery suddenly blurted flame. The crash of French 75's was overtoned by the metallic stutter of machine-guns and the crackle of rifle fire. As salvos and volleys swept the harbor, Braddy snatched the TBS and passed the signal. "Play Ball!" BERNADOU'S six 3-inchers and five 20 mm. guns let out a roar. The game was on.

Bad luck at the start. The destroyermen had been equipped with a magnificent pyrotechnic extravaganza which was to have made an aerial burst over the harbor. The item was a parachute flare which, when fired aloft, would unfurl an American flag. The parachute would then drift over Safi, with the flare illumining the Stars and Stripes. It was believed this dramatic display might have an agreeable influence on the sentimental French.

Instead, gun-flame jabbed the darkness, and both BERNADOU and COLE were straddled by salvos. Firing pointblank at the flashes, range 1,500 yards, BERNADOU's gunners answered with a hot barrage. Destroyer MERVINE also opened up on this target, which was identified as the Batterie des Passes some 2,000 yards north of Safi. Apparently BERNADOU's 3-inchers registered a direct hit. About six minutes after the firing began, the Batterie des Passes was silenced.

The invasion ships then came under fire of the Batterie Railleuse—four 130 mm. naval rifles emplaced on a headland about three miles northwest of Safi. These big enemy guns lobbed some heavy salvos into the harbor before they were knocked out. Battleship NEW YORK, cruiser PHILADELPHIA, and destroyers MERVINE and BEATTY were straddled, but not hit. An answering salvo temporarily silenced this coastal battery, and it was finally muzzled about 0715.

Meantime the landings went forward in the predawn dark. At 0430 BERNADOU's bows touched land and her load of assault troops went overside on Green Beach. The special troops carried by COLE (Lieutenant Commander G. G. Palmer) landed on the merchandise pier where they handily seized the loading cranes. Going alongside the enemy dock, COLE tied up with the precision of an excursion boat discharging holiday passengers at a beach resort. The ship came through the Safi adventure without a scratch, but one of her men was shot through the lungs. (He returned to duty a month later.) BERNADOU, deliberately run up on the beach, suffered only minor damage.

In recognition of sterling amphibious work, BERNADOU and COLE were each awarded a Presidential Unit Citation. For their part in the Safi invasion, destroyer captains Braddy and Palmer were awarded the Navy Cross.

Safi Wind-Up

About 0930 the troops going ashore at Yahudi Beach ran into some sharpshooting, and the COLE jockeyed around to furnish fire-support for the skirmishers ashore. According to her war diary:

> At about 1000 a request was received . . . to open fire with 3-inch 50-caliber gun on the signal station located on the hill overlooking the docks. Intense sniper fire from this building had been hampering the advance. The ship was moved under its own power until gun No. 6 could bear. Four 3-inch point detonating shells were fired from gun No. 6; the first, a near miss, passed over the roof, the second struck the tip of the roof, and the third and fourth completely demolished the upper story of the building. The building surrendered and was captured by the Army.

By 1300 in the afternoon of November 8 the three Safi coastal batteries were out of the game, and at 1400 the transport LAKEHURST moved in to tie up alongside the captured mole. At the close of D-Day the invasion troops were in full control of the port, and the Safi beachhead was secured.

On the morning after D-Day the French struck back with a brief and futile air attack. A plane from the escort-carrier SANTEE bombed Marrakech airfield without orders, and dispersed a column of French troops on the road east of Safi. The French attempted to retaliate, but only one plane got through the overcast. The plane was shot down. Later that day the battleship NEW YORK, escorted by high-speed mine-sweepers (ex-DD's) HAMILTON and HOWARD, steamed northward up the Moroccan coast to join the task group off Fedala in the Casablanca area.

At Safi, American tanks were rumbling off the mole, and American troops were striking northward to round up French forces in that neighborhood.

On November 10 the carrier SANTEE, some 60 miles offshore, was fired upon by an enemy submarine, but fortunately both hostile torpedoes missed.

Not long after the underwater salvo was fired, a plane from PHILADELPHIA spied and bombed a Vichy French submarine near Cape Cantin. Later that day another "PHILLY" pilot spotted probably the same sub beached ten miles north of Cape Blanco. Ordered out of Safi to investigate this submersible, destroyer DORAN made a fast run to the spot. The submarine was sitting it out, a doleful wallflower. DORAN fired a few rounds at the half-sunk vessel, then became aware it was abandoned. Captured without trouble, the sub proved to be French, and her name was MÉDUSE.

That evening the PHILADELPHIA, screened by destroyers KNIGHT and COWIE, steamed up the coast to Mazagan. COLE and BERNADOU also joined this minor expedition. The cruiser and her screen were to provide fire-support for the Army advancing along the coast road. COLE escorted six landing craft and military supplies, and BERNADOU followed with troops and supplies.

But early in the morning of November 11 Admiral Davidson received word that French resistance had ended at Casablanca. The Navy's guns were not needed at Mazagan, and the "ball game" on Safi field was over.

Disastrous French sortie from Casablanca. As in this case, a coast defense fleet fighting in its own ports generally is trapped and defeated. An inferior French force of one light cruiser, several destroyer leaders and destroyers, engaged our invading Armada and was vanquished. Only one vessel was undamaged. Photograph shows three warships grounded (above), one capsized.

Hambleton was torpedoed amidships off Fedala in November, 1942. Effective damage control kept her afloat. After temporary floating drydock repairs, including the removal of 29 damaged frames, she steamed safely home.

Admiral Ingersoll awards the Presidential Unit Citation to personnel of the destroyers Bernadou, Cole, and Dallas. These daring destroyermen performed outstanding amphibious service against the French at North Africa.

Admirals Hewitt and Hall read an important dispatch as General Patton leaves the ship. Cooperation and coordination between our superior Army and Navy forces was one of the decisive factors leading to victory overseas.

Immobility of a Safi target aids naval gunnery. A battery of four French coastal guns had their fire-control tower, shown in picture, smashed by our shells.

Bernadou (top) and Cole were converted into assault destroyers for amphibious attack on Safi harbor. Their hull alterations reduced their vulnerability.

Communications influence war. Quick, accurate information contributes to combat success. Here the Rowan passes orders to our transports off Fedala.

The unfinished, immobile French battleship Jean Bart lies damaged at her berth in Casablanca harbor, after a hammering from American guns and bombs.

Attack on Mehdia (Task Group 34.8 Takes the Field)

While the Southern Attack Group was bearing down on Safi, the Northern Attack Group was approaching the port of Mehdia, 65 miles north of Casablanca. Commanded by Rear Admiral Monroe Kelly, the group included the flag battleship TEXAS, cruiser SAVANNAH, small seaplane tender BARNEGAT, and destroyers ROE, LIVERMORE, KEARNY, ERICSSON, PARKER, HAMBLETON, MACOMB, DALLAS, and EBERLE. A pair of minesweepers accompanied the group, and eight transports carrying some 9,000 Army troops were in the convoy.

The fortified harbor of Mehdia lies at the mouth of the Oued Sebou, a sultry river which is navigable for some distance inland. Nine miles upstream is Port Lyautey with its airfield. This airfield was the prize in the Mehdia bag.

Mission of Task Group 34.8 was to land the Army forces at Mehdia, provide fire-support for military operations if necessary, and aid in the seizure of the airfield at Port Lyautey. The airfield's defenses were known to be sketchy—a few anti-aircraft and mobile guns. If assault forces could get upstream, Port Lyautey should be easy to take. But getting upstream was the rub. The Sebou River was shallow, sluggish, and meandering. A sullen stone fort guarded the estuary. The approaches to Mehdia on the south bank were under the guns of a battery of French 75's and a 138.6 mm. battery. Not far to the south, the Moroccan capital of Rabat contained a sizable garrison which could be rushed to Mehdia's defense.

By the afternoon of November 7 Admiral Kelly's task group was not far from its destination. At 1900 the destroyer ROE (Lieutenant Commander R. L. Nolan) was sent ahead to contact the American submarine SHAD, which had been stationed off the Sebou River entrance to serve as a beacon ship. Search high and low as she would, the destroyer was unable to locate the submarine. Thereupon ROE solved her dilemma by locating herself with a radar fix, after which she guided the Northern Attack Group to the waters directly off Mehdia.

The clocks were at 2321 when the group reached attack position. Three main beachheads (altogether there were five beaches) had been marked for the Mehdia landings. One lay three miles below the river mouth; another was located four miles north of the estuary; the third hugged the jetty on the south side of the entrance channel. While assault troops seized Mehdia, destroyer DALLAS was to steam up the Sebou to Port Lyautey with a Ranger Detachment on special mission to capture the Lyautey airfield.

H-Hour for Mehdia was set for 0400 in the morning of November 8. By 0100 the transport area was a-bustle with landing craft. Troops were going over ships' sides on cargo nets, and clambering down to bull-nosed LCP's. Jeeps and war gear were being stowed on blunt little ferries. Army Rangers, disembarked from transport SUSAN B. ANTHONY, crossed the water to board destroyer DALLAS. The sea was as smooth as undulant velvet under a night sky in which contented clouds were pastured. Mehdia slept.

At 0411 fire-support destroyers KEARNY, ROE, and ERICSSON took their respective stations. KEARNY (Commander A. H. Oswald) was positioned on the north side of the Sebou estuary. Lieutenant Commander Nolan maneuvered ROE into her assigned place south of the river mouth. ERICSSON (Lieutenant Commander C. M. Jensen) was stationed offshore in the backfield.

Landing operations, delayed, did not begin until about 0500. At that hour the first assault waves on their way in to the beaches passed the fire-support DD's. Before the watch at Mehdia woke up, the troops had landed on the target beachheads. Then the amphibs were spotted by a searchlight which speared down from the fort above Mehdia. A rash of rifle fire broke out along the dim parapets.

As at Safi, the assault forces had been instructed to make every effort to avoid battle with the French. But when a shore battery hurled a salvo at the landing craft going in to Green Beach, destroyer EBERLE, control vessel for this center group of boats, was ordered to return the fire. For two minutes the destroyer's guns boomed. The echoes clattered off into silence, and the Green Beach landings went full speed ahead.

Then at 0629 the shore batteries opened fire on destroyer ROE. She was immediately ordered to shoot back. ROE zigzagged and reversed course to dodge the salvos, meanwhile returning the fire at about 5,000 yards range. The French guns then went silent, and ROE enjoyed a breather. But the respite was brief. About 0650 enemy aircraft skimmed across the sun-painted horizon, and ROE was strafed by a pair of French fighter planes. The bullets furrowed the sea around her—no hits.

LATER KEARNY and ERICSSON opened AA fire on planes which strafed near-by landing craft. A plane machine-gunned KEARNY, wounding a bluejacket. By way of reprisal KEARNY's gunners shot down a bomber. The scuffle at Mehdia became an all-out fight.

The fort which crowned the native Kasbah proved a stumbling block to the American forces. It was an old-time affair, but its 138 mm. batteries badgered the landing craft and kept the channel under fire. In an effort to protect the transports, cruiser SAVAN-

NAH, with destroyer ROE as her screen, flung salvo after salvo at the stronghold. But the fort was a tough nut to crack. Skirmishing up to the battlements, Army troops were repulsed. The Legion garrison was reinforced, and the Kasbah guns continued to menace the river front. So long as the Mehdia fort remained in action, destroyer DALLAS would have a hot time steaming up the Sebou with the Rangers assigned to capture Lyautey airfield.

But every hour of delay undermined the invasion effort, so DALLAS was ordered to start upriver, fort or no fort. A heavy barrage finally silenced the guns on the Kasbah heights, but another stumbling block barred DALLAS' advance. A net and a large boom had been stretched across the river entrance. Working in darkness slashed by enemy rifle fire from the river bank, a Navy crew from one of the transports hacked down the net and partly cleared the channel. About noon, DALLAS steamed in and tried to ram the boom. Hot fire from the French shore batteries drove her back.

Early in the morning of November 9, the Foreign

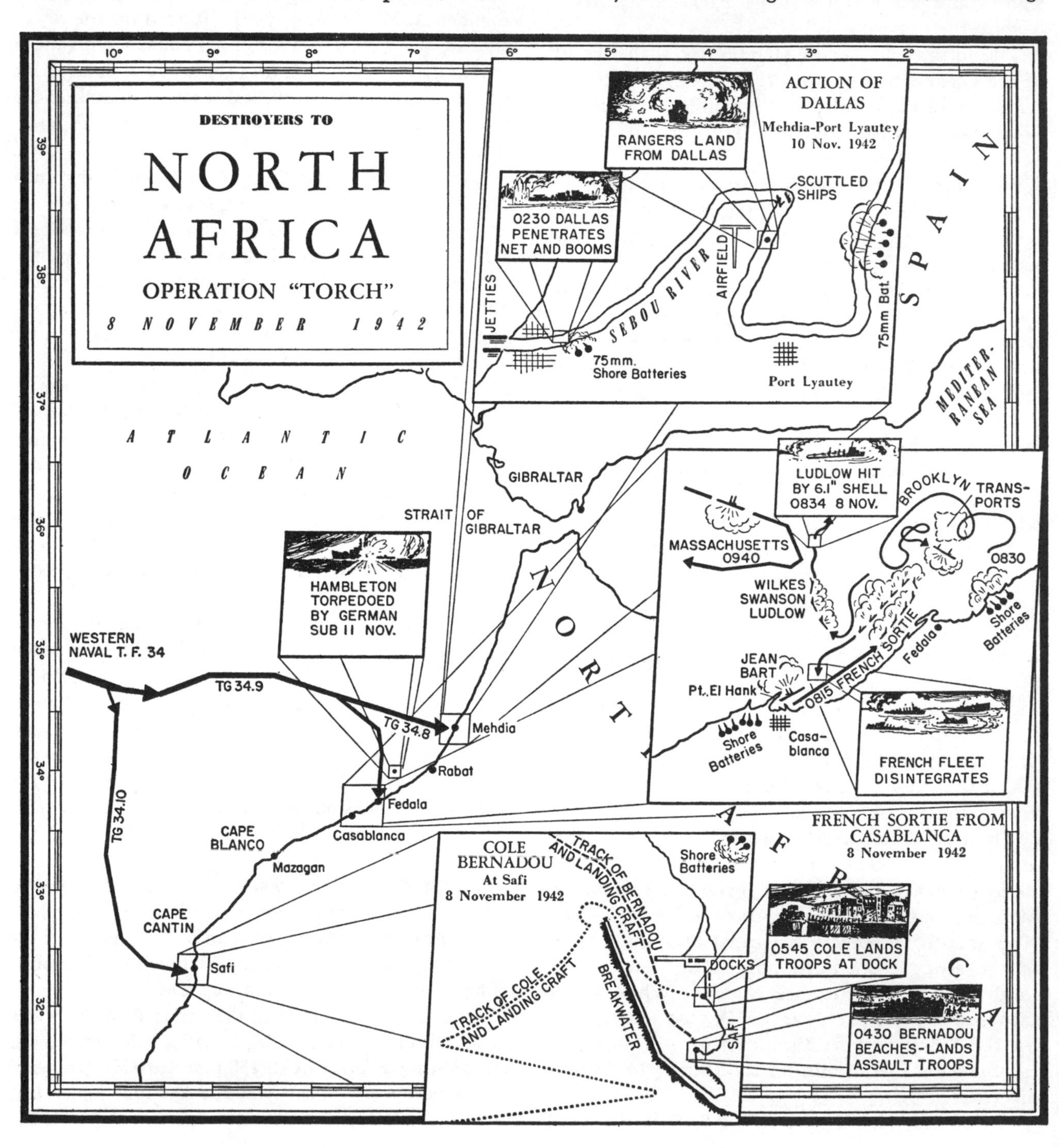

Legionnaires from the fort counter-attacked, and the assault troops were once more driven back. About 0900 of that morning a column of enemy tanks was spotted coming down the road from Rabat. Gunfire from SAVANNAH and aircraft from SANGAMON repulsed the advancing tanks. But the Mehdia garrison stubbornly held the fort, and DALLAS was still denied the river by the boom. It was not until 0230 in the morning of the 10th that the boom was finally cut.

Another stymie! The boom was cut on the north side where the channel was too shallow for DALLAS. She had to ram the cable in deeper water, and in trying to do so, she ran aground. She got off by working the engines at full power and chugging slowly through the river-bed mud. While she was struggling like a mired carabao, the Kasbah guns opened fire. And just as DALLAS neared the boom, a big shell raised a geyser dead ahead, and a near miss aft lifted her stern out of the muck. Lunging at 18 knots, she struck the cable midway between two floats, and brushed it aside. So DALLAS "lowered the boom."

Attack on Port Lyautey (Dallas Steals a Base)

But the river still lay ahead. And not only did the river meander around a score of bends convenient for ambush, but its channel was as shallow as a dishpan, and lumpy with shifting mud bars.

While Lieutenant Commander Robert Brodie, Jr., the skipper, looked after things in general, Lieutenant John N. Ferguson, Jr., the destroyer's "Exec," did the navigating across the treacherous entrance bar. Thereafter the DALLAS was piloted by René Malavergne, a Free French volunteer, who had been chief pilot on the Sebou before the war, and who knew every inch of the tricky channel.

Slowly, warily, DALLAS advanced up the waterway. The banks closed in and the French opened fire. While 75 mm. shells splashed close aboard, and machine-gun bullets zipped across the bow, the river bed grabbed at the destroyer's keel. She scraped bottom most of the way to Port Lyautey, her propellers churning chocolate mud. At one point of the journey, when the screws were turning at a rate which should have produced 25 knots, the ship was crawling at a 5-knot snail's pace. But in spite of mud under keel and gunfire from the Sebou's banks, she made Port Lyautey without damage or personnel casualties.

Squeezing between a pair of scuttled river steamers, the DD halted in mid-stream, and the Rangers went overside into rubber boats. Just as the Rangers were tumbling ashore, a battery of French 75's beyond a bend upstream let go with a vindictive salvo. The shells missed DALLAS by a scant ten yards. She was answering with her 3-inchers when a covering plane from the SAVANNAH sighted the enemy battery and demolished it with a brace of depth charges.

Not long after the local 75's were eradicated, the Rangers captured the airfield, and the special mission up the Sebou was accomplished. With the Lyautey field in hand to serve as an air base for American Army planes, the Mehdia area was bound to fall.

Fall it did the following day (November 11), after a Hollywood finish at the Kasbah fortress above the harbor. While the Rangers were seizing Lyautey airfield, American assault troops surrounded the citadel, and cruiser SAVANNAH bombarded the walls. And when SANGAMON bombers joined the attack, the fort surrendered. At 2200 in the evening of the 10th hostilities at Mehdia were ended.

As at Safi, casualties were astonishingly light. Not a ship in action in the Mehdia area suffered a damaging hit, and the only man harmed by all the shooting was the bluejacket injured when a plane strafed destroyer KEARNY.

And for successful accomplishment of its *mission extraordinaire*, the DALLAS received the Presidential Unit Citation, and Commanding Officer Brodie and Executive Officer Ferguson were awarded the Navy Cross.

Attack on Fedala (Task Group 34.9 in Action)

Timed to coincide with the Safi and Mehdia operations, the move on Fedala in the Casablanca area began late in the evening of November 7 when the Center Attack Group of the Western Task Force approached Cape Fedala. Commanded by Captain R. R. M. Emmet, the Center Attack Group contained cruisers AUGUSTA, BROOKLYN, and CLEVELAND, carriers RANGER and SUWANNEE, and destroyers WILKES, SWANSON, LUDLOW, MURPHY, BRISTOL, WOOLSEY, EDISON, TILLMAN, BOYLE, ROWAN, ELLYSON, FORREST, FITCH, HOBSON, and CORRY. Fifteen transports and cargo vessels were in the convoy, and minesweepers steamed in the van. The big assignment was to land about 20,000 Army troops on the beaches of Fedala, and to furnish whatever fire-support was necessary.

Fedala was a fortified strongpoint covering the approaches to Casablanca Harbor about a dozen miles distant. Four French batteries guarded the little port. At Chergui, three miles to the north, there was Pont Blondin with a heavy battery of four 138.6 mm. coastal guns. At the seaward end of Cape Fedala there was the Batterie des Passes—two French 75's. At the base of the cape was the Batterie du Port, with a pair of 100 mm. guns trained on the harbor. Directly below the town was a mobile AA battery of 75's. With all guns going, the French could raise a considerable storm at this Moroccan beach resort.

Making a cat-footed advance through the darkness, the invasion ships closed in on the Moroccan coast about midnight. Then while ships and landing craft maneuvered in the transport area, a little convoy composed of a French coastal steamer and a small corvette came puffing around the headlands of the cape and almost touched off a premature explosion.

The two little ships were heading straight for the transport area. To steer this unexpected traffic on a detour, the destroyer-minesweeper HOGAN ran across the water to intercept and divert the corvette. Unhappily enough, the French lieutenant skippering the corvette refused to be diverted. Not only that, but he tried to ram the HOGAN. As the little warship came defiantly on, there was nothing the American destroyermen could do but open fire. A machine-gun volley whipped across the corvette's bow. The craft staggered to a halt, her captain and nine of her crew lying dead on deck.

HOGAN, satisfied that the unhappy Frenchmen would lie to, resumed her anti-submarine patrol.

As at Safi and Mehdia, the local Vichy forces insisted on contesting the landings.

Destroyers WILKES, SWANSON, LUDLOW, and MURPHY were among the first invasion ships at Fedala to come under fire. Control vessels for the landing operations, they were stationed close in to the beachheads as guides for the boat-waves.

At 0604 the French shore batteries at Chergui and Fedala suddenly opened up on the American ships. Division Commander Durgin promptly ordered his DesDiv 26 destroyers to proceed to their fire-support stations. Flag destroyer WILKES (Lieutenant Commander J. B. McLean) and the SWANSON (Lieutenant Commander L. M. Markham) hurled answering salvos at Fedala. MURPHY (Lieutenant Commander L. W. Bailey) and LUDLOW (Lieutenant Commander L. W. Creighton) duelled with the big Blondin battery at Chergui.

At 0620 the "Play Ball!" signal was spoken, and the ships of Task Group 34.9 bore down on the offensive. One minute after the signal was flashed, MURPHY reported that she was being straddled, and requested fire-support from cruiser BROOKLYN. SWANSON joined in the bombardment of the Blondin battery at 0645. The big coastal guns of this stronghold flung booming salvos at the American cruiser and the DD's, and about the time SWANSON trained her guns on this enemy, MURPHY was hit.

The shell thunderbolted into MURPHY's after engine-room. Three men were slain by the explosion; seven were wounded. An excerpt from MURPHY's War Damage Report states:

> Immediate damage-control measures taken by the ship consisted in stuffing the exterior hole with a mattress, flooding magazines, and steam-smothering the engine-room. The Engineer Officer, Lieutenant Commander Robert W. Curtis, in utter disregard of his own safety entered the engine-room after it had filled with steam and smoke and had risen to an insufferable temperature; he tripped the still-running generator and thereby took electrical power off the arcing switchboard; thereafter he endeavored to insure that none of his men remained below.

Pounded by shells from BROOKLYN, SWANSON, LUDLOW, and MURPHY, the Blondin guns were finally silenced. In the meantime destroyers WILKES, SWANSON, LUDLOW, BRISTOL, EDISON, and BOYLE traded intermittent salvos with the coastal guns at Fedala.

The big threat to the Fedala landings came at 0825 when two French destroyer leaders and five destroyers sortied from Casablanca and steamed along the coast, heading for the TG 34.9 transport area. Destroyers WILKES, SWANSON, and LUDLOW fell back on BROOKLYN and AUGUSTA to engage the oncoming enemy.

In an exchange of shots with the French warships, LUDLOW was hit forward by a 6.1-inch armor-piercing shell. The blast wounded four men and started a blaze. The fire was quickly extinguished, the wounded were hustled to the sick bay, and LUDLOW was sent off to join the transport A/S screen. Coming under the fire of BROOKLYN and AUGUSTA, the French ships reversed course and started back on an evasive swing toward Casablanca. While maneuvering, they were intercepted by the warships of the American Covering Group. As will be seen, the unfortunate Frenchmen paid dearly for their sortie in behalf of the ambiguous Vichy Government.

Naval gunnery was ended in the Fedala area at 1140 when the Army forces ashore signalled for a cease fire.

Although naval casualties were heavier at Fedala than at Safi and Mehdia, the local fighting for the beachheads was soonest ended. And by the afternoon of November 10 more than 16,500 soldiers were landed with their battle gear in the area.

In the D-Day action, destroyers with the assault forces bore the brunt. Stationed far offshore during the landing operations, the Air Group had little to do at Fedala. Screening the aircraft carrier RANGER and light cruiser CLEVELAND, destroyers ELLYSON, CORRY, and HOBSON enjoyed what amounted to a doldrum. So did destroyers FORREST and FITCH, screening the escort-carriers SUWANNEE and CHENANGO. The Air Group DD's made several sonar contacts, sighted some real or imagined periscopes, and dropped a few depth charges. But for them the ball game was an unexciting one—no hits, no runs, no errors.

The big-league match on D-Day was at Casablanca where the French fleet steamed into action.

Attack on Casablanca (Task Group 34.1 Plays Ball)

The mission of the Western Task Force Covering Group was to hold the French fleet at bay in Casablanca Harbor and give such support to the landings as might be required. Commanded by Rear Admiral R. C. Giffen, the Covering Group contained flag battleship MASSACHUSETTS, cruisers TUSCALOOSA and WICHITA, and destroyers WAINWRIGHT, MAYRANT, RHIND, and JENKINS.

If the French at Casablanca showed fight, MASSACHUSETTS was to take care of the coastal battery at Point El Hank and knock out the French battleship JEAN BART. The cruisers were to bombard the Table d'Aoukasha and El Hank shore batteries and attend to the French submarines or other naval vessels that might attempt a sortie from Casablanca. The destroyers, units of Captain Moon's DesRon 8, were to provide an A/S screen for the heavy ships; to hunt down enemy submarines; to put up an anti-aircraft defense if needed; and to fire at such enemy warships and shore targets as would be designated.

The shooting began at daylight when French AA guns opened fire and French aircraft attacked the American spotting planes sent in to Casablanca on reconnaissance detail. Giffen ordered the task group's guns into action, and the DD's joined the heavy vessels in putting up an anti-aircraft curtain. One French plane was shot down; another flew off at a tangent, apparently hit.

At once the big guns on Point El Hank roared salvos at the American naval vessels. Then JEAN BART commenced firing from her berth in Casablanca Harbor. Hurled at 10-mile range, the French battleship's 15-inch projectiles threw up geysers ahead of the MASSACHUSETTS. MASSACHUSETTS answered at 0704, and the giant duel sent thunderclaps hammering across the seascape.

Cruiser TUSCALOOSA opened up on the Casablanca submarine berths and shelled the El Hank battery. Flung by JEAN BART and the El Hank battery, a spate of heavy salvos smashed into the sea several hundred yards from MASSACHUSETTS and her consorts.

The destroyers maintained their screening stations under this enemy fire—a nerve-wracking experience, as the DD's were unable to return the long-range shots. And then at 0815, while the big guns were roaring, the French ships came out. They were destroyer leaders MILAN and ALBATROSS, and destroyers FRONDEUR, FOUGUEUX, BRESTOIS, and BOULONNAIS.

The Frenchmen headed for the American anchorage at Fedala. From his flagship Admiral Hewitt flashed an order to the Covering Group and the carriers farther out, directing them to intercept. Before the ships of Task Group 34.1 could head off the Frenchmen, AUGUSTA, BROOKLYN, and destroyers of the Attack Group off Fedala moved southward to intervene.

Destroyers WILKES, SWANSON, BRISTOL, and BOYLE engaged the French destroyers, when a salvo from the destroyer MILAN splashed in the sea some yards short of WILKES, and LUDLOW was temporarily disabled by a hit. Gunnery lasted for about ten minutes before the French DD's broke off the long-range duel to retire the way they had come.

Beating a retreat to Casablanca, the French ships ran into fire from the big guns of the Covering Group and bombs from RANGER's aircraft. Punctured and set afire by shell hits from WILKES, the MILAN was driven in to the beach. BOULONNAIS, staggered by a hit that wrecked her steering gear, was sunk by salvos from MASSACHUSETTS. Multiple hits from MASSACHUSETTS and TUSCALOOSA sent the destroyer FOUGUEUX to the bottom.

The action became a furious melee when the light cruiser PRIMAGUET and more French destroyers steamed out at 1000 to engage the American ships. Rocked by a tornado of fire, destroyers BRESTOIS and FRONDEUR were fatally disabled by direct hits. AUGUSTA and BROOKLYN closed in on the PRIMAGUET and the remaining enemy destroyers. One by one the Frenchmen were driven into port or disabled. WAINWRIGHT fired a long-range torpedo shot at the French ships, but results were not observed. Smoke rolled across the water as the destroyers laid covering screens and the cruisers dodged angry salvos.

During the action French shells struck MASSACHUSETTS, BROOKLYN, and WICHITA, wounding some 20 American Navy men. But the French force was almost annihilated. Smothered by shellfire from AUGUSTA and a DD, and strafed by RANGER's aircraft, the BRESTOIS was mortally wounded. Destroyer leader ALBATROSS was driven to the beach. FRONDEUR was demolished. Of the ships that steamed out of Casablanca, only a single destroyer, the ALCYON, survived the unfortunate sortie.

There remained a number of French submarines and the battleship JEAN BART in Casablanca Harbor, and the stubborn Vichyite Vice Admiral F. C. Michelier refused an armistice until the afternoon of November 11, when the JEAN BART had been beaten into silence and American assault troops were at Casablanca's gates.

But it was the Nazis who made the final play in

the Casablanca area. Striking in the wake of the French surrender, Axis submarines slashed at American invasion shipping along the Moroccan coast. Within a two-day period immediately following the Casablanca armistice, four United States transports were sunk off Fedala, and three other American ships, including the destroyer HAMBLETON, were torpedoed.

Torpedoing of U.S.S. Hambleton

HOSTILITIES IN FRENCH MOROCCO HAVE CEASED BE ESPECIALLY VIGILANT AGAINST AXIS SUBMARINES

To American naval forces at Safi, Mehdia, Fedala, and off Casablanca the foregoing message with its explicit warning was broadcast shortly after the French capitulated. All A/S screens were alerted, and lookouts kept a sharp watch for tell-tale periscope "feathers."

Somehow the enemy subs got in. At Fedala Roads their torpedoes struck the Western Task Force a ferocious smash, and the American invasion fleet suffered its only losses off Morocco. The subs were the U-173 and the U-130, members of the wolfpack concentration which had missed the invasion fleet in the Atlantic. Now they had caught up.

Down went the transports JOSEPH HEWES, HUGH L. SCOTT, EDWARD RUTLEDGE, and TASKER H. BLISS. Fortunately all troops and most of the cargo had been sent ashore. But crashing warheads dealt death and injury to crews, and four transports constituted a heavy ship toll.

The fleet oiler WINOOSKI was also torpedoed in the Fedala roadstead. Not too badly damaged, she remained afloat.

The freighter ELECTRA was torpedoed about 17 miles north of Fedala on the 15th, an indication that the Nazis did not immediately retire from the area. U.S.S. COLE steamed to the cargoman's rescue, and picked up survivors from the disabled ship.

Destroyer HAMBLETON (Commander Forrest Close), flagship of DesDiv 19, was struck early in the evening of November 11, just after JOSEPH HEWES and WINOOSKI were torpedoed.

In company with the MACOMB, the HAMBLETON had served as screen for escort-carriers SANGAMON and CHENANGO during landing operations at Mehdia. About 1650 on November 11, the two destroyers were ordered to Fedala to fuel from the WINOOSKI.

The two DesDiv 19 destroyers arrived off Fedala about 1900, and anchored in the transport area, planning to fuel at daybreak the following morning. At 1955 the transport JOSEPH HEWES and the tanker WINOOSKI were rocked by torpedo explosions. A moment later HAMBLETON was hit.

The torpedo struck the destroyer on the port side amidships, and the blast almost blew the vitals out of the vessel. But mangled though she was, HAMBLETON did not go down.

"We were determined to save her," one of her officers said in postwar reminiscence. "It looked as though she might go under, but every hand on board worked to keep her afloat. They held her on the surface by the scruff of her neck, you might say. And they got her into port."

Here it is in the official language of the destroyer's War Damage Report:

> HAMBLETON absorbed a tremendous amount of damage. Her survival was possible because of the general excellence of the damage-control measures, adequate stability characteristics, and the ruggedness of her hull. Favorable weather conditions and the proximity of a port were important factors. Temporary repairs at Casablanca not only were ingenious but also were soundly conceived and executed.

HAMBLETON was placed in the floating drydock at Casablanca on January 19, 1943. The "ingenious" repairs in reference consisted of removing all structure between frames 87 and 116, moving the stern section forward 38 feet, and then connecting the bow and stern by a fairing section 12¾ feet long. That these repairs were "soundly conceived and executed" was evidenced by the fact that the repair plan required the minimum docking time of all schemes proposed, and the surgical engineering put HAMBLETON back on her feet. The work was completed on May 8, 1943, and the following day she steamed out of Casablanca and headed for home. With only the port propeller to go on, she made the Atlantic crossing in good time, arriving at Boston Navy Yard on June 26. There she underwent permanent repairs and alterations, and she was back in service on November 15, 1943. Remarkable recovery for a ship which had been literally truncated, shortened, sewed together again, and sent home with one amputated propeller.

Some people like to talk about their operations. Veteran destroyermen talk about HAMBLETON's.

Woolsey, Swanson and Quick down U-173

During the forenoon of November 16, destroyers WOOLSEY (Commander B. L. Austin), SWANSON (Lieutenant Commander L. M. Markham), and QUICK (Lieutenant Commander R. B. Nickerson) were patrolling as units of the A/S screen off Casablanca. Then at 1135 WOOLSEY's sonar registered sudden contact with an underwater target, range 700 yards. The echo, coming in "sharp and firm," called for an urgent attack. With neither time nor space to draw a bead on the target ahead, Commander

Austin swung the destroyer to deliver a starboard K-gun broadside.

Two starboard projectors were fired. Into the sea lobbed the depth charges to rouse the water with their deep-bellied detonations. As was shown by the DRT (Dead Reckoning Tracer) plot, these were the only charges that could reach the detected submarine. That they reached it was a fact immediately evidenced by an upwelling of oil which spread a lush black carpet across a considerable yardage of the ocean's surface. Large air bubbles came popping up like little balloons. Interested observers on board the Woolsey expressed an elated opinion. The consensus was: "We got her!"

But you never could tell from a first gush of oil and air. Here was a case in point. After Woolsey launched her urgent attack, the target was traced on the move. By 1149 the sub, as indicated by the DRT plot, had made a complete circle and was now back on its original course, traveling at snail's pace.

At 1149, then, Woolsey attacked again. This time the destroyer flailed the sea with a pattern of four depth charges. About one minute after the charges boomed, two or three distinct explosions of a timbre unlike depth-charge blasting vibrated the ship. In the wake of this barrage the sea was once more effervescent as the depths spewed up globules of oil and pingpong balls of air. For 15 minutes the oil and air continued to rise. To Woolsey it looked like the death throes of a stricken submersible.

Contact with the target was regained at 1214. The DRT plot showed the sub was lying inert. Commander Austin conned Woolsey directly over the target, and four more depth charges were dropped. They must have landed on the sub's conning tower—if it still had a conning tower—but the only evidence of a hit was another display of violent bubbling.

On orders from Captain J. B. Heffernan, ComDesRon 13, Woolsey then headed in to Casablanca to obtain urgently needed fuel. Swanson and Quick stepped in to deliver the death blow to the undersea enemy.

Taking over the contact, Swanson dropped two depth-charge patterns on the spot where the bubbles continued to rise. The explosions produced still more bubbles. Finally Quick, with a positive signature on her ASMD (Anti-Submarine Magnetic Detector), maneuvered in to drop a single charge set for bottom explosion. If the enemy submariners had been "blowing bubbles" for the purposes of trickery, that final blast put an end to the game.

This submarine kill had several unique features. Unusual was the fact that Swanson and Quick thought they were attacking some "sunken hull." It was a "sunken hull," all right. But Woolsey was the only DD certain that the contact was a sub, and, as Nazi records disclosed, she made the most of that certainty.

The submarine downed by Woolsey, Swanson, and Quick was the U-173, the very U-boat which had sunk the Hewes, damaged the Winooski, and all but killed the Hambleton. Now these torpedoings were well avenged.

North African Drive

About 0200 in the morning of November 8, the Anglo-American assault forces in the Mediterranean began landing operations on the coast of Algeria. In the Oran and Algiers areas there was some sharp opposition, but French resistance was halfhearted, and the amphibs were solidly in possession of important beachheads by November 10.

On that date Admiral Jean Darlan, Commander-in-Chief of French North African forces, was induced to abandon his pro-Nazi position and switch to the Allied side. On the 11th Hitler's armies swept into Vichy France, and most of the former Vichy holdouts in North Africa promptly joined the Allies. Not long after the Nazis marched into southern France, French Navy commanders scuttled the residual fleet at Toulon. Already the light of "Operation Torch" was falling across Europe.

So the DesLant Force earned its full share of encomiums for its part in the amphibious effort, the first continental invasion conducted by United States forces in World War II. American destroyermen could always look back on Morocco with satisfaction. At Safi, at Mehdia, at Fedala, at Casablanca—and all the way across the Atlantic—they carried the "Torch."

DALLAS OFF PORT LYAUTEY

CHAPTER 13

DESTROYER WARFARE IN THE ALEUTIANS

The Birthplace of Bad Weather

On June 6–7, 1942, the Japanese landed on American soil. It was the first time that soil had been trod by a foreign army since the War of 1812.

The Japanese came with ships, guns, planes, troops—all the bag and baggage of conquest. True, they landed on America's farthest outward fringe—but they were bent on territorial seizure and occupation.

Extending 1,100 miles westward from the Alaskan mainland, the Aleutians are a long way from the continental United States. Nevertheless the tramp of enemy boots on those remote Aleutian shores reverberated through the United States like a seismic shock. Japanese aircraft had bombed the U. S. Naval base at Dutch Harbor. Japanese submarines had been prowling off Kodiak. Now the Rising Sun flag was on Alaska's doorstep.

Anxious citizens consulted globes and geographies to acquaint themselves with the Aleutians. They learned that this arc of islands separated the North Pacific from the Bering Sea. That the western Aleutians lay nearer to Siberia than to North America. And some Americans remembered that Air Corps General William E. ("Billy") Mitchell had once stated: *"If Japan seizes Alaska, she can take New York."* So it seemed as though the Japanese had picked up strategic aces when they suddenly grabbed the western Aleutian islands of Kiska and Attu.

United States Army and Navy heads had been fully aware that the Japanese might make a lunge into the Aleutians. Anticipating an attack on those strategically valuable islands, the War Department and the Navy Department had pushed the construction of naval and air bases at Dutch Harbor, Kodiak, and other Aleutian strongpoints. At the Pacific War's outbreak reinforcements were moved to the Alaskan frontier, and aircraft, warships, and those old submarine S-boats affectionately called "Sugar Boats" and "sewer pipes" began patrols through the Aleutian Archipelago.

Navigation in those waters was an adventure in peril; many of the island approaches were uncharted, channels were blocked with saw-toothed reefs, and bays were ulcerous with shoals and submerged rocks. Crazy currents and racing tide rips coiled and swirled through the archipelago. When the islands weren't smothered in fog, they were whipped by screeching "williwaws" that kicked up monstrous seas and reduced visibility to "less than zero." A calm and sunny morning could deteriorate by noon to a foaming, ship-smashing norther. Nightfall might bring a black sleet storm, or a blinding, featherbed blizzard. With good reason the native Aleuts had named this wild archipelago "The Birthplace of Bad Weather."

Contrary to the initial impression left on the American public by the move, the Japanese High Command was not planning an invasion of continental Alaska. The Aleutian offensive was aimed at two strategic objectives. On the one hand, it was intended as a diversion to fool the Americans into rushing their Navy northward when Yamamoto struck at Midway. And on the other hand, seizure of the Western Aleutians would prevent the United States from using the archipelago as a causeway to Northern Japan.

Destroyers found that the forbidding Aleutian coast specialized in navigational hazards. Even eternal vigilance could not keep a ship off the rocks. Assigned to transport an Army detail from Adak to Amchitka, U.S.S. Worden successfully carried the troops in. Leaving Constantine Harbor, she was caught by the rocks off Kiriloff Point. *For her ultimate fate, see the next page.*

In the Battle of the Komandorskis: Salt Lake City (top) draws Jap fire. Dead in the water (bottom), she is being screened by the destroyer Dale. What looked like easy victory had developed into a battle for life against superior forces.

U.S.S. Bailey led the attack by three American destroyers against the Jap cruisers. Although she was stopped four times by shellfire, her torpedo attack helped to save the crippled Salt Lake City. Her sister DD's received little damage.

Worden (top) hard and fast on Amchitka's rocks. Her crew was rescued (center), but the ship was lost. Racked by heavy seas, she broke in two.

Relaxing after the Battle of the Komandorskis. Officers in the wardroom of Salt Lake City discuss the only conventional daylight surface action of the Pacific War without air support on either side. The torpedo officer of Monaghan tells of his amazingly lucky attack against the enemy cruisers. Just before he reached torpedo range, the Japs retired and the battle was over.

According to the postwar testimony of Captain Taisuke Ito, staff officer of the Imperial Fifth Fleet:

The primary objective of the Aleutian Operation was to occupy Adak as a northern base for patrol planes, which, in conjunction with Midway, could cover the northern approach across the Pacific to Japan. When the Battle of Midway went unfavorably, Admiral Yamamoto was against occupying any of the Aleutian Islands. However, Vice Admiral Hosogaya, Commander Fifth Fleet, argued strongly for the occupation of Kiska as a position from which to neutralize Dutch Harbor and prevent an advance toward Japan via the Aleutian Islands.

So Rear Admiral Kakuji Kakuta led the invasion fleet to the Aleutians. The invaders steamed to within 150 miles of Unalaska. Dutch Harbor was treated to an air raid, the Army base at Fort Mears was bombed, and then the Jap task force fell back to put troops ashore on Kiska and Attu.

Alaska's defenders were not too surprised by the enemy offensive. Rear Admiral Robert A. Theobald, commander of all United States and Canadian forces in the North Pacific theater, had readied his air groups and positioned his main naval force in the Gulf of Alaska. On June 1 the defenses were alerted. As of that date Admiral Theobald's forces consisted of 52 naval vessels (including five cruisers, eleven destroyers, and six submarines), and some 170 planes (mostly Army aircraft). However, as a result of the smashing Jap setback at Midway, Admiral Nimitz was able to speed reinforcements to the North Pacific.

The Jap occupation troops were soon cowering in foxholes pelted by bombs and projectiles. A week had not gone by before the Japanese commanders were worrying about the logistics problem.

American bombers flailed at the convoys approaching Attu and Kiska and blasted shipping in the enemy-held harbors. On July 4 the American submarine TRITON sank the Japanese destroyer NENOHI off Aggatu, and a few hours later the submarine GROWLER torpedoed three Jap DD's off Kiska Harbor, disabling two, and sinking the destroyer ARARE. The Aleutian campaign was on.

For the Japs, it developed into a tooth-and-claw holding operation—a desperate struggle to retain a grip on the captured islands. For the Americans the campaign became one of attrition—a fight to cut the Kiska and Attu supply lines and to isolate and crush the occupying garrisons.

And both invader and defender fought a gruelling war with the weather.

Kiska Bombardment

On July 22, U.S. Task Group 8.6, under command of Rear Admiral W. W. Smith, set out to bombard the invader's positions on Kiska. Kiska Harbor was the immediate objective. The American warships were to steam to the entrance waters of Vega Bay, and blast away at Jap installations which had been photographed by PBY reconnaissance. The bombardment was to be timed with an air raid for a simultaneous strike from sky and sea.

Admiral Smith's task group was composed of the heavy cruisers INDIANAPOLIS (flagship) and LOUISVILLE, light cruisers NASHVILLE, ST. LOUIS, and HONOLULU, four destroyers, and the minesweeper (converted destroyer) ELLIOT. The DD's in the group were CASE (Commander R. W. Bedilion), REID (Commander H. F. Pullen), GRIDLEY (Lieutenant Commander F. R. Stickney), and McCALL (Lieutenant Commander W. S. Veeder). With his flag in CASE, Commander Wyatt Craig (ComDesDiv 6) was in command of the destroyers. Riding in GRIDLEY as ComDesDiv 11 was Commander Frederick Moosbrugger.

Fog, fog, and more fog impeded the task group's advance. For a week the archipelago's waterways were smothered; the islands were buried in mist. The task group closed the invisible Kiska shoreline once, and then thought better of it. In the vapor destroyers brushed each other and those in the van were in danger of shaving their keels on uncharted reefs. Admiral Smith ordered a withdrawal to deep water.

Later that day the aerologists reported a possibility of clearing weather. As afternoon waned the mist thinned somewhat, and Task Group 8.6 headed for the entrance of Vega Bay. There would be no bombardment support by Army aircraft—the land planes were solidly grounded—but the cruiser planes took wing, and the warship gunners determined to give the enemy a sufficient taste of TNT.

However, as the task group advanced on Vega Bay the fog once more closed in.

Above the fog the cruiser planes circled and hovered, trying to pick out their mother ships and find an opening for a nearby landing. Hazardous for the naval pilots, this fog-hopping. The Japs spotted the planes and opened fire with anti-aircraft batteries. A Zero fighter rose to the attack. One of the two planes from INDIANAPOLIS vanished—she may have been struck by ack-ack or bullets from the Zero, or she may have crashed somewhere in the fog.

But the other INDIANAPOLIS plane had spotted a hole in the fogbank, a broad opening which afforded a good view of Kiska Harbor. Similar reports from other spotting planes sent the task group speeding to the clearing. Destroyers CASE, REID, GRIDLEY, and McCALL covered the formation's right flank. Light cruisers ST. LOUIS, NASHVILLE, and HONOLULU steamed in center column. INDIANAPOLIS and LOUISVILLE came in some distance astern, on the left. Minesweeper ELLIOT steamed ahead of the cruisers with her "broom."

Then at 1943, the destroyers, bearing in on a line between Vega Point and Bukhti Point, emerged suddenly from the fogbank into dazzling sunshine. Ahead lay Kiska with its emerald hills and snowcapped volcanic cone.

Following a predetermined firing course, the ships of the task group executed a maneuver which was culminated when the three columns were turned to the right and the DD column, inshore, had closed the range to 14,500 yards.

Tufts of fog still drifted around and over Kiska Harbor, but the shoreline presented a number of visible targets, and several Japanese ships could be seen. At 1955 the DD's opened fire. A moment later the light and heavy cruisers followed suit.

Apparently the bombardment caught the Japs on Kiska completely by surprise. Perhaps they took the naval aircraft for Army reconnaissance planes. Perhaps they believed American warships would be unable to penetrate the offshore fog. At any rate, Jap aircraft were rather slow on the counterattack. And the Japanese shore guns did not reply to the bombardment until 2005, when a single battery opened fire.

Shells straddled the ELLIOT, and a Kawanishi bomber picked on the minesweeper, evidently taking the old four-stacker for a cruiser. Four bombs landed in ELLIOT's weaving wake. The near misses peppered the ship with shrapnel, but she managed to dodge away, and salvos from NASHVILLE soon silenced the barking shore battery.

The destroyer CASE got in some fast shots at what looked like a Jap DD off the harbor mouth. CASE's lookouts reported a hit on the fleeting target—they had only a glimpse of the silhouette—then the ship disappeared behind a headland. The fog continued to plague the task group's fire-controlmen and gunners. Tons of steel were hurled into Kiska Harbor, but the spotting planes could neither verify hits nor ascertain damage done to military installations.

Suddenly ELLIOT's lookouts spied a feather on the water, and the serpent's-head of a Jap periscope. Submarine! The minesweeper flashed the alarm, and the American light cruisers executed an emergency turn to avoid torpedo attack. The turn brought the light cruisers squarely across the bows of heavy cruisers INDIANAPOLIS and LOUISVILLE, forcing the heavies to cease fire abruptly and turn hard right. With this maneuver (time: 2018) the bombardment was broken off. All units except the CA's had completed their regular bombardment schedule.

CASE fired one of the last shots. Leading the DD's, she was off Little Kiska Island and turning southeastward when a spiteful Zero buzzed down out of the gloaming. The Jap plane dived on the destroyer's port quarter and dropped a bomb. A miss! Fire from CASE's anti-aircraft batteries lashed the plane. The Zero staggered away in the dusk and bored into a fog-cloud.

Behind the whole Kiska bombardment operation hovered a doubtful question mark. Even as Task Group 8.6 steamed away, Admiral Smith was impelled to wonder if results justified the effort. Task Group casualties had been unexpectedly light—one cruiser plane lost and minor damage to minesweeper ELLIOT. But, then, enemy resistance had been light. And the attack on the island had been hair-raisingly risky for the fog-blinded warships. If some shore installations were demolished, there was no evidence that the enemy's Kiska defenses were vitally softened, or even more than temporarily impaired.

Admiral Smith concluded in a critical report:

> *The bombardment of Kiska by a surface force of heavy ships of questionable value unless followed by landing of troops. Results to be expected by indirect bombardment do not balance the risk to heavy ships under difficult conditions of approach in mineable waters, where enemy destroyers and submarines may be encountered in low visibility. On completion of the airfield now under construction, the enemy unquestionably will operate dive-bombers and torpedo planes from Kiska if the character of the field permits.*

Radio Tokyo, with its usual penchant for exaggeration, announced that a tremendous gun duel had been fought between an American fleet and Kiska's shore batteries. The fleet (declared Radio Tokyo) had been driven off by crack artillery fire which sank a United States "four-stack cruiser."

But the minesweeper ELLIOT had been merely scratched by shrapnel. And it was not the Japs, but the Aleutians themselves that frustrated the American task group—with fog.

Reid And Aircraft Kill RO-61

On the morning of August 31, the destroyer REID (Lieutenant Commander H. H. McIlhenny) was about ten miles southeast of Cape North, Atka, proceeding to conduct an anti-submarine patrol off the Nazan Bay harbor entrance.

At 0930 a Navy PBY droned into view out of nowhere. The plane—a unit of PatWing 4—raced toward the REID and signalled "Sub!" McIlhenny sent the crew to battle stations, and **Reid dashed into action.**

The PBY led the DD to the target, a Jap submarine which had suffered from a bombing by the airmen. The plane dropped a smoke float on the oil slick left by the damaged sub, and Reid steamed to the spot to try for the underwater bull's-eye.

The destroyer established sonar contact and McIlhenny ordered a depth-charge attack. Overside went the TNT, and up came the thunder. There was no sign of debris, and the "ping jockey" (sonar operator) reported the sub was still down there. At 1110 the Executive Officer, Lieutenant Commander Robert D. McGinnis, was given the conn. Because of disturbed water, it was 37 minutes before propeller noises were again heard. However, Reid was led to the quarry by an oil slick, and she managed to obtain an echo-range at 500 yards. The contact was again lost, and McIlhenny stopped Reid's engines to pause and listen. At 1217 the mushy echo of a wake was picked up, and propeller noises were heard.

A depth-charge barrage was dropped at 1219. After the first charge was dropped, the fathometer indicated Reid was passing over the sub. The barrage brought the enemy floundering to the surface. The submarine broached at a sharp angle, then lolled helplessly in the sea, her bow slanted skyward, stern under water. Frantic seamen fought their way out of the conning tower as Reid's gunmen opened fire with 5-inch 38-caliber and 20 mm. batteries.

The destroyer marksmen riddled the submarine's conning tower, and punched shells through the up-angled bow. After about eight minutes of this sharp-shooting, the sub capsized and sank by the stern. Seventeen survivors were counted in the swirling sea; the destroyermen were able to rescue but five.

The shivering submariners identified their demolished boat as RO-61. The obliteration of this undersea invader was remarked by a veteran destroyer-force commander as *"an excellent example of cooperation between a DD and a plane."*

Adak Operation

During the last week of August, 1942, the naval forces of Rear Admiral W. W. Smith picked up a convoy of several freighters, some fishing vessels, a couple of barges, and a sailing schooner, and escorted this seagoing miscellany down the archipelago to Adak island in the western Aleutians.

Destroyers ran A/S interference for the convoy, and such heavier warships as were available guarded its flanks. Making the most of high water and low visibility, the Navy led the expedition into Kuluk Bay, Adak, and the Army quietly went ashore to occupy the island.

So unexpectedly and expeditiously was the occupation accomplished that it took the Japs entirely by surprise. They had originally intended to seize the island themselves. Kuluk Bay could accommodate a fleet, and there was terrain suitable for an airfield. But it was the Stars and Stripes that were flying (or at least PBY's were flying) over Adak on August 30.

The Americans had stolen a base on the Japanese.

Loss Of U.S.S. Worden

Late in the autumn of 1942, Admiral Nimitz began to study plans for an advance on Kiska. Occupation of Adak had given the Catalinas a base 250 miles from the invader's easternmost foxholes. But a move from Adak to Amchitka still further west would put the PBY's within virtual "spitting distance" of the enemy.

The island was swampy—the low tundra afforded little protection against the williwaws—the soggy marshland militated against the construction of an airstrip. American scouts discovered that a Jap exploring party had visited Amchitka, and had apparently reported the island a quagmire not worth the taking. But CinCPac thought otherwise, and the occupation of Amchitka was scheduled for mid-January 1943.

D-Day was set for January 12. Landings were to be made on the beaches of Constantine Harbor. Troops were carried by the Coast Guard transport Arthur Middleton. And the destroyer Worden (Commander W. G. Pogue) was assigned to transport from Adak Island and land at Amchitka the Advance Security Detail of the Army.

The night of January 11-12 was as black as anthracite, the weather clearing and calming after a storm. Closing the harbor entrance, the destroyermen obtained a glimpse of outlying rocks and headland. Radar checked the picture, and the DD started in. After ticklish maneuvering between a great bed of kelp and a cluster of rocks, Worden managed the hazardous approach on the beach without misadventure, and quietly anchored off shore. In the darkness before the subarctic dawn she lowered her boats and landed the Army detachment. By 0720 of the 12th the last man was on the beach, and the destroyermen were congratulating themselves on a mission handily accomplished.

About 0730 Worden was once more under way, heading seaward. The bridge watch was vigilant. The lookouts scanned the water for signs of treachery. No man on watch was asleep on his feet. But the island was to exact a toll of these visitors, vigilance despite.

The destroyer was almost free of the bay's embrace when there was a crash, a grinding snarl under the keel, and the ship was snagged by a jagged rock. She tore free from the clutch of this conccaled snare, only to find herself trapped in a nest of rocks, with an outcropping of granite directly abeam. WORDEN had apparently been set to northwestward when she ran into this mist-veiled trap. She had hit hard, under the engine-room. Water spurted through her torn bottom-plates, and the engine-room spaces flooded rapidly.

Splashing about in the murk, the damage-controlmen fought to stem the rising flood. All available pumps were put into action, but the ocean came in, and the damage-controlmen were driven out. The engine-room was "partially abandoned."

With power lost, the ravaged DD drifted at the mercy of ground swells which drove her toward the jutting rocks abeam. Commander Pogue ordered the anchor dropped to hold the bow and prevent the ship from going broadside into the rocky tumulus. Her keel clear of the bottom, WORDEN rode at anchor until daylight. Had the sea remained lenient, the destroyer could undoubtedly have been extricated from the shoals.

But just as daylight began to dissolve the gloom, the harbor was roughened by a rising wind, and WORDEN's stern began to grind and pound submerged rock. A battering surf came breaking around the stranded ship. All hands were put to pumping and jettisoning operations, but WORDEN's stern could not be gotten off.

In answer to a distress call, the destroyer DEWEY (Lieutenant Commander Joseph P. Canty) steamed to WORDEN's aid. A tow line was rigged, and Dewey tried to pull WORDEN clear. There ensued a tug of war between straining destroyer and obdurate Aleutian rock, with WORDEN's life as prize. The rock won.

The contest had hardly begun when the tow line parted with a detonation like a gunshot. As the broken cable backlashed like a monster bullwhip, WORDEN lurched and listed to starboard. She began to settle, and the list increased as buffeting surf assailed her exposed beam. Driven against the rocks, the destroyer lay helpless and aground, and savage seas ran in to give her a beating.

Throughout the forenoon they slammed her against the rocks. Flogged her hull. Swept up over her deck to flood her hatches. The ship was floundering and groaning when Commander Pogue gave the order to abandon. A whaleboat was lowered into the boiling sea. Life rafts were launched. In the turmoil of wind and wave, seamen were thrown headlong into the water. The ship lurched and listed 35 degrees. Watching rescue operations, Commander Pogue was clinging to the splinter shield of a 40 mm. mount when a wave struck like a shell-burst and he was knocked overboard, unconscious.

Rescue operations under Commander G. R. Cooper (ComDesDiv 1 in DEWEY) were as hazardous as they were urgent. Whaleboats from DEWEY and the

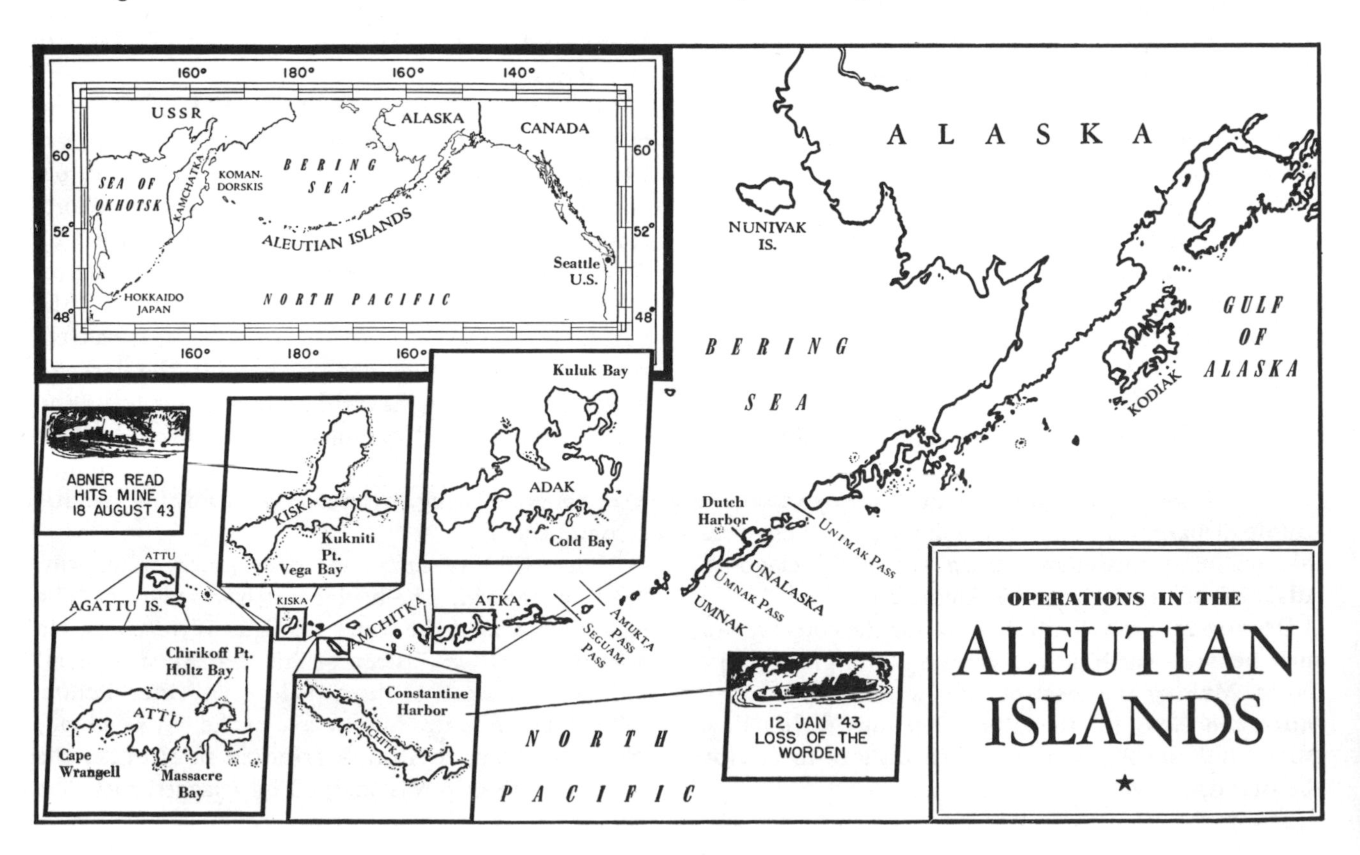

landing boats from the transport MIDDLETON came sweeping through the shoals to pick up WORDEN's survivors. In the furious water a number of the destroyermen were injured. Several were drowned. Rabid seas continued to pound the stranded destroyer. At 1225 the ship's hull broke in two, and she sprawled on the rocks, a halved carcass.

By evening a williwaw was blowing full force. The wind built up to 60 knots, and the whistling gale sent the transport MIDDLETON dragging her anchor across the bay. In dark bedlam the transport grounded and sprained her back. Desperate damage-control measures kept out the wild sea, but the ship remained hard aground. Eighty-four days would pass before the salvage crews finally had her afloat.

The same storm, followed by a blinding blizzard, swamped landing craft and disabled small boats. When the blizzard swirled off into Aleutian oblivion and the weather finally cleared to visibility, the date was January 17. The rocky teeth in the mouth of Constantine Harbor were bare. The WORDEN wreckage had been swallowed.

On August 10, 1943, four Mark VI depth charges, fitted with electrical exploder devices, were lowered in the sea where WORDEN went down. The charges were set off. The sea roared. The sunken ship was laid to rest, secure from all possibility of salvage by an inquisitive enemy.

Aleutian Blockade

By the end of January some 4,000 American troops had been transported to Amchitka. Defenses for the island were installed, the airbase was completed, and the enemy in the Western Aleutians found himself staring into the muzzle of the American pistol.

But the Japanese garrisons on Attu and Kiska had been in an unenviable spot for six months. Whereas the U.S. Navy could (and did) move a steady stream of supplies to such advance bases as Adak and Amchitka, the Imperial Japanese Navy could do little more than send an occasional supply ship to Attu and Kiska. Reason: the blockade established by Army and Navy Air and by the naval forces under Rear Admiral Smith and maintained by the naval forces under his successor, Rear Admiral Charles H. McMorris.

In mid-February Admiral McMorris's task group of blockaders set out to tighten the tourniquet that was paralyzing the Jap arm in the Aleutians. Admiral McMorris's force consisted of the light cruiser RICHMOND (flagship), the heavy cruiser INDIANAPOLIS (Captain Nicholas Vytlacil), and four destroyers. The destroyers in this group were BANCROFT (Commander J. L. Melgaard), CALDWELL (Commander J. F. Newman, Jr.), GILLESPIE (Commander C. L. Clement), and COGHLAN (Commander B. F. Tompkins). The group was searching for Jap shipping which had been reported off Holtz Bay by an American submarine. The report proved erroneous, but the blockaders, taking advantage of favorable weather conditions, went on to lob some shells into Chicagof Harbor and Holtz Bay. Then, late in the following afternoon (February 18) the warships proceeded to conduct an offensive patrol to the westward of Attu. The group divided into two sections—RICHMOND, CALDWELL, and BANCROFT; INDIANAPOLIS, COGHLAN, and GILLESPIE. Spreading out to sweep a broad field, the two sections steamed on the lookout for enemy forces which had been reported as approaching the Aleutians from the Jap homeland or the Kuriles. Mission: To intercept and destroy.

The Bering's waters were smooth and steely. Evening brought a cold, white moon, and the warships hunted across an empty, arctic seascape that might have been on the other side of the moon itself.

Then, about 2200, the destroyer COGHLAN (in the INDIANAPOLIS section which was some miles north of the RICHMOND section) picked up a radar "pip."

COGHLAN passed the word to INDIANAPOLIS, and Captain Vytlacil sent the heavy cruiser and the two DD's on a top-speed run for the target. COGHLAN took position ahead; GILLESPIE astern. About five minutes later—

"Smoke dead ahead!" came the lookout's call.

A half hour's run, and the vessel was in full view. INDIANAPOLIS challenged by blinker. The vessel's answer was, as Captain Vytlacil bluntly put it, "unsatisfactory." It came in Japanese code.

Cruisermen and destroyermen had been rushed to battle stations. At 2315 the gunners opened fire, range about 7,000 yards. Almost with the first salvo the guns were on target.

The luckless *maru* answered with a few rounds from a deck gun and some feeble machine-gun bursts, all shots falling short. A direct hit struck the Jap, tossing fragments of superstructure aloft. Then a thunder-burst rolled across the seascape. Trailed by another. And another.

An orange smudge enveloped the vessel. Exploding munitions cargo sent up spurting flares. Battered by multiple hits, the *maru* and its crew came to a dead end, and at 0125 next morning the wreck disappeared in a spurt of fire, going down stern first.

COGHLAN was ordered forward to pick up survivors. The destroyermen could not find a living soul. Of the ship—AKAGANE MARU, bound for Attu with a platoon of troops, stores, and materials for an airstrip—only an empty lifejacket, some indiscriminate lumber, a scattering of debris, and a bamboo life raft remained. There were no sailors on the life raft.

Scratch another blockade-runner.

Battle of the Komandorskis

> *Unique in the naval history of the Pacific War, the Aleutian campaign provided at the Komandorski battle the only conventional daylight gun duel between opposing surface forces in which air attack was not made.*
>
> *The Campaigns of the Pacific War*

As suggested by the foregoing statement, the Battle of the Komandorski Islands was an old-fashioned naval engagement, a hammer-and-tongs shooting match in which the opposing sea fighters sighted each other, engaged at close range, feinted, chased, sparred, duelled, and dodged. The involved cruisers zigged and zagged at high speed to evade enemy salvos. The action featured audacious torpedo attacks by charging destroyers, and the laying of defensive smoke screens. Neither dive-bombers nor submarines were on the scene.

Commanded by Rear Admiral C. H. ("Sock") McMorris, Task Group 16.6 was composed of the heavy cruiser SALT LAKE CITY (Captain B. J. Rodgers), the light cruiser RICHMOND (Captain T. M. Waldschmidt), and the following four destroyers of DesRon 14 under Captain R. S. Riggs: BAILEY (Lieutenant Commander J. C. Atkeson), COGHLAN (Commander B. F. Tompkins), DALE (Commander A. L. Rorschach), and MONAGHAN (Lieutenant Commander P. H. Horn). Admiral McMorris had his flag in RICHMOND, and Captain Riggs rode in BAILEY.

During the third week in March, 1943, this task group was patrolling the seas west of Attu, not many miles from the spot where McMorris and his blockaders had blasted the munition-carrying AKAGANE MARU into icy extinction. To the majority of the crews the waters off Attu must have resembled the freezing approaches to World's End.

But Admiral McMorris and the other Aleutian veterans in TG 16.6 were aware that the Attu area could prove hotter than it looked. Sooner or later the Japs would have to send supplies to their Attu and Kiska garrisons or the invading forces would lose their toehold on that tenebrous archipelago and meet defeat through the simple process of starvation.

In anticipation of just such a strong convoy and escorting naval force, Admiral McMorris with Task Group 16.6 patrolled the western approaches to the Aleutians.

"That Aleutian patrolling was drudgery," a destroyerman recalled later. "Half the time you couldn't see your hand in front of your face, for the fog. And when the williwaws were blowing, you couldn't see anything for the spume and spray. When you weren't soaked to the skin, you were frozen to the marrow, and it was cold enough to freeze a brass monkey. Every month was January, and there wasn't any thaw."

Narrating the adventures of the destroyer BAILEY, that warship's historian wrote:

> *The North Pacific, with its blasts that sometimes reach velocities well above 100 knots and which roll up unbelievably gigantic seas of 50 to 70 feet from trough to crest, was the global war's most rugged theatre from the climatic standpoint, and . . . a proving ground for both ships and men.*

The flagship of DesRon 14 had been on duty on that Aleutian proving ground since late September '42. On March 21, 1943, while serving with COGHLAN as a screen for RICHMOND, she fired her first shots at the Japanese invader—a float plane which came snooping over TG 16.6 as it steamed west of Kiska. BAILEY's anti-aircraft fire drove off this enemy scout, but not until after she had undoubtedly reported the presence of Task Group 16.6.

Actually the Japanese naval commanders had been aware of the task group's presence in the area ever since the summary destruction of AKAGANE MARU. The sinking of that hapless blockade-runner had been reported by a Jap picket boat, and several Japanese scout planes had subsequently sighted McMorris's blockaders. Given a fairly comprehensive idea of the opposition to be contended with, Vice Admiral Moshiro Hosogaya, commander of the Japanese Fifth Fleet, prepared to shatter the blockade with a superior naval force.

Hosogaya's plan to run a large convoy through to Attu was carefully laid. Three transports were assigned to the convoy. These were the 15-knot, 10,000-ton converted light cruiser ASAKU MARU, the 10,000-ton Army transport SAKITO MARU, and the slow, 4,000-ton Army transport SANKO MARU, The transports carried supplies, ammunition, war gear, and troops, and ASAKA MARU's burden included a staff and headquarters outfit.

For the escort force Admiral Hosogaya mustered all the Fifth Fleet units available. The force included the heavy cruisers NACHI (flagship) and MAYA, the light cruisers TAMA and ABUKUMA, and the destroyers WAKABA, HATSUSHIMO, IKAZUCHI, INAZUMA, and USUGUMO. As is apparent from the line-up, the cruisers of this formidable fleet outnumbered McMorris's cruiser force two to one. The Japanese destroyer force was one up on the American. The Jap warships were not equipped with radar, but this lack was at least partially offset by the three spotter planes carried by NACHI and by the Fifth Fleet's decidedly preponderant fire-power.

Hosogaya's strategic procedure was not ill conceived. The transports and the escort force were to rendezvous on March 25 at a point south of the Komandorskis and just outside the 600-mile radius from Adak—a meeting place beyond range of the area American Catalinas were searching at that time. From this rendezvous point the convoy would race to Attu. Once the success of the supply mission was assured, the Fifth Fleet was to undertake another important mission; if possible, it was to lure into battle, attack, and destroy the United States naval forces in the area. Certain that his fleet outweighed the American blockading force, Admiral Hosogaya was confident that both objectives of the dual enterprise could be attained.

However—and as might have been expected—bad weather threatened to maladjust the operation at the outset. Heavy seas slowed the transport SANKO MARU and her escort destroyer USUGUMO so that they were not at the rendezvous at the appointed hour.

But morning of March 26 brought flattening seas and a promise of improving weather. Visibility was unusually good. And Commander Miura on the flagship NACHI's bridge was scanning the horizon, on lookout for the laggard SANKO MARU and USUGUMO.

The Japanese ships, steaming in single column on a northerly heading, were led by NACHI in the following order: MAYA, TAMA, ABUKUMA, WAKABA, HATSUSHIMO, IKAZUCHI, ASAKA MARU, SAKITO MARU, INAZUMA. Sunrise was still some time away when Commander Miura turned his glasses southward and glimpsed a mast on the gilded horizon.

Voice of a lookout sang through the cold, *"Ship to starboard!"* And reported the bearing. The vessel was hull down, but Miura thought he recognized the USUGUMO's mast. Turning to a seaman, he snapped, "Notify the admiral the USUGUMO and SANKO MARU are joining up."

Miura's error—a case of hasty, and mistaken, identity. Admiral Hosogaya called for a column right through approximately 180 degrees, and by the time the maneuver was executed, four or five additional masts were visible to the south. American warships! The mast sighted by Miura was that of the U.S.S. COGHLAN.

McMorris's force had been steaming on a scouting line, the ships some six miles apart. Farthest north was the destroyer COGHLAN. Light cruiser RICHMOND was next in the formation. Then came destroyers BAILEY and DALE, heavy cruiser SALT LAKE CITY, and destroyer MONAGHAN.

BAILEY's historian described the enemy contact as follows:

> At 0730 on the morning of 26 March, BAILEY had just sounded drill general quarters for the morning alert when COGHLAN, on the extreme north end of the scouting line, reported at least two ships on her radar screen within an approximate range of 7 miles. Rear Admiral McMorris immediately ordered all ships to concentrate on his flagship and to form for battle at 25 knots. This was the call to battle which the crew of BAILEY had not experienced before—anxious faces scanned a horizon that was unusually clear. As the formation steamed on a northerly course to cut off the enemy, which was believed to be a supply convoy headed for Attu, the Jap ships appeared one by one in the distance until it was evident that the American forces were heavily outnumbered.

The enemy's numerical superiority came as something of an unwelcome surprise to Admiral McMorris. As his warships concentrated around RICHMOND, he led the task group at best speed toward the enemy convoy, which shaped up at first as two sketchily escorted *marus*. The Jap merchantmen turned and ran northwestward.

COGHLAN now reported five radar contacts; RICHMOND made three; and as dawn tinted the water, the enemy hove in view. About 0740, Combat Information Center gave the enemy's course, speed, bearing, and distance—the range was 21,000 yards.

McMorris promptly changed course to parallel the enemy's. He was determined to maintain contact, but he wanted to avoid closing the range until his group was better concentrated and the situation had clarified.

By 0820 RICHMOND's bridge personnel could count ten Jap vessels in the convoy, but the cruiser silhouettes were not yet identifiable. As Admiral McMorris phrased it, he *"still felt that a Roman holiday was in prospect."* A few minutes later the two Jap heavy and two light cruisers were identified. *"The situation had now clarified,"* Admiral McMorris stated in his battle report. And he went on to note, *". . . but it had also radically and unpleasantly changed."*

It seemed that the prospects of a Roman holiday remained, but there was a question as to who might do the celebrating. Even as that doubt arose on RICHMOND's bridge, it was apparent that the Jap warships were steaming eastward to come between the American task group and its base. Obviously the Japanese fleet was intent on closing the range and giving battle.

"Sock" McMorris prepared to slug it out, long odds or no. He set a course to pursue the fleeing Jap trans-

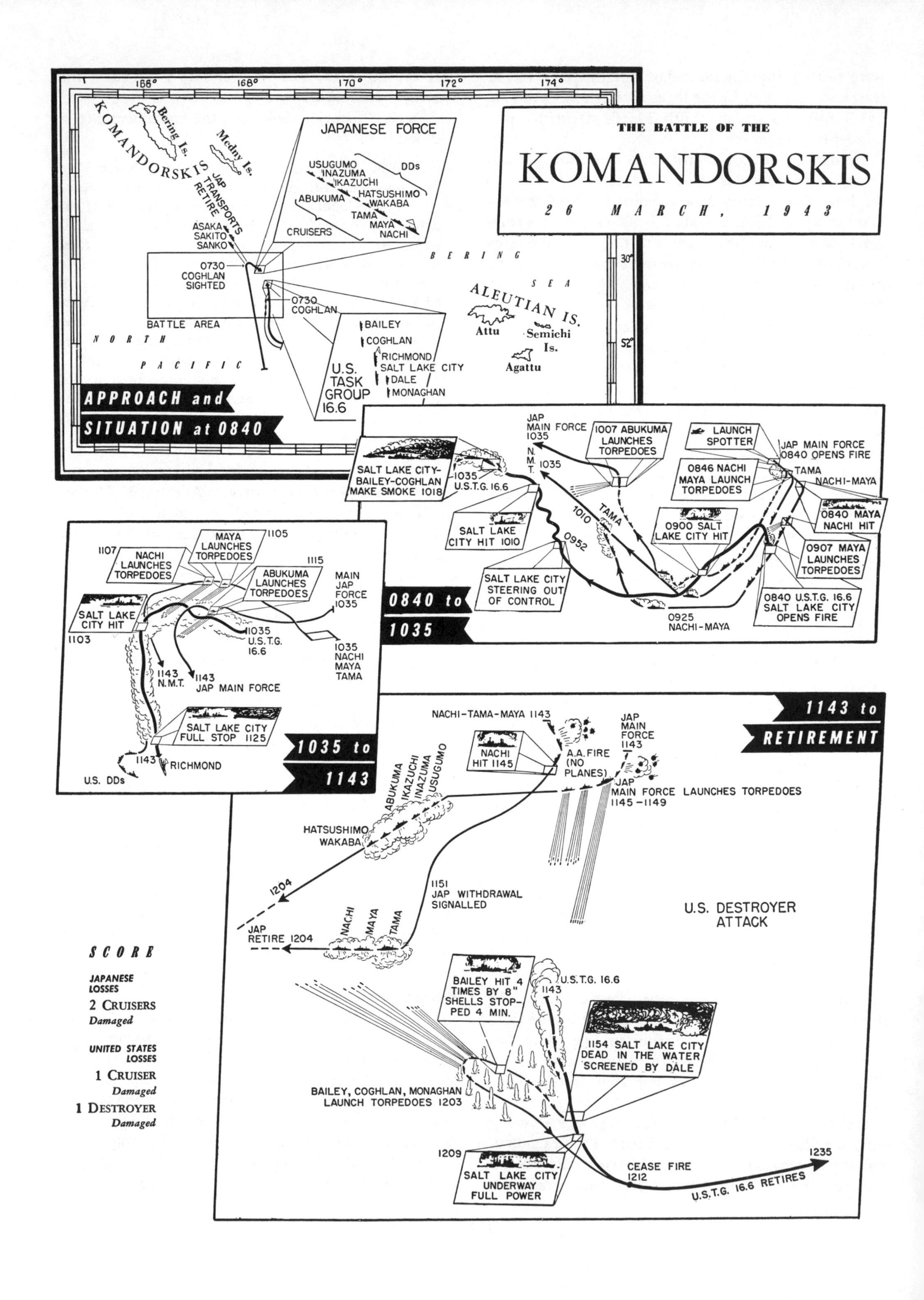
THE BATTLE OF THE
KOMANDORSKIS
26 MARCH, 1943
166° 168° 170° 172° 174°
KOMANDORSKIS
Bering Is.
Medny Is.
JAP TRANSPORTS RETIRE
ASAKA
SAKITO
SANKO
JAPANESE FORCE
USUGUMO
INAZUMA
IKAZUCHI
DDs
HATSUSHIMO
WAKABA
ABUKUMA
TAMA
MAYA
NACHI
CRUISERS
0730 COGHLAN SIGHTED
0730 COGHLAN
BATTLE AREA
BERING
SEA
ALEUTIAN IS.
Attu
Semichi Is.
Agattu
NORTH
PACIFIC
BAILEY
COGHLAN
RICHMOND
SALT LAKE CITY
DALE
MONAGHAN
U.S. TASK GROUP 16.6
APPROACH and SITUATION at 0840
JAP MAIN FORCE 1035
1007 ABUKUMA LAUNCHES TORPEDOES
LAUNCH SPOTTER
JAP MAIN FORCE 0840 OPENS FIRE
N. M. T. 1035
TAMA
NACHI-MAYA
SALT LAKE CITY-BAILEY-COGHLAN MAKE SMOKE 1018
1035 U.S.T.G. 16.6
0846 NACHI MAYA LAUNCH TORPEDOES
0840 MAYA NACHI HIT
1010
TAMA
0900 SALT LAKE CITY HIT
0907 MAYA LAUNCHES TORPEDOES
SALT LAKE CITY HIT 1010
0952
SALT LAKE CITY STEERING OUT OF CONTROL
0840 U.S.T.G. 16.6 SALT LAKE CITY OPENS FIRE
0925 NACHI-MAYA
0840 to 1035
1107 NACHI LAUNCHES TORPEDOES
MAYA LAUNCHES TORPEDOES
1105
1115 ABUKUMA LAUNCHES TORPEDOES
MAIN JAP FORCE 1035
SALT LAKE CITY HIT
1103
1035 U.S.T.G. 16.6
1035 NACHI MAYA TAMA
1143 N.M.T.
1143 JAP MAIN FORCE
SALT LAKE CITY FULL STOP 1125
1143
RICHMOND
U.S. DDs
1035 to 1143
1143 to RETIREMENT
NACHI-TAMA-MAYA 1143
JAP MAIN FORCE 1143
NACHI HIT 1145
A.A. FIRE (NO PLANES)
JAP MAIN FORCE LAUNCHES TORPEDOES 1145-1149
ABUKUMA
IKAZUCHI
INAZUMA
USUGUMO
HATSUSHIMO
WAKABA
1204
1151 JAP WITHDRAWAL SIGNALLED
U.S. DESTROYER ATTACK
NACHI
MAYA
TAMA
JAP RETIRE 1204
BAILEY HIT 4 TIMES BY 8" SHELLS STOPPED 4 MIN.
U.S.T.G. 16.6
1143
1154 SALT LAKE CITY DEAD IN THE WATER SCREENED BY DALE
BAILEY, COGHLAN, MONAGHAN LAUNCH TORPEDOES 1203
1209
SALT LAKE CITY UNDERWAY FULL POWER
CEASE FIRE 1212
1235
U.S.T.G. 16.6 RETIRES
SCORE
JAPANESE LOSSES
2 CRUISERS Damaged
UNITED STATES LOSSES
1 CRUISER Damaged
1 DESTROYER Damaged

ports. There was a chance that the Japanese might divide their forces in an effort to cover the retreating *marus*. The American task group closed up, RICHMOND and SALT LAKE CITY in column with the flagship leading, van destroyers BAILEY and COGHLAN off the light cruiser's port bow, and DALE and MONAGHAN off the heavy cruiser's starboard quarter. Determinedly the task group started a chase to overhaul the fugitive merchantmen, but the Japanese fleet commander was not tricked by the strategem. Instead of dividing forces, the Jap warships closed up and bore down for concentrated attack.

NACHI opened fire at 0840, range approximately ten miles. The Jap gunners were promptly on target, their salvos soon straddling the RICHMOND. But the blast of the opening salvo wrecked the two Zero spotting planes on NACHI's starboard catapult. In consequence, the spotters had to be jettisoned, and the Zero reconnaissance plane on the port catapult was the only one that managed to take off. Throughout the engagement, this seaplane served as a spotter. It was (according to post-war testimony by Miura) the only Jap aircraft in the battle area. The Americans had no spotters in the air.

Shortly after her opening salvo, NACHI and MAYA launched torpedoes. All ran wide of the mark. Such misses at extreme range might be expected, but a malfunctioning main battery created abnormal and serious trouble for the NACHI crew. After the first salvo was fired, loss of electric power left the battery inoperative. For 30 minutes the big guns remained at maximum elevation and could not be laid, thanks to low steam pressure at the generators.

Meantime RICHMOND and her consorts opened up a few seconds after NACHI's introductory salvo. The Americans gave as good as they got, and the gun duel went hot and heavy for the first quarter of an hour. MAYA shook RICHMOND with straddles, then turned her weapons on SALT LAKE CITY, the only American warship capable of trading heavyweight punches with the Japanese CA's. SALT LAKE CITY's 8-inchers volleyed and thundered as the range decreased and the Jap cruisers drove the American forces westward. The gunners on SALT LAKE CITY were not old salts, but they were seasoned enough to score hits on the enemy.

"In the first five or ten minutes of action," Commander Shigefuso Hashimoto, of Admiral Hosogaya's staff, testified later, *"the* NACHI *was hit at the after end of the bridge by a blue, dye-loaded shell, which killed five or six communications personnel and wounded twelve or thirteen others. A small fire which broke out . . . was soon extinguished."*

So the Americans apparently drew first blood. But the enemy's superior strength dictated an American retirement. If McMorris's task group steamed too far northwestward toward the Komandorski Islands, it might be cut off from home base—or, at least the approaches to Attu. The American task group would have to head eastward toward the Aleutians. Some fast maneuvers were called for.

But before the Americans could do much maneuvering, SALT LAKE CITY was struck and damaged. At 0910 a shell pierced her hull below the waterline, went through an alley housing a propeller shaft, and exploded in a fuel oil tank. Some pipelines carried away, and oil and water spurted into the after engine-room. The cruiser's damage-controlmen finally managed to control the flood, and the propeller shaft was not paralyzed. But the blow staggered the heavy cruiser, left her with a list, and inaugurated a series of troubles that seriously hampered her thereafter.

By way of reprisal, NACHI was hit and the light cruiser TAMA struck. Damage was superficial, however, and both warships joined the heavy cruiser MAYA and light cruiser ABUKUMA in a determined effort to blast the SALT LAKE CITY. Japanese salvos repeatedly straddled the American heavy cruiser as McMorris maneuvered the task group through a succession of radical course changes calculated to get his task group out of the enemy's reach. The American gunners scored several more hits on Hosogaya's flagship, and by 0950 NACHI was showing the signs of painful damage. In post-war testimony, the Japanese waxed eloquent concerning the American destroyers' gunnery. *"Their shells,"* said Commander Miura, *"landed aboard like rain."*

Over the TBS at 1010 went McMorris's order for a course change which would put the enemy astern.

At that very moment SALT LAKE CITY was struck another hard blow by a shell that stabbed through her main deck. A dud, but several compartments were flooded. Subsequent maneuvers brought the van destroyers into battle to cover the injured cruiser. Both BAILEY and COGHLAN opened fire on a Jap light cruiser, range about 15,000 yards. The destroyermen also fired heatedly at the Jap spotting plane which ventured overhead.

At 1018, SALT LAKE CITY, BAILEY, and COGHLAN commenced laying a smoke screen. Ten minutes later the Task Group Commander changed course 60 degrees to the left to take best advantage of the smoke screen, and shortly thereafter he directed Captain Ralph Riggs to assume tactical command of destroyers DALE and MONAGHAN, at that time up ahead with RICHMOND. Riggs ordered the DD's to join BAILEY and COGHLAN. Throughout the remainder of the engagement, DALE and MONAGHAN, BAILEY and

COGHLAN intermittently screened the cruisers with chemical and funnel smoke. Now and then the flanking Jap light cruisers would get around the end of the smoke, or make observation through gaps in the smudge, and the screen was, of course, unable to frustrate aerial observation. So the enemy kept up a more or less steady fire on the American warships. But the smoke furnished sufficient cover to prevent an annihilating number of hits, and the four DD's of DesRon 14 performed valiantly in screening the assailed cruisers.

At 1035 the four destroyers were some 800 yards apart and about 2,500 yards on the engaged side of SALT LAKE CITY. RICHMOND leading, the task group steamed at best speed to avoid another blizzard of 8-inch shells.

The Japs redoubled their efforts to demolish SALT LAKE CITY, and they made her the target of a relentless and murderous barrage. "Overs" and "shorts" splashed around the covering DD's, and the destroyermen could hear the big ones rushing through the air like invisible express trains.

To add to her difficulties, SALT LAKE CITY was badgered by steering casualties. At 0952 the concussions of her own salvos had thrown her steering gear temporarily out of control. Control was quickly regained, but only for the moment. At 1002 the gear went completely out of commission, and she no longer answered her helm. Her rudder stops had carried away. Shift was made to emergency steering, but she was limited to 10° rudder and consequent slow turns. SALT LAKE CITY was in trouble, but she continued to fight back with savage gunnery that made her tormentors keep their distance.

Now the light cruiser ABUKUMA and the DD's WAKABA, HATSUSHIMO, IKAZUCHI, and INAZUMA had closed on the starboard quarter. Between 1105 and noon, the Jap cruisers and two of the Jap destroyers launched torpedoes, but the range was extreme, and the "fish" failed to hit. Within that hour, MAYA, NACHI, and ABUKUMA got off a total of 16 torpedo shots; DD's WAKABA and HATSUSHIMO fired twelve.

For their part the American destroyers were desperately busy. At 1059 SALT LAKE CITY suffered another hit. A shell-burst clawed the cruiser's deck with shrapnel, wrecked her starboard catapult, wounded four men, and killed a bluejacket and an officer. At that time the task group was heading westward. Admiral McMorris decided the moment had arrived for a fast break-away to the south. The order to change course was spoken over the short-range radio. The DD's screened the turn with a serpentine smoke wall, but at 1103 SALT LAKE CITY was struck by still another shell. The hit jolted the cruiser. But it was internal injuries, suffered from the first hit she received in the battle, that now slowed her. At 1125 her after engines coughed to a stop. Frantically her repair parties worked the pumps, but the water was climbing in the engine-room spaces, and the lamed cruiser was in serious straits.

The Japs had followed the American task group's southward turn, and they were throwing everything at the crippled SALT LAKE CITY. As shell splashes geysered around the cruiser, Admiral McMorris ordered BAILEY, MONAGHAN, and COGHLAN to fend off the enemy with a torpedo attack. The three DD's received the order at 1130, and turned to face the oncoming foe. The range closed swiftly. The DD's bore in to shorten the gap. Jubilant Jap gunners aimed a blistering fire at DALE, the lone destroyer remaining with SALT LAKE CITY. Her skipper, Commander Rorschach, noted in a laconic report,

> Salvos landed short and kept walking up. They came up to 50 yards short, and then the CA's shifted fire to the other DD's.

Then, at 1138, before the destroyermen could launch their "fish," McMorris canceled the order for the torpedo attack. SALT LAKE CITY's engineers had managed hasty repairs, and the damaged cruiser had regained some of her speed. The destroyers fell back and continued their screening operations.

If Captain Riggs and his destroyermen had been tight-nerved, they were afforded no relaxation. At 1146 the Jap cruisers resumed the attack on SALT LAKE CITY. Simultaneously their anti-aircraft batteries opened fire on the overcast, and the sky above the enemy warships resembled a blossoming cotton field. American planes from Adak? Some of the destroyermen cheered. But radar sweeps dispelled this hope, and the officers of TG 16.6 knew the Japs were shooting at phantoms. Meanwhile 8-inch shells came lobbing in a steady rain over SALT LAKE CITY's smoke screen, and at 1154 the cruiser's engines shuddered to a stop. Salt water in the oil booster line to the boilers. As her boilers went out and she slowed to a drift, it looked like "curtains" for SALT LAKE CITY.

Now DesRon 14 was called upon to save the imperiled day. From Admiral McMorris the order went to Captain Riggs—DesRon 14 was to launch an immediate torpedo attack; one DD would remain behind to screen SALT LAKE CITY. Squadron Commander Riggs relayed the order to his little force DALE would screen the cruiser. BAILEY, COGHLAN, and MONAGHAN would execute the attack. Captain Riggs concluded the order with a directive, brusque and sharp:

"Get the big boys!"

The three DD's pointed their bows at the Japanese Fifth Fleet and started a run for the enemy cruisers. The odds were literally appalling—the men in BAILEY, COGHLAN, and MONAGHAN knew what they were up against. Here it is in the narrative of destroyer BAILEY's ship-history.

> *Apprehension was written on the faces of* BAILEY'S *crew when the order was received to make a torpedo run on the two heavy cruisers of the enemy's force. Complying with the order, she closed to 9,500 yards, firing her 5-inch guns as she came. Closer and closer she went, right into the teeth of the Rising Sun. Crew members even fancied they saw yellow faces peering over the side of the Jap warship—faces displaying no little scorn at the mouse that had dared to threaten the buoyancy of the lion. But* BAILEY *was making this a quick trip as she moved in for what she hobed would be the kill.*

But unbeknownst to the American command, the Japs had already decided to break off the action. Just three minutes before Captain Riggs received the attack order, Admiral Hosogaya had concluded that a retirement was the better part of valor. Evidently he was unaware of the damage dealt to SALT LAKE CITY, and it seems he feared an attack by American land-based bombers.

At any rate, the Japs were on the point of withdrawing, and the destroyer charge was entirely unexpected. With BAILEY, MONAGHAN, and COGHLAN bearing down on the booming cruisers, the battle took a surprising turn. At the rushing DD's the Jap heavy cruisers hurled a hurricane of 8-inch projectiles. Dodging and weaving, the destroyers raced forward through the exploding storm. NACHI's bridge personnel stared at the oncoming "cans" in awe and unbelief. In postwar testimony Commander Miura expressed admiration for the destroyer charge, and went on to declare, *"I do not know how a ship could live through the concentration of fire that was brought to bear on the leading destroyer."*

The three DD's were literally *"smothered with shell splashes."* Onward they raced, rushing in to launch their torpedoes. Driving in, COGHLAN fired furiously at the heavy cruiser MAYA. Little BAILEY and MONAGHAN hurled 5-inchers at the bellowing NACHI. The latter was ripped by several 5-inch hits.

But in making their sacrifice play, the DD's of Task Group 16.6 could not escape punishment. Zigzagging through a murderous pattern of shell splashes, van destroyer BAILEY was staggered by four successive hits. The first 8-incher pierced her like a bullet going through cardboard, and exploded in the galley passageway, wrecking the provision issuing room. One officer and three bluejackets were killed by the explosion, and another man, mortally wounded, died a short time later.

In the next moment NACHI's big guns punched another shell into BAILEY. This projectile punctured the destroyer's hull at the forward fireroom, waterline level. A fast-working repair crew plugged the hole, and the fire-and-bilge pump ousted the flood.

Then came a third hit, holing the destroyer at the forward engine-room. Water gushed into the ship, and it was necessary to secure and abandon the flooded compartment. Forward boilers No. 1 and No. 2 were secured. When shift was made from main to emergency feed—the steam supply from boilers No. 3 and No. 4 being temporarily suspended—BAILEY came to a four-minute stop. She went ahead at 15 knots, and when main feed was restored, about ten minutes later, she built up 18 knots on one engine, and dodged away through the shell-tornado.

The final hit—a dud—ricochetted from the base of a gun shield. No damage was done to the mount, but the caroming projectile grooved a 1-inch dent in BAILEY's steel.

The Japs were squarely on target, and all hands in BAILEY had reason to believe the destroyer's number was up. She was running on half an engineering plant in a crisis wherein she needed everything. But the enemy did not yet have the number of DD 492. On the assailed destroyer's bridge, Captain Riggs ordered the torpedoes fired. Lieutenant Commander Atkeson voiced the "Torpedoes away!" as the spread of five "fish" leapt from the tubes and went sprinting off in the direction of I.J.N. MAYA.

The fanning wakes were sighted, and MAYA maneuvered to evade the deadly war heads. Lookouts on BAILEY's bridge reported a torpedo hit on this Jap heavy cruiser, but MAYA's officers subsequently stated that the torpedoes were successfully dodged. Not so successfully did the NACHI dodge BAILEY's 5-inch fire. The destroyer's Control Officer reported numerous straddles as the DD's guns flashed defiant retort to the Jap flagship's wicked 8-inchers. Salvos were walked back and forth across the roaring cruiser, and NACHI was flailed by a succession of 5-inch hits.

BAILEY could deal it out, but she was also taking it. Another Jap shell—a near miss—shattered the starboard motor whaleboat and ruined the after davit. The previous hits had left her with five dead and a number of her crew painfully wounded. All hands sighed with relief when she finally came through the shell storm.

Miraculously, her team-mate MONAGHAN emerged from the scorching combat unscathed. COGHLAN, too, was singularly favored by Fortune. Attacking MAYA, Commander Tompkins' destroyer was brushed by 8-inch shells that missed her by the width of her paint. One projectile blasted close aboard, slashing the DD's superstructure with whistling fragments. Jagged shrapnel ripped into the director and put both radars out of commission. A flying scrap of iron struck the Executive Officer over the left eye and sent him reeling, to fall unconscious with blood masking his face. Two bluejackets were wounded. And one of COGHLAN's officers, stricken with shell shock, answered an order with a cataleptic stare, temporarily blinded and deafened by psychic trauma.

With four casualties, none fatal, COGHLAN plunged on through the tempest of 8-inch fire. Worst hurt of the three attacking destroyers, BAILEY limped out of it with all hands preparing to make a last-ditch stand.

But the Japanese Fifth Fleet did not follow through to easy victory. Aboard NACHI there was uncertainty and apprehension. Once more she was under SALT LAKE CITY's fire. The crippled American heavy cruiser was again under way, coaxing 15 knots from her engines, and lobbing shells at the Japanese flagship. Meanwhile Hosogaya's warships had expended so many rounds in the furious gun duel that the cruisers were running low on armor-piercing projectiles. Fuel was also running low in the Jap destroyer tanks. And Jap morale apparently had run low, thanks to the threat of air attack. Convinced that such an attack was imminent, Admiral Hosogaya gave the order to retire.

The retirement signal flashed through the Jap fleet only a few moments after BAILEY launched her torpedo attack. Strung out astern of BAILEY, the MONOGHAN and COGHLAN were given no chance to launch torpedoes; before they could reach the firing point, the Jap CA's had turned away. At 1205 SALT LAKE CITY ceased firing. At 1206 NACHI and MAYA turned northwestward, opening the range. At 1207 the Jap CA's shifted to westward, with the fleet's light forces conforming. On the bridge of every warship in TG 16.6, officers and men stared at the departing foe in incredulity.

"Damned if they're not heading for the horizon!"

"Our planes must be coming!"

But the Japs were running from ghost flyers in the sky—there were no American aircraft aloft in the battle area that noon.

By 1215 the lookouts of Task Group 16.6 had watched the last Jap warship dwindle over the western horizon. The way open to the Aleutians, TG 16.6 was heading for home base at best speed. The American warships were, in the salty terminology of SALT LAKE CITY's action report, "getting the hell out of there." And the Japs were doing the same in the opposite direction.

By 1230 all hands in the group knew the battle was over. For veterans and green crews alike it had been an excruciating contest—three and a half hours of touch-and-go, with SALT LAKE CITY and her destroyer screen bearing the brunt. For BAILEY that brunt had been particularly tough. After battle stations were secured, her exhausted hands had damage to fight. At 1335 her skipper ordered the depth charges jettisoned to correct a bothersome list, and the lamed destroyer, maneuvering with much difficulty, trailed the formation to Adak. She was temporarily repaired at Dutch Harbor; then, on April 2, she headed for Mare Island Navy Yard in company with the limping SALT LAKE CITY and the destroyer ELLIOT.

The Japanese Fifth Fleet had absorbed a similar amount of damage in the uneven combat. Hosogaya's flagship hobbled into Paramushiro with 15 dead and 27 wounded. Mangled by shell hits, the heavy cruiser went to Ominato for temporary repairs, and then to Sasebo for an overhaul. Light cruiser TAMA had only one casualty in her crew (a man wounded) but her topside damage presented the repair crews with a lengthy patch-up job.

Although outnumbering and outweighing the Americans, the Japanese had lost an unusual opportunity to wipe out the U.S. naval force in the western Aleutians.

This dramatic denouement led Admiral King to comment: *"No matter how bad your own situation appears to be, there is always the possibility that the situation of the enemy is much worse."*

The Commander in Chief also remarked the heroic action of Captain Riggs' DesRon 14, noting that *"the destroyers, due to bold and unfaltering conduct, contributed greatly to the protection of* SALT LAKE CITY." Undoubtedly, in pouring out their smoke and dashing to attack the enemy, they saved the life of the partially disabled heavy cruiser.

They also contributed to a naval effort that resulted in a major strategic setback for the Japanese. For the Fifth Fleet's primary mission had been to escort a convoy to the Aleutians. And the transports carrying reinforcements and supplies to the famished garrisons on Attu and Kiska never reached there.

BAILEY received a Naval Unit Commendation for her part in the Komandorski action, and Admiral Nimitz paid Captain Riggs and all units of DesRon 14 high tribute:

OUR DESTROYERS' GALLANT ATTACK IN THE FACE OF THE CONCENTRATED FIRE OF EIGHT ENEMY WARSHIPS AT THE BATTLE OF KOMANDORSKI DESERVES HIGH PRAISE.

CHAPTER 14

SOLOMONS CRUCIBLE

(THE GUADALCANAL CAMPAIGN)

(Part 1)

Green Hell in Molten Sea

Meanwhile in the Southwest Pacific the war had raged for 8 months. General MacArthur wanted to strike directly at Rabaul, the enemy's Southwest Pacific citadel. The Navy's strategists dissented. They pointed out that Rabaul was a power-house which could only be crushed by a large-scale offensive, and in the summer of 1942 the Navy had neither the ships nor men available for such an offensive.

Moreover the Japanese spearhead in the Solomons was a threat pointed straight at the Allied supply line to the New Hebrides and eastern Australia. This spearhead also guarded the eastern approaches to Rabaul. It would have to be blunted before an assault on Rabaul could be considered. So reasoned the Navy's leaders, and when the enemy landed on Guadalcanal Island early in July and began to construct an airfield, that settled it. The Joint Chiefs in Washington decided the Solomons should be the immediate target in a westward drive.

That the Navy's strategists were right in their estimates of Japanese strength was soon evident from the ferocious conflict which exploded at Guadalcanal. For the forces ashore—and particularly the Marines—the Solomons archipelago was a green-jungled hell. For the forces afloat—and especially the destroyers—it was a crucible.

Yet who, before the war, had ever heard of the Solomon Islands? To most Americans they might have been in the outer spaces of the cosmic void, peopled only by copra traders, pearl pirates, and cannibal blacks.

"There's a fair sort of port at Tulagi," better informed Australian pilots reported. "Some coconut plantations here and there, and a few missionaries. The rest of it is a pesthole, full of disease and fever. Half of the channels aren't charted, and most of those jungles have never been entered by a white man. If the heat doesn't kill you, the humidity will."

And then, of course, there were the Japs.

They chopped an encampment out of the jungle on the north coast of Guadalcanal at Lunga Point, and they cleared an airstrip for the Emperor's planes. Down from Tulagi they brought supplies and guns. And the naval forces of Rear Admiral Gunichi Mikawa, operating out of Rabaul, set out to support and maintain this forward outpost.

By the first week in August 1942, some 2,500 Japs, mostly construction workers, were sweating out the airfield. They were guarded by a contingent of tough, veteran jungle-fighters. The natives were merely rounded up and enslaved or shot.

On August 7 the United States Marines arrived on the scene—a landing force of the First Division under Major General A. A. Vandegrift. Storming ashore, they seized the airstrip (most of the Jap construction workers fled into the hills), and the following day it was named Henderson Field, after the Marine major who died leading a bomber squadron in the battle of Midway.

This was the first move in "Operation Watchtower," the Allied defensive-offensive designed to capture Tulagi, to expel the enemy from Guadalcanal, and to advance northwestward through the

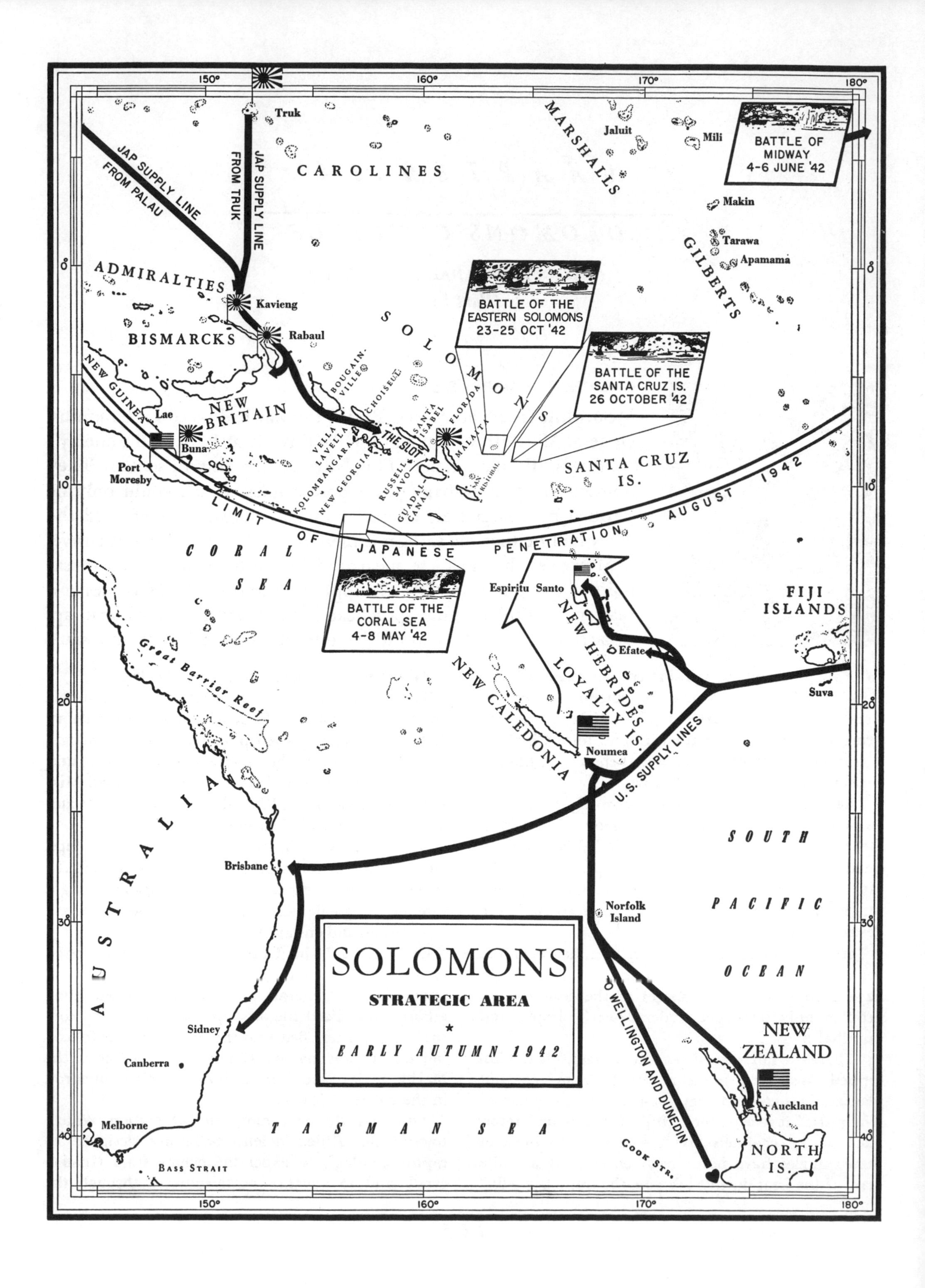

SOLOMONS
STRATEGIC AREA
EARLY AUTUMN 1942
BATTLE OF MIDWAY 4-6 JUNE '42
BATTLE OF THE EASTERN SOLOMONS 23-25 OCT '42
BATTLE OF THE SANTA CRUZ IS. 26 OCTOBER '42
BATTLE OF THE CORAL SEA 4-8 MAY '42
LIMIT OF JAPANESE PENETRATION AUGUST 1942
JAP SUPPLY LINE FROM PALAU
JAP SUPPLY LINE FROM TRUK
U.S. SUPPLY LINES
WELLINGTON AND DUNEDIN
CAROLINES
MARSHALLS
GILBERTS
ADMIRALTIES
BISMARCKS
NEW BRITAIN
NEW GUINEA
SOLOMONS
SANTA CRUZ IS.
CORAL SEA
NEW HEBRIDES
LOYALTY IS.
NEW CALEDONIA
FIJI ISLANDS
AUSTRALIA
Great Barrier Reef
SOUTH PACIFIC OCEAN
TASMAN SEA
NEW ZEALAND
NORTH IS.
Truk
Jaluit
Mili
Makin
Tarawa
Apamama
Kavieng
Rabaul
Lae
Buna
Port Moresby
BOUGAINVILLE
CHOISEUL
VELLA LAVELLA
KOLOMBANGARA
NEW GEORGIA
THE SLOT
SANTA ISABEL
FLORIDA
MALAITA
RUSSELL
SAVO
GUADALCANAL
Espiritu Santo
Efate
Noumea
Suva
Brisbane
Norfolk Island
Sidney
Canberra
Melborne
BASS STRAIT
Auckland
COOK STR.
150°
160°
170°
180°
0°
10°
20°
30°
40°

Solomons, with Rabaul as the ultimate objective. The drive was to be carried, supported, and maintained by Allied naval forces at that time under the direction of Vice Admiral R. L. Ghormley, Commander South Pacific Forces, headquartered at Auckland, New Zealand. Advance bases for warshipping were Espiritu Santo in the New Hebrides, and Nouméa on New Caledonia.

But the capture of Henderson Field was only the beginning of the Guadalcanal Campaign. The Japs struck back with tigerish fury. Recognizing the strategic value of this Solomons backwater, they rushed troops, planes, and warships to the area, and succeeded in establishing a line just west of Henderson Field across the Matanikau River. There ensued a desperate contest with the opposing land forces locked in a death-grip, and each side determined to reinforce and supply this Guadalcanal front while endeavoring to cut the opponent's transportation lines.

With a relatively short haul from Rabaul, Jap troop and supply convoys, heavily escorted, ran down through the Solomons to Guadalcanal with a regularity that won them the nickname "Tokyo Express." Their mid-archipelago route between Choiseul, Santa Isabel, and New Georgia became known as "the Slot."

For the Americans the long haul from Espiritu Santo up through Indispensable Strait acquired a variety of names, many of them unprintable, but all definitely descriptive of a passage to innermost Hades.

The code name for Guadalcanal was "Cactus"—an exceedingly apt name.

In the green hell of Lunga Point the Marines struggled in a limbo of mud, malaria, and murder. To the Americans the jungle fighting was peculiarly loathsome. Much of it was hand-to-hand—wrestling versus jiujitsu. The surprise raid, the ambush, the stab in the back featured large in this deadly tussle. Invisible Jap sharpshooters were everywhere. At night they screamed in cockatoo-like voices, taunting the Henderson defenders. "We kill you, Yankees! We kill you all!"

Over this festering coast Jap aircraft hovered like vultures over carrion. And the seas off the island bubbled and boiled with the crash of shellfire, the smash of air bombs, the blast of depth charges and torpedoes. In the seething heart of this crucible, Allied and Jap warships melted away like ingots in a swirl of molten lead.

It was remarked that destroyers were particularly beset in the crucible. During the seven months of the Guadalcanal Campaign, more United States destroyers were lost than any other type of combatant ship engaged, Japanese included. Fourteen American DD's went down in the Solomons. And another—ominous beginning—was lost at the very outset at Espiritu Santo.

Loss of U.S.S. Tucker

On August 4, 1942, the destroyer Tucker (Lieutenant Commander W. R. Terrell) was leading the cargo ship Nira Luckenbach into harbor at Espiritu Santo in the New Hebrides.

As she was heading into the western entrance, she was suddenly staggered by a shocking blast that sent a sheet of fire up her side and left her wallowing with a broken back, her hull almost torn in two at the No. 1 stack.

The entire steaming watch in the forward fireroom perished, and dazed men with bleeding hands and faces came stumbling topside from other compartments. Most of the destroyermen below decks managed to get out, but the U.S.S. Tucker was finished.

The broken destroyer gradually settled, a slowly folding jacknife. The crew abandoned, and near-by rescue vessels quickly recovered the survivors. Nothing could be done for the ship. The stern section of the wreck sank the following morning. A diving party scuttled and sank the jagged bow.

Tucker's loss was a blow to the DesPac Force, at that date trying to muster every available ship for the Guadalcanal showdown. Bad enough if she had been downed by the enemy, it was worse to have her downed, as was the case, by a friendly mine.

Entering Espiritu Santo, the hapless destroyer had steamed straight into the jaws of a minefield. Investigation disclosed that Tucker had been given no information on the field. Again somebody had failed to send the word.

Destroyers to Guadalcanal (Opening "Operation Watchtower")

The opening move in "Operation Watchtower" called for simultaneous Marine landings at Lunga Point on Guadalcanal, and on Tulagi and Gavutu islands in the embrace of Florida Island almost due north across Savo Sound. Landings were to be made by troops of the reinforced First Marine Division, 19,500 strong. They were to be carried to the beachheads by 23 transports screened by five American and three Australian cruisers, and accompanying destroyers. An Air Support Force, built around aircraft carriers Saratoga, Enterprise, and Wasp, screened by battleship North Carolina and numerous cruisers and destroyers, was to dominate the sky.

Vice Admiral Frank J. Fletcher commanded the assault forces. The amphibious force was under Rear Admiral R. K. Turner. The warships screening the amphibious force were under Rear Admiral V. A. C.

AIR SUPPORT FORCE

GROUP 1

PHELPS	*Lt. Comdr. E. L. Beck*
Flying the pennant of Capt. S. B. Brewer, COMDESRON 1	
FARRAGUT	*Lt. Comdr. H. D. Rozendal*
WORDEN	*Lt. Comdr. W. G. Pogue*
MACDONOUGH	*Lt. Comdr. E. V. Dennett*

GROUP 2

BALCH	*Lt. Comdr. H. H. Tiemroth*
Flying the pennant of Capt. E. P. Sauer, COMDESRON 6	
MAURY	*Lt. Comdr. G. L. Sims*
GWIN	*Comdr. J. M. Higgins*
BENHAM	*Lt. Comdr. J. M. Worthington*
GRAYSON	*Lt. Comdr. F. J. Bell*
Flying the pennant of Comdr. H. R. Holcomb, COMDESDIV 22	

GROUP 3

FARENHOLT	*Lt. Comdr. E. T. Seaward*
Flying the pennant of Capt. R. G. Tobin, COMDESRON 12	
LANG	*Comdr. J. Pollock*
Flying the pennant of Comdr. J. C. Pollock, COMDESDIV 15	
STERETT	*Comdr. J. G. Coward*
AARON WARD	*Lt. Comdr. O. F. Gregor*
STACK	*Lt. Comdr. A. J. Greenacre*
LAFFEY	*Lt. Comdr. W. E. Hank*

AMPHIBIOUS FORCE

FIRE-SUPPORT GROUP LOVE

Fire Section Four Comdr. W. Nyquist, COMDESDIV 1	
DEWEY *Flagship*	*Lt. Comdr. C. F. Chillingworth, Jr.*
HULL	*Lt. Comdr. R. F. Stout*
Fire Section Five	*Lt. Comdr. F. H. Gardner*
ELLET	*Lt. Comdr. F. H. Gardner*
WILSON	*Lt. Comdr. W. H. Price*

FIRE-SUPPORT GROUP MIKE

MONSSEN	*Comdr. R. N. Smoot*
BUCHANAN	*Comdr. R. E. Wilson*

SCREENING GROUP

DesRon Four Capt. C. W. Flynn, COMDESRON 4	
SELFRIDGE *Flagship*	*Lt. Comdr. C. D. Reynolds*
PATTERSON	*Comdr. F. R. Walker*
Flying the pennant of Comdr. F. R. Walker, COMDESDIV 8	
RALPH TALBOT	*Lt. Comdr. J. W. Callahan*
MUGFORD	*Lt. Comdr. E. W. Young*
JARVIS	*Lt. Comdr. W. W. Graham*
BLUE	*Comdr. H. N. Williams*
Flying the pennant of Comdr. L. B. Austin, COMDESDIV 7	
HELM	*Lt. Comdr. C. E. Carroll*
HENLEY	*Comdr. Robert Hall Smith*
BAGLEY	*Lt. Comdr. G. A. Sinclair*

Crutchley, R.N. Major General Vandegrift commanded the Marine landing forces. The carrier group was under Rear Admiral Leigh Noyes, and Rear Admiral J. S. McCain was in charge of a land-based air arm operating from the New Hebrides, New Caledonia, and other Allied islands within range of the Solomons. MacArthur's Army planes based on Australia and on New Guinea were to cooperate.

D-Day was set for August 7, 1942. The Guadalcanal beachhead was located just east of Henderson Field in a sector of coast between Lunga Point and Koli Point. The transports were to stand offshore in a roadstead, guarded by an arc of warships farther out.

The table above lists the destroyers assigned to duty with the Solomons invasion forces.

On paper the invasion fleet looked sizable. But size is a comparative matter. From Rabaul, Truk, and Kwajalein—three major bases, the farthest of which was only 1,200 miles away—the Japs could rush prompt military and naval reinforcements to the Solomons front. The nearest Allied major base was Pearl Harbor, full 3,000 miles distant. The U.S. Pacific Fleet was putting most of its eggs in the South Pacific basket. The Japs could match this commitment, and they had dozens of eggs in reserve. "Watchtower" to the Americans in the know was really "Operation Shoestring."

On July 26 the ships of Turner's Expeditionary Force made rendezvous south of the Fiji Islands and steamed down into the Coral Sea to approach Guadalcanal from the south. While Fletcher's carrier group waited south of the island, the invasion ships rounded the western end, and advanced on Lunga Point from Cape Esperance.

Early in the morning of August 7 the occupation forces were off the Guadalcanal beachhead. Shore

Savo Island debacle. The Australian cruiser Canberra (left), crushed by a Japanese hail of shells and hit by two torpedoes, is abandoned. The American destroyer Patterson (right), rescues remaining personnel. Grim as this defeat was for Allied naval units, it was worse for our precarious forces ashore on Guadalcanal, dependent on Allied sea power for their sole support.

Havoc's aftermath. Survivors of the Canberra are transferred by the Blue, one of the assisting destroyers, to U.S.S. Melville. The Naval War College analysis of this Savo action has provided valuable constructive criticism for professional students of naval warfare. A study of errors, where present, in past naval strategy and tactics may contribute to better decisions in the future.

We seized little Tulagi, located just off Florida Island and only a short distance from Guadalcanal, in August, 1942. Both sides realized the logistics importance of Tulagi's port in the coming bitter struggle for possession of the Solomons.

This view, taken from the U.S.S. O'Bannon, shows Tulagi harbor a year after we had gained possession. We gradually pushed our way up the Solomons chain and broke the Bismarck barrier, on our way to Leyte, Okinawa, and victory.

"Ironbottom Sound." Three Japanese merchant ships and one transport, below, helped create this name for the bloody waters off Guadalcanal.

bombardment was begun a little after 0600. The shelling obliterated the lone Japanese vessel on hand and made hash of a number of Jap seaplanes. The Jap labor battalions fled. The Jap soldiery, overwhelmingly surprised, fired a few hasty shots and retired.

In the afternoon of August 7 a flock of some 32 Japanese bombers from Rabaul delivered a counterattack. Carrier aircraft and AA fire from the screen blasted a score of these bombers from the sky. But not before the Japs shot down 12 American fighter planes, and damaged an American destroyer.

The victimized destroyer—the first to be scorched in the Solomons crucible—was the U.S.S. MUGFORD (Lieutenant Commander E. W. Young). At 1457 of that D-Day afternoon six Jap dive-bombers attacked the destroyer formation. MUGFORD's guns joined in the AA shooting match. Two bombers crashed in flames. Then the others roared down on MUGFORD, strafing and bombing as they came. A bomb crashed on the destroyer's deck, ripping up a section of the superstructure, and spraying her with fire and shards of iron. Seventeen of her crew were slain in this onslaught, and 17 men were wounded.

MUGFORD staggered under the impact of this sledgehammer blow, but kept on going. Her Executive Officer attributed her salvation to the valiant efforts of three courageous men. *"The heroic action of Lieutenant (jg) W. S. Farrel, Third Class Quartermaster R. H. Mooney, and First Class Gunner's Mate J. C. Huddleston, in fighting the fire in the vicinity of explosives with utter disregard for their own safety, no doubt saved the ship from fatal damage."*

The air attack on the 7th scarcely interrupted the Guadalcanal landings. By nightfall some 11,000 Marines were safely ashore.

On Tulagi and Gavutu the opposition was fairly stiff. The Jap troops holed up in dugouts and caves during the shore bombardment, then they counterattacked fiercely. But Marine rifles, air bombs, and naval artillery riddled the Imperial occupants, and by the afternoon of the 8th, these beachheads, too, were secured.

About noon of the 8th some 30 to 40 Jap torpedo-bombers came winging across Savo Sound. They were beaten off with heavy loss inflicted by the Navy's fighter planes and flak. However, a flaming Jap bomber crashed into the transport GEORGE F. ELLIOT, leaving the ship an inferno. And a Japanese torpedo stabbed the American destroyer JARVIS. The DD did not go down from this blasting. But, as will be seen, it was to result in her death.

So a transport was ruined and two destroyers were badly mauled in the opening round of "Watchtower." But by the afternoon of the 8th the enemy's unfinished airstrip at Lunga Point was in Marine possession, and the Japs on Guadalcanal were nowhere to be seen. The first amphibious operation undertaken by United States forces since the Spanish-American War had gone off swimmingly.

Unfortunately this was not to be a case of "well begun, half done." Almost immediately the Americans ran into a nightmare, one of the worst of the entire Pacific campaign. This Solomons nightmare materialized on the evening of August 8 in the near vicinity of Savo Island barring the entrance to Tulagi and Lunga Roads.

The Battle of Savo Island (A Tragedy of Errors)

Word of the Marine landings in the Solomons reached Japanese headquarters at Rabaul about 0700 in the morning of August 7. Admiral Mikawa, Commander Eighth Japanese Fleet and outer South Seas Force, promptly mustered his warship strength for a strike at the Allied invasion shipping. Late that afternoon he led a hastily assembled cruiser squadron out of Rabaul. This force consisted of heavy cruisers CHOKAI (flagship), AOBA, FURUTAKA, KINUGASA, and KAKO; light cruisers YUBARI and TENRYU; and destroyer YUNAGI, the only Jap DD then available in the area for battle duty.

Well aware that he was up against superior forces, Mikawa planned a fast hit-and-run strike to set the Allies back on their heels and clear the way across Savo Sound for a convoy of six troopships to be rushed from Rabaul to reinforce the Imperial Guadalcanal garrison. Mikawa timed the strike for the early hours of August 9. To reach the target in time, the run down through the Solomons archipelago had to be made during daylight of the 8th.

At the outset several B-17's of MacArthur's command sighted the cruisers on the move in St. George's Channel. The movement was reported, but the ships were too close to Rabaul for any indication of their intentions.

Then their sortie was spotted at 2000 in the evening of August 7 by the American submarine S-38 off Cape St. George. The sub was unable to attack the Jap warships, but she promptly reported the sortie of *"two destroyers and three warships of larger type"*—a fair estimate for a near-sighted periscope.

The following morning Mikawa's force was successively sighted at 1026 and 1101 off the northeast coast of Bougainville by a pair of Australian planes. Jap AA fire prevented the aircraft from making a close inspection. Unfortunately the "Aussie" who first sighted the Japs failed to make an immediate report. Out of Milne Bay on a search mission, the pilot was unwilling to break radio silence. Not until his return to Milne Bay late that afternoon did he report the Jap warships.

Due to a roundabout transmission relay (Milne Bay to Townsville to Brisbane) the word did not reach Admiral Crutchley, in command of the Allied screening force in Savo Sound, until 1839, over eight hours after the enemy ships were first sighted off Bougainville. The report was simultaneously sent from Brisbane to Pearl Harbor, where it was broadcast over the "Fox" system, by which means Admiral Turner, in command at Guadalcanal, received the word at 1845. As for the report from the pilot who sighted the Jap ships at 1101, it did not reach Admiral Turner until the next morning—after the shooting had started.

This snail-paced report was the first error in a series destined to make Savo a name no Navy man likes to remember. Less reprehensible than the delay, but equally disastrous, was the pilot's inaccurate identification of the enemy ships as *"three cruisers, three destroyers, and two seaplane tenders or gunboats."*

Because the airmen reported "two seaplane tenders" with the advancing Japanese force, Admiral Turner assumed the enemy contemplated an air attack rather than a surface strike. On Santa Isabel Island, 155 miles northwest of Savo, there was a bay perfectly suited for a seaplane base. Logic suggested the enemy force would put in there. Foul weather which had grounded the American land-based search planes that day abetted this logical assumption.

As for American carrier planes, Admiral Fletcher had precipitately withdrawn his carrier force from the Guadalcanal area in the evening of August 8, reporting to Admiral Ghormley that his ships were low on fuel and his fighter-strength dangerously reduced.

At the very hour that Fletcher's carriers were retiring, Mikawa's cruisers were steaming down the "Slot" toward Savo Sound. By midnight of the 8th, the Jap ships, undetected since that morning, were at a point about 35 miles from Savo Island.

On the same midnight, the submarine S-38, still patrolling off Cape St. George, intercepted the Jap troop convoy which had finally been sent from Rabaul on Mikawa's orders. The doughty old S-boat bored in and sank a transport. The other five troopships were immediately ordered back to Rabaul. Unfortunately this offstage victory had no direct influence on the Savo drama.

Meanwhile Admiral Crutchley had disposed his screening forces in positions calculated to cover the Guadalcanal and Tulagi beachheads. Savo Sound had been divided into three sectors. A Northern, a Southern, and an Eastern Force were stationed in the respective sectors. The Northern force was stationed inside a triangle immediately to the east of Savo Island, the Southern Force occupied a trapezoid to the south of Savo, and the Eastern Force operated in an area east of a line which extended from the western tip of Florida Island to Lunga Point.

Positioned to block the waters between Savo and Florida, the Northern Force consisted of U.S. cruisers VINCENNES, ASTORIA, and QUINCY, and destroyers HELM and WILSON. This force was under command of Captain F. L. Riefkohl in VINCENNES.

The Southern Force contained the Australian cruisers AUSTRALIA and CANBERRA, the U.S.S. CHICAGO, and destroyers PATTERSON and BAGLEY. Admiral Crutchley in AUSTRALIA was in immediate command of this force.

The Eastern Force, positioned below Florida Island, was composed of light cruisers SAN JUAN and H.M.A.S. HOBART, and destroyers MONSSEN and BUCHANAN. It was commanded by Rear Admiral Norman Scott whose flag was in SAN JUAN.

At Lunga Roads was Admiral Turner in flag transport MCCAWLEY, with 19 troop and supply ships which were to be unloaded that night, some at Guadalcanal, some at Tulagi. A miscellany of small vessels was on hand with this shipping.

An enemy trying to slip around Savo Island and get into the Sound for a crack at Tulagi or Lunga Roads would almost certainly be intercepted by the Northern or Southern Forces on patrol.

To tighten the guard, two picket destroyers were assigned to sentry beats outside the western entrances. Destroyer RALPH TALBOT patrolled a line to the northwest of Savo Island; destroyer BLUE patrolled a line to the southwest. Both RALPH TALBOT and BLUE carried SC radar. It was assumed that, making radar sweeps, they could detect and report any enemy forces which might attempt to pass north or south of Savo Island.

Analysts at the Naval War College have since pointed out that the disposition contained a number of serious flaws; that the picket screen of only two destroyers was weak; that their older-style SC radars had a reliable range of no more than 10 miles; and that when each destroyer was at the far end of her patrol line, the "center" was not covered. And Admiral Scott's flagship SAN JUAN, the only ship with the new SG surface radar, was located far in the eastern backfield.

Again, the picket destroyers were not stationed far enough west to give the forces to the east of Savo Island adequate preliminary warning in the event of a contact. Finally, the Allied cruiser groups were too far apart to support each other if an engagement developed.

But hindsight always sees a clearer picture than foresight. And the Allied sailors on duty in Savo Sound that evening were red-eyed from lack of sleep and exhaustion. Most of the crews had been at battle stations for 36 hours. Officers were fagged out, and Admirals Turner, Crutchley, and Scott, faced with the loss of carrier support, were compelled to improvise defense strategy at a speed which permitted no time for contemplative analysis.

Now occurred another of those events which undermined the Savo Sound defenses. At 2032 Admiral Turner summoned Admiral Crutchley to a conference at Lunga Point. Worried about the withdrawal of Fletcher's carriers, and convinced a seaplane attack was in the cards, he wished to discuss the situation with General Vandegrift and Admiral Crutchley. Crutchley steamed for Lunga Point in the AUSTRALIA, and there was one less ship on guard in Savo Sound.

So the stage was set and the curtain was rising on what was probably the Navy's worst performance of the war. Moving toward Savo Island were five Jap heavy cruisers, two light cruisers, and a single destroyer—eight ships in all. Available for the defense of Savo Sound were four United States heavy cruisers and a U.S. light cruiser, two Australian heavy cruisers and a light, and eight United States destroyers—a total of 16 ships. The Japs had the advantage of initiative; they could select the time and place for a thrust into the Sound. But the Allies had what should have been the overwhelming advantage of radar.

The night was sultry, overcast, and murky, with visibility varying between 4,000 and 12,000 yards. About half an hour before midnight a steamy rainsquall swept southeastward from Savo Island, drawing a watery curtain between the Northern Force and the Southern. All Allied ships were held at Condition II of readiness—half the crew on watch, the other half "in the sack," sleeping in exhaustion. Around 2345 when the mid-watch was pulling itself together to go on duty, there was the drone of planes in the sky.

The planes were Jap scouts catapulted from the approaching cruisers to search the Sound ahead. One was glimpsed and identified by destroyer RALPH TALBOT. Her skipper, Lieutenant Commander J. W. Callahan, immediately broadcast the alarm over TBS.

WARNING WARNING PLANE OVER SAVO HEADED EAST

To the southward, destroyer BLUE heard this alarm, and made radar contact with a plane. Cruiser QUINCY also made a radar contact, but thought nothing of it. And cruiser VINCENNES sighted aircraft, but her captain assumed they were Allied because their running lights were on. None of the ships in the Sound opened fire on the Jap scouts, and in consequence they were able to work without hindrance and to furnish Mikawa with a good picture of the Allied naval disposition.

But why had RALPH TALBOT's alarm been ignored?

Another of those bad breaks. The destroyer's voice radio was short-range, and weather conditions created static. The original alarm did not get through to Admiral Turner, only 20 miles away in flagship McCAWLEY. Receiving no answer from the top command, RALPH TALBOT's skipper spoke Division Commander Walker in destroyer PATTERSON. Walker tried persistently to relay the message, but PATTERSON's TBS did not get through, either. As a result, the senior commands failed to obtain the word.

Certainly everything conspired to favor the oncoming Japs. With the Allied cruiser forces located, and a fair idea of the shipping at Lunga Point and Tulagi, Admiral Mikawa squared away to strike. With his warships in an extended column—CHOKAI in the lead, followed by heavy cruisers, light cruisers, and destroyer YUNAGI as "tail-end Charlie"—he set a course to pass south of Savo Island, and ordered a high-speed advance on Guadalcanal.

Now occurred a break which was utterly fantastic. As the Japs came highballing down the track in the early morning of August 9, destroyer BLUE (the southern picket) was steaming toward the southwest end of her beat. Simultaneously, RALPH TALBOT (the northern picket) was beating well along in the opposite direction. Both ships had their fantails toward the approaching enemy. And apparently the destroyer lookouts, relying heavily on the radar watch, were concentrating on the waters ahead, and neglecting the waters aft.

At 0054 CHOKAI's lookouts sighted the BLUE. She was then about 5½ miles distant, and the Jap cruisermen were certain CHOKAI had been sighted in return. Pressing onward, the Japs trained their guns on the American destroyer and held their breaths. Then they relaxed. The American destroyer moved ploddingly away, paying no apparent attention. Racing on at about 25 knots, the Japanese cruiser squadron passed within some 500 yards of the BLUE—and remained undetected!

Mikawa, however, could not believe his luck. With every reason to think BLUE must have seen and reported him, he abruptly ordered a course-change to pass north of Savo Island. Then, as the column

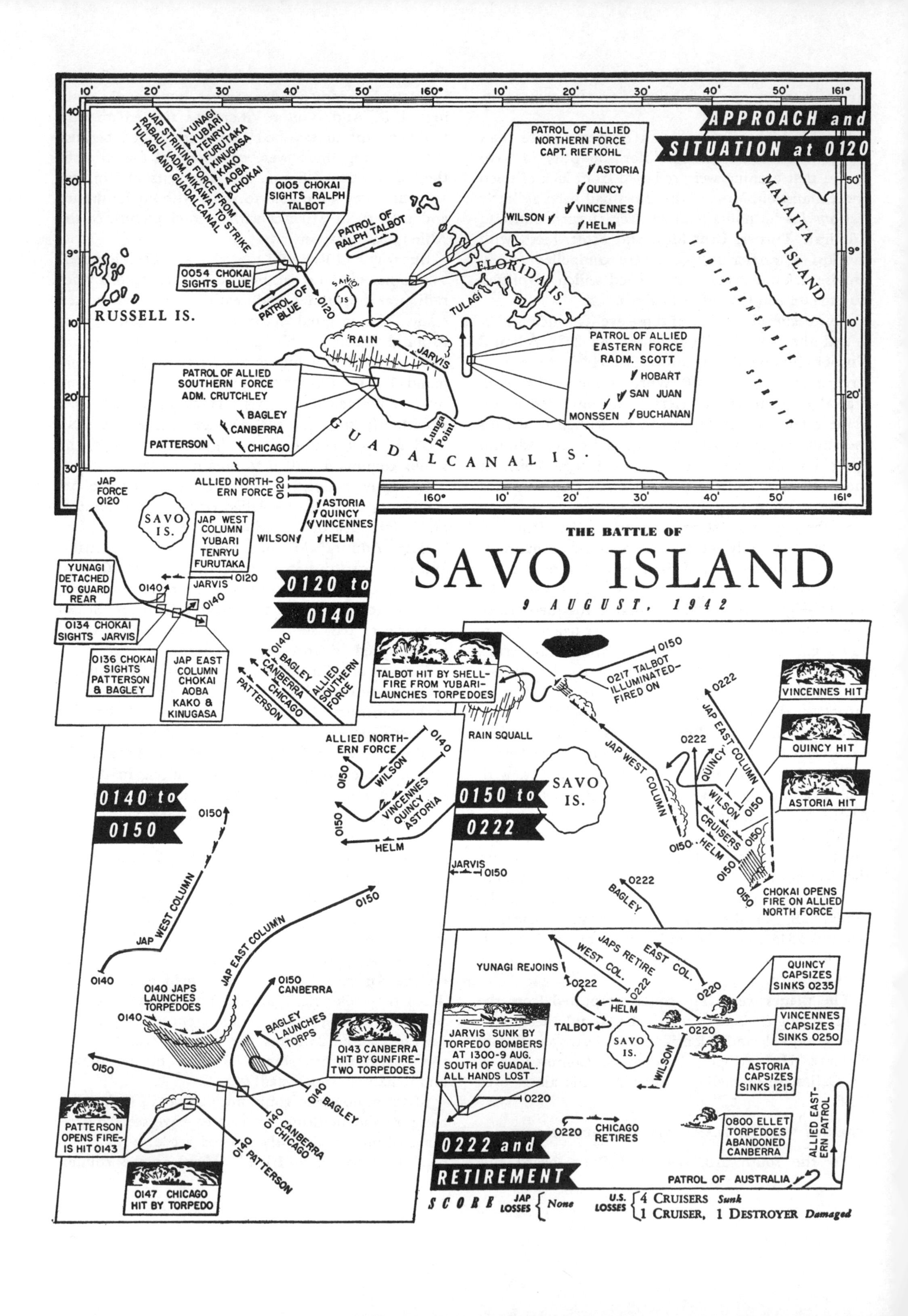

THE BATTLE OF
SAVO ISLAND
9 AUGUST, 1942
APPROACH and SITUATION at 0120
JAP STRIKING FORCE FROM RABAUL (ADM. MIKAWA) TO STRIKE TULAGI AND GUADALCANAL
YUNAGI
YUBARI
TENRYU
FURUTAKA
KINUGASA
KAKO
AOBA
CHOKAI
0105 CHOKAI SIGHTS RALPH TALBOT
0054 CHOKAI SIGHTS BLUE
PATROL OF BLUE
PATROL OF RALPH TALBOT
0120
SAVO IS.
RUSSELL IS.
PATROL OF ALLIED NORTHERN FORCE CAPT. RIEFKOHL
ASTORIA
QUINCY
VINCENNES
HELM
WILSON
FLORIDA IS.
TULAGI
MALAITA ISLAND
INDISPENSABLE STRAIT
RAIN
JARVIS
PATROL OF ALLIED SOUTHERN FORCE ADM. CRUTCHLEY
BAGLEY
CANBERRA
PATTERSON
CHICAGO
PATROL OF ALLIED EASTERN FORCE RADM. SCOTT
HOBART
SAN JUAN
MONSSEN
BUCHANAN
Lunga Point
GUADALCANAL IS.
0120 to 0140
JAP FORCE 0120
ALLIED NORTHERN FORCE
JAP WEST COLUMN YUBARI TENRYU FURUTAKA
YUNAGI DETACHED TO GUARD REAR
0134 CHOKAI SIGHTS JARVIS
0136 CHOKAI SIGHTS PATTERSON & BAGLEY
JAP EAST COLUMN CHOKAI AOBA KAKO & KINUGASA
ALLIED SOUTHERN FORCE
0140 to 0150
JAP WEST COLUMN
JAP EAST COLUMN
0140 JAPS LAUNCHES TORPEDOES
0150 CANBERRA
BAGLEY LAUNCHES TORPS
0143 CANBERRA HIT BY GUNFIRE-TWO TORPEDOES
PATTERSON OPENS FIRE-IS HIT 0143
0147 CHICAGO HIT BY TORPEDO
0140 CANBERRA CHICAGO
0140 PATTERSON
0140 BAGLEY
ALLIED NORTHERN FORCE
VINCENNES QUINCY ASTORIA
0150 to 0222
TALBOT HIT BY SHELL-FIRE FROM YUBARI-LAUNCHES TORPEDOES
0217 TALBOT ILLUMINATED-FIRED ON
RAIN SQUALL
JAP WEST COLUMN
JAP EAST COLUMN
VINCENNES HIT
QUINCY HIT
ASTORIA HIT
CRUISERS
CHOKAI OPENS FIRE ON ALLIED NORTH FORCE
JARVIS 0150
BAGLEY 0222
0222 and RETIREMENT
YUNAGI REJOINS
JAPS RETIRE
WEST COL.
EAST COL.
TALBOT
HELM
WILSON
QUINCY CAPSIZES SINKS 0235
VINCENNES CAPSIZES SINKS 0250
ASTORIA CAPSIZES SINKS 1215
JARVIS SUNK BY TORPEDO BOMBERS AT 1300-9 AUG. SOUTH OF GUADAL. ALL HANDS LOST
CHICAGO RETIRES
0800 ELLET TORPEDOES ABANDONED CANBERRA
ALLIED EASTERN PATROL
PATROL OF AUSTRALIA
SCORE JAP LOSSES { None
U.S. LOSSES { 4 CRUISERS Sunk
1 CRUISER, 1 DESTROYER Damaged

swung northward, CHOKAI's lookouts spied—or thought they spied—another destroyer. This could only have been the RALPH TALBOT. But according to her log, she was then about ten miles away. Yet the lookouts did report a ship, and Mikawa swung the column back on its original south-of-Savo course. Needless to add, RALPH TALBOT's lookouts did not see the Japanese ships.

So both of the American picket destroyers missed the enemy. Because of unfavorable atmospheric conditions and the background "interference" of Savo Island, the SC radars failed to pick up the Japanese column, and the eight Jap ships went by as though they wore invisible cloaks.

Mikawa's column entered the passage between Savo Island and Guadalcanal. And at 0134 the Jap lookouts sighted a third destroyer, range 3,000 yards, off the south coast of Savo Island, heading westward. Once again the Japs enjoyed fantastic luck. For this DD was the U.S.S. JARVIS, badly damaged during the previous day's air raid. As will be seen, she was off Savo at that hour by mere accident, and if she sighted the enemy, she had no means for communicating the alarm. Passing south of her, the Jap ships were safe. Mikawa detached the destroyer YUNAGI to protect his rear from BLUE and JARVIS. The column raced on through the passage. The foxes were in the henhouse!

At 0136 CHOKAI's lookouts glimpsed two destroyers directly ahead. These were PATTERSON and BAGLEY, screening cruisers CANBERRA and CHICAGO of the Southern Force.

On the port bow of CANBERRA, destroyer PATTERSON (Commander F. R. Walker) was the first Allied ship to sight the Japs. Instantly she radioed the alarm: *"Warning! Warning! Strange ships entering the harbor!"* But the time was 0143. Already the Jap cruisers had launched torpedoes. And now brilliant flares, dropped by Jap float planes, illumined the anchorage off Lunga Point and silhouetted CANBERRA and CHICAGO. Simultaneously CHOKAI and two other Jap cruisers opened fire.

A rain of shells fell on H.M.A.S. CANBERRA, and at the same time two torpedoes smashed into her starboard side. In an instant she was swaddled in flames and listing to starboard, disabled.

After flashing a repeat warning by blinker, PATTERSON's skipper had swung the destroyer hard left to bring her batteries to bear. The gunners fired starshell; then Commander Walker ordered a torpedo spread. The torpedo order went unheard, but the DD's guns opened up with a roar. An answering salvo smashed her No. 4 gun, put another gun out of action, and started a fire. The blaze was soon extinguished, and PATTERSON's guns kept on shooting as long as the enemy ships were in sight.

On CANBERRA's starboard bow, destroyer BAGLEY (Lieutenant Commander G. A. Sinclair) swung hard left to fire a starboard torpedo salvo at the enemy cruisers. So sudden was the attack that the torpedoes could not be readied for this salvo. BAGLEY continued to circle until the port torpedoes were brought to bear. The salvo was fired, but by that time the Jap cruisers were beyond range.

While BAGLEY's torpedomen were striving to insert primers into the starboard "fish," the Jap cruisers had turned northward and flung torpedoes at CHICAGO. At 0147 a torpedo smashed home, shearing off some of CHICAGO's bow. Her gunners fired starshells; the starshells were squibs. Unable to see any targets, CHICAGO floundered in uncertainty; then she spotted an enemy searchlight ahead. The light was from destroyer YUNAGI. CHICAGO opened fire; the Jap destroyermen snapped off their light. The damaged American cruiser ran blindly westward, and so on out of the battle.

Having dealt with the Allied Southern Force, the Jap cruiser column split up, racing northeastward. The split-up—unintentional, as the ships fell out of formation—left CHOKAI, AOBA, KAKO, and KINUGASA in column to the east of YUBARI, TENRYU, and FURUTAKA. Running on roughly parallel courses, the two Jap groups had the fabulous fortune to catch Captain Riefkohl's Northern Force betwixt and between.

The Northern Force had been steaming between Savo Island and Florida Island, following the legs of a square or "box patrol." The three American cruisers were in column, VINCENNES leading QUINCY and ASTORIA. Destroyers HELM (Lieutenant Commander C. E. Carroll) and WILSON (Lieutenant Commander W. H. Price) were screening ahead of VINCENNES.

Moving at 10 knots, the American ships were turning the southern corner of the square, and heading northwestward, when CHOKAI saw them and opened fire with torpedoes and shells. A moment later AOBA caught cruiser QUINCY smack on the quarter with a glaring searchlight. AOBA opened fire. Blazing guns, whistling projectiles, and dazzling searchlights stunned the Americans. General Quarters had been sounded, but battle stations were not yet fully manned. Gun-flashes had been seen far to southward, but Captain Riefkohl had assumed CHICAGO was shooting at aircraft. To add to the night's confusion, CHICAGO had failed to warn the Northern Force about the enemy cruisers.

So Riefkohl's force suddenly found itself in a

battle that exploded like a bolt from the black. Within a few minutes all three American cruisers suffered multiple hits. Riddled, ASTORIA burst into an inferno. Caught between the CHOKAI column and the inside Jap column, the QUINCY was soon shot into hopeless wreckage. Torpedoes and shells smashed into VINCENNES. Disabled and burning, the three American cruisers fought back. Their shells hit CHOKAI, AOBA, and KINUGASA, but the Japs, getting off with minor damage, left destruction in their wake.

For the American destroyers with the Northern Force the battle was a hellish scramble of blind-man's-buff. The enemy was here, there, and yonder, and the American cruisers were in the line of fire. Destroyer WILSON hurled some shots at CHOKAI, but her 5-inchers could not reach Mikawa's flagship. Bewildered in the melee, destroyer HELM had difficulty distinguishing friend from foe. She fired four rounds of 5-inch, then took off in pursuit of what proved to be a friendly ship—perhaps destroyer RALPH TALBOT. The Jap cruisers paid scant attention to WILSON and HELM; Mikawa was concentrating on American heavies.

By 0220 the Jap admiral was satisfied that he had done a *banzai* job. Ordering a withdrawal, he swung CHOKAI northwestward. The two Jap columns, going around Savo Island counter-clockwise, headed for Rabaul. Behind them they left the U.S.S. VINCENNES, ASTORIA, and QUINCY, and H.M.A.S. CANBERRA all sinking.

But there was one more target up ahead. Squarely in the path of the inside Japanese column was the picket destroyer RALPH TALBOT.

Damaging of U.S.S. Ralph Talbot

When RALPH TALBOT heard the alarm broadcast by destroyer PATTERSON, Lieutenant Commander Callahan headed his picket DD southwestward at top speed. Distant flashings in Savo Sound resembled the faraway flares of a thunderstorm, but the destroyermen knew a battle when they saw one.

The baleful flashings came closer. Then the glow of burning ships flushed the overcast. And then, about 0217, the blue-white ray of a searchlight swept across the water and focussed on RALPH TALBOT. An instant later she was target for a rain of shells that fell close aboard and showered her with colored splashes. A hit wrecked her No. 1 torpedo tube and killed two men. Callahan's hair went up. Those colored splashes were like American dye. He flashed recognition signals, and shouted the word over TBS. The firing abruptly stopped.

This first cluster of salvos may have been American, or they may have come from the Jap light cruiser TENRYU, at that time swinging northwestward around Savo Island. In any case RALPH TALBOT was passing dead ahead of the YUBARI-TENRYU-FURUTAKA column, like a Ford crossing the main line in front of the Limited Express. YUBARI now switched on her searchlights, and RALPH TALBOT was in for it.

Fire was opened at 3,300 yards, Japs and American destroyermen letting go in unison. YUBARI's gunners found the mark, and a shell smashed into the American destroyer's charthouse, partly wrecking the automatic gun control system. Another shell wrecked the wardroom. Still another shattered a torpedo tube, and a final hit knocked out the after 5-inch gun. The destroyermen fired four torpedoes, which missed, and they may have hit the cruiser with a shell or two. YUBARI's light went out, and the enemy ships raced by, their skippers doubtless thinking they had demolished another American vessel.

With flames pouring from her charthouse, her power and steering control gone, and her hull listing 20°, RALPH TALBOT was badly hurt. But she was far from demolished. A friendly rainsquall swept over her like a benison. Valiantly battling the damage, her engineers regained pressure in the after boilers, and she limped close in to Savo Island. There the fire was extinguished, the list taken off, and temporary repairs were made. Eventually, with 12 of her crew dead, two missing, and 23 wounded, she hobbled into port at Tulagi.

Savo Aftermath ("Ironbottom Bay")

The Japanese departure did not end the shooting.

About 0300 of that hectic morning of August 9, destroyer PATTERSON was ordered by CHICAGO's Captain H. D. Bode to go to the assistance of disabled CANBERRA. As PATTERSON jockeyed alongside the burning Australian cruiser, the latter's ammunition began to explode. And it was not until about 0400 that Walker and his destroyermen were able to aid the Australians in fighting the inferno.

It was soon evident that the fires could not be controlled in time for the cruiser to retire that morning with Admiral Turner's forces. The order was given to abandon. While the "Aussies" were going overside, an unidentified vessel came up out of the west in the darkness at 0510. PATTERSON challenged, and received no answer. After two more unanswered challenges, PATTERSON put a light on the stranger. The other opened fire. After an exchange of several salvos, Commander Walker thought he recognized CHICAGO's silhouette. Hurriedly he sent up emergency recognition signals. The stranger was indeed CHICAGO, and the gun duel was called off.

Destroyer BLUE came up at 0622 to aid CANBERRA, and she and PATTERSON took off the 680 Australian survivors, who were carried to the transport anchorage at Guadalcanal. About 0800, to prevent possible enemy capture, CANBERRA was torpedo-sunk by destroyer ELLET.

A flaming funeral pyre, cruiser QUINCY had capsized and sunk at 0235. Fifteen minutes later, the fire-gutted VINCENNES rolled over and went down. Some of the survivors of these two cruisers were picked up by destroyers BAGLEY and HELM.

BAGLEY also rescued some cruisermen from the ASTORIA, going bow-to-bow alongside the burning ship to take off sailors who were trapped on her forecastle. A little later the plucky destroyermen edged up to remove a party from the cruiser's fantail.

As ASTORIA remained afloat, 300 of her crew went back aboard to fight the fire. By daylight she was under tow of a minesweeper, and destroyer WILSON was on hand to aid the fire-fighting. Late in the morning WILSON and BAGLEY were relieved by destroyer BUCHANAN, whose men pitched into the ship-saving effort. But ASTORIA was too far gone to be saved. By noon her main deck was awash; the cruisermen abandoned; and at 1215 the ship capsized and sank.

To the Japanese forces at Savo the Fates had presented a stupendous victory. At the cost of minor damage to CHOKAI, AOBA, and KINUGASA, and an insignificant scratch on KAKO, the Jap warships had sent three United States heavy cruisers to the bottom; had fatally disabled an Australian heavy cruiser; and had left an American destroyer sorely crippled. On CHOKAI some 30 men had been killed, and 28 had been slain on the other Jap ships for a total of 58 dead. Some 53 Japs were wounded. The American death toll totaled 1,023 officers and men. And 709 Americans were wounded.

This shocking defeat for the Allied naval forces almost cut the ground out from under the Marines at Guadalcanal and Tulagi. Risking annihilation, Turner held his unprotected transports at Lunga Point and Tulagi long enough to unload munitions and five weeks' food supply; then the convoy retired to Nouméa. Watching the ships go over the horizon, the Marines must have wondered where next month's meal was coming from. Temporarily, at least, they were marooned.

By the hard-hit Navy, Savo Sound—graveyard of warships—would always be remembered as "Ironbottom Bay." And the Battle of Savo Island would be grimly remembered as a horror of fouled-up communications, fuddled tactics, mistaken moves, and atrocious breaks.

Facing the issue squarely, the Navy lost no time in conducting an investigation to find out what went wrong. Communications relays were rigorously overhauled, and numerous flaws which had interfered with fighting efficiency were ironed out. Among other things, the Navy learned it needed more training for night surface actions.

But the Japanese, too, had committed one major error at Savo. With the American screen wiped out and the American transports and supply ships naked to his attack, Mikawa retired to celebrate, thereby giving the beaten enemy a chance to recover. Mikawa's stated reason was fear of counterattack by air.

And as they steamed home to the Bismarcks in triumph, the Jap cruisers received one retaliatory crack from the American whip. They were almost within sight of Kavieng when they were waylaid by the American submarine S-44. And the old S-boat knocked off the cruiser KAKO.

But in the meantime the Japs had indirectly scored another Savo killing by sinking the American destroyer JARVIS.

Loss of U.S.S. Jarvis

JARVIS (Lieutenant Commander W. W. Graham, Jr.) was one of the destroyers screening the transport group at Lunga Roads when the Jap planes lashed at this shipping in the noon hour of August 8, 1942.

The transports were under way, and the ships maneuvered radically to dodge bombs and torpedoes. But some of the enemy bombers got in through the AA barrage. And a moment after the transport GEORGE F. ELLIOT was hit by a crash-diving plane, JARVIS was struck by a torpedo.

Fourteen destroyermen were killed, and seven were badly wounded in the explosion which ripped a ragged hole in the destroyer's hull. When the air attack was over, DEWEY moved in to assist the disabled vessels. She took the burning transport in tow (beyond salvage, this ship had to be sunk later) after towing JARVIS inshore.

Examination showed the destroyer's injuries had not left her entirely crippled; her engines were not wrecked, and Lieutenant Commander Graham was certain she could make port under her own steam. As the destroyer tender DOBBIN was at that time stationed in Sydney, Graham determined to lose no time in getting there with JARVIS so that she might be repaired and sent back into action as soon as possible.

This was a brave decision for Graham to make, for the ship would have to run a long gantlet in skirting Guadalcanal, and the severe damage she had suffered would reduce her speed. But the officers under him were undoubtedly eager to try it. As the hull was leaking, everything topside that could be jettisoned was thrown overside—boats and rafts included—to save weight. The engines were tested, and their performance was satisfactory. Admiral Turner was informed that the U.S.S. Jarvis could make Sydney under her own power.

Admiral Turner dispatched a message directing the destroyer to stand by for an escort and then to depart by an eastern channel. Apparently Lieutenant Commander Graham never received these orders. Either that, or the message was garbled and misunderstood. At any rate, at midnight Jarvis steamed away from Lunga without an escort, and headed westward for Cape Esperance—another fatal move in the baleful series of errors that dogged the Navy in the opening weeks of the Guadalcanal Campaign. For crippled Jarvis limped straight into the Battle of Savo Island.

At 0250 in the morning of August 9, the destroyer Blue, on picket duty off Savo, glimpsed the Jarvis rounding Cape Esperance to the southwest. Blue closed the range to identify the silhouette, and in so doing was diverted from the savage conflict at that hour raging in the Sound.

Blue noted that Jarvis was limping along at 8 knots, and trailing a long slick of oil. Satisfied as to the lamed ship's identity, the picket destroyer turned away at 0325. Jarvis passed out of sight, gamely going it alone.

Not long after daybreak Jarvis was sighted by a scout plane from Saratoga southwest of Guadalcanal at lat. 9-42 S, long. 158-59 E. The destroyer was in bad shape, down by the head and trailing oil. As she had passed through the thick of the Savo battle, analysts who studied that wild engagement concluded she could have been hit by fire from Chicago—a possibility, as she was within range of the cruiser's guns. It was remarked, however, that Chicago was probably firing on the Jap destroyer Yunagi, then in the vicinity. And Yunagi, in turn, may have disabled Jarvis. For the Jap DD reported an attack on a "light cruiser" heading westward—undoubtedly Jarvis.

In any event, the Saratoga scout plane was the last friendly eye to see the ship. Jarvis was never heard from again. It was presumed she had foundered, and her fate remained a mystery until Japanese records were inspected after the war. The records disclosed that Jarvis was attacked and sunk by torpedo-bombers of the Japanese 25th Air Flotilla at 1300 in the afternoon of August 9, 1942.

Acting on word from Yunagi that the damaged ship was in the area, the Jap planes combed the seascape and found the target. The aviators reported that they took her for a "light cruiser," and their onslaught was devastating. Jarvis never had a chance.

"Our Air Force," states Yunagi's War Diary, *"was ordered to attack and destroy the damaged destroyer which split and sank."*

Without lifeboats or rafts, Lieutenant Commander Graham and his men were doomed. All hands—some 247—were lost with the ship.

Loss of U.S.S. Blue

If any ship seemed to steam under an unlucky star, it was Blue. When the Enterprise force was setting out on its pioneer war cruise, Blue suffered the first casualty by losing a man overboard. At Savo Island she had missed a Japanese squadron only 500 yards distant. Again, she had been diverted from the scene of action by contact with crippled destroyer Jarvis. She was the only ship within 15 miles of Savo which did not fire a shot in that sorry battle.

Now, as though following some course predetermined by destiny, she approached the climax of an ill-starred career. It was the evening of August 21, 1942.

At that date and time destroyer Blue (Commander H. N. Williams) was steaming in company with destroyers Henley and Helm as escort for supply ships Fomalhaut and Alhena bound for Guadalcanal. The convoy was under Commander Robert Hall Smith, ComDesDiv 7, riding in Blue.

Indispensable Strait had been transited safely, and the convoy was off Taivu Point at the eastern reaches of Lengo Channel when Blue's "final orders" came. They came by way of a dispatch from Admiral Turner directing the Blue and destroyer Henley (Lieutenant Commander E. K. Van Swearingen) to leave the convoy and race ahead to Savo Sound where they were to intercept enemy naval forces bearing down on Lunga Point.

The two DD's peeled off as ordered, and sprinted at top speed for "Ironbottom Bay." By mid-watch, August 22, they were in that dark body of water. At 0324, when the destroyers were near the center of Savo Sound, Blue's radar and sonar instruments registered contact with an unidentified target. For the next eight minutes her radar and sonar operators intermittently maintained the contact. Henley was alerted, and the two destroyers moved this way and that at various speeds, like hounds sniffing an elusive scent. But the contact petered out; in the moonless dark nothing was seen; at 0346 the DD's slowed to 10 knots and patrolled at cautious pace, the lookouts tense and watchful.

Another suspicious radar and sonar contact was

A big-bellied enemy bomber makes a run on one of our warships. This was a familiar scene off Guadalcanal when for so long the opposing forces were about evenly matched. Geographic position favored the Japanese in their struggle for this strategic prize. But they made a serious blunder by underestimating the strength of air, sea, and land forces necessary to retain it.

This is how the battle looked from offshore. August 7, 1942, was a memorable Guadalcanal day, ashore and afloat. We struck first, landing Marines after preliminary shore bombardment. Then, in the afternoon, the Japanese struck back with a raid of 32 Rabaul bombers, shown here skimming in at low altitude, against our surface forces off Guadalcanal (background). This

was the beginning of a new type of warfare in which aircraft and ships developed new techniques offensively and defensively. Ship shown in background at the extreme right (probably the U.S.S. Mugford) is smoking from a bomb hit. Five months after this action our superior technology had produced the VT proximity fuse which substantially aided our defense against planes.

Japanese submarine I-15 scores success. She torpedoed both the North Carolina and the destroyer O'Brien. This picture shows the explosion of the enemy warhead against U.S.S. O'Brien's stern. Although this American escort group also lost the fast carrier Wasp to submarine attack, the convoy of United States Marines and aviation gasoline safely reached Guadalcanal's shores.

U.S.S. O'Brien sinking from the effects of a Japanese torpedo hit weeks before. Although the destroyer went to the bottom, she took not a man with her.

The O'Brien sinking off Samoa. After emergency repairs at Espiritu and Noumea she was permitted to cruise back to the States. This estimate of her seaworthiness proved incorrect. Her main girder collapsed and she broke up.

U.S.S. Duncan was a casualty at Cape Esperance. In this night action she was fatally damaged by an American salvo. These point-blank range battles off Guadalcanal understandably led to self-inflicted losses by both belligerents.

picked up by BLUE at 0355. She was then steaming eastward, about 400 yards ahead of HENLEY, and her electronic detection gear indicated the target as 5,000 yards distant on the starboard beam—a high-speed vessel of some sort, doing anywhere from "20 to 50" knots. HENLEY also made radar contact with this target, and off across the water a creamy wake was sighted.

Neither destroyer took a positive or offensive action. Continuing on her course at unchanged speed, BLUE brought her guns and torpedo tubes to bear, but she held her fire. HENLEY, too, held her fire. The range closed to 3,200 yards as the high-speed "stranger" approached.

Then, at 0359, shocked lookouts on board BLUE suddenly saw a spread of phosphorescent wakes reaching through the water toward the destroyer's stern.

"TORPEDO!"

The cry was drowned out by the roar of exploding war heads. Flame enveloped BLUE's stern; men, guns, and gear were flung skyward; and the destroyer reeled to a halt, dragging a shattered fantail.

HENLEY steamed forward to guard the paralyzed destroyer. At daylight she took BLUE in tow, and headed for Lunga Roads.

The tow was difficult, for BLUE's smashed and bogged-down stern made her balky. At 0709 the tow line snapped. HENLEY stood by while a Marine tank lighter and two other craft came out from Lunga to pass a line. At 1110 a dispatch from Admiral Turner was received, ordering the damaged vessel towed to Tulagi. HENLEY tried again and once more the tow line parted. Other boats, and destroyer MANLEY, came out to assist. The crews of both destroyers and boats labored with desperate industry, but it was the evening of August 22 before Tulagi was within reach.

It was a sad destroyer BLUE that crawled at rope's end toward the harbor—eight dead and 22 wounded among her complement, and nothing to show but her battle scars. Then even the gruelling haul for Tulagi was to go for naught. As a large Japanese force was approaching Guadalcanal that night, Destroyer Division Commander Robert Hall Smith recommended that BLUE be scuttled to prevent possible capture. Admiral Turner issued the order, and BLUE was sent to the bottom of "Ironbottom Bay."

Both Admiral Halsey and Rear Admiral Turner criticized destroyers HENLEY and BLUE for neglecting to develop the radar and sonar contacts made in Savo Sound, and for failing to pursue an aggressive course of action when the second target was contacted. But Nimitz softened this criticism by recognizing extenuating circumstances. He noted that the Division Commander on BLUE had thought the radar contacts might be a friendly patrol boat, and he was hoping, in any event, for a crack at larger game. It was evident his error was one of judgment—not the first such error committed in the Solomons.

So the destroyers missed a chance to deal with their assailant—the Japanese destroyer KAMIKAZE, which had just put a contingent of troops ashore on Guadalcanal. With the odds 2 to 1 in their favor, the American DD's hesitated. And BLUE was lost.

Battle of the Eastern Solomons

The Battle of the Eastern Solomons was an aerial explosion which detonated when the Japs unleashed their first all-out offensive to regain Tulagi and Guadalcanal. The Savo Island massacre had been followed by a fortnight's lull during which the Japs reinforced and supplied their Guadalcanal garrison, bombarded the Marine positions at Lunga Point, and chopped at the frayed Allied supply line with impunity. Ashore, the Marines fought off the enemy and held on by their fingernails. But the lull at sea was ominous.

Official congratulations to the contrary, Yamamoto had registered displeasure at Mikawa's failure to strike the Allied beachheads at Guadalcanal and Tulagi. Now he mobilized a powerful Occupation Force and a large Striking Force, drawing these warships from Rabaul, Truk, and other strongholds, and he dispatched these forces under Admirals Kondo, Nagumo, Mikawa, Abe, and others to blast the Allies out of the Solomons.

Allied aircraft saw it coming. In the morning of August 23 the Jap Occupation Force was sighted about 250 miles to the north of Guadalcanal. The enemy convoy, containing four transports, was screened by four ex-destroyers and a cruiser. About 100 miles to the east of these ships some of the Striking Force ships were sighted. This force included aircraft carriers SHOKAKU and ZUIKAKU, small carrier RYUJO, seaplane carrier CHITOSE, three battleships, a flock of cruisers, a flotilla of destroyers, and other vessels. A school of Japanese submarines scouted ahead. Evidently the Japanese First Team was taking the field!

As it happened, three United States task forces were steaming in the sea just northeast of the lower Solomons: Task Force 11, with SARATOGA; Task Force 16, with ENTERPRISE; Task Force 18, with WASP. Because of fuel shortage and confused intelligence reports, the WASP force steamed away from the field that morning. But the ENTERPRISE and SARATOGA forces were on hand like floating beehives, in good position to sting Yamamoto's finest.

The battle, which did not explode until the morning of August 24, was another of those air engagements in which planes did practically all of the fighting. Dogfights and dive-bombing featured the conflict as each side struck at the other from long range. Marine aircraft from Henderson Field and Army B-17's from Espiritu Santo joined the Navy's carrier planes in defensive and offensive actions. For two days the sky was livid with machine-gun fire and ack-ack, while the sea smoked and boomed under flailing bombs.

The destroyers serving with the SARATOGA force—PHELPS, FARRAGUT, WORDEN, MACDONOUGH, DALE, BAGLEY, DEWEY, and PATTERSON—did not get into combat. In the afternoon of the 24th, SARATOGA bombers located the small Jap carrier RYUJO, and bashed her to the bottom. But the enemy planes never "caught up" with SARATOGA.

The destroyers working with the ENTERPRISE force (which included the battleship NORTH CAROLINA) engaged in some hot anti-aircraft gunnery. They were:

BALCH	*Lt. Comdr. H. H. Tiemroth*
	Flying the pennant of
	Capt. E. P. Sauer, COMDESRON 6
MAURY	*Lt. Comdr. G. L. Sims*
BENHAM	*Lt. Comdr. J. M. Worthington*
GRAYSON	*Lt. Comdr. F. J. Bell*
	Flying the pennant of
	Comdr. H. R. Holcomb, COMDESDIV 22
MONSSEN	*Comdr. R. N. Smoot*
ELLET	*Lt. Comdr. F. H. Gardner*

About 1700 in the afternoon of August 24, enemy Zeros and bombers from SHOKAKU and ZUIKAKU sighted the ENTERPRISE force, and pounced. The Jap pilots who eluded the American fighter defense ran into such walls of aerial fire as had never before been seen. The American DD's joined battleship NORTH CAROLINA, cruisers PORTLAND and ATLANTA, and the "BIG E" herself in stoking this fire.

Jap planes came down in flakes, in fragments, in flames, in sparks, and in embers. Of the 80 which attacked, some 47 were shot down in dogfights and 23 were blown down by AA fire. Not a single torpedo plane penetrated the AA curtain. About 15 dive-bombers peeled off to strike, and only five or six gained striking distance.

In this furious battle the destroyers and other screening ships came through without a casualty to man or ship. But ENTERPRISE took three bomb hits which killed about 74 men, started fires, and left her flight deck badly mangled. She was able to keep going, however, which was more than could be said for the attacking Japs. Only three or four of the 80 planes from SHOKAKU and ZUIKAKU managed to get home.

Meantime planes from SARATOGA located the Jap group under Admiral Kondo, and gave the seaplane carrier CHITOSE a severe thrashing.

That night the ENTERPRISE and SARATOGA forces retired southward, while WASP and company steamed into position southeast of Guadalcanal to cover the area. After escorting battered ENTERPRISE to safe waters, the SARATOGA force raced back to the battle front. But the shooting was almost over.

Having lost a carrier, a destroyer, a transport, and almost half of the armada's carrier aircraft, Admiral Yamamoto had called off his dogs. Guadalcanal would have to wait.

Not a decisive victory for the Allies, the Battle of the Eastern Solomons gave the Marines at Guadalcanal and Tulagi a longer chance to hang on.

Commenting on the battle, Admiral Nimitz observed: *"So far the war in the Pacific has been featured by long-range carrier air duels. We have, however, suffered equal if not greater losses from submarine and surface ship attacks. We must use our surface ships more boldly as opportunity warrants."*

Savo Island was a case in point concerning attacks by enemy surface ships. And Japanese submarines were now in the offing.

Gamble Kills I-123

Ahead of the Jap armada which had set out for the Solomons arena was an Advance Expeditionary Force of submarines. This undersea contingent contained I-9, I-11, I-15, I-17, I-19, I-26, I-31, I-174, and I-175. Also with the armada were three submarines of Mikawa's command—I-121, I-123, and RO-34. In the wake of the Battle of the Eastern Solomons, these I-boats began to rear their ugly periscope heads in the waters east of Guadalcanal.

In the morning of August 25 destroyer GRAYSON (Lieutenant Commander F. J. Bell) sighted a surfaced submarine slinking across dusky water. Earlier that day the destroyer had been detached from the ENTERPRISE force and sent on a mission to search for pilots whose planes had run out of gas and crashed at sea some 40 miles to the northward. She was returning from this mission when she spotted the sub.

Relaying the word, GRAYSON's skipper maneuvered to attack. The sub ducked. Destroyers PATTERSON and MONSSEN presently teamed up in the game of hunt-and harry, and the trio gave the I-boat an all-day dose of depth-charging that its crew would not soon forget. The destroyers claimed a kill. But according to Japanese records, the I-9, although severely beaten up, escaped.

About the time these destroyers were loosening the rivets in I-9, a Navy plane was pulverizing the light bulbs in I-17. The pilot was certain of a direct hit, but the I-17 managed to limp home for repairs.

It remained for an old "four-piper," an ex-DD, to wipe out the first of the subs that went down in the enemy's Guadalcanal offensive. The old-timer was the U.S.S. GAMBLE. Converted into a destroyer-mine-layer, GAMBLE was on duty off Guadalcanal as an A/S vessel in a screen for Task Unit 62.2.4. At 0805 in the morning of August 29, her lookouts sighted the conning tower of a large submarine some 9,000 yards distant.

GAMBLE's skipper, Lieutenant Commander S. N. Tackney, snapped the crew into action. Though the old "four-piper" had taken up mine-planting as a vocation, she still carried depth-charge gear. She attacked the sub with "ashcans" at 0844, and kept at it for the next three hours.

After her last attack, made at 1147, a large quantity of oil surged to the surface, bearing in its dark tide the splintered remnants of deck planking. The kill was eventually verified by Japanese records opened for post-war inspection. In the bloodstained waters off Guadalcanal, GAMBLE had sunk I-123.

"Sara" Blasted! Wasp Sunk!

GAMBLE's killing of I-123, and the damage dealt I-9 and I-17, removed three Japanese subs from the seas off Guadalcanal. But other I-boats remained in the area. And while Japanese destroyers and troop convoys continued to run down through the "Slot" to Guadalcanal, and Jap aircraft hammered at Allied convoys bound for Lunga Point, the I-boats tried to set up an undersea blockade.

Surface and air actions centered in Savo Sound, and raged around the "Tokyo Express." In one battle, Marine dive-bombers stopped the Express cold by sinking a Jap destroyer and disabling two others. But the other Jap DD's in the transport service got through. In turn, Jap aircraft from Rabaul and the Upper Solomons sank the American destroyer-transport COLHOUN. And Jap warship raiders sank American destroyer-transports LITTLE and GREGORY.

Meanwhile the Jap submarines were active. And they had their periscopes trained on big game.

The day before GAMBLE sank I-123, airmen from the U.S. carrier WASP sighted and drove off an I-boat in the carrier's vicinity. Then, at 0330 in the morning of August 31, the SARATOGA force picked up an unidentified radar contact. Destroyer FARRAGUT peeled away from the screen to investigate. The contact disappeared in a manner suggestive of a submersible.

The task force went on its way, and the morning watch slid back into the well-oiled groove of routine. About 0746, while the SARATOGA men were lining up for chow, the routine was abruptly jolted out of the groove. The first jolt came when destroyer MACDONOUGH (Lieutenant Commander E. V. Dennett), screening on "SARA's" starboard bow, made an urgent sonar contact dead ahead.

The contact was hardly reported to the bridge before MACDONOUGH's lookouts sighted a periscope close aboard. By the time it took to get a shout out of a dry throat, the cobra-headed thing was only 30 feet from the destroyer's bow. In one split second (0746) the destroyermen hoisted the submarine warning signal; in another they shouted the word over TBS, "Torpedoes heading for carrier!"; and in another they dropped two depth charges. In the excitement, someone forgot to apply depth settings. And as the futile charges splashed into the water, something rasped like a giant piece of sandpaper against MACDONOUGH's hull. She had literally rubbed elbows with the Jap submarine.

Meantime, the sub—the I-26—had launched a spread of six "fish" at the SARATOGA. One of these jumped out of the water astern of MACDONOUGH. The others raced on toward the target.

With hard right rudder and a burst of speed, Captain D. C. Ramsey strove to swing the great ship to comb the wakes. It was like trying to move the Flatiron Building at moment's notice. One minute ticked away. Then another. Then came the big jolt as a torpedo smashed into the starboard side of the flattop abreast of the island, and a geyser erupted against the sky. *Boom!* Stabbed by a submarine at the very start of the war, "SARA" had been nailed again.

Luckily the blast did not cause severe structural damage. But it flooded a fireroom and fouled up the ship's electric power plant. With eleven of the crew injured and Admiral Fletcher wounded, the big carrier limped off for Tongatabu.

Destroyers MACDONOUGH and PHELPS went after the submersible with blood in their eyes. They probed and "pinged," made contacts, and executed depth-charge attacks. To no avail. Destroyer MONSSEN was detached from the task force screen and ordered to conduct a "hold-down" until nightfall. Commander R. N. Smoot and his MONSSEN men dropped a ton or two of TNT on the submerged I-boat, and happily reported her destruction. But I-26 survived the report.

With carriers ENTERPRISE and SARATOGA disabled, there was dense gloom in the Allied camp, and things were bound to worsen before they bettered. The reinforced Jap garrison on Guadalcanal was making it hot for the "Cactus" Marines. In mid-September,

Vandegrift's Leathernecks saved Henderson Field by hurling back the enemy at Bloody Ridge. But the "Tokyo Express" was arriving regularly with replacements from Rabaul, and American replacements from Espiritu Santo were gradually dwindling. Wanted were more Marines and more aviation gasoline. And more warships to screen the convoys, and carrier aircraft to protect the sea lanes.

On September 14, the day after the Bloody Ridge battle, a convoy of six transports, carrying the 7th Marine Regiment and 150,000 gallons of aviation gas, set out from Espiritu Santo for Guadalcanal. The convoy steamed under heavy escort. To maintain an aerial A/S patrol and guard the ship-train against attack by Jap carrier planes or heavy warships, Admiral Ghormley directed the WASP and HORNET teams to support the convoy.

The carrier task groups, unified into a support force, remained over the horizon as the convoy trudged on its way. But HORNET and WASP planes searched the seascape ahead, and the aircraft on the flat-tops were ready to go at first sign of opposition.

The opposition that materialized gave no sign. And it struck at the carrier force instead of the convoy. Early in the afternoon of September 15, while the WASP was making a routine turn, her lookouts sighted torpedo wakes to starboard. Before Captain F. P. Sherman could swing the ship, two Japanese "fish" hit her. A third torpedo glanced off the hull, and a fourth passed under the keel of destroyer LANSDOWNE.

WASP was fatally hit. The explosions tossed her planes in the air as though they were jackstraws. Fire burst from ruptured gasoline lines. Ready ammunition began to go off, and the ship assumed a dangerous starboard list. About half an hour after she was hit, a monstrous blast shattered the ship internally, and Captain Sherman was soon compelled to order her abandonment. That evening the flaming hulk was sunk by torpedoes from destroyer LANSDOWNE. Some 193 of the carrier's crew of 2,247 had perished in the molten ship.

The submarine which torpedoed WASP was the I-19. She was not alone on the field. With her was the I-15. And so the HORNET had a close call. She was about five miles northeast of WASP when the latter was struck. And within a few minutes of that blasting, torpedoes were racing toward HORNET.

Destroyer LANSDOWNE had voiced the alarm over TBS, but the word did not reach all of the ships in HORNET's screen. Lookouts on destroyer MUSTIN, on HORNET's port bow, were suddenly shocked by the sight of a torpedo wake. The deadly "fish" skimmed under MUSTIN's keel as the destroyermen stared, aghast. Then, seconds later, it smashed into battleship NORTH CAROLINA, some 500 yards away.

The blast killed five men in the battleship, and blew an enormous underwater hole in her port side. But the big "wagon" kept right on going at 25 knots, and eventually she steamed into port under her own power.

About two minutes after NORTH CAROLINA was slugged, a torpedo slammed into destroyer O'BRIEN. Several hundred yards on NORTH CAROLINA's quarter, the DD was right in line for a hit. Her lookouts sighted one wake in time for her captain, Commander T. Burrowes, to maneuver to dodge. As that "fish" sped by, a second was sighted by the ship's Gunnery Officer. From his station above the bridge he cried the alarm, but the torpedo was faster than the destroyer. The blast did not kill her, but it left her badly crippled. And her disablement eventually caused her untimely death.

The convoy carrying the 7th Marine Regiment reached Guadalcanal in safety. But the sinking of WASP at a time when ENTERPRISE and SARATOGA were on the binnacle list was a major disaster. HORNET was now the only Allied aircraft carrier left in the South Pacific.

Thus in a few minutes' time two enemy submarines had wrought more havoc with the Navy's South Pacific forces than Yamamoto's surface-air armada, off the Eastern Solomons, had accomplished in two days.

Apparently both submarines had had the great good fortune to be swimming directly in the path of the WASP-HORNET force. The water that day was laced with whitecaps—good cover for a periscope "feather" —and sea conditions were evidently unfavorable for long-range sonar detection. Firing long-range "browning shots" from outside the screen, the I-boats were not detected until their torpedoes were launched.

While the WASP sinking was subjected to some criticism, Admiral Nimitz, after studying the reports, concluded that *"No persons should be blamed or censured for the loss of* WASP." In that, there was some consolation.

Loss of U.S.S. O'Brien

The WASP's destruction by I-19 and the NORTH CAROLINA's torpedoing by I-15 were strong evidence of the lethal punch of the Japanese I-boats. Destroyer O'BRIEN, too, was battered to her knees on that afternoon of September 15, and the I-15 was to be credited with her knockout also.

The blow that struck O'BRIEN laid open her stem, leaving a tremendous gash from keel to hawsepipe—a jagged hole that forced the vessel to veer and shudder violently, slowing the ship.

O'BRIEN staggered as the shock vibrated her hull, wrenched her framework, jolted her internal machinery, and threw men headlong against bulkheads. Fortunately the blast did not start a fire, and the damage-controlmen were able to cope with the flooding. O'BRIEN's skipper, Commander T. Burrowes, reported that the engines were still running; the ship could do 15 knots.

At 1600 of that afternoon O'BRIEN was directed to proceed independently to Espiritu Santo, and she succeeded in making port the following day.

After emergency repairs at Espiritu, O'BRIEN limped on to Nouméa, where she was worked on by a tender. The tendermen patched her up, and a naval constructor signed her out as capable of a run to the States.

But the destroyer's injuries were more serious than they appeared to be. Torpedo explosion, and the vibrations thereby induced, had strained the principal ship girder and left the vessel with a weak back. She was in no condition for a long voyage when she set out from New Caledonia on October 10, in company with destroyer LANG and fleet oiler CIMARRON. The group reached Suva on the 13th, and went on from there on the 16th.

In the morning of October 19, 1942, when the home-bound group was off Samoa, O'BRIEN suffered something like a spasmodic seizure. While in this spasm, she began to break up. Literally she came apart at the seams. Deep fractures developed in the shell plating of the forward engine-room; a longitudinal crack opened in her hull; her keel snapped; and she pulled apart like a worn-out bushel basket.

Happily all hands got off in time, and there were no casualties.

The wreckage sank at 0759, and the hard-pressed Fleet had lost another destroyer.

Battle of Cape Esperance

Meantime in spite of numerous wrecks caused by Marine Corps bombers, the "Tokyo Express" continued to run down the "Slot" with depressing regularity. By the end of September, 1942, some 26,000 Imperial troops and a Jap naval contingent of 3,500 men were facing the Marines at Lunga Point. In the vicinity of Bougainville pagoda-masted warships were clustered in herds. Another Guadalcanal showdown was brewing.

At Nouméa 6,000 American soldiers prepared to embark for "Cactus." The HORNET task force took up a covering position to the west of Guadalcanal. A task force headed by battleship WASHINGTON moved into the seascape east of Malaita. For further protection Admiral Ghormley dispatched a newly-organized cruiser force from Espiritu Santo to the waters south of Guadalcanal, to cover the convoy's left flank. As it happened this force, designated Task Group 64.2 with code name "Task Force Sugar," was to shoulder most of the protection burden.

Under command of Rear Admiral Norman Scott, Task Force Sugar consisted of heavy cruisers SAN FRANCISCO (flagship) and SALT LAKE CITY, light cruisers BOISE and HELENA, and the following five destroyers:

FARENHOLT	*Comdr. E. T. Seaward*
	Flying the pennant of Capt. R. G. Tobin, COMDESRON 12
BUCHANAN	*Comdr. R. E. Wilson*
LAFFEY	*Lt. Comdr. W. E. Hank*
DUNCAN	*Comdr. E. B. Taylor*
MCCALLA	*Comdr. W. G. Cooper*

The force stood out of Espiritu Santo on October 7 and set a course toward Rennel Island. They were two days en route, and after getting there they cruised off the southwest coast of Guadalcanal for two more days. Then, in the afternoon of October 11, scouting American aircraft sighted a Jap force coming down the "Slot" about 210 miles from Guadalcanal. To intercept this force Admiral Scott led his ships around the western end of the island to Cape Esperance where they could cover the entry to Savo Sound.

The situation was somewhat similar to that which touched off the first Savo Island battle. Bearing down on Savo were three proud veterans of that engagement—units of Imperial Cruiser Division Six—the heavy cruisers AOBA, FURUTAKA, and KINUGASA. Accompanying these cruisers were destroyers FUBUKI and MURAKUMO. These ships composed a bombardment group under Admiral Aritomo Goto, on mission to blast American positions at Lunga Point. Behind them came a reinforcement group—seaplane carriers NISSHIN and CHITOSE, and six destroyers with troops and supplies for General Kawaguchi.

As on the first Savo occasion, information on the advancing enemy was sketchy, and the strength of the Jap striking force was underestimated. Again, the Jap cruisers made the run down the "Slot" unmolested, and gained the approaches to Savo Island by evening.

But this time there was a difference. Such information as he did receive from air scouts reached Admiral Scott in short order. In consequence the Americans were ready, and it was the Japs who were surprised.

Steaming off Cape Esperance, Scott's force had its eyes, ears, and guns cocked for bear. The evening was dark and humid, a thin moon setting, and the sea rippled by a sultry breeze.

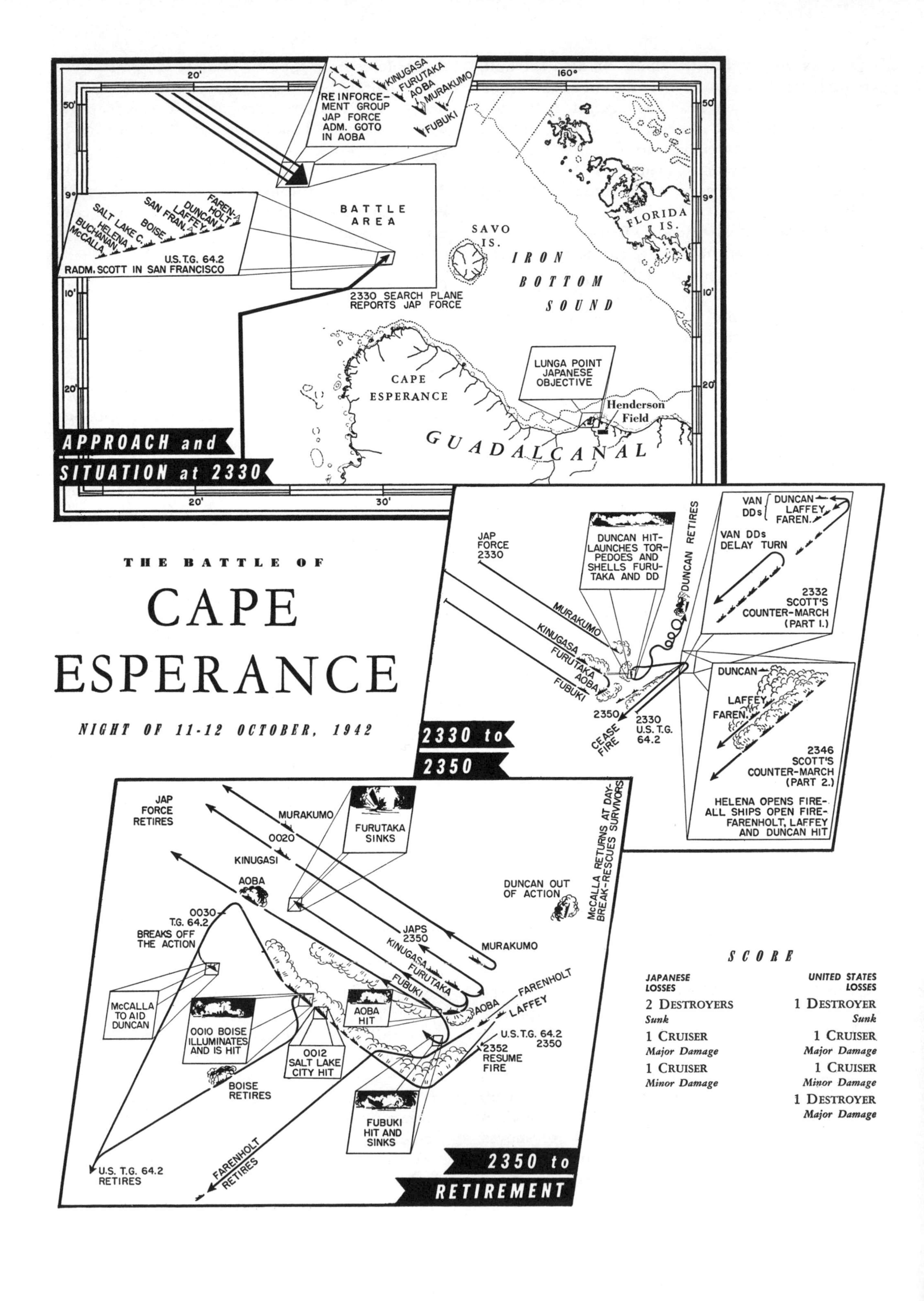

THE BATTLE OF
CAPE ESPERANCE
NIGHT OF 11-12 OCTOBER, 1942
APPROACH and SITUATION at 2330
KINUGASA
FURUTAKA
AOBA
MURAKUMO
FUBUKI
REINFORCEMENT GROUP JAP FORCE ADM. GOTO IN AOBA
FARENHOLT
DUNCAN
LAFFEY
SAN FRAN.
BOISE
SALT LAKE C.
HELENA
BUCHANAN
McCALLA
U.S.T.G. 64.2
RADM. SCOTT IN SAN FRANCISCO
BATTLE AREA
2330 SEARCH PLANE REPORTS JAP FORCE
SAVO IS.
IRON BOTTOM SOUND
FLORIDA IS.
CAPE ESPERANCE
LUNGA POINT JAPANESE OBJECTIVE
Henderson Field
GUADALCANAL
2330 to 2350
JAP FORCE 2330
DUNCAN HIT-LAUNCHES TORPEDOES AND SHELLS FURUTAKA AND DD
DUNCAN RETIRES
VAN DDs DUNCAN LAFFEY FAREN.
VAN DDs DELAY TURN
2332 SCOTT'S COUNTER-MARCH (PART 1.)
2350 CEASE FIRE
2330 U.S. T.G. 64.2
DUNCAN
LAFFEY
FAREN.
2346 SCOTT'S COUNTER-MARCH (PART 2.)
HELENA OPENS FIRE-ALL SHIPS OPEN FIRE-FARENHOLT, LAFFEY AND DUNCAN HIT
2350 to RETIREMENT
JAP FORCE RETIRES
MURAKUMO
0020
FURUTAKA SINKS
KINUGASI
AOBA
McCALLA RETURNS AT DAY-BREAK-RESCUES SURVIVORS
DUNCAN OUT OF ACTION
0030-T.G. 64.2 BREAKS OFF THE ACTION
JAPS 2350
KINUGASA
FURUTAKA
FUBUKI
MURAKUMO
FARENHOLT
LAFFEY
McCALLA TO AID DUNCAN
0010 BOISE ILLUMINATES AND IS HIT
0012 SALT LAKE CITY HIT
AOBA HIT
U.S.T.G. 64.2 2350
2352 RESUME FIRE
BOISE RETIRES
FUBUKI HIT AND SINKS
U.S. T.G. 64.2 RETIRES
FARENHOLT RETIRES
SCORE
JAPANESE LOSSES
2 DESTROYERS Sunk
1 CRUISER Major Damage
1 CRUISER Minor Damage
UNITED STATES LOSSES
1 DESTROYER Sunk
1 CRUISER Major Damage
1 CRUISER Minor Damage
1 DESTROYER Major Damage

Then, at 2325 U.S. cruiser HELENA made radar contact with the oncoming enemy. For some reason HELENA let 15 minutes elapse before reporting this contact. She was carrying new SG radar gear, and her captain evidently wanted to confirm the contact. However, at 2330 a SAN FRANCISCO search plane sighted enemy ships approaching Cape Esperance, and Scott knew the foe was in the immediate offing.

Task Force Sugar was at that time off the west coast of Savo Island, heading northeastward. The ships were in column with destroyers FARENHOLT, DUNCAN, and LAFFEY in the van, followed by SAN FRANCISCO, BOISE, SALT LAKE CITY, HELENA, BUCHANAN, and McCALLA, in that order. Intending to block the passage between Savo and Cape Esperance, Admiral Scott called for the column to reverse course.

The order "Left to course 230 degrees!" was voiced over the TBS. Led by flagship SAN FRANCISCO, the cruisers smartly executed the maneuver, as did rear destroyers BUCHANAN and McCALLA. But van destroyers FARENHOLT, DUNCAN, and LAFFEY, supposed to swing out as a separate column and then come down the flank of the cruiser column to regain head position, made a belated swing. They were thus left in the rear of the southbound cruiser column.

Squadron Commander Tobin now led the three DD's in a race down the starboard flank of the cruiser column in an effort to regain the van. But the battle exploded before Tobin's destroyers could get into the lead. FARENHOLT and LAFFEY were well abreast of the cruiser column when HELENA (time: 2346) opened fire on a target she had tracked by radar and then sighted some 5,000 yards to starboard.

The gunnery from HELENA was touched off by another of those freakish "breaks." When the HELENA, having made definite radar contact, requested permission to open fire, Admiral Scott's reply was, "Roger!" He meant he'd received the message. But HELENA's captain took the acknowledgment for permission to open fire.

Scott's captains had been supposed to open fire on their own discretion. But the Admiral doubtless would have restrained the cruiser guns until the destroyer situation cleared. Captain Tobin had advised him that the three destroyers were coming up to starboard, but Scott could not discern their exact position. And with the DD's somewhere between the American cruiser column and the enemy, their position was precarious, to say the least.

Moreover, DUNCAN had sheared out of line astern of FARENHOLT. While swinging on the hairpin turn, she had made radar contact with the enemy. Assuming that FARENHOLT was heading for the enemy, DUNCAN's Commanding Officer sent the DD on a westward run toward the target. LAFFEY was apparently following FARENHOLT on a course parallel to the cruiser column when HELENA's guns opened up. Then the other cruisers let go. Tobin's disrupted destroyer column was right in the line of fire.

But the Japs were in an even worse position.

Steaming along without benefit of radar, Admiral Goto's cruiser column was making a beeline for Savo Island just as Admiral Scott's cruiser column executed its hairpin turn. Goto had not even sent his gunners to battle stations, and in total darkness he led his ships head-on toward the American cruiser column. Captain E. G. Small, skipper of SALT LAKE CITY, said afterward, *"It was one of those things that naval officers wait twenty years to see. We crossed their T."*

They capped the Japanese "T" with a roaring broadside that sent a torrent of projectiles crashing around flagship AOBA. In that same burst of fire FURUTAKA was hard hit, and destroyer MURAKUMO was struck. Then, afraid that his cruisers were firing on Tobin's destroyers, Admiral Scott ordered a cease fire.

At this juncture Goto might have recovered somewhat, but the bewildered Jap Admiral was somehow under the impression that the Japanese transport group was firing at him. Blindly he swung his ships on a column right, intending to reverse course—a fatal move which exposed each ship in turn to American fire, much as targets coming around on a shooting-gallery belt are exposed to the fire of a row of marksmen. Some of Scott's captains did not hear the cease-fire order, and as AOBA made the turn a smacking salvo wrecked her bridge. It also wrecked Admiral Goto, who fell mortally wounded.

Admiral Scott now spoke with Tobin over the TBS, attempting to locate destroyers FARENHOLT, DUNCAN, and LAFFEY. Tobin informed him that the three DD's were coming up to starboard. Scott ordered them to flash recognition signals. When they did so, he ordered his cruisers to resume fire.

Destroyer DUNCAN had already been hit in the forward fireroom, perhaps by an American shell. As has been related, she had made a single-handed dash toward the enemy force. When the Jap column turned right, DUNCAN found herself less than a mile from I.J.N. FURUTAKA. Lieutenant Commander E. B. Taylor realized his ship was between two fires, and he did some desperate conning to bring his torpedo batteries to bear on FURUTAKA while dodging Jap and American shells.

For a starter DUNCAN shelled the Jap cruiser, then she shifted fire to an oncoming Jap destroyer (apparently MURAKUMO), then she fired two fast torpedo shots at FURUTAKA. At the same time she took hits which disabled her gun director, toppled her forward stack, and ignited the powder in her No. 2 handling room. A moment later DUNCAN was struck by what was evidently an American salvo. With her lights blown out, she staggered off in mortal disablement.

The Japs, meantime, had been lobbing a few salvos at Scott's cruiser column. These shots were answered with a rain of 6-inch shells. Floundering in a fog of smoke, the Jap heavy cruiser FURUTAKA was burning like a barn as she stumbled around the turn astern of AOBA. Flame-light and smoke-shadow gave her the appearance of a vessel bottoms-up. But she did not go down until 0040 the next morning.

The clock was nearing midnight when FURUTAKA rounded the fatal turn, and now another Jap warship was the recipient of a flogging. Bringing up the rear, KINUGASA made a wrong turn to the left instead of right—a lucky accident which saved her life. Destroyer MURAKUMO also made a lucky left turn. But the other Jap destroyer, I.J.N. FUBUKI, was not so lucky. Screening AOBA's starboard bow, she followed the right-turn maneuver. In doing so, she reached a position only three quarters of a mile from U.S.S. SAN FRANCISCO. The "FRISCO" men put a searchlight on her, and that was the end of FUBUKI. Every ship in Scott's column opened fire on the Jap destroyer. At 2353 the vessel blew up and went down.

With AOBA severely damaged, FURUTAKA disabled, FUBUKI sunk, and Admiral Goto dying, the Japs were in dismal straits. But they managed to strike back at the last and deal several nasty blows.

About the time DUNCAN was disabled, destroyer FARENHOLT was struck by what were probably American shells. Two bursts in her rigging raked her superstructure with flying iron. A third shell punctured her hull on the port side just above the waterline. A fourth ripped into her forward fireroom.

The shot through the hull wrecked her gunfire-control wiring and flooded her gun plot. The shot in the fireroom opened a leak in the main steam line of her No. 1 boiler, releasing a murderous jet which threatened to skin the crew alive. FARENHOLT's skipper, Lieutenant Commander E. T. Seaward, urged the fireroom watch to hold out as long as possible before it secured and abandoned. From the water tender in charge came the stalwart reply, *"We'll steam her into Tokyo!"*

They couldn't steam her into Tokyo, but they held on long enough to steam her out of dire trouble. Pressure was maintained on the No. 2 boiler while the engineering plant was cross-connected, except for fuel oil lines. So FARENHOLT limped out of danger. By dint of shifting fuel and water, and moving topside weights, the destroyermen contrived to list the ship to starboard, thereby raising the shell holes in her portside well above the water. Eventually she made Espiritu Santo under her own power.

In the meantime Admiral Scott had headed his cruiser column on a northwesterly course in an effort to maintain contact with the retiring enemy. Then BOISE picked up a radar "pip" and snapped on a searchlight. She immediately came under fire from KINUGASA and another warship, probably AOBA. Seven smashing hits put most of BOISE's guns out of action, and holed her below the waterline. As she staggered off, listing and afire, one of her magazines exploded, slaying many of her crew. The glare silhouetted SALT LAKE CITY, making her target for three damaging hits.

The American force now concentrated on KINUGASA, lashing her with shellfire as she fled northwestward. By 0020 the battle was over. Scott pulled his ships together, and sent destroyer MCCALLA out to round up and assist the cripples.

Under the leadership of Captain Edward J. Moran, BOISE's cruisermen fought the ship's battle-damage with a determination that quenched flames and had her engines doing 20 knots by 0240. At that hour, too, destroyer FARENHOLT was going on her own steam. But destroyer DUNCAN—the only American ship to die in the engagement—was going down.

Loss of U.S.S. Duncan

DUNCAN was mortally wounded when she reeled out of the battle around midnight. The ship's superstructure was a shambles. Her forward fireroom was wrecked. Her forecastle was in flames. Her radio was demolished. Coding room, radar-plotting room, gun plot, and gun-director platform were in ruins. Her interior communications and electrical lines were gone, and the only light below decks was cast by the fiery glare topside. Everywhere lay the dead—in the shattered charthouse, on the bridge, in smoke-choked passageways and blasted compartments, and on the burning forecastle. But her engines were still pounding and the ship was circling blindly at 15 knots.

Tongues of flame lapped around the bridge-wing, scorching the metal and licking hungrily at the paint. After a futile attempt to communicate with the crew aft, her captain, Lieutenant Commander E. B. Taylor, ordered the bridge abandoned. Fires were eating their way across the deck below, and the destroyermen on the bridge were compelled to go overside to save their lives. When the wounded were let down to rafts, the Commanding Officer and the others went over. DUNCAN circled off across the seascape, a burning death-ship.

Personnel of the Russell, right, gaze up at the towering heights of the burning Hornet, left. The Russell was one of the Hornet's destroyer screen which earned the commendation of Admirals Nimitz and Halsey for rescue, fire-fighting, and seamanship achievement. Hornet's loss caused the Bureau of Ships to stress the necessity for following directives as to fire hazards rigidly.

Our final large carrier loss of the war. U.S.S. Hornet sinks in the Santa Cruz action. Her remarkable hull toughness absorbed many enemy torpedo, bomb, and suicide plane hits and American torpedo and gunfire scuttling attempts. Four Japanese torpedoes finally destroyed her. Here Russell leads other American destroyers to the work of damage control, fire-fighting and rescue.

The Mahan, right, and another destroyer are shown steaming at high speed during the Santa Cruz action. Battle maneuvering often is difficult and dangerous. In this picture there is no collision course. However, shortly after this action the Mahan collided with the South Dakota as a result of a submarine alarm disrupting the force's formation. Both warships received damage.

Personnel rescued from the carrier Wasp are shown aboard the destroyer Lansdowne. Many lessons were learned from the loss of the Wasp. These included the necessity of cutting in all fire pumps during battles and of isolating damaged sections of the fire main. Also, the advisability of establishing a secondary damage control station and of further division of repair parties.

But there were still living men in that floating inferno—men topside and below decks who did not know the skipper had gone overside, or who thought everyone on the bridge had perished. Making his way to the after conning station, Ensign Frank A. Andrews succeeded in communicating with the Engineer Officer, Lieutenant H. R. Kabat. Assuming command as senior officer on board, Kabat ordered Ensign Andrews to beach the ship. Aided by Chief Torpedoman Boyd, Andrews strove to head the destroyer for Savo Island, to run her aground. Before they could get her inshore, the destroyer's bow was gutted by fire, and the engineers had to abandon the forward engine-room.

Then feed-water could not be pumped for the after fireroom. Lieutenant (jg) W. H. Coley, U.S.N.R., and Chief Water Tender A. H. Holt made a desperate effort to feed seawater into the boiler by a gasoline billy. The cold brine boiled away, and the pump became steam-clogged. Gradually the ship lost power and slowed to a stop.

About 0200 the ammunition began to explode, and the surviving members of the crew leapt overside. Clinging to powder cans, rubbish, anything that could keep them afloat, they swam away from the bursting destroyer. Her fiery hull was presently sighted by destroyer McCALLA (Lieutenant Commander W. G. Cooper), hunting for BOISE to the west of Savo Island.

Cooper maneuvered in carefully to investigate; then, satisfied that the burning vessel was not Japanese, he sent a boarding party under McCALLA's Executive Officer to determine salvage possibilities. The party chugged away in a whaleboat about 0300, and McCALLA steamed off to continue the search for BOISE.

Boarding the DUNCAN, the McCALLA men made an effort to fight the fire, but the ship was too far gone for ready salvaging. Cries from across the water led to the discovery of swimming survivors, and the McCALLA party shifted its attention to rescue work.

DUNCAN's survivors were in dire need of help. A school of sharks had caught the scent of blood. Around the huddle of floats and swimmers, the dark water had come alive with cruising dorsal fins and the gleam of slippery, white fish-bellies. Men and fish were engaged in a dreadful scuffling when the McCALLA party arrived on the scene. Rifle-fire broke up the shark attack only in time.

At daybreak destroyer McCALLA returned to search for survivors, and in a short time most of the living were picked up. A total of 195 officers and men were rescued. Most of the dead—some 48 or 50 of the crew—went down with the U.S.S. DUNCAN.

By 1130 of that morning the destroyer was a burned-out shell. She settled gradually in a shroud of billowing steam. By noon she was gone. She went down about six miles north of Savo Island—to stand picket duty, one might believe, for the United States warships not far distant on the bottom of "Ironbottom Bay."

Esperance Aftermath

"Esperance" means "hope." And the battle off this French-named cape did, indeed, bring a ray of hope to the Allies. Japanese ship casualties—a cruiser and a destroyer sunk, another cruiser severely damaged, and a third cruiser injured—considerably outweighed American ship casualties. BOISE and FARENHOLT had suffered heavy damage, but they could be repaired. SALT LAKE CITY's wounds were minor. Destroyer DUNCAN was the only ship lost.

The American victory in some measure squared accounts for the Savo Island debacle. More important, it gave the American Army convoy a chance to reach Guadalcanal unmolested.

But the Japs had not shot their Solomons bolt by any manner of means. On the night of October 13-14, battleships KONGO and HARUNA, a light cruiser, and accompanying destroyers raced into Savo Sound to hurl shells at the "Cactus" Marines. The big Jap guns demolished over half the aircraft on Henderson Field, and the Jap force retired without a scratch.

The following night came Admiral Mikawa in person, leading cruisers CHOKAI and KINUGASA to hammer at the Marine airfield. When that bombardment was ended, Henderson was almost blown off the map, and only a single Marine bomber was left intact.

On the morning of the 15th a Jap transport force came down the "Slot" and landed several thousand more troops just west of Lunga Point at Tassafaronga. It looked like curtains for the "Cactus" forces unless they were speedily reinforced and supplied.

The effort to supply them cost the life of the destroyer MEREDITH.

Loss of U.S.S. Meredith

For sheer horror the destruction of the DesPac destroyer MEREDITH surpassed anything thus far endured by destroyermen in that Solomons war of nightmares.

Her last voyage began in mid-October when she set out from Espiritu Santo with a gasoline convoy bound for Guadalcanal. By that date the aviation fuel shortage in General Vandegrift's camp had become extremely critical. Planes were grounded for thirst on Henderson Field, and only a dribble of high octane was getting through—a few loads flown in by Douglas Skytroopers, and a cargo spirited in by the submarine AMBERJACK.

Contemplating this grave situation, Admiral Nimitz was compelled to state,

> *It now appears that we are unable to control the sea in the Guadalcanal area . . . our supply of the positions will only be done at great expense to us. . . .*

A grimly determined service force prepared to pay the expense. So an emergency convoy was scraped together—attack cargomen BELLATRIX and ALCHIBA, PT-boat tender JAMESTOWN, and fleet tug (former minesweeper) VIREO, with destroyers NICHOLAS (Commander W. D. Brown) and MEREDITH (Commander H. E. Hubbard) for escort. Each cargoman towed a barge loaded with 1,000 barrels of gasoline and 500 quarter-ton bombs.

On October 15 the ships were off San Cristobal Island, a day's run from their objective. Daylight brought a Japanese scout plane, a mosquito hovering against the sky. It hovered long enough to make a gratifying inspection of the convoy; then it flew over the western horizon. The destroyermen knew what was coming. At 0608, in accordance with a dispatch from Ghormley, the barge towed by BELLATRIX was shifted to VIREO. NICHOLAS then shepherded the two cargo ships and JAMESTOWN in a hasty retirement. MEREDITH and VIREO trudged steadily forward.

At 1050 the "bogie" attack came—a pair of Jap planes pouncing on the destroyer and the tug. The planes made two assaults; were twice beaten off by crack-shooting AA gunners. Then MEREDITH received word that two enemy warships were in her vicinity, and Commander Hubbard ordered VIREO to reverse course.

It was soon apparent that the tug VIREO, panting in an effort to make 14 knots, would have to be abandoned or would fall prey to the nearing enemy. At noon Commander Hubbard ordered the tug's crew to quit the vessel. MEREDITH picked up the VIREO crew, and drew off to sink the tug by torpedo fire. The destroyermen were squaring away to fire the torpedo shot when (time: 1215) a flight of 27 Japanese planes from the carrier ZUIKAKU roared across the sky.

Caught in a thundering, screaming blizzard of bombs, torpedoes, and machine-gun fire, the MEREDITH was literally torn to fragments. Her desperate gunners shot down three planes. But the destroyer was a shambles, and the wreckage sank in a trice. And the MEREDITH survivors struggled in a sea of smoke, blood, burning flotsam, and flaming oil.

Some of the men tried to reach the abandoned tug VIREO, which had come through the attack without damage. But she drifted to leeward, maddeningly beyond reach, and only a few were able to board the vessel. Some of the MEREDITH men, clinging to mats of wreckage, floated away and were never seen again. Gradually the smoke cleared, the oil fires burned out, and a little huddle of swimmers and survivors on rafts remained adrift in an empty seascape.

On the rafts lay men who were wounded beyond hope and beyond the soothing lenitive of opiates—men with charred bodies, with crushed features, with riddled limbs. The strong supported the weak, and the maimed tried to comfort the blind. Among those dying on the rafts was MEREDITH's captain, Commander Harry E. Hubbard. At the Naval Academy in 1925 he had graduated at the head of his class.

There was not enough room on the rafts, and those who were able remained in the water, clinging to lifelines. When a wounded man died, a swimmer would take his place on the gratings. And so there was a final horror—sharks.

Attracted by the scent of blood, a school of sharks trailed the drifting rafts, and glided in to nip and slash at the swimmers hanging to the lifelines. Kicking and stabbing, the destroyermen fought them off. On one occasion a shark slithered aboard a listing raft to attack a bleeding man. Ensued a ghastly scrimmage in which the shark gnashed a bite of flesh from the victim's thigh before he was driven overside.

For three days and nights the Purgatory persisted. At last, on October 18, the survivors were sighted and picked up by destroyers GRAYSON and GWIN, and the tug SEMINOLE. A ghostly 73 destroyermen were recovered. Some 185 of MEREDITH's crew had perished. Of the VIREO crew, 51 were lost.

Although the gasoline convoy never reached Guadalcanal, the battle fought by MEREDITH off San Cristobal was not entirely futile. Standing her ground, she had drawn the enemy's fire, which might otherwise have smashed the ships retiring with NICHOLAS. This group beat off a seaplane attack and an onslaught by five dive-bombers, and made a safe return to Espiritu Santo. SEMINOLE took VIREO's barge in tow, and with GRAYSON and GWIN proceeded to Tulagi.

But the DesPac Force had lost another destroyer in the effort to supply the Marines on the Solomons front—an effort which might have dismayed those persons on the home front who were complaining about the gasoline ration that curtailed their Sunday motoring.

The MEREDITH survivors were picked up on a Sunday.

CHAPTER 15

SOLOMONS CRUCIBLE

(THE GUADALCANAL CAMPAIGN)

(Part 2)

Battle of Santa Cruz Islands

As of mid-October, 1942, the fierce Guadalcanal campaign had cost the Navy six destroyers: five downed in action, one sunk by a friendly mine. Not extravagant for a hammer-and-tongs struggle which had persisted without letup for nine weeks. In the impersonal statistics of warfare, six destroyers were a minor loss compared with the destruction of three U.S. cruisers and an aircraft carrier in the same period. But Japanese naval losses were not commensurate; the Solomons situation still balanced on a razor's edge; and the six DD's were sorely missed by a DesPac Force straining every rivet to meet the pressures of supply and demand.

New destroyers were coming into the South Pacific—FLETCHER-class ships manned by well-trained men—but as yet they couldn't keep pace with the reserves from Tokyo. Yamamoto was now for pitching every available Jap warship into the crucible, and he had available in the South Pacific five aircraft carriers, five battleships, 14 cruisers, and 44 destroyers. On the Allied side in the South Pacific were two carriers, two battleships, nine cruisers and 24 destroyers—37 warships against 68. Certainly "Operation Watchtower," the Allied effort to gain control of the Solomons area, had reached a crisis. And now, in a crucial four weeks' time, the Navy lost an aircraft carrier, two cruisers, and eight destroyers—seven of the latter in a battle which raged for three days. But the Japs were thrown back with a jolt which ripped their grip from Guadalcanal.

The first American destroyer lost in this Solomons tidal turn was the U.S.S. PORTER. She was sunk in the Battle of Santa Cruz Islands, and she went down in company with aircraft carrier HORNET.

A carrier duel fought by forces 250 miles apart, this battle exploded off those little islets which lie due east of the Lower Solomons and due north of the New Hebrides. Most of the combat took place in the sky, but PORTER was ambushed by an enemy submarine.

The battle occurred just one week after Vice Admiral W. F. Halsey replaced Admiral Ghormley as Commander South Pacific (ComSoPac). That was on October 18, and the Guadalcanal operation at that time was touch-and-go.

"Are we going to evacuate or hold?" he asked General Vandegrift.

"I can hold," Vandegrift said grimly, "but I've got to have more active support than I've been getting."

By way of a first installment Halsey sent the newly-repaired ENTERPRISE and the battle-hardened HORNET to a position off the Santa Cruz Islands. There the combined carrier forces could not be reached by Japanese land-based aircraft from Rabaul or the Solomons, but the ENTERPRISE and HORNET planes could strike the enemy if he moved on Guadalcanal. And, the way things looked, Yamamoto was preparing another large-scale move.

The looks were not deceiving. On the night of October 23-24 the Imperial troops on Guadalcanal hit the American line like a tornado. The Japs were determined to chop, stab, batter, blow, and blast their way to Henderson Field. All night the battle raged through the coconut groves west of Lunga Point. Jap cruisers and destroyers steamed across Savo Sound before dawn to join aircraft hammering the "Cactus" positions. The Americans hung on.

As the battle roared on throughout the 24th, a Japanese armada under Admiral Kondo maneuvered into the seascape northeast of the Solomons, and hovered off the Stewart Islands, waiting. It was waiting for word that General Kawaguchi's forces had seized Henderson Field. Upon receipt of this glorious intelligence Jap carrier planes were to fly to the captured airstrip. Meantime, Kondo's armada stood ready as ordered to "apprehend and annihilate" any Allied force or reinforcements in sight.

Kondo had a power-house task force for the job. It included two Japanese fleets—the Third Fleet, containing carriers SHOKAKU, ZUIKAKU, and ZUIHO, battleships HIEI and KIRISHIMA, five cruisers, and 15 destroyers; and the Second Fleet composed of carrier JUNYO, battleships KONGO and HARUNA, five cruisers, and 14 destroyers.

However, this armada could not steam around aimlessly forever, and as the hours went by the glorious news from Henderson Field failed to arrive. Yamamoto had to wait. And while the impatient Japanese Commander-in-Chief chewed on that bit of wormwood, United States Task Force 61 cruised into the Santa Cruz seascape. Under command of Rear Admiral T. C. Kinkaid, Task Force 61 contained two carrier groups—Task Force 16, with carrier ENTERPRISE, battleship SOUTH DAKOTA, two cruisers, and eight destroyers; and Task Force 17, with carrier HORNET, four cruisers, and six destroyers. The destroyer roster is listed in the next column.

Had Kondo's armada been fresh, the odds on a carrier duel would have weighed heavily against Kinkaid's task force. But the Jap warships were low on fuel by the morning of the 26th when the duel eventuated. Disappointed at adverse news from Guadalcanal, Kondo had already set his ships on a retirement course when ENTERPRISE search planes spotted them at the beginning of the forenoon watch. The enterprising airmen from ENTERPRISE dropped two 500-pounders on the stern of carrier ZUIHO, and the battle was on.

Almost at the moment the ENTERPRISE planes reported contact, Kondo's air scouts sighted and reported the American ships. Winging to the attack, a flight of planes from ENTERPRISE collided with a flock of oncoming Jap aircraft.

While this sky battle was going full blast, dive bombers from HORNET located the carriers of the Imperial Third Fleet, and attacked SHOKAKU. They dropped about half a dozen 1,000-pound bombs on

TASK FORCE 16

ENTERPRISE

PORTER	*Lt. Comdr. D. G. Roberts*
	Flying the pennant of *Capt. C. P. Cecil,* COMDESRON 5
SMITH	*Lt. Comdr. H. Wood, Jr.*
CUSHING	*Lt. Comdr. C. Noble*
	Flying the pennant of *Comdr. T. M. Stokes,* COMDESDIV 10
PRESTON	*Comdr. M. C. Stormes*
MAURY	*Lt. Comdr. G. L. Sims*
SHAW	*Comdr. W. G. Jones*
MAHAN	*Comdr. R. W. Simpson*
CONYNGHAM	*Comdr. H. C. Daniel*

TASK FORCE 17

HORNET

MUSTIN	*Comdr. W. F. Petersen*
	Flying the pennant of *Comdr. A. E. True,* COMDESRON 2
HUGHES	*Comdr. D. J. Ramsey*
RUSSELL	*Comdr. G. R. Hartwig*
ANDERSON	*Lt. Comdr. R. A. Guthrie*
MORRIS	*Lt. Comdr. R. B. Boyer*
BARTON	*Lt. Comdr. D. H. Fox*

the Jap flat-top—punishment which sent her to the repair yards for nine months. Other HORNET planes damaged the heavy cruiser CHIKUMA.

Meanwhile, Jap carrier aircraft attacked HORNET. About 1010 of that morning some 27 planes assaulted the carrier, and they hit her hard. A bomb gouged her flight deck. Then a "Val" made a suicide dive, smashing into HORNET's smokestack. Flinging a sheet of burning gasoline, the plane carommed off the signal bridge, crashed through the deck, and exploded. A moment later two "Kates" swept in, and launched torpedoes which burst in the carrier's engineering spaces. Blazing amidships, HORNET sloughed to a halt. As she wallowed in a mass of smoke she was hit by three more bombs and another suicide plane.

Desperately the carriermen fought the battle-damage while the ships in her task force circled slowly around her in a protective cordon. On board the burning flat-top the fire was fought with hand extinguishers and foamite. Destroyers MORRIS and RUSSELL moved alongside with pumps and hoses. By 1100 the flames were moderating.

Of the estimated 27 planes which pounced on the carrier, a known 25 were shot out of existence. Some were killed by Wildcat fighters, and a goodly number were downed by the tremendous barrage of flak flung skyward by HORNET's screen. Destroyer AA gunners did a lot of fast shooting in HORNET's defense, and they raised another iron thunderstorm when enemy aircraft lashed at the ENTERPRISE-SOUTH DAKOTA force.

ENTERPRISE and Company were attacked about 1115. Some 43 planes from SHOKAKU and ZUIKAKU delivered the attack, and most of them failed to survive the effort. They ran into something new in the Pacific War—40 mm. Bofors-type AA guns. ENTERPRISE and SOUTH DAKOTA carried thickets of these deadly weapons, and SOUTH DAKOTA alone shot down 25 or 26 of the attacking planes.

ENTERPRISE took three bomb hits which dealt injury with lavish violence to the crew but caused no severe structural damage to the ship. In a follow-up attack, bombs struck SOUTH DAKOTA and light cruiser SAN JUAN, causing minor damage. Oddly enough, it was two destroyers in Task Force 16 which were handed the hot end of the poker. First of these victims was destroyer PORTER, torpedoed by a Jap submarine at the start of the battle. Second victim was destroyer SMITH. She was hit during the torpedo plane onslaught on ENTERPRISE.

In the wake of the dive-bombing attack, some 14 "Kates" swooped at ENTERPRISE. Only nine of them got near enough to unleash torpedoes, and the attack was a washout. But the Jap pilots seem to have been in a *hari-kiri* mood that morning, and one of them flung his plane, torpedo and all, at the SMITH.

At the conn her skipper, Lieutenant Commander Hunter Wood, tried to wrench the ship out of the way. The suicide plane was faster. A stunning crash, a shower of flame, and the "Kate" had blown up on SMITH's forecastle.

At once the destroyer's bow was an inferno. Amidships and aft her gunners continued to blaze away at the Jap planes, but redhot fires spurted from the forecastle and drove men from the bridge. Wood dispatched Chief Quartermaster F. Riduka on the double to the steering-engine room, and raced to the after control station. By telephone he shouted steering orders to Riduka, who deftly ruddered the blazing destroyer through the milling task group and brought her flaming prow within a few yards of SOUTH DAKOTA's quarter.

As SMITH's stem sliced into the big battleship's foamy wake, a fount of spray swept across the destroyer's forecastle. The bow climbed a crest; thumped down into a trough; was buried in white lather. Again it rose, streaming water which sluiced across the deck, drenching hot steel and washing fiery wreckage overside. The destroyer's prow was sizzling like a flatiron when her Commanding Officer swung her away. But the dunking had laved her burns, and her AA guns were banging when the Japs came over again. Her battle casualties—28 dead and 23 wounded—would have been much heavier had she been incinerated. Quick thinking by an astute skipper and skilled work by an adept helmsman had saved another ship.

Over the horizon all hands in Task Force 17 were fighting to save HORNET. During the noon hour cruiser NORTHAMPTON had the damaged carrier in tow, and was hauling her across the water at a painful 3 knots. Mid-afternoon, destroyers RUSSELL and HUGHES stood in to take off the wounded and other carriermen who were ordered to leave the ship. Transfer was made by cargo nets, slings, and breeches buoys. By 1540 some 875 of HORNET's crew had been removed from the fire-blackened carrier.

The effort to save HORNET proved futile. About 1615 a flock of Jap dive-bombers and torpedo planes roared down on the disabled flat-top. They caught her without air cover. Misreading a signal, U.S. cruiser JUNEAU had steamed away to join the ENTERPRISE force—a blunder which left a large hole in HORNET's surface screen. As six torpedo-bombers swept in, NORTHAMPTON cut away from the tow and swerved to dodge a torpedo salvo. HORNET, a sitting duck, was struck by a fatal torpedo. A bomb put a period to this smash. With the sea plunging into her, HORNET listed heavily to starboard, and Captain Charles P. Mason ordered the carrier abandoned.

The Task Force 16 destroyers moved in to pick up the survivors. Captain Mason left the ship about 1730 to board destroyer MUSTIN. After the last of HORNET's men were picked up, MUSTIN was ordered to sink the abandoned vessel.

Standing a mile from the carrier's beam, the destroyer shot eight carefully-aimed torpedoes at the big ship. Only three of them hit. Two made erratic runs and the other three were defectives which probably ran deep or flooded their exploders. And the three which hit failed to sink the damaged carrier!

So destroyer ANDERSON squared away for a try. She fired her torpedoes at a range of less than a mile. Of her eight shots six struck the carrier squarely enough, but the dying ship absorbed the explosions as a feather bed would absorb kicks.

As HORNET remained afloat, the destroyers now resorted to gunfire. Into that punished hulk ANDERSON and MUSTIN fired over 400 rounds of 5-inch shell. The thrashed flat-top burst into flames, and by 2040 she was burning like a haystack. Still she floated, and it was time for the destroyers to go.

For the Japs had sighted the derelict, and Admiral Abe's warships were racing to get in on the funeral. They had hoped to capture the damaged flat-top and knock out the attendant American destroyers, but MUSTIN and ANDERSON did not linger for this denouement. With a Jap destroyer division at their heels, the two American DD's sprinted off in the night. Admiral Abe had only the sour satisfaction of burying the carrier which had placed Jimmie Doolittle's bombers within range of Tokyo.

Jap destroyers AKIGUMO and MAKIGUMO performed the obsequies with four torpedoes. About 0135 in the morning of October 27 HORNET boomed down under the sea.

Although the Santa Cruz engagement had cost the Americans 74 planes against a Japanese loss of about 100, Japanese ship-casualties were considerably lighter than the Navy's. Kondo retired with two carriers and a cruiser severely damaged, and two destroyers damaged. American ships damaged were ENTERPRISE, SOUTH DAKOTA, SAN JUAN, and SMITH; and HORNET and PORTER had been lost.

However, Admirals Nimitz and Halsey expressed satisfaction with the battle Kinkaid's force had put up against heavy odds. The destroyers in the HORNET and ENTERPRISE screens were commended for a stellar effort.

> *As on previous occasions,* Admiral Nimitz observed, *destroyers of both Task Forces exhibited a high order of seamanship in rescuing survivors. The seamanship of the destroyers was particularly notable in fighting fires on the* HORNET *and rescuing personnel.*

Admiral Halsey commented:

> *Throughout the action destroyer commanders handled their ships with assurance and efficiency. The manner in which destroyers were placed alongside* HORNET, *under hazardous conditions, and the promptness shown in rescue of survivors, denoted a high order of both courage and good seamanship which is most gratifying.*

But the undersea menace remained one for destroyer attention. While en route to Nouméa, Kinkaid's force caught a nasty backlash when a submarine alarm threw the ships out of formation and SOUTH DAKOTA and MAHAN collided. The big battleship received an ugly wound, and the destroyer was hurt—another tally, albeit indirectly scored, by the Japanese Submarine Force. And that was in addition to PORTER.

Loss of U.S.S. Porter

Death came for PORTER (Lieutenant Commander D. G. Roberts) at 1003 in the morning of October 26, 1942. Flagship of Captain C. P. Cecil, ComDesRon 5, the destroyer was working in the ENTERPRISE screen when enemy planes attacked Task Force 61 off the Santa Cruz Islands.

By mid-morning HORNET had been hit, and the ENTERPRISE screen was waiting with cocked guns for a glimpse of Jap aircraft. At 0958 a flight of "bogies" was reported about 30 miles away. PORTER's gunners tightened the chinstraps of their helmets and waited grimly.

At 1000 Roberts stopped his ship to pick up the pilot and gunner of an ENTERPRISE plane which had been shot down close aboard. The destroyermen were engaged in this rescue act when (time: 1002) a torpedo rushed through the sea 50 yards ahead of the ship. The alarm sent a shock through the destroyer. Then, before she could make an evasive swing, a second torpedo was sighted, lunging at the ship's port beam.

An ENTERPRISE pilot saw the deadly wake and came down in a power dive, lacing the water with machine-gun lead in an attempt to blast the war head. The "fish" beat the gun. Crashing into PORTER amidships, the torpedo exploded with a blast that wiped out both firerooms and instantly killed 11 destroyermen. PORTER staggered to a halt with steam pouring out of her wrecked boilers and oil spewing from her side.

At 1015 the enemy planes attacked ENTERPRISE. PORTER's gunners flailed at the flying "meatballs" while her damage-controlmen battled chaos below decks. Meantime, destroyer SHAW (Commander Wilber G. Jones), maneuvering to screen her disabled sister, made sonar contact with the submarine. Dropping depth charges, SHAW attacked furiously. But the undersea killer escaped.

At 1055 PORTER's predicament was seen as hopeless, and SHAW was ordered alongside to take off her crew. Circling away, SHAW then pumped gunfire into the half-sunk ship to speed her journey to the bottom. She took her dead down with her. Four of the nine men who had been wounded in the torpedo blast subsequently died.

The submarine responsible for this sinking was the I-21. But the score was soon to be evened as American destroyers downed one of the I-21's sisters.

Southard Kills I-172

It was early in the morning of November 10, 1942, and the I-172 was enjoying a breather on the surface near Cape Recherché, San Cristobal. The fresh night air was invigorating, and the batteries were charging beautifully, and wrist watches made in Japan timed the hour as 0230. Perched atop the conning tower, the Jap lookouts scanned the dark seascape. Perhaps the lookouts were sleepy. At any rate the night was suddenly smashed by a flash of flame, a crescendo whistle, and the blast of an exploding salvo. I-172 was under fire.

The sub had been sighted at 0231 by the U.S.S. SOUTHARD, an old "four-stacker" which had been pressed into South Pacific service as a minesweeper. Skippered by Lieutenant Commander J. G. Tennent, III, the ex-DD was en route to Aola Bay, Guadalcanal, with ammunition and rations for a Marine Raider Battalion.

WHEN SOUTHARD opened fire, the enemy sub made haste to submerge. But the old destroyer went after the target with sweeping sonar gear, and soon picked up the contact. At 0242 she attacked with depth charges.

Contact was lost in the turmoil; SOUTHARD was still searching at daybreak. At 0607 her "pinging" again found the sub, and once more she treated the target to depth charges. The treatment had to be repeated until SOUTHARD had delivered six attacks. Her sixth attack, a barrage of nine charges, brought I-172 to the surface, stern first.

Lieutenant Commander Tennent maneuvered SOUTHARD in for the kill. At 1003 the submarine's conning tower heaved up, and the destroyermen opened fire at 2,000 yards. A salvo crashed into the conning tower; the I-boat rolled at the blast, then thrust her bow toward the sky and plunged to the bottom for all time.

The Battle of Guadalcanal (November 13)

The three-day naval engagement, which came to be called the Battle of Guadalcanal, began on Friday, November 13, 1942. Friday the 13th. For the DesPac Force that was truly an unlucky day. Before it was two hours old, four American destroyers were sunk in combat, with heavy loss of life, and three were barbarously damaged. Destroyermen would always remember this conflict as perhaps the hottest surface action ever fought by destroyers..

Driven rabid by their inability to wipe out the American front on Guadalcanal, the Japanese War Lords had planned a supreme effort to regain the island.

On October 30 the U.S. cruiser ATLANTA and destroyers AARON WARD, BENHAM, FLETCHER, and LARDNER had arrived at Lunga Roads with a convoy carrying heavy artillery for the Marines. The DD's lingered in the area long enough to lend fire-support to a Marine drive on Point Cruz. Destroyers SHAW and CONYNGHAM steamed into this effort on the morning of November 2. Between them the two hurled 803 rounds of 5-inch shell at Jap gun positions in the jungles bearding the mouth of the Umasani River.

Five days later destroyer LANSDOWNE arrived at the "Cactus" front with 90 tons of ammunition for Vandegrift's troops. She joined a hunt for a Jap submarine which had torpedoed a Navy cargo ship off Lunga Point that day, but the I-boat got away.

Meanwhile, Halsey received word that Japanese war-shipping was concentrating at Truk, at Rabaul, and at various points in the upper Solomons. The shipping off Buin, Bougainville, and the Bismarcks was not for any run-of-the-mill "Tokyo Express." Something big was coming down the "Slot." And something bigger was coming down from Truk. To meet the threat some 6,000 additional Army troops and Marines were dispatched "special delivery" from Espiritu Santo and Nouméa to Guadalcanal. Admiral R. K. Turner's Amphibious Force warships did the delivering.

The convoy moved in two contingents. The first contingent was composed of three attack cargo ships under escort of a force commanded by Rear Admiral Norman Scott. This force consisted of flag cruiser ATLANTA, and the destroyers AARON WARD, FLETCHER, LARDNER, and MCCALLA, under Captain R. G. Tobin, ComDesRon 12, in AARON WARD. The contingent left Espiritu Santo on November 9 and reached Lunga Roads on the 11th.

The second contingent, commanded by Admiral Turner, contained four transports, including flagship MCCAWLEY, under escort of a task group composed of two cruisers and three destroyers. These ships left Nouméa on the 8th. When it arrived off San Cristobal Island on the 11th the convoy was joined by three more cruisers and five destroyers. All of the warships with Turner's contingent were units of Task Group 67.4, a Support Group under command of Rear Admiral Daniel J. Callaghan in flag cruiser SAN FRANCISCO. (The roster of Callaghan's Support Group is listed on page 190.)

When Scott's contingent reached Lunga Point it was promptly assailed by enemy dive-bombers. American fighters zoomed up from Henderson Field to intercept, and the Jap planes were able to do little damage. One attack-cargoman was injured. She was escorted back to Espiritu by destroyer LARDNER.

Arriving at Lunga Point on the 12th, Turner's contingent made haste to unload. Air and submarine alarms hurried the proceedings. At 1317 enemy aircraft were reported in the offing, and Turner led his ships out into Savo Sound where there was room for evasive maneuvering. The attacking Japs ran into American fighter planes and a storm of flak from seagoing AA batteries. Nearly all of the 25 Jap planes which struck at Turner's vessels were gunned down.

However, destroyer BUCHANAN (Commander R. E.

Wilson) took such a beating from friendly anti-aircraft fire that she had to be sent out of the battle area. And a Jap bomber, winged by gunfire from McCawley, made a suicide crash into cruiser San Francisco. The crash doused the deck with blazing gasoline, wrecked a gun director and the ship's fire-control radar, and killed 30 cruisermen.

This air assault on Turner's force was only a curtain raiser to the onslaught that was coming. Coming down from Truk and points north were Jap battleships Hiei and Kirishima, Jap light cruiser Nagara, and 14 of the Emperor's destroyers. Poised to come down the "Slot" from the Bismarck-Bougainville area was a group of ten transports and 12 destroyers. In the backfield to the north of the Solomons were Jap carriers Hiyo and Junyo. And there were more where these came from.

Turner knew his forces in Savo Sound were heavily outweighed and outnumbered. Compelled to cope with impossible odds, he sent his convoy steaming away out of danger.

At that critical hour the Enterprise force—the "Big E" had just returned after rush repairs—with battleships Washington and South Dakota was steaming northward from Nouméa. But these big guns were still a day away. Yet something had to be done to prevent a blasting of Henderson Field by the oncoming enemy battleships. To Callaghan's Support Group fell the defense of Guadalcanal.

In the twilight of November 12 Turner led his transports eastward, back toward Espiritu Santo. His ships were to be escorted to Espiritu by destroyers Buchanan (damaged), Shaw and McCalla (low on fuel), and old-timers Southard and Hovey (minesweepers). Callaghan's warships screened the convoy through Lengo Channel, then turned back to re-enter Savo Sound and cover the approaches to Lunga Point. The opening moves of this back-to-the-wall defense were left up to Admiral Callaghan.

The odds against Callaghan's force were appallingly long. The Japanese Striking Force which was advancing on Savo Sound included battleships Hiei and Kirishima, light cruiser Nagara, and 14 DD's. Somewhere behind it were two aircraft carriers, and up the "Slot" was a large transport group containing 12 DD's.

Against the Jap Striking Force and its potential reinforcements, the American force included heavy cruisers San Francisco (flagship) and Portland; light cruiser Helena, anti-aircraft (AA) cruisers Juneau and Atlanta, and eight DD's. The destroyers are listed in the next column.

Two heavy cruisers and three light cruisers against two battleships and a light cruiser. Eight destroyers against 14. So stood the American Support Group against the Japanese Striking Force. It was going to be a battle in which brains would have to make up for brawn.

Destroyers in

TASK GROUP 67.4

SUPPORT GROUP

Aaron Ward	*Comdr. O. F. Gregor*
	Flying the pennant of Capt. R. G. Tobin, COMDESRON 12
Barton	*Lt. Comdr. D. H. Fox*
Monssen	*Lt. Comdr. C. E. McCombs*
Fletcher	*Comdr. W. M. Cole*
Cushing	*Lt. Comdr. E. N. Parker*
	Flying the pennant of Comdr. T. M. Stokes, COMDESDIV 10
Laffey	*Lt. Comdr. W. E. Hank*
Sterett	*Comdr. J. G. Coward*
O'Bannon	*Comdr. E. R. Wilkinson*

Steaming westward through Lengo Channel in total darkness, the Support Group was strung out in a long serpentine column. In the van were destroyers Cushing, Laffey, Sterett, and O'Bannon. They were followed by cruisers Atlanta, San Francisco, Portland, Helena, and Juneau, in that order. Destroyers Aaron Ward, Barton, Monssen, and Fletcher brought up the rear. This sort of column had been favorably employed by Admiral Scott in the Battle of Cape Esperance. But on the present occasion the alignment, in respect to radar work, could have been better. Three cruisers and two destroyers which carried the new SG surface radar had been given rear positions. And some critics considered that the destroyers in the rear were positioned too far astern to aid the van in the event of a surprise encounter.

In command of the Japanese Striking Force, Vice Admiral Hiroaki Abe himself committed one or two errors in judgment on the eve of battle. He had been informed that a group of American warships were in the vicinity of Lunga Point, but he chose to assume that these men-of-war had retired eastward at sundown. And since his mission was to destroy Henderson Field, he loaded his guns with bombardment ammunition for that purpose and single-mindedly pressed forward into Savo Sound.

Early in the morning on Friday, November 13—a "Black Friday"—Callaghan's column was off Lunga Roads. Simultaneously the Japanese Striking Force steamed into the passage south of Savo Island. Americans and Japs were driving through the night on what amounted to a collision course.

At 0124 cruiser HELENA made radar contact with the enemy at 27,000 yards. Three minutes later Admiral Callaghan ordered his column to make a starboard turn which headed it straight for the enemy. In the meantime, destroyer O'BANNON made contact, and her skipper reported it over the TBS. As the range closed swiftly, the American TBS system became jammed with calls—a babel of range-and-bearing data, tactical orders, and requests for information. Once again the American communications apparatus was haywire, and the ships were plunged into battle with voice radios shouting in confusion.

Fortunately the Jap radiomen did not tune into this TBS uproar. However, the Imperial crews were at battle stations, the gunners ready to shoot the works at any target which came along. Henderson Field was in mind, but the lookouts had a wary eye on the black seascape.

Division Commander Stokes in lead destroyer CUSHING was also straining his eyes on the darkness ahead. When HELENA's contact report reached him, Callaghan had swung his column on a northward course, and the American ships were heading toward the center of "Ironbottom Bay." At 0141 Stokes suddenly sighted two Jap destroyers silhouetted in the starshine. They were I.J.N. YUDACHI and HARUSAME, screening ahead of Abe's battleship group. They were cutting directly across CUSHING's bow at a scant range of 3,000 yards.

CUSHING immediately radioed the word, and her skipper ordered a left turn to avoid headlong collision with the foe and to bring torpedo tubes to bear. The abrupt turn threw the rest of the van out of line, and cruiser ATLANTA had to sheer hard left to avoid ramming the turning DD's.

Callaghan's voice crackled over the TBS,

WHAT ARE YOU DOING

ATLANTA's captain answered,

AVOIDING OUR OWN DESTROYERS

Again the TBS circuit was jammed with inquiries from the other American ships—Where were the targets?—Should they open fire? While this medley of voices clogged the air waves, the two Jap destroyers snapped the word to Abe's flagship, and the Jap admiral squared away for action. Commander Stokes finally broke into the TBS clamor with a request to open torpedo fire.

Stokes was granted permission, but the word came too late. Destroyers YUDACHI and HARUSAME had not waited for this delayed-action order, and they were now beyond CUSHING's range. Meantime, Abe's heavy ships had pushed forward. And the other American captains were awaiting the firing order. From Callaghan the answer finally came at 0145, "Stand by to open fire!" Five tense minutes ticked by, Then, at 0150, a Jap searchlight flung its ray across the water and focussed squarely on cruiser ATLANTA.

With the range at 1,600 yards, the American cruiser opened fire. The Japs answered with a rain of salvos that were murderously accurate. Landing on ATLANTA's bridge, a heavy shell exploded with a blast that killed Admiral Norman Scott and felled the sailors around him right and left. Only one member of his staff survived this homicidal blow.

At this crucial moment Admiral Callaghan issued the order, *"Odd ships commence fire to starboard, even ships to port!"* Unfortunately some of the ships could not find targets on the designated hand, and the order did not allow for selective firing on vessels which were within range.

Results were chaotic. The American column ploughed headlong into the Japanese formation; both the American and the Japanese formations broke completely. All chance for a battle of maneuver went with the wind. What ensued was a ship-against-ship melee on the order of the Battle of Santiago—the kind of free-for-all described by Theodore Roosevelt as a "captain's fight."

It was a knockdown and dragout battle in every sense of the term—a conflict as wild as the Savo Island fray.

ATLANTA, the target for a sledgehammer fire from the Japs, was the first American ship battered out of action. Shortly after Admiral Scott was killed the ship was struck by one or more Japanese torpedoes. The blast almost heaved her out of the water. Listing and afire, she stumbled to a halt, ruinously damaged.

But the first American ship to go down was the destroyer BARTON.

Loss of U.S.S. Barton

BARTON (Lieutenant Commander D. H. Fox) was one of the rear destroyers in the American column which floundered into the Japanese formation off Savo Island at 0145 in that morning of November 13, 1942.

Her actions in the ensuing battle cannot be recorded with detail, for the column formation broke; it was every ship for herself, and BARTON remained in combat for a brief seven minutes. The doom which overtook her struck with terrible suddenness, and she was gone with most of her crew as though in a flash, leaving in her wake little more than the memory of a good ship manned by brave destroyermen.

At 0148 she heard the baffling order, "Odd-numbered ships fire to starboard, even-numbered ships fire to port." Simultaneously, searchlights blazed from

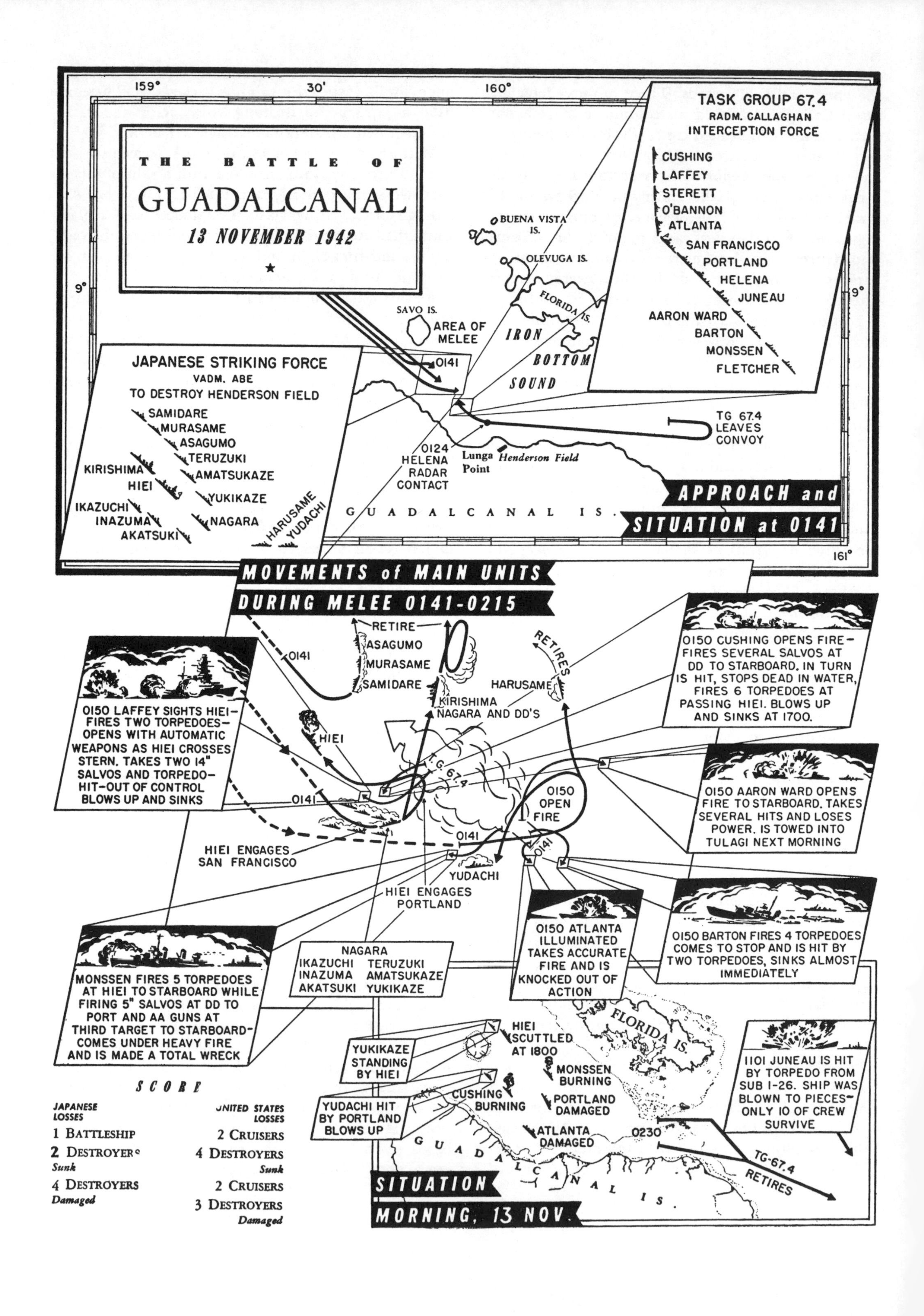
THE BATTLE OF
GUADALCANAL
13 NOVEMBER 1942
159°
30'
160°
161°
9°
TASK GROUP 67.4
RADM. CALLAGHAN
INTERCEPTION FORCE
CUSHING
LAFFEY
STERETT
O'BANNON
ATLANTA
SAN FRANCISCO
PORTLAND
HELENA
JUNEAU
AARON WARD
BARTON
MONSSEN
FLETCHER
BUENA VISTA IS.
OLEVUGA IS.
FLORIDA IS.
SAVO IS.
AREA OF MELEE
IRON BOTTOM SOUND
0141
JAPANESE STRIKING FORCE
VADM. ABE
TO DESTROY HENDERSON FIELD
SAMIDARE
MURASAME
ASAGUMO
TERUZUKI
KIRISHIMA
AMATSUKAZE
HIEI
YUKIKAZE
IKAZUCHI
INAZUMA
NAGARA
AKATSUKI
HARUSAME
YUDACHI
TG 67.4 LEAVES CONVOY
0124 HELENA RADAR CONTACT
Lunga Point
Henderson Field
GUADALCANAL IS.
APPROACH and SITUATION at 0141
MOVEMENTS of MAIN UNITS DURING MELEE 0141-0215
RETIRE
ASAGUMO
MURASAME
SAMIDARE
0141
RETIRES
HARUSAME
KIRISHIMA
NAGARA AND DD'S
HIEI
T.G. 67.4
0150 OPEN FIRE
0141
HIEI ENGAGES SAN FRANCISCO
YUDACHI
HIEI ENGAGES PORTLAND
0150 LAFFEY SIGHTS HIEI-FIRES TWO TORPEDOES-OPENS WITH AUTOMATIC WEAPONS AS HIEI CROSSES STERN. TAKES TWO 14" SALVOS AND TORPEDO-HIT-OUT OF CONTROL BLOWS UP AND SINKS
0150 CUSHING OPENS FIRE-FIRES SEVERAL SALVOS AT DD TO STARBOARD. IN TURN IS HIT, STOPS DEAD IN WATER, FIRES 6 TORPEDOES AT PASSING HIEI. BLOWS UP AND SINKS AT 1700.
0150 AARON WARD OPENS FIRE TO STARBOARD. TAKES SEVERAL HITS AND LOSES POWER. IS TOWED INTO TULAGI NEXT MORNING
0150 ATLANTA ILLUMINATED TAKES ACCURATE FIRE AND IS KNOCKED OUT OF ACTION
0150 BARTON FIRES 4 TORPEDOES COMES TO STOP AND IS HIT BY TWO TORPEDOES, SINKS ALMOST IMMEDIATELY
MONSSEN FIRES 5 TORPEDOES AT HIEI TO STARBOARD WHILE FIRING 5" SALVOS AT DD TO PORT AND AA GUNS AT THIRD TARGET TO STARBOARD-COMES UNDER HEAVY FIRE AND IS MADE A TOTAL WRECK
NAGARA
IKAZUCHI TERUZUKI
INAZUMA AMATSUKAZE
AKATSUKI YUKIKAZE
HIEI SCUTTLED AT 1800
YUKIKAZE STANDING BY HIEI
MONSSEN BURNING
CUSHING BURNING
PORTLAND DAMAGED
YUDACHI HIT BY PORTLAND BLOWS UP
ATLANTA DAMAGED
FLORIDA IS.
1101 JUNEAU IS HIT BY TORPEDO FROM SUB I-26. SHIP WAS BLOWN TO PIECES-ONLY 10 OF CREW SURVIVE
0230
TG-67.4 RETIRES
GUADALCANAL IS.
SITUATION MORNING, 13 NOV.
SCORE
JAPANESE LOSSES
1 BATTLESHIP
2 DESTROYERS
Sunk
4 DESTROYERS
Damaged
UNITED STATES LOSSES
2 CRUISERS
4 DESTROYERS
Sunk
2 CRUISERS
3 DESTROYERS
Damaged

near-by enemy vessels, and BARTON pitched in as best she could. She launched four port torpedoes at a fast-moving target, and made an abrupt stop to avoid collision. As her propellers were churning, bringing her to a halt, she was struck by two torpedoes.

The first torpedo blasted BARTON's forward fire-room. Hitting her a split second later, the second torpedo smashed into the forward engine-room. Torn in two, the ship went down almost instantly, drowning 90 per cent of her crew.

Lost with the ship was her captain, Lieutenant Commander D. H. Fox.

Destroyers Versus Battleship

Japanese Admiral Abe sent battleship HIEI booming southeastward toward the center of Savo Sound. KIRISHIMA, some 800 yards on the port quarter, came on firing. With his formation gone helterskelter, Admiral Abe pushed forward. As his flagship advanced he was astounded to discover she was under destroyer fire. At first he could not believe it, but such was the case. U.S. destroyers CUSHING, LAFFEY, STERETT, and O'BANNON were launching individual attacks on the bellowing battleship. The battleship struck back in berserk fury.

HIEI was an old-timer, vintage of 1916, but she had been designed by a British naval architect who knew how to build a dreadnaught. Like her companion, KIRISHIMA, she weighed 31,000 tons, carried thick armor, and packed 14-inch guns in her turrets. On the occasion in question, HIEI, like the other ships in Abe's force, had been caught with bombardment ammunition in the guns and on the hoists. But the Admiral made haste to shift to armor-piercing shells. And whatever the character of this battleship's slugs, they were heavy enough to down a destroyer.

A destroyer's chances against any battleship are somewhat comparable to those of a pistolman armed with a .22 against a foe armed with an elephant rifle. A quick pistol shot at close range might kill the larger adversary if it hit him in a vital spot, but almost any hit at all from an elephant gun would fell the pistolman. The destroyermen knew their chances. Their best chance lay in torpedo fire, and they maneuvered desperately to hit the battlewagon with "fish."

CUSHING and LAFFEY paid for valor with their lives.

Loss of U.S.S. Cushing

Bearing one of the Navy's proudest names, the U.S.S. CUSHING, van destroyer in the American column, was perhaps the first ship to strike the enemy in the Battle of Guadalcanal. She went in with her guns going, and they were going when she went out.

Deprived of a chance to hit the Jap detroyers she had sighted at 0141, CUSHING's gunners were bursting with impatience when the order to open fire finally came. It was then too late to torpedo the targets she had lined up, but by that time targets were everywhere in the offing, and she fired several fast salvos at another Jap destroyer glimpsed to starboard.

Then the melee broke around her, and the night became livid with gun flashes, the splattering incandescence of starshells, and the huge twinkle of explosions. Gusts of orange fire flared from torpedo hits, and red smoke billowed from burning hulls.

Several shells struck CUSHING amidships, and the blasting knocked out her power lines and slowed her to a crawl. Her captain, Lieutenant Commander E. N. Parker, conned her as best he could, the helmsman steering by hand. On the bridge Division Commander T. M. Stokes was trying to make order out of chaos and keep tabs on his scattered van division.

At 0154 Parker sighted the Japanese battleship HIEI looming up on the port beam. Parker swung his destroyer to the right to unleash a torpedo salvo. Shellfire from American cruisers and destroyers was lacing the Jap battlewagon, and she was plunging forward with thundering turret guns and growing larger as she came, like an expanding closeup on a movie screen. By the time CUSHING made her slow-motion turn, I.J.N. HIEI was only 1,000 yards away.

Parker gave the order, and six torpedoes, fired by local control, went leaping at the monster target. Three of the "fish" seemed to hit the bull's-eye; if they did, it was with tack-hammer thumps. They may have exploded prematurely. But HIEI's lookouts must have seen them coming, for the big ship swung her prow to the left and lumbered westward, disappearing in the smoke-haze.

At this juncture CUSHING, having steadily lost way, drifted to a stop and stood dead in the water, paralyzed. In dire jeopardy, with enemy ships rushing through the dark on either hand and Jap and American shells falling close aboard, the destroyermen struggled desperately to recover propulsion. Then, as the ship remained glued to the spot, an enemy searchlight struck her in the face.

An instant later CUSHING was rocked by a deluge of enemy shells. Pounded by hit after hit, her batteries were uprooted, her bridge was battered, her superstructure was torn to scrap. Flames sprang out of the wreckage. Successive hits tossed gear and machinery skyward. At 0220 Lieutenant Commander Parker ordered the burning vessel abandoned. The shells were still hailing down as the CUSHING men went overside.

Parker remained on board with a few last-standers

until 0315, but nothing could be done to save the ship. By that time the conflagration had eaten its way below the decks, and the power plant was ruined.

Looking back across the water, the survivors saw CUSHING drift away in a cloud of fire and bright smoke. In that inferno six officers and some 53 men were lost. Of the survivors who were picked up, 56 had been wounded, and ten of the wounded had received fatal injuries. CUSHING's crew had suffered severe punishment.

The destroyer burned throughout the morning, and she remained afloat, a redhot stove in a tide of debris, until late that afternoon. About 1700 the heat reached her magazines, and she blew up and sank.

Admiral Halsey wrote her obituary.

The destruction of the CUSHING *in no way reflects discredit on her gallant commander or the officers and men that fought her. The grim determination to effect maximum damage to enemy vessels against great odds is an inspiration to every one of us. Securing three torpedo hits on a battleship while being subjected to damaging gunfire, clearly points out the superb initiative and discipline of officers and crew of this ship.*

Unfortunately the hits in reference were illusory. But the initiative and discipline were all wool and a yard wide.

Loss of U.S.S. Laffey

In the group of van destroyers leading the American column into the Battle of Guadalcanal, the U.S.S. LAFFEY was the second ship in line. She was steaming in CUSHING's wake when the flag destroyer sighted the enemy, and she followed CUSHING's abrupt left turn into battle.

About the same time that CUSHING sighted the battleship HIEI, LAFFEY's lookouts saw the Jap behemoth ploughing up out of the night. White foam curled at the battleship's prow and her Oriental clipper bow towered against the stars like a cliff—an overhanging cliff advancing on LAFFEY with the speed of an avalanche.

LAFFEY's skipper ordered an abrupt swing which was made just in time to avert a collision. As the destroyer swung, two torpedoes were unleashed at the Japanese battlewagon. Both "fish" were seen to hit—and leap from the water at the battleship's bulge like playful bass. Fired at very close range, they had not had time to arm.

THE HIEI crossed LAFFEY's stern almost within pistol shot. Gritting their teeth, the destroyer gunners lashed at the great ship's bridge with all weapons that could bear. Ropes of 20 mm. and 1.1-inch fire flogged the Japanese pagoda, perhaps killing some of Admiral Abe's sailors and smashing some of HIEI's glass.

The battleship answered with a roar. Two 14-inch salvos smote LAFFEY, and almost simultaneously she was struck in the stern by a torpedo. The big shells demolished LAFFEY's power plant; the torpedo blast flooded her after compartments. Out of control, listing, she lay like a trampled basket in the middle of a crowded street. As a pillar of flame surged up amidships, her captain gave the command, *"Abandon ship!"*

The LAFFEY men went overside in good order. But as the survivors took their places on the rafts and the swimmers were adjusting kapok jackets, the destroyer's fantail with its depth charges blew up like a monstrous bomb. Showered with fire and wreckage, many of the survivors in the water were killed. The ruptured vessel sank immediately, pulling others of the crew down with her.

LAFFEY's casualties were excruciatingly heavy; nearly all of her crew were lost. Her captain, Lieutenant Commander W. E. Hank, went down with the destroyer. For his ship's courageous assault on Japanese battleship HIEI, he was posthumously awarded the Navy Cross.

Sterett and O'Bannon Versus Battleship Hiei

Destroyer STERETT, third in line in the van group, was one of the odd-numbered ships in the American column. Her captain, Commander J. G. Coward, strove to obey Admiral Callaghan's firing order, and STERETT's guns opened up on a Japanese warship glimpsed to starboard, range 4,000 yards.

Off to port destroyers CUSHING and LAFFEY were engaged in a death struggle with the mighty HIEI. But STERETT's skipper had his orders, and he kept up a rapid starboard fire for at least three minutes. Then a spate of Jap shells struck STERETT on the port side aft, wrecking her steering gear. A moment later a shell struck her foremast, bringing down her radar in a sparrow's-nest jumble. Momentarily out of control, the damaged ship swerved drunkenly. Only quick work on the part of destroyer O'BANNON, maneuvering astern of STERETT, prevented a collision.

Steering by means of the engines, Coward succeeded in bringing his ship into position for a torpedo attack on the HIEI. At a close range of 2,000 yards STERETT fired four torpedoes at the leviathan. Maybe they missed, or maybe they failed to arm and misfired.

While STERETT was thus striking at the Jap battlewagon, O'BANNON, sheering off to avoid Coward's injured destroyer, came right under the eye of the enemy Goliath. Commander E. R. Wilkinson promptly ordered his O'BANNON gunners to shoot the works at the HIEI. She was no more than 1,200 yards on the port bow when the destroyer opened fire.

Valiantly the 5-inchers blazed at the enormous target. And the Japanese giant was so close to little O'BANNON that her bellowing turret guns could not be depressed to draw a bead on the barking destroyer. For her part O'BANNON was shooting at the broad side of a barn. Shellfire spattered the great ship's pagoda, lighting her up like a carnival afloat. Then, as the destroyer gunners were pumping it in, a bewildering command came from Admiral Callaghan:

CEASE FIRING OWN SHIPS

Believing that the SAN FRANCISCO was mistakenly firing into the ATLANTA, Admiral Callaghan had ordered the cease fire presumably only for that ship; but whether or not this order had been intended for the flagship alone, it went out over TBS to all ships of the Force.

Some of the American ships received the word, some of them didn't. With HIEI's 14-inchers tearing through the air over his ship, Wilkinson ordered his gunners to hold their fire. But the Jap battleship was sliding by. Snapping into action, Wilkinson swung O'BANNON to bring her torpedo batteries to bear, and unleashed two "fish" at the HIEI. The wakes ribboned straight for the mark, but apparently the "fish" ran deep or failed to explode. However, multiple shell-hits were striking the Jap battleship, and flags of flame were flying from HIEI's superstructure when O'BANNON turned away to avoid collision with destroyer LAFFEY, lying helpless in her path.

O'BANNON's sailors flung life-jackets to the LAFFEY men as Wilkinson swung his ship hard over to steer clear of the sinking destroyer. The shout "Torpedo!" was raised by lookouts who sighted sizzling wakes ahead, and O'BANNON made another radical turn. Seconds later a huge undersea blast shook the maneuvering destroyer, jarred her engines, and jolted her electrical equipment. Across the water, LAFFEY had blown up.

Around O'BANNON all of Savo Sound seemed to be blowing up too. Unable to distinguish one ship from another, Wilkinson headed his destroyer southeastward in an effort to get his bearings and to identify enemy targets. Then, to intercept enemy transports which might have slipped in behind the warship group, he sent O'BANNON scouting toward the coast of Guadalcanal. So O'BANNON steamed out of the holocaust—one of the war's few destroyers to survive a pitched battle with a battleship.

Admiral Halsey was to note:

> *The* O'BANNON *gave an excellent account of herself, the ship was exceptionally well handled under the most trying conditions. The employment of both the 5-inch and torpedo batteries left little to be desired.*

STERETT—another DAVID—took a severe beating after her round with HIEI. With radar shot away and steering gear out of commission, she was left to fight her way through a crowd of HIEI's screen destroyers.

They ganged up on her as she limped out of the battle with the 31,000-tonner. At 0200 one of the Jap DD's hove up on STERETT's starboard bow. Commander Coward (no name for this skipper!) maneuvered for a torpedo attack on this new enemy—two shots at 1,000 yards. In return, his ship was subjected to a tempestuous shelling which knocked out all but two of her guns, set her ready-service powder afire, and turned her superstructure into an incinerator.

But her engines were pounding steadily, and by sporadic slowdowns to keep the wind from fanning the flames and flank-speed sprints to get the ship out of enemy range, Commander Coward brought her into the clear.

"Another example of the fighting spirit of the men in our destroyer force," Admiral Halsey commented. *"Only after having all offensive armament except forward 5-inch guns put out of action, and being completely ablaze aft, did the* STERETT *retire. Fire control and damage control* (exhibited by STERETT) *are considered outstanding."*

So STERETT, too, lived to tell about the battle with HIEI. But, heading for Lengo Channel, she left behind her two stricken companions—LAFFEY on the bottom, and CUSHING wrapped in a shroud of flames. Then, limping southeastward, she passed another victim of HIEI's vengeance, another destroyer which had dared the wrath of the Japanese battleship.

The destroyer was riddled, exploding in a crimson haze of fire—the U.S.S. MONSSEN in her death throes.

Loss of U.S.S. MONSSEN

Destroyer MONSSEN (Lieutenant Commander C. E. McCombs) had been next to last ship in the American column. She was directly astern of the BARTON when that destroyer, first to go down in the pellmell battle, was fatally torpedoed.

Searchlights were blazing, shells were crashing, and BARTON was going down before MONSSEN could grasp the situation. To make matters worse, if that were possible, MONSSEN's fire-control radar had been damaged during the previous day's air attack; she had to depend on vision and radio data for fire-control.

Then BARTON was torpedoed, and MONSSEN herself was under fire. A torpedo wake whisked through the water and passed under her keel. Maneuvering at high speed to evade, McCombs sent his ship racing ahead. Tragically enough, she plowed through a drift of flotsam from BARTON, killing unseen swimmers. Everywhere the darkness was exploding, and the flashes of fire and livid shell bursts created a kaleidoscopic play of glare and shadow that frustrated the lookouts.

But HIEI's silhouette was now plainly in view on MONSSEN's bow, about 4,000 yards to starboard. McCombs swung the destroyer, and five torpedoes were fired at the looming battlewagon. Another spread of five was launched at a target on MONSSEN's beam. Simultaneously her gunners were hurling 5-inch salvos at enemy ships dimly seen to port, and her 20 mm. batteries were flailing at a destroyer no more than a quarter mile distant to starboard.

Suddenly a swarm of starshells burst over MONSSEN, bathing her with brilliant light. Believing they had been fired by a friendly vessel which had fallen out of column, Commander McCombs flashed MONSSEN's recognition signals. Instantly a pair of searchlights fastened upon the destroyer. Within a matter of seconds she was reeling under a torrent of Japanese shells. A spread of torpedoes raced at her. The torpedoes missed, but the shells slammed home with deadly accuracy.

The destroyer's deck was torn up and her bridge was torn down. Shells crashed into her firerooms and engine-rooms. They wrecked her power lines and demolished her pumps. In the hurricane of explosions, 5-inchers were blown from their mountings, machine-guns were flung over the stacks, torpedo batteries were shattered, and depth charges were sent flying like bean cans. Altogether some 37 shells, at least three of them major caliber, struck the destroyer. When the firing subsided she was a total wreck, enveloped in searing flames.

The ship was abandoned at 0220. Trapped on the mangled bridge, the Commanding Officer and others of the conning party were compelled to leap overside from the rail. All were seriously injured.

Fighting their way out of the wreckage topside and the hell below, other officers and bluejackets escaped. But all too few survived this ship-slaughter. At least 130 of her crew perished in the MONSSEN.

Like CUSHING to the west of her, MONSSEN, a burning hulk, remained afloat. Clinging to life rafts and debris, the survivors in the water watched the flames chew their way through the abandoned ship. Then someone heard a cry for help. There were living men in that fiery ruin!

The cry reached across the water like an appealing hand. And it was grasped by a Bos'n's Mate and two seamen who contrived to put their raft alongside the ship at daylight. By that time the vessel was a crematorium. Any moment it might burst like a detonated mine, or make a sudden plunge under the water which boiled and steamed around its blistered hull. But men were trapped in the interior of that furnace. And C. C. Storey, Boatswain's Mate Second, and L. F. Spurgeon, Gunner's Mate Second, and J. G. Hughes, Fireman First, boarded the death-ship to get them.

Storey, Spurgeon, and Hughes—the Navy would remember their names. Would remember how they scaled the side of that oven-hot ship; how they clawed into the wreckage, and disappeared in a gulf of smoke. And how, after a wait that seemed beyond hope, they emerged from the gulf, bringing with them eight men—eight wounded shipmates who had been fastened in a compartment down below. No finer action was performed in the crucible of Savo Sound.

The wounded men and their valiant rescuers got away with little time to spare. About noon of that day the MONSSEN blew up and sank.

Damaging of Aaron Ward

Flagship of Captain R. G. Tobin, ComDesRon 12, AARON WARD, leading the rear destroyers, was directly astern of light cruiser JUNEAU in the American column. When the explosive storm broke around cruiser ATLANTA and Callaghan's column fell out of formation, Tobin tried desperately to unravel the tactical tangle. But he was soon aware that it was every man-of-war for herself, and the devil take the hindmost. Not to let his ship be taken hindmost, AARON WARD's skipper, Commander O. F. Gregor, headed at best speed for the battle's front.

AARON WARD opened fire on a target 7,000 yards on her starboard bow. On the tenth round she had to check fire as American cruisers steamed between her and the target. One of the cruisers—perhaps HELENA—came within a rope's throw of being rammed. By backing engines at full power, Gregor slowed his destroyer in time to prevent a crash.

For the next few minutes the destroyer groped for targets. Just as she lined one up, cruiser SAN FRANCISCO intervened. Then Japanese recognition signals glimmered from a vessel on AARON WARD's starboard bow. She fired at this self-identified target until the vessel obliged by blowing up. At least it seemed to blow up. Everywhere the night was splashed with enormous flares; whether they were Japanese, American, or illusory, it was impossible to determine.

Gregor now directed his ship's fire on enemy searchlights. In the bedlam astern, BARTON had been blasted to the bottom and MONSSEN was under fire. Far up ahead, CUSHING and LAFFEY, STERETT and O'BANNON were banging at HIEI in hopeless duel.

Fletcher—"tail-end Charlie" of the erstwhile American column—was off somewhere on her own. Callaghan's formation was now so disintegrated, and communications so broken down, that Squadron Commander Tobin was unable to cooperate with the cruisers. He let Aaron Ward have her head, and she went plunging into the vortex of the battle with blazing guns.

A sudden hit demolished her director, and her 5-inchers shifted to local control. Then a whistling cluster of projectiles struck Aaron Ward. The shells smashed her rangefinder, chopped down her radar antennae, blew out her searchlights, cut telephone cables, and wrecked her radar room. A lobbing shot sheared off her foremast above the stay ring. Another drilled her hull below the waterline. Altogether she took nine solid hits that finally brought the ship to a halt at 0235 with a flooded engine-room. For the rest of the night she wallowed, half-paralyzed, while her engineers labored in a desperate effort to muster steam. Twice she got under way, only to lose power after crawling a short distance.

After daybreak the tug Bobolink took the crippled ship in tow and headed for Tulagi. The battleship Hiei made a final effort to kill the escaping destroyer. But Aaron Ward, with 12 of her crew dead, three dying, and 57 wounded, deserved to escape. As Admiral Halsey stated:

> *The* Aaron Ward *gave another fine example of the fighting spirit of the men of our destroyer force. Though hit nine times by both major and medium caliber shells which caused extensive damage she nevertheless avoided total destruction by the apparently superhuman efforts of all hands. The superb performance of the engineers' force in effecting temporary repairs so that the ship could move away from under the guns of the enemy battleship largely contributed to saving the ship.*

And by that time Hiei herself was dying.

The Fighting Fletcher

One American destroyer emerged from that Friday-the-13th battle without a single abrasion on her paint. She was the U.S.S. Fletcher.

Rear ship of the American column, the Fletcher (Commander W. M. Cole) was last in line, but not least. She was carrying the new SG search radar, and when the formation ahead of her suddenly fouled up beyond recognition, Fletcher, in spite of the general mix-up, was able to put an accurate finger on the oncoming enemy ships.

She opened fire at once on the Jap vessel that speared Atlanta with a searchlight. Range was 5,500 yards, and shell bursts looked like solid hits. Then, noting that several other American ships were shooting at this target, Commander Cole shifted Fletcher's fire to another enemy man-of-war.

Fletcher's 5-inchers were going like triphammers when Callaghan's order to cease fire was received. Cole stopped his ship's guns for a moment, then aimed them at a target at longer range, and resumed fire.

Ahead of Fletcher, the Barton disappeared in a haze of bronze smoke, and then Monssen reeled away in a mantle of flames. Eager to use his ship's torpedoes, and seeking freedom for maneuver, Cole drove his destroyer in a northerly run to skirt the cruiser brawl and to get in on the Japanese flank. Somehow he conned Fletcher through the scramble of fighting ships, dodging shells from all sides and torpedoes from a dozen directions. Then, cutting back to the south, he sent Fletcher booming toward the enemy at 35 knots, her radar-informed gunners nailing one target after another with spikes of white-hot steel.

So Fletcher came smartly into position for a torpedo attack. Her radar picked up a large target; Cole tracked with precision and dispatch; ten torpedoes were launched at three-and-a-half mile range. The distance was too great for accurate observation. But the sky suddenly glowed over the target, and this bright aurora suggested destruction. Cole set a course for Sealark Channel, justifiably satisfied that Fletcher had done a good night's work.

Admiral Halsey stated,

> *The performance of the* Fletcher . . . *gives evidence of a high degree of organization and training. The deliberate, calculated attack on and probable sinking of a large enemy ship . . . in the face of constant danger of discovery and annihilation, typifies the offensive spirit so essential in present operations.*

Down Go the Big Guns (Death of the Hiei)

"We want the big ones—!" The voice was Admiral Callaghan's, broadcast by radiotelephone from the bridge of flagship San Francisco. The destroyers were already flailing at battleship Hiei, and I.J.N. Kirishima was due appropriate attention. The American cruisers turned their guns on both battlewagons. Then the column broke up as it stormed into the Japanese formation. Shells, apparently from San Francisco, slashed into disabled Atlanta, and Callaghan's abrupt cease-fire order crackled over the TBS.

As the cruisers checked their fire, a volley of Jap

salvos came whining across the sky. Some of the whines loudened into a deep-toned zoom, the aerial drone of 14-inch projectiles. Evidently they were fired by KIRISHIMA, far to SAN FRANCISCO's starboard.

Pinpointed by enemy ships on both sides, SAN FRANCISCO was hit more than a dozen times by major caliber projectiles, most of them 14-inch from HIEI, with whom she was closely engaged. One heavy shell striking the bridge overhead only a few feet away killed Admiral Callaghan and most of his staff; another killed Captain Cassin Young; others wiped out most of the ship's bridge personnel. A Jap destroyer close aboard on the port side flung shells into the flag cruiser's superstructure. Lieutenant Commander Bruce McCandless, wounded but miraculously alive amid the carnage, kept the conn for the remainder of the battle. For despite 25 fires aboard, her topsides a shambles and her steering gear damaged, and maneuvering with difficulty, SAN FRANCISCO continued to fight any enemy that could be identified and to lead what remained of the original column astern.

ATLANTA, too, was damaged and afire, out of action, but the other cruisers—PORTLAND, HELENA, and JUNEAU—still struck furiously at the enemy. And then in almost no time only PORTLAND and HELENA of the American cruisers were left fighting, for as JUNEAU waded into action with her guns going, she was stabbed by a torpedo. The blast shattered her forward fireroom, and probably snapped her keel. Fighting grievous damage, she crawled out of the battle.

PORTLAND and HELENA maneuvered into the storm center, firing at targets to port, starboard, and ahead. American and Japanese destroyers scrimmaged on either hand, and the two cruisers were compelled to dodge torpedoes from all directions. Had Admiral Abe but known it, this was the moment to deliver his knockout—when only two United States cruisers and three or four able-bodied destroyers stood between his battleships and Guadalcanal.

But the Japanese commander himself was confused by the violence of the American attack and the tactical turmoil. As though his battleship were some sort of gunboat, she was being peppered by small-caliber shells. Where were his screening ships? Where was cruiser NAGARA? Ships were everywhere, but silhouettes were distorted in smoke and signals were diffracted in glare. And now there were American cruisers where American destroyers should be, and American destroyers were on HIEI's flank where Japanese destroyers should have been. They were even shooting at the battleship with machine-guns!

To the neat little admiral all this must have seemed sheer delirium. And so, at about 0200 he ordered HIEI and KIRISHIMA to turn homeward. KIRISHIMA made the swing ahead of HIEI, came back in a long loop to lob a few shells at the American ships, then retired around the north coast of Savo Island. Behind her she left destroyer YUDACHI exploding like a fireworks display and battleship HIEI fighting off the American cruisers. KIRISHIMA received only one scratch in that night's engagement: she was grazed by an 8-inch shell.

HIEI, slow on the northward turn, and heavily hit by SAN FRANCISCO, had run into another blistering fire, this time from PORTLAND. The latter was struck by a torpedo which sheared off one of her screws and set her to weaving. But her forward turret guns drew an accurate bead, and Admiral Abe's flagship caught some heavy salvos. HELENA, too, may have hit the Jap battlewagon. And HIEI may have been struck by one of FLETCHER's torpedoes. Whatever the source, she was hit hard and often; her steering gear was injured and some of her guns were silenced. Altogether, about 50 shells struck her in the superstructure. Badly damaged, Abe's battleship made a half-circle turn below Savo, and went staggering northward along the east coast of the island.

The fighting in the Sound was almost over. But for the Americans the worst was to come as a sequel. About 0230 the HELENA led the SAN FRANCISCO and destroyer FLETCHER eastward through Sealark Channel. Destroyers STERETT and O'BANNON withdrew through Lengo Channel. Crippled JUNEAU had already retired eastward. Under command of Captain G. C. Hoover, who was HELENA's captain and senior officer present, this remnant force was pulled together for the run to Espiritu Santo.

Only HELENA and FLETCHER had emerged from the night's madness without injury. As the ships headed southeastward through Indispensable Strait, pace was set at 18 knots to accommodate the cripples. Destroyer O'BANNON, with damaged sonar gear but otherwise sound in wind and limb, was sent ahead to get off a radio message to Admiral Halsey. FLETCHER and limping STERETT were positioned 4,000 yards in front of the cruisers to serve as screen.

About 0950 STERETT made sudden sonar contact with an enemy submarine. Gamely she went after the unseen foe, dumping depth charges in an urgent attack. Commander Coward was unable to determine the results, and the ships could not wait to conduct a prolonged hunt.

They steamed into a deadly trap. Time: about 1100. Bridge personnel on SAN FRANCISCO glimpsed torpedo wakes racing across their bow, close ahead. The "FRISCO" men had no means of radioing the alarm, nor time to turn their ship away. Limping on

A picture taken after the Battle of Santa Cruz shows the damage to the forward gun mounts and forecastle of U.S.S. Smith done by a Jap suicide plane. With forecastle and bridge an inferno, the Smith's captain, conning from aft, pushed her nose into the foaming wake of the battleship South Dakota. The foam and spray cooled the flames, allowed fire-fighters to finish the job.

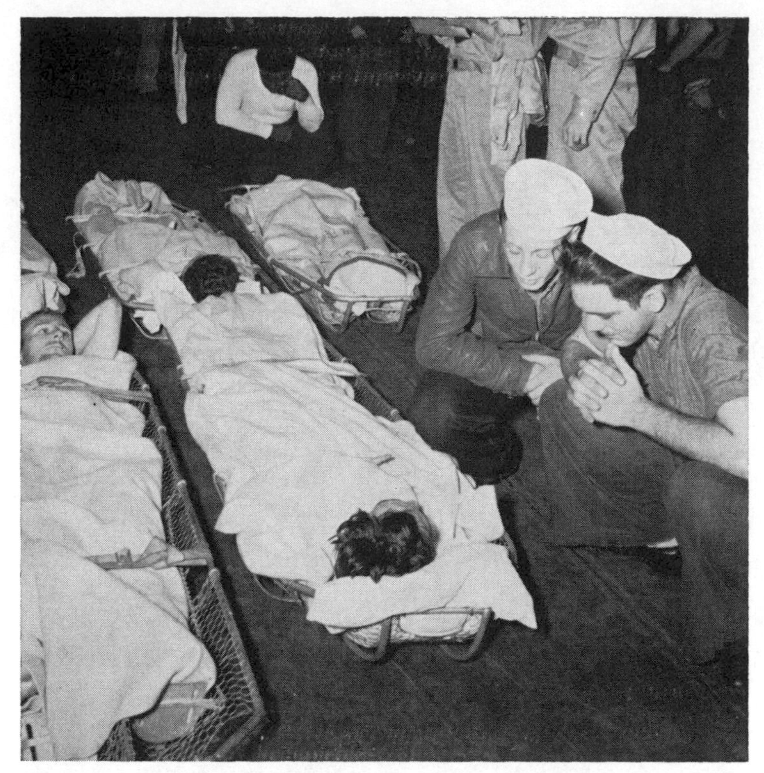

The Solace receives wounded American veterans of the Santa Cruz battle. Our Navy is indebted to the efficiency of the medical personnel of these seagoing hospitals for the survival of so many serious combat casualties.

We seized this Japanese submarine in the fall of 1945. Their torpeodoes had been superior to ours until 1943. Peacetime financial support of and technical progress in research and development lead to naval preparedness.

Japan suffered her first battleship losses in the Battle of Guadalcanal. Both the Hiei and her sister ship, the Kirishima, above, were sunk. Fighting these armored giants point-blank, U. S. destroyers took severe losses.

A Jap "Kate" crashes into the Smith's forecastle during the Battle of Santa Cruz. As the war progressed, the Japanese increasingly used these suicide tactics.

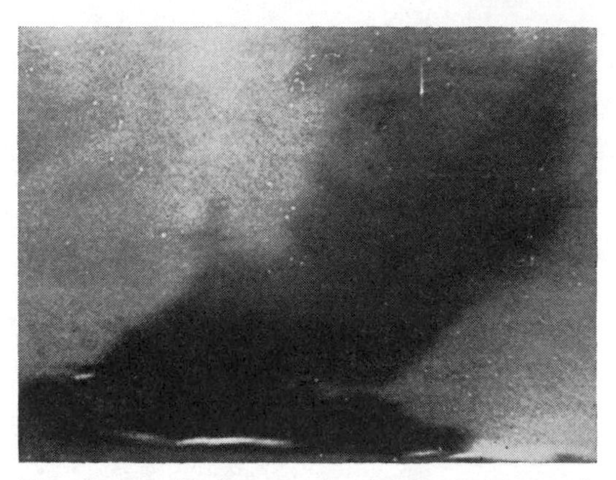

The U.S.S. Smith burns furiously after being struck, forward, by a Japanese suicide plane. But good U. S. seamanship was a match for Jap desperation.

Three of our destroyers were sunk while attacking the Japanese battleship Hiei. The O'Bannon, above, escaped alive after firing shells and torpedoes.

"FRISCO'S" starboard bow, cruiser JUNEAU was right in line for the shot.

At 1101 one of the torpedoes smashed into JUNEAU'S port side. The blast was utterly cataclysmic. Literally the ship was blown to fragments. When the mountains of fire and smoke dissolved, there was nothing but a few bits of flotsam where the ship had been.

Perhaps a hundred survivors were there in the flotsam, but Captain Hoover's group could not stop to pick them up. A Flying Fort saw the explosion, and was urged to report the sinking to Halsey. Somehow the message failed to reach Espiritu, and help did not come. Only ten of JUNEAU'S men survived. Some 700 of her crew perished in the disaster.

This savage blow, struck by the I-26, was not the final echo of that battle of the 13th. In Savo Sound, where there was mopping up to do, the Americans would strike the final blows.

After the Japanese retirement there had still remained on the field the cruiser PORTLAND (unable to steer), destroyer AARON WARD (unable to steam), cruiser ATLANTA (a charred wreck), and the fiery carcasses of CUSHING, MONSSEN, and I.J.N. YUDACHI. On the north side of Savo, HIEI was halted by an internal collapse, with destroyer YUKIKAZE squatting in near-by attendance.

Daybreak revealed Savo Sound as a steaming, debris-strewn sea in which the dead and dying vessels lay like flies in a pan of glue. In that cluttered seascape nothing moved. The water was motionless; on its yellow surface the ships remained fixed.

And now one of the vessels comes to life—the PORTLAND. Having halted for a moment to attempt a repair, she steams in a circle that brings her within range of the Jap destroyer YUDACHI. Six salvos are flung at the enemy hulk—to little avail, since the YUDACHI had been promptly abandoned after disablement, the crew taken off by I.J.N. SAMIDARE. But the hulk blows up and vanishes from the scene, a heartening display to American sailors watching from rafts.

Farther north, another sign of life on the water; the tug BOBOLINK from Tulagi steams into the scene. She has come to tow out the destroyer AARON WARD.

This stir of activity awakens the battleship HIEI. Thirteen miles distant, the wounded Japanese giant lets out a gruff roar. Another. Another. And again. Four heavy partial salvos come rumbling across Savo Sound, reaching for destroyer and tug. AARON WARD is shaken by one straddle, but sturdy BOBOLINK stands by, and at 0635 the damaged destroyer is on the haul eastward.

The thunder from HIEI awakens Marine Corps aircraft which come winging across "Ironbottom Bay" with a vengeance. It is curtains, now, for Admiral Abe's flagship. The Marines pelt her unmercifully. So do some Wildcats and Avengers, an advance group sent northward by ENTERPRISE to work with General Vandegrift's force.

While the planes are pounding the immobilized Jap battleship, Higgins boats from Lunga Point bustle into the Sound to rescue survivors and give PORTLAND and ATLANTA a hand. Later BOBOLINK returns. The two cruisers are pushed, shoved, and jackassed eastward; PORTLAND finally makes Tulagi, and ATLANTA is nudged to Lunga Point.

But there was no salvaging of battered ATLANTA. American cruisermen had to scuttle and sink her.

HIEI, too, was on her way to the bottom, although she was slower about going. Throughout the day American aircraft made intermittent attacks on the leviathan. They plastered her with bombs, holed her twice with torpedoes, practically melted down her pagoda, and left her reeling in crazy circles with a broken rudder. Some 300 of her crew perished in the shambles, and her engines expired. But the planes could not down the battlewagon. Late that afternoon Jap destroyers took off the survivors, and about 1800 they scuttled and sank the reluctant dragon, the first Japanese battleship to be sunk during the war.

By evening of the 13th most of the battle wreckage had been cleared from Savo Sound; the hulks were on the floor of "Ironbottom Bay," and a cleanly tide was sweeping rubbish and bodies in to the beaches of Savo Island and Cape Esperance.

Under the surface lay the residue of one of the fiercest sea fights in modern history. The 34-minute action had cost the U.S. Navy a light cruiser and four destroyers sunk, severe damage to two heavy cruisers and two destroyers, and a death toll which included two admirals and indeterminate numbers of American cruisermen and destroyermen. And JUNEAU'S destruction by a submarine below Indispensable Strait must be included in this grievous accounting.

With a battleship and two destroyers lost, four destroyers damaged, and a death toll far less than the American figure, Japanese casualties were relatively light. But the loss of HIEI left a king-size hole in the Japanese fleet. Above all, the Japanese were turned back unsuccessful in their all-out effort to deliver a Guadalcanal knockout.

But another day was coming. And so was the Jap transport force from the Bougainville area. And Mikawa's cruiser force from Rabaul. And Admiral Kondo's Main Body, including several aircraft carriers and two KONGO class battleships from Truk.

The naval battle for Guadalcanal was not yet over.

CHAPTER 16

SOLOMONS CRUCIBLE

(THE GUADALCANAL CAMPAIGN)

(Part 3)

The Battle of Guadalcanal (November 14-15)

Round One had gone to the Americans, but the Japanese did not abandon their try for a knockout. Fuming at Truk, Yamamoto ordered full speed ahead on the Guadalcanal offensive. Frightened by the assault on Admiral Abe's Striking Force, the Jap transport group had scurried back up the "Slot" toward Bougainville. But late in the evening of the 13th Mikawa's cruiser squadron from Rabaul bore down on Savo. Early next morning three of the cruisers and four destroyers steamed across the Sound, unopposed, and handed Henderson Field a savage bombardment. However, they were compelled to retire at 0205, their ammunition expended.

Mikawa's bombardment force did not escape unscathed. The ENTERPRISE task force was nearing Guadalcanal by that time. Not long after daybreak the carrier planes and aircraft from Henderson were on Mikawa's tail. Locating the Jap cruisers south of New Georgia, they proceeded to give them a pasting. Cruiser KINUGASA was sunk, and three other cruisers and a destroyer were damaged.

Then the ENTERPRISE planes caught the Jap reinforcement group—11 transports and 11 destroyers—as it made another try at coming down the "Slot." No "Tokyo Express" was ever derailed at greater speed. Before the trainwreckers were through, seven transports had been smashed to junk, and the remaining four severely damaged.

Meantime, up north of Florida Island, another striking force was getting set for a crack at Henderson Field. This force—it was designated a Bombardment Group—was under command of Vice Admiral Kondo. It contained the heavy cruisers ATAGO (Kondo's flagship) and TAKAO, battleship KIRISHIMA, two light cruisers, and a squadron of nine destroyers. Kondo's left flank was covered by a Screening Group composed of the light cruiser SENDAI and three destroyers. Air cover from the backfield was provided by a carrier group containing JUNYO and HIYO, battleships KONGO and HARUNA, heavy cruiser TONE, and screening destroyers.

Kondo's ships were sighted and reported by American planes and the submarine TROUT. Admiral Halsey sent a dispatch to the ENTERPRISE force, ordering battleships WASHINGTON and SOUTH DAKOTA and four destroyers to leave the carrier's screen. They were to steam hell-for-leather to intercept Kondo's warships and the remnants of the wrecked "Tokyo Express" approaching Savo Sound.

This interception force was under tactical command of Rear Admiral W. A. ("Ching") Lee in the WASHINGTON. The four destroyers were the U.S.S. WALKE (Commander T. E. Fraser), BENHAM (Lieutenant Commander J. B. Taylor), GWIN (Lieutenant Commander J. B. Fellows), and PRESTON (Commander M. C. Stormes).

The six American warships raced for Savo with bones in their teeth. By that evening of November 14 they were off the western end of Guadalcanal making a clockwise swing around Savo Island.

Lee was confident his big battleships could stop Kondo's cruisers and I.J.N. KIRISHIMA. At the same time he knew his interception force was burdened with several disadvantages. This was a new, unpracticed team going into action. The four destroyers were without a division commander, and they had been drawn from differing divisions, their selection dictated by the fact that each was well supplied with fuel. The force was strictly improvised for an emergency mission. And improvisation to counter planning is always hazardous.

However, the risk had to be taken, and Lee accepted it boldly. His ships were in an extended column with destroyers WALKE, BENHAM, PRESTON, and GWIN in the van some 4,000 to 5,000 yards ahead of battleships WASHINGTON and SOUTH DAKOTA.

They were all inside Savo Sound by 2215. The water was as still as stagnation. It was silent—too silent. Where was the enemy?

He had been coming down from the north, far distant on the American column's beam. But not so far abeam that lookouts on board I.J.N. SENDAI had not been able to discern through their excellent Japanese binoculars the silhouettes of Lee's ships to the southward. SENDAI had flashed the word to flagship ATAGO, and Admiral Kondo had lost no time in deploying his ships for battle. According to American tactical ideas, his deployment violated the tenet of "getting there fustest with the mostest," for he divided his force into four groups, thereby dispersing his strength.

The SENDAI group, split up in two sections, forked southward to cover the east and west side of Savo Island. Cruiser NAGARA and four destroyers were ordered to make a dash to the south of Savo and enter the Sound from the west. With his flank covered by the SENDAI group and his advance screened by the NAGARA group, Kondo would swing his big bombardment warships around the west side of Savo to strike at the Americans when opportunity presented. Kondo had the initiative, but he lacked accurate information. SENDAI had described the American force as *"two cruisers and four destroyers."*

For his part Admiral Lee had no current information. Unaware that enemy ships were trailing him into Savo Sound, he headed his southbound column on a beeline for Lunga Point.

Not far from the Guadalcanal coast Lee turned his column sharp right to follow the coastline toward Cape Esperance. The column was steaming due west when, at 2300, battleship WASHINGTON's radar picked up the Japanese scout group coming down the east side of Savo Island.

By radar, and then by telescope, WASHINGTON tracked the enemy. At 2317, she opened fire on the SENDAI. The Jap light cruiser and her destroyer companion fled. But destroyers AYANAMI and URANAMI, coming around the southwest coast of Savo, pressed forward. So did NAGARA and her consorts. Gunfire exploded as these ships encountered Lee's van destroyers. In the cyclonic battle which followed, three of those American destroyers went down fighting.

Exeunt PRESTON, WALKE, and BENHAM.

Loss of U.S.S. PRESTON

Leading the American column that morning of November 15, destroyer WALKE opened fire at 2322 on enemy ships detected 15,000 yards to starboard. BENHAM and PRESTON, next in line, quickly followed suit. Last in the destroyer line, GWIN fired starshells at the target detected by WASHINGTON.

The enemy just south of Savo returned shot for shot. The island in the background gave the Jap ships radar sanctuary and blurred their silhouettes. Firing at flashes, the American destroyermen scored a number of hits, but the Jap salvos came faster and harder.

Destroyer PRESTON was not the first American destroyer hit in this action, but she was first to receive a critical blow. Five minutes after the shooting started, her superstructure was burning fiercely, a torch for the enemy marksmen.

Those marksmen were manning the guns of the NAGARA. Virtually undetected, this Jap cruiser had closed in on Lee's column to strike at the van destroyers. Almost at pointblank range she opened fire on PRESTON.

Raked by gunfire, PRESTON rolled and shook under successive hits. Her gunners hurled steel at NAGARA, but the cruiser's salvos ripped the vitals out of the destroyer before she could punch home a solid blow.

One enemy salvo wrecked both firerooms. Down came PRESTON's after stack. A cluster of shells struck her fantail, and from amidships to depth-charge racks she burst into flames. By 2336 she was listing heavily to starboard and settling by the stern. Her captain, Commander M. C. Stormes, gave the order to abandon.

As the men were going overside, the ship rolled over on her beam, then slowly capsized and went down stern first. Her bow was slanted at the sky for about ten minutes before she slid under. Men came diving and tumbling down from her forecastle.

Commander Stormes was lost with the ship. So were three other officers and some 112 bluejackets of her crew. About 131 of her survivors were picked up the following day by the destroyer MEADE.

Loss of U.S.S. WALKE

Spearheading the American column, WALKE opened fire at 2322 on a Jap ship glimpsed against the dark foreshore of Savo Island. As Chief Fire Con-

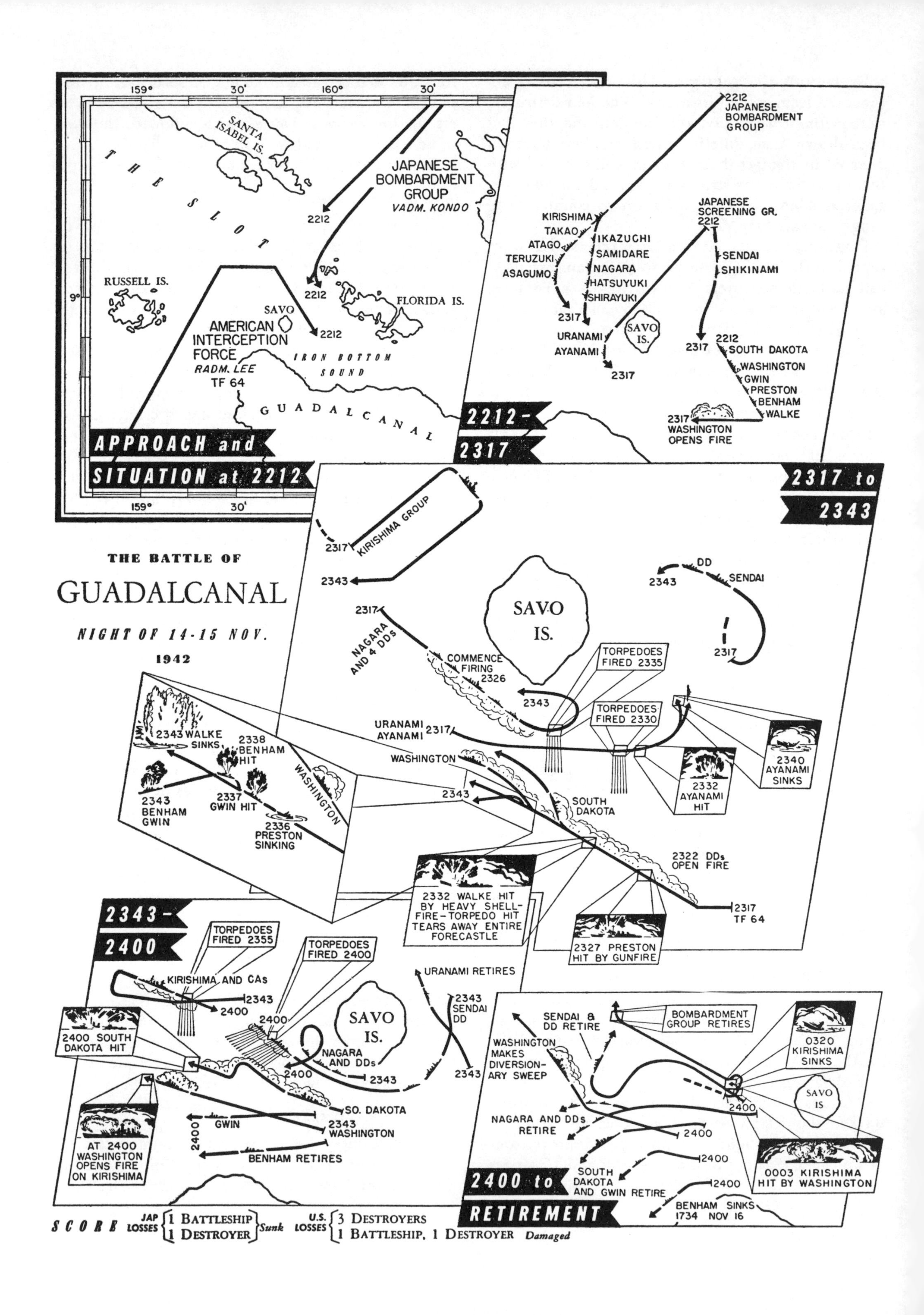

THE BATTLE OF

GUADALCANAL

NIGHT OF 14-15 NOV. 1942

SCORE JAP LOSSES {1 BATTLESHIP, 1 DESTROYER} *Sunk* U.S. LOSSES {3 DESTROYERS, 1 BATTLESHIP, 1 DESTROYER *Damaged*}

trolman R. P. Spearman recalled the encounter:

We opened up with a range of around 14,000 yards, but the ranges came down very fast. I don't remember what it was when we ended up, but I know it was pointblank. The Gunnery Officer said, "We'll take the bridge off that ship!" so we went through 250 rounds into that bridge. SOUTH DAKOTA *got three salvos out, and the third hit the magazines in the stern of the Jap. It looked to me like it went 500 feet up into the air.*

WALKE herself was scorched by furious shellfire. Her captain, Commander T. E. Fraser, tried to maneuver for a torpedo attack. But the ship fell off to port, and he could not bring the torpedo batteries to bear.

About ten minutes after she opened fire, WALKE was hit by a number of heavy shells, probably from cruiser NAGARA. Then she was struck by a torpedo. The explosion hurled her No. 2 gun a hundred feet in the air, slung men far out across the water, and tore away the entire forecastle. Bridge and after section were left foundering. At 2343 Commander Fraser ordered his sinking craft abandoned.

Only two life rafts could be launched, and many of the survivors going overside were compelled to tread water. They were swimming in oil, and splashing through flotsam when WALKE's stern section went under. As the fantail sank, depth charges which had been reported on "safe" began to explode. Many swimmers were slain by this blasting.

When the turmoil subsided WALKE's bow section was gone, and the water was strewn with debris and dead. The living paddled around the overburdened rafts, strong swimmers supporting those who were wounded or exhausted.

Lost with WALKE were some 75 of her crew. Among them was her skipper, Commander Thomas E. Fraser. "Ironbottom Bay" contained another DesPac grave.

Loss of U.S.S. BENHAM

Third American destroyer to go down in that battle of November 15, 1942, the BENHAM (Lieutenant Commander John B. Taylor) was in position 300 yards astern of WALKE. She opened fire on the target WALKE had sighted, then shifted to another enemy silhouette which emerged from Savo's shadowy shoreline.

Lieutenant Commander Taylor kept the guns going, but held his torpedoes in reserve for an opportune attack. Before the opportunity developed, BENHAM was hit by a torpedo.

The blow was struck at 2338. An enormous geyser deluged the destroyer's prow, and a portion of her bow disintegrated. The blast heaved BENHAM over to port, then she rolled back on her starboard beam. Then, shuddering and shaking, she came back to even keel, and steadied.

Destroyer WALKE was in flames by this time, and PRESTON was sinking. BENHAM's skipper thought his ship might be able to aid the distressed vessels. BENHAM couldn't make it. Her head was logy, and she slowed from 27 to 5 knots. As she headed sluggishly toward WALKE and PRESTON, the Japs flailed the two dying ships with a concentrated shelling. To save his damaged ship, Taylor had to leave the WALKE and PRESTON survivors shouting unanswered appeals from the flame-lit water.

Even so, BENHAM could not be saved. Although the crew stemmed the flood up forward, damage was progressive and cumulative. By 0100 the ship was fighting to keep under way, and Taylor was eventually forced to report that her condition was worsening. Admiral Lee then dispatched destroyer GWIN to escort the struggling BENHAM to Espiritu Santo. About 0300 GWIN joined her west of Guadalcanal, and the two ships started the "long voyage home" at 12 knots. The effort was too much for BENHAM. About 1500 in that afternoon of the 15th, when the ships were off the south coast of Guadalcanal, she began to break up. Taylor started the abandonment at 1537, the men going overside in good order. GWIN took off Taylor and his weary crew. The sinking destroyer was hurried under by GWIN's guns.

No lives were lost with the BENHAM. Miraculously enough, in the ferocious action off Savo only seven of her crew had been injured. For his determined attempt to save the badly wounded ship, Lieutenant Commander Taylor was awarded the Navy Cross.

Action of GWIN

Fourth of the van destroyers leading Lee's battleship column, the U.S.S. GWIN had fired starshells at SENDAI, then veered to shoot at the oncoming cruiser NAGARA. She found herself in a pitched battle with this menace, and probably gave as good as she got—which was a thrashing.

A shell burst in her engineering spaces. Another hit her in the fantail. Her skipper, Lieutenant Commander J. B. Fellows, sent her slugging forward while her engineers fought to keep the kettles boiling and all hell broke loose around her.

Ahead of her, PRESTON was sinking in a sudden gush of flames. Then WALKE's chopped hulk was silhouetted. BENHAM floundered off with a smashed bow, and GWIN was the only American destroyer in action on the field.

She had battleship support; the big shells were

zooming over her masthead, and crashing down on the enemy like missiles from Mars. But in the hurly-burly she was unable to attack NAGARA with torpedoes—a shell hit had jounced some of them out of the tubes—and her power plant was injured. She began to roll drunkenly, slopping her beam ends under.

Lieutenant Commander Fellows kept his destroyer firing until the enemy ships hauled out of range. They hauled out when SOUTH DAKOTA came roaring up the line with her turret guns thundering. So the battle rushed westward, leaving GWIN behind. The destroyer's skipper headed her for Cape Esperance.

Later, Admiral Lee directed GWIN to escort damaged BENHAM to Espiritu. That afternoon the mission ended lugubriously with BENHAM breaking up and GWIN called upon to sink the abandoned hulk.

GWIN fired her 5-inch 38's again, but this time at a friend and not an enemy. Their salvos swept the seascape clean, and she high-tailed south on her lonely run to the New Hebrides.

Battleship Finish

The three-day naval Battle of Guadalcanal ended as a battleship story. The details are too voluminous for a destroyer history, but this king-size conclusion merits brief recounting.

In the widespread combat, WASHINGTON and SOUTH DAKOTA boomed on into the waters west of Savo Island where they engaged Kondo's big Bombardment Group.

During the jockeying for position, SOUTH DAKOTA's radar went blind, and she fell afoul of KIRISHIMA and her pack of cruisers and destroyers. The Japs turned on searchlights, and lashed the big American with a heavy fire that damaged her No. 3 turret and killed about 40 of her crew.

As SOUTH DAKOTA retired southward, Lee sent WASHINGTON on a run northwestward past Kondo's force to divert its fire and hit it on the flank. For several minutes the KIRISHIMA force loped on parallel course in what began as a pursuit and ended in a flight. Hammered by 16-inch projectiles, the Japs soon had enough of U.S.S. WASHINGTON. In this running duel their cruisers and destroyers were not seriously hurt, but mighty KIRISHIMA took a first-class beating. Hit by nine 16-inch shells and a flock of 5-inchers, the Japanese battleship reeled out of action and began to chase her fantail in aimless circles.

That settled it for Admiral Nobutake Kondo. At 0125 he swung his unengaged ships to the eastward and ran for the open water north of Savo. A few minutes later Admiral Lee, satisfied he had driven off the enemy, turned WASHINGTON southward.

Off the northwest coast of Savo the KIRISHIMA continued to go in circles. As SENDAI and a couple of destroyers were standing disconsolately by, her captain sent the crew overside and ordered the battlewagon scuttled. With her sea valves open and some 250 dead on board, KIRISHIMA went down at 0320 not far from the grave of her sister, HIEI.

The blocking of Kondo's force had cost the Navy three destroyers and damage to a battleship and a fourth destroyer. But Japanese ship-casualties—a battleship and a destroyer sunk, and several cruisers and destroyers damaged—were considerably heavier. And loss of the battle was to cost them Guadalcanal.

Four of the Jap transports, residue of the large reinforcement group which had been wrecked the previous day, did manage to reach Guadalcanal. Driven by Rear Admiral Raizo Tanaka, this tattered convoy dodged into Savo Sound after WASHINGTON's departure. About 0400 the damaged transports were run in and grounded on the beach at Tassafaronga.

The Jap troops were wading ashore when Marine Corps planes from Henderson spotted the ships. Then destroyer MEADE (Commander R. S. Lamb) came steaming down from Tulagi to investigate.

MEADE was armed with new 40 mm. batteries, and, as this was her first time in action, she was eager to try them out. She proved their capabilities, and her own, in short order.

The first transport was shot to rubbish by 1121. Then one after another the other three were riddled to junk. Aircraft added bombs to MEADE's bombardment, and "Cactus" artillery joined in the shelling. No more than 2,000 of the large contingent of soldiery carried by the transports succeeded in getting ashore.

Having finished off the troopships, MEADE went on that afternoon to pick up the survivors of PRESTON and WALKE. She was assisted by landing and patrol craft, a PT-boat, and aircraft spotters. When her rescue effort was concluded she had saved 266 destroyermen.

A fitting finale for the naval Battle of Guadalcanal.

Guadalcanal Aftermath

Radio Tokyo proclaimed a stupendous victory. So did the American press.

There was no denying the fact that Lee's force routed Kondo's. Or the fact that Turner's reinforcement ships reached the "Cactus" front, whereas the Jap reinforcements were stymied. Or the fact that Japan's War Lords never made another all-out try for Guadalcanal, but instead decided to haul out of the Lower Solomons and retire to the Upper Solomons to make a stand in the Bougainville area. For the first time since the war's outbreak, Japan was definitely on the defensive. Admiral King flatly stated:

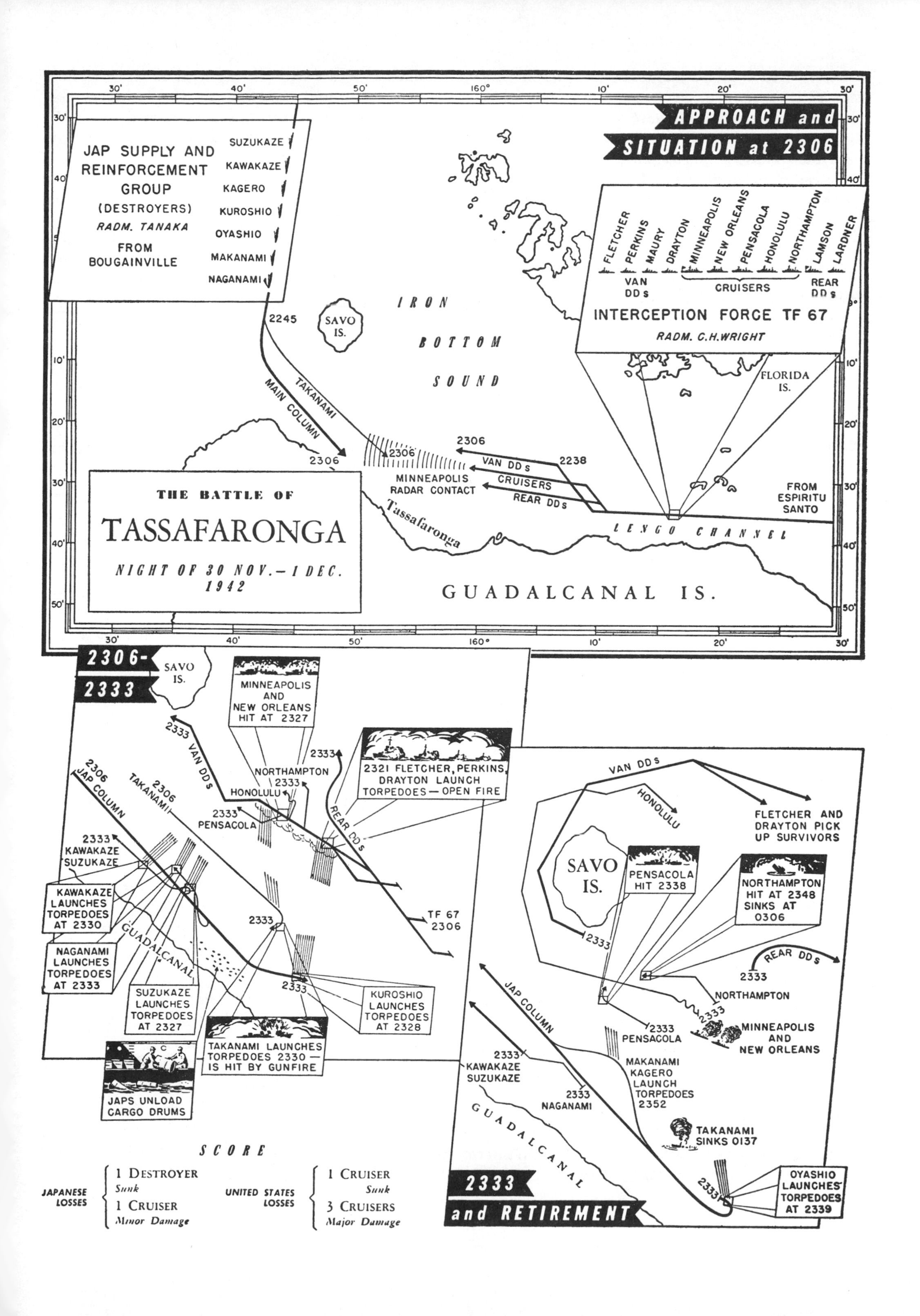

APPROACH and SITUATION at 2306
JAP SUPPLY AND REINFORCEMENT GROUP
(DESTROYERS)
RADM. TANAKA
FROM BOUGAINVILLE
SUZUKAZE
KAWAKAZE
KAGERO
KUROSHIO
OYASHIO
MAKANAMI
NAGANAMI
FLETCHER
PERKINS
MAURY
DRAYTON
MINNEAPOLIS
NEW ORLEANS
PENSACOLA
HONOLULU
NORTHAMPTON
LAMSON
LARDNER
VAN DDs
CRUISERS
REAR DDs
INTERCEPTION FORCE TF 67
RADM. C.H.WRIGHT
SAVO IS.
IRON BOTTOM SOUND
FLORIDA IS.
2245
TAKANAMI
MAIN COLUMN
2306
2306
2306
2238
VAN DDs
CRUISERS
REAR DDs
MINNEAPOLIS RADAR CONTACT
FROM ESPIRITU SANTO
Tassafaronga
LENGO CHANNEL
GUADALCANAL IS.
THE BATTLE OF
TASSAFARONGA
NIGHT OF 30 NOV.–1 DEC. 1942
2306–2333
SAVO IS.
MINNEAPOLIS AND NEW ORLEANS HIT AT 2327
2333 VAN DDs
2333
NORTHAMPTON 2333
HONOLULU
2333 PENSACOLA
2321 FLETCHER, PERKINS, DRAYTON LAUNCH TORPEDOES — OPEN FIRE
REAR DDs
2306 JAP COLUMN
2306 TAKANAMI
2333 KAWAKAZE SUZUKAZE
KAWAKAZE LAUNCHES TORPEDOES AT 2330
NAGANAMI LAUNCHES TORPEDOES AT 2333
GUADALCANAL
SUZUKAZE LAUNCHES TORPEDOES AT 2327
2333
2333
KUROSHIO LAUNCHES TORPEDOES AT 2328
TF 67 2306
TAKANAMI LAUNCHES TORPEDOES 2330 — IS HIT BY GUNFIRE
JAPS UNLOAD CARGO DRUMS
VAN DDs
HONOLULU
FLETCHER AND DRAYTON PICK UP SURVIVORS
SAVO IS.
PENSACOLA HIT 2338
NORTHAMPTON HIT AT 2348 SINKS AT 0306
2333
REAR DDs
2333
NORTHAMPTON
2333
MINNEAPOLIS AND NEW ORLEANS
2333 PENSACOLA
JAP COLUMN
2333 KAWAKAZE SUZUKAZE
MAKANAMI KAGERO LAUNCH TORPEDOES 2352
2333 NAGANAMI
TAKANAMI SINKS 0137
GUADALCANAL
OYASHIO LAUNCHES TORPEDOES AT 2339
2333
2333 and RETIREMENT
SCORE
JAPANESE LOSSES
1 Destroyer Sunk
1 Cruiser Minor Damage
UNITED STATES LOSSES
1 Cruiser Sunk
3 Cruisers Major Damage

The Battle of Guadalcanal, in spite of heavy losses we sustained, was a decisive victory for us, and our position in the southern Solomons was not threatened again seriously by the Japanese. Except for the "Tokyo Express," which from time to time succeeded in landing small quantities of supplies and reinforcements, control of the sea and air in the Southern Solomons passed to the United States.

And Rear Admiral Lee had this to say about destroyers WALKE, BENHAM, PRESTON, and GWIN:

In breaking up the enemy destroyer attack, our destroyers certainly relieved the battleships of a serious hazard and probably saved their bacon.

In reference to saving bacon, here is the story of a destroyerman who, cast adrift in enemy territory, saved his own. He was one of WALKE's survivors—Seaman Dale E. Land.

Separated from the group of rafts and swimmers, Land and a shipmate, Machinist's Mate Harold Taylor, struggled in the water for two days and nights. Finally they dragged themselves ashore on Guadalcanal, somewhere west of Tassafaronga.

The jungle was alive with Japs. But there were dead Japs in it, too. The bluejackets found an infantryman's rifle and cartridge belt. Subsisting on coconuts and Japanese biscuits, they worked their way eastward toward the American lines.

They hid by day and traveled at night, crawling through cesspool swamps and inching through festering thickets. Mosquitoes swarmed over them, and parrots flew at them, screaming. So did surprised Japs.

They shot up several Japanese patrols. Then Taylor was slain in a foray on an enemy outpost. Land eluded the search party which thrashed through the undergrowth on his track. Alone he trailed through the Jap-held jungle, hounded, sniped at. At last, on December 5, he sighted American pickets and tottered into the hands of a squad belonging to the 182nd Regiment. He was out of his head with a raving fever, mumbling incoherently, more ghost than human. But shreds of Navy clothing identified him as sailor, and in hospital he was soon able to speak for himself as a WALKE man.

It was such leaders as Admiral Lee at the top, and such bluejackets as Destroyerman Land down the line—such indomitable men as these who won the Battle of Guadalcanal. And saved the South Pacific for the Allies.

Tassafaronga Backlash

Tassafaronga was an anti-climax. It shouldn't have happened. It was a lacerating slash from a badly wounded tiger wasting strength in an effort to hold untenable ground. And the American hunters were not so reckless as they were unschooled in night tactics. In the bargain, they were up against an unusually cagey specimen.

In this instance the tiger was personified by Rear Admiral Raizo Tanaka, a very tough, very capable little man. Admiral Turner's counterpart, he was charged with the delivery of reinforcements and supplies to the Japanese front in the Lower Solomons. He had won the nickname of "Tenacious Tanaka" for driving the battered remnants of the "Tokyo Express" through to Tassafaronga while Savo Sound still echoed the shots of the Battle of Guadalcanal.

Tassafaronga had grown too hot for Japanese shipping. The destructive raid by destroyer MEADE guaranteed the heat wave. Then, on November 25, destroyer MCCALLA (Lieutenant Commander W. G. Cooper) visited Tassafaronga and shelled the stuffing out of 40 landing barges. Anyone but Tanaka might have despaired of landing perishable Jap cargo at this torrid terminal.

But Tanaka came up with a cool scheme. Run high-speed destroyers down to Tassafaronga at night, and toss the goods overside in watertight drums which would drift in on the tide to shallows where small craft and swimmers could recover the stuff. If a number of such runs were successfully made, the garrison could be supplied for a time.

The upshot of Tanaka's scheme was the Battle of Tassafaronga, which occurred late in the evening of November 30, 1942. From coast watchers, submarines, scouting aircraft, and other sources, Admiral Halsey learned that the enemy was going to make another attempt to reinforce Guadalcanal. He dispatched a task force under Rear Admiral C. H. ("Bosco") Wright to intercept and wreck this latest "Tokyo Express."

Admiral Wright's force (designated TF 67) as eventually constituted contained five cruisers—heavies MINNEAPOLIS (flagship), NEW ORLEANS, PENSACOLA, and NORTHAMPTON, and light cruiser HONOLULU—and six destroyers. The destroyers were:

LAMSON	*Lt. Comdr. P. H. Fitzgerald*
	Flying the pennant of Comdr. L. A. Abercrombie, COMDESDIV 9
FLETCHER	*Comdr. W. M. Cole*
PERKINS	*Lt. Comdr. W. C. Ford*
MAURY	*Lt. Comdr. G. L. Sims*
DRAYTON	*Comdr. J. E. Cooper*
LARDNER	*Lt. Comdr. W. M. Sweetser*

Admiral Wright, just arrived in the South Pacific, inherited this mission from Rear Admiral Kinkaid,

Our last damaged destroyer of the Guadalcanal campaign. The Nicholas, above, suffered both from enemy near misses and an accident. Japanese dive-bombers swooped down in an attack on this warship, which had no fighter cover, and damaged her steering gear. During the action, one 5-inch mount was wrecked, as shown, by a hang-fire. Even an enemy shell might have done less harm.

Task Force 67 just before the Battle of Tassafaronga. U.S.S. Fletcher is in the foreground, followed by other destroyers and, in the distance, cruisers. At Tassafaronga, Japanese Admiral Tanaka's destroyers gave us a lesson in torpedo skill. Our destroyer-cruiser tactics had not been advanced in peace to meet war exigencies of high-speed, limited-area surface night attack.

An LCT, foreground, transfers DeHaven survivors to the Fletcher (rear). The DeHaven was our fifteenth and final destroyer loss in the Guadalcanal Campaign. She was sunk by enemy planes.

U.S.S. Walke was one of three American destroyers lost in the Guadalcanal battle of November 15, 1942. Explosion of her own depth charges killed many struggling for survival in the sea.

The Japanese cruiser Nagara which fought the Walke and the Gwin in a short-range duel off Savo Island. 1942 produced more Pacific night naval battles than in all previous modern history.

One of the dozen enemy destroyers we sank off Guadalcanal. Salvage attempts were soon abandoned. Although we lost more major combatant craft than the Japanese, we won the logistics race.

who had been ordered to Pearl Harbor to take over another command. Kinkaid had already devised the operational plan, and Wright carried on with it. He was at some disadvantage, of course, stepping into hot action with a newly organized team.

Speed was imperative, and to save time Wright led his force from Espiritu Santo *via* Indispensable Strait into Lengo Channel and on westward into Savo Sound. His ships were formed in an extended column, destroyers FLETCHER, PERKINS, MAURY, and DRAYTON in the van, followed by cruisers MINNEAPOLIS, NEW ORLEANS, PENSACOLA, HONOLULU, and NORTHAMPTON, with DD's LAMSON and LARDNER bringing up the rear.

The column reached Lunga Roads about 2225 in the evening of November 30. Simultaneously "Tenacious Tanaka" with a force of eight Japanese destroyers steamed down into the channel between Savo Island and Cape Esperance. Japs racing east and Americans racing west met in a head-on crash.

Not only was the American force prepared for action, but it had a good set of operational plans. The van destroyers were positioned to use their radar to best advantage. They were instructed to hit the enemy upon encounter with a fast torpedo attack (provided the range was closed to 6,000 yards or less); then they were to haul out to the sidelines to give the cruisers a clear field. The cruisers were not to open fire until the DD's had launched their "fish" and pulled aside—the idea being to give the torpedoes a chance before gunfire alarmed the enemy. The cruiser-carried float planes stood ready to scout ahead and light up the enemy with flares if occasion presented. Searchlights were tabooed. Recognition lights were to be flashed only if one's ship were under friendly fire.

Thus Wright's ships went into action forewarned, forearmed, and rid of many of the wrenches that had fouled the machinery for the earlier battle-teams which had blazed the way at Savo. They had radar, and the Japanese had none. Above all, they had a tremendous weight advantage over the oncoming foe —five cruisers and six destroyers versus eight destroyers (of which six were encumbered with passengers and cargo).

A word of recognition is due here for Japan's DD's and the Japanese Destroyer Service. They were rugged little warships manned by rugged sailors with plenty of know-how in their sea bags.

For many months they had done the dirty work for Yamamoto's Imperial Fleet, going into waters where such mighty giants as KONGO and YAMATO feared to tread. If they were worn by hard usage, they were also as combat-hardened as alley cats, and they had learned some of the grimalkin's canny techniques for survival—how to make best use of cover; how to hit and run; and particularly, how to fight at night.

Moreover, they had one weapon which was blue murder—the souped-up Japanese torpedo.

And so, like tigerish alley cats, Tanaka's destroyers came prowling down into Savo Sound in the night. They were in column, NAGANAMI (flagship) in the van followed by MAKANAMI, OYASHIO, KURASHIO, KAGERO, KAWAKAZE, and SUZUKAZE. On NAGANAMI's port bow the TAKANAMI steamed as scout to feel out the way ahead. As the column entered Savo Sound, Tanaka slowed the pace to 12 knots and set a course to follow the Guadalcanal coastline down to Tassafaronga.

Meantime Wright had steered his American column northward toward the center of the Sound, then ordered a simultaneous ships' turn left which put his cruisers in line of bearing, and placed the van destroyer column on the starboard flank and the rear destroyer column on the flank to port. With a wide front the formation thus swept westward toward Cape Esperance.

The Sound was as black and silent as a pond at the bottom of a coal mine. The very air seemed dead. Then it livened up. At 2306 the radar watch on flag cruiser MINNEAPOLIS snared a suspicious "pip," range 23,000 yards, directly ahead. Wright immediately ordered a right turn which put his formation back into single column. The "pip" multiplied into a number of "pips," and there was the enemy. Swinging the column leftward, Wright set a course which was almost parallel to Tanaka's.

The van destroyers readied their torpedoes. FLETCHER, in the lead, probed the dark with acute radar. At 2316 the targets showed up on her port bow, range 7,000 yards. Over TBS FLETCHER's skipper, Commander Cole, asked permission to launch torpedoes. The Force Commander, dubious about the range, asked Cole if he considered it short enough. When Cole replied in the affirmative, Admiral Wright (time: 2320) ordered Cole to open torpedo fire. Cole instantly passed the word to the other van destroyers, and by 2321 FLETCHER's "fish" were unleashed in two salvos that sent a spread of ten torpedoes racing.

But neither time nor Tanaka had waited for Admiral Wright to issue the firing order. And while Commander Cole was waiting, the enemy targets slid past FLETCHER's beam, necessitating a rapid readjustment of the fire-control set-up. The range was lengthened, and when Cole finally received permission to shoot, the targets were going away on FLETCHER's quarter. Instead of broadside torpedo-fire with a favorable track-angle, she was compelled to get off a more difficult "up-the-kilt" shot.

Directly astern of FLETCHER, destroyer PERKINS flung eight torpedoes at the passing enemy. Destroyer MAURY, equipped with inferior radar, could not detect the Jap ships against the Guadalcanal coastline, so held her "fish" in check. DRAYTON also had weak radar; nevertheless, she got off two torpedo shots at a range of about 7,000 yards.

Twenty torpedoes went humming through the water in an undersea barrage at the enemy. And FLETCHER missed. PERKINS missed. DRAYTON missed. Not a single American torpedo found a mark. And worse still, lookouts on Tanaka's flagship sighted two oncoming wakes, and the foaming ribbons touched off the Japanese alarm.

Meantime, FLETCHER and the other DD's in the American van did their best to haul out (in accordance with plan) and give the cruisers a clear field. However, the cruisers opened fire within seconds of FLETCHER's final torpedo shot. Some of the cruisers fired starshells, and the battle was on. When the big guns started booming, FLETCHER, PERKINS, MAURY, and DRAYTON joined in with 5-inch gunnery. So did destroyers LAMSON and LARDNER at the tail-end of the column. Under all this heavy and medium fire Tanaka's eight destroyers should have been battered into trash.

Instead, they slipped out of the trap. Tanaka ordered a counter-attack with torpedoes. Aiming at the American gun flashes, the Jap destroyermen let fly. But the Japs were usually expert at this game.

TAKANAMI, the scout destroyer, unleashed her "fish" and swung hard right, reversing course. As she was out in front of the Jap column, she was exposed to the American gunnery, and she took a concentrated pounding. In a few minutes her own guns were out of action, her superstructure was thrashed to a shambles, she was afire and going down.

But TAKANAMI served as a decoy duck. While the Americans were hammering at this target, the other Jap ships were dodging. There was some confusion among them when the Squadron Commander signaled for a mass torpedo attack that required a column movement by each of the three divisions. Some of them steamed on toward Tassafaronga, their sailors busily tossing overside the floating cargo-drums. One or two missed the turn. But Tanaka reformed his column quickly, and in jig-time his ships were heading out of Savo Sound, and getting away. And getting away with murder.

For the Japanese torpedoes were running "true, hot, and normal" in a fashion only too fatal for the targets. FLETCHER and the other van destroyers, swinging around Savo Island in accordance with the battle plan, were out of danger. But at 2327 flagship MINNEAPOLIS was hit by two torpedoes. One struck her forward, and left 60 feet of her bow hanging like a dragging anchor. The other wrecked her No. 2 fireroom.

As she sheered off to avoid collision with the damaged flagship ahead of her, NEW ORLEANS was hit in the port bow by a torpedo. The explosion detonated two forward magazines, and NEW ORLEANS' bow was blown away.

Then PENSACOLA, maneuvering past the damaged ships, was hit. The blast let a Niagara into the after engine-room and ignited a horrible oil fire which cremated many of the crew.

HONOLULU, next cruiser in column, zigzagged off to starboard on the disengaged side of the column, and evaded the torpedo barrage. She was the only one of Wright's cruisers to escape unscathed. For, a few minutes later, NORTHAMPTON, last cruiser of the column, received the hardest blow of all. She had followed HONOLULU's northward turn, then swung back westward to bring her guns to bear on the enemy. Shortly thereafter she was struck by two torpedoes. The blasting tore a tremendous gash in her port side, burst her fuel tanks, and drenched her with blazing oil. With her mainmast burning like an enormous torch and her boat deck a mass of flame, NORTHAMPTON reeled out of action.

Steaming toward this pile-up of disaster and devastation, rear destroyers LAMSON and LARDNER were left to fend for themselves. LAMSON had endeavored to follow NORTHAMPTON's right turn, and while doing so, she had been shot at by one of the crippled cruisers. Whereupon her skipper had sagely decided to "get the hell out of there." LARDNER, too, was fired upon by the damaged American ships. She also evacuated at best speed.

It was now the first day of December, 1942. Admiral Raizo Tanaka, with seven of his eight destroyers intact, was high-tailing up the "Slot." In the dark passage between Savo Island and Cape Esperance, three United States cruisers were fighting serious damage and disablement, and a fourth was going down. The Battle of Tassafaronga was over.

Shortly after midnight Admiral Wright sent to cruiser HONOLULU a radio dispatch relinquishing his tactical command to Rear Admiral M. S. Tisdale. A hard-hitting officer who was to acquire a reputation for competence as ComDesPac, Admiral Tisdale sent HONOLULU steaming up the west coast of Savo Island in an effort to locate the retiring foe and the American van destroyers. The friends were easier to find than the foe. Some miles to the northwest, Tanaka was hitting for home at a clip that permitted no barnacles to gather under his keel.

Tisdale ordered the van destroyers to go to the assistance of the disabled cruisers. Then he headed HONOLULU southeastward around Savo to make a sweep of "Ironbottom Bay." And before the midwatch of that dark morning was over, the "Bay" had more iron on its bottom. At 0306 the heavy cruiser NORTHAMPTON went under.

Most of the cruisermen had abandoned at 0115 when it became apparent to Captain W. A. Kitts that the ship was doomed. By 0150 destroyers FLETCHER and DRAYTON were on hand to pick up survivors. The two DD's made a heroic job of it. For two and a half hours they groped about in the darkness, hauling man after man from the water. FLETCHER's motor-whaleboat rounded up rafts and boats, and towed them to the destroyer where nets were draped overside and strong hands were waiting for the cruisermen. First Class Fireman J. E. Howell swam out with lines to rescue swimmers who were in danger of drowning. So did Seaman Strickland and Thomas, and Torpedoman Krom. Ensign J. F. Ryan trudgeoned out from DRAYTON's whaleboat again and again to save men who were helplessly floundering. All told, FLETCHER picked up 600 men. DRAYTON picked up 128 survivors. This valiant work cut loss of life in the NORTHAMPTON disaster to 58—fatalities incurred, in the main, by fire and explosion. Lieutenant W. N. Pope, Medical Officer on board DRAYTON, labored nonstop for 30 hours to tend the wounded—another heroic lifesaving feat.

Meantime, destroyer PERKINS was standing by PENSACOLA to aid her crew in fighting the fires which scourged that ship. And destroyer MAURY was escorting damaged NEW ORLEANS to Tulagi. Destroyers LAMSON and LARDNER had remained shy of the battle area after being subjected to what is "laughingly" called friendly fire. Having been attached to Wright's column as Johnny-Come-Latelies, the two DD's had not been advised on the signals the task force was using, and they were naturally averse to inviting another barrage, however friendly. Division Commander Abercombie wisely remained on the sidelines with his two destroyers until directed to escort damaged MINNEAPOLIS to Tulagi.

By morning twilight the three damaged cruisers were in Sealark Channel, and the surface of "Iron bottom Bay" was once more cleared of wreckage. In a battle which had lasted about sixteen minutes, the enemy, although outweighed and outnumbered, had handily outfought the American task force. At the cost of one destroyer, the Japs had sunk a heavy cruiser and dealt such damage to three other cruisers that the injured ships would be out of action for a year. Small consolation was derived from the blocking of Tanaka's mission and the preventing of his express cargo from reaching Tassafaronga. At the cost of over 400 American lives, the investment was hardly worth the dividend.

Numerous reasons were given for this Tassafaronga defeat. American radar was nullified by the Guadalcanal background. The Navy lacked flashless powder. The cruiser planes, hampered by adverse sea conditions, were unable to get into the action. The Task Force Comander did not have sufficient time for thorough indoctrination of his subordinates.

Perhaps Admiral Nimitz cut to the core of the trouble with the trenchant observation that the Navy's combat crews needed *"training, training, and more training."* He also put in a word of acknowledgment of the pugnacity of the enemy's destroyers, and the skill with which Jap destroyermen delivered torpedo attacks.

Finally, it might be stated that at Tassafaronga the Navy encountered one of Japan's smartest admirals. Tanaka was good—as one destroyer officer phrased it, "damned good!" But as far as Guadalcanal was concerned, he was fighting a lost-cause battle. Yamamoto had already decided to pull out, and Tojo to pull back. And not again in World War II would the United States Navy suffer another Tassafaronga.

Tenacious Tanaka Tries Temerity

Tenacity is one thing, and temerity is another. In December Admiral Tanaka displayed an abundance of both in a final attempt to keep the "Tokyo Express" running to Tassafaronga.

The run from Jap-held New Georgia to Tassafaronga was something over 100 miles. On December 3 the Admiral's feline DD's came down the "Slot" on a high-speed dash. The column of ten destroyers was sighted by Allied coast watchers and intercepted by 15 bombers and torpedo planes from Henderson. But the Japs had fighter cover, and the air attack was frustrated. Jap destroyer MAKANAMI was damaged, but the train got through, delivered the cargo-drums, and retired without molestation.

Four days later Tanaka was back again with 11 destroyers. This time American aircraft sidetracked the "Express" long enough to give it a lambasting, and PT-boats joined the game. With I.J.N. NOWAKI badly crippled and another destroyer damaged, Tanaka pulled back up the "Slot."

He re-entered the Sound the following evening. And ran into a quartet of PT's which flung torpedoes and strafed the Jap destroyers with machine-gun fire. One PT made so bold as to close within 100 yards of destroyer OYASHIO. His own temerity outdone, Tanaka ordered a hasty retirement. Four PT-boats thus stopped a train which had previously wrecked a task force!

But Tanaka was as schedule-minded as a conductor with a new watch. On the dot he headed the "Express" down the "Slot" for the December 11 run. Right at the start it was struck off New Georgia by American aircraft, but the Jap DD's zigzagged out from under without damage.

The "Express" was next assaulted by PT-boats which waylaid the train off Cape Esperance. During the first hour of December 12, three of the PT's delivered a torpedo attack, and the Japanese destroyer TERUZUKI was holed and set afire. Worried about the PT onslaught, Tanaka sent his column on a fast reverse for New Georgia. But retirement came too late for TERUZUKI. At 0440 of that morning the burning destroyer blew up.

For the next three weeks the "Express" was held at bay by the moon—illumination which Tanaka could do nothing about. But as soon as the moon slimmed down, Tanaka tried again. On January 2, 1943, he started down the "Slot" with ten destroyers. The train was sighted by B-17 bombers, and the destroyer SUZUKAZE was disabled in consequence. The "Express" successfully evaded a PT attack off Cape Esperance, and raced on to Tassafaronga where the DD's dumped a considerable tonnage of cargo-drums and made good a fast retirement. All for nothing. The American PT-boats simply ran in among the floating drums and sank them with machine-gun fire.

Times were truly hard for the Japs on Guadalcanal at this juncture. With all supplies cut off, the Imperial garrison at Tassafaronga was starving. A despairing appeal for groceries went wailing out over the radio. Say it for Tanaka, the cry of hunger did not go unheeded. On January 10 he steamed down the "Slot" with a train of eight heavily-freighted destroyers.

Once more the "Express" was sighted and reported. Once more it was waylaid off Cape Esperance by eight PT-boats. Early in the morning of the 11th they gave it a warm reception. Two of the PT's were knocked out. In turn, the destroyer HATSUKAZE was holed by torpedo fire. Tanaka's train delivered the goods and steamed out to safety, but the PT's again overhauled and shot up the jettisoned cargo-drums.

The "Tokyo Express" of January 10 was the last freighter to run to Tassafaronga. The next "Express" (January 14) was a nine-ship passenger train carrying 600 troops sent to cover the evacuation of the starving garrison.

Mission to Munda

In December 1942 the First Marine Division was withdrawn from Guadalcanal and General Vandegrift relinquished his "Cactus" command to Major General A. M. Patch, U.S.A., and his soldiers.

At Munda Point on the northwest elbow of New Georgia Island the Japs were at that time rushing the completion of an airfield which threatened the "Cactus" positions on Guadalcanal. Admiral Halsey planned a strike at this airfield—a night bombardment.

Conduct of the Munda mission fell to Rear Admiral W. L. ("Pug") Ainsworth, whom Halsey had placed in command of Task Force 67, the force Tanaka had sloughed at Tassafaronga. An officer who had distinguished himself in the Atlantic as a destroyer squadron commander, and in the Pacific as ComDesPac, Ainsworth was precisely the driver to pull a beaten force together, and just the leader for the Munda foray.

The target date was set for January 4. Ainsworth's bombardment group (TG 67.2) contained the light cruisers NASHVILLE (flagship), ST. LOUIS, and HELENA, and destroyers FLETCHER (Lieutenant Commander F. L. Johnson) and O'BANNON (Commander E. R. Wilkinson). The destroyers were commanded by Captain R. P. Briscoe, ComDesRon 5, in FLETCHER.

While the bombardment group was striking Munda, a support group under command of Rear Admiral Tisdale was to maneuver off the southeast coast of New Georgia. The support group included light cruisers HONOLULU, ACHILLES, and COLUMBIA, heavy cruiser LOUISVILLE, and destroyers DRAYTON, LAMSON, and NICHOLAS. Catalina night-fighters of the newly organized "Black Cat" force scouted over and harassed Munda field on the two nights preceding the bombardment. These planes were also to act as spotters for Ainsworth's cruisers. The American submarine GRAYBACK took station off Munda to serve as a beacon ship for the bombardment group.

Night of January 4-5 was Stygian dark, an overcast sky releasing inky rain-showers. As Ainsworth's group approached Munda, the cruisers launched planes to drop flares if so ordered, and a radar-carrying Catalina searched ahead for Jap surface ships. At 0102 in the morning of January 5, NASHVILLE opened fire with her big batteries on Munda airfield. The other cruisers followed suit, and then Briscoe's destroyers slammed the target with a 5-inch barrage. The spotting planes reported excellent shooting. At 0150, the bombardment completed, Ainsworth led his ships eastward. Munda had been given a good plastering—about 3,000 rounds of 6-inch, and 1,400 rounds of 5-inch. The enemy shore batteries had fired a few salvos in return, hitting nothing.

But Tisdale's group, which joined up with Ainsworth's southwest of Guadalcanal that morning, was struck by Jap aircraft by way of reprisal. And cruiser ACHILLES took a bomb hit. In this action cruiser HELENA fired shells equipped with proximity fuzes, the first time these hard-hitting items were used in the Pacific.

The Munda raid boosted American morale in the South Pacific, and gave the Navy good practice in night operations. As Admiral Ainsworth commented:

> *The night bombardment of Munda is the first naval action against shore installations in which the most modern instruments, including our latest developments in radar, were available for navigation and fire-control purposes. It is also the first action in which our Navy has coordinated surface, submarine and aircraft units in a night bombardment. As an initial venture in this field of operations, this action may be taken as our first lesson in night amphibious warfare.*

Some Iron for the Japanese Diet

General Patch's "Cactus" forces lost no time in striking at the hungry enemy. While Patch's infantrymen stormed the Japs in their pillboxes, destroyers MUSTIN and PERKINS maneuvered off the mouth of the Matanikau, firing at designated targets. Together they pelted the Japs with about 2,000 rounds of 5-inch.

On January 12, 1943, destroyer REID steamed along the Guadalcanal coast near Cape Esperance, and plastered Japanese shore positions with 360 rounds of 5-inch.

Operating out of Purvis Bay near Tulagi, Captain Briscoe's "Cactus Striking Force"—destroyers NICHOLAS, O'BANNON, RADFORD, and DEHAVEN—stepped in to deliver a shore bombardment on January 19. On this occasion the four DD's pounded the Japs with over 2,000 rounds of 5-inch.

Destroyer FLETCHER contributed a bombardment on January 26. The target was near Visale—an enemy-occupied mudhole washed by the waters of Cape Esperance. FLETCHER carried a distinguished observer on this mission. Her passenger was General Patch, and one of his observations was an expression of high satisfaction with destroyer artillery.

On the banks of the Bonegi River, flanking Tassafaronga, the American vanguard encountered 600 troopers whom Tanaka had landed at that point to cover the garrison's retirement. Moving up to within a mile of the Bonegi's mouth, destroyers ANDERSON and WILSON turned their 5-inch 38 batteries on the beach, and gave the 600 Japanese a thorough blasting.

Meanwhile, the Japs had been working night and day to build an airfield at Vila, a coconut plantation on the southern coast of Kolombangara Island, opposite New Georgia on the west side of Kula Gulf. Early in the morning of January 24, Admiral Ainsworth led a bombardment group up the "Slot" to Kula Gulf, and down the Gulf to give this airstrip at Vila the Munda treatment. His bombardment force contained cruisers NASHVILLE and HELENA, and destroyers NICHOLAS, DEHAVEN, RADFORD, and O'BANNON.

While O'BANNON picketed the northern entrance of the Gulf, the rest of the group steamed down to Vila to give the airfield a gun-lashing. The cruisers pounded the field with some 2,000 rounds of 6-inch, and the DD's pegged about 1,500 rounds of 5-inch at the target. Jap shore guns replied with indifferent marksmanship. As Ainsworth's group steamed out of Kula Gulf and raced down the "Slot," Jap "Bettys" arrived on the scene. Using full radar control, destroyer RADFORD removed some of these from the night sky, and at daylight fighter planes from Henderson Field broke up the attack.

In this action RADFORD scored an interesting first. This was the first time a U.S. man-of-war shot down attacking aircraft with AA guns under full radar control (tracking and gunnery directed by radar), and without benefit of searchlight. The planes were not seen until four exploded like bursting meteors in the night.

As at Munda, the Japs soon repaired the damage at Vila, and the airfield remained a thorn in the American side until the enemy was ousted from southern Kolombangara.

Chicago Downed, La Vallette Damaged

Although the enemy had decided to evacuate Guadalcanal as soon as possible, his intentions were unknown to the Americans, and Patch's Army was heavily reinforced during the last week in January. A large troop convoy was dispatched from Nouméa under guard of Rear Admiral R. C. ("Ike") Giffen's Task Force 18.

The task force was composed of heavy cruisers WICHITA, CHICAGO, and LOUISVILLE; light cruisers MONTPELIER, CLEVELAND, and COLUMBIA; and an air support group built around escort-carriers CHENANGO and SUWANNEE. The force was screened by eight destroyers under command of Captain H. F. Pullen, ComDesDiv 41. The destroyer screen included DD's LA VALLETTE, WALLER, CONWAY, FRAZIER, CHEVALIER, EDWARDS, MEADE, and TAYLOR.

Late in the afternoon of January 29 the task force was some 50 miles north of Rennell Island. As the ships steamed northwestward into the sunset, a flock of Jap torpedo-bombers buzzed in on the attack. This first attack was broken up by an AA barrage, and one "Betty" came down afire, and others were probably damaged. The ships zigzagged out from under the rain of bombs with no damage. But at 1931 the "Bettys" were back. This time they penetrated the AA roof. A burst of tracer exploded one Jap plane not far from WALLER's fantail. A second torpedo-bomber smacked into the water off CHICAGO's port bow, and proceeded to burn like a magnesium flare. The cruiser was starkly silhouetted by this floating bonfire. And at 1945 a "Betty" skimmed in, and slammed a torpedo into the exposed ship.

The blast flooded an after fireroom and damaged the vessel's steering gear. As CHICAGO was rocking from this jolt, she was struck by a second torpedo, the explosion flooding the forward engine-room and knocking out the No. 3 fireroom. The cruiser staggered to a halt, her rudder jammed, her hull listing.

It was soon apparent to Admiral Giffen that the disabled ship would have to be towed out of bomber range. LOUISVILLE started the tow, and a course was set for Espiritu Santo. Early in the morning of January 30 the tug NAVAJO and the destroyer-transport SANDS were dispatched to CHICAGO's aid. About 0800 the tug took over the tow, and the cruiser was slowly hauled southward under heavy escort. At 1500 in the afternoon the cruisers were directed by Admiral Halsey to steam on to Efate. Guarded by a screen of five destroyers (including the APD), CHICAGO limped on her way, a wounded warrior borne off the field by a group of stretcher-bearers.

The screen was made up of destroyers, CONWAY (Commander N. S. Prime), LA VALLETTE (Commander H. H. Henderson), WALLER (Commander L. H. Frost), and EDWARDS (Lieutenant Commander P. G. Osler), plus destroyer-transport SANDS (Lieutenant Commander J. J. Branson). Division Commander Pullen rode in CONWAY.

But the little group never made it. At 1620 LA VALLETTE's lookouts sighted eleven Jap torpedo-bombers swooping down out of the clouds, range nine miles. CHICAGO's lookouts sighted them a moment later. But the big ship, crawling on a towline at 4 knots, could do little more than man her guns and pray.

At the time the planes were sighted the screen destroyers were some 3,000 to 5,000 yards from the disabled cruiser. The Task Force 18 cruisers were about 30 miles to the eastward, and the carrier group was farther to the southeast. Little help could be expected from the distant ships. The screen destroyers squared away to make it a fight.

But three DD's of the screen were on the unengaged side of CHICAGO, and LA VALLETTE was the only destroyer in position to block the high-speed attack. She opened fire at 10,000 yards; may have shot down two planes. CHICAGO's guns blurted when the planes were 8,000 yards distant; four or five of the "Bettys" were hit and compelled to drop their torpedoes outside the screen. A burning plane fell into the sea to starboard of CHICAGO, and another crashed in flames close aboard to port. Two more were shot down in the roaring battle, and then the combat patrol caught up with the rest of the Jap flock, which retired in a mad dogfight. The "Bettys" were fleeing when CHICAGO's lookouts glimpsed five torpedo wakes off the cruiser's starboard beam. So she was bitten, after all.

Unable to maneuver, she could only sit and take it. At 1624 four torpedoes hit the cruiser in chain-lightning succession. NAVAJO cut the towline, and the mortally stricken ship was immediately abandoned. She rolled over and sank at 1643.

Meantime, LA VALLETTE had been struck by one of the torpedoes dropped in the opening round of the battle. She had maneuvered smartly to evade the spread, but one "fish" was too fast for her. The war head burst into her forward engine-room. The forward fireroom was flooded, and water poured through a fractured bulkhead into the after fireroom. Lieutenant Eli Roth, the damage-control officer, and 20 men perished in the wreckage. Quick work by the other damage-controlmen stemmed the flood and set the pumps in action.

On board LA VALLETTE the hour for heroism had come. Men fought desperately to save the crippled ship and rescue crippled shipmates. The Executive Officer reported an outstanding case concerning M. W. Tollberg, Water Tender Second. At his post in the forward fireroom Tollberg had been frightfully burned by a spurt of escaping live steam. Blinded and in horrible agony, the man succeeded in climbing topside and reaching an oil-control valve which needed closing. He was clutching the valve and trying to turn it when found by the ship's Medical Officer. Tollberg died two hours later. It could certainly be said he gave his life in an effort to save his ship.

Two minutes after the torpedo struck, Commander Henderson had the ship moving forward on the after engine, and she crawled out of the battle under her own power. Later her feed-water failed, and she was towed by NAVAJO. On February 3 she reached Espiritu Santo. There she received temporary repairs, after which she was sent to the West Coast for a complete overhaul.

CHICAGO's survivors were picked up by EDWARDS, WALLER, SANDS, and NAVAJO, the four sharing in the rescue of 1,049 cruisermen. The Guadalcanal campaign had cost the United States Navy another fine cruiser and another heavy death toll.

And still another ship was to go down in the battle for "Cactus"—the U.S.S. DeHaven.

Loss of U.S.S. DeHaven

To block the enemy at Cape Esperance, General Patch dispatched an infantry battalion to Verahue Beach. The troops were carried to the beachhead by five LCT's and a seaplane tender under escort of Captain Briscoe's "Cactus Striking Force" from Tulagi—destroyers Fletcher, Radford, Nicholas, and DeHaven. Fighters from Henderson Field covered the landings, which were handily made in the early hours of February 1, 1943.

As luck would have it, the Japs had decided to begin their evacuation on this date. And their scout planes, looking down on Marovovo, evidently took the "Cactus Striking Force" for a group lying in ambush to intercept. The word was enough to bring a squadron of Aichi dive-bombers to the scene.

Winging over the horizon on the afternoon of February 1, the Jap airmen caught a glimpse of two destroyers and several LCT's about two miles southeast of Savo Island. The destroyers were Nicholas and DeHaven shepherding a trio of unloaded landing craft back to Tulagi. To the northwest of Cape Esperance, Fletcher and Radford were coming with the rest of the unloaded LCT's, but they were not spotted by the Japs.

The destroyers had been warned by Guadalcanal radio that the enemy was in the air and on the hunt. Radars and lookouts were watching the sky, and the destroyer and LCT gunners were waiting at hair-trigger. Unfortunately the American ships off Savo had not been furnished with fighter cover; all of the American fighter planes had remained with the Radford-Fletcher group. This neglect, whatever its cause, exposed Nicholas and DeHaven to a cyclonic aerial attack.

Some 14 "Vals" were in the sky. Nine of these were counted by DeHaven as the flight roared in at 5,000 feet. The ship's clocks timed the attack at 1457. Down came the lightning as six of the planes plummeted on the target destroyer.

DeHaven's anti-aircraft batteries rattled, banged, and flamed, smearing the sky with flak. The barrage was unable to stop the bombers. The screaming planes ripped through the AA curtain, and dropped three bombs squarely on the ship.

One bomb, smashing the destroyer's bridge, killed her captain, Commander C. E. Tolman. Men, guns, and deck gear were blown high in the air. A near miss, exploding near the bow, crushed in a section of the hull. With fires leaping from her mangled superstructure, DeHaven wallowed in agony, settling by the head. She went down as her frantic engineers were fighting their way topside out of the inferno, and sailors topside were desperately striving to launch rafts.

Meantime, destroyer Nicholas (Lieutenant Commander A. J. Hill) was beating off an attack by eight dive-bombers. Near misses killed two men and damaged the ship's steering gear, but otherwise she came through without hurt. Two of the landing craft shot down a plane.

The battle ended as abruptly as it had begun, and the planes winged away to report another United States warship on the floor of "Ironbottom Bay." The nearby LCT's circled in to rescue the DeHaven survivors. There were deplorably few to be rescued.

Of the ship's 14 officers, only four were found alive. One of the four was painfully wounded. And 146 men —38 of them wounded—were recovered. Altogether, 167 of the destroyer's complement had perished with the ship.

Adding DeHaven's name to the long, lugubrious list, the United States Navy could count her as the 15th destroyer lost in the Guadalcanal campaign.

Guadalcanal Conclusion

On that February afternoon of DeHaven's demise, Allied coast watchers and aircraft in the vicinity of Vella Lavella Island sighted the "Tokyo Express" advancing down the "Slot." Some 20 DD's were hooked into this train, and Tanaka had the throttle tied to the floor. The Allies did not know it, but this was the first section of a passenger special dedicated to "Operation KE"—the evacuation of the Emperor's Guadalcanal garrison.

It looked like a reinforcement effort, and the report sent 41 American planes into the air to intercept. About sundown they waylaid the train off Vangunu Island, and succeeded in "derailing" the destroyer Makinami. The rest of the train kept on going.

Three hundred mines were quickly strewn along the track between Tassafaronga and Cape Esperance by destroyer-minelayers Tracy, Montgomery, and Preble. An attack by waiting PT-boats drove the "Express" into the minefield with fatal results for destroyer Makigumo.

Then Captain Briscoe's "Cactus" force ran in to intercept. But Jap aircraft intervened, and destroyers Fletcher, Radford, and Nicholas were fended off.

American PT's struck at the "Express" time and again. Tanaka's train brushed them aside, and raced through to its Guadalcanal terminal. Early in the morning of February 2 it was northbound, loaded to excursion capacity. The Americans still did not know that the "Express" was picking up instead of delivering.

Two days later the train was southbound again. This time it was composed of 22 destroyers and a cruiser. As it came down the "Slot," it was met by aircraft from Henderson; destroyer MAIKAZE was all but swamped by near misses, and SHIRANUHI was hit by a bomb. But this time the PT's were evaded and the mines circumvented. Again the train reached its destination. Again (early morning of February 5) it was northbound with "standing room only."

No less successful was the third section of this "Tokyo Flyer," a string of 18 Jap destroyers which steamed down the "Slot" on February 7. Winging through bad weather, a group of American dive-bombers pounced on the "Express" and dealt minor damage to destroyers ISOKAZE and HAMAKAZE. As this train put in at Cape Esperance, the PT-boats and mines farther east had no chance to interfere.

The American forces on "Cactus" never had another crack at Tanaka's Guadalcanal special. It was "All aboard!" on that night of February 7-8; thereafter the run to Guadal was discontinued.

Pushing eastward from Verahue Beach and westward from Tassafaronga, General Patch's Army forces were surprised to come upon vacated camp sites, abandoned gear, and spiked guns. Aside from the shrieking cockatoos, the jungle was as silent as a grave. The only Japs who could be found were dead.

Accomplished in the face of strong potential opposition, the Japanese evacuation of Guadalcanal must go down in history as a masterpiece. In three nocturnal embarkations the Imperial Navy had removed from the island a total of 11,706 men, all in silence and secrecy. *"Only skill in keeping their plans disguised and bold celerity in carrying them out enabled the Japanese to withdraw the remnants of the Guadalcanal garrison,"* wrote Admiral Nimitz. Much of the skill and celerity in reference was attributable to the Japanese Destroyer Service and tenacious Admiral Tanaka, the "Casey Jones" of the "Tokyo Express."

But loss of Tulagi and defeat on Guadalcanal had cost the Japanese all chance of gaining control over the South Pacific, and had pulled a bastion out from under Rabaul and citadels west. *"I look upon the Guadalcanal and Tulagi Operations,"* said Admiral Nagano in gloomy postwar confession, *"as the turning point from offense to defense, and the cause of our setback there was our inability to increase our forces at the same speed that . . . (the Americans) did."*

Nagano's statement is overly broad, neglecting as it does the early weeks of the Guadalcanal campaign when the American ability to increase forces was certainly a futuristic one, and the American forces available were decidedly outweighed and outnumbered by the Jap. Something besides weight and number and the ability to increase these factors was responsible for the American victory.

It might be demonstrated that logistics—the old problem of maintaining and supplying front-line forces—was the key to the Japanese defeat. They were unable to keep open their extended communications arteries. When these arteries were cut, the front-line forces at Lunga Point and Tassafaronga "died on the vine." In fact, had the Japs had more little mouths to feed on Guadalcanal, the famine might have felled them sooner.

The American victory was purchased at a high price in life, limb, and material. Naval losses were particularly high. Ship for ship, the Japanese came out on the easier end of the bill, as the following table shows:

U. S. Navy and Imperial Navy
LOSSES
in the Guadalcanal Campaign
AUGUST 7, 1942 TO FEBRUARY 7, 1943

TYPE OF CRAFT	AMERICAN	JAPANESE
Battleships	0	2
Aircraft Carriers	2	1
Heavy Cruisers	5	2
Light Cruisers	2	2
Destroyers	15	12
TOTAL	24	19

The above table does not summarize the whole statistical story. Although the United States Navy suffered the heavier losses as compared to the Japanese Navy, the U. S. Marine Corps and the Army endured relatively light casualties compared to those suffered by the Japanese Army on Guadalcanal. Japanese aircraft losses were the heavier, and in other categories such as submarines and auxiliary craft their naval losses considerably exceeded the American.

The 15 American destroyers which went down in the Guadalcanal campaign were TUCKER, JARVIS, BLUE, DUNCAN, MEREDITH, O'BRIEN, PORTER, CUSHING, MONSSEN, LAFFEY, BARTON, WALKE, PRESTON, BENHAM, and DEHAVEN. All did not go down in Savo Sound. But it might be said that this squadron is permanently based on the bottom of "Ironbottom Bay." Every ship, with the exception of TUCKER, was a victim of enemy fire, and all contributed their services to the sinking of the Rising Sun in the Lower Solomons.

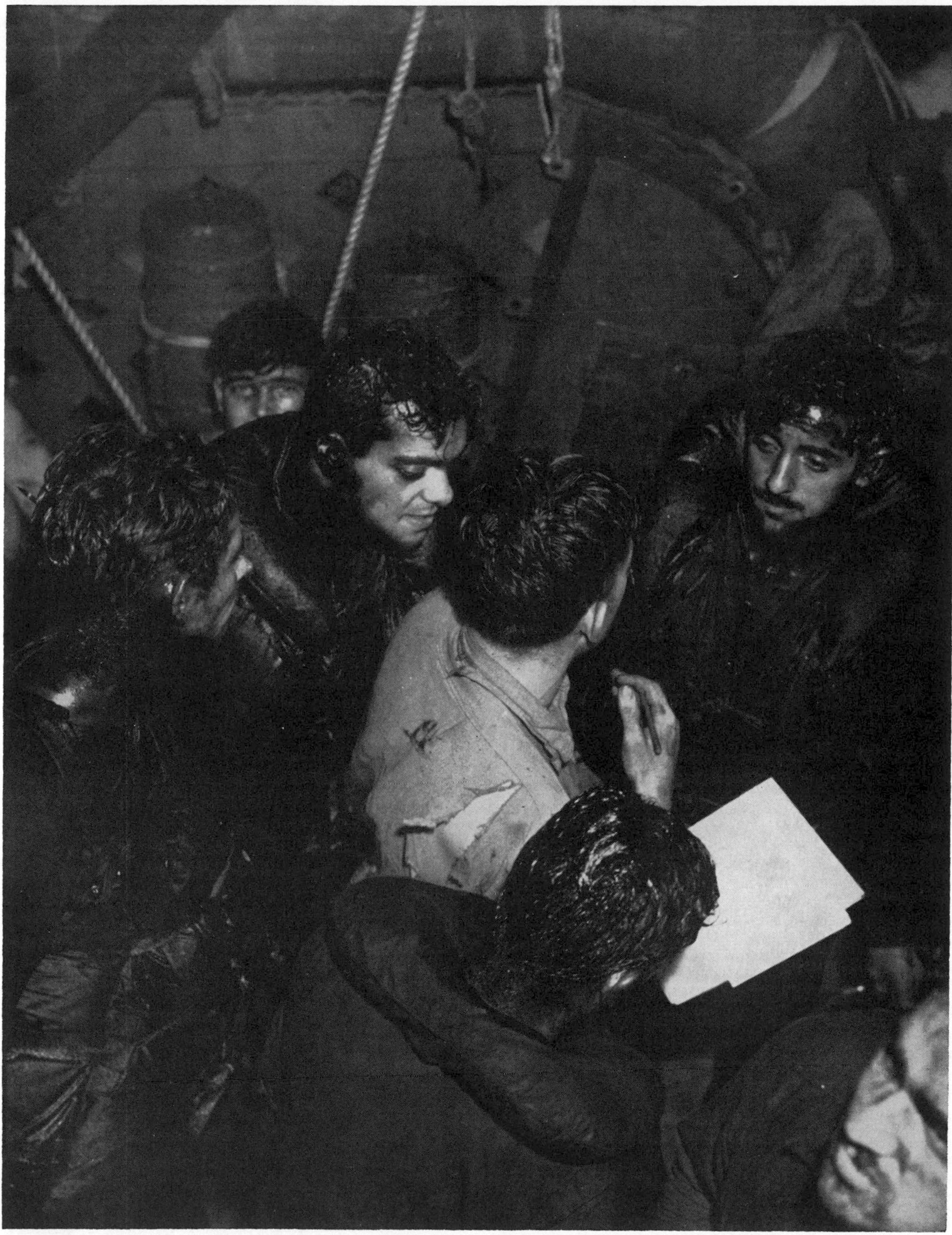

Destroyers to the rescue. The Nicholas picks up sodden, oil-soaked survivors of the U.S.S. Helena after that redoubtable cruiser came to her end from a Japanese "long lance" torpedo at the Battle of Kula Gulf. On a bombardment mission, U. S. ships intercepted a Jap troop convoy. In this night battle, the U.S. forces met Japan's best weapons, tactics, and destroyer skippers.

The morning after the battle—the U.S.S. Radford steams into Tulagi harbor in the Solomons with a deckload of survivors of the sunken cruiser Helena, and with the wounded filling all available space below. But even saved from drowning, the cruisermen had not finished with the battle, for the rescuing Radford, packed with survivors, met the Jap destroyer Amagiri in a slambang duel.

Taking off the wounded. Survivors of the Helena being transferred over the gangplank of rescue ship Nicholas after the Battle of Kula Gulf.

Part of the scrap heap of war—the crew of a U.S. destroyer stacking up empty shell cases after a night bombardment. The shell cases shown give a good idea of the midnight tempest that swept the Japanese airfield at Munda, July 4, 1943.

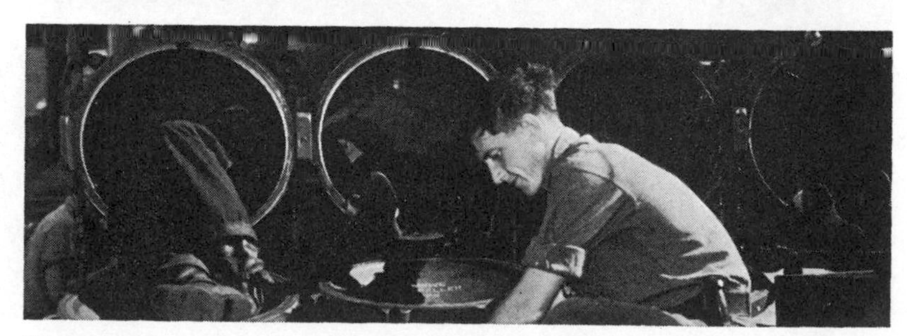

The torpedo gang of the U.S.S. Nicholas clean torpedo tubes after the Battle of Kula Gulf. A torpedo is such a delicate mechanism that even the slightest obstruction or foreign matter may cause a "cold" shot or erratic torpedo run.

CHAPTER 17

CENTRAL SOLOMONS SWEEP

(Part 1)

Stars on the Horizon

Ainsworth—Moosbrugger—Burke—three DesPac names indelibly enscribed on the waters of the Solomons Archipelago.

Rear Admiral Ainsworth, a one-time destroyer captain, then a Squadron Commander, eventually became ComDesPac (Commander Destroyers Pacific). Commander Frederick Moosbrugger came to the fore as a DesPac Division Commander who pioneered on the "Haul out with Halsey." Commander Arleigh A. Burke, another Division Commander, would lead the famous "Little Beavers."

To the foregoing names that of Rear Admiral A. S. ("Tip") Merrill could well be added; he was a task force commander who knew the Destroyer Service from "four-piper" days. On DD's in World War I, ComDesDiv 17 and ComDesRon 8 in the two years prior to World War II, he too was a "destroyerman's destroyerman." But his connection with the DesPac Force was somewhat more remote than the tie which brought Ainsworth, Moosbrugger, and Burke together in a bright destroyer constellation. And coincident with their ascendancy was the setting of the Rising Sun in the Solomons.

"Watchtower" versus "Operation I"

"Operation Watchtower" did not end with the American occupation of Guadalcanal. Capture of that strategic island was only a beginning. Often described as a ladder, the Solomon Islands extend northwestward to the gateway of the Bismarcks. Guadalcanal was only a "bottom rung."

The securing of Guadalcanal as a foothold in the Lower Solomons had been a hard fight. The climb through the Central and Upper Solomons was certain to be harder. As the Allies neared the Rabaul power-house, Japanese opposition was bound to stiffen—unless it could be softened by attrition.

But after eviction from Guadalcanal, the enemy did not sit idly by in supine despair. Admiral Yamamoto promised Emperor Hirohito that the Americans would be stopped dead in the Central Solomons.

How was this to be accomplished? By air power. Concentrate the Japanese air forces at Papua, New Guinea. Bring in Ozawa's Third Fleet with carriers ZUIKAKU, ZUIHO, JUNYO, and HIYO to put the head on a mighty sledgehammer with which to pound the Americans in the Lower and Central Solomons. Land-based aircraft from Rabaul in the Bismarcks, from Bougainville, Buka, and other Solomons bases, would weight the sledge.

On March 25, 1943, the Imperial War Council put the Japanese ideograph of approval on Yamamoto's aerial offensive. It was designated "Operation I." To conduct this operation Yamamoto installed his headquarters in Rabaul. Also headquartered in Rabaul was Vice Admiral Ozawa. The local command was held by Vice Admiral Kusaka, another air-minded exponent of "Operation I." Aviators and planes were rushed to Papua from all points of the Japanese compass, and the date for the offensive's grand opening was set for early April.

Fletcher and Naval Aircraft Kill RO-102

On February 11, 1943, destroyer FLETCHER (Lieutenant Commander F. L. Johnson) was steaming as a unit in an A/S screen working with Task Force 67.

The force was maneuvering about 100 miles south of Rennell Island when one of HELENA's planes sighted and bombed a Jap submarine about nine miles distant from FLETCHER. The sub was 75 feet under when the airmen dropped a 100-pounder, and in the wake of this blast it went deeper.

The plane planted a smoke pot to mark the spot, and FLETCHER was ordered to the scene to take a hand in the affair. The destroyer's sonar soon registered a clear, firm contact at a range of 2,900 yards. Johnson conned the ship in to launch a deliberate attack, and the destroyer let go with a 9-charge pattern. The charges were accurately placed, and all detonated.

Six minutes after the attack two deep-bellied explosions boomed under the sea. The turbulent rumble brought up a large air-and-oil bubble. Then a glistening slick. Five minutes later the FLETCHER was rocked by a stupendous undersea blast. For a moment the jolted destroyermen believed their ship had been torpedoed. The detonation, however, echoed from an exploding submarine.

Up came the ghastly trash—shattered deck-planking, chunks of cork, bits of jigsaw debris, and particles of this and that which bore undisputable evidence to the demolishment of submersible and submariners.

Johnson and company could now paint a Japanese naval flag on FLETCHER's scoreboard. And the Japanese Submarine Force could erase RO-102 from its roster.

Pushing the Japs Around (Vila and Munda Revisited)

Admiral Halsey, Commander Southern Pacific (ComSoPac), did not want to give the enemy a chance to regain his balance after the Guadalcanal setback. To his naval forces he dispatched the word, "Keep pushing the Japs around." Bombardments of the Japanese airstrips at Munda and Vila were designed to implement this program. Destroyers participated in the pushing.

Target date was the night of March 5-6, 1943. The Munda bombardment mission went to Captain Briscoe's "Cactus" team—destroyers FLETCHER, O'BANNON, RADFORD, and NICHOLAS. Early in the morning of March 6 the DD's were off the New Georgia base, at which they hurled some 1,600 rounds of 5-inch shells. But the Japs filled up the shell holes almost as soon as they were dug, and their planes were taking off from this field within 24 hours of the blasting.

The mission to Vila was somewhat more destructive. It was assigned to Task Force 68 under Rear Admiral Merrill. The force included light cruisers MONTPELIER (flagship), CLEVELAND, and DENVER, and three destroyers. The destroyers were WALLER (Commander L. H. Frost), flying the pennant of Commander A. A. Burke, ComDesDiv 43; CONWAY (Commander N. S. Prime), flagship of Commander H. F. Pullen, ComDesDiv 41; and CONY (Commander H. D. Johnston). Commander Pullen was senior destroyer officer present. The DD's were *"to provide protection against enemy submarines and PT-boats and silence enemy shore batteries, permitting cruisers to conduct bombardment unmolested."*

The sea was flat, the night as black as a funeral when the task force started up the "Slot." Three "Black Cat" planes, prepared to act as spotters, scouted the way ahead. At 2230 the sailors were put on their toes by a radio report from Guadalcanal advising them that two Japanese light cruisers or destroyers had steamed out of Faisi early in the evening and were heading southeast. The enemy ships were, in fact, DD's. Merrill, of course, did not know their destination, but then one of the "Black Cats" spotted the enemy vessels putting in at Vila.

The American ships entered Kula Gulf a few minutes after midnight. The ships navigated by SG radar, feeling their way down the New Georgia coast on the east side of the Gulf.

Destroyer WALLER was positioned 6,000 yards ahead of the cruiser column. CONWAY was 2,000 yards ahead. CONY steamed on the column's port quarter to guard the flank against PT-boat attacks. MONTPELIER, CLEVELAND, and DENVER steamed in the order named, keeping distance of 1,000 yards. With all guns manned the force forged southward at 20 knots.

At 0057 WALLER picked up radar contact with the enemy warships across the Gulf. From Merrill came the word, "Stand by to commence firing!" The clock was almost at 0101 when WALLER opened up with a salvo of five torpedoes, range about 3½ miles. Then the cruisers let go. And at 0101 WALLER's gunners opened fire.

Firing at flashes, the two Japanese destroyers answered with sporadic salvos that were not as accurate as the radar-aimed shots fired by the Americans. At 0107 a great explosion lit the sky over the coastal waters of Kolombangara. The blast was heard by the American destroyermen at Munda, 25 miles distant. One of the Jap destroyers, perforated by multiple hits, had been finished off by a torpedo from WALLER.

The second Jap destroyer was now afire, an easy mark for Merrill's cruisers. Shell after shell they threw into the burning target. By 0110 this DD, too, was on its way to the bottom, and its crew was swimming to the beach. Merrill's task force ceased fire at 0114, and he swung the column westward about five minutes later to bombard the Jap airstrip at Vila. Several enemy batteries returned the fire, but their aim was lackluster. One of them was silenced by a barrage from CONWAY.

For 16 minutes the American ships slammed shells into the Vila airstrip and adjacent appurtenances of Japanese aviation. At 0140 the bombardment was ended, and the task force high-tailed out of the Gulf. Behind it, in the cool waters of Kula, it left Japanese destroyers MURASAME and MINEGUMO on the bottom. On the Vila beach a lot of Japanese air equipment was burning.

The Vila raid evoked a word of commendation from Admiral Nimitz, who stated:

THE COMMANDER IN CHIEF, PACIFIC FLEET, CONSIDERS THAT TASK FORCE 68 GAVE A VERY CREDITABLE PERFORMANCE ON THE NIGHT OF 5-6 MARCH IN PICKING UP THE TWO ENEMY SHIPS AGAINST A CLOSE LAND BACKGROUND, OBTAINING A PROMPT FIRE CONTROL SET-UP, SINKING THE SHIPS IN A BUSINESS-LIKE MANNER AND THEN PROCEEDING WITH PLANNED BOMBARDMENT APPROXIMATELY ON SCHEDULE. THE OPERATION HAD ALL THE PRECISION OF A WELL-REHEARSED EXERCISE BY VETERAN SHIPS, WHICH THESE WERE NOT.

O'Bannon Kills RO-34

On April Fool's Day, 1943, Admiral Halsey received information which was nobody's practical joke. Scouting over the Upper Solomons, Allied aircraft had a glimpse of enemy activity which suggested a big aerial offensive in the making. A lot of supplies were being rushed in to enemy bases in the islands.

What the Allied flyers had glimpsed was the build-up for Yamamoto's "Operation I." Although unable to gauge the exact size of this Jap offensive, the Americans made prompt efforts to counter it.

Six times Admiral Ainsworth's force raced north of Kula Gulf, trying to intercept the Japanese, but each time the Jap convoys gave the American ships the slip. Reason: Jap snooper planes and submarines on picket patrol—a warning system which flashed the alarm to the nervous convoys, giving them adequate time to retire or take cover.

It was a good system while it lasted, but it cost the Imperial Navy another submarine. Early in the morning of April 5, Ainsworth's task force was up the "Slot," hunting contact with a reported convoy. The contact, tipped off, had made itself scarce. But destroyers STRONG and O'BANNON of the task force screen made radar contact at 0218 with one of the picket subs.

Initial range was 7,000 yards. O'BANNON reported the suspicious "pip," and her captain, Lieutenant Commander D. J. MacDonald, was ordered to conduct an immediate investigation. It took MacDonald about ten minutes to get his ship within sighting range and identify the submarine's silhouette as "made in Japan."

That was all the destroyermen needed. O'BANNON passed ahead of the sub at a distance of about 90 yards. Before the Jap deep-sea sailors knew what hit them, a hot 5-inch salvo was punched down the submarine's throat. MacDonald ordered a K-gun attack. Three portside projectors let fly. The charges straddled the submarine. As the smoke frazzled out of the K-guns, MacDonald conned the ship away and then closed the range to 150 yards, and the destroyermen raked the sub with 1.1-inch and 20 mm. fire.

MacDonald swung O'BANNON for another depth-charge salvo. Again the K-guns barked, lobbing charges at the wallowing undersea boat. A flash from the destroyer's searchlight showed the sub going under by the stern.

About 0319 O'BANNON's sonarmen obtained sound contact with the submerged target, and MacDonald conned the ship for a depth-charge run. An 8-charge pattern was dropped. It was noted that *"all charges functioned properly."* This was a technical way of saying that eight timed detonations were heard by the destroyermen, not to mention the submariners in the target submersible. Also, *"There was one particular very heavy explosion quite different in effect from a normal depth-charge explosion."* Evidently something bigger than a light bulb had popped within the submarine.

Twice more MacDonald ran his destroyer over the spot, but O'BANNON's sonar was unable to re-establish contact with the sub.

For the submarine had gone deep. Very deep. Flying over that locale the following day, American aviators sighted a large, undulant oil slick drifting on the surface of the "Slot." It was the last earthly remnant of the RO-34.

Loss of the U.S.S. Aaron Ward

About noon of April 7, 1943, Ainsworth's task force set out from Tulagi on mission to bombard Munda. The ships were just getting under way when Ainsworth received an air alarm broadcast from Guadalcanal. Turning his formation eastward, he headed for Indispensable Strait at high speed. This move was highly discreet on Ainsworth's part. Down the "Slot" were coming 67 "Val" dive-bombers and 110 "Zeke" fighters, most of them from Ozawa's Carrier Force. Yamamoto had pulled the trigger on "Operation I," and the biggest air raid since Pearl

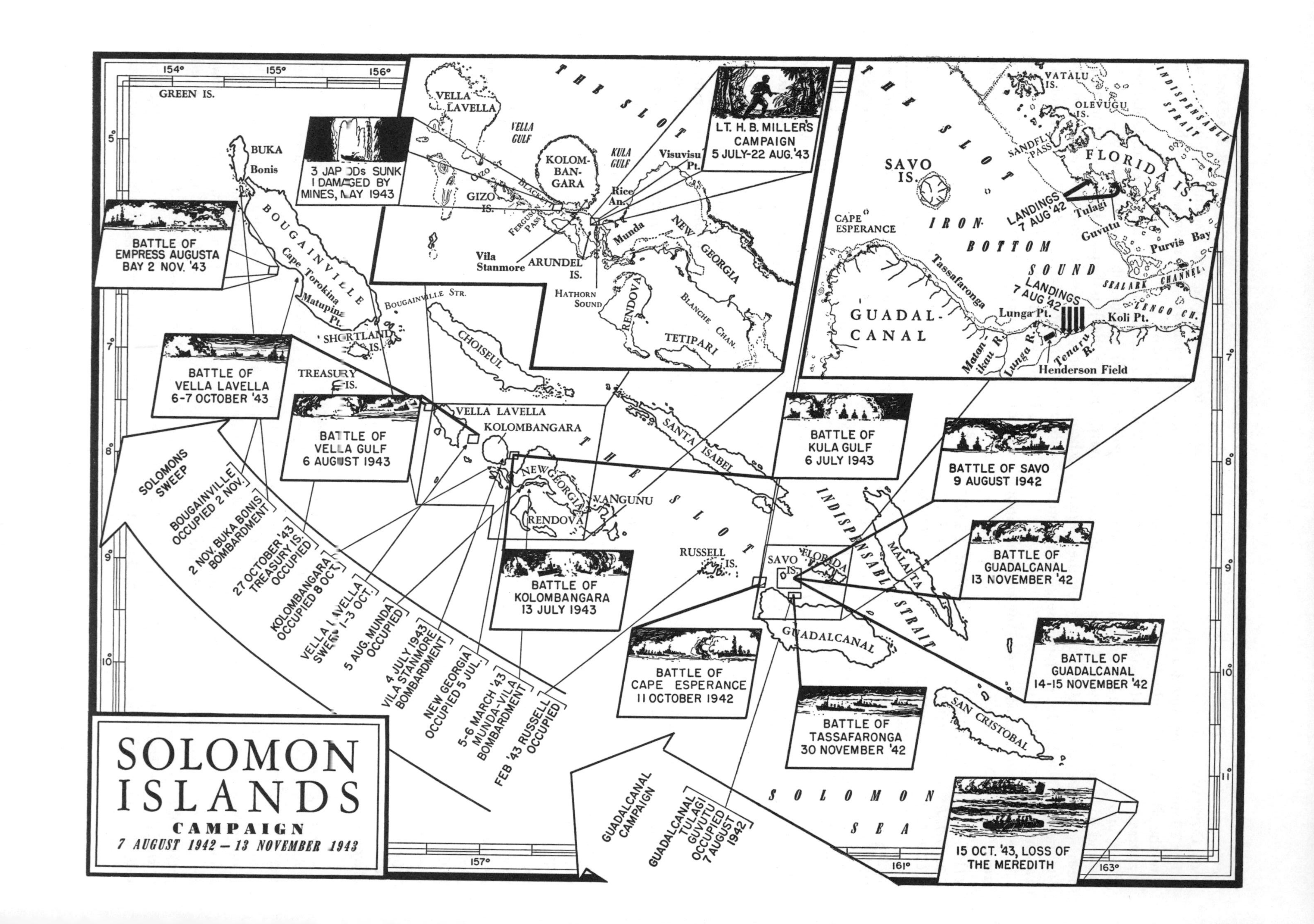

SOLOMON ISLANDS
CAMPAIGN
7 AUGUST 1942 – 13 NOVEMBER 1943
BATTLE OF EMPRESS AUGUSTA BAY 2 NOV. '43
3 JAP DDs SUNK 1 DAMAGED BY MINES, MAY 1943
LT. H. B. MILLER'S CAMPAIGN 5 JULY-22 AUG. '43
BATTLE OF VELLA LAVELLA 6-7 OCTOBER '43
BATTLE OF VELLA GULF 6 AUGUST 1943
BATTLE OF KULA GULF 6 JULY 1943
BATTLE OF SAVO 9 AUGUST 1942
BATTLE OF KOLOMBANGARA 13 JULY 1943
BATTLE OF GUADALCANAL 13 NOVEMBER '42
BATTLE OF CAPE ESPERANCE 11 OCTOBER 1942
BATTLE OF GUADALCANAL 14-15 NOVEMBER '42
BATTLE OF TASSAFARONGA 30 NOVEMBER '42
15 OCT. '43, LOSS OF THE MEREDITH
SOLOMONS SWEEP
BOUGAINVILLE OCCUPIED 2 NOV.
2 NOV. BUKA BONIS BOMBARDMENT
27 OCTOBER '43 TREASURY IS. OCCUPIED
KOLOMBANGARA OCCUPIED 8 OCT.
VELLA LAVELLA SWEEP 1-3 OCT.
5 AUG. MUNDA OCCUPIED
4 JULY 1943 VILA STANMORE BOMBARDMENT
NEW GEORGIA OCCUPIED 5 JUL.
5-6 MARCH '43 MUNDA-VILA BOMBARDMENT
FEB '43 RUSSELL OCCUPIED
GUADALCANAL CAMPAIGN
GUADALCANAL TULAGI GUVUTU OCCUPIED 7 AUGUST 1942
GREEN IS.
BUKA
Bonis
BOUGAINVILLE
Cape Torokina
Matupina Pt.
SHORTLAND IS.
TREASURY IS.
BOUGAINVILLE STR.
CHOISEUL
VELLA LAVELLA
KOLOMBANGARA
NEW GEORGIA
RENDOVA
VANGUNU
SANTA ISABEL
THE SLOT
RUSSELL IS.
SAVO IS.
FLORIDA
GUADALCANAL
MALAITA
INDISPENSABLE STRAIT
SAN CRISTOBAL
SOLOMON SEA
VELLA GULF
KOLOM-BAN-GARA
GIZO IS.
BLACKETT
FERGUSON PASS
Vila Stanmore
ARUNDEL IS.
HATHORN SOUND
KULA GULF
Rice An.
Visuvisu Pt.
Munda
BLANCHE CHAN.
TETIPARI
VATALU IS.
OLEVUGU IS.
SANDFLY PASS
FLORIDA IS.
LANDINGS 7 AUG '42
Tulagi
Guvutu
Purvis Bay
CAPE ESPERANCE
IRON BOTTOM SOUND
Tassafaronga
SEALARK CHANNEL
LENGO CH.
Lunga Pt.
Koli Pt.
GUADAL-CANAL
Matanikau R.
Lunga R.
Tenaru R.
Henderson Field
154°
155°
156°
157°
161°
163°
5°
7°
8°
9°
10°
11°

Harbor was bearing down on Guadalcanal and Tulagi.

Up from Henderson soared a flock of 76 U.S. fighter planes to intercept the aerial armada. The warning, "Condition Red!", had sent shipping in the area running for cover, alerted. Then, shortly after 1400, came the alarming broadcast, "Condition very Red!" The aerial storm broke about an hour later when a horde of "Zekes" flew into a crowd of American fighters over "Ironbottom Bay." During the wild dogfight that ensued, a number of "Vals" penetrated the American screen and struck at targets in the Sound.

One of their targets was destroyer AARON WARD (Lieutenant Commander F. J. Becton), veteran of the Guadalcanal campaign. That morning she had been escorting three LCT's from Russell Island to Savo. Then, as she drew in sight of Tulagi Harbor, a message came over the radio ordering her to leave the convoy and steam to the aid of LST-449, which was reported off Lunga Roads. The destroyer promptly reversed course, and a short time later she joined the LST off Togoma Point, Guadalcanal. With this ocean-going landing craft under her wing, she headed for Lengo Channel.

As the destroyer and the LST ran eastward, tugs VIREO and ORTOLAN and several small craft tagged along, eager to avail themselves of the DD's anti-aircraft cover. The little group of fugitives were hurrying along the Guadalcanal coast when the air battle exploded over Savo Sound. Then at 1512 three "Vals" burst from a cloud bank and came plummeting down a blinding shaft of sunlight.

Before Lieutenant Commander Becton could order an evasive maneuver, the bombers were on top of the ship. Becton called for flank speed and left full rudder. The portside automatic guns blazed at ranges between 1,500 and 2,000 yards. Three bombs, perhaps 500-pounders, came thunderbolting down. Two were near misses which showered the destroyer with jagged fragments. The third rocked the ship with a deafening blast.

Sixty seconds later three more bombers dived out of the sun and dropped two bombs. The flaming explosions, close aboard, scorched the destroyer's paint. All of the near misses landed within five yards of the ship.

AARON WARD was fatally injured, although the extent of her injuries was not immediately apparent. All electric power was lost on the 5-inch gun mounts. Shifting to manual and local controls, the gunners continued to bang away. The ship's hull plates were sprung by the blasting, and both firerooms were soon swamped. The forward engine-room bulkheads athwartships were ruptured, and water spurted into the compartment. Water also gushed into the after engine-room, welling through leaks in the port side of the hull.

The destroyermen fought the battle damage with every available means. Tugs ORTOLAN and VIREO took the ship in tow and started her toward Tulagi. Six hours after the bombing AARON WARD was still afloat, but she was now far over on her starboard beam. Despite desperate efforts to beach her, she sank that evening at 2135, going down three miles offshore in 40 fathoms of water. Down with her she took 27 dead. The remainder of her crew, including 59 wounded, were picked up by the accompanying tugs.

Bombed under with AARON WARD that day were a New Zealand corvette and the tanker KANAWHA. The Japanese paid for this success with 12 "Vals" and 9 or 27 "Zekes," the variation depending on point of view. The American point of view saw 27. Japanese records report 9. Seven Marine fighter planes were downed in the battle. Apparently Yamamoto was not too pleased with the assessment, for on April 16 he canceled "Operation I" and sent Ozawa's planes back to the flat-tops.

Two days later Yamamoto himself was canceled.

Brief Obituary of Japanese Admiral

This is not an incident of destroyer history. It is, however, an incident that was of more than passing interest to all DesPac destroyermen.

About the time of the "Operation I" strike at Guadalcanal, a tense conference took place in CinCPac's headquarters at Pearl Harbor. Subject of discussion was none other than Isoroku Yamamoto, Commander-in-Chief of the Japanese Combined Fleet.

It seemed that Yamamoto was planning to visit Bougainville in the Solomons. As Admiral Halsey subsequently wrote (in *Admiral Halsey's Story), "The Navy's code experts had hit a jackpot."* Unraveling a Japanese dispatch, they not only learned of Yamamoto's intended junket, but they discerned the time and place of his arrival. Traveling by air, he was due to fly over Ballale Island, just below Bougainville, at 0945 in the morning of April 18.

Here was a chance to take one of Japan's top War Lords on the wing. And aircraft from Henderson Field were assigned the role of executioner. The Admiral's plane was a little late, but not late enough to win him a reprieve. At 1135 in the morning of April 18, 1943, he was intercepted and shot down by American Lightning fighters over Buin, Bougainville.

Admiral Mineichi Koga replaced Yamamoto as

Commander-in-Chief of the Imperial Navy's Combined Fleet.

Mines for Blackett Strait

Early in May 1943 Admiral Halsey decided to plug the "Slot" with a minefield in Blackett Strait between Arundel Island and Kolombangara. The Tokyo Express had been racing through this narrow passage on dark nights, and a mine plant could be just the thing to wreck the train.

Accordingly, the Admiral mustered three destroyer-minelayers for the Blackett Strait mission. The ships—old "four-pipers" which had been converted into "three-stacker" DM's—were PREBLE (Lieutenant Commander F. S. Steinke), GAMBLE (Lieutenant W. W. Armstrong), and BREESE (Lieutenant Commander A. B. Coxe). Because their radar gear was not up to date, destroyer RADFORD (Lieutenant Commander W. K. Romoser) was detailed to shepherd the old-timers on the mine-laying junket. Romoser was placed in charge of the little task group.

The minelayers steamed out of Espiritu Santo on May 4. They paused at Tulagi to take fuel, and on the afternoon of the 6th headed up the "Slot" under RADFORD's leadership. Simultaneously Rear Admiral W. L. Ainsworth, with light cruisers HONOLULU, ST. LOUIS and NASHVILLE, and destroyers O'BANNON, STRONG, CHEVALIER and TAYLOR, proceeded to Vella Gulf to cover the mine-laying expedition.

The "miners" were up to a precarious enterprise. And the hazard was not reduced by the fact that GAMBLE was slowed by a leaky boiler tube which cut her top speed to 27 knots. Then, on the evening of the 6th, as they steamed in column toward Ferguson Passage (a tricky approach to Blackett Strait), Lieutenant Commander Romoser was dismayed to discover that radar and sonar sweeps showed the Passage was narrower by half a mile than indicated on the chart. Whereupon unkind Fate contributed extra difficulty by blotting out all visibility with an equatorial rainstorm.

Nevertheless, with RADFORD leading, the column steamed at 15 knots through Ferguson Passage. As RADFORD entered Blackett Strait, Romoser swung the group due north (time: 0005 in the morning of May 7).

Wheeling northward up the Strait, the three minelayers assumed echelon formation in line of bearing, with RADFORD in the van directly ahead of PREBLE. And on the turn PREBLE deposited the first "egg."

GAMBLE and BREESE followed suit with precision-machine timing. Three rows of mines were thus planted, the lines as beautifully parallel as railroad tracks. The trio of old-timers had trained months on end for this operation. Down went the "eggs" in perfect spacing, one every 12 seconds from each DM. In 17 minutes the field was sown with some 250 mines.

Remained the ticklish business of getting back to base. With Ainsworth's task group covering the retirement, the minelayers hit for home via Vella Gulf, a stretch of water considered "Japanese" until Ainsworth's ships invaded it that night (the first American men-of-war to do so). Soon after RADFORD and the DM's joined Ainsworth's group for the home run, a Japanese plane dropped a pretty flare in the wake of the retiring ships. Jap pyrotechnics and illuminations were consistently excellent throughout the war, but this particular flare must have seemed brighter than a sunburst to the sweating "miners." Somehow the engineers cranked 25 knots out of the old DM's, and they got out of there, one and all.

Now it was up to the mines. And mine-plants are notoriously uncertain. Sometimes they catch a ship immediately. Sometimes they sleep for weeks before claiming a victim. Again, they may be promptly detected and swept up by the enemy. However, the Blackett Strait minefield produced a bumper crop of victims in something like record time.

About dawn of May 8 a fast Tokyo Express highballed around the shoulder of Kolombangara and steamed into Blackett Strait. The Express contained destroyers OYASHIO, KAGERO, KURASHIO, and MICHISHIO. *Wham!* That was OYASHIO—first victim. *Crash!* That was KAGERO—victim No. 2. *Boom!* That was KURASHIO, getting hers about an hour later.

KURASHIO sank swiftly, but the other two remained afloat long enough to involve MICHISHIO in the mess. Having escaped the mines, this fourth destroyer hastened to the rescue of the cripples. To no avail. The rescue effort was spotted by an Australian coastwatcher who put in a call for Guadalcanal. So it was that 19 U. S. aircraft arrived on the scene that afternoon. Down went OYASHIO, struck by an aerial thunderbolt. Down went KAGERO. Unhappy MICHISHIO managed to escape, but not before she received a savage clawing by three Wildcats.

One destroyer badly damaged and three on the bottom the destroyer-minelayers responsible for this wreckage could congratulate themselves on a superb performance. Their minefield had dealt a harder blow to the enemy, and at less cost, than many a Solomons task force.

Mine-plants were not always that successful. On May 13, RADFORD led PREBLE, GAMBLE, and BREESE to Kula Gulf on another minelaying expedition. Again the "miners" were covered by Ainsworth's force. Luck militated against the operation on this occasion. While Ainsworth's ships were bombarding enemy airfields on Vila and New Georgia to detract attention, cruiser NASHVILLE suffered a serious turret explosion, a shell "cooked off" on board destroyer NICHOLAS and blasted a gun-mount, and cruiser ST. LOUIS was damaged by an anchor which carried away. The plucky DM's laid their mines with precision and dispatch, but the Japs came out within 24 hours and swept up the field.

But it remained for Davy Jones to sweep up the three Jap DD's on the floor of Blackett Strait.

Assault on Rendova Island ("Cans" Versus Cannoneers)

The Allied push into the Central Solomons had begun with the occupation in mid-February of the Russells, a flyspeck group 30 miles northwest of Guadalcanal. The Japs had already abandoned them, and the capture gave the Americans a good base for an airfield up the "Slot." The next rung up the ladder was not so easily gained. This was Rendova Island, south of New Georgia.

The capture of Rendova was put up to Rear Admirals R. K. Turner and T. S. Wilkinson, who were to direct amphibious operations. Vice Admiral A. W. Fitch was to provide air support. From his flagship at Nouméa, Admiral Halsey would exercise direct control of surface support. The Amphibious Force was composed of two large transport groups: the Western, under Admiral Turner (who was relieved by Admiral Wilkinson two weeks after the initial landings were made), and the Eastern, under Rear Admiral G. H. Fort. Not all of these forces were to go to Rendova. New Georgia Island was the prize at stake. But the outlying islands were to be seized in the general grab, and Rendova Island, five miles from Munda, was a key point to be taken.

Target date for Rendova: June 30, 1943. Admiral Turner in MCCAWLEY took personal charge of the landings. His transports were guarded by an Eastern and a Western destroyer screen.

The Eastern Screen was composed of destroyers WOODWORTH (Commander V. F. Gordinier), RALPH TALBOT (Commander J. W. Callahan), and MCCALLA (Lieutenant Commander H. A. Knoertzer). This screen was to cover the unloading transports against surface, submarine, and air attack from eastward.

The Western Screen contained the following destroyers: FARENHOLT (Commander E. T. Seaward), flagship of Captain T. J. Ryan, Jr., ComDesRon 12; BUCHANAN (Lieutenant Commander F. B. T. Myhre); GWIN (Lieutenant Commander J. B. Fellows, Jr.), flagship of Commander J. M. Higgins, ComDesDiv 23; JENKINS (Commander H. F. Miller); and RADFORD (Commander W. K. Romoser). This screen had three major tasks to accomplish: (a) As a group, it was to cover the transports in the unloading area against surface, submarine, and air attack from westward; (b) GWIN, JENKINS and RADFORD, under ComDesDiv 23, were to keep the air situation plotted, give timely warning to the task force, and direct American fighter cover—a paramount duty—with JENKINS carrying the fighter-director; (c) FARENHOLT and BUCHANAN were to serve as a fire-support unit. With Munda no more than five miles to the northwest across Blanche Channel, the Western Screen DD's could anticipate action.

As a preliminary to the Rendova landings, two small islands lying off Rendova were to be occupied. Early in the morning of June 30, destroyer-transport TALBOT and a minesweeper moved in to disembark troops on these islets. Foul weather fouled up this minor operation, and the sweeper became stranded on a reef. She was safely hauled off that afternoon by a tug, but the mishap was an ominous flounder on what was to prove a slippery ladder rung.

Another preliminary went wrong when destroyer-transports DENT and WATERS prowled into Rendova Harbor with assault troops who were supposed to snuff out the local garrison before the main landings were begun. The ships expected to find a beach marked with a signal light planted by an advance patrol. Unfortunately a rainstorm swept the harbor as the destroyer-transports maneuvered in. So the light was snuffed out, instead of the Japanese garrison. The ships could not find the right beach, and the troops went ashore "off the trail."

At daylight Turner's transports and screen destroyers moved into position off the harbor mouth. Sunrise tinted the water, and the landing craft, chugging shoreward, entered a tranquil bay which might have been somewhere among the Ten Thousand Islands of southern Florida. There was scarcely a sputter of Japanese opposition as the first wave of leopard-spotted troopers splashed ashore on a curve of flat beach. Several hundred Americans were on the sand before the enemy woke up at Munda.

The Munda gunners opened fire on the nearest targets, the destroyers of Turner's Western Screen patrolling in the channel. Right off the bat destroyer GWIN was straddled by a salvo, then struck by a 4.7-inch shell. The projectile slammed down on her main deck aft, killed three bluejackets and wounded seven, and knocked out the after engine. She was immediately directed by Squadron Commander Ryan to exchange stations with WOODWORTH in the transport area. Division Commander Higgins was ordered to assume command of the Eastern Screen.

Ryan then held fire-support destroyers FARENHOLT and BUCHANAN where they were, in an effort to invite the enemy's shots so that the location of the shore batteries could be discerned.

No sooner did the Jap guns pick on FARENHOLT and BUCHANAN than these two veterans of Cape Esperance picked on the Jap guns. And whereas the destroyers could shift from here to there in the channel on varying courses at various speeds, the Munda shore batteries could only stay put. Stationary targets being easier to hit than those on the move, the two destroyers had much the best of the shooting match. Before the duel was ended, seven Jap shore batteries were either knocked out or silenced. Neither destroyer was hit.

"Outwitting the Japs in this sport," wrote Captain Ryan, *". . . being able to thumb our noses at them while silencing their guns, was a thrill I shall never forget."*

The Japs were to have their Rendova innings, however. Late in the morning a flock of "Zekes" came down the "Slot" for a dogfight. They were speedily bitten and put to flight by American fighters. But the threat delayed unloading operations at Rendova, and gave Jap bombers time to reach the scene that afternoon. At 1500 Turner ordered a retirement. About an hour later the American ships were overhauled by 25 "Betty" torpedo-planes.

In the battle that ensued, the fighter-director team on board destroyer JENKINS put on a crack performance, pointing out targets to the American airmen aloft, and coaching the friendly fighter planes into action. FARENHOLT was struck by machine-gun lead and jolted by a dud torpedo. RALPH TALBOT and McCALLA shot their way out from under dive-bomber attacks, and brought down several "Bettys." More came blazing down when the DD's put up an umbrella of AA fire over the transports. Blanche Channel was littered with the corpses of Jap aviators when the battle was over. But one "Betty" bored through the screen and stabbed a torpedo into Turner's flagship McCAWLEY.

Known to a generation of American tourists as the S.S. SANTA BARBARA—and to the Navy's South Pacific forces as "WACKY MAC"—the 8,000-ton exliner was doomed. The Jap torpedo did not down her; it only wrecked her engine-room, flooded her after hold, and killed 15 of her crew. Destroyer RALPH TALBOT took off most of the survivors. Admiral Turner transferred his flag to the FARENHOLT. And transport LIBRA, then tug PAWNEE, strove to tow the damaged ship to Guadalcanal.

There was trouble with the tow, and the salvage party on board McCAWLEY could not stem the flooding. With night coming on, destroyer McCALLA took off the salvage party. Admiral Turner was wondering whether to scuttle or make another try at towing, when two torpedoes suddenly raced in out of the dark and blasted the ship. She went down in about 30 seconds. Some hours later TURNER learned that the torpedoes had been fired by American PT-boaters who mistook McCAWLEY for a Japanese vessel. Providentially, they did not draw a bead on the other American vessels in the vicinity.

As the only ship lost in the Rendova operation, the abandoned transport was not an extravagant exchange. A few hours after the beachhead was captured, American heavy artillery was emplaced and hurling salvos across Blanche Channel at Munda airfield. As has been related, Munda's shore batteries had already received a flogging from destroyers FARENHOLT and BUCHANAN.

Endorsing the Action Reports of those two warships, Rear Admiral Wilkinson had this to say:

> *The counter-battery firing of* BUCHANAN *and* FARENHOLT *was most effective and undoubtedly prevented what might have been embarrassing and perhaps damaging fire on the transport group.*

Not the first or last time in World War II that "cans" took the measure of cannoneers.

Radford Kills RO-101

While Army forces were digging in at Rendova, Marines were carried to Viru by destroyer-transports HOPKINS, KILTY, and CROSBY, and troops were landed on Vangunu and other islands of the New Georgia group. Destroyers WOODWORTH and JENKINS supported the Vangunu landings with a bombardment of Japanese trenches which flanked the beach. Rendova proved the only worthwhile prize in this grabbag, but the troops did not think it a fit bog for crocodiles.

Reinforcements, the second section of Turner's transport fleet, arrived with a rainstorm early in the morning of July 1. Everyone was cussing the weather, but this particular downpour was a disguised blessing. For the previous evening Admiral Kusaka had ordered five destroyers to intercept the American transports. The rainstorm washed out the attack by discouraging the Jap group commander, who turned back in the watery night. The rain also grounded air opposition, which did not develop at Rendova until the troops were solidly ashore.

By nightfall the transports were unloaded and on their way out of Blanche Channel. Some Jap float planes attempted a twilight attack, but were driven off. Then, as darkness deepened, another threat materialized in the form of a Japanese submarine. It was soon dematerialized by destroyer RADFORD.

A unit of the transport screen, RADFORD was at that hour conducting a sweep on the eastern side of Rendova. At 1948 the destroyer's SG radar registered contact with an unknown vessel about six miles distant. Deftly conning his DD, Commander Romoser closed range to 2,000 yards.

Time: 2008. The destroyermen snapped on a searchlight which caught a surfaced submarine full in the face. Instantly the silhouette was recognized as enemy, and in the same instant RADFORD's marksmen opened fire with all guns. A torpedo was also fired at the sub, but it was the shelling which did her in.

Right on target, the first three salvos whisked away the conning tower. Five-inchers and 20 mm. riddled the pressure hull. RADFORD closed the range to 1,500 yards. The sub lay in the sea like a waterlogged tree trunk, slowly foundering. Then it went under.

Romoser maneuvered his ship into position to ram if the sub happened to broach. It didn't happen. At 2012 he conned RADFORD over the submerged target, and an 11-charge pattern was deposited in the sea. Three minutes later the water was roiled by an undersea thunderclap that vibrated the cookpots in RADFORD's galley. Inquisitive searchlights were turned on the channel. The lights discovered lakes of dark oil, and a variegated clutter of debris which contained such items as strips of wood, hunks of cork, rags of fabric or clothing, and presumably segments of Jap.

Put them all together, they spelled RO-101. Another enemy removed from the Rendova area by destroyer warfare.

Bombardment of Vila and Bairoko Harbor

Early in the morning of July 5, 1943, American troops were landed at Rice Anchorage on the northwest coast of New Georgia Island. From Rice Anchorage the Army was to forge its way down the New Georgia shore to Enogai and Bairoko, jungly harbors which lay athwart the enemy's supply route from Vila to Munda. Halsey dispatched a task group under Rear Admiral Ainsworth to support the landings at Rice Anchorage by bombarding Vila-Stanmore and shelling the Jap defenses at Enogai and Bairoko.

Fourth of July evening found Ainsworth's task group well up the "Slot." In the group were light cruisers HONOLULU (flagship), HELENA, and ST. LOUIS, and four destroyers under command of Captain F. X. McInerney, ComDesRon 21. The destroyers were NICHOLAS (Lieutenant Commander A. J. Hill), STRONG (Commander J. H. Wellings), O'BANNON (Lieutenant Commander D. J. MacDonald), and CHEVALIER (Commander E. R. McLean, Jr.). Captain McInerney rode in NICHOLAS.

The Army convoy contained destroyer-transports DENT, TALBOT, MCKEAN, WATERS, KILTY, CROSBY, SCHLEY, and destroyer-minesweepers HOPKINS and TREVER, and it was screened by destroyers RADFORD, GWIN, MCCALLA, RALPH TALBOT, and WOODWORTH.

Ainsworth had no way of knowing that Jap Admiral Koga had decided to send a reinforcement of three Japanese destroyers to Vila on the very evening that the American transport group was to enter Kula Gulf.

About 0000, July 5, the American bombardment group arrived off Visuvisu Point, the northernmost tip of New Georgia. As the ships rounded the point and steamed into Kula Gulf, Ainsworth formed them in column. Destroyers NICHOLAS and STRONG moved up into the van, NICHOLAS about 3,000 and STRONG about 1,500 yards ahead of HONOLULU, HELENA, and ST. LOUIS. O'BANNON and CHEVALIER covered the cruiser column's rear.

The van destroyers were ordered to conduct a careful sonar and radar search of the Gulf ahead. They were not to open fire unless enemy shore batteries let go at the ships, or enemy searchlights demanded extinguishment. The night was humid and overcast, and drenched by sporadic rainsqualls. Under cover of this weather the bombardment ships made the run to Vila undetected, and at 0026 the cruisers began hurling shells at the enemy shore.

NICHOLAS and STRONG opened fire at Bairoko Harbor at 0030. Meantime, the transports quietly approached Rice Anchorage. They were off the Anchorage when the radar watch in RALPH TALBOT reported two "pips" on the screen. That was at 0031. The contacted vessels were coming westward. Nine minutes later they showed up as two unidentifiable ships steaming at 25 knots out of the Gulf on a northwest course.

At that moment (0040) the three cruisers, which had shifted fire to Bairoko, and destroyers STRONG and NICHOLAS, CHEVALIER, and O'BANNON, broke off the bombardment and headed north in column. Admiral Ainsworth was on the point of making a TBS inquiry about the vessels contacted by RALPH TALBOT when STRONG's Gunnery Officer sighted a torpedo wake sizzling toward his destroyer. "Torpedo!"—Lieutenant J. A. Curran scarcely had time to shout the alarm. Commander Wellings had no time to order an evasive maneuver. The torpedo struck home with a thunder-blast, and STRONG staggered out of line in mortal hurt.

All hands in the task group believed the ship had been torpedoed by an undetected submarine. Ainsworth detached destroyers O'BANNON and CHEVALIER to stand by the disabled STRONG, stationed near

NICHOLAS as picket, and led the cruiser column out of the Gulf to cover the entrance to the northward, prior to a fast retirement. At Rice Anchorage the landings went steadily forward. Destroyers GWIN and RADFORD silenced the batteries at the Anchorage, and by 0600 most of the transports were unloaded.

But the success had been achieved at cost of STRONG.

Loss of U.S.S. Strong

The torpedo which struck STRONG had burst her hull from port to starboard and left her sagging amidships like a hammock. The blast wiped out her forward fireroom, and water plunged into her engineering spaces, quickly swamping her vital machinery. The dead swirled uncaring through the flooded compartments as the living fought their way topside.

This doom had struck STRONG about two miles off Rice Anchorage. There she was found by CHEVALIER and O'BANNON. The rescue ships immediately stood in to her assistance. Commander Wellings, expecting aid, had held his crew on board.

Closing in on the disabled destroyer's port side, CHEVALIER thrust her bow into the wreckage. The thrust damaged the rescue ship's bow, but it enabled the CHEVALIER men to throw a web of nets and lines to STRONG's battered hull. The sea was flat, and the STRONG survivors were able to crawl across the span of cables and hemp. A number of the badly wounded were handed to safety, and all of the survivors might have gotten across had not the Jap gunners ashore suddenly spied the sinking ship.

No sooner spied than fired upon. An evil garden of starshells bloomed in the sky, lighting up the Gulf. A spate of salvos lobbed out from shore. The Jap artillerymen were soon on target. The shots came from Enogai Inlet and Bairoko. O'BANNON's gunners answered with furious fire while CHEVALIER rushed rescue efforts. Then a 150 mm. dud crashed on STRONG's deck. Some 240 of STRONG's crew were now on board CHEVALIER. Having held his ship alongside the sinking destroyer for seven minutes, CHEVALIER's skipper, Commander McLean, could no longer risk rescue operations. Two shells smashed into STRONG as CHEVALIER pulled away. The blasts ravaged the stricken vessel. A few survivors who had been left on board somehow managed to get overside.

The battered ship went under at 0122. As the wreckage sank, several 300-pound depth charges exploded in the water, killing and maiming swimmers. Pursued by Jap salvos, CHEVALIER and O'BANNON retired up the Gulf. In passing they asked the destroyers at Rice Anchorage to search for survivors.

The DD's of the transport group combed the water where STRONG went down. Among the lucky few recovered was Commander Wellings. But in the darkness which followed the shore gunnery, a huddle of swimmers drifted away to southward. Most of this group failed to reach land.

Seven officers and 39 men perished in the STRONG torpedoing. The torpedo which struck the ship was a Model 93 specimen fired by one of the two Japanese destroyers fleeing out of the Gulf to escape the bombardment group. It was an unbelievably long shot—another example of crack torpedo-work with a superior torpedo.

Commenting on CHEVALIER's rescue effort, Admiral Ainsworth wrote:

> *The* CHEVALIER *is to be commended for her splendid job in rescuing survivors of the* STRONG, *and the* O'BANNON *likewise rendered noble assistance in standing by and taking the annoying shore batteries under fire. During the rescue operations these batteries repeatedly illuminated the whole Gulf area with starshells and put in some very accurate practice on the* STRONG, *hitting her twice while she was sinking.*

And here is a story of self-rescue which has few parallels in the history of warfare.

Survival Story: The Stamina of Lieutenant Miller

When the depth charges exploded as the stricken STRONG went down, Lieutenant Hugh Barr Miller, U.S.N.R., was among those injured by the undersea blasts. Badly hurt though he was, he managed to tread water and remain afloat. Some 23 men were in a little huddle around him, clinging to life nets and pieces of raft.

The night was stygian—not a star visible—and it was easy for rescuers to miss this little group in the blind darkness. A current carried them away from their shipmates, and morning found them drifting in an empty world of gulf and sky. One after another men lost their hold on the flotsam which supported them, and slipped away into eternity. Four days after the torpedoing, when the flotsam drifted ashore on Arundel Island, about midway between New Georgia and Kolombangara, only six of the group remained. Lieutenant Hugh Barr Miller was among the six.

Two of these six survivors died of their injuries after they crawled ashore. The lieutenant and three bluejackets started to work their way through the coastal jungle. Miller was so weakened by internal bleeding that he thought he was going to die. On July 14 he suffered a severe hemorrhage which convinced him that his life was ebbing.

He told the three sailors with him that they would

have to leave him and try to reach friendly territory. He gave one lad his shoes; pressed his rainproof parka on the second; directed the third to take other articles of his clothing. Emergency rations were divided, and Miller kept for himself a broken pocket knife. The three men were reluctant to leave him in such fashion. Miller sent them on. Orders were orders.

But Lieutenant Miller didn't die. For a time he was in a semi-comatose state, but on the 17th a tropical downpour bathed and revived him. A few gulps of rainwater brought him to his feet, and he stumbled on through the jungle that fringed the beach.

Coral cut his bare feet, and vines and palm-thatch clawed his face and arms, while the sun blistered his shoulders and brought a salty thirst to his lips. But he was aware that the taste of blood was not so persistent in his mouth, and somehow the hemorrhaging had stopped.

Another night—another day—he found and broke open a coconut and chewed its meat. This was his first meal on Arundel Island, the first substantial food he had been able to swallow in two weeks.

Then he found something that startled him much as Friday's footprint shocked Robinson Crusoe. It was an old Japanese Navy blanket in the underbrush. Then, scouting forward on the alert, Miller found something else. He found a dead Japanese infantryman, complete with uniform, rations, and hand grenades.

Costumed, armed, and provided with solid food, Miller went on. On August 5, or thereabouts, he sighted a Jap patrol coming up the beach, evidently on the hunt for the party who had stripped the dead man. Miller ambushed the five-man patrol and killed the lot with a volley of grenades.

The battle provided him with more weapons and implements for survival. Also with more impetus to keep going. He built a lean-to in the jungle and set out to locate and raid the enemy camp. From his solitary base he staged a series of forays. When he was finally picked up after 43 days of existence on Arundel Island, he had lost 40 pounds, grown a scraggy reddish beard, and acquired the look of a wolf. But he was decidedly alive. And he had waged a one-man offensive against the Japanese occupants, killed about 30 Jap soldiers, and obtained a dossier of valuable military information. He was picked up by Luck—Major Goodwin R. Luck, U.S.M.C.R., who flew over the Arundel beach in a seaplane. Not long after that he was in hospital at Nouméa, where Admiral Halsey shook his hand, and he was recommended for the Navy Cross.

As a story of survival Miller's can scarcely be equalled. Physical stamina was partly responsible for his victory over death. Miller had been All-American quarterback at the University of Alabama, and his service in the Navy had not undermined a powerful physique. But man does not live by brawn alone. It takes drive, will to live, and Lieutenant Hugh Barr Miller had that in abundance.

Appropriately he served in a destroyer named STRONG.

The Battle of Kula Gulf

After the Vila-Stanmore bombardment and the brush with the enemy near Rice Anchorage, Admiral Ainsworth led his task group down the "Slot" to Savo Sound and eastward to Indispensable Strait. He was heading for a fueling rendezvous with a tanker south of San Cristobal Island. But before this rendezvous could be made, he received orders from Halsey directing him to reverse course. A fast "Tokyo Express" had been sighted on the southbound run from Bougainville, steaming for Vila-Stanmore with reinforcements. Ainsworth was to return to Kula Gulf on the double and intercept this train load of Japs.

At once he swung the column in a 180-degree turn, and headed back for Kula at 29 knots. As CHEVALIER had gashed her bow in going alongside the sinking STRONG, she was ordered to drop out with the STRONG survivors at Tulagi. Destroyers JENKINS (Commander H. F. Miller) and RADFORD (Commander W. K. Romoser), at that time loading fuel and ammunition at Tulagi, were hitched on to Ainsworth's formation as replacements. Full gun, Task Group 36.1 went racing northward up the "Slot."

About midnight Ainsworth, approaching the entrance of Kula Gulf, slowed the pace to 25 knots, and sent all hands to battle stations.

The night was another Solomons blackout—moonless and dark and sweating with humidity. Visibility, limited to about two miles, at times decreased to less than a mile when black rain swept over the water. It was a night just made for a collision with anything coming down the "Slot."

And coming down the "Slot" was the Jap reinforcement group, ten destroyers under command of Rear Admiral Teruo Akiyama. The enemy DD's were moving tandem in three groups. In the lead was a support unit composed of destroyers NIIZUKI, SUZUKAZE, and TANIKAZE. Next came a transport unit: destroyers MOCHIZUKI, MIKAZUKI, and HAMAKAZE. Then came a second transport unit: destroyers AMAGIRI, HATSUYUKI, NAGATSUKI, and SATSUKI. About 0025 in the morning of July 6, at the very time Ainsworth's ships were off Visuvisu Point, the Jap destroyers swung down into the Gulf.

Admiral Akiyama sent the first transport unit in-

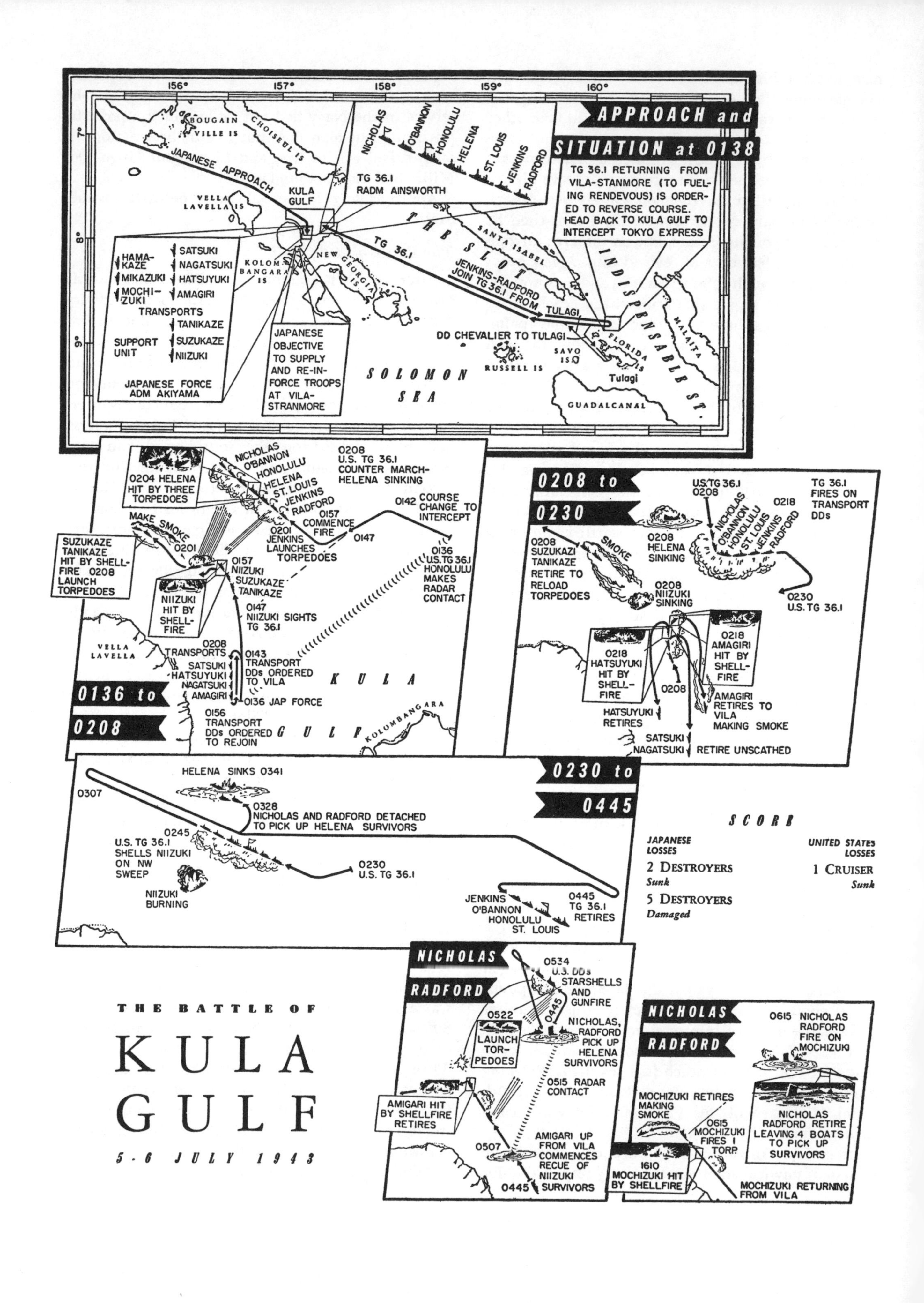
APPROACH and
SITUATION at 0138
TG 36.1 RETURNING FROM VILA-STANMORE (TO FUELING RENDEVOUS) IS ORDERED TO REVERSE COURSE. HEAD BACK TO KULA GULF TO INTERCEPT TOKYO EXPRESS
JAPANESE APPROACH
KULA GULF
TG 36.1
RADM AINSWORTH
NICHOLAS
O'BANNON
HONOLULU
HELENA
ST. LOUIS
JENKINS
RADFORD
THE SLOT
INDISPENSABLE ST.
JENKINS-RADFORD JOIN TG 36.1 FROM TULAGI
DD CHEVALIER TO TULAGI
HAMA-KAZE
MIKAZUKI
MOCHI-ZUKI
SATSUKI
NAGATSUKI
HATSUYUKI
AMAGIRI
TRANSPORTS
TANIKAZE
SUZUKAZE
NIIZUKI
SUPPORT UNIT
JAPANESE FORCE
ADM AKIYAMA
JAPANESE OBJECTIVE TO SUPPLY AND RE-INFORCE TROOPS AT VILA-STRANMORE
SOLOMON SEA
0136 to 0208
0204 HELENA HIT BY THREE TORPEDOES
0208 U.S. TG 36.1 COUNTER MARCH-HELENA SINKING
0142 COURSE CHANGE TO INTERCEPT
0157 COMMENCE FIRE
0201 JENKINS LAUNCHES TORPEDOES
MAKE SMOKE
SUZUKAZE TANIKAZE HIT BY SHELL-FIRE 0208 LAUNCH TORPEDOES
NIIZUKI HIT BY SHELL-FIRE
0157 NIIZUKI SUZUKAZE TANIKAZE
0147 NIIZUKI SIGHTS TG 36.1
0136 U.S. TG 36.1 HONOLULU MAKES RADAR CONTACT
0208 TRANSPORTS
0143 TRANSPORT DDs ORDERED TO VILA
0136 JAP FORCE
0156 TRANSPORT DDs ORDERED TO REJOIN
KULA GULF
0208 to 0230
U.S. TG 36.1 0208
TG 36.1 FIRES ON TRANSPORT DDs
0208 SUZUKAZI TANIKAZE RETIRE TO RELOAD TORPEDOES
0208 HELENA SINKING
0208 NIIZUKI SINKING
0230 U.S. TG 36.1
0218 HATSUYUKI HIT BY SHELL-FIRE
0218 AMAGIRI HIT BY SHELL-FIRE
HATSUYUKI RETIRES
AMAGIRI RETIRES TO VILA MAKING SMOKE
SATSUKI NAGATSUKI RETIRE UNSCATHED
0230 to 0445
HELENA SINKS 0341
0307
0328 NICHOLAS AND RADFORD DETACHED TO PICK UP HELENA SURVIVORS
0245 U.S. TG 36.1 SHELLS NIIZUKI ON NW SWEEP
NIIZUKI BURNING
0230 U.S. TG 36.1
0445 TG 36.1 RETIRES
JENKINS
O'BANNON
HONOLULU
ST. LOUIS
NICHOLAS
RADFORD
0534 U.S. DDs STARSHELLS AND GUNFIRE
0522 LAUNCH TORPEDOES
NICHOLAS, RADFORD PICK UP HELENA SURVIVORS
0515 RADAR CONTACT
AMIGARI HIT BY SHELLFIRE RETIRES
0507
AMIGARI UP FROM VILA COMMENCES RECUE OF NIIZUKI SURVIVORS
0445
0615 NICHOLAS RADFORD FIRE ON MOCHIZUKI
MOCHIZUKI RETIRES MAKING SMOKE
0615 MOCHIZUKI FIRES I TORP.
NICHOLAS RADFORD RETIRE LEAVING 4 BOATS TO PICK UP SURVIVORS
1610 MOCHIZUKI HIT BY SHELLFIRE
MOCHIZUKI RETURNING FROM VILA
SCORE
JAPANESE LOSSES
2 DESTROYERS Sunk
5 DESTROYERS Damaged
UNITED STATES LOSSES
1 CRUISER Sunk
THE BATTLE OF
KULA GULF
5-6 JULY 1943

shore to hug the Kolombangara coast on the run down the Gulf to Vila. The rest of the "Express" he took down the Gulf in column on a course farther out. The Americans were not acquainted with the fact that flag destroyer NIIZUKI carried new Japanese radar gear. Nor did they know the Jap DD's were equipped with enormous 24-inch torpedoes and special apparatus for the handling and re-loading of these three-ton whales. Not that the knowledge would have stopped an attack by Ainsworth. But the Japanese radar and the huge torpedoes somewhat offset the superior fire-power of the American cruisers.

With the clock nearing 0136, cruiser HONOLULU made the first radar contact with the Japanese ships at 22,000-yard range. Ainsworth immediately aligned his ships in single-column battle formation. In the van were destroyers NICHOLAS and O'BANNON. They were followed by HONOLULU, HELENA, and ST. LOUIS. Destroyer JENKINS steamed in ST. LOUIS's wake, and RADFORD was "tail-end Charlie."

At 0142, with radar "pips" multiplying on the screens, Ainsworth shifted course to come to grips with the enemy. One minute later Akiyama detached the second Jap transport unit and sent it in to Vila while he turned the support destroyers northward. Between Jap and American ships the range rapidly closed. Studying the radar picture, the Americans were momentarily baffled by the separation of Akiyama's column into two groups. When the Vila-bound group showed up as the larger of the two, Ainsworth ordered his rear DD's to join the three cruisers in gunning for this target. Van destroyers NICHOLAS and O'BANNON were directed to tackle the nearer, smaller group which was heading up the Gulf.

The clock ticked to 0154. Over TBS barked Ainsworth's order, "Destroyers commence firing!"

Destroyer Squadron Commander McInerney made inquiry: Did the Admiral mean gunfire or torpedo-fire?

Ainsworth meant gunfire. But now matters were developing in a fashion which dictated a tactical change. The larger target-group was swiftly opening the range, while the smaller was as swiftly drawing nearer. Ainsworth canceled his first gunnery order and directed his ships to concentrate on the oncoming target-group. They were then to make a simultaneous turn and *"get the others on the reverse course."*

At 0157, with the range closed to about 7,050 yards, Ainsworth snapped the order to fire. Steaming at 30 knots, the Japs were broad on the port beam. But they were not taken by surprise. NIIZUKI's lookouts had sighted and reported the American column. Admiral Akiyama had instantly rushed his crews to battle stations.

Even so, the American gunners got the jump. Squarely on target, the first cruiser salvo struck NIIZUKI a stunner. Holed, afire, her steering gear disabled, Admiral Akiyama's flagship floundered off course and started to settle.

Destroyers SUZUKAZE and TANIKAZE had better luck. Neither was stopped by the blizzard of heavy shells, and both were able to fling torpedoes at the American column—those supersize torpedoes with the double dose of dynamite in their war heads. While the torpedoes were racing away, SUZUKAZE was rocked by a couple of minor blows, and TANIKAZE caught a dud. Retiring behind smoke, these two DD's ran up the Gulf to reload for another torpedo attack.

And just as the Americans were ready to believe the first target-group had been annihilated, cruiser HELENA was hit by one of the long-range Jap torpedoes. Then she was hit by another! Then another! When the thunder echoed away and the smoke cleared, the cruiser was *in extremis*. Her bow had been slashed off, and she was buckled amidships, her fantail and her stump of forecastle thrust skyward to form a "V."

Meantime, Ainsworth had ordered the countermarch, aiming to engage the second target-group. He was unaware that HELENA had been hit, as the torpedoing was not sighted by the ships near her in formation. The first intimation of her plight came to Ainsworth when she failed to answer signals. By that time the Americans were battling the second Jap group, and HELENA's survivors had to wait.

Although Ainsworth succeeded in capping the "T" of both enemy groups, the Japs dodged the American salvos and escaped destruction. Destroyer HATSUYUKI was hit hard by three duds. Destroyer AMAGIRI was cut up a bit, but she got away behind a smoke screen. The other two DD's of the group ran for it. Reversing course, they ducked back to Vila anchorage, where NAGATSUKI, slightly injured, ran aground.

Ainsworth led his column in a westward sweep at 0227. As no targets were found, he swung back up the Gulf. About an hour later, after futile sweeps this way and that, he detached destroyers NICHOLAS and RADFORD to pick up the HELENA survivors, and led the rest of his force out to the "Slot." Round One of the Battle of Kula Gulf was over.

As usual, the Jap torpedoes had scored heavily. Contrast the American torpedo score. At the start of the engagement, van destroyers NICHOLAS and O'BANNON both held their gunfire in leash, the skippers hoping to open up with preliminary torpedo attacks. Neither ship was able to get in such an attack. Similarly, rear destroyers JENKINS and RADFORD delayed opening fire with guns while trying for a favorable torpedo set-up. At 0201 JENKINS finally flung a torpedo salvo. RADFORD was unable to follow suit until later. And when NICHOLAS, O'BANNON, and RADFORD belatedly fired torpedoes, O'BANNON shooting five at the second target-group as it retired, the score was a resounding zero. RADFORD'S "fish" hit nothing; JENKINS missed a torpedo shot, and fired at a "phantom."

As they swung up the Gulf several of the destroyers hurled shell at the sinking NIIZUKI. She was the only Jap warship killed in this round of the battle—poor recompense for HELENA. But Round Two was coming up. And in this climax two of the American DD's distinguished themselves.

The two DD's were NICHOLAS and RADFORD, detached to rescue HELENA'S survivors. The ship had gone down when the destroyers hove to at 0341 and lowered whaleboats to pick up the cruisermen. Shouts from the black water guided the rescuers to clusters of floats and swimming men. The sea was clotted with rafts and flotsam, and smeared with thick carpets of oil that gagged the swimmers and made them as hard to clutch as eels. The destroyermen were just making progress with the rescue work when (time: 0400) the radar watch in NICHOLAS reported a contact to the west, range 16,000 yards.

A moment later RADFORD'S radar snared a contact. The two DD's had to break off rescue operations and square away for action. Barking orders from NICHOLAS, Squadron Commander McInerney maneuvered the destroyers to meet the threat. Then the enemy in the west suddenly reversed course, and the "pips" flickered away.

Perhaps this turn was fortunate for RADFORD and NICHOLAS, handicapped as they were, and it was certainly lucky for the HELENA survivors. The oncoming enemy had been destroyers SUZUKAZE and TANIKAZE. Having finished their torpedo reloads, they were back down the Gulf looking for targets. Happily enough they failed to sight the two American DD's. The latter promptly resumed rescue work, and perchance missed a blasting by the long-range Model 93's.

At 0515 the American destroyers were alerted by another radar contact, range 13,000 yards. By this time they had picked up a large number of HELENA'S survivors, and they were ready to shoot. The enemy contacted was the Japanese destroyer AMAGIRI, which had come up the Gulf from Vila in search of the NIIZUKI survivors. The Japs had just begun rescue operations when their lookouts sighted the American ships. AMAGIRI put on steam to deliver a torpedo attack at the very moment NICHOLAS and RADFORD were doing the same.

At 0522 NICHOLAS fired a spread at 8,000 yards. AMAGIRI got off her torpedoes eight minutes later. Both spreads missed the marks. The Americans sent up starshells, and opened fire on the Jap's silhouette at 0534. They plunked a shell into AMAGIRI which demolished her radio room and knocked out her fire-control gear. Spouting a smoke screen, the damaged Jap fled. The Americans thought they had destroyed her. Actually they put a *finis* to some 300 of NIIZUKI'S survivors. These hapless sailors were never picked up, and lost with them was Admiral Akiyama.

Two other Jap destroyers at Vila Roads saw the gunfire to the north, and, having unloaded their troops, made haste to retire through Blackett Strait, the southern exit of Kula Gulf. A third destroyer, the MOCHIZUKI, was tardy in unloading. At 0600 the Squadron Commander on board decided to haul out through Kula Gulf. So MOCHIZUKI started northward, keeping close to the Kolombangara coastline. But she was not so close that the radar on NICHOLAS failed to spot her against the island's blur.

Once again NICHOLAS and RADFORD broke off rescue operations and made for the enemy. Reporting this action, Squadron Commander McInerney wrote: *"No better description can be given than the words of the Commanding Officer of the* NICHOLAS *as he stood toward the enemy ship at full speed.* IF THE SON-OF-A-BITCH WANTS TO FIGHT, I'LL GIVE HIM A FIGHT!"

Nice old ladies might blanche at this language, but nice old ladies never conned powder-scorched warships through fiery seas littered with the dead and dying.

MOCHIZUKI did not particularly want a fight, but she got one anyway. She unleashed a torpedo at the American ships at 0615, and they opened fire with 5-inch almost simultaneously. When several shells smacked the Jap, she laid smoke and ran for it. As daylight was making, and there was threat of air attack, McInerney also ordered a smoke screen to cover a retirement up the Gulf by NICHOLAS and RADFORD.

"Captain," someone reports, "we've picked up over 700 of HELENA'S men, but there are still several hundred in the water."

"We'll leave four boats to get them! Call for volunteers."

On board NICHOLAS and RADFORD volunteers were not lacking. The four boats circled off in the morning gloom as the two destroyers steamed on out of Kula Gulf. All told, the DD's carried 745 cruiser survivors out with them. As will be seen, the volunteer lifesavers picked up many of the remaining HELENA men, and DD's returned to recover a large party which drifted in to a hostile beach—one of the more heroic destroyer rescue exploits of the war.

Aside from the magnificent lifesaving effort of the destroyermen, the Americans accomplished nothing outstanding in the Battle of Kula Gulf. They failed to block the reinforcement of Vila-Stanmore, but they did sink one destroyer and damaged several others at the cost of a light cruiser. The wounded NAGATSUKI piled up on the beach near Vila, where she was found and demolished by American aircraft on the following afternoon. This could be counted as an indirect score for Ainsworth's group, as could the wholesale loss of the NIIZUKI crew, plus Admiral Akiyama.

And Ainsworth's task group was not through with Vila-Stanmore.

Taylor Kills I-25

The American ground forces ashore at Rice Anchorage and other New Georgia beaches swiftly beat aside the Japs on locale and drove through the jungle for Munda. They were supported by air assaults and by offshore bombardments delivered through the guns of Admiral Halsey's Third Fleet warships. (The designation "Third Fleet," now applied to Halsey's South Pacific forces, distinguished them from the "Seventh Fleet" naval forces operating in the New Guinea Area under General MacArthur's over-all command.)

While the Munda push rolled forward, Admiral Ainsworth's task group revisited Kula Gulf, supporting a reinforcement convoy bound for Rice Anchorage. Ainsworth's warships did not get into action on this night of July 11-12, but one of the two destroyers screening the transports did.

The screen destroyers were TAYLOR and WOODWORTH. Their run up the "Slot" and down the Gulf to Rice was uneventful, and so were the early morning landings. Uninterrupted, the landings were completed by 0430 in the morning of the 12th. And the emptied transports were heading northward up the Gulf, homebound for Guadalcanal, before trouble eventuated.

Action was sparked by a radar "pip" which showed up on the scope at 0450. TAYLOR sliced away from the convoy to investigate.

Four minutes later her lookouts spied the silhouette of a Jap conning tower 2,500 yards distant. Skippering the destroyer, Lieutenant Commander Benjamin Katz ordered on a searchlight and told the gunners to open fire. Down went the submarine and into the disappearing conning tower went several of TAYLOR's 5-inch shells.

Bursts of debris went helter-skelter; the water churned and frothed; the sub sloughed under. A pattern of nine depth charges was spread in the sea where the mangled sub had submerged. Two more depth charges were dropped at 0510. They raised a hubbub under the surface, and then all was still.

Daylight was diluting the dark, and TAYLOR's skipper hauled away, satisfied he had bashed the enemy to the bottom. His satisfaction was warranted. The Japanese submarine I-25 would never be seen in Kula Gulf or any other waterway again. Submersible and crew had gone to join Admiral Akiyama and the crew of destroyer NIIZUKI in that limbo which is beyond the range of human vision and, for that matter, any kind of detection gear.

THE BATTLE OF VELLA GULF

CHAPTER 18

CENTRAL SOLOMONS SWEEP

(Part 2)

The Battle of Kolombangara

To the Solomon Islanders, Kolombangara means "King of the Waters." The American sailors who fought the Japs off this island called it other and more sulphurous names. The Japanese, too, probably developed a distaste for the island. Bivouacked in the mud at Vila-Stanmore, they noted their rations were growing skimpy. It was the old story of logistics again. Although the "Tokyo Express" had a shorter run than previously, Kula Gulf was proving as nasty as Savo Sound. Japanese Destroyer Squadron 2 was still operating on the line, but Tenacious Tanaka had been removed as No. 1 Engineer. There was a new man in the cab as of July 12—Rear Admiral Shunji Izaki.

About 0530 in the morning of July 12 the "Tokyo Express" set out from Rabaul with reinforcements and supplies for the Jap garrison at Vila-Stanmore. It was composed of a support group containing the light cruiser JINTSU (flagship), and destroyers MIKAZUKI, YUKIKAZE, HAMAKAZE, KIYONAMI, and YUGURE. Passengers and freight were carried by destroyer-transports SATSUKI, MINAZUKI, YUNAGI, and MATSUKAZE.

Coast watchers and aircraft spied the Jap ships, and Halsey was tipped off. Out went a dispatch to Admiral Ainsworth; his ships were to make another dash to Kula Gulf to intercept. The "Slot" was becoming a groove for Ainsworth and his men. And now they were in it again. But this time Ainsworth's Task Group 36.1 was expanded by the addition of six destroyers. The force roster is listed on the next page.

Ainsworth received the order to head for Kula in the afternoon of July 12, and the task group stood northward from Tulagi at 1700. At 2300, when the force was about an hour's run from Visuvisu Point, the Admiral sent all hands to battle stations. Tonight there was a bright moon gilding the seascape and silhouetting the ships. With radar Ainsworth planned to beat the enemy to the punch. He was unaware that the oncoming Japs were equipped with novel radar detectors which enabled them to "intercept" the radar beams and plot the course of his approaching ships.

At 0036 in the morning of July 13, a "Black Cat" search plane contacted the Jap ships some 26 miles northwest of Ainsworth's force. The "Cat" reported a Jap cruiser and five DD's rat-racing toward Kula. Ainsworth immediately formed his night battle column—McInerney's destroyers in the van; cruisers next; Ryan's destroyers in the rear. He headed the column on a course that took it directly across the mouth of Kula Gulf.

At 0059 flag cruiser HONOLULU made first radar contact with the enemy, and at 0103 the lookouts on lead destroyer NICHOLAS spied the enemy's silhouette. Three minutes later Ainsworth swung his ships on a simultaneous 30° turn to the right to close the Jap warships. Suddenly the second ship in the Jap column laid a searchlight on the American DD's. Snapping the word over the TBS, Ainsworth ordered the destroyers to fire torpedoes at discretion.

McInerney's van destroyers let go at once, range about 10,000 yards. So did New Zealand cruiser LEANDER. Ryan's rear DD's had been crowding on steam to get in column formation when the firing order came, and they were badly bunched astern of

Out to derail the Tokyo Express. Here a U.S. destroyer (the Nicholas, DD 449) blasts the night with gunfire at the peak of the Battle of Vella Lavella, when U.S. destroyer forces intercepted the enemy trying to evacuate remnants of his troops from the Central Solomons. In such night actions, death could come suddenly from gunfire, from torpedoes, or from collision.

Laying down a smoke screen. Dense smoke pours from the U.S. destroyers Waller and Renshaw to make a protective screen for Cruiser Division 2, following close behind. Under the swirling smoke curtain the cruisers were poor targets for enemy bombs or shells, yet with radar they could pinpoint enemy targets with deadly accuracy. Few U.S. ships were sunk by enemy shore fire.

Hard to kill—the Chevalier, shown here with the Taylor. Torpedoed in the Battle of Vella Lavella—her bow blown off—and then rammed—the sinking Chevalier jettisoned all her torpedoes by firing them into a Jap destroyer.

Too tough to die—Lieutenant Hugh Barr Miller, U.S.N.R. Injured by his own ship's depth charges, he swam ashore to fight a one-man war there

TASK GROUP 36.1
Rear Admiral Ainsworth

DESTROYER SQUADRON 21
Captain Francis X. McInerney

NICHOLAS *Flagship*	*Lt. Comdr. Andrew J. Hill*
O'BANNON	*Lt. Comdr. D. J. MacDonald*
TAYLOR	*Lt. Comdr. Benjamin Katz*
JENKINS	*Lt. Comdr. Madison Hall*
RADFORD	*Comdr. W. K. Romoser*

CRUISER DIVISION 9
Rear Admiral Ainsworth
HONOLULU ST. LOUIS
H.M.N.Z.S. LEANDER
Replacement for HELENA

DESTROYER SQUADRON 12
Capt. T. J. Ryan

GWIN	*Lt. Comdr. J. B. Fellows* *Flagship of* *Comdr. J. M. Higgins,* COMDESDIV 23
RALPH TALBOT	*Comdr. J. W. Callahan*
BUCHANAN	*Lt. Comdr. F. B. T. Myhre*
MAURY	*Comdr. G. L. Sims*
WOODWORTH	*Comdr. V. F. Gordinier*

ST. LOUIS. These rear destroyers, it should be remarked, were all newcomers in Ainsworth's force. They were drawn from three unacquainted squadrons and had never worked in harness with each other. Yet with the exception of GWIN, all unleashed torpedo salvos. In spite of dense smoke from flashless powder, they avoided collision and made the turn safely. The trouble that came was the handiwork of the Japs.

As has been noted, the Jap ships carried radar-detectors. Admiral Izaki had seen the Americans coming, and about 0108 he had ordered a DD torpedo attack, thereby beating Ainsworth's by some 60 seconds. By jumping the gun, the Japs might have had a considerable advantage, but their only hit was a torpedo in the New Zealand cruiser LEANDER.

When the American destroyers in the van loosed their torpedoes, Jap cruiser JINTSU flashed a searchlight at them and opened fire with gun and torpedo batteries. Answering with rapid fire, Ainsworth's cruisers pumped shell after shell at JINTSU. In the action the Allied column had swung northwest, then southward on a wide loop. While it was swinging on this loop, the early-launched Jap torpedoes began to nip in. Cruiser LEANDER, overrunning the southward turn, was struck hard at 0122. Disabled by the blast, she fell out of action with 28 of her crew lying dead.

The Japs paid for this blow, and the price was the cruiser JINTSU. As they looped around to the southward, the American warships, one and all, flailed at JINTSU with shellfire. Centered in a tempest of flame and steel, JINTSU was literally melted down. While the cruiser was melting she was struck by a torpedo from the American van group. About 0145 she was torpedoed again, probably by a "fish" from Ryan's rear destroyers.

Admiral Izaki's flagship disintegrated. So did Admiral Izaki. So did some 483 Japanese cruisermen. JINTSU broke in two, and the flaming, exploding wreckage disappeared at 0148. Nearly all hands were either drowned, blown to pieces, or cremated.

Meanwhile, Ainsworth (at 0126) had ordered his van destroyers to peel away and pursue the Jap DD's reported by the Black Cat to be breaking off the action.

Heading northward in NICHOLAS, Captain McInerney shouted to Captain Ryan over TBS,

WE FOUR ARE ON COURSE 325 CHASING THE ENEMY
DON'T THROW ANYTHING AT US

I WOULDN'T DO IT FOR THE WORLD
GO TO IT AND GET THE BASTARDS X GOOD LUCK

was Ryan's reply.

More language to shock nice old ladies. But the ladies for whom this epithet was intended were neither old nor nice. Their names were MIKAZUKI, YUKIKAZE, HAMAKAZE, KIYONAMI, and YUGURE.

However, the order which sent McInerney's destroyers in pursuit of these Japanese destroyers proved unfortunate. NICHOLAS, O'BANNON, TAYLOR, and JENKINS were unable to locate the Jap DD's for the simple reason that the Japs had withdrawn to reload their torpedo tubes. All McInerney's destroyers could find was JINTSU's halved corpse, which they paused to bury with shellfire. While they performed this funeral service, the rest of the American force looped northward up into the "Slot" to support the pursuit. The van DD's thus became separated from Ainsworth's main body. Confusion resulted at 0156 when the American cruiser column was running northwest up the "Slot," and HONOLULU made radar contact with a group of ships on her port bow, range 23,000 yards. Were they Japs, or were they McInerney's?

Ainsworth was compelled to hold his fire until he could find out. The investigation cost time and a lot of talk over the TBS. Seven minutes ticked by. Then Ainsworth ordered his cruisers to fire starshells. When the eerie light flooded the seascape, the target ships were seen retiring at high speed. The retirement meant they were enemy. Ainsworth swung his cruisers on a right turn to bring their batteries to bear. But the Japs had fired first—and they had fired a barrage of Model 93 torpedoes.

Just as her gunners were about to fire, HONOLULU sighted one of the poisonous wakes. She flashed the alarm, but it was too late. Astern of her, ST. LOUIS was hit. The "fish" struck her forward, and bent her stem sideways like a broken nose. HONOLULU was also struck on the nose, and a dud smacked her in the stern. Each with a nose out of joint, the two American cruisers went floundering. Then GWIN, leading HONOLULU, caught a torpedo amidships. Instantly she was writhing in a bramble bush of fire. Those death-dealing Jap torpedoes had killed again.

The torpedoings threw Ainsworth's column into a snarl. Only destroyer RALPH TALBOT was able to launch torpedoes at the retiring Japs. They were long shots and they brought no results.

So the Battle of Kolombangara ended disastrously for Ainsworth's force. And disaster worsened when destroyer BUCHANAN sideswiped destroyer WOODWORTH in the jam which followed the torpedoings. The collision damaged WOODWORTH's port propeller, flooded three of her after compartments, and jounced her portside depth charges into the sea. Presumably the charges had been set on "safe," but one blasted off under BUCHANAN's bow. Fortunately, neither ship was disabled.

A destroyer sinking, three cruisers severely damaged, two destroyers bruised by collision—these were stiff casualties in exchange for the JINTSU. However, the "Tokyo Express" had been sidetracked, with consequent deprivation of the Japanese garrison at Vila-Stanmore. Ainsworth and company had fulfilled their mission.

But Kolombangara had been a costly engagement, all things considered. In honest retrospect, Ainsworth wrote to Admiral Nimitz: *"Looking over one's shoulder, one can always see how we should have done differently, and no one knows the fallacy of chasing Jap destroyers with cruisers better than I."*

Slowly and painfully, cruisers LEANDER, HONOLULU, and ST. LOUIS and destroyers WOODWORTH and BUCHANAN made their homeward way down the "Slot." Astern, they left destroyer GWIN sinking under the evil eye of Kolombangara, "King of the Waters."

Loss of U.S.S. Gwin

Doom struck the destroyer GWIN at 0214 in the morning of July 13, 1943. The torpedo which smote her was one of the Japanese supers, the type they called "long lance." Some 1,036 pounds of high explosive detonated to rip the vitals out of the ship, and she stumbled to a halt with oil spilling from her side and flames roaring up through her superstructure. The Japs had their vengeance for defeat at Kolombangara.

Men had been instantly slain in the destroyer's engineering spaces where the thunderbolt exploded. Others who were trapped in wrecked compartments died in gusts of live steam or were drowned by the inrushing sea. A brave effort was made by Ensign G. E. Stransky, U.S.N.R., and party to control a vicious ammunition and oil fire. Searing heat and suffocating oil-smoke scorched and blinded them, but they succeeded in squelching the flames.

Fortunately the destroyer did not break up. At dawn Jap aircraft came roaring down the "Slot" to strike at cripples. They were intercepted by American fighters from the Russell Islands, and beaten off. The attempt to save GWIN went on into the forenoon watch.

Offering all the help she could, destroyer RALPH TALBOT stood by. But gradually the flood rose below decks, dragging the GWIN deeper and deeper until she threatened to founder. About 0900 Division Commander Higgins, who was on board, saw the salvage effort was hopeless. RALPH TALBOT moved alongside to take off the survivors. Listing on her side, GWIN drifted in a haze of fumes. At Captain Ryan's direction, RALPH TALBOT stood off to sink the derelict. As someone on RALPH TALBOT recited the service for burial at sea, four torpedoes sent GWIN down under. Under with her she took the bodies of two officers and 59 men.

So ended the career of the only American destroyer to survive the battleship action which concluded the Battle of Guadalcanal. "She was a great ship," one of her crew said afterwards. "But we knew she'd been living on borrowed time. I guess all of us lived on that kind of time in the Solomons."

Destroyermen Rescue Helena Survivors

GWIN's loss was mourned by many of the survivors of the cruiser HELENA, who would always remember her as one of the destroyers which came to their rescue.

It would be hard to imagine a situation worse than the one which faced those survivors when their cruiser went down in Kula Gulf on that morning of July 6. The American task group had been forced to haul out and leave them behind. Ainsworth left boats with volunteers to pick up swimmers, but with Jap cannon to the right of them and Jap cannon to the left of them, where did they go from there?

The volunteers in the rescue whaleboats contrived to save 88 of HELENA's sailors, including her skipper, Captain C. P. Cecil. Three of the whaleboats were put to towing rafts and floats; they composed a miniature flotilla which reached an islet near Rice Anchorage that evening. Next day (July 7) destroyers GWIN and WOODWORTH had showed up off this landfall, expressly dispatched to Kula to hunt for the cruisermen. A blinker signal had brought the DD's in to the beach, and the 88 survivors had been rescued.

Meanwhile, about 200 of HELENA's left-overs had become separated from Captain Cecil's group. These survivors were clinging to HELENA's bow section as it drifted northward after the torpedoing. Fortunately a Navy Liberator spotted the flotsam and dropped four rubber boats and a scatter of life-jackets. The cruisermen succeeded in inflating three of the boats. Not much buoyancy for some 200 sailors, but enough to support the wounded and those who could not swim.

Strong swimmers played engine for the heavy-laden tow, and the group headed for the coast of Kolombangara. But wind and current swept the desperate huddle out into the "Slot." During the night a number of exhausted swimmers drowned, and some of the injured died. The following day the rubber boats drifted shoreward toward Vella Lavella Island, and most of the survivors reached the beach.

They were spotted by coast watchers who radioed the word to Guadalcanal. Friendly natives gave them shelter in the jungle. But the island was crawling with Japs, and 165 men could not easily remain under cover. Moreover, many of the wounded were in urgent need of medical aid. Would help arrive before the Japs found and massacred them?

Lying west of Kolombangara, Vella Lavella was only an air-jump from the Jap bases on Choiseul and Bougainville. Transports were required to take off the HELENA men, and the Japs were almost certain to spot any American ships which ventured that far up the "Slot."

Risky or not, the mission was to be undertaken. In the evening of July 15—barely 48 hours after the Kolombangara engagement—Captain McInerney led destroyers NICHOLAS, RADFORD, JENKINS, and O'BANNON up the "Slot." Three hours earlier a destroyer group under Captain Ryan, ComDesRon 12, had set out for Vella Lavella on a course which passed to the south of New Georgia and Kolombangara. In this group destroyers TAYLOR, MAURY, GRIDLEY, and ELLET escorted destroyer-transports DENT and WATERS. The lifesavers were on the way.

McInerney's group was spotted by Jap aircraft which had no trouble recognizing the American silhouettes in bright moonlight. But for some reason an all-out air attack was not launched, and the detected ships served to draw attention from the transport group approaching Vella Lavella from the south. Unmolested, Ryan's destroyers steamed into Vella Gulf. While her companion DD's patrolled off shore, destroyer TAYLOR felt her way into the reef-laced maw of Pareso Bay, leading the two transports. About 0200 in the morning of July 16 a light winked furtively from the beach. Going ashore in landing craft, the destroyermen picked up 61 survivors who had a Jap prisoner as mascot.

DENT and WATERS were then guided eight miles up the coast to another beach where 104 HELENA men were waiting. With them were 16 Chinese refugees. They were quickly carried out to the destroyer-transports. Then pouring on the coal, the eight destroyers and two destroyer-transports raced for Savo Sound. On the southbound run the ships stopped to pick up two Jap sailors found adrift in a motor whaleboat. The boat was a pathetic memento left by GWIN, and the two Japs were mementoes left by I.J.N. JINTSU. No, the HELENA survivors would never forget the destroyermen who were "ready to go to hell'n back for HELENA."

The Battle of Vella Gulf (Moosbrugger in Action!)

On July 15, 1943, Rear Admiral T. S. Wilkinson relieved Admiral Turner as Commander Amphibious Forces South Pacific. At that time Army and Marine troops were slugging their way toward Munda on New Georgia, fighting hard for that Central Solomons rung. The amphibious program was going forward full steam. But the disablement of three cruisers had almost left Ainsworth's task group on the beach, and the Japs had taken to running barges down the "Slot" to reinforce their Central Solomons front. Early in August Wilkinson received word that such a Japanese train was coming. He lacked heavy ships for the wrecking job in prospect, but there were some new destroyers in Tulagi. And with those destroyers was an officer named Moosbrugger.

Commander Frederick Moosbrugger had been sent to Tulagi to serve as ComDesDiv 12. His division consisted of destroyers DUNLAP (Lieutenant Commander Clifton Iverson), CRAVEN (Lieutenant Commander F. T. Williamson), and MAURY (Commander G. L. Sims).

On August 5 Munda fell. While it was falling Admiral Wilkinson sent Moosbrugger a dispatch ordering him to Vella Gulf to intercept the new "Tokyo Express." Moosbrugger was ordered to proceed by the southern route and enter the gulf via Gizo Strait between Kolombangara and Gizo Islands. Upon en-

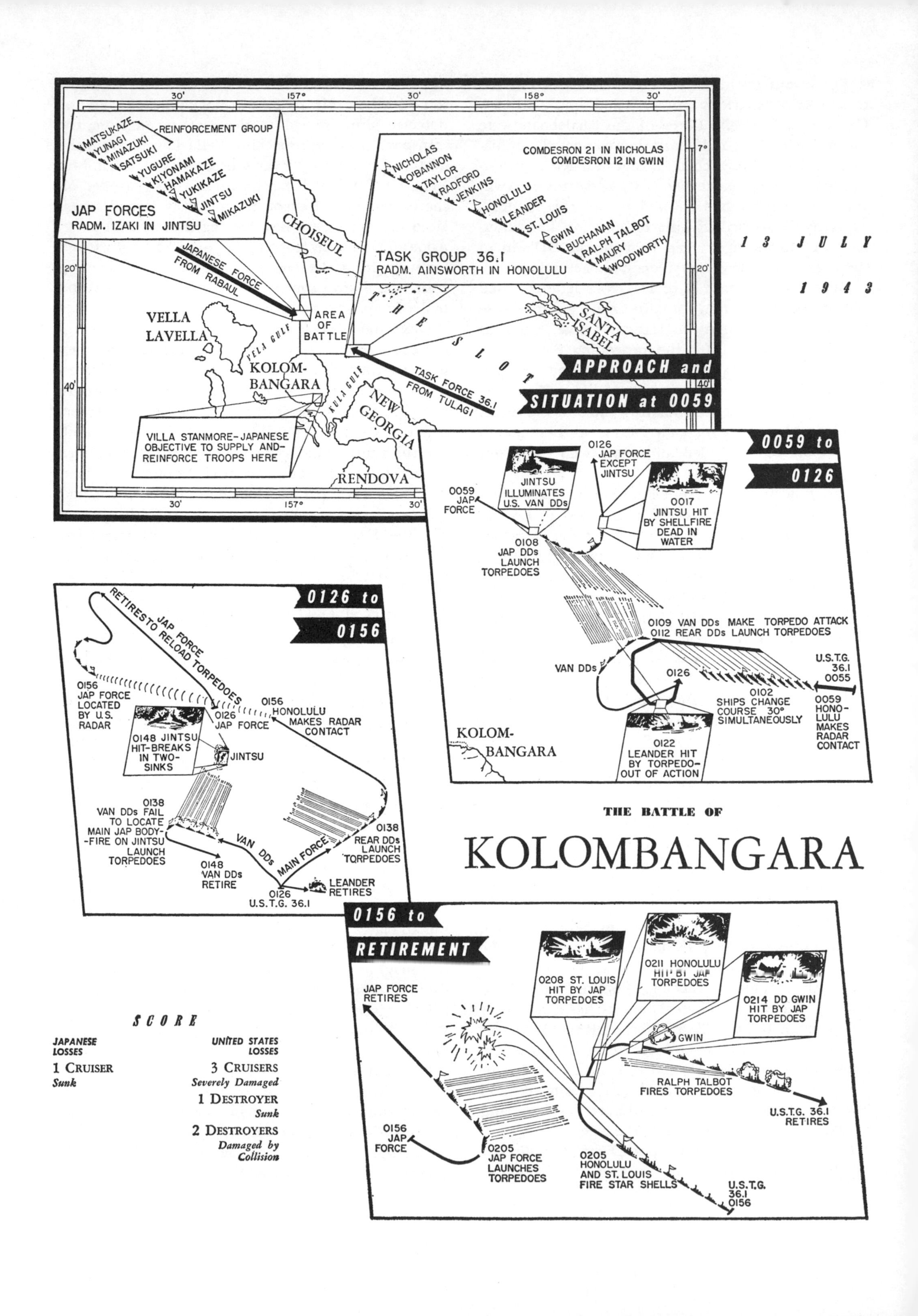

THE BATTLE OF

KOLOMBANGARA

SCORE

JAPANESE LOSSES	UNITED STATES LOSSES
1 Cruiser *Sunk*	3 Cruisers *Severely Damaged*
	1 Destroyer *Sunk*
	2 Destroyers *Damaged by Collision*

tering the Gulf he was to assume complete command of the operation and adopt whatever tactics he chose. He was to have daylight fighter cover, and cooperation of PT-boats in the Blackett Strait area. His force would include three DD's of Destroyer Division 15. These destroyers were LANG (Commander J. L. Wilfong), flying the pennant of Commander R. W. Simpson, ComDesDiv 15; STERETT (Lieutenant Commander F. G. Gould); and STACK (Lieutenant Commander R. A. Newton).

Here was the opportunity the DesPac captains had been waiting for. And Moosbrugger's outfit, DesDiv 12, had operated as a unit since May 1941. Further, their specialty was night torpedo attack under radar control.

Moosbrugger's plan was for the two destroyer divisions to steam up the Gulf in separate columns about two miles apart, Simpson's a little astern of Moosbrugger's. If the target proved to be a destroyer group, Moosbrugger's DD's would hit the first blow with torpedoes. If barges were encountered, Simpson's DD's, armed with new 40 mm. batteries, would open up with shells. Understood? Let's go!

At 1130 the six destroyers steamed out of Tulagi. About 2330 they entered Gizo Strait. Moonset turned the night into a coal-hole, and a rain-squall doused the darkness with shoe blacking. But the destroyers squeezed through the passage at 15 knots, probing the island coasts and the invisibility ahead with radar. As his ships entered Vella Gulf, Moosbrugger ordered them into battle formation. After probing the waters off Blackett Strait they headed due north, following the Kolombangara coast, with Simpson's DD's in the inshore position and Moosbrugger's on the outside track.

At 2333 DUNLAP made the first radar contact, a target in the mouth of the Gulf about ten miles distant. On the radar screen the "pip" quickly multiplied itself into four distinct "pips" which meant four enemy ships heading southward.

The enemy destroyers which had steamed into radar view were I.J.N. HAGIKAZE, ARASHI, and KAWAKAZE, chock-a-block with troops and supplies for the Emperor's garrison on Kolombangara, supported by SHIGURE, crammed with ammunition and torpedoes to be fired in the event of interference. These Jap ships did not carry radar, and they were unaware of Commander Moosbrugger and his destroyer team.

The range closed swiftly to good torpedo range. And Moosbrugger had tuned his torpedoes up by deactivating the cranky magnetic exploder device. Also his torpedo batteries were equipped with flash-hiders. These improvements were now to pay off.

At 2336 Moosbrugger passed the word over TBS to his leading division, "Stand by to fire torpedoes!" As DesDiv 12 came to course 335° T, the computed course to the torpedo firing point, Simpson's destroyers took station clear of the van division and headed for the enemy's disengaged bow, ready to launch torpedoes if opportunity presented. Moosbrugger barked the torpedo-firing order. DUNLAP, CRAVEN, and MAURY let go with spreads—eight torpedoes to a spread. As the "fish" raced off across the mouth of the Gulf, Moosbrugger swung his ships hard right to dodge Jap torpedoes, if any. Surface visibility was less than 4,000 yards, and no ship had as yet been sighted.

And now the Japs, having belatedly sighted the foaming torpedo wakes, were frantically trying to fire their own big "fish." All was uproar and confusion on HAGIKAZE's bridge. ARASHI and KAWAKAZE were also unprepared for action. Cracking the whip at the tail end of the column, SHIGURE was equally unready.

"Torpedo!" HAGIKAZE's lookouts screamed.

"Torpedo!" screamed the lookouts on ARASHI and KAWAKAZE.

"Torpedo!" screamed SHIGURE's lookouts.

Only the rear Jap destroyer escaped a blasting. HAGIKAZE was hit. Ditto for ARASHI. Double ditto for KAWAKAZE. Here is how it looked to an American witness.

"It seemed forever before the torpedoes hit," said Lieutenant E. H. Winslow, a gunnery officer on board LANG. "As soon as we saw the torpedoes hitting, all ships opened up with 5-inch 38's. One large ship was struck and began to burn. A destroyer blew up immediately; evidently the 'fish' struck her magazine. She went off the radar screen instantaneously."

Another Jap ship was hit. The sky went livid and the seascape resembled a forest fire. The Jap ships burned like clumps of dry brush.

While DesDiv 12's torpedoes were smashing home, DesDiv 15's shells were doing likewise. So torpedoed KAWAKAZE was blasted both above and below. Then STACK threw four torpedoes at the burning ship. KAWAKAZE capsized and went under. One down!

At 0010 in the morning of August 6, ARASHI blew up. "It looked," said another observer, "like a bed of hot coals thrown a thousand feet in the air." After this eruption, ARASHI went down like an iron grate. She was hurried on her way by torpedoes from DesDiv 15.

Meantime HAGIKAZE had erupted with a Vesuvius roar. She, too, went flaming down into the sea.

THE SHIGURE, sole survivor of this pogrom, had fired eight aimless torpedoes and taken to her heels. Alone the ship raced back to Bougainville to report

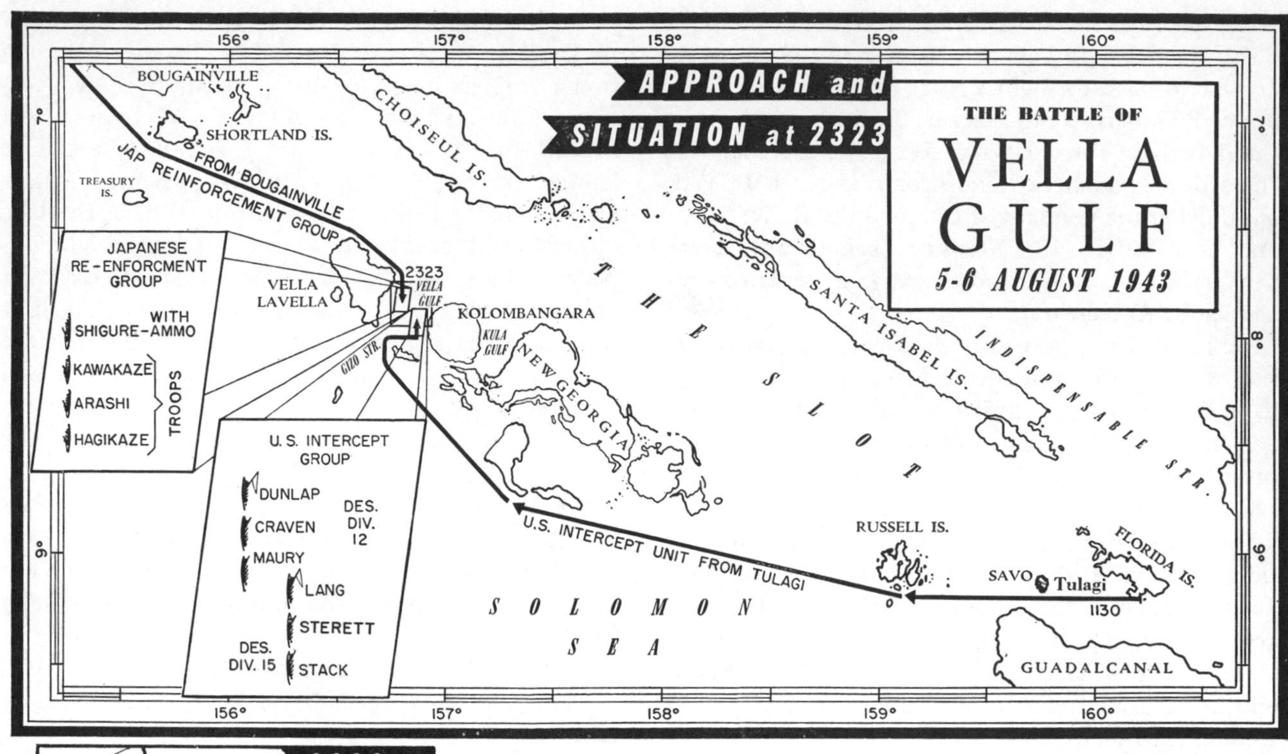
THE BATTLE OF
VELLA GULF
5-6 AUGUST 1943
APPROACH and
SITUATION at 2323
156°
157°
158°
159°
160°
7°
8°
9°
BOUGAINVILLE
SHORTLAND IS.
TREASURY IS.
FROM BOUGAINVILLE
JAP REINFORCEMENT GROUP
CHOISEUL IS.
THE SLOT
SANTA ISABEL IS.
INDISPENSABLE STR.
JAPANESE
RE-ENFORCMENT
GROUP
WITH
SHIGURE-AMMO
KAWAKAZE
ARASHI
HAGIKAZE
TROOPS
VELLA
LAVELLA
2323
VELLA GULF
KOLOMBANGARA
KULA GULF
GIZO STR.
NEW GEORGIA
U. S. INTERCEPT
GROUP
DUNLAP
CRAVEN
MAURY
DES.
DIV.
12
LANG
STERETT
STACK
DES.
DIV. 15
U.S. INTERCEPT UNIT FROM TULAGI
RUSSELL IS.
FLORIDA IS.
SAVO
Tulagi
1130
SOLOMON
SEA
GUADALCANAL

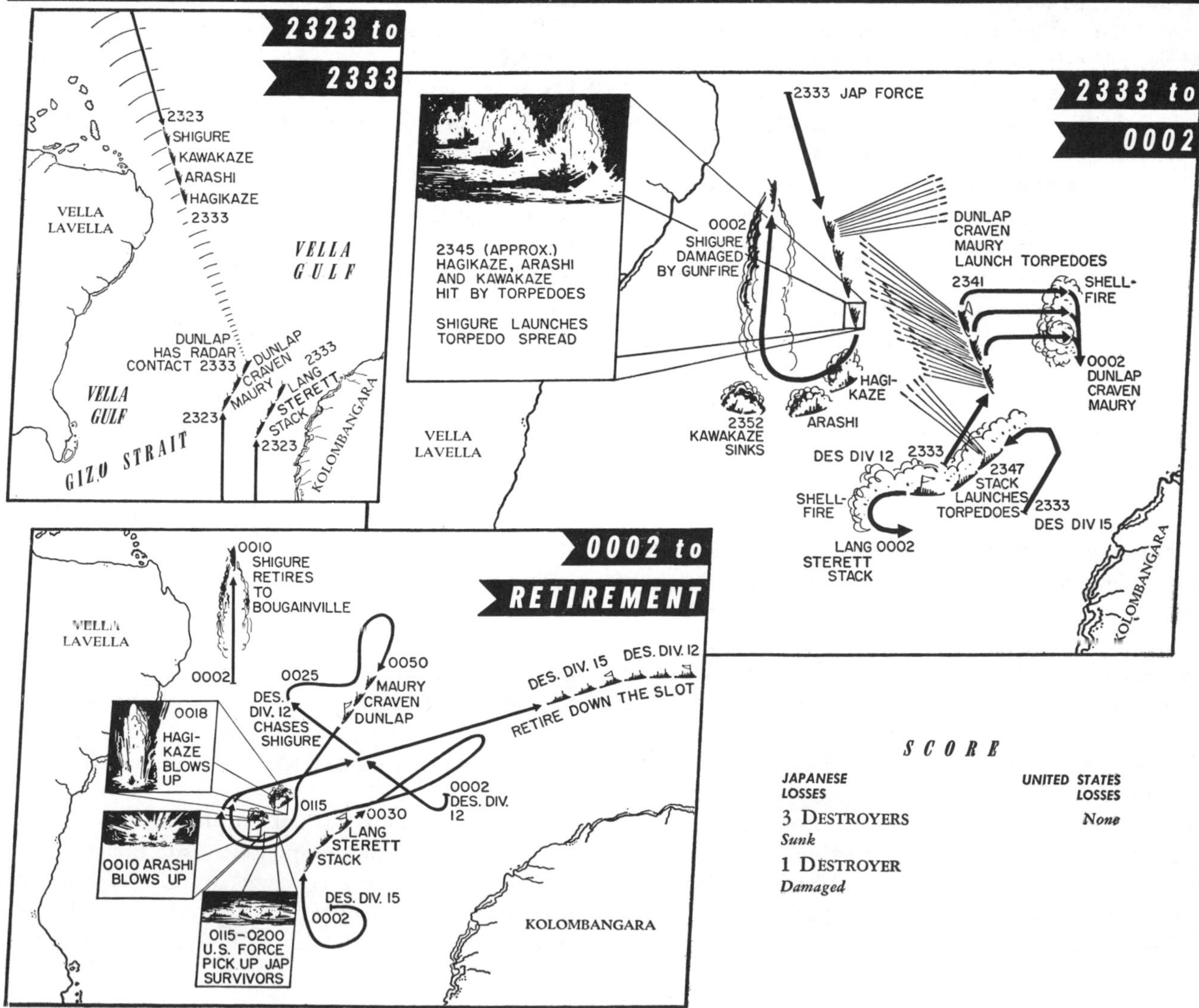
2323 to
2333
2323
SHIGURE
KAWAKAZE
ARASHI
HAGIKAZE
2333
VELLA
LAVELLA
VELLA
GULF
DUNLAP
HAS RADAR
CONTACT 2333
DUNLAP
CRAVEN
MAURY
2333
LANG
STERETT
STACK
2323
2323
GIZO STRAIT
KOLOMBANGARA
2333 to
0002
2333 JAP FORCE
2345 (APPROX.)
HAGIKAZE, ARASHI
AND KAWAKAZE
HIT BY TORPEDOES
SHIGURE LAUNCHES
TORPEDO SPREAD
0002
SHIGURE
DAMAGED
BY GUNFIRE
DUNLAP
CRAVEN
MAURY
LAUNCH TORPEDOES
2341
SHELL-
FIRE
0002
DUNLAP
CRAVEN
MAURY
HAGI-
KAZE
ARASHI
2352
KAWAKAZE
SINKS
VELLA
LAVELLA
DES DIV 12
2333
2347
STACK
LAUNCHES
TORPEDOES
2333
DES DIV 15
SHELL-
FIRE
LANG 0002
STERETT
STACK
KOLOMBANGARA
0002 to
RETIREMENT
0010
SHIGURE
RETIRES
TO
BOUGAINVILLE
VELLA
LAVELLA
0002
0025
0050
DES.
DIV. 12
CHASES
SHIGURE
MAURY
CRAVEN
DUNLAP
DES. DIV. 15
DES. DIV. 12
RETIRE DOWN THE SLOT
0018
HAGI-
KAZE
BLOWS
UP
0115
0002
DES. DIV.
12
0030
LANG
STERETT
STACK
0010 ARASHI
BLOWS UP
DES. DIV. 15
0002
0115-0200
U.S. FORCE
PICK UP JAP
SURVIVORS
KOLOMBANGARA
SCORE
JAPANESE
LOSSES
3 DESTROYERS
Sunk
1 DESTROYER
Damaged
UNITED STATES
LOSSES
None

the massacre of her companions. Moosbrugger led his destroyers in a footless chase of the fugitive, then circled back to look for Japanese survivors in the burning sea. Clots of Japs were found struggling in the water, but all refused rescue. At 0200 the rescue effort was called off, and DesDiv 15 headed southward down the "Slot" astern of DesDiv 12.

In the Battle of Vella Gulf, as this engagement came to be called, the enemy had not laid a hand on the American ships. The only casualty among these last was a broken feed pump in a destroyer. On board LANG a loader's hand was accidentally crushed. On the Japanese side three destroyers went down, two of them almost the latest thing in Jap construction. And with them went some 1,500 Jap sailors and their soldier passengers.

For anyone seeking answers, the Vella Gulf triumph was probably based on Dewey's recipe for success at Manila—"ceaseless routine of hard work and preparation." Or, as put by Admiral Nimitz, "training, training, training." And the leadership of Commander Moosbrugger.

Barging Toward Bougainville

Soured by the loss of several dozen assorted warships and a number of admirals, Japanese Commander-in-Chief Koga looked upon the Central Solomons with a jaundiced eye. He decided to discontinue the "Tokyo Express" run to the Central Solomons.

Of course this meant surrendering the right-of-way, and the loss of strategic bases on Kolombangara and Vella Lavella. Nothing could be done about it, and the decision was made. And the troops stranded at these bases would have to be ferried back to Bougainville by barges.

Thus, as of August 1943, Allied coastwatchers saw herds, flocks, and bevies of blunt-nosed Japanese barges creeping up and down the "Slot." By day they ducked into lagoons, or waited secretively in jungle-screened bays. By night they chugged and puttered along the channels, carefully hugging the shoreline. But they found no hiding place there. Over the "Slot" flew American aircraft, and up the "Slot" steamed American destroyers with no other mission than to intercept and destroy Koga's "canal" traffic. Just why the Japanese naval chief thought he could do with slow barges what he could not do with fast warships is a question unanswered in the record. Obviously barges were cheaper than warships, but why throw anything of value down a drain?

On the night of August 9-10 some barges in Vella Gulf were intercepted by Moosbrugger and his six-destroyer task group and shot to shards with rapid-fire gunnery.

A week later, off Choiseul, Captain Ryan, with NICHOLAS, O'BANNON, TAYLOR, and CHEVALIER, caught a good-sized convoy carrying troops to cover the exodus from the Kolombangara area. The convoy contained 17 barges, two auxiliary subchasers, and other small craft. And it was screened by three Jap DD's. When Ryan's destroyers piled in, the Japs fled back up the "Slot." The two subchasers, an armed boat, and two landing craft fell prey to American gunnery, and destroyer ISOKAZE was damaged.

On the night of October 1-2 a powerful American Striking Force and a strong support force under Admiral Merrill steamed into the waters off Vella Lavella to vacuum-sweep Jap evacuation traffic. Led by Captain W. R. Cooke, ComDesRon 22, the Striking Force was composed of destroyers WALLER (flagship), CONY, EATON, RENSHAW, SAUFLEY, RADFORD, GRAYSON, and LAVALLETTE. Built around two light cruisers, the Support Force contained destroyers CHARLES AUSBURNE (flagship of Captain M. J. Gillan, Jr., ComDesRon 23), DYSON, SELFRIDGE, SPENCE, and CLAXTON. At the cost of minor damage to SAUFLEY (but not minor to the two bluejackets who lost their lives), the sweepers swept 20 Jap barges into Davy Jones' dust bin. As will be related, destroyer EATON added an I-boat to the rubbish pile.

The following night Captain Cooke's Striking Force—destroyers WALLER, EATON, CONY, RALPH TALBOT, TERRY, and TAYLOR—encountered four Jap DD's evacuating Imperial forces from Kolombangara. Under Division Commander H. O. Larson, the TALBOT, TERRY, and TAYLOR opened long-range fire on the enemy. The Japs answered with hasty torpedoes and fled, I.J.N. SAMIDARE smoking from three shell hits. Cooke's force then lit into the smaller game. Down went a torpedo boat and 20 more barges.

The night after that NICHOLAS, CHEVALIER, and O'BANNON downed two more barges and a gunboat.

The Japs having lost some 46 barges and a miscellany of other craft in 60 days of feverish canal-boating, their garrisons on Vella Lavella, Arundel, and Kolombangara were trapped and starving. Accordingly, the Rabaul command decided to risk another full-size "Tokyo Express" in the evacuation effort. The result of their thinking was the Battle of Vella Lavella—another slam-bang destroyer action—to be discussed presently.

Meantime, the Japanese Submarine Force had been finding the Solomons Area most uncongenial. Four Imperial Navy submarines were downed by DesPac destroyers during the late summer-autumn period.

Patterson Kills I-178

Serving as A/S vessels, DesPac destroyers did not

have a particularly lively season in the South Pacific during the spring and summer of 1943. No fault of theirs. The reason was an increasing scarcity of game. The Japanese subs were growing gun-shy. Only a few I-boats were out convoy-hunting in the South Pacific during the period in question, and these few did not do very well. One which did very poorly was the I-178.

In the evening of August 25, 1943, destroyer PATTERSON (Lieutenant Commander A. F. White) was steaming along in the screen of Task Unit 32.4.7, at that hour on the road between Espiritu Santo and the Lower Solomons. At 1912 she picked up something on her radarscope and was promptly ordered to investigate.

Eleven minutes later, the range having closed to 4,000 yards, the "pip" suddenly vanished from the radar screen. This abrupt disappearance had all the ear-marks of a diving sub. Sonar substantiated the evidence by registering with the submerged target at 3,800 yards.

Maneuvering in on the run, PATTERSON steamed across the water, dropping depth charges. Follow-up attacks were made for the next two hours. At 2147 the last pattern went down. The TNT thumped far beneath the surface. Then (time: 2153) the destroyermen heard a deep undersea *boom* which sounded like blasting in a tunnel under a distant subway.

The detonation was too remote for accurate analysis, and PATTERSON "pinged" around on the usual search, but the contact was gone. She had never actually sighted the submarine; it was just a flicker on a screen, a whisper in the sound gear, and that final echo from deep under.

That—and a notation in the records of the Japanese Sixth (Submarine) Fleet, examined after the war. The notation disclosed that the submarine I-178 had disappeared on the night in question somewhere in the vicinity of lat. 12-57 S., long. 164-23 E. Which was the point where PATTERSON's depth charges, going deep, produced the deep-going *boom!*

Ellet Sinks I-168

I-168 arrived and departed in a manner similar to the coming and going of sister I-178. On September 3, 1943, the I-168 made the fatal mistake of nosing to the South Pacific surface in the vicinity of lat. 13 S., long. 165 E.

The sub's presence in the area was detected, and an A/S sweep was ordered by the naval authorities at Espiritu Santo. Evening of the 3rd found destroyer ELLET (Lieutenant Commander T. C. Phifer) on the job with a busy broom. Sweeping through the cobwebby gloom, ELLET snared a radar pip at 1935, range 13,000 yards. It was submarine I-168.

ELLET's skipper closed the range to about 5,000 yards. As the "pip" was unidentifiable, the destroyer challenged at that point with a blinker-gun. When the stranger made no reply, the destroyermen lit up the seascape with a starshell spread. The target disappeared at 3,400 yards, and the chase was on.

ELLET obtained sonar contact at 3,000 yards, and Lieutenant Commander Phifer conned the ship for a depth-charge attack. The first pattern was dropped at 2012, and the last one splashed into the sea at 2038. At 2040 sonar contact was re-established; then it was lost for good at 2059.

Hunt as she would, ELLET could find no further trace of the submarine. The destroyermen, trained to be skeptical in such matters, could not readily believe they had slain a sub in a depth-charge effort of only 26 minutes' duration. But such was the case. At daylight an extensive oil slick was sighted by a plane. Oil bubbles were seen, and a few scraps of debris were noted by the inquisitors.

The slick, the bubbles, the drifting scraps were the last earthly remains of Japanese submarine I-168. After the war her obituary was found in the Imperial Navy's records.

Saufley and Aircraft Down RO-103

Throughout the autumn of 1943, Japanese submarines continued to menace Allied communications lines in the Solomons Area, sniping at an occasional convoy in an effort to disrupt war shipping. Due in part to floundering Jap submarine strategy, the disruption effort was largely futile. American A/S work by patrol planes and convoy escorts contributed to the futility.

In company with the old minelaying "four-stacker" MONTGOMERY, the SAUFLEY (Commander B. F. Brown) was steaming southward from Port Purvis on September 15, 1943, with two merchantmen in convoy. About 11 o'clock in the morning the convoy was waylaid by a submarine at the lower end of Indispensable Strait.

First warning came when a torpedo whisked past one of the merchantmen in a near-miss. Apparently the Japs, over-hasty, had tried a long-range "browning shot." To the convoy the miss was as good as the proverbial mile. To the submarine it was fatal.

All hands on the alert, SAUFLEY began a search that found the target at 1251, range 3,000 yards. Maneuvering in on the attack, the destroyer steamed over the cowering submarine, and pelted the submersible with teardrops and ashcans.

Another round of this treatment. Another. And more. SAUFLEY kept the water booming and banging for about two hours. Then at 1443 the sub made

In the Battle of Vella Lavella the Jap torpedo packed a mighty punch. Chevalier lost her entire bow section forward of the bridge, was rammed by O'Bannon, and finally abandoned and sunk by an American torpedo. Selfridge (above) ran into a torpedo spread from Samidare and Shigure, lost her bow, but was able to get back to Purvis Bay, where this photograph was taken.

Bow trouble: O'Bannon (above) shows the great hole caused by her collision with Chevalier. Buchanan (below) is shown returning to Tulagi after the Battle of Kolombangara, in which she collided with Woodworth.

Frederick Moosbrugger, ComDesDiv 12, at Vella Gulf sank three Jap destroyers without losing one American sailor. He had the equipment and he knew how to use it.

U.S.S. Gwin was hit by a "long lance" Jap torpedo at the Battle of Kolombangara while screening the cruiser Honolulu. The destroyer had to be sunk by Ralph Talbot after all attempts to save her had failed. At last the sea claimed victory in a seven hour struggle against the only American destroyer to survive the battleship action which concluded the Battle of Guadalcanal.

the mistake of broaching in broad daylight within 2,000 yards of the DD.

As the submersible's prow came up, streaming foam, followed by the founting conning tower—an RO-boat!—the destroyer opened fire with all batteries. Machine-gun bullets crackled around the sub's bridge and shells struck the gray pressure hull, flinging up bouquets of smoke and confetti showers of debris.

Almost at the same instant, over the seascape and into the gun-roar winged a plane of Patrol Squadron 23, bent on dropping two depth charges near the surfaced sub. The Catalina gave the destroyermen an anxious moment as she made her bombing run at 100-foot altitude, hopping over SAUFLEY's 5-inch shell splashes like an eagle skimming a briar patch.

But the brambles did not hook the bird, and she laid her iron eggs where best intended. In a spouting cauldron of fire and water the submarine sank. Two minutes later the destroyermen heard the climactic explosion. The time was 1446. Gone was another RO-boat.

Evidence of this particularly futile Jap submarine effort bobbed to the surface in the form of oil slicks, shattered gratings, splintered planks, and kindling wood.

The submarine was to be identified as the RO-103. And very shortly she would have a successor on the missing list.

Eaton Kills I-20

EATON (Lieutenant Commander E. F. Jackson) was a member of Captain W. R. Cooke's Striking Force which steamed up the "Slot" on the night of October 1-2, 1943, to intercept barge traffic. As the group passed the mouth of Kula Gulf, the radar screens began to shimmer like television flaked with "snow." At 2248 EATON opened fire at a plump "pip" which blossomed on her radar, range 3,000 yards.

A barrage of starshells shed light on the target which was promptly identified as a Japanese submarine running on the surface. It did not run fast enough to escape EATON's gunnery. The first salvos were right on. And the next three nailed the conning tower and pressure hull of the hapless submersible. The submarine rolled over on her back and put her propellers in the air.

EATON's gunners planted a few more shells in the vessel's belly. For a minute or two the sub drifted like a dead whale. At 2251 the carcass sank from view. It had taken the killers exactly three minutes to slay this specimen. They went on to exterminate a few barges for good measure.

The submarine blown to the bottom was the I-20, a veteran of the Guadalcanal campaign. She went down in almost the exact center of the "Slot," midway between Choiseul and Kolombangara. There were no survivors.

The Battle of Vella Lavella

The task of evacuating the remnant Japanese garrison on Vella Lavella was detailed to Admiral Matsuji Ijuin. The Rabaul command scraped up a sizable force for this emergency job. It was composed of nine or ten DD's and a flotilla of small boats and sub chasers, a train reminiscent of the heyday of the "Tokyo Express." Early in the morning of October 6, 1943, this force stood southward from Rabaul. It skirted the northern coast of Bougainville, and by twilight it was steaming down the "Slot."

The progress of Ijuin's train was duly reported by search planes. But only three DD's were flying the American flag in the Vella Lavella vicinity. Admiral Wilkinson dispatched these immediately to the waters off the northwest coast of the island, and then detached three more destroyers from a convoy below New Georgia and ordered them to rush northward to reinforce the first three.

The first destroyers to reach an intercepting position were units of Captain Frank R. Walker's Squadron 4—destroyers SELFRIDGE (Lieutenant Commander G. E. Peckham), CHEVALIER (Lieutenant Commander G. R. Wilson), and O'BANNON (Lieutenant Commander D. J. MacDonald). The destroyers racing up from New Georgia were under Commander H. O. Larson—RALPH TALBOT (Lieutenant Commander R. D. Shepard), TAYLOR (Commander Benjamin Katz), and LAVALLETTE (Lieutenant Commander R. L. Taylor). Six American destroyers could have given Ijuin's nine or ten a good run for their money. But three against the Japanese gang was not such a happy circumstance. Yet that was the circumstance Captain Walker found himself up against when the "Tokyo Express" came over the dark horizon.

Ijuin's force had been advancing in three groups—a support group of six destroyers, a transport group of three destroyers, and a flotilla of subchasers and landing craft. His lookouts had sighted the three American destroyers at 2100—a glimpse which had caused the Jap admiral to order his destroyer-transport group to retire. With his support group and small flotilla he had tangented this way and that, waiting for the American patrol to withdraw. It did not withdraw.

At 2231 SELFRIDGE, leading Walker's three-ship column, made radar contact with the enemy up the "Slot." Walker headed his DD's toward the targets to investigate. By 2240 the enemy was in binocular range—six destroyers in two groups.

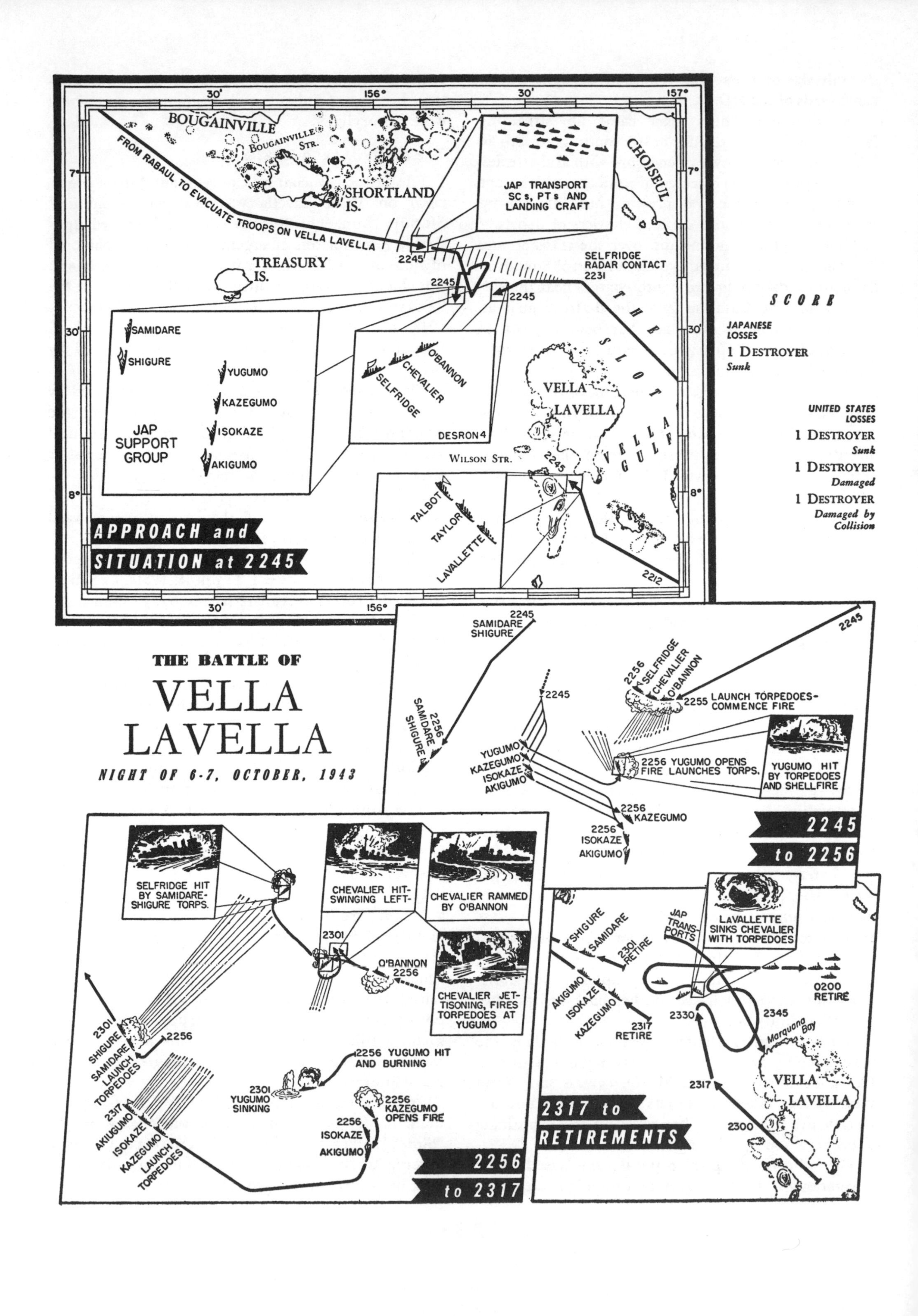
THE BATTLE OF
VELLA LAVELLA
NIGHT OF 6-7, OCTOBER, 1943
APPROACH and SITUATION at 2245
BOUGAINVILLE
BOUGAINVILLE STR.
SHORTLAND IS.
CHOISEUL
FROM RABAUL TO EVACUATE TROOPS ON VELLA LAVELLA
JAP TRANSPORT SCs, PTs AND LANDING CRAFT
TREASURY IS.
SELFRIDGE RADAR CONTACT 2231
THE SLOT
SAMIDARE
SHIGURE
YUGUMO
KAZEGUMO
ISOKAZE
AKIGUMO
JAP SUPPORT GROUP
SELFRIDGE
CHEVALIER
O'BANNON
DESRON 4
VELLA LAVELLA
VELLA GULF
WILSON STR.
TALBOT
TAYLOR
LAVALLETTE
2212
SCORE
JAPANESE LOSSES
1 DESTROYER Sunk
UNITED STATES LOSSES
1 DESTROYER Sunk
1 DESTROYER Damaged
1 DESTROYER Damaged by Collision
2245 to 2256
LAUNCH TORPEDOES-COMMENCE FIRE
2256 YUGUMO OPENS FIRE LAUNCHES TORPS.
YUGUMO HIT BY TORPEDOES AND SHELLFIRE
2256 to 2317
SELFRIDGE HIT BY SAMIDARE-SHIGURE TORPS.
CHEVALIER HIT-SWINGING LEFT-
CHEVALIER RAMMED BY O'BANNON
CHEVALIER JETTISONING, FIRES TORPEDOES AT YUGUMO
SAMIDARE LAUNCH TORPEDOES
2256 YUGUMO HIT AND BURNING
2301 YUGUMO SINKING
2256 KAZEGUMO OPENS FIRE
KAZEGUMO LAUNCH TORPEDOES
2317 to RETIREMENTS
JAP TRANSPORTS
LAVALLETTE SINKS CHEVALIER WITH TORPEDOES
2301 RETIRE
2317 RETIRE
0200 RETIRE
Marquana Bay

The foes having sighted each other after continuous aircraft information, there was no surprise to the action—unless Admiral Ijuin was surprised that three American DD's would assault a force mustering six. Captain Walker, himself, must have been a little worried about the odds. A moment after sighting the enemy, he put in a call for Larson's ships over the TBS. Some 20 miles away, Larson was beyond range of radio-telephony, and the call drew a blank.

Walker then might have hauled away to stall for time. Instead, he pressed forward to strike while the iron was hot. As Ijuin's support group came steaming southward in two columns, the four-ship column—AKIGUMO, ISOKAZE, KAZEGUMO, and YUGUMO—missed a chance to cap Walker's "T." To the starboard of Ijuin's main column, SHIGURE and SAMIDARE were on the disengaged side when the Americans, racing in at 33 knots, opened torpedo fire. Range was 7,000 yards, and the Japs were swinging sharp left in line of bearing when Walker ordered his ships to launch torpedoes. A barrage of 14 went leaping from the American tubes at 2255, and a split minute later Walker snapped the order for gunnery.

Put on the inside track by Ijuin's maneuver, the destroyer YUGUMO was not only presenting her beam to the American torpedoes, but she was also interfering with counterfire from her companions. Then at the crucial moment she veered off to deliver a torpedo attack on her own hook, swinging northward to close this range. By so doing she jaywalked right into a barrage of torpedoes and shells from SELFRIDGE, CHEVALIER, and O'BANNON.

Ijuin pulled out of the muddle by ordering his ships back into column and swinging them southward behind a smoke screen. KAZEGUMO got in a couple of salvos on the turn, but ISOKAZE and AKIGUMO were as yet unable to fire a shot. As for YUGUMO, she was out of it. Having collected an American torpedo and a swarm of 5-inchers, she was squatting disabled in the water and vomiting flames that were seen by Larson's destroyers miles to the south.

Now Ijuin was running westward in fast retreat. The flotilla of Jap small-craft was legging it in to Vella Lavella (eventually it did slip into Marquana Bay where, according to Jap report, it succeeded in evacuating 589 men). And Walker still had five Jap DD's and a mess of Jap "fish" to deal with.

In an effort to deal with the DD's, he sent his column westward in enthusiastic pursuit. In the lead, SELFRIDGE was firing at SHIGURE and SAMIDARE. CHEVALIER and O'BANNON, after pegging shots at YUGUMO's blazing hulk, also shifted attention to the two-ship column. The gun smoke was dense, and O'BANNON, astern of CHEVALIER, was racing through acrid fog. CHEVALIER was on the point of illuminating the targets ahead when her captain was notified that a pair of small craft were making a high-speed approach from starboard.

On CHEVALIER's bridge Lieutenant Commander Wilson ordered a swing to the left. Evidently the small craft were motor torpedo-boats from the Jap group to the north. Wilson intended to bring his 1.1-inch guns to bear on these vicious speedboats while keeping his 5-inchers trained on the two DD's in the west.

Just as CHEVALIER was swinging she was struck in the port bow by a torpedo. Then she was rammed by O'BANNON. Then SELFRIDGE up ahead was torpedoed. All this in a matter of moments.

Loss of U.S.S. Chevalier

It was Japanese destroyer YUGUMO that flung the torpedo which struck CHEVALIER at 2301 in the evening of October 6, 1943. At the moment CHEVALIER's skipper, Lieutenant Commander George R. Wilson, was maneuvering to attack several Jap torpedo boats when the ship was hit. The war head smashed into a portside magazine, and the resulting blast ripped off the destroyer's bow as far aft as the bridge.

All hands on the bridge were thrown from their feet by the thunderclap explosion. Lieutenant Commander Wilson was knocked momentarily unconscious. When he dragged himself upright, he found himself clutching the rail and staring, dazed, at a yawn of swirling water where the destroyer's forecastle should have been. Oil and debris spewed from the mangle of broken framework and machinery under the bridge. Off in the dark somewhere swimmers were shouting, and the sea was hazed with smoke.

Wilson had a glimpse of that, and then he saw something else. What he saw was destroyer O'BANNON's bow looming up directly astern. He shouted to Chief Signalman Crudele to flash a blinker warning. The engineroom telegraph was damaged, and the skipper sent Ensign McQuilkin on a rush below decks to order the engines backed full power—the turbines were still drumming, and the pushing propellers were driving the ship's wrecked forward end down into the sea.

Then men on the fantail were yelling. Someone squalled, "We're going to be raaaamed!" Before the decapitated vessel could be turned or backed, she was struck amidships by O'BANNON. When his lookouts cried the warning, Commander MacDonald of the O'BANNON tried desperately to swing his destroyer aside. Too late. Momentum carried O'BANNON squarely into CHEVALIER's starboard side.

There was the crunch of metal chewing metal. The

disabled destroyer shuddered and heeled. Again some of her crew went spinning and somersaulting across the deck. In the dark after passageways wounded men cried out. Smoke gushed from the wreckage, and bluejackets came climbing topside, coughing.

O'BANNON's screws had been churning to pull her back when her stem gnashed into CHEVALIER. The bite was not deep, but it was deep enough to let the sea into the disabled ship's after engine-room and start copious leakage in both firerooms. With her forecastle torn away, her hull gashed, her power-plant half wrecked, and water rising to swamp her boilers, CHEVALIER leaned on her side, mortally injured.

Bent on saving the destroyer, however impossible the odds, Wilson ordered the crew to jettison everything topside that could be jettisoned. The torpedoes were deliberately aimed and launched at YUGUMO's burning hulk, and the CHEVALIER men had the satisfaction of seeing the enemy ship blown under. Meantime, O'BANNON had been backed off, and MacDonald lowered boats to pick up CHEVALIER's stretcher cases.

While O'BANNON was jockeying about, destroyer SELFRIDGE, five miles up the "Slot," had run into a fan of torpedoes spread by SAMIDARE and SHIGURE. Swinging to comb the wakes, she caught another Model 93. When the thunder and smoke ebbed away, SELFRIDGE had lost most of her bow.

The SELFRIDGE blast put an exclamation point finish to the Vella Lavella destroyer battle. The Japs raced north, leaving mayhem and manslaughter behind them. Commander MacDonald maneuvered O'BANNON into position to cover SELFRIDGE as well as CHEVALIER, and two O'BANNON boats paddled close to Wilson's sinking ship to rescue the crew. Wilson still had hopes of salvaging the hulk, but she was settling as though in quicksand.

By 2330 Larson's three destroyer's were on the scene. They had sighted the gun flashes and had raced at top speed to reach the arena. It was all over but the damage control when they got there, but Larson sent his DD's scouting along the coast off Marquana Bay in the hopes of flushing the enemy. At 0020 in the morning of October 7, Larson gave up the chase and ordered his ships in to the aid of SELFRIDGE and CHEVALIER.

Wilson was now ready to concede his case as hopeless, and CHEVALIER was abandoned. Those who were able dived overside and swam out to O'BANNON's boats. The wounded were gently passed by hand. A Japanese float-light glowed on the water, unintentionally aiding the rescue work. In O'BANNON's wardroom the wounded were skilfully tended by Lieutenant R. C. Manchester, U.S.N.R., the ship's Medical Officer. Among others, CHEVALIER's captain and her "Exec" were both in line for bandaging.

Destroyer TAYLOR moved up to take off the SELFRIDGE crew. These had jettisoned such topside weights as could be dumped into the sea, and damage-control parties had shored up the foreward bulkheads to keep out the flood. As the engines were unharmed, the ship was able to move through the water at about 10 knots. Lieutenant Commander Peckham, determined to stick it out, remained on board with a salvage party. Most of the crew and Squadron Commander Walker were taken off by the TAYLOR. With gun crews manning her undamaged weapons, SELFRIDGE steamed slowly down the "Slot" under her own power. She was screened by RALPH TALBOT and TAYLOR.

LAVALLETTE was ordered to sink wrecked CHEVALIER. At the range of one mile she fired a single torpedo. A great balloon of fire rolled up into the sky, and then nothing was left of the broken warship.

Lost with CHEVALIER were 53 bluejackets and an officer.

Bougainville Invaded ("Operation Shoestring 2")

With New Georgia, Kolombangara, and Vella Lavella in Allied hands, only Bougainville remained as a major barrier to the "Watchtower" drive on Rabaul. Dominating the Upper Solomons, Bougainville is the largest of the Solomon Isles.

Occupying the island in 1942, the conquering Japs had installed a garrison at Buin on the south coast, and built air bases at near-by Kahili and Kara. Outposts were established in the Shortlands and Treasury Island just to the south, and on Buka Island just to the north. The Japs considered Bougainville very secure.

They considered it less secure after the Allies swept into the Central Solomons. Japanese Imperial Headquarters determined to defend the island at any cost. Early in October Admiral Koga dispatched carrier reinforcements to Rabaul. Troops were rushed to Bougainville. More planes were sent to Rabaul. The bases on Bougainville were bolstered with every man and gun available.

The Japs read aright the Allied intention to assault their Upper Solomons stronghold. Flying from New Guinea, American long-range bombers were already striking at the Bismarcks. Given bases on Bougainville for fighters and light bombers, the Allies would have Rabaul in an aerial nut-cracker. Halsey planned the offensive against Bougainville for the express purpose of acquiring these advanced airfields.

The Third Fleet had been strengthened by some rebuilt units and warships released from the Atlantic and "Torch" fronts. Rear Admiral F. C. Sherman was on hand with a strong carrier force which contained newly repaired SARATOGA and the light carrier PRINCETON. Admiral Wilkinson's amphibs were given added muscle, and convoys carried ground reinforcements to Guadalcanal in a steady stream.

To soften up the opposition, the Allies launched a series of air assaults in mid-October. Biggest of these was aimed at Rabaul by General MacArthur, who was in over-all command of the area. On October 12 a massive fleet of 349 Army planes raided the enemy's Bismarck citadel. MacArthur publicized his air offensive as "taking out Rabaul," but although tons of bombs were dropped on Simpson Harbor, only a few small Jap vessels were sunk and a handful of Jap planes destroyed.

The western shore of Bougainville was selected for the landings—beaches at Cape Torokina on the northern point of crescent-shaped Empress Augusta Bay. Here the coast was virtually unexplored jungle. There were few inhabitants, black or white. The shore bled off into the sea in a quagmire of stagnant lagoons and swamps. The shallows were uncharted.

The invasion was scheduled for the first week in November. By way of preliminaries, shore bombardments were conducted, and American troops landed on Treasury Island.

The Japs were caught off guard in the Treasury group when the Americans steamed in on the morning of October 27. The Treasury garrison fired mortar shells at the American landing craft, but the mortars were quickly silenced by destroyer PHILIP (Lieutenant Commander W. H. Groverman). At 1530 in the afternoon some 25 "Vals" swept in to attack the landing craft. Destroyers CONY (Commander H. D. Johnston) and PHILIP maneuvered at high speed to dodge the rain of bombs. CONY, carrying a fighter-director team, called for air help, but the "Vals" were not intercepted. Two bombs struck CONY on the main deck aft, putting her out of action with a flooded engine-room, and killing eight of her crew. Next day she was towed to Tulagi by the tug APACHE.

On the last evening of October, Rear Admiral Merrill led his Task Force 39 to the northernmost rung of the Solomons ladder to bombard the Jap airfields on the Bonis peninsula and on Buka Island. His force included four light cruisers and Captain Arleigh A. Burke's Destroyer Squadron 23, a DD team soon to shoot its way into headlines as the "Little Beavers."

The "Little Beavers" and Merrill's cruisers began shooting at the Buka-Bonis targets at 0021 in the morning of November 1. Jap aircraft promptly attacked the bombardment ships, but hit nothing, whereas hundreds of well-aimed cruiser and destroyer shells landed on Jap airstrips, Jap planes, and Japs.

Having hashed up the enemy's air defenses at the northern end of Bougainville, Merrill rushed his task force to the southern end to repeat the performance in the Shortland Islands. As he described it, his ships "made a dignified retirement at 30 knots." Then they bombarded the Shortland airstrips with dignity.

November 1, 1943 was D-Day for the Bougainville landings. To guarantee a reduction of air opposition, Rear Admiral F. C. Sherman took his carrier group northward to launch follow-through strikes at the Buka-Bonis airstrips. Planes from the "SARA" and PRINCETON bombed these bases on that day and the next. When they were through, Jap aircraft from Buka and Bonis did not contest the Bougainville landings, nor were Jap planes from the Shortlands in evidence.

The first troops put ashore on Bougainville were some 13,300 Marines, and the convoy of 12 transports was screened by 11 destroyers under Commander Ralph Earle, ComDesRon 45. The destroyers were: FULLAM, GUEST, BENNETT, HUDSON, ANTHONY, WADSWORTH, TERRY, BRAINE, SIGOURNEY, CONWAY, RENSHAW.

At Cape Torokina the Japs had one 75 mm. artillery piece and a company of less than 300 men. For a short time this force put up savage resistance, but it was soon whittled down and chased into the jungle. A few Jap aircraft from Rabaul struck at 0735, D-day morning. Planes from Vella Lavella and Munda scattered the attack, the only ship casualty resulting from a near miss that shook up destroyer WADSWORTH and killed two of her crew.

During D-day afternoon about 100 Jap carrier planes roared down from the Bismarcks. They, too, were intercepted by American fighter planes. The Americans were coached into position by a fighter-director team in destroyer CONWAY. No ships or landing craft were hit by the attacking Japs.

By late afternoon General Turnage's Marines were on the beaches of Torokina with supplies and battle gear. The situation was well in hand, and Wilkinson pulled his transports out of Empress Augusta Bay before nightfall, anticipating a furious reaction from Japanese air and surface forces at Rabaul. His anticipations were to be realized in the Battle of Empress Augusta Bay.

The Battle of Empress Augusta Bay (Arleigh Burke in Action!)

When word reached Admiral Koga at Truk that the Americans had dared to put foot on Bougainville, he radioed instructions to strike the interloper and strike hard. Rabaul's air strength was mustered, and with air power to back him up, Rear Admiral Sentaro Omori set out from Rabaul late in the afternoon of November 1 with a bloodthirsty surface force. Mission: to blast the Americans at Cape Torokina.

In Omori's force were heavy cruisers MYOKO and HAGURO, light cruisers SENDAI and AGANO, and six destroyers. Five troop-carrying assault transports sortied with the force, intending to land a thousand soldiers on the Torokina beaches to give battle to the U.S. Marines. But these APD's were late for the rendezvous, and after an American sub was sighted near St. George Channel, Omori was glad to send them home. He wanted freedom for fast maneuver.

He needed it. Halsey had the word on his sortie, and ComSoPac had lost no time in dispatching Rear Admiral Merrill's task force to intercept the southbound Japs. When Merrill received this flash assignment his cruisers were off Vella Lavella, enjoying a breather after the strenuous bombardment work of the previous day. Commander B. L. ("Count") Austin was on hand with DesDiv 46. Captain Arleigh Burke's DesDiv 45 was refueling in Hathorn Sound at the entrance of Kula Gulf, but these destroyers topped off with dizzy speed, and by 2315 in the evening of November 1, Merrill's force was racing headlong to meet the warships of Admiral Omori.

Omori did not expect to encounter a cruiser-destroyer force. He expected, perhaps wishfully, to encounter a transport group. Bearing down on Empress Augusta Bay, he had his Imperial naval vessels disposed in a simple formation with heavy cruisers MYOKO (flagship) and HAGURO in the center; light cruiser SENDAI and destroyers SHIGURE, SAMIDARE, and SHIRATSUYU to port; light cruiser AGANO and destroyers NAGANAMI, HATSUKAZE, and WAKATSUKI to starboard.

Merrill's force was disposed in line-of-bearing of unit guides. In column to starboard were Burke's van destroyers: CHARLES AUSBURNE (Commander L. K. Reynolds); DYSON (Commander R. A. Gano); STANLY (Commander R. W. Cavenagh); and CLAXTON (Commander H. F. Stout). In center column steamed cruisers MONTPELIER (flagship), CLEVELAND, COLUMBIA, and DENVER. To port steamed Austin's rear destroyers: SPENCE (Commander H. J. Armstrong); THATCHER (Commander L. R. Lampman); CONVERSE (Commander D. C. E. Hamberger); and FOOTE (Commander Alston Ramsay).

Omori's force suffered the first blow when an American plane, detecting the Jap approach, planted a bomb in the superstructure of heavy cruiser HAGURO. That was at 0130 in the morning of November 2. Lamed by the hit, HAGURO reduced the formation's speed to 30 knots. Then one of that cruiser's planes reported Merrill's task force coming up. The airmen erroneously notified Omori that one cruiser and three destroyers were in the offing. When, a few minutes later, he was informed by another air scout that a fleet of transports was unloading in Empress Augusta Bay, he sent his formation racing southeastward, hot for a massacre. Apparently the "transports" sighted were destroyer minelayers BREESE, GAMBLE, and SICARD, at that time working along the coast under escort of destroyer RENSHAW.

The night was black as carbon. Several of Omori's warships carried radar apparatus, but he put more reliance on binoculars. American "Sugar George" radar was to out-see Japanese vision on this occasion.

Merrill's cruisers made the initial radar contact at 0227. He had already decided to maintain his ships in a position that would block the entrance to Empress Augusta Bay. Once action was joined, he intended to elbow the enemy westward, thereby gaining sea room which would enable him to fight a long-range gun battle with least chance of danger from Jap torpedoes. But his destroyers were to open proceedings with a torpedo attack, and the cruisers were to hold their fire until the "fish" had opportunity to strike the foe.

These plans were carefully laid, and they were known, chapter and verse, by Captain Arleigh Burke, leader of Des Div 45. Commander Austin and DesDiv 46 were not so well versed in the detail. They were new to Task Force 39, and Austin was not thoroughly acquainted with Merrill's battle techniques.

As soon as radar contact was established, Merrill headed his formation due north. After a brief run, Burke's van destroyers sliced away northwestward to deliver a torpedo strike as planned. Merrill then ordered a simultaneous turn to reverse course. Austin's destroyers were instructed to countermarch, and then hit the enemy's southern flank with torpedoes as soon as they could reach firing position.

While Merrill's cruisers were swinging around the hairpin turn, Burke's destroyers were tacking in on Omori's portside column. At 0246 Burke shouted the word over TBS, *"My guppies are swimming!"* But the Japs had sighted Merrill's cruisers, and Omori was turning his formation southwestward. Because of this sudden turn, the barrage of 25 "guppies" sailed on into silence and oblivion, and Burke's briskly executed attack failed to score.

Meanwhile, the SENDAI column launched torpedoes at the American cruisers. But Merrill had not waited for this counterfire. When C.I.C. informed him of Omori's southwestward turn, he ordered his cruisers to let go with gunnery. I.J.N. SENDAI was chief target for this booming fusillade. She caught a cataract

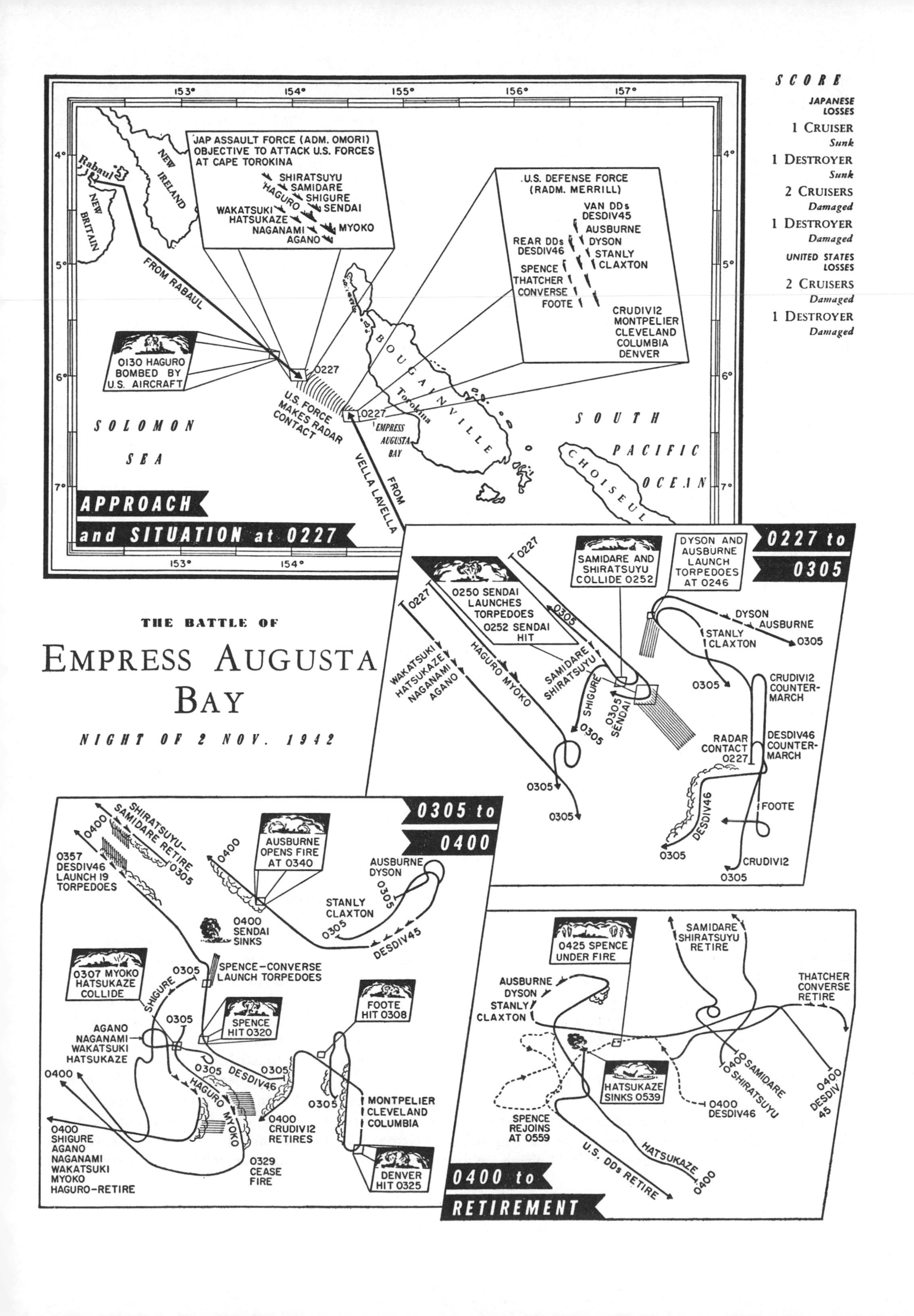
SCORE
JAPANESE LOSSES
1 CRUISER Sunk
1 DESTROYER Sunk
2 CRUISERS Damaged
1 DESTROYER Damaged
UNITED STATES LOSSES
2 CRUISERS Damaged
1 DESTROYER Damaged
THE BATTLE OF
EMPRESS AUGUSTA BAY
NIGHT OF 2 NOV. 1942
APPROACH
and SITUATION at 0227
JAP ASSAULT FORCE (ADM. OMORI)
OBJECTIVE TO ATTACK U.S. FORCES
AT CAPE TOROKINA
SHIRATSUYU
SAMIDARE
SHIGURE
HAGURO
SENDAI
WAKATSUKI
HATSUKAZE
NAGANAMI
MYOKO
AGANO
U.S. DEFENSE FORCE
(RADM. MERRILL)
VAN DDs
DESDIV45
AUSBURNE
DYSON
STANLY
CLAXTON
REAR DDs
DESDIV46
SPENCE
THATCHER
CONVERSE
FOOTE
CRUDIV12
MONTPELIER
CLEVELAND
COLUMBIA
DENVER
0130 HAGURO
BOMBED BY
U.S. AIRCRAFT
FROM RABAUL
U.S. FORCE MAKES RADAR CONTACT
0227
FROM VELLA LAVELLA
Rabaul
NEW IRELAND
NEW BRITAIN
SOLOMON SEA
BOUGAINVILLE
Torokina
EMPRESS AUGUSTA BAY
SOUTH PACIFIC OCEAN
CHOISEUL
153°
154°
155°
156°
157°
4°
5°
6°
7°
0227 to 0305
0250 SENDAI
LAUNCHES
TORPEDOES
0252 SENDAI
HIT
SAMIDARE AND
SHIRATSUYU
COLLIDE 0252
DYSON AND
AUSBURNE
LAUNCH
TORPEDOES
AT 0246
WAKATSUKI
HATSUKAZE
NAGANAMI
AGANO
HAGURO MYOKO
SAMIDARE
SHIRATSUYU
SHIGURE
SENDAI
DYSON
AUSBURNE
STANLY
CLAXTON
CRUDIV12
COUNTER-
MARCH
RADAR
CONTACT
0227
DESDIV46
COUNTER-
MARCH
FOOTE
DESDIV46
CRUDIV12
0305
0305 to 0400
SHIRATSUYU-
SAMIDARE RETIRE
0357
DESDIV46
LAUNCH 19
TORPEDOES
AUSBURNE
OPENS FIRE
AT 0340
AUSBURNE
DYSON
STANLY
CLAXTON
DESDIV45
0400
SENDAI
SINKS
0307 MYOKO
HATSUKAZE
COLLIDE
SPENCE-CONVERSE
LAUNCH TORPEDOES
SPENCE
HIT 0320
FOOTE
HIT 0308
AGANO
NAGANAMI
WAKATSUKI
HATSUKAZE
SHIGURE
HAGURO
MYOKO
DESDIV46
0400
CRUDIV12
RETIRES
MONTPELIER
CLEVELAND
COLUMBIA
0400
SHIGURE
AGANO
NAGANAMI
WAKATSUKI
MYOKO
HAGURO-RETIRE
0329
CEASE
FIRE
DENVER
HIT 0325
0400 to RETIREMENT
0425 SPENCE
UNDER FIRE
SAMIDARE
SHIRATSUYU
RETIRE
THATCHER
CONVERSE
RETIRE
AUSBURNE
DYSON
STANLY
CLAXTON
HATSUKAZE
SINKS 0539
0400 SAMIDARE
0400 SHIRATSUYU
0400 DESDIV46
0400 DESDIV 45
SPENCE
REJOINS
AT 0559
U.S. DDs RETIRE
HATSUKAZE
0400

of shells just as she was swinging to starboard, and the explosions blew her innards right out through the overhead.

SENDAI's abrupt come-uppance threw her column into a jumble. In the ensuing confusion, destroyers SAMIDARE and SHIRATSUYU collided full tilt, and went reeling off in precipitous retirement. That left the SHIGURE all by herself, and she chased southward to join the Jap cruiser column.

MYOKO and HAGURO made a blind loop that tangled them up with the AGANO column. Although Jap starshells had turned the night into a dazzle, the heavy cruisers failed to sight Merrill's ships, and they maneuvered right into a tempest of American shell-fire. Steaming in a daze, MYOKO slammed into destroyer HATSUKAZE and ripped off a section of that DD's bow.

Meantime, Burke's "Little Beavers," having launched torpedoes, became separated. And they did not get back into battle until 0349, when AUSBURNE spotted SENDAI and hurried the vessel under with a volley of shots. Then SAMIDARE and SHIRATSUYU, the two DD's which had collided, showed up on the radar screen. Burke took off after these departing enemies at top speed.

Commander Austin's DesDiv 46 destroyers had run into hard luck. Destroyer FOOTE misread Merrill's signal to turn, and fell out of formation. While racing to rejoin Austin's column, she was hit in the stern by a Jap torpedo which had been aimed at the American cruisers. Cruiser CLEVELAND swerved just in time to miss the disabled DD by 100 yards. But destroyer SPENCE, farther down the line, was not so lucky. Swinging hard right to give the cruiser column a clear line of fire, she sideswiped destroyer THATCHER. The 30-knot brush sent sparks and sweat-beads flying, and removed a wide swath of paint, but both DD's kept on traveling at high speed. Then at 0320 a Jap shell punctured SPENCE's hull at the waterline. Salt water got into a fuel tank, contaminating the oil, and this slow poison soon reduced the destroyer's speed. As if this were not enough misfortune for one division, Austin's DD's lost a fine chance to strike at MYOKO and HAGURO with torpedoes. When his flagship sideswiped THATCHER, Commander Austin dashed out on the bridge to see what was what. Some bright "pips" blossomed on the radar screen; Austin would have fired torpedoes at 4,000 yards or so, but the C.I.C. officer reported the targets were American. So the little scrape with THATCHER cost something more than a paint job.

A moment later SPENCE made contact with cruiser SENDAI. At that time the Jap vessel was a staggering merry-go-round, but her guns were still firing, and she was as dangerous as a wounded leopard. Austin maneuvered for torpedo fire, and SPENCE and CONVERSE flung eight "fish" at the cripple. They did not sink her—Burke's destroyers would presently perform that chore. Austin's three DD's raced on northwestward in an effort to catch SAMIDARE and SHIRATSUYU.

By 0352 SPENCE, THATCHER, and CONVERSE had overhauled the two Jap DD's, and 19 American torpedoes were fanning out to catch each by the fantail. The 19 torpedoes scored a perfect zero. Some may have been improperly adjusted, but the zero probably had its source in improper fabrication.

In counterattack, SAMIDARE and SHIRATSUYU flung shells and "fish" at Austin's three destroyers. If the Jap "fish" missed, the marksmen at least had an excuse for poor torpedo work—the two Jap DD's were dodging to escape a tempest of shell fire, and both ships had been badly damaged by collision.

Now SPENCE was running low on fuel, and what little she had was contaminated by salt water. Austin relinquished his tactical command to THATCHER's skipper, Commander Lampman, and veered away with SPENCE to disengage. The maneuver brought his flag destroyer into line for a salvo from Arleigh Burke's fast-shooting division. At 0425 a pack of projectiles slammed into the sea around SPENCE.

Over the TBS Commander Austin shouted a plea to Burke.

WE'VE JUST HAD ANOTHER CLOSE MISS HOPE YOU ARE NOT SHOOTING AT US

Captain Burke's answer was a classic of Navy humor.

SORRY BUT YOU'LL HAVE TO EXCUSE THE NEXT FOUR SALVOS THEY'RE ALREADY ON THEIR WAY

Austin made haste to get SPENCE out of the vicinity. In dodging Burke's ebullient fire, SPENCE picked up a good target in Jap destroyer HATSUKAZE.

HATZUKAZE was the DD which MYOKO had rammed, and she was in no condition to dodge well-aimed salvos. SPENCE closed the range to 4,000 yards while her gunners pumped shells into the disabled Jap. HATSUKAZE was soon flaming and wallowing, her engines dead. Austin yearned to finish off this foe, but SPENCE's ammunition was running low, so he put in a call for Burke's destroyers to complete the execution. Thereupon an avalanche of 5-inchers from DesDiv 45 buried HATSUKAZE. About 0539 the ship rolled over and descended into the grave.

SPENCE joined up with DesDiv 45 as Burke ordered a retirement. Unable to catch SAMIDARE and SHIRATSUYU, destroyers THATCHER and CONVERSE were also retiring. As day was making, Admiral Merrill had already headed his cruiser column eastward. While

Destroyers of Task Force 16.7 head out of Kuluk Bay, Adak, for patrol off Attu. Japanese operations in the Aleutians had been planned as a diversion at the time of the Battle of Midway and as a means of preventing Allied attacks via the northern route. Rock-studded, uncharted channels and possibly the world's worst weather discouraged major operations by either side.

The only warship casualty in the Kiska operation, Abner Read struck a floating Japanese mine while on patrol off the island. A terrific explosion tore off the destroyer's stern and left her helpless, drifting down onto the rocks, until Bancroft and Ute came to the rescue. With a jury rudder, shown above, Abner Read was safely navigated to the Puget Sound Navy Yard for repairs.

U.S.S. Hulbert shown on the beach after digging out operations at Attu. This ship had served as a tender for PBY's operating at Nazan Bay, Atka Island, and Kanaga Island. The usual Aleutian weather interfered with navigation on the sea and above it, but the PBY's were able to obtain photographs and conduct bombing missions during the annihilation of the Jap forces on Attu.

his DD's were trying to tag fleeing Japs, Merrill's cruisers had been maneuvering across the seascape in a duel with the Jap heavies. For over an hour the opposing formations had dodged about like gamecocks in a pit, neither side able to score a death-dealing blow. Convinced that he had tangled with no less than seven heavy cruisers, Omori pulled out at 0337 and fled northwest up the coast of Bougainville. The American cruisers chased until daybreak, then Merrill turned back, anticipating aircraft from Rabaul.

Around 0500 Burke's voice came cheerfully over the TBS. His destroyers were still to the west of Merrill's cruisers, and he requested permission to pursue the fleeing Japs. According to Captain Briscoe, Merrill's answer to this was,

ARLIE THIS IS TIP FOR GODS SAKE COME HOME WE'RE LONESOME

So Burke came steaming south with his seven DD's to keep the cruisers company.

"We were glad when those destroyers showed up," another cruiserman recalled. "As we pulled away from Empress Augusta Bay the radar screens broke out in a rash of aerial pips. It looked like a blizzard coming down from Rabaul."

Destroyer Foote, with her stern blown open, constituted a problem at this crisis. Claxton was ordered to take the disabled ship in tow, while Ausburne and Thatcher steamed as escorts. Vectored into position by a fighter-director team, 15 Allied aircraft flew to intercept the Jap planes racing down from the Bismarcks. Some 100 Jap carrier planes were too much for the Allied 15, and bulk of the defense fell upon Merrill's weary gun crews.

About 0800 the Jap aircraft attacked the retiring ships. The formation roared right over damaged Foote, some ten miles astern of the cruisers. Lamed though she was, Foote put up an umbrella of flak. No bombs were dropped upon her, and she saw a plane plunge into the sea.

Five minutes later, the Jap birds swooped down on Merrill's task force. He had the force disposed in a circular AA formation. As the bombers came over, he maneuvered to bring main batteries to bear, and the destroyers opened up with AA fire at about 14,000 yards.

Merrill described it in his Action Report:

> The scene was of an organized hell in which it was impossible to speak, hear, or even think. As the ships passed the first 90 degrees of their turn in excellent formation, the air seemed completely filled with bursting shrapnel and, to our great glee, enemy planes in a severe state of disrepair. . . . Planes were in flames as they passed over the flagship, exploding outside the destroyer screen. . . . Ten planes were counted in the water at one time, and seven additional were seen to crash well outside the formation.

At the height of the battle, Merrill ordered a 360° turn which kept the warship carousel steaming clockwise. All the gunners seemed to be catching prizes from the air. Three Japs bailed out in parachutes and landed almost in the center of the wheeling formation. "Bettys" blew up in the sky and exploded in the water. Of the 70 or 80 planes which attacked, perhaps two dozen were shot down (Jap figures were never forthcoming). The Japs landed only two hits on cruiser Montpelier, damaging a catapult and wounding one man. At 0812 they broke off the attack and ran northward, pursued by Allied fighter planes.

The Battle of Empress Augusta Bay and its aerial epilogue were over. On the sea and in the air the enemy had taken a colossal thrashing. A light cruiser and a destroyer sunk, two destroyers disabled, heavy cruiser Myoko dented by collision, heavy cruiser Haguro severely damaged—Omori's force slunk home in sorry defeat. In Merrill's force destroyer Foote was the one serious casualty, and even she would live to fight again. Cruiser Denver and destroyer Spence, with minor damage, would lose little time on the binnacle list.

Commenting on this smash-hit victory, Admiral W. S. Pye of the Naval War College wrote:

> *The destroyers were not tied in close to the main battle line and held there within gun range. They were loose, well removed from the cruisers, with freedom of action. They were used offensively instead of defensively. . . .*

Offensively—that was the way Captain Arleigh Burke and his "Little Beavers" liked to work.

Augusta Bay Aftermath

Early in the morning of November 4 a convoy carrying reinforcements sailed from Tulagi for the Cape Torokina beachhead. The eight APD's (destroyer transports) and eight ocean-going LST's were escorted by six destroyers of Captain J. E. Hurff's DesRon 22. These escorts were Waller, Saufley, Philip, Renshaw, Eaton, and Sigourney. Merrill's indefatigable Task Force 39 covered the convoy formation. The ships reached Torokina unmolested.

A second section of this reinforcement lift followed in with infantry and artillery. This convoy was escorted by Commander Ralph Earle's DesRon 45 and a group of minesweepers. During the landings Jap aircraft pitched into the picture, but the assault was speedily disrupted by U.S. fighter planes. That evening the Jap bombers came back for another try.

The transports had hauled out under cover of a convenient rainstorm. But the beady-eyed airmen found another target.

This target was a task group commanded by Rear Admiral L. T. DuBose. At dusk the group was steaming off Mutupina Point at the southern end of Empress Augusta Bay, covering the retirement of the unloaded transports. DuBose's group consisted of light cruisers SANTA FE (flagship), BIRMINGHAM, and MOBILE, and four destroyers under Captain E. M. Thompson, ComDesRon 25. These DD's were JOHN RODGERS (Commander H. O. Parish); HARRISON (Lieutenant Commander C. M. Dalton); MCKEE (Commander J. J. Greytak); and MURRAY (Commander P. R. Anderson). Thompson rode in JOHN RODGERS.

Buzzing in on the attack, the Japs found the American ships in anti-aircraft disposition, the cruisers centered as a hub in a wheel of destroyers. From dusk until moonset (1900 to 2015) the Jap torpedo-bombers, perhaps 30 in number, and accompanying planes kept after the warships. And, it should be added, the warships kept after the aircraft.

The Japs made ferocious bombing runs, skimming in over the cruiser and destroyer mastheads. High speed maneuvering and hot AA gunnery saved the Americans serious damage. BIRMINGHAM was hit hard by enemy missiles. But she was the only vessel to suffer in the onslaught, and the Japs lost about nine planes. Halsey commended the group for a "highly gratifying" performance that reflected good training.

The air battle fought by DuBose and company occurred on the evening of November 8. A somewhat similar action was fought by Merrill's task force off Empress Augusta Bay on the night of November 12-13. In this battle, cruiser DENVER was severely damaged by a "fish" from the low-flying Japs. At least six Jap carrier planes were gunned down.

After the assault of the 13th, Admiral Koga discontinued "Operation RO," although he announced it as a tremendous victory. In fact the Imperial Navy officially announced the destruction of 5 battleships, 10 carriers, 19 cruisers, 7 destroyers and what not off Bougainville. The truth was decidedly different. About 70 per cent of Koga's Third Fleet carrier planes which flew out of Rabaul had been lost. The Japanese Eleventh Air Fleet had suffered similar losses.

A number of things contributed to the frustration of Koga's anti-Augusta Bay blitz. One was the VT proximity-fused projectile. Introduced in the South Pacific by cruiser HELENA the preceding January, this item of ammunition was widely distributed in Halsey's fleet by November, 1943. (A word about the VT device. In effect it worked as a miniature radio transmitter-receiver. Affixed to an anti-aircraft shell, the contrivance sent out radio waves which were reflected back from a plane when it passed within 70 feet of it. The returning impulse exploded the shell. Shrapnel did the rest. Deadly for AA work, the projectile could also be used against surface targets. Destroyer TERRY had found VT ammunition just the thing to shoot at thin-skinned barges.)

Director-controlled 40 mm. fire also wrought the downfall of Koga's air campaign. The twin and quad 40's were much in evidence by November, 1943, and a 40 mm. barrage could deal a dive-bomber pilot a splitting headache. Ditto for the pilot of a torpedo-plane or a Jap fighter.

Destroyers carrying fighter-director teams were another big help at Empress Augusta Bay, as were the Army, Navy, and Marine planes on the job.

And so was the initiative a help. By the time Wilkinson's amphibs reached Cape Torokina, the whole Pacific Fleet was going on the offensive. The top of the Solomons ladder had been reached. The Allies were through with shoestring operations from here on out. A new, aggressive spirit spurred the Allies.

The Japanese were inspired by no such spirit.

Contrast the following incident with the episode concerning Lieutenant Hugh Barr Miller, whose will to live brought him out of a grave in the Central Solomons.

In the afternoon of November 10 Merrill's Task Force 39 was operating in an area west of Treasury Island. Six of Burke's destroyers were working with the force, and as usual the "Little Beavers" stirred up something. On this occasion destroyer SPENCE did the stirring. Here is the story as recorded in her Action Report by her skipper, Commander H. J. Armstrong:

> At 1545 the SPENCE sighted and, as requested, was ordered to investigate a life float. On approaching, several bodies were noted in the float as it passed close aboard down starboard side. Seven men who had been feigning death sat up and started talking in Japanese. One, apparently an officer and pilot, broke out a 7.7 mm. machine-gun (evidently salvaged from a plane). Each man in succession placed the muzzle of the gun in his mouth, and the Jap officer fired a round, blowing the back of the man's head out. The Jap first to be killed showed great reluctance to be included in the suicide pact. One man held him while another wielded the machine-gun. All of the bodies toppled over the side and sank, followed closely by sharks. The Jap officer, alone on the raft, gave a short farewell speech or harrangue to the Commanding Officer, then shot himself. Total time was only about five minutes.

The Japanese pilot's farewell address makes a fitting curtain-line for the last act of the Solomons drama.

CHAPTER 19

ALEUTIAN CONCLUSION

The Battle for Attu

Up in the Aleutians the bitterest fighting occurred at Attu. The Joint Chiefs of Staff had been determined to expel the Japanese from the Aleutians ever since the day the invader landed. In January 1943, Admiral Nimitz presented to Rear Admiral Thomas C. Kinkaid and Rear Admiral Francis W. Rockwell over-all plans for a drive on Kiska. A joint staff composed of Army and Navy officers was formed to work out the details. Training exercises for amphibious operations were immediately begun in California. Destroyers ABNER READ, MACDONOUGH, and PHELPS participated with battleships IDAHO, NEVADA, and PENNSYLVANIA in practice landings which were as realistic as live ammunition and daredevil dive-bombers could make them.

But cargo ships and attack transports were urgently needed elsewhere. The shipping shortage compelled Admiral Kinkaid to recommend that the Kiska operation be deferred in favor of a springtime smash at Attu. There the enemy garrison (some 2,200 men) was about half the size of the force occupying Kiska. Attu's defense installations were presumably weaker than Kiska's. Moreover, seizure of Attu at the seaward end of the Aleutian chain would put American forces in a position to intercept all reinforcements for Kiska, and that island would, in effect, be surrounded. Weather factors, too, favored the Attu objective.

Attu, then.

Rear Admiral Kinkaid was in over-all command of the operation. Rear Admiral Rockwell (of Corregidor, and since then Commander Amphibious Force Pacific Fleet) was to command the attack force. The Army forces were under Major General Brown, Commanding General 7th Division. Target date was set for May 7.

As March thawed into April, Admiral Rockwell's task force assembled in the waters of Cold Bay. The attack force was composed of the battleships PENNSYLVANIA, NEVADA, and IDAHO, the escort carrier NASSAU, twelve destroyers under Captain R. E. Libby, four transports, two seaplane tenders, and five minesweepers. Submarines NARWHAL and NAUTILUS bobbed up in the attack force roster carrying Army scouts.

Captain Libby's twelve destroyers were the following:

PHELPS	*Lt. Comdr. J. E. Edwards* *Flagship of* *Capt. R. E. Libby,* COMDESRON 1
ABNER READ	*Comdr. Thomas Burrows*
AMMEN	*Lt. Comdr. Henry Williams, Jr.*
AYLWIN	*Lt. Comdr. R. E. Malpass*
DALE	*Lt. Comdr. C. W. Aldrich*
DEWEY	*Lt. Comdr. J. P. Canty* *Flagship of* *Comdr. G. R. Cooper,* COMDESDIV 1
EDWARDS	*Lt. Comdr. P. G. Osler*
FARRAGUT	*Comdr. H. D. Rozendal*
HULL	*Lt. Comdr. A. L. Young, Jr.*
MACDONOUGH	*Lt. Comdr. E. V. E. Dennett*
MEADE	*Comdr. R. S. Lamb*
MONAGHAN	*Lt. Comdr. P. H. Horn*

The attack force was screened by two cruiser-destroyer covering groups under command of Rear Admirals C. H. McMorris and R. C. ("Ike") Giffen.

The Southern Covering Group (Rear Admiral McMorris) was composed of the light cruisers DETROIT, RICHMOND, RALEIGH, and SANTA FE, and the following five destroyers:

GANSEVOORT	*Comdr. E. A. McFall*
	Flagship of *Capt. R. S. Riggs,* COMDESRON 14
BANCROFT	*Comdr. J. L. Melgaard*
CALDWELL	*Lt. Comdr. H. A. Lincoln*
COGHLAN	*Comdr. B. F. Tompkins*
FRAZIER	*Lt. Comdr. Frank Virden*
	Flagship of *Comdr. H. F. Pullen,* COMDESDIV 27

The Northern Covering Group (Rear Admiral Giffen) consisted of the heavy cruisers LOUISVILLE, SAN FRANCISCO, and WICHITA, and the following four destroyers:

MORRIS	*Lt. Comdr. E. S. Burns*
	Flagship of *Comdr. H. R. Holcomb,* COMDESRON 2
BALCH	*Comdr. H. H. Tiemroth*
HUGHES	*Lt. Comdr. H. H. Marable*
MUSTIN	*Lt. Comdr. E. T. Schreiber*

The target date had to be postponed. Usual reason, foul weather. First there was fog. Then mountainous seas. Then high surf. But finally (on the evening of May 10) the invasion forces were maneuvering off Attu—in a fog as opaque as cotton batting.

The main landings were to take place on the northern side of the island in the Holtz Bay area, and on the southern side at ominously named Massacre Bay. H-Hour was set for the following morning.

The "northern" and "southern" landing forces groped for position. The fog thickened.

So the ships were compelled to play a silent blindman's-buff in the vapor. A dangerous game. Groping through the mist, the destroyer-minelayer (DM) SICARD (Lieutenant Commander W. J. Richter) rammed blindly into the MACDONOUGH. A muffled cry, a crash, and SICARD's bow sliced into the destroyer, overturning MACDONOUGH's No. 1 torpedo mount. The sea plunged through the gash in MACDONOUGH's hull, and with engine-room and after fireroom rapidly flooding, she started to settle as SICARD backed off. The destroyermen managed to keep MACDONOUGH afloat as the DM's frantic crew passed a line. SICARD was ordered to tow the disabled MACDONOUGH to Adak. A close call for both warships, and one that took them out of the Attu operation.

One of the first destroyers to reach Attu—and one of the busiest operators thereafter—was the PHELPS (Lieutenant Commander J. E. Edwards). Stealthily moving in through the fog-smother, she led eight landing boats carrying an advance party of Aleut scouts into Beach Red in the Holtz Bay area.

PHELPS then escorted the landing barges when Combat Team 17-1 went in to Beach Red at H-Hour. The troops were disembarked from the transport BELL, and the destroyer had a ticklish time of it guiding the barges in through the churning fog.

Lieutenant Commander "Johnny" Edwards and crew made three ship-to-shore tours with the soldiery. After which they had to conduct a search for some 28 unloaded barges which had become lost in the sceneless murk. One by one PHELPS found the barges and herded them back to the BELL.

On the island's south coast the ships at Massacre Bay were also imbedded in dense fog. Escort for landing craft going in to Yellow Beach and Blue Beach, the destroyer-minelayer PRUITT (Lieutenant Commander R. C. Williams, Jr.) had to beckon to the blinded landing craft with her searchlight. The PRUITT lacked SG radar's "seeing eye," and she had to work blindfolded. Groping shoreward, she was guided by directions from the destroyer DEWEY's radar watch.

Fortunately the Japs did not contest these fogbound landings. American shock troops were solidly ashore and probing inland before they encountered sniper bullets and mortar fire. Committed to a *harikiri* stand, the Japs had taken to the hills and dug deep into the badlands muskeg.

Step by step the American combat teams fought their way through dripping canyons and up the flanks of foggy hills, the worst sort of terrain. Jap guns blazed from hidden emplacements. The Americans hurled grenades at ghosts, and were sniped at by spectres. Down from a ridge, half mist, half moonlight, might shrill a parrot-like screech: "Come and get it, Yankees!" Attu had that "bad dream" quality of the Solomons-New Guinea fighting—a struggle with devils in the dark.

The 1,000 men landed at Holtz Bay and the 2,000 landed at Massacre Bay were not enough. Continuous fog prevented the employment of aircraft to blast out the cunningly emplaced enemy artillery, and the entrenched Japs repulsed one assault after another. A week of savage fighting ended in a stalemate until reinforcements were called in. Ultimately it became necessary to land 12,000 troops on Attu.

Admiral Rockwell's forces covered the initial and succeeding landings with shore bombardments, and conducted A/S patrols, mine sweeping, and reconnaissance. The destroyer gunners hurled tons of shells at the evil island. By May 15 the destroyer PHELPS, serving with the bombardment group at Holtz Bay, was almost out of 5-inch ammunition. Destroyer ABNER READ covered a landing with fire at Holtz Bay the following day. On the 19th PHELPS delivered a bombardment that helped to clear the enemy from the bay's East Arm. After the amphibious work was completed, PHELPS, MEADE, and destroyer AYLWIN stood by to lend fire support to the Army's advance.

Three days later PHELPS steamed around to Chirikoff Point to screen transports retiring from Massacre Bay and to conduct an A/S patrol. Patrolling the Holtz Bay entrance on the afternoon of May 22, she was on the fantail end of a strafing by Jap torpedo planes which had been rushed to Attu through clearing skies. PHELPS and her companion, the gunboat CHARLESTON, flung a storm of ack-ack at the torpedo-bombers. At least one of the aircraft staggered off to crash and burn in the distance.

Dissolving fog had given Army Lightnings and PBY's an occasional chance to bomb and strafe the Jap positions in the Attu interior. By the evening of May 28 the last-stand troops of Colonel Yasuyo Yamazaki were pocketed.

As the Americans closed in, the Japs made a mad attempt to break out of the trap. Down from the heights they came in a maniacal *banzai* charge that almost carried through to the beachheads of Massacre Bay.

Within a mile or so of that aptly named bay, the screaming rush came to a dead end. Point blank, the Japs hurled themselves at the American machine-guns. Others, facing capture, impaled themselves on bayonets. Scores blew themselves to oblivion with a last hand grenade. With the exception of 28 prisoners, the garrison (about 2,200 strong) was wiped out to a man.

The operation cost 552 American lives. Some 1,140 Americans were wounded.

Navy personnel casualties were limited to minor injuries, and not a warship was lost. Considering the difficulties of the amphibious landings, the complex covering, minesweeping, and bombardment missions, and the fact that at least three Jap submarines were prowling off Attu, as well as others off Kiska, the Navy's performance stands out as decidedly able.

Frazier Kills I-31

One of the destroyers blockading Kiska that June was the FRAZIER (Lieutenant Commander E. M. Brown). Japanese submarines had been reported in the area, and American forces were on the lookout for the undersea blockade-runners.

At that date, Dutch Harbor headquarters assumed that the Japs would make an effort to bolster their Kiska defenses. There were indications that the Kiska garrison was preparing to make a last-ditch stand in keeping with the suicide action at Attu. American Intelligence had no way of knowing that the Imperial High Command had decided to evacuate the troops on Kiska and thereby terminate the Aleutian campaign.

For the Japs for once had sanely reasoned that their troops could better serve the Emperor in the Land of the Living than in some mythical Netherworld populated by Honorable Ancestors. Preparations for Kiska's defense were planned as so much camouflage to hide a clandestine withdrawal. Fifteen I-boats were assigned to this extraordinary evacuation.

On June 13, FRAZIER was plodding on patrol off Point Sirius, Kiska. At 1758 her radar picked up a miniscule "pip" at a range of 7,000 yards. FRAZIER headed for the contact at 20 knots. It faded from the radar screen, then was regained at 3,000 yards. The "pip" looked like business, and Lieutenant Commander Brown rushed the crew to battle stations and slowed down to 15 knots. At 1809, Sound reported contact, at 1,500 yards. The DD held radar contact as the range closed to 600 yards. At 1815 the destroyer's lookouts sighted twin periscopes close aboard, range 100 yards.

The destroyermen let fly with two starboard projectors, and then opened fire with main battery and machine-guns. As explosions dug holes in the smooth sea, and 5-inch shells struck the periscopes, the sub went under. The ashcans went down and fountains of water erupted. At 1825, the destroyermen unleashed still another depth-charge attack. The explosions trailed off in watery thunder, and a streak of oil and a large bubble appeared on the heaving surface.

Five minutes later Brown directed a final depth-charge onslaught. The ashcans raised an undersea rumpus, and brought up a gurgling gusher of oil. Combing the area, FRAZIER's destroyermen noted a spreading carpet of Diesel fuel and a great clutter of oil-scummed debris—splintered gratings, chunks of cork, scraps of paper, etc.

As the destroyer reported it,

NO FURTHER CONTACT

The demolished submarine was the I-31.

Monaghan Kills I-7

Three days prior to the sinking of I-31, an American patrol craft (PC 487) had downed the I-9 in Kiska's waters. And nine days after FRAZIER's kill off

Point Sirius, the destroyer MONAGHAN (Lieutenant Commander P. H. Horn) took a hand in wrecking the I-boat effort to evacuate Kiska.

Early in the morning of June 22, MONAGHAN was patrolling south of Kiska Island. At 0135 she made contact with her "Sugar George" radar, picking up a "pip" at range of 14,000 yards. Horn sent his destroyer steaming forward to investigate.

After about an hour's tracking, MONAGHAN had closed the range to 2,300 yards. Was the contact a sub? The night was thicker than coagulated ink; the target remained invisible. Time: 0230. Horn snapped the order to commence firing. As MONAGHAN's guns flashed and roared, the unseen foe replied with a chattering automatic. Bullets whined over MONAGHAN's superstructure. The destroyer's salvos sent echoes booming across unseen water. The blind duel lasted for ten minutes, then DD and the enemy ceased firing and jockeyed for position.

Ensued a swift game of blindman's-buff. Then, at 0310, with the range closed to 2,030 yards, Horn ordered MONAGHAN's gunners to resume fire. The enemy answered with a pugnacious fusillade. Such duelling was reckless on the part of a thin-skinned I-boat. After eight minutes of lively shooting, MONAGHAN's bridge personnel saw a crimson glow mushroom in the darkness where the target was positioned. The hot flush waxed and waned as though some astrological stoker had opened and closed a furnace door in the night sky.

"That," said one of MONAGHAN's destroyermen, "was a submarine explosion."

But the target was still there on the radar screen, and the gun battle continued until MONAGHAN's captain broke off the engagement. She was then about a mile south of Zaliva Point, and Lieutenant Commander Horn ordered a sharp change of course to avoid the unfamiliar and dangerous coastline. The stricken I-boat was headed for an ugly "giant's causeway" indicated as a marine snare on the chart and named "Twin Rocks." Horn had no wish to tangle with this invisible menace.

Evidently the battered submarine was unable to handle the twins. At any rate, aerial photographs of Twin Rocks, taken some time later, disclosed an I-boat piled up on one of the granite pinnacles like a dead whale. The submersible's flanks were under water, and only a portion of her foredeck and conning tower showed. Before abandoning, the Japs had wrecked the sub internally with demolition charges.

The MONAGHAN's expert marksmanship is evidenced by the fact that the entire action was fought in pitch darkness, visibility at no time exceeding 300 yards. The guns were directed by full radar control, and, except for the glow of the explosion caused by a hit, the destroyer gunners never caught a glimpse of the target.

So the Japs lost another transport submarine in the Aleutian fiasco. And the demolishment of I-7, swiftly following the destruction of I-31, caused the Japanese naval lords to revise their Kiska withdrawal plan.

The deep-sea blockade-runners had managed to evacuate some 700 of the Kiska garrison between the forepart of May and June 10. But this surreptitious submarining proved another of those extravagances that bankrupted the Japanese venture in the Aleutians. As a Japanese Fifth Fleet officer ruefully declared in postwar testimony, *"Since the operation became too costly in submarines, the plan was changed to one which would effect the evacuation by a dash by surface ships."*

In removing I-31 and I-7 from the Japanese submarine roster, destroyers FRAZIER and MONAGHAN forced the enemy to burn his fingers as he pulled his Kiska chestnuts out of the fire.

Kiska Occupation (Disaster Strikes Abner Read)

August 15, 1943, was set as D-day for the American landings on Kiska. Vice Admiral T. C. Kinkaid, Rear Admiral F. W. Rockwell, and Major General C. H. Corlett worked out the details with scrupulous care.

The enemy positions on Kiska were known to be heavily fortified. Shallows treacherous with barrier reefs, uncharted rocks, and pinnacles made the island's approaches most hazardous. Kiska's beachheads were narrow and could be easily defended by the enemy. The island's interior was a trap of volcanic wasteland, rocky and unexplored—terrain worse than Attu's.

Fog hung over the island like a shroud of mystery. Reconnaissance and aerial observation had been unable to penetrate the forbidding recesses of Kiska's foreshore, unable to discern the enemy's activity.

Admiral Kinkaid's warships repeatedly shattered the deep Kiska silence with a series of shore bombardments to soften the enemy's defenses. Tons of steel were hurled at the island's fog-dimmed face. The explosions clattered away like echoes in an empty cavern. The American warships might have been small boys with bean-shooters shooting at the Sphinx.

On July 28, the Japanese radio on Kiska went off the air. Thereafter the island was as quiet as the evening after the Last Day. Everyone believed the occupants had gone into hiding, and a tooth-and-nail campaign to root them out—another Attu battle—was in prospect.

So a large invasion force was assembled. About 35,000 troops—some 5,000 of them Canadian—were assigned to the operation. A naval armada, its attack force to be commanded by Admiral Rockwell, was organized. The armada consisted of nearly 100 vessels, including three battleships, a heavy cruiser, a light cruiser, nineten destroyers, five attack transports, one attack cargo-vessel, ten transports, three freighters, several minesweepers, minelayers and naval tugs, and numerous landing craft.

The exact composition of these forces is of no present consequence. But the destroyers who participated are listed in the adjacent column.

At dawn of the 15th the armada lay off Kiska, and the landing forces moved in to selected beachheads while battleships, cruisers, and destroyers blasted the island's ominous coasts with a covering bombardment. Japanese shore batteries remained mute.

Probing inland, the tense-nerved scouts expected an ambush. Any moment a blast of gunfire might slash out, a *banzai* charge might come screaming down from the foggy rocks. But the only rifle fire resulted from nervous trigger-fingers and accidental exchanges between the scouting parties. Not a living Jap could be found in Kiska. Nineteen days before the Americans landed, the Japs had pulled up bag and baggage and abandoned!

The Japanese evacuation of Kiska, accomplished by means of submarines in June and surface forces in July, must remain one of the more remarkable exploits of World War II. Where undersea blockade-running had proved over costly, Japanese surface forces, operating under cover of night and fog, had succeeded in getting in and out through the blockade undetected. This in spite of watchful American patrols and search radar!

However, Admiral Kinkaid expressed no apologetics when he stated that the occupation of Kiska was a highly successful move.

> *We got what we set out to do. The lives saved by the withdrawal of the enemy made it even more successful.*

It might be added that in all probability such a fade-away by the enemy could only have happened in the weird Aleutians. And, after all, there was a sufficiency of danger in the island's investment—enough, perhaps, to satisfy hindsight critics who did not risk their lives in the operation. The price the occupation forces might have paid had the enemy resisted is suggested by the token payment made by the destroyer ABNER READ. The Japs collected this gratuitous toll on August 18, long after their abandonment of Kiska.

Early in the morning of the 18th, ABNER READ was steaming along on A/S patrol off Kiska's dark coast.

DESTROYERS AT KISKA

HUTCHINS	*Lt. Comdr. E. W. Herron*
	Flagship of Comdr. K. M. McManes, COMDESRON 24
PHELPS	*Lt. Comdr. J. E. Edwards*
	Flagship of Capt. R. E. Libby, COMDESRON 1
AMMEN	*Lt. Comdr. Henry Williams*
ABNER REED	*Comdr. Thomas Burrowes*
BACHE	*Comdr. F. M. Adamson*
BEALE	*Comdr. J. B. Cochran*
BROWNSON	*Comdr. J. B. Mayer*
FARRAGUT	*Lt. Comdr. E. F. Ferguson*
	Flagship of Comdr. G. R. Cooper, COMDESDIV 2
AYLWIN	*Lt. Comdr. R. E. Malpass*
MONAGHAN	*Lt. Comdr. P. H. Horn*
DEWEY	*Lt. Comdr. J. P. Canty*
HULL	*Lt. Comdr. A. L. Young*
DALE	*Lt. Comdr. C. W. Aldrich*
BUSH	*Lt. Comdr. T. A. Smith*
	Flagship of Comdr. W. F. Petersen, COMDESDIV 48
DALY	*Comdr. R. G. Visser*
MULLANY	*Comdr. B. J. Mullaney*
BANCROFT	*Lt. Comdr. R. M. Pitts*
	Flagship of Capt. H. F. Pullen, COMDESDIV 28
COGHLAN	*Lt. Comdr. B. B. Cheatham*
CALDWELL	*Lt. Comdr. H. A. Lincoln*

Operating with the invasion fleet's two covering groups were the following DD's:

GANSEVOORT	*Lt. Comdr. M. L. McCullough, Jr.*
	Flagship of Capt. W. Craig, COMDESRON 14
MORRIS	*Lt. Comdr. E. S. Burns*
	Flagship of Capt. H. R. Holcomb, COMDESRON 2
EDWARDS	*Lt. Comdr. P. G. Osler*
FRAZIER	*Lt. Comdr. E. M. Brown*
MEADE	*Lt. Comdr. J. Mulholland*
MUSTIN	*Comdr. E. T. Schreiber*
HUGHES	*Lt. Comdr. H. H. Marable*
RUSSELL	*Lt. Comdr. W. H. McClain*
ANDERSON	*Lt. Comdr. J. G. Tennent, III*

★

At 0150 the destroyer was executing a turn when a stupendous explosion jolted the ship with a gigantic leverage that drove her bows deep in the tide. A deafening blast. A fountain of flame and water. With that fiery thunderclap the destroyer's fantail heaved, and she fell back with a tremendous shudder, disabled. A floating mine had blown up her stern.

Flung from their bunks, men who had been sleeping in the aftermost compartment found themselves struggling in a jagged jungle of interior wreckage. Belowdecks was in utter darkness. Caught in a trap of buckled bulkheads and twisted steel, injured men cried out and the unconscious lay in grotesque postures. Groping through the pitch dark, the men made their way to ladders and hatches; their knowledge of the ship's layout and compartments served them well. Water rose steadily in the dark compartments, and asphyxiating fumes began to surge through the passageways. In orderly fashion—the calmness with which old hands meet emergency—the men made their way topside. But the thickening fumes tried every man's nerves.

On the bridge the destroyer's captain, Commander Thomas Burrows, sent out a distress call. The disabled destroyer, powerless and listing, was caught by a muscular tide that was carrying her toward the rocks of a Kiska beach.

Plates, decks, and framework ruptured and broke as the ship's stern section settled. Many survivors on the fantail found the deck almost too hot to stand on barefooted. Worse was the smudge that enveloped the stern. Choking officers reported to the bridge that the fumes were becoming unbearable. Men staggered blindly through this suffocating vapor, stumbling, gagging, with hands to throat.

Veterans shouted to tell the rookies that the fog was not enemy gas, but chemical smoke—the destroyer's smoke generators were damaged and the FS tanks were fuming. FS liquid, a compound of sulphur trioxide and chlorsulphonic acid, combines immediately and violently with water or moisture in the air. If consistently inhaled, the fumes can prove toxic and painful. Spraying from ABNER READ's damaged smoke generators, these fumes enveloped the ship with a vapor that was almost as anguishing as phosgene. Commander Burrows described the ordeal in his report:

> The FS smoke was the most depressing single defect of the disaster that the men had to cope with. It blinded them, but worse yet it strangled them. It appeared to immobilize their respiratory muscles, so that they could neither breathe in nor out. After a few whiffs of smoke, their mental outlook became one of forlorn abandon. They lay down and waited for the ship to sink. Some leaned fruitlessly over the lifelines desperately gasping for air. About four climbed up on top of No. 5 gun mount, where they caught not over one or two whiffs of fresh air before the stern sank. Sinking of the stern brought great relief to all men on it by way of escape from FS smoke. Water was cold and covered with fuel, but such was a minor consideration compared to the terrifying effects of the smoke.

Fortunately the fantail did not sink with a plunge. The stern section broke away gradually and went down slowly, and a number of the survivors had a chance to grab for a floater net that drifted clear of the wreckage. The water was thickly carpeted with oil, but that was preferable to the FS fumes.

With her stern under the sea, ABNER READ drifted closer to the snarling rocks. Her distress had become dire emergency when the destroyer BANCROFT (Lieutenant Commander R. M. Pitts) came to the rescue. Shortly before 0300, BANCROFT took the disabled ABNER READ in tow and jockeyed her away from the Kiska reefs.

An hour later BANCROFT was relieved by the salvage tug UTE. And by daylight the crippled destroyer, towed by UTE, was well on her way to Adak.

All hands in ABNER READ commended the rescue work of BANCROFT and UTE. *"They kept us off the beach,"* Commander Burrows said simply.

But it was a silent crew of destroyermen who took ABNER READ from Adak to the States for ultimate repairs. Seventy-one of their shipmates had been lost in the mine explosion, and 34 others had been injured. The ABNER READ was the only warship casualty in the Kiska operation.

Gilmore Sinks I-180

The Aleutian fiasco cost the Japanese Army something more than the regiments squandered at Attu and the equipment abandoned at Kiska. And it cost the Imperial Navy something more than some twenty surface ships, five submarines, and face.

Nor did it hold the American Navy from more critical areas, as the Japanese had originally planned. Instead, the bulk of the United States North Pacific Force was quietly shifted from the Aleutians area to the Central Pacific. Admiral Nimitz was preparing to strike the tropical Gilberts. To strike Tarawa and Makin—the Marshalls—and Truk.

Meantime, completely deceived, the Japanese frantically began strengthening their Kurile Island defenses, certain that the American assaults on Attu and Kiska were but preliminary to a great northern offensive via the Aleutians.

The Americans encouraged them in this belief. American long-range bombers struck from the Aleutians, and American submarines from Dutch Harbor (and Pearl Harbor) harried Jap shipping in the Kuriles. These raids had every appearance of an overture to a major offensive—but actually little more than a skeleton force remained in the Aleutians.

Throughout the winter of 1943-44 the Japs in the Kuriles remained on tenterhooks. Zero scout planes could not reach the Aleutians. Nor could surface reconnaissance penetrate the fogs which screened the archipelago. Therefore, to obtain information, the intelligence-hungry Japanese Fifth Fleet commander dispatched a submarine or two to scout the Aleutian Islands. And late in April the submarine I-180 was prowling in the waters east of Dutch Harbor.

This I-boat was intrepid, if nothing else. On April 25, 1944, she had reached a position off the south coast of the Alaskan peninsula, about 120 miles from Kodiak Island. And in the evening of that day she was coolly charging batteries on the surface. One might say the I-boat was "asking for it." But Jap submersibles, in common with other types of that period, were compelled to surface for a battery charge whenever the occasion seemed propitious. In this instance the I-boat's timing was poor. She surfaced in waters destined to lie within radar range of a destroyer-escort named GILMORE.

The DE GILMORE was named for Commander W. W. Gilmore, who lost his life when the LEXINGTON was sunk in the Battle of the Coral Sea.

Aleutian duty did not seem to promise the DE GILMORE action, however. Throughout the winter of 1943-44, storms had been the only enemy encountered in the bleak archipelago. On the evening of April 25, it was the same routine. GILMORE, in company with destroyer-escort EDWARD C. DALY, was engaged in convoy duty (serving in CortDiv 14 under Commander L. F. Sugnet), escorting a cargoman from Dutch Harbor to Kodiak. A monotonous run. On GILMORE's bridge, her captain, Lieutenant W. D. Jenckes, U.S.N.R., was bored by the tedium. Below decks the men off watch yawned over cards, wrote letters, or idled in their bunks. When radar picked up a "pip" at 2230, range four miles, the off-watch had time to finish a few technicolor dreams. But there was action on the bridge. ComCortDiv 14 (in DALY) was notified by TBS. Course was changed toward the target.

It might be a derelict—an Aleut fishing boat—anything. GILMORE challenged the target by light. No reply. "General Quarters" galvanized the crew into action. Acey-deucy, letters, dreams went into the discard as men raced to man their battle stations.

At 2235, range two miles, the target disappeared from the radar screen.

"Wow! That looks like a diving submarine!"

"A sub? Holy Joe! Can we get him?"

The answer reached the bridge at 2238. Sound contact at 2,600 yards!

Lieutenant Jenckes started his ship on a run for the invader, ordering an attack with A/S Mark 10 projector. As the range closed, the sub maneuvered radically to evade, and Jenckes widened the range to gain better attack position.

At 2252 GILMORE's destroyermen opened fire with a hedgehog salvo. At 2307 they again fired hedgehogs. They sent another hedgehog salvo splashing into the sea at 2336.

No hits, and it was twelve o'clock, and all wasn't well. Jenckes decided to dig out the deep-submerged enemy with depth charges. At 0027, the destroyermen distributed 13 depth charges in a barrage calculated to obtain results. But the underwater blasts failed to produce visual or sonic evidence of a hit.

Shortly before one o'clock GILMORE made a run over the target, and obtained a fathometer reading of 47 fathoms. At 0107, Jenckes ordered another barrage of 13 depth charges. Six minutes later, a volcano seemed to explode deep in the sea, violently shaking the DE.

The concussion which thus jarred the GILMORE must have pulverized the target submarine. Neither sound nor radar contact could be regained after the huge explosion, and GILMORE's destroyermen were justifiably confident of a kill. Their handiwork was certified when a Kingfisher from Kodiak sighted a heavy oil slick spread across the sea where the A/S battle had been fought. Vice Admiral F. J. Fletcher, Commander North Pacific Force, subsequently noted that the oil slick was still present in the area as of May 16, 1944.

After the war, that disillusioned Japanese Fifth Fleet staff officer, Commander Hashimoto, recalled that five I-boats were lost in the Aleutians. And he based the failure of the I-boat effort on the fact that the boats were unwieldy, the skippers lacked aggressiveness, and the evasion tactics were poor. Hashimoto's memory was short one boat—the I-180. (Which raised the casualties to six.) And he failed to mention the most important cause for their failure. That was the A/S war waged by the force responsible for the sinking of at least four of the six I-boats in mention—the American Destroyer Force in the Aleutians.

If Japanese I-boats (as Hashimoto stated) obtained very little intelligence, and if Japan's Fifth Fleet remained on tenterhooks in the Kuriles throughout 1944, the cause could be traced to such hard-hitting destroyermen as manned the destroyer-escort GILMORE.

CHAPTER 20

SOUTH SEAS MOP-UP

Destroyer Operations, New Guinea (DD's with the Seventh Fleet)

In 1942 the Japs had triumphantly invaded New Guinea. The world's second largest island (only Greenland being larger), it was a prize much coveted by the Tojo-Yamamoto team.

Coinciding with the Solomons drive, the Japanese invasion began as a walkaway. Sailing down from their Bismarck citadel, the Japs swept across narrow Dampier and Vitiaz Straits and landed on the northeastern coasts with the greatest of ease. They established bases at Wewak, Alexishafen, and Madang. Planted the Rising Sun flag at Saidor, Finschhafen, and Lae on the Huon Peninsula. Strutted eastward down the coast to Salamaua and Buna. Then, probing past Buna, they headed for Milne Bay. By the end of 1942 they had seized nearly all of the miniature island continent off the northeast doorstep of Australia.

But the invaders were unable to swallow whole the 300,000 square miles of beach and mountain and jungle that was New Guinea. They bit at the rind, so to speak, but they could not swallow the interior. Nor could they seize the eastern stem—the Papuan peninsula which projects into the Coral Sea. Reaching out, they made a grab for Milne Bay at the southeastern tip, and for Port Moresby on the southern side of the peninsula. The greedy reach for Milne was delayed when they jerked back burnt fingers from the Battle of the Coral Sea. General MacArthur, the "Aussies," and the Owen Stanley Mountains frustrated the grab for Port Moresby.

In August 1942 the invaders made another try for Milne Bay. Beaten off, they sent their destroyers back in September to bombard the Allied defense installations. And on the 11th of that month American destroyers were on the scene.

The DD's were units of Destroyer Squadron 4, under command of Captain C. W. Flynn—SELFRIDGE (Lieutenant Commander C. D. Reynolds) flying the pennant of Captain Flynn; BAGLEY (Commander G. A. Sinclair); HENLEY (Lieutenant Commander E. K. Van Swearingen), and HELM (Lieutenant Commander C. E. Carroll). On orders from Rear Admiral V. A. C. Crutchley, R.N., Task Force Commander, the squadron steamed northward from the Coral Sea in an attempt to intercept the Jap warships. The attempt was unsuccessful. Making a high-speed retirement, the Japs ran back to where they came from.

For the rest of 1942 the Japs were compelled to devote most of their energies to Guadalcanal. New Guinea remained in their hands as a bastion protecting the approaches to the Netherlands East Indies. Perhaps "on their hands" would be a better term. New Guinea's climate and terrain were worse than anything in the Solomons. And the Owen Stanley Mountains proved impassable for the Japs, who were thrown back and across those jungly crags by hard-fighting Australians. January 1943 found the invaders retreating through Buna, and by February American-Anzac forces were in possession of that advance base.

Given Milne Bay and Buna for springboards, MacArthur plotted an offensive aimed to clear the Japs from the northeast coast of New Guinea. The offensive was to consist of a series of amphibious drives that would go leap-frogging westward along the coast and scoop up such enemy bases as Lae, Salamaua, Finschhafen, and Wewak. A major operation, this offensive was timed to mesh in with Halsey's advance in the Solomons. American-Australian troops would do the New Guinea land fighting. Army Air would play a leading role. And the Navy would carry the offensive by sea—"Navy" meaning the United States Seventh Fleet, as organized by Cominch on February 19, 1943. Or, more specifically, the Seventh Amphibious Force under command of Rear Admiral D. E. ("Uncle Dan") Barbey.

The enemy saw it coming and made frantic efforts to reinforce their New Guinea front. From the Netherlands Indies and from the Bismarck Archipelago they dispatched the usual barge-fleets, naval craft, and jerry-built convoys with every man, bullet, biscuit, and oil can they could spare.

In March 1943 a patrolling B-24 spied a Japanese convoy New Guinea-bound in the Bismarck Sea. Six troop transports, two freighters, and an auxiliary under escort of eight destroyers—very pretty! The B-24 flashed the word. Bad weather and black night delayed immediate attack. But the night was not too black for a patrol of Navy "Black Cats"—coal-colored Catalinas that tracked the ships through Vitiaz Strait and kept Allied Air Headquarters informed.

At daybreak on the following morning American Army and Australian aircraft caught the Japanese convoy 60 miles from Salamaua. For the next two days the Allied planes pounded the Jap ships. It was a wholesale execution. All six transports were sunk. Both freighters were battered under. The auxiliary vessel was obliterated. Four of the Jap destroyers were blasted to the bottom. About 50 Jap planes were shot out of the sky. After a desperate struggle to pick up survivors, the four remaining Jap DD's—the ARASHIO, ASASHIO, SHIRAYUKI, and TOKITSUKAZE—fled for their lives. When the carnage—called the Battle of the Bismarck Sea—was over, the New Guinea convoy was nonexistent. So were some 3,600 hapless Japanese.

With a flying start, then, the Allied offensive to regain New Guinea was well under way. Late in June—at the time of the landings on New Georgia and Rendova—Army troops went ashore on the Woodlark and Trobriand Islands, and an exploratory force seized a beachhead on the New Guinea coast ten miles south of Salamaua.

The Japs fired a few shots, then retired into the coastal jungles—some 56,000 Japs, waiting. Allied Intelligence estimated about a fifth of the total force was camped in the Lae-Salamaua area.

MacArthur and Admiral Barbey (who commanded all Seventh Fleet naval units in the operation) readied their forces. In August 1943 the drive for Lae was launched.

American destroyers spearheaded the push, setting out from Milne Bay two weeks before the landing date. Their mission was to sweep the Lae approaches and wipe Jap shipping out of the coastal waters between Salamaua and Finschhafen. For this task Admiral Barbey selected four DD's of Destroyer Squadron 5, commanded by Captain Jesse H. Carter.

Destroyers in this group were PERKINS (Lieutenant Commander G. L. Ketchum) flying the squadron Commander's pennant; CONYNGHAM (Commander J. H. Ward); SMITH (Lieutenant Commander R. A. Theobald, Jr.); and MAHAN (Lieutenant Commander James T. Smith). Steaming across the waters between Salamaua and Cape Cretin, the DD's bombarded enemy installations at Finschhafen for ten minutes without retaliation.

Early in September the Lae Task Force, under command of Admiral Barbey, stood out of Milne Bay. Destroyers in this invasion force were the CONYNGHAM (Commander Ward); FLUSSER (Lieutenant Commander J. A. Robbins), PERKINS (Commander Ketchum); SMITH (Commander Theobald); MAHAN (Commander Smith); LAMSON (Commander P. H. Fitzgerald); MUGFORD (Lieutenant Commander H. G. Corey); and DRAYTON (Lieutenant Commander R. S. Craighill).

Riding in CONYNGHAM was Admiral Barbey. Captain Carter in PERKINS commanded the DD's of DesRon 5. The destroyermen were primed for a redhot battle. During the latter part of August, Allied aircraft had pulverized Jap airstrips at Wewak, Alexishafen, Madang, and Hansa Bay, but there was every likelihood of attack by Jap air fleets from Rabaul in the Bismarcks. Ahead of the Lae Task Force, destroyer REID (Commander H. H. McIlhenny) was dispatched to take station as a radar picket off Cape Cretin. On board REID was a fighter-director team prepared to vector Allied aircraft into combat with enemy planes. A new duty for destroyers.

In the pre-dawn dark of September 4 CONYNGHAM scouted the Lae coastal area for a look-see. On the destroyer's bridge Admiral Barbey passed the word, the task force moved up, and the amphibious landings were begun.

Destroyers PERKINS, SMITH, and MAHAN covered the landing craft at "Beach Red." LAMSON and FLUSSER performed similar service at "Beach Yellow." Both beaches were dealt a brisk preliminary bombardment by the covering destroyers. The enemy fired a few random return shots, and after sunrise a flight of seven Mitsubishis and three Zeros roared over to shower the LCI's and LST's with bombs.

Later in the day a serious air threat developed. About 1300, REID, sweeping the Huon Gulf approaches with her radar, picked up three large groups of Jap aircraft bearing down from Rabaul. The planes were about 60 miles distant. Flashing the alarm, REID brought 48 Lightning fighters over the horizon and directed them into intercepting position. In the resulting battle 23 Jap planes were destroyed and the remaining 50 or so were dispersed. Admiral Barbey lauded the picket DD with:

> *Not only did* REID *do a splendid job of air warning and fighter directing, but she well defended herself. . . . Three Val bombers made near misses; one bomber was definitely destroyed.*

Ashore Jap resistance was little more than token. By nightfall of the 4th about 8,000 troops were solidly ashore at "Red" and "Yellow."

Salamaua fell to the Allies on September 11. Five days later Yanks and "Aussies" skirmished into Lae. The securing of Lae blighted the last Japanese hope of conquering eastern New Guinea. Outnumbered at sea and in the air, and unable to reinforce their New Guinea garrisions with anything more than driblets, the Japs pulled back to Finschhafen.

The American-Australian offensive followed hard on the enemy's heels. Assault date for Finschhafen was advanced to September 22.

It was during operations to secure this New Guinea strong point that the Seventh Fleet suffered its first destroyer loss of the war.

Victim was the U.S.S. HENLEY.

Loss of U.S.S. Henley

Steaming from Buna on the morning of September 21, 1943, the U.S.S. HENLEY (Commander Carleton R. Adams) headed westward to engage in what was destined to be her final campaign. Veteran of Pearl Harbor—pioneer on the New Guinea front—the DD that had buried NEOSHO after the Battle of the Coral Sea, and had stood by BLUE after the latter was torpedoed in the Battle of the Eastern Solomons—this destroyer had seen her full share of war in the South Pacific.

Yet Fate had enscribed her name on the slate of doom. Departing from Buna, she sailed toward that bourne from which no traveler returns—that misty destination which cannot be avoided, failing, as it does, to appear on the chart.

When she left Buna on the 21st, HENLEY was one of five DD's accompanying a herd of sixteen LCI's bound for a Finschhafen beachhead. Leading this assault force, Admiral Barbey scouted ahead in CONYNGHAM. The force stopped at Lae to pick up an Australian infantry brigade. Four destroyers which had preceded the convoy to the Lae area also attached themselves to the amphibian body. Thus augmented, the little armada pursued its northwestward course, and in the early-morning dark of September 22 the ships reached Cape Cretin.

Zero hour was timed for the gray-before-dawn of 0445. At 0433 destroyers LAMSON (Commander P. H. Fitzgerald), DRAYTON (Lieutenant Commander R. S. Craighill), MUGFORD (Lieutenant Commander H. G. Corey), and FLUSSER (Lieutenant Commander J. A. Robbins) moved in to thrash the beach with a preliminary bombardment. Concealed in jungle, Jap machine-gunners opened fire from the north end of the beach, and the LCI's ran into some sharp fusillades. But the landing craft went stubbornly in, the enemy machine-gun nest was quickly obliterated, and the hard-fighting "Aussies" had a firm footing on the beachhead by 0930 of that morning.

Angry Jap aircraft counter-attacked. Once more destroyer REID, acting as air picket and fighter-director, brought Allied aircraft overhead to intercept. The Army planes roared in and shot down 37 of the enemy before the Japs broke through the air defense and slashed at Admiral Barbey's amphibs as they retired from Scarlet Beach. The onslaught occurred around noon, just as the last of the unloaded LST's and accompanying DD's were heading away from the area. Ten Jap torpedo planes came roaring across the water. Destroyers CONYNGHAM, PERKINS, REID, SMITH, MAHAN, and HENLEY, under group command of Captain J. H. Carter, were picked as targets. They returned the compliment with interest.

Ordering full speed from all turbines, Captain Carter sent the DD's circling the LST's counterclockwise. Simultaneously the destroyers put up a canopy of 5-inch fire that blasted two of the attacking planes before they could launch their torpedoes, and wrecked a third in mid-air as it made the drop. Seven torpedoes were flung at the convoy; all missed. The destroyers in turn gave the bombers a lesson in marksmanship. Before the AA batteries stopped barking, five more Jap planes had been shot down by sharpshooting DD gunners. The scrimmage ended abruptly when the two remaining Jap bombers, eschewing demolishment, fled in the direction of Rabaul.

HENLEY emerged from this hot engagement unscathed. And throughout the ensuing week the destroyer was a busy unit in the amphibious machine that maintained and sustained the Australian troops battling southward from the beachhead.

On October 3, in company with destroyers REID and SMITH, the HENLEY was ordered to conduct an offensive A/S sweep off Cape Cretin. Under tactical command of Commander H. H. McIlhenny, the three destroyers commenced the sweep late that afternoon. The duty seemed anti-climactical after the Finschhafen battle. Not an enemy plane showed up on the radar scope, nor were enemy surface craft discernible along the Finschhafen foreshore.

However, having lost Finschhafen, the Japs were indisposed to surrender Vitiaz Strait without a battle. To the Cape Cretin area they dispatched a naval vessel to contest the Allied supremacy—a naval vessel that defied both binocular and radar detection. Operating submerged, this I-boat (or RO-boat) was not spotted by the three DD's that steamed northwestward into Vitiaz Strait. The destroyers were moving at 20 knots. REID and SMITH were able to work their echo-ranging gear at this speed, but HENLEY's sonar equipment was ineffective at 20 knots, and she was not "pinging." In the destroyer's path the Japanese submarine remained undetected. Apparently chance placed it in an intercepting position. In any event the sub was there. For destroyer HENLEY this was zero hour.

At that moment destroyer SMITH sheered out of column with a sudden swerve to starboard. As the ships had previously been ordered to form a scouting line at sunset, HENLEY, following the directive, swung to port to form the line. And just as his destroyer heeled, Commander Adams, on HENLEY's bridge, sighted two foaming torpedo trails whipping through the sea like streaks of underwater lightning, aiming for his DD.

Jap submarine torpedoes were practically wakeless —no more than a glimpse, and the thunderbolts would strike. Adams responded instantly, snapping a "Left full rudder!" that swung the ship on the arc of a tight circle. As the destroyer swerved to comb the wakes, the first torpedo whisked by, clearing the bow by some 30 yards. The second missed close astern. But a third torpedo, centered in the spread, struck the vessel a shattering smash on the port side, amidships.

Bursting in at the No. 1 fireroom, the torpedo exploded with a blast that stopped the ship dead in her tracks with a broken back. Spouting smoke and steam, the destroyer immediately began to settle. In less than four minutes the main deck was awash. At 1818 Commander Adams ordered the ship abandoned.

Men who had raced topside to escape the inrushing flood now made a fast grab for floats or rafts, or calmly stepped overside into the water. At 1826 the last raft was clear of the ship. Last to leave the HENLEY was her skipper, Commander Adams, who quit her bridge without a minute to spare. Barely a quarter of an hour after the torpedo wakes were sighted, the destroyer went down with a rush. One moment her bow was tilted high against the sky; then it slid under, leaving on the surface a pall of steam. About 60 seconds later the shocked survivors heard two tremendous underwater blasts—probably caused by exploding boilers. HENLEY was gone.

Destroyers REID and SMITH searched for the submarine, dropped depth charges, lost contact, and turned to the task of recovering the HENLEY survivors —18 officers and 225 men. Eight of the surviving officers and 44 of the men were wounded. Two of the wounded men died after they were picked up. One officer and 14 men went down with the stricken ship.

HENLEY's loss left a hard-to-fill gap in the destroyer roster of the Seventh Fleet.

Destroyers Versus Aircraft off Finschhafen

Flanking the northeast coast of New Guinea, the Jap-held Bismarck Archipelago loomed over the battle area like a smoldering Vesuvius. Any day or hour Rabaul on New Britain might emit swarms of warships or clouds of aircraft to scorch MacArthur's forces. From Rabaul undoubtedly came the Japanese submarine that sank HENLEY. From Rabaul came Jap bombers to raid the Allied positions around Finschhafen. Most of these raids were of nuisance caliber, and easily brushed aside. But on the night of October 19-20 a Jap submarine and some 60 Jap planes made a large-scale strike at American warships and landing craft in the Finschhafen area.

In action on the American side was Destroyer Squadron 5, composed of the following DD's:

PERKINS — *Lt. Comdr. G. L. Ketchum*
Flying the pennant of
Capt. Jesse H. Carter, COMDESRON 5
MAHAN — *Comdr. James T. Smith*
DRAYTON — *Lt. Comdr. R. S. Craighill*
SMITH — *Lt. Comdr. R. A. Theobald, Jr.*
Flying the pennant of
Comdr. C. D. Reynolds, COMDESDIV 10
MUGFORD — *Comdr. H. G. Corey*
REID — *Comdr. H. H. McIlhenny*

This destroyer squadron was in the Finschhafen area on an escort mission which involved the transport of troops and supplies to Langemak Bay. Supplies and troops were going ashore in LCI's and LST's during the night of October 19-20 when the Jap submarine entered the picture. The sub was more or less expected. In accordance with usual procedure, the destroyers, after dropping the convoy at Langemak, formed a scouting line to go sub-hunting while the convoy was unloading. Action came around 0120 shortly after the hunt was begun.

Destroyer REID made sound contact almost as soon as she was on station, and promptly went after the

sonar-detected enemy. The sub evaded the depth charges and fired a torpedo that streaked the sea close aboard the destroyer DRAYTON.

PERKINS then stepped in from stand-by position, and made a vigorous attack. When contact evaporated, Captain Carter considered a sinking probable, but the search was continued by the scouting line.

The destroyers steamed across the seascape, brooming the area with radar sweeps and probing the sea with echo-ranging "pings." No contact. The undersea tiger—perhaps the killer which ambushed HENLEY—got away.

October 20 broke bright and clear. New Guinea's mountains trooped across the background scene in dark silhouette. Offshore the destroyers continued their A/S sweep. About 0300 the squadron was 10 miles to the northeast of the landing area, where operations were proceeding smoothly. But trouble was brewing.

From the beginning of the sub-hunt, Jap snooper planes had been flitting on the fringe of the area. Usually the snoopers kept their distance; if they came too close a burst of AA fire would send them kiting. Tonight, however, the enemy observation planes soared around like hungry buzzards. Then they dropped ominous float lights. Finally, at 0300, a large group of Jap aircraft came out of the northeast. Faint at first, swiftly loudening, the drone cut through the stillness. The sub-hunt was over. Here were the bombers!

"Bogies on the port beam!"

General Quarters!

Destroyermen racing to battle stations.

Gunners jamming on their helmets as they leapt to man the AA batteries—the 20- and 40 mms., the 5-inch 38's.

Bathed in moonlight, the destroyers were beautiful targets for aircraft. Squadron Commander Carter elected to make them the world's hardest targets to hit. He ordered the ships into column formation, the DD's spaced 1,000 yards apart. Defenses called for expert seamanship, for crack radar work, for radical high-speed turns, for smoke.

Between the hours of 0300 and 0600, five groups of Jap aircraft made successive attacks on Destroyer Squadron 5. Wheeling overhead, they dropped ladders of bombs. But their block-busters fell in the sea. Their bombs raised picturesque fountains, and showered the moonlight with shrapnel. They gouged tons of foam from the wakes of high-balling destroyers and showered brine and dead fish on heeling destroyer bows. But nothing more.

MAHAN escaped. DRAYTON escaped. SMITH, MUGFORD, and REID came through without injury. They came through by laying dense smoke screens that coiled and curved across the water until the seascape resembled a forest afire. Dashing through the smoke, the ships made 90° right or left simultaneous turns—some sixty turns in all—maneuvering at top speed with the precision of figure skaters.

In closed mounts and behind splinter-shields, the gun crews fired a few sharp bursts that made some of the bombers sheer off. Several of the ships fired a few rounds of 5-inch 38 AA in radar control. But they did not shoot down any planes.

What worried the Japs was a ruse contrived by Captain Carter. He had reason to believe that the destroyer fighter-circuit voice call had become known by the Japanese. The code call was "Duckbutt." Why not put it on the air on the off chance it would mislead these attacking bombers? It was worth a try, and at 0445 the DD's fighter director began to issue calls to a mythical Allied air squadron supposedly racing to join the battle. It worked. The Japs bit on "Duckbutt" and finally took off. And at 0550, with daylight coloring the sky, it was over. The last Jap plane retired. The smoke drifted away. About 0645 genuine Allied fighter cover appeared. The reinforcements were welcome, but the big bout was concluded. Intact, Destroyer Squadron 5 had come through.

The enemy bombers had failed to score a single hit. Only one ship had suffered injury—flag destroyer PERKINS, slightly damaged by a near miss that clawed her with flying shrapnel, killed one of her men and wounded several others.

Among the wounded, Shipfitter R. C. Stamler was cited for "outstanding performance of duty." His leg slashed by a shrapnel fragment, Stamler remained on his feet as a member of the repair party. Aiding the removal of his wounded shipmates, he refused treatment for himself until they had been cared for in the battle dressing-station.

Other destroyermen of Squadron 5 merited commendation, every DD in the action deserved applause. In all probability the squadron's smoke screen drew the Jap planes away from the landing craft in Langemak Bay. By attracting the flock of bombers and bearing the brunt of the onslaught, Carter's destroyers averted a massacre on the New Guinea beach.

Admiral Kinkaid subsequently commended Captain Carter for the record.

Commander Seventh Fleet considers that Commander Destroyer Squadron Five handled his destroyers during this attack with outstanding skill.

But tragedy was to stalk the flag destroyer of Carter's squadron and strike her down when the blow was least expected. PERKINS was the second American destroyer to be lost during the drive to take northeast New Guinea.

Loss of U.S.S. Perkins

She was not a battle casualty. Hers was the fate perhaps hardest on heroes—to survive the storm's vortex and the fury of battle, only to go down through freakish mishandling.

Tassafaronga — Gifu — Lae — Finschhafen — those were the names on PERKINS' war record. From those actions she emerged with colors flying, wearing only the scars from the battle off Finschhafen. A little less than six weeks after that savage encounter with Jap aircraft, the destroyer was scrap on the dark sea-bottom near Cape Vogel, New Guinea.

Disaster struck in the early-hour darkness of November 29. An hour as black as the New Guinea coastline to port, smudged by the ink of bad weather. Bound from Milne Bay to Buna, and proceeding independently, PERKINS was steaming through the gloom when, around 0145, her radar picked up a ship about six miles dead ahead. PERKINS' Executive Officer, who was navigator, kept tabs on the contact as radar tracked the target to within 8,000 yards. The "Exec" then went to the pilot-house and asked the Officer of the Deck (whom he was about to relieve) if he could see the oncoming ship, which was obscured in the murk. Somehow the nearing vessel faded from view—

there was one of those strange moments of physical or psychological blindness which seem to precede such catastrophes—then the "Exec" suddenly sighted the ship bearing down close aboard. Steep as a cliff the vessel's prow loomed out of blackness—a churn of froth at the cutwater—iron eyes looking down. And exactly at four bells the destroyer was rammed full tilt by the Australian troopship H.M.A.S. DUNTROON.

The transport's bow sliced into the destroyer's No. 2 fireroom. There was a clangorous crash, the crunch of buckling metal, a torrential roar of water, and the scalding hiss of steam.

With churning propellers DUNTROON backed away. The destroyer flooded rapidly as the crew struggled topside. When he saw her case was hopeless, PERKINS' captain, Lieutenant Commander Ketchum, gave the order to abandon. The destroyermen went overside in good order to await rescue by the Australian trooper.

Twenty-five minutes after the ramming, PERKINS sank. She broke in two just before going down. Nine of her crew were lost with her. Squadron Commander Jesse H. Carter, Commanding Officer Ketchum, and 228 others of the ship's company were saved.

A Court of Inquiry found the captain, the navigator, and the Officer of the Deck at fault for the collision.

Convoy to Empress Augusta Bay

While the "Aussies" were mopping up around Finschhafen, the Marines were digging in at Bougainville. Outflanked in his Bismarck citadel, Vice Admiral Kusaka faced Halsey in the Solomons and MacArthur in New Guinea. Although stunned by the punishment which Halsey had dealt Rabaul in the opening days of November, Kusaka made a strenuous effort to dislodge the Marines from their Bougainville beachheads. Down from New Britain and New Ireland jumped Japanese aircraft to blast the Marine positions and bomb supply shipping. And on several occasions the Japs gave the American vanguard in the Upper Solomons a nasty mauling.

Early in the morning of November 17, 1943, a squadron of some eight or ten torpedo planes pounced on an American convoy approaching Empress Augusta Bay, and a hot time was had by all. The battle featured a combination of destroyer seamanship, crack destroyer marksmanship, and heroic destroyer rescue work.

Under command of Captain G. B. ("Chick") Carter, the convoy was composed of the following units:

Task Group 31.6, consisting of the destroyer RENSHAW (Lieutenant Commander J. A. Lark) flying the pennant of Captain Carter; high-speed transports STRINGHAM, TALBOT, WATERS, DENT, KILTY, CROSBY, WARD and MCKEAN; fleet tug PAWNEE; and eight LST's. And a screen containing destroyers WALLER (Lieutenant Commander W. T. Dutton) flying the pennant of Captain J. E. ("Jack") Hurff, ComDesRon 22; SAUFLEY (Commander B. F. Brown); SIGOURNEY (Commander W. L. Dyer); PRINGLE (Lieutenant Commander G. DeMetropolis); and CONWAY (Lieutenant Command H. G. Bowen), flying the pennant of Commander J. R. Pahl, ComDesDiv 44.

The ships steamed in formation as follows: the LST's in three center columns; PAWNEE in the middle column, the transports in a protective cordon around the landing ships; RENSHAW, SIGOURNEY, WALLER, PRINGLE, and CONWAY on the convoy's flanks as an outer screen; SAUFLEY seven miles ahead, guiding the formation. Group Commander Carter anticipated a torpedo attack by Jap planes, and his ships were disposed for best mutual defense, and gunners alerted accordingly.

The convoy was off the southwest coast of Bougainville when the enemy struck. Ships' clocks were at 0300. Out of a star-powdered sky washed with tropic moonlight the Jap planes swooped into view.

"Bogies astern!"

All hands in the convoy made a concerted dash for battle stations.

Because the tactic would have hindered the LST's in maneuver, and hampered AA fire, the destroyers did not lay smoke. Shoals on either flank of the convoy formation prevented a radical course-change, but the ships had enough "elbow room" for individual evasive action. Visibility would give a good view of the attacking aircraft, and a well directed fire would be the best defense.

The opening round was auspicious. Sighting the convoy, the Japs dropped a brilliant float-light and two flares. This carnival glow seemed to dazzle the pilot of the first attacking plane, which came in on a crazy dive toward PRINGLE, and crashed blindly near that destroyer's bow. A perfect dud of a performance, for the "Betty" was not under fire on the one hand, and it failed to let fly at the target on the other.

The second attacking plane came in at 0336. As the bomber roared in to strike, the destroyer CONWAY and the leading LST's opened up with a 20 mm. barrage. Banking through curtains of tracer, the "Betty" caught a fatal hit, swerved wildly, burst into flame, and went torching into the sea some 500 yards astern of CONWAY. Two torpedoes dropped by this bomber scooted through the foam between destroyer RENSHAW and the leading LST's.

About two minutes later the destroyer-transport MCKEAN was torpedoed. Positioned at the convoy's rear, the ship was attacked by a bomber that came in

Forces for the Kiska landings are assembled in Adak. It appeared that American and Canadian troops embarked for the invasion of the last Jap stronghold in the Aleutians would be up against worse terrain and more heavily defended positions than on Attu. But the Japs had been whipped. They evacuated the island and were glad to be gone from such inhospitable territory.

When the Allies landed on Kiska, the coastline was obscured by heavy fog. American destroyers are shown screening the landing craft moving in for the attack. Over 100 vessels and 35,000 troops participated. Lack of opposition hinted at ambush, but the warriors of Nippon had pulled out nineteen days before the attack was made. Not a living Jap could be found on Kiska Island.

Another victim of Aleutian fury, the destroyer King goes on the beach at the end of runway "B" at Adak. The King, an old fourstacker, helped fight off the aerial attack on Dutch Harbor.

U.S.S. Monaghan ties up in an Aleutian port after battling a Japanese sub. In a surface engagement on the pitchblack night of June 22, 1943, the destroyer mortally injured her foe, the I-7.

The Bristol-class destroyer Bancroft (DD 598) is part of the screen off Kiska on D-day. In the background is the 14,000-ton transport Harris. Nineteen destroyers took part in the operation.

on the port flank, crossed the formation, and circled to strike from starboard. Blasted and burning, the McKean listed over and began to settle.

Furiously the destroyers blazed away at the oncoming bombers with 40 mm. and 20 mm. fire, as the 5-inchers could not at first be kept on target by means of radar control. While the screen was banging away, destroyer Sigourney (Commander Dyer) and destroyer-transport Talbot (Lieutenant Commander C. C. Morgan, U.S.N.R.) were ordered to stand by the stricken McKean. Closing in, the rescue vessels found the torpedoed troopship burning like a haystack. Crew and passengers fought desperately to escape this floating inferno; the oil-carpeted water was littered with rafts, rubbish, and shouting men.

Illuminated by the fiery wreck, the two rescuers were at once exposed to attack, and the bombers bore down on them with a vengeance. For the next two hours the Jap planes wheeled and dipped like vultures over the dying transport and the rescue ships. During intervals of respite, Sigourney and Talbot maneuvered close to the sinking McKean to pick up survivors. Then the bombers would come back, roaring, and the destroyer and companion transport would spray the sky with lead and tracer to drive the attackers off.

Again and again the destroyers' guns raised an aerial tempest that forced the planes to dodge away or drop their lethal "fish" at long range. Two torpedoes missed the DD. Sigourney's marksmen were better. With a burst of 20 mm. her gunners riddled a bomber and brought it down close aboard. A direct 5-inch hit sent another Jap plane plummeting into the sea. Still another bomber was severely if not fatally damaged by the DD gunners.

Talbot, too, performed in four-star fashion. Aboard the fire-swept transport the casualties were agonizing, but they could have amounted to virtual annihilation had it not been for the valiant work of Talbot and Sigourney.

At 0550 American fighter planes arrived on the scene, and the surviving Jap airmen—or, most of the survivors—fled. Seven, who had ditched, were taken prisoner by the destroyer Waller.

Steaming into Empress Augusta Bay, the Bougainville convoy counted the loss of one transport and numerous casualties. By way of reprisal, however, the convoy's defenders had shot down at least three, and probably four, of the attacking planes, and one bomber had come a-cropper for good measure. The Japanese could ill afford these aircraft losses on the Upper Solomons front. But neither could they afford to let seven United States transports arrive safely in Empress Augusta Bay.

For their part in the action, the crews of Sigourney and Talbot won special commendation.

"The all-around performance of Sigourney *was excellent,"* Screen Commander Hurff lauded the DD. *"The* Talbot *is not under my command, but an excellent performance by that vessel was noted."*

"This action," Admiral Halsey commented, *"serves to emphasize the urgent need for night fighters."*

Studying the pertinent battle reports, a destroyer officer remarked conclusively, *"When night fighters aren't available, as in this specific case, DD's have to fill in. This is another instance of the versatility of the destroyer, the handiest ship afloat."*

The Christening of "31-Knot" Burke

Some officers of the Regular Navy are known by sobriquets they acquired in boyhood. Many possess nicknames bestowed upon them while at the Naval Academy. A number win informal appellations while at sea or elsewhere on active duty. And of these last a few are awarded that type of sobriquet, usually unusually colorful, distinguished as a "war name" or *nom de guerre*. None of those originating in World War II will be better established in legend than the one conferred on Captain Arleigh Burke, extraordinary leader of extraordinary Destroyer Squadron 23.

This is the story behind that famous *nom de guerre*.

During the third week in November 1943, Burke's DD's, busiest destroyers in the Solomons, were engaged in offensively sweeping the Bougainville area. As of this date DesRon 23 was composed of flag destroyer Charles Ausburne (Commander L. K. Reynolds); Claxton (Commander H. F. Stout); Dyson (Commander R. A. Gano); Converse (Commander D. C. E. Hamberger), flying the pennant of Commander B. L. Austin, ComDesDiv 46; and Spence (Commander H. J. Armstrong).

On the 24th the five destroyers put in for fuel at Hathorn Sound in Kula Gulf, New Georgia Island. They were loading their tanks to capacity ("topping off," in Navy parlance) when Intelligence dispatched the interesting information that the Japs planned to evacuate important aviation personnel from the battered Buka-Bonis airfields. As Jap destroyers and high-speed transports would probably attempt the evacuation, it seemed logical that American destroyers, if they also moved at high speed, could frustrate the evacuation effort. Halsey's flagship advised Burke's flag destroyer accordingly.

Burke was directed to finish topping off at top speed, then to steam to "Point Uncle"—a point off the southwest coast of Bougainville. There he was to report his time of arrival. And if the evacuation eventuated, DesRon 23 was to "take care of it."

Burke was away from Hathorn Sound with a celerity that let no moss grow under keel. He reported that his squadron would arrive at "Point Uncle" about 2200, via a route south of Treasury Island. This and a subsequent report indicated that his destroyers were making 31 knots—a fact which brought an exclamation from Captain R. H. Thurber, Halsey's Operations Officer and one-time squadron mate of the fast-moving Burke. According to one story, Thurber cried:

"Thirty-one knots! And he recently advised us he could make only 30 knots formation speed!"

When Halsey's next order was dispatched it was worded as follows:

THIRTY-ONE KNOT BURKE GET ATHWART THE BUKA-RABAUL EVACUATION LINE ABOUT 35 MILES WEST OF BUKA X IF NO ENEMY CONTACTS BY 0300 . . . 25TH . . . COME SOUTH TO REFUEL SAME PLACE X IF ENEMY CONTACTED YOU KNOW WHAT TO DO

Historic message! Flashing from ComSoPac to ComDesRon 23, it sent Burke's destroyers steaming into the waters between Buka and New Ireland to fight the classic Battle of Cape St. George. And it endowed Captain Burke with a *nom de guerre* destined to stay with him for the duration of naval history—"31-Knot" Burke.

The Battle of Cape St. George

About 0130 in the morning of November 25 the five destroyers of "31-Knot" Burke began their fateful patrol in the waters between Buka and New Ireland. Burke had his two divisions ranged in two-column echelon formation—CHARLES AUSBURNE in the lead, followed by DYSON and CLAXTON, with CONVERSE and SPENCE trailing on parallel course to port.

The night was overcast and moonless, its 3,000-yard visibility blurred by sporadic rainsqualls. Burke ordered a patrolling speed of 23 knots through warm seas that were greasy-smooth and heaving. *"An ideal night,"* he noted, *"for a nice quiet torpedo attack."*

At 0141 through the propitious quietude came the first tally-ho—radar contact by destroyer DYSON on a target 22,000 yards to the northeast. Commander Gano passed the word over voice radio, and Burke's reply by TBS was as informal as it was informative.

HELLO DS 23 HANG ON TO YOUR HATS BOYS HERE WE GO

The Squadron Commander's next order was:

DIVISION CORPEN 85 COMDESDIV 46 HOLD BACK UNTIL YOU GET YOUR PROPER BEARING . . . THAT IS 225

This order headed the squadron for the enemy, the DesDiv 45 column in the lead, and the DesDiv 46 column trailing to starboard in backfield position.

As the destroyers sprinted toward Target No. 1, a second "pip" showed up on the radar screen. Then, as the range decreased, a third "pip" glimmered into view on the scope, and the radar watch thought they had three Jap ships in the immediate offing. Actually one of these "pips" was an electronic phantom—an illusion. The squadron was bearing down on two Jap men-of-war which were serving as a screen for the evacuation ships astern and to the east. These other ships were detected in due time—three more "pips" snared by the Americans' radar to make a total of five goodly targets in all. Although Burke formed no positive opinion as to the type of enemy ships ahead, some of the destroyermen believed they were cruisers, and Burke counted the enemy force as six. Perhaps it was just as well that the Jap ships numbered five, and that they proved to be destroyers instead of cruisers. Not that the larger size and number would have deterred Captain Burke and company. But the five American DD's would have been heavily outweighed had the Jap force included several CL's.

As it was, the combatants were evenly matched as to weight; and for Burke's scrappy destroyers an even match was tantamount to a sizable advantage. Given radar's all-seeing eye, the American advantage became overwhelming. Deployed in two columns (screening pair, and trio astern), the Japs were taken completely by surprise, and forced to fight blindly against a foe with long-range vision.

Failing to detect the approaching Americans, the two Jap DD's in screening position were steaming on a steady course when Burke's van destroyers closed the range to 5,500 yards. The Japs were blissfully unaware of what was coming. AUSBURNE, CLAXTON, and DYSON had time to maneuver into position for a sharpshooting torpedo set-up. "31-Knot" Burke drew a bead, so to speak, and ordered his DesDiv 45 DD's to let fly.

Five port torpedoes were fired by each attacking destroyer—a barrage that sent fifteen deadly "fish" in a school toward the Japanese targets. A lengthening wait stretched suspense to the limit of endurance, and then the TNT thunderstorm exploded across the distance. Orange flame spouted against the sky as detonations boomed across the seascape. One target sent up a ball of fire 300 feet in height. Explosions hurled up burning towers of debris. In that livid climax one of the Japanese destroyers crumpled in ruination and sank. The other staggered about in solitary desolation, a burning wreck.

Immediately after the torpedoes were fired Burke's

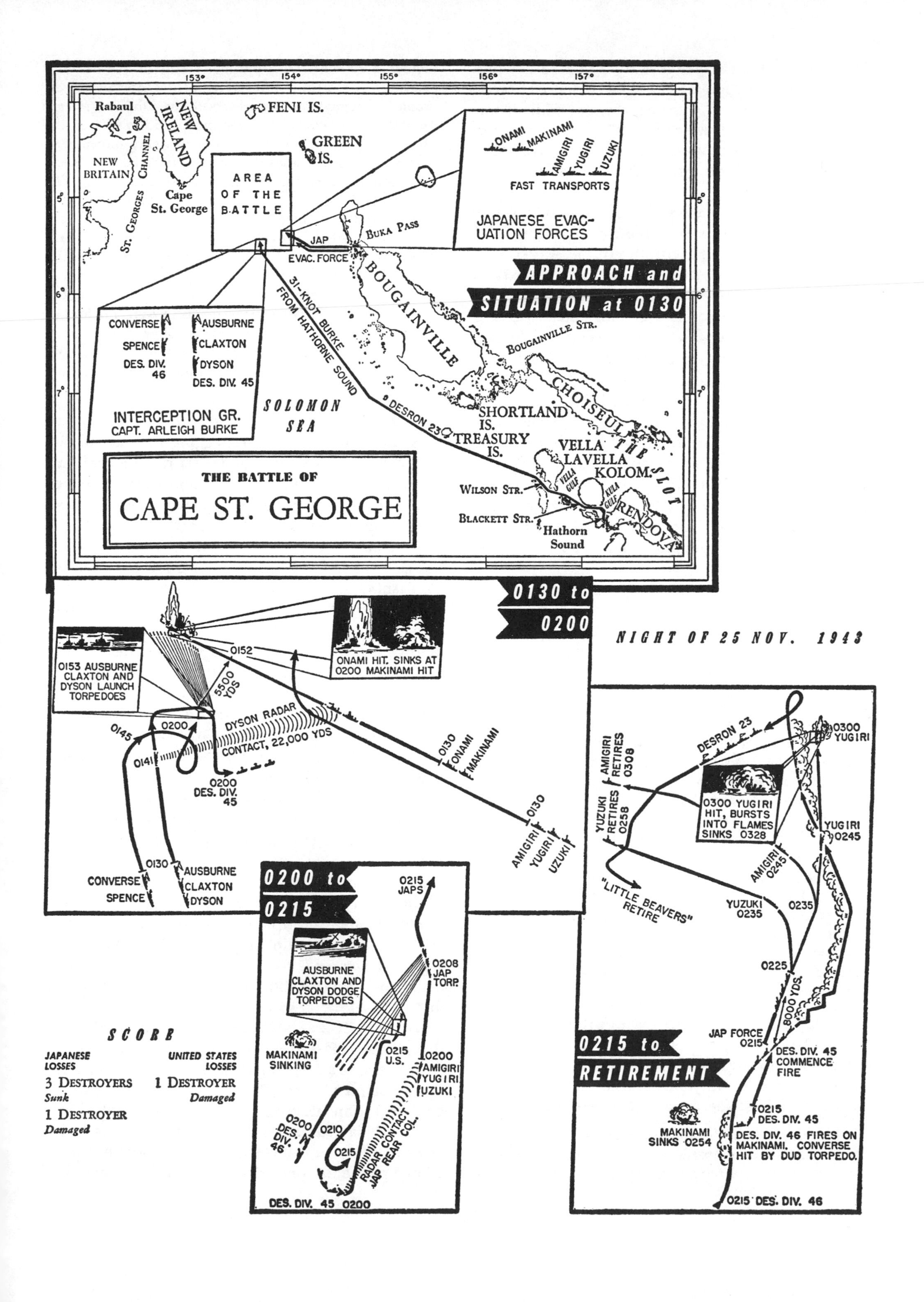

THE BATTLE OF
CAPE ST. GEORGE
APPROACH and SITUATION at 0130
Rabaul
NEW IRELAND
NEW BRITAIN
ST. GEORGES CHANNEL
Cape St. George
FENI IS.
GREEN IS.
AREA OF THE BATTLE
ONAMI
MAKINAMI
AMIGIRI
YUGIRI
UZUKI
FAST TRANSPORTS
JAPANESE EVACUATION FORCES
BUKA PASS
JAP EVAC. FORCE
BOUGAINVILLE
31-KNOT BURKE FROM HATHORNE SOUND
CONVERSE
SPENCE
DES. DIV. 46
AUSBURNE
CLAXTON
DYSON
DES. DIV. 45
INTERCEPTION GR.
CAPT. ARLEIGH BURKE
SOLOMON SEA
BOUGAINVILLE STR.
CHOISEUL
THE SLOT
SHORTLAND IS.
DESRON 23
TREASURY IS.
VELLA LAVELLA
KOLOM.
VELLA GULF
KULA GULF
WILSON STR.
BLACKETT STR.
Hathorn Sound
RENDOVA
0130 to 0200
NIGHT OF 25 NOV. 1943
0153 AUSBURNE CLAXTON AND DYSON LAUNCH TORPEDOES
ONAMI HIT. SINKS AT 0200 MAKINAMI HIT
0152
5500 YDS
DYSON RADAR CONTACT, 22,000 YDS
0145
0200
0141
0200 DES. DIV. 45
0130
0130 ONAMI MAKINAMI
0130 AMIGIRI YUGIRI UZUKI
CONVERSE
SPENCE
AUSBURNE
CLAXTON
DYSON
0200 to 0215
0215 JAPS
0208 JAP TORP.
AUSBURNE CLAXTON AND DYSON DODGE TORPEDOES
MAKINAMI SINKING
0215 U.S.
0200 AMIGIRI YUGIRI UZUKI
0200 DES. DIV. 46
0210
0215
RADAR CONTACT JAP REAR COL.
DES. DIV. 45 0200
SCORE
JAPANESE LOSSES
3 DESTROYERS Sunk
1 DESTROYER Damaged
UNITED STATES LOSSES
1 DESTROYER Damaged
0215 to RETIREMENT
DESRON 23
0300 YUGIRI
AMIGIRI RETIRES 0308
YUZUKI RETIRES 0258
0300 YUGIRI HIT, BURSTS INTO FLAMES SINKS 0328
YUGIRI 0245
AMIGIRI 0245
"LITTLE BEAVERS" RETIRE
YUZUKI 0235
0235
0225
8000 YDS.
JAP FORCE 0215
DES. DIV. 45 COMMENCE FIRE
0215 DES. DIV. 45
MAKINAMI SINKS 0254
DES. DIV. 46 FIRES ON MAKINAMI. CONVERSE HIT BY DUD TORPEDO.
0215 DES. DIV. 46

DD's had executed a 90-degree right turn to side-step any counter torpedo-attack. The defensive tactic proved unnecessary in this instance, but while it was being made the radar watch picked up the second Jap column, 13,000 yards astern of the first. AUSBURNE, CLAXTON, and DYSON promptly wheeled to attack these new targets.

Alarmed by the blasting of Column No. 1, the second Jap column ran. Ordering CONVERSE and SPENCE to demolish the enemy cripple, Burke sent DesDiv 45 in hot pursuit of the fugitives—targets that finally materialized as three destroyers.

The three Jap destroyers hiked for home base with their fantails between their legs. Racing northward, they built up a speed of 32 knots. Ordering all the turns the engineers could make, "31-Knot" Burke coaxed 33 knots out of his pursuing DD's.

The Japs had a long head start, however, and DesDiv 45 could not overhaul for torpedo attack. A stern chase is invariably a long one, and this one seemed interminable to the sweating American destroyermen. For a time it seemed as though it might go on until the whole "kit and boiling" ended up in a Jap backwater of Simpson Harbor. No matter—DesDiv 45 kept on going.

At 0215 Burke, acting on a sudden hunch, ordered a radical course-change to the right to avoid a possible salvo of Jap torpedoes. The division steadied, and a moment later came back to its base course. Intuition—whatever it was—Burke's hunch-move apparently paid off. As he reported it:

> No sooner had the . . . division come to course . . . than three heavy explosions were felt by all ships. The explosions were so heavy the ships were badly jarred and the Squadron Commander could not resist the temptation to look at the bow to see whether or not it was still there. CHARLES AUSBURNE did not slow, and it was felt that at least one of the ships astern had been hit by torpedoes. Each one of the ships astern thought that one of the other ships had been hit. Fortunately the explosions were merely Japanese torpedoes exploding at the end of their runs or as they crossed our wakes. It may be that the short jog to the right threw the Division out of torpedo water. If so, it was one of the most fortunate of the many lucky breaks the Squadron experienced.

At 0222 the pursuing DD's were within gun-range, and Burke snapped the order to open fire. The destroyers opened up with their forward guns at a range of about 8,000 yards. Burke penned a colorful description of the action which ensued.

> The enemy from this time on made several changes of course and also returned our fire. A large amount of smoke covered the retreating Japanese force which was either a smoke screen purposely laid or powder and stack smoke resulting from incidental operations. As soon as enemy fire was observed the Division started to fishtail, weaving back and forth within 30° of the base course. The enemy salvos were well grouped. Patterns were small and they came close, but for some unaccountable reason there were no direct hits. The nearness of the enemy projectiles is best demonstrated by the fact that there were two inches of water on the CLAXTON's bridge caused by the splashes of the shorts. Some of the enemy salvos landed short, some over. They were not consistent in their missing.
>
> Hits were observed on the targets almost at once, but they seemed to have no effect. There were no fires in the beginning, the targets did not slow, and in spite of the magnificent efforts of the gunners of the 45th Division, we seemed to be conducting a futile gun-practice.

As the American 5-inchers continued to blaze and bark, the Jap destroyers, zigzagging like jackrabbits, took divergent courses. The fastest raced ahead on a base course of 350°T, and the other two tangented on either side. This split-up occurred at 0225, three minutes after the Americans opened fire. And presently it was apparent that the American gunnery was not as futile as Burke had feared. Shots from DesDiv 45, flashing and twinkling through the smoke which shrouded the fleeing ships, had hit the enemy some savage blows. At 0300 one of the jackrabbiting Jap destroyers burst into flame and went reeling.

Burke led his pursuing division in a column past this disabled warship. In passing, AUSBURNE, CLAXTON, and DYSON punched shell after shell into the target. Soon the assailed vessel was flaring like a fireworks display. To complete the destruction, Burke brought his division circling back on the exploding hulk. Destroyer DYSON was directed to sink the wreck with a torpedo salvo, but before the torpedoes could strike the mark the Jap DD went down of its own accord.

Meanwhile, CONVERSE and SPENCE were attending to the vessel previously crippled. Five torpedoes from CONVERSE and multiple shell-hits from both DD's laid this Jap warship on the sea floor. While engaged in this endeavor, CONVERSE was struck by a malignant torpedo, but the enemy war head was a dud.

By dawn it was all over but the obituaries. Although two of the five Jap ships had managed to escape, Burke's DesRon 23 had every right to hoist the broom of victory. To the bottom (at 31 knots) it had sent Jap destroyers YUGIRI, MAKINAMI, and ONAMI. A Jap sub from Rabaul rescued YUGIRI's survivors. But down in MAKINAMI and ONAMI had gone a large passenger complement of that important aviation personnel whose evacuation from Buka had incited this water carnival. More important, of course, was the destroyer destruction which seriously impoverished the enemy force hanging on by the skin of its teeth at Rabaul. All this without a single American fatality, and no casualties other than a few ruptured eardrums and several cases of battle fatigue.

Famous when it entered the engagement, DesRon 23 emerged from the fray with a celebrity's reputation. If Squadron Commander Arleigh Burke had made a new name for himself, so, too, had his champion squadron acquired a new name. Thenceforth Burke's DD's would sail through history as the "Little Beavers"—a sobriquet of risible implications, with its source in wardroom humor, but clearly associated with "busy."

Indeed, off Cape St. George these five destroyers had been so busy that the Japs who escaped reported an attack by *"a cruiser division, a destroyer division, and several PT-boats."*

Well might the "Little Beavers" of "31-Knot" Burke claim a lion-sized victory. They had fought an engagement to be characterized by the Naval War College as *"the almost perfect surface action."*

Sundown in the Bismarcks (Destroyers Go to New Britain)

In December 1943, to Kusaka's despair, the Allies came up from down under and landed on the underbelly of New Britain. Arawe on the south coast, to be exact—a spot some strategists believed would make a limber springboard for a direct leap at Rabaul. The Japanese in their Bismarck citadel could do little to prevent the seizure. And they did that little too late.

Sea forces under over-all naval command of Vice Admiral T. C. Kinkaid (late that November appointed Commander Seventh Fleet) carried the invaders, covered the landings, and established the supply lines to the beachheads. Admiral Barbey's Seventh Amphibious teams blazed the trail and opened up the front.

Assembled at Buna, New Guinea, the invasion force set sail for Arawe, New Britain, on December 14. Led by "Uncle Dan" Barbey in destroyer CONYNGHAM, the convoy consisted of the Australian transport WESTPHALIA, destroyer transports HUMPHREYS and SANDS, an LSD (Landing Ship Dock), and an escort unit of destroyers. The DD's in this unit were SHAW (Commander R. H. Phillips), DRAYTON (Lieutenant Commander R. S. Craighill), BAGLEY (Commander T. E. Chambers), and MUGFORD (Commander H. G. Corey). SHAW was flying the pennant of Captain Jesse H. Carter, ComDesRon 5. With the invasion force was a bombardment group composed of destroyers REID (Commander H. H. McIlhenny), flagship of Commander C. D. Reynolds, ComDesDiv 10, SMITH (Commander R. A. Theobald, Jr.), LAMSON (Commander J. R. Rubins), FLUSSER (Commander J. A. Robbins), and MAHAN (Commander J. T. Smith).

A covering force of two Australian heavy cruisers, three light cruisers, and four destroyers ranged east of Arawe to block possible Jap surface force interference from Rabaul. But enemy warships did not show.

About 0400 in the morning of the 15th the invaders were off Arawe. A Japanese float plane attacked and missed REID with a shower of bombs, and the battle for New Britain was begun. Enemy resistance at Arawe was spotty, but tough in those spots. At "Blue Beach," about three miles to the east, transport SANDS and supporting destroyer SHAW ran into a hornet's nest. The troops going ashore in rubber boats were severely lashed and thrown back by concealed Jap guns. SHAW treated the jungle-screened gunners to eight rounds from her 5-inch 38's. The Jap sharpshooters retired. But the landing force was so badly cut up it was unable to gain this beach. Fifteen rubber boats from SANDS had started in. Twelve had been riddled and sunk in a bloody wallow.

At the main landing beach the enemy's shore defenses were subjected to a sunrise bombardment delivered by REID, SMITH, LAMSON, FLUSSER, and MAHAN. After raking the bush with this preparatory barrage, the destroyers stepped aside to let two DUKW's (amphibious trucks) wade in and scorch the enemy with bazooka-fired rockets—something new in the Pacific. Flayed by these novelties as well as by the destroyers' 5-inch shells, the Japs at Arawe retired to interior defense positions. A few fusillades peppered the shore-going American troops, but the beachhead was secured by 0900. Then, at 0930—

"Vals and Zekes!"

The alarm sent gun crews leaping to man their batteries on destroyer CONYNGHAM. Last DD to leave Arawe Harbor, Admiral Barbey's flagship was picking up "Blue Beach" survivors when the Jap aircraft came over. Thirty-six enemy planes! The destroyer got a move on, and her guns were racketing as the Zekes and Vals hurtled overhead. Three bombs missed CONYNGHAM by a sufficient 50 yards. As that distance is no more than 150 feet, the sufficiency was not exactly comfortable. All hands breathed easier when a flight of P-38's locked horns with the foe. Hitting her stride, CONYNGHAM galloped out from under.

Six days later the American invaders captured weed-grown Arawe airstrip. Arawe itself was of little value to either side, but its capture by the Allies was significant. As the Rising Sun came down on this jungly patch of New Britain, the Japs must have known they were through in the South Pacific. With aircraft here and submarines there they could still strike a few more blows in the South Seas theater, but it would cost an exorbitant price in planes and submarines at a time when Imperial Japan could no longer afford such extravagance.

Griswold Kills I-39

The day before Christmas 1943, the destroyer-escort GRISWOLD (Lieutenant M. C. Walley, U.S.N.R.) was patrolling off Lunga Point. To GRISWOLD's destroyermen the area was about as devoid of Christmas atmosphere as Hades. Westward in the murky, before-dawn dark, Guadalcanal lay in sinister silhouette. In a few moments GRISWOLD's decks, under an equatorial sun, would be as uncomfortable underfoot as those in a steamer's fireroom, and her firerooms would be all but intolerable.

"Can you imagine tomorrow's Christmas?" a seaman mutters. "That anywhere there's snow?"

"In these latitudes there ain't no Santy Claus."

Yet GRISWOLD was to obtain a Christmas present—of sorts. In the Solomons one could not be too fussy.

At 0856 the DE received a dispatch from a shore station that a Jap sub had been spotted in the vicinity of Koli Point. Lieutenant Walley headed his ship for this trespasser on the double.

About 25 minutes later Sound reported an underwater contact which spelled "submarine." GRISWOLD's crew went to battle stations, and the DE squared away to deliver the attack. Hedgehogs first—the projectiles soaring like iron birds, and spattering the surface with their pattern. Then depth charges splashing in to throw up hummocks of sea.

For almost four hours the GRISWOLD kept at it—attacking, searching, attacking—harrying the undersea foe as a hunting dog would harry a badger in a bush. Some of the salvos scored hits early in the battle; when their watery thunder grumbled away, the sea was simmering with air bubbles and streaked by an iridescent oil slick.

At 1318 a periscope was sighted about 800 yards distant, thrust up from the eddying water like a cobra's head. GRISWOLD wheeled to crush the submersible, bombing the sea with a TNT barrage that literally tore the I-boat to pieces.

Boiling to the surface came wooden gratings, lengths of shattered planking, fragments of cork, fragments of unidentifiable debris, and fragments of Jap. Like the Emperor's troops before them, the Japanese submariners in I-39 had learned that Guadalcanal was an unhealthy neighborhood for Imperial intrusion.

Evil territory at best, the Solomons. Atmosphere about as far removed from Christmas as anything can be. But the American destroyermen on board the DE GRISWOLD could sigh with some relief—at least, they were not there for eternity. And back at base there would be letters and remembrances from home, and maybe time for a little celebrating. And words of congratulation, such as the visual dispatch flashed to Walley's DE by Commander Flotilla 25 in H.M.N.Z.S. MATAI:

MY OPINION IS THAT YOU MADE A CLEAN KILL YESTERDAY X CONGRATULATIONS ON A GOOD CHRISTMAS PRESENT

Drive on Northern New Britain (DD's to Cape Gloucester)

With Arawe in American hands, MacArthur's strategists urged a landing on the northwest extremity of New Britain, vicinity of Cape Gloucester. The move would put Allied forces inside the Bismarck Archipelago.

Once more the transport and landing operations were shouldered by Barbey's Seventh Amphibious, and the Force was en route to Cape Gloucester on Christmas Day, 1943.

The transports carried United States Marines, veterans from Guadalcanal. In the invasion force were destroyers CONYNGHAM, FLUSSER, MAHAN, SHAW, DRAYTON, BAGLEY, BEALE, LAMSON, MUGFORD, HUTCHINS, BROWNSON, DALY, REID, SMITH, BUSH, AMMEN, BACHE, and MULLANY—DesRon 5 under Captain Jesse H. Carter, and DesRon 24 under Captain K. M. McManes.

Also with the force were American cruisers PHOENIX and NASHVILLE, and Australian cruisers SHROPSHIRE and AUSTRALIA.

Destination was a patch of shore on the northern fringe of Borgen Bay and near-by Cape Gloucester beaches. The Japs knew what was coming, but they did not know precisely when or where, and they were not on hand at "Beaches Yellow" when the invaders moved in on the morning after Christmas.

Smart destroyer work by FLUSSER (Commander J. A. Robbins), MAHAN (Lieutenant Commander E. G. Campbell), and the Japanese destroyer MIKAZUKI (captain unknown) paved the way for the invaders. Entry to the Borgen Bay area required navigation through a maze of uncharted bars and coral reefs—a treacherous snare extending along the coast in the vicinity of Cape Gloucester. Destroyers FLUSSER and MAHAN were selected to "sound out" the channel through these sharktooth barriers and blaze the trail with buoys. Just another commonplace detail to versatile destroyermen.

Accompanied by a pair of minesweepers and two subchasers, the pathfinders probed their way in through the sticky darkness of an overcast night. They were compelled to make a landfall on Cape Gloucester by radar, and to locate the channel by "pinging." The Sound men in this instance were probing for coral barriers. Reefs revealed by deflected sonar beams were carefully noted for avoidance. Thus the channel was discerned by destroyer "ping jockies" in a manner which would have astounded the seamen of an earlier day.

The exploratory job was made doubly ticklish by the time element imposed. FLUSSER and MAHAN had to work with utmost speed, for the transports and LCI's were following them hard astern, and the schedule called for a swift advance and happy landings. Spurred by this urgency, the two DD's steamed toward the ugly reefs.

Here the previously mentioned Jap destroyer entered the proceedings. This DD was lodged on a reef some 9,000 yards northeast of Cape Gloucester, where it had been stranded and abandoned in the early days of the Japanese occupation. Beaten by weather and ravaging sea, the vessel was as forlorn a wreck as the HESPERUS. But the pathfinders found it a lifesaver—a radar landmark as handy as a lighthouse. Making radar contact with the wreck, the two DD's were able to fix their positions with neatness and dispatch. It was their primary and almost only navigational aid in those nasty waters. MIKAZUKI's erstwhile captain might not have appreciated the performance, but no Japanese destroyer ever served more efficiently as a beacon ship.

FLUSSER found the opening in the barrier and led the task unit through the passage. The minesweepers deftly planted the buoys as directed, and the path through the reefs was marked in jig-time. Even before the buoy-planting was completed, the heavy cruisers outside the reefs had begun to fire on the enemy shoreline.

The Allied cruisers also spotted the wrecked destroyer with radar. With the "pip" on the radar screen the cruisers were able to fix their offshore positions for their bombardment detail. And once again the defunct MIKAZUKI performed yeoman service as a beacon ship—perhaps the only ghost destroyer to operate in such fashion with the Seventh Fleet.

At 0730 in the morning of the 26th the Marines hit the beach near Borgen Bay without opposition. But that afternoon the enemy struck back hard. He could not then or later dispossess the landed Marines, but he dealt the invasion force a vicious blow that cost the Seventh Fleet the destroyer BROWNSON.

Loss of U.S.S. Brownson

In company with DD's HUTCHINS, DALY, and BEALE, the BROWNSON (Lieutenant Commander J. B. Maher) had escorted a troop and supply convoy from Cape Cretin, New Guinea, to the Cape Gloucester objective. This escort group was under Captain K. M. McManes, ComDesRon 24, pennant in HUTCHINS.

After reaching the landing area BROWNSON was ordered to conduct an independent patrol outside the reefs. For two hours, nothing to report. Then, at 1419, with the ship about eight miles north of Cape Gloucester, BROWNSON's radar picked up several enemy planes. They were members of a flock endeavoring to break through the Allied air screen for a strike at the invasion shipping. High in the clouds a fierce dogfight was going on—P-38's tangling with "Vals." Searching the sky with glasses, BROWNSON's skipper saw two Jap planes hurtle down through the ceiling like smoking meteors. But nine or ten of the enemy eluded the Allied fighters and roared down to bomb the ships. Senior Destroyer Commander Captain Carter disposed the DD's to meet the attack, and they were maneuvering to do so when two "Val" dive-bombers swooped down on BROWNSON's stern.

BROWNSON's gunners lashed at the planes with 40 mm. and 20 mm. fire. One of the "Vals," scorched by tracer, went floundering off on a tangent. But the other ripped through the AA fusillade. Two bombs struck the BROWNSON near the base of her No. 2 stack. The destroyer staggered under a cloud of smoke and debris, then slumped in the sea mortally injured and afire.

BROWNSON was not the only ship blasted in this lightning attack. SHAW was badly maimed by the explosion of a 500-pound bomb which fell close aboard, and the shrapnel of near misses gave MUGFORD and LAMSON a clawing. The Jap air armada of some 80 planes paid dearly for the strike—at least half of the "bogies" were shot down by intercepting American fighters and AA gunnery—but BROWNSON was a heavy toll in exchange.

Lieutenant Commander Maher remarked BROWNSON's damage as devastating. *"I rushed out of the pilot-house,"* he reported afterward, *"and saw that the entire structure above the main deck, and the deck plating from the center of No. 1 torpedo mount aft to the No. 3 five-inch mount, was gone."* The ship's back was broken. As she buckled amidships, her bow and stern came up like the folding blades of a jackknife.

Stunned bluejackets clung to the fantail and forecastle, and others struggled out of the wreckage amidships as the flood poured in below decks. Through smoke-choked hatches the wounded were dragged to safety. Rafts and floats were flung overside to swimming men.

On the forecastle Coxswain F. P. Mora and eight seamen stood by as a salvage party ready to take over if the ship's stern broke away and the bow section stayed afloat. When the bow assumed a dangerous list Maher shouted from the bridge, ordering the men to jump. With Chief Signalman Uranowich and Chief Yeoman Andrews at his side, the destroyer captain remained on the bridge until a sickening lurch underfoot gave the final warning.

At 1450 Lieutenant Commander Maher gave the order to abandon. Nine minutes later the destroyer sank. Some of her depth charges exploded as she went down. The detonations churned the water with blasts that killed two of the swimmers who were struggling to reach the lifeboats.

Destroyers DALY and LAMSON moved in to rescue survivors. They found the sea a bloodstained welter where BROWNSON had gone under. Huddled on floats and clinging to rafts were the remnants of the destroyer's crew—those lucky enough to live through a blasting which exacted a final-count death toll of some 108 lives. Among the survivors there were men blinded, maimed, sick; men suffering from burns and shock.

One of the survivors was the ship's doctor, Lieutenant C. F. Chandler, MC-V(G), U.S.N.R. Among the last to leave the BROWNSON, Chandler was picked up by the destroyer DALY. He had been struck by flying shrapnel which lacerated his right forearm—a searing wound that left him partially incapacitated.

"You've got to take it easy," someone told him.

But the lieutenant who wore a doctor's insignia refused to take it easy. In spite of his crippled arm he worked throughout that afternoon and late into the night, tending the emergency cases on board DALY.

Chandler's performance was indicative of the fine practitioner skilled in the arts of medicine and surgery and dedicated to the service of his fellow man in the hour of need. Such devotion to duty was, and is, typical of the profession many concede to be the finest in the world. For the Chandlers who saw action in the Navy during World War II the citation valued even above any medal or ribbon was the one voiced by the ship's company itself.

"He was a good Doc."

Buchanan Kills RO-37

GO TO THE ASSISTANCE OF USS CACHE TORPEDOED LAT 12-08 S LONG 164-33E

That, in substance, was the message flashed to the destroyer BUCHANAN as she was proceeding from Purvis Bay to Espiritu Santo in the morning of January 22, 1944. Her skipper, Commander F. B. T. Myhre, immediately called for top speed, and the destroyer headed for the disaster scene with her engines humming. The CACHE had been ambushed by a submarine not far from San Cristobal Island.

At 2005, when BUCHANAN was about 25 miles from the torpedoed ship's reported position, the destroyer's SG radar registered a "pip" at 12,750 yards. The shimmering indication was bright and sharp, and there was good reason to believe it was "enemy."

Commander Myhre sent the DD's gunners scrambling to their mounts as BUCHANAN sprinted on through the moonless and murky tropic dark. When the range closed to 2,000 yards Myhre determined to identify the unknown craft, which might conceivably be friendly. Although such illumination was always risky, the identification was imperative, for a hunter-killer vessel was known to be in the vicinity, and this was a shipping lane. So he ordered the searchlight crew to open up with a 36-incher.

The white light swept across the seascape and caught the target, bull's-eye. A conning tower nestling down into the sea. Astern of this Japanese silhouette there was the froth of churned water and a luminous, curving wake, broad as an avenue. Before the destroyermen could open fire the target had sunk from view; the submarine was burrowing deep.

Then, at 1,250 yards, BUCHANAN's sonar instruments gained contact. Myhre jockeyed the destroyer into attack position and directed the launching of a depth-charge pattern. The first charge splashed into the sea exactly 30 minutes after the radar contact that instigated the search. Two hours later the destroyer circled in to commence a final attack. The depth charges walloped the water at 2241, and after this booming turmoil subsided BUCHANAN's sonarmen were unable to locate the sub.

Combing the area, the BUCHANAN discovered a great spread of floating oil. Through the humid darkness drifted a pungent smell that reminded the destroyermen of kerosene. Sunrise confirmed this evidence of a submarine's liquidation by revealing a seascape strewn with kindling, chunks of cork, and nondescript debris. BUCHANAN's oarsmen boated across the water to obtain samples of this flotsam—specimens that were eventually identified as samples of an RO-boat.

The Imperial Japanese Navy had lost another submarine. Post-war inquest divulged the "name and serial number" of BUCHANAN's victim. Myhre and his men had accounted for the RO-37. Incidentally,

When destroyers of Squadron 45 shelled the Shortland Islands, they came under the fire of a Japanese shore battery of 3-inch guns. Bennett was their target at ranges of 6,000 to 1,900 yards, and Halford also came under heavy fire. But the Jap Navy had vacated those waters, leaving behind many a garrison that soon began devoting itself to agriculture rather than warfare.

To prepare the way for the leapfrog tactics of Allied forces leaping up the island chains toward the Philippines, U.S. destroyers and cruisers blasted Japanese shore bases heavily, while U.S. carrier planes hammered enemy airfields far inland. This picture is a gun-flashlight photo of a night bombardment of Buka, off Green Island, last stepping stone toward the Bismarcks.

This Hubuki-class destroyer is a sister ship of Yugiri, which was sunk, and Amagiri, which was routed, in the battle of Cape St. George. These 2,000-ton cans had a top speed of 34 knots.

Arleigh Burke's famous flagship, Charles Ausburne, takes on fuel from the cruiser Columbus. In her Burke led his squadron in the "almost perfect surface action" of the Southwest Pacific.

Under "31 knot" Burke, the "Little Beavers" sank three Jap cans off Cape St. George. Burke's five busy destroyers were reported by the enemy as cruiser and destroyer divisions plus PT-boats.

CACHE got away from Davy Jones, so the submarine's score was double zero.

Green Islands Raiders

Off the northwest tip of Bougainville lies Buka, and 37 miles northwest of Buka lies the atoll cluster of Green Islands, the last Solomons steppingstone on the road to the Bismarck Archipelago. Infested by the Jap invader when Tojo and Yamamoto were on the march as conquerors, these islands were on the agenda for Allied counter-invasion early in 1944. This miniature offensive, one of the last of the Upper Solomons campaign, was designed to put Halsey's forces on the doorstep of Kavieng and Rabaul. United States destroyers, assisted by a spotting plane, spearheaded the thrust.

To keep the Japs in hot water, destroyers ANTHONY (Commander B. VanMater), flagship of Commander E. B. Taylor, ComDesDiv 90, and PRINGLE (Commander G. DeMetropolis) conducted an offensive sweep in Bougainville Strait between Choiseul Bay and the Shortlands on the night of January 20-21. Sweeping, they broomed up a flotilla of Jap barges, shot them to pieces, and brushed the clutter into Davy Jones' dustbin. Another Solomons house-cleaning job.

Sizable Jap garrisons still occupied northern Bougainville and outlying islets. These marooned armies were to be by-passed, but, in passing, Halsey's Third Fleet units indulged in target practice. On the night of January 8, 1944, Task Force 38 shot up targets in the Faisi-Shortland area. Destroyers with the force, which was commanded by Rear Admiral W. L. Ainsworth, were BUCHANAN (Commander Myhre), FARENHOLT (Commander A. G. Beckman), flying the pennant of Captain Rodger W. Simpson, ComDesRon 12, LANSDOWNE (Commander F. J. Foley), flagship of Commander F. H. Ball, ComDesDiv 24, LARDNER (Lieutenant Commander O. C. Schatz, Jr.), and WOODWORTH (Lieutenant Commander C. R. Stephen).

To Green Islands then, went the "Green Raider Detachment" to probe the defenses. Composed of New Zealanders and American Navy men, the detachment was carried to the objective by Task Group 31.8 (Captain Ralph Earle, Jr.). The group included destroyer transports TALBOT, WATERS, and DICKERSON, under escort of destroyers FULLAM, BENNETT, GUEST, and HUDSON. They were off the island early in the morning of January 31.

Covered by darkness, the ships closed the jungle-cloaked beach, and the "Anzacs" and Navy specialists went ashore to reconnoiter. Pushing inland, one reconnaissance party was ambushed. A spatter of shots —four men slain by sniper fire—then silence.

Offshore the warships waited. The sun blazed on the horizon and the island's lagoons began to steam. Evening, and still no sign of shore batteries or defending aircraft. Where was the enemy? Had he abandoned?

The Jap garrison was on the other side of the island. But the Imperial Navy was preparing an ambush—or, at least, one unit of that navy was creeping in for a strike at Captain Earle's task group. Only the strike was frustrated by destroyers GUEST and HUDSON.

Guest and Hudson Down I-171

NO ENEMY ACTIVITY.

That was the report from Task Group 31.8 on January 31, 1944. Such reports were subject to change without notice.

On February 1, 1944, this group was engaged in evacuating the Green Islands raiders, when, at 0411 of that morning, FULLAM, Captain Earle's flagship, picked up a radar "pip" that revealed the presence of a strange vessel in the waters off the Green Islands. Target range: 10,500 yards.

Task Group Commander Earle ordered GUEST (Lieutenant Commander E. K. McLaren) and HUDSON (Lieutenant Commander R. R. Pratt) to peel off and investigate. The two DD's closed in on the stranger. The destroyers held their fire, however, for American PT-boats were known to be operating in the vicinity. As the range closed, GUEST's destroyermen made a flash sweep with a searchlight. Nothing in view. Then, at 3,500 yards, the target glimmered out on the radar scope. A diving submarine!

A few minutes later both HUDSON and GUEST picked up the sub's trail with their sound gear. Tracking swiftly, GUEST was first to reach attack position. Lieutenant Commander McLaren directed two depth-charge runs. Over the target sailed the destroyer, dumping lethal quantities of TNT. Four minutes after the last charge was dropped, the destroyermen heard two muffled, tumultuous explosions that blended in a prolonged, rolling roar. Not the basso boom of depth charges, but the tympanic din of a bursting pressure hull, collapsing framework, and tearing steel.

Then HUDSON's destroyermen heard a deep-sea explosion in the near-by depths, and Lieutenant Commander Pratt ordered a depth-charge salvo. Evidently the two charges dropped by HUDSON gave the submarine the *coup de grace*. As of that date another I-boat was erased from the roster of the Imperial Navy.

Japanese records verified the kill. The submarine

downed by destroyers GUEST and HUDSON off the Green Islands on February 1, 1944, was the I-171.

Rabaul Knockout

Allied strategy had called for the elimination of Rabaul. But as the Central Pacific offensive was rolling westward in high gear, Allied leaders decided to neutralize Rabaul by by-passing—a move in space which would save time and also conserve lives, ships, aircraft, and ammunition. Surrounded, the supply lines cut, the Japanese Rabaul base would "die on the vine."

Already the Bismarck Gibraltar was considerably withered, supplied only in driblets by submarines *via* Kavieng. And Kavieng was not doing so well as a feeder base. One reason was the Christmas Day blasting delivered by a carrier task group led by Rear Admiral F. C. Sherman. The group included carriers BUNKER HILL and MONTEREY under escort of destroyers BRADFORD, BROWN, COWELL, BELL, CHARRETTE, and CONNER. And on January 4, 1944, Sherman's task group repeated the operation. In the wrecked Kavieng harbor they found little to bomb. The place was practically deserted by shipping.

Halsey now jabbed a thumbtack into Rabaul and ordered its bombardment by surface forces. The shelling was delivered by Destroyer Squadron 12 (Captain R. W. Simpson) on the night of February 17-18. A night sullenly overcast, visibility obscured by cloudbursts. Nothing to spoil destroyer gunnery, however.

The DD's of DesRon 12—FARENHOLT, BUCHANAN, LANSDOWNE, LARDNER, and WOODWORTH—staged a shooting-gallery foray. Squadron Commander Simpson led the destroyers past the target in column formation, and the main batteries hurled a blizzard of shells into the enemy harbor. Almost 4,000 five-inch projectiles blasted the citadel. Shipping in Keravia Bay was treated to a blasting by fifteen torpedoes. Blindly shooting back, the shore batteries failed to score a hit on the fast-moving destroyers. In turn, the destroyer gunners hammered Rabaul as though it were an anvil. When General Tojo (no less) and Admirals Nagano and Shimada inspected the Bismarck base on February 22, they found it a junkyard.

Kavieng, too, was shelled with impunity. The final shooting-up was done by "31-Knot" Burke and his "Little Beavers." Attacking at sunrise on February 18, destroyers AUSBURNE, DYSON, STANLY, CONVERSE, and SPENCE subjected the harbor to an hour's blasting that must have loosened its hold on the map. The "Beavers" were not satisfied until 6,681 shells were lobbed into the anchorage and shore installations. Two enemy planes tried to counterattack. Without success.

Even then the "Beavers" were not content. After steaming to Purvis Bay to refuel and replenish the ammunition supply, they were off on an offensive sweep of the enemy's shipping lanes between Kavieng and Truk. As no enemy ships were encountered, they returned to Kavieng to resume the bombardment.

Off the northwest coast of New Ireland the indefatigable "Beavers" shot up a Jap auxiliary and a small minelayer-destroyer. AUSBURNE captured 73 prisoners, most of them aviation personnel—a good catch for Intelligence to catechize.

"Not all of the Japs wanted to be taken prisoner," Burke reported later. *"Many of them cut their throats in the water. Some deliberately bashed their heads against wreckage. Others tried to drown themselves."* Oddly enough, a number who preferred life to *hari-kiri* were presently offering to pass ammunition when AUSBURNE, DYSON, and STANLY moved in on the night of February 22-23 to bombard Duke of York Island off New Ireland.

It may be seen that Japanese morale in the Bismarcks had crumbled. The very islands were crumbling when the "Beavers" ranged along the New Ireland coast to blast the enemy with a concluding barrage. With their backs to a falling wall, a few of the Japs at Kavieng manned desperate guns. BUCHANAN and FARENHOLT were hit by shells, and several DD's were scratched by near misses. But the fight was knocked out of Kavieng.

And Rabaul was at the end of a frayed rope. While the "Beavers" were gnawing the foundations out from under Kavieng, two American destroyer divisions were threshing the wreckage at Rabaul. The final shellings were delivered by Destroyer Squadron 45 (Captain Ralph Earle, Jr.)—destroyers FULLAM, BENNETT, GUEST, HALFORD, HUDSON, ANTHONY, BRAINE, TERRY, and WADSWORTH; and Destroyer Squadron 22 (Captain W. F. Petersen)—destroyers WALLER, PHILIP, RENSHAW, SAUFLEY, CONWAY, EATON, SIGOURNEY, and PRINGLE. When the shooting was over, Rabaul was not only neutralized, it was virtually pulverized.

PART IV

COMING OF THE HUNTER-KILLERS

Howl, Ye ships of Tarshish
For your strength is laid waste.
ISAIAH XXIII.i

CHAPTER 21

HOLDING THE TRANS-ATLANTIC LINE

(JANUARY-APRIL 1943)

U-Boat Counter Offensive

New Year's 1943—and to most Americans the eastward horizon seemed promisingly bright. The U.S. Army was driving across Algeria. The U.S. Navy was operating in the Mediterranean. Rommel's Afrika Corps was certainly beaten. The Russians were standing like a rock at Stalingrad. Everywhere the Axis was on the defensive—everywhere with the exception of the Atlantic.

The American public was not generally aware of this exception, and an optimistic impression prevailed that the U-boats were on the run and the anti-submarine war was practically won. Even in naval circles some of the more hopeful were encouraged to think that the U-boat menace was nearly liquidated.

But withdrawing from the Western Atlantic, the U-boat Force was merely gathering muscle for offensive blows at Allied shipping in mid-ocean. Following the flare-up of "Operation Torch," the Nazi wolfpacks struck Allied convoys some of the hardest smashes of the war—blows well timed to hit when and where they could do the most harm.

The U-boats failed to stab their torpedoes into troop transports running to North Africa. But the hard-working, relatively slow cargo transports were in for some mauling, particularly on the North Atlantic run.

In the cold oceanic reaches between "Westomp" and "Eastomp," the Battle of the Atlantic went on full blast, and the Navy was compelled to do its best with the A/S forces available. CinCLant and ComDesLant counted destroyers as the desperately needy count pennies, but there weren't enough to go around. They were needed for Central Atlantic convoys running to North Africa. They were needed in the Mediterranean. They were needed for coastal defense. They were needed for training duty. And in the winter of 1942-43 the wolf was at the Navy's North Atlantic door—a fact all too evident in Allied and neutral shipping losses due to U-boat action in the Atlantic and Arctic Areas during the winter of 1942-43. After it was over, the Navy Department's Fleet Operations Statistical Section compiled a depressing table.

MONTH	NUMBER OF SHIPS SUNK	GROSS TONS
November 1942	106	636,907
December 1942	54	287,730
January 1943	29	181,767
February 1943	50	312,004
March 1943	95	567,301
TOTAL	334	1,985,709

Within five months' time, almost 2,000,000 tons of shipping were torpedoed and sunk, most of it by wolfpack submarines operating in North Atlantic Convoy Areas. Balanced against the loss of 334 torpedoed ships, Nazi sub losses in the Atlantic for that period totaled less than 50, from all causes. If the wolfpacks were not squelched in the near future, Hitler would win the Battle of the Atlantic.

But the wolfpacks *could* be squelched—that was the conclusion drawn by Captain P. R. Heineman, U.S. Navy. Former captain of the destroyer MOFFETT, and veteran escort commander, Captain Heineman was thoroughly acquainted with anti-submarine warfare. In February 1943, when Ocean Escort Unit A-3 took the field, Heineman was in command. Fighting a four-day North Atlantic U-boat battle, Escort Unit A-3 gave a demonstration of teamwork that served as a guide for subsequent A/S operations. "Heineman's Harriers" pioneered the way for the A/S task groups of the future.

Heineman's Harriers

When Ocean Escort Unit A-3 formed up for convoy duty, one of the stormiest winters in history was lashing the North Atlantic into a state of chronic fury. Throughout January, gales and blizzards had alternately buffeted and blinded the ships at sea. Veteran navigators could not recall such weather. Sunless days when a sextant was useless. Nights that seemed to be chopped from black ice. And a perpetual tumult of hell and high water. In this heaving wilderness of wind and froth, merchantmen were rolling their beam ends under—and sometimes failing to regain even keel. Some 166 Allied merchantmen were lost through accident and wreck that winter.

But the cargoes had to reach England; the trans-Atlantic convoys had to go across. Then the ships had to return to the States for another load—and getting back was as perilous as going over.

Appointed guardian of west-bound Convoy ON-166 (United Kingdom to Halifax), Captain Heineman's Ocean Escort Unit A-3 joined the convoy train at "Eastomp" around noon on February 12, 1943. The convoy numbered 63 merchant ships. Ocean Escort Unit A-3 was eventually composed of eight naval vessels.

The set-up—one escort for eight merchantmen—would have provided better-than-average numerical coverage for that period of the war, had the ships been available in a body. But the eight escorts were not simultaneously on hand with the convoy. Heineman's force contained but one destroyer, and this DD did not join the escort group until the 22nd. Two United States Coast Guard cutters were the only American ships in the little task group. One British and four Canadian corvettes constituted the remainder of the escort force.

"Heineman's Harriers," then, lined up as follows:

The 1540-ton Polish destroyer Burza *(which did not join the group until February 22).*

U.S.C.G.C. Spencer *Comdr. H. S. Berdine, U.S.C.G.*
U.S.C.G.C. Campbell
Comdr. J. A. Hirschfield, U.S.C.G.
H.M.S. Dianthus H.M.C.S. Rosthern
H.M.C.S. Chilliwack H.M.C.S. Trillium
H.M.C.S Dauphin

For the first three days the convoy bucked into a nor'wester which slowed the advance to an average 4-knot pace. However, the escorts managed to fuel from three tankers in spite of a 50-knot wind, and there were only two stragglers during the first week. Then, on February 18, "Huff-Duff" bearings indicated that submarines were in the offing. "Heineman's Harriers" tightened their belts, adjusted their life-jackets, and prepared for combat.

By midnight of the 20th all hands knew that zero hour had arrived.

Spencer Kills U-225

Shortly after midnight, radar contact was reported. Spencer, in the convoy's van, ran forward to investigate. At 0038, the Coast Guard cutter's lookout sighted a conning tower, range 5,000 yards. At 0045, the submarine dived. A few moments later, Sound reported contact at 1,500 yards. Then contact evaporated at 200 yards. The U-boat was within 600 feet of the Coast Guard cutter, and Spencer was forced to strike at a vanished target. Blind-man's-buff in the dark!

Spencer's skipper, Commander Berdine, reacted immediately. Just three seconds after contact was lost, he ordered a depth-charge attack. Firing on "recorder time," the Coast Guard cutter dropped a 9-charge pattern that blew up tons of water in her wake.

After the thunder of this barrage faded out, Sound was unable to regain contact. A box search was promptly conducted, but contact remained unobtainable. Estimating the submarine's probable position, Berdine ordered the dropping of two 600-pound charges, set for 100-foot depth. The explosions blasted up a mound of water. The foam-topped mound collapsed. After a few minutes' futile probing with detection gear, Spencer steamed off to rejoin the convoy.

Berdine and his Coast Guard crew were not certain of a kill. Subsequently they learned they had finished off U-225.

Convoy Under Fire

Spencer's fray with U-225 was only a curtain raiser. While Berdine and his Coast Guardsmen were scuffling with the undersea foe, the convoy was stalked by other invisible assailants. "Huff-Duff" gave the escorts several fixes, and U.S. Coast Guard cutter Campbell made two or three attacks after sound contact.

Campbell was no novice at this deadly game of hide and seek. Early in the war she had steamed into dangerous waters off Greenland, and in November 1941 she had served as ocean escort with Convoy HX-159. Her skipper, Commander Hirschfield, was an experienced Coast Guardsman. Aboard Campbell was an all-Negro 20 mm. gun crew that had won a reputation for marksmanship and was all-out All-American. A tough little craft, the CAMPBELL.

Late in the afternoon of February 21 SPENCER and DIANTHUS ran a 10-mile race to team up with an R.A.F. Liberator that was attacking a trio of submarines off the convoy's starboard quarter. Assailed by the two escort vessels and the plane, the U-boats were driven down. And while this scrimmage was taking place, the corvette ROSTHERN made radar contact with two surfaced U-boats. ROSTHERN tried to run them down, but the U-boats made off at top speed and escaped.

But the worst was yet to come, for Convoy ON-166 had now voyaged beyond the range of air cover by the land-based Liberators.

And the U-boats were waiting. Ghostly and vengeful, they closed in around the convoy, cloaked spectres creeping through the blackout. The opening assault came at 2135, perhaps seven Nazi submarines ganging up on the convoy's van. At that hour on the evening of February 21, only four escorts were near at hand. The Polish destroyer BURZA had not yet joined Heineman's team. SPENCER was eight miles on the starboard quarter, rejoining. CAMPBELL was eight miles astern, rejoining. And DIANTHUS was 10 miles astern, rejoining. The four corvettes in the convoy's vicinity had a battle on their hands.

Outnumbered though they were, the Canadian corvettes dispersed the attacking U-boats. Only one of the wolves managed to get its fangs into prey. This U-boat fired a spread of torpedoes at the lead ship in the convoy's second column, the S.S. EMPIRE TRADER. The warheads struck the target; the merchantman staggered to a halt, disabled.

Early the following morning came another torpedo attack. The escorts bunched forces to fight off the wolfpack, but a second freighter was stricken. At 0151 this vessel was torpedoed in the stern by a U-boat which penetrated the screen. Carrying out a night search, the escorts illuminated the seascape with starshells, but the U-boat escaped detection. CAMPBELL closed the sinking ship, and picked up all survivors. The battle's hide-and-seek went relentlessly on. About 0530, two submarines were sighted dogging the convoy's stern, and DIANTHUS peeled off to drive away this pair with hedgehog salvos.

By that hour "Heineman's Harriers" were taut-nerved and red-eyed from lack of sleep. It had been necessary to detach the corvette DAUPHIN and send her to escort the disabled EMPIRE TRADER back to British waters—a futile effort, for the TRADER was so badly damaged that the Admiralty ordered her abandoned and sunk before she made port. To add to Heineman's worries the weather was too rough for fuelling at sea, and the corvette H.M.S. DIANTHUS reported her fuel tanks running low. And a three-day run through open seas without air cover remained to be logged.

But the day of February 22 brought some relief. Over the horizon came O.R.P. BURZA, running to join the escort group. Wind and seas shifted a little, and the convoy was able to make 9 knots. And the U-boats, following the familiar *Rudeltaktic,* kept their distance that day.

The respite, however, was the lull before the storm. BURZA (the name means "Squall") joined up that afternoon, and the "Harriers" were cheered by the destroyer's arrival. But darkness promised more U-boats, and the Coast Guard and corvettemen tightened their belts for another night of it.

They did not have long to wait. About an hour and a half after sundown the attack exploded.

Campbell and O.R.P. Burza Kill U-606

All day U-606 had been trailing the convoy like a shark trailing a lonely group of dories. By nightfall she was closing in for the strike. Nightfall—the hour between sundown and moonrise when the dusk had gone and the seas were all but invisible. Time: around 2000. Closing on the convoy's port flank, U-606 planed to the surface and ran in for the strike.

Accounts vary as to the details of the action that followed. The submarine pumped torpedoes into three ships on the convoy's flank. The explosions flared in the night, and merchant seamen died in fiery engine-rooms and drowned in a muddle of capsized lifeboats and tangled lines. "Heineman's Harriers" immediately counterattacked. Apparently the corvette H.M.C.S. CHILLIWACK sighted the retiring U-boat and went after it with depth charges. CHILLIWACK lost contact, and at that juncture, according to some reports, BURZA stepped in with a depth-charge attack. Conflicting reports say that she did not arrive on the scene until the battle was over and the U-boat was battered into submission. At any rate the battering was done by the U.S. Coast Guard cutter CAMPBELL.

According to CAMPBELL's War Diary and Commander Hirschfield's action report, the Coast Guard cutter's radar screen picked up the enemy "pip" at 2016, range 4,600 yards. Not long after contact, the U-boat silhouette was sighted off the Coast Guardman's starboard bow.

Ordering right full rudder and 18 knots on the line, Hirschfield set a collision course to ram the enemy. At about 200 yards, the CAMPBELL gunners manning the forward 3-incher opened fire.

After it was over some of the Nazi submariners

stated they had come to the surface because of battle damage received from depth charges a few minutes before CAMPBELL's attack. Whether previously damaged or no, the submarine was due for a bashing from CAMPBELL. Guns blazing, the cutter loomed over the U-boat's flank. Nazi gunners fell riddled on the cigarette deck; the U-boat skipper on the bridge was killed; the conning tower was drilled. All that in a flash of time, and then *crash!* Under the impact of collision, the submarine rolled and floundered, mortally hurt.

CAMPBELL herself was damaged by the smash. At the moment before collision, the U-boat veered, and the submarine's diving planes knifed into the cutter's side, slashing a deep gash in CAMPBELL's hull. Water spurted through the incision, flooding the engine-room. At 2025 the engines were stopped, and the engineers scrambled topside.

On deck, CAMPBELL's gunners were pouring a withering fire at the wallowing U-boat, and Hirschfield had ordered two 600-pound ashcans rolled from the racks. At 2028, he gave the "cease-fire" order—the sub was lying helpless, her conning tower knocked all acockbill. Two minutes later, all of CAMPBELL's electrical power went out, short-circuited in the flooded engine-room.

About this time the submariners decided to abandon. CAMPBELL saw the flutter of water-lights off to starboard, but the cutter was too busy with her own trouble to go to the assistance of the U-boat crew. Once the damage was under control, however, Hirschfield sent a boarding party to inspect the disabled submarine and pick up survivors.

High seas prevented the rescue of those still in the submarine. U-606 was slowly foundering, settling sluggishly as swooping waves slopped over her conning tower and poured successive Niagaras down into her control room.

At 2220 (according to CAMPBELL's report) the destroyer BURZA arrived to screen the damaged cutter. At 2255 CAMPBELL's small boat returned with five of the U-606 survivors. Meantime BURZA lowered a boat and picked up some half dozen shivering Germans. Some time around midnight the punished U-boat sank with the remainder of her Nazi crew.

The Long Voyage Home

The following morning, CAMPBELL transferred some of her crew and all of her German prisoners to BURZA. H.M.C.S. DAUPHIN had rejoined the group, and this hard-working corvette relieved BURZA of the duty of screening crippled CAMPBELL. Hirschfield and a skeleton crew kept their cutter going, and on February 26 the tug TENACITY showed up out of the West and took CAMPBELL in tow. On March 3, the battle-weary Coast Guardsmen reached St. Johns, Newfoundland.

CAMPBELL's disablement left "Heineman's Harriers" seriously shorthanded, and the abbreviated escort group had a lot of fighting on its hands after the sinking of U-606. Early in the morning of February 23 the wolfpack struck again. Corvettes ROSTHERN and TRILLIUM beat off that attack, and the U-boats failed to score.

The seas roughened that day, slowing the convoy again, and prevented fuelling operations. H.M.S. DIANTHUS reported that her tanks were nearing the empty point, and Heineman was compelled to order the corvette to proceed ahead on her own, lest she run out of oil while maneuvering with the convoy and become an encumbrance. Shortly before midnight of the 23rd the British corvette pulled away. As it was, she had to make a tight squeeze to reach St. Johns. *"We emptied 120 gallons of Admiralty Compound into Number 6 tank,"* the corvette's captain reported later. *"Also all gunnery oil, paint mixing oil, and two drums of special mineral oil. This increased fuel remaining by approximately half a ton, and eventually enabled me to get in."*

Coming in the wake of CAMPBELL's disablement, the departure of the British corvette left Heineman's group up against it. And the U-boats struck again in the dark before dawn of February 24. Torpedoes smashed into another merchantman, and the convoy suffered its sixth ship-loss.

Still another ship was torpedoed in the darkness of the following morning when the U-boats made their sixth attack on the convoy. And the U.S. Coast Guard cutter SPENCER three times narrowly missed being torpedoed.

"Heineman's Harriers" were a haggard company when Convoy ON-166 finally gained the shelter of air cover and home water. For five days running, the wolfpack battle had been touch and go. The iron-nerved escort group had fought off six attacks and downed two U-boats. And only seven ships of the slow convoy had been torpedoed and sunk. But seven lost were seven too many, and the one-sided battle had worn Ocean Escort Unit A-3 down to the nub.

Rear Admiral R. M. Brainard, Commander Task Force 24, commented on the ordeal:

> *This convoy was shadowed and attacked by one of the largest concentrations of submarines yet encountered. Unfortunately during the period of the attacks the convoy was out of range of effective air cover.*

And Captain Heineman summarized the experience

of Ocean Escort Unit A-3 in a report which contained a number of pertinent suggestions and recommendations.

(a) Tremendous value of HF/DF in determining strength and movements of U-boats near convoy.

(b) Need for an escort unit HF/DF officer, such as is carried in British groups.

(c) Great value of long-range aircraft as demonstrated by excellent air coverage given to convoy as far out as 1,000 miles from the British Isles by planes of the 4-engine type, such as are lacking in the Western Atlantic.

(d) Urgent need for air coverage during forenoons, especially after U-boats have attacked the night before and have surfaced to report results; also at dusk to spot shadowers and attack groups.

(e) Lack of sufficient escorts to properly screen a large convoy. This was further aggravated by casualties and damage to escorts, searches for U-boats, and screening and rescue work.

(f) Great handicap in escort operations due to lack of high-speed escorts.

(g) Once shadowed and attacked, routine evasion by convoy failed to shake off shadowers or frustrate attacks, and it was necessary to make radical course changes of about 80° from the base course in order to evade with any success.

(h) At least three of the escorts performed in a very outstanding manner: the SPENCER, ROSTHERN, *and* TRILLIUM, *who by their aggressive actions prevented at least five additional attacks on convoy and did yeoman duty in screening and rescue work, equipping tankers for fueling, etc.*

Captain Heineman concluded with a recommendation that convoys be accompanied by tankers properly equipped for fuelling escorts at sea—a rarity at that period of the war.

So the fight put up by Ocean Escort Unit A-3 was not without its lessons. But "Heineman's Harriers" were not to ship their oars and rest on their laurels. Ocean Escort Unit A-3 had hardly entered the embrace of Argentia Harbor when it was ordered out for a trans-Atlantic crossing with an eastbound convoy.

The Ordeal of SC-121

The convoy "Heineman's Harriers" were to escort was a ship-train from the Western Atlantic to the British Isles—Convoy SC-121.

Ocean Escort A-3 had shrunk. It was now composed of the Coast Guard cutter SPENCER (Commander H. S. Berdine, U.S.C.G.), the destroyer GREER (Lieutenant Commander T. H. Copeman), H.M.S. DIANTHUS, H.M.C.S. ROSTHERN, H.M.C.S. TRILLIUM, and H.M.C.S. DAUPHIN. To the veterans of the ON-166 crossing it must have seemed as if they had survived the frying pan only to go into the fire.

From the Argentia take-off, the tired "Harriers" had tough going. Foul weather kicked the Atlantic into a foaming tantrum. The ships bucked into high seas, and from March 4 to March 12 they struggled against continuous westerly and southwesterly gales.

There were 56 ships in the convoy, in a formation of 14 columns, which gave the convoy a front about seven miles across. The boisterous seas opened gaps in the formation, and some of the merchant captains were unable to close up. At the time Escort Unit A-3 took over, there were already three stragglers far astern. By the 12th of March there were 16 straggling vessels.

Captain Heineman urged the convoy commodore to shorten the convoy's front by reducing the formation from 14 to 11 columns. Unfortunately the British commodore, while agreeing with the suggestion, wished to wait for improved weather. The ships were all over the seascape when the U-boats made their first attack. Thereafter the voyage was a free-for-all, much like the westward passage of ON-166.

Between midnight March 6 and midnight March 10 the running wolfpack battle went on. Wary of radar, the U-boats attacked from periscope depth—or so it appeared from lack of radar contacts. On several occasions the escorts were decoyed away from the convoy by deceptive "Huff-Duff" transmissions, and once the Germans cut in on the TBS to lure the escorts offside with a voice message in English.

For Escort Unit A-3 the voyage became a nightmare—detection apparatus went dead; DAUPHIN's engines gave out. Six ships were torpedoed and sunk, and another was severely damaged. Furious seas impeded rescue work, and after one ugly sinking, steep waves prevented the destroyer GREER from picking up survivors. Bitterly the destroyermen had to watch the laden rafts and lifeboats drift away in the blowing spume—human flotsam lost in the Atlantic wilderness.

Heineman's request for a tighter convoy formation was not acted upon until five days after it was made. The change came too late to save the British commodore, who lost his life when his own ship was sunk. Another ship that went down was the escort oiler.

That the overworked escorts did manage to hold down ship losses to six was something of a miracle. Perhaps "phenomenon" is a better term for an effort resulting from phenomenal grit, endurance, fighting spirit, and seamanship.

Nazi 750-ton submarine U-175 sunk by U.S.C.G.C. Spencer on April 17, 1944. After eluding wolf-packs for two days while steaming south of Iceland, Convoy HX-223 seemed past the worst danger when one ship was sunk. Later that morning Spencer made contact and began stalking her prey. Finally a mousetrap barrage did the trick. Details of action are shown on the following page.

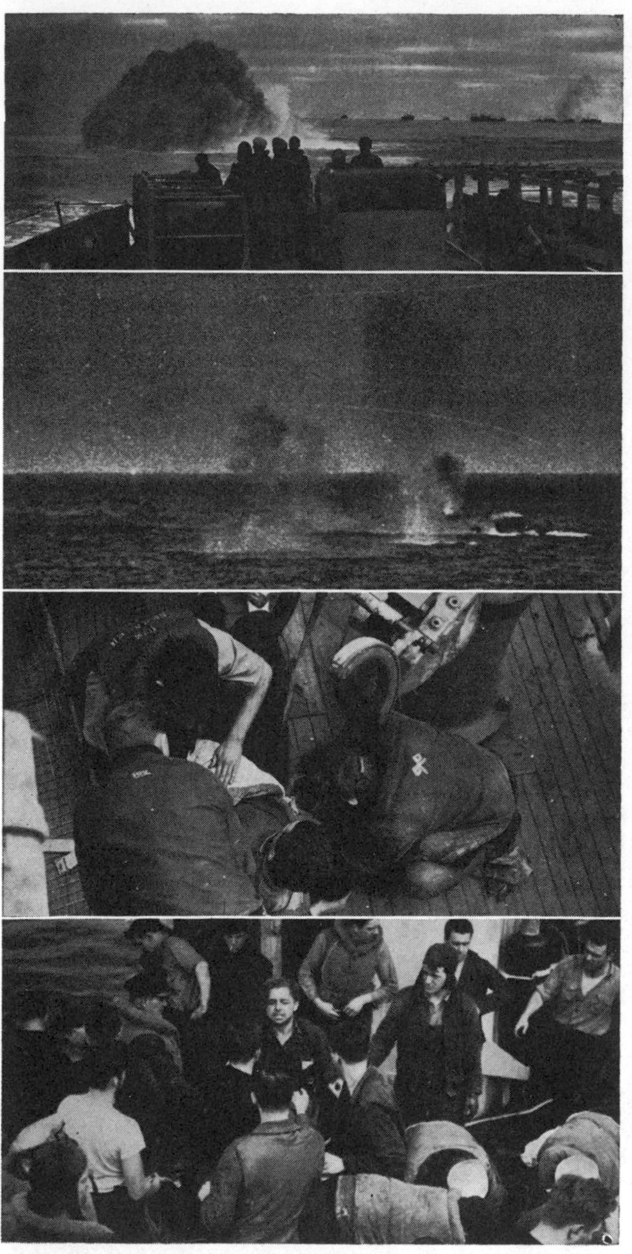

(From top to bottom) 1. Spencer blows U-175 to surface with depth charges. 2. Spencer shelling U-boat. 3. Coast Guardsman wounded by sub's gun. 4. Nazi prisoners of war on board Spencer.

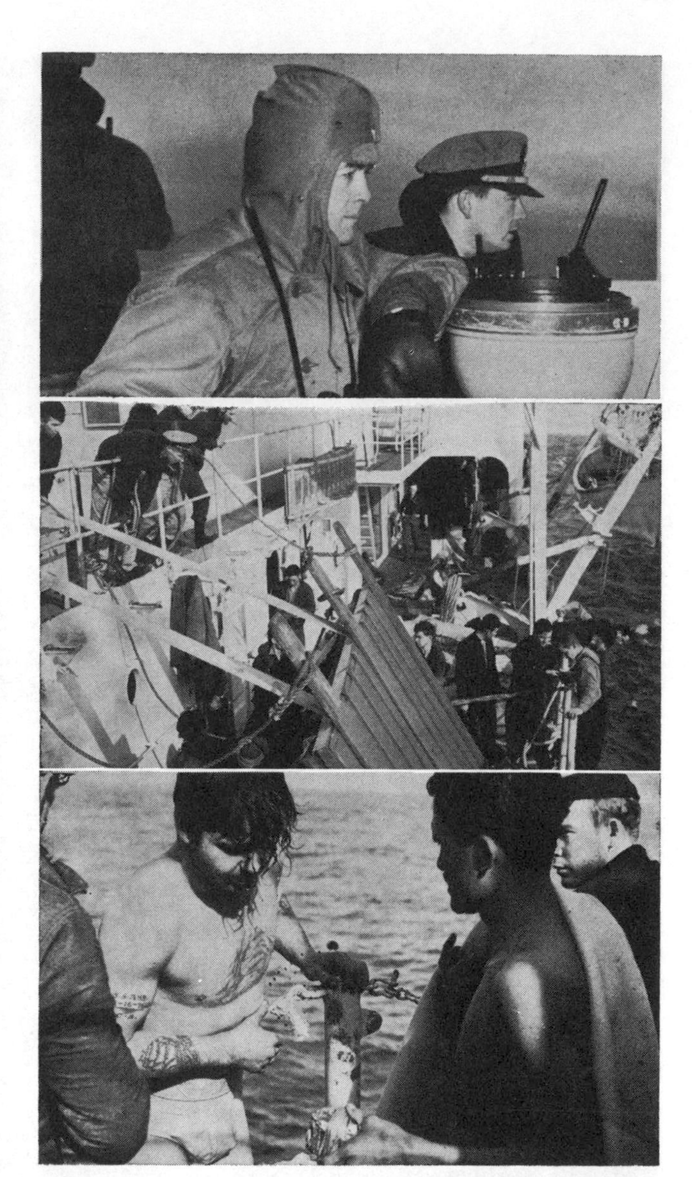

Campbell's skipper, leaning on pelorus, was wounded while routing six U-boats in one day. Ramming a sub damaged the cutter, but a coffer dam and over-the-side repair party kept her afloat.

Captain Paul R. Heineman of "Heineman's Harriers" discusses U-175 action with Commander Harold S. Berdine, skipper of the cutter Spencer. The Coast Guardsmen had also killed the U-225.

Survivors of torpedoed transport Mallory are picked up by the Bibb. Enroute to Iceland with hundreds of servicemen, the Mallory sank with the loss of 300 soldiers, sailors, and Marines.

After it was over Captain Heineman put on record a few more pertinent observations and recommendations:

(a) Inconsistency of HF/DF intelligence which was used to anticipate the direction from which attacks would be made, with the actual direction from which U-boats did appear to make attacks. This leads to the conclusion that U-boats may be using decoys to transmit from directions other than where S/M do attack.

(b) Indications that U-boats penetrated the escort screen at periscope depth to make attacks on the convoy. (This had reference to the night attacks which the U-boats apparently made submerged in order to avoid radar detection.)

(c) Failure of U-boats to attack down wind and sea in many instances. (LantFlt A/S W officers commented: "This is added evidence that the wolfpacks of the North Atlantic are resourceful and well led.")

(d) Urgent need for more air coverage when flying conditions permit.

(e) Lack of sufficient escorts to properly screen a large convoy.

(f) Impracticability of maintaining reasonable A/S screen with few escorts while convoy presents an excessively wide front. Also indoctrination of convoy commodores to reduce convoy front to the smallest number of columns practicable.

(g) Urgent need for better matériel upkeep of escorts, especially in detection devices. At one time two out of three HF/DF sets were inoperative. Similarly, four of eight escorts had their radars out of commission, while the Asdic sets of three of the eight ships present were defective.

The Ides of March

Few Americans outside of official Washington and Navy Headquarters realized how crucial the U-boat situation was in March 1943. For obvious reasons of military security, facts and statistics concerning the Battle of the Atlantic were carefully concealed, and most Stateside Americans were unaware of the grim harvest reaped by the U-boats in the first quarter of 1943.

March was the season's worst month. The ordeal of Convoy SC-121 was typical. Convoy SC-122 had similarly hard going, lost nine ships on the submarine-haunted passage. At the same time, in those embattled seas, Convoy HX-229 lost eleven ships.

Navy bluejackets, Coast Guardmen, and merchant seamen put up a heroic fight. But torpedo after torpedo crashed home. In blasted hulls and boiling seas scores of good merchant seamen lost their lives. Morale not unnaturally melted in this crucible. Crews abandoned in disorder, and lifesaving gear was neglected. Some ships were not properly equipped with fire-fighting and damage-control apparatus, and their despairing men went overside at the first hit. In Convoy HX-229 the crew of the American freighter MATTHEW LUCKENBACK deliberately voted to straggle when the ship-train came under wolfpack attack and the convoy commodore did not signal a change of course. Attempting to evade in this fashion, the straggling freighter was torpedoed and sunk.

Result of such desperate melees could only be heavy casualties. Altogether, between March 1 and March 20, the Atlantic wolfpacks downed 85 merchantmen for toll of over half a million tons. And only a single U-boat was destroyed in that period—sunk by a Liberator flying from Iceland.

The obvious (but not easy-to-achieve) solution was mid-ocean air cover for the convoys. Escort-carriers were coming. But in the meantime the surface escorts had to fight it out. In April "Heineman's Harriers" were at sea again.

Spencer Kills U-175

On April 12, 1944, Ocean Escort Unit A-3 picked up a Western Atlantic-to-British Isles convoy off St. Johns. The seas had flattened somewhat after their equinoctial rampage, and a forecast of fair weather promised a fast and successful voyage.

Convoy HX-233 contained 57 ships disposed in 11 columns. The merchantmen were steaming in good order, and the convoy's tight front facilitated the screening job.

Heineman's group was composed of the following eight escorts:

U.S.C.G.C. SPENCER	*Comdr. H. S. Berdine, U.S.C.G.*
U.S.C.G.C. DUANE	*Capt. H. B. Bradbury, U.S.C.G.*
H.M.C.S. SKEENA	H.M.S. BERGAMOT
H.M.C.S. WETASKAWIN	H.M.S. BRYONY
H.M.S. DIANTHUS	H.M.C.S. ARVIDA

First indication of wolfpack activity came on April 15 when four U-boat transmissions were intercepted. The next day SPENCER made sound contact with a sub, and attacked with depth charges, with negative results. Convoy course was shifted to evade a nearing wolfpack, and these anti-sub measures frustrated attack on the 16th.

On the 17th the convoy was steaming due south of Reykjavik, vicinity of lat. 48-00 N., long. 21-00 W. Four British destroyers joined the escort in this submarine zone—formidable protection that might be expected to give the convoy a breathing spell.

The breathing spell proved illusory. About 0505, the freighter FORT RAMPART staggered out of line. At 0530, a near-by merchantman saw the freighter displaying a red light. FORT RAMPART's davits were outboard, lines were down, and her boats were in the water. In the gloaming of 0505 she had been torpedoed. Curiously enough, the stealthy attack had been as silent as a dagger blow in a featherbed.

Captain Heineman reported:

> No explosion was heard, no signal made nor rocket fired at the time, and no report received from Commodore or the ships. Escorts present considered at the time that the ship was falling out due to defects. Accordingly, no search was ordered or conducted by escorts.

Later that day FORT RAMPART broke in two. The derelict sections were sunk by destroyers of the support force.

About the time this ship was torpedoed, SPENCER, patrolling in the convoy's van, sighted a dark object off the bow, ahead. She passed the word to DIANTHUS, and the two peeled off to investigate. That was the beginning of a busy morning for Ocean Escort Unit A-3.

For SPENCER and her veteran crew the morning proved particularly busy. At 1050 she was patrolling along as usual when Sound reported another contact —range, 1,500 yards.

Berdine's Coast Guardsmen sprang into action. At exactly 1052 SPENCER's depth charges started rolling. Eleven charges exploded in a thundering pattern. And then another 11-charge pattern was dropped at 1058. Ten minutes later SPENCER, maneuvering between columns 6 and 7 of the convoy, was working to regain sound contact. While she probed with her detection gear, she coached her sister Coast Guard cutter DUANE into the hunt.

At 1117 the contact was reestablished; range 1,700 yards. Berdine ordered a mousetrap barrage. The rocket projectiles soared away and silently plunged into the pellucid sea.

About 15 minutes later the submarine broached, breaking water astern of the convoy and some 2,500 yards from SPENCER. The sub was U-175, a 750-ton specimen. Badly hurt by the depth-charge barrage, she had plunged to 38 fathoms before regaining depth control, and then, blowing all ballast, she had surfaced like a bale of cork. With decks awash she turned to run. SPENCER rushed her with blazing guns.

The crippled U-boat circled about helplessly. DUANE opened fire. Armed Guard crews on the merchantmen open fire. SPENCER's gunners were knocking the U-boat's conning tower into junk. Somehow a submarine gun crew got topside and fired a few rounds in return. During this savage exchange a shrapnelburst raked SPENCER's deck and eight of her crew were struck. J. T. Petrella, Radioman Third, was mortally wounded.

Berdine set a collision course to ram. But the assailed submariners had had enough, and they were seen abandoning as the Coast Guard cutter closed in. At 1145 SPENCER's gunners were ordered to hold their fire. With DIANTHUS screening, SPENCER and DUANE moved in to recover survivors. Forty-one of the Nazi undersea warriors were recovered.

Captain Heineman dispatched a SPENCER boarding party to examine the U-boat with an eye to possible salvage. Especially trained for such duty by Lieutenant Commander John B. Orem, U.S.C.G., the boarding party went alongside the wallowing submarine. Salvage was found to be impossible. U-175's conning tower had been punctured like a tin can on a boy's rifle range; her pressure hull was ruptured and leaking. At 1220 (five minutes after the boarding party was ordered off) the damaged submersible began to sink. At 1227 the sub's bow angled skyward, and the hulk slid down under the sea, stern first. Another U-boat done for.

Convoy HX-233 was about 600 miles off Land's End when this battle occurred. Aircraft from England soon arrived on the scene, and from there on in the convoy marched along under a canopy of planes. With aircraft aloft, the U-boats went under and stayed under.

En route, the ocean escorts had fuelled 17 times from four tankers. All fuelling, both alongside and astern, was carried out satisfactorily and expeditiously. Aside from the sinking of FORT RAMPART and the collision of two American merchantmen during convoy maneuvers, the ship-train got through without casualty. And the U.S. Coast Guard cutter SPENCER had two U-boats to her credit.

The Battle of the Central Atlantic

While anti-submarine warfare raged in the North Atlantic in the first quarter of 1943, a similarly violent conflict stormed across the more temperate latitudes of the Western Ocean. The weather in these latitudes was comparatively mild, but the warfare was not. The fighting raged from the Azores to Morocco and from Madeira to the Caribbean island of Curaçao. The prize at stake was the American trans-Atlantic supply line to North Africa, the shipping artery that carried sustenance to the United States Army driving against Rommel.

Actually (as in the North Atlantic) there were several of these shipping arteries. Cargo after cargo had to go across to the American forces in North Africa. Thousands of tons of guns and ammunition—

tanks, jeeps, and half-tracks—battle gear and K-ration—thousands of tons of everything an Army needs at the fighting front. To keep the fires of "Operation Torch" burning—that was the Navy's transport mission in the Central Atlantic sector.

And the "Torch" burned oil. Millions of barrels of oil. Literally millions of tons. All those Army planes, tanks, jeeps, and armored vehicles consumed oil and gas in enormous quantities that created an unparalleled supply problem. The problem called for new pipe lines from America, and in January 1943 three new convoy routes were established for the carrying of oil to the North African front. The first of these new routes ran between Curaçao and the United Kingdom. The second, between Curaçao and Casablanca, with a Gibraltar branch line. The third, New York-Norfolk to Casablanca. Royal Navy escorts cooperated on the Curaçao-United Kingdom haul. But the new trans-Atlantic runs to Casablanca were largely under operational control of the United States Navy, and much of the problem's weight fell on the shoulders of Destroyers Atlantic.

One of the first A/S battles in the Central Atlantic that season was fought by U.S. destroyers EARLE and PARKER, steaming as escorts with Convoy GUF-3, bound for the States from Casablanca. A fast convoy, GUF-3 contained 24 ships disposed in 7-column formation. The escort group included the battleship NEW YORK and light cruiser PHILADELPHIA, and seven DD's in addition to EARLE and PARKER. Rear Admiral L. A. Davidson, ComCruDiv 8, in PHILADELPHIA, was Escort Commander. Captain C. C. Hartman was Screen Commander. The convoy left "Casa" on December 29, picked up Gibraltar and Oran sections on the 31st, and was well at sea on New Year's Day.

By evening of January 3 the convoy was beyond the covering range of land-based air. And then, with explosive suddenness, the going was hot.

Action began when destroyer EARLE made radar contact with a submarine. EARLE's captain, Commander H. W. Howe, was none other than the naval officer who had captained the destroyer ROPER when she scored DesLant's first war-time U-boat kill. Howe sounded "General Quarters"; the destroyer raced forward on the attack, and with a sweeping searchlight she caught the surfaced submarine full in the face. Howe ordered the gunners to open fire, and he was certain of two hits before the submarine submerged.

PARKER (Lieutenant Commander J. W. Bays) raced up to join EARLE in searching and depth-charging. The enemy's silhouette had been that of an Italian. The submarine, however, managed to escape. It was luckier than the U-boat caught by EARLE the following night.

This time radar contact was made at 8,700 yards. Pouring on the coal, Howe drove the destroyer at the target in a top-speed rush. At 2355 the range was cut to 3,300 yards. Howe swung the destroyer to starboard to bring her port battery to bear, and turned on the searchlight to sweep the seascape. The spot picked up a U-boat, and the destroyer's gunners instantly opened fire, smothering the silhouette with shrapnel explosions, and lashing the conning tower with tracer. EARLE's FD radar operator was able to trail the projectiles straight to the target. At least a dozen 5-inch shells were seen to hit close aboard the submarine. Immediately after opening fire on the sub, Howe directed a torpedo shot that missed close aboard. For five minutes the destroyermen kept the guns going. When the cease-fire order was given at midnight, 34 rounds of 5-inch, three rounds of 40 mm., and 360 rounds of 20 mm. had been shot at the submarine. The U-boat dived a few seconds before the guns went silent; then she broke water like a porpoise, made a splash, and went under. The searchlight picked up some scraps of wreckage, but a post-war search of German records failed to verify a U-boat loss at that time and place. Evidently the submarine was only damaged.

ComDesLant, Rear Admiral Deyo, described EARLE's attack as ". . . *a classic example of aggressive action in which radar control was used to best advantage.*" This, of course, was early in 1943. (By the autumn of that year, confidence in radar had so increased that it became the accepted practice to open fire on radar contact alone.)

But if EARLE failed to sink a U-boat on the night of January 4, the enemy was at least driven off. And the U-boats failed to sink any of the ships in convoy GUF-3. Only one convoy lost ships to Nazi torpedoes on the newly established routes during the first quarter of 1943. The luckless convoy was UC-1, running from the British Isles to Curaçao.

Convoy UC-1 contained 33 ships. Most of the vessels were tankers, on their way to the Caribbean for a refill. The convoy was escorted by six British corvettes and the American destroyers MADISON, HILARY P. JONES, CHARLES F. HUGHES, and LANSDALE. On the night of February 23-24, the convoy, off the Azores, was attacked by a large wolfpack. In spite of the strong defensive screen five tankers were torpedoed. Three went down. Among those lost was the American Esso BATON ROUGE.

On the 25th a radio dispatch from London informed the convoy that direction-finder bearings pointed to some ten U-boats lying in the convoy's path. Alerted, the escorts tightened their defensive screen. The ships were moving in nine columns. Four thousand yards ahead of the convoy, three British corvettes covered the convoy's front. Destroyers MADISON and HUGHES patrolled on either bow of the formation. A corvette patrolled on either beam. Off port and starboard quarters, the destroyers HILARY P. JONES and LANSDALE patrolled as rear guard. Directly astern of the convoy a British corvette trailed the center column.

That evening a U-boat, trying to penetrate the screen on the convoy's port quarter, was driven off by HILARY P. JONES. Not long after that the same destroyer sighted and fired upon another submarine. Attempting to make a third attack, still another U-boat was driven off. Thereafter the Nazi submarines gave Convoy UC-1 a wide berth, and the ship-train made Curaçao without further misadventure. Commending the American destroyers for their A/S work, the British escort commander wrote: *"No escort group has ever been better supported."*

Three merchantmen were lost through wolfpack onslaughts on the cargo transport run, New York to Casablanca, late in January. These were stragglers from Convoy UGS-4.

The Ordeal of Convoy UGS-6

The second week in March, 1944, Convoy UGS-6 was trudging eastward on the main line, New York-to-Casablanca. The ships had reached that lap of the voyage which entered hot submarine water in the vicinity of the Azores. Consisting of 45 vessels, all laden to the Plimsoll-mark with military supplies, the slow convoy must have looked appetizing to enemy periscopes observing its heavy-footed advance.

And the periscopes were watching. However, the greedy-eyed U-boats took a second look before endeavoring to attack these tempting targets. Convoy UGS-6 was under escortage of seven U.S. destroyers. This escort group, under the leadership of Captain Charles Wellborn, Jr., contained the following DD's:

WAINWRIGHT *(Flagship)*	*Comdr. R. H. Gibbs*
TRIPPE	*Lt. Comdr. R. C. Williams*
CHAMPLIN	*Lt. Comdr. C. L. Melson*
Flagship of Comdr. B. R. Harrison, COMDESDIV 32	
MAYRANT	*Comdr. E. K. Walker*
ROWAN	*Lt. Comdr. R. S. Ford*
RHIND	*Lt. Comdr. O. W. Spahr, Jr.*
HOBBY	*Lt. Comdr. E. Blake*

These destroyers carried the latest in radar gear. Each was equipped with SG, SC, and FD radar, plus the QC projector. They were not supplied with HF/DF instruments. Cominch, however, obtaining cross-bearings from D/F stations ashore, was able to track and report to them the movements of near-by wolfpacks.

Apparently the Germans at this time were unaware that their U-boat radio transmissions were subject to pinpoint direction-finding. But the wolfpacks in the Azores area might have suspected that UGS-6 was receiving a continuous tip-off, for the convoy made numerous course-changes to side-step ambush off the Azores. And the destroyers frequently peeled away on high-speed sweeps off the convoy's flanks, blocking the approach of stalking U-boats.

But even radar cannot eliminate the Luck factor in warfare. On March 7 an unescorted Norwegian freighter, traveling independently, steamed over the horizon and blundered into the convoy's midst. WAINWRIGHT made strenuous efforts to divert this vessel, but the Norwegian either misread the signals or failed to see them. As a result she collided with a cargo transport. The crash sank the Norwegian, disabled the cargoman, and necessitated the leaving of a merchantman behind for rescue operations.

In spite of this nasty incident the convoy, depleted by two ships, made scheduled time, maintaining a 9-knot pace. As it neared the Azores Islands it came under submarine surveillance. The scouting U-boats relayed the word to pack leaders, and the subs farther eastward ganged up to intercept. Then, on the evening of March 12, the U-boat onslaught began.

Champlin Sinks U-130

The evening twilight had faded into darkness, and Convoy UGS-6 had reached the vicinity of lat. 37-00 N., long. 40-00 W., when the destroyer CHAMPLIN obtained an SG radar contact on an enemy submarine. Time: 2150. Range: 4,020 yards. CHAMPLIN's skipper, Lieutenant Commander Melson, sounded "General Quarters," and drove the destroyer for the target.

At 2158 the submarine's phosphorescent wake was sighted about 2,000 yards off. A moment later the conning tower was visible. Melson gave the order to open fire. CHAMPLIN's gunners opened up, but were unable to spot hits. CHAMPLIN was almost on top of the U-boat—150 yards—when the Nazi skipper "pulled the plug." Squarely into the bull's-eye of the swirling water CHAMPLIN dropped two depth charges.

The sea heaved skyward and crashed in a spreading sprawl of foam. Melson and crew followed through with four more depth-charge attacks, the last at 0158 of March 13. Thereafter the destroyer was unable to contact the submarine. A vigorous search plan was adopted and continued until daylight. At 0645, CHAMPLIN's lookouts sighted a number of oil slicks. Examination disclosed them to be the lifeblood of a submarine, and CHAMPLIN was able to report a kill.

CHAMPLIN's victim, identified by post-war records, was the U-130. This was the submarine that had got in under the screen at Fedala Roads on March 12, 1942, and torpedoed the transports HUGH L. SCOTT, EDWARD RUTLEDGE, and TASKER H. BLISS, with a consequent loss of 108 American lives. CHAMPLIN had killed a killer.

UGS-6 Versus Wolfpack

While CHAMPLIN was finishing off U-130, the other destroyers were busy driving off other submarines. The wolfpack continued to shadow the convoy throughout the daylight hours of March 13. Around 2030 of that evening a straggler was torpedoed and sunk about 50 miles astern of the convoy. The destroyers made high-speed sweeps from bow to quarter—tactics which were employed just before the twilight faded, and which may have disrupted a wolfpack attack.

Similar sweeps were made on March 14, and the convoy made several course changes to throw off the trailing wolfpack. But that night the U-boats loped forward on the surface, to strike at the convoy's rear. Again the DD's radar screen proved effective, and the pack was driven off. The following day Cominch reported that at least four U-boats were trailing UGS-6. That afternoon HOBBY and MAYRANT made high-speed sweeps to a distance of 10 miles off the convoy's port and starboard flanks to drive the U-boats away.

At 1830 on the evening of the 15th, WAINWRIGHT's hydrophone picked up the whisper of a stalking sub. The trace was evanescent, and after a fruitless 15-minute search of the immediate area, WAINWRIGHT resumed her normal patrol station. At 1852, the S. S. WYOMING was torpedoed by a U-boat which slipped under the screen from ahead. Executing a short-range, submerged attack, the sub opened fire at about 650 yards to slam two deadly fish into the target vessel. CHAMPLIN picked up survivors while HOBBY screened and simultaneously made a sweep for the killer. At 2304 HOBBY gained an SG radar contact, range 9,000 yards, but the sub escaped as the DD sent up starshells. Late in the afternoon of the next day, more U-boat contacts were made—this time ahead of the convoy—and at sunset another merchantman was torpedoed and sunk. Other ships in the convoy were narrowly missed by torpedoes. At 1903, RHIND had sound contact; she veered to avoid a torpedo, and thrashed the water with depth charges, but failed to kill her assailant.

On March 17, at sunset, a fourth merchantman was torpedoed and sent down. The stricken vessel, the S. S. MOLLY PITCHER, was struck by one torpedo in the port bow—the lucky shot of what appeared to be a four-torpedo spread fired by a sub at extreme range on the convoy's port quarter. The destroyer ROWAN searched astern of the convoy for the U-boat, but the slippery foe escaped. The next day the convoy made large, evasive course-changes in the late afternoon to frustrate ambush. Patrolling well ahead of the convoy's front (a tactic employed to force down lurking U-boats), one of the destroyers put up an effective screen. Since the evening of March 17, however, UGS-6 had been provided with continuous air cover, and from there on in the voyage was untroubled. Loss of four ships was serious, but fatalities were unusually light. Only six men were lost in the ships sunk while steaming with the formation. Loss of life aboard the straggler was considerably heavier.

Comments by Captain Heineman

Captain P. R. Heineman, Atlantic Fleet Anti-Submarine Warfare officer, submitted an interesting critical review of the tactics employed by the escort group and the enemy during the voyage of UGS-6.

Referring to WAINWRIGHT's use of blinker tube in her effort to divert the Norwegian freighter which wandered into the convoy, Captain Heineman wrote:

> Use of a signal searchlight, loud hailer, herding, or gun-fire I believe preferable in situations of this nature where the merchant vessel does not respond readily to a blinker tube.

The destroyers with UGS-6 made sound contact on 11 occasions. Concerning this feature of the escorts' effort, Captain Heineman observed:

> On four occasions sound contact was regained for one additional attack, but only once was sound contact held while three or more attacks were delivered. . . . The record of our A/S vessels . . . points unmistakably to greater emphasis on training to regain contact. It is considered that a larger percentage of kills will be achieved sooner if increased attention is paid to maintaining the contacts that are made.

On March 13 the straggler (which was subsequently torpedoed) had been trailing along after the convoy contrary to instructions to follow a straggler's route. By such trailing the straggler may have given the U-boats a clue as to the convoy's main line of advance. Remarking this episode, Captain Heineman noted that a radical course-change by the convoy might have proved effective.

No enemy transmissions were heard on medium frequencies, but transmissions had been registered on high frequencies. With regard to this matter, Captain Heineman observed:

> UGS-6 had no HF/DF equipment with which to evaluate these transmissions. If HF/DF bearings could

have been obtained, the radical change of course might have been made in the right direction and would have had a good chance of being effective. A radical course alteration could have been made anyway, and the laws of probability should have given it a 50-50 chance of success.

Concerning the wolfpack battle as it developed, Captain Heineman noted:

A shift in type of U-boat attacks was (on March 14) very possible after the failure of their night surface approaches. . . . This could only mean submerged approach, and the problem became one of time. Submerged daylight attacks had not been too successful, especially against an efficient destroyer sound screen. More success had attended the twilight attacks at dawn and dusk. With an east-bound convoy the dusk attack is the more dangerous. The U-boat would then have the convoy silhouetted against the setting sun. The moon would also be up at this time. The sound screen, therefore, should have been effective and more alert than before, since radar had been 100% successful at detecting surface approaches.

With reference to the action of March 16:

The convoy course-change of 15° to port in the late afternoon appears to have left a U-boat on the starboard flank instead of ahead. The course-change was small enough, however, for the submarine to close to firing position by using high submerged speeds. . . . The actual value of the high-speed sweeps cannot be determined because they produced no sightings or contacts. It can be stated that the U-boat tactics appear to have changed. It would have been logical to assume that submerged attack at sunset would be repeated, since it had been used with success. In the absence of any firsthand HF/DF intelligence, it does not appear to have been feasible to vary the system of sweeps used for the past three days. Additional sweeps at different times during the day might have helped. For the daylight period, an escort at visibility distance on each bow was desirable, with all other escorts in a sound screen ahead of the convoy. Improved sound screen coverage was the most apparent requirement. With no additional escorts available, sound coverage could be increased only by increasing the patrolling speed of the escorts already on station. In addition, a more radical course-change late in the afternoon should have proved most helpful in upsetting planned sunset attacks of the U-boats.

With reference to a long-range torpedo attack made on the convoy on March 16, and the convoy's evasive actions, Captain Heineman remarked:

The convoy made eight course-changes in three hours and ten minutes, and the U-boat undoubtedly felt that in the growing darkness a long-range torpedo salvo was the only chance left for firing. . . . The radar screen was still effective. The sound screen had been efficient, although it did not prevent this attack. . . . It seems to have been more than ever desirable to place an escort at visibility distance on each bow during the dawn to dusk period. . . . It can be said that the shift in U-boat tactics had been successful on two successive days. No reason appears that would forecast a shift in these tactics which were proving satisfactory. . . . U-boats shifted their approach tactics as soon as they realized the one they were using had failed. . . .

An escort stationed well ahead of the convoy was more effective than bow-to-quarter sweeps in late afternoon. . . . Sweeps should be based on first-hand HF/DF intelligence in order to make them most effective.

Captain Heineman concluded:

Evasive course-changes, when a convoy is shadowed, should be large, radical alterations. The length of time each alteration is held should not be too short. . . .

End of a Bad Winter

American and Allied trans-Atlantic convoys took a beating in the winter of 1942-43 to the tune of 334 merchantmen, nearly two million tons of shipping.

Admiral Jonas H. Ingram tersely told the story in an informal report on the A/S campaign submitted to Secretary of the Navy Forrestal a year or so later, Admiral Ingram wrote:

"The mission of the Atlantic Fleet was to keep the sea lanes open, to make an effective blockade of the Axis powers in the Atlantic, and also protect neutral shipping and Allied shipping. The Battle of the Atlantic is going to go down as one of the decisive battles of the war, because if the Battle of the Atlantic had not been won, war in Europe would not have gone on. In early 1943, when the Germans had as many as 450 submarines available, it was just nip and tuck, and if they had kept on at the rate of sinkings of early 1943 for the remainder of that year, I doubt if there would have been any invasions in the Mediterranean or Normandy, or any Great Britain."

But the Germans did not keep on at that rate. By the spring of 1943, the counter to the wolfpack menace was in the making. Working hand in glove with destroyers and other A/S vessels, land-based aircraft had cooperated to form teams that had virtually driven the wolfpacks out of American and United Kingdom coastal waters. If such sea-air teams could operate in the mid-Atlantic, the U-boat problem would be solved. That solution was on the way.

By April 1943, strong destroyer reinforcements were emerging from American shipyards, and air umbrellas for convoys in mid-ocean were coming into being. These new A/S teams' influence on the Battle of the Atlantic will be detailed in subsequent chapters.

CHAPTER 22

THE GANG BUSTERS

(MAY 1943-DECEMBER 1943)

The Coming of the Hunter-Killers

The answer to the mid-ocean wolfpack was the escort-carrier (CVE) and the destroyer-escort (DE)—warships which were relatively inexpensive; which could be constructed on a mass production basis; and which could be rushed into the Battle of the Atlantic to supplement the hard-working destroyer and other A/S forces engaged in the war against the U-boat.

The escort-carrier to carry aircraft within striking distance of those oceanic reaches where the wolfpacks had roamed with comparative impunity; the destroyer-escort to screen the CVE and cooperate with the carrier aircraft in search and attack—these new warships would add a lot of weight to the Allied anti-submarine effort. They would help to shoulder the convoy burden heretofore borne in the main by the Navy's destroyers. On convoy duty, the CVE and accompanying DD's and DE's would pick up a fleet of transports on the perimeter of a protected area, and escort the ship-train through more perilous submarine water until it reached the relative safety of foreign or home waters beyond the danger zone. Escort-carriers, destroyer-escorts, and destroyers would also team up to form far-ranging, hard-hitting task groups capable of raiding wolfpack hunting grounds and conducting offensive missions against submarine rendezvous areas. Teamwork was the weapon with which the CVE-DD-DE "hunter-killers" would crush the U-boat menace.

But the construction of escort-carriers and destroyer-escorts took time. So did the training of crews which were to specialize in the hunting and killing of submarines. Not until the summer of 1943 did the "hunter-killer" campaign go into high gear.

However, during the second quarter of 1943, German Admiral Doenitz's wolfpacks failed to equal their success of the year's first quarter. Clement spring weather, lengthened days, air reinforcements, and revised A/S measures aided the trans-Atlantic convoys.

The difficulties of joint United States-British convoy operations were alleviated that spring by placing the responsibility for the North Atlantic run entirely in the hands of British and Canadian escort forces, while the U.S. Navy assumed entire responsibility for convoying in the Central Atlantic, and for the oil lines running from Curaçao to the United Kingdom.

Due to the factors mentioned and to others to be presently discussed, in April the Atlantic U-boats sank only 44 Allied and neutral ships—less than half the number downed in March. In May the figure dwindled to 41—a significant score. In that same month exactly 41 U-boats were downed, even-Stephen. And no one knew better than Doenitz that the U-boat Force could not afford to fight it out on a 50-50 basis.

Of that Maytime score two U-boats were downed by Destroyers Atlantic. The first was sunk by the U.S.S. MACKENZIE.

Mackenzie Kills U-182

On May 16, 1943, the destroyer MACKENZIE (Commander D. B. "Dan" Miller) was en route to Casablanca in company with destroyer LAUB, whose captain, Commander J. F. Gallaher, was senior officer of the two-destroyer task unit. At 0350 MACKENZIE had a radar contact on her SG radar, range 7,800 yards. At 2,700 yards the radar contact was lost, but a good sound contact was established at 1,600 yards.

MACKENZIE made a run on the submarine, dropping a 10-charge pattern at 0439. While the destroyer turned to make a second attack, Sound reported contact at 500 yards. Miller ordered five more depth charges dumped upon the enemy. The barrage raised the usual geyser followed by a spreading maelstrom, then silence.

For some time thereafter MACKENZIE and LAUB searched in the vicinity. But attempts to regain contact with the target proved futile. However, at 0458 and at 0503 both destroyers heard marine explosions, similar to the blast of deep depth charges.

The destroyers searched for wreckage—found nothing. No scraps of submarine; no oil slicks. Turning their bows for Casablanca, the destroyers proceeded on their way.

The wreck left by MACKENZIE's handiwork was not located until after the war, when it was found in the vicinity of lat. 33-55 N., long. 20-35 W.—in the German Navy's records. The submarine that disappeared in that locale early in the morning of May 6, 1943, was the one sunk by MACKENZIE.

The records identified the victim as U-182.

Moffett, Jouett, and Aircraft Kill U-128

In May 1943, destroyers MOFFETT and JOUETT, veterans of the South Atlantic Force (recently designated the Fourth Fleet), took care of a U-boat in the warm waters off the hump of Brazil, about 200 miles southeast of Recife.

Submarine activity in Brazilian coastal waters had quieted down somewhat after the attack on Convoy BT-6 in March. In April a program of barrier-sweeps by aircraft flying out of Natal had been inaugurated, and, on the 15th of that month, planes of Squadron VP-83 had caught and sunk the Italian submarine ARCHIMEDE.

The destroyers of DesRon 9, under Commander A. H. Oswald—DAVIS, WINSLOW, MOFFETT, JOUETT, and SOMERS—operating with the Fourth Fleet, had made few contacts in March and April. But consistent support from land-based air presaged a livening hunting season. And about sundown on the evening of May 16, two patrolling aircraft of Squadron VP-74 sighted a Nazi sub charging its batteries on the surface. Out went the call, and destroyers MOFFETT (Commander J. C. Sowell) and JOUETT (Commander F. L. Tedder) were rushed to the reported position.

The DD's had a long run of it. While they were on the way, the two planes bombed, strafed, and hounded the undersea invader. The scrimmage between airmen and submariners outlasted the evening of the 16th and continued throughout the early hours and tropical morning of the following day. At 1246 of the 17th, the destroyers sighted the U-boat on the surface, 10 miles distant. They opened fire at 1303, range 5,500 yards.

Two minutes later the DD's ceased firing. Under a storm of shell bursts the submarine had disappeared. But a moment later the U-boat's conning tower was again in view, and the MOFFETT and JOUETT gunners were immediately on target. Straddles were observed, and several smashing hits were seen. At 1309 the punctured submarine went under, leaving a cluster of frantic swimmers in her wake.

JOUETT covering MOFFETT, the DD's ran forward to pick up the survivors. They found most of the submarine's crew paddling and splashing around in an otherwise clean sea. No debris—no litter—no mess of oil. Fifty live U-boaters and one dead man were taken aboard the destroyer MOFFETT. The sunken submarine was identified as U-128. The German commander reported only three of the crew missing.

The Tenth Fleet

In May 1943 the Tenth Fleet was organized. Actually it was a fleet in name only. Operating through the Fleet and Sea Frontier commands, it exercised coordinating control over the Navy's anti-submarine forces. Its business in this regard was wholly administrative. It was an agency dedicated to the development of A/S weapons and measures, and to the coordination of the A/S effort. In charge of the anti-submarine program, the Tenth Fleet contained the Scientific Council described in Chapter 5. And among its other duties, it developed and had control over the forthcoming hunter-killer program.

Admiral King, as Commander-in-Chief United States Fleet and Chief of Naval Operations, assumed command of the Tenth Fleet. Rear Admiral Francis S. ("Froggy") Low, assistant Chief of Staff in charge of anti-submarine warfare, became Chief of Staff of the Tenth Fleet, directly under King.

Introducing the Escort-Carrier

The vessel's christened name was S.S. MORMACMAIL. She was a Diesel-powered, C-3 type freighter which the Navy had acquired from the Maritime Commission for experimental purposes. The experiment? Conversion of this cargo ship into a small flat-top—a "baby" aircraft carrier which could be employed as an A/S escort for convoy duty, or as an aircraft transport, or, if need arose, as a substitute for a first-line carrier.

Her conversion reminiscent of the job that turned the veteran collier JUPITER into the Navy's first carrier LANGLEY, the "baby flat-top" came down the ways early in 1941 as the original escort-carrier LONG ISLAND. This new CVE (C for carrier; V for heavier than air; E for escort) was a much stouter ship than the ex-collier "OLD COVERED WAGON" of 1922. LONG ISLAND's successful performance established her as a prototype for the fleet of "baby flat-tops" rushed from American building yards to fight the Battle of the Atlantic. Contracts for mass conversions were let in the spring of 1942. And as the U-boat battle roared into high gear in the summer and autumn of that year, the escort-carrier building program was eventually expanded to include "tailor-made" CVE's, constructed from the keel up. Leader in this new construction was Henry J. Kaiser, the bottleneck-breaking industrialist whose yards brought the "tailor-made" CVE's off the line.

The escort-carriers created for the Navy another training problem. Aviators in particular needed considerable drill in take-off and landing techniques, for the flight deck of the "baby flat-top" was neither as roomy nor as stable as the flight deck of a full-sized carrier. As a Navy flyer with previous carrier experience explained it: "Looking down on a CV, you had the feeling you were going to land on a shingle. Looking down on a baby flat-top, you had the feeling you were going to land on a playing card—and it was probably the joker, at that."

For the special training of aviators and crews, two Great Lake steamers were converted into CVE's, and the CVE CHARGER, commissioned early in March 1942, was assigned to training duty. Then the first new escort-carrier on A/S duty in the Atlantic was U.S.S. BOGUE (Captain G. E. Short). Launched in Puget Sound, and commissioned in September 1942, BOGUE steamed eastward through the Canal in November of that year, and early 1943 found her on the Newfoundland-Iceland run in the North Atlantic. She was trailed through the Canal by U.S.S. CARD (Captain A. J. "Buster" Isbell). These two were presently followed into the Atlantic by CORE, BLOCK ISLAND, SANTEE, CROATAN, and other "baby flat-tops."

So the U-boat skipper saw aircraft winging across the No-Man's-Land sky of mid-ocean where only Lindbergh and a few others had previously flown. And then, some time after diving, he was glaring amazedly through the periscope at a new and menacing silhouette. A stubby vessel that resembled a freighter bereft of its superstructure—a flat-topped craft that was rolling like a barn adrift, and aircraft buzzing up from that pitching deck like angry hornets leaving a hive.

The U-boater who spotted the first American escort-carrier was in for a decidedly unpleasant surprise. The CVE was quarterback of a team, a destroyer group devoted solely to the enterprise of sinking Nazi submarines with gunfire, hedgehog projectiles, depth charges, or whatever A/S weapon was available. Any U-boat that got close enough to sight a baby flat-top and her companions would find it advisable to go deep and rig for depth charges.

Entering the Battle of the Atlantic, the CVE-DD team set out early in 1943 to turn the tide against the voracious wolfpack.

BOGUE began operations on St. Valentine's Day in the North Atlantic. She scattered a wolfpack of 11 U-boats and scored her first kill late in May. The British convoy she was escorting on that occasion made the trans-Atlantic run unscathed. Dispatched to the Central Atlantic, BOGUE then joined forces with CARD and SANTEE, hunting submarines on the sea lanes to Africa.

The U-boats were hard to find that June. Alarmed by the mounting casualties from air attack, Commander-in-Chief Doenitz was calling home his *unterseebooten* to arm them with anti-aircraft guns. So the U.S. Navy's new CVE-DD teams had to beat the bushes for game. And beat the bushes they did, driving deep into the U-boat's mid-Atlantic territory. Striking in the Azores area in June, BOGUE flushed a wolfpack, and her aviators downed another Nazi sub. At the same time, SANTEE's planes broke up a U-boat concentration in the Azores vicinity.

These raids on the mid-Atlantic "milk cow" meadows came as a decided shock to the German Submarine Command. No longer could the "tanker submarines" browse around the Azores in bucolic peace. The thirsty wolfpacks would now have to fuel on the fly. And already, on April 11, Admiral Doenitz had reported to Hitler, *"I fear that the submarine war will be a failure if we do not sink more ships than the enemy is able to build."* And in June 1943 the U-boats sank only 19 merchantmen!

From the high crest of March 1943 to the low trough of June 1943, the graph of Allied shipping losses seemed to indicate that the U-boat Force had shot its bolt. But in the summer of 1943 the U-boats made a desperate comeback, equipped with anti-aircraft batteries and radar-detection devices.

Anti-aircraft batteries or no, a surfaced U-boat was hardly able to cope with a group of Grumman Wildcats or Avengers flying from a baby flat-top. Nor could U-boats hope to shoot it out with gunning

DD's. Put together, the aircraft-destroyer combination was a submarine Nemesis against which the Nazis had no countermeasure.

Badger Kills U-613 (With a Footnote by Edgar Allen Poe)

On July 23, 1943, while serving as screen for BOGUE, the BADGER (Lieutenant T. H. Byrd, U.S.N.R.) made sound contact with a submarine. The time: 1106. The place: lat. 35-31 N., long. 28-40 W. Range was 1,100 yards.

BADGER did not have much opportunity for preliminary sparring. Lieutenant Byrd drove the destroyer in a rush at the enemy, and with great skill and alacrity gave the submarine a going-over.

BADGER's first depth-charge attack brought up nothing but the usual tons of salt water. A second run produced the same negative result—a roar of undersea explosions and a tremendous geyser on the surface, but no sign of submarine. Byrd maneuvered the old four-piper back into position for another barrage at a different level. Ashcans and teardrops splashed the sea, the TNT volleyed and thundered, the water thrashed and calmed. Evidently the submarine had gone deeper than the usual dive.

Lieutenant Byrd determined to dig out the U-boat, whatever its depth. Ordering a new setting on the charges, he directed the firing of a fourth barrage. Commenting on this attack, Rear Admiral Deyo observed later:

> *The estimate of deep submergence, and the use of his equipment available to obtain this estimate, indicates that the Commanding Officer,* U.S.S. GEORGE E. BADGER, *understood and clearly analyzed the attack problem. A more uniform depth spread in the depth-charge pattern will obviously make an attack more potent. However, the results of this attack leave nothing to be desired in so far as its potency is concerned.*

Those results could only have come from a direct hit. In BADGER's wake the sea erupted with a roar, and with the upheaval a swirling litter of wreckage, debris, and human remains gushed to the surface.

Searching through this residue of destruction and death, the destroyermen managed to identify their victim as the U-613. One of BADGER's crew delved into the ghastly flotsam and came up with a dripping book. Appropriate volume for the scene and the occasion, it was a German translation of *The Murders in the Rue Morgue.*

Watercolor in Brazil Area

During the summer of 1943, nine "milk cow" submarines were killed in their mid-ocean pastures by the combined efforts of hunter-killer groups led by BOGUE, SANTEE, CARD, and CORE. Perhaps as a diversion, or possibly in response to one of Hitler's intuitive inspirations, Doenitz launched a midsummer submarine drive against Allied shipping in the coastal waters off Brazil.

But Admiral Ingram, in command of the American-Brazilian naval forces in the South Atlantic, was prepared to meet the U-boat threat. Flying from shore bases and tenders at Fortaleza, Natal, Recife, Balina, and Ascension, Navy air patrols guarded the Brazilian sea frontier. The Fourth Fleet stood ready. German submarines were asking for trouble when they approached the Brazilian coast.

Some 15 U-boats asked for it. Seven got it. Showing up off the Brazilian coast in July 1943, the invading wolfpacks immediately came under fire of the air patrols. On July 9, one U-boat was sunk and another damaged by a converted B-24 off Recife. On the 19th one more was sighted and sunk by aircraft. Then, late in July, destroyers and aircraft teamed up to fight one of the war's more colorful anti-submarine battles.

Moffett and Aircraft Kill U-604

This aircraft-destroyer versus U-boat contest began on July 30 when the U-185 was sighted off the Brazilian coast by a PV-1 plane. The aircraft dropped bombs on the U-boat, and radioed the word to Admiral Ingram's Fourth Fleet. U-185 won the first round by eluding the aircraft during the last day of July. But the contest was only begun. The destroyers soon arrived on the scene, and they teamed up with the planes to conduct one of the war's most persistent U-boat hunts. U-185 and her pack-mate, U-604, were spotted early in the first week of August. Thereafter the pair were marked submarines.

For five days the two Nazi subs were kept on the run by bombs, gunfire and ashcans. They could hardly make a daylight periscope exposure without inviting attack, and when they surfaced at night to charge batteries they were spotted by radar's all-seeing eye.

By the evening of August 5 the fugitive U-boats had retreated far to the west of Fernando de Noronha. But hard on their weary heels came the pursuit—long-range aircraft and the destroyer MOFFETT. The destroyer, captained by Lieutenant Commander G. H. Richards, was finding the chase exciting enough for any DD. Twice, while running through the night, she was mistaken for a U-boat by friendly planes and subjected to a lively strafing.

Fortunately the aircraft found the right target on August 6, and U-604 was put on the receiving end of a strafing by two sharpshooting planes. The planes also dropped bombs on the exhausted foe, and MOFFETT raced into the fray in time to sight the submarine before the U-boaters were able to take her down.

Rushing to the spot where the sub went under, the destroyermen followed through with a series of depth-charge attacks. The enemy did not reappear after this going-over. MOFFETT made a diligent search, but was unable to regain contact. Disappointed, the destroyer finally abandoned the hunt. There was no evidence to suggest a kill, and modest MOFFETT did not report a "probable."

The submariners in U-604 reported something else again. Staggering out from under the depth-charge barrage, the U-boat managed to elude the finger of MOFFETT's detection gear. But it was a severely injured submarine that eventually struggled to the surface and opened its hatches to gasp for air.

Not long after that, U-604 got off a message to U-185, urgently requesting assistance. A rendezvous was eventually arranged. On the 11th of August, U-185 and U-172 managed to meet U-604 at the designated point some 800 miles off the Brazilian coast. The men in U-604 were a haggard company of Germans. By dint of desperate damage-control measures they had kept the submarine afloat. But the pressure hull was leaking dangerously; drenched electrical installations had shorted and burned out; batteries were cracked; the diving machinery was out of kilter. The battered submersible was at the end of her rope, and the German pack-commander ordered the crew to scuttle.

Before U-604 could be abandoned, a long-range Liberator sighted the trio of submarines and swooped down on the attack. The Nazis opened fire with anti-aircraft guns as the bomber roared in. A lucky hit struck home, and the Liberator plunged into the sea. All hands aboard the bomber were lost.

Few of the submariners who witnessed it would live to tell of this triumph. For the crew of U-604, in particular, was this a Pyrrhic victory. After the Liberator was shot down, the U-604 crew was taken aboard U-185, and the submarine was scuttled. Thus, on August 11, U-604 expired—sunk, in effect, by aircraft bombs and the depth charges dropped by MOFFETT on the 6th.

And the full price was yet to be paid. Playing host to the U-604 crew, U-185 was an overcrowded submarine. Overcrowding in a submarine can create numerous difficulties—bad air, short rations, jarred elbows, jangled nerves. And in the event of emergency the escape hatches can be too narrow and too few.

Jammed like "sardines in a tin." The phrase is hackneyed, but it best describes the crews of U-185 and U-604 all in the same boat. Running home, the crowded submarine got as far as the waters off the Azores. There, on August 24, it was caught by aircraft from the escort carrier CORE.

Four of CORE's planes attacked. Down came the tracers and TNT. Riddled by bullets and blasted by bombs, U-185 plunged to the bottom. For the crew of U-604 it was the last round of a contest told in installments—a grim undersea drama for a German War Diary:

> U-boat attacked in Brazilian waters by aircraft and destroyer on August 5, 1943.
>
> U-boat severely damaged by depth charges on August 6th.
>
> U-boat abandoned and scuttled on August 11th. Crew transferred to U-185.
>
> U-185 attacked and sunk in Azores area by aircraft on August 24th.

Point-Counterpoint

With the Brazilian campaign a fiasco—seven U-boats lost, and the remainder fleeing home in various stages of despair and disrepair—the outlook in Doenitz's headquarters went from pessimism to gloom. During July and August, 1943, some 62 Nazi submarines had expired in the Atlantic Battle, in the Mediterranean, and elsewhere. Only 44 Allied and neutral merchantmen had been torpedoed and sunk. At this rate of exchange the German submarine effort would soon be bankrupt.

The Germans' radar-detection device was a flop. And the arming of U-boats with anti-aircraft guns was worse. True, a lucky hit might stop a plane, but in a surface duel with A/S forces the U-boat usually went down for the count. The torpedo was the submarine's best weapon, and Doenitz made a mistake in trying to arm the U-boats with formidable guns.

He now attempted to cancel the error with an improved torpedo. For some time the German scientists had been working on an acoustic torpedo which was capable of "homing" on the noise of a ship's screws. This wizardish model was issued to the U-boat Force in September 1943—an extremely ingenious and efficient secret weapon. Going into action, it worked beautifully, and it caught the Allies more or less by surprise. September and October shipping losses increased alarmingly. Then the Seven Day Wonder was exploded—by the simple device of noise-makers towed in the target vessel's wake.

Borie Kills U-405 ("Scratch One Pig Boat—")

BORIE was one of those old flush-deck four-pipers the sailors referred to as "cans." High-ranking naval officers frowned at the term, but its use was common in the Fleet, and certainly those in the destroyers never made objection. BORIE was BORIE, whether one referred to her as a destroyer (officially DD 215) or a "can."

In the autumn of 1943 BORIE was a unit of the task group built around the escort-carrier CARD. On CARD's bridge stood Captain A. J. ("Buster") Isbell. On BORIE's bridge stood Lieutenant Commander Charles H. Hutchins, U.S.N.R. But they stood as one in the resolution to sink U-boats whenever and wherever found.

On the evening of November 1, the task group was cruising in high water some 700 miles north of the Azores. In came word from one of CARD's scout planes —submarine! BORIE was off on the scent, steaming on ahead of the group through seas that mounted higher as the hour grew late and the night thickened.

Then a "pip" appeared on the radar screen—and another. Two U-boats in the offing! Hutchins sent BORIE boring in on the attack. Sighting the nearer U-boat, the destroyermen opened up with an accurate fire that promptly drove the enemy under. Hutchins followed through with a depth-charge onslaught. Hard to tell in those jumping seas whether shells and ashcans were on target, but explosions sounded like hits and the submarine seemed to evaporate. Hutchins sent CARD a terse report:

SCRATCH ONE PIG BOAT AM SEARCHING FOR MORE

The search turned out to be a chase. Loping away in the night, the second U-boat had run for the cover of a blinding rainsquall that swirled through the darkness like blowing ink. The ink failed to impair radar's all-seeing eye. Hutchins drove his old four-piper in top-speed pursuit. Swinging uphill and down dale through 15-foot seas, the veteran BORIE—an old-timer from the days of World War I—overhauled one of Doenitz's new submarines, and caught the enemy on the surface! Not only caught the big U-boat, but spotted her in the white glare of a searchlight. A second later the livid breath of gunfire scorched the darkness, and the battle was on!

This U-boat was one of the specimens equipped with heavy deck-batteries. And her skipper, throwing discretion to the winds, decided to duel. So began one of the war's strangest battles—a battle as ferocious as it was unorthodox. As BORIE closed in with booming salvos, the U-boat opened fire. Her guns spat in the night, and BORIE was shaken by two hits, one amidships and one on the bridge.

For nearly an hour the gun battle continued, the destroyer and the submarine circling each other "like tomcats in the dark," as a commentator expressed it. Now the U-boat's gunners were driven from their mounts by a fusillade of machine-gun fire from BORIE. Now the destroyermen were under the fire of salvos and bursts of tracer from the submarine.

Neither ship was large as warships go, and both were buffeted by the plunging seas, showered with stormy spray, and flayed by the wind as they jockeyed and maneuvered about. The wonder was that either Nazi or American gun crews could keep their feet. But the shell-passers kept the weapons fed, and pointers and trainers found the mark as the guns traded shot for shot.

Finally Hutchins saw the opening he wanted, and stepping up the speed to 25 knots, he drove BORIE in to ram. There was a crash and then a grinding din as the old DD slammed into the U-boat and rode up on the submarine's afterdeck, shearing through the pressure hull as though it were so much cardboard. Her own bow damaged by the collision, BORIE was for the moment held fast, even as she pinned the enemy's stern under water. For a full ten minutes the thrashing destroyer and struggling submarine were locked together—a panther with teeth fastened in the hindquarters of a crocodile.

The Nazis came boiling up from below to make it a fight. Forward of the conning tower, the submarine's deck-gunners clung to their mounts, and the U-boat's bridge personnel sniped wildly at the destroyer's bow. BORIE's searchlight poured down its blinding glare. At such close quarters the destroyermen were unable to bring their big guns to bear, and they bore down with every other weapon available.

Pistols barked and rifles spanged. Hot-shell men flung empty shell cases. A German gunner sprinted down the submarine's sloped foredeck—someone hurled a sheath knife at him from the destroyer's bridge. Other Nazis had Lugers shot out of their hands. A BORIE man opened fire with a Very pistol, and the U-boat's bridge was showered with pyrotechnic stars. Volleys of rifle fire riddled the submarine's conning tower; a burst from a machine-gun brought smoke spurting from the structure, and a moment later it was spouting flame.

As an American described it afterward, *"That battle was like a riot in a shooting gallery. The boys hit that Nazi U-boat with everything but the kitchen range. They didn't need to throw that when the sub's conning tower took fire. Why carry coals to Newcastle?"*

So the submarine was a burning wreck when the heavy seas, which had wedged the vessels firmly together, suddenly washed them apart, permitting DD and sub to break their death-grip. As the U-boat stumbled away, mortally hurt, Hutchins learned that his own ship was severely injured, her forward engine-room taking water. But the foe was not yet downed, and Hutchins drove the damaged destroyer in dogged pursuit.

Unable to risk a dive, the submarine crawled away on the surface, her skipper exerting every effort to elude. BORIE, painfully crippled, hung on the trail. Once, tracking with radar, Hutchins tried to stop the fugitive with a torpedo attack. Again, he closed in to ram, and BORIE missed the submarine by the width of her paint. Then the U-boat turned with guns snapping and barking, and made a frenzied attempt to ram the lamed destroyer. With a salvo of shallow-set depth charges, the destroyer stopped the U-boat's wild rush, and once more the gunners were firing pointblank. Again the sub slipped away, and again the destroyer failed to hit the enemy with torpedoes.

The end came suddenly when the BORIE gunners got on target with their main battery. A salvo hit the U-boat's charred conning tower, reducing it to a shattered mangle. The exhausted Nazis fired pyrotechnic stars in signal of surrender. When BORIE's searchlight spotted the submarine, the Germans were going overside in rubber boats and the U-boat was going down.

"Scratch one pig boat," Hutchins had advised at the end of the action with the first U-boat. As it turned out, he had been overly optimistic; he had damaged but not finished off that first one, and it got away. But BORIE did not miss on the second one, the U-405. Shell fire—machine-gun fire—rifle fire—empty shell-cases—a sheath knife—Very stars—depth charges. And, of course, old BORIE herself, veteran destroyer, DD 215, "can," or whatever one chose to call her.

Loss of U.S.S. Borie

After the battle BORIE rolled all night long in the rising seas, barely able to keep her screws turning. She had conquered the U-boat, but she could not beat back the Atlantic. Strive as they would, the damage-control parties were unable to stem the flood in the forward engine-room. By morning, when CARD's planes found her, the old four-piper was in deep distress.

The Task-group Commander, Captain Isbell, dispatched the destroyers GOFF (Lieutenant Commander H. I. Smith, U.S.N.R.) and BARRY (Lieutenant Commander H. D. Hill, U.S.N.R.) to assist the wounded warship. Throughout the daylight hours of November 2, BARRY and GOFF, themselves old-timers, stood by while Hutchins and crew fought BORIE's battle-damage.

It was a losing fight. The maimed engines were beyond first aid, and the destroyer's hull, crushed at the bow below the waterline, was letting in the sea at a rate which pumps and bucket brigades were unable to contend with. As the afternoon grayed into dusk, 20-foot waves were crashing over BORIE's fantail, and it was all she could do to keep her stern to the gale.

At nightfall it was evident that the vessel was sinking. Commander Hutchins signalled his intention to abandon, and summoned the men up from below. As though determined not to be cheated of this victim, the seas climbed higher as BARRY and GOFF closed in to take off BORIE's crew. Tragically enough, 27 of BORIE's crew were lost in the rabid seas. Expert rescue work by GOFF and BARRY, and the superb courage of all hands from BORIE, prevented a greater loss.

The destroyer went down, but she had sent U-405 ahead of her.

Badger, Clemson, Dupont, Ingram, and Bogue Kill U-172

On December 12-13, 1943, a CVE-DD team fought an anti-sub battle that was to stand as a fine prototype for cooperative effort between the surface and air units of a hunter-killer group. Here was synchronized teamwork as successful as it was exemplary.

The group (Task Group 21.13) was composed of the escort-carrier BOGUE (Captain J. B. "Joe" Dunn) and the veteran destroyers GEORGE E. BADGER (Lieutenant E. M. Higgins, U.S.N.R.), DUPONT (Commander J. G. Marshall), CLEMSON (Lieutenant W. F. Moran, U.S.N.R.), and OSMOND INGRAM (Lieutenant Commander R. F. Miller, U.S.N.R.). Led by Commander E. W. Yancey, the quartet of old four-pipers teamed with BOGUE to form a crack hunter-killer outfit under over-all command of Captain Dunn.

Conducting an offensive anti-sub patrol, the group was steaming en route from Casablanca to the States, and it had reached the vicinity of lat. 26-19 N., long. 29-58 W., when December 12 came up on the calendar. The date was not all that came up on that day.

Action began when BOGUE's scouting aircraft spotted a skulking U-boat. The enemy submerged, and the hunt was on. Racing to the area where the sub had been discovered, CLEMSON made sound contact with the U-boat and promptly spread a pattern of depth charges over the appropriate spot. While the water boiled, a plane from BOGUE took station overhead to watch for bubbles or debris.

Meanwhile, BADGER, DUPONT, and INGRAM steamed forward to join CLEMSON in the hunt. Deep under the surface, the U-boat engaged in those evasive maneuvers which are the speciality of the submarine under fire—playing doggo with motors cut off; drifting this way and that; quietly fishtailing off in the hope of finding some foxhole under a density layer that will deflect the hunter's probing "ping."

But the American destroyers were not to be eluded. For the remainder of that day and throughout the succeeding night they remained on the deep-sea enemy's track. Intermittent sound contacts kept the DD's in touch. Circling and "pinging," they located the U-boat time and again. Down went the depth charges, hurling up voluminous geysers and tumbling the surface in the attacking destroyer's wake. The persistence of the DD's and the violence of barrage after barrage forced the U-boat captain to the surface during the night in a frantic effort either to charge batteries or gulp fresh air. Instantly the destroyers opened fire on the submarine's silhouette, and the U-boat was forced to submerge and endure another prolonged depth-charge ordeal.

Then BOGUE's impatient airmen rejoined the battle at 0400, and the implacable hunt went on in the dawn's early light. Shortly after 0800, one of the flyers —Lieutenant (jg) H. G. Bradshaw—sighted a telltale oil slick, and called the destroyers to the spot. Thereafter the sound gear was practically superfluous; the injured U-boat was leaking oil and leaving a trail as plain as the slime-track of a snail.

Following the oil slick, CLEMSON and INGRAM thrashed the adjacent and subjacent waters for an hour with a steady rain of depth charges. Then another hour—and still another hour. By that time—and the clock well past mid-morning—both destroyers were short of teardrops and ashcans. And it looked as though their target would succumb to nothing less than a direct hit.

Then, just as American patience was giving out along with the anti-sub ammunition, the U-boat climbed to the surface and ran for it. One of BOGUE's aircraft spied the sub as she broke water, and the aviator shouted the word over voice radio. Two Wildcats zoomed from BOGUE's flight deck and bulleted to the target, whipping machine-gun fire at the U-boat. With three planes strafing the conning tower, and the destroyers closing in, the Nazi submariners opened the hatches and dived overside. The aircraft held their fire and veered off, believing the U-boaters were abandoning ship.

But not all of the U-boaters abandoned. Apparently those who leaped into the water were panic-stricken or mutinous; the Nazi captain and some of the crew rushed to man the deck guns, and the U-boat gunners opened fire. One shell struck INGRAM's quarterdeck. The explosion killed a destroyerman and wounded eight others of the crew.

The DD's answered the Nazi's fire with deadly gunnery that soon had the U-boat wheeling helplessly in circles. Six minutes of this shooting match, and the submarine's decks were awash. As the Germans flung themselves from her bridge, the battered U-boat plunged for the last time. The captain, executive officer, and 33 other survivors were fished from the littered sea by the American hunter-killers.

The submarine destroyed by Task Group 21.13 was the U-172, one of Nazi Germany's largest and newest specimens. The stubborn resistance put up by this submersible, and its ability to absorb the shock of aerial bombs, strafing, prolonged depth-charging, and bursts of gunfire in a going-over of nearly 24-hour's duration, testified as to how tough these new U-boats were. As a matter of fact it was crew morale which first succumbed. The pressure hull sustained damage and leaked some oil, but it was the nerve of the embattled crew which apparently drained away. The submariners caved in—not the submarine.

Hunter-killer teamwork had achieved a great success. But perhaps the moral which highlights this A/S episode concerns persistence.

If the U-boat was stubborn, the hunter-killers were more so. The patience and perseverance which moves mountains had removed from the Atlantic another Nazi submarine.

Schenck Kills U-645

While the BOGUE hunter-killers were patrolling the convoy route to Casablanca, other A/S groups were making the North Atlantic unsafe for the wolfpacks. One of these was Task Group 21.14 built around the previously mentioned escort-carrier CARD and Captain A. J. ("Buster") Isbell. They were out on the hunt the week before Christmas 1943.

But they found no festive holly, no gay Yule log in that foam-blown area of the gray North Atlantic, vicinity of lat. 45-00 N., long. 21-00 W. Rather, the seas were wind-whipped and icy, and the spirit in the task group was expressed by tense vigilance, gritted teeth, and anything but peaceful intentions.

For Task Group 21.14 was after one of Doenitz's wolfpacks a pack of such numerical size that it amounted to a U-boat concentration. At least 30 submarines were known to have foregathered in the target area.

The battle exploded the day before Christmas.

On the night of December 23-24, SCHENCK (Lieutenant Commander E. W. Logsdon) was operating as screen on CARD's port bow. At 0216 on the morning of the 24th the destroyer picked up a radar contact, range 10,100 yards. As SCHENCK rushed for the submarine, the "pip" faded on the radar screen. But at

2,500 yards the U-boat was sighted in the act of submerging, her stern toward the DD.

Logsdon ordered a swift change of course to avoid a possible homing torpedo, then shifted rudder after swinging 50°, and slowed to 15 knots to probe with sonar where the U-boat had gone under. Sound reported contact at 800 yards, and at 0250 SCHENCK dropped the first depth charges of a pattern. The destroyer rolled and veered as fountains boomed in her wake. The battle was on.

Thirty minutes of this, and then a "pip" showed up on the radar screen, range 4,000. As Logsdon drove his destroyer at this target (probably the U-boat which had been depth-charged), radar contact was lost at 2,500 yards. But Sound regained contact at 1,900, and at 0327 SCHENCK sowed another depth-charge pattern across the sea.

About two minutes after the last charge exploded, a rumbling blast welled up from the deep with a detonation that shook the destroyer. Up came a great billow of oil that spread a dark carpet across the water. There could be no doubt of a kill, and post-war records verified the U-boat's destruction. However, SCHENCK's destroyermen were unable to make immediate verification. As Logsdon was preparing to get a sample of the Nazi sub's lifeblood, a call came in over the TBS. The destroyer LEARY had been torpedoed!

Logsdon wasted no time in post-mortem oil examination. Ordering the engine-room to "pour on the coal," he sent SCHENCK racing to LEARY's rescue.

Loss of U.S.S. Leary

As the first United States destroyer to make radar contact on an enemy submarine, the U.S.S. LEARY had acquired a distinction unique in American naval history.

She had earned her radar reputation while on "short-of-war" convoy duty in November 1941.

Escorting convoys during the succeeding months of the shooting war, LEARY had suffered no dearth of "pips" on her radar screen, and had dropped her full share of depth charges on the elusive *unterseebooten.* In the summer of 1942 she had served with nine escorts under group leadership of Commander P. R. Heineman, conducting Convoy ONS-102 across miles of hot submarine water. On that particular run LEARY participated in a six-day U-boat brawl that kept the destroyermen at battle stations until all were ready to unravel from strain and fatigue.

LEARY, then, knew these U-boat infested waters, and she had been bucking along through the December seas with a crew hair-triggered for action. The night of the 23rd-24th was typical of the season—frosty whitecaps leaping in the dark, and a boreal wind brooming up gusts of spume and spray that stung a lookout's face like shots of salt.

Midnight on the clock, and LEARY was driving along in the blackout, making radar sweeps. The calendar entered December 24, and the watch went about the usual routine. Then the monotony was jolted by a sharp report from the radar watch. Contact! Submarine off the bow!

Time: 0158. LEARY's captain, Commander James E. Kyes, rushed all hands to battle stations, and the destroyer went after the U-boat. While tracking, she momentarily established a sound contact at close range. Before her crew could unlimber depth-charges, the destroyer was struck and staggered by two torpedoes that smote her on the starboard flank, well aft. The rapid explosions blended into a single roar. Men were thrown from their feet as the LEARY lurched and veered, hard hit. Twelve minutes had elapsed between the time of radar contact and this mortal blow.

LEARY's men fought her battle-damage with the quiet desperation of seamen who know their ship is *in extremis.* There was no holding back the icy seas that plunged with a roar through the breach in the destroyer's hull. About 0225, Commander Kyes gave the order to abandon. The men lined up in their kapok jackets and went over the side.

About 0237, the sinking destroyer was convulsed by two more explosions. Survivors believed that LEARY was struck by a third torpedo which hit her amidships, causing the internal blasts. A moment before this volcanic eruption, LEARY's captain, Commander Kyes, was glimpsed in the act of handing his kapok life-jacket to a mess attendant. He refused to abandon ship until those who served under him were safely off, and this valiant conduct was to cost him his life. Her hull ruptured by those two final explosions, LEARY sank almost immediately, taking her captain down with her.

Commander Kyes' sacrificial heroism was matched by the heroic efforts of CARD's captain to rescue the LEARY's survivors. For the rest of that night Captain Isbell sent his flat-top zig-zagging and circling through the darkness, while SCHENCK combed the surface for LEARY's destroyerman. With but one destroyer, the DECATUR, remaining to serve as screen for CARD, the CVE was a set-up target for the U-boats in that vicinity. Nevertheless Isbell refused to call in CARD's other guardian until the last LEARY survivor was rescued from the freezing sea.

Thanks to Captain Isbell and the good work of SCHENCK and other units of the task group, many of LEARY's crew were saved. By final count, some 97 of the stricken destroyer's complement were lost. It was a painful blow for the DesLant Force on that day before Christmas, but one that left in memory the silhouette of a fighting ship and the name of two valiant captains—Commander Kyes, who gave his life-jacket to a messman, and Captain Isbell, who risked an escort-carrier to rescue a good company of destroyermen.

LEARY was the third United States destroyer to go down to U-boat torpedoes in the Battle of the Atlantic. And she was the last.

Inventory 1943

Grand Admiral Karl Doenitz, Commander-in-Chief of the German Navy, was a worried Nazi on New Year's Eve, 1943. He had just been running over the figures of his U-boat campaign for the past year and checking them against those of the previous war years. And his troubles were as obvious as the simple arithmetic of profit and loss.

SUBMARINE WAR STATISTICS

In 1939 (four months of war): 9 U-boats lost, 810 Allied ships sunk.

In 1940: 22 U-boats lost; 4,407 Allied ships sunk.

In 1941: 35 U-boats lost; 4,398 Allied ships sunk.

In 1942: 85 U-boats lost; 8,245 Allied ships sunk.

In 1943: 237 U-boats lost; 3,611 Allied ships sunk.

On the Allied side of the ledger, some interesting merchant marine statistics were on hand for perusal at the end of 1943. The table at the bottom of the page tells the story of British-American shipbuilding during the war to that date.

Remarking upon the statistical summary at war's end, Admiral King noted in his report (*The U.S. Navy at War*) that the figures revealed important features of the Battle of the Atlantic.

(a) Until the closing months of 1942 the German submarines were continuing to reduce the available total of Allied tonnage;

(b) Antisubmarine operations resulted in the sinking of an average of 12 German submarines per month after 1 January 1943, or a total of 480 in the two years 1943-44;

(c) American shipyards alone produced an average of a million tons per month of new merchant ships after 1 January 1943, or a total of 24,000,000 tons in two years.

So much for the statistical features of the Battle of the Atlantic as of December 31, 1943.

But Doenitz promised himself a comeback. Under construction in German yards were new and formidable submarines—prefabricated jobs that could be mass produced. Of the two new U-boat types projected, Type XXI, a 1,600-tonner, was a submersible calculated to put all previous models in the shade. Radically streamlined, this 251-foot submarine was powered by a stepped-up drive that gave it a submerged speed of approximately 18 knots. It was reported that the craft could dive to the unheard-of depth of 700 feet. Some time would pass before production problems could be ironed out, but Type XXI was well past the blueprint stage, and would be launched when the production bottle-neck was broken.

Another surprise Doenitz had up his sleeve was *Schnorkel*. In fact, this famous "breather device" was already emerging from his cuff.

But neither *Schnorkel* nor the Type XXI U-boat was a *fait accompli* by the end of 1943. *Schnorkel* would not go into action until 1944, and Type XXI did not enter the war until 1945. And neither of these submarine innovations could turn the war-tide. *Schnorkel* might replace old-style U-boat gear; Type XXI's might replace lost U-boats. But neither could replace the expert submarine crews who had gone down in the Battle of the Atlantic. Neither could revive the expert wolfpack captains—the Priens, the Schepkes, the Guggenbergers—who went out and failed to return.

And, speaking of U-boats early in that year, Secretary of the Navy Frank Knox had observed, *"Each time they go out, there will be a sharply increasing likelihood that they will not come back."*

NEW CONSTRUCTION (TONS)

DATE	U.S.	BRITISH	TOTAL	NET GAINS OR LOSSES
1939	*101,000*	*231,000*	*332,000*	*— 478,000*
1940	*439,000*	*780,000*	*1,219,000*	*— 3,188,000*
1941	*1,169,000*	*815,000*	*1,984,000*	*— 2,414,000*
1942	*5,339,000*	*1,843,000*	*7,182,000*	*— 1,063,000*
1943	*12,384,000*	*2,201,000*	*14,585,000*	*+10,974,000*
TOTALS	*19,432,000*	*5,870,000*	*25,302,000*	*+ 3,831,000*

These men are submarine killers! Crew of Borie being transferred to Card, after their destroyer sank one sub and rammed another. Riding over the starboard bow of the Nazi submarine, Borie suffered damage which opened up her port side and flooded her forward engine-room. Forced to abandon ship in a storm, three officers and 27 men were lost transferring to Barry and Goff.

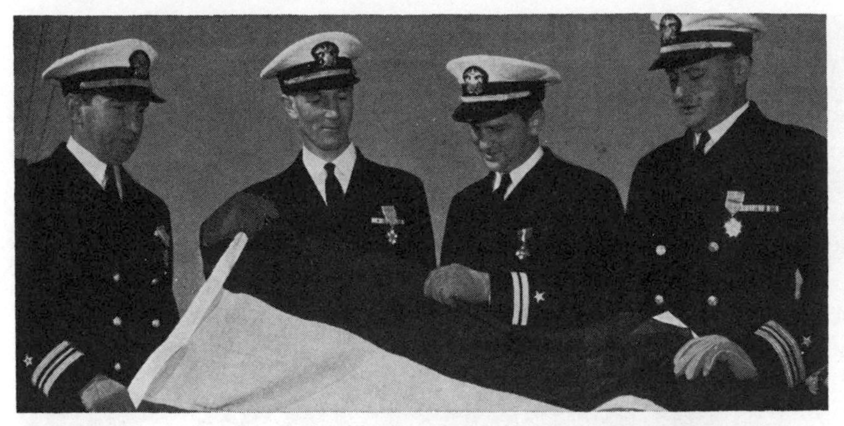

Task Unit Commanders examine Presidential Unit Citation pennant awarded the CVE-DD group built around U.S.S. Card. Destroyermen and naval aviators had developed tactics that changed A/S war from the defensive to the offensive.

Card group sends another Nazi sub to Davy Jones' locker. Destroyers picked up 44 survivors who swarmed from the sinking U-boat.

U-185 sinks with her own crew and that of U-604 after attack by planes from Core, August 24, 1943. The crew of the crippled U-604 had scuttled and transferred to U-185 800 miles off the Brazilian coast. But destiny caught up with them off the Azores.

The end of the Borie. Listing heavily and leaking oil, the abandoned destroyer is sunk by bombs from planes of the carrier Card.

One of the hunter-killer groups was led by the jeep carrier Santee. Bainbridge (DD 246) was doing plane guard duty when Ensign Thomas Edward D'Ansen went into the drink, and returned him to his ship. The carrier was one of four Cimarron-class fleet oilers, 11,000-ton vessels, that had been converted in 1942. The hunter-killer campaign went into high gear in the summer of 1943

CHAPTER 23

THE GANG BUSTERS (Continued)

JANUARY 1944-APRIL 1944

Schnorkel

Probably the most important submarine innovation of the war was the variously spelled *"Schnorkel"* device which permitted a submarine to operate its Diesels (and thus charge its batteries) while submerged. This ingenious funnel or extension stack could be thrust up periscope-fashion by the submarine beneath the surface. Aptly described as a "breather tube," it served as an air intake and an exhaust for the Diesel engines, and the U-boat equipped with the device might remain under water for weeks at a time, presumably beyond the easy reach of radar discovery.

Schnorkel was developed and exploited by the Germans, but it was not a German invention. Parenthetically it might be noted that Nazism, with its insistence on conformity and regimented thinking, was not disposed to foster scientific cerebration. Many of the nation's top-ranking scientists had been driven into exile before the war. The physicists and chemists who did remain on the home front were for the most part assigned to Army and Air Force projects. The German naval effort suffered accordingly. Not until the end of 1943 was Admiral Doenitz able to set up an experimental staff similar to the Scientific Council created by Admiral King.

To the learned Karl Kuepfmuller, appointed head of this research body, Doenitz dourly confessed, *"For some months past the enemy has rendered the U-boat war ineffective. . . . He has achieved this object not through superior tactics or strategy, but through his superiority in the field of science (which) finds its expression in the modern battle weapon, detection. By this means he has torn our sole offensive (naval) weapon in the war against the Anglo-Saxons from our hands. It is essential to victory that we make good our scientific disparity and thereby restore to the U-boat its fighting qualities."*

The Admiral's jeremiad was, of course, inspired by search radar, the detector that put the finger on the surfaced U-boat. *Schnorkel* was rushed into production as the answer.

The *Schnorkel* stack was Dutch in origin. It was invented some time around 1935 by Commander J. J. Wichers of the Royal Netherlands Navy. By early 1939 the *"Snuiver,"* as the Dutch termed the device, was being installed in all new Netherlands Navy submarines.

When the Nazis invaded Holland in May, 1940, the invading Germans found some scuttled *Snuiver* submarines in Dutch construction yards. The *Snuiver* apparatus was promptly salvaged, and Doenitz had an ace card in his U-boat deck. Fortunately for the Allied A/S effort, matériel priorities were hard to obtain for German naval purposes, and *Schnorkel* did not appear on German submarines until 1944.

By that date the U.S. Navy's hunter-killers were on the rampage, and the U-boat Force was never able to recover the initiative. The *Schnorkel* gear was hard to sight, but it did not provide the submarine with an invisible cloak. Aircraft spotted the *Schnorkel* "feather," even as they spied the wake of a slinking periscope. And, of course, the U-boat's pressure hull was still vulnerable to air bombs and depth charges.

So *Schnorkel* did not overcome the Allies' head start in scientific submarine detection and destruction.

Somers and Jouett Versus Blockade-Runners

The *Schnorkel* conversion program created another hiatus in the U-boat effort. Submarines could not be at sea and in drydock acquiring a windpipe at one and the same time. Wherefore the transition from non-*Schnorkel* to *Schnorkel* removed many U-boats from active duty. And large areas of Atlantic Ocean were free of Nazi submarines in the winter of 1943-44.

One such area was the oceanic triangle off Brazil. Submarine game was notably shy in these South Atlantic waters in the last quarter of 1943, and the U.S. Fourth Fleet's routine patrols had grown tedious, if not boresome. The Navy PB4Y's based on Ascension Island far out in the South Atlantic found much of the going duller than ditchwater. So did the DD's and other Fourth Fleet units which had occasion to visit that flinty flyspeck in mid-ocean.

Almost equally isolated was the island of Fernando de Noronha, several hundred miles off the coast of Brazil. American air patrols and DD or cruiser-destroyer task groups pacing the dreary reaches between Ascension, Fernando de Noronha, and the coast began to feel they were operating in a vacuum.

But, as someone once remarked, war is an endurance contest in waiting, and sooner or later one side can't wait. In this particular case the Germans couldn't. For months Hitler's *Wehrmacht* had been scraping along on *ersatz,* and the Nazi war effort was desperately in need of rubber. Tin, tungsten, and other items were also on the "must get" list. So German vessels, wearing all sorts of disguises, had been striving to reach the far-off ports of Indonesia where the precious raw materials were obtainable from the Japanese conquerors—and then trying even harder to sneak their cargoes home by the only two routes left open, around Cape Horn or around the Cape of Good Hope.

So, on New Year's Day 1944, the monotony in the South Atlantic was broken. It was broken when Lieutenant M. K. Taylor, U.S.N.R., flying a patrol from Ascension, sighted an unescorted merchant ship steaming along on the ocean's blue. Lieutenant Taylor took his Liberator down to scrutinize the vessel. She was too fast for a tramp and too ordinary-looking to be anything else.

Taylor circled the ship to investigate, and challenged her by blinker. The vessel hoisted a four-flag call, but hauled it down before the plane could read it. Closing in, Taylor buzzed the freighter; was able to discern a small nameboard on the bridge. Ostensibly she was a Britisher, the S.S. GLENBANK. Again Taylor challenged. When the ship failed to hoist an answering call or make satisfactory reply, he sent a shot across her bow at close range. Whereupon the "Limeys" opened up with a savage fire. Three shots struck the Liberator, damaging the No. 2 engine and wounding one of the bomber's crew, who had been photographing the ship.

"Limeys, hell! Those birds are Krauts!"

Heading the injured bomber for Ascension, Taylor radioed the word to whom it might concern.

It concerned the destroyer SOMERS (Commander W. C. Hughes, Jr.) and another Liberator (Lieutenant R. T. Johnson, U.S.N.R.), on patrol in the area. Johnson made a beeline for the blockade runner; ran into thickening darkness; kept going until his fuel supply went low. Then he winged for home to pick up gas and wait for morning. Destroyer SOMERS raced on through the night, hot for the quarry.

The following morning Johnson's Liberator roared up from astern, streaked over the DD, and sped on over the horizon. Not long after that, a radio message came back from the bomber. The plane had located the Nazi vessel. But the blockade-runner's anti-aircraft batteries had put several shots through the Liberator as it swooped in on the attack. Although his plane had been struck twice in the tail and a wing, Johnson remained on station to home the SOMERS and the other two planes of his search group to the target. Then he sent word that the hits had caused a gas leak. His aircraft in trouble, Johnson was turning back for Ascension.

The injured Liberator presently reported that one engine was dead. A few moments later Johnson radioed that another engine was gone. Seventy miles from Ascension, the bomber was flying in on a wing and a prayer. It didn't make it. Rescue planes took off from the Ascension base, but somewhere in the vastness of the South Atlantic the Liberator with Johnson and nine crew members disappeared without trace. The rescue planes abandoned the hopeless search at nightfall. Score one for the spurious "S.S. GLENBANK."

Aboard the U.S.S. SOMERS all hands determined to get that blockade-runner. Racing through the evening of January 2, the destroyermen "lighted off all burners." A short time later the lookouts had the enemy in sight—a rakish silhouette in the moonlight.

The Nazi strove with everything in her to escape the oncoming DD. Her engines were fast, but not fast enough. SOMERS closed the range to 7,000 yards. At 2302 Hughes ordered his gun crews to open up, and shells from the DD began to splash around the target. Zigzagging frantically, the Nazi freighter ran like a jackrabbit. Her guns were no match for those of the destroyer, and the DD's fire was not returned. Stabbing shells into the freighter, SOMERS closed in. The blockade-runner reeled under the impact of multiple hits. Shrapnel smashed her deck machinery and ripped up her bridge. Her funnel went askew. Down came her wireless mast. Her taffrail was blasted. Her decks littered with dead and dying Germans, her superstructure torn to pieces, the disintegrating vessel sloughed to a stop.

From seven lifeboats and a raft SOMERS retrieved 17 officers and 116 men. A good haul. At 0030 in the morning of January 3, the target sank. The Germans identified the vessel as the S.S. WESSERLAND. So the conquerors of ODENWALD added a second blockade-runner to their score sheet.

Like certain species of big game, German blockade-runners sometimes ran in pairs. Witness the fact that on January 4, 1944, a scout plane from the light cruiser OMAHA (flagship of Rear Admiral O. M. Read, ComCruDiv 2) sighted a furtive merchantman steaming across the South Atlantic seascape not many miles from the spot where WESSERLAND had met her end. Unable to satisfactorily identify herself, this vessel was soon brought to book by OMAHA and companion destroyer JOUETT (Commander J. C. Parham, Jr.). The Nazi's doom was sealed. In a running gun battle with the cruiser and the destroyer, she was smashed to the bottom. The sailors who lived identified her as the S.S. RIO GRANDE.

And now the Fourth Fleet was presented with a real bonanza. The RIO GRANDE had hardly gone to the bottom of the South Atlantic, when OMAHA received word from a plane of the Natal patrol that an unidentified freighter was skulking along the horizon in that sector. So it came about that on January 5 the OMAHA-JOUETT team had another blockade-runner hull down on the horizon. As the warships closed in, the Germans threw up the sponge, and scuttled. They were waiting meekly in lifeboats and on rafts when the destroyers WINSLOW and DAVIS, the Brazilian minelayer CAMORIN, and the Brazilian merchantman POTI finally arrived to pick up survivors. The scuttled ship was the S.S. BURGENLAND.

The liquidation of these three blockade-runners cost the Nazis a good 21,000 tons of shipping, and an enormous quantity of rubber, the No. 1 want in Germany at that time. And Hitler's loss was Uncle Sam's gain. The freighters went down, but the rubber floated. The Navy's salvage tugs recovered enough rubber *"to make tires for 5,000 bombers."*

Loss of U.S.S. Turner

Early in the morning of January 3, 1944, the U.S.S. TURNER maneuvered into an assigned anchorage off Ambrose Light, and dropped the hook. A new destroyer, commissioned on April 15, 1943, she had just made the long voyage home after a routine escort job as a unit of Task Force 64. Tired seamen turned in with the usual "channel fever" which takes a ship's company after an arduous passage brings the vessel within easy reach of port, while the watches went about their regular duties. The destroyer swung quietly in the darkness—all the usual routine.

Then, at 0616, just as the night was graying to eastward, TURNER was shaken by a violent explosion. Men were jostled from their feet and thrown from their berths. As all hands rushed to emergency stations, some thought the destroyer had been hit by a torpedo, or had been struck by a drifting mine. But the blast had hurled up a fan of light in the vicinity of No. 2 mount; the explosion was internal, probably caused by defective ammunition. Flames leapt up through open hatches, exposing deck and turret in holocaustal light. TURNER had been badly damaged, and she was burning fiercely.

Having sighted the blast, the destroyer SWASEY and other vessels of Task Force 64 closed in to aid TURNER, and pilot boats and small boats were soon standing by for the rescue. TURNER's decks were hot when the rescuers reached her anchorage. Neither foamite nor bulkheads seemed able to contain the flames, and flash after flash had turned the destroyer into a floating inferno.

She burned until 0742, when the fire evidently reached her magazines and a volcanic eruption burst her smoke-wrapped hull. TURNER went down almost immediately, rolling over to starboard and sinking stern-first in a shroud of lethal fumes and steam. As the waters closed over the stricken vessel, the rescuers ran in to pick up survivors.

TURNER's captain, Commander H. S. Wygant, Jr., went down with the ship. Two officers and about 165 men were saved. To the DesLant Force the destroyer's loss came as a severe shock. Fatalities were unusually heavy, and the violence of the initial explosion and subsequent flash fire consumed evidence as to the exact cause of the disaster.

Enter the Destroyer-Escort

The destroyer-escort was a tough little warship. Averaging 1,140 to 1,450 tons, she was designed to do the A/S work of the full-sized destroyer engaged in normal anti-sub duty, and she was given sufficient punch to enable her to trade hard blows with surface and air attackers if necessary. Although the DE lacked the speed, fire power, and armor of the DD, her depth charges were equally as destructive, and anti-submarine warfare was specifically the destroyer-escort's business. To that end she was equipped with the latest detection devices and the newest of A/S weapons.

All DE's were in one of six different design groups. Their armament varied from three 3-inch 50-caliber dual-purpose guns and one 40 mm. quad to two 5-inch 38-caliber dual-purpose guns, one 40 mm. quad, and three 40 mm. twin mounts. They were variously powered by turbo-electric plants, Diesel engines, or geared-turbines. Their shaft horsepower ran from 6,000 to 12,000; their speed from some 20 to 24 knots—which is about 15 knots less than that of a modern DD. But horsepower was not the destroyer-escort's big talking point. As a submarine hunter she enjoyed one considerable advantage over the DD—the advantage of a tight "turning circle" that gave the DE an agility or maneuverability which was envied by veteran destroyermen and feared by enemy submariners.

Contracts for the first destroyer-escorts were let in November 1941. However, as early as the previous June of that year, Rear Admiral J. W. S. Dorling, R.N., heading the British Supply Council in North America, had discussed with Naval Secretary Knox the need for such a warship as the destroyer-escort. Dorling proposed that Lend-Lease funds be used for the building of DE's. The U.S. Navy's Bureau of Ships already had a suitable design available, and the Royal Navy requested 100 of the vessels on a ten-per-month construction schedule.

But merchant ships and landing craft for amphibious operations had the priority, and Diesel engines and steel were not available to the DE builders for months to come. So the first destroyer-escort was not delivered until February 1943, when the U-boat situation was alarmingly critical.

To the Royal Navy went two of the four DE's launched that February from American yards. But the two which entered the United States Navy—U.S.S. DOHERTY and U.S.S. AUSTIN—were followed by a dozen more that spring, and by July 1943 the DE building program was going full gun. Then, to quote Lewis Carroll, "thick and fast they came at last, and more and more and more." Seventeen building yards were engaged in the construction effort, among them Brown Shipyards of Houston, Texas, the Dravo Corporation of Neville Island, Pennsylvania, and the Tampa Shipbuilding Company of Tampa, Florida. Navy Yards at Boston, Philadelphia, Mare Island, and Puget Sound also put their shoulders to the DE construction job. And as mass production methods and techniques went into high gear, destroyer-escorts came off the line with a rapidity that approached conveyor-belt speed. Between February 1943 and War's end, 467 destroyer-escorts were produced by American builders. The Royal Navy received 78 of these warships; eight went to the Brazilian Navy, and six went into the service of the Free French.

Like destroyers newly commissioned, many of the Navy's new DE's were named after naval heroes, officers and men who had lost their lives in heroic action during the opening months of World War II—such as the TOMICH for Chief Water-Tender Tomich of the stricken UTAH at Pearl Harbor; the MUIR for Lieutenant (jg) Kenneth Muir, U.S.N.R., Armed Guard officer of the torpedoed freighter NATHANIEL HAWTHORNE; and the BORUM for Lieutenant (jg) John R. Borum, U.S.N.R., who achieved hero stature in the burning tanker BRILLIANT. Along with these modern heroes the new destroyer-escorts commemorated such Old Navy heroes as Reuben James and Jacob Jones.

By the end of June 1943, there were twenty-two 1,140-ton destroyer-escorts and thirteen large 1,450-ton DE's available for duty. The smaller DE carried a complement of about 200 officers and men. The larger averaged about 216 crew members. The majority of DE captains and crews were drawn from the Naval Reserve. The schooling of these destroyermen marked a new high in Navy Training. Rushed through basic, specialist, and operational schools, the DE crews engaged in A/S training at Key West, Bermuda, and elsewhere, and went out to do able battle with the enemy after the briefest of shakedown cruises.

Only a few of the DE's were available for service with DesLant forces in the summer of 1943. The need was urgent, particularly for convoy duty. Experience demonstrated that the U-boats in a wolfpack attacking a convoy usually outnumbered the escorts two to one. CinCLant and ComDesLant hoped to overcome this disparity by assigning at least two extra destroyers or DE's to a task group. Given these additional escorts, the Escort Commander could detail one or several DE's to run down a contact and stay with it, conducting a persistent hunt, without leaving a dangerously large gap in the convoy's escorting cordon.

Meantime, destroyer-escorts were also needed in the Pacific, and the Navy had to meet the exigencies and pressures of a two-ocean war. It was not until the autumn of 1943 that DE's appeared in the Atlantic in anything like the desired number.

But by December of that year destroyer-escorts were showing up on the flanks of trans-Atlantic convoys and as screens for baby flat-tops leading groups of hunter-killers on offensive A/S missions.

Already the CVE-DD teams had blown large holes in Doenitz's wolfpacks. The CVE-DD-DE teams would knock the ultimate bottom out of the Nazi U-boat effort.

Thomas, Bostwick and Bronstein Kill U-709

March 1944 was the month in which the DE's made their first U-boat kill. Sharing the honors were the destroyer-escorts THOMAS (Lieutenant Commander D. M. Kellogg, U.S.N.R.), flying the pennant of Commander G. A. Parkinson, U.S.N.R., ComCortDiv 48; BOSTWICK (Lieutenant Commander J. H. Church, Jr., U.S.N.R.); and BRONSTEIN (Lieutenant S. H. Kinney). These DE's were units of Task Group 21.16, built around the new escort-carrier BLOCK ISLAND, under the driving command of Captain Logan C. Ramsey. The baby flat-top's screen included the destroyer CORRY and the DE BREEMAN, but these two did not get into the action which exploded late in the evening of February 29.

Action had been brewing for several days, for BLOCK ISLAND and her team of hunter-killers were operating in wolfpack water, vicinity of lat. 49-00 N., long. 26-00 W., where at least 18 Nazi submarines were reported to be holding rendezvous.

Steaming as screen on the port bow of BLOCK ISLAND, destroyer-escort BRONSTEIN made the radar contact, range 6,500 yards, at 2208. Then, as BRONSTEIN raced for the target, the flare of a depth-charge marker lit up the seascape. DE's THOMAS and BOSTWICK, developing their own contacts, were silhouetted by one of their markers as they bore in on a coordinated attack. The three destroyer-escorts boxed the target, but the submarine remained unsighted until 2213, when BRONSTEIN fired an illumination spread. The light sprayed a downward glare that caught the enemy full in the face—a surfaced U-boat.

Evidently the Nazi submariners were concentrating on THOMAS and BOSTWICK, for they seemed unaware of BRONSTEIN's rush until Kinney ordered his gunners to open fire. As BRONSTEIN's guns roared and spat, there was a scramble on the U-boat's bridge. Shells from the DE's 3-inch 50-caliber battery dug holes in the sea close aboard the submarine, and tracers from BRONSTEIN's 40 mm. twin mount whipped across the U-boat's conning tower. With 40 mm. shells bursting against the U-boat's superstructure, the sub captain called for a dive, and "pulled the plug."

BRONSTEIN made two hedgehog attacks, pelting the sea with pattern after pattern. Then BOSTWICK and THOMAS followed through with runs, spattering the submerged enemy with hedgehog barrages and deep-thundering depth-charge bombardments.

For five hours the DE's kept at it, tracking and bombing, tracking and bombing. There was no respite for the Nazi submarine, no let-up.

It was all up with the U-709. About 0320 of that March morning, destroyer-escort THOMAS was laying a pattern of depth-charges set for a deep barrage. Down went the ashcans. Up came the rumble of explosions deep under. Then, at 0324, the surface heaved with the detonation of a blast that left a maelstrom in the DE's wake. The eruption could have had but one meaning—a U-boat had blown up.

But U-709 (identified by post-war records) was not the only U-boat sunk by the DE hunters on that spot and date. While THOMAS and BOSTWICK had been concentrating on their quarry, BRONSTEIN had found other fish to fry.

Bronstein Sinks U-603

Commissioned on December 13, 1943, BRONSTEIN had completed her shakedown period only three weeks before this North-Atlantic U-boat battle. But lack of experience did not prevent her sonar operator from recognizing a brand new echo in his gear as distinctly different from the intermittent depth-bombing THOMAS and BOSTWICK were giving the U-709.

Skipper Kinney of BRONSTEIN immediately went to work—and high time, for when contact was made at 0137, the range was a perilously short 450 yards. In exactly one minute Kinney had the depth charges going. After the TNT went overside, Kinney sent the DE veering about in an effort to regain sound contact. Fifteen minutes of patient searching by the DE followed, with the U-boat somewhere down below, playing "it" in this lethal game of tag.

At 0155, with all hands in a vise of tension, Kinney directed the dropping of a pattern of 18 depth-charges, set to go deep. The barrage was still thundering down under when a tremendous explosion boomed in the sea. There could be little doubt that the submarine's pressure hull had burst, but Kinney was taking no chances. At 0236 he ordered a full 18-charge pattern. The echoes of this barrage died away into a silence which convinced the DE's Sound crew that the submarine under fire had also died away.

Post-war records revealed that BRONSTEIN's target on this occasion was U-603. Score two for BRONSTEIN. And her maiden cruise was not yet over.

Loss of U.S.S. Leopold

In March 1944, Convoy CU-16 was trudging across the North Atlantic under escort of Task Group 21.5. Among the units of TG 21.5 were the destroyer-escorts LEOPOLD and JOYCE. Both comparative newcomers, the pair were running along on the convoy's flank like shepherd dogs guarding a plodding herd.

On the 9th of March the convoy was in the vicinity of 58-00 N., 25-00 W., about 540 miles southwest of

Iceland. No waters of the Atlantic were more dangerous. In this area, about a third of the way between the British Isles and Newfoundland, the U-boat blitz had raged at its height in the winter of 1942-43. Here such convoys as HX-217, HX-218, and HX-219 had fought bitter battles with the ravening wolfpacks. Scores of Allied merchantmen had been torpedoed and hundreds of seamen had been killed by fire and explosion in these waters, or had drowned in wintry seas which averaged around 30° Farenheit.

Now, treading the path across this submarine zone, destroyer-escort LEOPOLD picked up a radar contact at 1950 in the evening. The DE's skipper, Lieutenant Commander K. C. Phillips, U.S.C.G., rushed all hands to battle stations, and drove LEOPOLD forward to investigate.

About 1955, LEOPOLD's TBS excitedly voiced the message:

THIS LOOKS LIKE THE REAL THING

Destroyer-escort JOYCE (Lieutenant Commander Robert Wilcox, U.S.C.G.) was ordered to assist her sister DE. But before JOYCE could get there, the battle was on. About 2000, two starshells soared from LEOPOLD's deck, and as the pyrotechnic bursts illumined the seascape, the DE's guns opened fire at the enemy's silhouette.

The U-boat fired a spread of torpedoes. Before Phillips could swing his ship to comb the wakes, two of the deadly fish smote the DE, blasting her portside compartments B-1 and B-2. Bounced by the explosions, the destroyer-escort staggered to a halt. There was a dreadful rending of metal, the creak and crunch of buckling plates. LEOPOLD's back was broken.

When JOYCE reached the scene at 2015, LEOPOLD was dead in the water, jackknifed, with bow and stern up-angled, and screws in the air. After a fruitless search for the enemy sub, JOYCE began rescue operations. At midnight she was still picking up survivors. Hazardous work, for the U-boat remained in the vicinity long enough to fire two torpedoes at the second DE. JOYCE spotted the oncoming fish, and managed to evade. The submarine was driven down, and rescue work went forward.

At 0045 of the following morning, a gush of sea rode over the half-swamped vessel, and LEOPOLD's stern section tore loose and sank. Going under, the DE's depth charges exploded. Men died wretchedly in this eruption of fire and water, and JOYCE had a difficult time locating swimmers in the littered swirl.

Man after man was fished, shivering and oil-smeared, from the churning sea. But the count was depressingly brief. By morning only 28 survivors had been recovered from the stricken destroyer-escort. Not a single officer was found, and it was evident that Lieutenant Commander Phillips had been lost aboard his ship.

When the last survivor was picked up by JOYCE's willing hands, the sea was cleared of the living, and only the stump of LEOPOLD's bow could be seen adrift. After daybreak revealed that further search was useless, JOYCE was ordered to sink this residue with gunfire and depth charges. JOYCE performed this grim task at 0745, and LEOPOLD was gone. She was the first destroyer-escort downed in the war.

But the DE's avenged her loss many times over. And only two more destroyer-escorts would go down to U-boat torpedoes in the Atlantic Battle—a remarkable record for the months of unceasing A/S warfare that engaged the DE's in the Atlantic until VE-Day.

Hobson, Haverfield, Prince Rupert, and Aircraft Kill U-575

The psuedo-science of numerology endows the number 13 with influential properties, mostly unlucky.

But to the officers and men of Task Group 21.11, the 13th of March must have seemed a fortuitous date, whereas the Nazi captain and crew of U-575 must have considered it precisely the opposite. Much depends on a point of view.

Task Group 21.11 was a hunter-killer group led by escort carrier BOGUE under Captain J. B. Dunn. It included the destroyer HOBSON (Lieutenant Commander K. Loveland), the destroyer-escort HAVERFIELD (Lieutenant Commander J. A. Mathews, U.S.N.R.), H.M.C.S. PRINCE RUPERT, and three aircraft squadrons—British 172 and 206 and American VC-95. The Normandy invasion was on the planning table when these hunter-killers were dispatched to raid a U-boat rendezvous off the Azores, and all hands were out to do a sweeping job.

Action began late in the morning of the 13th when one of BOGUE's planes sighted an oil slick. The plane sent out a call for surface craft, and dropped a sono-buoy. The buoy signalled the presence of a submarine in the vicinity, and the hunt was under way.

At 1151, destroyer-escort HAVERFIELD arrived on the scene. After searching for about two hours, she made sonar contact at 1,700 yards, and at 1417 she fired a hedgehog salvo. She followed through with a second and third hedgehog attack, and at 1447 she unleashed a depth-charge barrage. The explosions brought a cluster of black oil bubbles to the surface.

Meantime, H.M.C.S. PRINCE RUPERT arrived on the field of battle. The Canadians delivered a depth-charge attack and let fly with a hedgehog pattern. HAVERFIELD laid still another depth-charge pattern at

1538, and followed through with a full pattern of hedgehogs at 1551. PRINCE RUPERT continued the depth-charging at 1601, and at 1629 unleashed a full pattern of depth-charges. The Canadian remained "to the left of contact" to conn HAVERFIELD into firing position. At 1632 HAVERFIELD dumped 13 depth charges down on the target when PRINCE RUPERT signalled on bearing.

At this juncture destroyer HOBSON steamed onto the scene of action. She stood by as HAVERFIELD made a run at 1704, dropping a deep barrage. At 1732 HAVERFIELD tried yet again, sending the charges deep under. Then at 1759 HOBSON opened fire with a full depth-charge pattern, following through with another barrage at 1833, on a bearing given by HAVERFIELD.

No submarine could survive this sort of bombardment, and the Nazi specimen in question was not the exception. Two minutes after HOBSON's second attack, the U-boat broached. As the submarine's hull broke water, HAVERFIELD opened fire. PRINCE RUPERT's gunners lashed at the sub with a 20 mm., and HOBSON immediately joined the shooting match. While shells and bullets were riddling the U-boat's conning tower, a plane from BOGUE dived into the fray, dropped two bombs on the target, circled, and fired rockets into the port side of the battered submarine.

By 1843 the submarine's conning tower was in flames, fire was spouting from a forward hatch, and frantic Germans were fighting for a chance to leap overside. Settling slowly on an even keel, the U-boat gradually submerged. Then, with the water lapping over her decks, she suddenly thrust her bow at the sky and slid under the sea, stern-first.

HAVERFIELD picked up seven survivors. HOBSON recovered sixteen, including the U-boat captain "and one corpse."

This victim, the U-575, was the first *Schnorkel*-submarine killed by American A/S forces. But already it was too late for *Schnorkel*. The hunter-killers already had the U-boat Force by the throat.

Corry and Bronstein Kill U-801

The "milk cows" were back in the old pasture that March, and TG. 21.16 got the word. Their morale high from their recent victories in the North Atlantic, the U.S.S. BLOCK ISLAND (now under command of Captain F. M. Hughes) and her associate hunter-killers steamed at top speed for the target area, which was located northwest of the Cape Verdes.

Scouting ahead, aircraft from BLOCK ISLAND went ranging over the enemy's refuelling ground. And on the morning of St. Patrick's Day the BLOCK ISLAND scouts spotted a U-boat, vicinity of lat. 16-42 N., long. 30-28 W.

The attack fell to the destroyer CORRY (Lieutenant Commander G. D. Hoffman) and destroyer-escort BRONSTEIN (Lieutenant S. H. Kinney). BRONSTEIN was the same DE that had won distinction on the night of March 1 by single-handedly sinking one U-boat and participating in the destruction of another. The destroyer CORRY was an old hand in the Atlantic Battle, with experiences ranging all the way from service stripes with the British Home Fleet to icy North Atlantic and humid Caribbean patrols. With her and BRONSTEIN and BLOCK ISLAND that March day were THOMAS, BREEMAN, and BOSTWICK.

Promptly on word from the BLOCK ISLAND, BRONSTEIN and CORRY peeled off and made for the target. Guided by the tracking aircraft, they maneuvered to box the U-boat in. Earlier that morning, while conducting an independent search, CORRY had made radar contact with what turned out to be radar decoy balloons. After shooting up these futile novelties, the destroyermen had continued the sub-hunt with whetted appetite. When BRONSTEIN joined the search at 0705, an oil slick was visible on the surface. Ensued the usual game of tag, the two hunters veering this way and that as the submarine dodged down below, and contact was lost, regained, lost again, and again regained. Down went the ashcans and teardrops, to be followed by thunderous upheavals of water and a flotsam of dead fish.

Then, at 1318, U-801 came plunging to the surface like a wounded whale. As the submarine broached, both CORRY and BRONSTEIN opened fire. For about five minutes the DD and DE flung 5-inch and 20 mm. fire at the struggling sub. Hits struck the U-boat's deck and conning tower, scattering the sea with debris. Then the submarine's hatches burst open and the crew came boiling up from below.

The Nazi submariners were given no chance to man the deck guns. They had only time to abandon ship. At 1326 CORRY was clasing in to ram, when the battered U-boat went abruptly down, stern first. Forty-seven of the crew of U-801 were picked up.

That afternoon of March 17, 1944, there was jubilation aboard the BRONSTEIN. Within 17 days she had participated in three U-boat kills, a record which many a veteran A/S vessel might well envy.

But her captain's action report was as modest as it was laconic. With deference Kinney wrote,

> It should be noted that the BRONSTEIN was on her first duty following her shakedown period which ended 7 February, 1944, on which date she reported for duty. Credit is reflected upon the Destroyer Escort Shakedown Group, Bermuda, which prepared this ship to take her place in the fleet, ready to fight, in a very short period.

Kinney's report concluded with this comment:

> The entire task group contributed to the sinking of this submarine. The result was the product of teamwork that realized fully the mission of CVE groups by combining every weapon, air and surface.

As for CORRY, she steamed into action two days later when planes from BLOCK ISLAND sent another U-boat to the bottom. Ordered to pick up survivors of an aircraft which had been downed, and to rescue any U-boat personnel remaining on the scene, the destroyer made a fast 70-mile run as a life-guard. She got there in time to save one U.S. naval aviator and fish eight Nazi submariners from the sea. Then she joined BOSTWICK and THOMAS in a midday attack on another submarine, which escaped. But the previous target was heard from. Before leaving this battle scene, the CORRY men recovered the body of a dead U-boat sailor. Burial services were held for the latter late in the afternoon.

Attack—rescue work—burial at sea. All in a warday's work for the destroyermen.

Champlin and Huse Down U-856

Not many U-boats were risking their necks in the waters of the Western Atlantic in the spring of 1944. By that date the Nazi Submarine Force had acquired a respect for radar that amounted to a nervous allergy. Such ingenious countermeasures as decoy balloons festooned with tails of tinfoil, and search receivers for the detection of search radar, were proving as futile as earlier attempts to frustrate sonar by coating the U-boat with rubber and sprinkling its wake with *pillenwerfer*.

Also the latest U-boat models, equipped with *Schnorkel* and high-speed Diesels, and capable of going deeper than 600 feet, were slow in coming off the ways, and were earmarked for duty in European waters. Only a few submarines were sent westward across the Atlantic.

One of these was U-856. Early in April 1944 she was roaming the sea lanes about 500 miles south of Halifax, and risking her life every time she ran up her periscope.

On April 7, DesDiv 32 (Commander C. L. Melson in flagship BOYLE), accompanied by destroyer-escort HUSE, was on the hunt. At dawn the sub had been spotted in the vicinity of lat. 40-00 N., long. 62-00 W. The destroyer group spent the morning combing the area. Contact was not made until 1542 when destroyer CHAMPLIN (Commander J. J. Schaffer) detected the deep-sea intruder with sound gear.

A veteran with one U-boat already to her credit, CHAMPLIN was joined by the destroyer-escort HUSE, and the pair made several depth-charge and hedgehog attacks. The onslaught went on for a little over an hour. Then the tormented U-boat lunged to the surface to fight it out.

As the submariners scrambled up from below to man the deck guns, CHAMPLIN's gun crews opened up, slamming shells into the enemy's conning tower and whipping her bridge with machine-gun fire, and then her skipper hurled her forward to ram. CHAMPLIN's port bow glanced off the U-boat's stern and the rammed U-boat rolled and wildly veered off, just in time to be struck by a burst of gunfire from DE HUSE.

But in the heat of the battle, a 20 mm. projectile from the CHAMPLIN's port bridge mount had struck the open top of the near-by ready-box and exploded. The shrapnel-burst felled CHAMPLIN's captain and injured three men. Commander Schaffer was mortally wounded. The Pharmacist's Mates were carrying him below when a shout went up from the destroyer's deck—the U-boat was sinking.

The submarine plunged at 1714, and a moment later CHAMPLIN and HUSE were shaken by a deep-sea explosion. U-856 had blown up.

Destroyers NIELDS and ORDRONAUX recovered 28 German survivors. The sole American fatality was CHAMPLIN's captain, Commander John J. Schaffer, who died of his wounds the following morning.

In the time-old tradition of the Navy his body was commended to the deep.

Pillsbury, Pope, Chatelain, Flaherty and Aircraft Kill U-515

Captain D. V. ("Dan") Gallery's new escort carrier GUADALCANAL had her prow pointed for Madeira that first week of April 1944. Nazi submarines were foregathering in those familiar waters, and Gallery intended to be in on the rendezvous.

So Task Group 21.12, consisting of GUADALCANAL, plus destroyer-escorts PILLSBURY (Lieutenant G. W. Casselman, U.S.N.R.), POPE (Lieutenant Commander E. H. Headland), CHATELAIN (Lieutenant Commander J. L. Foley), and FLAHERTY (Lieutenant Commander M. Johnston, Jr.), steamed for the area at top speed. The DE's were under group leadership of Commander F. S. Hall, riding in PILLSBURY.

Gallery's task group introduced a new feature into the book of anti-submarine warfare tactics. GUADALCANAL's pilots had been doing some experimental night flying. Hazardous enough on a full-size carrier, night take-offs and landings on a baby flat-top called for aviation of a high order. And on the night of April 8-9 the aviators who flew by starlight produced results.

About half an hour before midnight, searching air-

Skipper of the U-515 leads survivors aboard a DE after the hunter-killer group of the Guadalcanal had given the Nazi submarine a fifteen-hour going over. This kill in April, 1944, saw the first successful employment of night hunting from a jeep carrier. Planes had located the sub on the surface at midnight. It escaped, was relocated in the morning, and killed by the DE's.

Corry charges in on the sinking U-801, which disappeared under the waves, leaving 47 survivors, before the destroyer could ram. Spotted by the Block Island's scouting planes, the Nazis found it impossible to escape the hunter-killer team.

Nazi blockade runners Burgenland (top) and Rio Grande (bottom) are scuttled by their crews when attacked by Jouett and Omaha.

Boxed in by Pillsbury, Flaherty, Chatelain, and Pope, U-515 was caught in a death trap. Blasted to the surface, the Nazis tried to fight their way out. Chatelain and Flaherty were on target, however, and were shortly rescuing 43 survivors.

(Above) Captured Nazi sub captain Werner Henke of the U-515. (Below) The submarine beset by shells and torpedoes of U.S. DE's.

Gandy, Joyce, and Peterson sink U-550 while the tanker Pan Pennsylvania, which the sub had torpedoed, stood by to see herself avenged. Depth charged, shelled, and rammed, the U-550 was scuttled. Her skipper and eleven of his crew survived. Her shakedown cruise just over, Gandy had been on escort duty only eight days. She was one DE that "went to war in a hurry."

craft sighted a U-boat loitering on the surface. The planes attacked, and the U-boat opened fire with tracer, then made a dive to duck a rain of bombs. The submarine escaped, and around 0625 the nervy U-boat was once more sighted on the surface. Again she dived out from under, after pausing to return the fire of the attacking planes. A tough customer! It was time to call up the DE teams.

Gallery dispatched destroyer-escorts PILLSBURY and FLAHERTY to the scene. The DE's commenced searching with their sound gear around 0710, and PILLSBURY made contact about five minutes later. Lieutenant Casselman ordered two hedgehog attacks. The water was figuratively boiling when CHATELAIN steamed up to lend a hand. Not long after that, POPE arrived. Boxed by the four DE's, the U-boat was trapped.

But it was some time before the hunters were able to flush the quarry. The process involved the usual depth-charge runs, hedgehog attacks, deep and deeper barrages. First one, then another DE attacked, coached into position by a team-mate. The day heated into noon, and the seascape thundered as K-guns, racks, and hedgehog batteries released their salvos.

At 1405 there was a gush of white water close aboard CHATELAIN, and the U-boat snorted to the surface. The sub, determined to fight it out, was no novice. Hatches snapped open, gunners spilled out on deck, and German bullets were flying almost as soon as CHATELAIN's gunners opened fire. The roar of gunnery echoed across the sea, and the other DE's veered to CHATELAIN's aid.

FLAHERTY opened fire as soon as she had a clear bearing. She also launched a torpedo at 1,200 yards, which missed ahead of the dodging submarine. The U-boat gunners directed a savage fire at FLAHERTY, but were unable to score hits. CHATELAIN and FLAHERTY were on target, however, and several shell bursts staggered the U-boat. At 1408 an internal explosion shook the sub; smoke poured from her conning tower hatch; the crew came fighting up from below. Eight minutes after the explosion, the U-boat sank in a swirl of water strewn with struggling Germans.

Of the U-boat's complement of six officers and 53 men, 37 men and all the officers were picked up. They identified the downed submarine as U-515.

Among the submariners captured was the U-boat's skipper, Herr Kapitan Werner Henke, complete with Knight's Cross of the Iron Cross, plus oak leaves. He was aboard the GUADALCANAL the following day when a trio of the CVE's planes sank the U-68 in the waters off Madeira.

And Henke's capture seems to have given Captain Gallery an idea. If a CVE-DD-DE team could bag a U-boat skipper who wore the Knight's Cross of the Iron Cross, plus oak leaves, why couldn't it bring an entire U-boat back alive?

The dramatic upshot of Captain Gallery's thinking is recorded in a subsequent chapter.

Gandy, Joyce and Peterson kill U-550

Early in the morning of April 16, 1944, the merchant tanker PAN PENNSYLVANIA was ambushed and torpedoed about 100 miles off New York. Units of Task Group 21.5, the destroyer-escorts GANDY (Lieutenant Commander W. A. Sessions, U.S.N.R.), JOYCE (Lieutenant Comander Robert Wilcox, U.S.C.G.), and PETERSON (Lieutenant Commander S. M. Hay, U.S.C.G.R.) were at that time engaged in escorting the ships of a convoy which was forming in the area. The three DE's were ordered to get the submarine invader and rescue the crew of the stricken tanker.

At top speed the DE's raced to the tanker's aid. Obviously the wallowing vessel was hard hit, but her crew had the situation in hand, and the destroyer escorts commenced an immediate hunt for her assailant.

JOYCE presently made sound contact with the enemy. Lieutenant Commander Wilcox directed a depth-charge attack, and the DE sowed her teardrops and ashcans with such speed and accuracy that the first pattern disabled the submarine and brought it lunging to the surface.

The U-boat broached and made a lame run for it. All three DE's opened fire. The submarine gunners tumbled topside and fired back. A shell-burst sprayed shrapnel across GANDY's foredeck, wounding four of her men. In answer Lieutenant Commander Sessions ordered the DE full speed ahead, and sent her charging at the foe. Hot on the heels of her shells the DE rammed the U-boat and sent her reeling.

As GANDY veered away, JOYCE and PETERSON resumed fire. Boxed in, the battered submarine staggered and rolled in the vortex of a shrapnel tempest. Evidently her pressure hull was punctured, her control room was flooding, and her machinery was crippled, for she could neither dive nor run away. Her skipper gave the order to scuttle. Only a few of the U-boaters managed to abandon as the scuttling charges exploded within the submarine. The muffled blasts opened her seams, and she went down with a rush.

JOYCE picked up the swimming survivors—a dozen Germans, all told, including the Commanding Officer. He identified the sunken submersible as U-550.

"That U-boat had the book thrown at her," one of the destroyermen of TG 21.5 said afterward. "She was depth-charged, shelled, and rammed so fast she must have thought the whole U.S. Navy was on top of her. No wonder her skipper scuttled."

The fight with U-550 was the GANDY's baptism of fire. She had completed her shakedown cruise less than two weeks before, and had been on duty no more than eight days when she went into battle.

"That," observed a captain in Atlantic Fleet destroyers, *"was going to war in a hurry."*

Frost, Huse, Barber, and Snowden kill U-488

Along came another baby flat-top—the CVE CROATAN under Captain J. P. W. ("Johnny") Vest. She led another group of sharpshooting hunter-killers: Task Group 21.15, composed of the destroyer-escorts INCH (Commander C. W. Frey, U.S.N.R.), FROST (Lieutenant Commander J. H. McWhorter, U.S.N.R.), HUSE (Lieutenant Commander R. H. Wanless, U.S.N.R.), BARBER (Lieutenant Commander E. T. B. Sullivan), and SNOWDEN (Lieutenant Commander N. W. Swanson, U.S.N.R.). Riding the CROATAN was Commander F. D. Giambattista, division commander of these sub-hunting escorts. Destination: a U-boat pasture in the balmy April seas to the west of the Cape Verdes. The "milk cows" were on the range, and Task Group 21.15 was on the wolfpack trail.

So it happened that in the morning mists on April 26, 1944, HUSE and FROST were investigating a sound contact with inquisitive detection gear. And at 0555 FROST fired a hedgehog salvo that was presently echoed by three muffled deep-sea explosions. Then silence. The DE "ping jockies" worked their instruments as the destroyer-escorts roamed the area. The Sound men at the phones were all ears. No answer. Straining lookouts and CROATAN's sharp-eyed planes searched the seascape for signs of U-boat flotsam. Nothing. Was it a kill?

Two days later a persistent CROATAN hunter spied a dark carpet of oil floating on the sea's warm surface. Destroyer-escorts SNOWDEN, FROST, and BARBER raced to the spot to conduct a hunt.

The DE trio probed the deep, and dropped depth charges. After several depth-charge attacks, two undersea explosions were heard. Then a silence that drifted off into nothing. If a U-boat had been down there, it was no longer operating.

Post-war inquiry revealed that U-488 had vanished somewhere west of the Cape Verdes late in April 1944. Doenitz's headquarters had written her off as *Sperlos Versenkt*—"sunk without a trace." But evidence indicates that she was sunk in the vicinity of lat. 17-54 N., long. 38-05 W., by action of destroyer-escorts FROST, HUSE, BARBER, and SNOWDEN.

From Menace to Problem

Northern seas, or waters warmed by the equator—whatever the latitude or longitude, the Atlantic Ocean during the winter of 1943-44 had become too hot for the U-boat Force. The *unterseebooten* were unable to cope with the CVE-DD-DE teams that combed the Atlantic as hunter-killers.

Kills that winter were spotty because game was scarce. In the South Atlantic waters off Brazil, in the Caribbean area, in the region of the Grand Banks, Nazi submarine raiders were few and far between. In Central Atlantic waters and along the North Atlantic convoy runs, the wolfpacks had grown gun-shy. And many U-boats had been called home to have *Schnorkel* installed. But German naval bases on the Baltic and U-boat pens on the Atlantic coast of Europe were under fire by the time the *Schnorkel* stack went into production, and so were factories which produced various elements of the device.

Spearheaded by the CVE-DD-DE task groups, the Allied A/S Forces had the Nazi submarines on the run by the spring of 1944. With radar, Huff-Duff, and hedgehog, with synchronized teamwork and ruthless persistence, the hunter-killers were winning the Battle of the Atlantic. Winning it while American convoys were transporting scores of thousands of men and cargo after cargo of equipment to the British Isles for the invasion of Fortress Europa.

The war-tide had turned. Its turn was registered in Tenth Fleet Headquarters by a set of simple statistics.

FOR EACH U-BOAT DESTROYED IN 1941, ABOUT 16 ALLIED VESSELS WENT DOWN. FOR EACH U-BOAT DESTROYED IN 1942, THE ALLIES LOST ABOUT 13 VESSELS. IN 1943, THE ALLIED FIGURE WAS REDUCED TO 2. AND BY THE SPRING OF 1944, A U-BOAT WAS GOING DOWN FOR ALMOST EVERY ALLIED VESSEL SUNK.

The tidal turn was also remarked by Admiral Ernest J. King, Commander-in-Chief United States Fleet, when he made the following report to Secretary of the Navy Frank Knox on March 1, 1944:

"Submarines have not been driven from the seas, but they have changed status from menace to problem."

CHAPTER 24

SWEEPING THE WESTERN OCEAN

(MAY 1944-SEPTEMBER 1944)

Escorting Operation Overlord

In the spring of 1944 some 2,500 transports and legions of men were assembled in English waters for "Operation Overlord," the drive to crack Hitler's West Wall. The majority of those ships and men were American. As such, they'd had to journey across a good 3,000 miles of Atlantic Ocean to reach this springboard to Adolph's Fortress Europe. Day after day, week in, week out, they had steamed into Londonderry, Northern Ireland, and down to Falmouth, Plymouth, Brixham, and other southwest ports of Wales and England.

This vast concentration of men and transports arrived in convoys—ship-train after ship-train that crossed the Atlantic on main-line schedule. And they arrived only because of the escortage furnished by the U.S.N. and the British Navy, and the anti-submarine campaign waged by the British and American A/S forces. Every U-boat downed by escort groups or hunter-killers increased the safety factor for the convoy system. Obviously the submarine sent to the bottom in January was not on hand to torpedo the convoy that sailed in March. And the Werner Henke, captured in March, could not contribute his skills to the U-boat effort in May.

The part played by DesLant in this vast transport effort has been suggested in episodes relating to destroyers on convoy duty and their participation in the hunter-killer program. And the work of the destroyers in the anti-submarine war went on throughout the spring and summer of 1944, while the guns thundered on the beachheads of Normandy. There was no cessation in the Battle of the Atlantic or the dangers thereof—as witness the following episodes.

Loss of U.S.S. Parrott

There was something of brutal irony in the fate that befell the destroyer PARROTT. The retreat from the Philippines—the Java Sea campaign—the desperate retirement from Tjilatjap—PARROTT lived through them all. She was one of the five old Asiatic Fleet four-stackers to survive the whirlwind Japanese offensive and reach Australia after the fall of the Malay Barrier. Scarred and salty from long duty on the Pacific front, a veteran of many battles, and brushed by many a close shave, she returned to the States for repairs and recuperation.

In the spring of 1944 she was at Norfolk, Virginia. With her was her veteran skipper, Commander J. N. Hughes, and many of her original complement—men of the old Asiatic Fleet who had fought the war under Admiral Hart and shot it out pointblank with the invasion forces from Tokyo.

On the afternoon of May 2, the destroyer received orders to move. She was backing clear of her berth at the Naval Operating Base, Norfolk, when at 1636 there was a shout; a shadow loomed over her like a cliff rising out of fog, and a crash shook the old DD from stem to stern. She had been rammed by the merchant ship S.S. JOHN MORTON.

Three of her men dead. Seven wounded. And PARROTT, her hull half buckled, was fatally hurt.

At 1655 the disabled destroyer was beached by tugs. Later she was towed to the Navy Yard at Portsmouth, Virginia. Repair crews looked her over, and reported extensive damage. She was decommissioned on June 16, 1944.

Buckley and Aircraft Kill U-66 ("Stand By To Repel Boarders!")

Here is the story of a DE-submarine battle that featured a command the like of which had not been heard in the Navy for over a century. The destroyer-escort was the BUCKLEY, commissioned as recently as April 30, 1943. The submarine was a Nazi model, the U-66. The battle occurred in the Central Atlantic on May 6, 1944. And the command, quoted in the above heading, had not been heard by United States Navy men since the day of the Tripolitan Wars.

But the story's beginning is modern enough—a hunter-killer team (Task Group 21.11) led by the new escort-carrier BLOCK ISLAND (Captain F. M. Hughes) in a foray to the Cape Verdes area. There, in the Arquipélago de Cabo Verde, the wolfpacks had been reported again, with their migrant "milk cows" driven far south of Madeira and the Azores. Sailing from Norfolk on April 22, the BLOCK ISLAND team was to relieve the CROATAN group which had been operating in the Cape Verdes area.

Including the escort-carrier, the BLOCK ISLAND group was composed of four 24-knot "black oil" DE's: the destroyer-escorts AHRENS (Commander M. H. Harris, U.S.N.R.), BARR (Lieutenant Commander H. H. Love, U.S.N.R.), BUCKLEY (Lieutenant Commander B. M. Abel, U.S.N.R.), and EUGENE E. ELMORE (Lieutenant Commander G. L. Conkey, U.S.N.R.). The DE's were under the leadership of Commander H. Mullins, Jr., whose pennant was in AHRENS.

At 1555 on April 29, the BLOCK ISLANDERS relieved the CROATAN team on station, and the offensive sub-hunt was under way. Two days later the group was given a "Huff-Duff" fix on a submarine in the offing. A search plane made radar contact and attacked the U-boat with depth charges. When the sub evaded, the BLOCK ISLAND team commenced intensive hold-down tactics which continued for the next five days.

Under that sort of pressure the U-boaters usually made a desperate rise for air and a battery-charge. As expected, the U-boaters hunted by TG 21.11 did just that.

On the fifth day of the hunt the DE's AHRENS and ELMORE were sent to a position some 60 miles ahead on the submarine's projected track. Destroyer-escorts BUCKLEY and BARR remained behind on the projected track. By the evening of May 5, the hunter-killers were some 500 miles to the west of the Cape Verdes, making radar sweeps for the hidden submarine. BUCKLEY (Lieutenant Commander Abel) was steaming along as screen for BLOCK ISLAND.

A fine night for cruising on a sea laved with silver from a full May moon. Flying fish and phosphorus twinkling in the water and all the rest of it. The war could seem remote on such a night in those balmy latitudes. Were it not for the blackout and the drone of scouting aircraft, a sailor standing lookout might think the world at peace.

All hands in TG 21.11 knew that the sub was in the vicinity; at 2122 her "pip" had showed upon the radar screens. The contact had glimmered out, and at midnight the seascape looked as peaceful as a painting. But at 0216 the next morning one of BLOCK ISLAND's night-flying scouts reported radar contact. Some 20 miles from BUCKLEY the U-boat was prowling along on the surface.

Aided by a stream of information voice-radioed from the plane, BUCKLEY ran the contact down. The DE's lookouts sighted the sub at about 2,500 yards, sharply silhouetted in the moon-path and making no apparent effort to avoid detection. To the surprise of Lieutenant Commander Abel and others on the destroyer-escort bridge, the U-boat defied both convention and BUCKLEY by making herself more conspicuous with a pyrotechnic display of three red flashes.

Whether the flares were a challenge, a signal to some companion submarine, or a Nazi trick, Abel had no time to learn. At 2,200 yards he ordered his gunners to open fire. Washed with carmine light, the target was a set-up for the DE marksmen and they were on it with first salvo. Replying with deck batteries, the U-boat returned the salvo and pulled away to open the range. Abel called for high speed, and the DE raced in.

There was a moment wherein BUCKLEY and U-66 were running neck and neck, leaving parallel wakes that streamed astern in the moonlight like silver railroad tracks. Not 20 yards apart, the American and Nazi gunners were firing hammer-and-tongs. Then, at Abel's order BUCKLEY's helmsman threw her over. Veering sharply, the DE swung at top speed and rammed the submarine.

The collision sent BUCKLEY's bow riding high over the U-boat's deck, and the two were locked in a tight embrace. It was the BORIE-U-405 battle all over again, with a few unusual refinements. Neither BUCKLEY nor U-66 could bring their guns to bear. But the Nazis in this instance showed more pugnacity than the U-405 crew. Scrambling out of the hatches and mounting the conning tower, they let fly with a fusillade of small-arms and rifle fire. For a moment those on BUCKLEY's bow and bridge were forced to take cover. And then the destroyermen were astounded to see the submariners clambering up the DE's bow, coming hand over fist in a squalling assault to board.

STAND BY TO REPEL BOARDERS!

Above the tumult and shouting, the crackle of pistol fire, the din and clang, that command seemed to linger in the gunsmoke as an echo from the past. Imagination, perhaps. But there was nothing imaginary about the Nazi charge and the defensive fight put up by BUCKLEY's crew.

A man on BUCKLEY's bow saw a Teutonic face in the smoke, and struck it with a knotty fist. The Nazi foemen kept coming. The infuriated destroyermen hurled empty shell-cases, coffee mugs, spitkits, anything and everything that could serve as missiles. Rifles and hand grenades reached the defenders up forward just as the DE broke away and slid clear of the submarine's hull. A splash and a roll, and BUCKLEY and U-66 were grappling beam to beam, frigate-fashion.

A grenade curved like a baseball from the DE's bow and exploded in a submarine deck-hatch. The U-boat veered to port, then swung hard right to ram the destroyer-escort. Jarred by a glancing blow, BUCKLEY swayed and veered away, then swung back toward the submarine. Another pitched grenade hurtled from the DE's deck and curved into the enemy's conning tower hatch. A savage explosion, a fiery glare, and a gush of smoke—and the U-boat went stumbling down under the sea.

Abel followed up with the usual A/S maneuvers. BUCKLEY was a little prankish about answering her helm, for her bow below the waterline was bent a bit to port, in the shape of a plowshare. The U-66, too, must have been cranky about answering her helm—unless the steersman in her control room was deliberately following a course to Valhalla. The silence in her wake was the hush of extinction. The sea swept away the watery swirl where she had plunged, and she was erased.

Damaged, but far from disabled, BUCKLEY was detached from the BLOCK ISLAND group at midnight on the 7th, and directed to proceed independently to New York *via* Bermuda. She carried with her a unique distinction. She was the first U.S. naval vessel since the day of Decatur obliged to repel boarders.

Elmore and Ahrens Kill U-549 (Block Island's Last Battle)

After BUCKLEY was damaged in the fierce scrimmage with U-66, the DE's AHRENS and ELMORE were recalled to serve as screen for BLOCK ISLAND. Engaged in this activity, ELMORE made sonar contact with an enemy sub and attacked with a depth-charging that may have lamed the unseen U-boat. For the next six days the BLOCK ISLANDERS conducted an air and surface 'round-the-clock hold-down, but they were unable to flush the submarine. On May 13 the group was relieved by the BOGUE team (Task Group 22.2), and BLOCK ISLAND led her huntsmen to Casablanca.

If the BLOCK ISLAND hunter-killers did a little celebrating ashore, they were more than entitled to festivity. The little flat-top was No. 2 scorer in the CVE fleet. This distinction had won her the title "FIGHTING BLOCK ISLAND," abbreviated to "U.S.S. FBI," a *nom de guerre* that expressly suited her proclivities as a gang-buster.

On May 23 the gang-busters, reinforced by destroyer-escort ROBERT I. PAINE (Lieutenant Commander D. Cochran, U.S.N.R.) were out again. With Captain F. M. Hughes on her bridge, the BLOCK ISLAND led her team straight to the troubled Canary area—the vicinity of Monaco Deep, where the bottom lies at 3,441 fathoms—and where U-boats were known to be foregathering.

For four days the cruising task group conducted routine search operations. Then, shortly after midnight on May 28, one of BLOCK ISLAND's Grummans made a radar contact which the pilot interpreted as a surfaced sub. The CVE-DE team raced to the spot, and hold-down tactics were begun.

But the contest was not always one-sided. The submerged submarine retained the advantage of invisibility, and given a favorable opening she might capitalize on that advantage by launching a torpedo attack. An unseen foeman with an underwater dagger, the U-boat, especially when cornered, could prove exceedingly dangerous. As was evidenced by the submarine strike at the BLOCK ISLAND task group on the evening of May 29.

The battle exploded with the suddenness of chain lightning. The gloaming had thickened into darkness, the hunter-killers were on the alert, but the U-boat lying in ambush was not spotted until a moment too late. Unseen, the submarine upped a furtive periscope, and opened fire. Time: 2015. Two torpedoes struck BLOCK ISLAND, their explosions melting into a single thunderclap and a volcanic blast of orange flame.

Destroyer escort ELMORE spotted the enemy's periscope at 2022, and started a full-gun dash for the sub. One minute later a third torpedo struck BLOCK ISLAND. Within the following sixty seconds, ELMORE let go a depth-charge barrage, a full pattern that tossed up foaming haystacks of sea, but failed to destroy the enemy beneath. Now AHRENS came running in. And the PAINE. About 3,000 yards from BLOCK ISLAND, the destroyer-escort Barr headed in on the attack. At 2033 BARR was struck in the stern by a torpedo.

All this in less than 20 flying minutes—an escort-carrier mortally stricken and a DE torpedoed and disabled. BARR would remain afloat, but "FIGHTING BLOCK ISLAND" was going under. Listing and afire, the CVE was sinking rapidly. And it speaks headlines for the rescue work of destroyer escorts AHRENS and PAINE that of BLOCK ISLAND's crew only the six men killed by the torpedo explosion went down with the ship. About 40 minutes after she was struck, the escort-carrier sank, a smoking mass of buckled steel and wreckage. But AHRENS saved 674 survivors, and PAINE rescued 277.

Meantime the destroyer-escort ELMORE was battling it out with the enemy. At 2038 she dodged a torpedo, and at 2110 she picked up a sound contact previously made by AHRENS. At 2113 ELMORE's captain, Lieutenant Commander G. L. Conkey, ordered a hedgehog salvo. He followed through with another. And another. Thrashing the water into a miniature storm, the hedgehog barrage scored a hit. The sea tumbled and boomed from U-boat explosions. Four minutes later the destroyermen heard the crackly, tearing noises and harsh rumble that mean a submarine is breaking up like a crushed bushel basket.

The battle was over—a murderous action for the record. BLOCK ISLAND sunk—BARR disabled so that she had to be towed to Casablanca—it was a sea fight the hunter-killers of Task Group 21.11 would never forget.

To the A/S forces loss of the BLOCK ISLAND was a severe blow. But the "U.S.S. FBI" was to be replaced by another BLOCK ISLAND.

And the "FIGHTING BLOCK ISLAND" did not go down alone. With her in Monaco Deep went her attacker, sunk by ELMORE—the U-549.

Francis M. Robinson Kills RO-501 (Thereby Downing a U-Boat)

German Vice Admiral Paul H. Weneker arranged the deal in Tokyo. Weneker was in charge of blockade-running by submarines between Japan and Germany. A number of U-boats reached the Java Sea and Singapore late in the war, and several made Japan. One or two Japanese submarines managed to run from Japan to Germany.

Weneker did not think much of Japanese submarines. *"They were too big for easy handling when under attack,"* he asserted, *"and consequently they were easily destroyed. Then the Asdic and sonic and radar equipment was very far behind in development."*

However, Weneker cooperated fully with Admiral Miwa, and the Nazi U-boaters did their best to aid and abet the Nipponese submariners. Weneker arranged for a Japanese submarine crew to be sent to Germany for training. *"They had, I think, very good training in German boats and German attack methods. But unfortunately they got caught in the North Atlantic in early 1944 while returning to Japan."*

Evidence indicates that Admiral Weneker's information was essentially correct, but his date was slightly off. His account, therefore, was not quite as accurate as the report submitted by Lieutenant Commander J. E. Johansen, U.S.N.R., captain of the destroyer-escort FRANCIS M. ROBINSON.

The DE was a screening unit for BOGUE in Task Group 22.2, the hunter-killers who had relieved the BLOCK ISLAND team in the Cape Verdes area where BUCKLEY had won her memorable battle. Not to be outdone by their predecessors, on the very day they took over from the BLOCK ISLANDERS the BOGUE team stirred up a submarine.

The date was May 13. The enemy was located northwest of the Cape Verdes, only a few miles from the spot where BUCKLEY downed U-66. The play fell to the FRANCIS M. ROBINSON.

The seascape was painted with sunset (time: 1900) when the ROBINSON made sound contact at 825 yards. In a flash the hedgehogs fired. As the scattered projectiles splashed the water, a salvo of depth charges went lobbing overside—Mark 8 magnetics set to blow the moment they were "influenced."

Seven seconds after the projectiles were fired, two distinct explosions indicated a couple of hedgehog hits. Then came the deep-throated thundering of three depth-charge explosions, booming with a rumpus of upthrown water. Two or three minutes after the last depth charge explosion there was a muffled roar that sounded like a bursting pressure hull. This was followed by a deep-sea blast that must have killed fish a quarter of a league away.

The destroyermen presumed they had polished off a U-boat. As indeed they had—the U-1224. It was not until after the war that they learned that the selfsame U-boat was also the RO-501. There in the Atlantic the FRANCIS M. ROBINSON had sunk a Japanese submarine!

The records in Doenitz's German Navy Headquarters and the testimony of Admiral Weneker in Tokyo explained the paradox. The U-1224 had been turned over to a Japanese crew in Germany, renamed the RO-501, and entered into the service of the Emperor. Then, en route to Japan, she was removed from the Emperor's service by the deft handiwork of destroyer-escort FRANCIS M. ROBINSON.

The DE's skipper summed up the matter tersely:

HEARD SUB SANK SAME

Chatelain, Jenks, Pillsbury, and Aircraft Capture U-505 ("Away Boarders!")

Ever since the capture of the much decorated Kapitan Henke, the idea had intrigued "Dan" Gallery. If you could bag a U-boat skipper caparisoned with medals, why not an entire U-boat? And at this stage of the war, when Doenitz was equipping his submarines with all manner of highly secret gadgets, a specimen U-boat would provide the United States Tenth Fleet with a wealth of valuable information.

The captain of the escort-carrier GUADALCANAL had little difficulty in justifying an enterprise to capture a U-boat. When his team put in at Norfolk in the spring of 1944, Captain Gallery went straight to his superiors with the point, and Navy heads liked the idea as much as he did. When the GUADALCANAL hunter-killers (Task Group 22.3) sailed from Norfolk late in May, the group had special permission to "bring one back alive."

Task Group 22.3 contained the following units:

CVE GUADALCANAL	*Capt. D. V. Gallery*
DE PILLSBURY	*Lt. Comdr. G. W. Casselman, U.S.N.R.*
DE FLAHERTY	*Lt. Comdr. M. Johnston, Jr.*
DE POPE	*Lt. Comdr. E. H. Headland*
DE JENKS	*Lt. Comdr. J. F. Way*
DE CHATELAIN	*Lt. Comdr. D. S. Knox, U.S.N.R.*

The five DE's were under division leadership of Comdr. F. S. Hall

All hands were instructed on the "Frank Buck" objective of the enterprise, and it loaned an exciting flavor to a hunt which might otherwise have followed tedious routines.

"Remember," Captain Gallery stated in effect, "we're out to bring back a U-boat, bag and baggage. That means we've got to snare her on the surface and seize the crew before they can touch off demolition charges or plant booby-traps."

Everything, then, depended on timing. And speed and teamwork were of the essence. Let the Nazi skipper or Chief of the Boat get below decks long enough to touch off a fuse, or perhaps push a button, and the whole exploit would be sabotaged. The hunters would have to pounce with all kinds of celerity to make a seizure.

Keyed-up, the GUADALCANAL team was hair-triggered for action when it reached the submarine-infested area northeast of the Cape Verdes. On June 4 the hunters were about 100 miles off the African coast, on the parallel that marks the boundary of Rio de Oro and French Mauretania.

The date—two days before the Normandy landings—was propitious for this high enterprise. Day broke with a pleasant sky; the sea was rumpled and touched here and there with lazy whitecaps, but nothing to interfere with the hunting project. At 1110 in the morning the destroyer-escort CHATELAIN made the first sound contact that touched off the action.

The DE's had been steaming ahead and off both bows of the escort-carrier. At the middle of the right flank, CHATELAIN was about a mile from the GUADALCANAL when she picked up the contact. Evidently the submarine was trying to slip through the screen for a headlong torpedo strike at the CVE. CHATELAIN's captain, Lieutenant Commander Knox, got off the report,

AM STARTING TO ATTACK

and at 1116 he ordered a hedgehog salvo.

Upon receiving CHATELAIN's report, Captain Gallery launched GUADALCANAL's planes as fast as they could take off. Skimming over the seascape in a Wildcat, Ensign J. W. Cadle, U.S.N.R., sighted the sub running under the surface. A moment later a brother Wildcat pilot, Lieutenant W. W. Roberts, U.S.N.R., glimpsed the shadowy U-boat. Splashing the sea with machine-gun fire, the two pilots pointed out the quarry to CHATELAIN and to DE's JENKS and PILLSBURY rushing to the spot.

The submarine glided in a roundabout turn to present its stern tubes toward the flat-top. This scorpion-like maneuver, the prelude for a stern torpedo shot, cost the submarine the initiative. Following directions given by the aircraft, and tracking by sound, CHATELAIN dashed to an intercepting position and lambasted the U-boat with a full pattern of shallow-set depth charges. The barrage was launched at 1121. At exactly 1122½ the submarine broached within 800 yards of ready CHATELAIN. This was fast action. From salvo to barrage, it had taken the DE less than 13 minutes to gouge the submarine out.

Fast as was that piece of work, the ensuing action was even faster. As the U-boat floundered to the surface, the CHATELAIN gunners opened fire with a small caliber fusillade hot enough to make Jerry keep his head down, but not so withering as to wreck the submarine. Scrambling up out of the hatches, the U-boaters were able to snap back with a few wild shots. But when PILLSBURY and JENKS joined the shooting match with long-range (but light) gunnery, the Nazis promptly threw up the sponge. With bullets whistling across the slender decks and ricochetting off the conning tower, the submariners went overside like bullfrogs. Division Commander Hall in PILLSBURY had opportunity to count the jumpers and ascertain the fact that the U-boaters had summarily abandoned. Amazingly enough the U-boat's screws were still churning, and the expected thunder of demolition charges failed to come.

Yet the Nazis might have left the submarine fused and set to blow up like a mammoth time-bomb. Or one or two of the crew might have remained below to open flood valves and go down with the U-boat. Wallowing on the surface, the sub was a thing of mystery and menace not to be taken lightly. There were some quickened pulses among the destroyermen when Commander Hall gave the "Go get 'er" order.

To CHATELAIN and JENKS:

PICK UP SURVIVORS

To PILLSBURY:

WE ARE GOING TO BOARD AWAY BOARDING PARTIES LOWER AWAY WHALEBOATS

Here was another drama reminiscent of old Navy days—a small boat hauling away to come alongside the prize and put a boarding party on the enemy's deck. Not an easy task under the immediate circumstances. The abandoned U-boat was making about 7 knots, and traveling in a circle. The PILLSBURY men had a time of it trying to overhaul and catch the vagrant craft. When the DE closed in and made an effort to get lines aboard, the sub swung alongside and slashed PILLSBURY's hull with sharp bow planes. The destroyermen might have been trying to lasso a giant shark.

But at length the boarding party managed to overhaul, and the party's leader, Lieutenant (jg) A. L. David, U.S.N.R., accompanied by S. E. Wdowiak, Radioman Second, and A. W. Knispel, Torpedoman Third, clambered up the slippery hull. They were met on deck by a dead man who watched them with a sightless stare. No use trying to interrogate this submariner; if he knew the answers, he wasn't going to talk. And time was ticking. If bombs were also ticking, this silent sub was on the verge of blowing up like an exploding cigar; there was no moment to be wasted in dreary imaginings.

"All right, boys. Let's go."

Down through the open conning tower hatch. Down to the evacuated control room. The murky atmosphere redolent of oil, grease, and body smell; the periscope shaft and complex instrument panels; the passageways that were a jungle of water and air lines, pipes, cables—to Lieutenant David, an old submariner, at least these things were familiar. He found the right controls, and managed to stop the Diesel engines. With the engines stopped, the submarine went logy; evidently the 7-knot pace was all that had kept her from sinking by the stern. Another lurch and she might head for the bottom. The boarders rushed to the seacocks and shut out the flood just in time.

And so it was done. The U-boat neither sank nor exploded. GUADALCANAL sent a boarding party to take over the sub; a tow line was passed to the CVE; Captain Gallery boarded the prize to examine her interior and adjust her jammed steering mechanism. Minor repairs were managed then and there; the submarine was battened down and prepared for a journey.

Altogether it was quite a bag. While destroyer-escort PILLSBURY had been roping and hog-tying the prize, destroyer-escorts JENKS and CHATELAIN had picked up the crew: five officers, including the captain, and 53 men. Only one of the crew had been killed. And the only man wounded was the U-boat's skipper, *Oberleutnant zur See* Harald Lange.

Probably he suffered as much from injured feelings as from bodily hurt when he saw his submarine, the U-505, led off into captivity with the Stars and Stripes floating over the conning tower. However, he could have assuaged his chagrin with the knowledge that his U-boat had been bagged by one of the champion CVE-DE teams on the Atlantic. DE's CHATELAIN and PILLSBURY had already acquired repute as A/S experts, and GUADALCANAL was one of the top flat-tops in the fleet. What chance had an ordinary U-boat when hunted by these naval Nimrods?

There remained for the victors the long voyage home, a 2,500-mile haul to Bermuda, with U-505 trailing meekly on the end of a tow line. Tenth Fleet experts at Bermuda were waiting in a high pitch of excitement and curiosity.

While *Oberleutnant zur See* Harald Lange and his crew were interrogated by Intelligence officers, the U-505 was gone over by trained examiners. The prisoners of war were noncommittal. But U-505 divulged some of Doenitz's most cherished secrets. Needless to say, this inside knowledge greatly enhanced the Navy's A/S effort.

For this invaluable contribution to that effort Captain Gallery's CVE-DE group was awarded the Presidential Unit Citation.

Frost, Inch, Huse, and Aircraft Down U-490

In June 1944 one of the newer Nazi submarines went down to what at that date must have been close to a record depth. The submarine was the U-490, a large "refueler" sent out for the specific purpose of rendezvousing with thirsty U-boats and supplying them with Diesel oil.

Dangerous duty! Refueler subs were marked for immediate attention by Allied hunter-killers. Obvi-

Down the hatch! Cornered by the escort-carrier Guadalcanal and destroyer-escorts Pillsbury, Flaherty, Jenks, Pope, and Chatelain, the U-505's crew had scuttled her before abandoning —or so they thought. But risking a probable death trap, these daring U.S. sailormen dived below, closed the seacocks, pumped her out, and brought her back with all her latest U-boat secrets.

Above, the boarding party secures a tow line to the U-505. Below, the U-boat's after torpedo room which was suspected of being a booby trap.

U-boat captors—Captain Gallery of the Guadalcanal and Lieutenant (jg) David of the Pillsbury. Captain Gallery planned the job and checked for booby traps; Lieutenant David salvaged the sinking U-boat for her trip into captivity.

The U-1229 (above, with schnorkel) was sunk by U.S.S. Bogue before she could land saboteurs. Below, the Buckley's bow, bent from ramming U-66.

Result of one torpedo. The stern of the destroyer-escort Barr after she was torpedoed by the U-549 in the same wolfpack battle in which U.S.S. Block Island was sunk. Block Island's killer was sunk in turn by DE's Frost and Inch.

Happy to be alive. A survivor of the refueler U-490, sunk by CVE Croatan and DE's Frost, Inch, and Huse, smiles as he is hoisted to safety.

The other side of the picture. U.S. destroyer-escort Fiske, her back broken by a torpedo, begins to sag before breaking apart in the middle. No echo of sound warned her sonarmen, no eye saw the track of the torpedo that killed her.

ously a wolfpack submarine would be in dire distress if it reached a rendezvous with drying oil tanks, only to find itself roaming in an oceanic desert wherein the oasis had faded like a mirage. It was the express purpose of the Navy's A/S teams to create exactly that situation as often as possible. Not only did the destruction of a refueler cost the Germans a large sub and a lot of Diesel oil, but it imperiled the wolfpack in the area. The mortality of "milk cow" submarines was accordingly high.

To reduce the losses, the master minds of the U-boat Forces assigned deep-diving submarines to refuelling operations, in the hope that they might thereby frustrate attacking hunters. However, in the advanced stage of June 1944 the Navy's hunter-killers stayed on a job until it was done. They did not break off an attack after sighting a few bubbles, as did the overconfident Japanese, nor did they readily abandon the hunt if the enemy's trail faded out. Wherefore a spotted U-boat might be hounded 'round the clock for days on end, and the extreme depth at which it took cover was of no particular consequence. The Navy's hunter-killers simply remained "on locale," basing their search tactics on the reversed axiom, "Whatever goes down, must come up."

The destruction of U-490 furnishes a specific case in point. In June 1944 she was operating in the old rendezvous area northwest of the Azores. General Eisenhower's drive on Fortress Europa was in full swing at the time, and so the wolfpacks were concentrating on the Atlantic convoy routes for obvious reasons. Every cargo transport that could be deleted would weaken the Anglo-American drive, and submarine warfare along the communication lines would create a diversion. Hence the presence of U-490 in the waters off the Azores during the second week of June 1944. Also the presence of an American hunter-killer group in the same area.

The A/S team was led by the escort-carrier CROATAN (Captain J. P. W. Vest). It included the destroyer-escorts FROST (Lieutenant Commander J. H. McWhorter, U.S.N.R.), INCH (Lieutenant Commander D. A. Tufts, U.S.N.R.), and HUSE (Lieutenant J. H. Batcheller, Jr.), Leading the DE division, in FROST, was Commander F. D. Giambattista.

On June 10 the group received word from CinCLant that a U-boat was in the Azores vicinity. "Huff-Duff" fixes were obtained at 1231 that afternoon and at 2236 in the evening. Hot on the trail went the CROATAN team.

FROST picked up the first sound contact on the morning of the 11th. Thereafter sonar contact was made intermittently until 2000 that evening. Synchronizing their efforts, FROST, HUSE, and INCH made numerous runs in an effort to blast out the submarine. All day they kept the ashcans crashing, trying to catch the U-boat with a neat "tic-tac-toe" of patterns. They blew up tons of salt water, but could find nothing to indicate a blown-up submarine.

Evidently the sub had found a foxhole, and was lying low. With midnight approaching, the DE hunter-killers decided to try a new game. The play called for a ruse—a simulated retirement. Withdrawing to a position five miles from the last point of contact, the three destroyer-escorts waited and watched. This interesting variation of "come out, come out, wherever you are!" produced surprisingly dramatic results.

FROST, INCH, and HUSE had hardly taken up station when the U-boat's "pip" was registered by FROST's radar. Lieutenant Commander McWhorter sent the DE steaming for the target. As the range closed, he fired starshells, and at 3,000 yards FROST had the submarine silhouetted in the glare of her searchlight. The DE opened fire with all batteries. INCH, racing up, followed suit. Wildly zigzagging, the U-boat ran for it. By stepping up speed and changing course, the DE's remained on target and held range to about 1,600 yards. At 1,200 yards, the target vanished from the radar scope.

A few minutes later, the racing destroyer-escorts were at the spot where the U-boat had disappeared. The water seemed to be alive with screaming men. A searchlight sweep revealed floundering swimmers and yellow rubber rafts. No sign of the submarine. But as the destroyermen maneuvered to pick up survivors, a stupendous deep-sea explosion was heard. The blast was followed by the crunching sound of buckling metal and disintegrating machinery. Far under the surface, sea pressure was tearing the U-boat to fragments. The hour was 2210 in the evening of June 11.

The submarine thus demolished was the U-490, the refueler introduced at the beginning of this account. She had been in commission no more than six months. Loaded with Diesel oil and provisions, she had arrived at the appointed rendezvous, only to make a rendezvous with death. The CROATAN killer group had overtaken her before she could fuel or provision a single U-boat.

U-490 had received some slight damage from a hedgehog attack the previous day, but nothing that her damage controlmen could not handle. In an effort to elude the continuous depth-charging, her skipper had taken her down to a depth below 700 feet. At this whale-hole level she had escaped the ashcans. But after the deep dive for cover, and after 17 hours' submergence under fire, both her oxygen and the nerve of her crew had reached the point of exhaustion. It was this critical state of affairs that caused the U-boaters to surface as soon as they thought the hunter-killers had left the vicinity.

Sixty prisoners, including the captain—the submarine's entire complement—were fished from the sea, little the worse for wear. But U-490 was totally erased, and the wolfpack U-boats in the area would have to fend elsewhere for fuel.

Inch and Frost Kill U-154

In July the CROATAN hunter-killer group was again in action, beating the oceanic bushes to the east of the Azores. Captain J. P. W. Vest was on CROATAN's bridge; Commander F. D. Giambattista was in charge of the DE's; FROST (Lieutenant Commander J. H. McWhorter, U.S.N.R.) and INCH (Lieutenant Commander D. A. Tufts, U.S.N.R.) were there on the team.

At 0911—a typical day—INCH made sound contact with a submarine. At 0914 FROST hustled forward to assist. At 0916 INCH's lookouts sighted two torpedoes coming, and the DE veered with neatness and dispatch to let the "fish" race by. At 0917 INCH let fly with hedgehogs.

Meantime FROST made several sonar contacts; lost them; came back on the hunt. At 1026 INCH attacked with a depth-charge barrage. FROST followed through with more depth charges at 1039. The team was working like a precision machine, and the submarine was caught. At 1050 the DE's were shaken by a stunning undersea explosion. That was it!

Half an hour later the two destroyer-escorts sighted a great mess of oil and floating debris. Combing through this rummage, they picked up life-jackets, coats, shattered wood, cork, and other bits of wreckage. Realistic American hunter-killer commanders were reluctant to credit a kill unless the *corpus delicti* was in evidence. In this particular case there was no lack of that sort of evidence.

Post-war records identified the victim of INCH and FROST as the U-154. The gang busters had scored again.

Baker and Thomas Sink U-233

Indicative of the jeopardy risked by a U-boat when it ventured to trespass in American waters in the summer of 1944 was the end which overtook U-233.

This Nazi submarine was a minelayer, newly equipped with some of the latest undersea novelties. Across the North Atlantic she came *Schnorkeling* to sow her lethal fields in the shipping lanes of the Eastern Sea Frontier. As she sowed, so she was to reap.

For all her new apparatus and *Schnorkel* gear U-233 was detected in the Gulf Stream off Cape Sable. The detectors were units of the CARD hunter-killer group (Task Group 22.10) under Captain R. C. Young. This group included the destroyer-escorts BAKER (Lieutenant Commander N. C. Hoffman, U.S.N.R.) and THOMAS (Lieutenant Commander D. M. Kellogg, U.S.N.R.). Leading the DE division was Commander G. A. Parkinson, U.S.N.R., in THOMAS.

Steaming about 100 miles south of Sable Island, BAKER made sound contact at 1907 in the afternoon of July 5. The DE dropped her first depth-charge pattern at 1913, and dropped a second at 1920. Caught in the thundering barrage, the U-boat pitched and rolled down under. Then at 1931 the submarine came up like a snorting hippopotamus.

As the U-boat's bow broke water in a splashy broach, BAKER's gunners let go with all batteries, flaying the target with a scorching fusillade. Commander Hoffman simultaneously directed the firing of two torpedoes. The torpedoes looked like perfect hits, but the range was too short for arming, and the war heads did not explode.

Dashing forward, BAKER passed ahead of the sub, and as she did so, the destroyermen let fly with K-guns. The lobbed depth-charges straddled the U-boat's bow, smothering the foredeck with a barrage that would have blown a less hardy submersible to the bottom then and there. This U-boat was tough enough. As she kept on coming, BAKER launched a full pattern of 13 depth charges squarely in the submarine's path. The blast hurled up a hill of water that fell down with the roar of an earthquake. And the submarine, half swamped but still under way, came ploughing through this avalanche.

However, the U-boaters were not quite so obdurate as the U-boat. As the conning tower pitched and rolled, a number of submariners dived overside and others were seen struggling to get out of the hatches. Destroyer-escort THOMAS was now bearing down, peppering U-233 with shells and bullets. Damaged, punctured, bleeding oil, the undersea minelayer tried to drag herself out of range. But she was boxed. Driving his DE forward at top speed, Lieutenant Commander Kellogg set a collision course, and THOMAS rammed the sub, slicing into the pressure hull about 20 feet abaft the conning tower. A rending of metal, a bedlam of swirling sea and screaming men—and the U-boat plunged for the bottom.

The destroyermen rescued 30 half-drowned, wholly wretched Germans. Thirty-nine of the submarine's crew went down to those depths which lie beyond the reach of rescue.

No, *Schnorkel* was not infallible. Neither were those other items (Admiral Ingram called them "fancy gadgets") installed in the newer Nazi submarines. Doenitz might improve the subs, but he could do little to improve the war situation and nothing whatever to improve the durability of submariners. A man can take just so much.

The U-boaters were learning that the way of the transgressor (especially in the Western Atlantic) remained hard.

Loss of U.S.S. Fiske

The second destroyer-escort lost in the Battle of the Atlantic, the U.S.S. FISKE (Lieutenant J. A. Comly, U.S.N.R.) was operating in the summer of 1944 as a unit in Task Group 22.6, a hunter-killer team led by the escort-carrier WAKE ISLAND.

On the morning of August 2, the group was combing a North Atlantic area about midway between Newfoundland and the British Isles. *Schnorkel* subs had been reported on this old battleground, and the WAKE ISLANDERS (group included five DE's) were on the hunt. At 1157 the destroyer-escort FISKE, accompanied by her companion DE DOUGLAS L. HOWARD (Lieutenant Commander W. Stokey, U.S.N.R.), peeled off to investigate a contact.

Racing across a seascape burnished with noon, the two DE's reached the vicinity of lat. 47-11 N., long. 33-29 W. With the chronometers at 1223, the contact was identified as a submarine. At 1235, sonar range 1,075 yards, FISKE was suddenly stunned by a tremendous underwater explosion. The blast shattered her hull amidships, left her listing and disabled. No torpedo had been heard by the sonarmen, the lookouts had seen no telltale wake. It is possible that FISKE was hit by a "wakeless" electric, a model that could sometimes strike like a bolt from the blue.

At 1240 the disabled DE was convulsed by an internal explosion somewhere forward. Through a haze of steam and smoke the men below decks groped their way topside. Lieutenant Comly gave the order to abandon, for the vessel's back was broken, her forward engine-room flooding. Although many of the crew were badly injured, the men went overside in good order. Close at hand, the destroyer-escort FARQUHAR (Lieutenant Commander D. E. Walter, U.S.N.R.) moved in to pick up survivors.

In the heaving sea FISKE broke in two. The flooded bow section sank at 1342. With screws awash, the stern section remained afloat until sunk by gunfire from the HOWARD later in the afternoon.

FISKE suffered painful losses: 33 dead or missing, and 52 injured among the 183 survivors. By 1620 all survivors were recovered by FARQUHAR, and the injured were in the good hands of doctors and Pharmacist's Mates.

The U-boat responsible for this disaster escaped immediate reckoning. But the payment would not be long deferred. The U-boat Force was losing heavily to American hunter-killer groups that season. And German torpedoes would sink but one more American destroyer-escort before VE-Day, whereas American destroyer-escorts would send a continuing procession of Nazi submarines to sea-bottom.

Cloak and Dagger

In August 1944, plotting behind padded walls of secrecy, Admiral Doenitz conspired with Nazi Intelligence to land a party of saboteurs on Long Island. And if it could be done on Long Island, why not Maine, Florida, and elsewhere along the American east coast? Put ashore by *Schnorkel* submarines, the saboteurs could burrow into the American seaboard like so many termites. After lying low presumably secure in hide-outs arranged by secret agents and Nazi sympathizers, the saboteurs could emerge with demolition gear to blow up ammunition factories, wreck railroads, and terrorize the American populace generally. It was all very wonderful. But the cat got out of the bag, and the Allies got word of the fine Hollywood plot. Hence the presence of hunter-killer groups in various waters where the *Schnorkeling* saboteurs were expected.

So it came about that on August 20 the BOGUE hunter-killer team was at the right place at the right time. Along came U-1229, sneaking on tiptoe in true submarine villain fashion, the periscope with a wicked gleam in its eye. The DE's with BOGUE did not get in on the kill, but they screened the flat-top while her aircraft pounced on the melodramatic sub. Crushed by these bombers, the invader ended up on the sea floor.

A couple of other *Schnorkels* managed to get through the Sea Frontier fence and land saboteur parties on the eastern beaches of Long Island and Florida. There the secret invaders were promptly picked up by Coast Guard patrols and the famous G-Men of J. Edgar Hoover. So another Doenitz enterprise came to naught.

The destroyer forces which participated in sabotaging the Nazi sabotage effort were merely living up to their role as gang-busters.

A/S Assessment

By the end of summer, 1944, the U-boat effort was practically squelched. It was utterly vanquished insofar as cutting the American supply line to the European front was concerned. The huge tonnages necessary to feed, fuel, and supply the United States legions in Normandy were crossing the Atlantic on schedule. Torpedo warfare flared along the ship lanes, and some smitten cargomen went down, but convoys protected by American and Allied A/S forces crossed the ocean in a steady parade and delivered the goods for the continuing drive of "Operation Overlord."

In turn the "Overlord" drive spiked the U-boat effort by depriving German submarines of French and Netherlands ports. One after another the submarine pens were captured or demolished as the liberators advanced. Before the planes and guns of the U.S. and Allied vanguards the U-boaters fell back. Eventually they were compelled to retire to bases in the Baltic and along the coast of Norway.

Admiral Doenitz would make a final desperate try with the long-range, streamlined Type XXI's and improved *Schnorkels.* The try was a submarine swan song. The U-boats got into the Atlantic once more, but there were not enough of them to carry on as packs. And even if there had been enough, wolfpacking as practiced by the Nazis was obsolete.

The *Rudeltaktik* was done for. Sunk by search radar and hunter-killer teams composed of CVE's, DD's, and DE's.

"REPEL BOARDERS"–BUCKLEY VERSUS U-66

PART V

DESTROYERS TO EUROPE

The trident of Neptune
is the sceptre of the world.
JOHN ADAMS

CHAPTER 25

DESTROYERS TO SICILY

(DD SUPPORT OF "OPERATION HUSKY")

Destination Sicily

By January 1943 the Axis was on the defensive on all fronts. In the Pacific the United States Navy had begun the long drive for Tokyo. In the Atlantic the U-boats were gradually giving way. In Eastern Europe the Russian Army had broken the back of the German Sixth Army at Stalingrad. In North Africa Rommel's Afrika Korps had retreated to Tunisia, and Allied forces were marching eastward through Morocco and Algeria for a showdown with the badly singed "Desert Fox." Allied strategists found the global situation auspicious.

Italy was the weak link in the Axis chain—that was obvious. Reports indicated that the Italian people were unhappy over the Nazi partnership. The Germans in Italy struck a domineering attitude which was cordially resented. The wholesale losses suffered by the Fascist Army in the war had clad the nation in mourning and black defeat. The time was ripening for a drive on the Fascist homeland.

At a conference held in Casablanca (January 14-24, 1943) Roosevelt and Churchill met with Allied military leaders to plan future war moves. The Russians, staggered by huge casualty lists, were openly demanding a second front in Europe. But Hitler's "West Wall" was too formidable for immediate storming. Italy, the midriff of what Churchill called the "soft underbelly of Europe," was the logical target. A smash at Italy had a good chance of knocking the Fascists out of the war; also a large German army might be trapped on the Italian boot. Seizure of Italy would place the Allies at the back door of occupied France. And it would give them control of the Mediterranean Sea—the vital passage to Suez, India, China, and the East Indies.

So priority on the invasion program went to Italy. But Sicily, the stumbling block at the toe of the Italian boot, had first to be taken care of. Capture of this mountainous island would remove a barrier lying athwart the sea road from North Africa to Italy, and at the same time it would give the Allies a strategic base on Italy's southwest flank. Sicily, then, was item No. 1 on the 1943 invasion agenda.

The Germans in North Africa had yet to be contended with, and in mid-February they launched a savage counteroffensive. The Americans staggered back, recovered, and a few weeks later resumed the Tunisia push. On May 8 the British Tommies fought their way into Tunis and the G-I Joes battered down the gates of Bizerte. The "Desert Fox" and a few of his choice field commanders managed to escape to Europe. Cornered in northeast Tunisia, the Nazi-Fascist African Army surrendered on May 11.

During May and June the Allies assembled forces and rushed preparations for the invasion of Sicily. Tunisia provided them with front-line ports for the staging and maintenance of a drive across the narrow waist of the Mediterranean. From Algerian and Moroccan bases came parades and processions of troop and supply convoys that had steamed down from the British Isles or made the Atlantic passage from America. And all this war-shipping meant convoy duty for destroyers; screening duty for destroyers; an escort program, and an A/S campaign, and anti-aircraft work that grew hotter and heavier as the calendar approached the target date.

The escort of Allied invasion convoys through the Straits of Gibraltar to points east in the Mediterranean was no easy task. Mussolini had striven to turn the great sea into a Fascist lake. Aided by Nazi might and the connivance of Franco Spain, this project had almost been realized. The British had held their Gibraltar-to-Suez lifeline by the skin of a bulldog's teeth, and Axis domination had been frustrated. But in the spring of 1943 U-boats still roamed the waters below Gibraltar; German torpedo-planes flew from nests on the Azure Coast, Sicily, and the Italian boot; and *Il Duce's* naval forces struck when and where they could.

The Italian Navy was represented, even by the Nazis, as a "fleet-in-being," remarked for its menace value rather than its fighting qualities. Whether this Nazi scorn for Italy's surface fleet was warranted or not, such derision for the Italian submarine service would not have been justifiable. Italian submarines were not to be taken lightly. In the prewar decade the Fascists had built a large undersea force. Appearing in the Atlantic from time to time, Italian subs had undoubtedly torpedoed a fairly sizable tonnage of Allied shipping, and they joined the U-boats in the Axis effort to hold the Mediterranean.

American destroyers fought Italian submarines during the build-up for the Sicilian invasion. So far as is known, the Fascist submariners did not sink any American ships during this period. But American destroyermen operating off the coast of Algeria demolished an Italian submarine.

Nields Kills Submarine Gorgo

Early in the afternoon of May 21, 1943, seven destroyers of Captain T. L. Wattles' DesRon 16 steamed out of Mers-el-Kebir, Algeria, and headed for patrol sectors off Oran Harbor. A member of this busy squadron, destroyer NIELDS (Lieutenant Commander A. R. Heckey) was assigned the easternmost station of the patrol area.

NIELDS reached her station at 1515. The patrol was so much routine until 1650, at which time Heckey's destroyer received a "sub sighted" signal from a British observation plane. The aircraft led NIELDS to the point where the submarine was spotted, and at 1710 the plane dropped a depth charge. Then flares were dropped by this and a second plane. Six minutes later the destroyer made sound contact with the target at 400 yards.

At 1718 NIELDS attacked, spreading a pattern of nine depth charges. Sound contact was again established at 1723, and Heckey and company treated the target to another 9-charge pattern at 1724. Maneuvering for a third attack, the destroyermen fired two forward K-guns on sound contact at 1731. They followed through with three portside K-guns at 1741, firing at a contact that was dim and whispery. The barrage thunder ebbed off into silence—the quietude of a deep-sea grave.

Circling the area, NIELDS continued the sonar search until 0700 of the following morning, when she moved to take up station off Oran to cover the sortie of a convoy. By that hour the submarine's destruction was confirmed by splintered deck planking and oil streaking the sea's surface over a three-mile expanse—and by the Italian records, after the war.

The records identified the victim as the Italian submarine GORGO. She was one of the two Fascist subs sunk by United States ships during the war. The second sinking would come during the Sicilian invasion. That, too, was the work of an American destroyer.

"Operation Husky"

By July over 3,200 Allied ships, craft, and boats, 4,000 air craft, and 250,000 troops were assembled in staging areas for the Sicilian invasion. As of that date, this was the greatest armada ever mustered in world history. Allied Commander-in-Chief was General Eisenhower, with headquarters at Malta. Admiral Sir Andrew Cunningham, R.N., headed the combined fleet. The American naval task force of some 1,700 vessels was under command of Vice Admiral H. K. Hewitt, U.S.N.

The operation, appropriately titled "Husky," called for a simultaneous attack on Sicily by British and American task forces. The American Western Task Force would put General Patton's American army ashore on the southwestern coast of the island. The British Eastern Task Force would land an army division on Sicily's east coast. The troops were to drive for a junction in the mountainous hinterland while the naval forces patrolled the coasts and cut the sea arteries to the Italian mainland. D-Day was set for July 10, 1943.

A rough campaign was in prospect. Enemy strength on Sicily was estimated at four or five first-rate Italian divisions, five coastal defense divisions, and at least two German divisions. Powerful *Luftwaffe* units were on Sicily, and reinforcements could be rushed from Italy. Doenitz's U-boats and Italian naval units could be counted on to harry invasion shipping.

Vice Admiral Hewitt's United States task force—the naval complement of the Western Task Force—was composed of three separate attack forces which were to land American invasion troops on beachheads at Licata, Gela, and Scoglitti. These attack forces were given the code names "Joss," "Dime," and "Cent."

The British task force came down from England; the American set out from North African ports. A large group of ships stood eastward from Oran on July 5. This group was joined by invasion ships from Algiers. Steaming on to Tunis and Bizerte, the fleet picked up waiting flotillas of landing craft—new "amphibs" out to get their baptism of fire in this Sicilian operation.

Upon departing from Tunis on July 8, the Allied armada headed southward from Cape Bon on a deceptive course calculated to baffle enemy observers. In the van was the British Eastern Task Force. To the rear were American attack forces "Cent," "Joss," and "Dime." The great fleet's formation was more than a mile wide and 60 miles long.

The following morning radio listeners intercepted a Nazi broadcast concerning the invasion fleet. So the enemy was alerted. Even so, he could not be certain of the fleet's destination.

As the ships steamed toward the objective, they bucked high winds and foam-bearded seas. Nasty weather could not delay "Operation Husky," however. Already Allied saboteurs had parachuted into

OPERATION "HUSKY"
10 July 1943

Sicily, Allied planes were bombing Sicilian and mainland-Italian airfields, paratroopers were taking off for a drop behind enemy lines.

By 0000 D-Day the American attack forces were maneuvering into position off Licata, Gela, and Scoglitti. Fire-support groups of cruisers and destroyers were drawing a bead on designated targets. Destroyers and other A/S vessels were conducting anti-submarine sweeps to safeguard heavy warships and protect the vessels in the transport areas.

H-Hour was set for 0245. Foul weather delayed the assault, but by dawn of July 10 the "Joss," "Dime," and "Cent" troops were all fighting their way across Sicilian beachheads, and the Allied fist had landed on Europe's "soft underbelly."

But there was nothing soft about Sicily.

"Husky was a rugged deal," a destroyerman said afterward. "We went in through a gale; we shot it out with shore batteries; we traded punches with the *Luftwaffe*. We had plenty to do. We even got called on to do business with some enemy tanks. The cans worked their heads off at Sicily."

"Joss" at Licata

The "Joss" Attack Force (TF 86) was led by Rear Admiral R. L. Conolly, an officer who had climbed to the top on destroyer ladders. The force contained the amphibious force flagship BISCAYNE, cruisers BROOKLYN and BIRMINGHAM, two ocean-going LSI's (Landing Ships, Infantry), over 200 ocean-going landing craft of other types, eight mine vessels, 33 patrol craft, several auxiliaries, and the following DD's of Destroyer Squadron 13:

BUCK	*Lt. Comdr. M. J. Klein*
Flying the pennant of Comdr. E. R. Durgin, COMDESRON 13	
WOOLSEY	*Lt. Comdr. H. R. Wier*
LUDLOW	*Lt. Comdr. L. W. Creighton*
EDISON	*Lt. Comdr. H. A. Pearce*
BRISTOL	*Comdr. J. A. Glick*
WILKES	*Lt. Comdr. F. Wolsieffer*
Flying the pennant of Comdr. V. Huber, COMDESDIV 26	
NICHOLSON	*Comdr. L. M. Markham, Jr.*
SWANSON	*Lt. Comdr. E. L. Robertson, Jr.*
ROE	*Lt. Comdr. R. L. Nolan. Jr.*

Mission of the "Joss" Attack Force was to place assault troops ashore on beaches near Licata, and capture and secure that port with its local airfield. About 0200 on D-Day morning the landing craft started in through darkness that was bituminous-black and pitching, but all landings were made successfully on the proper beaches according to the planned time-interval schedule.

Licata was considered the best-defended Sicilian port in the Western Task Force Assault Area, but no ship or craft was fired on during the approach. The shore guns did not open up until the assault amphibs had hit the beaches. The surprise was complete.

Worst antagonist at the start was the weather. Landing craft were bounced and kicked about in foaming breakers, several of the amphibious boats were swamped, and gear was lost in the shallows.

Offshore in blind darkness, destroyers SWANSON and ROE collided at 0255 while steaming to investigate two unidentified surface contacts. The crash left the destroyers reeling and crippled with damage that eventually sent them home to the States for repairs. Expert damage-control measures, however, kept the injured DD's going, and subsequently each shot down a German plane off Licata.

The enemy in the "Joss" area opened up about 0400, and the American fire-support ships let go at coastal targets. At dawn the sea and shore in Licata's vicinity were roaring. There was trouble at Red Beach where enemy guns were lashing at the boat waves going in. Two destroyers were ordered close inshore to screen the boat lanes with smoke.

Excerpt from Admiral Conolly's Battle Report:

> At 0725 WOOLSEY and NICHOLSON commenced laying smoke screen on Red Beach as directed. At 0728 Beachmaster Red Beach reported fire support excellent, that no enemy fire had landed on the beach for fifteen minutes. Situation was clearing on Red Beach. Fire support and smoke screen laid by destroyers was very effective in supporting and screening the landing of the LCT's.

Excerpt from report by Admiral Hewitt:

> The most notable use of smoke during the operation was made in the Joss Area during the early hours of daylight on D-Day. The destroyer WOOLSEY placed a very effective smoke screen on the left flank of one of the beaches using 5″-38 white phosphorous projectiles, thus hiding the beach and craft from shore batteries firing from Licata.

As the morning advanced, DesRon 13 destroyers on bombardment detail added their 5-inch 38 salvos to the cruiser barrage hammering the Licata batteries. One after another the enemy guns were silenced. Admiral Conolly noted that the fire-support groups performed their missions most efficiently and the gunnery was excellent.

Equally efficient was the anti-aircraft defense put up by destroyer and other warship gunners when Axis aircraft struck at the "Joss" force.

By 1605 in the afternoon of D-Day the Sicilian port of Licata was in American hands. Naval casualties were unexpectedly light: a few landing craft damaged; 23 sailors lost; 118 wounded.

"Cent" at Scoglitti

The "Cent" Attack Force (TF 85) was commanded by Rear Admiral A. G. Kirk, U.S.N. It was the largest of the three American attack forces in "Operation Husky." "Cent" contained the amphibious force flagship ANCON, U.S. cruiser PHILADELPHIA and British monitor ABERCROMBIE, 18 transports (APA's and AKA's), 28 ocean-going landing craft of various types, 16 mine vessels, four patrol craft, several auxiliaries, and the 19 destroyers listed below:

MERVINE — *Lt. Comdr. D. R. Frakes*
Flying the pennant of
Capt. C. C. Hartman, COMDESRON 15
DAVISON — *Lt. Comdr. J. D. Collett*
QUICK — *Lt. Comdr. P. W. Cann*
BEATTY — *Comdr. F. C. Stelter, Jr.*
TILLMAN — *Comdr. F. D. McCorkle*
COWIE — *Comdr. C. J. Whiting*
Flying the pennant of
Comdr. R. B. Nickerson, COMDESDIV 30
KNIGHT — *Lt. Comdr. J. C. Ford, Jr.*
DORAN — *Lt. Comdr. H. W. Gordon, Jr.*
EARLE — *Comdr. H. W. Howie*
PARKER — *Lt. Comdr. J. W. Bays*
Flying the pennant of
Capt. T. L. Wattles, COMDESRON 16
LAUB — *Comdr. J. F. Gallaher*
KENDRICK — *Comdr. C. T. Caufield*
MACKENZIE — *Lt. Comdr. D. B. Miller*
CHAMPLIN — *Lt. Comdr. C. L. Melson*
Flying the pennant of
Comdr. B. R. Harrison, Jr., COMDESDIV 32
BOYLE — *Lt. Comdr. B. P. Field, Jr.*
NIELDS — *Lt. Comdr. A. R. Heckey*
DESDIV 60
COLE — *Lt. Comdr. B. Chipman*
BERNADOU — *Lt. Comdr. B. L. E. Talman*
DALLAS — *Lt. Comdr. A. C. Roessler*

Mission of the "Cent" Attack Force was to put assault troops ashore on beaches near Scoglitti, to secure the beachhead area, and to capture the near-by airfields of Comiso and Biscari.

A good picture of destroyer work in "Operation Husky" is limned in the following sketch by Captain T. L. Wattles, briefly recording the activity of Squadrons 15 and 16 before, during, and immediately after the "Cent" attack.

On 5 July DesRons 15 and 16 sortied from Mers el Kebir with ships of NCF-1 (TF 85). At about 1745, 6 July, CruDiv 8 (3 CL's) and DesRon 16 became the Covering Group (TG 80.7) under Rear Admiral L. A. Davidson, U.S.N., whose mission was to cover passage of UK Convoy KMF-18 and U.S. Convoy NCF-1 during transit along the northern coast of Africa and through the Tunisian War Channel. TG 80.7 was dissolved on 9 July (it sank several floating mines but sighted no enemy forces, and DesRon 16 rejoined the screen of TF 85 (2nd Section of Convoy NCF-1). At 2215, 9 July, the transports of TF 85 divided into two Assault Units, screened by DesRons 15 and 16, and approached the landing beaches off Scoglitti. At 2255 heavy AA fire was noticed ashore.

At 2330 DD's shifted from screening to approach stations. Friendly planes passed overhead. Fires burned along the beach as a result of earlier bombing attacks. Flares and AA fire were sighted, probably directed at our transport and bombing planes. Many tracers were observed, red, green, white, and blue, producing a 4th of July fireworks effect. A flight of our own bombers passed overhead at a low altitude, probably less than 600 feet, heading south. These planes turned on their running lights, and fortunately all ships withheld their fire—they were so close we could have hit them with spuds. Three large AA searchlights on the beach swept to seaward periodically, but apparently the beams extended beyond the vision of the operators because no action was taken by the shore batteries against the assembled ships. H-Hour was delayed one hour.

At 0330, 10 July, boat waves left the transports. H-Hour was at 0345 at which time fire-support ships commenced shore bombardment according to plan. The searchlights and an air beacon were knocked out. No naval opposition materialized. DesRon 15 performed mostly fire-support duties while DesRon 16 screened the transport area; some ships of the latter—LAUB, MACKENZIE, and CHAMPLIN—relieved DesRon 15 DD's when their ammunition supply ran low. Enemy aircraft dropped bombs on the Cent transport area at various times and dog-fighting took place overhead; sneak bombing attacks were made on the beaches. The enemy air effort, however, was too weak to disrupt proceedings. Shore-based machine-guns and batteries put up no opposition to the initial landings. There was slight opposition by shore batteries after daylight but it was quickly silenced. On orders of CTF 85, DD's up sun were directed to make smoke from 1958 to 2010 on 10 July. At 1430 on 11 July CTF 85 ordered screening DD's to move out to 10,000 yards from transports to enable a minefield to be laid. Some of the DD's left the area on the afternoon of 12 July to escort empty combat loaders to Oran. At about 1220, 13 July, PARKER, COWIE, and MACKENZIE conducted A/S operations against a reported sub about eight miles from Cape Scalambri Light with no apparent results. At 1800 Convoy CNF-3, consisting of remaining transports, escorted by remaining DD's, left the area for Oran.

During the amphibious assault on the Scoglitti beachheads, the "Cent" fire-support ships were notably successful in knocking out enemy shore batteries. Salvos from PHILADELPHIA, rocket boats, and supporting destroyers scoured the beaches with flame and steel. The destroyer and cruiser barrages reached several miles inland to knock out enemy battery emplacements.

About 1350 on D-Day afternoon, destroyer CHAMPLIN was ordered to bombard a battery in the village of San Croce, Camerina. As reported by Division Commander Harrison, the destroyer

> fired one four-gun salvo. While (CHAMPLIN was) waiting for a spot, the Shore Fire Control Party ordered cease firing and a few minutes later reported that the village had surrendered. This target had previously been under heavy bombardment by the PHILADELPHIA, but the report amused everyone and the crew was certain the CHAMPLIN's salvo was the reason for the surrender.

As has been noted, enemy planes attacked in the "Cent" area. They made bombing runs on the transport area and their "eggs" fell close to the DD's and the cruiser PHILADELPHIA. Anti-aircraft fire from the DD's expanded the ack-ack umbrella that frustrated the Axis aviators. No "Cent" ships were damaged by air bombs, and none was struck by enemy salvos from shore.

Army casualties were not too painful on the beachheads, and the landings went forward on schedule in spite of weather which was so atrocious that Admiral Cunningham could not believe the amphibs would get in at Scoglitti. Referring to the Scoglitti assault in his book, *Crusade in Europe,* General Eisenhower relates that Cunningham *"promptly took off in a destroyer to see what had happened. He came back and reported that landings in the 45th Division sector constituted one of the finest exhibitions of seamanship it had been his pleasure to witness in forty-five years of sailoring."*

Scoglitti fell at 1415, D-Day afternoon. As at Licata, naval casualties were unexpectedly light: 12 men lost; 164 wounded. Most of the injuries were caused by shell and bomb fragments. It would seem that expert seamanship and marksmanship paid off.

Admiral Kirk subsequently reported:

> Prisoners and captured documents indicate that naval gunfire was overwhelming. Throughout the assault and until the 45th Division had moved inland beyond the range of naval guns, various supporting fires were laid down on call, with excellent results.

General Clark also made some complimentary remarks about the destroyers at Sicily, and observed that their gunfire was right on target. He said it must have been good, because the infantry hadn't complained, and they usually claimed that the artillery had shot short.

"Dime" at Gela

Commander of the "Dime" Attack Force (TF 81) was Rear Admiral J. L. Hall, Jr., U.S.N. This attack force consisted of eight transports (APA's and AKA's) including Admiral Hewitt's flagship MONROVIA, force flagship SAMUEL CHASE, two ocean-going LSI's, cruisers BOISE and SAVANNAH, 35 ocean-going landing craft of various types, eight mine vessels, ten patrol craft, several auxiliaries, and the following destroyers:

NELSON — *Lt. Comdr. M. M. Riker*
Flying the pennant of
Capt. D. L. Madeira, COMDESRON 17
MURPHY — *Lt. Comdr. L. W. Bailey*
GLENNON — *Comdr. F. C. Camp*
JEFFERS — *Lt. Comdr. W. T. McGarry*
MADDOX — *Lt. Comdr. E. S. Sarsfield*
BUTLER — *Lt. Comdr. M. D. Matthews*
GHERARDI — *Lt. Comdr. J. W. Schmidt*
Flying the pennant of
Comdr. J. B. Rooney, COMDESDIV 34
HERNDON — *Lt. Comdr. G. A. Moore*
SHUBRICK — *Lt. Comdr. L. A. Bryan*
McLANAHAN — *Lt. Comdr. H. R. Hummer, Jr.*
Relief flagship for Vice Admiral Hewitt
Operating in "Dime" area.
ORDRONAUX — *Lt. Comdr. R. Brodie, Jr.*
Operating with "Dime" area screen

Mission of the "Dime" Attack Force was to land assault troops on beachheads near Gela, expand the captured area and seize the near-by airfield at Ponte Olivo. Gela, "center beach" of the Western Task Force assault sector, was flanked on the left by the "Joss" area and on the right by the "Cent" area.

The first assault waves struck the Gela beaches about 0245 on D-Day morning. Plunging in through the breakers, the shock troops encountered negligible opposition. But the follow-up waves were raked by furious shellfire. Spotted by the blue-white glare of searchlights, landing craft were lashed by shrapnel. Three LCI's were lacerated, and the shallows were strewn with dead.

As soon as troops were ashore, destroyers SHUBRICK and JEFFERS opened counterfire on the offending batteries. Hurling accurately-aimed salvos, they blasted the shore guns and blew out searchlights. Cruisers SAVANNAH and BOISE began harassing fire on designated targets at 0400. The cruisers catapulted spotting planes at dawn (around 0430), and about the same time all fire-support ships plugged into communication with shore fire-control parties. An earth-quaking naval barrage smote the beaches of Gela.

As darkness waned, Axis aircraft joined the battle. Flying out of the Acate River valley on the eastern border of the "Dime" area, they winged along the coast, bombing and strafing ships, landing craft, and beaches. One of these dive-bombers, flitting over the "Dime" transport area, loosed fateful lightning on an American destroyer.

Loss of U.S.S. Maddox

Death came for the destroyer MADDOX with thunderbolt suddenness at 0458 in the morning of July 10, 1943. One minute before the fatal moment she was serving in a screen for American vessels off Gela. Two minutes after death struck she was deep under the sea.

Her captain, Lieutenant Commander E. S. Sarsfield, and those at battle stations topside heard the plane. A penetrating drone overhead, faint, loudening. The aircraft was unseen.

Then a bomb came hurtling down; there was a deafening crash of a near miss which showered the ship with water and flying iron. An instant later she was struck by one or two bombs on the fantail. In a gust of flame, smoke, and debris the destroyer's stern was blown open.

Evidently the ship's watertight integrity was immediately dissolved. Her after compartments were inundated before many of the men below decks could escape. She went down in less than two minutes, sinking in a whirlpool of smoke, fire, and steam.

Few warships stricken in action went under with such instantaneous finality. A nearby tug, racing in to the rescue, could find but 74 survivors. Lost with the destroyer were 202 men and eight officers, including Lieutenant Commander Sarsfield, who went down with his ship.

MADDOX's Commanding Officer was posthumously awarded the Navy Cross for extraordinary heroism.

WHILE HIS SHIP WAS EFFECTIVELY SUPPORTING THE ASSAULT AT GELA, LIEUTENANT COMMANDER SARSFIELD . . . MAINTAINED ALERT AND ACCURATE DIRECTION OF GUNFIRE UNTIL THE MADDOX WAS GRAVELY DAMAGED. . . . GRIMLY STANDING BY TO SUPERVISE ABANDONMENT OF THE RAPIDLY SINKING VESSEL, HE WAS RESPONSIBLE FOR SAVING THE LIVES OF NINE OFFICERS AND 65 MEN OUT OF A TOTAL OF 284 ON BOARD.

Apparently the dive-bomber which sank MADDOX was a German plane—probably a Focke-Wulf or a Heinkel. But in return the MADDOX's sister destroyers at Gela avenged in considerable measure her sinking. Destroyers GHERARDI and SHUBRICK each shot down a *Luftwaffe* specimen the following day. And it was at Gela that American destroyers helped to smash up a German counterattack by tanks of the vaunted Hermann "Göering" Division.

Destroyers Versus German Tanks

Had some prewar class in destroyer gunnery been informed that DD's might one day tangle with enemy tanks, skeptics might have answered with an incredulous, "Oh, yeah?" Yet as World War II progressed, destroyer gunners found themselves shooting at practically everything on the sea, under the sea, in the air —and on land. Even tanks.

In the American sector of southwest Sicily the Germans had available some 60 tanks. Around 0830 of D-Day morning about 30 of these crawling armored monsters—members of the famous Hermann Göering Panzer Division—were spotted on the upland roads above Gela, lumbering down from the foothills, eager to gore and chew their way across the "Dime" area beachheads.

Spotting planes flashed the alarm. And "alarm" was the word for it. At that hour the assault forces had not yet landed their anti-tank guns or the heavy artillery to cope with such tanks. Nor did the Army at that date possess weapons which could readily demolish these Hermann Göering models. In the path of this rumbling herd, troops of the American 1st Division were directly threatened. Something had to be done to stop the enemy tanks, and stop them soon. The call went out for Navy gunfire.

Cruiser BOISE and destroyer JEFFERS took the leading tanks under fire at 0830. The cruiser's salvos ruined at least one tank and perhaps disabled others. However, some of them, scattering, nosed steadily forward until they reached Gela's outskirts, and others debouched across the coastal plain at the mouth of the Acate Valley.

Then destroyer SHUBRICK (Lieutenant Commander L. A. Bryan) hurled shells at a tank column on the Gela-Ponte Olivo road. Other "Dime" destroyers, moving to firing positions some 800 yards off the beach, blazed away at the Herman Göering specimens. Not long after the destroyers opened fire, the tanks turned tail and retired, leaving several burned out hulks behind them.

They were back again the morning after D-Day. To the destroyers BOISE relayed the word from her spotter, and the DD's once more squared off for a tank-shoot.

This time the anti-tank gunnery featured the marksmanship of destroyers LAUB (Commander J. F.

Gallaher) and COWIE (Commander C. J. Whiting). On fire-support mission in the joint "Dime-Cent" fire-support area, the two DD's flung pinpoint salvos at the Göerings as they came snorting across the Gela plain.

Scorched by shellfire, the tank group turned this way and that in a desperate effort to find cover. Several tanks were exploded by hits. Others, disabled, sat down on their haunches and burned. Fourteen demolished tanks were counted on the field by the time the enemy retreated and the cruiser-destroyer barrage was over.

LAUB was credited with the destruction of at least four tanks. COWIE was also commended as a big-game hunter. And "Nimrod" honors were divided among the other destroyers in on the shooting.

So Gela, in American hands by D-Day afternoon, remained in American hands. Excerpt from the Action Report of Admiral Hewitt:

> The amphibious assaults (at Sicily) were uniformly successful. The only serious threat was an enemy counter-attack . . . against the 1st Infantry Division when a German tank force drove across the Gela plain to within one thousand yards of the Dime beaches. The destruction of this armored force by naval gunfire delivered by U.S. cruisers and destroyers, and the recovery of the situation through naval support, was one of the most noteworthy events of the operations.

Destroyers Versus Aircraft at Gela
(Lesson in Gunnery)

Tanks were not the only enemy at Gela. In the morning twilight Axis aircraft struck the "Dime" area with cyclone fury. During this raid, the transport BARNETT was hit, and two other transports were clawed by fragments.

About 1415 the enemy again roared over the coast. And later in the afternoon a flight of Heinkels and Focke-Wulfs attacked. Liberty ship ROBERT ROWAN, heavy-laden with ammunition, was hard hit. Destroyer MCLANAHAN steamed to the rescue of survivors. About two hours after she was disabled, the ROWAN blew up like a gargantuan bomb, and part of her wreckage, in shallow water, served as a flaming beacon for enemy bombers that evening.

Between 2150 and 2300, Axis aircraft struck in a series of vicious attacks. The planes dropped magnesium flares to light the targets, and bombs fell on the "Dime" ships in cascades, clumps, and clusters. Cruiser BOISE and every destroyer in the area, with the exception of JEFFERS, were shaken by close straddles. Shrapnel of a near miss closely shaved destroyer MURPHY, and MCLANAHAN was shaved by a close one that bounced her stern out of the water.

Mindful of the doom which smote MADDOX, the destroyer gunners manning the AA batteries put up a sky-searing aerial barrage. GHERARDI and SHUBRICK scored during this battle.

Another destroyer in the thick of the action was BENSON. In company with PLUNKETT and NIBLACK, she had that afternoon been screening some minelayers while they buoyed a minefield off Gela. At sunset she joined the destroyer screen around the threatened transport anchorage. At 2155 enemy planes dropped three flares directly astern of the destroyer, brilliantly illuminating the BENSON and several nearby transports.

At once the ships in the vicinity opened fire on the flares with close-range automatic weapons. In the heat of excitement, elevation safety-angles were disregarded. Hot steel sang, whipped, and ricochetted around the ships in a wild fusillade that endangered all hands. BENSON's main battery director-shield was struck by a stray 20 mm. projectile, and the blast knocked out her FD radar. Unable to see any planes, BENSON's gunners restrained their fire, if not their vocabulary.

BENSON's Action Report was eventually endorsed with this warm notation:

> The indiscriminate use of 20 mm. guns at unseen targets or targets out of range has resulted in injuries to personnel and material in adjacent ships. . . . Strict fire discipline is necessary and must be continuously stressed.

About 2200 several medium bombs blasted close aboard BENSON, slashing her starboard side with shrapnel. The destroyer's captain, Lieutenant Commander R. J. Woodaman, and 18 of the crew were wounded in this and a succession of dive-bomber onslaughts which ensued. BENSON fought off the planes and was still shooting at 2306 when all destroyers in the area were ordered to lay smoke screen—a measure which brought down the curtain on that night's air battle.

Grimed and sweaty, the Navy gun crews had learned a basic law of gunnery—that friendly projectiles, recklessly fired, can be as dangerous as enemy bombs.

The terrible impartiality of projectiles was demonstrated again in the early hours of the 12th, when 24 Allied planes through error were shot down by American naval batteries and shore guns. By a ghastly blunder the planes had been sent on a course which differed from the one that had been announced—a fatal error which cost the lives of many British paratroopers.

While "Operation Husky" was featured by crack sharpshooting, it also emphasized the drastic need for careful gun-handling, target recognition, and a strict adherence to scheduled moves through zones otherwise subject to friendly fire.

Action Off Palermo (Damaging of Mayrant and Shubrick)

By the evening of July 12 the Americans had a solid foothold on southwest Sicily, the British "Husky" forces were equally well established on the island's eastern coast, and the emptied transports were starting the return run to North Africa. Then, as American and British troops battled their way inland, Allied warships moved around the perimeter of the island to hammer at shore installations and to prevent the Italians from landing any reinforcements.

From captured Pozzallo, Noto, and Syracuse, General Montgomery's British and Canadian divisions hooked northward toward Mount Etna. A wing of Patton's army drove westward along the coast to Marsala. Another wing pushed directly northward into Sicily's mountainous interior. And a third raced all the way across the island to seize the strategic port of Palermo on the north coast. When the troops reached Palermo on July 22 they slammed shut an Axis escape-hatch, and American destroyers were rushed to the port to keep it locked.

Off Palermo in the afternoon of July 25 arrived Task Group 80.2 under command of Captain C. Wellborn, Jr., ComDesRon 8. The task group contained destroyers WAINWRIGHT (Commander R. H. Gibbs); MAYRANT (Commander E. K. Walker); ROWAN (Lieutenant Commander R. S. Ford); and RHIND (Lieutenant Commander O. W. Spahr, Jr.). The group's roster included 12 mine vessels and four patrol craft, the "miners" assigned to the important task of sweeping the approaches to Palermo. Captain Wellborn rode in WAINWRIGHT.

Upon arriving in the Palermo area, the group immediately took station on a patrol line off the seaport, and the mine group began exploratory sweeping. Evening and night of the 25th proved quiet. But the destroyermen suspected this was the lull before the storm.

In the morning of July 26 the storm broke. MAYRANT saw it coming at 0931 when her radar picked up aircraft five miles distant. In a few minutes the planes were in view—three Junker 88's.

As the destroyer steamed across the water her gunners opened fire with two ready 5-inch 38's. One of the Junkers broke up into shards. Another flew off at a tangent, dragging a long tail of smoke. The third plane came on.

MAYRANT's Action Report vividly describes the destroyer-versus-Junker battle that ensued.

> Speed was changed to flank speed 25 knots, and the rudder was put over to full right. Before the ship had even begun to swing, a stick of 3 or 4 bombs was dropped on the starboard side, distance about 150 yards, by a plane approaching from astern, which had not been previously sighted. This was immediately followed by a plane attacking from the port quarter, which had also not been previously sighted. This was followed by a stick of one or two bombs dropped approximately 500 yards ahead of the ship by one of the three planes in the initial contact group. At this time it is believed that all guns which were manned were firing on the initial contact on the port bow. However, one of these planes dropped his stick of 4 bombs which straddled the MAYRANT. One bomb landed approximately 5 feet off the port beam at frame 102½. A second bomb landed off the starboard beam at a distance of about 40 yards. At that instant the ship was accelerating and had swung through approximately 50 degrees of her turn. The ship listed heavily to port and nearly all personnel were thrown to the deck or against bulkheads.

All main and auxiliary steampower lost, MAYRANT was sorely hurt, dead in the water without steerageway, her forward engine-room and after fireroom completely flooded, and the forward fireroom and after engine-room flooding rapidly. The emergency Diesel generator took over the ship's electrical load for a minute or two, then all electrical power was lost as the generator's cooling system failed.

Helping the wounded, men groped their way out of the black passages and flooded compartments below. Water engulfed the after engine-room at 0945 and simultaneously rose in the forward fireroom to within four feet of the waterline. Commander Walker, at 0953, ordered the whaleboat overside, and directed the jettisoning of all topside guns and gear that could be torn loose.

But the destroyermen did not abandon. Although the ship had no more than 14 inches of freeboard and a 4 degree list, the compartments which were not flooded showed no sign of leakage, and the vessel remained stubbornly afloat.

When WAINWRIGHT and RHIND came up to stand by, MAYRANT's seriously wounded were transferred by whaleboat to Captain Wellborn's flagship. After the wounded were transferred, the boats fetched pumps and hoses from RHIND, WAINWRIGHT, and minecraft SKILL and STRIVE which were on the scene.

At 1046 STRIVE snugged up alongside the disabled destroyer to furnish power for the pumps and for MAYRANT's 5-inch and 40 mm. guns. The SKILL also came up to give a hand.

With STRIVE alongside and SKILL tugging on a tow line, the half-sunk destroyer was started for Palermo at 6 knots. But three more enemy bombers came drilling down the sky at just this critical time, and once more MAYRANT's gunners raced to their mounts.

Roaring over at high noon, the planes picked WAINWRIGHT and RHIND for targets, and bombs fell close aboard the zigzagging DD's. The destroyermen elevated a fiery canopy that burnt the wings of one aircraft and brought it down crashing—a kill credited to RHIND.

It would seem the bombers missed an opportunity by failing to attack disabled MAYRANT. Perhaps not. Although her engines were paralyzed, her AA guns were not, and they were firing all-out when the enemy fled.

Mid-afternoon found MAYRANT off the entrance to Palermo, after a 15-mile tow. STRIVE and a subchaser jockeyed her into the harbor. Reporting the episode, MAYRANT's Commanding Officer made special mention of the *"fine seamanship and invaluable assistance"* which STRIVE contributed that day. He concluded that without help from the minecraft, the destroyer might have gone down.

MAYRANT's battle casualties were two men lost, 13 wounded. Among the wounded was a young lieutenant, Franklin D. Roosevelt, Jr. A large segment of the American public remained unaware of the fact that the President's son had been injured while serving as a two-striper in a destroyer off Palermo.

Also serving in MAYRANT were Lieutenant (jg) Donald E. Craggs, U.S.N.R., and Chief Machinist's Mate Harold M. Steeves. When the bombs struck the ship, the blast wrecked the forward engine-room. F. F. Decker, a Machinist's Mate, was hurled across the floor with a violence that broke his legs. Water plunged over him as he lay stunned and helpless. And Decker would have drowned had not Lieutenant Craggs fought his way across the swirling, steam-choked compartment to drag him to safety. At the same time Chief Steeves clawed through the wreckage to rescue R. W. Peterson, a Machinist's Mate who was trapped in a snare of smashed machinery, plunging water, and scalding steam.

Steeves, Craggs, young Roosevelt—these were the men who kept MAYRANT on the surface. These, and the men who manned her gun-batteries, her pumps, her bridge. And her skipper, Commander Walker.

Then there were the destroyermen who manned the U.S.S. SHUBRICK. She was the second American DD to undergo a severe blasting at Palermo.

During a raid delivered on August 1, enemy bombs set fire to an ammunition ship, blew up a cargo of gasoline drums stored on the wharf, and damaged destroyer MAYRANT under repair at the dock. Another raid hit the port about 0400 in the morning of August 4th. At that date and time the warships of Task Force 88 were anchored in the outer harbor. Among those present was destroyer SHUBRICK (Lieutenant Commander L. A. Bryan).

When the alert was sounded, Bryan got his ship under way to occupy a screening station on the starboard bow of cruiser SAVANNAH as the latter headed for open sea. As related in SHUBRICK's Action Report, here is the account of her ordeal:

> Various speeds (5 to 10 knots) were used to maintain position while endeavoring to avoid creating a phosphorescent wake. During this period aircraft flares were being dropped on all sides. Occasionally aircraft motors were heard, and numerous bombs dropped near-by, close enough to shake the ship markedly. It was impossible, however, to see the aircraft, and AA fire was directed at the sound.
>
> At 0430 a plane was heard diving from the starboard side, and was accordingly taken under fire. Immediately after it passed over, a stick of three bombs landed, one short, one hit, one over. The ship shook violently and it was at once apparent that the hit was a serious one. The bomb, estimated to be either 500 pounds or 1,000 pounds, struck just aft of the torpedo tube, at frame 101, three feet to port of the centerline, direction of travel to port about 30° from the vertical. It penetrated the main deck just inside the electrical workshop and detonated in the vicinity of the shell plating at the turn of the bilge, about 5 feet forward of the bulkhead between forward engine-room and after fireroom. The explosion ruptured this bulkhead, creating a hole about 15 feet by 10 feet in the shell plating. Both spaces flooded immediately. Steam lines were ruptured in both spaces, severely burning all personnel present.
>
> All light and power was lost immediately. Due to split-plant operations, the flooding of the two engineering spaces and the intense heat of the escaping steam, it was impossible to effect sufficient repairs to use the port engine. The ship was therefore dead in the water, although the bulkheads held water out of the forward fireroom and after engine-room and steam was bottled up in boilers one and two. No further air attack on this ship developed.

Medical assistance was rushed to the disabled destroyer from cruiser PHILADELPHIA and destroyer KNIGHT. Nine of SHUBRICK's crew had perished in the blasting. Of the 17 men who were injured, 14 were wounded critically; seven would die in the hospital.

But, as in MAYRANT's case, the SHUBRICK remained afloat. A mine vessel and a subchaser tugged the disable destroyer into the inner harbor where she was tied up to the MAYRANT alongside the salvage vessel CHAMBERLIN.

When the blockbuster struck, the SHUBRICK's after fireroom was transformed into a torture chamber. Live steam, invisible and murderous, spurted from broken pipes. Men slipped, slid, and floundered in blindness . . . sea water rushed in with a roar . . . they were trapped, suffocating, drowning.

Chief Water Tender J. W. Daugherty, U.S.N.R., went to their assistance. A blackout device blocked his way. He cut down this gear, and forced an entry into the fast-flooding, steam-fogged compartment. Shouting orders and encouragement, he reached the imprisoned men. For this heroic endeavor, Chief Dougherty was awarded the Navy Cross.

He was joined in the rescue effort by Chief Water Tender J. J. Dennison, and Machinist's Mate W. W. Pemberton. Together these men braved scalding and drowning to fight their way into the fireroom and release their shipmates.

This rescue might have been impossible but for the action of Chief Machinist's Mate F. M. Borcykowski, whose quick-thinking and damage-control work met emergency requirements immediately after SHUBRICK was bombed.

And all of the critically wounded might have died but for the skill and professional acumen of Lieutenant G. M. Caldwell, U.S.N.R., ship's Medical Officer. The destroyer's light had been extinguished. Sterile water was lacking. There were no hospital anesthetists . . . no laboratory facilities . . . no operating room. Caldwell improvised. Someone fetched blankets. Someone held lights. Someone scrubbed a shipmate's arm, preparing it for injection. Quickly and expertly he treated the burned, the maimed, those suffering from shock. Seven of the desperately wounded pulled through.

But there were many of that kind of men in the Navy's Destroyer Service. The foregoing episodes were related in some detail to give an inside picture of destroyer damage and ship-saving which was typical rather than exceptional. Typical of both the ships and the men who served in them.

Buck Kills Submarine Argento

While American Army and naval forces clamped down on the northwestern coast of Sicily, Allied convoys from North Africa continued to pour troops and supplies into the southern sector despite Axis attempts to stop them.

On August 2 destroyer BUCK (Lieutenant Commander M. J. Klein), a member of Task Force 86, was engaged in patrolling the approaches to Licata. About 1400 that afternoon she took station with destroyer NICHOLSON as escort for a convoy of six Liberty ships, bound for Algiers from Sicily.

Off the Island of Pantelleria that evening, BUCK's radar detected a sharp little "pip" indicating an intruder on the seascape some 5,500 yards distant. The "pip" vanished at 2257, range 2,800 yards. At the conn, Lieutenant Commander Klein took appropriate steps to investigate this phenomenon, which had all the aspects of a diving submarine.

By 2300 the submersible was identified as such by sonar contact at 700 yards. Klein and BUCK pitched in to dig out the undersea rover. Klein maneuvered the destroyer to the target, and BUCK unleashed a depth-charge barrage.

Circling off, the destroyer squared away for a second attack which was delivered at 2311. Contact was lost during the deep-sea upheaval, and not recovered until after midnight. BUCK made a third depth-charge attack at 0019 in the morning of August 3. One minute later, her radar registered a "pip" at short range. The sub had broached and was blundering around on the surface.

Three minutes after the "pip" came in, BUCK's lookouts glimpsed the enemy's silhouette. That was all the destroyermen needed. Klein snapped the order, and the gunners opened fire with all batteries, lambasting the target with everything in the book.

For 24 minutes BUCK blazed away like a shooting gallery; then the sub was observed to be sinking, and the crew abandoning her in haste.

Klein ordered a whaleboat overside, and 46 prisoners, including the submarine captain, were fished from the sea. One of the men died of wounds after he was taken on board the destroyer.

These hapless submariners were Italians. They informed BUCK's Commanding Officer that he had sunk the Italian submarine ARGENTO. This was the second Fascist sub downed by American depth charges in World War II. For his skillful direction of the attack Lieutenant Commander Klein was awarded the Navy Cross.

The Road to Messina (DD's Meet E-boats)

From late July until mid-August, Task Force 88 roamed the north coast of Sicily, supporting Patton's 7th Army as it slugged its way eastward from Palermo on a drive that was to take it to Messina.

The hard-bitten Nazis fought tooth and nail. Allied cruiser and destroyer bombardments helped to batter down the enemy's road blocks, blast his rear guard, and shatter his gun emplacements. And keeping step with the Army's advance, the TF 88 warships ferried artillery and supplies, landed troops on beaches, and conducted expeditions against outlying islands. The road to Messina was amphibious all the way.

Commanded by Rear Admiral L. A. Davidson, Task Force 88 contained three light cruisers, flotillas of landing craft, PT-boats and patrol vessels, and numerous DD's. Operating with it at various times

Part of the greatest armada in history—units of **DesRon 15** *in the port of Mers-el-Kebir, Algeria, before* **Operation Husky**, *the invasion of Sicily. At center of the picture is* **U.S.S. Mackenzie**. *The armada of 3,200 Allied ships, craft, and boats formed a column sixty miles long and a mile wide, and transported 250,000 troops. Over three dozen U.S. destroyers participated.*

High and dry. Here on the beach at Palermo where they had been blown by the explosion of an ammunition ship are two enemy freighters. Moored at the left is one of the U.S. destroyers which screened the armada, fought off enemy bombers, and gave gunfire support in the landings. Palermo was an important escape hatch for Axis troops, and U.S. destroyers raced to shut it.

U.S.S. Biscayne (AVP-11), left, operated as amphibious force flagship during landings in Sicily. She is shown with two DDs, probably Doran and Cowie.

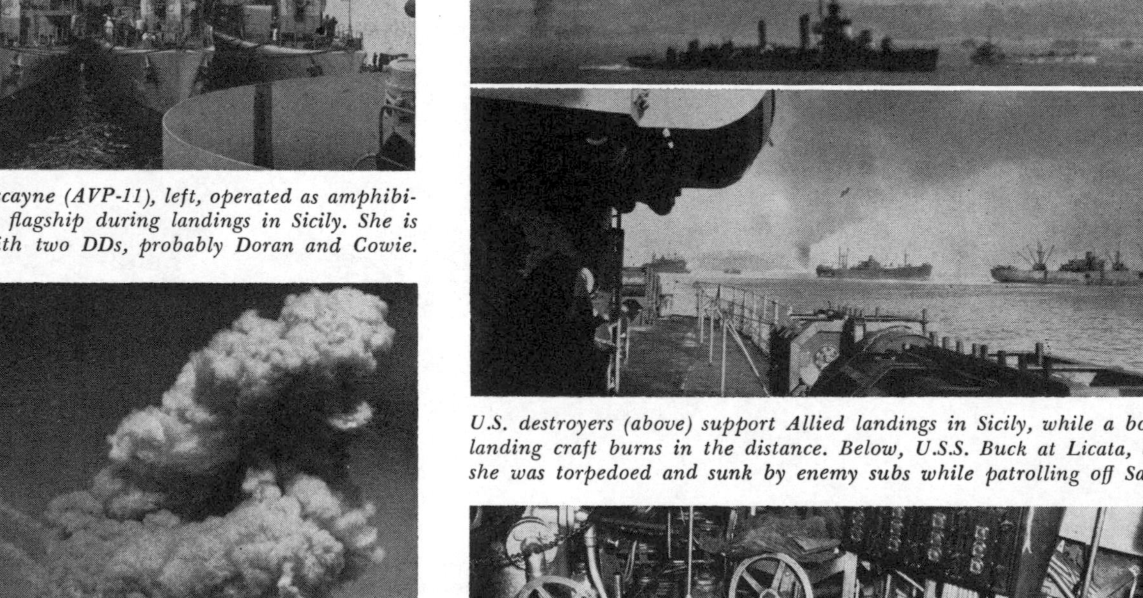

U.S. destroyers (above) support Allied landings in Sicily, while a bombed landing craft burns in the distance. Below, U.S.S. Buck at Licata, before she was torpedoed and sunk by enemy subs while patrolling off Salerno.

Man-made volcano. A U.S. ammunition ship blows up when struck by an enemy bomb in the Sicilian invasion. Aircraft were the destroyers' biggest enemy.

The men behind the men behind the guns. Members of the Wilkes' engine-room gang snatch a bit of sleep between calls for flank speed. These men worked 48 hours without stopping in order to get into the action at Licata.

were destroyers WAINWRIGHT, RHIND, ROWAN, TRIPPE, GHERARDI, BUTLER, GLENNON, HERNDON, PLUNKETT, GLEAVES, BENSON, NIBLACK, COWIE, LUDLOW, BRISTOL, and EDISON. MAYRANT and SHUBRICK had been attached to this stalwart force.

Typical of destroyer work during the Messina campaign was the mission accomplished on the night of August 3-4 by GHERARDI (Lieutenant Commander J. W. Schmidt) and RHIND (Lieutenant Commander O. W. Spahr, Jr.). The destroyers were under the leadership of salty Commander J. B. Rooney, ComDesDiv 34, who rode in GHERARDI.

On the night in question GHERARDI and RHIND were ordered eastward from Palermo to conduct an offensive sweep against enemy shipping along the north coast of Sicily and then to bombard the enemy's seaward flank on the coast road a mile west of St. Agata.

A dangerous assignment. The beaches bristled with Axis artillery, and in the dark coves and coastal waters hostile landing craft or German torpedo boats —E-boats—might be encountered. Packing heavy machine-guns and torpedoes, and with tremendous speed and maneuverability, the E-boats were vicious antagonists.

The two destroyers steamed out of Palermo at 1900 in the evening and headed eastward at 25 knots, GHERARDI inshore, with RHIND keeping pace 2,000 yards on her port beam.

After a run of about three hours, the radar snared a "pip," range 7,300 yards. RHIND swung over to fall in astern of GHERARDI on orders to form column and shoot when GHERARDI opened fire. Rooney had decided beforehand that if action developed, each ship should fire a full starshell salvo to illuminate the target. Thereafter only one gun would fire starshells as needed.

"This was done," Commander Rooney explained, *"to size up the opposition and to use visual spotting if full radar control was not satisfactory."*

The starshell barrage disclosed three enemy vessels slinking across the water ahead. One was a large landing craft, a ship of the "F" type. This vessel was under escort of the other two, which were E-boats.

Rooney gave the order, and at 2223 GHERARDI opened fire at a range of about 4,000 yards. The targets were clearly exposed, and the destroyer used visual spotting. Aiming at the largest target, the gunners pumped a devastating fusillade into the vessel. Shells smashed home with mercurial flashes that tore ragged gaps in the landing ship's silhouette. Smoke belched from the vessel's deck. Three minutes after the first salvo from the destroyer, the F-ship blew up with a blast that rivalled the eruptions of Stromboli. Later it was learned that the vessel was probably carrying land mines.

Meanwhile, RHIND was hurling salvos at one of the torpedo craft at 3,000 yards. Desperately the E-boat veered and raced in an effort to dodge. The craft could not escape the ruthless starshell light, or the shells which were loaded with explosive. A burst of flame, a gush of smoke, and the E-boat was out of existence.

The destroyers then opened up on the second E-boat. The craft was racing at 25 knots. It whipped a torpedo at the DD's, then fled. GHERARDI sighted the phosphorescent wake streaking across the water like a luminous chalkline. Both destroyers avoided it to parallel the torpedo track and comb a possible spread.

Although doused with shell splashes, the second E-boat got away, disappearing inshore where radar was ineffectual and the Sicilian coast was sketched in charcoal. The destroyers ceased fire at 2230, and continued their sweep eastward.

About an hour later they almost shot their way into a disaster when they opened up on new targets detected ahead. The craft in this instance were American PT-boats which had been sent to comb the eastern reaches of the sweep area.

By dodging away at high speed behind smoke screens, the PT's managed to escape without damage. Lucky fellows. On their tail were DD's, the modern descendants of torpedo-boat destroyers—the very ships designed to hunt down the smaller torpedo-craft. It was no hour for PT's to make an unscheduled appearance on the warpath.

Having carried out their first assignment, the destroyers headed back for Palermo and the bombardment of the St. Agata road. On this detail GHERARDI pounded the coastal pike with 189 rounds of 5-inch 38-caliber common shell. After which, Rooney led his destroyers into Palermo Harbor.

When the campaign was over, Admiral Davidson wrote that the *"sweeps were generally unproductive of contacts except in the case of ComDesDiv 34* (Commander Rooney)." But he concluded: *"It is believed there was no evacuation of German troops and equipment by boat to the northward of the Straits of Messina."*

"Husky" Conclusion

Not far off the northern coast of Sicily lies the Island of Ustica. It is a small island, a modest island, an island quite willing to let the rest of the world go by. Even the equipping of some of the local fishermen in Blackshirt uniform did not greatly disturb the inhabitants since they did not take Fascism any too seriously. And they made no resistance when on August 5, 1943, two American warships materialized off the foreshore and one of them dropped a boat overside.

Flocking to the beach, they stared at the boat which came shoreward under a white flag. The boat motored directly in to the mole. From it stepped a United States naval officer and sailors.

And Ustica surrendered, cheerfully and unconditionally, to Commander G. L. Menocal, ComDesRon 7, who had arrived to conduct the ceremony with destroyers PLUNKETT (Lieutenant Commander E. J. Burke) and GLEAVES (Lieutenant Commander B. L. Gurnette). Representing the local garrison was Capitano De Maria Antonio, who politely proffered his sword, a fellow officer, 84 soldiers, and 13 sailors to the American Commander.

Admiral Davidson subsequently noted that Commander Menocal carried out his task with firmness, discretion, and a praiseworthy humanitarian approach. When the destroyermen departed from the island, they left the population *"friends rather than a fearful, vanquished group."*

Thus Ustica had its historic episode—one unique, at least, in destroyer history.

On August 17 Messina fell, and "Operation Husky" was over; Sicily was in Allied hands. The operation had been costly, with the land forces bearing the brunt. Naval casualties were relatively light, with the destroyer forces bearing the heaviest losses.

With the island's fall, Italy was wide open for invasion. The very day Messina was captured, a naval force, which included four American destroyers, set out to bombard the toe of the Italian boot. And during the Allied approach on Messina, Benito Mussolini had been ousted and lodged in prison.

But in spite of the Allied vise on Sicily some 88,000 German troops had escaped eastward across the Straits of Messina to the mainland. Reinforcements were pouring down through the Alps, and the Nazis were preparing to turn Italy into a cockpit.

The Italians awaited liberation.

AFTER FIREROOM OF THE SHUBRICK

CHAPTER 26

DESTROYERS TO ITALY

(SUPPORTING OPERATIONS "AVALANCHE" AND "SHINGLE")

Prelude to Invasion

Messina and Sicily fell to the Allies on August 17, 1943. On that same day the islands of Stromboli and Lipari, north of Sicily in the cobalt Tyrrhenian Sea, were captured by American naval forces. And at 1945 that evening, Task Force 88 (Rear Admiral L. A. Davidson) steamed eastward from Palermo on mission to bombard the mainland of Italy.

Admiral Davidson's bombardment force consisted of flag cruiser PHILADELPHIA, cruiser BOISE, and destroyers PLUNKETT (Lieutenant Commander E. J. Burke), BENSON (Lieutenant Commander R. J. Woodaman), NIBLACK (Lieutenant Commander R. R. Connor), and GLEAVES (Lieutenant Commander B. L. Gurnette). The DD's were led by Commander G. L. Menocal, ComDesRon 7, with his pennant in PLUNKETT.

Steaming under a gondolier's moon, the warships passed between Lipari and Stromboli, then formed two groups to separate and head for the twin targets, Palmi and Gioia Taura. BOISE, NIBLACK, and GLEAVES were assigned the Palmi bombardment. The other three ships went to Gioia Taura.

At 0145 in the morning of August 18, the natives of these dusty little seaports were awakened by thunderous crashings on the foreshore—blasts that centered around a bridge some distance from Gioia Taura, and jolted the switchboxes of a railway electric-power station on the outskirts of Palmi. Italy was under fire.

Each of the light cruisers fired 300 rounds of 6-inch ammunition. Each destroyer fired 100 rounds of 5-inch. At 0159, the bombardment completed, Admiral Davidson headed his ships for Palermo at 25 knots.

On the face of it, this minor naval blow might seem picayune; Allied bombers had already been flailing at Italian seaports, smashing Axis ship traffic and military installations. But the shell bursts which awakened Palmi and Gioia Taura also reverberated in Rome and were heard in such distant capitals as Berlin and Tokyo. Of special interest was the fact that for the first time in history United States men-of-war had bombarded the European Continent.

On August 19, American warships treated Gioia Taura to another shelling. Even as this barrage was falling, secret envoys of Italian Field Marshal Badoglio, who had replaced Mussolini as Premier, were meeting with Eisenhower's representatives in Lisbon to discuss surrender terms. Italy wanted to get out of the Axis partnership.

But Hitler's forces held Italy in a relentless grip. And there were still blackshirt zealots who hoped to pull Mussolini's chestnuts out of the fire.

Italian Army surrender negotiations, inaugurated by the fall of Sicily, did not go through. So the Allied war leaders were compelled to prosecute the invasion of Italy with all vigor. The invasion called for British and American landings at the lower end of the boot. By a sweeping slash across southern Italy the Allied armies would try to cut off the German forces which had slipped across the Straits of Messina from Sicily. Then they would head for Rome.

The Sicilian campaign had lasted 38 days. The

battle for southern Italy, one of the hardest campaigns of the war, was to last 38 weeks.

American destroyers were in it from the beginning at Gioia Taura to the ending on the banks of the Tiber.

"Operation Avalanche"

Invasion of Italy began in the dark before dawn of September 3, 1943, when two divisions of Montgomery's British Army jumped across Messina Strait and landed without opposition on the point of Italy's toe. In the following week British forces swept around into the instep of the boot to seize Taranto, the large naval base on the inside of the heel. They were soon at Brindisi and Bari on the Adriatic below the boot-spur.

Meantime, the main invasion assault was aimed at the Gulf of Salerno, where a British-American naval force was to land the Fifth Army of Lieutenant General Mark Clark. Once Salerno was secured, the invaders were to make a swift thrust to Naples—one of the largest seaports of southern Europe—35 miles to the northward, and then an eastward drive across the boot. The Salerno operation was given the code-name "Avalanche."

To "Operation Avalanche" the Navy assigned many of the warships which had been engaged in Sicilian "Husky." As Commander-in-Chief Mediterranean, British Admiral Cunningham remained in over-all command of the "Avalanche" naval effort. Vice Admiral Hewitt headed the Salerno invasion fleet, which was divided into a Northern Attack Force and a Southern Attack Force.

The Southern Attack Force was under Rear Admiral Hall, whose flag was in the U.S.S. SAMUEL CHASE. Admiral Hewitt was with this force, flying his flag in ANCON. The Force contained a Fire-Support Group under Rear Admiral Davidson. Mission of this force was to land and support the Army on an eight-mile stretch of foreshore which extended from the south bank of the Sele River to Agropoli.

United States destroyers which operated with the Southern Attack Force are listed opposite.

The Southern Attack Force Fire-Support Group (TG 81.5) included the flag cruiser PHILADELPHIA, U.S. cruiser SAVANNAH, and the British monitor ABERCROMBIE under escort of Dutch gunboat FLORES.

Commanded by Commodore G. N. Oliver, R.N., the Northern Attack Force assayed the mission of landing and supporting British troops on beaches which lay north of the Sele just below Salerno.

The Northern Attack Force contained four British cruisers, an anti-aircraft ship and a monitor, 18 destroyers, about 40 minecraft of various types, and over 300 landing craft. A Support Carrier Force built around five aircraft carriers, and a Covering Force containing eight British battleships and screen, operated with the Salerno invasion fleet, which was loaned a United Nations complexion by the inclusion of two Polish destroyers, a Greek destroyer, and a couple of Dutch gunboats.

D-Day was scheduled for September 9. From Oran, from Algiers, from Bizerte, from Tripoli, from ports as far east as Alexandria, and from Palermo, the ships of the "Avalanche" armada set out. The convoys from North Africa converged off the northwest coast of Sicily, and the Palermo group joined the main body about 100 miles off the Italian coast. This mass movement of invasion shipping did not go unremarked by the enemy. At the very hour of sailing a horde of German bombers struck at the North African harbors where the ships had assembled. Navy gun crews were busy at the invasion's outset.

At 0630 in the evening of September 8, while the

DESTROYERS IN SCREEN

PLUNKETT — *Lt. Comdr. E. J. Burke*
Flying pennant of
Comdr. G. L. Menocal, COMDESRON 7

NIBLACK — *Lt. Comdr. R. R. Connor*
BENSON — *Lt. Comdr. R. J. Woodaman*
GLEAVES — *Lt. Comdr. B. L. Gurnette*
MAYO — *Lt. Comdr. F. S. Habecker*
WAINWRIGHT — *Lt. Comdr. R. H. Gibbs*
Flying pennant of
Capt. C. Wellborn, Jr., COMDESRON 8

ROWAN — *Lt. Comdr. R. S. Ford*
KNIGHT — *Lt. Comdr. J. C. Ford, Jr.*
Flagship of
Capt. C. L. Andrews, Jr., COMMANDER DIVERSION GROUP

COLE — *Lt. Comdr. B. Chipman*
BERNADOU — *Lt. Comdr. B. L. E. Talman*
DALLAS — *Comdr. A. C. Roessler*

DESTROYERS IN SCREEN AND FIRE-SUPPORT GROUPS

WOOLSEY — *Lt. Comdr. H. R. Wier*
Flying pennant of
Comdr. E. R. Durgin, COMDESRON 13*

BRISTOL — *Comdr. J. A. Glick*
EDISON — *Lt. Comdr. H. A. Pearce*
LUDLOW — *Comdr. L. W. Creighton*
NICHOLSON — *Comdr. L. M. Markham, Jr.*
TRIPPE — *Lt. Comdr. R. C. Williams, Jr.*
RHIND — *Lt. Comdr. O. W. Spahr, Jr.*

*Relieved on 15 September by Comdr. Harry Sanders.

armada was off the Gulf of Salerno, General Eisenhower broadcast the stunning announcement that Italy had capitulated. Explaining the broadcast, he subsequently wrote that the *"action did not by any means change our invasion plans."* Actually, Italian Premier Badoglio had been temporizing. And the announcement was put on the air to force Badoglio's hand (he officially acquiesced an hour and a half later) and to confuse the Germans. In Allied Headquarters some officers hoped the broadcast might induce the Italian soldiery to turn on the Nazis. But intelligence reports indicated that the Germans had already disarmed many Italian garrisons, taking over military defenses, and were preparing to fight to the last Italian ditch.

Such, indeed, was the case at Salerno. Apparently well informed on the "Avalanche" objective, German Field Marshal Albert von Kesselring had rushed reinforcements to the Sele estuary, installed strong defenses on the neighboring beaches, and planted artillery on the ridges dominating Salerno Gulf. The Gulf was a lion's mouth waiting to snap when the Allied invasion fleet arrived.

Bloody Salerno

Through darkness which was warm and fragrant, the invasion fleet entered a gulf as calm as Peace. The Italian coastline was a silhouette in black velvet. The water inshore lay almost breathless, its gentle swells like the quiet breathing of untroubled sleep.

On schedule the first assault waves moved in. The second waves soon followed, meeting indifferent opposition. Then, as the third waves approached the shore, the Salerno volcano exploded.

From hidden pillboxes, redoubts, and gun emplacements, the Nazis poured shot and shell at the LCI's, the DUKW's, and other landing craft in the shallows. Troops on the beaches were flayed by machine-gun crossfire. Big Krupp guns let out a basso roar and Mark VI tanks charged out of nowhere.

On some of the beaches the American and British troops, enfiladed, were driven back to water's edge. On several, the combat teams were slaughtered to a man. Nazi aircraft swept over to bomb and strafe the reeling landing forces. By mid-morning the Salerno shallows were a crimson sludge, and it appeared as though the invaders might be literally blown from the beachhead.

At this point Admiral Davidson's First Support Group stepped in. The bombardment ships had been held at bay by the maze of minefields, and so they were late in taking station in their assigned fire-support areas. But about 1000 of that critical D-Day morning the cruisers and destroyers moved shoreward, and by noon they were all in position. They were just in time.

By that hour the Salerno beaches looked like death-traps. Nazi artillerymen had rolled forward big batteries which included 88 mm. guns, and these rifles, emplaced on ridges, were pounding the sands with a devastating barrage. General Clark described the Germans as *"looking down our throat."* On one beach a herd of Nazi tanks had advanced to within 200 yards of the American foxholes. And at Green Beach counterattacking Nazis broke through and gained foxholes only 80 yards from the water.

Then the fire-support ships opened up. The cruisers and destroyers were unable to repeat their sharpshooting "Husky" performance. Shore fire-control (SFC) parties had become scattered in the bedlam of battle. Some of the SFC men had been killed; some had lost their gear, or been marooned with damaged radio sets. However, two cruisers and one destroyer managed to establish communication with fire-control parties ashore.

And in spite of the fact that most of the bull's-eyes were not spotted with exactitude, cruiser and destroyer salvos began to land on target. Nazi machine-gun emplacements were wiped out. Mobile guns were blown off their wheels, and heavy artillery units were put out of action. A railway battery was either knocked out or silenced. Crashing in from the sea, naval shellfire stopped Nazi tanks in their tracks, blowing a goodly number out of existence.

By D-Day evening the Nazis were falling back. Although the Naval fire support could not be scored in precise statistics, its effectiveness was certified by the following message from General Lange (5th Army) to Admiral Davidson:

THANK GOD FOR THE FIRE OF THE NAVY SHIPS X PROBABLY COULD NOT HAVE STUCK IT OUT AT BLUE AND YELLOW BEACHES X BRAVE FELLOWS X PLEASE TELL THEM SO

Even as the "Avalanche" forces pounded on the doorstep to Naples, a small diversionary force steamed northward to capture a small chain of islands in the Gulf of Naples some 40 miles west of the great seaport.

The diversionary force was led by Captain C. L. Andrews, Jr., in the destroyer KNIGHT (Lieutenant Commander J. C. Ford, Jr.). It included two Dutch gunboats, and enough men to capture the islands of Ventotene, Ponza, Procida, Ischia, and the postcard Isle of Capri.

On Ventotene the Italian garrison cheerfully surrendered. A force of some 90 Germans elected to fight, but were soon either dead or captured. KNIGHT and Company quickly scooped up the other islands, and the Navy had a base in hand for the Naples drive.

At Salerno the assault forces gained ground on the morning after D-Day, although the *Luftwaffe* unleashed an almost continuous series of air raids. Allied carrier aircraft and Sicily-based Army fighters dog-fought the German planes. Again the Navy moved in with fire-support for the ground troops.

Admiral Davidson's group had lost the services of H.M.S. ABERCROMBIE; the ship had been disabled by a mine on D-Day. During the action on September 10, H.N.M.S. FLORES was crippled by bomb explosions close aboard. These were the group's only ship casualties. By the evening of the 10th it seemed feasible to assign 11 of the American destroyers in the group to convoy duty. At 2215 they took screening positions around Convoy SNF-1 to escort the formation to Oran—a task which was to prove infinitely more dangerous than the fire-support mission.

The day after Davidson's task group was broken up, Vice Admiral Hewitt's flagship ANCON entered Salerno Bay, and General Clark and staff went ashore. The beachhead now seemed well in hand. Unfortunately, the situation was deceiving. During evening twilight of the 13th, Nazi reinforcements stormed into the area. Once more the U.S. VI Corps was fearfully mauled and nearly dislodged from the beachhead.

This time the Navy's cruisers and destroyer MAYO moved up to pump salvos at the enemy's tanks, troops, and guns. General Eisenhower now ordered the Strategic Air Force to defer inland railroad bombing and to join the beachhead battle. Air bombings supplementing naval barrages, the Nazi counterattack was battered into a Nazi retreat. Salerno would not be secured for several more days, but Kesselring's forces could no longer hope to reverse the tide of "Avalanche."

Again, the destroyer accomplishment at Salerno remains difficult to assess. As in Operations "Torch" and "Husky," the DD's working in "Avalanche" were members of a great amphibious organization containing all types of ships on all manner of missions. But something of the size and efficacy of their fire-support effort is indicated by the following excerpt from a report by Admiral Hewitt:

> *The enemy was ready and waiting for the Allied assault when the landings were made at Salerno. Without the support of naval gunfire, the assault of the beaches could not have carried, and the Army could not have remained ashore without the support of naval guns and bombing aircraft. On D-Day alone fire-support ships engaged a minimum of one hundred thirty-two targets. Ammunition expenditure was reported on only seventy, or 53% of the targets, but the weight of explosives hurled at about one-half of the targets more than equaled the weight that twenty-two batteries of 105-mm. howitzer, firing 400 rounds per battery, could have fired had they been ashore and in position. The Army position was precarious on D-Day, and continued so until after the heavy air and naval bombardment on D plus 6 and 7, and until the beachhead was secured on D plus 8. Naval gunfire continued on a heavy scale until the 19th of September. By the 28th of September, more than the equivalent of 71,500 105-mm. field artillery projectiles had been fired at 556 or more targets.*

No less an authority than the German military savant, Sertorious, attributed the loss of Salerno to General Von Kesselring's inability to cope with naval bombardments.

By the end of September, Salerno had been won. But the Allies had paid a heavy price for the prize. Some 7,000 British and 5,000 American soldiers had been slain in the fighting. And two United States destroyers had been downed in action. First victim was the U.S.S. ROWAN.

Loss of U.S.S. Rowan

Late in the evening of September 10, 1943, the destroyer ROWAN (Lieutenant Commander R. S. Ford) took station in the screen which was forming around the empty transports and cargo vessels of Convoy SNF-1, bound from Salerno to Oran.

Over the inner reaches of Salerno Gulf the night sky was flushed by the crimson breath of angry guns. The distant foreshore resembled a dark grid on which embers smoldered, while smoke coiled and fumed over the glowing coals. The ridges above the shore were charred backlogs festooned with splashes of flame. By contrast the outer reaches of the Gulf seemed cool, the channel there was quiet and shadowy, and a ship, heading seaward, might draw a deep breath of relief.

ROWAN had joined the convoy screen at 2240. At midnight she was pacing along—nothing to report. A moment later her startled lookouts glimpsed a phosphorescent streak racing through the water on the ship's bow.

TORPEDO!

The alarm sent all hands to battle stations. The torpedo passed harmlessly ahead. Lieutenant Commander Ford turned the destroyer on the proverbial dime, and drove her down the torpedo's track.

As ROWAN charged across the water, a flicker of "pips" appeared on her radar screen—E-boats in the offing. Firing by full radar control, the destroyer opened up on the enemy. Guns blazing, she closed the range on one target to 2,000 yards. Then, while swinging in a fast turn, she was apparently struck in the port quarter by a torpedo.

Crash of the explosion was instantly followed by a ship-shattering blast that ripped open the destroyer's stern and blew segments of deck and superstructure skyward. The first detonation had exploded the after magazine.

Men and officers were hurled into the sea. Gunners who had been standing at their mounts found themselves clinging to mats of wreckage. Sailors found themselves swimming desperately through glutinous oil in a fog of steam. ROWAN was nowhere in sight. The destroyer had vanished. Forty seconds after the explosion, the ship was under the sea.

Loss of life in this sinking was excruciatingly heavy. Rescuers speeding to the scene could find only too few survivors, and many of these were wounded. Heroic lifesaving work by destroyer BRISTOL could not prevent a tragic death toll. She picked up 72 of ROWAN's complement.

It has never been ascertained that ROWAN was torpedoed by an E-boat. One of her signalmen declared that he sighted the killers through a spyglass, but no one else saw or heard them. Although an E-boat torpedoing seemed highly probable, there remained the possibility that the ship had struck a mine.

Among the ROWAN survivors was her captain, Lieutenant Commander Ford. Reporting the disaster, he praised the initiative of a bluejacket, Torpedoman Second W. F. Garrigus, who had managed to set the depth charges on safe. The man's quick action undoubtedly saved the lives of many swimmers struggling in the swirl where the ship went under.

ROWAN was the first American destroyer lost in "Operation Avalanche." In the embattled seas off Salerno she was to have company.

Loss of U.S.S. Buck

Not far from the spot where ROWAN went down, destroyer BUCK was patrolling the approaches to Salerno. This was the night of October 8-9, 1943. The Americans had entered Naples on October 1, only to find the harbor a shambles. Retreating, the Nazis had blown up wharves, demolished docks and marine machinery, and blocked the bay with a sargasso of sunken ships. And while this wreckage was being cleared, invasion shipping continued to make port at Salerno. Hence the patrol in that locality by such destroyers as U.S.S. BUCK.

Midnight, and all was well. The watch changed with mechanical precision. Down in the after engineroom an ensign listened attentively to the good drone of dependable turbines. Radar and sonar crews concentrated on their instruments.

Then suddenly all was changed. A surface radar contact had been made. BUCK's captain, Lieutenant Commander M. J. Klein, sounded General Quarters. And whatever the preoccupation of those on or off watch at that hour—coffee, or sleep, or odd job, or reminiscence—all hands sprang as one man to battle stations. These were the same men who had taken the measure of Italian submarine ARGENTO.

But while BUCK was tracking the enemy that morning of October 9, the foe drew a deadly bead on the destroyer. Destroyermen thought they saw a dim silhouette across the water—a ghostly conning tower. Two torpedoes struck the destroyer's bow with killing violence. Smashing explosions burst the ship's hull plates, wrecked her forward compartments, and let in the flood.

In a turmoil of smoke, flame, and steam, the ship sloughed to a halt. Four minutes after she was hit, BUCK plunged for the bottom. A depth-charge explosion blasted the swirl where the vessel sank. Then thunder and tumult were abruptly swallowed by the sea. Wreckage and oil spread across the surface, and with it drifting rafts, and the gagged shouts of swimming men.

Steaming to the rescue, destroyer GLEAVES and British LCT 170 picked up 57 survivors. Lieutenant Commander Klein was not among the rescued. In an action that had taken the lives of some 150 of BUCK's good company, the captain had gone down with his ship.

On the chart ROWAN's grave is marked at lat. 40-07 N., long. 14-18 E. Near-by, within 15 miles, lies BUCK. Two destroyers lost in the Salerno campaign.

But the invasion of Italy was only getting under way. Within a fortnight the effort would claim still another American DD.

Loss of U.S.S. Bristol

In mid-October, 1943, all roads led to Rome. In particular, all transport highways in the Western Mediterranean were leading to Rome. The Rome haul was a long haul and a tough haul, beset all the way by brigandage and murder and war's legalized high piracy. In early autumn of 1943 the nearest Allied terminal was Salerno. But the Rome haul would eventually get through, largely aided by the work of such stalwarts as the U.S.S. BRISTOL.

On the night of October 12, 1943, BRISTOL (Commander J. A. Glick) was with a destroyer squadron steaming as screen for a transport division. The convoy was on a Mediterranean road which followed the coastline of Algeria. The evening was fine—clement weather and placid seascape under a sky powdered with stars.

At 0400 in the morning the convoy was off Cape Bougaroun, about midway between Algiers and Tunis. The fine night had, if anything, improved. A golden moon, high, full, and bright, laid a luminous path across the water. Visibility was excellent.

Patrolling at 15 knots on the port side of the formation, BRISTOL paced like a restless lion. Topside lookouts scanned sky and water with steady scrutiny. At their sensitive instruments, radar and sonar operators watched and listened. For eternal vigilance was the price of safety on this Mediterranean road.

Yet vigilance and all the detection devices of modern science were sometimes frustrated—and when least expected—by the cunning enemy. Under some conditions of water density and temperature, sonar's "echo-ranging" beams might peter out or be deflected. From undiscovered ambush a submarine might fire with deadly suddenness, its presence first betrayed by a streaking torpedo wake, or—as in BRISTOL's case—a whisper in the sound gear.

At 0423 the destroyer's sonar watch heard the hydrophone effect of a torpedo. The low, rushing whistle of an oncoming 88 mm. shell might have given the ship more warning. Scarcely was the alarm flashed topside when, ten seconds after it first was heard, the torpedo struck BRISTOL.

Smashing in on the ship's port side at the forward engine-room, the blast stopped the destroyer dead with a broken back. Men, guns, fragments of gear and machinery were strewn by the violent explosion. Mortally stricken, BRISTOL sagged in the moon-washed sea, and began to settle under a surge of smoke.

There was time to launch life rafts, to give the wounded a hand, to get overside in "Mae Wests." Not much time. A few minutes after she was struck, BRISTOL broke in two and sank. WAINWRIGHT and TRIPPE soon arrived to rescue survivors. Dawnlight presently aided the rescue work, and the lifesaving went swiftly forward. All told, 241 men were saved. But in spite of brave work by survivors and rescuers, casualties were heavy. Fifty-two of the crew were lost with the ship.

The submarine responsible for the sinking was never sighted, and so far as is known it eluded the hunt and escaped. It may have fired a long-range shot from periscope depth, and then gone deep into some whale-hole ambush to lie in wait for another convoy.

The road to Rome was a hard and dangerous road for the Destroyer Service, as loss of ROWAN, BUCK, and BRISTOL is evidence. And before the autumn was out another American destroyer would go down on that death-stalked "Appian Way." The killers were German aircraft and their victim was U.S.S. BEATTY.

Onslaught on Ship-Train for Naples

By November, 1943, engineers and Seabees laboring like giants had cleared some of the Naples wreckage. Booby-traps had been exploded, a few port facilities had been replaced, others were repaired, and channels were open in the bay. Naples was shaping up as a base for the Allied ground forces fighting their way through Italy.

Bound for Naples in the first week of November was a great Allied ship-train, Convoy KME-25A, transporting tons of war supplies and thousands of troop reinforcements for the Army of General Mark Clark. Assembled in the United Kingdom, the convoy contained 15 American and eight British transports. These heavy-laden vessels were screened by a powerful destroyer task group, TG 60.2 under command of Captain C. C. Hartman, ComDesRon 15. American destroyers in the screen were:

DAVISON	*Lt. Comdr J. D. Collett*
	Flagship of Capt. Hartman
BEATTY	*Lt. Comdr. W. Outerson*
MERVINE	*Lt. Comdr. D. R. Frakes*
TILLMAN	*Lt. Comdr C. S. Hutchings*
PARKER	*Comdr. J. W. Bays*
	Flying pennant of Capt. C. J. Carter, COMDESRON 16
LAUB	*Lt. Comdr. A. G. Hay*
MCLANAHAN	*Lt. Comdr. N. C. Johnson*

In addition to the seven American DD's, the screen included three British destroyers, two Greek destroyers, and the anti-aircraft vessel H.M.S. COLOMBO. After the convoy entered the Mediterranean and headed eastward for the Tunisian War Channel, the task group was augmented by two American destroyer-escorts from Mers-el-Kebir. The DE's were FREDERICK C. DAVIS (Lieutenant Commander O. W. Goepner, U.S.N.R.), and HERBERT C. JONES (Lieutenant Commander A. W. Gardes).

Steaming along the Algerian coast, the convoy followed the sea road which led to the narrow waist of the Mediterranean. Too large to pass through the Tunisian War Channel in columns of three ships each—the favored formation—the convoy was strung out in less maneuverable seven- and nine-ship columns.

The convoy's vulnerability became all too manifest on November 6, as the ships, having left Algiers far astern, were approaching Philippeville. Traveling at

The calm before the storm: destroyers at Salerno before Operation Shingle. At far right is Plunkett, flying the pennant of ComDesRon 7. The destroyers' primary duty in the Anzio operation was to provide anti-aircraft protection for the invasion shipping. There was an average of three air raids a day for ten straight days. Several ships were sunk, including H.M.S. Spartan.

Mopping up on Plunkett (DD 431) shortly after she was hit by a bomb off Anzio. While desperate hands fought the fire and explosion, Plunkett continued firing at the Nazi planes. Some 53 men were killed, 20 wounded, in the action.

Smeared with blood and oil, these three survivors of Rowan (DD 403) are awaiting medical attention. Their ship had sunk in 40 seconds after her stern had been ripped off by an E-boat torpedo or a mine during the Salerno operation.

One of the "flat stacks," probably Charles F. Hughes, under German attack during the Allied invasion of Nettuno Bay, some thirty miles south of Rome. Invasion shipping had assembled at Naples for this jump around the Nazi flank.

The Murphy transports the King of Arabia and his retainers to meet President Roosevelt at the Suez Canal. The King's tent was erected on deck.

Night anti-aircraft firing at Salerno protects the landing forces from enemy planes. Nazi defeat was hastened by effective naval bombardment.

12 knots, they had reached a point on the road not far from Cape Bougaroun, the scene of the BRISTOL ambush, when the enemy struck. Time: 1800. Visibility poor. Diving out of the dark and the daylight, the *Luftwaffe* descended like a flock of vultures on unsuspecting game.

This game, though, could fight back, with sweeping scythes of anti-aircraft fire.

A mixed force of some nine bombers and 16 torpedo planes, the Nazi aircraft attacked at 1804. Speeding in at low altitude, a plane slipped a sharpshooting torpedo into the water, and at 1805 American destroyer BEATTY was fatally hit.

In the ensuing battle the screen destroyers of Task Group 60.2 put up a worthy defense. The attackers—destroyermen identified at least one Heinkel 111, a Dornier 217, and three Junker 88's—ran into aerial thickets of ack-ack. DAVISON shot down a plane. PARKER shot down a plane. TILLMAN shot down a plane. Destroyer-escort H. C. JONES shot down a plane. So did British destroyer HAYDON and one of the transports in the convoy.

Poor visibility favored the aircraft, however, and they had the advantage of high-speed raiders versus large, slower moving targets. They struck at the van destroyers of the screen, at ships on the convoy's port flank and on its quarters. Then they concentrated on the quarters of the formation.

Fire-spitting AA guns broke up the attacks. They brought down a half dozen aircraft. They forced torpedo planes to make long-range drops, and bombers to remain at a high level. But bombs and torpedoes were not the only weapons wielded by the fast-flying enemy. In this onslaught on Convoy KMF-25A the Germans unleashed a new killer.

At first glimpse, destroyer gunners who had never seen it before took the thing for a midget airplane. Then, at close range, it resembled a winged rocket, a streak of red light with a flaring green tail. Released from a high-flying bomber, these phantasmal comets would swoop across the sky, then abruptly plummet down on a target in a screaming dive. Radio-controlled glider bombs!

First employed on Allied invasion shipping at Salerno, the glider bombs had appeared as a lethal menace to anchored vessels. Now they gave Convoy KMF-25A and Captain Hartman's task group some spine-chilling moments. They did not strike any ships, but they came devilishly close.

Dangerous as were the glider bombs in the battle off Cape Bougaroun, aircraft torpedoes were the weapons which wrought the havoc. Before the Nazi planes were finally beaten off, two Allied transports were fatally torpedo-stabbed—the S.S. SANTA ELENA and the S.S. ALDEGONDE. When the aircraft droned away in the dark they left behind them a sea splotched with fire and wreckage—burning ships and demolished planes.

Six planes for three ships. Numerically in the convoy's favor, this battle-score weighed many tons in favor of the *Luftwaffe*. And although the defense put up by the screening destroyers was stout, Rear Admiral C. F. Bryant, who analyzed and endorsed Captain Hartman's Action Report, severely criticized some features of the convoy. His remarks are quoted herewith.

> In my opinion this convoy was not properly organized and controlled by the British.
>
> The convoy commodore and the screen commander should have been members of the same service, preferably British as this was a British controlled convoy operating in areas controlled by them.
>
> Convoy speed was unnecessarily slow. Troop ship convoys should steam at maximum speed of slowest ship and rendezvous should be arranged accordingly. It is folly to have ships carrying 4,000 to 7,000 troops each steam at speeds of 12 knots merely to make a rendezvous.
>
> Convoy should have been split into two groups after entering Mediterranean—into a fast and a slow group. There were included in this convoy a number of large ships capable of eighteen knots or better. . . . It is inviting disaster unnecessarily to have the MONTEREY, carrying 7,000 troops and capable of 20 knots, steam at 12 knots. . . .
>
> Air coverage was withdrawn before dark.

After the battle a call for assistance was flashed to Algiers. From that port on November 7, Destroyer Division 32, under Commander J. C. Sowell, steamed to the scene to conduct rescue and salvage operations. This division contained flagship CHAMPLIN (Commander C. L. Melson), and destroyers BOYLE (LIEUTENANT Commander B. P. Field, Jr.), NIELDS (Commander A. R. Heckey), and ORDRONAUX (Commander R. Brodie, Jr.).

The two transports which had been torpedoed remained afloat until the 7th. But the ships were not to be saved. Nor did the rescuers arrive in time to save destroyer BEATTY. Long before they reached the battle scene, she had gone beyond all possible salvage.

Loss of U.S.S. Beatty

When BEATTY was hit, she was maintaining her position in the convoy formation. Stationed on the starboard quarter of the rear ship in the right-hand column, and about 3,000 yards out, the destroyer was target for the first attack which roared in through the twilight.

Lieutenant Commander W. Outerson and others topside scarcely had time to set their teeth before the killing torpedo struck the ship. With a stunning blast the warhead burst against the starboard side at the after engine-room. BEATTY shuddered to a halt and sagged in the water with a broken keel.

She did not go down off Cape Bougaroun without a fight. Below decks her damage-controlmen fought fire, steam, and flood with every measure available. Topside, her gunners battled the *Luftwaffe*.

Torpedoes rushed past her, bombs thundered in the water near-by, and glider bombs rocketed overhead. But though BEATTY could beat off her assailants, she could not win the fight for buoyancy. Steadily the water rose below decks, stifling her power plant, drowning vital machinery.

Her damaged hull could not stand the strain of flooding. With a sudden lurch the ship broke in two. Under a pall of smoke the fore and aft sections sank. The time was about 2305.

BEATTY's crew had abandoned smartly, with opportunity to launch rafts and floats, and to make good use of lifesaving gear. Casualties were consequently few. Eleven bluejackets were lost with the ship, and a wounded man died after rescue. The other wounded —an officer and six enlisted men—recovered from their injuries.

Rescuers found the BEATTY men a tough, enduring lot. Perhaps the pace for endurance and pluck was set by Sam S. Poland, Radarman 3c, U.S.N.R. Manning his battle station at a starboard depth-charge thrower, Poland had been standing practically on top of the spot where the torpedo smote BEATTY. Hurled overboard by the blast, he was flung into the sea with a double compound fracture of the left leg. All evening and all night he remained afloat, in spite of his broken leg. When his cries were finally heard, and he was sighted by destroyermen of the U.S.S. BOYLE, Sam Poland was swimming—typical of the never-say-die spirit of the Destroyer Service.

Wainwright and H.M.S. Calpe Kill U-593

By December 1943 the Mediterranean was no longer a potential Fascist lake. But the Nazis were doing their best to keep the Swastika flying over (and under) its waters. While they concentrated on the Tyrrhenian storm center, they did not neglect Algiers and Gibraltar traffic lanes.

However, the U-boat and *Luftwaffe* menace was gradually being stifled by an unremitting A/S and anti-aircraft campaign. This dual campaign entailed continuous sweeps and round-the-clock patrols which, often unproductive in the Algiers and Gibraltar areas, were particularly tedious for destroyermen on the U-boat hunt.

"You worked your shirt out at the elbows and you seemed to accomplish nothing," a destroyerman said. "Most of those anti-sub patrols off North Africa were as boresome as a cop's beat in Flatbush. But Murder Inc. was out there. You had all the excitement you could use when you ran into those gunmen."

In mid-December destroyer A/S teams killed two U-boats in the Western Mediterranean. The first was downed on the 13th by U.S.S. WAINWRIGHT and British destroyer CALPE.

The two DD's were conducting a sub-hunt in company with destroyers NIBLACK and BENSON. They were sweeping an area northwest of Algiers and about midway between the North African coast and the coast of Spain when WAINWRIGHT left the group to investigate a "sub sighted" report. That was at 0120 in the morning of December 13.

Aware that they were "it" in a game of hide-and-seek, the U-boaters promptly ducked. WAINWRIGHT steamed this way and that, probing with sonar, but her electronic fingers were eluded by the needle in the haystack. At 0229 H.M.S. CALPE arrived on the scene to team up on the hunt.

The search continued through daybreak and sunrise—no success. Doggedly the two destroyers kept at it while the clock ticked through the morning, through noon, into afternoon. Persistence paid off. At 1408 WAINWRIGHT's sonar instruments registered a contact. Her captain, Commander W. W. Strohbehn, directed a booming depth-charge attack. CALPE picked up the contact at 1423 and promptly let go with depth charges. WAINWRIGHT regained sound contact at 1435, and coached her British team-mate up to the target. CALPE distributed a pattern of depth charges at 1440, and this blasting rang the bell.

Seven minutes after the last depth charge was dropped, a U-boat came spouting to the surface some 1,800 yards from WAINWRIGHT. The American destroyer opened fire. Two minutes of that, and the German submariners came out of the conning tower to abandon.

As the Nazi crew sprang overside, Strohbehn ordered the destroyer gunners to cease fire. Then he sent a party across the water to pick up survivors. The destroyermen had time to board the damaged U-boat and bring out men who were calling, *"Kamerad!"* CALPE joined in the rescue of these frantic submariners who preferred a Prisoner-of-War camp to entombment in a sunken U-boat.

At 1530 the two destroyers with their prisoners set a course for Algiers. Behind them on the bottom they left the U-593.

Woolsey and Trippe Kill U-73

On the afternoon of December 16, 1943, a U-boat

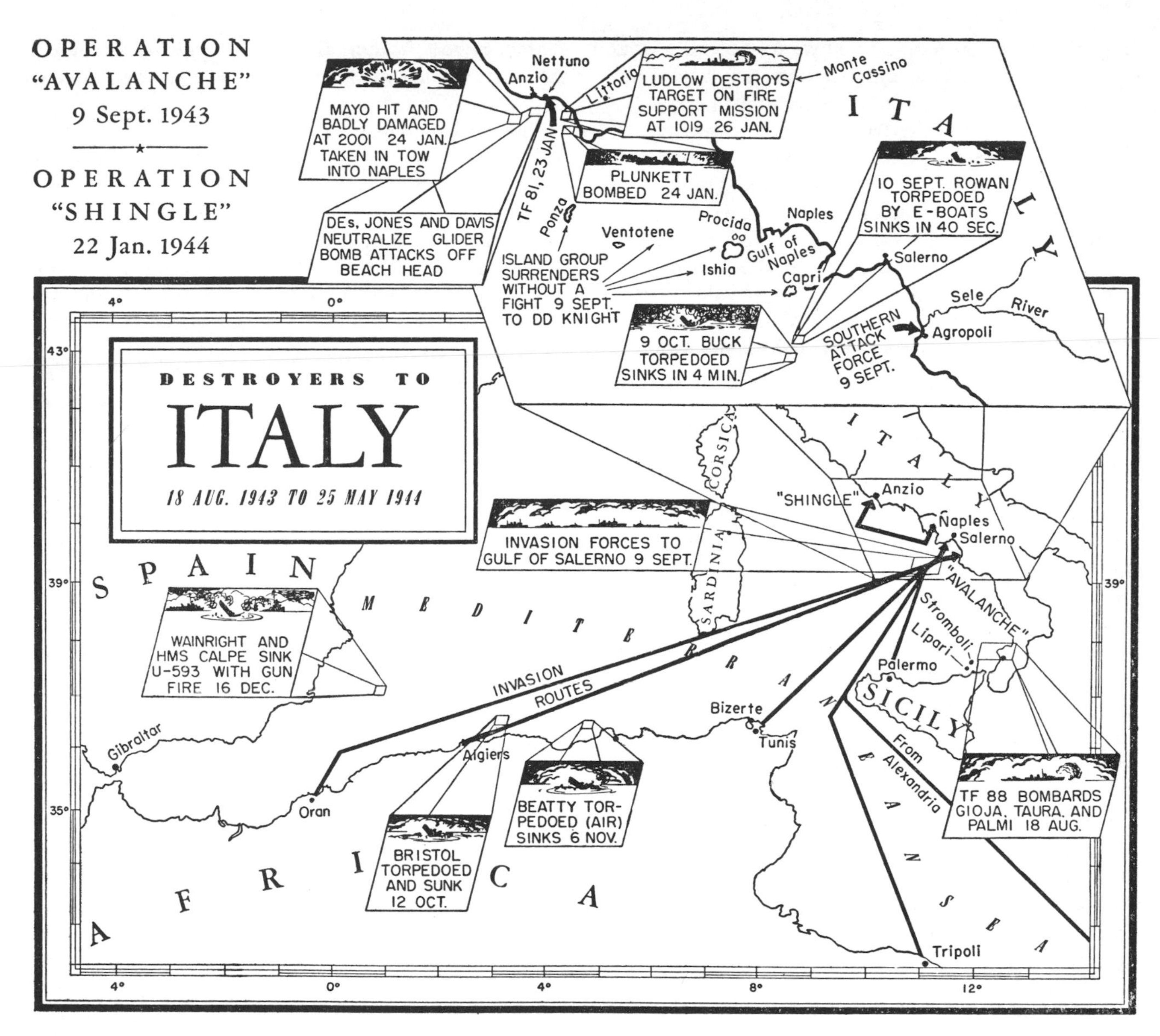

ambushed a convoy off Cape Falcon, Algeria. Torpedoes smashed into the S.S. JOHN S. COPLEY, and there was death in the afternoon. Then American destroyers steamed out of Mers-el-Kebir to track down the sub.

Under command of Captain H. Sanders, ComDesDiv 13, the destroyers were WOOLSEY, TRIPPE, and EDISON. The last named did not get in on the U-boat kill, but she assisted in screening and in picking up the U-boat survivors. Sanders' flagship, the WOOLSEY (Commander H. R. Wier), and destroyer TRIPPE (Commander R. C. Williamson) did the shooting.

They reached the vicinity of the torpedoing about 1715, and started the A/S search about 1730. Within 45 minutes of the hunt's beginning WOOLSEY's sonar put the finger on the skulking enemy.

As the destroyer jockeyed in on the attack, the contact evaporated, and the hunters held their depth charges in leash, waiting for a sharper materialization of the target. At 1837 WOOLSEY regained sound contact, and the destroyermen were able to execute a deliberate attack.

Thundering around the submarine, WOOLSEY's depth charges dished in the hull, pulverized light bulbs, and knocked out various electrical fixtures. The blasting also caused leakage, a casualty obviously fatal to a submarine if not soon mended. But persistent leaks may paralyze a submarine long before they flood it. A salty spray shooting in through a damaged gasket may wet the vessel's electrical cables and cause arcing, flashing, and the worst sort of fires and fumes. Sooner or later a leaking submarine must go down permanently or be brought to the surface. The captain of leaking U-73 ordered the crew to blow all ballast and take her to the surface.

Whereupon WOOLSEY's SG radar snared a "pip"

dead ahead at a range of 1,900 yards—precisely what WOOLSEY and TRIPPE had been waiting for. They shot the ray of a powerful searchlight across the water. As the spotlight fastened on the submarine, the Nazi gunners opened fire. Hot steel whistled across WOOLSEY's deck; two bluejackets were wounded. The submariners were to regret this folly, for both destroyers immediately replied with a hot and accurate fusillade that lashed the U-boat into sinking wreckage. Some 27 Nazis went down with the boat. The destroyermen picked up 34 survivors.

Thus another Mediterranean marauder was eliminated. There were more where that one came from. But the Allies were driving forward, and the calendar was moving into 1944, and the days of Hitler's U-boats were numbered.

The Battle for Anzio ("Operation Shingle")

Sicily had been tough. Italy was a lot tougher. Nazi General Kesselring pulled his troops out of the southern end of the peninsula and established the rock-ribbed "Gustav" and "Adolph Hitler" lines athwart the peninsula to block the Allied drive for Rome. Fighting northward from Naples, the American Army crashed into the defenses at Monte Cassino, and was brought to a halt. On the Adriatic side of the peninsula the British were stopped at the Sangro River. As the year turned on 1944 the Allied invasion was stalled.

Meantime, German paratroopers had snatched Mussolini from prison, and the Allies had suffered a catastrophic setback at Bari, where the *Luftwaffe* (on December 2, 1943) smashed the Adriatic port with a lightning raid that sent 16 transports to the bottom of the harbor.

With Naples and the important southern air base at Foggia in possession, American strategists were inclined to favor a holding action, but Churchill argued persuasively for a continued offensive in Italy. Because head-on attacks against the enemy's "mountain line" were proving extravagantly costly, the British Prime Minister promoted an amphibious landing on the Tyrrhenean coast at Anzio. Such a move would outflank the Nazi position at Monte Cassino, and put Allied troops 55 miles behind the "Gustav" line at a point only a few miles south of Rome.

Eisenhower cautioned that the move would be risky, but Churchill's strategy prevailed. Reinforcements were found for the Anzio operation, which was given the code-name "Shingle." As General Eisenhower was leaving for England to become Supreme Commander, Allied Expeditionary Forces, British General Sir Henry Maitland Wilson assumed the over-all Mediterranean command, hence was in charge of the Italian theater. "Operation Shingle" was to go full speed ahead. D-Day was set for January 22, 1944.

The landings were to take place on beaches in a sector which extended from Nettuno, a holiday resort some 30 miles south of Rome, to a point just below the Tiber estuary. Bull's-eye in this target sector was the little port of Anzio.

The invasion shipping assembled in the Naples area, the U.S. Navy and the Royal Navy teaming up with that cooperation which had brought them from the coast of Canada to this Italian littoral. The American naval forces (Amphibious Task Force 81) were commanded by Rear Admiral F. J. Lowry. British naval forces were under Rear Admiral Thomas Troubridge, R.N. The "Shingle" armada contained many of the amphibious vessels and fire-support warships which had carried the Allied invasion to Sicily and Salerno. Newcomers were also in the invasion fleet. A number of French, Dutch, and Greek warships, out to give the gunfire a United Nations tone. And two American destroyer-escorts, soon to show all and sundry that bantam DE's could put up a giant-size battle.

American destroyers and destroyer-escorts which operated with Task Force 81 are listed below.

PLUNKETT — *Comdr. E. J. Burke*
Flying the pennant of
Capt. J. P. Clay, COMDESRON 7
WOOLSEY — *Comdr. H. R. Wier*
Flying the pennant of
Capt. H. Sanders, COMDESRON 13
WAINWRIGHT — *Comdr. W. W. Strohbehn*
TRIPPE — *Comdr. R. C. Williams*
NIBLACK — *Comdr. R. R. Connor*
GLEAVES — *Comdr. B. L. Gurnette*
EDISON — *Comdr. H. A. Pearce*
LUDLOW — *Comdr. L. W. Creighton*
MAYO — *Comdr. A. D. Kaplan*
*CHARLES F. HUGHES — *Lt. Comder. J. C. G. Wilson*
Flying the pennant of
Comdr. V. Havard, Jr., COMDESDIV 14
*HILARY P. JONES — *Comdr. F. M. Stiesberg*
*MADISON — *Comdr. D. A. Stuart*
*LANSDALE — *Lt. Comdr. D. M. Swift*
H. C. JONES — *Lt. Comdr. R. A. Soule, III, U.S.N.R.*
FREDERICK C. DAVIS
Lt. Comdr. R. C. Robbins, Jr., U.S.N.R.
**Arrival off Anzio between 7-19 February.*

Mission of Task Force 81 was to establish Army Forces ashore on beaches near Cape D'Anzio for an attack on the rear of the enemy's right flank. The warships were to cover the landings, furnish all necessary fire-support, and bolster the attack wherever possible.

Following a misleading course which headed in the general direction of Corsica and then swung back toward Cape D'Anzio, the invasion fleet approached Anzio about midnight of January 21. H-Hour was set for 0200, morning of the 22nd.

Closing the coast, the ships moved in on headlands and foreshore that looked as quiet as scenery in a painting.

The dark foreshore remained fixed and silent as the landing craft started in. Just before the troops reached the shallows, rocket boats sprayed the beaches with a preparatory barrage. By 0400 the vanguard had a solid footing on the beachhead, and scouts were probing inland. Still no reaction from the enemy.

Watching from offshore, sailors who remembered Salerno Gulf were surprised and pleased by this phenomenon. Unfortunately the picture was bound to change. With the morning light, gunfire began to thud and sputter behind the beaches. Presently the *Luftwaffe* put in an appearance. The battle for Anzio was on.

Yanks and Tommies skirmished into Anzio and Nettuno on D-Day afternoon, but the seizure of these little coast towns was only a beginning. Caught off base, the Nazis rushed men, guns, and planes to the area to contain the invaders. German 88 mm. shells began to pound the Anzio-Nettuno beaches, and clouds of Swastika aircraft came roaring down the sky over the cape. As Admiral Lowry stated: *"Initial bombings during D-Day were light, but increased in intensity from D plus one. The first ten days had approximately seventy red alerts, of which thirty-two resulted in bombing attacks."*

An average of three air raids per day for ten straight days. The destroyers screening Task Force 81 had their fill of anti-aircraft work. More than their fill. Morning and night the gunners were kept jumping by dive-bombing and high-level bombing onslaughts. Heaviest raids were at evening twilight, at which time the *Luftwaffe* generally struck with dive-bombers, torpedo-planes, and glider bombs—a vicious combination. They managed, however, to get in only one surprise attack.

Meantime, the Army on D-Day had begun to call for fire-support, and the destroyers had begun to give it. Singly and severally, and sometimes in company with heavier warships, they moved along the coast to shoot at targets designated by shore fire-control parties.

Confusion might have resulted from the fact that American shore fire-control parties were operating with British warships, British shore fire-control parties were working with American warships, and U.S. Army Air Corps fighter pilots, using Army artillery procedure, were spotting for both British and American ships. But communications were exchanged with a glibness that brought results better than satisfactory.

In his report Admiral Lowry stated:

> *As revealed by dispatch from VI Corps Commander to Commander Task Force 81, prisoners of war reported that naval gunfire . . . was very effective and demoralizing to German troops. . . . Probably the most important type of fire delivered by naval support units was in the form of interdiction fire on road junctions, highways, crossroads and bridges. By denying the use of certain strategic points to the enemy, our forces were able to organize their position before enemy reserves could be assembled to challenge the beachhead.*

One of the first destroyers to give fire-support at Anzio was the U.S.S. MAYO (Commander A. D. Kaplan). On D-Day she steamed in to bombard enemy positions on the right flank of the Anzio beachhead. On the following day (January 23) she was still at it. The Germans had moved up heavy guns to lambaste the Anzio beaches, and under this cover a Nazi force was trying to fight its way across the Mussolini Canal. Thanks to MAYO, the Nazis were stopped on the towpath of this waterway. *"The speed and accuracy of her fire,"* Admiral Lowry noted, *"kept the Germans from counterattacking across Canale Mussolini."*

MAYO continued to shell Nazi targets until the evening of January 24, when she was disabled by an underwater explosion of unknown origin. The blast, which occurred at 2001, may have been the work of a mine or an unseen, circling torpedo. The explosion mashed in the starboard side of the vessel, wrecking and flooding the after engine-room and after fire-room, rupturing the bulkhead between the two compartments, bulging the main deck, and breaking the starboard propeller shaft. With six men killed, a man missing, and 25 wounded, the MAYO crew fought her battle-damage, and kept her above water. She was towed to Naples for temporary repairs, and eventually sent home to the States.

Another destroyer which contributed hot fire-support service to "Shingle" was U.S.S. LUDLOW (Commander L. W. Creighton). At 1019 in the morning of January 26 she answered a call to shoot up a Nazi strongpoint in Littoria. Steaming to the area, she opened fire and lobbed 267 rounds at the target—enough to win her the message: "Nice going. No more Littoria."

LUDLOW, too, was struck at Anzio. On February 8, while steaming off the coast, she was hit on the director deck by a 6-inch (or larger) shell. Luckily the projectile was a dud. But before it stopped spinning about the deck, it injured a bluejacket, exploded some ready ammunition, and a fragment of the rotating band slashed Commander Creighton's leg, felling him with a severe wound. The hot projectile, which was spilling its explosive charge, was picked up and heaved overside by Chief Gunner's Mate James D. Johnson—a nervy action which prevented more damage. LUDLOW went on her way with Lieutenant P. Cutler, U.S.N.R., assuming temporary command of the ship.

Sufficient evidence of the able fire-support loaned the "Shingle" effort by the destroyers may be found in the records of the U.S.S. EDISON (Commander H. A. Pearce). In action at Anzio this destroyer fired 1,854 rounds of 5-inch 38 ammunition at 21 separate targets. With 101 rounds fired on January 29, she turned a parade of Nazi trucks and armored vehicles into a roadside junk pile. From exuberant shore fire-control parties she received one congratulatory message after another. Here are some verbatim extracts.

FIRE EFFECTIVE VERY VERY GOOD BRASSED OFF A BUNCH OF KRAUTS

MANY ENEMY TROOPS KILLED BY YOUR FIRE GOOD WORK

PILOT SAID YOUR FIRE WAS VERY EFFECTIVE YOU WERE HITTING RIGHT ON THE ARTILLERY PIECES YOU WERE FIRING AT

EFFECT OF FIRE MACHING-GUN EMPLACEMENT IN BUILDING TOTALLY DESTROYED.

YOUR LAST TARGET WAS A TOWER BEING USED AS AN OBSERVATION POST YOU DEMOLISHED IT COMPLETELY

Air Raids at Anzio (Damaging of U.S.S. Plunkett)

Bombardment missions were not the only ones deftly accomplished by destroyers at Anzio. As was usual in an amphibious operation, they did all sorts of jobs, some routine, some odd. For instance, some were conducting A/S sweeps around the transport area, and keeping an eye out for possible E-boats. Some destroyers were guiding incoming traffic, and some were escorting empty convoys over the seaward horizon. These latter destroyers in Task Group 81.6, under Captain J. P. Clay, ComDesRon 7, were dealt duties as various as versatility itself. A paramount duty was the covering of invasion shipping with anti-aircraft protection. Most of the destroyers participated in this effort at one time or another.

In fact, this task kept the destroyermen busier than any other detail at Anzio. German artillery and the *Luftwaffe* constituted the chief opposition. The big Krupp guns did not arrive until late in the campaign, but the *Luftwaffe* was already on the job. Enemy air raids averaged three a day for the ten days immediately following D-Day.

Destroyers watched the sky with vigilant radar, hammered the raiders with flak, and rushed about laying smoke screens to cloak threatened shipping. All ships and craft in the area had some sort of smoke-making apparatus. It was used to good effect during twilight and after-dark raids when flashing AA batteries might otherwise silhouette the ships. German aviators, stunting through heavens of fire, were forced to drop their bombs more or less at random on seas of smudge.

But the Heinkels, Junkers, and Dorniers got in a few savage licks. Early in the battle against the *Luftwaffe,* Captain Clay's flagship, detroyer PLUNKETT, was hit. The ship, which was skippered by Commander E. J. Burke, was sorely wounded.

The attack occurred on January 24 in the shadows of evening—the *Luftwaffe's* favorite hour. It was one of those triple-threat onslaughts which featured torpedo-planes, dive-bombers, and glider bombs. Some eight or ten aircraft participated. The planes sighted were identified as Junker 88's. PLUNKETT's Action Report describes the attack's development:

> The action opened when two glider bombs were observed coming in on the port beam. They were identified by a pale green light which marked their trajectory. Almost simultaneously two Junker 88's were observed at a 50 foot altitude, one to port and one crossing ahead from starboard to port. Fire was opened and speed increased to 27 knots. A turn was made toward the glider bombs. These bombs hit the water about 200 yards astern of the ship.
>
> From this time on the ship was turned so as to keep pointed at the low flying planes. The forward 20 mm. gun crews reported seeing a plane at low altitude drop a torpedo at about 800 yards range which paralleled the track of the ship. During the next ten minutes these planes were intermittently sighted trying to obtain favorable positions and at least five bombs fell, missing the ship from 20 to 200 yards. These bombs were believed to have been dropped by dive-bombers although the bombers were not seen.
>
> The silhouette of the ship must have been outlined by the continuous firing at the low level planes. One enemy plane was seen to crash about 1,000 yards on the port beam and another 1,000 yards on the starboard bow. One was seen heading away trailing smoke. About twelve minutes after the action started this ship was hit on the 1.1-inch gun mount by a bomb. . . .

Estimated to be a 250-kilo job, the bomb detonated with a huge explosion that swept the deck with molten iron and fire. Men perished instantly in the face of this blast; a number were hurled overside or slain by flying debris. The flames touched off ready 1.1-inch and 20 mm. ammunition near the gun mount, and the wild fusillade added to the carnage. Her port engine disabled, the destroyer staggered and veered. The starboard engine was stopped to prevent the wind from fanning flames over depth charges aft.

While desperate hands fought fire and explosion, the gunners at the forward 5-inch and 20 mm. mounts blazed away at the attacking aircraft. For five more minutes the ferocious battle continued; then the holocaust aft was brought under control, and simultaneously the planes sped off in the night. Barbarously mutilated, PLUNKETT limped out of the battle area. Some 53 destroyermen had lost their lives in the blasting; 20 were wounded. Under escort of destroyer NIBLACK the maimed warship was sent to Palermo. Captain H. Sanders, ComDesRon 13, in WOOLSEY, assumed command of Task Group 81.6.

PLUNKETT was not the only *Luftwaffe* victim at Anzio. A number of other ships were damaged and several were sunk, including H.M.S. SPARTAN. But losses were relatively light when balanced against the weight of air bombs, torpedoes, and glider bombs which the Nazi aircraft flung at Allied shipping in the first three weeks of "Shingle." And it was at Anzio that a pair of DE's nipped the glider bomb in the bud.

DE's Versus Glider Bombs ("Frau Maier" Squelches the Robots)

Hatched in dark secrecy in the recesses of Nazi Germany, the glider bomb—it might have been more appropriately called a robot jet—was a dwarf descendant of the murderous "buzz bomb." It did not have the "buzz bomb's" range, nor carry as big an explosive charge, but militarily it was far more dangerous, and its potentialities were appalling.

The big "buzz bomb" was a demolition weapon with enormous destructive power, but it was as senseless as a berserk butcher. The glider bomb, on the other hand, could be aimed. In effect, it operated as a small "buzz bomb" having rocket propulsion and a sentient control-mechanism which answered the directives of a radio signal. Launched by a high-level bomber, it could be guided by remote control, and sent into a meteor-like dive straight for the target. That this weapon possessed great propensities for slaughter was obvious to those who saw its introduction at Salerno and its use against Convoy KMF-25A. Something had to be done to counter it. But what?

Anti-aircraft guns were not the answer. Like comets the robots came rocketing down the sky, too fast for accurate AA fire, too small for snaring in a net of flak. At Salerno the only antidote seemed to be an aircraft counterattack on the high-level bombers which launched the glider bombs. Convoy KMF-25A, without air cover, had been compelled to sweat out the robot onslaught.

It may be remembered there were two DE's in the task group which escorted that embattled convoy—destroyer-escorts HERBERT C. JONES and FREDERICK C. DAVIS. In company with the other vessels in the screen, the two little ships did their share of sweating when the glider bombs skimmed into view. Originally constructed as A/S vessels, destroyer-escorts were not as a type dedicated to anti-aircraft, much less anti-glider bomb, warfare. It appeared, however, that this pair was dedicated to that specific endeavor, for the Action Report of FREDERICK C. DAVIS, contains the following:

> On 21 January this vessel departed from Naples. . . . At this time and for three months previously, this vessel together with H. C. JONES had comprised Task Group 80.2 whose mission was the investigation and development of countermeasures against radio-controlled bombs. As visualized in advance, therefore, the primary function of these vessels in Operation Shingle was the protection of shipping from this type of missile.

When DAVIS (Lieutenant Commander R. C. Robbins, Jr., U.S.N.R.) first reported for duty with the Eighth Fleet, an interceptor unit (Y-team) was placed on board for service in connection with the investigation of glider bombs. This team was composed of three Army men, enlisted men who were technicians in the radio field. Why radio technicians? Because the rocket glider-bomb was radio-controlled. Radio was the key to the robot's performance, the "brain" which worked the steering mechanism and sent the bomb diving down on the target. And someone with quick perception had seen that this "brain" could also be an Achilles' heel.

For that which was guided by radio might also be *misguided* by radio—by jamming the air waves with broadcasts that would throw its radio-directed steering gear out of true.

Hence special intercepting and jamming equipment was rigged on board the F. C. DAVIS; the Y-team was prepared to scotch the robot's signals, if that were possible.

A Y-team with similar gear was placed on board destroyer-escort H. C. JONES (Lieutenant Commander R. A. Soule, III, U.S.N.R.). Captain Sanders' flagship, destroyer WOOLSEY (Commander H. R. Wier), also carried this type of apparatus. No one was certain that jamming would do the trick, but all hands involved in the effort were determined to make the try.

So "Shingle" found destroyer-escorts FREDERICK C. DAVIS and H. C. JONES stationed at the anchorage off Anzio beachhead. Day after day, raid after raid, they were there on duty with their peculiar equipment. Other ships flung up spectacular screens of AA fire. DAVIS and JONES were in there firing, too, but their most effective barrages were invisible. Whereas other warships were spraying the sky with TNT, these destroyer-escorts were spraying it with radio transmissions. And while the TNT was bringing down Nazi aircraft, the radio broadcasts were bringing down glider bombs.

WOOLSEY participated in this special work, but her Y-team equipment was not as effective as that on board the DE's. JONES and DAVIS fought the lion's share of the weird battle. They also starred as air raid wardens, detecting the *Luftwaffe's* approach and issuing warnings. Complimenting the DAVIS Y-team on its performance, Lieutenant Commander Robbins stated, "*. . . it should be said that the work of one of these men was truly remarkable, with the result that, prior to the establishment of shore-based radar,* DAVIS *was much the best and most reliable source for early warnings against enemy aircraft attack.*"

But the master accomplishment of DAVIS and JONES at Anzio was the frustration of the glider bomb—as is indicated by excerpts from the battle reports of Task Group Commander Sanders:

> During the period 22 January-2 February, 1944, there were some 26 bombing attacks by the German Air Force. Radio-controlled bombs were dropped during four of these attacks. . . . The efficiency with which F. C. DAVIS and H. C. JONES jammed radio-controlled bombs is an outstanding achievement on the part of these vessels.
>
> During the period of this report (2-7 February, 12-14 February, 1944) there were some thirteen bombing attacks in the Anzio area. . . . Radio-controlled bombs were noted in two of these attacks. No ships were hit. . . . A feature of the glider bomb attacks was the effective deflection of the bombs by jammers in F. C. DAVIS and H. C. JONES and to a lesser extent by WOOLSEY. On the last attack two glider bombs were seen to suddenly break off from their flight path and plunge into the sea.

The above are samples. Between the lines one may discern some nerve-wracking drama: the tense moment when the DE's first tried the jamming gear—the cheering when a bomb was deflected—the sober faces of men who realized that a DE with her radio prattling could stand out like a sore thumb. What if those Nazi bombers got the idea these little ships were throwing a wrench in the robot machinery?

One day when the *Luftwaffe* was in the sky, a radioman of the DAVIS Y-team overheard an enemy pilot call to a squadron mate, *"Let's all concentrate on Frau Maier."* A knowledge of everyday German sent the listener's hair up. "Frau Maier" is slang for "old gossip." The listening radioman had an idea that "old gossip" was the FREDERICK C. DAVIS.

And no sooner had the intercepted message been reported to the bridge than four enemy planes peeled off and made for the DE. Thirteen bombs fell around her in a tight circle, ringing the ship with geysers. DAVIS rolled and shook. Not a bomb hit her, but flying shrapnel left her with the only casualty she was to suffer during 142 days of "Shingle."

"Frau Maier" continued her gossiping. She was attacked by torpedo planes; she was dive-bombed; she was strafed. She was jolted by near-misses. She was given a close shave by practically every aircraft weapon except one—the glider bomb. FREDERICK C. *("Frau Maier")* DAVIS simply talked the robot down.

Excerpt from endorsement on F. C. DAVIS Action Report by Captain J. P. Clay, Commander Destroyers Eighth Fleet:

> After the Anzio landing, the F. C. DAVIS or H. C. JONES remained at the anchorage off the beachhead most of the time. Many enemy aircraft bombing and radio-controlled missile attacks were delivered on the convoys and beachhead anchorage while these destroyer-escorts were present. Their work in investigating frequencies and jamming the radio bombs has been outstanding.

Then the punch line:

> As a result of the counteraction against the weapon, the Germans practically ceased using it in this area after February.

Last Mile to Rome

Raging at the Anzio beachhead, German General Kesselring managed to pin the Allied forces to the Anzio-Nettuno vicinity. Late in the winter huge 280 mm. railroad guns were moved up by the Nazis to hold the line. Abetted by these Big Berthas, the German forces in the area dead-stalled the Anzio invaders.

Finally, when winter melted into spring, the stalemate was broken by mass Allied air raids which smashed up German communications lines as far north as Florence, and virtually obliterated Monte Cassino. Storming forward, the Fifth and Eighth Armies linked up near Anzio on May 25, 1944.

The Allied armies marched into Rome on June 4. Fall of the first Axis capital shook the world. For the Allies, ultimate victory was now within sight. For Nazi Germany and Samurai Japan, defeat loomed on the horizon. As for Italy, Fascism was in its grave.

American destroyers and destroyermen had played no small part in bringing about that dramatic victory.

Destroyers played an active part in the amazing amphibious invasion of Normandy, which included shore bombardment, clearing the way to the beaches, putting troops ashore, supporting the landings with defensive and offensive gunfire, and protecting the artificial harbors which were to handle the follow-up shipping. Here a DD bombards the French coast in Operation Neptune.

Operation Mulberry: The amphibious assault was only a first step on the road to the lair of the Nazis. Before Allied power could roll, it was necessary to build up advanced bases. This picture of massed shipping gives some idea of the urgency, magnitude, and vulnerability to air attack of the logistic support. DD's did a vital job in keeping the Allied war machine moving.

U.S.S. Harding off the invasion coast. As the hulk in the background testifies, Allied shipping was in constant danger from mines, shore batteries, and the Luftwaffe during the assault on Festung Europa. Four thousand ships had engaged in the Channel crossing. Eight American destroyers were assigned to each major task force and 17 were with the reserve fire-support group.

This monster Nazi gun emplacement is typical of the massive installations on the French coast overlooking the invasion beaches. Concrete walls 13 feet thick protected four 10-inch guns.

An oddity among the first prisoners transported to England from the front by naval forces were some Mongolians fighting for the Nazis in France. Most German captives were a surly lot.

CHAPTER 27

DESTROYERS TO NORMANDY

(FIRE SUPPORT FOR THE DRIVE ON FORTRESS EUROPE)

Festung Europa, 1944

The downfall of the first Axis capital filled Berlin with a horror matched only by the chill inspired by the news from the eastern front where the Russian steamroller was steadily advancing.

Nazi generals and Nazi admirals saw the bastions of Fortress Europa crumbling in the south and collapsing in the east. They saw the holes in the vaunted "Atlantic Wall" even as Hitler declared it impregnable.

To shore up that wall against the Allied storm—a storm which had long been gathering forces in the British Isles—the Nazi generals rushed troops and guns from east to west. In so doing they weakened their Russian-assailed front. Recalling troops from Italy, they exposed the south of France to an Allied drive. For months American and British air forces had been chopping down the *Luftwaffe,* blasting German industrial centers, blowing up captive oil refineries, hammering at Baltic and Channel ports. Austria, the Balkans, and the Fatherland itself were half in ruins. Where were the West Wall reinforcements to come from?

To defend the threatened Channel approaches, the Nazi admirals dredged bottom for ships and men. During the winter of 1943-44 Admiral Doenitz had called in his U-boats for hasty *Schnorkel* fittings; had pulled the residual German Navy together to guard the French coast. But the *Schnorkel* subs were too late, the surface warships too few, to offer the American and British fleets anything more than last-ditch resistance.

The Channel ports were massively fortified, the beaches protected by dense minefields and miles of underwater snares, miles of redoubts, miles of pillboxes and artfully emplaced guns. These coastal defenses were but the facade of another, a Germanic Maginot Line. The Germans themselves had proved the vulnerability of static land defenses.

They could defend the beaches for a time, perhaps. But they lacked the air and naval power to block amphibious invasion and prevent landings. They had lost the Battle of the Atlantic, and Eisenhower's armies were mustered in England, practically on France's threshold.

Afterwards Doenitz blamed it all on *Der Fuehrer.* *"Germany was never prepared for a naval war. . . ."* Doenitz complained in rueful retrospect. *"A realistic policy would have given us a thousand U-boats at the beginning."*

Doenitz's laments were seconded by Nazi Fleet Admiral Hermann Boehm, who wrote: *"The German Navy knew quite well that a world war is in essence a sea war, and that no matter what great battles might occur on land, sea power is the deciding factor. Whether German statesmen and war leaders were equally clear about this, I somewhat doubt."*

So Grand Admiral Doenitz, knowing a thousand submarines were necessary, could muster no more than a couple of squadrons in the spring of 1944 to defend the coast of France. So Fleet Admiral Boehm, aware that sea power was the deciding factor, could not gather together the ghost of a high seas fleet for the showdown. The U-boat Force had been whittled to the skeleton by attrition and malnutrition; many of its Channel bases were untenable; *Schnorkel* was not in adequate supply. As for the High Seas Fleet, most of it was on the bottom of the North Sea, the Atlantic, and the Mediterranean. A few remnants were cowering in the Baltic; a few were in the fiords of Norway, trapped by a blockade which had held them prisoner for many months.

Without anything like adequate naval support, the Nazi War Lords were compelled to rely almost wholly on infantry, artillery, and Panzer divisions, plus a smattering of the *Luftwaffe,* for defense of the threatened French coast. They were not as confident as the Master Mind in Berchtesgaden about the outcome. Their doubts were expressed by excited quarreling in Headquarters, by wrangles over strategy and policy, by angry recrimination, by a rash of inter-command jealousy and politicking and suspicion.

There was no such atmosphere in the Allied camp.

Channel Crossing ("Operation Neptune")

At Casablanca the decision was made; at Quebec in August 1943 the Combined Chiefs of Staff presented the plan to Roosevelt and Churchill; at Teheran in November 1943 Stalin was informed. It was agreed that British and American armies would crash into France. The Red Army would cooperate by launching a monster drive from the east. Nazi Germany would be crushed as in a giant vise.

Since early 1943 troops in southwest England had been intensively training for an amphibious campaign. Simultaneously Army Air and the R.A.F. were pounding Germany and Nazi bases in occupied Europe, and, in 1944, the Channel coast of France and the Lowlands. This concentrated bombing of the Channel area gave the Germans a general idea of what was coming. Information from espionage agents and U-boats confirmed the suspicion. A huge Allied armada was massing in the British Isles, and an all-out cross-Channel drive was impending.

But neither Nazi spies nor U-boats could inform the German High Command as to the invasion date or the point at which the battering-ram would strike.

By deduction the German War Lords concluded the Allies would make their main landing effort in the Calais region on Dover Strait where the Channel jump was shortest, the beaches were best for amphibious work, and foothold would place the Allied armies relatively close to the German border. This conclusion was exactly the one Eisenhower wished the enemy to draw. Deliberately the Germans were encouraged to rush reinforcements to the Calais sector; misleading maneuvers were made in that direction; Calais was all but openly named as the objective.

Confident that the enemy was convinced concerning Calais, the Combined Chiefs marked the Norman coast for the landings. The shock troops would go ashore in a 50-mile sector located about midway between Cherbourg and Deauville, with the western end of the sector lying on the Cotentin Peninsula. A push across this peninsula would isolate Cherbourg, and the inevitable fall of that important seaport would give the Allies a maritime door to Western Europe. For the immediate accommodation of invasion shipping, artificial harbors were to be installed on the captured coast as soon as the beachheads were secured.

The target sector was divided into three sections. The beaches lying in the eastern section near Deauville were to be taken by British forces. The center, designated "Omaha Beach," and the western section on the Cotentin Peninsula, designated "Utah Beach," were to be seized by American forces.

Under over-all command of General Eisenhower, Supreme Commander of the Allied Expeditionary Force, the projected invasion of Europe—an offensive to be culminated by an assault on Nazi Germany—was given the code-name "Operation Overlord." This text cannot attempt to detail the vast machinery and intricate workings of that gigantic triphibious plan nor can it do more than outline the labyrinthian complex of "Operation Neptune," the Normandy effort involved in "Overlord."

Objective of "Neptune" was the capture and securing of the fore-mentioned Normandy beaches by invasion troops totaling close to a million men. The operation called for the transport and landing of this Allied host—a dual mission involving an enormous convoy project and a stupendous amphibious program. Shipment of the Allied armies and their war gear occupied hundreds of merchantmen and escorts. All manner of naval vessels were employed in the amphibious program, which included clearing the way to the beaches, putting the troops ashore, covering and supporting the landings with defensive and offensive fire, and installing and protecting the artificial harbors which were to handle follow-up supply shipping.

Each one of these "Neptune" tasks was a colossal undertaking. Notoriously treacherous, the Channel presented tricky problems in convoy navigation—problems composed of high winds, soupy fogs, and jumpy seas that could easily wreck a great ship-train. Off the Norman coast the naval forces in the van would have to pick their way through lethal fields of magnetic, contact, electrical, and other tricky mines. Sweeping in, they would come to shallows rigged with traps and obstacles—concrete pylons, sawtooth underwater barricades of iron and steel. The landing forces would contend with miles of coast defenses, and the Navy's fire-support groups would be required to knock out pillboxes, casemated coast artillery, heavy Krupp guns concealed far inland, and rapidly shifting mobile batteries. To be constructed of sunken ships, floating steel caissons, and pontoon causeways, the great artificial harbors called "Mulberries" and the harbors for landing craft ("Gooseberries") had to be towed in through tumbling surf and shoal water, and set up with circus-lot celerity. All this in the face of enemy opposition—possible U-boats in the Channel, *Luftwaffe* overhead.

Altogether more than four thousand ships were assembled for "Operation Neptune." Allied Naval Commander-in-Chief Expeditionary Force was Admiral Sir Bertram H. Ramsay, R.N. The huge armada contained five task forces—three British, under Rear Admiral Sir Philip L. Vian, R.N., and two American, under Rear Admiral A. G. Kirk. Because the landings were to be on open beaches, D-Day was set for late May or early June when demolition teams and assault forces could take advantage of low springtides and an expected stretch of fair weather.

An ungodly weather-turn delayed "Overlord" just as the operation was started on June 5. A sudden gale, an abrupt turnback, and a 24-hour postponement failed to disorganize "Neptune," in spite of the fact that its immense machinery had been set in motion. On June 6 "Overlord" was again thrown into gear, and the "Neptune" invasion fleets were under way.

The "Neptune" forces sortied from widely separated bases in the United Kingdom and converged on an assembly area below the Isle of Wight. Down from Belfast, Northern Ireland, came the heavy warships of the Fire Support Group. American transports and escorts steamed from harbors on the southwest coast of Britain. From the Thames Estuary, Southhampton, and other southeast ports of Britain came the British forces.

Through an intricate system of scheduling, the various forces and task groups of this huge armada made rendezvous in the Channel assembly area, and then headed for Normandy in predetermined formation.

Ahead went the minesweepers and special demolition teams to clear the paths to the beaches and blaze the way with lighted dan buoys. Four paratroop and glider-borne infantry divisions swept in with the vanguard to strike behind the foreshore, seize local airfields, and sever inland supply roads. Then came the light attack vessels and herds of landing craft bearing the assault forces—groups which would move in to a Line of Departure some 3,000 yards offshore. Next came troopships and supply vessels—convoys bound for Transport Areas some 12 to 14 miles off the target beaches. With these troop and cargo carriers were the combat ships of the Fire-Support Group—men-of-war which would take station in Fire-Support Areas flanking the Transport Areas. These were followed by troopships bearing reserves, by heavy cargo transports, by hospital ships, by the innumerable auxiliaries and escorts attendant upon such convoys.

Well off the Norman coast the invasion armada split three ways, British and Canadian forces heading for the eastward beaches, American Task Force "O" heading for "Omaha Beach," American Task Force "U" heading for "Utah Beach."

Task Force "O" was commanded by Rear Admiral J. L. Hall. Rear Admiral D. P. ("Don") Moon commanded Task Force "U." Both forces composed the Western Task Force, under Rear Admiral Kirk. Task Force "O" was given fire-support by a fire-support group under command of Rear Admiral C. F. Bryant. This group included battleships TEXAS (flagship) and ARKANSAS, light cruisers GLASGOW, MONTCALM, and GEORGE LEYGUES, eight American destroyers, and three British destroyers. Task Force "U" was given fire-support by the fire-support group under command of Rear Admiral M. L. Deyo. This group consisted of the old battlewagon NEVADA, British monitor EREBUS, heavy cruisers TUSCALOOSA (flagship), QUINCY, and HAWKINS, two British light cruisers, Dutch gunboat SOEMBA, and eight American destroyers. A reserve fire-support group was composed of Admiral Kirk's flagship AUGUSTA, British light cruiser BELLONA, and 17 American destroyers.

The American destroyers which served in the "O," "U," and reserve fire-support groups are listed on the following page. Also listed are the American DE's in the Western Task Force. Destroyer operations were so interwoven through the "Neptune" tapestry that a panoramic picture of the Normandy landings may be acquired from the Action Reports of the destroyers and DE's involved.

June 6, 1944. That was the morning of D-Day, the morning of the landings Hitler had sworn would be repelled in *"exactly nine hours."* Sighting that dark and sombre coastline, the American destroyermen in "Neptune's" vanguard were not at all sure *Der Fueher's* boast would prove idle. But destroyermen would not forget Admiral Kirk's emphatic pre-battle statement:

I AWAIT WITH CONFIDENCE THE FURTHER PROOF IN THIS THE GREATEST BATTLE OF THEM ALL THAT AMERICAN SAILORS AND SEAMEN ARE FIGHTING MEN SECOND TO NONE

U. S. DESTROYERS IN

FIRE-SUPPORT GROUP "O"

DESRON 18

FRANKFORD *Lt. Comdr. J. L. Semmes*
Flying the pennant of
Capt. Harry Sanders, COMDESRON 18
CARMICK *Comdr. R. O. Beer*
DOYLE *Comdr. J. G. Marshall*
McCOOK *Lt. Comdr. R. L. Ramey*

BALDWIN *Lt. Comdr. E. S. Powell, Jr.*
Flying the pennant of
Comdr. W. J. Marshall, COMDESDIV 36
HARDING *Comdr. G. G. Palmer*
SATTERLEE *Lt. Comdr. R. W. Leach*
THOMPSON *Lt. Comdr. A. L. Gebelin*

U. S. DESTROYERS IN

FIRE-SUPPORT GROUP "U"

DESDIV 34

BUTLER *Comdr. M. D. Matthews*
Flying the pennant of
Comdr. W. L. Benson, COMDESDIV 34
GHERARDI *Comdr. N. R. Curtin*
HERNDON *Comdr. G. A. Moore*
SHUBRICK *Lt. Comdr. W. Blenman*

DESDIV 20

HOBSON *Lt. Comdr. K. Loveland*
Flying the pennant of
Comdr. L. W. Nilon, COMDESDIV 20
FORREST *Comdr. K. P. Letts*
FITCH *Comdr. K. C. Walpole*
CORRY *Lt. Comdr. G. D. Hoffman*

U. S. DESTROYERS IN

RESERVE FIRE-SUPPORT GROUP

DESDIV 119

BARTON *Comdr. J. W. Callahan*
Flying the pennant of
Capt. W. L. Freseman, COMDESRON 60
WALKE *Comdr. J. C. Zahm*
LAFFEY *Comdr. F. J. Becton*
O'BRIEN *Comdr. W. W. Outerbridge*
MEREDITH *Comdr. G. Knuepfer*

DESDIV 33

JEFFERS *Lt. Com. H. Q. Murray*
Flying the pennant of
Capt. A. C. Murdaugh, COMDESRON 17
NELSON *Lt. Comdr. T. D. McGrath*
MURPHY *Comdr. R. A. Wolverton*
GLENNON *Comdr. C. A. Johnson*
PLUNKETT *Comdr. W. Outerson*

DESDIV 19

ELLYSON *Comdr. E. W. Longton*
Flying the pennant of
Capt. A. F. Converse, COMDESRON 10
HAMBLETON *Comdr. H. A. Renken*
RODMAN *Comdr. J. F. Foley*
EMMONS *Comdr E. B. Billingsley*

DESDIV 18

SOMERS *Comdr. W. C. Hughes, Jr.*
Also Acting COMDESDIV 18
DAVIS *Comdr. W. A. Dunn*
JOUETT *Comdr. J. C. Parham, Jr.*

U. S. DESTROYER-ESCORTS IN

WESTERN TASK FORCE

AMESBURY *Lt. Comdr. A. B. Wilbor, U.S.N.R.*
Flying the pennant of
Comdr. A. B. Adams, Jr., COMCORTDIV 19
BORUM *Lt. Comdr. J. K. Davis, U.S.N.R.*

MALOY *Lt. Comdr. F. D. Kellogg, U.S.N.R.*
BATES *Lt. Comdr. H. A. Wilmerding, Jr., U.S.N.R.*
RICH *Lt. Comdr. E. A. Michel, Jr.*
BLESSMAN *Lt. Comdr. J. A. Gillis, U.S.N.R.*

And there ahead was Normandy. The clock was ticking toward H-Hour. With the vanguard at "Utah Beach," destroyers HOBSON, FITCH, and CORRY moved in.

Action of Hobson, Fitch, and Corry

They were DD's of Commander L. W. Nilon's DesDiv 20—flagship HOBSON (Lieutenant Commander K. Loveland); FITCH (Commander K. C. Walpole); and CORRY (Lieutenant Commander G. D. Hoffman). A companion destroyer, FORREST, did not accompany them. Assigned as Fire-Support Unit 3 in Task Force "U," the trio sortied from Tor Bay, England, about noon on June 5.

They found the Channel baring its white teeth to the whip of ill-tempered weather, but they plodded stubbornly through the chop to take up screening positions with a convoy bound for the Cotentin Peninsula. Despite the ugly weather and surly seas they made the crossing on schedule.

About midnight the destroyer lookouts sighted the spatter of anti-aircraft fire against the sky, and the flush and flutter of bomb explosions. The Allied planes which had passed overhead like flocks of migrant geese were now on target. For miles the skyline was festooned with twinkling aerial bursts, brilliant spokes and sprays, and vivid gusts that shuttled like rapid passages of sheet-lightning. Gun flashes lit the lower darkness, and here and there the night was burned through by a steady blaze.

Presently you could hear the rumble, an insistent monotone grumbling that seemed to vibrate in the air—as though some giant train were trundling across an invisible trestle, distant in the night. Snatches of buzz-saw droning drifted from the sky where unseen aircraft squadrons were going over. A thousand smokes were going up, a thousand thunders shaking the air. Inside and around, fast boats, barges, all description of craft chugged and circled and maneuvered—dim, half-seen silhouettes, trailing foamy wakes. On the tide flares floated, illumining the current, and lights winked. And there was smell of the land, and of smoke, and of burnt powder.

This was "Utah Beach." The destination of Force "U," it was considered the easiest of the Normandy landing objectives. And certainly it was easier than "Omaha Beach" in the center and the British strip to the east. The British and Canadian amphibious teams had to fight their way in through rocky, surf-battered shallows. "Omaha Beach" was dominated by steep bluffs which gave enemy guns every chance to rake the flat, shingly foreshore. In contrast, "Utah's" was a terrain of low ground which could be swept by rocket and artillery fire and flailed by creeping barrages of naval salvos. Moreover, the enemy here was least prepared to meet attack.

The "miners" were sweeping in when DesDiv 20 reached the Transport Area. Enemy mines were imbedded in the waters of this littoral like raisins in a cake. Here the ships had to walk with the caution of cats on eggs. So while "Utah" was easy (the term is an admitted euphemism) for the Army, for the Navy this Cotentin beach was a thorn patch.

U.S.S. HOBSON, FITCH, and CORRY reached the Transport Area at 0110 in the morning of June 6. There they lay to for three hours while the minesweeping of the Transport Area was completed.

At 0410 the three DD's maneuvered into the boat lane to lead the first boat wave in to the offshore Line of Departure. This shoreward procession moved at slow speed, "walking softly to go far." Evidently because of low visibility and unpreparedness, the Germans had not yet sighted the advancing ships.

At 0530 the trio of lead destroyers turned away from the boat lane and headed for their assigned fire-support stations, which were located some 4,000 yards off "Utah Beach" at a point about two miles from the St. Marcouf Islands. Just as they were clearing the boat lane, FITCH and CORRY were fired upon by shore batteries. Sudden flashings—muffled thunder—the drilling whine of big projectiles—the crash and surge of near misses founting around the ships. The world was lurid and noisy with the din of battle.

At once FITCH and CORRY answered the challenge. Noting the location of the flashes, the two destroyers replied in unison, firing what were probably the first defensive naval shots of "Operation Neptune." Apparently the destroyer gunners found the target, for at 0550 the offending batteries went silent.

Meantime, flag destroyer HOBSON had opened up on scheduled targets. FITCH followed suit at 0550, and CORRY entered the bombardment program at 0600.

At this hour the "Neptune" battering-ram struck full force against the entire Normandy sector. As dawn dispelled the darkness, dozens of combat ships unleashed a barrage that shook the French coast from the Cotentin shore to Deauville. Flight after flight of Allied aircraft stormed across the sky to join in the bombardment. At "Utah Beach" the Allied bombers and Force "U" warships delivered a steel hurricane that seemed to blow the shoreline loose. Mountains of smoke surged up from the peninsula. Landfalls appeared to dissolve into smudge. Dunes heaved and flattened and were whisked away in cyclonic gusts.

Yet here and there in the heart of that inferno German gun crews sweated; officers shouted; cannon spat and recoiled and returned to battery, spilling

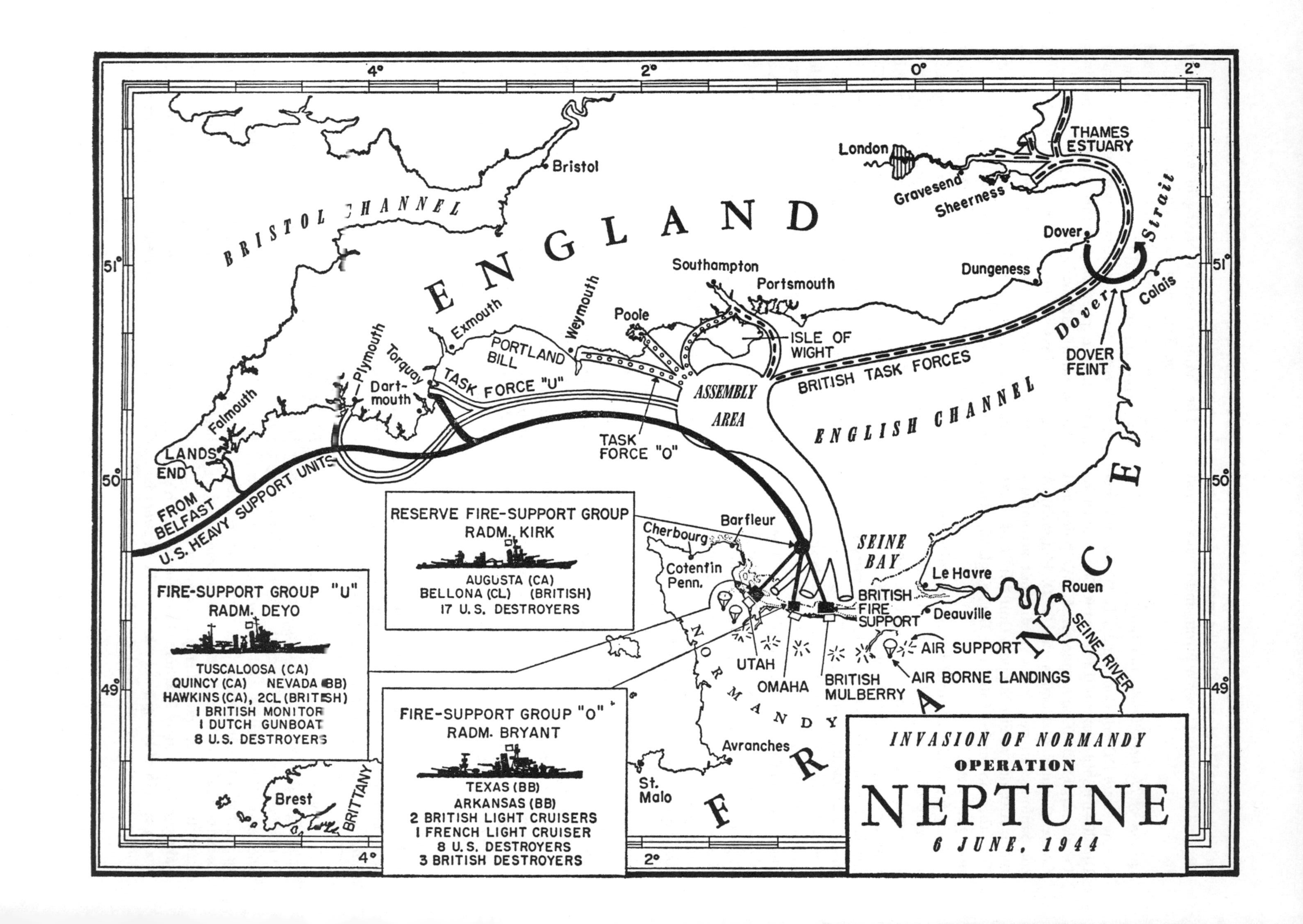
INVASION OF NORMANDY
OPERATION
NEPTUNE
6 JUNE, 1944
ENGLAND
FRANCE
NORMANDY
BRISTOL CHANNEL
ENGLISH CHANNEL
Dover Strait
SEINE BAY
ASSEMBLY AREA
THAMES ESTUARY
London
Gravesend
Sheerness
Dover
Dungeness
DOVER FEINT
Calais
Bristol
Southampton
Portsmouth
ISLE OF WIGHT
Poole
Weymouth
PORTLAND BILL
Exmouth
Torquay
Dartmouth
Plymouth
Falmouth
LANDS END
FROM BELFAST
U.S. HEAVY SUPPORT UNITS
TASK FORCE "U"
TASK FORCE "O"
BRITISH TASK FORCES
Cherbourg
Barfleur
Cotentin Penn.
Le Havre
Rouen
SEINE RIVER
Deauville
BRITISH FIRE SUPPORT
AIR SUPPORT
AIR BORNE LANDINGS
UTAH
OMAHA
BRITISH MULBERRY
Avranches
St. Malo
Brest
BRITTANY
RESERVE FIRE-SUPPORT GROUP
RADM. KIRK
AUGUSTA (CA)
BELLONA (CL) (BRITISH)
17 U.S. DESTROYERS
FIRE-SUPPORT GROUP "U"
RADM. DEYO
TUSCALOOSA (CA)
QUINCY (CA) NEVADA (BB)
HAWKINS (CA), 2CL (BRITISH)
1 BRITISH MONITOR
1 DUTCH GUNBOAT
8 U.S. DESTROYERS
FIRE-SUPPORT GROUP "O"
RADM. BRYANT
TEXAS (BB)
ARKANSAS (BB)
2 BRITISH LIGHT CRUISERS
1 FRENCH LIGHT CRUISER
8 U.S. DESTROYERS
3 BRITISH DESTROYERS
4°
2°
0°
51°
50°
49°

their own smokes and spent shell-cases. Spotters screamed into telephones, directing the fire of 75's and 88's and bigger Krupp guns. They spotted the destroyer FITCH in the offshore dimness, and at 0608 a shell smashed the water about 600 feet from the DD's starboard quarter. Commander Walpole rang up 20 knots to get his ship out of range, and the shells nipped at her heels as she sprinted, one salvo landing about 300 feet astern.

As FITCH steamed for the southwest corner of the Fire-Support Area, Walpole and his lookouts strained their glasses in an effort to locate the sharpshooting battery. But the shore was now fogged with so dense a haze that flashes were difficult to discern. And Allied planes, trailing smoke, were laying screens that concealed the ships of Force "U" from enemy view. By 0615 FITCH and all but one ship in the area were behind the smoke curtain. Exposed in front of the smoke was the destroyer CORRY.

Anchored at "short stay," Lieutenant Commander Hoffman's destroyer came under a concentrated fire that figuratively blistered her paint. By dint of flank-speed spurts, quick stops, backing right full rudder and left full rudder, she managed to dodge the Nazi salvos, but it was touch and go.

While CORRY was jockeying about, her guns and those of her companion DD's blazed away at enemy batteries which hurled sudden salvos in their direction. Farther out, the battleships, cruisers, and other destroyers of the Fire-Support Group were shelling the beach, smashing gun emplacements, raking the redoubts with the new VT-fused ammunition—the type politely labeled "anti-personnel." The clocks touched H-Hour. At 0631 a swarm of landing craft let go with a rocket barrage. The sands of "Utah" erupted, exploded, churned, founted, and roared. Seaward rolled drifts of acrid smoke and dust, and under this hot fog the shock troops streamed shoreward. The landings were under way.

The DD's of DesDiv 20 were in the center of the inferno—HOBSON firing, CORRY firing, FITCH firing. In the latter's Action Report, Commander Walpole subsequently jotted some interesting comments on the performance of his ship's Combat Information Center:

> *The performance of C.I.C. was of inestimable value in handling the ship during the engagement. All navigation of the ship was accomplished from C.I.C. When the ship originally came under fire, bearings were taken on the flashes, sent to C.I.C. and then from there data selected on known targets and the probable batteries taken under fire, using the gunnery officer as spotter. For the scheduled bombardment of the shore positions C.I.C. furnished the data and controlled the indirect fire, using the gunnery officer only for the spotter. When the air bombardment commenced and there was considerable flak from AA batteries, C.I.C. was able to give advice as to whether flashes were from known gun locations or whether it was probable AA fire. This information was of great value in preventing the taking of needless targets under fire.*

This glimpse into FITCH's C.I.C. affords a general picture of the workings of that organization in Navy destroyers at that stage of the war. Maintaining a continuous comprehension of the tactical situation—what might be called an omniscient observer's view of the battle—C.I.C. was the warship's brain-center, the cortex which received the sensory impressions, and radiated appropriate impulses to the vessel's various controls.

Unfortunately there were agents of warfare beyond C.I.C.'s powers of perception. For example, a mine stirred up by a rush of high-speed maneuvers, or by the turbulence of water thrashed by propellers and tossed by shell hits.

At 0633 CORRY struck such a mine.

Loss of U.S.S. Corry

The mine let go under CORRY's engineering spaces, crushing her bottom plates as though they were cardboard, and rending her hull. *"There was a fearful explosion,"* one of her officers remembered. *"We seemed to jump clear of the water."*

The sea plunged into the forward engine-room and forward fireroom, swamping vital machinery and flooding fires. A moment later the after fireroom was inundated. All electric power went out, and the ship's compartments were in darkness. As engineers raced topside, beating the rush of water and deadly steam, the destroyer traveled the arc of a tight circle with her rudder jammed at hard right.

At 0637—four minutes after the blast—all steam was lost in the after engine-room, and the ship's propulsive power expired. Drifting, she slowed to a stop. It was evident that her case was desperate; she was still under enemy fire, and the mine explosion, which had stifled her turbines, had also snapped her keel and opened a great fissure in her main deck and hull. Still, there seemed a chance of saving her. Boats were lowered, and men stood ready to rig a tow to prevent her from drifting ashore into enemy hands. As the boats went overside, CORRY hoisted the distress signal: *"This ship needs help."*

She needed more than help. At 0639 the waves were lapping her main deck, and she lolled sway-backed in helpless paralysis. She was sagging amidships, sinking. The word had been given to abandon. Below decks the inrushing water boomed; there was a din of crunching metal, a screech of breakage, a great hissing of live steam. And in the forward fireroom a Water Tender was trapped under the grating of the upper level—a dim figure swimming in a swirl of water and fuel oil.

Lieutenant (jg) John O. Parrott, Damage Control Officer and First Lieutenant, answered the man's outcry. Clawing his way through a hatch, he went down into the jungle of the fireroom. In that cavernous compartment, its deck-plates tilted at a crazy angle, its darkness a-whistle with scalding steam, Lieutenant Parrott forced his way under the grating and pulled the oil-smeared Water Tender to safety. Navy Cross for Lieutenant Parrott.

For those who escaped the flooded destroyer, the ordeal was only beginning. As she settled slowly, her stacks leaned together, her bow and fantail made the "V" of a folding jackknife, and the Nazi gunners continued a wicked fire that maimed survivors in the water, and slashed at the broken ship. A hit ruptured the smoke-screen generator on CORRY's fantail, releasing a torrent of FS vapor that swirled out over the flotsam, blinding and choking the swimmers and boat crews. Another shell struck one of the 40 mm. gun tubs, exploding the projectiles that were at ready stowage.

In the midst of carnage, CORRY's survivors hung on, fighting through blood and oil and debris. One raft was carried in a complete circle around the drowned ship. As the survivors passed between wreck and shore, a near-miss from a German salvo lashed them with shrapnel, creating fresh casualties. Water temperature was 54°F., and several men died of exposure. But in spite of shellfire, toxic fog, adverse currents, and bitter immersion, most of CORRY's complement remained alive.

Ordered by Admiral Deyo to pick up CORRY's survivors, destroyer FITCH made a fast run to the scene. By 0729 she had her first haul of survivors on board. She spent the ensuing hour and a half pulling men from the sea and lambasting the Nazi artillery on the beach.

Then HOBSON moved in to assist. She had been covering the landings in her assigned area, blasting scheduled targets and bombarding the flank of a beach where troops were storming ashore. Now, steaming to the aid of CORRY's crew, HOBSON continued the bombardment on one hand while conducting rescue work on the other. As Lieutenant Commander Hoffman noted in CORRY's Action Report:

> The FITCH and HOBSON entered the survivor area with all guns firing at the shore batteries on one side of their respective ships, while lowering boats and cargo nets on their other sides.

After saving her share of lives, HOBSON returned to her bombardment station to resume gun-work on a scheduled target, strong point and road block. Meanwhile, the destroyer BUTLER (Commander M. D. Matthews) had joined FITCH in rescue operations, and PT 199 had run in to help. At 0854 HOBSON was relieved on station by BUTLER, at which time the DesDiv 20 flagship was ordered to take over CORRY's fire-support mission.

By 0900 the last of CORRY's survivors were picked up. As they left the scene of battle, HOBSON came steaming down the line to serve as replacement. Behind them, U.S.S. CORRY was on the bottom at six fathoms. She was down, but not yet under. Her mast, her director, the top of her bridge, and her tilted prow remained visible.

Lost with CORRY were 21 men and an officer. Most of her survivors—260 officers and men, including 33 wounded—were placed on board the transport BARNETT which sailed for Portland, England, at 1300 that afternoon. FITCH and HOBSON accompanied the BARNETT convoy on the west-bound passage.

In the vanguard of the Normandy invasion, those three DD's had been the spearpoints on "Neptune's" trident. They had gouged a hole in Hitler's "Atlantic Wall."

Destroyers to "Omaha Beach"

For the amphibs the "Omaha" landings were a hell of fire and water. That was the place where, as Field Marshal Montgomery phrased it, *"the American troops held on by their eyelashes."*

The main assault point, it was a terrible beach. In the shallows the Nazis had planted a maze of tetrahedrons and hedgehogs interlaced with barbed wire and set with cunning traps. Fighting in through this horror of obstacles, the Navy's Underwater Demolition Teams lost nearly half their men through mine explosions and vicious fusillades from the shore. LCI's and LCT's, advancing along dangerously narrow lanes, were bounced and shaken by combers as well as projectiles. And by D-Day, H-Hour, the German defenders were thoroughly aroused, and the shock troops and Rangers of the First Army, struggling shoreward, were met by a tornado barrage from the Nazi guns.

Battleships ARKANSAS and TEXAS and companion warships of the Force "O" Fire-Support Group slugged the enemy's gun positions with a thunderous bombardment. Some of the casemated shore batteries were knocked out, but the big Krupp guns nested in the chalk bluffs overlooking the beach were not to be immediately eradicated. And in spite of furore and confusion in Nazi Headquarters, the beach defenses were formidably stiffened in short order. Panzers and field pieces were rushed to the embattled shore. Raked by a murderous fire from coast artillery, mobile guns, machine-gun nests and rifle pits, the first wave of American troops went down.

All morning the Germans held the Americans pinned down to the water's edge. Only a few of the assault companies managed to reach inshore foxholes and the gully-cleft bluffs. Attempting to fight their way into ravines and valleys, they were riddled by enfilading fire from redoubts and concealed pillboxes. It appeared that the "Omaha" invasion might be thrown back.

That was the critical hour when the Germans should have seized the initiative, throwing every tank, every Panzer gun, every machine-gun squad in the area to the fore. Indeed, at that hour the roads to "Omaha" were crawling with Panzers, with infantry caravans, with all manner of military traffic. But much of this traffic could not get through. Nearing the coast, it jammed.

It jammed because of a stupendous naval bombardment which struck the Nazi front at "Omaha" on D-Day afternoon. That bombardment would never be forgotten by the Nazis who lived to remember it. Or by the Navy men who delivered it—particularly the destroyermen who shared in its delivery.

Time: about noon. Admiral Deyo's Fire Support Group had been standing inshore, blasting at the Nazi positions with everything. Battleships ARKANSAS and TEXAS heated their turrets now. So did the Allied cruisers working with Force "O." As for the Fire-Support destroyers, they pushed so close inshore that, as Admiral Kirk expressed it, *"they had their bows against the bottom."*

The American destroyers which had their "bows against the bottom" at "Omaha" were the U.S.S. DOYLE, FRANKFORD, MCCOOK, THOMPSON, BALDWIN, CARMICK, and EMMONS. Most of them had been fighting since dawn, firing at "targets of opportunity." Also in on the bombardment were British DD's MELBREAK, TALYBONT, and TANATSIDE.

Throughout noon hour and the rest of the afternoon the destroyermen kept up a pointblank bombardment, sweeping the enemy's beach guns and bluff guns with shellfire. Dealing out salvo after salvo, they blasted pathways for the invasion troops to follow from water's edge to bluffs. Hurling shells at the escarpments, they brought guns down in chalky avalanches; pulverized pillboxes; blew Nazis out of dugouts. In the maw of ravines and valleys open to the sea the German guns were emplaced for cross-fire. The destroyers got them by the simple expedient of pounding both sides of a ravine or valley until the walls threatened to collapse.

Farther offshore, the heavy ships, aided by specially trained RAF spotters and Navy fire-control parties working with Army units, sledgehammered the enemy's gun positions and concentration points inland. A rain of shells, 8-inch and up, blasted shore roads, abolished bridges, crashed down on herds of Nazi tanks, and blew Nazi infantry out of existence.

By 1700 the Nazi reinforcements bound for "Omaha" were stalled on roads blocked with wrack and ruin. Nazi guns no longer dominated the coast, and the American Army was going steadily ashore. The situation at "Omaha Beach" was in hand.

After it was over, Field Marshal Von Rundstedt glumly attributed the German defeat on the Norman coast to *"the power of the Allies' naval guns, which reached deep inland . . . making impossible the bringing up of reserves needed to hurl Allied invasion forces into the Channel."* To an interrogator who questioned him after his capture, he said bluntly, *"Your naval artillery was terrific."*

Destroyers Versus Nazi Mines

Unable to take advantage of the carnage at "Omaha," the Germans strove desperately to harry the invasion forces with E-boat strikes and destroy offshore shipping with a mine barrage.

During the afternoon and night of D-Day a considerable number of German planes winged across the "Utah Beach" area, dropping mines. This activity was at once detected. But the Allied minesweepers were unable to cope with the situation that night, as they were moved inshore to block a possible E-boat sortie from the Carentan River estuary. As a result the mines were widely distributed by the Channel current, and the following morning the minesweepers had their work cut out for them.

Early that morning of June 7 an American minesweeper group stood in to clean up the shallows. They were sweeping for O-type moored mines. They failed to brush up any of this type. But the American minesweeper TIDE disturbed another sort of mine. The explosion blew the ship literally out of the water. She was the second U.S. naval vessel sunk by mine explosion off "Utah Beach."

Again the German minelaying planes skimmed over, scattering their deadly marine eggs. That night the heavy-laden troopship SUSAN B. ANTHONY, steaming along the eastern fringe of the "Utah" area, struck a mine. Most of her passengers and crew were rescued, but she was another ship downed by mine warfare.

Because the tidal currents in the "Utah" area flowed parallel to the coastline of the Cotentin Peninsula, mines dropped near the St. Marcouf Islands on the northwest border of the "Utah" area might drift in a few hours to the "Omaha" region. On the reverse current, mines dropped in the "Omaha" locality might drift across the "Utah" front to the St. Marcoufs. It was in the vicinity of these islands that the Nazi mines took their heaviest toll.

During the first nine hours of the morning of June 8, United States destroyers MEREDITH and GLENNON and destroyer-escort RICH were sunk by mines off "Utah Beach."

Loss of U.S.S. Meredith

At about 0110 in the morning of June 8 the destroyer MEREDITH, serving with the Force "U" Fire Support Group, arrived in her assigned screening area near the cruiser TUSCALOOSA off "Utah Beach." These ships were units of a task group working in the northwest waters of "Utah." MEREDITH's skipper, Commander George Knuepfer, set the destroyer on course for a vigorous patrol, screening to the northward of numerous heavy ships on locale.

The dark was lively with spray and choppy water. A fresh breeze blowing under low, wet clouds occasionally unravelled them to reveal a pallid moon. Patrolling in the area were a half-dozen Allied DD's and several DE's. They were keeping a sharp lookout for, among other things, a new German secret weapon.

For weeks German scientists and technicians had been working with frantic speed to produce a secret weapon in time to meet the Allied invasion. Guided missiles! The first of these new flying bombs made their uncanny appearance during the Normandy landings. Tipped off on their production, the Allies had been looking for them. Now, early in that morning of June 8, several were sighted by the American destroyer JEFFERS (Lieutenant Commander H. Q. Murray), flagship of Captain A. C. Murdaugh, ComDesRon 17. JEFFERS was in the northwest "Utah" patrol area, and steaming about a mile distant from MEREDITH.

Although MEREDITH's lookouts did not sight any guided missiles, about five minutes after the ship commenced screening operations, a covey of planes droned into view. Some of the heavy warships and their screening units opened fire on the aircraft. MEREDITH held her fire because she could not pick up a target which was definitely identifiable as an enemy.

That the planes were German "miners" was almost a certainty. The Nazi airmen had taken to the mission with enthusiasm, making it a practice to drop their magnetic and contact specimens after dark. And it was a good night for such an endeavor. With the clock no later than 0152, MEREDITH struck a mine.

Hearing the thunder, JEFFERS' crew thought MEREDITH had been hit by a guided missile. She was probably blasted by a mine of the submerged contact type. Excerpts from the Action Report submitted by her Commanding Officer give interesting details of the fatal episode:

> A violent explosion shook the ship, appeared to lift her up and throw her forward. A huge geyser of water drenched the entire forward part of the ship and falling debris rained upon the open bridge area. The personnel on the bridge were thrown to the deck and against the sides of the open bridge. There was a total absence of any flash, smoke, or flame from this explosion. As the cloud of water settled, only steam rushing from the after stack area was evident, and this subsided rapidly.
>
> The explosion appeared to have occurred deep down in the ship on the port side amidships. It vented itself upward and outward on the main deck and ship's side over the after fireroom. All power and lighting were lost immediately; the ship stopped dead in the water, turning slowly to starboard; all communications were lost with the engineering spaces and the after part of the ship. . . .
>
> At about 0220 the ship appeared to settle deeper in the water, the list increased to 12° and the starboard side of the main deck was awash. All hands were ordered to the main deck to stand by the life floats and nets. At about 0230, after having received a complete report of the damage sustained and reports of injured, I decided to transfer all personnel to near-by ships for their own safety. The ship was drifting towards the enemy shore, and with the increased settling in the water this appeared to be the best decision. The major damage was confined to the area of free flooding in the forward engine-room, after fireroom, and after engine-room. These areas had a gaping hole 65 feet wide on the port side, open to the sea. . . . The ship had reached a position of static balance and would remain in this condition if the huge bulkheads on either side of these spaces would hold. . . . In my opinion the ship could be saved by salvage operations and the salvage equipment available in the area. Therefore decided to evacuate all personnel to near-by ships and to place my key officers and men and myself aboard one of the ships and to return aboard the MEREDITH at dawn, or prior to that time if the salvage tugs arrived sooner.

When the mine struck, Chief Machinist's Mate Brady L. Bryan was in charge of the watch in MEREDITH's after engine-room. Bryan and the men about him were hurled off their feet and the engine-room went into complete darkness.

Then all hell broke loose. Before a man could get his bearings he was struck in the face by a steel bar, or a scalding jet of steam, or a flash of hot grease or oil. He was struggling in a swirl of water that swept him across tilted floor-plates, perhaps sucked him through a hatch, or smashed him against a bulkhead. He might be trapped under a grating, or wedged in a vise of shattered machinery; might find his arm pinned behind him by an invisible hook, or his pants leg caught in a snare.

Deafened, stunned, Chief Machinist's Mate Bryan groped through the dark, found the portside ladder. Dimly aware of the effort, he scrambled up the greasy rungs. He went through the after engine-room hatch with a lunge, and stumbled along the portside passageway to the fantail.

Out in the open—fresh air; a reassuring glimpse of men and officers hurrying about the business of seamanship and damage-control; the exhilarating feel of safety. Brisk commands. Crews at their stations. Boats, gear, and sea in familiar order. Perhaps Bryan's first thought was, *"I made it!"*

Perhaps not. But if it was, his next thought was for his shipmates. The hands who had stood watch with him down there in the after engine-room—they weren't here on the fantail! They hadn't made it!

That was all Bryan needed. That, and a flashlight. He retraced his journey through that dark portside passageway to the engine-room hatch, and down that slippery ladder to the inky limbo below.

The flood had climbed to within four feet of the overhead, and the whirling water was scummed with oil and clots of grease, and littered with bits of flotsam. But in that swirling cistern, Bryan found four injured men. Badly wounded, they were clinging to handholds, fighting for breath, treading water. Working his way through the topsy-turvy of murk and shadow, the Chief went after them. He got them.

Recommending Brady L. Bryan for the Navy Cross, Commander Kneupfer noted that had it not been for Bryan's act the four injured men would have gone down with the ship. Kneupfer concluded the citation with the following:

HE CARRIED THESE MEN OUT OF THE AFTER ENGINE-ROOM TO THE FANTAIL, KEPT THEM TOGETHER, AND SUBSEQUENTLY ASSISTED IN PUTTING THEM ABOARD A SHIP THAT CAME ALONGSIDE TO REMOVE THEM. THESE MEN WERE ALL BADLY INJURED AND WERE HOSPITALIZED FOR BURNS, FRACTURES, AND LACERATIONS. BUT ALL OF THEM ARE ALIVE AND WILL RECOVER FROM THEIR INJURIES.

But valor—and it was not wanting in other members of MEREDITH's complements—could not save the stricken destroyer. About 40 minutes after MEREDITH was mined, the destroyer-escort BATES (Lieutenant Commander H. A. Wilmerding, Jr., U.S.N.R.) arrived to take off survivors. PC 1263 and PC 1232 joined in this detail. Destroyer JEFFERS came up to stand by. After all hands were removed from the disabled destroyer, Commander Kneupfer boarded the DE, and BATES and JEFFERS mounted guard over the abandoned ship.

MEREDITH did not go down. But as morning advanced, she drifted to a point within range of enemy guns guarding Cape Barfleur on the northeast head of the Cotentin Peninsula. As his destroyer stubbornly remained afloat, Captain Murdaugh, ComDesDiv 17 in JEFFERS, decided to put a party on board to determine salvage possibilities. When volunteer boarders reported the ship's condition favorable, JEFFERS maneuvered alongside, and salvage work was begun.

By means of jettisoning, MEREDITH's 15 degree list was reduced; a tow was rigged, and JEFFERS hauled the disabled ship out of enemy gun-range. Two salvage tugs (Commodore Sullivan, Salvage Officer) arrived on the scene about 0515 to relieve JEFFERS of the tow. Not long after the tugs came up, Commander Knuepfer and 52 of his crew returned on board MEREDITH. She was then towed to the Advanced Transport Area where she was anchored not far from Admiral Moon's flagship BAYFIELD.

During the tow, MEREDITH's list increased several degrees. But all compartments and bilges forward and aft of her damaged mid-section were found to be dry, so another effort was made to lighten ship. Torpedoes were removed and light guns dismantled, a salvage crew from the tug BANNOCK assisting MEREDITH's men in the work.

That afternoon the MEREDITH was towed by BANNOCK to a new anchorage about three miles off the beach in the vicinity of Grandcamp. There BANNOCK tied up alongside, and salvage work was continued.

The destroyermen on board MEREDITH were relieved by a security watch about 2030 that evening. They had put in an exhausting day. But their ship was still on her feet, and it looked as though they had pulled her through.

But early in the following morning (June 9) a flock of Nazi aircraft raided the "Utah" area. These Swastika planes roared over MEREDITH's anchorage, dropping 2,000-pound bombs. One of the blockbusters landed about 800 yards off the port bow. The blast shook the ship, jarring her stern sideways.

Tug BANNOCK returned alongside at 0730 that morning. A thorough check revealed no additional damage to the disabled destroyer. But the stress and strain of that block-buster blast had inflicted fatal injuries not at once apparent.

At 1010 in the morning, without preliminary warning, the MEREDITH broke in two amidships, and went down with a plunge. The BANNOCK cut her lines to clear the side, and stood off to recover survivors. All hands of the security watch jumped or lowered themselves from the sinking ship, and were rescued.

Lost with MEREDITH at the time she was mined were two officers and 33 men. Due to efficient emergency measures and the courageous action of Chief Machinist's Mate Bryan and others, 322 officers and men, including 26 wounded, survived the disaster.

MEREDITH was the third ship to carry that name on the Navy's roster—and the second MEREDITH to be sunk during World War II.

Loss of U.S.S. Glennon

While MEREDITH was drifting in mortal disablement off Cape Barfleur, a second American destroyer was blasted by a mine in the "Utah" area. The destroyer was the U.S.S. GLENNON (Commander C. A. Johnson).

Disaster smote GLENNON off Quineville, a clutter of cottages and fishing smacks on the Cotentin coast about ten miles below Barfleur. For with the coming of the Nazi hordes the Normandy village had been ruthlessly transformed into a Nazi strongpoint. Barbed wire fenced the beaches, and, from the dunes overlooking them, casemated guns poked their ugly snouts from the embrasures of concrete pillboxes.

On the morning of June 7 a naval barrage was erasing some of this as American troops closed in on pillboxes and guns. And among these American troops were shore fire-control parties spotting targets for Navy attention. Offshore a trio of American destroyers were steadily shelling the designated targets.

Engaged in this bombardment were destroyers BUTLER (Commander M. D. Matthews), Flagship of Commander W. L. Benson, ComDesDiv 34; JEFFERS (Lieutenant Commander H. Q. Murray), flying the pennant of Captain Murdaugh, ComDesDiv 17; and GLENNON. The GLENNON had arrived on station at sunrise, ordered to furnish close fire-support for troops advancing from the eastward. After hurling 200 rounds at the day's first target, the GLENNON gunners were pleased to hear that they had found the bull's-eye; the target was demolished.

Next they bombarded a 6-gun 155 mm. battery which had previously straddled the BUTLER. They could not see the target, but they treated the heavy battery to 100 fast rounds. In this shooting match GLENNON was unable to knock out the battery with her 5-inch 38 guns, but the enemy's answering salvos came no closer than 500 yards, and the duel was a draw. After stepping in to relieve GLENNON, destroyer JEFFERS withdrew when a near miss ripped her with fragments and wounded five men.

Late in the afternoon of that day GLENNON received another target designation. A Nazi force estimated at two divisions was counterattacking in the Quineville vicinity. GLENNON was to block the advance at one point with a defensive barrage. Her fire had to be closely controlled, or she would hit American troops on the beach. The destroyer gunners met the marksmanship requisite by lobbing 200 rounds on the exact location ordered. Elatedly, the fire-control spotter reported the enemy in full retreat.

At 2300 that evening GLENNON was directed to join the screen for the heavy ships farther offshore. This was quiet duty until about 0230 in the morning of June 8, when aircraft buzzed over the immediate area. Because no planes were positively identified as hostile, GLENNON held her fire. The aircraft disclosed themselves as enemy by dropping a few bombs. One landed about 50 yards off the GLENNON's port bow, spraying her with salt water and fragments. No damage.

Thus far GLENNON's activity at "Utah" was more or less typical of DD operations in the Battle for the Beachheads. Daylight bombardment missions; screening duty at night. She had fired at coastal batteries and military installations; had covered the landings, and supported the troops skirmishing ashore; had come under enemy fire in return. And she had experienced a brush with Nazi aircraft.

But the hour of ordeal was now upon her, and the blow was unexpected. Time: 0802. She was steaming at one-third speed, maintaining position in a swept channel two miles west of the Area Screen. She was under the guns of Nazi shore batteries at Quineville, but for the moment they were not bothering her. Her lookouts were maintaining vigilant watch; her degaussing coils were set. Time: 0803. Explosion!

As described in Commander Johnson's Action Report:

> The effect was violent throughout the ship. All power was lost due to the tripping of circuit breakers, but regained in about three minutes. The force of the explosion had been of such magnitude as to throw two men, who were standing on the fantail, 40 feet in the air, landing them in the water. One of these men was later recovered with both legs broken and possible internal injuries. A 600-pound depth charge was torn from the stern racks and thrown 50 feet, landing on the torpedo platform abreast No. 3 5-inch gun-mount. A 150-pound cement dan buoy anchor was thrown 125 feet from the fantail to the port 20 mm. gun nest, torpedo platform. Water rose to a height of 25 feet about equally on the port and starboard quarters.
>
> General Quarters was sounded. A boat was lowered to pick up 16 men who had been thrown into the water.

Repair parties assembled for rescue and salvage work. After an immediate report of damage, word was passed over the loudspeaker circuit: "The ship will not sink, all hands remain on board, repair parties proceed with rescue and salvage work." . . . Use of engines was not attempted because such action would have been useless, causing further damage to plant. An anchor was not dropped because set of current was favorable.

Immediately following the explosion there was the usual aftermath of pandemonium—the topside rush from flooded compartments, the oil-smeared, blood-smeared, staggering procession of men who were dazed, men who were sick, men dragging broken limbs.

At the moment of the blast Frank A. Spiller, Coxwain, was asleep in his bunk. The explosion flung him headlong through a jagged fissure in the overhead. He fell back through the break and landed sprawling in a black dungeon crammed with scrambled junk, a-swirl in a tide of ink.

With the coming of comprehension—an awareness of sounds, smells, pain and danger—Spiller's first reaction was probably the normal impulse for self-preservation. But there were men around him, wounded, crying in the dark. The Coxwain pulled himself upright; forgot the pain of sprain and laceration; plunged about in the ink and froth, hunting his shipmates.

"Although wounded," says the officially worded record, *"with great presence of mind he aided three other wounded men out of the rapidly sinking stern section, through the break, onto the deck of the forward section, thereby saving their lives."* Coxwain Frank A. Spiller was recommended for the Navy Cross.

Commander Johnson and all able hands pitched in to save their disabled ship. About 0830 minesweepers STAFF and THREAT came up to assist. A tow line was passed to STAFF; THREAT maneuvered ahead to sweep a path, and GLENNON prepared for a haul to the Transport Area.

While the tow was being rigged, the destroyer-escort RICH approached from eastward, to inquire if assistance were needed. The reply was sent immediately,

NEGATIVE X CLEAR AREA CAUTIOUSLY DUE MINES

The DE circled astern of GLENNON, and headed away at five knots.

Meantime, the destroyer's disablement was noted by Nazi binoculars, and just as RICH turned away a Quineville battery opened fire. A thumping 4-gun salvo smote the water some 200 yards from the GLENNON's stern. Commander Johnson immediately spoke Admiral Deyo's flagship by TBS, requesting a covering fire. The Germans added urgency to the radiotelephone call by straddling GLENNON in range with a salvo that whacked the sea a scant 150 yards astern. Then Deyo's cruisers opened up with some salvos of their own, and the shore battery went silent. As the gun-thunder ebbed away, there was a deafening explosion from the RICH, at that time about 1,500 yards from the GLENNON. The DE had struck a mine!

GLENNON's bridge personnel saw the smaller ship break in two as though the hull were made of wet clay. A moment later there was a second detonation. The DE's bow section presently disappeared. As a minesweeper and numerous small craft were near the RICH, there was no need for the disabled destroyer to offer assistance. She herself was in much distress, for her whole stern was down at a 30 degree angle, her shattered after section had settled to the bottom, the starboard propeller was apparently anchored fast, and STAFF was unable to budge her.

Commander Johnson appealed for a salvage tug. While waiting, GLENNON's crew made a strenuous attempt to lighten the ship's stern and shift weight to the bow. Salvage tug KIOWA came alongside about 1100. She had negotiated a precarious approach. Moving ahead of the tug, a pair of sweepers had abolished an acoustic mine and a magnetic mine. The local waters were poison, and the Quineville shore batteries contributed an ugly threat to the menace.

KIOWA's journey was useless; strive and sweat as she would, the powerful tug could not move the inert destroyer. At 1430 the towline was slipped, and the tug anchored off GLENNON's port bow. At 1630 a message was received from Task Force Commander Moon—salvage attempts were to be abandoned; GLENNON's bow was to be anchored to prevent her forward section from drifting ashore if she broke in two during the night; code books and all similar material were to be removed, and the survivors to go aboard an LST.

By 1800 the work had been accomplished. Commander Johnson, however, remained convinced that his ship could be salvaged. The Executive Officer, Engineering Officer, and eight men were left on the GLENNON. Accompanied by the Salvage Officer, Lieutenant Commander McClung, U.S.N.R., Johnson visited the BAYFIELD to confer with Admiral Moon.

The Admiral agreed to continue the salvage effort. Johnson returned to his ship the following day, and all that day (June 9) he and his destroyermen worked with the salvage crew to get GLENNON off. But time and tide were against them, and so were the Germans.

About sunrise on June 10 the Nazi guns at Quineville opened up. Their second salvo hit GLENNON aft, wrecking the after engine-room. A third salvo straddled forward, one shell smashing into the forecastle, and a near miss flaying the deck with shrapnel and injuring two men. GLENNON could not fight back; all power was lost as a result of the first hits. Commander Johnson ordered the ship abandoned.

As captain and crew members boarded an LCM, shells were hitting on all sides, bursting on impact with the surface. GLENNON suffered more thrashing before the Germans ceased. After the shelling was over, the "Exec" and a party boarded the battered DD to inspect the damage, seal the ship, and remove any secret or special gear left aboard. They noted the destruction wrought by about a dozen direct hits. Near misses had left numerous punctures in the hull. GLENNON's condition was hopeless.

At 2145 that evening the destroyer leaned over on her beam with a list of exhaustion. She had taken a lot of punishment. She was done. The dark waters presently closed over her, and she was under.

Lost with GLENNON at the time of her mining were 25 men. Some 267 officers and bluejackets—among them 38 wounded—survived the mine blast and subsequent shelling.

Loss of U.S.S. Rich

When destroyer-escort RICH steamed to the aid of the disabled destroyer GLENNON on that ill-omened morning of June 8, her skipper, Lieutenant Commander E. A. Michel, knew the DE was entering dangerous water. RICH had been patrolling to seaward of the Task Force 125 Bombardment Group—NEVADA, QUINCY, TUSCALOOSA, and H.M.S. BLACK PRINCE—when she was ordered by Admiral Deyo to lend GLENNON a helping hand. Not only was the sea in GLENNON's vicinity a probable mine-nest, but it was also within range of the Quineville shore batteries. However, the DE's skipper did not hesitate. In the dry, official language of the Navy he *"proceeded in his vessel with utmost dispatch, with disregard of the danger from enemy gunfire and possible mines, and stood by close aboard the stricken ship to render assistance."*

As she neared the GLENNON, the destroyer-escort lowered a motor whaleboat which headed for the disabled ship. At that point, as related in the GLENNON story, the destroyer signalled RICH that her assistance was unnecessary, and warned her to beware of mines.

Observing that the GLENNON was in no need of immediate help, Lieutenant Commander Michel turned the DE close under the destroyer's stern, and, passing GLENNON's starboard side, headed away. Recall was signalled to the whaleboat, and seamen stood ready to hoist the craft aboard.

RICH's captain was taking every precaution—slow speed; the ship squared away for emergency; all hands topside instructed to maintain a sharp lookout for enemy planes and drifting mines. But there were undersea mines which a lookout could not detect—mines which drifted deep under in the tidal currents, and were set to explode by "influence" when they entered a ship's magnetic field.

Time: about 0920. RICH was about 300 yards from the minesweeper STAFF, which was then engaged in taking GLENNON in tow. The minesweeper and the DE had passed through these waters not long before; they were clean enough, then. But now—

A stunning explosion burst the sea about 50 yards off RICH's starboard beam. The seaquake shook the DE from stem to stern; sent sailors stumbling from their stations; tripped the circuit breakers, and knocked out the ship's light and power. Three depth charges in their arbors were flung from their projectors into the water, and two others hurtled to the deck. But the charges did not explode, and there was no serious damage from the mine blast. The forward engine-room reported "light and power regained, ready to answer all bells." Some gauge lines had suffered injury, and instrument glasses had been shattered. Nothing worse.

But that was only a beginning. About three mintes after the offside blast, a mine exploded directly under the ship. Men on the DE's bridge were thrown to the deck. A 50-foot section of the ship's stern was torn off and set adrift. Survivors clung to this floating wreckage and swam desperately in the debris-strewn water. At the break where the fantail had been amputated, wounded men crawled in a thicket of broken scrap and uprooted gear. A series of emergency reports reached the bridge: several torpedoes were making hot runs in their tubes; the main deck had sagged, vicinity of No. 2 engine-room; compartments forward of the engineering spaces had suffered only minor damage.

Before this information could be assessed, the disabled DE was blasted by a third mine. The explosion occurred about two minutes after the second blast. In his Action Report, Lieutenant Commander Michel mentioned that the final explosion hurled him from the bridge. He recalled a sensation of flying through the air, then blackout unconsciousness.

His graphic account continues:

> Upon regaining consciousness, I found myself on the deck some ten or fifteen feet from my usual station on the flying bridge, and got to my feet with some difficulty to survey the damage. The flying bridge was completely demolished, with the mast lying across the debris; all personnel appeared dead or unconscious except myself

and Ensign W. D. Cunningham, Assistant Gunnery Officer, but upon going to the side, a few more could be seen moving on the decks below. The force of the explosion and its effect on material and personnel were terrific. . . . It is believed that the mine exploded approximately under the ice machine room. . . . The ship began to settle slowly by the bow. The forward fireroom was severely damaged and had to be abandoned; the after fireroom lost pressure and was forced to secure. . . . Personnel casualties were heavy, the force of the explosion having thrown men as much as fifty feet or more, and it is believed that not more than two or three men who were forward of the mast survived without more or less severe head, back, or leg injuries. Considering the damaged condition of the ship, the immediate and urgent task appeared to be to remove the injured to small craft before the ship should sink. . . . Life rafts were cast loose. Attempt was made to hail alongside all PT, British ML, and Coast Guard patrol craft in the vicinity, and these vessels sent men and blankets aboard to move the injured off. . . . All these worked unstintingly to remove the wounded to the small craft that came alongside, and left only when the ship started its final plunge. It is estimated—very roughly—that the ship floated for about fifteen minutes, starting its final plunge slowly by the bow, but gathering momentum and turning on its starboard side as it settled. Men who had been working to remove the injured stepped off with the last injured men as their deck went under. All cleared the ship, swam free of the turbulent waters, and were picked up by a Coast Guard patrol craft from which we were delivered to LST-491 for treatment and later transfer to hospitals in the United Kingdom.

RICH was the last DesLant ship to go down to Nazi mines off Normandy. Her forward section sank at a point about three miles from the San Marcouf Islands; the after section sank in the same watery burying ground. Compared with the casualties suffered by CORRY, MEREDITH, and GLENNON, the little DE's losses were very heavy. Of a complement of 215, some 89 officers and men were lost with the ship; 73 survivors were wounded.

FOR EXTRAORDINARY HEROISM AND DEVOTION TO DUTY AS COMMANDING OFFICER OF THE U.S.S. RICH . . .

so reads the citation which conveyed the Navy Cross to Lieutenant Commander Edward A. Michel, Jr. Reviewing his effort to aid the GLENNON, the citation concludes:

. . . WHILE ATTEMPTING TO ASSIST THAT SHIP, HIS OWN VESSEL STRUCK AND WAS DESTROYED BY THE EXPLOSION OF TWO ENEMY MINES. LIEUTENANT COMMANDER MICHEL, DESPITE SEVERE INJURIES, INCLUDING A BROKEN LEG, STEADFASTLY REFUSED TO LEAVE HIS SHIP, AND DIRECTED AND ASSISTED IN THE REMOVAL OF ALL POSSIBLE SURVIVORS UNTIL HIS SHIP SANK BENEATH HIM. BY HIS ACTION AND EXAMPLE, ALL ABLE-BODIED SURVIVORS ON BOARD WERE INSPIRED TO REMAIN WITH THE SHIP AND ASSIST IN THE RESCUE OF THE GREATEST POSSIBLE NUMBER OF MEN.

It is interesting to note that in his Action Report, Lieutenant Commander Michel made no mention of his broken leg.

He had taken that in his stride.

Destroyers Versus E-Boats

As the Navy had learned in the Mediterranean, the German E-boat could be a thorn in the side of an invasion force. Similar to a PT-boat, it was speedy, agile, hard-hitting, and hard to hit. Its strategy and tactics were those of surprise raid—night attack. Its arms were 40 mm. machine-guns and torpedoes. Like the panther it possessed a savagery out of all proportion to its size, and leaping forward, it could slay a victim twenty times its weight if its fangs found a vital mark.

Twenty-seven or thirty E-boats were reportedly based at Cherbourg and on the east coast of the Cotentin Peninsula. A possible seven Nazi destroyers based at Brest, Cherbourg, and Le Havre constituted another menace to be guarded against. Accordingly, the Area Screen guarding the Western Naval Task Force was on the alert from the crack of D-Day.

The mission of the screen was *"to protect vessels of the Western Naval Task Force against attack by enemy surface forces and submarines, and assist in the protection against air attack."* E-boats were the No. 1 surface threat, and the waters immediately menaced were those of the "Utah Area."

Units of the Area Screen were instructed to *"investigate and identify all unidentified contacts. A continuous all around surface radar guard was to be maintained. Illumination was to be by starshell. Ships were to remain in swept areas if possible but were to cross unswept areas if own forces were endangered. All contacts in the Mountain Area, that is, eastward of the Peninsula to line bearing 026°T from position 'MD,' were to be considered as enemy. . . ."*

On the night of June 8-9 the Area Screen was composed of 13 American destroyers, three American destroyer-escorts, five British SGB's and eight American PC's, mounting guard on the "Dixie Line," and 12 PT-boats and two PC's stationed on the "Mason Line." Backing up the "Dixie Line" were four American destroyers, three British destroyers, and a British destroyer-escort.

The 13 American destroyers on the "Dixie Line" were FRANKFORD, HERNDON, BUTLER, EMMONS, SAT-

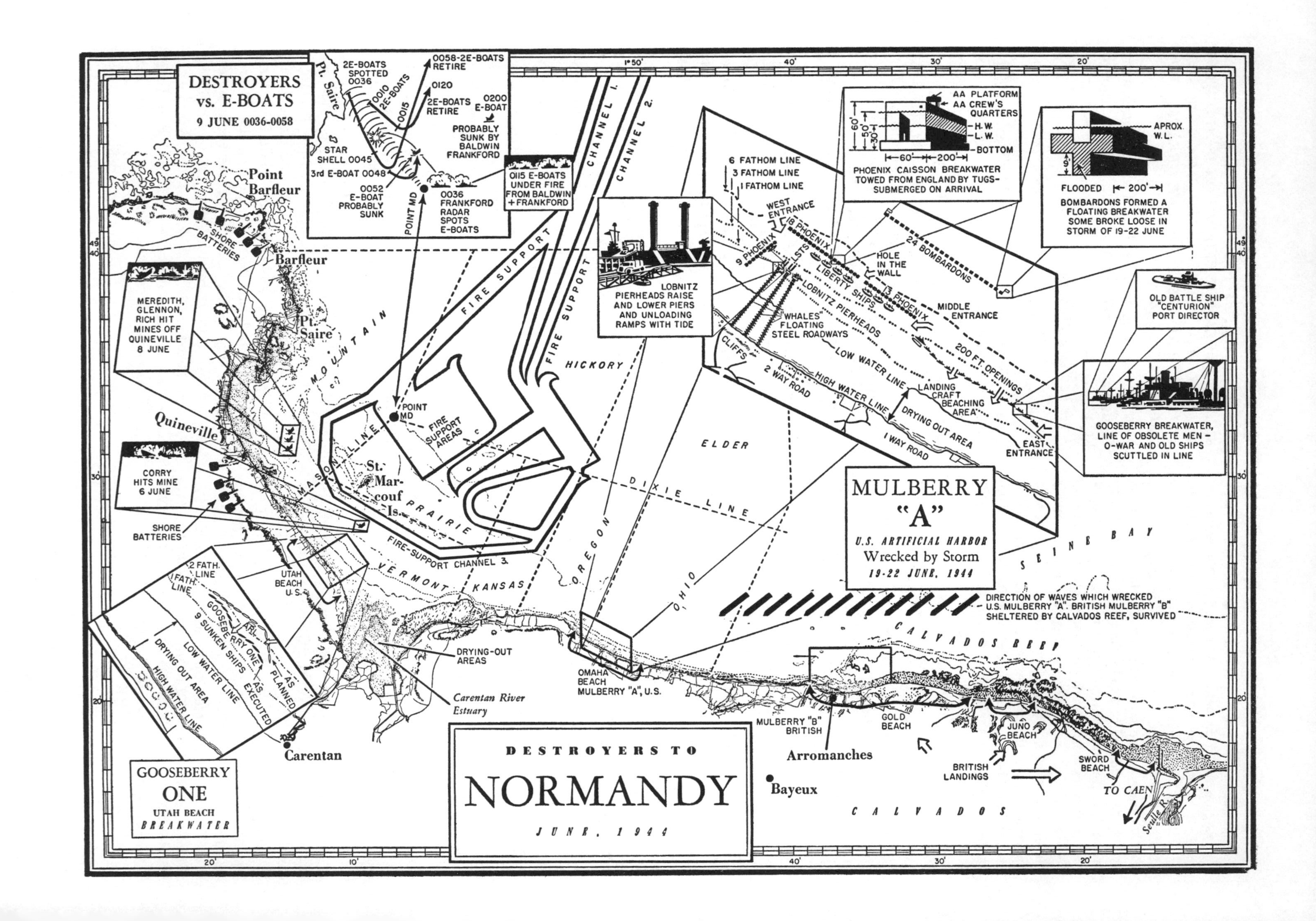
DESTROYERS TO
NORMANDY
JUNE, 1944
DESTROYERS vs. E-BOATS
9 JUNE 0036-0058
2E-BOATS SPOTTED 0036
0010 2E-BOATS
0015
0058-2E-BOATS RETIRE
0120
2E-BOATS RETIRE
0200 E-BOAT
PROBABLY SUNK BY BALDWIN FRANKFORD
STAR SHELL 0045
3rd E-BOAT 0048
0052 E-BOAT PROBABLY SUNK
0036 FRANKFORD RADAR SPOTS E-BOATS
0115 E-BOATS UNDER FIRE FROM BALDWIN + FRANKFORD
POINT MD
Pt. Saire
Point Barfleur
Barfleur
SHORE BATTERIES
MEREDITH, GLENNON, RICH HIT MINES OFF QUINEVILLE 8 JUNE
Quineville
CORRY HITS MINE 6 JUNE
SHORE BATTERIES
MOUNTAIN
MASON LINE
St. Marcouf Is.
PRAIRIE
FIRE SUPPORT AREAS
FIRE SUPPORT
FIRE SUPPORT
CHANNEL 1.
CHANNEL 2.
FIRE-SUPPORT CHANNEL 3.
HICKORY
VERMONT
KANSAS
OREGON
OHIO
ELDER
DIXIE LINE
UTAH BEACH U.S.
2 FATH. LINE
I FATH. LINE
GOOSEBERRY ONE
9 SUNKEN SHIPS
AS PLANNED
AS EXECUTED
LOW WATER LINE
DRYING OUT AREA
HIGH WATER LINE
GOOSEBERRY ONE
UTAH BEACH
BREAKWATER
Carentan
DRYING-OUT AREAS
Carentan River Estuary
OMAHA BEACH MULBERRY "A", U.S.
LOBNITZ PIERHEADS RAISE AND LOWER PIERS AND UNLOADING RAMPS WITH TIDE
6 FATHOM LINE
3 FATHOM LINE
I FATHOM LINE
WEST ENTRANCE
18 PHOENIX
9 PHOENIX
LSTS
LIBERTY SHIPS
HOLE IN THE WALL
24 BOMBARDONS
13 PHOENIX
MIDDLE ENTRANCE
LOBNITZ PIERHEADS
"WHALES" FLOATING STEEL ROADWAYS
CLIFFS
2 WAY ROAD
HIGH WATER LINE
LOW WATER LINE
200 FT. OPENINGS
LANDING CRAFT BEACHING AREA
DRYING OUT AREA
1 WAY ROAD
EAST ENTRANCE
AA PLATFORM
AA CREW'S QUARTERS
H. W.
L. W.
BOTTOM
60'
50'
30'
60'
200'
PHOENIX CAISSON BREAKWATER TOWED FROM ENGLAND BY TUGS-SUBMERGED ON ARRIVAL
APROX. W.L.
9'
FLOODED
200'
BOMBARDONS FORMED A FLOATING BREAKWATER SOME BROKE LOOSE IN STORM OF 19-22 JUNE
OLD BATTLE SHIP "CENTURION" PORT DIRECTOR
GOOSEBERRY BREAKWATER, LINE OF OBSOLETE MEN-O-WAR AND OLD SHIPS SCUTTLED IN LINE
MULBERRY "A"
U.S. ARTIFICIAL HARBOR
Wrecked by Storm
19-22 JUNE, 1944
SEINE BAY
DIRECTION OF WAVES WHICH WRECKED U.S. MULBERRY "A". BRITISH MULBERRY "B" SHELTERED BY CALVADOS REEF, SURVIVED
CALVADOS REEF
MULBERRY "B" BRITISH
Arromanches
GOLD BEACH
Bayeux
BRITISH LANDINGS
JUNO BEACH
SWORD BEACH
TO CAEN
Seulle R.
CALVADOS
1°50'
40'
30'
20'
10'
49°40'
30'
20'

This famous picture suggests the tremendous size of Operation Overlord, for here is only a segment of the shipping that was required to keep the trans-Channel invasion rolling. It was up to the destroyers to help defend these reinforcements and supplies so that they would flow ashore in an uninterrupted stream. The Omaha and Utah beaches were their special responsibility.

Glennon, shown in a convoy bound for France, met her doom off Utah Beach. After a busy day and night of silencing Nazi shore batteries, she struck a mine off Quineville and her shattered stern sank enough to anchor her to the bottom within easy range of German gunners. When efforts to pull her off failed, she was abandoned. She sank under Nazi gunfire that night.

View of the destruction in the harbor at Port-en-Bassin after the Allied invasion. Military installations and shipping were the primary targets, but in the process of driving out the Nazis many buildings were bombarded to bits.

An Allied destroyer caught this Nazi minesweeper (top) shown washed up on the beach. Part of the defense of the Le Havre U-boat pens (bottom).

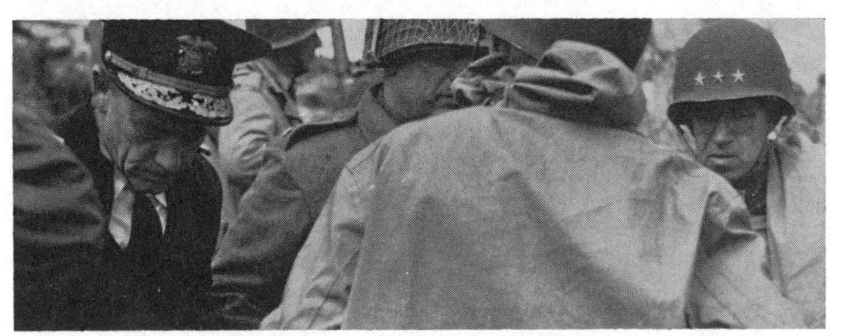

Admiral Kirk and General Bradley: High level talk on the Normandy sands shortly after D-day. Only with difficulty were Winston Churchill and other Allied leaders discouraged from endangering themselves in premature visits.

U.S.S. Carmick (DD 493) was a member of Fire-Support Group "O" assigned to Omaha Beach. She was one of the destroyers that pushed right in to the beach with her bow practically aground, and shelled the Nazis at pointblank range.

Blockships at "Mulberry A" (top) before the storm struck. Waves, which destroyed the harbor, break over the old British battleship Centurion.

terlee, Baldwin, Thompson, Carmick, Davis, Rodman, Hobson, Somers, and Jouett. The three DE's were Blessman, Borum, and Amesbury. The four American destroyers supporting the screen were Hambleton, Gherardi, Nelson, and Forrest.

The action which eventuated that night involved destroyers Frankford, Hambleton, and Baldwin.

Frankford was the flagship of Captain Harry Saunders, who was serving in dual capacity as Area Screen Commander and ComDesRon 18. The destroyer was captained by Lieutenant Commander J. L. Semmes. Hambleton, sturdy veteran of "Torch" fame, was skippered by Commander H. A. Renken. Baldwin's Commanding Officer was Lieutenant Commander E. S. Powell, Jr., and she flew the pennant of Commander W. J. Marshall, ComDesDiv 36, another veteran outfit.

The Area Screen took station at nightfall, and the forenamed destroyers commenced the usual routine patrol. Evening darkened into a mild night—easy sea swells, sky overcast, but visibility good.

Flag destroyer Frankford was stationed at the "MD" junction of the "Mason-Dixie Line." The following is a condensation of Lieutenant Commander Semmes' Action Report:

> At 0036, 9 June, 2 or 3 targets were picked up by radar bearing 323°T, distance 13,600. These targets were near the Cherbourg Peninsula south of Pt. Barfleur. They were tracked and their course determined to be about 150°T, speed 20 knots. At 0045 Frankford fired a spread of 2 starshells, target range 8,000 yards, bearing 314°T. The C.O. and bridge personnel were able to distinguish 2 E-boats which increased speed but continued southward. At 0045½ Frankford commenced firing full radar control (FD radar) on the E-boats at a range of 4,560 yards. These boats turned away and laid a smoke screen to cover their retirement. One of the boats returned the fire with what appeared to be a 40 mm. gun—evidently using the DD's gun flashes for a point of aim—and several of the projectiles fell near the Frankford. At 0047 the DD ceased firing. In the meanwhile her CIC picked up a 3rd target which had trailed the other two in at very close range. "Control" was given the target and fire was resumed, full radar control, at 0050, target bearing 350°T, range 2,000 yards. The target turned northward but appeared to slow. Radar operators stated that all salvos appeared to be landing on the target. At 0052 the target disappeared from all radar screens at 3,660 yards and is believed to have been sunk. The other E-boats escaped to the northward—contact on them was lost at about 14,000 yards. During this action Frankford got way on and proceeded to the northward of Point "MD."

While Frankford was thus chasing Nazi panthers, destroyers Baldwin and Hambleton dashed through the screen to engage the enemy.

At 0110 another target was picked up. Apparently there were two E-boats in this group, and when they were taken under fire by Frankford and Baldwin they retired with dazzling speed.

Around 0200 Hambleton and Baldwin picked up an E-boat contact about four miles north of the "Dixie Line." Both ships lashed the target with hot gunfire. And the "pip" disappeared with a suddenness that indicated another E-boat sent to the bottom.

At 0240 Frankford fired on a blurry contact which was made along the peninsular shoreline, range about 11,000 yards. This target fled northward and vanished from the screen. For the time being, at least, the E-boat shoot was over.

For that night's shooting, destroyer Frankford had used AA common shell with fuses set to burst at the target. Hambleton used AA common with fuses set on safe. Concerning the action, Frankford's Executive Officer made some interesting comments in the ship's Action Report:

> The many hours of haranguing the SG operators not to get too interested in one target finally paid dividends. If the SG operators had not put into effect this training it is quite possible that the E-boat which came in astern of the leading two on the first approach would have torpedoed us after the leading two had turned north.
>
> The employment by protective screens of air bursts against E-boats is felt to be very sound. The purpose of the screen was to "drive off" and destroy if possible. Since E-boat captains are seldom aggressive in the face of illumination and gunfire, an air burst would have a much more discouraging effect on morale than splashes in the water. E-boats are very lightly armored and 5" shrapnel would no doubt cause a great deal of damage while a 5" shell might just go through the boat and do relatively minor damage.

But the E-boats had not yet shot their bolt. The "Utah" raid of June 9—their first attempt to strike the Western Task Force—was followed two nights later by a slashing attack on shipping in the "Omaha Area." During this foray the E-boats torpedoed the American destroyer Nelson.

Torpedoing of U.S.S. Nelson

It was a good night for E-boating—water calm; wind negligible; sky darkly overcast, with visbility about 2,000 yards; the seascape as black as carbon.

The date was June 12, 1944. The hour: 0100. At that time the destroyer Nelson (Lieutenant Commander T. D. McGrath) was anchored at her screening station on the "Dixie Line" boundary of the "Omaha Beach" assault area. Other units of the Area Screen in Nelson's vicinity were destroyers Laffey (Commander F. J. Becton) and Somers (Commander W. C. Hughes).

Nelson was not at her best, for she could not use her port engine for propulsion. Her port shaft and propeller had been removed after she had fouled a buoy at Plymouth, England. Despite this handicap she had steamed across the Channel to carry on in "Operation Neptune."

The following terse account is from the destroyer's Action Report:

> At 0105 C.I.C. reported contact bearing 358°T at six thousand yards. Shortly thereafter reported target course 190°T, speed twenty. The ship was alerted and F.D. (radar director controlling 5-inch battery) coached to target by C.I.C. At 0107 battery was reported on. As required by operation order, signalman challenged, and about fifteen seconds later ship opened fire at four thousand yard range, with entire battery in full radar control. Contact slowed, turned away and separated into three distinct targets. Anchor had been heaved in and chain was up and down. About ten salvos had been fired when at about 0109 ship was hit. There was an explosion aft and ship heeled sharply to port and then resumed an even keel. Electric power was lost momentarily but regained in a short time. Chain was veered; repair parties rescued personnel and checked flooding. Ship was reported in no danger at 0122. The next day she was towed to Portsmouth, England.

Nelson was harder hit than the above summary would suggest. The torpedo blast blew off the stern and No. 4 mount; the starboard shaft was bent downward and, with propeller attached, it dragged water at a depth of 52 feet. Crew casualties were severe. Some 24 of the ship's complement were lost; nine were wounded.

At the time of the E-boat attack, destroyer Laffey was stationed on the "Dixie Line" about 1,600 yards ahead of Nelson. Somers was about the same distance astern. At 0051, a good 14 minutes before Nelson detected the enemy, Laffey picked up a small, hazy "pip" on her surface radar, bearing 005°T, range 8,800 yards.

The range closed slowly. And the cloudy "pip" developed into five or six small, distinct targets. When first discerned, they were traveling at 15 knots. Gradually they slowed to 9. They were advancing at a 5-knot crawl when Nelson reported herself torpedoed. Whereupon the targets on Laffey's radar appeared to reverse course and beat a rapidly accelerating retirement.

There was now no doubt about their E-boat identity. Screening ships to westward opened fire on the fleeing craft, and Laffey went after them in hot pursuit. When the other ships ceased fire, she continued the chase, working up to 32 knots. Illuminating with starshells, she fired AA common at the raiders. The pursuit and shooting lasted until 0125, when the enemy dashed in close to an Allied convoy and Laffey ceased fire to avoid hitting friendly ships.

Somers also had made contact with E-boats, picking up the targets at 0105, range 8,000 yards. She opened fire about the same time Nelson did, illuminating with starshell and blazing away with common service ammunition. At 0115 she lost contact and ceased fire, noting that Laffey had taken up the chase.

Although both Laffey and Somers detected the approaching enemy, neither reported the contact to other ships in the Area Screen—or, if they did, Nelson failed to get the report. Had Nelson received a report from Laffey, she could have squared away to meet the attack some 14 minutes sooner than she did. And perhaps a prompt burst of starshell and gunfire would have driven the E-boat off, or caused the Nazi torpedomen to miss.

In regard to the matter of showing lights, Nelson's Action Report made this pertinent comment:

> It is felt that the ship was hit by an E-boat torpedo. This was fired at the signal light when the challenge was made. Where using a fixed screen around an area, vessels approaching should bear the burden of proving their friendly character. Challenging imposes too great a penalty on the screening vessels. If this ship could have opened fire as soon as control reported on target without challenge, she probably would not have been hit.

The Bombardment of Cherbourg

Cherbourg was the objective of the American Army landed on "Utah Beach." In *Crusade In Europe*, Eisenhower points to this port as the crux to the Normandy invasion. *"Unless we could soon seize Cherbourg, the enemy's opportunity for hemming us in . . . might be so well exploited as to lead to the defeat of the operations."*

Of key importance, then, in the "Overlord" plan, the capture of this big French seaport became an emergency "must" after the Channel treacherously sided with Hitler and sabotaged the Allied invasion effort with the worst storm in four decades. Giving the lie to fair weather forecasts, the blow struck on June 19. Three days later, when wind and seas abated, the Normandy coast was strewn with the wreckage of some 300 small craft and the fragments of what had been the artificial harbor at "Omaha Beach."

Destruction of this "Omaha" harbor placed a backbreaking load on the "Overlord" transportation system. Supplies for the American troops in that area had to be detoured through the British sector to the east. To relieve this traffic jam and open an adequate supply artery for the Allied invasion armies, it was necessary to capture Cherbourg with the utmost dispatch.

German counterattack on Britain added urgency to this American drive. On June 12, 1944, the first V-1 flying bomb had crashed into London. This secret weapon—a small robot plane loaded with a tremendous explosive charge—struck the British capital a nerve-shattering blow. Worse was to come in the form of the supersonic V-2 rocket; the launchers for this terrible weapon were already being installed on the French coast. If "Overlord" failed, a frightful reprisal was in store for Britain. Everything hinged on the Cherbourg campaign.

Fighting through hedgerows and scrub, General Collins' U.S. VII Corps reached the southern outskirts of Cherbourg on June 24. Simultaneously advancing on Cherbourg from the sea was Task Force 129 under command of Rear Admiral M. L. Deyo. Its mission was to reduce German forts and shore batteries flanking the port, and to directly support Collins' troops by shelling Nazi artillery and military targets as directed by shore fire-control parties and aircraft spotters.

There were some big Krupp batteries guarding Cherbourg—casemated guns up to 280 mm. caliber. But Cherbourg had to fall, and the Navy's services were requested. The target date was set for June 25, bombardment to begin at noon.

Admiral Deyo's force was composed of three American battleships, two American cruisers, two British cruisers, and 11 American destroyers. He divided it into two task groups.

Group one, under Deyo's tactical command, contained cruiser TUSCALOOSA (flagship), battleship NEVADA, cruisers QUINCY, H.M.S. GLASGOW and H.M.S. ENTERPRISE, and the following six destroyers:

ELLYSON	*Comdr. E. W. Longton*
Flagship of Capt. A. F. Converse, COMDESRON 10	
HAMBLETON	*Comdr. H. A. Renken*
RODMAN	*Comdr. J. F. Foley*
EMMONS	*Comdr. E. B. Billingsley*
MURPHY	*Comdr. R. A. Wolverton*
GHERARDI	*Comdr. N. R. Curtin*

Group Two, under command of Rear Admiral C. F. Bryant, contained battleships TEXAS (flagship) and ARKANSAS, and the following five destroyers:

BARTON	*Comdr. J. W. Callahan*
Flagship of Capt. W. L. Freseman, COMDESRON 60	
O'BRIEN	*Comdr. W. W. Outerbridge*
LAFFEY	*Comdr. F. J. Becton*
HOBSON	*Lt. Comdr. K. Loveland*
Flying pennant of Commander L. W. Nilon, COMDESDIV 20	
PLUNKETT	*Comdr. W. Outerson*

Steaming in company to a point north of Cherbourg, the two task groups separated to begin the approach, then converged on an inner Fire-Support Area off Cherbourg where the ships were to conduct a 90-minute neutralization fire on targets designated by General Collins. They were instructed not to open up in the outer areas unless they were first fired upon. As the task groups were to learn, there were two formidable Nazi forts to the west of Cherbourg, and a third to the east. These constituted priority targets for bombardment.

The Germans held their fire until the ships were well within range; that is, until they reached the inner Fire-Support Area. Both Group One and Group Two had timed their advance to bring them into this area at noon. Group One was on the leg going due south—the minesweepers ahead, H.M.S. GLASGOW, H.M.S. ENTERPRISE, NEVADA, TUSCALOOSA, and QUINCY in column, and the destroyers on the flanks—when the Krupp guns let go. Deyo dispersed the column to give his big ships maneuvering room; the destroyers laid smoke screens; and the duel was on.

"Information was not complete as to location of our front lines," Admiral Deyo reported later, *"and concern was felt lest we fire into our own troops. Finally all ships were ordered not to fire at any targets more than 2,000 yards in from the shoreline unless directed by a shore party."*

Word from the spotters came in, and the ships fired salvo after salvo. Navy men serving with Army units on the heights behind the city were delighted to recognize the billowing crimson bursts of battleship and cruiser shells. Deyo's ships did excellent shooting. On the roads far inland, naval projectiles landed on Nazi tank squads and blew them into scrap. German pillboxes were powdered, and gun emplacements tossed skyhigh. All this in the teeth of a scorching return fire from the shore batteries—a rain of shells that thrashed the sea around the warships.

"Although all enemy batteries were never silenced during the three hours of bombardment," Deyo noted, *"they could not prevent our general mission or the final success of the action. They did, however; prolong the action and interfere to a considerable extent with the work of assisting the Army. . . ."*

Although NEVADA and the cruisers were slashed by

near misses and closer shaves, H.M.S. GLASGOW was the only Group One vessel more than superficially damaged. Two hits and a blast close aboard wounded but did not cripple the British cruiser. The destroyers in Deyo's group were all narrowly missed, but to destroyermen that was as good as a mile.

Group Two, however, was viciously punished by the enemy shore batteries on the east side of Cherbourg. Battleship TEXAS took a hit on the top of her conning tower, and was forced to make a temporary withdrawal. Destroyer LAFFEY was slugged by a dud. Destroyer BARTON was holed by a ricochetting 8-inch shell that punctured her hull as though it were made of tin. And destroyer O'BRIEN was staggered by a 205 mm. smash that killed 13 and wounded 20 of her crew.

On the approach to Cherbourg, O'BRIEN had been steaming in the wake of the minesweepers which scoured the path for Task Group Two. Her orders were to cover the sweepers with smoke, and to support them with gunfire if they were fired upon. The sea was dead calm that noon. And the ships advancing from the eastward were perfectly visible to Nazi gunners, although the French coast, hazed with smoke, was not so clearly discernible from the sea.

Battleship ARKANSAS opened fire at 1208 while TEXAS awaited a target designation from her shore fire-control party. The Nazi batteries waited for the range to close, then they roared like hungry beasts. Excerpts from Admiral Bryant's account graphically detail the destroyer action:

> At 1228, while steaming . . . at 10 knots on base course 251°T and conforming to Approach Channel No. 4, the Task Group and minesweepers were taken under fire by the enemy coastal defense batteries. The first salvo landed among the sweepers ahead and near the O'BRIEN. The BARTON located flashes of the shore batteries at 1229 and both the BARTON and O'BRIEN opened counter-battery fire immediately. . . . About 1231 a salvo of major caliber projectiles straddled the stern of the BARTON in column directly ahead of the TEXAS. The BARTON was immediately directed to draw further ahead to permit the TEXAS to increase speed and maneuver and was also directed to be prepared to make smoke. The TEXAS came hard right, increased speed and maneuvered evasively during the remainder of the engagement. . . . The ARKANSAS conformed in general to the movements of the TEXAS.
>
> The BARTON was hit by a 240 mm. AP ricochet which went through her hull sideways instead of end-on—this was from the salvo which straddled her about 1231. The shell failed to detonate and was picked up and thrown over the side. At 1232 a salvo landed ahead of LAFFEY, one shell striking very close to the port bow and ricochetting into the waterline just forward of the anchor. Fortunately it failed to explode.
>
> Most of TEXAS' and ARKANSAS' fire was directed at Target No. 2 which was also frequently under the fire of two or more DD's simultaneously. At 1255 the HOBSON and PLUNKETT screened the battleships while the minesweepers retired to the northward under screen laid by BARTON, O'BRIEN, and LAFFEY, and augmented by their own smoke. At 1250 a heavy 3-gun shore battery (estimated 205 mm.) took the O'BRIEN under fire. The first salvo landed 600 yards over, the second about 300 yards over, and the third straddled, one of the shells hitting the DD in the starboard after corner of CIC (bridge superstructure) where it exploded. The immediate effect of this direct hit was to put CIC, all radars, and one 40 mm. twin mount out of commission. At 1256 enemy fire ceased for a short time, possibly because the ships were screened from view and his radar was being jammed simultaneously. By 1314 the enemy fire had become extremely heavy and accurate again, and at 1316 the TEXAS was hit. . . . The TEXAS was immediately ordered to withdraw to the northward to open the range until damage could be assessed.

Captain C. A. Baker and his "Texans" continued to fire as the battle wagon pulled away. Destroyers HOBSON and PLUNKETT were ordered by Division Commander Nilon to lay smoke. It caused the Nazi gunners to cease fire at 1325.

TEXAS came booming back on the bombardment path at 1454, a few minutes before the time scheduled for the task group's withdrawal. Again the shore batteries bent a concentrated fire in her direction. Again the destroyers intervened with a curtain of smoke. Behind this curtain TEXAS and ARKANSAS retired northeastward. The enemy batteries went silent. Its Cherbourg mission concluded, Task Group Two headed for Portland, England, as directed by Admiral Deyo.

Commenting on this bombardment and fire-support effort, Admiral Deyo made some observations which could apply to such missions in general:

> The German shore defense batteries, when resolutely manned, are very formidable. They are so located that only direct hits close to or on the guns themselves or on their communications will disable them. . . . A preliminary phase of long-range bombardment with plane spot under favorable conditions is necessary to silence temporarily or longer the larger batteries. . . . Direct fire or indirect fire without spot are not very effective against well placed shore batteries (though they may have a moral effect). Either good air spot or shore parties are required. When strong currents add to the navigational problem this is even more true.

In respect to the outcome of the Cherbourg mission, Admiral Deyo considered it gratifyingly successful. He noted:

> Much regret is felt at the damage and casualties suf-

fered by this force. It is believed, however, that under the circumstances we got off very lightly indeed and that the results attained were such that the Army was probably saved a good deal of damage which would otherwise have been received.

Admiral Bryant, Commander of Task Group Two, took a somewhat dimmer view of the operation. His conclusions follow:

> A major caliber, heavily casemated or turreted, and well dispersed coast defense battery cannot be silenced by bombardment without excess expenditure of ammunition and great risk to the bombarding force unless the firing can be carried out from a blind bearing or from a greater range than that of the shore battery. . . . Such a mission should not be undertaken unless its successful accomplishment is of sufficient importance to justify unrestricted expenditures of ammunition and the risk of serious damage to the bombarding force. . . .

Perhaps the Navy units at Cherbourg were unusually fortunate. Certainly casualties were light for such an operation—14 American Navy men dead, and 35 wounded. More than half the ships in Task Force 129 had been hit or peppered by shell fragments. But only TEXAS, H.M.S. GLASGOW, and destroyer O'BRIEN were materially damaged.

On June 27, Cherbourg itself fell, and the success of "Operation Overlord" was assured.

"Neptune" Postscript

It had been a costly effort for the DesLant Force. Spearheading "Operation Neptune," the Destroyer Service had suffered the only major combat-ship losses inflicted by the enemy during the Battle for the Beachheads. CORRY, MEREDITH, GLENNON, and destroyer-escort RICH were warships from truck to keel, and they would not be easily replaced.

But the landings had been successfully made and the beachheads secured. By early July Allied troops, guns, and war supplies were pouring into France through Cherbourg like floodwater through a breach in a dyke. This invasion flood swept southwest to the Bay of Biscay, trapping a German army in Brittany. It swept eastward to reinforce the British drive on Falaise. It plunged across central France toward Paris. And eventually it swept across the Lowlands to extinguish those V-bomb launchers which were dealing death to England.

SERVING THE GUNS OFF CHERBOURG

CHAPTER 28

WINNING THE MEDITERRANEAN

(DESTROYERS TO SOUTHERN FRANCE)

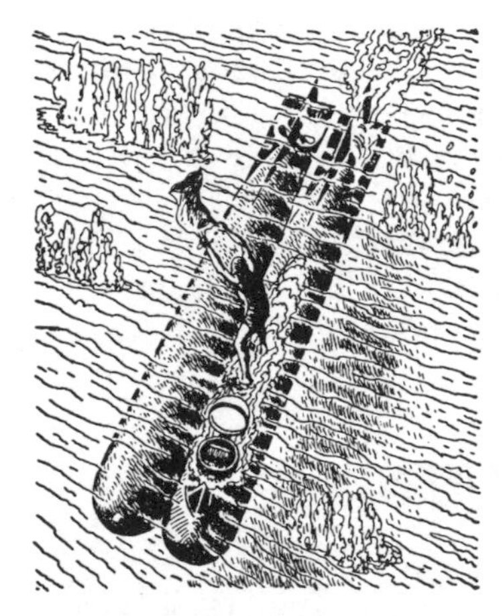

War Comes to the Azure Coast

While the European spotlight was on Normandy, the Allies rushed preparations for the invasion of Southern France. The target area embraced the great seaport of Marseilles, the naval base at Toulon, and the pastel beaches of the French Riviera—the "Azure Coast."

In the watercolor bays and delightful coves of this tourist playground, the Germans had secreted E-boats and other warcraft. Krupp batteries had been planted in the gardens behind summer casinos, and Tiger tanks were flocked along the picturesque shore roads. From the Golfe de Lyon prowled U-boats, and from Riviera airfields flew Swastika bomber squadrons that consistently harried Allied shipping in the Western Mediterranean.

During the prolonged Anzio deadlock, which lasted from January until June, 1944, Allied convoy escorts had fought life-and-death battles on that sea-going road which entered the Mediterranean through the Straits of Gibraltar, trailed along the coast of North Africa, squeezed through the Tunisian War Channel, and swung northward through the Tyrrhenian Sea. These Mediterranean battles did not make front-page news, but they were all part and parcel of the effort that loosened the Nazi grip on Italy and Southern Europe.

After the Allies captured Rome, Churchill advocated a Balkan offensive—a push up the Adriatic into Jugoslavia, or a drive into Greece. American strategists favored an invasion of Southern France. At least one valid reason for the Azure Coast priority may be discerned from the following accounts of the enemy onslaught on Convoys UGS-36, UGS-37, UGS-38, and GUS-38—an onslaught which sank Allied cargoes, killed Allied sailors, and cost the Navy's Destroyer Force three hard-fighting warships.

Attack on Convoy UGS-36 (Lesson in Gunnery)

One of the larger convoys to run the Mediterranean gantlet was UGS-36. Bound in the spring of 1944 from the U.S.A. to Bizerte, this convoy contained 90 ships—72 merchant vessels and 18 ocean-going LST's. It was guarded by a powerful task force (TF 64) which typified the escort provided for a large ship-train at this period of the war. A decided contrast to the escort groups available in the lean days of 1942, Task Force 64 was composed of the warships listed on the next page.

Steaming in the Western Mediterranean, the ships of this minor armada were ranged in 13 columns, with the LST's in the rear. Destroyers WHIPPLE, ALDEN, and JOHN D. EDWARDS were stationed astern as rear guard. Destroyer-escort MILLS paced along on the starboard quarter of the formation. Escort Group 37, less BLACK SWAN and AMETHYST, formed an outer A/S screen 12,000 yards ahead of the guide. The rest of the DD's and DE's in the task force formed an inner screen.

The port flank, regarded as the more exposed, was supported by the mine vessel SPEED, by BLACK SWAN and AMETHYST (ships equipped with heavy AA guns, radar-controlled), and by the fighter-direction ship COLOMBO. SPEED was stationed on the port bow, COLOMBO on the port quarter.

TASK FORCE 64

ESCORT FOR

CONVOY UGS-36

Destroyer DECATUR
Lt. Comdr. D. G. Wright, U.S.NR.
Flying the broad command pennant of
Capt. H. S. Berdine, U.S.C.G., Com. Task Force 64

DESTROYER-ESCORTS (CORTDIV 23)

SELLSTROM *Comdr. W. L. Maloney, U.S.C.G.*
Flying the pennant of
Comdr. F. P. Vetterick, U.S.C.G., COMCORTDIV 23

RAMSDEN *Lt. Comdr. S. T. Baketel, U.S.C.G.*
MILLS *Lt. Comdr. J. S. Muzzy, U.S.C.G.*
RHODES *Lt. Comdr. E. A. Coffin, Jr., U.S.C.G.*
SAVAGE *Comdr. O. C. Rohnke, U.S.C.G.*

DESTROYERS (DESDIV 57)

WHIPPLE *Lt. Comdr. S. E. Woodard*
Flying the pennant of
Comdr. E. W. Yancey, COMDESDIV 57

ALDEN *Lt. Comdr. W. Herkness, II*
JOHN D. EDWARDS *Lt. R. A. Norelius, U.S.N.R.*

DESTROYER-ESCORTS (CORTDIV 7)

TOMICH *Lt. C. B. Brown, U.S.N.R.*
SLOAT *Lt. Comdr. W. A. Cashman, U.S.N.R.*

ESCORT GROUP 37

H.M.S. JOHAN MAURITS *(flagship)* H.M.S. AMETHYST
H.M.S. FRISO H.M.S. DEPTFORD
H.M.S. BLACK SWAN H.M.S. CAMPION
H.M.S. COLOMBO
(JIG and Fighter-Direction ship)*
H.M.S. SPEED
(Minesweep—JIG ship)*

* JIG—special jamming gear.

So large a ship-train could hardly escape detection by the enemy, and the Germans were soon informed of the convoy's presence in the Mediterranean. They struck with a prompt, combined air-submarine attack. The submarine attack was launched late in the evening of March 31, when the convoy was about midway between Oran and Algiers. The air attack was a *Luftwaffe* onslaught delivered early in the following morning of April 1.

Destroyer-escort TOMICH picked up a sharp sonar contact at 2213 on that last evening of March, and Lieutenant C. B. Brown, U.S.N.R., took appropriate steps to counterattack the U-boat. The DE was assisted by H.M.S. BLACK SWAN. Although a kill was not scored, the enemy was beaten off. So the submarine strike missed.

The *Luftwaffe* strike was somewhat more effective. Timing was good—the attack was made in the darkness of 0400, about an hour and a half after moonset, while the convoy was still a considerable distance (about 56 miles) west of Algiers. At that time TOMICH and BLACK SWAN were just rejoining the convoy, and the enemy may reasonably have supposed that the U-boat attack had disrupted the screen formation.

Some 20 Nazi planes roared in on the strike. One minute they were looking down on a sea of darkness. A moment later they were stunting over an area that blazed like the blast-furnace district of Pittsburgh.

An excerpt from the Action Report of Task Force Commander Berdine describes the vivid battle:

> The attack opened . . . with a string of flares over column eleven near the head of the column, followed at short intervals by additional illumination over the starboard quarter, port bow, and outer screen. Low-flying planes could be heard faintly above the sound of the AA guns and machine guns, and all escorts except one had brief glimpses of these planes, apparently two-engined torpedo-carrying bombers. COLOMBO and ComDesDiv 57 reported sighting what was believed to be sticks of bombs from high-level bombers, the former placing the splashes from the port flank toward the center of the convoy, the latter, from the center toward the starboard quarter. The reaction of the convoy to the attack was immediate and surprising.
>
> If the enemy had required illumination prior to the attack, none was required 30 seconds later, for the whole convoy was solidly outlined, with tracer streaming from every gun.

Two Nazi planes were shot down by this tempestuous barrage. Dragging a flaming tail, a third plane batted off across the sky. A fourth plane may have been fatally scorched. The rest got out of there.

The convoy suffered no personnel casualties, but two destroyermen in the escort contingent were wounded at their battle stations by 20 mm. fragments. The merchant ship JARED INGERSOLL was struck by an aircraft torpedo. It caught her on the port bow at the No. 1 hold, the explosion started a nasty fire. The crew abandoned ship. Destroyer-escort MILLS quickly picked up the INGERSOLL men, then Lieutenant Commander Muzzy placed his DE alongside the burning freighter to fight the conflagration. Through this action by MILLS, and efforts of the British tug MINDFUL, the INGERSOLL was salvaged and much of her cargo was saved. Thus the Nazi score was practically reduced to zero.

In addition the escorts for Convoy UGS-36 learned a lesson. Instead of shooting at the aircraft, many of the gunners had opened fire on the flares. The barrage was spectacular, but the enemy profited by the spectacle. As Vice Admiral Hewitt, criticizing the action, subsequently noted:

> The importance of fire discipline at night is emphasized in connection with a point of aim for enemy aircraft. Although illumination may be bright, its main purpose is to provide silhouettes, and the latter are greatly affected by the use of smoke. The bomber aircraft above the illumination do not get a good point of aim unless ships resort to gunfire. Indiscriminate 20 mm. fire is very dangerous because it affords a good point of aim.

In the lean days of 1942 it had been enough for a convoy escort to serve as a shield. By the spring of 1944 it was expected to wield a sword, as well.

There could be no compromise with the enemy. Witness the attack he delivered on the next eastbound convoy to Bizerte—

Attack on Convoy UGS-37

Convoy UGS-37, bound from Norfolk for Bizerte, was not so large as its forerunner. But in ratio of escort per ship in convoy, it was under a considerably heavier guard.

The convoy consisted of 60 merchant vessels and six LST's. It was escorted by Task Force 65, under command of Captain W. R. Headden. This task force contained the naval vessels listed on this page.

The convoy needed every gun of this heavy guard. As usual, the Germans were informed of this shiptrain's arrival in the Mediterranean, and the *Luftwaffe* struck late in the evening of April 11, 1944, when the convoy was about seven miles off Cape Bengut, Algeria.

The night was as fine as good weather could contrive—sky cloudless, sea as calm as a millpond, water silvered by the light of a three-quarters moon. Steaming at 7.5 knots, the ships were in good formation, aligned in 12 columns, 600 yards between columns, each ship in column 400 yards from the next.

The escorts were disposed around the convoy in positions 3,000 yards from the convoy's perimeter. DesDiv 66 had the stations astern on the "down moon" side. Destroyer LANSDALE, equipped with glider-bomb jamming gear, and four DE's of CortDiv 58 were on the port side of the convoy. Four escorts were to starboard. Cruiser DELHI was stationed on the port quarter between the convoy and CortDiv 58 ships. Destroyer-escorts HOLDER and FORSTER paced ahead of the convoy's front.

At 2245 one aircraft was reported in the convoy's vicinity. Twenty minutes later some five to ten aircraft were hovering in the offing. The clan was gathering.

At 2318 a white flare was dropped about five miles ahead of the convoy. More flares were dropped ahead and to port. Watching in sweaty fascination, destroyer lookouts gripped their binoculars, and gunners waited tight-nerved.

At 2332 Captain Headden ordered various escorts to make smoke. Two minutes later, about a dozen planes were in the vicinity, and flares blazed over the convoy. At 2335, flag DE STANTON opened fire on a plane which came in from port and crossed her bow. The battle was on.

The escorts in Task Force 65 put up a formidable barrage. That the *Luftwaffe* had its first team in the field was evident from the cool deliberation with which the onslaught was launched, and the determination with which it was pushed. Some 15 to 26 aircraft delivered the assault. The planes were Dornier 217's and Junker 88's.

Early in the battle, destroyer-escort HOLDER was torpedoed by one of the low-flying bombers. Striking

TASK FORCE 65

ESCORT FOR

CONVOY UGS-37

DESTROYER-ESCORTS

Temporarily assigned to DesDiv 66

STANTON — *Lt. Comdr. P. J. Tiffany, U.S.N.R.*

Flagship of Task Force Commander Headden

SWASEY — *Lt. Comdr. H. M. Godsey, U.S.N.R.*

DESTROYERS (DESDIV 66)

BRECKENRIDGE — *Lt. Comdr. F. R. Arnold*

Flying pennant of

Comdr. A. M. Kowalzyk, Jr., COMDESDIV 66

BLAKELEY — *Lt. Comdr. R. J. Brooke, U.S.N.R.*

BIDDLE — *Lt. Comdr. R. H. Hopkins, U.S.N.R.*

BARNEY — *Lt. H. D. Sprenger, U.S.N.R.*

DESTROYER-ESCORTS (CORTDIV 58)

PRICE — *Lt. Comdr. J. W. Higgins, Jr., U.S.N.R.*

Flying pennant of

Comdr. E. E. Garcia, COMCORTDIV 58

STRICKLAND — *Lt. Comdr. A. J. Hopkins, U.S.N.R.*

FORSTER — *Lt. Comdr. I. E. Davis, U.S.N.R.*

STOCKDALE — *Lt. Comdr. R. W. Luther, U.S.N.R.*

HISSEM — *Lt. Comdr. W. W. Low, U.S.N.R.*

HOLDER — *Lt. Comdr. W. P. Buck, U.S.N.R.*

Destroyer LANSDALE — *Lt. Comdr. D. M. Swift*

H.M.S. DELHI *(AA Cruiser)* — H.M.S. NADDER *(Escort vessel)*

H.M.S. JONQUIL *(Escort vessel)* — H.M.S. MINDFUL *(Rescue tug)*

H.M.S. VAGRANT *(Rescue tug)*

Task Force 65: While escorting 60 merchant vessels and six LST's in the Mediterranean in April, 1944, the task force effectively fought off a persistent night attack by Nazi bombers. Not a single member of the convoy was hit, but destroyer Biddle suffered casualties and destroyer-escort Holder was shattered by an aerial torpedo. The DE's first fight proved to be her last.

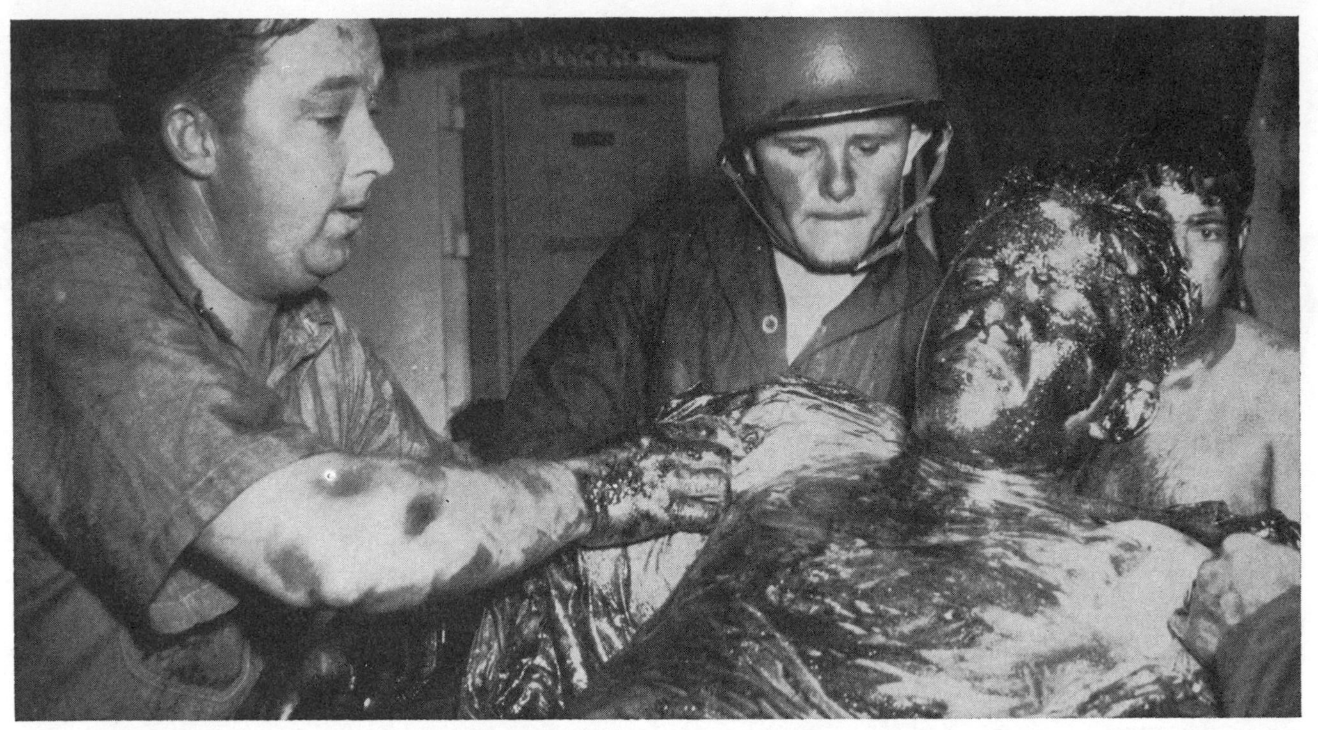

A survivor of Lansdale is picked up by a sister destroyer off the coast of North Africa. Equipped to jam radio-controlled glider bombs, the veteran fighter fulfilled her special mission with success but could not escape a swarm of Heinkel bombers which attacked the convoy she was guarding off Cape Bengut, Algeria. Her back broken by a torpedo, Lansdale tore apart and sank.

Some of the 235 survivors of Lansdale (DD 426) who were taken aboard Newell and Menges. Lansdale (bottom) was a veteran of Atlantic patrols and Mediterranean invasions, including Anzio.

Two damaged DE's become one fighting ship. By a miracle of shipyard surgery, the torpedoed Holder and Menges, the first hit from the air and the other by a U-boat, are made a new Menges.

This boy was not as fortunate as his ship. He died in the torpedoing of Menges. Thirty of his fellow crew members were also slain by an explosion which ripped away both props and rudder.

through the barrage, the planes made repeated attacks thereafter. At 2349 destroyer LANSDALE reported there were indications the enemy was using radio-controlled missiles. At 2350 a plane dropped a stick of bombs close aboard STANTON. Midnight, and the attackers were still coming. Destroyer-escort SWASEY dodged an aircraft torpedo at 0010. The battle's tempo moderated at 0013, and it was all over by 0030.

When the firing ceased, Task Force 65 could sigh in relief. It had spent a long, hard hour. Admirably it had defended the convoy; not a merchant ship or LST was hit. But, with the exception of two "possibles," the assailants had escaped retribution.

Captain Headden later criticized destroyer LANSDALE for *"a most regrettable poor performance,"* because she fired only five rounds of 40 mm., and expended no 20 mm. or 5-inch ammunition. Vice Admiral Hewitt did not agree with this sharp criticism. *"The remarks regarding the poor performance of the* LANSDALE *are not concurred in,"* he wrote. *"On the contrary, the fire discipline of the* LANSDALE *appeared excellent and in conformity with lessons she had learned from her war experience in the Mediterranean."*

Admiral Hewitt, in turn, criticized Captain Headden for being too slow in ordering his smoke screen. *"If order to make smoke had been issued when first flare was sighted* (2318), *the convoy should have been fairly well covered by 2334."* And he did not agree with Captain Headden's opinion that *"for best protection against torpedo attacks, smoke should be so placed that the horizon on bearings favorable for attack is obscured."* Instead Hewitt stated: *"The observation of horizon is immaterial. Planes are on instruments and do not have to see horizon. Automatic weapons should not fire unless planes are within range and can be seen."* He concluded: *". . . It is again pointed out that the main result of illumination is to produce ship silhouettes. This is directly affected by smoke. An accurate point of aim for the enemy is necessary to produce effective hitting, and it is believed that this point of aim is usually indicated by ships' gunfire."*

So more smoke had been in order, and perhaps less fire. And although Convoy UGS-37 was unharmed, the escorting task force suffered casualties. On board destroyer BIDDLE seven men had been wounded by fragments of a 20 mm. shell which was sloppily fired by another ship. And destroyer-escort HOLDER was hard hit.

Loss of U.S.S. Holder

Destroyer-escort HOLDER (Lieutenant Commander W. P. Buck, U.S.N.R.) was one of the UGS-37 escorts ordered to make smoke just before the *Luftwaffe* attacked. HOLDER was on her first operational voyage after a shakedown, but she went into battle like a veteran.

Between 2323 and 2332 her radar picked up two enemy planes. At 2335 she let go with her smoke generators as directed, and began to build a wall of fog across the convoy's menaced front. A few minutes later she sighted a Nazi plane skimming across the water.

As reported by HOLDER's skipper:

> At 2339 a plane of a type not positively identified was sighted off the port beam and fire was opened with all guns that could bear. As plane approached, flying very close to the water, it was observed to launch a torpedo at a range estimated at 300-400 yards. The torpedo wake was clearly visible and strong hydrophone effect was picked up and reported from the Sound Hut. As soon as torpedo was sighted, flank speed was ordered and full left rudder applied. At 2340, before the order to increase speed had taken effect, the torpedo struck amidships on the port side below the waterline with two distinct heavy explosions. They were a fraction of a second apart and seemed of almost equal intensity. A yellow flash accompanied the explosions. The ship settled and took on a four degree list to starboard.

HOLDER's power-plant was paralyzed. The sea plunged into Compartments B1, B2, and B3, and an ugly oil fire broke out in B3. While the flames were being smothered with foam, the ship's guns went on firing.

The destroyer-escort FORSTER (Lieutenant Commander I. E. Davis, U.S.N.R.) was ordered to go to the disabled DE's assistance. At 0113 she edged up alongside HOLDER and took off twelve critically injured men. Sixteen of the crew had perished in the torpedoing.

Destroyer-escort PRICE (Lieutenant Commander J. W. Higgins, Jr., U.S.N.R.) transferred a doctor to the battered DE. At 0230 in the morning of April 12 the ship was taken under tow by the rescue tug MINDFUL. About eight hours later she reached the harbor of Algiers.

After a temporary repair job, concluded on May 24, HOLDER was towed out by the tug CHOCTAW to join a convoy bound for the States. On June 9, 1944, the crippled destroyer-escort arrived in New York Navy Yard. There she was carefully examined by expert repair crews whose verdict was a headshake. Battle damage was too extensive to warrant overhaul and rehabilitation. The DE's first fight had been her last.

On September 13, 1944, the U.S.S. HOLDER was placed out of commission.

By dint of tremendous fire-power, plus a bit of luck, Convoys UGS-36 and UGS-37 had come through with relatively light ship-casualties. Not so fortunate was Convoy UGS-38. Another large Hampton Roads-to-Bizerte convoy, this ship-train was struck by the enemy off Cape Bengut, Algeria, not far from the spot where UGS-37 had been intercepted.

Attack on Convoy UGS-38

The convoy consisted of 85 merchant vessels, two Navy tankers, and the Coast Guard cutter DUANE. It was escorted by Task Force 66 under command of Captain W. H. Duvall. The warships which composed this escort force are enumerated below.

TASK FORCE 66

ESCORT FOR

CONVOY UGS-38

C.G.C. TANEY — *Comdr. H. J. Wuensch, U.S.C.G.*
Flagship of Task Force Commander Duvall

DESTROYER-ESCORTS (CORTDIV 21 AND CORTDIV 46)

JOSEPH E. CAMPBELL — *Lt. Comdr. J. M. Robertson*
Flying the pennant of
Comdr. L. M. Markham, Jr., COMCORTDIV 21

LANING — *Lt. Comdr. E. A. Shuman, Jr., U.S.N.R.*
FECHTELER — *Lt. C. B. Gill*
FISKE — *Lt. J. A. Comly, U.S.N.R.*
MOSLEY — *Lt. Comdr. J. A. Alger, Jr., U.S.C.G.*
PRIDE — *Comdr. R. R. Curry, U.S.C.G.*
FALGOUT — *Comdr. H. A. Meyer, U.S.C.G.*
LOWE — *Comdr. R. H. French, U.S.C.G.*
MENGES — *Lt. Comdr. F. M. McCabe, U.S.C.G.*
Flying the pennant of
Capt. R. E. Wood, U.S.C.G., COMCORTDIV 46

NEWELL — *Comdr. R. J. Roberts, U.S.C.G.*
CHASE — *Lt. Comdr. G. O. Knapp, II, U.S.N.R.*
FESSENDEN — *Lt. Comdr. W. A. Dobbs, U.S.N.R.*
Destroyer LANSDALE — *Lt. Comdr. D. M. Swift**
H.N.M.S. HEEMSKERCK *AA Cruiser** — H.M.S. SUSTAIN* *(Minesweep)*
H.M.S. SPEED* *(Minesweep)* — H.M.S. VAGRANT* *(Tug)*

* Joined convoy in Mediterranean.

Approaching Cape Bengut on the evening of April 20, 1944, the convoy was steaming in 10-column formation. Three destroyer-escorts were stationed in the outer screen. Other DE's formed the inner screen which covered the front and both flanks of the convoy. One DE was in "caboose position" astern.

Three British submarines were in column, traveling with the convoy. The Dutch AA cruiser HEEMSKERCK and the American destroyer LANSDALE were also on the convoy's port beam. Mine vessel SPEED was directly ahead of the convoy; SUSTAIN was on the starboard flank. (HEEMSKERCK joined Task Force 66 at Gibraltar. Among other things she was responsible for fighter-direction, air-warning guard, and maintenance of contact with fighter sectors. LANSDALE, SUSTAIN, and SPEED joined at long. 2 W. They carried special jamming equipment.)

In conformance with Vice Admiral Hewitt's directives, Captain Duvall emphasized the gunnery doctrine to be observed by Task Force 66 on the Mediterranean haul. *"Doctrine this area directs escorts to fire machine-guns only at seen targets at night and only when satisfied own ship's position is known to plane. At longer ranges main-battery controlled fire only will be used."*

The code word for an aircraft alarm was "Whoopee." There were several daytime "whoopees" as the ship-train, steaming at 7.5 knots, approached Cape Bengut. But after dark the attackers were not detected until they were almost on top of the ship-train.

Excerpt from Captain Duvall's Action Report:

> The attack was well planned. . . . The enemy employed twilight and shore coverage to the fullest advantage, and further escaped detection by flying low over the water. Only torpedoes were used by the attacking planes, all of which apparently made straight runs. Numerous explosions were heard by the various escorts. These explosions may have been from depth charges which were dropped by PRIDE for reasons unknown to Task Force Commander. . . . No shooting was done by the aircraft. No flares were used by the attacking planes. . . . No concerted attempt at smoke-laying was made by the escorts. . . .

Captain Duvall also stated, *"Effective fighter protection was apparently totally lacking in the vicinity of the convoy."*

The attack came from ahead on a bearing about 100° true, the planes barely skimming the water and employing the dark shoreline as background to blur their silhouettes and to frustrate radar. Destroyer-escort LOWE sighted five of the oncoming aircraft at 2103. In the gloaming they had appeared with the suddenness of a flight of bats. It was "Whoopee!" then, and no mistake.

The onslaught was delivered in three waves. The first wave, about nine Junker 88's, veered away from the shore background and struck from dead ahead. Torpedoes, probably fired by the leaders of this group, crashed into the S.S. PAUL HAMILTON and

S.S. SAMITE. The HAMILTON was fatally hit. So swift and unexpected was this attack that the DE's in the screen failed to fire on the leading Junkers. Some of the ships in the convoy got off a few rounds, and the cruiser HEEMSKERCK shot at the leaders as they retired. The "tail-end-Charlies," however, were the target for a tornado barrage set up by most of the convoy and all of the escorts. Several of the planes were undoubtedly hit.

The second attack wave, seven Junker 88's, came in swiftly behind the first. The group split up, and three or four of the Junkers raced down the convoy's starboard flank. S.S. STEPHEN T. AUSTIN and S.S. ROYAL STAR were torpedoed during this attack. Destroyer-escorts LOWE and TANEY did some fast footwork to side-step torpedoes which sizzled close aboard.

The third attack wave, perhaps five Heinkel 111's, struck at the convoy's port bow. During this attack HEEMSKERCK's lookouts sighted three torpedo wakes. Ships swerved, maneuvering to avoid, as anti-aircraft gunners hurled flak at the dimly-glimpsed assailants. The gunners of destroyer LANSDALE knocked down one plane and were credited with two "possibles." Then, with shattering violence, a torpedo crashed into the destroyer, and LANSDALE, too, was out of it.

As suddenly as it had begun, the battle was over; the *Luftwaffe* was gone. But Convoy UGS-38 had received a hard blow. It might have been even harder but for the fact that the enemy air squadron had, earlier that evening, attacked a Corsica-Africa convoy located some 100 miles to the northeast of UGS-38. The Nazis had struck at this convoy with glider bombs as well as torpedoes, and they were either out of robot ammunition when they reached Cape Bengut, or they were out of patience with the robots. For the control signals had been intercepted by destroyer LANSDALE and mine vessel SPEED, whose operators had promptly jammed the glider-bomb transmissions. Four minutes after this long-range interference the bombers ceased using the robots.

It was noted the enemy did not use flares while attacking Convoy UGS-38. In reference to which, Vice Admiral Hewitt observed:

"It is emphasized that the enemy did not illuminate. In this case it did not appear necessary. In the twilight or early darkness, the enemy apparently relies on the individual ship's gunfire for his point of aim. If the planes were visible at 7,000 yards, it is still considered that effective smoke would have been of value. . . . All practicable steps should be taken to improve the anti-aircraft batteries of destroyer-escorts."

Obviously the *Luftwaffe* scored heavily in this foray. While an estimated six planes were shot down in the battle and five more damaged, these shootings hardly compensated for the casualties suffered by the convoy. Torpedoed and sunk were the merchant vessels PAUL HAMILTON and ROYAL STAR. Two other merchantmen were severely blasted. And destroyer LANSDALE had been sent to the bottom. The sinking of this veteran Mediterranean-fighter is described herewith.

Loss of U.S.S. Lansdale

LANSDALE (Lieutenant Commander D. M. Swift) had been attached to the escort force guarding Convoy UGS-38 when that ship-train entered the Mediterranean. Equipped with apparatus for detecting and jamming radio-controlled glider bombs, LANSDALE was operating as an anti-robot specialist. But she was a salty veteran as well, whose skill as a fighter had been remarked by Admiral Hewitt after her previous service with Convoy UGS-37.

The glider-bomb detail was by way of extra duty, but LANSDALE handled the job with neatness and dispatch. She was at it early in the evening of April 20, 1944, when the eastbound convoy was approaching Cape Bengut, Algeria. Some 100 miles over the northeast horizon enemy planes were attacking another convoy. At 2045 LANSDALE heard glider-bomb transmissions. So did mine vessel SPEED, another specialist carrying anti-robot equipment. Promptly the operators on both LANSDALE and SPEED went to work to jam the air waves and befuddle the radio-controlled robots. The Germans quit using these weapons, frustrated by convoy escorts 100 miles away!

The same Nazi aircraft struck Convoy UGS-38 off Cape Bengut at 2103. About 2104 the third attack wave—a group of Heinkel 111's—swept in on the convoy's port bow. In the center of this onslaught, LANSDALE was assailed from both port and starboard. Her AA guns put up a double-barreled defense, but she could not fend off the two-sided attack. At 2105 a Heinkel torpedo smashed into the destroyer.

The blast wrecked the ship's forward fireroom and broke her back. Valiantly the LANSDALE crew fought her battle-damage, but with her vital machinery swamped, the destroyer leaned helplessly in the sea, smoke and steam pouring from her breached hull. About 2122, fearing that the vessel might capsize, Lieutenant Commander Swift ordered the ship abandoned.

Not long after the destroyermen went overside, the ship tore apart amidships, and the wreckage sank. Some 235 survivors (two fatally injured) were picked up by destroyer-escorts NEWELL and MENGES. Forty-seven of the crew were not recovered.

So the Navy's Destroyer Force lost another warship on the Nazi-menaced Mediterranean run. And within a little over a fortnight the Force was to lose still another. Before this next victim was downed, however, some of her companions on that embattled sea road slew a U-boat marauder.

Pride, J. E. Campbell, Sustain, L'Alcyon, Senegalais, and H.M.S. Blankney Kill U-371

There was little rest for the Navy's escort forces on the main line of the Western Mediterranean. Take Task Force 66, for example. Hardly had it conducted eastbound Convoy UGS-38 into Bizerte, when it was ordered out on the reverse run with westbound GUS-38. Leave and liberty were short-term items on the site of ancient Carthage.

GUS-38 was a big convoy. It contained 107 merchantmen formed in 16 columns. The escort included 12 DE's, a large Coast Guard cutter, and the British AA cruiser DELHI.

Task Force 66, steaming westward with Convoy GUS-38, had reached the dangerous waters below the southeast coast of Spain by morning of May 3, 1944. In this area, where the Mediterranean bottle narrows into a neck, the Nazi enemy was ready and waiting for GUS-38. And in the early hours of May 3 a submarine torpedo crashed into destroyer-escort MENGES, flagship of Captain R. E. Wood, U.S.C.G., ComCortDiv 46.

MENGES had been patrolling 3,000 yards astern of the convoy. Shortly after midnight her radar spotted a target six miles astern. Captain Wood ordered the DE to investigate. MENGES' skipper sent the crew to battle stations, and the ship streamed "foxer" (false targets) to outfox acoustic torpedoes. About 0050 the DE began to zigzag. At 0104 she increased speed to 20 knots to close the range. The target disappeared, but a new spatter of "pips" flickered on the radar screen to confuse the issue. At 0115 MENGES' speed was slowed to 15 knots to facilitate sonar search. And three minutes after that a torpedo hit her in the stern.

The blast carried away both propellers and rudders, and wrecked the after compartments of the ship. Thirty-one of the crew were slain in the explosion, and 25 were injured. The DE wallowed logily in the sea, paralyzed and almost defenseless. With the exception of her forward batteries and four 20 mm's. near the stack, all her weapons had been put out of commission.

At 0140 Task Force Commander Duvall ordered two destroyer-escorts to leave the convoy screen, go to MENGES' assistance, and hunt down her assailant. These DE's were PRIDE (Commander R. R. Curry, U.S.C.G.) and JOSEPH E. CAMPBELL (Lieutenant J. M. Robertson), flagship of Commander L. M. Markham, Jr., ComCortDiv 21.

At 0255 PRIDE picked up the submarine contact near MENGES, and the two able-bodied DE's closed in to trap and exterminate the U-boat. It was soon apparent they were up against a wily customer.

Tracking down the contact, PRIDE delivered two depth-charge attacks. An hour later the target was still on hand, so PRIDE and CAMPBELL executed a creeping attack. PRIDE did the coaching, and CAMPBELL dropped a lot of depth charges. But they did not execute the enemy.

With daylight tinting the dark, the two DE's maneuvered in for another creeping attack, which was delivered at 0600. This time CAMPBELL coached and PRIDE dropped the charges. Down went more "dynamite" from PRIDE at 0627. This blasting brought a swarm of bubbles popping to the surface, and the hunters were confident they had damaged the U-boat. But the contact evaporated. The enemy might be playing 'possum.

So another creeping attack was started at 0807, and at 0833 a pattern of magnetic depth charges was dropped. Then the contact "got lost" and stayed lost.

But the Division Commander was persistent. Picturing the sub snugged down in the mud of some deep-sea foxhole, Comander Markham ordered CAMPBELL and PRIDE to go over the area with a fine-tooth comb.

The two DE's combed until 1030. No trace of the target—the U-boat might have dissolved like a lump of sugar in a cup of coffee. Yet the sub could not have disintegrated in such fashion without leaving a deposit of scum on the surface—residue of some kind. And an undetected escape through the sonar net was highly unlikely. Commander Markham was convinced the U-boat was alive on the bottom. The hunt was continued along the lines of a systematic search.

H.M.S. BLANKNEY joined the search team that forenoon. And at 1225 the American mine vessel SUSTAIN and the French destroyers L'ALCYON and SENEGALAIS entered the game Throughout the afternoon of May 3, and all evening, the five hunters cut intricate patterns across the seascape, probing for the enemy down under. At midnight the search was still going on.

By 0200 of the 4th it was no longer hide-and-seek, but a game of come out, come out, wherever you are. No submarine could endure much more than a day's submersion, and the hunted U-boat had now been under a good 24 hours. The crew would either suffocate or—

At 0315 SENEGALAIS made radar contact with a surfaced submarine. The French destroyermen fired starshells, spotted the U-boat's silhouette, and blazed away with ready guns. Meantime, CAMPBELL and PRIDE were closing in at full speed, and maneuvering to block the sub's escape to the north. BLANKNEY and SUSTAIN blocked escape to the west. Moving at about 12 knots, the sub headed southwest. At 0359 the U-boat submerged. Five minutes later SENEGALAIS was struck in the stern by a torpedo. The blast smashed her fantail, but she remained afloat, more durable than her mortal enemy.

At 0433 some shouting Germans were glimpsed in the water by lookouts on board the SUSTAIN. The mine vessel steamed forward to investigate. In all, 41 men and seven officers were picked up. Five of their fellows had gone down with the submarine, which had been abandoned at 0409. She was the U-371—one of the toughest Nazi subs to be sunk in the Mediterranean.

But the crew's ability to endure depth-charge barrages, fouling air, nerve strain, and claustrophobia could not re-charge the sub's electric batteries. Nor could human stamina make a U-boat invulnerable to surface gunfire. Tough as was U-371, she could not beat such a 'hold-down" as was clamped on her by persistent Commander Markham and his destroyermen.

Unfortunately the killing of this U-boat did not end the attack on Convoy GUS-38. The following day, destroyer-escort FECHTELER was torpedoed.

Loss of U.S.S. Fechteler

One of the escorts for westbound Convoy GUS-38, destroyer-escort FECHTELER (Lieutenant C. B. Gill) plodded on with the slow ship-train which took an evasive course after the submarine attack on U.S.S. MENGES. The convoy swung southward toward Oran, then headed west. Early in the morning on May 5, 1944, it was approaching the island of Alboran, a Spanish flyspeck in the center of the Mediterranean's bottle-neck.

About 0315, destroyer-escort LANING (Lieutenant Commander E. A. Shuman, Jr., U.S.N.R.) made radar contact with a strange vessel 13 miles distant. Presently the "pip" disappeared; the vessel had submerged. The submarine alarm was flashed, and the convoy made several course-changes, maneuvering to evade ambush.

At 0345 FECHTELER, covering a sector between the convoy and the sub's reported position, was swinging right to follow a new course. The ship was still turning when she was rocked by a thunderclap explosion. On the topside men were thrown from their footing on the bridge and at gun mounts. In the compartments below decks engineers and firemen were hurled against bulkheads or pitched into a jungle of shattered machines. Water spouted in through the smashed hull, and the destroyer-escort wallowed in helpless disablement.

There were the usual acts of heroism—sailors plunging through steam and oil to rescue wounded shipmates; all hands doing their utmost to save each other and the ship. But the torpedoed DE was beyond saving. A few minutes after she was hit, the ship began to crack up. All hands abandoned at 0415. Then the ship snapped amidships and folded until bow and stern were almost perpendicular. About 0500 the wreckage exploded and sank.

Some 186 survivors were picked up by the destroyer-escort LANING and a rescue tug. The rest of FECHTELER's crew either perished in the torpedo blast or went down with the wreckage.

The submarine responsible for this sinking may have been the one detected by LANING's radar 30 minutes before the strike. Or it may have been a companion undersea-boat, fortuitously positioned in the convoy's path. And there was still another possibility: the FECHTELER sinking could have been the handiwork of a renegade Italian submarine.

U.S. DD's and British Aircraft Kill U-616 ("Operation Monstrous")

Dealing death to destroyer-escort FECHTELER and severe damage to destroyer-escort MENGES and French destroyer SENEGALAIS, the submarine onslaught on Convoy GUS-38 raised the temperature in Allied headquarters to thermite heat. When the undersea enemy struck again on May 14, ambushing Convoy GUS-39 and disabling two merchantmen by torpedo fire, the lid blew off. Determined to squelch the marauders operating in the waters between Spain and Algeria, Commander in Chief Mediterranean (CinC-Med) instituted one of the biggest submarine hunts ever staged in that sea—a hunt appropriately designated "Operation Monstrous."

Launching the campaign, Allied commanders in the area tightened the A/S defenses and accelerated the A/S sweeps. British Coastal Command aircraft flew needle-eyed patrols, and American warships from Algiers and Mers-el-Kebir beat the undersea bushes for a trace of the enemy. It was a reckless U-boat commander who would dare to prowl in these precincts while this heat was on.

Such a boat was the U-616.

No sooner was the submarine detected on May 14, 1944, than the wheels of the hunt went into motion. The search brought into action the aircraft of British Squadron 36. The destroyers, teamed up under squadron command of Captain A. F. Converse, included the following ships:

Ellyson	*Comdr. E. W. Longton*
	Flagship of Capt. Converse
Nields	*Comdr. A. R. Heckey*
Gleaves	*Comdr. B. L. Gurnette*
Hilary P. Jones	*Lt. Comdr. F. M. Stiesberg*
Macomb	*Lt. Comdr. George Hutchinson*
Hambleton	*Comdr. H. A. Renken*
Rodman	*Comdr. J. F. Foley*
Emmons	*Comdr. E. B. Billingsley*

All of these DD's were veterans. And one of them, Commander Renken's Hambleton, had a particularly long U-boat score to settle. She, it may be recalled, was the destroyer torpedoed in Fedala Roads during "Operation Torch"—the DD that, having been cut in two, foreshortened, and sewn together again, had gone home under her own power to be overhauled and re-lengthened. Then, at Oran on May 4, she was ordered to Djijelli, Algeria, to pick up survivors of the torpedoed destroyer-escort Menges. As one of her crew described it, she went out on the sub-hunt on May 14 "with blood in her eye."

Hambleton was not the only destroyer out for a kill. Ellyson took first crack at the foe. She made a high-speed run to the point of first contact, which the aviators had marked with flares. After picking up sonar contact, Ellyson pitched in with a depth-charge attack. She treated the target to a full pattern, set to explode at "shallow."

In Ellyson's wake the sea vomited and heaved, but it failed to disgorge any submarine. Unable to regain sonar contact, the destroyermen began a box search, but to no avail. But they did detect a strong smell of Diesel oil. And in the morning of the 15th the lookouts sighted an undulant slick which extended across the water for ten miles. The sea had belched up something, after all.

Or, rather, the submarine had. The U-boat was still in existence, for a search plane spotted her on the surface some 10 miles west of the point of Ellyson's attack. Captain Converse immediately raced Ellyson to the locale. The sub did not wait, and another box search for the undersea beast was begun.

From morning until midnight of the 15th the destroyer squadron pursued the trail, hunting in two groups. The DD's swept in to the Spanish coast the following day, combing the waters off Cap de Santa Pola. U-616 was not there. Her skipper had decided to run northeast, and that evening of the 16th the sub was loping along on the surface, heading toward the Riviera.

At 2356 the U-boat was sighted by a British Wellington bomber about 50 miles distant from Converse's destroyers. The airmen passed the word, and the contact report was intercepted by both hunter-groups. They headed for the target at once, steaming at top speed on converging courses.

At midnight the sub was racing for her life, with the two groups of huntsmen in hot pursuit. "This U-boat was not an ordinary one," a Hambleton man recalled. "The Nazi skipper used every trick of the trade to throw us off, and when he ran out of old ones he invented some new ones. But he couldn't shake us that night. We were right on his heels, and he was running down a dead-end street."

Aware that his sub had been spotted from the air, the U-boat skipper released a number of decoy-radar balloons. *"They were quite effective,"* Captain Converse reported. *"However, his own pip was stronger, steadier, and identifiable by the speed he was making."* So the hunters relentlessly closed in.

Macomb was the first DD to sight the target. Opening up with her searchlight, she speared the gray conning tower at 2,400 yards. Mistaking the destroyer's light for that of an aircraft, the submariners opened fire with 20 mm. deck guns. Macomb's 5-inch 38's answered with an authoritative roar. The sub made a running dive, and Macomb was on top of the target with depth charges at a rush. She dropped them deep, and followed with a pattern set to explode at 600 feet.

Now Gleaves arrived on the spot, and a creeping attack was begun, with Macomb coaching. As sonar contact could not be regained, the attack went uncompleted.

At 0145 Nields stepped in to drop a pattern. Emmons followed suit. Contact petered out entirely after these attacks, and another box search was set in motion, seven DD's participating.

For four days the enemy had led the hunters in a chase all around Robin Hood's Barn. And now, although they had him in the barn, he succeeded in hiding somewhere in the hay.

Around and around the hunters circled, determined to smoke out the quarry. Somewhere deep under, the sub glided and drifted with motors cut off, then ran for a moment to regain momentum, then slid silently to another level. But coast and fishtail as he would, the enemy could not shake the pursuit overhead.

At 0645, with daylight on the seascape, Hambleton made the electrifying sonar contact about ten miles south of the point where contact had been lost at 0230. Commander Renken conned the ship through two fast depth-charge runs, laying deep patterns set for 500-600 feet. Ellyson and Rodman closed in for a go at the target, and the other destroyers formed a circle with a four-mile radius encompassing the three DD's at the hub.

About 0710, while HAMBLETON, ELLYSON, and RODMAN were probing for contact, there was a swirl of water at the center of the circle. With a swoosh of spray the U-boat came up right in the bull's-eye. At once the three ships opened fire, range 2,500 yards. As 5-inchers hit the U-boat's conning tower, the Nazi submariners hit the deck. Wildly waving dungarees and shirts, the U-boat crew dived overside in one of the fastest abandonments ever beheld. As the Diesel engines were in high gear, the sub raced on across the water, leaving the survivors strewn astern.

The destroyer gunners lashed at the deserted sub, avoiding the residue of swimmers. They were somewhat more humane than the U-616's skipper who, it appeared, had made a "crash dive" the previous night, leaving a crew of deck-gunners on the surface of the Mediterranean to sink or swim. They were the only fatalities of U-616. The rest of the crew—53 in all—were fished from the water by destroyers ELLYSON and RODMAN. Only one of their number was injured —a man with a shrapnel wound in his hip.

The U-boat, however, went down, punctured by a score of direct hits. About three minutes later the water echoed to a thunderous boom. A few items of debris swirled to the surface. "Operation Monstrous" was over.

Speaking of this operation, the Task Unit Commander stated: *"I cannot speak too highly of the cooperation in this operation by all concerned; with particular reference to Coastal Command Aircraft who fulfilled every request to the limit of their ability."*

Returning to Oran with their prisoners-of-war, the destroyer complement of this persistent hunter-killer group were treated to several barrels of free beer and a bushel of congratulations for a job well done.

Niblack, Ludlow, and British Aircraft Kill U-960 ("Monstrous 2")

Sequel to the abolishment of U-616 was the pursuit and punishment of U-960, a fellow member of the Doenitz Mediterranean mob.

If the actions of U-616 had been reckless, those of U-960 were positively suicidal. For this undersea-boat had the nerve to fire at several of the destroyers of Captain Converse's killer squadron, even as those DD's were returning in triumph from the U-616 kill. Among the targets was Captain Converse's flag destroyer ELLYSON. The spread of three torpedoes missed, but the wakes were arrows pointing to the enemy's whereabouts. Destroyer GLEAVES sighted something that looked like a periscope, and the spot was marked for immediate reference.

Presently DesDiv 25—WOOLSEY, MADISON, BENSON, and LUDLOW—arrived on the scene to relieve Captain Converse's destroyer. Division Commander R. B. Ellis in WOOLSEY took charge of the proceedings. Then another DD joined the hunt.

Top speed from the vicinity of Mers-el-Kebir raced destroyer NIBLACK (Commander R. R. Connor). To the area flew aircraft of British Squadrons 36 and 500. One good sub-hunt deserved another, and this team was out to substantiate the adage.

The enemy was lurking in that favorite U-boat haunt, the waters about midway between Ténès, Algeria, and Cartagena on the southeast coast of Spain. At 1900 of May 18 the hunters were ordered by CinCMed to work in two groups—WOOLSEY, BENSON, and MADISON in one; NIBLACK and LUDLOW in the other. At 0240 in the morning of the 19th a plane reported suspicious radar contact some ten miles from NIBLACK. The British flyers had tagged the spot with a marker.

NIBLACK and LUDLOW highballed over to investigate. They sighted the marker at 0251. Thirty minutes later LUDLOW's sonar instruments registered the presence of a submarine in the vicinity. NIBLACK made sonar contact a few minutes after that, and the two DD's pitched in to dig out the U-boat.

As senior officer present, Commander Connor in NIBLACK directed the blasting, and the two destroyers roiled the water with a total of eleven depth-charge attacks. The barrage was right on target. The sun came up, and so did the U-boat.

At 0708 the submarine broached, popping to the surface, stern first. The U-boat's tail was still silhouetted against the sky when the destroyermen opened fire. At 0712 a British plane dived on the floundering sub, pelting the water with bombs that landed close. A moment later shells from NIBLACK and LUDLOW smashed into the conning tower. Centerpiece in a bouquet of shrapnel-bursts, the U-boat sank.

NIBLACK sprinted forward to treat the sinking sub to a 10-charge pattern. Once again the U-boat was blown to the surface. Then, with stern thrust skyward, the submersible made a final dive. At 0721 NIBLACK and LUDLOW moved in to pick up the 20 survivors of the U-960—another Nazi submarine that was *kaput*. The participating destroyermen called the operation "Monstrous 2."

"Operation Anvil"

Destruction of U-371, U-616, and U-960 more or less squared accounts for the loss of HOLDER, LANSDALE, and FECHTELER. But it did not square accounts for other torpedoings, or for the ship-casualties inflicted by the *Luftwaffe* on Allied convoys in the Western Mediterranean that spring.

The Germans had given up all hope of a win in the Mediterranean. But as long as they held Southern France they could strike vengefully at all Allied forces and convoys within reach. They were fighting for a stalemate—a draw that would weary the Allies or wear them out.

So "Operation Anvil"—an Allied assault on the Nazified Azure Coast—was in the cards. Sooner or later the Germans would have to be dislodged from this Riviera littoral—and the sooner it was done, the better the chance of ruining Hitler's stalemate strategy.

Devised as a follow-up for "Neptune," "Operation Anvil" would not only liberate Southern France and relieve pressure on the southern flank of Eisenhower's armies in Normandy, but it would put Allied armies on Kesselring's Italian Riviera flank. It would give the Allies one of Europe's largest seaports—Marseilles. It would open the Rhone Valley for a drive on Paris. And, finally, it would practically eliminate the U-boat-*Luftwaffe* menace in the Western Mediterranean.

About the middle of May the Allied Strategic Air Force began to bomb the highways, railroads, tunnels, and bridges on the fringe of the target area. "Anvil" D-Day was set for August 15, 1944, on the assumption that by this date Eisenhower's forces would be well on their way across Normandy, and the Allies would be firmly established in Rome.

Vice Admiral Hewitt was to command the "Anvil" naval force. Mission of this force was to land the American Seventh Army and the assault troops of the recently organized French Expeditionary Corps on three beachheads east of Toulon. Fire-support and the usual amphibious services were to be included in the naval mission. Also to be included were some services decidedly unusual.

By way of acquiring an advanced base, Free French forces seized Corsica in the autumn of 1943. On June 19, 1944, French Army forces and an Allied naval task force captured neighboring Elba. Dominating the southern reaches of the Ligurian Sea, these islands were stepping stones to the French Riviera.

By late July the "Anvil" invasion fleet was assembling. Small craft were staged from the newly-captured Corsican ports and from Naples. Down from Cherbourg came American fire-support ships—AUGUSTA, TEXAS, TUSCALOOSA, and the others which had bombarded that key Channel port. In from the Atlantic came U.S. cruisers, U.S. battleships, and carriers KASAAN BAY and TULAGI, and others. Seven British escort-carriers joined the fleet. So did British battleship RAMILLIES and seven British cruisers. So did French battleship LORRAINE and five French cruisers. From Oran, Algiers, and Bizerte, from Palermo and Naples came troop ships, supply ships, and men-of-war. When the armada was finally assembled it contained a total of 880 ships and craft, and 1,370 ship-borne landing craft. This was truly a United Nations fleet. Its complement included 515 United States war vessels, 283 British, 12 French, seven Greek, and 63 merchant ships of various nationalities.

The destroyer representation (83 DD's) was typically international—47 United States; 27 British; 5 French; 4 Greek. There were 8 American and 5 French DE's in the fleet (listed on next page).

Some idea of the multitudinous duties assigned to the "tincans" may be obtained from Admiral Hewitt's Operational Plan (OP Plan No. 4-44).

> *DD's and DE's played an important role in this operation. DD's served in the Gunfire Support Group of each of the three Attack Forces (TF's 84, 85, and 87) and of the Support Force (TF 86), and in the screen of the Aircraft Carrier Force (TF 88). By far the greatest number, however, were assigned to the Anti-Submarine and Convoy Control Group (TG 80.6) under Captain J. P. Clay, ComDes, 8th Fleet, who had 41 DD's (14 United States, 21 British, 6 French) and 13 DE's (8 United States, 5 French) under his command. . . .*
>
> *The tasks of TG 80.6 were to escort convoys to assault area. To establish and maintain protective screen for the defense of shipping in the beach assault areas against submarine and E-boat or other surface attack. To provide "jammer" protection to important units. To provide relief DD's to Fire Support Groups as required by Attack Force Commanders. To assign DD's for diversionary and other special tasks as required. To conduct return Convoy Control, organizing convoys and escorts in general conformity with Convoy Plan. To give particular attention to movements of special-use LST's and shuttles. And to maintain positive communications with U.S. Naval Liaison Beach Control Group to insure receipt of timely information of required diversion of incoming convoys to newly-opened beaches. . . .*
>
> *Additional radio transmitters were installed and additional communication officers, radio and signal personnel were embarked to handle the huge volume of traffic. Destroyer* JOUETT *(Commander J. C. Parham, Jr.) was used as the operational flagship of Captain Clay.*

From the foregoing it can be rightfully deduced that the destroyermen who participated in the invasion of Southern France had their work cut out for

Preparations for Operation Anvil: Destroyers rendezvous at a port in Southern Italy with other ships of the task force assembled for the invasion of Southern France. Forty-seven American destroyers and eight American destroyer-escorts assisted the American Seventh Army and Free French assault troops on three beachheads east of Toulon. Allied shipping totalled 880 units.

An American destroyer and the French cruiser Georges Leygues are bracketed by Nazi salvos during the Allied naval bombardment of Toulon. Gunfire support had earned the respect of the Nazis in Sicily and again at Salerno. Once more warship barrages hastened the success of the Allied forces. DD diversionary attacks had diverted the Nazi attention from the true landing area.

A destroyer lays a protective smoke screen for U.S.S. Quincy while the cruiser fires by radar control at the Nazi defences in Toulon. British, French, and Greek ships were numbered among those participating in Operation Anvil.

A human torpedo like the ones sunk by Ludlow and Madison. Madison holds the record with four kills and one probable. Some pilots were captured.

Luckily, it was a dud! When Endicott was hit by a dud shell from a Nazi corvette, one of her crew carried the live shell topside and heaved it overboard. The hit didn't put the destroyer out of action. See page 377 for details.

Some units of Italy's fleet which surrendered at Taranto. Midget and sea-going subs (top), and midget sub, MAS boat, and destroyers (bottom).

U. S. DESTROYERS AND DESTROYER-ESCORTS
participating in
"ANVIL"

DESTROYERS

Jouett	McCook	Rodman	Champlin
Plunkett	Baldwin	Emmons	Nields
Benson	Harding	Macomb	Ordronaux
Niblack	Satterlee	Forrest	Woolsey
Madison	Thompson	Fitch	Ludlow
Hilary P. Jones	Livermore	Hobson	Edison
C. F. Hughes	Eberle	Parker	Somers
Frankford	Kearny	Kendrick	Gleaves
Endicott	Ericsson	MacKenzie	Murphy
Carmick	Ellyson	McLanahan	Jeffers
Doyle	Hambleton	Boyle	Butler

Gherardi   Herndon   Shubrick

DESTROYER-ESCORTS

Tatum	Runels	Marsh	F. C. Davis
Haines	Hollis	Currier	H. C. Jones

them. Only the highlights of their effort can be recounted herewith.

Destroyers Versus Nazi Corvettes (Including a Dramatic Diversion)

The "Anvil" landings were scheduled for 0830, D-Day morning. All through the night of August 14-15 the Allied invasion ships were closing in on the French Riviera. Three main target beaches were located near the resort towns of St. Tropez, St. Maxime, and St. Raphael. Meantime, action developed on the flanks of the target area where, on the one hand, enemy surface craft were unexpectedly encountered, and on the other, a diversion was intentionally created.

A few miles south of Port Cross and Levant Islands, destroyer Somers (Commander W. C. Hughes, Jr.) was conducting a patrol, on the lookout for enemy submarines and surface craft. She was also on duty as a fire-support ship for an advance force which had gone ashore on the Isles d'Hyeres and on the mainland near Toulon. These troops went in at 0130. But H-Hour for "Anvil" was set for 0830, and Somers would have preferred to hold her fire until that time, lest a premature blast awaken the Nazi defenses and ruin the chances for a tactical surprise.

In consequence Commander Hughes had a knotty problem on his hands when the radar watch, at 0347, reported two unidentified ships in the offing. Hoping they were friendly PT-boats known to be somewhere in the area, Hughes decided to track the "unknowns" at a distance, maintaining position to intercept should they turn toward the target beaches where invasion shipping was located.

At 0430 the vessels were heading in a direction which promised trouble. Hughes ordered Somers forward to close the range, and at 0440 the destroyer challenged with signals flashed from her 12-inch searchlight. No answer. Making a showdown decision, Hughes ordered Somers' gunners to open fire. A full salvo caught the first jaywalker with a solid hit. The gunners then shifted fire to the second vessel, the larger of the two, and broke it in half with a smashing fusillade.

Fire was then concentrated on Vessel No. 1. In a short time the ship was dead in the water, blazing. As the enemy crew abandoned, Commander Hughes sent a party across the water to board the burning hulk. The Somers men made a rapid and efficient search, and got off just in time. Three minutes after they left the deck, the flaming derelict sank.

The vessels summarily demolished by destroyer Somers were the German corvettes Camoscio and Escaburt. After the shooting, the destroyermen

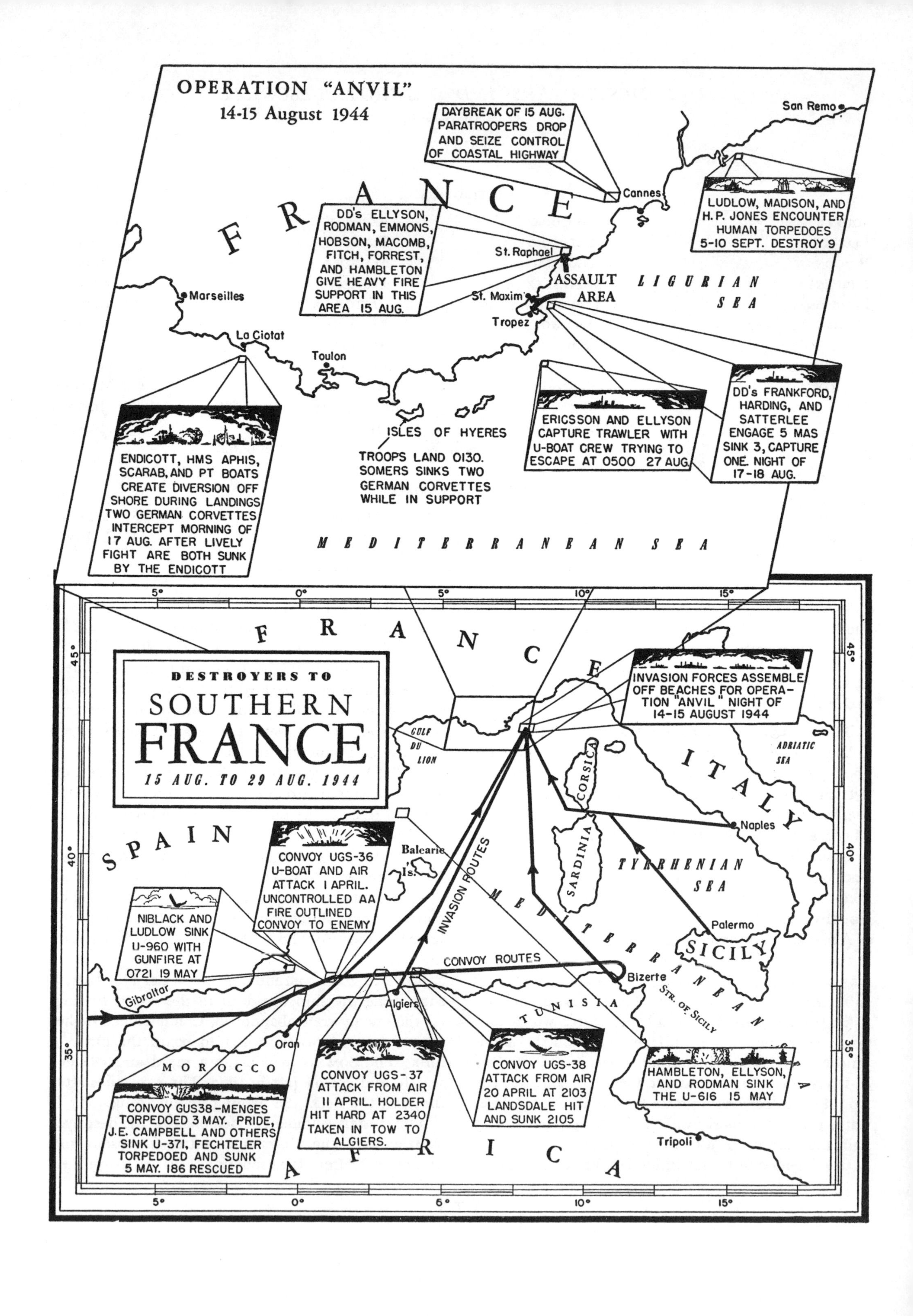

OPERATION "ANVIL"
14-15 August 1944
DAYBREAK OF 15 AUG. PARATROOPERS DROP AND SEIZE CONTROL OF COASTAL HIGHWAY
San Remo
Cannes
FRANCE
LUDLOW, MADISON, AND H.P. JONES ENCOUNTER HUMAN TORPEDOES 5-10 SEPT. DESTROY 9
DD's ELLYSON, RODMAN, EMMONS, HOBSON, MACOMB, FITCH, FORREST, AND HAMBLETON GIVE HEAVY FIRE SUPPORT IN THIS AREA 15 AUG.
St. Raphael
ASSAULT AREA
LIGURIAN SEA
Marseilles
St. Maxim
Tropez
La Ciotat
Toulon
ERICSSON AND ELLYSON CAPTURE TRAWLER WITH U-BOAT CREW TRYING TO ESCAPE AT 0500 27 AUG.
DD's FRANKFORD, HARDING, AND SATTERLEE ENGAGE 5 MAS SINK 3, CAPTURE ONE. NIGHT OF 17-18 AUG.
ISLES OF HYERES
TROOPS LAND 0130. SOMERS SINKS TWO GERMAN CORVETTES WHILE IN SUPPORT
ENDICOTT, HMS APHIS, SCARAB, AND PT BOATS CREATE DIVERSION OFF SHORE DURING LANDINGS TWO GERMAN CORVETTES INTERCEPT MORNING OF 17 AUG. AFTER LIVELY FIGHT ARE BOTH SUNK BY THE ENDICOTT
MEDITERRANEAN SEA
DESTROYERS TO SOUTHERN FRANCE
15 AUG. TO 29 AUG. 1944
FRANCE
INVASION FORCES ASSEMBLE OFF BEACHES FOR OPERATION "ANVIL" NIGHT OF 14-15 AUGUST 1944
GULF DU LION
ADRIATIC SEA
ITALY
CORSICA
SPAIN
Balearic Is.
SARDINIA
Naples
TYRRHENIAN SEA
CONVOY UGS-36 U-BOAT AND AIR ATTACK 1 APRIL. UNCONTROLLED AA FIRE OUTLINED CONVOY TO ENEMY
INVASION ROUTES
MEDITERRANEAN
NIBLACK AND LUDLOW SINK U-960 WITH GUNFIRE AT 0721 19 MAY
Palermo
SICILY
CONVOY ROUTES
Gibraltar
Algiers
Bizerte
STR. OF SICILY
TUNISIA
Oran
MOROCCO
CONVOY UGS-37 ATTACK FROM AIR 11 APRIL. HOLDER HIT HARD AT 2340 TAKEN IN TOW TO ALGIERS.
CONVOY UGS-38 ATTACK FROM AIR 20 APRIL AT 2103 LANDSDALE HIT AND SUNK 2105
HAMBLETON, ELLYSON, AND RODMAN SINK THE U-616 15 MAY
CONVOY GUS38-MENGES TORPEDOED 3 MAY. PRIDE, J.E. CAMPBELL AND OTHERS SINK U-371, FECHTELER TORPEDOED AND SUNK 5 MAY. 186 RESCUED
Tripoli
AFRICA

picked up 99 survivors. Perhaps more valuable than this haul were the charts and documents which the boarding party had obtained. If Commander Hughes had been worried about tangling with the two corvettes, his doubts were dispelled by Rear Admiral Davidson's endorsement of SOMERS' Action Report.

The decision to open fire and disclose the presence of Allied ships offshore was a difficult one to make. It is considered that the Commanding Officer of the SOMERS *took prompt and decisive action, displaying courage and initiative and sound reasoning, and that he conducted the action with outstanding professional skill. The accuracy and volume of fire from the* SOMERS *was overwhelming. The return fire from the* CAMOSCIO, *as viewed from the flagship, was of short duration.*

The boarding party under the command of Lieutenant (jg) Hamblen carried out their search of the CAMOSCIO *with diligence and thoroughness in the face of grave danger from the ship capsizing and exploding. The charts of cleared channels in local water secured by this party were of great immediate value to the Task Force Commander.*

While SOMERS was discreetly shooting troublesome corvettes, a United States destroyer and consorts a few miles west of Toulon were indulging in some purposely indiscreet gunnery. This destroyer was the U.S.S. ENDICOTT. In her company were British gunboats APHIS and SCARAB and several rambunctious PT-boats.

If silence and blackout were imposed on the "Anvil" forces waiting for H-Hour to the east, there were no such restraints to inhibit this little group to the west. Their mission called for an excursion in the coastal waters midway between Toulon and Marseilles, and when they reached a point off the beach at La Ciotat they were to create a five-alarm disturbance with no sounds barred.

The purpose of this naval charivari was, of course, to attract attention, rattle the local area command, and convince the enemy that landing forces were about to swarm ashore at this point. While this storm in a teacup was diverting the Nazis, the real hurricane would strike the Riviera to the eastward.

In over-all command was Captain H. C. Johnson of Rear Admiral Davidson's staff. Skippering destroyer ENDICOTT was Lieutenant Commander John D. Bulkeley, who had starred as a PT-boater in the Philippines. The two British gunboats were under command of another well-known star, Lieutenant Commander Douglas Fairbanks, Jr. Serving as Special Operations Officer on Admiral Hewitt's staff, Fairbanks had himself written the plan for the La Ciotat diversion. Now, on board H.M.S. APHIS, he was to act in the dynamic skit he had authored.

The group went in to raise a rumpus, and they raised it. As ENDICOTT and the gunboats smashed the quietude with a beach bombardment, the PT's raced shoreward in a frenzy, making all the motions of an assault.

The local reaction was immediate—wild volleys from startled sentinels, and a general view-halloo. To keep the pot boiling, ENDICOTT and her consorts moved in the following night to plaster the Ciotat beach with another barrage. But the enemy did not counterattack until early in the morning of the 17th, when two large Nazi corvettes arrived on the scene just as the "invaders" were retiring from the area. In the dusk before daybreak the British gunboats were intercepted, and there was nothing sham about the battle that ensued.

The corvettes were ugly specimens—an ex-Egyptian craft by name of KEMID ALLAH, and an ex-Italian, the CAPRIOLO. Both out-weighed the British gunboats, and the CAPRIOLO carried torpedo tubes and 4.7-inch guns.

The scrimmage promptly went against Fairbanks and his Britons. APHIS and SCARAB were outgunned to begin with, elderly to go on with, and low on ammunition to end with. Raked by shellfire, they fled southward. The corvettes chased. At 0545 the ENDICOTT received a call for help.

Bulkeley headed the destroyer for the scene of action at 35 knots, and soon began throwing salvos at KEMID ALLAH, the larger of the two enemy vessels.

ALLAH was fast, pugnacious, and fairly powerful. Still she would have been easy prey for ENDICOTT had the destroyer's main batteries been in working order. But only one 5-inch 38 was working. ENDICOTT's other three 5-inchers were out of kilter with jammed breech-blocks—casualties caused by over-heating from fast and furious fire during the simulated assault on La Ciotat.

There was also CAPRIOLO to be dealt with. Both corvettes hurled shells at ENDICOTT, and she dodged through numerous straddles. A dud drilled through her hull, whistled into a forward compartment, and set fire to some bedding. Shipfitter L. J. Ashe helped to plug the hole and smother the fire. Then he carried the live shell topside and tossed it overboard with his blessing.

But in spite of close shaves, dud-damage, and handicapped batteries, ENDICOTT pressed forward to close the range and keep the corvettes engaged. And early in the action a couple of ENDICOTT projectiles slammed into the ALLAH's engine-room, slowing that vessel to a crawl. The destroyer then shifted fire to

CAPRIOLO, the more dangerous of the two corvettes. By this time ENDICOTT's gunners had one or two of the other 5-inchers operating, and the moment a gun could function it was fired at the foe.

At 0648 the ex-Egyptian, slopping along with a port list, began to explode. The Nazi crew abandoned forthwith. CAPRIOLO now shot her bolt by firing two torpedoes at the ENDICOTT. As Bulkeley maneuvered his ship to avoid, two of the PT-boats, which had been screening ENDICOTT, dashed in to launch torpedoes at CAPRIOLO.

A blistering fire drove the PT's back, and their underwater shots missed the mark. Then ENDICOTT, at a range of 3,200 yards, fired two torpedoes which missed. It remained for gunboats SCARAB and APHIS to tag the ex-Italian with a telling punch. Fairbanks brought them back into the battle with guns blazing, and at 0700 one of them staggered CAPRIOLO with a direct hit.

The ALLAH sank at 0709. A few minutes later CAPRIOLO was foundering in a fiery shellstorm. Overside scrambled as many Nazis as could make it, and the vessel sank at 0830. The destroyermen picked up 169 prisoners; the gunboats grabbed 41.

As seen against the panoramic holocaust of the "Anvil" offensive, the corvette battles fought by SOMERS and the ENDICOTT group may seem like match-flare actions. But minor actions can be important.

As has been noted, the information obtained through the SOMERS exploit was of decided value to Rear Admiral Davidson's Support Force. And undoubtedly the sham assault on La Ciotat by ENDICOTT and company threw some of the Nazis off balance and helped to draw their attention from the real landings. Only at St. Raphael did the assault teams meet stiff opposition, and that was more or less impromptu.

The Nazis were certainly looking in the wrong direction when "Anvil" struck the beaches east of Toulon. It could be that they were watching the drama at La Ciotat—a British-American production directed by Henry C. Johnson, starring John D. Bulkeley and Douglas Fairbanks, Jr., with a cast of Royal Navy gunboat sailors, American PT boaters, and DesLant destroyermen.

DD's Versus MAS Torpedo-Boats, Schnellbooten, et Cetera

At daybreak of the 15th the "Anvil" assault forces were ready. In the earlier hours of that morning thousands of paratroopers had been dropped inland to seize the main coastal highway from Toulon to Cannes. By sunrise the target beaches were practically sealed off.

In many sectors the Germans, aware that reinforcements would not be forthcoming, took to their heels. In a few sectors, notably at St. Raphael, the defenders stood their ground. Then Army and carrier aircraft went to work, and the "Anvil" fire-support ships opened up.

Among the latter were destroyers ELLYSON, RODMAN, EMMONS, HOBSON, MACOMB, FITCH, FORREST, and HAMBLETON. Pillboxes, stone walls, cottages, villas, boathouses, yacht clubs, hotels—anything within range which might afford cover for a Nazi was lambasted with 5-inch and 40 mm. fire.

Meanwhile, the landings went steadily forward. Because the water off the Azure Coast is deep, the beach approaches could not be obstructed by such mine plants and underwater snares as blocked the shallows at "Utah" and "Omaha." But the pretty little harbors were infested with MAS torpedo boats, Nazi *Schnellbooten,* explosive boats, armed trawlers, and other virulent warcraft of peculiar ilk and kidney.

To destroyermen fell the job of sweeping up some of this naval ragtag and bobtail, the leftovers of the French and Italian fleets. But the Italian MAS torpedo boat and the German *Schnellboot,* Axis versions of the PT-boat, were fast, agile, and dangerous as all torpedo-carrying craft are dangerous. On the night of August 17-18 destroyers FRANKFORD, HARDING, CARMICK, and SATTERLEE had a brush with five of the MAS specimens. And FRANKFORD (Lieutenant Commander J. L. Semmes), flagship of Captain H. Sanders, ComDesRon 18, had a close shave.

Action began at 2324 when the destroyers, operating in the outer line of the beachhead screen, made radar contact with four MAS boats racing through the dark. HARDING (Commander G. G. Palmer) immediately gave chase. FRANKFORD joined the pursuit, leaving the other destroyers to maintain the screening line.

The chase ran through midnight, the MAS boats pairing off as they fled. The destroyers overhauled. As they closed the range, HARDING was skimmed by a machine-gun burst (no damage), and FRANKFORD was jolted by what was probably a dud torpedo. Dealing swift reprisal, HARDING blew up the first of her pair by gunfire, and rammed the second to the bottom. FRANKFORD shot the third MAS boat to fragments, and captured the fourth, which was in sinking condition.

Incidentally, while HARDING was about it, she came within an ace of ramming a Royal Air Force rescue-boat which accidentally became embroiled in the embroglio. Contacting this craft at close quarters, HARDING flashed a challenge, and the boat failed to answer. Taking her for another MAS specimen, the destroyer's skipper maneuvered to ram, and only at the last moment was friendly recognition established.

As it turned out, there was another MAS boat in the vicinity that night. But its presence in the area was of brief duration. It was spotted by destroyers CARMICK (Commander R. O. Beer) and SATTERLEE (Lieutenant Commander R. W. Leach). Shortly thereafter its existence was terminated by gunfire from these DD's.

However, MAS boats and other craft of the E-boat type remained a menace throughout the Riviera landings, and on the night of August 20-21, three Nazi *Schnellbooten* got loose and threatened to penetrate the area screen.

They were detected by destroyer CHARLES F. HUGHES (Lieutenant Commander "JC" G. Wilson), flagship of Commander V. Havard, Jr., ComDesDiv 14. Chasing these marauders, the destroyermen had to tie on the knots. Which is to say, the HUGHES sprinted at high speed. She sank one *Schnellboot* with gunfire, and damaged the other two, which were run aground and abandoned. The HUGHES was assisted in this chase by destroyers HILARY P. JONES, CHAMPLIN, and BOYLE, companions who blocked the sidelines to present the enemy's escape. The destroyer NIELDS later searched along the shore in an attempt to find and demolish the craft which had been beached. Even *Schnellbooten* which had been run aground could take up a destroyer's valuable time.

But an alert watch for these venomous nuisances paid off with something else on the night of August 26-27. On that night destroyer ERICSSON (Lieutenant Commander B. H. Meyer) was patrolling off the St. Tropez sector. At 0050 in the morning of the 27th she made a suspicious radar contact. Companion destroyer HAMBLETON fired starshells to illuminate the seascape, but ERICSSON could not see the target. However, it was sighted by destroyer ELLYSON, and this DD put on steam to track it down.

The craft was finally overhauled by both ERICSSON and ELLYSON. A few salvos from the destroyers brought an answering display of red Very stars from the target vessel, which turned out to be a fishing trawler. The craft surrendered readily as the destroyers closed in. As a ship it was not much of a prize, but it contained some very interesting fish.

On deck were four Nazi naval officers and 46 men, the entire crew of a U-boat. It seemed that this submarine, the U-230, had gone aground in the d'Hyeres Islands off Toulon the week before. Unable to budge the stranded sub, the crew had scuttled her, then abandoned in rubber boats. They were trying to sneak out of Toulon in the trawler when captured.

MAS boats and *Schnellbooten* continued to plague the "Anvil" invasion fleet, and while destroyers chased these pests around, another type showed up. This was the explosive boat—a shallow-draught racer about 18 feet long, with a 5-foot beam, carrying a 500-pound explosive charge. The boat had twin screws, no rudder, and a cockpit where the operator crouched over his instruments. He would drive the craft at top speed toward a target, then drop overside on a life raft as the boat rushed in to strike. A contact charge would sink the boat when it hit the mark, and an exploder device touched off the main charge four seconds later when the boat was a few feet under.

Destroyers GLEAVES (Lieutenant Commander W. M. Klee), while patrolling off the Italian Riviera between San Remo and Oneglia, encountered a trio of these barracuda-like craft. About 0327 in the morning of October 2, the destroyer's lookouts sighted a wake approaching from the port bow. It looked like a torpedo. Then, as Lieutenant Commander Klee took the conn and the destroyer swung to avoid, the wake passed clear astern, and a second wake—clearly that of a racing boat—came foaming in on the starboard beam.

The starboard battery was brought to bear, and a K-gun was fired. The depth charge boomed in the water ahead of the boat; the gunners riddled the craft; and the boat vanished in a blurt of flame.

Within the next ten minutes, two more explosive boats were sighted on the ship's port bow. One passed about 300 yards astern, and one zipped down the port side, no more than 50 feet away. Making hairpin turns, the two boats took position on either side of GLEAVES' wake and came racing along at the destroyer's heels. As they appeared to be gaining, Lieutenant Commander Klee called for top speed. An "ashcan" was rolled from the rack, and a K-gun was fired. The first charge failed to detonate, but the second blew the pursuing boats into matchwood.

After daylight GLEAVES returned to the vicinity of this water carnival and picked up two of the explosive-boat operators. She also captured an undamaged explosive boat, gingerly picking up this novelty with her davits and stowing it on deck as Exhibit A for future examination. The captive operators were much chagrined at having failed to hit the destroyer.

Another and even more dangerous naval novelty made its appearance off the Riviera early in September. As a destroyer officer put it, "This was one for the book!" Certainly it was one for a destroyer history. It was the "Human Torpedo!"

Destroyers Versus Human Torpedoes

What induces a man to become a human torpedo?

The question is not entirely academic, for this suicidal stunt was of more than passing interest to the Navy when the performance was staged during "Operation Anvil."

Was it a desperate measure of bankrupt defense forces turning to last resorts? Or was it the manifestation of a bankrupt Nazidom indulging the psychology of *Götterdammerung?*

In any event the German twilight had set in, and out of this twilight came the human torpedo. One of the earliest encounters with these fantastic freaks involved the American destroyer Ludlow (Lieutenant Commander W. R. Barnes).

On the morning of September 5, 1944, Ludlow and the French light cruiser Le Malin were patrolling off Cape Forrat near Monte Carlo. Operating as a fire-support group, the two warships were waiting for calls from shore fire-control parties advancing with American troops along the Riviera toward Menton.

Then, about 0810, a lookout on board Le Malin spied a queer-looking object rippling along through the sun-glazed water. An object that looked incredibly like a bubble containing a human head.

The captain of Le Malin fixed fascinated binoculars on the object. The thing was now about 1,200 yards away, moving through the water at 6 or 7 knots, and leaving a thin, lacy wake. *"It was,"* stated Captain Ballande, *"a glass—or plexiglass—dome, about 20 inches long and 20 inches high. . . . We identified this object as the lookout station of a human torpedo."*

The French light cruiser was of a type classified as an anti-torpedo-boat ship, but the target in focus was not common to her experience. Le Malin immediately treated it to 20 mm. and 40 mm. fire. Captain Ballande's statement continues: *"With my binoculars I could see very distinctly the head of the pilot in the torpedo when the splashes did not conceal the glass dome. At 0819 the dome of the human torpedo slowly settled in the water. No hits were observed."*

Meanwhile, word had been passed to Ludlow over the TBS, and the destroyer now made a high-speed run to drop depth charges on the spot where the weird target had submerged. The water was still booming when lookouts sighted a man swimming about a half mile away. Ludlow sidled over and picked up Seaman Joseph Schwarz of the German Navy.

This capture was made at 0830. And while the Nazi was being hoisted from the sea, Le Malin reported more human torpedoes in the vicinity. At 0848 Ludlow's lookouts sighted one dead ahead. The thing was crossing Ludlow's bow, and Lieutenant Commander Barnes ordered full speed ahead for a depth-charge attack. The target sank, then reappeared in the form of a swimmer who seemed anxious to get out of the way when the destroyermen, aiming to detonate any near-by underwater weapon, fired a depth-charge salvo at 300 yards range. At this the swimmer wildly waved his arms in signal of surrender.

While Ludlow was stopping to capture this second torpedo-pilot, a third human torpedo was spotted some 2,500 yards ahead. As French cruiser Le Malin was in line of fire beyond the target, Ludlow's gunners were deprived of a chance to sharpshoot, and the destroyer once more dashed forward to attack with depth charges.

As the range closed, the glass "bubble" could be plainly seen. And so could the occupant, who was making frantic efforts to extricate himself from this transparent trap. When the destroyer was about 500 yards away, the torpedo-pilot managed to break out of the plexiglass dome and get clear. The torpedo's tail jutted out of the water, then the thing sank harmlessly as the pilot shouted for rescue. He was picked up as a prize by cruiser Le Malin.

According to the captured pilots, the specimens downed by Ludlow and Le Malin were human torpedoes of the "one man" type. Evidently some of the breed had two heads. It may have been one of these two-headed specimens that Hilary P. Jones demolished off Menton on September 10. Because the torpedo was submerged when spotted, and the human element was killed, the make-up of the thing was hard to determine.

There were about a dozen human torpedoes operating in the area that morning. Working as a fire-support ship for Army forces ashore, the Jones could not devote immediate attention to these Nazi freaks. She was in the firing area shooting at shore targets, and her gunners were hard at it when a shore fire-control party reported a midget submarine off the Menton breakwater.

A PT-boat was sent to deal with this trouble-maker, but the PT crew could not locate the sub. They did, however, sight and chase a human torpedo. And apparently they chased it toward Hilary P. Jones. For as soon as her firing mission was over, Jones received word from the shore fire-control party that an underwater target was now in her vicinity.

The destroyer's lookouts could see nothing. But the shore fire-control party, perched on the side of a mountain, could see the object clearly. As directed by the spotter ashore, Jones' skipper, Lieutenant Commander F. M. Stiesberg, maneuvered the destroyer to close the range.

The destroyermen were still unable to see the target, but with information from the spotter ashore they opened fire. After two spots from the men on the mountainside, the human torpedo appeared on the surface, and direct fire was opened on the target. The salvos must have hit the glassy bull's-eye, for the torpedo disappeared, leaving in its wake a swimming survivor, who headed for the beach. He never made it. JONES fired a final salvo to finish off the torpedo, and it finished off the "human," as well.

The shooting off Menton was unique in respect to both target and gunnery. The human torpedo may have been a larger-than-usual specimen. And this was probably the first time in history that a warship fired on a sea-going target while a fire-control party ashore called the shots.

But the Nemesis of the human torpedoes that day was destroyer MADISON (Commander D. A. Stuart). Operating off Cape Martin in the Menton area, she ran into a school of these queer fish. The first was sighted at 0718. The fish-eye globe was only 500 yards distant, and Commander Stuart directed speedy maneuvering to avoid. Then MADISON's gunners sprayed 40 mm. and 20 mm. fire at the target. A nearby PT-boat simultaneously shot at the glass dome. The torpedo went under, and the PT-boat captured the half-drowned operator.

At 0743 a scouting plane from the cruiser BROOKLYN sighted another human torpedo south of Cape Martin. MADISON and the PT-boat raced to the spot. Gunfire from the PT and depth charges from MADISON disposed of this item.

An hour or so later, while MADISON was delivering a shore bombardment, a third human torpedo was sighted. At 0900 MADISON opened fire at about five-mile range. Two salvos were seen to straddle. The target disappeared, and was scored as a "probable."

Eight minutes after that, another of these contrivances showed up on the seascape. MADISON attacked with depth charges and gunfire, sank the torpedo, and picked up the injured pilot.

She nailed a fifth human torpedo shortly after noon, having sighted the "bubble" some 1,000 yards distant to starboard. A few 5-inch salvos and a couple of depth charges put an end to the affair.

With four certains and a probable on her record, MADISON was the champion human-torpedo shooter of the "Anvil" destroyer fleet. And after her field-day performance, the torpedo-pilots evidently gave up trying to die for Hitler the hard way.

The human torpedoes were menacing enough, and their freakish effort could not be discounted as one primarily designed for a spectacular display of *hari-kiri.* Potentially the torpedo contraption was dangerous. His head in a plexiglass cupola, the pilot crouched in a watertight housing or cabin astride the torpedo. Literally riding the torpedo, he could aim it, then detach it from the housing, and let it rip.

According to the captured operators, the torpedoes were electric, and left no wake. They could dive to 100 feet (if the pilot had the nerve), and in effect they were miniature midget submarines.

Still, the device was wholly impractical when used as a weapon against warships, as the Riviera demonstration revealed. Anchored shipping might have been vulnerable, if unprotected. Against a man-of-war the merman-torpedo had no chance.

The pilots complained that they couldn't aim the torpedoes at fast-moving targets. To aim at anything they had to get their glass domes above the surface, and a single machine-gun bullet could smash it.

The captured operators confessed to a fear of gunfire, but claimed they were unafraid of depth charges —an assertion hardly substantiated by their hasty surrenders when depth charges or shells were thrown.

There remains the question of what induces a man to become a human torpedo to begin with. Consider one of the characters captured by the U.S.S. LUDLOW. Hauled to the deck, he is seen as a young man wearing blouse and shorts, swimming shoes, life jacket, and some sort of rescue breather. On his thigh is the holster of a fine Luger pistol which he has readily surrendered along with himself. He is exhausted; dripping. But when presented to LUDLOW's Commanding Officer, he stands rigid, heels together, eyes front.

Name? He answers to the absolutely improbable name of Parsival Heller.

Rank? *"Steurmaun's Obergefreiter."*

Serial number? "W18894/42."

Other questions, too, he answers willingly enough—about the number of human torpedoes in the area; their make-up, speed, diving depth, and so on. His testimony contributes to the evidence that the German commanders were desperately using last-resort measures against the ships off the Riviera.

But as to why such characters volunteered for the duty—who knows?

"Girl trouble," a destroyer officer suggested. "I've heard that men used to join the French Foreign Legion because they were disappointed in love."

One could imagine a Parsival Heller admitting as much. "I became a Foreign Legionnaire because I was disappointed in love. *Und* I became a human torpedo because I was disappointed in the Foreign Legion."

Destroyers in "Anvil" Chorus (Featuring Madison and H. P. Jones)

The destroyers in "Operation Anvil" did not spend all or even a great part of their time chasing the corvettes, MAS boats, *Schnellbooten,* explosive boats, and human torpedoes that came rat-racing out of the Riviera waterfront. Covering the landings and the movements of the forces ashore, the fire-support DD's were particularly busy with shore bombardments.

MADISON, for example, was in on the siege of several of the coast towns. During one tour of duty which lasted from August 17 to September 25, she fired steadily in support of the Allied left and right flanks, expending 1,426 rounds of 5-inch 38 ammunition. In all she conducted 31 shore bombardment missions.

HAMBLETON, LUDLOW, ELLYSON, ERICSSON—these and other destroyers were similarly occupied during the invasion of Southern France. Perhaps one of the best examples of destroyer-work in an invasion operation comes from the industrious DD which was skippered by Lieutenant Commander F. M. Stiesberg. Here is a page from the war diary of the HILARY P. JONES.

During period 8-30 September, 1944, a total of 38 successful fire-support missions were fired for the First Airborne Task Force on targets as follows:

(a) Troops and gun positions.
(b) Flak wagon destroyed.
(c) Self-propelled gun destroyed.
(d) Ammunition dumps destroyed.
(e) German Headquarters badly damaged.
(f) Observation post, covered.
(g) Bridge cut.
(h) Bridge damaged.
(i) Vehicles destroyed.

In the same period, the following targets were engaged while standing by in fire-support area or during bombardments of St. Remo and Maurizio harbors:

(a) Coastal freighter, 200-foot—destroyed.
(b) Three "F" lighters loaded with ammunition destroyed.
(c) Three large MAS destroyed.
Nine small MAS destroyed.
Two MAS damaged.
(d) Tug damaged by direct hit.
(e) Two or three small motorboats destroyed.
(f) Four or five small scows destroyed.
(g) Explosive boat destroyed.
(h) Two human torpedoes destroyed.
(i) Midget sub accurately attacked, believed destroyed.
(j) Railroad car destroyed.
Two railroad cars damaged.
(k) Three vehicles destroyed.
(l) Two 88 mm. guns knocked out.
(m) Eight coastal or heavy flak batteries silenced.
(n) Three ammunition dumps blown up.
(o) Small power-house destroyed.
(p) Highway bridge cut.
(q) Tunnel blocked.
(r) Railroad cut retainer-wall destroyed.
(s) Large oil storage tank destroyed.
(t) Eight large fires on jetty and of combustible stores in harbor area.

Ammunition Expended: 3,450 AA Common; 80 Common; 22 Smoke; 11 Star—Total, 3,563 rounds.

It is clear the men in HILARY P. JONES were not sitting on their hands. Neither were any of the destroyermen who worked in "Operation Anvil."

Mediterranean Finale

Marseilles and Toulon were in Allied hands by August 29. Toulon furnished the Allies with a fine naval base, and the great seaport of Marseilles was the door to Southern France—a portal for troops and supplies which could go up the Rhone Valley, special delivery, to General Eisenhower.

Two weeks after the Riviera landings, the vanguard of General Patch's Seventh Army reached Lyons on the main line to Paris. Meantime, the French Forces of the Interior came out from underground and harried the retreating Nazis. The whole German defense system in South and Central France was crumbling. Even before the capture of Marseilles and Lyons, the French Partisans in Paris had risen to smite their would-be conquerors. On August 25 French troops under Major General Jacques Leclerc marched down the Champs Elysee, and the trapped Germans surrendered.

Along the eastern Riviera the scuffling would continue throughout the autumn. And in Northern Italy the Nazis would hang on. But the *Wehrmacht* had started its retreat for the Rhine. In the east the Russians were driving implacably forward; in the west Eisenhower's armies were smashing ahead; the "Thousand Year Reich" was doomed. For the Germans could no longer operate in the Mediterranean, and the whole southern frontier of their *Festung Europa* was exposed to invasion.

The American destroyers which had fought their way from North Africa to Southern France could now devote full time to the Atlantic where wolfpacks were still on the prowl. Doenitz was promising to launch a great *Schnorkel* offensive—as soon as he had enough *Schnorkels.*

But he never had enough. After the "Anvil" chorus boomed out, the U-boat effort in the Atlantic was a swan song.

ALBERT W. GRANT AT THE BATTLE OF SURIGAO

PART VI

DESTROYERS TO ASIA

Perhaps more valid Armes,
Weapons more violent when next we meet,
May serve to better us, and worse our foes,
Or equal what between us made the odds.
In Nature none: . . .

PARADISE LOST

CHAPTER 29

CENTRAL PACIFIC PUSH

(FROM THE GILBERTS TO SAIPAN)

DD's to the Gilberts (Battle for Tarawa)

While the destroyers of Burke, Moosbrugger, Simpson, and their contemporaries were chasing Japanese warships, *marus,* and barges out of the Upper Solomons, in the Central Pacific, Admiral Nimitz had decided that the time had come to excise the Gilbert Islands from the Japanese Empire.

It would not be the first time Pacific Fleet destroyers visited the Gilberts area. On October 22, 1942, destroyers LAMSON (Lieutenant Commander P. H. Fitzgerald), flagship of Commander L. A. Abercrombie, ComDesDiv 9, and MAHAN (Commander R. W. Simpson) had raided enemy shipping in that area.

The Gilberts raid of the two destroyers called for a deep penetration of enemy sea territory. Small in land area, the Gilberts are spread out over a Pacific expanse the size of Texas. Jap warships were at that time all over the lot. But the destroyer raiders struck boldly, shot accurately, and left behind them on the bottom a Jap schooner laden with gasoline, and the ex-Jap gunboat HAKKAISAN MARU, which had probably been fuelling the Emperor's submarines.

Endorsing Commander Abercrombie's Action Report, Admiral Halsey wrote: *"The subject raid was well planned and efficiently executed."*

Thereafter, American submarines took over the Gilbert blockade, and further surface action there waited on the development of the Fast Carrier Task Force. Outgrowth of the original carrier force of 1942 and early 1943, the Fast Carrier Task Force eventually included three or four task groups, with each group composed of some five aircraft carriers, several battleships, a half dozen cruisers, and about twenty destroyers.

By September, 1943, the Fast Carrier Task Force had matured and was ready for the invasion of the Gilberts. The operation was designated "Galvanic." Landings on Makin, Tarawa, and Apamama were scheduled for the morning of November 21. The first assault on strongly fortified enemy atolls in the Central Pacific, the "Galvanic" operation would employ a force of 118 warships and a large fleet of transports, supply ships, and auxiliary vessels. Invasion forces were placed under the command of Vice Admiral R. A. Spruance. The Assault Force was led by Rear Admiral R. K. Turner. The carriers were under Rear Admiral C. A. Pownall. Additional air support was furnished by Rear Admiral J. H. Hoover's shore-based air forces.

Altogether some 54 DesPac destroyers and six DE's served with the forces dispatched to the Gilberts. For the most part the destroyermen had little to do. At the southern end of the Gilbert group, Apamama fell easily into the hands of a small company of Marines landed on the beach by the submarine NAUTILUS and the destroyer GANSEVOORT (Lieutenant Commander J. M. Steinbeck). At the northern end Makin was swiftly taken. Tarawa, in the center, was tough—a porcupine of barbed wire entanglements, redoubts, pillboxes, and Japs who seemed immune to air bombs.

Tarawa is essentially the story of the Marines, and the details of their struggle on the beaches and amid the palms will be accorded heroic treatment in any history of land or amphibious warfare. For the most part the destroyers, after delivering the preliminary bombardment, played the role of bystanders. Two destroyers, however, were more prominently involved. They were RINGGOLD (Commander T. F. Conley, Jr.), flying the pennant of Commander H. Crommelin, ComDesDiv 50, and DASHIELL (Commander J. B. McLean). These ships composed Fire Support Section Four of Rear Admiral H. F. Kingman's Support Group operating with the Southern Attack Force under Rear Admiral H. W. Hill. On the night of October 19-20 RINGGOLD was sent ahead to locate a point on the approach course between the two atolls of Tarawa and Maiana.

Then, at 2100, RINGGOLD's radar, which had just picked up Tarawa, detected a surface target at seven miles range. On the radar screen the "pip" resembled nothing so much as an enemy patrol vessel. Over TBS Commander Conley reported the contact. After a similar report from several other ships, Admiral Hill gave RINGGOLD's skipper permission to open fire. Conley lined up the target and fired two "fish." One seems to have prematured. The other made a circular run. The target slowed down but kept on going.

Thereupon, the destroyermen opened up on the target with 5-inch. Cruiser SANTA FE joined the shooting. After nine minutes of gunnery the target disappeared. It looked like a "sunk," and the Task Force Commander signalled RINGGOLD a

WELL DONE

However, for submarine NAUTILUS (Commander W. D. Irwin) and 78 U.S. Marines, the shooting was not so good. The big V-boat had been on her way to Apamama with the Leathernecks, and somebody had failed either to send or to get the word. At any rate, Admiral Hill's Attack Force had not been advised of the submarine's presence in the waters between Tarawa and Maiana, and when RINGGOLD picked up NAUTILUS on her radar, she naturally identified her as "enemy."

Luckily the only hit scored on NAUTILUS was a 5-inch projectile that slammed into her conning tower and failed to explode. Also a near miss ruptured a water line as the NAUTILUS frantically submerged. But aside from these injuries and a bad case of nerves, the big transport submarine got away without serious trouble. But as one naval officer subsequently remarked, "It's better not to count on luck. It's safer to get the word!"

RINGGOLD herself was damaged when she entered Tarawa lagoon that morning about 0700 to support a pair of minesweepers which were working in-shore, and to lend fire support to assault troops. Accompanying RINGGOLD was destroyer DASHIELL. Jap shore batteries were flinging hot salvos at the minesweepers, and the two DD's opened up with a shattering return fire. At one point DASHIELL went so close to the beach that, as a sailor expressed it, the Japs could have hit her with rocks. Firing pointblank, the destroyers hurled a tremendous weight of ammunition at the enemy gun emplacements. RINGGOLD fired 1,755 rounds of 5-inch; DASHIELL fired 1,800 rounds. In return RINGGOLD was slashed by two 5-inch shells. One of them smashed into the after engine-room. As a stream of water shot into the compartment, Lieutenant W. A. Parker, ship's Engineer Officer, looked desperately for a plug to cork the hole. Finding none, he flung his shoulder into the breach, plugging the leak in this fashion until conventional material was rushed in.

The chief stumbling block at Tarawa was Betio Island at the southwest extremity of the atoll. Ultimately some 15,000 Marines were landed on this islet before the 3,000 Japs of the garrison could be rooted out. While the battle for Betio was going on, a Japanese torpedo-bomber broke through the AA barrage and stabbed three torpedoes into the light carrier INDEPENDENCE.

But all in all, the destroyer AA gunners had a relatively easy time of it. The hot fight was ashore, and the biggest menace to the Navy at Tarawa was the omnipresent threat of enemy submarines.

Frazier and Meade Sink I-35

Six Japanese I-boats, dispatched to the Gilberts, did not arrive in time to intercept the invasion forces, but two of them managed to get themselves intercepted.

In the afternoon of November 22, while screening the heavy units of a cruiser division about nine miles northwest of Betio, destroyer MEADE (Lieutenant Commander J. Munholland) put a "pinging" finger on an undersea target. MEADE's report brought destroyer FRAZIER (Commander E. M. Brown) on the run to join the hunt.

The destroyers jockeyed into attack position; the "ashcans" were sent rolling; patterned explosions thudded under the sea. The sub, when detected, was at shallow depth, and the blasting must have hampered her diving capacity. Up came a great swirl of oil which clogged the air with fumes. The DD's immediately deposited four more depth charges on the fringe of the oil slick.

Results were prompt. The sub came thrashing to the surface, and Japs scrambled out of the conning tower. Both destroyers opened fire as the I-boat broached. Pummeled by 5-inch and 40 mm. fire, the submarine pitched and rolled in a torment of TNT. Then FRAZIER raced in to ram. Like a ploughshare, the destroyer's bow sliced into the sub's pressure hull just aft of the conning tower. FRAZIER backed off, and the I-boat, with the sea pouring into its vitals, plunged to the bottom.

Two survivors, fished from the sea, identified the sunken sub as the I-35.

Radford Kills I-19

The submarine which had torpedoed WASP on September 15, 1942, and which may have been responsible for the torpedoing of NORTH CAROLINA on that same date, was the Imperial Navy's I-19. But this ship-killer met her match on the evening of November 25, 1943, when she surfaced in the waters off Tarawa. At that hour she ran into two hard-hitting Radfords—Rear Admiral A. W. Radford, Commander of Task Group 50.2, and destroyer RADFORD (Commander G. E. Griggs).

Rear Admiral Radford's group had just repelled a torpedo-plane attack when destroyer RADFORD's surface radar detected the killer sub. The time was 2049. The range was about eight miles. RADFORD, in the van, was ordered to peel off and do the investigating.

At 2130 the "pip" disappeared from the screen—meaning submarine. Ten minutes later RADFORD tagged the submerged target with her sonar gear, and her skipper conned the destroyer for seven runs over the target. Several of the runs were "dry," but enough of them were of the type which liquidates submarines. Down went the "ashcans" and up came the rubbish. The destroyermen smelled Diesel oil for the rest of the night, and an expansive oil slick was sighted. The following morning, aircraft noted a great strew of flotsam which included wood, cork, and various indefinable remnants of submarining.

A post-war examination of Japanese records disclosed the number of RADFORD's victim—I-19. This was RADFORD's second submarine kill of the year, her first being RO-101. And the kill came just in time to offset somewhat a staggering smash dealt the Navy by an I-boat on the previous day. That smash had sent to the bottom the escort-carrier LISCOME BAY.

"Galvanic" Conclusion (Liscome Bay Lost; Gilberts Won)

About 0505 in the morning of November 23, a submarine alarm sent the crew of Rear Admiral H. M. Mullinix's flagship, the "jeep carrier" LISCOME BAY, to General Quarters. Steaming with her in formation were carriers CORAL SEA and CORREGIDOR, battleships NEW MEXICO and MISSISSIPPI, cruiser BALTIMORE, and screen destroyers FRANKS, HUGHES, MORRIS, MAURY, GRIDLEY, and HULL. The ships were members of Rear Admiral Turner's Northern Attack Force, and when the submarine alarm clanged in the early morning dark they were about 20 miles off Makin Island.

Ordered to investigate the contact, a destroyer sliced away from the formation and raced off through the gray darkness. The other DD's strained their electronic eyes and ears in an effort to detect the intruder. But the sub was already within striking distance. A luminous wake streaked the water near LISCOME BAY. Someone shouted, "Torpedo!" The carrier was given no time to dodge. In a matter of seconds the "Long Lance" torpedo with its souped-up war head struck home, sending a wave of flame leaping through the vessel's interior. With a sea-quaking roar the carrier's top blew off. A pillar of fire shot a thousand feet in the air. Debris landed on ships over a half-mile away. Twenty-five minutes later LISCOME BAY lurched over on her beam and sank in a sea of blazing oil. Of the thousand officers and men who had manned her, some 650 perished with the ship; with one blow the enemy sub had killed almost as many Americans as were slain in the battle for Tarawa beachhead. Lost with the ship were Admiral Mullinix and her skipper, Captain I. D. Wiltsie.

The LISCOME BAY sinking was a stunner to the Navy. But not until the spring of 1945 would the Imperial subs sink another major American warship.

The capture of the Gilbert Islands marked the Navy's first move in an all-out offensive that was to take the Allied forces through the Marshalls to the Carolines and Marianas, through the Southwest Pacific to the Philippines, through Japan's inner defense line to the heart of Tokyo Bay. As Admiral Spruance stated in a post-war address made in London, England:

"The Gilberts operation was important to us in that our plans for it established, basically, the organization and the pattern that were used thereafter as a basis for future operations in the Central Pacific. Our task organization gave us: a Fast Carrier Force; a Joint Expeditionary Force; and a force which had the operational control of the shore-based aircraft and shore bases within the area of operations and of the Mobile Service Squadron which was to furnish our advanced base logistic support."

The destroyers and destroyer-escorts which served with the "Galvanic" forces are listed on the following page.

DD's to the Marshalls ("Operation Flintlock")

Lying north of the Gilberts, the Marshalls are

DESTROYERS AND DESTROYER-ESCORTS IN THE GILBERT ISLANDS OPERATION

MUSTIN	HUGHES	BAILEY	LAVALLETTE
KIMBERLY	DALE	FRAZIER	NICHOLAS
BURNS	CALDWELL	GANSEVOORT	TAYLOR
DEWEY	BANCROFT	MEADE	BOYD
HULL	COGHLAN	ANDERSON	BRADFORD
MAURY	JOHN RODGERS	RUSSELL	BROWN
GRIDLEY	SIGSBEE	RINGGOLD	FLETCHER
PHELPS	HEERMANN	DASHIELL	RADFORD
MACDONOUGH	HAZELWOOD	SCHROEDER	JENKINS
MORRIS	HARRISON	IZARD	BULLARD
HOEL	MCKEE	CHARRETTE	KIDD
FRANKS	MURRAY	CONNER	CHAUNCEY

ERBEN	STACK	WILSON
HALE	STERETT	EDWARDS

DESTROYER-ESCORTS

WHITMAN	LEHARDY	CHAS. R. GREER
WILEMAN	W. C. MILLER	H. C. THOMAS

sprinkled across a vast area of ocean. This expanse of Pacific water gave Spruance's fleet plenty of elbow room for maneuvering, and it afforded Nimitz a number of choices when it came to selecting a channel for invasion and a target for attack. Conversely, it gave the Japanese an enormous "frontier" for defense. They were faced with this problem: If they stretched their defenses to cover the area's perimeter, they would only have a smattering of strength at any point. If they concentrated at one point within the area, they would leave immense gaps in the perimeter. They chose to concentrate.

Original plans for "Operation Flintlock"—the seizure and occupation of the Marshalls—had called for assault on the eastern atolls. But after the Gilberts capture Nimitz decided to by-pass Wotje, Maloelap, Jaluit, and Mille and strike straight for Kwajalein, the western stronghold. He assumed such a blow would take the Japs by surprise. And his assumption, based on sound information, was right.

The Kwajalein assault was scheduled for February 1, 1944. During January the Marshall approaches were probed, reconnoitered, photographed, and thoroughly studied by the usual pre-invasion methods. At Pearl Harbor forces were massed, sharpened up, and loaded up for the Kwajalein attack. By the last week in January Spruance's Fifth Fleet, weighing in at something like two million ship-tons, was assembled in the Marshall-Gilberts area. The fleet, designated Task Force 50, included six task forces. Carrying 84,000 expeditionary troops, Rear Admiral Turner's force contained about 300 ships. Fast Carrier Force 58, under Rear Admiral Marc Mitscher, was composed of six large carriers, five light carriers, eight battleships, six cruisers, and 36 destroyers. The other task forces were similarly powerful.

For 48 hours preceeding D-Day, Mitscher's aircraft and Spruance's battlewagons treated Kwajalein and neighboring atolls to a tremendous bombing and bombardment. In the meantime the defenders were thrown off base by a divisionary strike at Wotje. The Wotje bombardment, dealt on January 30, was delivered by a task group under Rear Admiral J. B. Oldendorf. Oldendorf's group included cruisers LOUISVILLE (flagship), SANTA FE, MOBILE, BILOXI, and six destroyers. The destroyers were MORRIS (Commander G. L. Caswell), flagship of Captain E. A. Solomons, ComDesRon 2, ANDERSON, HUGHES, FLETCHER, MUSTIN, and RUSSELL.

At 0630 the group, steaming along the eastern coast of Wotje, opened fire at 8,000-9,000 yards range. As the group came abeam of the island's center, Jap shore batteries roared at the leading destroyers—flag destroyer MORRIS and ANDERSON (Commander J. G. Tennent, III). The first Jap salvos were on in deflection but short by some 200 yards. As the column maneuvered to open the range, a heavy shell smashed into the ANDERSON's Combat Information Center. The explosion wrecked the radar installation and killed Commander Tennent, two other officers, and three men. Fourteen of the C.I.C. team and crews at near-by stations were wounded. Immediately taking command of the destroyer, Lieutenant G. E. Alexander, U.S.N.R., kept her firing. Captain Solomons reported:

> *His excellent performance of duty in this critical situation . . . is to be commended. The U.S.S.* ANDERSON *. . . was an outstanding ship of DesRon 2.* ANDERSON *could be depended upon to carry out any assigned mission with assurance that it would be well done.*

Oldendorf's ships continued to shell the island until noon. Shore batteries were silenced and at least two ammunition dumps were sent up in smoke. And while this was going on, Kwajalein was receiving what came to be called a "Spruance haircut." The atoll was literally flattened to copra pulp. Not a palm tree was left standing. About three-fourths of the 8,600 Japs who manned the garrison were piled up with the cord wood. The island *"looked as if it had been picked up to 20,000 feet in the air and dropped"* —so it was described by an officer who inspected the bombardment's handiwork.

Not all of the shots fired during this phase of the Kwajalein assault were aimed at the atoll. On January 29 the destroyer BURNS (Commander D. T. Eller) was ordered to leave formation and pick up three aviators reported adrift in the area. About three hours later she had the grateful flyers stowed safely aboard. After a badly injured airman was transferred to battleship SOUTH DAKOTA, the DD steamed off to rejoin her group screening Task Group 58.3 some 85 miles southwest of Kwajalein.

At 0025 in the morning of the 30th, BURNS' radar registered contact with a suspicious vessel about 21,000 yards distant. The "pip" divided into two blobs as she closed the range. At 0107 Commander Eller hailed the targets over TBS. When the answer came in a blank of silence, the destroyer opened fire at 9,000 yards. As she was shooting at the invisible ships, her radar picked up several other targets. The destroyer's gunnery started some large bonfires in the night. At 0151 two burning vessels were in view. Apparently the *marus* constituted a convoy which the Japs had neglected to screen. Circling about, BURNS swept the water with a searchlight. Oil and wreckage were sighted, as was a freighter which burned to the water and a tanker which flamed like a torch.

The following day destroyer HARRISON (Commander C. M. Dalton), operating with the Southern Fire Support Group, was screening to seaward of SAN FRANCISCO when the latter ordered her to intercept and destroy a Jap tanker which was trying to escape from Gugegive Island lagoon. At 0853 the DD had her guns trained on the fugitive. At 0933 the tanker was afire and sinking.

The islets of Kwajalein Atoll form a loose loop about a lagoon whose entrance on the north is guarded by the islets of Roi and Namur. Early in the morning of January 31, Task Force 53 was prying open the channel between these islands. Off nearby Ennuebing Island stood destroyer PHELPS (Lieutenant Commander D. L. Martineau), serving as a fire-support ship and senior control boat at the line of departure for landing craft going in. While acting in this capacity she lobbed shells at Jap guns on Roi.

H-Hour was set for 0900. Choppy seas delayed the landings for half an hour; then, supporting minesweepers, PHELPS entered the lagoon through Mellu Pass. Just before dark several of the atolls were assaulted and captured. Roi and Namur were bombarded all night long. Inside the lagoon the PHELPS was joined by the LAVALLETTE (Lieutenant Commander R. L. Taylor), and both vessels remained at anchor throughout the night to lend fire support and assistance to landing craft maneuvering in the lagoon. They had ringside seats (in the middle of the ring) to one of the war's most devastating bombardments. Admiral Nimitz observed that it *"exceeded in duration and intensity anything previously known to warfare except possibly that at Verdun in World War I."*

Both Roi and Namur were secured by Marines before the evening of February 3. Kwajalein was declared secured by the 5th. Of the thousands of American troops put ashore, only 368 were killed. About 150 Japs survived the "Spruance haircut" and the Marine and Army massage. And PHELPS, when she entered Kwajalein lagoon, had been the first Allied vessel to drop the hook in Japanese territorial water since the war's beginning.

Walker Kills RO-39

While Kwajalein was being blown out of the Japanese Empire, Task Unit 50.15.2 was operating in the eastern Marshalls, hammering Jap airfields on Wotje and Taroa. Working as a screen for SALT LAKE CITY were destroyers ABBOT and WALKER. The ships concluded a shelling of Wotje at 0327 in the morning of February 2, 1944. At 0418 WALKER's radar picked up a surface target at 13,300 yards range. Her skipper, Commander H. E. Townsend, closed the range to 6,000 and ordered a starshell spread. Silhouetted in the eerie light was the conning tower of a Jap submarine.

The sub dived before WALKER's gunners could open fire. But the sonar crew had the contact directly at 2,500 yards. Townsend conned the ship for a depth-

DESTROYERS AND DESTROYER-ESCORTS IN THE MARSHALL ISLANDS OPERATION

BLACK	STEPHEN POTTER	DUNLAP	DALE
BULLARD	HICKOX	FANNING	LAVALLETTE
KIDD	HUNT	CASE	AYLWIN
CHAUNCEY	LEWIS HANCOCK	CUMMINGS	JOHN RODGERS
WALKER	LANG	REMEY	HAZELWOOD
ABBOTT	STERETT	MACDONOUGH	HAGGARD
ERBEN	STACK	HUGHES	FRANKS
HALE	IZARD	ELLET	SCHROEDER
C. K. BRONSON	CHARRETTE	FLETCHER	HAILEY
COTTEN	CONNER	MORRIS	MCKEE
DORTCH	BELL	ANDERSON	STEVENS
GATLING	BURNS	MUSTIN	BAILEY
HEALY	BRADFORD	RUSSELL	FRAZIER
COGSWELL	BROWN	PORTERFIELD	MEADE
KNAPP	COWELL	HARADEN	COLAHAN
CAPERTON	WILSON	JOHNSTON	MURRAY
INGERSOLL	MAURY	HOPEWELL	HARRISON
OWEN	CRAVEN	PHELPS	RINGGOLD
MILLER	GRIDLEY	FARRAGUT	SIGSBEE
THE SULLIVANS	MCCALL	MONAGHAN	BANCROFT

COGHLAN CALDWELL HALLIGAN

DESTROYER-ESCORTS

GREINER LOVERING SANDERS

charge run. Five charges were dropped. The ship circled off, maneuvering to start a second run. A second was unnecessary. Under the sea there was a clap of thunder that trailed off into the valleys of the deep. After the thunder ebbed away, sonar contact could not be regained.

WALKER searched the area, and her lookouts sighted a large carpet of oil on the water. Ordinarily a destroyer did not sink an ocean-going submarine with a single depth-charge run, but WALKER's was the exceptional performance that proved the rule. After the war the sunken sub was located in the records of the Japanese Sixth (Submarine) Fleet. She was the RO-39.

Charrette and Fair Down I-21

The Japanese submarine I-21 had an interesting, and to the Jap point of view, distinguished career. She was in the vanguard of Vice Admiral Nagumo's Striking Force at Pearl Harbor. And she was the sub which probably sank the destroyer PORTER during the Battle of the Santa Cruz Islands. But her own destiny overtook her on February 4, 1944.

On that date destroyer CHARRETTE (Commander E. S. Karpe) was operating with Rear Admiral F. C. Sherman's Task Group 58.3 (built around the carriers BUNKER HILL, MONTEREY, and COWPENS). At 2203 in the evening of the 3rd, battleship NEW JERSEY reported radar contact with an enemy vessel 21 miles distant. CHARRETTE was ordered to leave her station in the Sound screen and track down the target. The "pip" disappeared at 10,300 yards.

At 0003 in the morning of February 4 the destroyer put a "pinging" finger on the sub. Running in, CHARRETTE dropped an 8-charge pattern. She followed through with several approaches, but lost sonar contact as the sub scuttled away and went deep. Commander Karpe reported a conviction that the sub was damaged, and destroyer-escort FAIR (Lieutenant Commander D. S. Crocker, U.S.N.R.) was sent to the scene to aid the hunt.

The DD and the DE worked like a long-practiced team. Nine minutes after FAIR reported for duty, CHARRETTE coached her into position for a hedgehog attack. The DE let fly at 0040. The projectiles splashed in the sea, and a moment later four detonations were counted. These hits were followed by a roulade of exposions which signalled the farewell of the enemy submersible. About three minutes after the hedgehog salvo, the roulade was concluded by a deep-sea thunderclap. The war had caught up with I-21.

The destroyermen were, of course, unaware of their victim's identity. Behind her she left nothing but an oil slick and a smell of Diesel. But her obituary was written in the records of the Japanese Submarine Force. CHARRETTE and FAIR had settled an old score.

Taking the Tuck Out of Truk

By now Admiral Mineichi Koga, in Truk, was alarmed. He had been uneasy ever since his promotion to Imperial Navy Commander-in-Chief as replacement for Admiral Yamamoto. Disaster in the Solomons. Disaster in the Gilberts. Disaster in the Bismarck Archipelago. And now disaster at Kwajalein.

Perhaps better than any other personage alive, Koga realized that Truk was an illusion, a hollow shell, a Gibraltar built on sand. For two years this island bastion had fooled the Allies, but Truk had never been and never would be able to live up to its reputation as a mid-Pacific stronghold. Now that the U.S. Navy was approaching, the mirage was about to be literally exploded.

Sweating on the bridge of his flagship MUSHASHI, Koga pulled out of Truk on February 4, and set a course for Tokyo. Out of Truk ahead of him had gone the carriers of Admiral Jisaburo Ozawa on the run for Singapore. Trailing Ozawa went Kurita with the Japanese Second Fleet, all hands eager to reach the relative safety of the Pelews. This general retirement beat an American attack that battered Truk into another Kwajalein.

The attack was delivered by Task Force 58 in mid-February. Admiral Mitscher's hellcats and succeeding waves of Navy bombers and torpedo-planes caught a mess of *marus* in the Truk lagoon. It was like dropping rocks on a basket of eggs. A number of fugitive ships, including the light cruiser NAKA, were nailed outside the "fortress" by carrier planes.

While Truk was being blasted from the air, a striking force personally led by Vice Admiral Spruance swept counter-clockwise around the island to trap escaping ships. Spruance's force was composed of the new battleships NEW JERSEY and IOWA, heavy cruisers MINNEAPOLIS and NEW ORLEANS, and four destroyers. The destroyers were IZARD (Lieutenant Commander E. K. Van Swearingen), flagship of Captain C. F. Espe, ComDesRon 46; CHARRETTE (Commander E. S. Karpe); BRADFORD (Lieutenant Commander R. L. Morris; and BURNS (Commander D. T. Eller).

In the afternoon of February 16, Spruance's force sighted a group of three ships northwest of North Pass. Simultaneously a Japanese destroyer was glimpsed on the horizon.

DESTROYERS WITH

TASK FORCE 58

JANUARY-FEBRUARY, 1944

TG 58.1

C. K. BRONSON
Flagship

COTTEN	COGSWELL
DORTCH	CAPERTON
GATLING	KNAPP
HEALY	INGERSOLL

TG 58.2

OWEN
Flagship

MILLER	LEWIS HANCOCK
THE SULLIVANS	LANG
STEPHEN POTTER	STERETT
HICKOX	STACK

HUNT

TG 58.3

IZARD
Flagship

CHARRETTE	BRADFORD
CONNER	BROWN
BELL	COWELL
BURNS	WILSON

TG 58.4

MAURY
Flagship

CRAVEN	DUNLAP
GRIDLEY	FANNING
MCCALL	CASE

CUMMINGS

A small freighter which was lying dead in the water was the first target attacked. With shells eating into her, the freighter got underway, but she didn't get far. Struck by 5-inch fire from a battleship, the *maru* blew up.

The next ship caught was the cruiser KATORI. Already damaged by aircraft bombs, the warship was swiftly polished off by fire from Spruance's cruisers. Also damaged and dead in the water was the Jap destroyer which had been sighted. The U.S.S. IZARD attacked this sitting duck first, and then the Jap DD was swamped by fire from the American battleships, cruisers, and all four destroyers. Down went the I.J.N. MAIKAZE.

"The accuracy of fire," observed Admiral Mitscher, "especially by the destroyers of the screen, was very gratifying." This is a scene of the Jap effort to repulse Operation Cherry Tree, a carrier strike at the Marianas on February 21-22, 1944. Note the Japanese plane which appears as a dark rectangle just above the horizon line near the right hand edge of the photograph.

Finis! A Japanese bomber crashes into the sea in flames, shot down by screening destroyers (at left) and the carrier's own guns. A total of eight Jap attackers were destroyed and the raid on Saipan was pushed through as planned.

Truk, during the second bombing. This "island bastion" proved to be practically a hollow shell, quickly smashed. The Japs withdrew in a hurry.

For eleven hours Task Force 58 fought off the best the Japs in the Marianas could throw at it. Bronson made the first kill. The Jap planes attacked in groups of two and three—which made it good shooting for the destroyermen.

American destroyers catch Maikaze fleeing from Truk, February 16, 1944. Taking mortal hits (top), the Jap destroyer goes up in smoke (bottom).

A Jap torpedo bomber attacks the task force during a raid on Truk. Caught in an embarrassing moment, 93 of the 104 planes on Truk were destroyed during the second American raid on that island. Jap pilots were getting worse fast.

Task Force 58 caught this Jap cruiser trying to escape from Truk. Slowed by aircraft bombs, Katori was caught by Admiral Spruance's surface force and polished off by his cruisers. Then American destroyers helped finish a Jap DD.

These photographs show the devastation and destruction on the Pacific atolls caused by Allied bombardment: Tarawa, Roi, Kwajalein, Namur.

The task group continued its circuit of the island. At 1810 another target was discovered—the Japanese sub-chaser SC 24. Destroyer BURNS was ordered to demolish this craft. Commander Eller conned his ship into range, and BURNS' gun crews blazed away. By 1834 the sub-chaser was sub-chasing to the bottom. Eight prisoners were fished up, but a number of others screeched angrily at the destroyermen, refusing rescue.

The blasting dealt Truk abolished a bogie of two years' standing. And even as this bugaboo dissolved in smoke, Mitscher headed Task Force 58 for the distant Marianas, and American forces swept into the westernmost Marshalls to seize Eniwetok Atoll.

Phelps and Sage Sink RO-40

PHELPS (Lieutenant Commander D. L. Martineau) was one of the escort vessels assigned to the Southern Group of the Eniwetok Expeditionary Group which Rear Admiral H. W. Hill rushed westward. The group steamed out of Kwajalein at daylight on February 15, 1944. At 1742 of the following day, PHELPS made sonar contact with a target at 1,700 yards.

The destroyer executed a deliberate attack, dropping a full pattern of depth charges. While the destroyer was attacking, Captain E. R. McLean, Commander of the Southern Group, riding in PHELPS, turned the formation away. Two ships joined the subhunt—destroyer MACDONOUGH and minesweeper SAGE. The SAGE (Lieutenant F. K. Zinn, U.S.N.R.) was a little 700-tonner, but she followed up the contact and launched a depth-charge attack on the undersea foe.

The contact evaporated after SAGE made her attack. The ship searched until sunset, and then PHELPS and SAGE were ordered to rejoin the formation. MACDONOUGH continued the hunt for some time with negative results. An oil slick was sighted by other vessels in the area, but the destroyermen and the "miners" could not believe they had downed a sub in an action which lasted only a few minutes.

But there the RO-40 was on the bottom, and her obituary was found in the records of the Japanese Submarine Force at the end of the war.

Nicholas Kills I-11

Early in the morning of February 17, 1944, destroyer NICHOLAS (Commander R. T. S. Keith) was escorting three merchantmen from Pearl Harbor to Kwajalein. The convoy was about halfway between Hawaii and the Marshalls when NICHOLAS picked up a radar contact with a surface target 24,000 yards distant.

Commander Keith sent the DD racing to close the range. At 2,800 yards the target vessel appeared to be submerging—obviously a submersible. NICHOLAS immediately opened fire with main battery guns, and flashes indicated several hits. The 5-inch salvos hurried the submarine's dive, but she did not go down fast enough to escape sonar detection.

Conning the ship deftly, Commander Keith ran NICHOLAS in for an urgent depth-charge attack. She followed through with three deliberately laid patterns. About ten minutes after the third attack a basso explosion boomed in the deep. The blast sent to the surface a swirl of oil and a litter of shattered planking. This residue was all that remained to mark the grave of the Imperial Navy's I-11. Destroyer NICHOLAS had reason to be happy about the kill. Just three weeks before, while at Pearl Harbor, she had been presented the Presidential Unit Citation by Admiral Nimitz.

Action at Eniwetok

Eniwetok was Kwajalein all over again. In the atoll the Japs had established an aircraft base and a stage for naval shipping. The bull's-eye target was the islet of Engebi where the Japs had installed some heavy guns. To get at Engebi the invasion forces had to pass Eniwetok Island and Parry Island.

D-Day was February 17, 1944. Spearheading the assault, destroyer PHELPS, with Captain E. R. McLean on her bridge, served as flagship for the southern section of Rear Admiral Hill's Expeditionary Group. At sunrise McLean ordered the landing craft and support ships into column, and they steamed into the lagoon. The advance was delayed long enough to let SAGE sweep up and explode a moored mine; otherwise the ships might have been entering an American harbor.

Meanwhile, the Northern Group arrived off Eniwetok and Parry islands. This group contained heavy cruisers PORTLAND and INDIANAPOLIS, and in Fire Support Section Three were destroyers TRATHEN (Commander F. L. Tedder) and HOEL (Commander W. D. Thomas). The islands were pounded with a heavy shelling, and by afternoon the channel was open. At 1300 TRATHEN and HOEL entered the lagoon.

HOEL's boat picked up several downed aviators and returned them to INDIANAPOLIS. At 1521 the destroyer shelled Japanese troops on Parry. She also shelled and abolished some Jap boats on the beach. At 1945 TRATHEN started throwing shells at Parry and Eniwetok. For the next several days the two DD's remained in the lagoon lending fire-support to the landing forces.

In the morning of February 19 destroyer HAGGARD (Commander D. A. Harris) anchored off Eniwetok.

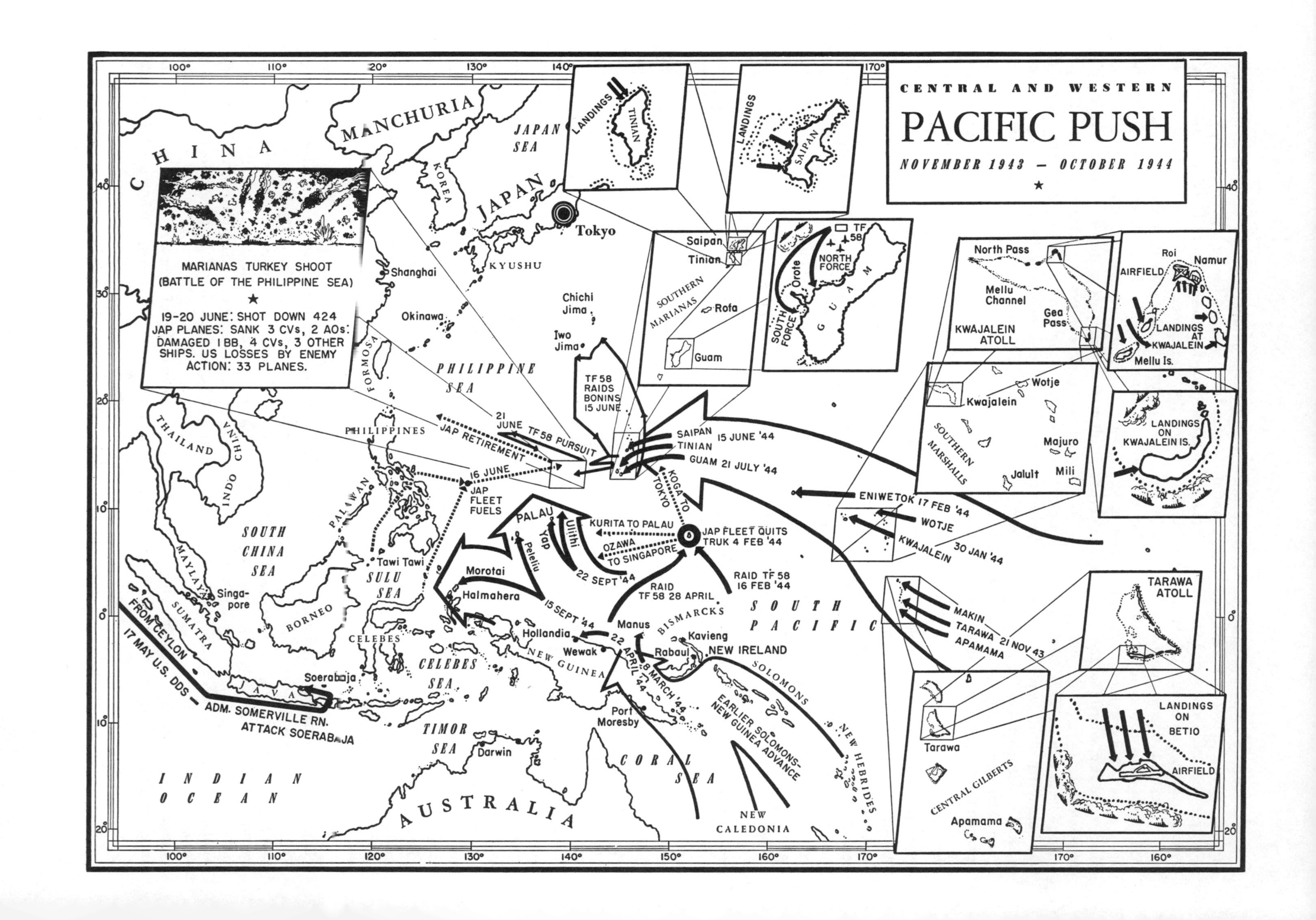
CENTRAL AND WESTERN
PACIFIC PUSH
NOVEMBER 1943 – OCTOBER 1944
MARIANAS TURKEY SHOOT
(BATTLE OF THE PHILIPPINE SEA)
19-20 JUNE: SHOT DOWN 424 JAP PLANES: SANK 3 CVs, 2 AOs: DAMAGED 1 BB, 4 CVs, 3 OTHER SHIPS. US LOSSES BY ENEMY ACTION: 33 PLANES.
CHINA
MANCHURIA
KOREA
JAPAN
JAPAN SEA
KYUSHU
Tokyo
Shanghai
Okinawa
FORMOSA
PHILIPPINE SEA
PHILIPPINES
THAILAND
INDO CHINA
SOUTH CHINA SEA
PALAWAN
MAYLAYA
Singapore
SUMATRA
BORNEO
Tawi Tawi
SULU SEA
CELEBES
CELEBES SEA
JAVA
Soerabaja
FROM CEYLON
17 MAY U.S. DDS – ADM. SOMERVILLE RN. ATTACK SOERABAJA
INDIAN OCEAN
TIMOR SEA
Darwin
AUSTRALIA
Port Moresby
CORAL SEA
NEW CALEDONIA
EARLIER SOLOMONS-NEW GUINEA ADVANCE
NEW HEBRIDES
SOLOMONS
NEW IRELAND
Kavieng
Rabaul
BISMARCKS
Manus
22 APRIL '44
8 MARCH '44
NEW GUINEA
Hollandia
Wewak
Halmahera
Morotai
15 SEPT '44
Peleliu
PALAU
Yap
Ulithi
22 SEPT '44
KURITA TO PALAU
OZAWA TO SINGAPORE
JAP FLEET QUITS TRUK 4 FEB '44
RAID TF 58 16 FEB '44
RAID TF 58 28 APRIL
KOGA TO TOKYO
SOUTH PACIFIC
16 JUNE
JAP FLEET FUELS
21 JUNE
TF 58 PURSUIT
JAP RETIREMENT
Chichi Jima
Iwo Jima
TF 58 RAIDS BONINS 15 JUNE
SAIPAN 15 JUNE '44
TINIAN
GUAM 21 JULY '44
ENIWETOK 17 FEB '44
WOTJE
KWAJALEIN
30 JAN '44
MAKIN
TARAWA
APAMAMA
21 NOV 43
LANDINGS
TINIAN
LANDINGS
SAIPAN
Saipan
Tinian
SOUTHERN MARIANAS
Rota
Guam
TF 58
NORTH FORCE
SOUTH FORCE
Orote
GUAM
North Pass
Mellu Channel
Gea Pass
KWAJALEIN ATOLL
Roi
Namur
AIRFIELD
LANDINGS AT KWAJALEIN
Mellu Is.
Wotje
Kwajalein
SOUTHERN MARSHALLS
Majuro
Jaluit
Mili
LANDINGS ON KWAJALEIN IS.
TARAWA ATOLL
LANDINGS ON BETIO
AIRFIELD
Tarawa
CENTRAL GILBERTS
Apamama
100° 110° 120° 130° 140° 150° 160° 170° 170° 160°
40° 30° 20° 10° 0° 10° 20°

She opened fire on the island at 0822 and during the next 23 hours she pounded enemy shore positions with 919 rounds of 5-inch.

Firing at Parry Island, the bombardment ships might have been on a practice mission. The 1,800 Jap defenders could only crouch in foxholes and await massacre. They did not have long to wait when four American battleships, three cruisers, and destroyers HALL, AYLWIN, MACDONOUGH, MONAGHAN, JOHNSTON, and MCCORD opened up with their main batteries trained at Parry. The ships delivered interdiction fire at ranges anywhere from 3,200 to 4,500 yards. On the evening of February 21 MCCORD, flying the pennant of Captain A. G. Cook, Jr., ComDesRon 47, and skippered by Commander W. T. Kenny, moved in on the beach for pointblank fire delivered at ranges as close as 1,222 and 1,600 yards.

By February 27 Eniwetok Atoll was securely in American hands. Some 3,400 Japs had manned the garrison. About 65 survived the assault. American casualties (dead and wounded) totaled 716. And, except for some mopping up in the eastern islands, the Marshalls campaign was over. Japan's outer Pacific defense line had been liquidated.

Strike at the Marianas ("Operation Cherry Tree")

Immediately after the Truk smash Admiral Mitscher sent the following message to the ships of Task Force 58:

I CANNOT TELL A LIE D-DAY IS WASHINGTON'S BIRTHDAY
LET'S CHOP DOWN A FEW NIP CHERRY TREES

The D-Day in reference had to do with "Operation Cherry Tree," a carrier air strike at Saipan in the Marianas. It was Spruance's idea. Keep the enemy off balance. Let the Navy's Fast Carrier Task Force strike all over the Central Pacific, keeping the enemy in ignorance as to where the lightning would strike next.

Task Force 58 raced westward. Mitscher had hoped to catch Saipan off guard, but by bad luck a Jap scout plane happened to sight the force, and at 1930 in the evening of February 21 the carrier admiral messaged his ships over TBS:

STAND BY FOR A FIGHT TO THE FINISH

The Jap air attack developed at 2030. Swarming out of the Marianas, the enemy planes descended in a cloud on Rear Admiral A. E. Montgomery's Task Group 58.2. This group contained carriers ESSEX, YORKTOWN, and BELLEAU WOOD, battleships SOUTH DAKOTA and ALABAMA, cruisers SANTA FE, MOBILE, BILOXI, and OAKLAND, and eight destroyers. The destroyers were: C. K. BRONSON (Lieutenant Commander J. C. McGoughran), flagship of Captain S. R. Clark, ComDesRon 50; DORTCH (Commander R. C. Young); GATLING (Commander A. F. Richardson); HEALY (Commander J. C. Atkeson); COGSWELL (Commander H. T. Deutermann), flying the pennant of Commander C. F. Chillingworth, Jr., ComDesDiv 100; CAPERTON (Commander W. J. Miller); INGERSOLL (Commander A. C. Veasey); and KNAPP (Commander F. Virden).

Reported at 2245, the first attacking plane was shot down at 2308 by flag destroyer BRONSON. Jap aircraft flailed at the task group for the rest of the night. Fortunately the Japs attacked in groups of two and three, which gave the American AA crews a chance to cut down the enemy piecemeal. But it was a busy night for the destroyermen; the formation was constantly maneuvering, and all hands remained at battle stations hour after hour. It was a hot initiation for the DD's of DesRon 50 engaging in their first action.

"Bogies" haunted the group the following day while the air strikes at Saipan were carrying on. At 0910 in the morning of the 22nd, C. K. BRONSON teamed up with MOBILE to knock down a "Betty." About the same time, several destroyers—probably CAPERTON and INGERSOLL—joined OAKLAND in bagging a "Betty." Navy fighters in the CAP (Combat Air Patrol) shot down a number of planes. The attacks gradually subsided as Jap aircraft hit the water and American bombs hit the airdromes on Saipan. All told, Task Group 58.2 shot down eight planes.

"The accuracy of fire," observed Admiral Mitscher, *"especially by the destroyers of the screen, was very gratifying."*

Manlove and PC-1135 Down I-32

For reasons best known to the strategists of the Imperial High Command, the Japs tried to maintain a foothold on some of the atolls of the eastern Carolines. By so doing they provided the U.S. Navy with some excellent gunnery and anti-submarine practice.

On March 24 a hunter-killer team was dispatched to waters east of the Marshalls to intercept a Japanese transport submarine bound with supplies for the garrison on Wotje. The team contained destroyers HALSEY POWELL (carrying the Officer in Tactical Command) and HULL, and destroyer-escort MANLOVE. Operating with these ships was PC-1135.

Rendezvousing at Erikub Atoll on March 23, the team searched around Wotje for three nights, but remained out of sight from shore during the daytime. At 0335 of the 24th MANLOVE made radar contact with the waiting destroyers. The ships steamed to take up position for a box search. But the search proved unnecessary.

At 0422 on March 24 the DE and PC moved out to investigate a target detected by radar. The range was about five miles. The night was moonless, but apparently the destroyer-escort and her companion were sighted by Jap eyes at 3,000 yards. At any rate the "pip" vanished, and MANLOVE promptly acquired sound contact. Skippering the DE, Lieutenant Commander J. P. Ingle, U.S.N.R., jockeyed in for a hedgehog barrage. The PC, captained by Lieutenant W. S. O'Kelly, U.S.N.R., was coached in for a one-two attack. This coordinated attack produced results.

MANLOVE fired four hedgehog salvos, and rolled an ashcan pattern. The PC let fly with four mousetrap salvos. This was one of the few instances in the war wherein American mousetraps caught a rat. A few seconds after the fourth mousetrap snapped, there were several explosions. Four minutes later the hunters heard two distant, deep explosions. After this final blasting neither ship was able to regain contact. With their usual methods, the hunter-killer team continued the search. To no avail. Daylight provided an answer—the seascape was smeared by an oil slick that extended for five miles. From the waters off Wotje the destroyer-escort MANLOVE and PC-1135 had removed one submarine, the I-32.

Shelling the Eastern Marshalls

In the southeastern reaches of the Marshall group lie Mille and Jaluit islands. Centered in the eastern fringe are Wotje and Maloelap. These islands all became targets for Navy guns and Navy bombs after the Japanese war-tide ebbed westward. The garrisons marooned on these landfalls were virtually condemned to execution by Navy firing squads of aircraft and warships.

On March 18 the Bombardment Unit of Task Group 50.10 under Rear Admiral W. A. Lee, Jr., headed for Mille. Mission to bombard the island was part of a training exercise for LEXINGTON's new air group. Battleships IOWA and NEW JERSEY were in need of target practice. Destroyers DEWEY (flagship of Captain E. R. McLean, Jr., ComDesRon 1), HULL, MACDONOUGH, and PHELPS participated.

It was highly realistic practice. Enemy shore guns returned an accurate fire, and DEWEY was twice bracketed by 3-gun straddles. IOWA was hit by two 6-inch shells. Jap planes struck at the American ships, and three of these aircraft were shot down by AA fire. The warships took it out on buildings, ammunition dumps, pillboxes, gun emplacements, and small craft. Mille was thoroughly smashed.

In May, destroyer-escort CLOUES (Lieutenant Commander T. K. Dunstan, U.S.N.R.) reconnoitered Jaluit, Wotje, Mille, and Maloelap. Native scouts visited each island, paddling ashore under cover of darkness and discussing the situation with native islanders. Twenty-four hours later they would paddle seaward to be picked up by CLOUES.

During the last week in May, four destroyers of Task Group 57.8 bore down on Mille for target practice. The DD's were FRAZIER (flagship of Captain R. N. Smoot, ComDesRon 14), GANSEVOORT, CALDWELL, and MEADE. The ships opened up at a range of 11,000 yards. The Japs answered with an accurate fire that appeared to be director-controlled, and the destroyers retired. *"This type of operation as an exercise does not warrant the risk involved,"* reported Captain Smoot. *"Approaching the problem as an exercise precludes taking decisive and aggressive action."*

American aircraft continued to blast Mille and the other eastern Marshalls. On June 9 destroyer GANSEVOORT (Lieutenant Commander J. M. Steinbeck), while cruising on blockade patrol off Mille, received word that an aviator was in the sea near the southwest corner of the island. Lieutenant Commander Steinbeck sent the ship's whaleboat to pick up the flyer. Under Lieutenant G. E. Craig, U.S.N.R., the boat started in at 1400. As the little craft chugged along, it was spotted by the enemy. The Jap batteries roared. GANSEVOORT's guns flamed in angry reply. After 24 salvos from the ship the Jap artillery went silent. At 1538 the whaleboat was back, bringing Captain Judson Bell, U.S.M.C. Aviator saved!

Long after the eastern Marshalls had lost all strategic value, the Japanese garrisons hung on. Perhaps they hung because there was no way for them to get off. As late as September, 1944, the marooned Japs were in an aggressive mood. On the 7th of that month the destroyer FLUSSER (Lieutenant Commander T. R. Vogeley) was fired upon by a shore battery when she steamed within 4,000 yards of the Wotje beach. Exploding close aboard, one salvo raked the ship with shrapnel and wounded nine of the crew. Retiring behind smoke, FLUSSER hit back with her after 5-inchers. Thereafter the DD's gave Wotje a wider berth, and it was left "to die on the vine."

Punch at Palau

Late in March, 1944, Task Force 58 struck at the Pelews (sometimes called the Palau Islands) in the western Carolines. This strike took Mitscher's planes within 500 miles of the Philippines. Meantime, Nimitz and Spruance were planning an invasion of the Marianas similar to "Operation Flintlock." With the invasion of Saipan the Japanese sun would go down to the western horizon.

Admiral Koga saw disaster coming, but he died in a plane smash somewhere off Palau before he could do anything about it. His epaulets passed to Admiral Soemu Toyoda, who had no better success.

CHAPTER 30

GANG BUSTERS, PACIFIC

(APRIL 1944 - JUNE 1944)

Sinking the Emperor's Subs

The Japanese submarine effort was in some respects like buckshot. It went off with a great, thundering bang, and then sprayed all over the place, losing force through dispersal.

Japanese submarines were used for all manner of missions. So were United States submarines. But the versatile American subs never neglected their primary mission—that of being both commerce raider and warship.

As the Pacific War progressed, the U. S. Submarine Forces devoted more and more time to ship-sinking. They might have concentrated on this enterprise from the first had they not been hampered by a munitions shortage and defective torpedoes. Conversely, the Japanese submarines got off to a fast start, but, after the sinking of the U.S.S. LISCOME BAY in the Gilberts, they failed to down a single major United States combatant ship until the tag-end of the war.

A chief reason for the slump, of course, was the impenetrable screen put up by American naval escorts and the devastating anti-submarine campaign waged by American and Allied A/S forces in the Pacific. The toll exacted from the Japanese Submarine Force by DD's, DE's, planes, and submarines did much to undermine the Japanese submarine effort and reduce it to a stage approaching impotence. But another important reason for the slump was the aforementioned dispersed nature of the effort itself. Imperial Navy heads did not seem to know exactly what to do with Admiral Miwa's submarines. Asked who controlled operations when Japanese submarines were supplying Imperial Army troops, Admiral Miwa declared, "It was undecided."

As a result there was no Japanese wolfpack campaign comparable to the German; no attrition offensive dedicated to the destruction of Allied merchant or naval shipping. The Jap submarines were kept busy running errands for the Army, or hauling oil from some remote Borneo port to the homeland. Now and then they torpedoed an Allied ship—in passing, so to speak—but in 1943 and 1944 they spent more time evading than attacking.

In consequence the American A/S forces in the Pacific were not called upon to fight such an undersea war as engaged their counterparts in the Atlantic. Concentrations of force were not continually required to counter opposing concentrations, for the Japanese subs seldom operated in offensive groups. And as fighting units, the I-boats and RO-boats were decidedly inferior to the U-boats. Miwa boasted that the Japanese had invented a "breather" device similar to *Schnorkel,* but material bottlenecks impeded its production. Radar was not installed in Japanese submarines until June 1944. The large plane-carrying I-boats were slow divers, and the smaller I- and RO-specimens were not as sturdy as their Nazi accomplices.

However, the Japanese sub could be a dangerous foe, and there was nothing buckshot about the Jap torpedo. The Emperor's Submarine Force maintained the menace of a "fleet in being." And U. S. Navy hunter-killer teams were organized in the Pacific to reduce that menace. A fine demonstration of co-operative A/S work was staged by destroyers and aircraft in the Truk area on April 30, 1944.

Macdonough, Stephen Potter, and Aircraft Down I-174

Late that month, while the Navy's forces solidified their positions in the Marshalls and MacArthur's troops swept across Hollandia, U. S. Task Force 58 paid a second hit-and-run visit to Truk. Among the numerous visitors were the light aircraft carrier MONTEREY (Captain S. H. Ingersoll) and the destroyers MACDONOUGH (Commander J. W. Ramey) and STEPHEN POTTER (Commander C. H. Crichton).

This Truk strike came as a result of the Hollandia victory in which Admiral Mitscher's Fast Carrier Task Force had participated. When that objective fell like an overripe tomato, Task Force 58 was left with "time on its hands." It occurred to the energetic Mitscher that a side-swipe at Truk might go a long way toward completing the neutralization of that already semi-neutralized stronghold. Into conference he called his new Chief of Staff, Captain Arleigh ("31-Knot") Burke of destroyer fame. Burke had the plans worked out in less than an hour's time, and TF 58 was soon steaming for Truk at 31 knots.

As with the previous strike, this one was an air show. The "impregnable" stronghold had not yet recovered from the February pulverizing. Nevertheless Mitscher's planes were peppered with the hottest ack-ack they had yet encountered. Twenty-seven were shot down. The Japs, however, lost 93 out of their 104 Truk aircraft, and the island was given a monstrous blasting. Meanwhile, MONTEREY, MACDONOUGH, and STEPHEN POTTER, on picket station 60 miles south of Truk, bagged their I-boat.

MACDONOUGH made the contact at 0621 in the morning of April 30—a radar indication, range 12,600 yards. Commander Ramey rushed the destroyer for an intercepting position. At 1,760 yards the target vanished from the screen in a fast dive. Sonar took up where radar left off, and the submerged I-boat was promptly detected.

Ramey directed the dropping of a depth-charge pattern. Overside went the ashcans and teardrops. Up came the water-thunder. A few minutes later the DD's lookouts sighted a glistening oil slick. The I-boat was bleeding.

At this juncture STEPHEN POTTER steamed up to lend a hand. And down from the distance came a Grumman to join the proceedings. The POTTER made a run, depositing a pattern of depth charges. Then the aircraft got in its licks at the slicks, after which MACDONOUGH made a second depth-charge attack.

When the barrage quieted down and the waters calmed, a great patch of oil spread across the sea and a litter of debris came bobbing to the surface. Deep-bellied rumblings were heard. After these explosions, the sonar operators were unable to regain contact with the submarine. Like Truk, it had been blown out of the war.

Japanese records indicated later that this victim was the I-174.

Haggard, Franks, and Johnston Kill I-176

Another highly efficient I-boat hunt began on May 12, 1944, when DesDiv 94 (Commander J. H. Nevins, Jr.) steamed out of Blanche Harbor in the Treasuries to track down a Jap sub spotted by a plane off Buka.

The hunting division consisted of DD's HAGGARD (Commander D. A. Harris), HAILEY (Commander P. H. Brady), FRANKS (Commander N. A. Lidstone), and JOHNSTON (Commander E. E. Evans). HAGGARD, HAILEY, and JOHNSTON had been in action together at Eniwetok. FRANKS, a veteran of "Operation Galvanic," had witnessed the terrible death throes of LISCOME BAY. With that horror fresh in memory, Commander Nicholas Lidstone and his crew were doubly determined to remove the reported submarine from the Buka area.

Early in the morning of May 16 the hunters arrived in the waters northwest of Buka where the I-boat had been spotted. The search was begun. Not long after sunrise, four destroyers of DesDiv 93 (Captain I. H. Nunn) arrived on the scene. Under Captain Nunn's direction the search intensified.

To the submarine crouching in the depths the whisper of screws loudening, fading, and coming back with a roar of static, and the hour-after-hour tension of waiting in helpless inertia, must have created an accumulation of nerve-strain approaching the unbearable. As the day dragged on, the air in the I-boat fouled to gas; the humid heat within the pressure hull became stupefying. All that the sweating, stupefied Japanese crew could do was to wait for their hour to come.

For the submarine I-176 that fatal hour arrived at 2145, twenty hours after the beginning of the "hold-down," when the destroyer HAGGARD, after making sound contact, dropped a full depth-charge pattern on the hiding submersible. The stunned submariners got their I-boat out from under, but they could not escape the trap.

Destroyers JOHNSTON and FRANKS closed in. At 2213 HAGGARD's sonar again picked up the I-boat, and Commander Harris immediately treated the sub to another full depth-charge pattern.

At this point HAGGARD's gyrocompass went out of

commission. But JOHNSTON promptly stepped in, and Commander Evans let the target have a full depth-charge pattern. Again the I-boat edged clear, but it was a doomed submarine.

At midnight JOHNSTON turned over contact to destroyer FRANKS. Lidstone and crew had been impatiently waiting their chance, and at 0015 in the morning of May 17 they made the most of opportunity. Down upon the target FRANKS dropped a full depth-charge pattern. When the thunder finally died away, the silence in the sea was that of a grave. Buried in that grave was I-176.

In the morning the "gravemarkers" were drifting on the surface—bits of sandalwood, chunks of cork, some fragments of wrapping paper marked with Japanese ideographs.

Duly inscribed in Imperial Navy records, the obituary of the I-176 was found by American investigators after the war.

England and the RO-Boats (Prologue to a Six-Part Serial)

In the spring of 1944, Admiral Soemu Toyoda assembled the Japanese Combined Fleet in the Philippines at the old American fleet anchorage of Tawi Tawi. There he sat down to wait. For what? Toyoda himself was not sure.

United States forces were going to drive westward across the Pacific, that much was certain. But from which direction would they drive? And which sector of the Empire's crumbling defense perimeter was marked for the sledgehammer blow? In the Central Pacific a United States armada was gathering muscle in the Marshalls. In the Southwest Pacific MacArthur's troops were firmly installed on the New Guinea coast at Hollandia and Aitape. Would the American fleet drive from the Marshalls to strike Guam and Saipan in the Marianas? Or would MacArthur's forces drive from New Guinea to strike the Japanese stronghold of Palau in the western Carolines? At Tawi Tawi in the Philippines, Admiral Toyoda would have given a good deal to know the answer.

The Japanese were not strong enough to defend both sectors at once. Only by concentrating forces on either the Marianas or the Pelews could they hope to contain the United States offensive. It was therefore essential that Toyoda anticipate the American objective. Centrally positioned at Tawi Tawi, the fleet could be thrown either way, but advance information of American plans would be invaluable.

Studying charts, piecing together intelligence reports, Toyoda finally concluded that the island of Manus in the Admiralties was being rigged by the Americans as the springboard for a great drive at Palau.

The Americans were indeed building Manus into a staging base. Crowding into the island's spacious Seeadler Harbor were Allied transports and warships. At near points on New Guinea, MacArthur's troops were massing. Toyoda's conclusions concerning Palau were not wholly unwarranted.

The Admiral did not risk a jump at this conclusion. Convinced though he was, he sought substantiating evidence. For an American drive at the Marianas still remained a possibility, and Toyoda wanted to know with absolute certainty which way the cat was going to leap.

So Admiral Toyoda appealed to Headquarters Japanese Submarine Force. What the Admiral wanted was a submarine scouting line to cover the southern approaches to the Pelews; a line that would extend from the waters south of Truk to the waters some distance west of Manus. He wanted the submarines so placed along this line that an invasion fleet moving westward would inevitably be detected.

The subs were provided. Assigned to the vital mission was a select division of war-built RO-boats: RO-104, RO-105, RO-106, RO-108, RO-116, and RO-117. Southward they went in mid-May to take their stations in the scouting line. No doubt Toyoda realized they were flimsy pickets in a precarious fence. But they were the only pickets available. And if the American fleet advanced on Palau, six Jap subs would surely last long enough to relay the word. If they didn't last? That, too, could be taken as evidence of an all-out American drive from Manus. So reasoned Toyoda, apparently forgetting that circumstantial evidence might be misleading.

Now it happened that while Toyoda and other Japanese naval heads were juggling grand strategy, a little DE was fussing around in the far-off eastern Solomons—on May 18, to be specific, she was at Purvis Bay, Florida Island. The destroyer-escort ENGLAND, commissioned on December 10, 1943, was a newcomer in the Southwest Pacific.

ENGLAND was captained by Lieutenant Commander Walton B. Pendleton. Her Executive Officer was Lieutenant Commander John A. Williamson. They were trained naval officers and experienced shiphandlers, but in common with the rest of ENGLAND's crew, they had as yet to hear the explosion of hedgehog projectiles against an enemy submarine's pressure hull.

At Purvis Bay ENGLAND was assigned to Escort Division 39, which included destroyer-escorts GEORGE (Lieutenant Commander Fred W. Just, U.S.N.R.), and RABY (Lieutenant Commander James Scott, II). Commander Hamilton Hains, the Officer in Tactical

Command, rode in GEORGE. Commander C. A. Thorwall, U.S.N.R., the second escort division commander in the group, rode in ENGLAND. The three DE's were attached to the new escort-carrier HOGGATT BAY for A/S duty.

On the morning of May 18 there were no indications of high drama in the making for destroyer-escort ENGLAND. No star fell across her bow, nor did an albatross visit her as a sign. A Jap submarine was reported heading south from Truk with supplies for Bougainville, and the DE division was ordered out to intercept. Just another job—nothing to suggest that in future histories of the Destroyer Service, and in future conversations of destroyermen, the name ENGLAND would take on an eternal glory.

England Kills I-16 (First Installment)

Report of the I-boat from Truk had reached the U. S. Third Fleet flagship on the evening of May 17. Ever since Bougainville had been cut off and by-passed, Jap submersibles had been trying to supply the large garrison isolated at Buin. Obviously the sub in question was Buin bound. Accordingly, ENGLAND, GEORGE, and RABY were dispatched to waters northwest of Bougainville to waylay this undersea supply boat.

The DE's employed the familiar technique of plotting the submarine's assumed course from start to destination, and then proceeding on this course to meet the advancing sub. Spaced 4,000 yards apart, the three ships steamed in a line, making sonar sweeps calculated to detect the I-boat if it passed anywhere in the vicinity. By a blend of estimate and algebra, the destroyermen deduced they would meet the enemy submarine sometime in the afternoon of May 20. But the sun was high on the 19th when ENGLAND made sound contact in the vicinity of lat. 05-10 S., long. 158-17 E.—a point not far from the passage between Bougainville and Choiseul. The time was 1325. The sub was seven miles east of the expected point, and 24 hours ahead of schedule!

The Sound man reported an "underwater object." He was an inexperienced hand, but ENGLAND's skipper would not risk a delay to replace him. Commander Pendleton ordered an immediate attack. Executive Officer Williamson and crew snapped into action. A cautious trial run—a "dry run"—convinced Sound the "object" was a submarine. Then Pendleton ordered a hedgehog salvo. ENGLAND maneuvered into firing position. The projectiles soared away and spattered the surface.

No luck on the first attack. But the DE's second attack produced results. Somewhere under water there was a sharp explosion, not much louder than a door-bang. ENGLAND's captain and crew had heard their first hedgehog hit. Up came a cluster of bubbles. The turbulence subsided; the ship swung around; Pendleton drove ENGLAND on another run. The sub was fish-tailing, and the destroyermen tried again with hedgehog. Altogether ENGLAND made five runs, firing hedgehog. On the fifth run—time: 1433—she hit the winning combination.

Twelve seconds after the projectiles splashed water, the depth re-echoed the thud of several muffled explosions. A flash at 54 fathoms was registered on the fathometer as the ship passed over the submarine. About two minutes later came the deep-sea climax, a blast that jolted the ship.

Executive Officer Williamson stated, *"This explosion was so violent that it knocked men off their feet throughout the ship. At first we thought we had been torpedoed."*

About 20 minutes later the destroyermen sighted the evidence of a kill. Up came a slow seepage of oil which gradually developed into a gusher that spread across acres of the ocean's surface. Up with the oil came kindling wood and other items of debris. I-16 was an ex-submarine. And ENGLAND was on her way to stardom.

England Kills RO-106 (Second Installment)

The sinking of I-16 puzzled the hunter-killers. According to calculations, the supply sub from Truk should not have shown up until the following afternoon. Was the present victim an unexpected interloper? ENGLAND lowered boats to examine the debris. GEORGE cooperated in the watery inquest. Several life jackets, an oily mattress, and splinters of furniture were combed from the sludge, but no bodies were found.

Finally the searchers fished from the sea a large sack of rice—typical cargo of a supply submarine. Still, Commander Hains and his group were reluctant to take anything for granted. The contact had been made a day ahead of time and about seven miles off the estimated course. On the assumption that they had bagged a Japanese "stray," the hunters continued on the line they had originally set out to follow. So they made another day's run toward Truk.

While the DE's were thus engaged, a plane from Manus spotted one of the subs (apparently RO-117) in the Japanese scouting line. The plane dropped bombs; the undersea scout went deep; the pilot radioed the word to Admiral Halsey's flagship. This report convinced Halsey that the enemy had established an undersea scouting line off the Admiralties. Halsey himself favored such submarine tactics, and the reported contact—one of several—prompted in-

A battle-scarred veteran comes home showing her scars and wearing her decorations. This is the famous England which destroyed Toyoda's scouting line by sinking six Jap subs in twelve days. Note the kills recorded on her bridge. Twelve days after she set the record, England herself was blasted by a kamikaze. This picture shows her arrival at a West Coast port for repairs.

Robert I. Paine, sister ship of the destroyer-escort England, was with the Block Island group when that jeep carrier was torpedoed, and rescued 277 of the Block Island crew. This type of ship was armed with 3-inch guns, had a complement of 220 men, and could make a maximum speed of 24 knots with her turbo-electric drive. She was 1400 tons with an overall length of 306 feet.

Types of Japanese submarines. In the foreground are two-man midget subs. Beyond these are the RO-boats, 239 feet overall, with one 3-inch gun and four 21-inch torpedo tubes, capable of 16 knots on the surface, 9 knots submerged.

Walton B. Pendleton, skipper of England at the time that destroyer-escort killed six picket RO-boats and ruined the Japanese defensive plans.

An early Japanese I-boat: The I-5 was typical of the big sea-going enemy submarines. Displacing about 2500 tons, armed with a 5-inch gun and six 21-inch torpedo tubes, she made 17 knots on the surface, 9 knots submerged.

These giant Jap subs, captured at the end of the war, were designed to carry aircraft in a hangar on deck, but were underpowered and unwieldy.

vestigation. Since his big board showed ENGLAND, RABY, and GEORGE in the suspected scouting line's vicinity, Halsey immediately dispatched the DE trio to the area where the RO-boat had been sighted.

Early in the morning of May 22, destroyer-escort GEORGE reported radar contact, range 14,000 yards. The three DE's headed for the target. ENGLAND picked up the "pip" at 15,000 yards, and closed in with GEORGE on the attack.

At 0410 GEORGE swept the seascape with her searchlight. ENGLAND's bridge personnel glimpsed the sub—a ghostly shadow in the offing. GEORGE's bridge gang failed to spot the ghost, but ENGLAND's had a good look at 4,100 yards. The phantom immediately faded, and its "pip" vanished from the radar screen. But as the enemy submerged, GEORGE made sound contact and Commander Just fired hedgehog.

The salvo missed. GEORGE lost contact. However, ENGLAND obtained a clear sound contact at 2,500 yards. Pendleton maneuvered in, and the hedgehogs soared. No hits! The sub was fishtailing. But ENGLAND got another "bead," and at 0444 Pendleton ordered another hedgehog salvo. Eighteen seconds later came three sharp explosions. At 0451, while ENGLAND was making a third run, all hands heard a thunderstorm under the sea. The rumbling shook the DE and vibrated the teeth of her sister ships. The booming came from an exploding submarine.

In the morning an oil slick was sighted. Also scraps of debris. This was the residue of RO-106.

England Kills RO-104 (Third Installment)

Twenty-four hours after ENGLAND scored her second sinking, the group picked up a new contact. Time: 0604 in the morning of May 23. Destroyer-escort RABY caught the "pip" on her radar screen, and dashed forward as the target disappeared. Promptly RABY obtained sound contact; and Commander Scott directed a hedgehog attack. The salvo missed. RABY tried again. Another miss. For the next half hour she made runs and attacks, relaying ranges and bearings as she did so to let the other DE's plot positions. She riddled the water with a hedgehog barrage, but she failed to hit the detected submarine.

For this Jap sub was skippered by an artful dodger. Foxy, he "pinged" back at the "pinging" DE's to muddle the electronic recorders. Having expended 50 minutes and most of her hedgehog ammunition, frustrated RABY gave over to GEORGE.

GEORGE picked up the contact, ran in, and let fly with hedgehog. The salvo missed. Then ENGLAND stepped up to bat. Sound had difficulty obtaining distinct echoes, so ENGLAND's marksmen held their fire to let GEORGE do it. GEORGE executed four more attacks—no hits. She retired again to the sidelines, and ENGLAND took over.

At 0819 ENGLAND fired a full hedgehog salvo. She followed through with another at 0834. About 22 seconds after this salvo went rocketing, the subjacent water boiled and boomed like a witch's cauldron.

Apparently a dozen projectiles had found the mark, for the undersea din was prodigious. So was the eventual silence. Pendleton sent his DE running over the spot, and the submarine's destruction was certified by a pattern of 13 depth charges set to blow deep. They blew, and the fragmentary rummage of RO-104 swam to the surface.

Score another kill for ENGLAND.

England Kills RO-116 (Fourth Installment)

About an hour after ENGLAND slew her third Jap submersible, Hains' hunter-killer group made still another submarine contact. The DE's were unable to run this one down. But it assured Hains that the Japanese had indeed established a scouting line southwest of Truk. And the group leader was in something of a quandary. His ships were running low on fuel and hedgehog ammunition. Should they chance it toward Truk, or head for Manus? The decision was to head for Manus on the line they were already following. They could not have taken a more fortuitous tack.

They were patrolling down the line—interval eight miles—when they made their next contact. Early in the morning of May 24 GEORGE caught the "pip" on her radar screen, range 14,000 yards. The "pip" soon vanished, but at 0150 ENGLAND had Sound contact with the submerged submarine.

ENGLAND at once headed for the sub. But the enemy executed some cagey evasion tactics. *"This submarine was by far the trickiest we had encountered,"* Pendleton noted. *"We were forced to make two dry runs before our firing run, on which we hit."* Projector Mark-10 charges were thrown. At least three struck the target. No undersea uproar at this time. Nothing more than a muffled grumble followed by deep silence. But the silence had the sound of extinction. The echo-rangers could find nothing to "ping" on.

And in the morning ENGLAND's whaleboat, searching a sea burnished with sunrise, discovered several small ponds of oil in which drifted shattered pieces of deck-planking. The next afternoon extensive oil slicks were sighted. The oil and the planking were all that was left of RO-116—another submarine deleted from the Japanese scouting line.

England Kills RO-108 (Fifth Installment)

May 26, 1944—by that day ENGLAND's reputation had soared to a point that embarrassed her modest captain and crew. Modesty, however, would not restrain her from pursuing her sensational career—which she did on the evening of May 26.

Spaced at 16,000 yards, ENGLAND, GEORGE, and RABY were patrolling across dark seas toward Seeadler Harbor. At 2303 RABY picked up radar contact, range 14,000 yards. One minute later ENGLAND had the contact. She headed for the target. The Jap sub submerged when the range closed to 4,100 yards. Too late. At 2315 ENGLAND's sonar crew reported contact, range 1,700 yards. The DE slowed to 10 knots; maneuvered into position; fired a hedgehog salvo at 2323. The salvo was echoed by basso explosions.

ENGLAND moved to the sidelines, and her teammates took over with detection gear. RABY and GEORGE conducted a retiring search to the sub's "7-hour circle," but they were unable to locate the target. Reason: there was no target left to locate.

At daybreak the destroyermen discovered evidence of ENGLAND's deadly marksmanship. Greasy bubbles were blubbering to the surface at the spot where the sub had broken up. Boating through the bubbles, RABY's men found a piece of mahogany with a brass fitting (perhaps part of a chronometer case), deck planking, some hunks of cork, and other nondescript items of debris. One item found was a meat chopping block—a grim *memento mori*. The victim was eventually identified as RO-108.

So ENGLAND had done it again. Five submarines within a week! Toyoda's scouts were suffering like the Ten Little Indians in the nursery rhyme. No. 1 had been ousted by the plane from Manus. ENGLAND had carried on as recounted. And then, as in the rhyme, that left only one.

England, George, Raby, Hazelwood, and Spangler Kill RO-105 (Last Installment)

At this stage of the ENGLAND campaign, Halsey decided to send HOGGATT BAY to the scene. On May 30 the escort-carrier (Captain W. V. Saunders) was in the waters off Manus. With her were destroyers HAZELWOOD (Commander V. P. Douw) and MCCORD (Commander W. T. Kenny).

The destroyer-escort SPANGLER (Lieutenant Commander D. J. McFarlane, U.S.N.R.), had already been dispatched from Tulagi for a rendezvous with ENGLAND, GEORGE, and RABY at Manus. She was waiting with a supply of hedgehog ammunition when Hains' hunter-killer group came in on the afternoon of the 27th.

So the three DE's found a sizable reception committee on hand at Seeadler Harbor. They stayed overnight; loaded; took on fuel. Late afternoon of the 28th they were out again, SPANGLER included.

Early in the morning of May 30 the destroyer HAZELWOOD, sweeping with radar, picked up a "pip" at 15,000 yards. Time: 0144. At 0153 the "pip" evaporated, but the destroyer immediately obtained sonar contact. HAZELWOOD attacked with depth charges. Damage was probable, but she failed to flush the sub. She maintained contact until 0435, at which time she was relieved by GEORGE and RABY, called in to assist. The two DE's had been echo-ranging in formation with ENGLAND and SPANGLER. The latter pair, under Commander C. A. Thorwall, U.S.N.R. (ComCortDiv 40, riding in ENGLAND), continued the search.

GEORGE established contact; made several attacks: finished off with a run at 0630, firing a full hedgehog pattern. Three explosions indicated hits. RABY followed through with several attacks. These the wounded sub evaded. The two DE's spent the rest of the day trying to track the sub. By evening it was apparent that she was playing 'possum in a foxhole.

Shortly after sunset three underwater blasts thundered in the sea. But evidence of destruction did not bob to the surface. The explosions were baffling. Had a tricky submarine skipper detonated torpedoes to deceive the hunters? So it seemed, for the DE's presently regained contact with the submersible. RABY and GEORGE were ordered to maintain the contact. The following morning they renewed the attack.

Meanwhile, ENGLAND and SPANGLER, overhearing TBS dialogue between RABY and GEORGE, steamed to the attack area. Arriving on the scene at 0500, they took position on the 5,000 yard circle. SPANGLER presently maneuvered in to add her hedgehogs to the barrage. Her salvos missed. And at that juncture the DE's were warned by Halsey's flagship that they might be attacked by air and had better clear out.

Pull out and let the cornered submarine escape? *"Oh, hell,"* Commander Hains exclaimed over the TBS, *"Go ahead,* ENGLAND*!"*

So ENGLAND went ahead. At 0729 she obtained sonar contact. Six minutes later Pendleton ordered the firing of a full salvo. The hedgehogs soared, dug in, and hit. Initial explosions were climaxed by a ship-shaking blast.

Soon the surface was blotched by a spew of debris. Reporting the matter, Lieutenant Commander Pendleton wrote: *"It is believed this submarine was destroyed. It seems that practice does make perfect."* He need not have qualified these statements. RO-105 had come to the end of the line. And ENGLAND had polished off her sixth submarine.

England and the RO-Boats (Epilogue)

Six enemy submarines in 12 days! In recognition of a feat unparalleled in Navy history, destroyer-escort **England** was awarded the Presidential Unit Citation.

But **England**'s *phenomenal* A/S score was by no means the sum total of her accomplishment. Pendleton and his crew had done something more than annihilate six Japanese subs. They had wiped out a scouting line—one of the more important scouting lines of the Pacific War.

Only one of the six RO-boats of the line escaped **England**'s deadly hedgehogs. That submarine—RO-117—was spotted by a PBY south of Truk lagoon, and done in forthwith. The others were done in by **England**.

Even in the barest of summaries the record is impressive.

She killed I-16.
She killed RO-106.
She killed RO-104.
She killed RO-116.
She killed RO-108.
And she finished off RO-105.

With that Toyoda's scouting line was totally abolished. In consequence, the Commander-in-Chief of the Japanese Combined Fleet at Tawi Tawi failed to get word which might nave made all the difference between victory and defeat in the Battle of the Philippine Sea.

For the word he did get was the gloomy intelligence that his scouting line had been sunk to the last sub. Not unnaturally he assumed that a great armada was assembling in the Manus area and that his undersea scouts had been obliterated by a horde of Allied warships. This assumption was never officially admitted, but in post-war statements Toyoda acknowledged that he thought the Allies were aiming their next drive at Palau. It would seem he based this deduction on the A/S activity south of Truk.

In any event, Toyoda bobbled a command decision and rushed 71 Jap planes from Guam to the Pelews. And, of course, those 71 planes were ultimately needed for the defense of Guam.

If Toyoda's decision *was* influenced by the destruction of his Truk-Manus scouting line, **England** and her companions had indeed done something more than sink six RO-boats. All unknowing, they had achieved what amounted to a major feint—a strategic feint that threw Toyoda's defenses off base two weeks before the American drive for the Marianas.

ATTACK TEAM ON THE ENGLAND
"ALL HER EQUIPMENT WORKS!" HOW DID WE DO IT? WE PULLED OUT THE PINS!

CHAPTER 31

WESTERN PACIFIC PUSH

Destroyers Westward Ho!

By the spring of 1944 the bastions of Japan's inner Pacific defense line were crumbling like rotten ice. Like a tidal wave the war was rushing westward toward Japan, toward the Philippines, and toward the Netherlands East Indies. Off the Japanese home islands, and deep within the seas of the Co-Prosperity Sphere, American submarines were tearing the Empire's transportation lines to ribbons. Allied aircraft were pounding at such bases as Saipan, Palau, and Hollandia, New Guinea. Allied A/S teams were sinking Jap submarines in droves. And Allied fleets, including specifically American destroyers and destroyer-escorts, were daring the Imperial Navy to fight.

The Kuriles, for example. Early in March they were visited by a United States task force from the Aleutians. The force was composed of the cruiser RICHMOND (Rear Admiral W. D. Baker) and eight destroyers. The DD roster included PICKING (Commander R. S. Lamb), flagship of Captain H. F. Gearing, ComDesRon 49; WICKES (Commander W. Y. Allen, Jr.); SPROSTON (Lieutenant Commander M. J. Luosey); YOUNG (Commander G. B. Madden); W. D. PORTER (Commander W. A. Walter); ISHERWOOD (Commander R. E. Gadrow), flying the pennant of Commander H. Wood, Jr., ComDesDiv 98; KIMBERLY (Commander Harry Smith), and LUCE (Commander H. A. Owens).

The force sortied from Massacre Bay, Attu, on the evening of March 1, and entered the Sea of Okhotsk about 0200 in the morning of the 4th. Mission: to search for a convoy reported in the vicinity of Musashi Wan, and then bombard beaches in the area.

Poor visibility and wild seas interfered with the search. If the convoy was there, it probably received a battering from the weather which equalled anything the warships could have handed out under the circumstances. Force 6 wind and foaming waves compelled Admiral Baker to abandon the search and cancel shore bombardments.

Retiring from the Okhotsk area, the ships were buffeted by a storm that started RICHMOND leaking and sent two destroyers into drydock for repairs. The other six DD's made port with topside damage. ISHERWOOD was worst off of the squadron. Butting head seas, she cracked a main injection casting.

Four months later another task force sortied from Attu to take a crack at the Kuriles. This force—Task Force 94, under Rear Admiral E. G. Small—was considerably larger than Admiral Baker's. It was composed of cruisers CHESTER (flagship), PENSACOLA, and CONCORD, and nine destroyers. Eight of the DD's were veterans of the March raid. The newcomer was the C. J. BADGER, captained by Lieutenant Commander J. H. Cotten. ISHERWOOD was skippered by Lieutenant Commander L. E. Schmidt, and carried Commander W. G. Cooper, ComDesRon 98. W. D. PORTER was captained by Commander C. M. Keyes.

In the last week of June the force steamed westward to bombard Jap air installations on Kurabu Zaki on the southeast point of Paramushiro. As some 257 planes were stationed in the area, the American force, which had no air cover, utilized the cover of a weather front. Excellent reports from a Navy weather plane called the turn. Admiral Small led his ships out of Attu on June 24, and the force steamed into low visibility and foggy seas. Objective was reached on the 26th. The target was bombarded for 20 minutes, and the destroyers sank several picket boats and shot up other small craft. Evidently Jap planes tried to locate the warships, for numerous "bogies" showed up on the radar scopes. But the ships retired across a vaporous seascape, and returned to Attu without incident. This was one time the North Pacific weather (accurately forecasted) aided and abetted the Navy's raiders.

The North Pacific strikes were geared in with Central Pacific raids and the general advance along the equator. In the South Sea islands the Navy's forces were marching in step with those in the Carolines and the Kuriles. Operating in the Bougainville area, some old hands were engaged in ringing down the curtain in the Solomons theater. Excerpt from report by Admiral Nimitz:

Throughout March, destroyers of Divisions 42, 43, 44, 45, 89 and 94 were active in the support of Army operations ashore. They operated under the direction of the Commanding General, XIV Army Corps, and provided counter-battery fire, bombarded enemy troops or installations ashore, and gave fire support for our troops as requested. In addition, they inaugurated a series of patrols coordinated with motor torpedo boats and LCI gunboats, supporting the smaller craft in their interdiction of enemy barge traffic.

The destroyers in reference, nearly all of them war-scarred veterans of the Solomons campaign, are listed below in the next column.

Although the war had swept on past the Solomons to the Admiralty Islands 500 miles to the westward, there were anti-climactical (and furious) battles fought on Bougainville. Major General O. W. Griswold's forces which had been landed on Cape Torokina would have been in serious difficulty but for the support of Admiral Ainsworth's cruisers, American aircraft, PT-boats, landing craft, and the destroyers enumerated. Among those DD divisions were Burke's famous "Little Beavers," Petersen's veterans, and Earle's case-hardened "cans." The destroyers of Captain W. F. Petersen's Squadron 22 (flagship WALLER) were the big guns of General Griswold's "Bougainville Navy". These destroyers performed yeomen service supporting the forces ashore and the strangulation blockade that had been thrown around the island.

One of the last actions fought by destroyermen in the Bougainville area was dated August 5, 1944. On that day destroyer-escort BOWERS (Lieutenant Commander F. W. Hawes) approached the estuary of the

---

DesDiv 42

FLETCHER — JENKINS
RADFORD — LAVALLETTE

DesDiv 43

WALLER — SAUFLEY
PRINGLE — PHILIP
RENSHAW

DesDiv 44

CONWAY — EATON
CONY — SIGOURNEY

DesDiv 45

STANLY — AULICK
CHARLES AUSBURNE — CLAXTON
DYSON

DesDiv 89

HALFORD — BENNETT
GUEST — FULLAM
HUDSON

DesDiv 94

HAGGARD — HAILEY
FRANKS — JOHNSTON

Jaba River to shell a batch of Japs who had driven off Fiji troops the previous June. BOWERS' gunnery convinced these recalcitrants that farming was better than fighting. At war's end the Japs on Bougainville were tending some of the nicest gardens in the South Pacific.

Destroyermen Up the Ladder (Leadership Story)

As someone once said, there are three kinds of naval leadership—good, indifferent, and bad. This text would not presume to analyze the leadership qualities of the Navy's destroyer captains, division commanders, and squadron commanders who fought the battles of World War II. Actions speak louder than words, and the records of these commanders and skippers speak eloquently in their behalf.

The record of Captain Arleigh ("31-Knot") Burke could be seen, then, or perhaps it would be better to say "heard," as an oration on good leadership. For nine months his DesRon 23 had been slugging it out in the Solomons, and they had practically worked themselves out of a job. Here is the story as told by "31-Knot" Burke:

On the 23rd of March we returned to Purvis, where I received orders that I was to be detached from DesRon 23 and was to report to Commander

Carrier Division 3 (Admiral Mitscher) as Chief of Staff. This nearly broke my heart because I knew that I would never again get a command like this destroyer squadron. Never again would there be so many fine captains in one organization. Not only that, but I was leaving some of my very best friends.

However, the whole squadron was going to join Task Force 58. The hunting in the South Pacific was nearly over. There was not much game left for our ships. The Japanese had not sent any surface craft to amount to anything out to Rabaul or Kavieng since our last sweep. Our ships were roaming at will around the Admiralties. There was nothing more for us to do in the Solomons, so we thought that perhaps this new duty would be pretty good.

Military literature is loaded with dissertations on leadership. But it is doubtful that all their maxims, aphorisms, and formulae state the case any better than these plain words of that same "31-Knot" Burke quoted from *Battle Report,* by Walter C. Karig:

It happens to so many people who have been in battles for a long time. Their ideas of what is important change rapidly. Things that used to be very important were completely unimportant now. Good food was important. A glass of beer was important. What your shipmates thought of you was important. But what was written down on a piece of paper, or what somebody who was not fighting thought about how you were fighting, that was completely unimportant. He didn't know what he was talking about. We knew that. It was obvious from some of the letters, too, although nobody had criticized us. But we could read criticism of other people's action, and we commenced to believe that it took a combat man to analyze another combat man's action. And even then it can't be done because nothing can ever be completely written in action. The reason why a commander made the decision that he did make is probably obscure.

I've tried keeping logs on the bridge, keeping yeomen to write down all the reasons why I was going to do a certain thing. But then when the stress came I would probably think of a half dozen reasons very quickly. The yeoman would perhaps be asleep and I would hate to wake him up, and I'd let it go. Or perhaps he didn't even have time to write it down. In any case I made the decision and hoped it was right. But I never recorded all the reasons why I made it or why I did not make some other decision. The same thing is true with everybody. Without the stress and the strain and the limit on time, nobody can actually duplicate the strain that a commander is under in making a decision during combat. Consequently it's a brave man, or an incautious one, who criticizes another man for the action which he took in battle unless it is obviously an error caused by lack of character.

There is a veteran destroyerman speaking. And he says a lot between the lines.

Saufley Kills I-2

After the Battle of Cape Esperance (October 11-12, 1942), a Jap submarine had attacked the destroyer McCalla, which was combing the waters north of Savo for survivors. The sub which had made that frustrated effort was the I-2.

The I-2 was still in the Solomons area in the spring of 1944. That was her last season on that or any front. On April 7, DesDiv 43 (Renshaw, Saufley, Pringle, and Philip) was patrolling in the vicinity of Mussau and Emirau Islands. At 0630 Saufley's sonar tagged a submarine 1,350 yards distant. Lieutenant Commander D. E. Cochran conned the ship for a depth-charge run.

At 0645 Saufley dropped a conventional 9-charge pattern. Thirty minutes later she dropped another of the same. Eight minutes after that a couple of heavy deep-sea explosions shook the ship. Sonar contact evaporated. Saufley "pinged" all over the seascape to no avail. Then, at 1120, an expanding oil slick was located about four miles from the scene of the last depth-charging. The oil was analyzed and found to be Diesel. By sunset the slick was 14 miles long. It marked the grave of I-2, Saufley's No. 2 submarine kill.

American Epaulets on the Admiralties

Just west of the Bismarcks lie the Admiralty Islands, the next stepping stone on the Allied road through the Southwest Pacific to the Philippines. Annexed by Germany in Bismarck's day, the Admiralties were taken over by Australia after World War I, and seized by Japan in 1942. The Japs built airfields on Los Negros and at Seeadler Harbor, Manus. On February 29, 1944, MacArthur's forces went ashore on Los Negros. Reconnaissance had been sketchy, and Intelligence underestimated the Jap garrison. As a result, a bitter battle exploded on the beachhead.

Kinkaid's Seventh Fleet forces provided heroic support for the hard-pushed Army troops. A task group under Rear Admiral W. M. Fechteler spearheaded the assault. The group was composed of Captain Jesse H. Carter's veteran DD's—Reid, Flusser, Mahan, Drayton, Smith, Bush, Welles, Stockton, and Stevenson. High-speed transports Humphreys, Brooks, and SANDS carried the expeditionary pioneers. The approach was covered by cruisers PHOENIX and NASHVILLE and destroyers DALY, HUTCHINS, BEALE, and BACHE, under Rear Admiral R. S. Berkey.

The landing ships were met by heavy artillery fire, but the troops went doggedly ashore. Reinforcements were brought in, and in three weeks the Los Negros garrison was subdued. Simultaneously, Manus Island was invaded. Into Seeadler Harbor on March 8 went transport destroyers LONG and HAMILTON, escorted by the WILKES and the SWANSON. Supporting the Admiralty beachheads, some of the destroyers, such as DesDiv 26, encountered ferocious enemy salvos.

The destroyers of DesDiv 26 were: WILKES (Commander F. Wolsieffer), NICHOLSON (Commander W. W. Vanous), SWANSON (Commander E. L. Robertson, Jr.), and SMITH (Lieutenant Commander F. V. List). The division was commanded by Commander A. J. Greenacre, riding in WILKES. The ships arrived off Hyane Harbor, Los Negros, on March 4, 1944. The group was directed by Captain Carter (ComDesRon 5) to relieve four other DD's which had been patrolling the harbor.

In the daytime the ships maintained an A/S screen. During the night they patrolled independently, keeping watch for barge traffic, and delivering shore bombardments on call. On the morning of the 6th, NICHOLSON was ordered to Seeadler to draw fire from shore batteries and thus determine their location.

Not only did NICHOLSON succeed in drawing fire, but she located and blasted the batteries which exposed themselves. In so doing she was hit by a shell from a naval gun which put her No. 2 gun out of action, killed three men, and seriously wounded two.

Rear Admiral Fechteler lauded DesDiv 26 for *"an excellent performance."* He remarked, *"Fire support units on call in the immediate assault area contributed materially to the progress of forces ashore."* Other destroyers which contributed to that progress in the Admiralties were MULLANY and AMMEN, and H.M.A.S. WARRAMUNGA.

Seeadler Harbor gave the Seventh Fleet an exceptionally good anchorage, and Manus soon developed into a major Southwest Pacific base for Allied operations. With the Admiralties in Allied hands, Rabaul was sealed off. The war rushed on past the Bismarcks, and the Rabaul citadel became about as useless as a decaying castle in Spain.

In mid-March the MacArthur steamroller was flattening such New Guinea bases as Wewak. Seventh Fleet destroyers joined Army air in pounding this Jap outpost. On March 18-19, Task Group 74.5 raided the Wewak-Hollandia area. The group was composed of destroyers DALY (flagship of Captain K. M. McManes, ComDesRon 24), HUTCHINS, BEALE, MULLANY, and AMMEN. Shipping in Wewak Harbor was shelled and several small craft were sunk. A few "bogies" were picked up, but no air attacks developed. The raid advised the Japs that their hold on northwest New Guinea was slipping.

In April the Japs on Java and Sumatra received similar advices. On the 19th of that month the East Indies were visited by forces from Trincomalee, Ceylon. Crossing the Indian Ocean, an Allied fleet under Admiral J. F. Somerville, R.N., struck at Sabang, Sumatra. Operating with this force from India were American destroyers CUMMINGS, DUNLAP, and FANNING. A month later (May 17) the same force delivered an air attack on Soerabaja, Java.

Meanwhile, MacArthur's forces, carried by Seventh Fleet amphibs, had gone leapfrogging to Aitape and Hollandia. Task Force 58 was called south to provide air cover for the Hollandia drive, but the big Central Pacific carriers enjoyed something of a holiday, and they were released almost immediately to conduct strikes against Truk and Panope. By June MacArthur troops were entering Geelvink Bay near the western end of New Guinea. The Japs in the Geelvink area put up a savage fight, and destroyers were called upon to bombard Biak Island lying athwart the mouth of the bay.

Destroyer REID (Commander S. A. McCornock) off Biak was lacerated by near misses when Jap aircraft attacked on June 3. In company with destroyers MUSTIN and RUSSELL she was on duty in the mouth of Geelvink when Jap planes dived out of the clouds at about 1100. In the battle that ensued the destroyer was bombed and strafed by "Tonies" and "Tojos." REID shot down two planes, and sent two others veering off with smoke pouring from their tails. Anywhere from 15 to 20 Jap aircraft had struck at the ship. Remarkably enough, she fought her way out from under with no more damage than four small holes in her superstructure and superficial injury to her SG radar antenna. One sailor was killed and some six were wounded in the furious action.

On the night of June 8-9 an Allied force containing cruisers H.M.A.S. AUSTRALIA (flagship) and PHOENIX, and DesDivs 47, 48, and 49, plus two Australian destroyers, made contact with a Jap reinforcement convoy of five destroyers off Biak. The Japs fled northwestward as the Allied force "poured on the coal" to close the range. The American destroyers chased, hurling long-range salvos at the fleeing ships. The enemy destroyers returned the gunfire and unleashed some torpedoes at their pursuers. No ship on either side was hit in this action. As a veteran DD commander noted, "Gun action at or near maximum range is usually wasted effort. All one can hope for is a lucky hit."

By mid-September the heavy ships of the Seventh Fleet were bombarding the airfields of Halmahera Island and the beachheads of Morotai. Army troops waded ashore on Morotai on September 15. MacArthur's vanguard was less than 350 miles from Mindanao. But the big shock to Tokyo was the Battle of the Philippine Sea and the American invasion of the Marianas. All of which happened that June.

Destroyers to Saipan and Tinian (Marianas Campaign)

The Battle of the Philippine Sea (June 19-21, 1944) featured American submarine work, Navy Air, antiaircraft gunnery, and the blasting of Toyoda's "Plan A-Go." Participation by Destroyers Pacific was more or less limited to A/S screening, AA gunnery, and the usual jobs detailed to destroyers serving with a Fast Carrier Task Force. The complex moves of this battle cannot be covered in a text devoted to destroyer warfare. Toyoda's planning has been discussed in the previous chapter. As was related, the submarine-massacre staged by destroyer-escort ENGLAND and her companions did much to scramble the Japanese "A-Go" plan. When Nimitz's invasion forces approached the Marianas during the second week in June, 1944, Toyoda was unprepared to throw his full strength into the defense of the archipelago. By the time he got Kurita's battleships into the Philippine Sea, Ozawa's carriers had been detected in the area, Saipan had suffered a tremendous bombardment, and Marines were going ashore on the island's southwest coast.

As the Jap Combined Fleet raced eastward from the Philippines to plug the leaky Mariana defenses, Task Force 58 took position in the waters off the archipelago, and squared away to have it out with the oncoming Japs. At 1000 in the morning of June 19, Task Force 58 groups were attacked by Jap naval and land-based planes. That was the beginning of what came to be called the "Marianas turkey shoot." Before the end of the day nearly 400 Jap planes had been shot out of the sky by AA fire and American fighters. The Japs landed one bomb on battleship SOUTH DAKOTA, and a crashing plane dealt minor damage to the INDIANA. Some 27 American aircraft were lost. So was the battle, for the Japanese.

Immediately after the "turkey shoot," Admiral Spruance ordered Mitscher's carrier forces to run westward and attack the Imperial Fleet. But the Jap fleet was already hauling out for Japan at best speed. American submarines had ambushed several of Ozawa's finest carriers. The Jap ships were out of pilots, out of gas, and out of confidence. Naval aircraft caught up with them, however, and then they were out of the carrier HITAKA, a destroyer, and a fleet oiler. Navy bombs dug holes in three more flat-tops, and damaged a battleship, three cruisers, and three tankers. Toyoda had lost control of the sea, and the Imperial Navy was now a reluctant dragon with its wings badly clipped as it raced for home and sanctuary at 20 knots.

Almost immediately afterward the Japs received more bad news from the Marianas front. Saipan, Tinian, and Guam in this bastion of the Empire were strongly defended by land batteries, land-based air, and large garrisons. But they could not hold out against the Central Pacific steamroller, once control of the surrounding seas was lost. It was lost, as has been noted, in the Battle of the Philippine Sea.

The forces which undertook the Saipan invasion were organized along the lines of the "Flintlock" forces that took the Marshalls. Vice Admiral Turner's Expeditionary Force contained 535 ships and carried some 127,500 Marines and Army troops to the Marianas beachheads. The invasion troops were opposed by about 50,000 Japanese, over half of whom garrisoned Saipan. Chief objective on Saipan was the large airfield on the southern end of the island. As this field was within range of heavy artillery on Tinian, that island also had to be taken. Guam also was on the agenda—former American territory due for recapture.

American destroyers fought hard battles in the Marianas campaign. Early on the scene were destroyers BURNS and COWELL, serving as picket ships for Task Group 58.1 conducting the first Marianas strike. About noon on June 11 the destroyer team went into action, reporting a "bogie" and vectoring CAP (Combat Air Patrol) planes to intercept. That and several other Jap planes were shot down before evening. Typical picket duty for typically sharp DD's.

Bombarding Tinian Harbor on June 14, destroyer BRAINE (Commander W. W. Fitts) silenced several enemy batteries. She took a direct hit which killed three men and wounded 15, but escaped other salvos by radical maneuvering.

Off Saipan on June 15, destroyers BOYD and CHARRETTE, under Commander W. M. Sweetser, ComDesDiv 92, trapped and sank the Jap cargoman TATSUTAGAWA MARU. The *maru*, carrying Jap "laborers," was en route from Saipan to Yokosuka. She was detected about 30 miles from Task Group 58.1 and attacked by aircraft. Division flagship BOYD requested and received permission to gun down the ship. She and CHARRETTE shelled the vessel around noon, and

Destroyer at work with an Underwater Demolition Team: Robinson pours 40 mm gunfire onto the beach at Peleliu Island to cover the demolition squad clearing away obstacles for the landing scheduled to take place next day. Transporting, covering, and recovering UDT's was only one of many special assignments carried out by destroyers in the Allied sweep across the Pacific.

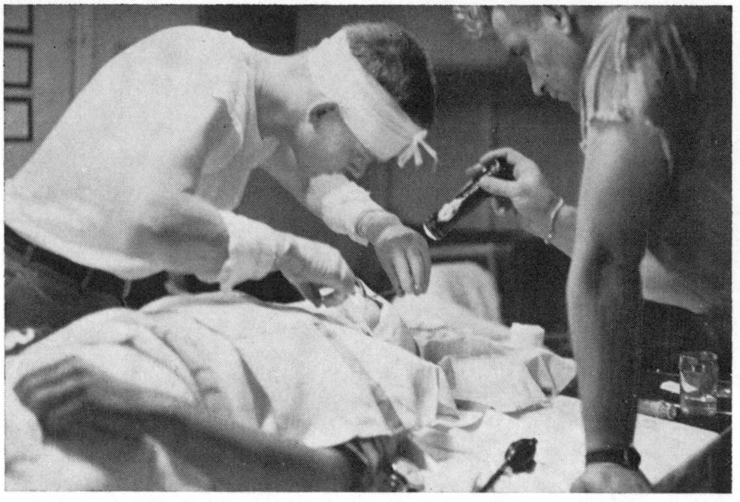

A destroyer's wardroom is used for more than serving meals, playing card games, and holding courts-martial. During the battle for Saipan, medical aid is given aboard Monssen (DD 798) while supporting the landing forces.

Off Guam, east of Agano, Farragut shells Jap caves and gun emplacements at pointblank range—and while she was doing it, her stateside mail was delivered aboard. Marianas assault forces included 159 DD's and DE's.

Marianas Turkey Shoot. In the two-day battle almost 500 Jap planes were destroyed, stripping the Japanese fleet of most of its experienced naval aviators. U. S. losses included 130 planes, but only 76 aviation personnel.

Destroyers work over the Japs on Saipan. The bottom photograph shows McNair with her flock of transports and merchantmen off the Marianas after D-day.

Kalk helps refloat stranded LST's at Biak with her wash from a high-speed run close to the Beach, and (bottom) supports the landings at pointblank range.

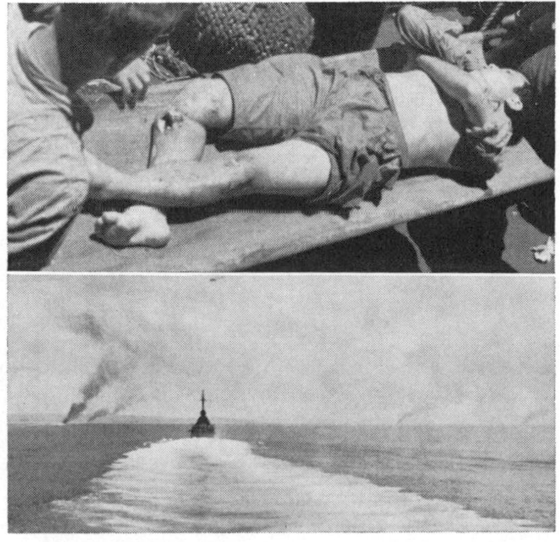

A Jap survivor of the Turkey Shoot picked up by Healy (top). The pillars of smoke (bottom) are from Jap merchantmen of a 32-ship convoy that was sunk.

DESTROYERS AND DESTROYER-ESCORTS IN THE MARIANAS OPERATION

VESSELS WHICH PARTICIPATED IN ASSAULT
(SHIPS IN GARRISON ECHELONS OMITTED)

DESTROYERS

Abbot
Albert W. Grant
Anthony
Aylwin
Bagley
Bailey
Bancroft
Bell
Bennett
Bennion
Black
Boyd
Bradford
Braine
Brown
Bullard
Burns
Callaghan
Caperton
Capps
Case
Charles Ausburne
Charrette
Chauncey
Clarence K. Bronson
Coghlan
Cogswell
Colahan
Conner
Converse
Conway
Cony
Conyngham
Cotten

Cowell
Craven
Dale
Dashiell
David W. Taylor
Dewey
Dortch
Downes
Dyson
Eaton
Edwards
Ellet
Erben
Evans
Farragut
Franks
Fullam
Gatling
Gridley
Guest
Haggard
Hailey
Hale
Halford
Hall
Halligan
Halsey Powell
Haraden
Harrison
Healy
Helm
Heywood L. Edwards
Hickox
Hudson
Hull

Hunt
Ingersoll
Izard
John D. Henley
John Rodgers
Johnston
Kidd
Knapp
Lang
Lansdowne
Lardner
Lewis Hancock
Longshaw
Macdonough
Marshall
Maury
McCall
McCalla
McDermut
McGowan
McKee
McNair
Melvin
Mertz
Miller
Monaghan
Monssen
Mugford
Murray
Newcomb
Norman Scott
Owen
Patterson
Paul Hamilton
Phelps

Philip
Porterfield
Prichett
Pringle
Ralph Talbot
Remey
Renshaw
Ringgold
Robinson
Saufley
Schroeder
Selfridge
Shaw
Sigourney
Sigsbee
Spence
Stack
Stembel
Stephen Potter
Sterett
Stevens
Stockham
Terry
Thatcher
The Sullivans
Tingey
Twining
Wadleigh
Wadsworth
Walker
Waller
Williamson
Wilson
Yarnall

DESTROYER-ESCORTS

Acree
Bangust
Baron
Canfield
Dionne

Elden
Fair
Hilbert
Lamons
Manlove

Mitchell
Riddle
Samuel S. Miles
Sederstrom
Swearer

Tisdale
Waterman
Weaver
Wesson
Whitman

Wileman

in less than seven minutes the *maru* rolled over and sank. CHARRETTE picked up 112 unhappy survivors.

One of the busiest DD's on the Saipan front was PHELPS (Lieutenant Commander D. L. Martineau). On duty off Saipan from June 15 to June 22, she performed dozens of missions. During the evening of June 19, while alongside the repair ship PHAON, she loaded ammunition from small boats while repairing battle damage and dealing out a shore bombardment with her forward guns. Answering call fire, she expended a total of 958 rounds. This ambidexterous performance followed a shooting match which took place during the morning watch—a duel with a shore battery in which PHELPS was struck by two medium-caliber shells. One hit below her bridge, and the other struck on the starboard side near the base of her No. 2 stack. Sixteen men were wounded (one fatally) by the explosions. PHELPS had gone alongside PHAON for repairs when she went into evening action as related.

On December 16 destroyer SHAW and high-speed transport GILMER shot up some Jap shipping off the southwest end of Saipan. During this action GILMER was peppered by machine-gun fire from a small *maru*, or "sea truck." Five of these wooden vessels had been detected. Four were gunned down by GILMER, one by SHAW.

Perhaps the hardest destroyer action in the Mariana campaign was fought by Fire Support Unit Three —battleship COLORADO (Rear Admiral T. D. Ruddock, Jr.), cruiser CLEVELAND and destroyers REMEY (flagship of Captain J. G. Coward, ComDesRon 54), NORMAN SCOTT, and MONSSEN. During the assault on Tinian on July 24 these ships conducted a diversionary demonstration off Tinian Town. Camouflaged Jap batteries opened fire about 0740. COLORADO and NORMAN SCOTT were hard hit. Six 6-inch shells slammed into the SCOTT before she could dodge away. The blasting killed 19 men and wounded 63. Among those killed was the destroyer's skipper, Commander S. D. Owens. *"The conduct of the* NORMAN SCOTT," wrote Admiral Oldendorf, *"reflects great credit upon . . . its complement and upon the courageous name which it bears."*

June, 1944, was also a bad month for Admiral Miwa's submarine fleet. Nine ocean-going subs were abolished by Allied A/S work that month. United States Navy destroyermen were responsible for six of the nine abolishments.

Taylor Downs I-5

Destroyer TAYLOR (Commander N. J. F. Frank) was a screening ship with Captain W. V. Saunders' Task Group 30.4, built around escort-carrier HOGGATT BAY. The group was engaged in a hunter-killer patrol north of the Admiralty Islands. In the afternoon of June 10, 1944, one of the "jeep carrier" planes sighted a long oil slick trailing across the seascape, and TAYLOR was detailed to make an investigation.

The destroyer steamed for the spot at 1341, and in a short time picked up sonar contact. Commander Frank directed two depth-charge attacks. While maneuvering for a third attack, TAYLOR saw the submarine lunge to the surface dead ahead, at a range of 2,400 yards. Immediately the ship opened fire on the I-boat. Shells slammed around the enemy conning tower, and smoke rolled across the sea as the sub submerged. Steaming to the spot where the I-boat went under, the destroyer launched three more depth-charge patterns. About nine minutes after the third pattern was dropped, and eleven minutes after the submarine dived, the sea was roiled by underwater demolition.

The explosions sent the usual litter to the surface—deck planking, chunks of wood, and oil. The kill was made about 180 miles off the Admiralty Islands. The dead submarine was eventually identified as the Japanese I-5.

Bangust Kills RO-111

On the night of June 10-11, 1944, the destroyer escort BANGUST (Lieutenant Commander C. F. MacNish, U.S.N.R.) was steaming independently from Pearl Harbor to Kwajalein Atoll. She was about 60 miles east of Roi when her radar registered a suspicious "pip." Time: 2325.

At 2342 a vessel was sighted emerging from a rain-squall. The silhouette was blurred in the streaky dark, and immediate identification was impossible. But by the time BANGUST had closed the range to 3,000 yards the stranger had the look of a small surface craft or a submarine. Commander MacNish challenged twice. Deigning to offer no reply, the stranger turned away and submerged.

BANGUST was on the trail like a mongoose after a cobra. Tracking, sonar contact, search and attack followed the usual pattern. The DE unleashed three hedgehog salvos with negative results. A fourth salvo was nothing if not positive. A spatter of explosions amplified into a huge undersea blast. After which the listening sonar crew heard in the sea an effervescent hissing, bubbling, and gurgling. Diesel fumes came drifting across the water. The destroyermen searched the area until 1700 in the afternoon of June 11. BANGUST never regained sonar contact with the sub. The submersible had gone beyond "pinging" range. In its wake it had left a telltale oil slick and a strew of diced cork. Post-war inquest divulged the sub's identity. BANGUST had killed RO-111.

Melvin Sinks RO-36

Cruising off Saipan on June 13, 1944, an RO-boat unluckily met up with the destroyer MELVIN (Commander W. R. Edsall). MELVIN was a member of Rear Admiral Oldendorf's Task Group 52.17.

At 2202 the Task Group Commander sent MELVIN to investigate an unidentified radar target. Within four minutes the destroyer had the contact at 6,000 yards. Closing to 4,000, the DD opened up with gunnery, using full radar-control salvo fire. A brilliant flash indicated a hit by the second salvo. The target promptly disappeared from the radar scope.

At 2239 sonar contact was obtained, range 2,900 yards. Commander Edsall conned MELVIN into position for a depth-charge attack, and a full pattern was sent rolling at 2245. Swinging away from the exploding charges, the destroyer passed through a fog of Diesel fumes. Evidently the sub had been hard hit by the 5-inch barrage.

A second and third depth-charge attack was delivered on the undersea target. When contact could not be regained, MELVIN was ordered to abandon search and rejoin the task group formation. The time was 2331. In something like an hour and a half the destroyer had come, seen, and conquered. The victim was RO-36. And, as will be noted, MELVIN was just warming up.

Burden R. Hastings Kills RO-44

Early in the morning of June 16, 1944, the destroyer-escort BURDEN R. HASTINGS was proceeding independently to Pearl Harbor from Eniwetok. She was about 120 miles east of the atoll when she picked up a long-distance radar contact (range 20,000 yards). By 0337 she had closed the range to 5,000 yards. Unable to identify the target, the DE's skipper, Lieutenant Commander E. B. Fay, U.S.N.R., challenged with Aldis lamp. Upon receiving no reply, he ordered a starshell spread. Under a spray of light the stranger's silhouette was seen to submerge.

The DE had the sonar contact at 0354. Steaming forward on the attack, she opened fire with hedgehog. The second salvo scored a thunderous explosion at shallow depth, and phosphorescent lightning flashed and fluttered through the water. The HASTINGS cruised over the spot where this luminous display flared and faded, and four depth charges were flung overside. About five seconds after these charges exploded, there was a blast which shook the DE from stern to stem. The jolt threw out the circuit-breaker on the forward main motor and caused a loss of gyro power for about 15 minutes. In the wake of that thunderclap sonar contact was gone for good.

At sunrise the DE's lookouts saw an interesting smear of oil and debris. Out of this litter some anatomical scraps were picked up, and the boat crew found a varnished oak boxtop tagged with an aluminum name-plate. The plate identified the exploded submarine as the RO-44.

Wadleigh and Melvin Sink RO-114

On June 17, 1944, Oldendorf's task group was sharing the seascape about 100 miles west of Saipan with another RO-boat. The area was not big enough for both of them, so the RO-boat had to go. It went, after destroyer MELVIN obtained radar contact with the surfaced sub at 7,400 yards. The sub went under as MELVIN closed the range, but she did not go deep fast enough.

Visibility was practically zero, but after the submarine dived, vision did not matter. MELVIN's sonar detected the submersible at 2,500 yards. This contact was made at 0115. Commander W. R. Edsall launched a deliberate attack, and a full pattern of depth charges was sent deep. The destroyer followed through with two "dry" runs. She had only 12 charges left, and was keeping her powder dry. Destroyer WADLEIGH (Commander W. C. Winn) was thereupon dispatched by ComDesRon 54 to take over the attack.

WADLEIGH took over by dropping four patterns. In the booming wake of this 4-charge pattern the sea echoed to a blast which sent vibrations through the destroyers "upstairs." Thereafter, sonar contact was unobtainable.

The destroyers terminated their hunt when sunrise revealed on the water an extensive smear of oil and a variety of debris. The sub's obituary notice was eventually found in Admiral Miwa's records. WADLEIGH and MELVIN had destroyed the RO-114. This was MELVIN's second kill in four days.

Newcomb and Chandler Sink I-185

Destroyer NEWCOMB (Commander L. B. Cook), flagship of ComDesRon 56, and destroyer-minesweeper CHANDLER (Lieutenant Commander H. L. Thompson, Jr.) were members of a screen for transports which were maintaining a flow of supplies and troops to Saipan. In the morning of June 22, 1944, NEWCOMB acquired a sudden sonar contact at 0903. Commander Cook conned the ship for an urgent attack. Depth charges were dropped at 0906. Fast work!

At 0907 the ex-"four-piper" CHANDLER teamed up with NEWCOMB on the attack. The two ships were "pinging" for the target when, at 1023, the sea echoed to two rumbling explosions. Sixty seconds later

CHANDLER made sound contact with the target, and dropped an 8-charge pattern. Up came a pungent oil slick and a mess of debris. Spelling each other off, NEWCOMB and CHANDLER depth-charged the water which was spewing this oily rubbish. At 1144, after a last attack by CHANDLER, there was a final deep-sea explosion.

"Debris in area of attack included cork slabs, wood, Diesel oil, and human entrails."

The end had come for Imperial Navy submarine I-185.

She was the sixth submarine downed by American destroyermen in the Pacific during the month of June, 1944. With July coming up on the calendar, the A/S campaign went ahead in high gear.

Riddle and David W. Taylor Kill I-10

Independence Day, 1944, was a dark day for Japanese submarine I-10. She was keeping her head down that evening, but not down far enough when Task Group 50.17 (a fuelling group consisting of six oilers and an escort-carrier) cruised by. Screening units in this group were destroyer-escort RIDDLE (Lieutenant Commander R. H. Cramer, U.S.N.R.) and destroyer DAVID W. TAYLOR (Commander W. H. Johnsen). The ships were minding their business in waters off the Marianas when RIDDLE, at 1707, made sonar contact with the I-boat at 6,000 yards.

While the formation maneuvered to avoid the "skunk," the DE dropped an embarrassing barrage of depth charges. At 1732 she let fly with hedgehog. Three minutes later the TAYLOR was sent by ComDesRon 51 to assist. While the DD was heading for the scene of action, RIDDLE fired two more hedgehog salvos, and followed through with a depth-charge run.

TAYLOR had sonar contact at 1822, and dropped an 11-charge pattern four minutes later. All charges exploded boisterously. At 1828 both ships heard and felt a stupendous undersea blast. A flock of bubbles rose to the surface, and TAYLOR came upon a large pond of oil and flotsam. The ships continued the search for about 20 hours, but they could find nothing more.

And they had found enough. On the sea bottom, her pressure hull burst and her compartments probably flooded, lay the I-10. Evidently she was downed by the old one-two—staggered by RIDDLE, and floored by DAVID W. TAYLOR.

William C. Miller Kills I-6

At 2120 in the evening of July 13, 1944, an A/S plane spotted a Jap sub submerging about 78 miles west of Rorogattan Point, Saipan. Dispatched on hunter-killer mission by ComDesRon 56, Commander of the Saipan Transport Area Screen, destroyer-escort WILLIAM C. MILLER (Lieutenant Commander D. F. Francis, U.S.N.R.) and high-speed transport GILMER arrived on the scene at 0022 in the morning of the 14th.

The two ships searched until well after sunrise before the target was located. Then at 0720 the MILLER made sonar contact at 1,700 yards. Her skipper conned the DE in for a run, and she laid 13 charges in a neat pattern across the seascape. Lieutenant Commander Francis opened the range; contact was regained at 1,500 yards; another 13-charge pattern was fired. The MILLER started a third attack, but broke off the approach when the lookouts saw chunks of wood popping to the surface. A moment later the destroyermen heard a series of underwater *booms.* The sea churned and boiled. Thirteen charges were dropped into the swirl. Much debris rose with a spew of oil.

The destroyermen fished up a fur-lined cap with Jap naval insignia attached. Also fished up were several bits of something which appeared to be human lung tissue. These were the last earthly remains of the crew which manned the Imperial Navy's I-6.

Wyman Kills RO-48

Destroyer-escort WYMAN (Lieutenant Commander E. P. Parker, U.S.N.R.) was one of four DE's screening HOGGATT BAY. The hunter-killer group was on the prowl for bear along the convoy routes between Eniwetok and Saipan. On July 19, 1944, they had good hunting.

At 0024 WYMAN peeled off to track down a surface target picked up by radar at eight miles range. Twenty minutes later the "pip" flickered out on the radar screen, and WYMAN's sound crew immediately reported sonar contact. This was the familiar submarine affair, and WYMAN gave it an ending equally familiar. By 0051 Lieutenant Commander Parker had the ship in attack position, and she fired a full pattern of hedgehogs. The projectiles missed. Thirty-one minutes later the hedgehogs were flying again. A crackle of explosions assured the destroyermen they had found the mark.

At 0130 a number of deafening explosions roared into the DE's sound gear. Lost in the wake of this bombilation, contact could not be recovered. WYMAN was presently joined by destroyer-escort REYNOLDS (flagship of ComCortDiv 49), and the two ships ran the legs of a retiring-search plan. After daylight they picked up oil samples and specimens of debris. While WYMAN's whaleboat was combing through the flotsam, the little craft was attacked by eager aircraft from HOGGATT BAY, the airmen mistaking the boat for a surfaced sub. Two destroyermen were injured by the strafing planes before "recognition" was made. Fortunately WYMAN's boat did not join RO-48 on the ocean floor.

Wyman and Reynolds Kill I-55

Late in July the HOGGATT BAY group added another submarine to the month's A/S score. The ships responsible were destroyer-escorts REYNOLDS (Lieutenant Commander E. P. Adams, U.S.N.R.), flagship of Commander R. E. Lockwood, ComCortDiv 49, and WYMAN.

At 1733 in the evening of July 28, 1944, the two DE's steamed away to track down a sub which had been sighted by WYMAN's lookouts and simultaneously reported by HOGGATT BAY. When spotted, the submarine was 12½ miles from the hunter-killer group. As the two DE's headed for the submersible, she made haste to submerge.

At 1805 WYMAN's Sound men reported contact, and nine minutes later Lieutenant Commander Parker had the ship in attack position. She fired a full pattern of hedgehogs straight to the mark. The sea boomed and banged, and the rataplan was concluded by a great deep-sea roar.

REYNOLDS stepped in to fire a full hedgehog pattern. The projectiles sank in silence, and silence was reported by the DE Sonarmen. As was so often the case, this sonar silence was golden. It was followed by the discovery of an oceanic oil well, shattered planking, and scraps of woodwork. The woodwork was stamped with Jap ideographs. After the war this rubbish was identified as the residue of Japanese submarine I-55.

In sinking the I-55, destroyer-escort WYMAN made herself something of a record. As Commander Lockwood noted in endorsing her Action Report, the U.S.S. WYMAN *"had two sound contacts, fired a total of three hedgehog salvos, and destroyed two subs."*

Footnote to the A/S campaign: Of the six Jap submarines downed in July, 1944, American destroyermen accounted for four.

Destroyers to Morotai

By September, 1944, the Army-Navy amphibious team had cut the Bismarcks, the Admiralties, and New Guinea out of the Japanese Empire. The way to the Netherlands East Indies lay open, and the ground was cut from under the Jap-held Philippines. MacArthur's Army forces and Kinkaid's Navy forces were now prepared to slash their way to Mindanao.

Between New Guinea and the southernmost Philippine Islands, Halmahera reared its bulk as a stepping stone. Off this Celebes land mass the Japs had established an outpost on the island of Morotai, and had strongly fortified it with artillery and a sizable garrison. But MacArthur had marked it for a fall. And D-Day was set for September 15, 1944.

The Morotai defenses had not been too well analyzed, and the landing forces had a tough fight on their hands before the Japs were put down. Operating with the Amphibs were the destroyers of Rear Admiral R. S. Berkey's Task Group 77.2. These DD's were HUTCHINS (flagship of Captain K. M. McManes, ComDesRon 24), DALY, BEALE, BACHE, ABNER READ, BUSH, AMMEN, MULLANY, H.M.A.S. ARUNTA, and H.M.A.S. WARRAMUNGA.

Destroyers to the Pelews

Timed to coincide with landings on Morotai were the U.S. landings in the Pelews of the Caroline group. The invasion fleet sent to Palau contained some 800 ships, the First Marine Division, and Army forces. D-Day was set for September 15, 1944. As usual, the drive for the beachheads was spearheaded by destroyers.

A tooth-and-claw fight was in prospect, for the enemy would not readily surrender this base within 500 miles of the Philippines.

The occupation began with the biggest bombardment yet seen and heard in the Southwest Pacific. The DesPac DD's had their work cut out for them at Peleliu. Typical duty was undertaken and accomplished off that beachhead by destroyer ROBINSON (Commander E. B. Grantham, Jr.), flagship of Captain T. F. Conley, Jr., ComDesDiv 112. From September 12 to September 29, ROBINSON operated nonstop as a unit of the Peleliu fire-support group. Here are some of the assignments which were on her busy agenda.

(a) September 12-14: provided close fire support for UDT's.
(b) September 15-16: on call fire missions.
(c) September 19-20: furnished night illumination and harassing fire.
(d) September 21-22: night illumination fire and call fire.
(e) September 22-23: night illumination fire and call fire.
(f) September 24: shelling enemy barges.
(g) September 26-27: night illumination and harassing fire.
(h) September 27-28: night harassing fire mission, and bombardment of Ngesebus.
(i) September 28-29: night illumination fire.

Perhaps ROBINSON's most interesting mission involved close fire support for the Underwater Demolition Teams. Covering the "frog men" at their hazardous work, the destroyer hammered enemy machine-gun emplacements, pillboxes, trenches, and sniper hide-outs with 40 mm. and 5-inch. On September 22 she shot it out with a number of Japanese tanks which came crawling out of the undergrowth, her fire spotted by a keen-eyed plane from cruiser INDIANAPOLIS.

The minesweeping job in the Pelews was no mean task. The destroyers in the thick of it were WADLEIGH (Commander W. C. Winn) and BENNETT (Commander P. F. Hauck). On September 15 WADLEIGH reported for duty as a radar picket off Kossol Passage. The following morning she took station astern of three sweepers to act as mine-demolition vessel while the eastern entrance of Kossol was being cleared. By 1235 of that day the destroyer had demolished 11 mines. She took care of another early in the afternoon. Then at 1428 she fouled a mine to starboard. The blast shattered her forward engine-room; her rudder was damaged; all power was lost. The sea poured into her engineering spaces, and the ship assumed a five degree list. Three men were killed by the explosion, and 15 were injured. Taken in tow by destroyer BENNETT, the badly damaged vessel was hauled to safe anchorage, and valiant repair measures kept her afloat.

"Ordinarily destroyers are not to be used as mine disposal vessels. . . . The importance of establishing Kossol Passage as a seaplane base and temporary fleet anchorage justified the use of any ships available to free this area of the mine hazard." So stated Vice Admiral T. S. Wilkinson, who comanded the invasion fleet.

Commenting on the episode, ROBINSON's captain stated in his report: *"The Commanding Officer knows of nothing more sinister looking than a moored mine some ten feet below the surface and close aboard his vessel. When once again in safe waters, all hands relaxed and, in spite of the intense heat, consumed much coffee."*

In on the barge shooting at Peleliu was destroyer HEYWOOD L. EDWARDS (Commander J. W. Boulware). Early in the morning of September 24 the Japs sneaked a large barge convoy into the lagoon. EDWARDS fired starshells, and then with her main battery joined a number of landing craft in blasting the targets. When EDWARDS ran low on starshells, she turned a searchlight on the lagoon. Barges were exploding and sinking all over the scene. As far as is known, the entire reinforcement convoy was sunk—14 barges and several companies of soldiery abolished.

"The H. L. EDWARDS," wrote Rear Admiral Oldendorf, "*. . . never served more effectively than on the night of September 24, when she destroyed numerous enemy barges attempting to reinforce Peleliu."*

Although the First Marine Division secured the southern end of Peleliu and the local airfield within two days, it took ten weeks and cost heavy Marine casualties to secure the entire island.

Angaur Island was handily captured. The troops which had been assigned to that mission were transported to Ulithi Atoll to capture that base. About 350 miles northeast of Palau, Ulithi provided the Navy with a fine anchorage. The Japs had pulled out when the Americans arrived, and the atoll was by way of a "gift." It was cheerfully "accepted" on the morning of September 22 when Rear Admiral R. W. Hayler's fire-support group, containing cruiser DENVER and destroyers ROSS (Commander Benjamin Coe) and BRYANT (Commander P. L. High), steamed into the lagoon. Nearby Yap Island was occupied at the same time. By October, 1944, Nimitz's forces were firmly based in the western Carolines within easy striking distance of the Philippines.

For an operation of such magnitude, destroyer casualties had been extremely light. On October 28 destroyer-escort DEMPSEY (Lieutenant Commander J. A. Weber) was lashed by machine-gun fire from a barge which slipped through the Peleliu screen. None of DEMPSEY's crew suffered injury, and the barge was sunk for its pains.

Hardest hit in the Palau battle was the crew of destroyer BAILEY (Commander M. T. Munger). While on night picket station off Peleliu, the destroyer, acting as fighter-director ship, was mistaken, attacked, and strafed by American planes. Nine of her crew were killed and sixteen wounded.

McCoy Reynolds Sinks I-175

While fleets, armies, and air forces were battling for possession of the Pelews, a little destroyer-escort was doing something about Miwa's Submarine Fleet, and doing it independently and with dispatch. The DE was the U.S.S. McCOY REYNOLDS, skippered by Lieutenant Commander E. K. Winn, U.S.N.R.

On September 26, 1944, while making a solitary run from Palau to Guam, the DE picked up radar contact at 0203 with a surface target, range 9,200 yards. When the DE challenged, the target answered by vanishing from the radar scope. Submarine!

McCOY REYNOLDS had sonar contact at 2,500 yards, and Winn maneuvered her in to fire hedgehog. The first salvo, uncorked at 0218, missed the mark. The second, a full pattern fired eight minutes later, produced a volley of detonations. The DE let fly with two more hedgehog salvos. Then Winn directed a depth-charge attack.

Apparently the "ashcans" missed. So another hedgehog barrage was fired. Crackling thunder echoed this salvo, and about seven minutes later a deep-sea blast shook the ship. Thereafter, sonar contact was unobtainable. But twenty minutes after the thunderclap, an odorous spew of Diesel oil spread across the ocean's surface, along with splintered deck planking and fragments of office or cabin furniture. Japanese submarine I-175 was no longer in the Land of the Living.

Loss of U.S.S. Shelton (and Sinking of Seawolf)

Always dangerous for the surface, air, and undersea forces were areas of joint operation where safety lanes and attack zones were frequently shifted with the tide of battle, and security from friend and foe alike depended on a rapid relay of accurate information. In such a joint operational area two factors placed friendly forces in constant jeopardy. First, the enemy might invade the defined safety lane, thereby obtaining temporary sanctuary. Second, someone might fail to "get the word," and open fire on a friendly unit detected in an area designated as safe. Early in October, 1944, these two adverse factors linked up to produce for the Seventh Fleet forces a tragic hour that cost the Navy a hard-working destroyer-escort and an ace submarine.

In the morning of October 3, 1944, a Seventh Fleet Task Group was steaming in the seascape off Morotai, on the road from New Guinea to the Philippines. The task group, built around the carriers MIDWAY and FANSHAW BAY, was screened by destroyer-escorts EVERSOLE, EDMONDS, RICHARD M. ROWELL, and SHELTON.

A new submarine safety lane, wherein American submarines would presumably be immune from attack by friendly forces, had recently been established in that area. On the morning in question, four American subs were working in these "safe waters." So was a Japanese submarine.

Here was the set-up for dire trouble. The American hunter-killers on the surface and in the air were prohibited from attacking any sub detected in the safety lane because it presumably would be "friendly." In consequence, the I-boat invader had that temporary sanctuary which at least would have compelled the hunters to make a positive identification before opening fire. The Japanese I-boat skulking off Morotai took advantage of this situation, and ambushed the hunter-killers.

At 0807 the sub fired a long-range spread. Target was destroyer-escort SHELTON (Lieutenant Commander L. G. Salomon, U.S.N.R.). The ship's lookouts glimpsed an oncoming wake at 900 yards, but before the DE could sprint away, a second "fish" struck the ship astern, blasting her starboard screw. Two officers and 11 men were killed by the explosion, and 22 of the crew were wounded.

Destroyer-escort ROWELL was directed to stand by the disabled DE and search for the submarine. While ROWELL was circling SHELTON, the injured ship's listening gear heard the whisper of a submarine propeller. The word was passed to ROWELL. At once ROWELL's skipper ordered a depth-charge salvo, and a pattern of "ashcans" went booming down into the sea.

At 1130 two planes took off from the escort-carrier MIDWAY to search the area. One of these planes sighted and dived on a submarine, bombing the submersible as it went down. The sighted sub was well within the safety lane, but the pilot who made the attack had not been properly informed on this detail.

The plane marked the spot with dye, and destroyer-escort ROWELL was sent racing to the scene—a run which took her 18 miles from the spot where SHELTON had been torpedoed. At 1310 ROWELL made sound contact with the submarine. The DE let fly with hedgehogs. As she circled off after this unsuccessful attack, she heard faint signals from the submarine. The stuttering dots and dashes bore no resemblance to friendly recognition signals. And ROWELL's skipper decided that an enemy sub was trying to "jam" the DE's sound gear.

So the DE made a second pass, throwing hedgehog projectiles. In the wake of this attack, four or five explosions were heard. A large air bubble ballooned to the surface. Up came a small scatter of debris, and the DE's lookouts saw what appeared to be a section of periscope. ROWELL was convinced she had downed a Jap submarine.

Meanwhile, the disabled SHELTON had assumed a list, and efforts to stem the flood proved unavailing. Her crew, transferred to ROWELL, was certain their fellow destroyermen had killed SHELTON's assailant. Affairs took a bad turn that evening when destroyer LANG arrived to take SHELTON in tow. With destroyer STEVENS screening, the long trek to port was begun. But SHELTON was too far gone for salvaging. At 2145, while under tow, the damaged vessel capsized.

As the hull remained adrift, Captain J. L. MELGAARD, ComDesDiv 4, in LANG, ordered the destroyer to sink the DE. About 2200 the destroyer's guns roared, and the SHELTON sank under a storm of fire.

This brought the curtain down on a tragic drama. For the submarine sunk by RICHARD M. ROWELL was not Japanese. The story emerged when the U.S.S. SEAWOLF, which had been en route from Manus to

Samar with a group of Army specialists, failed to arrive in the Philippines. Eventually it was learned that the famous SEAWOLF had been passing through the safety area at the fatal hour of the ROWELL attack. Bucking heavy seas, the American submarine had been running a day behind schedule. She had informed the Commander of Task Force 72 of that fact, and the information had been promptly relayed to the Commander of the Seventh Fleet. But someone failed to get the word. The A/S forces off Morotai never received this vital information. And, as has been related, the aviator from the MIDWAY was unaware that he had bombed a sub in a safety lane.

In view of the grim evidence, the Submarine Force could only draw the unhappy conclusion that SEAWOLF had been sunk by the aircraft bombing or by the hedgehog attacks delivered by RICHARD M. ROWELL. A Board of Investigation held it unlikely that a submarine would try to jam the sound gear of an A/S vessel by transmitting signals. ROWELL's Commanding Officer was censured for failing to make an effort to identify the signalling submarine. However, the Board recommended that no disciplinary action be taken, as the DE captain's action was considered *"due to over-zealousness to destroy an enemy."* And the major error was obviously a blunder in the communications system. Repeat: Somebody failed to get (or pass) the word.

What of the submarine that torpedoed SHELTON? She was identified after the war as Japanese submarine RO-41. After delivering the attack off Morotai, this RO-boat eventually returned to Japan. But the RO-41 herself was not on hand at war's end to testify in her own behalf. As will be seen, in the spring of 1945 she had one DE encounter too many.

Convoy Shoot Off Mindanao

Meanwhile, the Allied noose was steadily tightening around the Japanese neck in the Philippines. In the South China Sea, Seventh Fleet submarines were on the rampage. Around Luzon the wolfpacks of the Pacific Fleet increased the pressure of a numbing blockade. Afloat and ashore the Japs were pounded by carrier aircraft, and Tojo's forces in the archipelago's interior were harassed by relentless Filipino guerillas. By September, 1944, the Jap defenses were going soft.

About 0900 in the morning of September 9, scouting U.S. aircraft reported a ship-train of some 32 *marus* steaming south along the Mindanao coast. The convoy was made up of small freighters, oilers, and sampans, varying from 200 to 700 tons displacement, and they were hugging the shoreline timidly.

At the time the report was received, Task Unit 38.3.3, under Rear Admiral L. T. DuBose, was operating with TG 38.3 some 60 miles east of Sanco Point, where the convoy had been spotted. DuBose's task unit was composed of light cruisers SANTA FE (flagship) and BIRMINGHAM, and destroyers LAWS (Commander L. O. Wood) flagship of Commander M. Van Metre, ComDesDiv 110; PRICHETT (Commander C. T. Caufield); MORRISON (Commander W. H. Price); and LONGSHAW (Commander R. H. Speck). DuBose was directed to intercept and attack the convoy. Air cover was furnished the group by the carrier LANGLEY.

When the warships arrived off Cape Sanco they found the convoy already scrambled by the bombs of carrier aircraft. As DuBose's ships steamed into range, planes were diving on the targets, five *marus* were burning, and some of the Jap vessels were racing to reach the shelter of Bislig Bay.

The cruisers and destroyers opened fire at high noon, shelling all of the Jap craft. For an hour and forty-five minutes the American warships cruised off the coast "holding target practice on the enemy." DuBose tersely reported, *"All visible targets were sunk or otherwise wrecked."*

Apparently the convoy was unprotected by escorts, and if the *marus* carried weapons no one bothered to fire them. When DuBose's ships ceased fire and headed away to rejoin the task group, some 9,000 to 15,000 tons of Japanese shipping had been destroyed at no more cost than the expended ammunition.

As a consequence, somewhere in the Philippines one more Jap garrison tightened its belt and went on short rations. Or perhaps somewhere in the home islands another gas tank went dry because an oiler failed to show up with Borneo petroleum. In any event this convoy-slaughter off Mindanao furnished the cruiser and destroyer participants with a glimpse into the future. The Philippine Islands were soggy. With Nimitz's forces closing in from the north and center, and MacArthur's forces coming up from the south, it would not be long before the Philippines would be out of the Japanese Empire.

Operation "King Two" was in the making.

CHAPTER 32

RETURN TO THE PHILIPPINES

(LEYTE GULF, SURIGAO)

"King Two" Versus "Sho-Go"

During September 1944 Halsey's Third Fleet flyers bombed Jap installations in the Philippines all the way from Davao Gulf to Manila Bay. In so doing they obliterated about 900 enemy planes and some 70 Japanese ships. Convinced that enemy defenses were crumbling, Halsey recommended that the Philippine "return" be scheduled at once instead of in December, as planned. Nimitz concurred. Halsey went on to propose that the invasion forces should by-pass Mindanao (where MacArthur wanted to land) and go ashore on Leyte in the central Philippines. Concurrently meeting with Roosevelt and Churchill in Quebec, the Joint Chiefs of Staff, informed by Admiral King of this proposal, readily approved. Thereupon "Operation King Two" was advanced on the Allied agenda.

For "King Two" the Allies mustered the largest invasion armada yet assembled in the Pacific. The operation called for a drive from the south by MacArthur's forces, which included Admiral Kinkaid's Seventh Fleet. Simultaneously Halsey's Third Fleet would strike at the northern Philippines and support the Leyte invasion with Navy Air. Tremendous gun and air power would be brought to bear, for the better part of the Atlantic Fleet had now been transferred to the Pacific, and the Allies had a powerhouse available. Under Halsey's command were 9 heavy and 8 light carriers, 5 battleships, 14 cruisers, and 58 destroyers. General Walter Krueger's Sixth Army, reinforced by the 24th Army Corps from Hawaii, was to be put ashore on Leyte by the Third Fleet Amphibious Force. Admiral Kinkaid's Seventh Fleet contained 6 old battleships, 18 escort-carriers, 11 cruisers, 86 destroyers, 25 destroyer-escorts, and scores of smaller vessels. When they "returned" to the Philippines, the Allies intended to stay.

To meet this massive invasion threat, Admiral Soemu Toyoda, Japanese Commander-in-Chief, could muster 9 battleships, 23 cruisers, 63 destroyers, and 4 carriers. The carriers were manned by green airmen who had been rushed through flying school and graduated before they were capable of deck-landings at night. For that matter, their daytime landings were not up to snuff, and once they took off they were liable to be gone for good.

The Japanese battle plan for the defense of the Philippines—"Plan Sho-Go"—was another halfbaked affair. Much of it was spur-of-the-moment, devised in an atmosphere of hysteria and haste. The word "Sho" is Japanese for "conquer." Applied to a hasty (or any) defense plan, it seems decidedly incongruous.

"Sho-Go" called for a do-or-die stand by Kurita's weary Second Fleet. It called for a suicidal feint by Ozawa's crippled Carrier Force. And it called for a *hari-kiri* effort by Imperial airmen. Fantastically enough, it came within an ace of disrupting the Leyte landings.

As of October, 1944, the Imperial Navy's forces were at both ends of the shrinking Empire. Ozawa's Carrier Force was at home base in Japan. Kurita's Second Fleet (built around the twin giantesses, MUSHASHI and YAMATO) was at Lingga, near Singapore. In the Pescadores, off Formosa, lay a cruiser squadron under Admiral Shima. "Sho-Go" was to bring Ozawa down from the north; to bring Kurita up from the south; and to leave Shima in a fog. Its more intricate workings will be detailed presently, but the general idea was the defense of Leyte Gulf.

While Toyoda was fumbling with the awkward intricacies of the "Conquer" plan, Halsey's carrier groups were implementing "King Two" with strikes to maladjust Japanese thinking. Such a strike was the one delivered on Marcus Island. Destroyers participated.

Bombardment of Marcus Island (DD's Undertake Deception)

BOMBARD MARCUS ISLAND IN ORDER CREATE DIVERSION AND DESTROY ENEMY INSTALLATIONS X TARGETS ARE RADIO AND WEATHER STATIONS SUPPLY DUMPS AND BUILDING AREAS

Issued to Rear Admiral A. E. Smith's Task Group 30.2, the foregoing order destined Marcus Island for a blasting on October 9-10, 1944. Primary purpose of this mission was to draw Japanese attention from larger forces which were aiming a strike at Okinawa.

Task Group 30.2 consisted of three cruisers and six destroyers. Led by Captain H. P. Smith, ComDesRon 4, the destroyers were DUNLAP (Lieutenant Commander C. R. Welte), FANNING (Commander J. C. Bentley), CASE (Lieutenant Commander R. S. Willey), CUMMINGS (Commander P. D. Williams), CASSIN (Commander V. J. Meola), and DOWNES (Commander R. S. Fahle).

By employing numerous deceptive devices Admiral Smith contrived to give the diversionary bombardment the appearance of an invasion effort. At dawn of October 9, CUMMINGS took station 15 miles east of Marcus, made smudges to resemble a convoy's smokes, laid a smoke screen, and released aerographers' balloons carrying radar targets. Every effort was made to convince the Marcus garrison that a large fleet was hovering beyond the horizon.

During the night of October 9-10, Smith divided his task group into three units. These units bombarded three widely separate sectors of the Marcus foreshore. The ships fired 8-inch shells, 5-inch illuminating, white phosphorus, and AA common. Upon completion of a 45-minute bombardment, they set adrift several radar targets and three floats bearing flashlamps. As the floats rose and fell in the ground swell, the lamps flickered and blinked in simulation of ship lights.

Admiral Smith was dubious about the value of these delusive contrivances. While the warships were shelling the designated targets, the Marcus shore batteries answered with a vigorous fire. Although taken by surprise, the Japs did not seem unduly alarmed by the foray.

As Admiral Smith pointed out, it would be difficult to put across a mock assault on such an outpost as Marcus without the employment of carrier aircraft and "sham" transports. Admiral Halsey, however, expressed satisfaction with the operation. *"It was brilliantly executed and accomplished the desired purpose of creating a diversion, as well as inflicting damage upon enemy installations."*

Leyte Preliminaries

While Krueger's expeditionary troops and Kinkaid's invasion fleet were assembling at various New Guinea bases and at Manus, Halsey's Third Fleet Air squadrons aimed diverting strikes at Okinawa and Formosa. Neither of these islands ("home soil" to the Nipponese) had previously been hit by the Navy's bombs. The mid-October air strikes sent a seismic shock through Imperial Headquarters in Tokyo. On Formosa, the epicenter of the shock, some 300 Japanese aircraft were shattered to chopsticks, and local harbors and airdromes were smashed.

Hitting back, Jap planes from Formosa succeeded in torpedoing the new American cruisers CANBERRA and HOUSTON. Both ships had to be towed to Ulithi. A crippled torpedo-plane grazed the cruiser RENO, and destroyer PRICHETT was scarred by friendly ack-ack. That was the sum total of damage to the Third Fleet.

But the Formosa airmen reported a colossal victory. Shrilling over the microphone, Tokyo Rose cried, *"All of Admiral Mitscher's carriers have been sunk tonight—instantly!"* This roseate broadcast touched off a great celebration in Tokyo. Amazingly enough, some high Japanese naval commanders, among them Admiral Shima, believed the news. It was not substantiated by Halsey's ironic message to Admiral Nimitz:

ALL THIRD FLEET SHIPS REPORTED BY TOKYO RADIO AS SUNK HAVE NOW BEEN SALVAGED AND ARE RETIRING IN THE DIRECTION OF THE ENEMY

This irony was both typical of the naval commander who uttered it, and typical of the actual facts in the case.

If Imperial Headquarters was celebrating on October 17, the festivities were soon canceled. On that day Kinkaid's vanguard landed several Ranger battalions on the beaches of Leyte Gulf. Before the defenders could recover from this surprise, minesweepers, Underwater Demolition Teams, and a covering force of battleships, cruisers, and destroyers under Rear Admiral J. B. Oldendorf moved in. For three

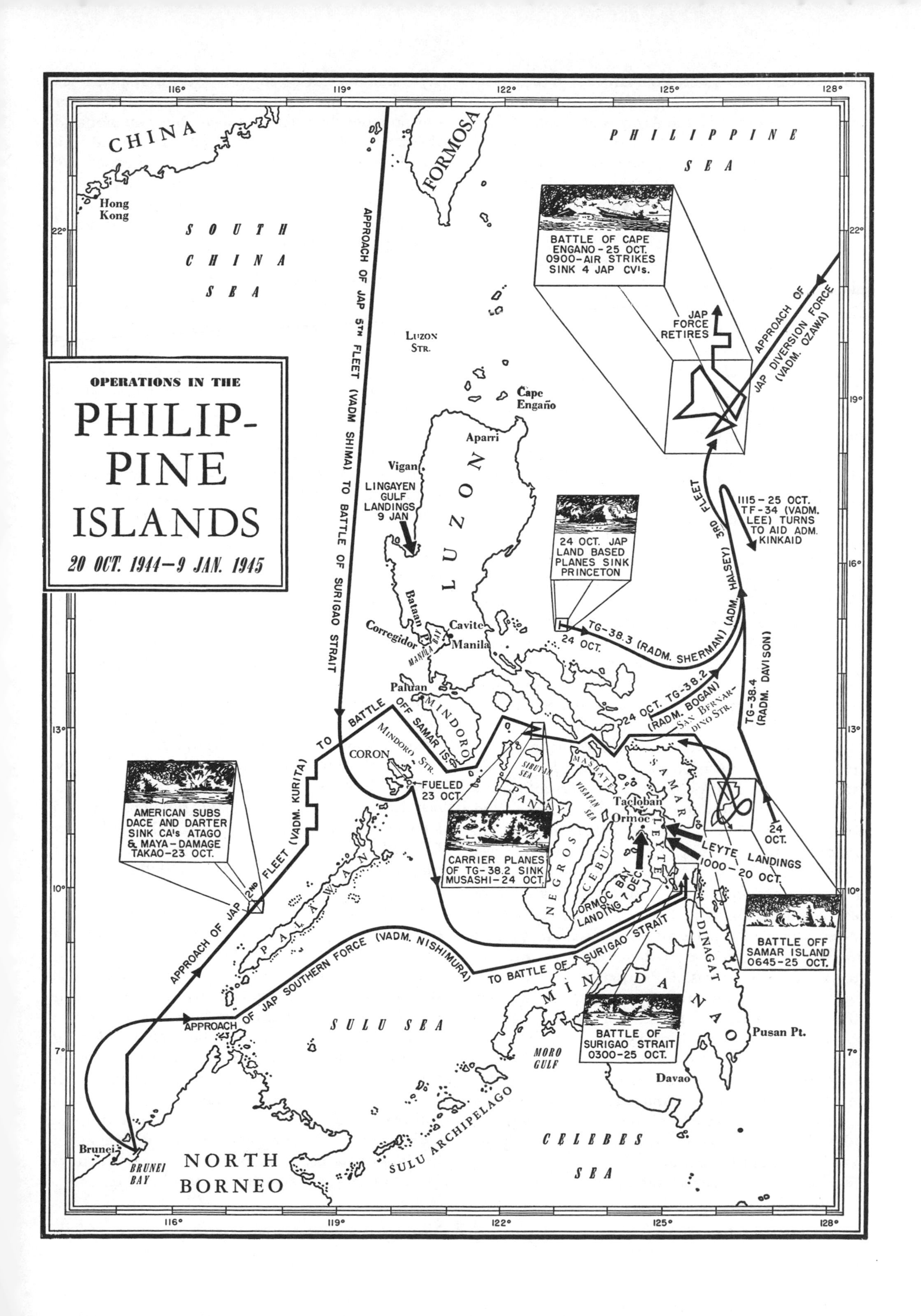

OPERATIONS IN THE
PHILIPPINE ISLANDS
20 OCT. 1944—9 JAN. 1945
CHINA
Hong Kong
SOUTH CHINA SEA
FORMOSA
PHILIPPINE SEA
LUZON STR.
Cape Engaño
Aparri
Vigan
LUZON
LINGAYEN GULF LANDINGS 9 JAN
Bataan
Corregidor
Cavite
Manila
MANILA BAY
Paluan
MINDORO
MINDORO STR.
CORON
FUELED 23 OCT.
SIBUYAN SEA
PANAY
MASBATE
VISAYAN SEA
NEGROS
CEBU
SAMAR
LEYTE
Tacloban
Ormoc
ORMOC BAY LANDING 7 DEC.
LEYTE LANDINGS 1000—20 OCT.
SAN BERNARDINO STR.
DINAGAT
MINDANAO
MORO GULF
Davao
Pusan Pt.
SULU SEA
SULU ARCHIPELAGO
CELEBES SEA
PALAWAN
NORTH BORNEO
Brunei
BRUNEI BAY
APPROACH OF JAP 5TH FLEET (VADM SHIMA) TO BATTLE OF SURIGAO STRAIT
APPROACH OF JAP 2ND FLEET (VADM. KURITA) TO BATTLE OFF SAMAR IS.
APPROACH OF JAP SOUTHERN FORCE (VADM. NISHIMURA) TO BATTLE OF SURIGAO STRAIT
APPROACH OF JAP DIVERSION FORCE (VADM. OZAWA)
BATTLE OF CAPE ENGANO—25 OCT. 0900—AIR STRIKES SINK 4 JAP CV's.
JAP FORCE RETIRES
3RD FLEET (ADM. HALSEY)
1115—25 OCT. TF-34 (VADM. LEE) TURNS TO AID ADM. KINKAID
24 OCT. JAP LAND BASED PLANES SINK PRINCETON
TG-38.3 (RADM. SHERMAN)
24 OCT.
24 OCT. TG-38.2 (RADM. BOGAN)
TG-38.4 (RADM. DAVISON)
24 OCT.
AMERICAN SUBS DACE AND DARTER SINK CA's ATAGO & MAYA—DAMAGE TAKAO—23 OCT.
CARRIER PLANES OF TG-38.2 SINK MUSASHI—24 OCT.
BATTLE OFF SAMAR ISLAND 0645—25 OCT.
BATTLE OF SURIGAO STRAIT 0300—25 OCT.
116° 119° 122° 125° 128°
22° 19° 16° 13° 10° 7°

days the local beaches were bombarded. On the morning of the 20th the landing ships went in through storm-tossed water, and the Army waded ashore. Jap artillery fired a few shots, the U.S.S. HONOLULU was holed by an aerial torpedo, and an attacking Jap plane crashed H.M.A.S. AUSTRALIA. But before the day was over MacArthur took the microphone to say, "I have returned!" and the invasion of Leyte was begun.

Somewhat belatedly Admiral Toyoda now put "Plan Sho-Go" into effect, sending Kurita's Second Fleet steaming up the South China Sea, and bringing Ozawa's carriers chugging down from Japan. Ozawa was under orders to play decoy duck in the north while Kurita barged through the Philippines to strike at the Leyte invaders.

Heading northward, Kurita put in at Brunei, Borneo, to pick up fuel. He left Brunei on the 22nd to make a northeast run past Palawan Island, then swing east through the center of the Philippines, and steam on out through San Bernardino Strait. With the usual Japanese penchant for dispersal of forces, Kurita split his fleet after leaving Brunei. Detaching a squadron under Admiral Shoji Nishimura, he sent these ships across the Sulu Sea to strike at Leyte Gulf through Surigao Strait. The American invasion fleet in the Gulf was thus to be caught in a pincer composed of Nishimura's Southern Force and Kurita's Main Body, while Halsey's fleet was lured far afield by decoy-duck Ozawa. This triple threat was supposed to confuse the United States Navy, and for a time it did. It also confused the Imperial Japanese Navy.

While the "Sho-Go" forces were steaming into play, the "King Two" invasion and covering forces were disposed off the Philippines with the Seventh Fleet ranged across the Gulf mouth between Mindanao and Samar and the Third Fleet off Samar and Luzon. Supporting the landings, Third and Seventh Fleet carrier groups were on the move, delivering air strikes. On October 23 the Third Fleet groups of Rear Admirals Davison, Bogan, and Sherman were located at their proper stations. Ozawa had by that time reached the marge of the Philippine Sea, and Kurita's Main Body was off Palawan.

At this point some other forces were heard from. Early in the morning of the 23rd two American submarines ambushed Kurita's force off Palawan, and Kurita's Main Body lost the services of three heavy cruisers. This was an ominous beginning for the "Sho-Going" Japs. American submarines off Japan had also detected and reported Ozawa's sortie, and Halsey's ships were braced for a major engagement in the Philippine Sea.

For their part, Japanese submarines rushed to the Leyte area did not do so well. Every available I-boat and RO-boat had been dispatched to the Leyte front. But no more than ten were available. One not available was I-364. Another, the I-362, was downed while asserting its availability. Both subs were erased from the picture by American DE's. Through the efforts of these DE's and other energetic sub-hunters, the Imperial Navy lost five of the ten Jap submarines dispatched to Leyte Gulf.

Princeton-Birmingham Disaster

Rear Admiral F. C. Sherman's Task Group 38.3 was sighted by a Japanese search plane shortly after daybreak of October 24. With characteristic exaggeration, the Jap pilot reported that he had located the whole American fleet. As a result, Imperial aircraft took to the sky from most of the strips on Luzon, and Ozawa's carriers launched their one-way bombers. Task Group 38.3 was in for trouble.

Fortunately the first enemy attack wave arrived just as Sherman's planes were warming up for a takeoff. All set to go, the Navy pilots zoomed to meet the radar-detected Japs. The U.S. Hellcats were outnumbered, but they clawed into the enemy hawks and chased them all over the sky.

Then a single "Judy" broke through the defense and dropped out of the clouds to strike at carrier PRINCETON. The plane unleashed a bomb which hit squarely amidships, plumping into the hangar. The hit would have caused little damage had not the bomb smashed a loaded plane. Fire and explosions ravaged the carrier. By mid-morning she was swaddled in dense smoke, and dead in the water.

Working with PRINCETON were cruisers BIRMINGHAM and RENO and destroyers MORRISON (Commander W. H. Price), GATLING (Commander A. F. RICHARDSON), IRWIN (Commander D. B. Miller), and CASSIN YOUNG (Commander E. T. SCHREIBER). At once they moved in to aid the flat-top. With luck she might have been saved.

But at 1002 a thunderous explosion convulsed the carrier, bursting the flight deck and turning the vessel into a furnace. CASSIN YOUNG closed the stern to rescue men who were struggling in the water, while RENO, IRWIN, and GATLING circled the ship, maintaining air guard. Three minutes later another fiery explosion ruptured the carrier's bow. Going alongside to port, IRWIN took off some of the carriermen and stood by to fight the flames. Pounding against PRINCETON's hull, the destroyer suffered topside damage which soon forced her to stand clear. The two light cruisers were also prevented from standing alongside by the searing heat and ugly sea. At 1245 destroyer MORRISON snugged against the burning ship, only to become wedged fast between PRINCETON's stacks. Scorched and badly bruised, she spent a precarious two hours trying to wrench free. Just in time she managed to escape.

A number of enemy aircraft badgered the struggling ships, and about 1330 a "Zeke" was driven off by AA gunnery. At that hour the fires on the flat-top seemed under control, and PRINCETON's Captain W. H. Buracker was encouraged to believe he could salvage the vessel. BIRMINGHAM was ordered alongside to give PRINCETON a tow.

But a rising wind fanned the flames. And while PRINCETON's hands were passing several lines to BIRMINGHAM, a huge explosion shattered the carrier's stern. BIRMINGHAM was engulfed by an avalanche of fire and raked by enormous chunks of torn steel. When the cruiser staggered away, her decks seemed to be bleeding, and her starboard-side superstructure was perforated as though by a barrage. Some 233 dead sailors lay in the wreckage. Of the surviving crew, 211 were seriously wounded; 215 had suffered minor injuries. The BIRMINGHAM's casualties were far higher than those on board PRINCETON.

Fearing that another explosion would smite the rescue vessels, Captain Buracker finally ordered the carrier abandoned. On orders from Admiral Sherman, cruiser RENO and destroyer IRWIN fired torpedoes into the molten hulk. After PRINCETON went down, destroyers MORRISON, GATLING, and IRWIN escorted BIRMINGHAM to Ulithi. It was a sad little cortege which steamed southward. Destroyer IRWIN was mangled, MORRISON was badly damaged, GATLING limped with an injured screw, and BIRMINGHAM was a death-ship.

All hands in Task Group 38.3 had battled valiantly to save PRINCETON. Concerning the efforts of the destroyermen, BIRMINGHAM's Executive Officer wrote: *"The performance of all three destroyers left nothing to be desired. They were all handled promptly and expertly in all respects."*

The loss of PRINCETON and the frightful punishment dealt BIRMINGHAM were severe blows to the United States Third Fleet. But they were nothing to the blows about to fall upon the Imperial Navy. While Sherman's ships off Luzon were undergoing the ordeal just related, Third Fleet aircraft were striking Kurita in the Sibuyan Sea. Catastrophe—for the Japs—was in the making.

The Battle of Surigao Strait

When Kurita's elephantine main body lumbered into San Bernardino Strait, the wheels of Toyoda's "Sho-Go" machine clashed into high gear. Already several teeth were missing, and the cogs did not quite mesh. Deprived of three heavy cruisers off Palawan by American submarines DACE and DARTER, Kurita was in trouble. Not only was his main body minus the services of these ships, but fleet communications were thrown out of joint. While transferring his flag from sinking ATAGO to superbattleship YAMATO, the Jap admiral failed to transfer some of his communications staff. A number of these officers boarded a destroyer which accompanied the damaged cruiser TAKAO back to Brunei. The Japanese equivalent of the Combat Information Center on Kurita's new flagship was accordingly shorthanded. And apparently some of the code books were lost. Thereafter the system went so much to pot that Kurita lost touch with his Southern Force, with Ozawa's Carrier Force, and for a time with Toyoda's headquarters.

However, the three-legged naval juggernaut went forward. Through the central Philippines went Kurita. Down from Formosa Strait steamed Admiral Shima's so-called Fifth Fleet—three cruisers and four destroyers. Around the northern end of Borneo went Admiral Nishimura's Southern Force—battleships YAMASHIRO (flagship) and FUSO; heavy cruiser MOGAMI; and destroyers MICHISHIO, ASAGUMO, YAMAGUMO, and SHIGURE. The mission of this Southern Force was to penetrate Surigao Strait and strike at the American invasion shipping in Leyte Gulf. Shima's "fleet" was supposed to join Nishimura's in this endeavor. But Shima's orders seem to have been fuzzy; at least they were far from clear in this Vice Admiral's mind. Steaming southward, he was under the impression that he would encounter and mop up "the remnants" of Halsey's force—the left-overs of a disastrous sea-air battle.

Shima's first surprise came by way of a radio message from Nishimura, who stated that he was already in Surigao Strait engaging strong American forces. At that hour Shima's ships were some 30 miles from the scene of action—another nasty surprise, for Nishimura was to have waited for Shima to join up.

Interestingly enough, a matter of naval punctilio was involved. Shima was Nishimura's senior in grade. But in years he was Nishimura's junior. Evidently Nishimura was disinclined to be outranked by a younger man. Refusing to relinquish tactical command, he deliberately raced into Surigao Strait ahead of Shima, bent on hogging the glory of a victory. Under any circumstances such foolish play for prestige invited disaster. As it was, the move proved fatal.

Speeding into Surigao Strait at 0245 in the morning of October 25, 1944, Nishimura rushed into a trap. The trap was the work of Rear Admiral Jesse B. Oldendorf. Unencumbered by unwieldy battle-plans and intra-service jealousy, Oldendorf was able to concentrate on the art of naval warfare. Informed by submarine and air scouts that the Japs were headed eastward, Admiral Kinkaid's Seventh Fleet flagship had a good idea of what was coming, and Oldendorf, operating in Leyte Gulf, was forewarned and fore-armed. On October 24 he sent a flotilla of 30 PT-boats down to the southern entrance of Surigao Strait to act as reception committee. Across the Leyte Gulf end of the Strait he "deployed the force in battle disposition with guide in center of battle line."

On the right flank (off the coast of Leyte) were stationed destroyers HUTCHINS (flagship of Captain K. M. McManes, ComDesRon 24), BACHE, DALY, H.M.A.S. ARUNTA, BEALE, and KILLEN. Cruisers H.M.A.S. SHROPSHIRE and U.S.S. BOISE and PHOENIX were positioned as shown on next page. Also off the Leyte coast were three DD's of "DesDiv X-Ray"—CLAYTON, THORN, and WELLES.

Directly in the center were destroyers NEWCOMB (flagship of Captain R. N. Smoot, ComDesRon 56), RICHARD P. LEARY, and ALBERT W. GRANT, with destroyers ROBINSON (flagship of Captain T. F. Conley, Jr., ComDesDiv 112), HALFORD, and BRYANT located to the north, and destroyers HEYWOOD L. EDWARDS, LEUTZE, and BENNION to the south. Farther south, and athwart the passage, were destroyers REMEY (flagship of Captain J. G. Coward, ComDesRon 54), MELVIN, MCGOWAN, MCDERMUT (flagship of Commander R. H. Phillips, ComDesDiv 108), and MONSSEN.

Due north of Hibuson Island were cruisers LOUISVILLE (flagship of Admiral Oldendorf), PORTLAND, MINNEAPOLIS, DENVER, and COLUMBIA. Positioned north of these cruisers were three destroyers of "DesDiv X-Ray"—AULICK, CONY, and SIGOURNEY.

Then there were the six battleships, under Rear Admiral G. L. Weyler—the PENNSYLVANIA, CALIFORNIA, TENNESSEE, MISSISSIPPI, MARYLAND, and WEST VIRGINIA.

Advancing northward in Surigao Strait, impetuous Nishimura was charging right into the jaws of the trap. Even with the support of Shima's three cruisers and four destroyers, his force would have been overwhelmingly outnumbered. As it was, he was throwing two aged battleships, a reconditioned cruiser, and four DD's against six battleships, eight cruisers, and 26 DD's.

Late in the evening of the 24th the Japs were ambushed by the PT-boats. They brushed off this attack. Then, around 0300 next morning, Nishimura's van destroyers ran into Captain Coward's eastern attack group, and the main fight was on. By 0301 the American DD's of DesRon 54 had fired a total of 27 torpedoes at the enemy, and had retired, zigzagging and making smoke. The Japs snapped on searchlights, and opened fire. Near-by shoreline blurred their radar, and they failed to get on target, although they managed a number of straddles.

About 0309 destroyers MCDERMUT and MONSSEN of the western attack group launched 20 torpedoes at the oncoming foe. Again Jap salvos futilely straddled the retiring American ships.

Meanwhile, American torpedoes ploughed into the enemy. Old battleship FUSO, struck hard by two "fish," floundered in mortal hurt. Also fatally struck in this opening round was Jap destroyer MICHISHIO. Score two for DesRon 54!

Nishimura plugged doggedly forward—straight into a torpedo and gunfire barrage from the DD's of DesRon 24 strung along the Leyte coast. The Japs answered with furious but inaccurate gunnery. For their part, the Americans punched four torpedoes and a fusillade of 5-inch into battleship YAMASHIRO.

Apparently the torpedoes which struck the venerable battleship were launched by destroyer KILLEN. Her skipper, Commander H. G. Corey, had recognized the Jap battleship and quickly ordered a torpedo depth of 22 feet. After the war, the captain of I.J.N. SHIGURE stated that YAMASHIRO was hit by deep-running torpedoes which blasted her keel and broke her back. Corey's fast readjustment of the firing set-up evidently accomplished this execution. Blasted at 0400, YAMASHIRO sank in about 15 minutes. Scouting to the bottom ahead of her went Jap destroyer YAMAGUMO, torpedoed at 0330. Shortly before YAMASHIRO went down, Nishimura issued his last order from the battleship's bridge:

YOU ARE TO PROCEED AND ATTACK ALL SHIPS

But with battleships YAMASHIRO and FUSO and two destroyers now out of the battle, there was not much Southern Force left to do the specified "proceeding and attacking."

Nevertheless, cruiser MOGAMI and destroyers ASAGUMO and SHIGURE plodded ahead. By so doing, they waded into gunfire and torpedo fire from Captain Smoot's DesRon 56. These centrally positioned destroyers attacked in three sections. Section 2 (destroyers ROBINSON, HALFORD, and BRYANT) and Section 3 (H. L. EDWARDS, LEUTZE, and BENNION) launched their torpedoes at 0355 and 0358 respectively. The ships ran through a storm of Jap salvos, but none was hit. Retiring smartly behind smoke, the two sections cleared the channel.

Now destroyers NEWCOMB, R. P. LEARY, and A. W. GRANT, led by Captain Smoot in NEWCOMB, steamed in to launch torpedoes. Attacking from ahead, these DD's were in sizzling water. Smoke billowed in the

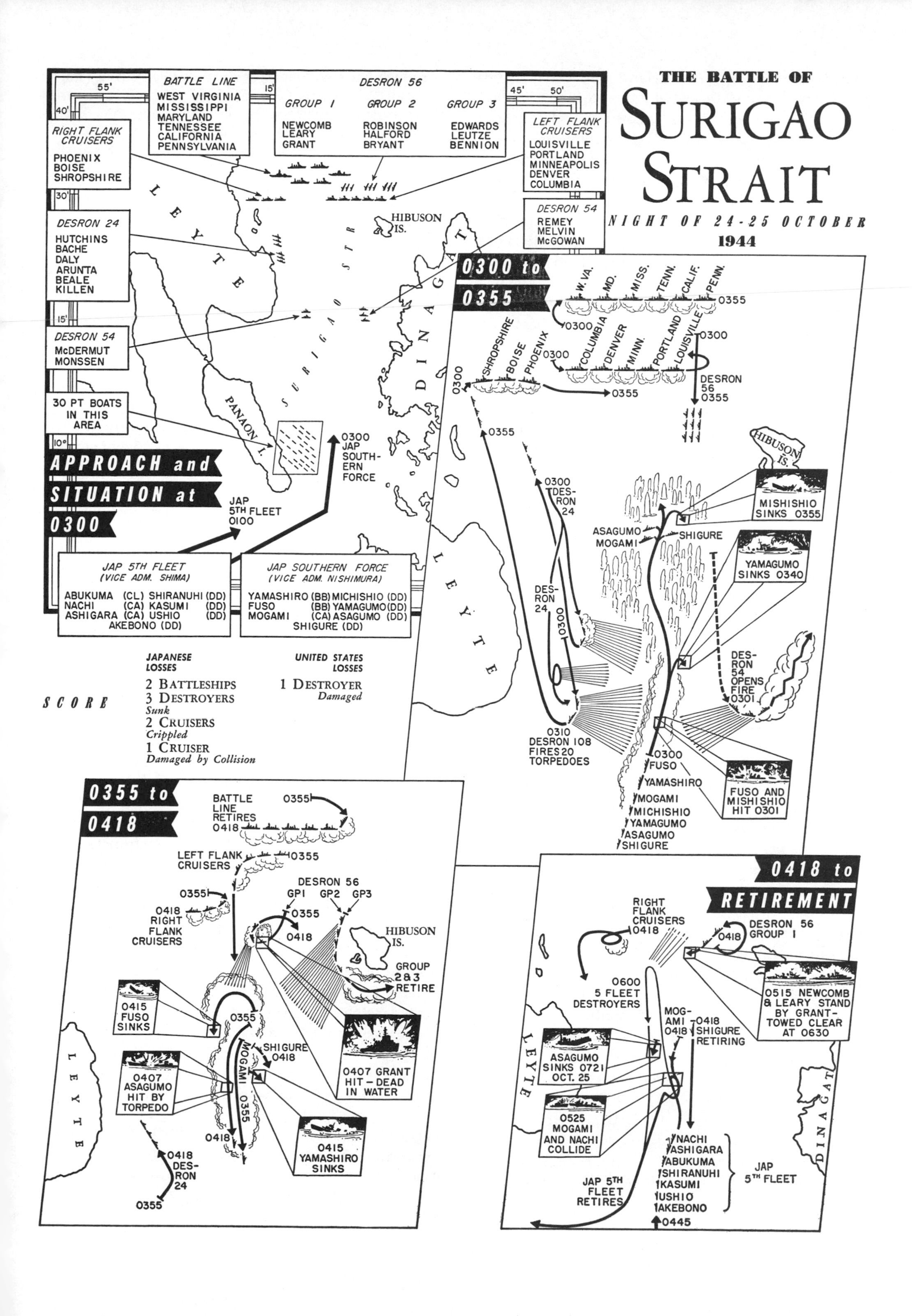
THE BATTLE OF
SURIGAO STRAIT
NIGHT OF 24-25 OCTOBER 1944
APPROACH and SITUATION at 0300
BATTLE LINE
WEST VIRGINIA
MISSISSIPPI
MARYLAND
TENNESSEE
CALIFORNIA
PENNSYLVANIA
DESRON 56
GROUP 1
NEWCOMB
LEARY
GRANT
GROUP 2
ROBINSON
HALFORD
BRYANT
GROUP 3
EDWARDS
LEUTZE
BENNION
RIGHT FLANK CRUISERS
PHOENIX
BOISE
SHROPSHIRE
LEFT FLANK CRUISERS
LOUISVILLE
PORTLAND
MINNEAPOLIS
DENVER
COLUMBIA
DESRON 54
REMEY
MELVIN
McGOWAN
DESRON 24
HUTCHINS
BACHE
DALY
ARUNTA
BEALE
KILLEN
DESRON 54
McDERMUT
MONSSEN
30 PT BOATS IN THIS AREA
LEYTE
SURIGAO STR
DINAGAT
PANAON I.
HIBUSON IS.
0300 JAP SOUTHERN FORCE
JAP 5TH FLEET 0100
JAP 5TH FLEET (VICE ADM. SHIMA)
ABUKUMA (CL) SHIRANUHI (DD)
NACHI (CA) KASUMI (DD)
ASHIGARA (CA) USHIO (DD)
AKEBONO (DD)
JAP SOUTHERN FORCE (VICE ADM. NISHIMURA)
YAMASHIRO (BB) MICHISHIO (DD)
FUSO (BB) YAMAGUMO (DD)
MOGAMI (CA) ASAGUMO (DD)
SHIGURE (DD)
SCORE
JAPANESE LOSSES
2 BATTLESHIPS
3 DESTROYERS
Sunk
2 CRUISERS
Crippled
1 CRUISER
Damaged by Collision
UNITED STATES LOSSES
1 DESTROYER
Damaged
0300 to 0355
W. VA.
MD.
MISS.
TENN.
CALIF.
PENN.
0355
0300
SHROPSHIRE
BOISE
PHOENIX
COLUMBIA
DENVER
MINN.
PORTLAND
LOUISVILLE
DESRON 56 0355
0355
0300 DESRON 24
MISHISHIO SINKS 0355
ASAGUMO
MOGAMI
SHIGURE
YAMAGUMO SINKS 0340
DESRON 24
DESRON 54 OPENS FIRE 0301
0310 DESRON 108 FIRES 20 TORPEDOES
FUSO
YAMASHIRO
MOGAMI
MICHISHIO
YAMAGUMO
ASAGUMO
SHIGURE
FUSO AND MISHISHIO HIT 0301
0355 to 0418
BATTLE LINE RETIRES 0418
LEFT FLANK CRUISERS
DESRON 56
GP1 GP2 GP3
0418 RIGHT FLANK CRUISERS
GROUP 2&3 RETIRE
0415 FUSO SINKS
0407 ASAGUMO HIT BY TORPEDO
SHIGURE 0418
MOGAMI 0355
0407 GRANT HIT – DEAD IN WATER
0415 YAMASHIRO SINKS
0418 DESRON 24
0418 to RETIREMENT
RIGHT FLANK CRUISERS 0418
DESRON 56 GROUP I
0515 NEWCOMB & LEARY STAND BY GRANT–TOWED CLEAR AT 0630
0600 5 FLEET DESTROYERS
MOGAMI 0418
0418 SHIGURE RETIRING
ASAGUMO SINKS 0721 OCT. 25
0525 MOGAMI AND NACHI COLLIDE
NACHI
ASHIGARA
ABUKUMA
SHIRANUHI
KASUMI
USHIO
AKEBONO
JAP 5TH FLEET
JAP 5TH FLEET RETIRES
0445

narrows between Dinagat Island and Leyte; ships were here, there, and everywhere, and target identification was almost impossible. Radio crackling—shells banging—radar "pips" from all directions—in this bedlamite confusion, sorting out enemy targets was on a par with selecting hornets from a swarm of honey-bees. However, when flashes of gunfire indicated the position of Jap warships turning from a northerly to a westerly course, Captain Smoot turned his DD's westward to parallel. At 0405 he ordered torpedoes fired to port at targets 6,300 yards distant. Evidently the spreads were not fired in vain, for Jap destroyer ASAGUMO was struck by a "fish" soon after these were launched.

Captain Smoot had intended to continue across the channel and retire along the Leyte shoreline. But a difficult and dangerous situation had developed. Having come under heavy fire from the Japs, Smoot's ships were faced with a Hobson's choice for retirement. They could turn directly away from the enemy and retire up the middle of the Strait—a tactic which would present the enemy with the smallest target angle, would open the range fastest, and would afford best smoke-cover. But such a mid-channel run would bring them spearing into the American ships maneuvering to the north, and would expose them to fire from the heavy ships athwart the northern end of the Strait. Yet a westward dash across the Strait and a run up the Leyte shoreline, while clearing the American line of fire in short order, would expose the DD's to Jap fusillades.

NEWCOMB's skipper, Commander L. B. Cook, decided to turn directly away from the Japs. With Captain Smoot's advice and approval, he swung the flagship northward. Destroyer LEARY followed the swing. A storm of Jap and American shells descended on the wheeling ships. Last in column, ALBERT W. GRANT was hit before she could make the turn.

At 0403—three minutes before NEWCOMB swung up the channel—GRANT had fired a half-salvo of torpedoes at the enemy. A shell struck her at 0407. Several more hit her just as she was on the point of heading northward to follow NEWCOMB and LEARY. GRANT's skipper, Commander T. A. Nisewaner, now realized she would have been hit whether she had started to turn north or had continued westward. Aware that GRANT might be sunk, he ordered the rest of her torpedoes flung at the enemy. By the time these spreads were fired, the DD was sorely hurt.

Excerpt from GRANT's Action Report:

0408½—Additional shell hits began to riddle ship. Hit forward at waterline flooded forward storeroom and forward crew's berthing compartment. Hit in 40 mm. No. 1 exploded 40 mm. ammunition and started fire. Hit through starboard boat davit exploded, killing ship's Doctor, Lieutenant C. A. Methieu, five radiomen, and almost entire amidships repair party. Other hits in forward stack, one hit on port motor whaleboat, one hit and low-order explosion in galley. One hit in scullery room, one hit in after crew's berthing compartment, and one additional hit in forward engine-room. All lights, telephone communications, radars, and radios out of commission. Steering control shifted aft.

Struck by no less than seven Japanese 4.7-inch projectiles and eleven American 6-inch armor-piercing shells, GRANT was a floating catafalque. Desperately Commander Nisewaner flashed a call for help over blinker gun.

WE ARE DEAD IN WATER TOW NEEDED

Ravaged by fire and explosion, the ship drifted helplessly. Topside and below decks the dead lay everywhere, and the agonized cries of the wounded penetrated the roar of combat, the screech of shells, the blast-splash of near misses, and the clangor of broken machinery.

When a companion Pharmacist's Mate was killed, burden of tending the injured fell upon First Class Pharmacist's Mate W. H. Swaim, Jr. Swaim did the work of a full-fledged physician, surgeon, and specialist. Maintaining his own battle dressing station in the "head" aft, he also supervised the sick bay amidships and the dressing station forward. He was aided by Chief Commissary Steward L. M. Holmes, who labored in the wardroom, and by a Sonarman, J. C. O'Neill, Jr., who skillfully administered morphine and tended several sailors who had fallen at their posts with an arm or leg shot away.

Almost every officer and man in the shell-butchered vessel was cited in GRANT's Action Report for valiant conduct. There was R. H. Parker, Machinist's Mate First Class. Dodging explosions, and slipping in puddles of blood, Parker raced from the fantail to cut off steam escaping in the engineering spaces forward—an act that saved the lives of the watch trapped below. There was Ensign F. D. Case, who, although painfully wounded, served as a stretcher bearer. And Lieutenant B. B. V. Lyon, Jr., Engineer Officer, who rushed below to check the boilers and remained in a black, steam-choked compartment to direct the work of a repair crew. Braving live steam and flood, Commander Nisewaner himself forced his way into the forward engine-room to rescue several injured sailors. And no man in the GRANT, at least, would ever forget Radioman First Class, W. M. Selleck. His obituary was written as follows by the ship's Executive Officer:

A single Jap bomb, which exploded a loaded plane on the hangar deck, proved fatal to the carrier Princeton in the opening action of the Battle for Leyte Gulf. Destroyers rescued many carrier-men, even at extreme danger to themselves. The worst catastrophe occurred when a great explosion inflicted over 650 casualties on Birmingham, which had come alongside to aid Princeton.

Destroyers come to the aid of Birmingham. Morrison, Gatling, and Irwin escorted the stricken cruiser to Ulithi after the disaster alongside Princeton had killed 233 of Birmingham's crew.

Cassin Young, from which this picture was taken, picks up survivors of Princeton from the water. Morrison was wedged for two hours between the carrier's stacks during rescue operations.

Vengeance for the Battles of Savo Island and Guadalcanal: Night firing in the Battle of Surigao. The Jap battleship Yamashiro was sunk by torpedoes fired by Killen, as Nishimura's and Shima's forces were almost annihilated that night in the trap set by Admiral Oldendorf. The Japanese attempt to break through at the southern end of the line dissolved in complete frustration.

American cruiser finds the target at Surigao. The two Jap Admirals had a total of two battleships, four cruisers, and four DD's to attack our six battleships, eight cruisers, and 26 DD's.

C.I.C. team on Albert W. Grant, the only U. S. ship damaged at Surigao. This picture was taken during bombardment of Brunei Bay for Australian landings. Australian officer is at far left.

BOTH LEGS BLOWN OFF, AND NEAR DEATH FROM LOSS OF BLOOD, SELLECK WENT OUT A HERO. HIS LAST WORDS AS HE LAY ON THE WARDROOM TABLE . . . WERE, "THERE'S NOTHING YOU CAN DO FOR ME, FELLOWS. GO AHEAD AND DO SOMETHING FOR THOSE OTHERS."

So, held on the surface by little more than the courage of brave men, ALBERT W. GRANT remained afloat. Word of her predicament reached the flagship at 0410, and the Officer in Tactical Command immediately ordered the heavy ships to cease fire. At 0515 NEWCOMB and LEARY steamed back down the channel to aid the crucified ship. NEWCOMB's Medical Officer and two Corpsmen were placed on board the GRANT, and by 0630 the crippled vessel, towed by NEWCOMB, was on her way out of Surigao Strait.

Death made one last swipe at the GRANT—and missed. While the destroyermen were struggling to rig the tow, torpedo-wakes came streaking up the dark channel. These shots had been fired by the warships of Admiral Shima, the ambiguous Japanese Fifth Fleet which had at last arrived on the scene.

Upon entering the south end of the Strait, Shima's column had been attacked by the waiting PT squadron. The fierce little speedboats plunked a torpedo squarely into cruiser ABUKUMA, putting her out of action directly. With cruisers NACHI and ASHIGARA, and destroyers SHIRANUHI, KASUMI, USHIO, and AKEBONO, the befuddled Shima pushed on up the Strait. A destroyer came tearing southward like a bat out of Hades. Flagship NACHI challenged. The fleeing DD identified herself as I.J.N. SHIGURE—"And who are you?" NACHI flashed her name, and the ships passed in the night. Apparently Shima did not question the SHIGURE. Had he done so, he would have learned that she was the last vessel of NISHIMURA's Southern Force able to steam anywhere at any kind of speed.

A few minutes later Jap cruiser MOGAMI was in view—a carnival float veiled in pink smoke and festooned with fiery aureoles. Other ship bonfires were now visible, and it was evident to Admiral Shima that Nishimura had come a cropper. Hoping to avoid a like fate, Shima ordered his four destroyers ahead for a torpedo attack, and turned his two cruisers to fling torpedoes at a dim radar contact to the northeast. The "fish" fired by the Jap DD's may have been the ones which missed GRANT, NEWCOMB, and LEARY. In any event, this Jap torpedo attack missed. The one ship struck in this action was cruiser MOGAMI. She was struck by her sister NACHI, who rammed her on a high-speed turn. As a result of this collision, MOGAMI was doubly disabled, and NACHI was badly hurt.

That was enough for Shima. Recalling his four destroyers, he headed southward to get out of Surigao at best speed. Best speed wasn't fast enough. Both ABUKUMA and MOGAMI were caught and finished off in the Mindanao Sea by American aircraft. On November 5 NACHI was sighted and sunk by Navy planes. Only the ASHIGARA and two of Shima's destroyers managed to reach Japan. They, with destroyer SHIGURE, lone survivor of Nishimura's force, were the only Jap ships to escape the Surigao debacle.

The last shots of the Surigao Strait battle were fired after daylight in the morning of October 25. At 0640 Rear Admiral R. W. Hayler was ordered to take two cruisers, screened by destroyers ROBINSON, BRYANT, and HALFORD, down the Strait to sink Jap cripples. One such was sunk with celerity. By 0730 the battle was over, and Surigao Strait was registered in history as a smashing American victory.

When Toyoda heard the news he must have been stunned. At the cost of ten warships, the maladjusted Nishimura-Shima team had failed to sink a single American man-of-war. All told, they had landed no more than seven hits, and those, in company with American shells, had fallen on battered ALBERT W. GRANT. Even so, the GRANT had remained unsinkable. She was the only United States warship damaged in the five-hour engagement.

An awe-inspiring series of blunders had brought disaster upon the Japs in Surigao Strait. The only error (if it may be so called) on the American side was the shelling hurled at GRANT. In the smoke and radar-blur of a wild melee, such accidents are almost inevitable. And GRANT's misfortune was the single tragedy in a destroyer performance that was a tactical masterpiece. Launching what was probably the war's greatest topedo-attack, the American DD's spearheaded the victory at Surigao Strait. In downing two battleships and several destroyers, and crippling a cruiser—all this without loss of an American DD—they set a record rare in naval annals.

The Surigao drama ended with a flash of alarm. At 0727 word was received that an escort-carrier group off Samar was under attack by a Japanese battleship force. Oldendorf turned his ships in Leyte Gulf to meet this ominous threat.

CHAPTER 33

BATTLE OFF SAMAR

SMALL BOYS VERSUS GIANTS

Battle Off Samar

At the time that Nishimura's force was racing eastward across the Sulu Sea en route to disaster, Kurita's main body entering the Sibuyan Sea barged into trouble. It was discovered, about mid-morning of the 24th, by scout planes from the U. S. carrier groups of Admirals Davison and Bogan. For the rest of that day Kurita's ships were treated to an unmerciful hammering. By nightfall his five battleships were bomb-scorched and smoking. Heavy cruiser MYOKO, disabled, was crawling down the South China Sea for Singapore. A destroyer had been sent to the bottom. And the monster battleship MUSHASHI was a monster junk-pile on the sea floor. Struck by at least 16 bombs and 19 aerial torpedoes, the mighty battlewagon and 1,100 sailors had rolled over and gone down.

Down, too, had gone Kurita's enthusiasm for "Plan Sho-Go." With darkness setting in, he reversed course and headed westward. This retrogression seems to have been directly contrary to Toyoda's previous battle order. At any rate, when Toyoda heard of it, he directed Kurita to turn about and head once more for San Bernardino Strait. The Commander-in-Chief's directive was couched in poetic terms. It read:

ADVANCE COUNTING ON DIVINE ASSISTANCE

Obediently Kurita ordered a turn-about, and headed his punished force eastward for San Bernardino. About midnight the Jap big guns reached the Pacific end of the Strait. The force was six hours behind schedule as it debouched in the Philippine Sea and steamed southward along the east coast of Samar, bound for Leyte Gulf. By 0600 in the morning of October 25, the ships were about halfway between the San Bernardino exit and the Gulf of Leyte. Had Kurita but known it, he could indeed have thanked Providence for permitting his advance. He could also have thanked Admirals Ozawa and Halsey.

For Ozawa, in the north, had been wandering around with his "decoy ducks" in the most attractive fashion, breaking radio silence, making smoke, and doing everything possible to invite attention. And Halsey needed no engraved invitation. He was of course unaware that the enemy carriers off Cape Engano were deliberate lures. Convinced that the Jap flat-tops had to be kept away from Leyte at all cost, he had drawn off the task groups of Bogan and Davison and sent them on a top-speed run to intercept.

Halsey's move left the San Bernardino gateway open at the very time Kurita was hoping to slip through. For this reason the departure of the U. S. Third Fleet from the Samar area was subjected to considerable post-war criticism. Halsey's answer to the critics was the destruction of Ozawa's Carrier Force with a series of aerial hammer-blows at that date unparalled in the history of naval warfare. It seems, however, that he failed to inform Admiral Kinkaid of the Third Fleet's northward run. In consequence, Kinkaid did not know that the Samar approaches to Leyte Gulf were left wide open. His first intimation of this dangerous gap came when Rear Admiral C. A. F. Sprague's Northern Carrier Group called for help from the waters off southern Samar.

Sprague's group was composed of escort-carriers

FANSHAW BAY (flagship), SAINT LÔ, WHITE PLAINS, KALININ BAY, KITKUN BAY, and GAMBIER BAY, screened by three destroyers and four DE's. The destroyers were HOEL (Commander L. S. Kintberger), flagship of Commander W. D. Thomas, Screen Commander; HEERMANN (Commander A. T. Hathaway), and JOHNSTON (Commander E. E. Evans). The destroyer-escorts were DENNIS (Lieutenant Commander S. Hansen, U.S.N.R.), JOHN C. BUTLER (Lieutenant Commander J. E. Pace), RAYMOND (Lieutenant Commander A. F. Beyer, U.S.N.R.), and SAMUEL B. ROBERTS (Lieutenant Commander R. W. Copeland, U.S.N.R.).

At 0645 Kurita's force detected the American ships. About the same time, the Japs were detected by American aircraft.

ENEMY SURFACE FORCE OF FOUR BATTLESHIPS SEVEN CRUISERS AND 11 DESTROYERS SIGHTED 20 MILES NORTH OF YOUR TASK GROUP AND CLOSING AT 30 KNOTS

Shouted down from the sky, this message from Ensign W. C. Brooks sent a shock through FANSHAW BAY. Unable to believe this foul intelligence, Admiral Sprague demanded verification. He was informed that the ships had pagoda masts. A splatter of AA fire above the northern horizon convinced him. At once he ordered a course-change, flank speed, and the launching of all aircraft.

A moment later the Japs opened fire at 17 miles. Sprague's ships, which had been on a northerly course, ran eastward, laying smoke. Planes buzzed away from the "jeep carriers" to strike at the oncoming Japanese battleships and cruisers. Justifiably alarmed, Sprague reported the situation in plain language, urgently requesting help.

Help was not immediately available. Halsey's Third Fleet was far to the north. In Leyte Gulf, Oldendorf's force was low on fuel, weary from the Surigao battle, and almost out of ammunition. In any event, it could not reach Sprague before afternoon. Southeast of Sprague's group Rear Admiral F. B. Stump's escort-carrier group was stationed. Stump alone could be counted on for ready aid. And the two escort-carrier groups were the only American naval forces standing between Kurita's battleship force and Leyte Gulf.

So the immediate defense-burden fell like an avalanche on Sprague's escort-carriers. On them, too, like an avalanche would fall shellfire from the Japanese heavy ships. Those ships included the KONGO, the HARUNA, the NAGATO, and the monster YAMATO, sister-ship of the dead MUSHASHI. The giantess was out for revenge, and no American baby flat-top would be able to endure her 18-inch salvos. As for destroyers, the American DD's were never made to withstand normal battleship fire, much less the shells of a super BB. Such shots, of course, would burst a DE as a pistol-volley would burst an egg.

Sprague could only run hell-for-leather, and run he did. With most of his planes in the air, he turned his ships southward for a lengthy sprint, and then shifted the course southwestward toward Leyte Gulf. A friendly rainsquall offered a few minutes' cover. But the same cloudburst gave the pursuing Japs a measure of protection from air assault.

It was Kurita himself who provided the desperate Americans with a break. Instead of sending his ships due south to cut off the approach to Leyte Gulf, he split his force three ways in an effort to box Sprague's formation on three sides. Piling on best speed, the Jap cruisers raced across the rear of the American formation, and then closed in from the east. The Jap destroyers swung westward to take the Americans from that direction. Down through the center boomed the Imperial battlewagons.

Kurita's tricky maneuvering gave Sprague a momentary breathing spell. But the cruiser threat from the east proved mortally dangerous, for it prevented the carriers from turning into the wind to launch planes. And as the Jap cruisers gained, the threat of a "box" compelled drastic counteraction. The action was taken by Sprague's destroyers and destroyer-escorts, and it remains an epic in the drama of destroyer warfare. In the Aleutian theater, in the Solomons arena, and at Surigao, U.S. destroyers had attacked cruisers and battleships. But never before had American DD's rushed in to trade blows with such a force of heavies as bore down on Sprague's carriers that morning of October 25. And never anywhere had little DE's presumed to exchange blows with cruisers and battleships. Never, anywhere, had DE's *or* DD's faced such a mastodon as the 63,000-ton YAMATO.

First destroyer to attack the nearing enemy was the U.S.S. JOHNSTON (Commander E. E. Evans). At 0720 she peeled away to rush a heavy cruiser. Evans and his men got off a full torpedo salvo. A cyclone of enemy shells hit the attacking JOHNSTON and she reeled through the water with her speed reduced to 17 knots. Then, taking one hit after another, she maintained a hot fire on the Jap cruisers, shooting at ranges as short as 5,000 yards.

Meanwhile, Sprague ordered the DD's and DE's to spread smoke, and his flat-tops were soon covered by a cotton-thick screen. As the Jap fire slackened, Sprague ordered the screening ships to form up for two torpedo attacks.

At 0727, destroyer HOEL (Commander L. S. Kintberger) rushed out of the smoke to launch a half-salvo at a battleship 9,000 yards distant. She was hammered by shells, but she managed to get off another half-salvo at 0735—a spread that apparently damaged a heavy cruiser. And the fight was just beginning.

Destroyer HEERMANN (Commander A. T. Hathaway) made her attack at 0754. Racing out of the smoke-fog, she flung seven torpedoes at a heavy cruiser. Six minutes later she threw three torpedoes at a battleship. Then, bold as brass, she exchanged gunfire with a pair of heavy cruisers. Lucky HEERMANN! With tons of projectiles crashing in the sea around her, she came through the action only slightly damaged.

The relatively slow destroyer-escorts had been instructed to launch their torpedo attack after the three destroyers stepped out. Another rainsquall swept the seascape as the DE's squared away to tackle the enraged enemy. Maneuvering in sheeting rain and dense smoke, the DE's were unable to coordinate their torpedo strikes. Blinded, they dashed across the water, and several of them nearly collided. But they threw the Japs off stride.

Closing to within 4,000 yards of a heavy cruiser, destroyer-escort SAMUEL B. ROBERTS (Lieutenant Commander R. W. Copeland, U.S.N.R.) unloosed a spread of torpedoes at a heavy cruiser. Between 0805 and 0855, the ROBERTS engaged the Jap heavies, firing pointblank at ranges as short as 6,000 yards. The little DE was struck by a shell at 0851—the first lash of a terrible flogging.

At 0759 destroyer-escort DENNIS (Lieutenant Commander S. Hansen, U.S.N.R.) closed the enemy and fired three torpedoes at a range of 8,000 yards, after a gun-battle begun at 0740. After throwing torpedoes, she continued to blaze away with her gun batteries until 0920 when she reeled out of action, savagely mauled.

Destroyer-escort JOHN C. BUTLER (Lieutenant Commander J. E. Pace) did not launch a torpedo attack. After engaging a heavy cruiser and a destroyer with gunfire, she was ordered ahead of the carriers to lay smoke.

DENNIS retired behind JOHN C. BUTLER's smoke-screen.

Destroyer-escort RAYMOND (Lieutenant Commander A. F. Beyer, U.S.N.R.) opened fire on the foe at 0730. Closing the Jap cruiser column to within 5,700 yards, she slammed something like 16 shells into the superstructure of one vessel. At 0808 she flung three torpedoes at the enemy ships. Hers was a charmed life. In the thick of battle for two hours and 20 minutes, she emerged without a scratch.

JOHNSTON, HOEL, HEERMANN, SAMUEL B. ROBERTS, DENNIS, JOHN C. BUTLER, RAYMOND—the names of these warships were indelibly written that morning in the Navy's Log of Fame. The history of naval warfare contains few actions which match the battle fought by these DD's and DE's against the heavy-weight men-of-war of the Imperial Navy.

"Small boys," Admiral Sprague had called them, ordering them to cover his carriers. *"Small boys form for our second attack!"*

Small boys, they pitched in—literally no bigger than midgets against the giants of the Japanese Navy. Five-inch guns against 8- and 16- and 18-inchers. Unarmored ships against capital vessels clad in coats of steel.

Despite their suicidal efforts, they were unable to save all the carriers. The Japs got close enough to land four 8-inch shells on the FANSHAW BAY. The KALININ BAY was rocked by 15 shells. And GAMBIER BAY, hit below the waterline and disabled, was torn to pieces and sunk by Jap cruiser fire. But these blows serve to indicate what could have happened to Sprague's force if the DD's and DE's had not intervened.

That intervention fended off Kurita's force and gave Admiral Stump's aircraft time to arrive on the scene. It also gave Sprague's aircraft time to reload and refuel on Leyte and fly back into the battle. It also gave Seventh Fleet bombers from the waters off Mindanao a chance to reach the battle area in time. By 1130 these air reinforcements had convinced Kurita that the American flat-tops were not worth the risk of further pursuit, and the way into Leyte Gulf was barred. Their defense had been so magnificent that he thought he had encountered ESSEX-class carriers with cruiser escorts! With victory almost in his grasp, he opened his hand and ordered a general retirement northward. If the "small boys" were not entirely responsible for Kurita's frustration, they were to be credited with a large share of that responsibility.

But, as was expected, the DD's and DE's took a frightful beating. DENNIS limped out of the battle with her superstructure a shambles, six of her crew slain, and 19 wounded. HEERMANN's damage was light, but the term meant little to her five dead and nine wounded. The ships that suffered untold agony were destroyers JOHNSTON and HOEL, and destroyer-escort SAMUEL B. ROBERTS. All three were riddled by the enemy's fire. All three went down. And each fought undaunted to the end.

First to go was the U.S.S. HOEL.

U. S. S. HOEL

★

About 0725, while Commander Leon Kintberger was maneuvering his ship in an effort to get in a torpedo attack, the HOEL took her first hit, a smash on the director platform. She kept on going at high speed. Targets were hard to distinguish in the surging fogs of white and black smoke and the torrential downpours which blotted the seascape. But HOEL's C.I.C. team had its multiple eye on the leading Jap battleship, which happened to be the I.J.N. KONGO. Closing the range to 9,000 yards, Kintberger ordered a half-salvo of five torpedoes thrown at this booming menace. The "fish" were away at 0727. About 0728 a 14-inch shell thunderbolted into the ship's after engine-room, blowing the port engine to scrap. A moment later another 14-incher struck aft, uprooting guns and damaging the electric steering apparatus.

HOEL shifted to hand steering, and plugged ahead on one engine as Kintberger aimed a torpedo strike at the Jap cruiser column. Loss of electrical power forced the Torpedomen to train their batteries by hand, but at 0735 another half-salvo was launched. Geysers jumped around the target cruiser, possibly I.J.N. KUMANO. The ship roared and turned away. If she were indeed the KUMANO, brave HOEL could be credited with striking a blow that crippled the vessel and set in motion a chain of events which ultimately resulted in her death.

For this valiant blow, HOEL was to pay dearly. "With our ten 'fish' fired,"one of her officers stated afterward, "we decided to get the hell out of there." But getting out proved many times harder than getting in. Eight thousand yards on the port beam loomed Kurita's battleships. On the starboard quarter at 7,000 yards loomed the Jap heavy cruisers. Cannon to the right of them, cannon to the left of them, Kintberger and crew had to fight their way out with two forward guns—guns which were difficult to train on pursuers. A rain of heavy shells fell on the little ship as she zigzagged madly to escape the gantlet. Five-inchers, 8-inchers, and 14-inch sledgehammers struck the ship aft and amidships. Flame burst from her fantail. Her superstructure was torn, chewed, and pulverized by successive explosions. Still the forward gunners kept firing. They fired to the end.

It came at 0855 in the morning of October 25, 1944, after two excruciating hours in which the HOEL had been pounded by some forty hits. Only a few of her crew survived this crimson thrashing. And almost every man who escaped the molten vessel was wounded. On the bridge Screen Commander William D. Thomas and Destroyer Captain Kintberger were with her to the last. Around them the disintegrating decks were strewn with dead and crawling with wounded. Men had to be sent forward to compel the gun crews to leave their mounts and abandon the sinking ship. Already listing and down by the stern, HOEL was a fiery skeleton when she capsized to port and went under. Lost with the ship were 253 destroyermen. Fifteen of the wounded later succumbed.

Only a few destroyers in the war suffered as did U.S.S. HOEL. Only a few accepted such heavy odds, and did so much with so little.

U. S. S. SAMUEL B. ROBERTS

★

SMALL BOYS FORM FOR OUR SECOND ATTACK

When the order from Admiral Sprague rasped over the TBS, the DE's—smallest of the "small boys"—were racing through the smoke and rain, some of them pegging shots at the enemy. SAMUEL B. ROBERTS (Lieutenant Commander R. W. Copeland, U.S.N.R.) had opened fire at 0655. Now, at about 0800, she dashed toward a dimly seen heavy cruiser; closed the range to less than 4,000 yards; swung, and threw a spread of three torpedoes at the pagoda-masted foe. One war head struck home—a flash and a waterspout. The cruiser's guns flamed, and straddles raised fountains around the little ship. Other cruisers roared at ROBERTS. Like a terrier barking at mastiffs, the DE dodged in to fire 5-inch at these monster, steel-clad opponents.

At 0851 ROBERTS was struck by the first shell of a fusillade that was to batter her into a blind and bleeding wreck. But staggering through a tornado of flame and steel, she struck fierce blows in return. For 50 minutes she endured hit upon hit. Enduring, she threw shell after shell at her tormentors. Ranges shifted between 7,500 and 6,000 yards as DE and enemy cruisers zigzagged across the smoky seas in death-battle. Against the massive batteries of the enemy, the assailed destroyer-escort had but two 5-inch guns—and one of these was presently silenced by a crushing salvo. With one hand thus figuratively tied behind her, this "small boy" fought on.

Out of the thunder, the smoke, the incinerating blast of shells, the clangor and outcry of the ship's ordeal, came another saga of men who met that definition of heroism which describes it as "the accomplishment of the impossible." Typical was the fight put up by Gunner's Mate Third, Paul Henry Carr, gun captain of the DE's No. 2 mount. His story was told by ROBERTS' Action Report and by Lieutenant W. S. Burton, one of the ship's surviving officers.

According to Lieutenant Burton:

That gun in less than an hour expended something in excess of 300 rounds of 5-inch ammunition, including starshells when all Common and AA projectiles were gone. . . . The rapid and continuous fire from Gun 2 was an inspiration to every man on the ship. We had to maneuver radically in order to avoid the oncoming salvos, and although we operated with very little fire-control equipment, Carr was able to obtain a great many hits on a Japanese cruiser. We positively knocked out their number three 8-inch gun turret, demolished their bridge, and started fires aft under their secondary control tower. . . . After we had been in action perhaps 50 minutes, we received our first hits. At that time Carr's ammunition hoist went out of commission. That did not delay his rate of fire in the least.

Excerpt from ROBERTS' Action Report:

After all power, air, and communications had been lost, and before the word to abandon ship was passed, the crew of No. 2 gun, who as a crew distinguished themselves throughout the entire action, loaded, rammed, and fired six charges entirely by hand and with a certain knowledge of the hazards involved due to the failure of the gas-ejection system caused by the air supply having been entirely lost.

While attempting to fire the seventh round, the powder charge cooked off before the breech closed, wrecking the gun and killing or wounding all but three crew members, who were critically injured and two of whom were blown clear of the mount and the ship as a result of the explosion.

The first man to enter the mount after the explosion found the gun captain, Carr, on the deck of the mount holding in his hands the last projectile available to his gun, even though he was severely wounded from his neck down to the middle of his thighs. He was completely torn open and his intestines were splattered throughout the inside of the mount. Nevertheless, he held in his hand the 54-pound projectile, held it up above his head and begged the petty officer who had entered the mount to help him get that last round out. You must appreciate that the breech of the gun had been blown into an unrecognizable mass of steel. The mount, itself, was torn to pieces. He was the only man capable of physical movement within the mount and yet his only idea was to get out that last round.

The petty officer, who entered the mount, took the projectile from Carr and removed one of the other men, who was wounded and unconscious, to the main deck in order to render him first aid. When he returned to the mount, there was Gunner's Mate Carr again with the projectile in his hand, still attempting, although horribly wounded, to place the projectile on the loading tray and thereby utilize his last chance to do damage to the Japanese.

Carr died a few minutes after he was dragged from the gun mount. All told, he and the other marksmen who served in the SAMUEL B. ROBERTS fired 608 rounds from the ship's 5-inch 38's. But by 0907 some 20 Jap heavy shells had smitten her, and the vessel herself was disemboweled. She could take little more, and that she had survived over two hours of hammer-and-tong fighting with the enemy cruisers verged on the miraculous. As was usual in such extraordinary cases, the miracle was compounded of grit, skill, and luck. By "chasing salvos" ROBERTS ducked tons of Jap steel; the small Jap patterns helped, and much of the cruiser shooting was excited and inaccurate.

Twenty hits, however, were enough to crush the valiant DE. About 0935, Lieutenant Commander Copeland shouted the order to abandon. All who could make it went overside. In the water were 50 wounded men, many burned, others frightfully mutilated. Seven of these subsequently died. Also charred and mutilated, the SAMUEL B. ROBERTS sank at 1005.

Lost with the ship were some 89 of the crew.

She was the second "small boy" to go down off Samar during the morning of October 25, 1944. The Navy would always remember her as the destroyer-escort that fought like a battleship.

U. S. S. JOHNSTON

★

First destroyer into action, U.S.S. JOHNSTON (Commander E. E. Evans) was the last "small boy" to go down in the Battle off Samar. Like HOEL and ROBERTS, she fought until her hull was riddled, her engines were wrecked, her superstructure was chopped to a shambles, and her guns knocked out.

She was hit just after she unleashed a spread of ten torpedoes at the nearest Jap cruiser, range 8,000 yards. Launched at 0720, the torpedo salvo was answered by a stupendous barrage, Imperial battleships and cruisers roaring in chorus at the pint-sized warship which had dared to bar their way and test their might. Boring through the air with an express-train whoop, three 14-inch shells struck the leaping destroyer. The monstrous blows sent the little ship stumbling through the sea, and they were echoed by the minor blasts of three 6-inch shells.

About this time Admiral Sprague ordered the destroyers to form up for a coordinated torpedo attack. Although her torpedoes were gone and she was crippled by damage that slowed her to 17 knots, JOHNSTON swung in astern of HOEL and HEERMANN in an effort to support them with gunfire. And support them she did. Driving in on the enemy's flank, Commander Evans closed the range to 5,000 yards while the JOHNSTON gun crews pumped 5-inch at the Japanese cruiser column. Bringing their batteries to bear, the cruisers hurled a blizzard of 6-inch at Evans' destroyer. The one-sided duel could have only one outcome.

For over an hour JOHNSTON blazed away at the Jap heavies, trading 5-inch salvos for 6-inch barrages that gradually hammered her superstructure to rubbish and turned her hull into a stove. Below decks men were cremated in clogged passages, or roasted in red-hot compartments. Topside, they vanished in incandescent splurts of high explosive. By 0830 only two of JOHNSTON's guns were fully operative. With injured engines hammering their best, the ship could make no more than 15 knots. From forecastle to fantail the decks were littered with wreckage. And in whatever shelter they could find, the wounded and dead huddled together in pitiful companionship.

Through the battle's din came Sprague's order over the hoarse TBS.

SMALL BOYS ON MY STARBOARD QUARTER INTERPOSE WITH SMOKE BETWEEN MEN AND ENEMY CRUISERS

The "men" in reference were the escort-carriers. The "small boys" were the DD's and DE's ripping this way and that across the seascape in the path of the oncoming Jap men-of-war. The "small boys" laid smoke—funnel smoke, and FS fumes. Black and white clouds rolled across the water, blinding destroyermen and Japs alike. JOHNSTON was trailing smoke when she was hit by a fatal salvo.

The destroyer died hard. On her bridge Commander Ernest Evans fought his ship to the last. Struck by a burst of shrapnel, he was bleeding as though from the volley of a firing squad. A cuff of his jacket was blood-soaked—two fingers of that hand had been slashed away. He refused to quit his post.

Lunging out of the smoke, destroyer HEERMANN passed close to JOHNSTON. HEERMANN's skipper, Com-

ROBERTS HEERMANN HOEL DENNIS CHOKAI TONE CHIKUMA

mander A. T. Hathaway, later reported: *"It was obvious that the* Johnston *was badly damaged and couldn't make the speed we could. The radar was hanging down on her yardarm, and Evans sent me a signal, 'Only one engine, no radar, and no gyros.'"* Not long after that, Heermann, executing a fast maneuver, almost collided with Evans' crippled vessel. It was evident that Johnston could not last long.

She fought until 0945. Then the order to abandon was spoken, and the survivors struggled to get overside. At 1010 the shattered destroyer sank. Adrift in her wake she left 101 wounded men. Lost with the ship were 184 of the crew and Commander Evans.

So was slain the third "small boy" to die in the Battle off Samar—a battle that made of October 25, 1944, a crimson-letter day for the DesPac Force. But if the day was crimson for American destroyermen, it was fatal for the sailors of the Imperial Navy. As has been related, the "small boys" caused Kurita to hesitate. Hesitating, he was lost.

Writing of the Johnston sacrifice, Admiral Kinkaid commented: *"That the* Johnston *should have been lost was among the calculated risks of such an undertaking. This ship did not go down in vain; largely through its efforts and those of the other ships the Japanese force was slowed down and turned back. What the Japanese had planned as an American naval disaster was turned into a Japanese rout. The part played by the* Johnston *in this cannot be over-estimated."*

Samar Aftermath

When Kurita turned northwestward at 0920 in that morning of October 25, his striking force was still pretty much intact. His leviathans had taken a few hits, but the only warship seriously damaged was the heavy cruiser KUMANO, struck by a destroyer torpedo. Before him Sprague's force lay practically helpless, and beyond it the whole fleet of American transports and landing craft. Yet monster YAMATO, KONGO, NAGATO, and HARUNA turned tail.

Of course, help for Sprague was coming up. Although Admiral Stump had decided not to enter the surface action, he threw his air squadrons over the horizon into the battle. Up from the south Seventh Fleet forces were racing. And Sprague's desperate calls for help had started the carriers of Vice Admiral J. S. McCain on a high-speed rush for the Samar area. But most of these reinforcements would not arrive until afternoon, and they were balanced, if not equalled, by the aid given Kurita when Jap aircraft from Luzon pounced on Rear Admiral T. L. Sprague's Southern Carrier Group which was operating off Mindanao. While "Cliff" Sprague's Northern Group was battling Kurita's fleet, "Tom" Sprague's Southern Group was fighting death from the sky. A suicide plane smashed into the carrier SANTEE. Another suicider crashed the carrier SUWANNEE. Carriers SANGAMON and PETROF BAY were barely missed by suicide planes. And in the midst of this furious scrimmage, the disabled SANTEE was torpedoed by a Jap submarine. Had Kurita pushed on to Leyte Gulf, he would have had little trouble from this group.

Then, about 1100, the Jap aircraft, returning from their strikes in the Leyte area, pounced on "Cliff" Sprague's battle-scorched ships. Carriers SAINT LÔ and KITKUN BAY were struck by diving planes. Despite the fact that she was already crippled, KITKUN BAY absorbed a smashing from two "Zekes." But the plane which crashed SAINT LÔ touched off a series of explosions which gutted that vessel from stem to stern. Afire and bursting, the flat-top rolled over and went down. That noon the door to Leyte Gulf was practically pried open. But Kurita and his force were fleeing northward.

By that time he had reason to flee. Stump's aircraft had caught up with the Jap cruiser force. A bombing had blasted SUZUYA and left her in a sinking condition. Lambasted from the sky, cruisers CHIKUMA and CHOKAI were reeling in helpless disablement. Unaware of what had happened farther south, Kurita decided that a run to Leyte Gulf was out of the question. He ordered his destroyers to sink the disabled heavy cruisers, and he headed the rest of his force north to "search for Halsey." The quotes are Kurita's. When he reached the approaches to San Bernardino, he lost his desire for the search, and led his ships westward into the strait. By nightfall his force was steaming at best speed for the Sibuyan Sea.

On Toyoda's heels was Task Group 34.5—battleships IOWA and NEW JERSEY, cruisers VINCENNES, BILOXI, and MIAMI, and eight destroyers—led by Rear Admiral O. C. Badger. The destroyers in this Third Fleet group were TINGEY (flagship of Captain J. P. Womble, Jr., ComDesRon 52), OWEN, MILLER, THE SULLIVANS, HICKOX (flagship of Captain W. T. Kenny, ComDesDiv 104), HUNT, LEWIS HANCOCK, and MARSHALL. At 1623 in the evening of October 25, Halsey had sent this task group racing to intercept Kurita's retiring battleship force. Unfortunately Kurita beat Badger to San Bernardino, thereby jumping out of the bag.

But Badger's group did not go empty-handed. At 0028 in the morning of October 26, while sweeping along the coast of Samar, LEWIS HANCOCK (Commander W. M. Searles) made radar contact with a Jap vessel which was fleeing westward at 30 knots. The cruisers and DesDiv 103, ordered to engage this enemy, closed the range from 29,000 yards to shooting distance. The cruisers opened fire at 16,000 yards, and the destroyers let go at 11,000 yards. Within six minutes the target ship's speed was reduced to 2 knots. A moment later it slowed to zero knots. A bright orange fire blossomed on the seascape. Destroyers OWEN (Commander C. B. Jones) and MILLER (Lieutenant Commander D. L. Johnson) were ordered in to douse this illumination.

Five-inch salvos and a brace of five torpedoes from OWEN liquidated the burning vessel. At 0136 the seascape was again a blackout. OWEN sent up a few starshells to verify the target's vanishment. Task Group 34.5 then swept on down the coast of Samar, but all they could find were eleven American aviators who had been downed at sea, and a few swimming Japs who were willing to be saved.

The ship sunk that night by Badger's interceptors was a Kurita straggler, the destroyer NOWAKI. YAMATO and her remaining consorts reached the Sibuyan Sea in relative safety. From there they had a long voyage home. Crippled KUMANO, trying to sneak up the west coast of Luzon, was ambushed by four American submarines. The subs fired a total of 23 torpedoes at the vessel. KUMANO was a durable hulk! The subs drove her into the beach, but they failed to down her. It took a bombing by naval aircraft to finish off the job Sprague's destroyers off Samar had begun. Less durable was battleship KONGO, waylaid in Formosa Strait by the U.S.S. SEALION. A spread from this submarine blew the home-running

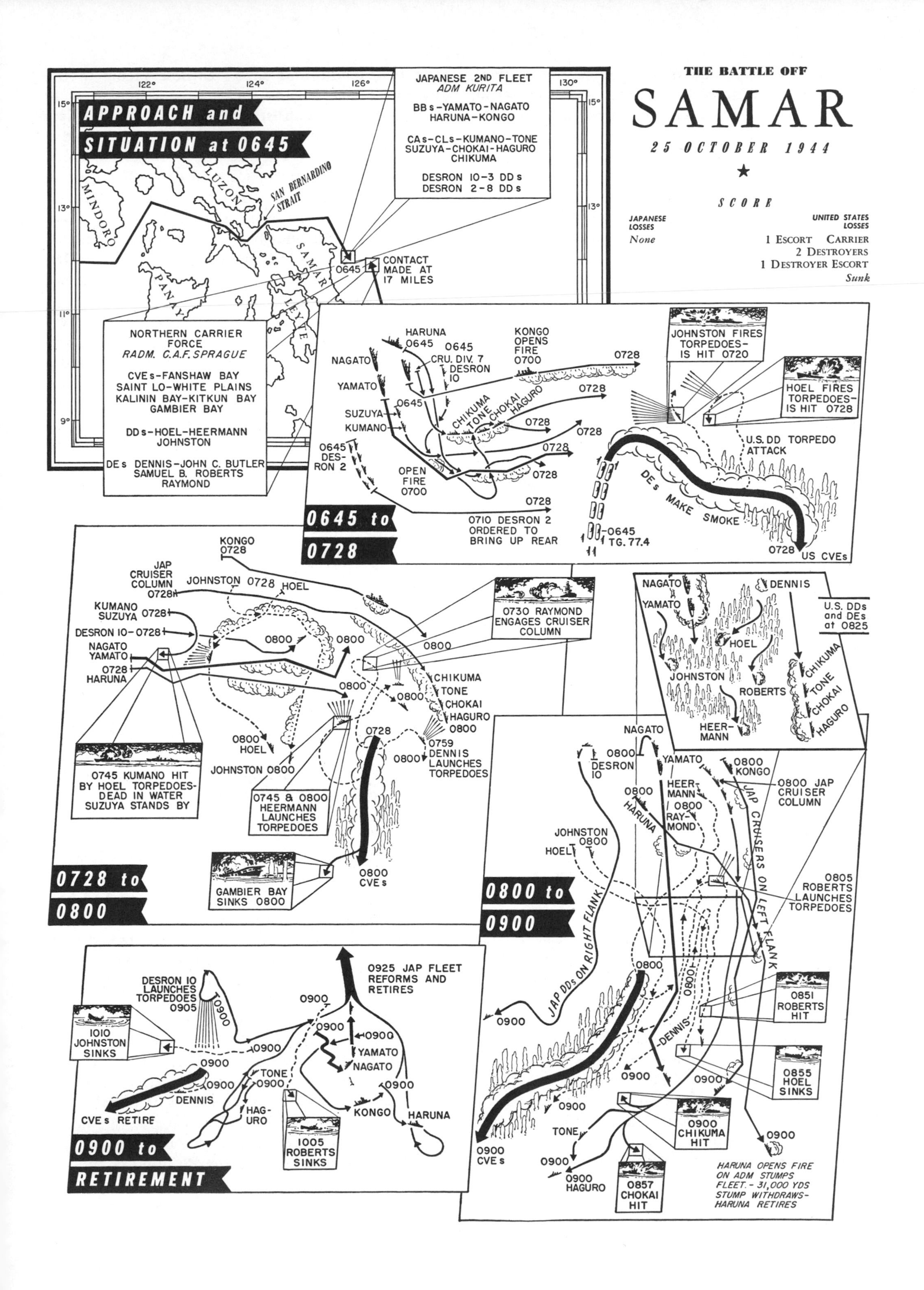
THE BATTLE OFF
SAMAR
25 OCTOBER 1944
SCORE
JAPANESE LOSSES
None
UNITED STATES LOSSES
1 Escort Carrier
2 Destroyers
1 Destroyer Escort
Sunk
APPROACH and
SITUATION at 0645
JAPANESE 2ND FLEET
ADM KURITA
BBs-YAMATO-NAGATO
HARUNA-KONGO
CAs-CLs-KUMANO-TONE
SUZUYA-CHOKAI-HAGURO
CHIKUMA
DESRON 10-3 DDs
DESRON 2-8 DDs
CONTACT MADE AT 17 MILES
NORTHERN CARRIER FORCE
RADM. C.A.F. SPRAGUE
CVEs-FANSHAW BAY
SAINT LO-WHITE PLAINS
KALININ BAY-KITKUN BAY
GAMBIER BAY
DDs-HOEL-HEERMANN
JOHNSTON
DEs DENNIS-JOHN C. BUTLER
SAMUEL B. ROBERTS
RAYMOND
MINDORO
LUZON
SAN BERNARDINO STRAIT
SAMAR
PANAY
LEYTE
0645 to
0728
JOHNSTON FIRES TORPEDOES-IS HIT 0720
HOEL FIRES TORPEDOES-IS HIT 0728
KONGO OPENS FIRE 0700
CRU. DIV. 7
DESRON 10
DESRON 2
OPEN FIRE 0700
U.S. DD TORPEDO ATTACK
DEs MAKE SMOKE
0710 DESRON 2 ORDERED TO BRING UP REAR
0645 TG. 77.4
US CVEs
0728 to
0800
JAP CRUISER COLUMN 0728
DESRON 10-0728
0730 RAYMOND ENGAGES CRUISER COLUMN
0745 KUMANO HIT BY HOEL TORPEDOES-DEAD IN WATER SUZUYA STANDS BY
0745 & 0800 HEERMANN LAUNCHES TORPEDOES
0759 DENNIS LAUNCHES TORPEDOES
GAMBIER BAY SINKS 0800
0800 CVEs
U.S. DDs and DEs at 0825
0800 to
0900
JAP DDs ON RIGHT FLANK
JAP CRUISERS ON LEFT FLANK
0800 JAP CRUISER COLUMN
0805 ROBERTS LAUNCHES TORPEDOES
0851 ROBERTS HIT
0855 HOEL SINKS
0900 CHIKUMA HIT
0857 CHOKAI HIT
HARUNA OPENS FIRE ON ADM STUMPS FLEET.- 31,000 YDS STUMP WITHDRAWS-HARUNA RETIRES
0900 to
RETIREMENT
0925 JAP FLEET REFORMS AND RETIRES
DESRON 10 LAUNCHES TORPEDOES 0905
1010 JOHNSTON SINKS
1005 ROBERTS SINKS
CVEs RETIRE

battleship skyhigh, and took a Jap destroyer simultaneously skyward! When the left-overs made Japan, the Imperial Navy was all but wiped out. It had lost the Battle of Surigao Strait and the Battle off Samar. And the Battle off Cape Engano—

Cape Engano Mop-Up

At 0205 in the morning of October 25, an INDEPENDENCE scout plane, winging across the sea about 85 miles ahead of Task Force 38, made an interesting radar contact. In the Philippine Sea northeast of Cape Engano steamed a group of Japanese ships. At 0220 a second Japanese group was detected 40 miles astern of the first. Halsey's Third Fleet was in contact with Ozawa's Carrier Force!

There they were—large carrier ZUIKAKU, light carriers CHITOSE, CHIYODA, and ZUIHO, carrier-battleships ISE and HYUGA, light cruisers TAMA and OYODO, and eight destroyers. Their presence in the area was no surprise. Halsey had been informed that they were approaching northeast Luzon. In effect, this information had been transmitted by Ozawa himself, in his role as decoy duck.

Unaware of the enemy's almost complete lack of planes and pilots, Halsey expected a carrier duel and perhaps a big-gun duel, and he maneuvered carefully into position for a dawn attack. Mitscher's search planes took off to inspect and keep tabs on the enemy, and at 0630 the first striking groups were away. A few Jap fighters rose to intercept the Hellcats. They were promptly shot down. By 0900 the American planes, diving through canopies of anti-aircraft fire, were flailing at the Jap flat-tops with heavy bombs and torpedoes.

Throughout the day the strikes continued. Ozawa was certainly a successful decoy. But the strategem was one of the most extravagant ruses in the history of naval warfare. Down went the ZUIKAKU. Down went CHIYODA. ZUIHO went down. They were escorted to the bottom by the destroyer AKITSUKI. At graveside wallowed the carrier CHITOSE, paralyzed by bombs. And by mid-afternoon Ozawa had run his course and was fleeing northward with his surviving warships.

Somewhat incongruously (after the deliberate sacrifice of the flat-top) he detached the cruiser TAMA and a pair of destroyers, ordering them to stand by the sinking CHITOSE. This irrational gesture gave Halsey's surface forces a chance for action.

By that hour the Third Fleet commander, satisfied that Ozawa's carriers were out of the war, had dispatched Bogan's task group and a battleship-cruiser force under Vice Admiral Lee to the Samar front. To wipe up the Ozawa remnants, he sent a cruiser force under Rear Admiral L. T. DuBose racing to the waters off Cape Engano.

DuBose's force consisted of cruisers SANTA FE (flagship), MOBILE, WICHITA, and NEW ORLEANS, and a dozen destroyers. The destroyer roster included PORTERFIELD (flagship of Captain C. R. Todd, ComDesRon 55, and senior DD officer present), CALLAGHAN, C. K. BRONSON (flagship of Captain E. R. Wilkinson, ComDesRon 50), COTTEN, DORTCH, HEALY, COGSWELL (flagship of Captain W. J. Miller, ComDesDiv 100), CAPERTON, INGERSOLL, KNAPP, PATTERSON, and BAGLEY.

At 1625 that evening the dying CHITOSE was sighted, lined up in the sights, and under cruiser fire. When the wreck burst into flames DuBose ordered a destroyer division to sink the ruin. But the ruin saved them the trouble by capsizing and heading for the bottom.

At 1840 radar contact was made with TAMA and her consorts. The Jap cruiser and two DD's ran northward. DuBose's warships overhauled. After a long chase, Captain Miller was ordered to close in with COGSWELL, INGERSOLL, and CAPERTON for torpedo attack. At 2011, with the range closed to 6,800 yards, the three DD's each fired a half-salvo. Then the nearer target, a destroyer, was struck by cruiser shells. By 2046 this ship was dead in the water and burning. Destroyer PORTERFIELD headed in to finish off the vessel. Before she could do so, the ship blew up. She was later identified as the destroyer HATSUTSUKI.

By 2100 the other two Jap ships were 46 miles to the northward, and running like jackrabbits. Because his destroyers were low on fuel and time was lacking, DuBose broke off the chase. As it was, cruiser TAMA ploughed into a submarine ambush, and she too was on the bottom before midnight.

"King Two" Checkmate

The day after the Surigao-Samar-Cape Engano debacle, Jap cruisers KINU and NOSHIRO and destroyer URANAMI were caught in Philippine waters and battered under by Navy planes. On October 27 destroyers FUJINAMI and SHIRANUHI were bombed to the bottom. The Imperial Navy was now little more than a ghost of its former self—a bugaboo soon to be forever dispelled.

Decisively, and with dispatch, the naval elements of "King Two" had checkmated "Operation Sho." Fighting the Battle for Leyte Gulf, the U.S. Navy had lost one light carrier, two escort-carriers, two destroyers, and a destroyer-escort. The Imperial Navy had lost three battleships, four carriers, six heavy cruisers, four light cruisers, eleven destroyers, and all possible chance of holding the Philippines and defending Japan. *"After this battle,"* mourned Vice Admiral Ozawa, *"the surface force became strictly auxiliary."*

But Japanese soldiery, Jap submariners, and Japanese airmen were still to be dealt with. A long, hard road lay between Leyte and Manila.

The Durability of U.S.S. Ross

A memorable example of destroyer durability was furnished the U. S. Fleet by the U.S.S. Ross (Commander Benjamin Coe). Early on the Leyte scene, this DD absorbed a dose of punishment that would have downed a less hardy warship. That she stood up under it as she did spoke eloquent testimony for the naval architects who designed her class, the builders who constructed her—and the men who manned her.

Here is the story in graphic extracts from her Action Report:

> During the period from October 17 to November 1, 1944, the U.S.S. Ross participated in the Leyte Operation, undergoing and surviving a series of hazards which has seemingly been endless. Up to October 19, the Ross rode out a storm, conducted a bombardment, and drove off several enemy planes in the normal course of events. At 0133 on the 19th, the ship struck a mine which put the forward fireroom and engine-room out of commission and killed several men. This was only the start of our misfortune. At 0155, while all hands were attempting salvage operations, another mine hit under the after engine-room, flooding it as well as fuel oil service tanks, living compartments, magazines, and the workshop aft, and killing and injuring more personnel. The ship listed to 14° and the port side aft was under water.
>
> Ross remained adrift in the minefields while salvage work, removal and shifting of topside weights, care of the wounded, and initial preparations for abandonment went on simultaneously. When it was determined that the list had stopped at 14° and the ship continued to recover from rolls, the Commanding Officer . . . announced to the crew that the ship could and would be saved. All ideas of abandoning were given up and full salvage efforts were continued.
>
> The tug CHICKASAW arrived on the scene promptly, took the Ross in tow and headed toward Homonhon Island. As we proceeded away from the minefield, apprehension of hitting a third mine faded into the background. We anchored close to Homonhon Island, and further efforts reduced the list to 5° and brought the stern about 18 inches out of water. At this point an enemy plane dived over the hill near-by on Homonhon and scored a near miss which critically injured two men and put a few minor holes in the ship. This accentuated a growing desire to move the Ross nearer to friendly ships and planes. CHICKASAW, in her constantly fine and helpful manner, promptly accomplished this, the ship anchoring south of Mariquitdaquit Island, about eight miles south of the northern transport area.
>
> The next two days were punctuated by brief but determined air attacks, in which this vessel fired its few remaining workable guns at planes which had hit the U.S.S. PRESERVER and the U.S.S. HONOLULU. By this date the moon began to get brighter at night, and the objective of Jap air attacks shifted once more to isolated cripples and weakly defended ships. A move to the center of the transport area was indicated, and was accomplished. . . . Our position within the transport area . . . gave us much comfort. Air attacks increased in intensity, but our salvage work went on between periods of repelling the enemy air. By this time two 5-inch and most of the 20 mm. and 40 mm., plus directors and plot, were back in commission. Morale lifted from grim determination to high confidence when the Ross shot down one of three "Lilies" on her first salvo, started a second down before any other ships had opened fire, and assisted in damaging a third.
>
> The next two days were marked by air attacks day and night, and by the anxiety felt for our squadron in particular and the fleet in general as they engaged the enemy. The large number of enemy planes seen to be shot down by AA and by our fighters, plus a definite assist on another Jap plane, kept our spirits high. A typhoon on the 27th of October came almost as a welcome relief, since enemy air was grounded during the night, and everyone was confident that the ship could now ride out a storm . . . which it did. Events from then up to the present date (November 1) consisted of air attacks followed by more air attacks, day and night.

Twenty-three of Ross's crew were slain in action during her tour of duty on the Leyte front, and many of the ship's company were wounded. Her Pharmacist's Mates worked as long and valiantly as her gun crews and repair parties. And with equal skill.

Early in 1945 the ship reached Pearl Harbor under tow. March found her in Mare Island Navy Yard where she underwent overhaul and refit. On June 26 she was once more at sea, a man-of-war ready to enter combat.

Commenting on Ross's hardihood, Commander Coe observed:

> One fact which was clearly demonstrated is that the 2,100-ton destroyer is extremely sturdy and well constructed. Not only did the ship structure hold up remarkably well, but the equipment installed stood terrific shocks with little damage other than that which occurred in the near vicinity of the explosions.

Samuel S. Miles Sinks I-364

On October 3, 1944, destroyer-escort SAMUEL S. MILES (Lieutenant Commander H. G. Brousseau, U.S.N.R.) was steaming with a hunter-killer group off Palau. The group was composed of the escort-carrier HOGGATT BAY and four DE's of CortDiv 8. The morning watch had just come on when the MILES obtained radar contact with a sub, range 16,800 yards. She was promptly ordered by the Task Group Commander, Captain W. V. Saunders, to track the target down.

At 0440 the surfaced sub was sighted and identified as Japanese. When MILES closed the range to 6,000 yards, the enemy I-boat decided it was time to dive. MILES ran in to peg hedgehog at the diving "pig boat." On the second run the projectiles hit the mark. Two explosions were trailed by an underwater thunderclap that jolted the destroyer-escort like a collision. The DE's radar, sound gear, and TBS went out of commission. For a moment some of the sailors thought, with apparently good reason, that the ship had been torpedoed.

Needless to say, the undersea blast which could jolt a DE in such fashion would wreck the submersible from which it emanated. At daybreak a mess of flotsam and a spread of oil were sighted. Two days later the carpet of Diesel oil was still expanding. The oil was the lifeblood of I-364—another Jap sub destroyed by fast DE work.

Richard M. Rowell Kills I-362

RICHARD M. ROWELL (Commander H. A. Barnard, Jr.) was attached to Task Unit 77.4.13, the screen for Rear Admiral T. L. Sprague's carriers. On the morning of October 24, 1944, these ships were providing close air support for the Leyte landings. A Sound man had to be a sharp operator to "hear" a submarine while a DE was ranging through the wakes of a group of escort-carriers steaming in formation. Such an operator was working in the crew of destroyer-escort ROWELL.

At 0833 the sonar contact was picked up directly astern of the formation. Turbulent water made the contact doubtful. Nevertheless, Commander Barnard directed a hedgehog attack at 0908. A few seconds after the pattern was fired, one charge exploded. About 40 seconds later another explosion rumbled up from deep under. At 0913 Sound heard still another explosion. Then came a peal of undersea thunder that vibrated the ship. The sinking thunder was suggestive of a down-going submarine. Thirty minutes later ROWELL made a final attack, but the contact was faint and results were negative. However, this final effort was superfluous.

Diesel oil was already gurgling to the surface. And in the vicinity of this marine gusher the destroyermen found telltale debris—splintered wood, cork, and a small glass ampoule labeled with Japanese characters. Sunk by ROWELL was I-362. Her obituary was found in records of the Japanese Sixth (Submarine) Fleet.

Helm and Gridley Kill I-54

Destroyers HELM (Commander S. K. Santmyers) and GRIDLEY (Commander P. D. Quirk) were attached to Task Unit 38.4.3, the screen unit for Rear Admiral Davison's task group which was supporting the Leyte occupation on October 28. The task group was in circular cruising disposition when HELM's sonar gear registered a contact at 600 yards.

The contact was made at 1228. The DD unleashed an urgent attack. Ordered to assist, GRIDLEY joined in at 1232. About 20 minutes later HELM launched a second attack with depth charges, and the booming "ashcans" struck oil. The up-welling oil was seen by an aircraft which had been ordered to assist. The sub was hit and bleeding.

HELM executed another attack at 1330. Up came a cluster of air bubbles. Now GRIDLEY was ready to fire. Fire she did at 1342. HELM followed through with a fourth attack at 1414. The depth-charge barrage was echoed by deep-sea thunder. Oil, cork, and shattered timber floated on the troubled water. To assure a "positive kill," GRIDLEY made two more depth-charge runs. HELM delivered a final attack at 1508. For the next half-hour the destroyermen boated about, fishing up debris. Among the items recovered were *"three pieces of teak deck planking, and two fresh human lungs."*

Deleted from the Japanese submarine effort at Leyte was the Imperial Navy's I-54.

Loss of U.S.S. Eversole

EVERSOLE (Lieutenant Commander George E. Marix) cleared Leyte Gulf in the evening of October 27, 1944, to rendezvous with Rear Admiral Sprague's task force at daylight the following morning. At 0210 in the morning of the 28th, the destroyer-escort made radar contact with a vessel five and a half miles distant.

About 18 minutes later the ship's sonar watch reported contact with a target at 2,800 yards. Thirty seconds after contact was made, EVERSOLE was struck by a torpedo. The ship staggered and canted in a 15° list. A moment later she was struck by a second torpedo which crashed inboard through the hole blasted by the first torpedo. The explosion dealt death and destruction below decks, and the mortally stricken DE assumed a 30° list. Lieutenant Commander Marix ordered the ship abandoned at 0240.

The crew scrambled overside as best it could, and the sea was soon clotted with crowded life rafts and swimmers. The EVERSOLE sank within 15 minutes. About 0300 the Japanese submarine opened fire on the survivors. For 20 minutes the desperate men were target for this ruthless gunnery; then the sub submerged. A few minutes later the sea was erupted by a murderous blast which killed or wounded everyone in the water. Casualties exacted by torpedo explosions, strafing, and underwater blast were tragically high. Some 139 of EVERSOLE's crew were rescued.

EVERSOLE's captain believed the final blast was caused by some sort of anti-personnel bomb deposited in the sea by the submarine. The DE's depth charges (according to claim) had been all set on safe, and the ship had gone down at least 30 minutes before that final explosion. Undoubtedly fatalities would have been close to total had not destroyer-escorts RICHARD S. BULL and WHITEHURST soon arrived on the scene. With the following results—

Whitehurst Sinks I-45

Shortly after EVERSOLE went down, destroyer-escort WHITEHURST received over the TBS word from destroyer-escort BULL that their sister DE had been torpedoed and sunk. WHITEHURST was operating at the time with Task Unit 77.7.1, which had the mission of feeding fuel and ammunition supplies to units of the Seventh Fleet supporting the Leyte landings.

After relaying the word on EVERSOLE, destroyer-escort BULL requested a DE to act as A/S screen while she rescued survivors. WHITEHURST was thereupon dispatched to the scene of the sinking. Her skipper, Lieutenant J. C. Horton, U.S.N.R., took the ship through a search pattern around the area. The search had almost been completed when WHITEHURST picked up a sonar contact at 0545. Ten minutes later she reached firing position, and let fly with a full hedgehog salvo. Results were negative. At 0608, 0635, and 0648 she delivered hedgehog attacks. Eleven seconds after the fourth salvo splashed into the sea, a series of explosions echoed up from below. The rataplan ended in a thunderous detonation which ebbed away with a prolonged rumble. The undersea blasting was violent enough to knock out WHITEHURST's "pinging gear."

Thereupon BULL was asked to continue the search. After a fruitless effort to gain contact, BULL's skipper reported over TBS,

FROM THE SOUND OF THE EXPLOSIONS WHERE I WAS THREE MILES AWAY I DON'T THINK THERE IS ANYTHING LEFT OF THE SUB

His implication was correct. However, the destroyermen, making a daylight search of the area, discovered some submarine residue. Splintered teak, a wooden damage-control plug, chunks of painted wood, and what not. After the war these items were attributed to the submarine I-45, the sub which probably sank EVERSOLE.

WHITEHURST had lost no time in tracking down and exterminating the Japanese killer.

DAMAGE CONTROL PARTY ON THE ROSS

CHAPTER 34

ENTER THE SUICIDERS

DD's Versus Death-Divers at Leyte

On November 1, 1944, the Japs made an "all-out" effort to blast the Seventh Fleet's Covering Forces out of Leyte Gulf. By that date the Imperial Navy was finished. But the Japanese air forces—land-based and carrier remnants—constituted a hawk which retained deadly talons. As the American warships in Leyte Gulf learned on the first day of November.

Covering Leyte on that date was Task Group 77.1, under Rear Admiral G. L. Weyler. The group consisted of battleships MISSISSIPPI, CALIFORNIA, and PENNSYLVANIA; cruisers PHOENIX, BOISE, NASHVILLE, and H.M.A.S. SHROPSHIRE; and, when fully complemented, 19 destroyers. The destroyers were NEWCOMB (flagship of Captain R. N. Smoot, Screen Commander, and ComDesRon 56), KILLEN, ABNER READ (flagship of Captain J. B. McLean, ComDesDiv 48), AMMEN, LEUTZE, ROBINSON (flagship of Captain T. F. Conley, Jr., ComDesDiv 112), BRYANT, CLAXTON, FLUSSER (flagship of Captain W. M. Cole, ComDesRon 5), MAHAN, SMITH, JENKINS, DRAYTON, and EDWARDS. Destroyers BUSH, BENNION, H.M.A.S. ARUNTA, HEYWOOD L. EDWARDS, and RICHARD P. LEARY—members of the task group—were stationed as A/S guards and radar pickets at the entrance to Leyte Gulf.

The mission of this powerful aggregation of ships was *"to cover, protect, and defend Leyte Gulf and the invasion forces and ships engaged in the Leyte operations against attack by enemy surface forces."* As far as Japanese surface forces were concerned, most of those in the Philippines theater were currently resting on the bottom, but Weyler's task group had some anti-aircraft work on its hands.

Early in the morning of November 1 the group was cruising in the Gulf entrance. Several snoopers approached the formation. An all-night air alert strained the nerves of the American sailors, and daybreak did not relieve the tension. It was obvious that the enemy was gathering information and muscle for a strike.

At 0916 in the morning the air alert was re-broadcast as the radar watches reported Jap planes in the offing. Zigzagging, the task group stepped up speed to 15 knots, and the screen contracted. All ships were at Condition of Readiness to repel air attack, with the gun crews tense at their mounts and C.I.C. teams working at full speed, when the plot indicated enemy aircraft on various bearings, closing rapidly.

Action began at 0940 when destroyer BUSH (Commander R. E. Westholm), on patrol in South Surigao Strait, opened fire with all batteries on a "Betty" which came in on the ship's starboard beam. Dropping a torpedo, the plane veered off to the right. With a fast dash and hard right rudder, BUSH avoided the torpedo. A burst of 40 mm. fire hit the plane.

Four minutes later another "Betty" attacked BUSH. Roaring in on the destroyer's port beam, the plane flung a "fish" at 800 yards. BUSH dodged by swerving left with hard rudder, and her guns brought the plane down in a swirl of fire 100 yards from the ship.

At 0951 a third "Betty" attacked BUSH. The destroyer gunners poured fire into the plane, but the aircraft got close enough to drop a 500-pound bomb

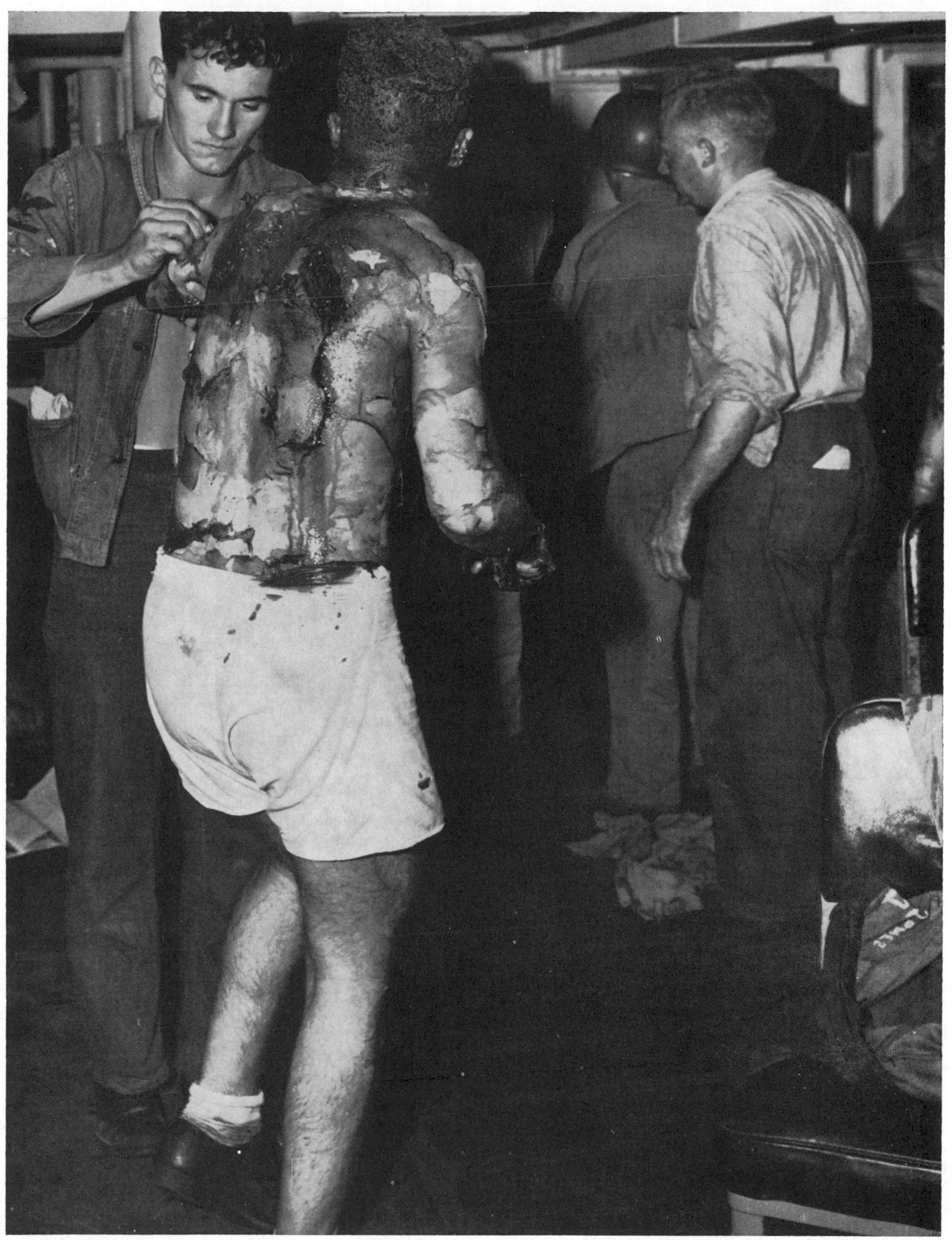

Battles are fought by men. The score, in terms of ships sunk and damaged, determines the winner and loser. The score in terms of pain and anguish is without winner or loser but tells the story of heroism and dedication at the level of the individual. The magnificent sacrifice of American sailors in the execution of duty is shown in this man's personal ordeal by fire.

Here is a battle which, for sheer courage in the face of tremendous odds, may well rank with the greatest of all time. The major Japanese effort to turn back the invasion of the Philippines had been launched. Only a handful of jeep carriers screened by "small boys" stood between Kurita and the Leyte beach. Interposing themselves between the carriers and the Jap

capital ships, a few heroic destroyers and a clutch of destroyer-escorts engaged the enemy at almost pointblank range. This picture shows destroyer-escorts in the van of the carrier group laying a protective smoke screen. Splashes from the Jap gunfire may be clearly seen. So effective was the defense that Kurita thought he was up against Essex-class carriers and cruisers!

Guns like the 5-inchers of Eugene E. Elmore (DE 686) were not intended to engage the 18-inch rifles of Yamato. This DE, which sank the U-boat that sank the Block Island, is a sister ship of those which so gallantly fought Kurita's fleet off Samar. With turbo-electric drive, the 1450-ton destroyer-escort could make 24 knots. She was 306 feet long, and carried 220 in her crew.

Wadleigh (DD 689) exploding mines in Kossol Passage, Palau. After she had exploded twelve successfully, she fouled a thirteenth. The explosion shattered an engine-room, killed three men, and put the ship out of action.

Shown steaming as part of Task Group 38.4, Cooper was later lost during a night action at Ormoc Bay. After helping to sink a Jap DD, she was hit, probably by a submarine torpedo, and sank with heavy loss of life.

One of the first destroyers to be hit by a kamikaze: Haraden (DD 585) in the western Mindanao Sea. Except on individual initiative, suicide tactics were not used by the Japs until after the Philippine invasion in 1944.

Destroyers supporting the amphibious push across the Pacific: (From top to bottom) Morotai, with La Vallette in foreground; Anguar, Palau; Mariveles Harbor, P.I., under guns of Picking; Hollandia; Lingayen Gulf; Palawan, with Drayton in foreground; Leyte Gulf, with Cony in foreground. These pictures show typical destroyer support.

which exploded about 60 feet from the ship's starboard quarter. Flying shrapnel gave the ship a clawing. The plane also escaped.

At 1007 BUSH dove off a fourth "Betty." At 1044 two more "Bettys" attacked the destroyer, and the ship dodged another aerial torpedo. One of the "Bettys" roared down BUSH's starboard side, the tail gunner lashing at the vessel with machine-gun fire. Two sailors fell wounded. But the plane got a belly full of automatic fire for her pains.

Ten minutes later two "Zekes" pounced on the DD. After she hit one of them with 5-inch, the pair hit for the clouds. At 1100 a "Zeke" (apparently the one which had been hit) came down in what appeared to be a suicide dive on the ship. The plane dropped a small bomb which missed. BUSH's sharpshooters did not miss. Riddled, the "Zeke" plunged into the sea 50 yards astern.

At 1111 the indomitable BUSH drove off still another "Betty." This was her last air battle of the day. The skies over her vicinity cleared at noon, and her crew took time out to mop fevered brows. That had been a busy morning for BUSH. A "Betty" and a "Zeke" shot down, two "Bettys" badly damaged, a "Betty" moderately damaged—three torpedoes dodged—not a bad day's work before lunch! In fact, it was such a good day's work that Commander Rollin E. Westholm won special commendation from Rear Admiral Weyler. BUSH's performance also won special mention by Tokyo Rose. Going on the air with her daily broadcast on November 2, that siren of the mike paid BUSH this compliment: *"Our aircraft attacked a lone American destroyer which had automatic 5-inch guns."*

Meantime, Weyler's task force in Leyte Gulf fought a battle royal against attacking Jap aircraft. The Gulf battle began at 0950, ten minutes after the first onslaught on BUSH. A flight of Jap torpedo-planes winging over the Gulf drew a thunderstorm AA barrage from the ready warships. Two planes were shot down, and an attack on cruiser SHROPSHIRE was beaten off. One of the planes which attacked the Australian ship, however, climbed into a cloud, and then dropped like a meteor on destroyer CLAXTON (Commander M. H. Hubbard).

CLAXTON's gunners lashed the plane with 40 mm., forcing it to take a tangent which brought it down into the sea. But the plane struck close aboard and exploded with a shattering blast which killed four of CLAXTON's crew, wounded 24, and severely damaged the ship. In spite of these injuries, the DD stayed in the fight, and by 1200 was able to steam at 15 knots, thanks to efficient damage-control measures.

At 0951 destroyer KILLEN was struck by a bomb. With fire topside and flood below, the KILLEN fell out of formation. Her skipper, Commander H. G. Corey, and her crew fought extensive battle damage with extensive grit. And the ship, escorted by destroyer ROBINSON, steamed to a safe anchorage in the Gulf. Three or four Jap planes were seen to go down under fire from KILLEN's guns.

Then, at 0952, destroyer AMMEN (Commander J. H. Brown) was crashed by a Jap plane. As will be seen, this smash was probably a deliberate suicide. When, early in the afternoon, a plane smashed into ABNER READ, the suicide tactic was obvious. The Navy's Pacific destroyermen realized they were up against something new in the grim book of warfare—the *Kamikaze.*

Loss of U.S.S. Abner Read

The aerial onslaught on Rear Admiral G. L. Weyler's Task Group 77.1 gave the Seventh Fleet destroyermen a bitter taste of what was to come—the employment of self-destruction as a combat tactic. And by November 1, 1944, the curtain was rising on a horror drama that had no equal in the bloody history of warfare.

The Jap aircraft which was riddled by CLAXTON's 40 mm. fire and crashed close aboard, blasting the destroyer, may have been a suicider. The Jap "Frances" which crashed into AMMEN seems to have been more deliberate. But the strike on ABNER READ, which occurred early in the afternoon, seems to have been undoubtedly purposeful.

Screening damaged CLAXTON, ABNER READ (Commander A. M. Purdy), flagship of Captain J. B. McLean, ComDesDiv 48, was conducting a circular patrol. About 1339 the radar watch reported two enemy aircraft about 11 miles distant, and coming fast. ABNER READ opened fire with main battery and automatic guns. Down from the sky plunged a "Val" dive-bomber, dragging a tail of smoke. Evidently hit by ABNER READ's scorching fire, the plane was burning, but the pilot drove straight for the destroyer.

It happened fast—three minutes after the initial radar contact. ABNER READ's guns were slamming, chattering, and roaring. It seemed impossible that an aircraft could penetrate the lacework of flame, machine-gun lead, and flak. All hands on the bridge watched in a freeze of dread as the dive-bomber came on, nearer and nearer, growing in size as eyes stared in dilated appallment.

Someone shouted, "Oh, my God!"

Men were thrown to the deck as the "Val" crashed into the destroyer's starboard side, smashing in a splatter against the after stack. A wave of fire blew across the superstructure. Blazing gasoline showered the wreckage with flame. At once the ship was an inferno topside. Then the conflagration ignited a magazine. Ready ammunition exploded near a gun mount. Sailors were struck down by flying shrapnel and whistling scraps of debris. The flames ran below decks and touched off a series of explosions. ABNER READ, listing and shaken by interior blasting, lay dying in the sea. Torpedoes were jettisoned, and damage-control parties fought a desperate battle to save the ship, but the flood swept in through her ruptured hull, and her abandonment had to be ordered. Thirty-six minutes after the plane crash, ABNER READ plunged for the bottom of Leyte Gulf. For several hours an ugly oil fire burned on the sea where she went down.

Lost with the ship were 19 men and three officers. Among the survivors picked up by the rescue vessels were a wounded officer and 55 injured men. While rescue work was going forward, the air battle raged on. A suicide plane plummeted at destroyer RICHARD P. LEARY. Torn to pieces by AA fire from LEARY and CLAXTON, this plane crashed in the sea. The attack indicated all too clearly that Japan's airmen were in a *hari-kiri* mood. The suspicion of deliberate suiciding was confirmed that evening by the report that destroyer ANDERSON (Lieutenant Commander R. H. Benson, Jr.) had been crashed by a plane in Cabalian Bay.

After fighting off numerous air attacks near Panaon Island that day, ANDERSON had been struck at 1812 by one of three attacking Jap fighters. The plane crashed into the ship's motor whaleboat aft, and the shattering of the boat undoubtedly absorbed much of the blast. As it was, ANDERSON suffered 18 fatalities, and 21 of the crew were wounded. The ship's boilers were damaged, it was necessary to jettison the torpedoes, and the crew had a hard fight extinguishing wild fires and keeping the ship under way. Destroyer BUSH stood by to screen the damaged vessel and offer medical aid. At 2030 ANDERSON fought off an attacking torpedo-plane. Pluckily she made San Pedro Bay under her own power.

Altogether, November 1 was a rough day for the destroyermen in the Leyte area. Six ships were struck, of which four—CLAXTON, AMMEN, ANDERSON, and ABNER READ—were victims of suicide onslaughts. Of these ABNER READ was the first United States destroyer to die at the hands of the homicidal Japanese suiciders.

Leyte Backlash (Collett in Action; Aulick and Saufley Damaged)

Throughout November the Third Fleet continued to strike the enemy's airdromes and harbors in the northern Philippines. The Japs could not catch up with fast-moving McCain and Halsey, but on the evening of November 19, four "Bettys" pounced on destroyer COLLETT (Commander J. D. Collett) as she patrolled a picket station some 20 miles from the center of Task Force 38.

The planes launched a two-section coordinated attack. Speeding up to 30 knots, COLLETT shingled the sky with flak, and dodged a torpedo that was dropped at 800 yards. The destroyer shot down one "Betty" and drove another off wobbling. The third plane crossed COLLETT's stern and dropped a torpedo at 1,500 yards. As the DD swerved hard right to avoid, her portside automatic guns crashed this "Betty" at 500 yards. The fourth plane, discouraged, flitted away in the dusk.

"COLLETT," wrote Admiral McCain, *"forcefully demonstrated the invaluable service rendered by . . . destroyer strike-pickets in disorganizing enemy air attacks threatening the main body of a task force, and in giving early warning of the approach of the attacking planes."*

Evidently the "Bettys" which struck at COLLETT were not suicidally inclined, but in the Leyte Gulf area the homicidal self-killers subjected Seventh Fleet destroyermen to a number of ferocious assaults. On the evening of November 29, destroyers AULICK and SAUFLEY fought off a nasty suicide attack.

Patrolling between Homonhon and Dinagat Island the ships were on A/S guard at the entrance to Leyte Gulf. At 1750 AULICK (Commander J. D. Andrew) made radar contact with a flight of Jap aircraft. Six "Oscars" were sighted and taken under fire. Diving at the ship, one of the planes clipped the SC radar antenna, and crashed in the sea about 20 yards off AULICK's port bow. Another plane, roaring in, struck the starboard guy on the mast and slammed into the windshield of the bridge. The aircraft and its bomb exploded just above the main deck near the wardroom. The blast killed 32 of AULICK's crew, wounded 64, and tore ragged gaps in the ship's superstructure.

Meantime, SAUFLEY was hot in action. She shot down what looked like two "Vals" and a "Zero." By agile maneuvering, her skipper, Commander D. E. Cochran, dodged one suicide-diving "Val" which struck close aboard. The explosion in the sea gave the ship a scorching. Sixty seconds later SAUFLEY was hit by a "Zero" which struck her a glancing blow on the port side near the forward boat davit. About 1759 another "Val" swooped in astern and released two bombs which exploded close aboard, sent a wave of green water over the starboard weather decks, and injured a number of the crew. Struck by bursts of fire, the "Val" crashed in the sea about 50 yards to starboard. With minor damage and 21 wounded, SAUFLEY dodged away.

AULICK continued her patrol until relieved by destroyer PRINGLE, after which she limped off to San Pedro Bay. SAUFLEY remained on the A/S job. And as December came up on the calendar, the American destroyermen in the Philippines were grimly aware that Leyte Gulf was only the first round of a knockdown, drag-out death match.

Nicholas Kills I-37

Early in the evening of November 12, 1944, the destroyer NICHOLAS (Commander R. T. S. Keith), in company with destroyer TAYLOR, was escorting the cruiser ST. LOUIS from Ulithi to the Pelews. At 2003, NICHOLAS made radar contact with a surface target at 21,300 yards. Steaming to investigate, NICHOLAS saw the "pip" disappear from the radar screen as the range closed to 8,100 yards. This disappearance had all the earmarks of a diving submarine, and the destroyer picked up sound contact at 2047.

Between 2053 and 2230 NICHOLAS delivered two deliberate depth-charge attacks on the submersible. Five minutes after the last barrage went down, a great explosion roared under the sea. Tangible evidence of a submarine's demolition was found on the surface the following morning. The evidence consisted of the usual flotsam, in which was found a piece of lung tissue. (This anatomical item was frequently found in the wake of an exploded submarine.)

Post-war inquest disclosed the identity of NICHOLAS' victim. The submarine was the I-37. She was the second I-boat downed by this destroyer, a veteran DD with a distinguished battle record.

Rockford and Ardent Sink I-38

The day after NICHOLAS sank I-37, a frigate and a minesweeper followed through with arithmetical progression far across the Pacific to get the number of I-38.

The two ships were escorts conducting a convoy from Pearl Harbor to San Francisco. Frigate ROCKFORD (Commander D. H. Bartlett, U.S.C.G.) was a 1,430-tonner. Minesweeper ARDENT (Lieutenant Commander A. D. Curtis, U.S.N.R.) was an 890-tonner. The submarine in question weighed almost as much as these two ships put together.

ARDENT made the first sonar contact at 1225, range 2,100 yards. She delivered three hedgehog attacks. When the patterns sank in silence, ROCKFORD stepped in (at 1308) to fire a salvo. Three explosions echoed ROCKFORD's shooting. Then the minesweeper fired a fourth salvo at 1315. Hit by the frigate's hedgehogs, the submarine exploded with a detonation that littered the sea with rubbish. ROCKFORD thereupon dropped thirteen depth charges, perhaps to suit the date—which was November 13, 1944. Bottom up, the sub rose to the surface, then sank like a dead whale. Its number—I-38—was found in the records of the Japanese Submarine Force after VJ-Day.

Lawrence C. Taylor and Aircraft Kill I-26

From Ulithi on November 4, 1944, sailed a hunter-killer team built around the escort-carrier ANZIO, flagship of Captain P. W. Watson, ComTaskGroup 30.7. Five DE's steamed with the ANZIO. The DE's were led by Commander A. Jackson, Jr., U.S.N.R., ComCortDiv 72, whose pennant flew in LAWRENCE C. TAYLOR. The TAYLOR was skippered by Commander R. Cullinan, Jr. On November 18, this task group was conducting an A/S patrol around the perimeter of the Third Fleet fuelling area.

Turn the calendar back to the last day of August, 1942. Put the clock at 0330. And shift the scene to the Coral Sea. At that date, time, and place, battleship NORTH CAROLINA and carrier SARATOGA made radar contact with what might have been a submarine. Destroyer FARRAGUT, sent to investigate, could find nothing but empty sea. But in that same vicinity at 0706 a Japanese periscope had its eye trained on the "SARA." At 0746 a torpedo jumped from the foam in destroyer MACDONOUGH's wake, and a second later a submarine grazed the destroyer's hull. That same submarine pumped a torpedo into the SARATOGA. And, escaping reprisal, that submarine, on November 13, 1942, sank the light cruiser JUNEAU. The number of that deadly undersea boat was I-26.

Coincidence—at about 0330 in the morning of November 18, 1944, an ANZIO plane reported radar contact with a submarine on the surface which promptly dived. A second ANZIO plane was vectored to the position. Float lights were dropped, and so were sonobuoys. The latter registered definite submarine indication, and the planes bombed the spot.

Meanwhile, destroyer-escorts LAWRENCE C. TAYLOR and MELVIN R. NAWMAN were rushed to the scene. At 0559 TAYLOR established sound contact with the submersible, and fired hedgehogs, which missed. TAYLOR stood in to throw a second salvo, which produced one explosion. A third attack netted three medium explosions and a huge blast which jarred the teeth of TAYLOR's crew. She followed up with four more attacks on a doubtful contact which finally faded into oblivion. By that time daylight was on the water, and so was a large blotch of oil as well as cork, deck planking, and shards of red-lacquered wood.

In an action described by a veteran destroyer officer

as *"a fine example of cooperation between air and surface craft."* Anzio's airmen, teamed up with Taylor, had settled the score for Saratoga and Juneau. At the bottom of the Philippine Sea off Samar lay the bones of the I-26—a burial long overdue.

Conklin and McCoy Reynolds Kill I-177

When the "Aussies" were playing leapfrog along the New Guinea coast in December, 1943, they bypassed 12,000 Jap troops encamped in a coastal mudhole at Sio, and pushed on to capture an airstrip at Saidor. A Japanese submarine was dispatched as a taxi to carry General Hatazo Adachi from Madang to Sio where the General was to extricate the surrounded garrison. But at Sio four American PT-boats detected the underwater hack, and she escaped a depth-charge thrashing by the skin of her teeth. The sub finally got into Sio, and General Adachi marched the local garrison down the coast to Gali, hoping to find evacuation ships. Instead, he found the beach bombarded on January 8, 1944, by destroyers Reid, Mahan, Beale, and Mugford. On the 15th the beach was once more shelled, destroyers Bush, Ammen, and Mullany doing the job. What was left of the haggard garrison and weary General was left in the bush, stranded and forgotten. As for the I-177, in evading the depth charges at Sio, she had only deferred her demise.

On November 19, 1944, Task Unit 57.18.14, composed of destroyer-escorts Conklin (Lieutenant Commander E. L. McGibbon, U.S.N.R.) and McCoy Reynolds (Lieutenant Commander E. K. Winn, U.S.N.R.), was anchored at Kossol Passage, Palau. At 0914 that day both these ships were ordered to speed to a position outside of the western passage to participate in a hunter-killer action against a sub which had been sighted at 0858. The ships reached the scene at 1055, and cruised across the seascape "echo-ranging." Aircraft were already searching.

The hunt went on through the noon hour—on into mid-afternoon. At 1500 McCoy Reynolds and Conklin put sonar fingers on the hiding sub. For the next two hours the DE's pelted the target with hedgehog, McCoy Reynolds delivering the first three attacks with negative results, then Conklin following up with attacks four and five. The fifth salvo thrown by Conklin missed. Reynolds' next attack was a hit. Up came an enormous air bubble; then, at 1700, the sea echoed to a monstrous explosion.

The blast put Reynolds' sound-gear out of tune. Three minutes later she dropped charges set for a deep-sea level. Dull explosions clambered up out of the deep. A gush of oil and debris rose to the surface, and fragments of a human body.

The submarine thus disposed of was the forementioned I-177. This was the McCoy Reynolds' second kill of that autumn. As one destroyerman lauded her, she was "the real McCoy."

Waller, Renshaw, Saufley, and Pringle Sink I-46

Late in November, the remnant Imperial Navy tried to establish a "Tokyo Express" between northern Philippine bases and invaded Leyte. Reinforcement trains were sent chugging down through the archipelago to Ormoc Bay on Leyte's west coast. Supply and transport submarines were enlisted for this service. Coast watchers promptly reported the activity at the Ormoc terminal, and the Seventh Fleet was called upon to put a stop to this Jap interference.

On November 27, 1944, DesDiv 43 was dispatched to Ormoc Bay to bombard shore installations and to sweep through the Camotes Sea on an anti-shipping mission. The Division consisted of Waller (Commander H. L. Thompson, Jr.), Renshaw (Commander G. H. Cairnes), Saufley (Commander D. E. Cochran), and Pringle (Lieutenant Commander J. L. Kelley, Jr.). Officer in Tactical Command was Captain Robert Hall Smith, ComDesRon 22, riding in Waller.

The passage through Surigao Strait was made without incident. The ships ran into Ormoc Bay and showered the designated targets with 5-inch shells, after which they swept westward across the Camotes Sea.

Meanwhile, a PBY patrol plane had reported a Japanese submarine approaching Ormoc Bay.

At 0127 next morning, DesDiv 43 was cruising north of Ponson Island, when Waller made radar contact with a surface target at 10,200 yards. The destroyer lit up the seascape with starshells, the Division headed directly for the sub, and the four ships took the silhouette under fire. Recklessly enough, the I-boat stayed on the surface to return the shots. The submarine gunners missed the DD's, and in turn took a pounding which damaged the submersible.

At 0138, when Waller set a course to ram, the sub was seen to be badly damaged, and Captain Smith decided to shoot it out with the wounded undersea boat. Accordingly, Waller passed the sub at a range of 50 yards abeam, while the DD gun crews pumped 40 mm. armor-piercing shells into the conning tower and pressure hull. Under this fierce barrage the I-boat became an incandescent mass of explosions.

Coming about for a second run past the sub, Waller saw her target make a sizzling dive for the bottom. Bow slanted against the sky, the I-boat stood on her tail, and then slid under, stern first. Half a dozen Jap swimmers in the water might have been picked up, but several made threatening gestures with what looked like hand grenades. Captain Smith did not delay to discuss the matter with the hostile swimmers. The Division had been ordered to quit the Camotes Sea by 0330, and it seemed more sensible to follow this directive than argue with illogical Japs.

The submarine gunned to the bottom of that sea was the I-46.

Midget Sideshow at Ulithi

Not long after the Battle for Leyte Gulf, Admiral Miwa tried to divert American attention to Ulithi. The diversion featured a special type of miniature submarine—a model described by Miwa as a "one-man torpedo sub." Apparently the one-man torpedo sub was a 1944 innovation—an undersized midget packed with high explosive and an expendable operator. This sea-going "sewer pipe" was carried to the target area by a large submarine. Released from the undersea transport, the torpedo-sub was thereafter on its own. It seems to have differed from the "human torpedo" in one minor aspect—the operator had an infinitesmal chance to abandon through an escape hatch. Miwa sent eight of these aquatic dwarfs to Ulithi.

The eight Lilliputians were piggy-backed to the objective by two I-boats. They were released off Ulithi some time during the night of November 19-20, and nine minutes before sunrise an American lookout sighted one of the periscopes off the channel entrance.

It so happened that at that moment U.S. Task Group 57.9 (three heavy cruisers and four DD's) was outside the lagoon, just getting under way for Saipan. The submarine alarm sent all hands to General Quarters, and excitement mounted when destroyers CUMMINGS (Lieutenant Commander W. J. Collum, Jr.) and CASE (Lieutenant Commander R. S. Willey) rushed a periscope which was slipping through the water near cruiser PENSACOLA. At 0538, CASE rammed this menace. There was a watery crash, and the dwarf went plunking to the bottom.

Inside the lagoon the anchorage was crowded with shipping—war-battered vessels in for repair, tenders, transports, and the supply ships of Commodore W. R. Carter's service fleet. At 0550 the tanker MISSISSINEWA, anchored inside the lagoon, was stabbed by a torpedo. With a great shattering roar the oiler blew up, flinging a cloud of flame against the sky. One of Miwa's freaks had scored.

The blast touched off one of the liveliest A/S hunts of the Pacific War. Outside the channel entrance destroyers CASE and CUMMINGS were combing the seascape. Now, in response to a general TBS summons from destroyer COTTEN, three DE's began a search for a dwarf detected in the vicinity of the cruiser MOBILE at anchor in the lagoon. The destroyer-escorts were U.S.S. RALL (Lieutenant Commander C. B. Taylor, U.S.N.R.), flagship of Commander H. Reich, U.S.N.R., ComCortDiv 61; HALLORAN (Lieutenant Commander J. G. Scripps, U.S.N.R.); and WEAVER (Lieutenant Commander W. A. Taylor, U.S.N.R.), flagship of Commander R. H. Groff, U.S.N.R., ComCortDiv 32.

Presently RALL's lookouts sighted a swirl in the water near the MOBILE. The DE dropped one depth charge set to blow at 50 feet and two charges set for 75 feet. HALLORAN and WEAVER also dropped shallow-set charges. Stacks of brine rose and fell, and two Jap faces were seen in the churning foam. They were not there for long. The sub (or subs) spotted near the MOBILE simultaneously vanished. The dwarf attack on Ulithi was over.

Compared with the Battle for Leyte, the Ulithi "diversion" was a picayune affair, but it did cost the Service Force an oil tanker, and the Navy considerable effort, fuel, and time. For this Miwa seems to have paid several one-man subs, for that same morning two American patrol planes bombed and sank what looked like another midget sub in Ulithi waters. An oil slick marked the grave of this specimen, and a boxlike object bobbed to the surface as a target token. And three days later the body of a Japanese sailor (undoubtedly a submariner) was fished up in a berth near the scene of the MOBILE attacks.

But coming up shortly on the calendar were events which for neither side could be called a "diversion."

Breaking into Ormoc Bay

The Japs had a powerful ally—General Weather.

Ordinarily Nature refuses to take sides, but in the late autumn of 1944 the forces of Nature operated to the advantage of the Japanese. In November the monsoon rains set in, and MacArthur's troops on Leyte bogged down in a quagmire. And while American aircraft were grounded by the sluicing downpour and while Krueger's infantrymen struggled through drowned jungles, the Japs ran a steady stream of reinforcements down to the invaded island.

The Navy worked 'round-the-clock to cut the enemy's supply lines to Leyte and slow the transport of Yamashita's reinforcements. American submarines maintained non-stop China Sea patrols, but Jap transports and warships scuttled down through the islands with persistent frequency, landing troops on the western coast of Leyte. So U.S. destroyers were sent through Surigao Strait to sweep enemy shipping out of Ormoc Bay.

These were hazardous missions. And the fourth Ormoc sweep, conducted by DD's early in December, cost the Seventh Fleet a fighting ship.

In the evening of December 2, 1944, three destroyers left Leyte Gulf and headed through Surigao Strait for Ormoc. The destroyers were ALLEN M. SUMNER (Commander N. J. Sampson), flagship of Commander J. C. Zahm, ComDesDiv 120; MOALE (Commander W. M. Foster), and COOPER (Commander M. A. Peterson). The ships were ordered to seek out and destroy five Japanese vessels which had been reported landing troops in the Ormoc area.

Entering Ormoc Bay early next morning the destroyers were immediately attacked by enemy aircraft, and air attacks continued without let-up until the following morning. The Division fired intermittently at radar-detected surface targets, at Jap planes, and at shore installations. They sank the Jap destroyer KUWA, downed several small *marus,* and shot nine or ten Jap planes out of the air. In return, destroyers SUMNER and MOALE suffered minor damage, SUMNER being injured by a near miss and strafing, and MOALE losing two men from a strafing which also wounded 22. Harassed by aircraft, fired at by naval guns and shore batteries, and menaced by submarines, the ALLEN M. SUMNER and MOALE finally battled their way out of the redhot spot. And, commenting on the action, MOALE's Commanding Officer wrote:

> *Operations of this sort should not be entered into unless air coverage is assured. Enemy planes continually tracked and attacked our group for one hour prior to the surface engagement until one hour after our retirement. The enemy was thoroughly alerted and had only to wait until our arrival to fire torpedoes at us. This strike was designed as an offensive; however, there was a strong feeling of being on the defensive throughout.*

As proof of his words there was the fact that only SUMNER and MOALE had returned. Behind them they had left COOPER forever.

Loss of U.S.S. Cooper

Entering Ormoc Bay with SUMNER and MOALE, the COOPER had made surface contact with a target at 12,200 yards range just minutes after midnight. Commander M. A. Peterson gave the order to open fire. For nine minutes the destroyer's guns pumped 5-inch at the target. Then the ship, evidently a large destroyer, was seen to be burning—sinking under a cloud of flame. This was the Jap DD KUWA. She had been transporting reinforcements for Yamashita's Leyte garrison. Many of those infantrymen never made it. About 250 of them floated in to the Ormoc beaches for hasty burial.

COOPER immediately shifted fire to a second target, but was unable to learn the results of her gunnery, for only a minute or two later she was struck by an undersea weapon just as she completed a turn.

A huge explosion heeled the COOPER on her side. Fire and water swept over her superstructure, and within 30 seconds of the blast she broke in two. The survivors swam in swirling oil and hot foam under a fog of smoke. Division Commander Zahm on SUMNER was faced with a bitterly difficult decision—to risk air attack and fire from shore batteries in an effort to save COOPER's men, or pull out to assure the safety of his two remaining ships. Reviewing the case, an experienced destroyer officer wrote: *"It was a tough decision. But, in deciding not to make the rescue attempt, the Division Commander did the right thing."*

Most of the COOPER survivors were picked up between mid-afternoon and dusk of that day by U.S. Navy "Black Cat" planes. While swimming in the Bay, the afflicted destroyermen noted the fire of heavy shore batteries. They also saw several submarines sneak out through the entrance. The presence of subs in Ormoc Bay suggested that COOPER might have been the victim of a giant "Long Lance" torpedo. Down with the ship went 10 officers and 181 men. Some 168 of COOPER's crew were saved.

Amphibs to Ormoc

By the opening days of December, Yamashita's garrison on Leyte had been increased by some 30,000 troops, but this transport effort had cost the Japs eight destroyers, a cruiser, six smaller warships, and at least ten transports.

Soon after the sweep conducted in Ormoc Bay by DesDiv 120, the Navy was called upon to undertake an amphibious landing at Ormoc; the ulcer was to be cut out of the Jap defense system. On short notice, Rear Admiral A. D. Struble was ordered to Ormoc Bay with Task Group 78.3. The group consisted of eight fast transports and 43 landing craft, carrying General A. D. Bruce's 77th Division. Admiral Struble flew his flag in the destroyer HUGHES (Commander E. B. Rittenhouse). Twelve destroyers screened the task group. They were: BARTON (flying the broad command pennant of Captain W. L. Freseman, ComDesRon 60), WALKE, LAFFEY, O'BRIEN, FLUSSER (flagship of Captain W. M. Cole, ComDesRon 5), DRAYTON, LAMSON, EDWARDS, SMITH (flagship of Captain H. F. Stout, ComDesDiv 10), REID, CONYNGHAM, and MAHAN.

The way into the harbor was cleared by a minesweeping unit, and a Control and Fire-Support Unit abetted the amphibious work. After a 20-minute shore bombardment by DD's and rocket craft, the troops started in at 0707 in the morning of December 7. Opposition to the landings was *nil*. But the retiring ships were attacked by enemy aircraft.

The air assault began about 0820. U.S. fighters flew to intercept the Jap planes, but a number of Japs broke through the CAP cover and dodged the AA barrage. By midday several ships had been hit by crash-diving suicide planes. Among those struck were destroyer MAHAN (Commander E. G. Campbell), destroyer-transport WARD (Commander R. E. Farwell, U.S.N.R.), and destroyer-transport LIDDLE (Lieutenant Commander L. C. Brogger, U.S.N.R.). Four landing ships were also damaged, one of them fatally. The suicide attacks proved a horror to the destroyermen. MAHAN's Commanding Officer noted that it was probably the first time the death-diving Japs unleashed multiple suicide attacks while employing torpedo-plane tactics.

The attacks continued throughout the day. About 1400 a plane plummeted on destroyer LAMSON (Commander J. V. Noel, Jr.), and crashed forward of the stack. Twenty-one men were killed by the smash and 50 were wounded. As flames roared through LAMSON's superstructure, destroyer FLUSSER (Commander T. R. Vogeley), flagship of Captain Cole, stood by to cover the stricken vessel. While FLUSSER's gun crews hurled flak at enemy aircraft, the rescue tug ATR-31 assisted the LAMSON men. All hands were forced to leave the burning ship, but the rescue tug finally succeeded in extinguishing the flames, and LAMSON was saved. FLUSSER picked up about 20 men (most of them wounded) who had jumped off the bridge and director platform when the plane ploughed into the ship. Later beating off an air attack, she shot down a "Dinah." This efficient work won for FLUSSER a word of high commendation from Admiral Kinkaid.

At 1745 the Japs made their final air attack; after this onslaught the battle was over. Having fought off 16 air raids since that morning, Struble's men welcomed the advent of nightfall. At 2130 the task group was joined by destroyers ALLEN M. SUMNER, MOALE, HOPEWELL, and PRINGLE. Thus reinforced, the tired warships made the run back to San Pedro Bay in safety.

In the waters off Ormoc, Struble's ships had taken gruelling punishment. Destroyer-transport LIDDLE had been crippled. Destroyer LAMSON, paralyzed, had to be towed into Leyte Gulf. LSM-318 had been downed. And an ex-DD and a DD had been lost.

The ex-DD was destroyer-transport WARD. Sorely hit, she had to be abandoned, and her burning hulk was buried in the sea by friendly gunfire. The task was assigned to destroyer O'BRIEN—a strange turn of fate. O'BRIEN's captain, Commander W. W. Outerbridge, was the same Outerbridge who had been skipper of the WARD when she fired the first Jap-killing shot of the Pacific War at Pearl Harbor. And that shot, which sank a midget submarine off the harbor entrance, had been fired just three years previously to the day.

The destroyer which was fatally damaged by a Jap suicide plane, and which had to be abandoned and sunk in Ormoc Bay by friendly fire, was the U.S.S. MAHAN. Here is the MAHAN story—

Loss of U.S.S. Mahan

Serving in the Escort Unit of Rear Admiral Struble's Ormoc Attack Group, MAHAN was one of the two fighter-director ships in amphibious Task Group 78.3. When, shortly after the troops began going ashore in the Ormoc landings, enemy planes were detected, MAHAN's fighter-director team had gone to work the moment the Jap planes appeared on the radar screen. She was joined in this work by the team on board destroyer SMITH (Commander F. V. List). Captain Freseman, the Escort Commander, reported that the two ships *". . . turned in an outstanding performance."*

For MAHAN the performance was all too brief. About 0948 her gunners opened fire on a flight of nine enemy bombers escorted by four fighter planes. While the destroyermen banged away with AA weapons, three U.S. P-38's were guided in to the attack. The American planes shot down three Jap fighters and damaged two bombers. Four Jap planes were shot down by MAHAN's guns. But the enemy airmen, launching a coordinated suicide assault, penetrated the defense. Skimming in across the water, three of the Jap planes crashed into MAHAN.

The ship shuddered and reeled under the impact of these stunning blows. Drenched with burning gasoline, the destroyer's wrecked superstructure was enveloped in flames. Fire vomited from the exploding forward magazine. Thirteen minutes after the third crash, Commander E. G. Campbell, MAHAN's skipper, ordered the crew to start abandoning. By 1025 the last man was off. Destroyers WALKE and LAMSON moved in to pick up the survivors, thirteen of whom were seriously wounded or burned. Five men and an officer had disappeared in the burning ship.

Nothing could be done to save the wrecked and exploding destroyer, and at 1150 MAHAN was sunk by gun and torpedo fire from destroyer WALKE.

About the performance of his officers and men MAHAN's captain had this to say:

The strain of standing there and battling back as one after another of the bombers came roaring in was terrific. Even so, not a single man jumped overboard to escape what at times looked like inevitable death. . . . The fact that four of the nine planes were shot down, that no one abandoned ship until the word was given, that the entire Engineering Force stayed at their stations throughout the action, in spite of no information . . . that the damage control parties continued to function . . . that gun captains shifted promptly to local control when the main-battery director was disabled, and that the ship was abandoned in an orderly manner, all testify to the high state of discipline and courage displayed by the entire crew.

Loss of U.S.S. Reid

Ormoc Bay claimed still another Seventh Fleet destroyer, the U.S.S. REID (Commander S. A. McCornock). On December 11, the REID was operating with Task Unit 78.3.8, a re-supply echelon which was dispatched to the Ormoc beachhead. The task unit, under command of Captain J. F. Newman, Jr., ComDesRon 14, contained 13 landing craft and six destroyers. The destroyers were CALDWELL (flagship of Captain Newman) REID, CONYNGHAM, SMITH (flagship of Captain H. F. Stout, ComDesDiv 10), COGHLAN, and EDWARDS.

Carrying vital and urgently needed supplies to the land forces in the Ormoc area, the ships hauled out of Tarraguna and raced through Surigao Strait. About 1700 in the evening of the 11th a flight of 12 "Jills" attacked. Newman's ships had fighter cover of only four Corsairs. Guided by fighter-director ship SMITH, they shot down two planes. But the leading planes broke through the defense and swooped down at REID and CALDWELL. The assailed DD's lashed at the "Jills" with AA fire. In the ensuing scrimmage four planes were shot down by the destroyer barrage, and at least four others were damaged. But five of the "Jills" crash-dived.

Four of the diving planes concentrated on the REID. One "Jill" raced in and hooked a wing on the destroyer's starboard whaleboat, then collided at the waterline abreast of the No. 2 gun, the smash detonating the aircraft's bomb. A moment later a second plane caromed off the No. 3 gun, skidded into a 40 mm. tub, and exploded. The explosions set off the after magazines. Her superstructure aflame, her lower compartments gutted by internal blasts, the REID heeled over and went down by the stern. The ship sank swiftly; two minutes after she was hit by the first plane, she was rumbling down under the sea. Loss of life, heavy in this action, was typical of the toll exacted by suicide crashes. Some 152 of REID's crew escaped death.

The battle was fought off Limasawa Island near the western end of Surigao Strait. After shooting its way out from under the aerial assault, Newman's task unit steamed on to arrive at the Ormoc beachhead about midnight. They were continually harried by enemy aircraft, and after daylight another full-scale air attack developed. Bombers pelted the destroyers in conventional fashion, and then the suiciders dived in. A plane crashed into CALDWELL's radio room; 29 of her crew were killed, and 40 were wounded, four of the wounded dying later. The blasting put her forward guns out of commission, and started a conflagration, which swept her forecastle. But the fires were eventually extinguished, and she managed to get home under her own power.

REID was the last destroyer lost in the battle for Ormoc. She had been at Pearl Harbor when the Japanese thunderbolt struck from the blue to start the war. Since that day she had participated in 13 landings, 18 shore bombardments, and innumerable missions. She had shot down 12 Japanese planes, sunk a Japanese submarine, and bagged eight Jap prisoners. All told, she had fired nearly 10,000 rounds of 5-inch at enemy targets. And it cost the Japs seven planes to sink her.

REID was one of DesPac's ace destroyers—a "small boy" with a man-sized war record.

Mugford, Drayton, and Hughes Versus Suiciders

While the battle for Ormoc Bay was going on, supporting forces were landed at Baybay, on the Leyte west coast, by Task Unit 78.3.10, under command of Captain W. M. Cole, ComDesRon 5. The task unit included the DD's of DesDiv 9—FLUSSER (Commander T. R. Vogeley), Captain Cole's flagship; DRAYTON (Commander R. S. Craighill); LAMSON (Commander J. V. Noel, Jr.); and SHAW (Lieutenant Commander V. B. Graff). Eleven landing craft were in the convoy.

The equipment was unloaded at Baybay without difficulty, and the ships set out on the return run for San Pedro Bay at 0300 in the morning of December 5. Just before daybreak an enemy bomber scored a near-miss which killed two men and caused minor damage on board DRAYTON. After daylight, friendly fighter cover arrived. But at 1100, eight Jap bombers roared down out of the clouds. They were undetected by radar, and they gave the task unit a rough going over.

Two destroyers, stationed as pickets in Surigao Strait, joined the assailed unit. These DD's were MUGFORD (Commander M. A. Shellabarger), flagship of Captain K. F. Poehlmann, ComDesDiv 12, and LAVALLETTE (Commander W. Thompson). The latter shot down one plane. Another was shot down by FLUSSER. The assault was broken up by sharp destroyer gunnery, and the unit continued its eastward run.

That afternoon the Jap aircraft tried again. At 1715 an enemy suicide plane made a strafing run on MUGFORD and then crashed into the port side of the ship. Two men were killed instantly. Eight subsequently died of burns, and 16 others were agonizingly burned. A fierce conflagration ravaged the destroyer. But the flames were quelled within half an hour, and the battered ship finally made port under her own steam.

"The MUGFORD,*"* wrote Captain Cole, *"was handled with skill. . . . Even though damaged and burning, she maintained gunfire against enemy planes that were threatening the task unit. This command has only praise for her vigorous and intrepid actions."*

DRAYTON also had been grazed by a suicide plane which sideswiped her during the morning battle. She steamed out of action with eight dead and 19 wounded.

Another destroyer to suffer damage from a suicide assault that December was the HUGHES (Commander E. B. Rittenhouse). The ship was patrolling a station off Dinagat Island on the Leyte front on the 10th, when the Jap planes glided in on bombing runs and straddled the ship with five bombs. One of the bomb-carrying planes crashed on the destroyer's port side amidships. The blast killed 18 men and wounded 22. Showered with blazing gasoline and burning wreckage, HUGHES was severely damaged. After the crash several Jap planes hovered over the ship, eyeing the destruction. Apparently satisfied that the destroyer was done in, they flew away.

HUGHES had been operating without fighter cover. After she was struck she radioed for cover, and American fighters came to her support at 1715, a little late. Expert damage control by the destroyermen quickly quelled the fires, and that evening destroyer LAFFEY came up to take the disabled ship in tow. That night the tug QUAPAW arrived, and the tugmen completed the tow to San Pedro Bay.

HUGHES' Commanding Officer noted that long hours of drill paid off in short hours of emergency repair work and fire-fighting. His report also emphasized three other measures that paid off—insistence that the crew wear helmets, life jackets, and long-sleeved shirts when topside. He reported that a man in a kapok jacket blown overside by a blast which flung him 300 yards from the ship, managed to swim back to the destroyer *"under his own power."* Another man had his helmet split down the middle—something better than having a similar split in his head. And long sleeves saved more than one man from serious flash burns.

Courage was a common denominator supporting the HUGHES crew.

Excerpt from the destroyer's Action Report:

> Carl D. Baumeister, Water Tender First Class, remained on his station as checkman in the after fireroom after the plane had crashed through the deck, starting a large fire and cutting live steam lines. He was badly burned by steam and flames caused by the burning plane. In spite of this he secured his feed check valve and tried to secure fire main cut-out going aft because he thought it was probably shot away aft in the forward engine-room. Finding this jammed, he ran to the forward fireroom while his clothes were in flames, and informed personnel in the forward fireroom of the damage. He told them to secure everything going aft. He then attempted to return to the after fireroom to fight the fire, but was forcibly restrained while the fire on his clothes was put out. He then ran topside and was on his way down into the after fireroom when he collapsed. His quick action saved much valuable equipment and aided in saving the ship. This was accomplished while enemy planes were still in attacking position and reattack was expected. He was seriously burned and was in critical condition for two days before he began to recover.

ACTION ON THE HUGHES

CHAPTER 35

TYPHOON—MANILA BAY CONCLUSION

Typhoon!

While the Mindoro invasion was going forward, the Third Fleet stood off the Philippines to send carrier aircraft roaring westward in a series of strikes at targets in the Manila area. Halsey planned to fuel his ships on December 17 and to launch a three-day strike series on the 19th. But the day chosen for fuelling operations proved one of the darkest in Third Fleet history. Trouble began during the forenoon watch of the 17th. When the calendar turned on December 19, the Third Fleet had lost three ships, 790 men, and about 200 planes. Twenty-eight ships were damaged, and nine of the damaged were so badly battered they had to be sent into port for major overhauls. The enemy was that "Ole Devil Sea."

On the morning of the 17th the ships were about 500 miles east of Luzon. Begun during the forenoon watch, fuelling work was made increasingly difficult by a moderate cross-swell and rising winds which varied from 20 to 30 knots. The destroyers were soon harassed by the jumping seas. Attempting to take on oil from the New Jersey, destroyer Spence was hard put to it to avoid collision, and the forward and after hoses snapped. Alongside the Wisconsin, destroyer Collett had similar difficulty, both fuelling hoses carrying away. Stephen Potter, Lyman K. Swenson, Preston, and Thatcher were unable to fuel. And the Mansfield had to give up the attempt.

Upon receiving word that the weather would worsen, Halsey ordered the fuelling operation suspended, and headed the Fleet northwestward to evade the storm, which was advancing from the east. Later that afternoon the storm changed course, and so did Halsey in another effort to evade. That night the Third Fleet ran southwest. But the storm, strangely vindictive, refused to take the expected tack, and gradually caught up with the retiring ships. During the morning of December 18 the weather relentlessly deteriorated. An attempt to fuel, begun at 0700, had to be canceled. The glass fell steadily, and by 0830 the storm had grown into a monster typhoon, its center only 150 miles from the ocean-blown Third Fleet.

For the remainder of that morning and most of the afternoon, the Third Fleet fought a battle against an enemy which neither guns nor bombs could quell. Throughout this combat in which marksmanship had no part, only seamanship and leadership were of avail. Buffeted by 70-foot seas, the American battleships rolled like canoes in a rapids. Light carriers Monterey and Cowpens, heaving like hammocks, suffered damage when aircraft broke loose, and spurting gasoline started fires. Fire broke out on the flight deck of escort-carrier Cape Esperance. Escort-carrier Kwajalein lost steering control. Escort-carrier Rudyard Bay went dead in the water. By mid-afternoon the wind was shrieking at 93-knot velocity. At 1358 the typhoon's center was only 35 miles distant, and the sea and sky were berserk.

Rough on battleships and carriers, the typhoon was unmitigated hell for the destroyers, some of which, low on fuel, had pumped out water ballast preparatory to fuelling and were consequently riding high in the water. During the peak of the storm, a number of the DD's were rolled on their beams and pinned down with their stacks almost flat against the sea. In such a roll to leeward, destroyer DEWEY lay over in a cant which registered 75° on the ship's inclinometer. The AYLWIN, another FARRAGUT-class destroyer, rolled 70°. With their beam ends buried and giant waves sweeping over forecastle and superstructure, the destroyers endured excruciating moments of jeopardy. Water plunged into ventilators and intakes. Electrical installations were swamped and short-circuited. With loss of electric power, lights gave out, steering gear failed, and the ships, without means of communication, were left to wallow feebly in deaf-and-dumb desolation.

The destroyermen could only batten down, lash such items of unstable gear as could be captured and hogtied, and cling to handholds and bulkheads. On the pounded decks, life rafts were swept away, lines were snapped, boats were ripped out of their davits, antennas were twisted into bedsprings, and deck gear was uprooted. Typical damage was suffered by the destroyer HICKOX (Commander J. H. Wesson), whose skipper reported her steering motors out of commission, her main switchboard and emergency Diesel boards ruined, power panels wrecked, radar antenna torn away, a searchlight stripped, and a depth-charge rack smashed like a stepped-on tinker toy. Salt water "poisoned" one of the ship's boilers; the overhead of the after deckhouse was buckled; the carpenter shop and another compartment aft were flooded; and the motor whaleboat was whisked overside.

Destroyers BRUSH, FRANKS, CUSHING, MADDOX, COLAHAN, and MANSFIELD were among the DD's which suffered minor storm damage, while riding out hell and high water. The little DE's with the Third Fleet dug in and hove to as best they could—orphans of the tempest. But one of the destroyer-escorts did more than that—a whole lot more. She was the U.S.S. TABBERER (Lieutenant Commander Henry L. Plage, U.S.N.R.). And she ran to the rescue of the three Third Fleet ships which were lost in the typhoon—three destroyers.

Loss of U.S.S. Hull, U.S.S. Spence, and U.S.S. Monaghan

They come under the same heading, for theirs was a common grave.

HULL	*Lt. Comdr. J. A. Marks.*
SPENCE	*Lt. Comdr. J. P. Andrea.*
MONAGHAN	*Lt. Comdr. F. B. Garrett, Jr.*

Somewhere in the immediate vicinity of lat. 14-57 N., long. 127-58 E., they were erased by mountainous seas—battered under by a foe more relentless than any human agency.

HULL and MONAGHAN were screening vessels for a Third Fleet fuelling unit which was servicing Task Force 38. SPENCE was a screening vessel attached to Halsey's fleet. When the typhoon struck on that morning of the 18th, HULL had 70 per cent of her fuel capacity aboard; MONAGHAN's tanks contained 76 per cent. Both ships were without water ballast. SPENCE, carrying only 15 per cent of her fuel capacity, and caught with only a little water ballast, was riding like an empty tanker.

The storm came howling down from the north; the ocean surged up to meet the sagging sky; the seascape blurred out in a gray-white opacity of flying spume. And somewhere in that screaming limbo of wind and water the three ships went down. Apparently first to go, SPENCE capsized after her rudder jammed full right shortly after 1100. Only 23 of her crew lived to tell the story of her final hour. Lost with his ship was Lieutenant Commander Andrea.

HULL went down during the noon hour. The wind had driven her over on her starboard side until her inclometer went "out of sight." A sudden gust forced her beyond the point of recovery; a hill of water avalanched across her decks; she rolled over and sank. Fifty-five men and seven officers, among them Lieutenant Commander Marks, managed to escape the vessel and survive the raving ocean.

The exact moment of MONAGHAN's demise is unknown, but she went down at midday in company with HULL and SPENCE. About 300 officers and men went down with the ship when it capsized. Lost with the destroyer was Lieutenant Commander Garrett. Only six of the crew survived.

About 1400 of that dark day the weather began to mend. By 1600 the wind had decreased to 35 knots and the barometer had climbed to 29.46. Halsey had word of the missing ships, and a search for survivors was begun before darkness set in. After nightfall there were several reports of lights glimpsed and whistles heard, but destroyers dispatched on the hunt were unable to locate the sources of these signals in the blowing dark.

Throughout that night and the ensuing two days, the ships and planes of the Third Fleet conducted what Halsey described as *"the most exhaustive search in Navy history."* Four ships were believed lost, for the destroyer-escort TABBERER had disappeared and did not answer radio calls. Here and there a few swimmers were picked up, and several rafts were located. Then word came in from the TABBERER. The little DE had lost her foremast. Her radio had been knocked out and her radar ruined. But she was very much afloat, and she was bringing with her 55 destroyermen, survivors she had rescued from the typhoon's wrath. A number of these survivors—men from the HULL—said they had never seen such seamanship as that exhibited by TABBERER's skipper when he jockeyed his ship through giant seas to snatch drowning men from the water. That skipper, Lieutenant Commander Plage, promptly received from Halsey the message, *"Well done for a sturdy performance."* Recalling the incident in *Admiral Halsey's Story,* the leader of the Third Fleet remarked that he expected to learn that Plage was a veteran mariner who had "cut his teeth on a marlinspike." Halsey was overwhelmed to discover that Plage was a Reserve Officer at sea for his second cruise—a sailor who had "cut his teeth" in the ROTC at Georgia Tech.

From the survivors rescued by TABBERER, by destroyer-escort SWEARER, destroyer BROWN, and other lifesavers, the Navy learned the details of the HULL, SPENCE, and MONAGHAN sinkings. Typical were the stories told by Lieutenant (jg) A. S. Krauchunas, U.S.N.R., sole surviving officer of SPENCE, and Water Tender Second Class Joseph C. McCrane, U.S.N.R., highest ranking of the six MONAGHAN survivors.

Lieutenant (jg) Krauchunas recalled the ordeal in the following testimony:

The typhoon began its fury on the (18th) . . . and it was impossible . . . to fuel. Orders were given to ballast ship at 0900 since the ship had only 12 per cent fuel and was rolling heavily. These rolls exceeded 50 degrees. At 1100 the power was gone due to water seeping into the fireroom through vents. The ship was caught in the huge swells. The first huge swell rolled the ship 75 degrees, from which it recovered, but the next one rolled her over, trapping all those below the main deck, passageways, radio shack, C.I.C., wardroom, and so forth. Fifty to 60 men managed to get off into the water from their stations topside. They clutched to life rafts, floater nets, life jackets or whatever they managed to get ahold of. The wind blew them out of sight of ship within a few minutes. None saw the ship sink, and it was last seen floating upside down. The gale lasted for another eight hours before it subsided, and during this time many were drowned, being in a shocked and dazed condition. The gale, approximately 115 knots, subsided that evening to about 15 to 20 knots. There were four groups of men floating in the darkness, some in the water, some on a life raft, and some on a floater net.

Krauchunas stated that the nine men on the floater net

had many unusual experiences. The men began to suffer from the hot sun that burned any exposed areas of the skin. The floater net had two kegs of water, no flare, no medicine kit, and no food kits, all of which broke off during the vicious typhoon. Water was given out once every three hours in order that it would last longer. A can of vegetable shortening was picked up and spread over the men's sunburned areas. Two search planes flew overhead but did not see us. One of the men became unconscious and slipped from the net several times before he was missed. Of the three men to die, he was the first. His name was Ensign George W. Poer. At midnight, December 20, 1944, Lieutenant (jg) John Whalen slipped from the net. The other man had become unconscious some time before, but was held on the net by Charles Wohlleb, Water Tender Third Class, but it became necessary to let him go.

At 0300 on the morning of December 20, an aircraft carrier slipped into view on the horizon.

The men on the net shouted, whistled, and waved.

The carrier heard us and dropped smoke bombs and flares to mark our approximate position, and it continued on its way. Within a half an hour, a destroyer appeared from the other direction but we were not successful in attracting its attention. Shortly another ship appeared and it found the flares which the carrier had dropped. This ship was the U.S.S. SWEARER, which eventually picked us up.

Another group of men, unknown to us at this time, were drifting some distance away. One man distinguished himself by saving men on five different occasions, but lost his own life when he attempted to save the last man. He was Henry Oliver Tagg, First Class Machinist's Mate, and he has been recommended for citation.

Three other men were picked up after having drifted for two days and nights. They were tied together with five life jackets, lines, and floater ring. Two of them had been unconscious for some time but were held by David Moore, Steward First Class, who is credited with saving their lives. U.S.S. TABBERER was the rescue ship.

William Keith, Seaman First, was picked up by the U.S.S. GATLING after he had been floating by himself for two days and nights. He was delirious, and his . . . experience . . . was interesting. He claimed that drowning was not his way of dying . . . and that a Japanese torpedo was floating by, and he chased it for some time. He wanted to set it off and blow up with it. . . .

Water Tender McCrane of the MONAGHAN tells this stark story:

. . . I went back to the engineers' compartment and the ship was rolling so heavy that all of us decided to go topside into the after gun shelter. . . .

I managed to work myself to within about ten feet of the door on the port side. There were about 40 men in the shelter. One of the fellows was praying aloud. Every time the ship would take about a 70 degree roll to starboard, he would cry out, "Please bring her back, dear Lord, don't let us down now." We must have taken about seven or eight rolls to the starboard before she went over on her side. When the ship went over some of the fellows tried to get the door open on the port side. It was a difficult job because the wind was holding and the waves were beating up against it, but they did get it opened and we started out. All the fellows kept their heads and there was no confusion or pushing and everyone was trying to help the other fellow. A Gunner's Mate by the name of Joe Guio, with absolutely no thought of his own safety, was standing outside of the hatch pulling everyone out. . . .

McCrane, himself, was knocked off the shelter into the churning sea. Swimming through the watery smother, he finally reached a raft. Guio also got to the raft. The Gunner's Mate was injured and shivering—suffering from shock. His clothing had either been discarded or torn from his body, and McCrane held him in his arms to keep him warm. The wounded man lapsed into unconsciousness, while McCrane chafed his wrists and hands. Then—

Guio awoke and asked me if I could see anything, and when I told him I could see the stars, he said that he couldn't see anything. He then thanked Melroy Harrison, Seaman Second, for pulling him aboard the raft and then he thanked me for trying to keep him warm. He laid his head back on my shoulder and went to sleep. About a half-hour later I had a funny feeling come over me and I tried to wake him up only to find that he was dead. I told the rest of the fellows and we decided to hold him a little longer before we buried him. In about 20 minutes we had our first burial at sea. We all said the Lord's Prayer as he was lowered over the side. . . .

. . . We were in shark-infested waters and were completely surrounded by them; we were plenty scared of them, too. Every time we opened a can of Spam, more sharks would appear.

That evening there were two more burials. And by the evening of the 20th most of the men were in delirium. *". . . they thought they saw land and houses."* One man swam away from the raft and disappeared in the dark. He was never seen again. On the raft another man died, and the survivors consigned his body to the deep.

McCrane's testimony goes on:

We saw a large onion floating about 25 feet from us, and we tried to get to it. We almost had it when a shark about eight feet long had the same idea, so we decided to let him have it.

Several ships were sighted, and the little party on the raft cried itself hoarse and gestured madly in an effort to attract the distant vessels. At length the raft was spotted by two search planes.

We were so happy we were almost speechless, so we could think of nothing better to do than to thank God, so we all said a prayer of thanks. . . .

Not long after the aircraft contact, McCrane and his five companions were picked up by the destroyer Brown.

In rescuing the survivors of Hull and Spence, the Tabberer men risked their own lives in more ways than one. It was not easy to maneuver the little DE in the teeth of the storm. At one point the ship, struggling to make 10 knots, was caught in the deep valley of a trough, and forced over on her beam in a roll of 72 degrees. They almost caught an exhausted swimmer who, unable to reach a life ring, was treading water while Tabberer stood by. Suddenly an enormous shark slid down a wave and glided toward the man. Sighting the deadly fin, Tabberer's sailors opened fire with rifles. The shark passed within six feet of the swimmer, then was driven off by the sharpshooting destroyermen. The DE's "Exec," Lieutenant Robert M. Surdam, U.S.N.R., plunged overside to secure a line around the fainting man. The exhausted swimmer was hauled aboard and quickly revived.

Another Tabberer lifesaver, L. A. Purvis, Bos'n's Mate, First Class, almost lost his life while struggling in the water with a half-drowned swimmer. Too much slack was left in his line, and a bight caught on the underwater sound dome when the DE rolled. Purvis was dragged under the ship. Realizing what had happened, he wrenched off his kapok jacket, swam under the ship, and came up on the other side. Only his presence of mind and his skill as a swimmer saved him from a fatal keel-hauling.

Concerning kapok jackets, Tabberer's Commanding Officer noted that *"Out of the 55 men rescued, 54 had kapok jackets. It is believed many were drowned during the storm because of the inadequate support given by the belt-type life jacket."*

The typhoon of December 18 was one of the worst

encountered in the Pacific. During the Okinawa campaign in the spring of 1945, a raging typhoon would again strike the Third Fleet a devastating uppercut. Destroyer McKee and destroyer-escort Conklin would be whipped by the backlash of this storm off Formosa. In this same tempest, other ships would receive severe damage; the vessels in mention were only moderately injured. Later in 1945 a typhoon would delay the Japanese surrender. But no Pacific tantrum struck the Navy a harder blow than the one which downed Hull, Spence, and Monaghan. Only two other destroyers were storm-sunk during the war; Truxtun, driven aground by a North Atlantic, blizzard-blinded gale, and Warrington, swamped by a Caribbean hurricane.

There were contributing factors to the December 18 tragedy. The typhoon was not accurately predicted, the immediate signs of it in the operating area were not heeded early enough, and it traveled a capricious path. One of the stricken ships was low on fuel and the others lacked water ballast. In reviewing the disaster, Admiral Nimitz noted that the three ships lost had been maneuvering to the last in an attempt to maintain station. It might have been better had they disregarded station-keeping in an effort to ride out the storm. *"The time for taking all measures for a ship's safety is while able to do so,"* wrote Admiral Nimitz. *"Nothing is more dangerous than for a seaman to be grudging in taking precautions lest they turn out to be unnecessary. Safety at sea for a thousand years has depended on exactly the opposite philosophy."*

As Admiral Nimitz observed, the storm "took charge." And when a typhoon takes charge, the forces of man are all too puny against the forces of Nature. In conclusion, Admiral Nimitz stated that the December 18 typhoon caused *"the greatest loss that we have taken in the Pacific without compensatory return since the First Battle of Savo."*

The Road to Manila

During the last days of December, 1944, and the first two months of 1945, the Allied forces in the Philippines forged their way toward and into Manila Bay. And by an odd complexity of events, the drive for Manila involved almost every feature of destroyer warfare. On the road to Manila the destroyers served as scouts, as escorts, as screening ships, as rescue vessels, and as pickets. They conducted shore bombardments and anti-shipping sweeps. They provided fire support for amphibious landings. They fought large submarines and midget subs, underwater snares and mines, conventional air attacks and suicide assaults. An example of just one phase of this work was the RO-boat sunk by Fleming as far away even as the Central Pacific.

Fleming Kills RO-47

This was the first submarine kill of the war year 1945 for the DesPac Force. During the second week in January, the Fleming (Lieutenant Commander K. F. Burgess, Jr., U.S.N.R.) was one of the two escorts for a pair of merchant tankers bound for Eniwetok from Ulithi. Late in the evening of the 18th she made radar contact with a surface target 14,000 yards distant, and challenged it.

The challenge went unanswered, and the "pip" vanished from the DE's radar scope at 1,900 yards. Sonar promptly picked up the vessel's undersea trail; Burgess maneuvered Fleming into assault position; the DE delivered a depth-charge attack. She followed through with four hedgehog attacks, spattering the sea with neat patterns. Attack No. 4 did the trick. Sharp explosions were echoed by a grumbling basso blast that shook the DE and damaged her sound gear. A pungent odor of Diesel oil drifted across the dark water, and various bits of wreckage were sighted in the vicinity—the last vestiges of one more Japanese submersible.

Post-war inquest disclosed that the submarine downed by Fleming was the RO-47.

Conklin, Corbesier, and Raby Kill I-48

Late in the evening of January 21, 1945, a plane sighted a Japanese sub on the surface 18 miles due west of Ulithi. The alarm brought sprinting from Ulithi a hunter-killer team composed of destroyer-escorts Conklin (Lieutenant Commander E. L. McGibbon, U.S.N.R.), Corbesier (Lieutenant H. V. Jones, Jr., U.S.N.R.), and Raby (Lieutenant J. L. Slade, U.S.N.R.). Conklin, two months before this hunt, had teamed up with McCoy Reynolds to sink the I-177 off Leyte. Raby had been a member of the All-American England team which had staged the greatest sub-slaughter of the war.

The three ships conducted an expanding search that lasted all day and night of the 22nd. At 0310 in the morning of the 23rd, Conklin and Corbesier made radar contact with the sub. Shortly thereafter the submarine submerged, and Corbesier promptly tagged her with sonar contact. Conklin and Raby stood off to let Corbesier attack. The latter made six hedgehog tries without result. When the contact then faded out, the ships swung into an expanding box search. Again Corbesier's sonar tagged the elusive sub (time: 0902), and the DE tried a seventh-inning hedgehog attack. When the projectiles sank in silence, Conklin stepped in with a hedgehog salvo. This time the projectiles did not silently sink, and neither did the sub. At 0936 there was an undersea explosion of such violence that a 1400-pound safe in the ship's office on board CONKLIN was kicked from its welded base and sent eight feet across the deck.

The blast was the last of I-48—another Japanese submarine stowed in Davy Jones' Locker.

Bell, O'Bannon, Jenkins, and U. M. Moore Down RO-115

The next submarine sinking in Philippine waters was a prime example of the streamlined teamwork now exhibited by the DD's and DE's.

The destroyers involved were the BELL (Commander J. S. C. Gabbert), O'BANNON (Lieutenant Commander J. A. Pridmore), and JENKINS (Commander P. D. Gallery). The destroyer-escort was the ULVERT M. MOORE, captained by Lieutenant Commander Franklin D. Roosevelt, Jr., U.S.N.R.

Date: January 31, 1945. On that day BELL and O'BANNON were steaming in the screen of Rear Admiral F. B. Stump's Task Group 77.3, which was operating to the west of Mindoro on mission to intercept Jap transports on the run to Luzon. Destroyers JENKINS and LAVALLETTE and destroyer-escorts GOSS and U. M. MOORE were rejoining Stump's formation from the north where they had been hunting the submarine which had torpedoed the attack transport CAVALIER.

Action began that evening as dusk darkened the South China Sea.

Time: 1955: Cruiser BOISE reported a surface radar contact.
1956: BELL snared same contact at 9,250 yards.
2000: BELL and O'BANNON were ordered to investigate.
2001: Radar contact disappeared at 5,500 yards.
2005: BELL obtained sound contact at 2,900 yards.
2012: Making depth-charge run, BELL dropped pattern.
2020: O'BANNON attacked with depth charges.
2034: BELL reported to ComTaskGroup that contact was temporarily lost, and requested a DE be sent to assist. (A DE, because that type carried superior A/S equipment.)
2035: ULVERT M. MOORE was detached for job. Peeling off, she joined BELL and O'BANNON.
2041: Meanwhile, O'BANNON reported passing through an oil slick.
2042: BELL regained sonar contact with target.
2050: BELL launched depth-charge attack.
2051: ComTaskGroup ordered JENKINS to relieve BELL and take charge of sub-hunt operation.
2122: JENKINS joined hunter-killers conducting "Operation Observant."
2223: BELL sighted oil slick, and noted strong smell of same. (Evidently BELL and O'BANNON had wounded the quarry before JENKINS and U. M. MOORE arrived on scene.)
2225: While the three destroyers circled the bull's-eye, destroyer-escort MOORE stepped into the ring and fired hedgehog.
2228: MOORE delivered another hedgehog attack. The projectiles soared and splashed. Three explosions crackled under the sea.
2259: MOORE let fly with a third hedgehog barrage. The projectiles sank in silence, but bubbling noises and muffled detonations continued to echo the previous salvo.
2319: MOORE's Sound men heard still another gruff explosion. (Obviously things were cooking in a smitten submarine.)
2337: Maneuvering into attack position, the DE unleashed another hedgehog salvo. Two loud detonations boomed up from below.
0015: With the calendar 15 minutes into February, MOORE made her fifth hedgehog attack. The projectile barrage produced two more smacking explosions. (If the sub were not already dimpled, dented, and dished in, these last shots dealt the damage.)
0019: The hunting ships were jolted by a prodigious deep-sea blast. Goodbye Japanese submarine!

In the wake of that final bombilation, Sound contact was permanently lost. So was the RO-115. Behind her the submarine left the usual spew of oil and flotsam. And Admiral Miwa scratched another number from his Sixth Fleet roster.

Commenting on the kill, a DesPac officer wrote: *"The Commanding Officer of* JENKINS *was smart in letting the DE do the attacking with hedgehogs, while the three DD's circled the area of attack to prevent the sub's escape."*

Thomason Sinks RO-55

By war year 1945 the Imperial Navy's submariners must have realized that their chances of returning from a patrol were definitely slim. They were nonexistent for RO-55 when that reckless submersible tried to patrol at periscope depth on the evening of February 7, 1945.

On that evening a task unit composed of destroyer-escorts THOMASON (Lieutenant Commander C. B. Henriques, U.S.N.R.) and NEUENDORF were hunter-killering in the vicinity. At 2307 THOMASON made radar contact with the skulking sub. Range 3,500 yards. She made a dry run, and did not open fire until her second run, which was executed at 2327. The hedgehogs soared, splashed, and about one second after they struck the water five or six of them detonated simultaneously. Blending into a single blast, the explosions flashed like lightning playing under the surface. This watery fireworks display illuminated the death-throes of the RO-boat.

Excerpt from THOMASON's War Diary:

"After range was closed to about 300 yards, a white luminous outline was seen which did not disappear as did the white foam from breaking seas. At firing range this luminous water had taken a long, oval shape and was definitely the outline of a submarine which could not have been more than 25 to 50 feet deep, perhaps at periscope depth."

After the aqueous pyrotechnics, the spectral sub disappeared. A carpet of oil spread across the water. The two DE's searched the area for the next nine hours, to no avail. RO-55 was beyond mortal contact.

Finnegan Kills I-370

Late in February, destroyer-escort FINNEGAN (Lieutenant Commander H. Huffman, U.S.N.R.) was one of four ships escorting a convoy of nine transports from Iwo Jima to Saipan. Just before daybreak of the 26th, when the convoy was about midway between the Volcano Islands and the Marianas, FINNEGAN's radar registered a contact with a surfaced submarine.

Eight minutes later, with the range closed to 6,700 yards, the "pip" vanished from the radar scope. After passing over the spot where the target had disappeared, FINNEGAN commenced "Operation Observant." Presently she had sonar contact, and at 0659 she let fly with hedgehog. The projectiles missed. Four more hedgehog patterns were fired in vain. At 0800 Commander Huffman realized the sub must have gone deep. So he tried for her with a pattern of 13 depth charges.

The charges boomed down, but nothing came up. Then the DE's fathometer indicated that the sub was swimming at varying levels between 20 and 30 fathoms. At 0925 FINNEGAN fired another hedgehog barrage. Silence. At 1000 she maneuvered in and dropped a full pattern of depth charges set to blow at "medium." About five minutes after the first "ashcan" rolled from the rack, a thunder-blast roared under the sea. It was echoed by muffled rumbling and regurgitative bubbling sounds. The explosion was way down under, and the ocean's surface remained unruffled. FINNEGAN had really reached for that one.

Oil and debris kept coming up for the rest of the day. The oil smeared an area four miles long and two miles wide. Thirty-one pieces of shattered timber were picked up by the destroyermen. Some of it was marked with Japanese ideographs. I-370 was the sub's number.

Unlocking Luzon (The Drive to Lingayen Gulf)

Japanese Vice Admiral Shigeru Fukudome, Commander Imperial Second Air Fleet, headquarters Manila, was surprised when the American invasion force by-passed Manila Bay and landed at the Lingayen Gulf back door instead.

For the Lingayen operation Admiral Kinkaid had mustered an attack force of some 850 vessels. Amphibious groups under Vice Admirals Wilkinson and Barbey would land some 200,000 Sixth Army troops on the beachhead. Fire-support ships under Vice Admiral Oldendorf; surface cover by vessels under Rear Admiral Berkey; air cover by escort-carrier units under Rear Admiral Durgin; Rear Admiral Conolly's reinforcement ships—to Lingayen went an armada that could have mowed down the Japs even in their heyday.

The Lingayen landings were scheduled for January 9. Kinkaid's forces expected little trouble from the Imperial Navy, but they frowned apprehensively at the sky. With increasing frequency one word was uttered with grim emphasis by ship captains and muttered uneasily by gun crews. The word was "suicide."

Destroyermen heard and spoke it often after the Battle for Leyte. Destroyers and DE's were particularly vulnerable to this Japanese suicide plane attack, and all hands were acutely aware of that vulnerability.

Late in December destroyer GANSEVOORT got it. Captained by Commander J. M. Steinbeck, the ship was working as a unit of a Resupply Echelon which was off the Mindoro beachhead. With her were eight other DD's. On the afternoon of December 30 the ships were patrolling the transport area when a number of Jap suiciders dived from the sky. Several vessels were hit; then GANSEVOORT was struck by a hell-bent plane. The crash killed 16 of her crew, injured 15, and left the ship listing, exploding, and afire. Only fast and efficient damage-control by her men, and fire-fighting aid from destroyers PHILIP (Commander J. B. Rutter, Jr.) and WILSON (Commander C. J. Mackenzie), kept the stricken destroyer afloat. But she was out of the war for months to come. The suiciders had struck another scoring blow.

Seven days later they scored again. This time they knocked out the destroyer-escort STAFFORD. Steaming with an escort-carrier group that was a part of the Luzon Attack Force, STAFFORD (Lieutenant Commander V. H. Craig, Jr., U.S.N.R.) was one of five

Typhoon! The Japs weren't the only foe in the Pacific. These destroyers survived, but the Fleet suffered severe casualties more than once when struck by monstrous storms. On December 17, 1944, off the Philippines, twenty-eight ships were damaged and three destroyers, Spence, Monaghan, and Hull, foundered. There was a total of fewer than 100 survivors from the three ships.

Battle for Lingayen Gulf: The full fury of the kamikaze attack is here shown as a Japanese suicider crashes into the battleship California, at left, in one of the earliest attacks involving intentional, mass suicide tactics. Here is graphic proof of Admiral Ainsworth's remark, "When at grips with the enemy on the sea, under the sea, or in the air, no Task Force Commander ever had

*enough destroyers." This photograph of destroyers screening heavy units of the task force was taken from the Colorado, whose **crashing** guns vibrated the camera in a manner which gives an illusion of the actual intensity of the scene. Destroyers suffered the heaviest casualties from the kamikazes; the armored ships could generally shrug them off with less **damage.***

Five were shot down, but six got through. Helm, shown shooting down one of the kamikazes, was one of the ships to be hit. A carrier, two cruisers, and two other destroyers were damaged.

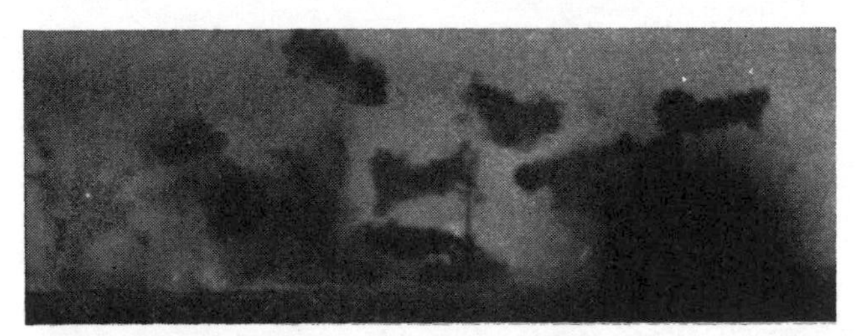

Stafford (DE 411) suffers major damage from a kamikaze. This destroyer-escort, hit during the January 5, 1945, raid off Mindoro, was fortunate to have only two men killed in this attack.

Radford strikes a mine while going to help the La Vallette which had also struck a mine. These destroyers were damaged while supporting minesweepers opening Mariveles Harbor, Bataan.

The "Divine Wind" begins to blow: Ammen (DD 527) is hit by a "Frances." This curtain-raiser of the kamikaze onslaught occurred off Leyte, November 1, 1944. She survived the attack.

In the great typhoon of December, 1944, Taberrer, radio and radar knocked out, was thought lost. Actually, she was busy at the unbelievable feat of picking up 55 survivors from the Hull.

Hopewell (DD 681), photographed three minutes after she had taken a direct hit from Jap guns on Corregidor, February 14, 1945. Hit by four shells, she had seven men killed, eight wounded.

Survivors of Lamson are being picked up by the destroyer Flusser, Ormoc Bay, December 7, 1944. Lamson, victim of attacks by suiciders and torpedo planes, is seen burning in the distance.

First U.S. ship sunk by a kamikaze, Abner Read plunged to the bottom of Leyte Gulf, November 1, 1944, only 36 minutes after she was hit by a Jap "Val" in the suicide attack on T.G. 77.1.

DE's screening the carrier TULAGI. In the afternoon of January 5, 1945, the group was struck by Jap aircraft off Mindoro. This was the third strike of what had proved a warm day, and the Jap planes broke through the tired Combat Air Patrol (CAP) defenses. Five suiciders were shot down by AA gunnery, but six made good their *hari-kiri* dives. Carrier MANILA BAY, cruisers LOUISVILLE and H.M.A.S. AUSTRALIA, destroyers HELM and H.M.A.S. ARUNTA, and destroyer-escort STAFFORD were struck in this meteor-rain of crashing planes. The bigger ships managed to shrug off the blastings, but STAFFORD was badly hurt. Fortunately crew casualties were light—two killed; 12 wounded—and the little DE, although crippled, limped gamely along in the wake of the Lingayen-bound group.

Approaching the objective, the Attack Force encountered only a shadowy surface opposition. There were, however, a number of submarine alarms. And on January 5, destroyer TAYLOR (Commander N. J. F. Frank), patrolling in advance of the San Fabian Attack Force, put the finish to the minor career of a midget. This undersized sub discharged two torpedoes at the light cruiser BOISE. The torpedoes missed. TAYLOR saw the wakes, and maneuvered to avoid. Later the destroyer's lookouts spied a periscope, lobbed depth charges at close range, then rammed the damaged midget hard amidships. The midget submarine went down with a drowning gurgle.

Racing boats loaded with high explosives also threatened the American invasion forces. Jabbing out of Luzon's jungly backwaters, these ugly little craft struck at the armada's vanguard. But Jap aircraft bent on suicide were the chief threat, and the menace mounted with every mile as the invaders approached Lingayen Gulf.

In the forefront of this battle against death from the sky were the destroyers of Squadrons 60 and 56—screen for the Bombardment and Fire Support Group which covered the preliminary mine-sweepings and the landing operation. The destroyer roster included the DD's listed on this page.

DESRON 60

BARTON
Flagship of
Squadron Commander, Capt. W. L. Freseman

WALKE — LAFFEY — O'BRIEN

ALLEN M. SUMNER
Flagship of
Comdr. J. C. Zahm, COMDESDIV 120

MOALE — INGRAHAM — LOWRY

DESRON 56

NEWCOMB
Flagship of
Squadron Commander Capt. R. N. Smoot

BENNION — R. P. LEARY
H. L. EDWARDS — LEUTZE

IZARD
Flagship of
Capt. T. F. Conley, Jr., COMDESDIV 112

KIMBERLY — BRYANT — W. D. PORTER

Australian destroyers ARUNTA *and* WARRAMUNGA *also served with the Bombardment and Fire Support Group.*

As they steamed northward toward Lingayen Gulf, the destroyers experienced one air attack after another. On one day, January 6, the assaults were almost continuous, and the Jap suiciders scored a total of 16 scorching hits or near-misses.

Patrolling isolated stations off the beachhead that day, the destroyers were target set-ups for the hell-divers. WALKE (Commander G. F. Davis) was attacked simultaneously by four Jap planes. Her desperate gun crews shot down two suiciders, and, after she was crashed by a third, they got the fourth with an AA burst. The smashing plane blasted the ship's superstructure, killed 12 of the crew, and wounded 35. Among the wounded was Commander Davis. Although in agony, he refused to leave his post or submit to medical treatment until the attacks were over and his ship was out of danger. He died that afternoon.

After disabling WALKE, the suiciders fell upon the ship which relieved her—destroyer O'BRIEN (Commander W. W. Outerbridge).

The plane struck like a lightning bolt. O'BRIEN reeled from the blow and crawled out of action with a section of her superstructure knocked all acockbill. Luckily her crew escaped with few casualties. Meanwhile, destroyer SUMNER was crashed by a plane that blasted her deck and left her disabled. With 14 dead and 29 wounded, the ship endured the day's heaviest casualties.

On that same day RICHARD P. LEARY was damaged by a suicider which grazed her forward 5-inchers; NEWCOMB was blistered by a near miss, the blast of which killed two men and wounded 15; and LOWRY, jolted by a near miss, was damaged by friendly fire. All these destroyers had been engaged in covering minesweepers inshore. Their AA fire broke up the Jap attack and undoubtedly saved the mine-vessels from abolishment. Destroyers INGRAHAM and BARTON threw some hard blows at the Jap planes, as did BENNION while escorting minesweepers on the 7th.

On the day of the landings four DE's of Escort Division 69, under Commander T. C. Phifer, were stationed in the protective screen of the Attack Force. These destroyer-escorts were RICHARD W. SUESENS (Lieutenant Commander R. W. Graham, U.S.N.R.), flagship of Commander Phifer; OBERRENDER (Lieutenant Commander S. Spencer, U.S.N.R.); LERAY WILSON (Lieutenant Commander M. V. Carson, Jr., U.S.N.R.); and GILLIGAN (Lieutenant Commander C. E. Bull, U.S.N.R.). Three of these ships were not on duty long.

On January 10 LERAY WILSON was struck by a suicider. The blast killed six men, injured seven, and wrecked half the vessel's superstructure. Although charred by a gasoline fire, the DE remained on patrol until evening, when she joined a task unit bound for Leyte. On the 12th GILLIGAN was struck by a "Betty" which her sharpshooting AA gunners had turned into a blowtorch. The flaming plane struck a 40 mm. mount aft, killed 12 men and injured 13. About 30 minutes later, RICHARD W. SUESENS was damaged by a suicider as she was searching the water for men blown overside from GILLIGAN. Riddled by SUESENS' automatic guns, the plane skimmed over the DE and plunged into the sea close aboard.

For a suicide variation, Jap speedboats made a try in Lingayen Gulf in the dark before dawn of January 10. The hard-to-see, hard-to-hit demolition boats blasted two landing craft, severely damaged a transport and an LST, and bruised destroyer ROBINSON (Commander E. B. Grantham, Jr.). Destroyer PHILIP (Commander J. B. Rutter, Jr.) drove off several of these suicide boats with gunfire, and blew one of them to smithereens. Such *hari-kiri* craft were highly dangerous but the waters of Lingayen Gulf were soon cleansed of the pests.

And after the landings the suicide air assaults abated. On the 21st of January an echo crackled across the seas to the north of Luzon when suicide aircraft struck at Task Force 38 off Formosa. During the attack, the large carrier TICONDEROGA was badly hurt by two Jap suiciders. And destroyer MADDOX (Commander J. S. Willis) was briefly put out of action by a crashing "Zeke." The plane exploded on MADDOX's main deck, killing seven of her crew and wounding 33. The ship stood up well under the blast, and the conflagration topside was soon under control.

Commenting on the air smashes in Lingayen Gulf, Captain R. N. Smoot, ComDesRon 56, wrote:

> *As colorfully expressed by some of the commanding officers of this unit, defense against suicide attacks comes under three headings; i.e., Providence, Speed, and Gunnery. Of the first, no further comments are appropriate. As to speed and gunnery, it is generally conceded by those experienced in the matter that the ship should be maneuvered at high speed and in such a manner as to always put the broadside to the attacking plane. This serves three purposes: It provides the greatest concentration of gunfire; it presents the narrowest target in range; and it effects the greatest deflection movement from the point of view of the attacking pilot.*

Manila Bay Conclusion (DD's Fight War's Last Surface Engagement)

With appropriate, if accidental, symbolism the last major surface engagement of the Pacific War was fought off the entrance of Manila Bay.

The date was January 7, 1945. The American DD's involved were members of Task Unit 781.11, part of the San Fabian Attack Force which at that time was en route to Lingayen Gulf. The destroyers were CHARLES AUSBURNE (Lieutenant Commander H. W. Baker), flying the pennant of Captain T. B. Dugan, ComDesRon 23; SHAW (Lieutenant Commander V. B. Graff); BRAINE (Commander W. W. Fitts); and RUSSELL (Lieutenant Commander J. E. Wicks, Jr.). That January evening the four were steaming in column about five miles on the right flank of a transport group. All was quiet on a black seascape under a star-powdered sky. Then, at 2214, the destroyers were roused by radar contact with a ship or ships maneuvering at a range of 15,000 yards. The suspicious targets could only be Jap. Captain Dugan ordered his DD's to change course, put on speed, and investigate.

> *As the mission of the Unit was essentially defensive, and as the number and nature of the targets was uncertain, it was decided to illuminate at long range rather than attempt a surprise torpedo attack.*

With the range closed to 10,000 yards, AUSBURNE fired starshells. The pyrotechnic light disclosed a single ship, the silhouette of a Japanese destroyer. With one voice the American destroyer batteries roared, and the bellow sent the enemy fleeing eastward. AUSBURNE hit and slowed the ship before she could get her fantail back into Manila Bay. Pale flashes indicated torpedo-fire from the fugitive vessel, and the Americans changed course to avoid a possible spread. Thirty minutes after AUSBURNE's first salvo of starshells, a roulade of explosions echoed across the water. The Americans, only 2,000 yards away, saw the ship thrust her bow toward the stars and slide under the sea. Detailed to look for survivors, destroyer

RUSSELL searched the area, but could find nothing but wind and wave. The war's last surface engagement was over. After VJ-Day, investigators learned that the Imperial Navy's final sea battle had been fought—and lost—by the destroyer HINOKI. (The I.J.N. would make one last attempt in April, but the attempt would be nipped in the bud by Navy air.)

By February 4 American troops were slugging their way into the outskirts of the Philippine's capital. While the Battle for Manila was shaking the island, American amphibs and paratroops were battling to regain Corregidor. The struggle entailed a push into Mariveles harbor at the lower end of Bataan. While supporting minesweepers which were clearing the way into Mariveles, two Seventh Fleet destroyers were severely injured by mine explosion. Disabled were destroyers LAVALLETTE (Commander Wells Thompson) and RADFORD (Lieutenant Commander J. E. Mansfield).

The blasting occurred in the afternoon of February 14. LAVALLETTE was following the sweepers into the harbor, covering their advance and shooting at mines which were cut adrift, when a heavy explosion rocked the ship. The blast wrecked her No. 1 fireroom, let in a flood, and sent the destroyer reeling with six dead and 23 wounded. Destroyer RADFORD had been standing by outside the harbor. She moved in to take LAVALLETTE in tow. As she was nearing the disabled ship, RADFORD herself was stunned by a mine-blast. Three of her crew were slain and four were wounded. Both ships managed to clear the harbor under their own steam and limp to Subic Bay for repairs.

While supporting minesweepers which were clearing a channel north of Corregidor, destroyers FLETCHER (Commander J. L. Foster), flagship of Commander L. H. Martin, ComDesDiv 42, and HOPEWELL (Commander W. S. Rodimon), flagship of Captain J. K. B. Ginder, ComDesRon 21, were savagely mauled by enemy gunfire from the Rock. This blasting also occurred on Valentine's Day. Three shore batteries had the range. A roar of 6-inch salvos wrecked a minesweeper. HOPEWELL was hit by four shells. Seven men were slain by the explosions, and eight were injured. Struck by a single shell, FLETCHER lost six men, and five of her crew were wounded. The offending batteries were quickly silenced by a barrage of naval gunfire and a pounding from the air.

But the Rock proved a tough nut to crack. Its tunneled guns and interior corridors were almost as bomb-proof for the Japs as they had been for the original American defenders. Accordingly, naval artillery was brought in to add weight to the assaulting hammer. On February 16 Task Unit 78.3.5 was organized and assigned the express mission of pounding the Rock. Under command of Captain R. W. Cavenagh, ComDesDiv 46, this unit contained the following destroyers:

CONVERSE (Lieutenant Commander E. H. McDowell), flagship; THATCHER (Commander W. A. Cockell); DYSON (Commander L. E. Ruff); CLAXTON (Commander M. W. Firth); SAUFLEY (Lieutenant Commander F. W. Silk); and CONYNGHAM (Lieutenant Commander F. W. Bampton).

Most of the above-named DD's were veterans of the original DesRon 23, the "Little Beavers" of the famous Arleigh ("31-Knot") Burke. And from February 16 to February 28 they smote the Jap artillerymen on Corregidor hip and thigh. Army forces were also in there smiting. But the Japs on Corregidor died hard. And they took their time about it—as Captain Cavenagh observed in his Action Report.

> *This action is considered unique in that the destroyers were stopped for days at a time less than a thousand yards from the enemy ground forces, firing at pill boxes and caves, with spotting assistance from the beach. We could see plainly and report enemy troops. From the historical point of view at least the retaking of Corregidor was an event. It will be seldom that the Navy fire support will be so closely tied in with the activity of the Army.*

Another unique aspect of this fire-support effort was the fact that only one of Cavenagh's destroyers was scathed by return fire. SAUFLEY was lacerated by iron fragments when some 75 mm. shells landed close aboard.

Night and day the Corregidor pounding went on. By February 28 many of the survivors were in a state of catalepsy. The way into Manila Bay was cleared.

While Corregidor was in the nut-cracker, Manila was crumbling, and the Japanese sun was setting on the Philippine Archipelago. It was almost under the horizon when the Japanese Submarine Force made one last stab at the Seventh Fleet invaders. The ambush was staged off Siquijor Island. At 1059 in the morning of February 21—sea calm, visibility good—lookouts on board destroyer RENSHAW (Commander G. H. Cairnes) glimpsed a periscope off the ship's port beam. RENSHAW, one of the escorts of a convoy bound for Subic Bay, went to General Quarters on the double, and her skipper ordered full left rudder, intending to close the target. Just as the order was given, a torpedo wake was sighted less than 500 yards abaft the port beam. Before the destroyer could dodge, the "fish" struck her amidships.

Seventeen men perished in the blast which wrecked both engine-rooms and the after fireroom. With all power lost, RENSHAW sloughed to a halt. For a moment the sub's conning tower appeared on the surface, and the destroyermen lashed out with 40 mm. fire. Some who glimpsed the enemy identified the sub as an RO-boat, but it may have been a midget. Destroyers WALLER and SHAW searched the area for ten hours without detecting the submersible. Hard hit, RENSHAW remained stubbornly afloat. Torpedoes, depth charges, topside ammunition, provisions, and other heavy items were jettisoned during the fight for buoyancy. It was touch and go, but the ship was held on the surface, and destroyer SMITH towed her to Leyte.

Philippine Sundown

March, 1945—the Philippines were liberated. Coincident with the liberation was the finish of the Japanese Empire. Here and there in the Netherlands East Indies the Emperor's troops clung to patches of ground, but these troops were marooned. The Co-Prosperity Sphere was bankrupt. The Japanese Merchant Marine was wrecked. Most of the Imperial Navy was rusting on the floor of the Pacific. What was left of it lay at anchor for want of fuel.

Yet the hardest battle of the whole Pacific War was still in store for the United States Navy. Ahead of the Navy's destroyermen was perhaps their most gruelling ordeal.

Over the dark northern horizon lay Okinawa.

SINKING OF HULL

CHAPTER 36

PRELUDE TO OKINAWA

THE BACKGROUND—INCLUDING IWO JIMA

The Coming of the Kamikazes

In the Mediterranean, American destroyermen encountered human torpedoes. In the Pacific they encountered the midget sub which, crammed with high explosive, could be expended as a torpedo. Now, in the closing months of the Pacific War, they encountered the deadly *Kamikaze* suicide-plane, and the wicked *Oka,* a jet-propelled, human bomb. These diabolical weapons, in which a man was deliberately sacrificed as a part of the infernal machine, measured the barbarism and desperation of the Japanese war leaders who sponsored such devices. The *Kamikaze-Oka* onslaught gave the United States Navy what many consider its worst hour of World War II.

When Admiral Toyoda ordered Kurita's Second Fleet to turn about and head back into the Leyte battle, his order read,

ADVANCE, COUNTING ON DIVINE ASSISTANCE

Evidently the divinity in reference had to do with the Imperial Navy's Special Attack Corps—its newly devised *Kikusui* program featuring the suicide attack and the *Kamikaze* plane. *Kamikaze* means "Divine Wind."

But if Kurita counted upon this "Divine Wind" assistance at Leyte, he was self-deluded. The promised wind failed to blow with drastic force. The Special Attack Corps was not quite ready. Recruited from Ozawa's Carrier Fleet and from such outfits as Admiral Onishi's Manila-based Air Fleet, the human element was not as yet fully prepared for the sacrifice. Scores of Japanese naval pilots volunteered for *Kamikaze* duty, but even a suicide pilot needs special indoctrination and training. Moreover, the sacrificial planes were not mustered in sufficient number to lend Kurita decisive aid. And thanks to the American submarine assault on Japan's tanker fleet, they had to wait for gas. So at Leyte the "Divine Wind" was no more than a preliminary puff.

Nevertheless the Leyte *Kamikaze* attacks were an ominous beginning. By year's end destroyers MAHAN and REID and destroyer-transport WARD had been blasted to the bottom of Ormoc Bay by *Kamikazes;* escort-carrier OMMANEY BAY and three minesweepers had been downed by the same agency off Mindoro; and numerous vessels, including battleships NEW MEXICO, CALIFORNIA, and MISSISSIPPI, were reporting topside damage from crashing Jap planes. So it was evident that a concentrated suicide onslaught had been launched.

Actually, as the calendar entered 1945 the *Kamikaze* campaign was only getting under way. Throughout January the menace continued to mount. As has been related, carrier TICONDEROGA and destroyer MADDOX, while cruising off Formosa with Task Force 38, were both severely damaged by suicide air attacks. The results from Toyoda's point of view must have seemed most gratifying. In the first three months of the campaign some 121 *Kamikazes* had crashed into Allied ships, and 53 had scorched the targets with near misses.

Respecting life, liberty, and the dignity of the individual, Democracy abhors human sacrifice. Neither the United States nor any other civilized nation sponsors mass suicide or urges its loyal defenders to blow themselves deliberately to bits. But Japan's *Kamikaze* pilots were not only urged to commit suicide, they were given every opportunity to do so. The plane provided for the performance was crammed chock-a-block with high explosives. Conventional bombs were to be dropped or torpedoes launched if occasion presented, but above all the aircraft was to be rammed into the target—if possible, by a power dive. Teamwork by companion *Kamikazes* was recommended for a thorough blasting.

The *Kamikaze,* then, was in effect a huge projectile in which the pilot served as fire-control device and exploder mechanism. The *Oka* (Americans called it *Baka*—Japanese for "idiot") was even more on the order of a projectile. Powered by jet propulsion, it was a winged rocket with a warhead that contained 1,135 pounds of high explosive. Like the German glider-bomb, the *Oka* was carried to the scene of action by a mother plane, usually a medium bomber. But the Nazi glider-bomb was a radio-controlled mechanical robot, whereas the Jap *Oka* was controlled by a human robot who rode the rocket down to the target. There was no turning back once the flying bomb was launched from the release gear of the plane which carried it. The rocket ride was suicide.

So the *Kamikaze* and *Oka* pilots were sworn to court death, as were the other operators in the Special Attack Corps—the drivers of suicide speedboats, the submariners in the explosive midgets, the human torpedoes.

But Americans were unready to credit a campaign of mass *hari-kiri* and wholesale expenditure of troops. So Allied Intelligence, apparently applying Western morality and Western reason to the problem, failed to forecast the "Divine Wind" hurricane which struck the American invasion fleet at Okinawa. By the end of March, 1945, the *Kikusui* Special Attack Corps was ready and eager for the slaughter. Hundreds of *Kamikaze* pilots, dozens of *Oka* operators, and scores of aquatic suiciders were prepared for the offensive that was to make of the Okinawa seascape a lake in hell. The word had gone out from Imperial Headquarters—Okinawa was to be the "Last Battle." Japan's War Lords were determined to hold the island at all cost, and everything was to go into the showdown—Imperial Army, Imperial Navy, Imperial Air Force, everything. Okinawa was to be saved by that climactic sea-air battle in home waters which Yamamoto had always advocated for the destruction of the American fleet. True, the Imperial Navy was now no more than a fleshless skeleton, and the Imperial Air Force was all but grounded for lack of fuel. But there was still enough gas for one-way flights.

So it was that skies around and above Okinawa were fairly seared by the *Kamikazes.* And from the naval standpoint, the story of "Operation Iceberg"—the Okinawa campaign—is the story of the DD's and DE's that fought in the epicenter of the "Divine Wind" hurricane. Forty per cent of the American warships sunk at Okinawa were destroyers. Approximately forty per cent of the 368 vessels of all types damaged at Okinawa were DD's and DE's. Nowhere in the two-ocean conflict did destroyermen endure an ordeal worse than the *Kamikaze* offensive at Okinawa. That "Iceberg" did not melt away under the hot "Divine Wind" was largely due to the fight put up by those little gray ships that were called "small boys" and "tin cans." Against the champions of suicide, they fought a battle which has no equal in the annals of warfare—a battle described by no less an authority than Winston Churchill as *"the most intense and famous of military history."*

"Operation Iceberg"

The Nansei islands (also called the Ryukus) lie like a disjoined column of vertebrae between Formosa and Kyushu, Japan. A slash through the Nansei Shoto archipelago would sever Japanese communications with Formosa, the nation's last stronghold in the south; would give the Allies control of the East China Sea; and would bring Allied air within easy bomber range of Tokyo.

But in projecting a drive on the Nansei Shoto chain, the Allied leaders were after something more than a bomber base and a fueling station for blockaders. They were out to acquire a springboard for the invasion forces which would make the final great invasion of the Japanese home islands themselves. A base in the Nansei Shoto archipelago for the staging of that final drive was wanted; a place for the assembly of armada, supplies, and troops, and airdromes suitable for the bomber squadrons which must cover the invasion forces. Such a base was Okinawa.

Located midway between Formosa and Kyushu, Okinawa is the largest of the 55 Nansei islands. It is shaped something like a salamander, about 60 miles in length, 18 miles wide at its broadest point, and only two miles wide in the narrow strip which joins the lengthy northern head to the splayed southern tail. Although the beaches are hemmed with coral reefs, Okinawa bears no resemblance to the tropical atolls of the equatorial Pacific. The mountainous northern terrain is thickly forested; the hilly southern terrain is under green-thumb cultivation.

Strategically, Okinawa's relation to Japan was similar to that of Cuba to the southeast seaboard of

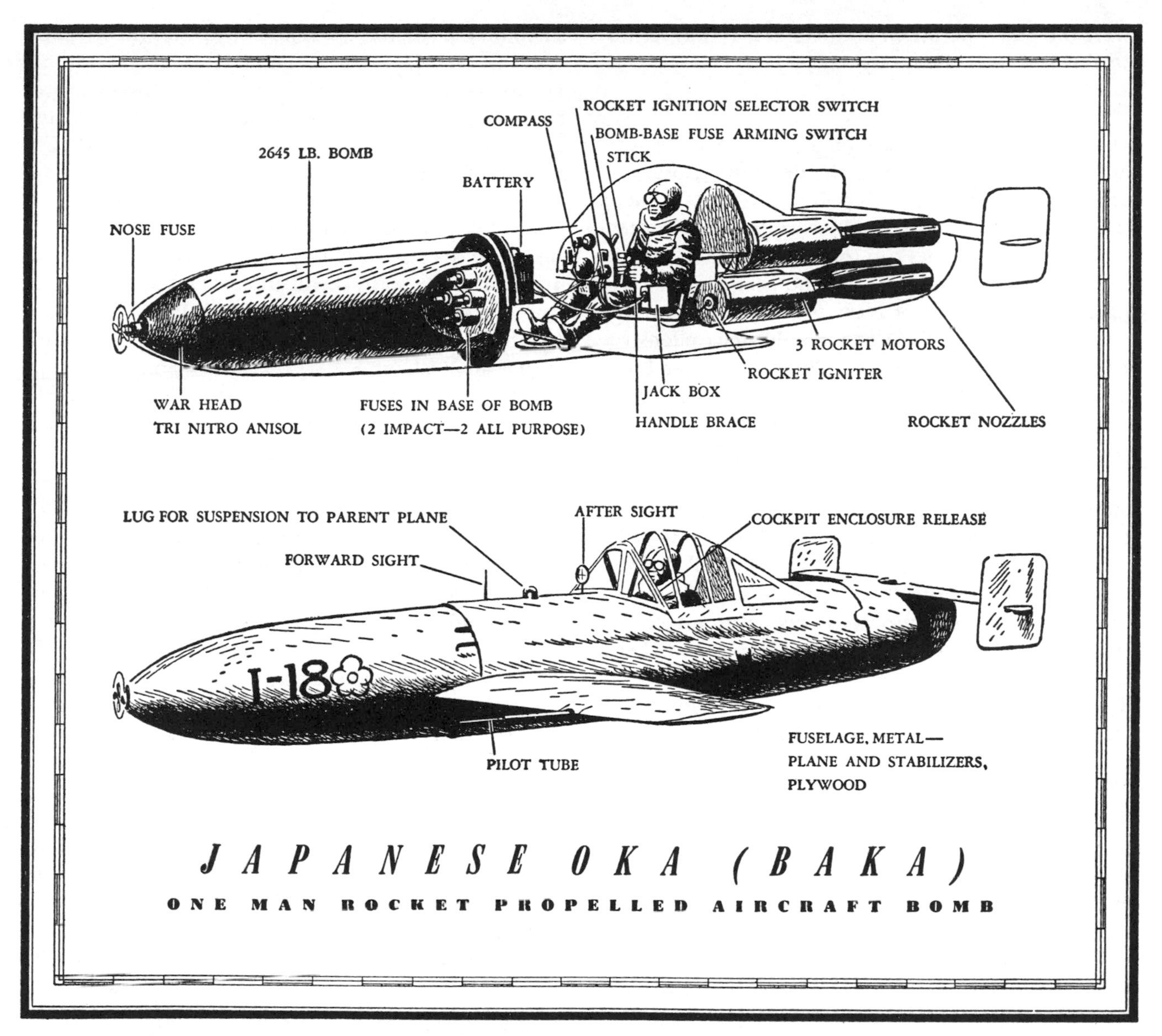

JAPANESE OKA (BAKA)

ONE MAN ROCKET PROPELLED AIRCRAFT BOMB

the United States; and as a bastion in Japan's inner defense perimeter, the island had been made a honeycomb of fortifications. Guns reared their snouts from the timber in the north and lay concealed in the ravines and crags of the south. Two large airfields—Yontan and Kadena—were located in the hinterland a few miles north of Naha. The island was pocked with caves and tunnels, pillboxes and blockhouses, and the coastal waters were seeded with mines.

Allied Intelligence considerably underestimated the island's strength. The Imperial Navy was correctly estimated as standing on its last legs, and Japanese carrier strength was correctly marked as negligible. But Intelligence was wide of the mark in the analysis of Okinawa's ground defenses. General Mitsuri Ushijima had on Okinawa over 120,000 men, with artillery in proportion. And Intelligence had no intimation of the *Kikisui* program.

It was realized, however, that the campaign would not be a mere picnic. The Imperial Fleet was still counted on for some interference, and the home-based Japanese Air Force was considered a major problem. And it was recognized that before the Okinawa invasion could be attempted, the Japanese air defenses would have to be whittled down.

Accordingly, a series of bomber raids on Japan's home airdromes and aircraft factories was projected. Before these raids could be fully launched, it was necessary to obtain a base close to Japan—airstrips for the fighter planes needed to protect the big Superfort bombers. The island of Iwo Jima, in the Volcano-Bonin Chain, 750 miles south of Honshu, was the answer. So the capture of Iwo Jima was planned as the first step in "Operation Iceberg." Late in January, 1945, Fleet Admiral Nimitz transferred his headquarters from Pearl Harbor to Guam to direct the dual operation, and Iwo D-Day was set for the third week in February.

Iwo Jima Overture

In the public mind Iwo Jima means Mount Suribachi and the Marines. But the dramatic capture of Suribachi was the peak-high point of the battle; there was fierce fighting before, and ferocious fighting afterward. And the Marines had to be transported, landed, supported, and maintained on the island.

Hence a great deal of Navy was involved, for Iwo demanded one of the largest amphibious offensives of the Pacific War. Some 110,000 troops under Lieutenant General Holland Smith, U.S.M.C., were carried to the target island. Commanded by Admiral R. A. Spruance, the invasion armada mustered over 1,000 ships. Vice Admiral Turner, veteran amphibious commander, was in charge of the 495 vessels allocated to the transport, landing, and inshore jobs. The Support Force under Rear Admiral W. H. P. Blandy contained 6 battleships, 8 escort-carriers, 5 cruisers, 20 destroyers, and 9 destroyer-escorts, plus minecraft, gunboats, and other vessels. Vice Admiral Mitscher's Fast Carrier Task Force spearheaded the offensive. Mitscher's force was now built up to a strength of 118 warships—17 carriers, 8 battleships, 16 cruisers, and 77 destroyers.

Long before the landings the five by two-and-a-half mile island had been subjected to a prodigious pounding by U.S. bombers. Day after day, for many weeks, carrier planes and land-based aircraft, including B-29's, had hammered Iwo. By February 15 nearly 7,300 tons of bombs had been dropped on the place; 7,300 *tons* of bombs. Additional tons of TNT had been hurled upon the island by surface ships which conducted seven "Spruance haircut" shore bombardments.

But the little volcanic island was an iron-hard mass of lava and granite. And the beaches were dunes of black volcanic ash deposited on the foreshore in that forgotten time when Mount Suribachi was active. In these ashy dunes aircraft bombs and naval projectiles fell as though on beds of sawdust.

As for the Japanese defenders, when the bombers came over they retired into a labyrinth of caves, dugouts, and underground burrows. In spite of the daily bombings, fortifications were strengthened, the two airfields remained in operation, and work went forward on the new airstrip. Some 20,000 Japanese troops were manning this stronghold when the invaders arrived, and those Japs were prepared to fight to the last man.

Of course Iwo was bound to fall ultimately. With the United States Fifth Fleet in possession of the surrounding sea, there was no escape once the invasion started. And Japanese General Kuribayashi was up against an insoluble logistics problem. An American submarine blockade had already put the isolated garrison on emergency rations. It would only be a matter of time before Iwo would have a bare cupboard.

But Spruance did not have that much time. April 1 had been selected as D-Day for Okinawa, and the Iwo Jima invasion was scheduled for February 19, only five weeks ahead. That was the situation which called for the 1,000-ship armada and 110,000 men to assault such a small island.

In the pre-invasion preliminaries of heavy air raids, shore bombardments, and the establishment of a blockade, U.S. Navy destroyers participated all around the clock. They were on duty as lifesavers ready to race to the rescue of downed aviators. They steamed with bombardment groups which shot at the island and its Volcano neighbors. They supplemented the submarine blockade with surface sweeps for supply and reinforcement shipping. As early as the first week in January, destroyers were operating in the Iwo area, paving the way for the big assault.

On January 5, destroyers DUNLAP, FANNING, CUMMINGS, ELLET, ROE, and DAVID W. TAYLOR were in the Volcanos on bombardment mission. Under command of Captain H. P. Smith, ComDesRon 4, these DD's spearheaded a task group which included cruisers CHESTER, PENSACOLA, and SALT LAKE CITY. Led by Rear Admiral A. E. Smith in CHESTER, the warships visited Chichi Jima, Haha Jima, and Iwo Jima, shooting up shipping and shore installations.

During the bombardment of Chichi Jima, DAVID W. TAYLOR (Commander W. H. Johnsen) fouled an enemy mine. The blast flooded a forward compartment; four men were drowned; the ship staggered out of action. FANNING (Commander J. C. Bentley) was holed by an enemy shell. Both ships were detached and sent in company to Saipan; from there the TAYLOR went home for a Navy Yard overhaul.

Destroyer HEYWOOD L. EDWARDS (Commander A. L. Shepherd) returned from an Iwo bombardment mission early in February with an interesting deception story. As told in the DD's Action Report:

> During one short bombardment . . . a Jap spotter on a frequency very close to the spotting frequency then in use called this ship, saying, "Right a little! Up a little!" Fortunately his accent was unmistakable, his procedure was incorrect, and he was not exactly on frequency, or he might have proven very disconcerting, if he did not altogether destroy communications.

The opposition roughened as the preliminary pace

Destruction of Halligan (DD 584) off Okinawa. Moving up to her station as a member of Fire Support Unit 2 to cover minesweepers along the southwest coast of the island, this destroyer was shattered by a terrific explosion. Only two junior officers and 166 men survived the catastrophe. For reasons unknown, she had steamed into an unswept area and probably hit a moored mine.

The Ides of March, 1945. Steaming up from Ulithi, Task Force 58 struck hard at the Japanese home islands to soften opposition and divert attention from the imminent invasion of Okinawa. The gunfire of this section and the planes of the carrier units were combined many times in the ensuing months to flatten a desperate enemy, who turned to suicide tactics as a last resort.

Franklin fights for her life off Kyushu. An early episode in the carrier's heroic saga saw Miller going alongside to remove the flag officers and their staffs. Later Hickox rescued men trapped on the carrier's fantail.

Another view of Halligan, showing her broken in two on the rugged coast of Okinawa. No senior officers survived to explain why the ship was in mined waters.

Hall (DD 483) is hit while engaged in fire support for the Iwo Jima landings. Destroyers participated all around the clock helping to pave the way for the big assault. Jap guns on Mount Suribachi made plenty of trouble.

Softening up Iwo Jima: Enemy installations being bombarded by naval units, as seen from Heywood L. Edwards, one of the destroyers in fire support group.

Murray (DD 576) transfers wounded to Hornet. An aerial torpedo had gone right through the bow of the ship and detonated in the water alongside. Note hole just under stretcher. One man was killed and four wounded.

Kamikaze hits Halsey Powell. The Jap suicide plane crashed completely through the destroyer's stern, but the DD had helped save the carrier she was guarding.

accelerated and the invasion date approached. On February 17 destroyer LEUTZE began the day as a fire-support ship for minesweepers combing the water off the eastern beaches. Then she moved inshore to support an Underwater Demolition Team. While covering the UDT's with a shore bombardment, she was struck during an exchange of shells with a Mount Suribachi shore battery.

An enemy shell—a 3- or 4-incher—hit the starboard side of the No. 1 stack, ripping open the stack and slashing the superstructure with shrapnel. LEUTZE's skipper, Commander B. A. Robbins, Jr., was seriously injured. And a dangerous fire broke out in the forward 40 mm. handling room.

Assuming command, Lieutenant L. Grabowsky, the ship's "Exec," kept the guns going, and closed the beach to flay the offending battery. Meantime, Gunners Mates, Third, Eugene Balinski and Warren H. Gurwell dragged fire hoses across the deck, opened the door of the burning magazine, and fought flames which threatened to set off a disastrous explosion. Then, the fire smothered, they threw a batch of hot powder containers overside. The ship remained on duty off Iwo until the evening of the 18th, when she steamed away in company with battleship NEW YORK for Ulithi.

On the night of February 17-18, three destroyers conducted a brisk anti-shipping sweep off Japan. The destroyers were the INGRAHAM (Commander J. F. Harper, Jr.), flying the pennant of Commander J. C. Zahm, ComDesDiv 120; BARTON (Commander E. B. Dexter); and MOALE (Commander W. M. Foster).

Two of these destroyers suffered a misadventure on the evening of February 16 while serving in the screen of Fast Carrier Task Group 58. The group was a little too fast for INGRAHAM when her TBS went out of commission and she missed a signal to start zigzagging. Promptly she was rammed by destroyer BARTON. The collision caused minor damage, and ignited a small fire, but repairs were quickly made, and there were no casualties.

The following evening the three DD's were detached from Task Force 58 and ordered to proceed as a unit to Saipan. Steaming in a scouting line, they retired along the track toward Iwo Jima. Around 2115 they made radar contact with two Japanese ships, and a few minutes later the destroyer gunners were on target. The Japs fled; the DD's overhauled. Closing the range to 1,300 yards, the three destroyers pumped shells into a *maru* which soon blew up with a tremendous bang. Then the second target, a patrol craft, went down riddled. Early in the morning of the 18th the destroyers contacted and trapped another *maru*. When the shooting ended, this ship also had blown her top. And as the clock was ticking toward 0400, INGRAHAM, BARTON, and MOALE headed southward to outstrip possible air reprisal. The two merchantmen and the escort vessel, probably acting as pickets, had undoubtedly radioed word of the attack to the home front.

Shooting holes in the enemy picket line off the coast of Japan was always a risky enterprise. Other destroyers with Task Force 58 encountered sentinel shipping that morning of the 18th. About 0530 destroyers PORTERFIELD (Lieutenant Commander D. W. Wulzen), flagship of Captain A. E. Jarrell, ComDesRon 55, and CALLAGHAN (Commander C. M. Bertholf) teamed up to demolish a 100-ton picket. Laced by 40 mm. fire, the patrol boat was reduced to junk before it could return a single shot. Eight Japanese Navy men were fished out of the debris which marked the grave of this shell-shattered vessel.

Some of the Japanese pickets were more pugnacious than the ones abolished by the forementioned sweepers. Early in the morning of February 26 a couple of the Task Group 58 destroyers off Tori Shima ran into a corker. PORTERFIELD was in this scrimmage, as was destroyer STOCKHAM (Commander M. G. Johnson) and cruiser PASADENA. The gunners were hampered by scudding rain and rolling seas. Because the enemy craft was in the center of the task group's screen, the three ships which closed in to finish off the Jap were compelled to limit their fire to 40 mm. The trapped enemy replied with blazing fusillades that gave PASADENA a clawing and wounded 12 men and killed a young ensign on board PORTERFIELD. Destroyer and cruiser shells tore the enemy to pieces, and STOCKHAM stepped in to pulverize the wreckage. But such minor actions could be costly. In addition to crew casualties, PORTERFIELD received damage which sent her to Ulithi for repairs.

Turner's transports were off the Iwo beachheads in the dark before dawn of February 19. The ships were deployed abreast of their assigned beaches in a line off the island's southeast coast. At daybreak the bombardment ships opened up. Shell fire, mortar fire, and rocket fire turned the foreshore into an incandescent strand that could not have been hotter when Suribachi's lava was flowing. Bombers flew in to contribute to the demolition. At 0900 the bombardment ended, and the Marines started in on schedule with their assault gear. The first boat waves ran into little opposition. But double trouble was in the offing.

It began when the landing craft went in through swooping combers and struck those beaches of sugar-soft volcanic sand. Troops leaping from the boats sank up to their ankles in the stuff. In this chemical sand the wheels of amphibian trucks bogged down to the hubs, and caterpillar half-tracks churned helplessly. The whole Iwo shore was as loose as ashes. And in no time the landing flotilla was piled up in a traffic jam of foundering boats and struggling machines and men.

Happily for the Marines, the preliminary shore bombardment had knocked out or demoralized the Jap batteries in the immediate vicinity. And while the assault troops were floundering on the ash-dump beaches, the destroyers and other warships of Blandy's Support Force unleashed a creeping barrage, stepping up the range by 200-yard increments to treat the coast to a bombardment which gradually climbed inland. This advancing curtain of fire held the enemy gunners at bay until U. S. bulldozers managed to chew some beach roads through the mushy dunes, and the crisis at water's edge had passed.

By nightfall some 40,000 Marines were ashore, battling their way toward the southern airfield, only to find that Iwo was a Bastille of pillboxes, blockhouses, and traps. Fifty-yard gains were to demand Marine casualties which made Tarawa seem a picnic in comparison.

The Navy offshore had a relatively easy time of it. Fire-support ships shelled targets on call, and carrier planes bombed Jap gun emplacements. The Japanese Air Force gave General Kuribayashi a smattering of support which was more spectacular than decisive. On February 21 a flock of 50 Jap planes struck "desperately" at the invasion fleet. Spectacularly enough, five *Kamikazes* smashed into aircraft carrier SARATOGA, wrecking her flight deck, blasting her hangar, killing 110 of her crew, and wounding 180. Brutally mauled, the "SARA" pulled out of the fleet and set a course across the Pacific for home. In the same attack escort-carrier BISMARCK SEA was struck by a suicide plane. The blast ignited a conflagration which exploded the ship's torpedoes. Bursting internally, the carrier capsized. Some 347 officers and men died in this disaster. The LUNGA POINT and the KEOKUK were also struck by *Kamikazes* during this raid. February 21, 1945, was the Navy's worst day off Iwo.

With the exception of AA gunnery and shore bombardments, the destroyers in the Iwo Jima area had little to do. Acting as lifeguards, they snatched a number of downed aviators from the sea, a rescue feat by GREGORY (Commander Bruce McCandless) being typical. In the morning of February 26 the GREGORY was patrolling a radar picket station off Iwo Jima. About 0900 the destroyer was directed to run at best speed to the rescue of three ENTERPRISE airmen adrift near-by in a rubber boat. The sea was misty under a lowering sky, and although four aircraft joined the hunt, it was mid-afternoon before the rubber boat was spotted. By that time the weather had cleared, and Jap batteries on Chichi Jima had sighted GREGORY. When a salvo landed 100 yards astern, the destroyer laid smoke and hiked seaward. The drifting airmen were sighted by a search plane at 1402, and GREGORY, maneuvering in, picked them up 40 minutes later. *"We have had a tendency to belittle Japanese gunnery,"* Commander McCandless observed. *"We would like to point out that there is one very hot battery . . . on Chichi Jima. There may be others."*

Destroyers COLHOUN and TERRY encountered some of these other "hot" batteries. Captained by Commander G. R. Wilson, COLHOUN was one of the destroyers off the island with Turner's transport fleet on "Dog Day" (February 19). Thereafter she worked like a dog as a radar picket, a fire-support ship, and an AA sharpshooter. Relieved of fire-support duty in the afternoon of February 27, the destroyer was attempting to clear a fouled anchor and get under way when she stumbled into a three-way collision with a transport and a freighter. COLHOUN staggered out of it with an ugly gash in her side. Emergency repairs were rushed by the crew as the ship lay at anchor off Tachiwa Point. And on the morning of March 1, while she was lying there, a Jap shore battery drew a bead and opened fire. Before COLHOUN could get under way, a shell struck her No. 2 stack, and a jag of shrapnel hit one torpedo, exploding its air flask. This blast caused considerable damage. Sixteen men were wounded, one of them fatally. Not that this destroyer did, but no ship could afford to ignore Japanese coast artillery.

Destroyer TERRY (Commander W. B. Moore) was hard hit by the gunners on Iwo. She participated in the invasion as a unit of Rear Admiral B. J. Rodgers' Task Force 54, a heavy gunfire and covering force. Early in the morning of March 1, TERRY was given a close shave by a Jap torpedo-bomber. The enemy, invisible in the dark, launched a "fish" which missed by a scant 50 yards. At sunrise TERRY steamed to a screening station off the north shore of Iwo. About 0720 she was suddenly fired upon by a concealed 6-inch battery which almost got her with the first salvo. TERRY tied on 27 knots to dash out of range while her gunners fired back at the flashes. At 0728 she caught a direct hit on the starboard side over the forward engine-room. The blast knocked out her starboard engine and damaged her steering controls. Eleven of the crew were slain and 19 wounded by the shell-burst.

By the evening of March 3, TERRY's wounds were patched and she was able to join a slow convoy bound for Saipan. With reference to the patching of

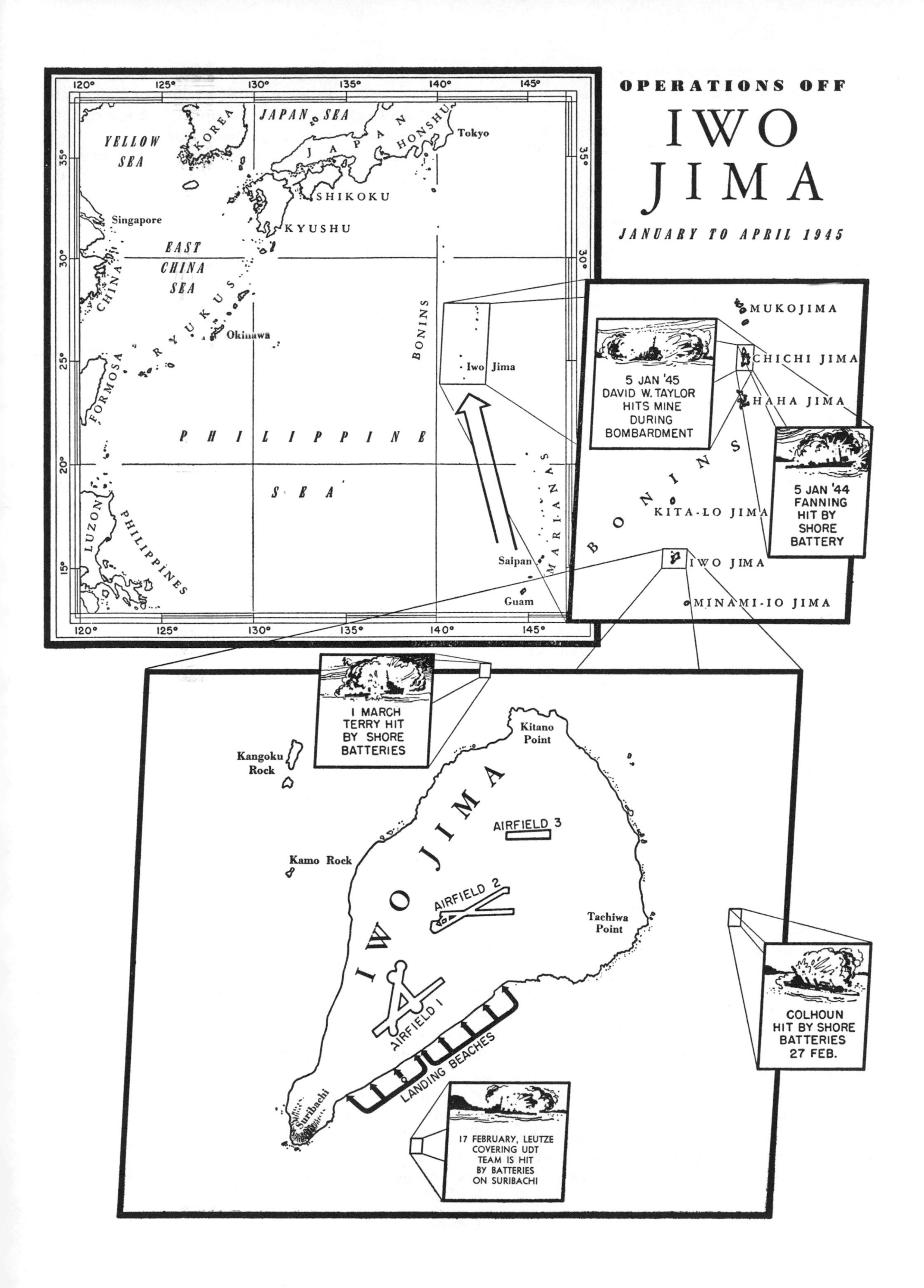

OPERATIONS OFF
IWO JIMA
JANUARY TO APRIL 1945
120° 125° 130° 135° 140° 145°
35° 30° 25° 20° 15°
YELLOW SEA
KOREA
JAPAN SEA
JAPAN
HONSHU
Tokyo
SHIKOKU
KYUSHU
Singapore
EAST CHINA SEA
CHINA
RYUKUS
Okinawa
FORMOSA
BONINS
Iwo Jima
PHILIPPINE SEA
MARIANAS
Saipan
Guam
LUZON
PHILIPPINES
MUKOJIMA
CHICHI JIMA
HAHA JIMA
KITA-LO JIMA
IWO JIMA
MINAMI-IO JIMA
5 JAN '45
DAVID W. TAYLOR
HITS MINE
DURING
BOMBARDMENT
5 JAN '44
FANNING
HIT BY
SHORE
BATTERY
I MARCH
TERRY HIT
BY SHORE
BATTERIES
Kangoku Rock
Kitano Point
Kamo Rock
Tachiwa Point
AIRFIELD 3
AIRFIELD 2
AIRFIELD 1
LANDING BEACHES
Suribachi
COLHOUN
HIT BY SHORE
BATTERIES
27 FEB.
17 FEBRUARY, LEUTZE
COVERING UDT
TEAM IS HIT
BY BATTERIES
ON SURIBACHI

wounded men, the destroyer's captain noted in the ship's Action Report:

> Particularly gratifying was the quality of the first-aid given the wounded by the crew members. This was remarked upon by the visiting Medical Officers as well as by our own. Time and again a doctor would get to a wounded man to find that his hemorrhaging had been checked, morphine given, and shock treatment skillfully applied. This degree of efficiency was achieved as a result of tedious hours of first-aid given to the whole crew in small groups over and over again. It paid off in human life.

But destroyer casualties were small compared to those of the Marines. By March 26, Marine casualties were close to 21,000, including some 4,900 slain. Secured as of that date, Iwo had cost the Corps the heaviest losses yet. Statistic: at Tarawa, Marine casualties had been 8.6 per cent; at Iwo Jima they were 32.6 per cent. Japanese losses at Iwo were close to 100 per cent. When the mopping up was over, the entire garrison, with the exception of some 200 prisoners, lay dead.

And U. S. Superforts were now flying from the island's airfields; Tokyo would soon be the target for fire raids that would turn the Japanese capital into a roaring bonfire. On one hand the Allies had gained a most important air base; on the other they had removed a menace from the Okinawa flank. "Operation Iceberg" could now go into high gear.

Late in March, 1945, the Fifth Fleet turned its bows toward the Nansei Shoto archipelago—and Okinawa.

Task Force Off Japan (DD's to the Rescue of Franklin)

The Ides of March found Task Force 58 steaming up from Ulithi to deliver a series of strikes on the Japanese home islands. The blows were calculated to clear the northern air for the "Iceberg" invasion fleet and to divert Imperial attention from Okinawa. Approaching Kyushu, Mitscher sent his planes in to bomb the daylights out of the Emperor's airdromes. The carrier airmen turned one field after another into a junkyard, and in the bargain wrecked a number of Jap warships which were lurking in the Inland Sea.

Hitting back at 0700 in the morning of March 19, Jap bombers caught Mitscher's task force about 50 miles off the Kyushu coast and dropped two 500-pounders on the carrier FRANKLIN just as her planes were taking off. One bomb went through the flight deck and burst in the hangar. FRANKLIN's aircraft began to blaze like blowtorches. Bombs and rockets started to explode. The detonations ruptured the ship's gasoline lines, and 40,000 gallons of high octane fed the flames. A magazine erupted. In a few minutes the vessel was a floating blast furnace.

Destroyers HICKOX, HUNT, MARSHALL, TINGEY, and MILLER, along with cruiser SANTA FE, stood in to the carrier's assistance. At 0800 MILLER (Lieutenant Commander D. L. Johnson) moved alongside the burning ship to take off Admirals Davidson and Bogan and their staffs for transfer to the carrier HANCOCK. While TINGEY mounted guard, the other DD's maneuvered around the FRANKLIN, rescuing men in the water.

Although FRANKLIN's predicament worsened by every minute of the morning, her skipper, Captain L. E. Gehres, rejected the idea of abandonment. SANTA FE drew alongside to aid the fire fighters, and Gehres directed her to stand off after some of the carriermen, acting without orders, leaped to the cruiser's deck.

At 1130 destroyer HICKOX was ordered to go alongside FRANKLIN's stern to rescue men trapped on the fantail. Flagship of Commander P. L. High, ComDesDiv 104, HICKOX made a neat job of it. Conned by her skipper, Commander J. H. Wesson, the destroyer advanced through a fog of smoke to nuzzle her bow against the hot ship.

Excerpt from HICKOX' Action Report:

> Put bow under after 40 mm. gun sponson to allow men to jump from FRANKLIN to HICKOX. Put mooring line from HICKOX bullnose to FRANKLIN after bitts to hold bow in. Rigged trolley line for stretcher between HICKOX No. 1 5-inch gun and FRANKLIN gun sponson. 11:45: HICKOX directed streams of water into after compartment on hanger deck level of FRANKLIN and appeared to extinguish major portion of fire. Observed numerous explosions on FRANKLIN which appeared to be ammunition exploding. 12:15: All men aboard from FRANKLIN's fan-tail. Two stretcher cases and 16 others. Backed clear. All fires seemed to be well under control. . . .

During the afternoon destroyer MILLER, again on the scene, went alongside the FRANKLIN to fight fires and take off wounded survivors. Jap aircraft put in an appearance, but the enemy bombers were driven off by fighter planes and an ack-ack barrage. The rescue work went steadily forward, with HUNT, TINGEY, and the other destroyers grabbing carriermen from the sea. All told, the DD's recovered about 850 of the FRANKLIN crew. Skippered by Commander J. D. McKinney, destroyer MARSHALL alone plucked 212 survivors from the water.

By evening the carrier's fires were almost smothered, the explosions were fizzling out, and cruiser PITTS-

BURGH had the charred ship in tow. The Navy and the American public would be thrilled by the story of FRANKLIN's survival—how she reached Ulithi, and from there traveled to Pearl and on to New York Navy Yard under her own steam. But it was a story saddened by her thousand casualties, including 832 dead.

HICKOX' Action Report furnishes another interesting glimpse into this life-saving effort:

> While HICKOX was lying to in an area where there were scattered survivors, use was made of the "bull horn" to tell the men whom we were not actually recovering that they were seen and would be picked up, and for them to start swimming slowly toward the ship but not to exhaust themselves. It is felt that this prevented some of the men from exhausting themselves by continued shouting or waving, or by trying to swim too fast toward the ship. . . .
>
> It was again well illustrated that if men who are forced to abandon ship make every effort to organize themselves in as large groups as possible, their chances of rescue are greatly increased. Aside from the morale effect they will have on each other, they will be seen at much greater distances, and their concerted shouting or whistle blowing will be very effective.

Commander Wesson also noted that his crew for the first time used "Flashburn Protective Cream" for the face and hands, and results were encouraging.

Minor as these last items may appear in the war panorama, they were of genuine interest to a destroyer Force which, at Okinawa, was soon to need every fire-fighting aid and rescue technique available.

"Iceberg" Opening Gun (DD's versus Kamikazes off Kerama Retto)

"Operation Iceberg" was bearing down on the Nansei Shoto archipelago throughout the last week in March, 1945. On the 24th the battleships of Task Force 58, under Vice Admiral W. A. Lee, treated the southeastern coast of Okinawa to a sledgehammer bombardment as minesweepers broomed the water inshore. This activity was a feint intended to draw enemy strength from the west coast beaches which were marked for the invasion landings.

Six days before invasion D-Day, an advance U. S. detachment under Admiral I. N. Kiland skirted the southern tip of Okinawa to seize Kerama Retto and the Keise Group, island clusters lying west of Naha. No more than 20 miles from Okinawa, Kerama Retto would provide the Navy with a seaplane base on the enemy's southern flank, and a sheltered anchorage for backfield invasion shipping.

Kiland's detachment steamed in with the 77th Infantry Division, and the local garrison, taken completely by surprise, burrowed into the hills and remained "underground" like a prairie dog colony—a situation which at once gave the invaders the upper hand. But the capture of Kerama Retto was not easy in any sense of the word. That morning the "Divine Wind" blew. Its hot breath scorched the destroyer KIMBERLY, the first DD to be thus blistered in the "Iceberg" campaign.

At 0615 in the morning of March 26, the KIMBERLY (Commander J. D. Whitfield) was proceeding to her radar picket station off Kerama Retto. As she steamed through the morning twilight, her lookouts sighted two Jap "Vals" apparently headed for the transport area. The destroyer opened fire on the planes, and they turned away. Commander Whitfield gave the order to cease fire. His Action Report goes on:

> Almost simultaneously with "cease firing," one of the Vals peeled off and began to close the range on a converging but nearly opposite course. Fire was immediately reopened and the rudder put over hard right to maintain all guns bearing as the relative target-bearing rapidly dropped aft. During this phase of the approach, the fire control problem was one of an extremely high deflection rate which the Japanese pilot further complicated by resorting to radical maneuvers including zooming, climbing, slipping, skidding, accelerating, decelerating, and even slow rolling. He continued to close the range on a circling course indicating his intention to get on "our tail," and further indicating to all observers his ultimate intention.
>
> By this time the range had closed to 4,000 yards and all bearing 40 mm. mounts opened fire. The plane was now in a vertical right bank, circling to come in from astern. The target seemed to be completely surrounded with 5-inch bursts and 40 mm. tracers. At about 1,500 yards range on relative bearing 170° he leveled off and came straight in at an altitude of about 150 feet, performing continuous right and left skids.
>
> The ship was still turning with full right rudder, but the target skidded to remain inside the ship's wake. At 1,200 yards all the bearing 20 mm. guns opened fire, and at about this same time the previously faint line of smoke coming from the plane became a positive stream of black smoke, but still the target kept coming.
>
> Now only the after guns would bear, and each 5-inch salvo blasted the after 20 mm. crews off their feet. In spite of this difficulty, at the instant the Val passed over the stern, the 20 mm. guns had managed to empty one complete magazine. The plane was now about 100 feet in the air and apparently headed for the bridge, with 40 mm. guns No. 3 and No. 5 still firing at maximum rate. Just as the plane reached a point above 40 mm. gun No. 5, it went out of control and fell nearly vertically between 5-inch mounts No. 3 and No. 4, crashing into the still rapidly firing guns of 40 mm. mount No. 5.

Intensity of the resulting explosion and nature of

the damage indicated that the plane was armed with a bomb, perhaps a 200-pounder, fitted with a virtually instantaneous fuze. Commander Whitfield summarized the blast-damage as follows:

> Ship's complement reduced by 18%. Two 5-inch 38 guns put out of commission; one 40 mm. gun missing; effectiveness of 20 mm. battery reduced by at least 30% (Mark 14 sights inoperative). All radar and fire control spare parts destroyed. Two K-guns and five roller-loaders out of commission. Smoke-screen generator controls and air supply demolished. Two fuel oil service tanks pierced and buckled.

In his report Commander Whitfield noted that *"the failure of the Val to reach a more vital part of the ship"* was directly attributable to the steadfast courage and crack marksmanship of the gunners who flailed at the plane as it roared in. All fires were extinguished within five minutes of the crash—fast work by damage controlmen. And half a minute after the *Kamikaze* hit the deck, the KIMBERLY gunners at undamaged batteries were training their weapons on the second "Val."

Intensive first-aid training proved invaluable. Although one of the ship's three Corpsmen was killed, the Medical Officer had previously trained a number of men for first-aid work. Several gunners administered morphine to badly injured shipmates. The crew of a 40 mm. saved the life of a man whose leg had been torn away. A Radarman successfully administered plasma without the benefit of previous experience. The 57 of the crew who were wounded found themselves in good hands.

Four men were slain by the *Kamikaze* blast. The death-toll would certainly have been higher but for preventive measures taken by the crew. As reported by Commander Whitfield:

> An agreement had been established between the First Lieutenant and the Chief Engineer in which the former was to notify the Engineer if a suicide attack appeared probable so that the Engineer could shut down all engine-room ventilation. The Engineer further planned that whenever he heard the 20 mm. guns fire, he would close off the ventilation without word from the First Lieutenant. As a result of this planning, the engine spaces ventilation supply was secured and undoubtedly saved the after engine-room control personnel from serious burns which would have undoubtedly been caused by flames being sucked down the ventilation intakes.

Altogether KIMBERLY acquitted herself well in this *Kamikaze* battle. In the afternoon of March 31 she steamed southward, Ulithi-bound for repairs. With her went destroyer O'BRIEN, another *Kamikaze* victim.

The O'BRIEN (Commander W. W. Outerbridge) was struck on the day after the Kerama Retto landings. Both ship and captain were hardened battle veterans, and some of the crew had been in the war since pioneer days. The *Kamikaze* off Kerama Retto was the toughest antagonist the destroyer had yet encountered.

At 0545 in the morning of March 27, O'BRIEN was detached from the screen at Kerama Retto and ordered to report to Fire Support Unit No. 3 off Okinawa. At 0618 she received a report of aircraft in the offing. All hands manned battle stations. About five minutes later a bevy of planes, flying in loose formation, drifted overhead. Some of the planes were identified as friendly. Then a dive-bomber peeled off and swooped down at the ship. Outerbridge called for hard right rudder, and the destroyermen opened fire with 40 and 20 mm. batteries. The plane crashed in the water close aboard the ship's starboard quarter.

At 0624 a second plane plummeted at the O'BRIEN and smashed into the destroyer's port side just above the main deck and aft of the No. 1 stack. The blast, evidently the work of a 500-pound bomb, sent the ship reeling. Flames lunged from the wrecked superstructure. All radars were put out of commission. The TBS was knocked out. The starboard twin 40 mm. was shattered; the port twin was crushed; the forward fireroom had to be abandoned by the steaming watch. The ship's sonar gear went out, as did the two torpedo directors. All facilities in the C.I.C. were thus incapacitated. Fifty of the ship's crew were killed, and 76 were wounded. Nothing short of miraculous damage-control work contained the fires topside and kept O'BRIEN going.

On March 31 the battered destroyer teamed up with KIMBERLY for the run to Ulithi. Endorsing the ship's Action Report, Captain B. R. Harrison, ComDesRon 6, made the following observation: *"This report again emphasizes the fact that lookouts must be constantly on the alert. The fact that friendly planes are sighted in the area is no guarantee that suiciders are not around. Early warning by lookouts of this type of attack offers the best chance of frustrating it."*

Two other "small boys" were struck by the mad suiciders off Kerama Retto. These were destroyer-escort FOREMAN (Lieutenant Commander W. J. Carey, Jr.), flagship of Commander F. W. Hawes, ComCortDiv 40, and destroyer PORTERFIELD (Commander D. W. Wulzen). PORTERFIELD had a hair-raising shave; skimming her bridge, a *Kamikaze* flicked off the SC radar antenna. FOREMAN's shave was even closer. In company with destroyer-escort WITTER, she was screening cruiser INDIANAPOLIS in a fire-support area about five miles north of Kerama Retto. Two enemy planes jumped the ships at 0623. Both *Kamikazes* were shot to Kingdom Come. But before that happened, the first plane, a "Val," headed for FOREMAN in a long, toboggan-slide dive that seemed to last for an hour. The plane grazed the DE's starboard bow, carried away a lifeline, and knocked one man off his feet. The Grim Reaper merely nicked the ship's chin.

Still another destroyer was damaged off Kerama Retto—the MURRAY (Commander P. L. De Vos). In the morning of the 27th, a "Jill" torpedo-bomber plunged out of a low cloud at a range of about 3,000 yards, and raced at the MURRAY. MURRAY's skipper ordered emergency full speed ahead; the destroyer sprinted across the water; the gunners laced the plane with 40 mm. At 200 yards the airman dropped a torpedo. Commander De Vos ordered full left rudder to evade the "fish" and the plane. The "Jill" missed the ship by inches, hopping over the superstructure to crash in flames about 200 yards on the port beam. But the torpedo struck hard—so hard that it passed through the ship like a bullet through a tin box, and exploded close aboard on the port side. Evidently, released at close range, it had failed to arm properly.

The luck did not hold for the MURRAY man who was killed and the four of her crew who were seriously wounded. But the destroyer, herself, got off lightly. Damage controlmen quickly plugged the holes in the hull, and the ship was able to maintain station until she was relieved at 0730.

So the "Divine Wind" howled at Kerama Retto in gusts which hinted of the storm to come. It would blow its hardest at Okinawa. But the first destroyer lost in "Operation Iceberg" was downed by an undersea weapon. Victim was the U.S.S. HALLIGAN.

Loss of U.S.S. Halligan

Destroyer HALLIGAN (Lieutenant Commander E. T. Grace) was a member of Fire Support Unit 2 working along the southwest coast of Okinawa. The unit's assignment was to bombard the Okinawa beach and cover minesweepers which were combing the waters inshore.

At dusk on March 26, HALLIGAN had orders to take a night patrol station located off the coast in that region. Minesweeping was still in progress between Kerama Retto and Okinawa, and all ships had been warned to give unswept areas a scrupulous avoidance. But doom struck HALLIGAN as she moved to her patrol station. At 1835 the destroyer was lifted half out of the tide by a monstrous explosion that sent a pillar of fire towering in the twilight. Men and scraps of deck machinery were hurled overside, and the ship's hull was split open by the blast. Below decks officers and men were slain outright, and many more were drowned as the sea engulfed the stricken vessel.

So swiftly did HALLIGAN go down that nearly half her crew went under with her. With the exception of two ensigns, the ship's entire officer complement—including her captain, Lieutenant Commander Grace—perished in the disaster. One hundred and sixty-six men survived the sinking.

The explosion that destroyed HALLIGAN was caused by a submarine torpedo, a drifting mine, or a moored mine—there could be no certainty as to which. But available evidence suggested a moored mine as the destructive agent. And the area in which the ship was steaming when she was blasted had not been declared swept.

There remains the question of why HALLIGAN steamed headlong into an unswept area. Was she there through navigational error? Investigating something? Somebody failed to get the word? The answer will never be known. All officers in a position to know were lost.

FRANKLIN RESCUE

CHAPTER 37

OKINAWA INVASION

(Iceberg: Destroyers' Hottest Mission!)

"Love Day"—D-Day for Okinawa—fell on Easter Sunday. Beautiful weather for the East China Sea. Cloudless sky; smooth, jade water; promise of a sparkling spring morning, with a hint of gardenia in the air. At home there would be the somnolent clang of church bells—sunrise services. But to the men in "Operation Iceberg" the day was just April 1, 1945— ironically designated "Love Day."

In the pre-dawn gloom the "Iceberg" expeditionary forces had taken up position off the Okinawa coast. Marked for the landings were beaches below Cape Zampa on the west shore. For five days these beaches had been "softened up" in the usual fire-and-iron manner by preliminary bombings and shore bombardments. Meanwhile, Underwater Demolition Teams had gone in to dynamite obstacles and cut away snares. A force of 75 minesweepers and 45 auxiliary craft had combed the entire perimeter of the island's southern coast. During all these preliminary activities Okinawa's shore guns were as silent as though they had been spiked; not a shot was fired in the island's defense. The shore remained in sinister silence.

The invaders did not know that General Ushijima had concentrated his forces in southern Okinawa on a line athwart the island, between the Hagushi beaches and Naha. They did not know that this line, with ancient Shuri Castle as its keystone, contained a system of deep tunnels and limestone caves reinforced with ferroconcrete that made a warren almost invulnerable to air bombardment and naval barrage. Nevertheless, the "Iceberg" leaders knew that Okinawa was a Japanese Gibraltar, and that its capture would be resisted to the last.

To subdue and secure this Nansei Shoto bastion, Admiral Nimitz had allocated some 1,450 United States vessels manned by well over half a million Americans. Operating at the southern end of the Nansei Shoto chain a British Carrier Force under Vice Admiral Sir B. M. Rawlings added its weight to the immense armada.

Directly off Okinawa Admiral Turner's amphibious force contained 1,213 ships carrying 182,000 assault troops under command of General Simon Bolivar Buckner, U.S.A. A total of 318 combatant vessels were on the "Iceberg" front. Several European invasions had covered wider fronts. But the Atlantic and Mediterranean transport hauls were relatively short compared with the trans-Pacific lifts which carried the "Iceberg" forces and their supplies from America, Hawaii, Espiritu Santo, Guadalcanal, and other distant bases to Okinawa. Altogether, "Operation Iceberg" employed the largest fleet yet assembled in naval history—over 40 carriers, 10 battleships, scores of cruisers, submarines, minesweepers, landing craft, patrol vessels, salvage vessels, and auxiliaries. And more than 148 American destroyers and destroyer-escorts were in the armada that fought the Okinawa campaign.

As has been stated, from a naval standpoint the story of that campaign is the story of those American DD's and DE's that bore the brunt of the sea-air battle. Allied carrier groups stood far offshore; bombardment groups came and went. On blockade duty,

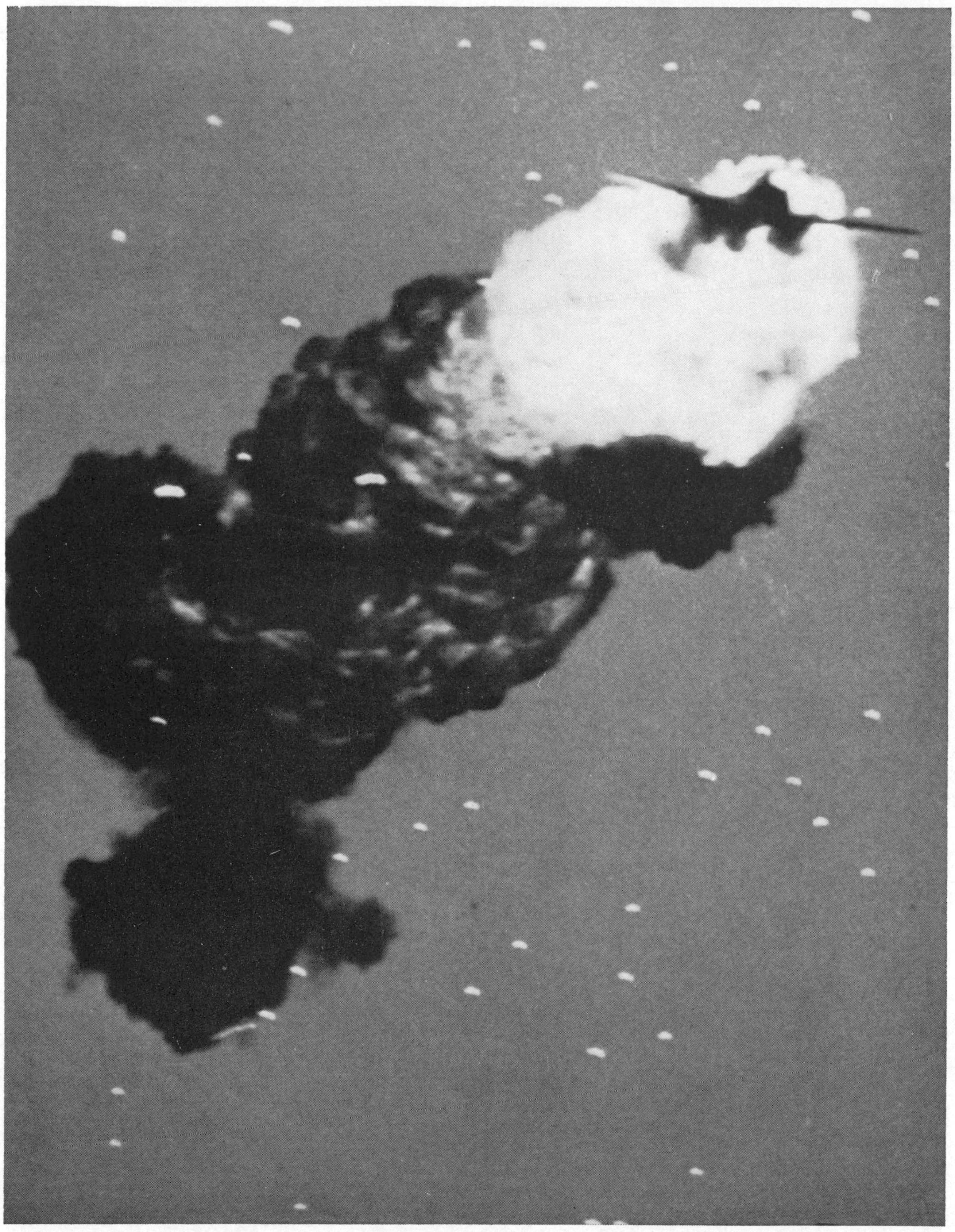

Even the kamikaze was not enough! . . . Here was the test, and Okinawa was the testing ground. The Japanese employed the most effective weapon against surface naval units that had been devised up to that time. Weapons will improve, but no guidance system is likely to surpass a living pilot. Despite all that, the Navy rolled with the punch and fought through to final victory.

Stranded on Ose Reef off Okinawa, Longshaw (DD 559) was pounded to pieces by concealed coastal batteries when the ship could neither fight nor run. For four days and nights this destroyer had supported the American troops ashore with call-fire bombardment of designated beach targets. Then, on the morning of May 18, 1945, somebody was careless in plotting the ship's

position and she grounded hard on the reef. Neither her own engines nor the added efforts of the tug Arikara could free her. The Jap guns found a sitting duck target. Eleven officers and 66 men perished with their ship; nine others died of their wounds. The ninth destroyer lost at Okinawa, Longshaw, a charred and shattered wreck, was sunk by friendly naval gun fire.

With her hull crushed by a kamikaze that exploded close aboard, William D. Porter flooded and sank, but not until the LCI's had taken off her entire crew.

This spectacular damage resulted from two kamikaze hits on Lindsey (DM 32). The punishment that these tin-clads took and survived attests to the heroic qualities of their crews and the toughness of the ships themselves.

Carriers were the prime target for the kamikazes. Although it looks as if the Bunker Hill must certainly be lost, neither she nor any other Essex-class carrier was sunk by the suiciders, thanks to superb damage control.

Detroyer guarding the kamikazed Intrepid. Over 2,500 Japanese pilots were sacrificed in suicide missions. Many were shot down, many found a target, but even methods of utter desperation could not turn the tide of battle.

Casualties from Bunker Hill are removed to hospital ship Bountiful. A high-speed turn dumped burning oil off her decks to save the carrier. Escorting destroyers in foreground are Hobby (DD 610) and The Sullivans (DD 537).

American submarines met practically no opposition. But the destroyer forces on the "Iceberg" front were in there fighting for days and weeks on end. The "small boys" got the man-size job at Okinawa. And they put up a giant-size effort to accomplish that job. The DD's and DE's which were engaged in that effort are listed on this page.

Most of the destroyers and destroyer-escorts on the "Iceberg" front worked as radar pickets or patrol vessels in the area screen. Covering the approaches to Okinawa, they mounted guard at radar picket stations positioned in a ring encircling the island, or patrolled the convoy approaches and served as A/S and anti-aircraft guards on a perimeter which embraced the transport area. These picket and patrol ships constituted Task Flotilla 5, under command of a veteran destroyerman, Commodore Frederick Moosbrugger.

The "Iceberg" mission of the DD's and DE's in Task Flotilla 5 is best detailed in the words of Commodore Moosbrugger, whose official summarization is quoted herewith:

(A) *Radar Pickets and Supports.*

Distant radar pickets were stationed between 40 and 70 miles from the transport area in the direction of the approach of enemy aircraft from the Japanese Island chain, China bases, and Formosa. Close radar pickets were stationed 20 to 25 miles from the transport area. In addition, stations in the outer and inner anti-submarine screen were designated as radar picket stations. Their special duty consisted of detecting, tracking, and reporting on aircraft in the vicinity of the transport area.

The function of the distant radar pickets was to give early warning of enemy air raids and surface craft, and to perform the duties of fighter direction. Specially equipped fighter-director destroyers with fighter-director teams embarked were used as fighter-director ships. These fighter-director destroyers controlled such units of the CAP as were assigned them by the central fighter-director unit embarked in the ELDORADO *or other headquarters ship. Initially a radar picket group was composed of one FD (fighter-director) destroyer and two LCS supports. Each LCS was stationed one third the distance to an adjacent radar picket station to increase the probability of detection of low-flying planes and barge or other surface movement along the island chain. In case of attack the supports closed the radar picket for mutual protection. This formation was later changed, and the LCS's were stationed with the picket as close supports.*

DESTROYERS AND DESTROYER-ESCORTS AT OKINAWA

(MARCH 26-JUNE 21, 1945)

Destroyers

Ammen	Gregory	Paul Hamilton
Anthony	Guest	Picking
Aulick	Hall	Porterfield
Bache	Harry E. Hubbard	Preston
Beale	Hart	Prichett
Bennett	Herndon	Pringle
Bennion	Heywood L. Edwards	Purdy
Boyd	Howorth	Putnam
Bradford	Hudson	Ralph Talbot
Braine	Hugh W. Hadley	Rooks
Brown	Hutchins	Rowe
Bryant	Hyman	Russell
Bush	Ingersoll	Shubrick
Caperton	Ingraham	Smalley
Cassin Young	Irwin	Sproston
Charles Ausburne	Isherwood	Stack
Charles J. Badger	Kimberly	Stanly
Claxton	Knapp	Sterett
Cogswell	Laffey	Stoddard
Colhoun	Lang	Stormes
Compton	Lansdowne	Thatcher
Converse	Laws	Twiggs
Cowell	Little	Van Valkenburgh
Daly	Lowry	Wadsworth
Douglas H. Fox	Luce	Walke
Drexler	Mannert L. Abele	Watts
Dyson	Massey	Wickes
Evans	Metcalf	Wilkes
Farenholt	Moale	Willard Keith
Fullam	Morris	Wilson
Foote	Morrison	Wm. D. Porter
Gainard	Mullany	Wren
	Mustin	

Destroyer-Escorts

Abercrombie	Gendreau	Riddle
Bebas	Gilligan	Samuel S. Miles
Bowers	Grady	Sederstrom
Bright	Griswold	Seid
Carlson	Halloran	Snyder
Connolly	Hemminger	Stern
Cross	Henry A. Wiley	Swearer
Crouter	La Prade	Tills
D. M. Cummings	LeRay Wilson	Tisdale
Edmonds	Manlove	Vammen
Eisele	McClelland	Walter C. Wann
England	Metivier	Wesson
Fair	Oberrender	Whitehurst
Fieberling	O'Neill	Willmarth
Finnegan	Paul G. Baker	Witter
Fleming	Rall	Wm. C. Cole
Foreman	R. W. Suesens	Wm. Seiverling

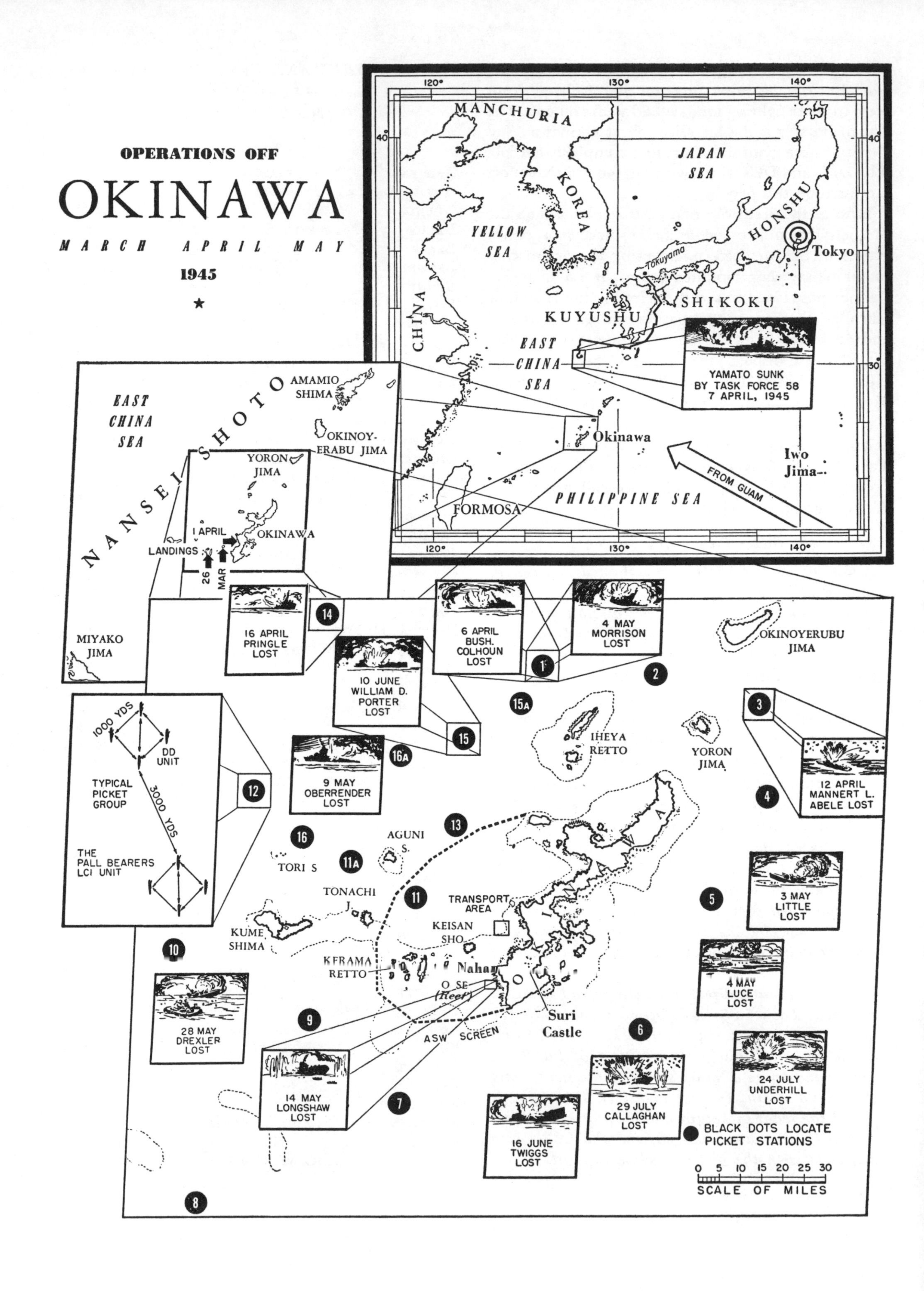
OPERATIONS OFF
OKINAWA
MARCH APRIL MAY
1945
MANCHURIA
JAPAN SEA
KOREA
YELLOW SEA
HONSHU
Tokyo
Tokuyama
CHINA
SHIKOKU
KUYUSHU
EAST CHINA SEA
YAMATO SUNK BY TASK FORCE 58 7 APRIL, 1945
Okinawa
Iwo Jima
FROM GUAM
FORMOSA
PHILIPPINE SEA
NANSEI SHOTO
AMAMIO SHIMA
OKINOY-ERABU JIMA
YORON JIMA
OKINAWA
1 APRIL
LANDINGS
26 MAR
MIYAKO JIMA
16 APRIL PRINGLE LOST
10 JUNE WILLIAM D. PORTER LOST
6 APRIL BUSH. COLHOUN LOST
4 MAY MORRISON LOST
OKINOYERUBU JIMA
IHEYA RETTO
YORON JIMA
12 APRIL MANNERT L. ABELE LOST
9 MAY OBERRENDER LOST
1000 YDS
DD UNIT
TYPICAL PICKET GROUP
3000 YDS
THE PALL BEARERS LCI UNIT
AGUNI S.
TORI S
TONACHI J.
TRANSPORT AREA
KEISAN SHO
KUME SHIMA
KERAMA RETTO
Naha
O SE (Reef)
3 MAY LITTLE LOST
4 MAY LUCE LOST
28 MAY DREXLER LOST
ASW SCREEN
Suri Castle
14 MAY LONGSHAW LOST
24 JULY UNDERHILL LOST
29 JULY CALLAGHAN LOST
16 JUNE TWIGGS LOST
BLACK DOTS LOCATE PICKET STATIONS
0 5 10 15 20 25 30
SCALE OF MILES

The vital importance of maintaining radar picket groups on station can be attested by the fact that the bulk of the defense of the Okinawa amphibious operation evolved around the raid reporting and fighter direction exercised by these exposed fighter-director ships and their supporting elements. It became apparent early in the operation that the brunt of the enemy air attacks would be absorbed by the radar pickets and units of the outer A/S screen, therefore it was considered necessary to increase the number of units on each radar picket station and provide a protective CAP over each radar picket. The possibility of reducing the number of occupied radar picket stations was seriously examined, but the number could not be reduced until after shore based radar stations were in operation.

During the first days of the operation there were insufficient destroyers available to assign more than one destroyer to each occupied picket station. This was occasioned by other required employment such as (1) the necessity of assigning destroyers to screen transport groups, tractor groups, and covering groups in night retirement; (2) assignment of destroyers to task groups in awaiting areas; (3) the necessity of having units available to meet emergencies. However, the strength of the radar picket stations was increased by assigning all available LCS, LSM(R), and PGM types as close supports. Later, when night retirement was discontinued and groups returned from awaiting areas, additional destroyers were assigned as radar picket supports. Beginning 10 April it was possible to assign two destroyers and four small support craft to the more exposed radar picket stations. Continued damage to units prevented increasing the strength further until reenforcements arrived from other areas and the number of picket stations was reduced. Finally on 19 May it became possible to maintain at least three destroyers and four LCS's on each of the five occupied stations.

Destroyer-escorts and similar type were considered as picket supports. Their inadequate anti-aircraft armament precluded exposing them to the vicious air attacks experienced on radar picket stations. None of the destroyer-escorts with the increased armament of two 5-inch, ten 40 mm. and ten 20 mm. guns were at the objective.

Continued efforts were made to obtain a protective CAP of from four to six planes for each picket station. This special CAP was to be employed solely for local picket protection, reporting directly to the radar picket on a special frequency. It was entirely separate from the regular CAP. Sufficient planes were not available at the objective to supply the desired, protective CAP, but commencing 14 April the TAF (Tactical Air Force) was able to maintain a two-plane protective CAP over three picket stations, and later over five stations.

In the early stages Radar Picket Stations 1, 2, 3, 4, 7, 10, 12, and 14 were filled, with number 9 later when more warning was thought necessary against low-flying planes approaching Kerama Retto from southwest. On 16 May, with the completion of shore-based radar installations on Hedo Saki and Ie Shima, the number of occupied radar picket stations was reduced to five (Stations 5, 7, 9, 15, and 16.)

Due to damage to fighter-director ships it was necessary to continuously equip additional ships with fighter-director radio and associated equipment, and in some ships, not so equipped, with suitable visual fighter-direction stations. . . .

A number of formations were used in the course of the operation. The typical normal cruising formation used with a group of three or more destroyers and four LCS's under the tactical command of a squadron or division commander consisted of a destroyer unit concentrated in an anti-aircraft circular formation with ships equally spaced, distance between ships 1,000 yards, and an LCS unit similarly disposed, with distance between ships 500 yards or less. The LCS unit under the direct tactical command of the senior LCS commander would patrol along a track designated by the officer in tactical command of the picket group. The destroyer unit would patrol as directed . . . keeping within 3,000 yards of the LCS unit. . . .

(B) *Outer Anti-Submarine Screen*

The outer A/S screen consisted of a closed area screen extending from Ie Shima around Kerama Retto to the southern tip of Okinawa. It further enclosed the southeastern half of Okinawa during demonstration and fire support activities in that area, and to the northward of Ie Shima during activities incident to its capture. This closed area screen permitted unescorted movement of ships between Hagushi, Ie Shima, Kerama Retto, and the Eastern Beaches. Since it also enclosed the bombardment ships it afforded the most economical assignment of screening ships. Ships of the outer screen were at a distance of from 20 to 25 miles from the transport area. This permitted timely detection of enemy aircraft that had successfully evaded the radar pickets and their CAP.

Warning given by the outer screen of the approach of enemy aircraft was of great value, espe-

cially at night, as it alerted the inner screen and transports and permitted blanketing the transports with a protective smoke screen in time. The outer screen served as an additional buffer against enemy air attacks. It was usual procedure for the enemy planes to expend their bombs, torpedoes, and themselves against the outer screen rather than against the ships in the transport area. Ships of this screen shot down many planes and absorbed much punishment. In their exposed positions, with 7,000 yards between units, they were out of mutual supporting range.

When it became apparent that the submarine threat was relatively minor, the outer screen was formed into what was designated as "Dusk AA Formation." In this formation, units of the outer screen concentrated in pairs or groups of three, and either patrolled their combined A/S stations in company or concentrated and headed toward a point in the transport area until at a certain distance from the inner A/S screen, and then resumed patrol in company parallel to the inner screening stations. "Dusk AA Formation" habitually was taken at one hour before sunset and normal stations resumed at one hour after sunset. This formation was also taken when heavy air attacks were expected.

(C) *Transport AA Screen*

When air attacks were expected, an anti-aircraft screen was thrown around the transport area. In effect, it consisted of two screens: one composed of destroyer types which had been in the transport area for logistics, maintenance, etc., and the second composed of LCI-LCS types not otherwise employed. The LCI-LCS types were equally disposed on, and patrolled on, an arc 700 yards to the seaward of the transports. The destroyer type patrolled on an arc 1,500 yards from transports. This was primarily a day screen. At night the LCI-LCS type took smoke stations or special anti-suicide boat patrols; the destroyer types anchored around the edge of the transport area.

(D) *Anti-Small Craft and Anti-Suicide Boat Patrols*

LCI and LCS patrols were maintained along shores of Okinawa to prevent enemy barge and small boat movement along the coast and to detect and destroy suicide-boats, motor torpedo-boats, and swimmers. A destroyer type patrolled a mile to the seaward of each group of four to five, in support and as a source of illumination. The Commanding Officer of the destroyer type acted as Officer in Tactical Command of the group. In addition to the above, a number of LCS's patrolled on a line approximately perpendicular to the shore line on the flanks of the transport areas. Small minesweepers were stationed as close inshore as practicable at critical locations, such as off Naha Harbor.

Twenty-three destroyers worked with the fire-support groups which bombarded the Okinawa beaches in the interval between dawn and H-Hour of D-Day. At 0830 the troops began to land on the designated six-mile stretch of Hagushi foreshore.

There was virtually no opposition. By nightfall of April 1 the advance guards had seized the Yontan and Kadena airfields. About 50,000 soldiers and Marines were ashore. "Love Day" had been practically bloodless. But by morning of April 2, Buckner's troops were clashing with the outposts of the Shuri Line. During the next three days the land battle steadily developed. And on April 6 the *Kamikaze* hurricane broke over the sea in full fury.

Down from Kyushu and the upper Nansei Shoto islands came the planes—"Vals" and "Zekes," "Bettys" and "Oscars" and "Jills." Some were new, and some had been modernized, but many were old-timers, aged and battle-scarred, rigged especially for suicide jobs and carrying just enough gas for a one-way trip to doom. As they approached Okinawa on April 6, many of these *Kikusui* pilots were shot down by intercepting planes. However, about 200 broke through the screen. Not to live, but hoping to die.

Weaving and skidding, barrel-rolling and looping, they descended on the "Iceberg" forces at Hagushi Beach.

The ordeal began on that day of April 6—a day which might well have been designated DD-Day—"Destroyer Day." At Okinawa the shore was afire. The sky was afire. The sea was afire. Plane after plane was blown to extinction by destroyer gunners fighting for their lives. One ship after another was blasted by the mad aviators of the Mikado, seeking death for the glory of the god-Emperor. Destroyer MULLANY was hit. NEWCOMB was hit. LEUTZE was hit. HOWORTH was hit. HYMAN was hit. MORRIS was hit. HAYNSWORTH was hit. Destroyer-escort FIEBERLING was hit. HARRISON was scorched by a near miss. And in this hell of fire and death, two destroyers, each struck by two or more *Kamikazes,* went flaming and exploding to the bottom.

The destroyers slain were the U.S.S. BUSH and the U.S.S. COLHOUN.

Loss of U.S.S. Bush

Leaving Leyte on March 27, 1945, the BUSH (Commander R. E. Westholm) steamed north, eventually to occupy No. 1 Picket Station, which was located 51 miles north of Okinawa. On April 2, the destroyer PRICHETT reported to relieve her, and BUSH proceeded to Kerama Retto for fuel. On the next day, word was received that the PRICHETT had been seriously damaged by a suicide plane. BUSH was at once ordered back on station.

From April 3 to April 5 the Japs gave the destroyer a nasty time. She succeeded in repelling the air attacks and in warning the task force of impending strikes. Her luck ended on April 6. During the early hours of that day the destroyer took four different targets under fire, shooting down one. But the attackers were persistent, and at midday they swarmed all over the ship.

Shortly after 1500, just when the third raid in half an hour was driven off, a lone Jap suicider came streaking in about 30 feet above the water. The pilot ran into a streak of bullets and shells. Fragments broke away from his plane. But accurate fire could not deter him. The *Kamikaze* crashed with a huge explosion at deck level on the ship's starboard side between No. 1 and No. 2 stacks. A torpedo or bomb exploded in the forward engine-room with such force that a six-foot section of engine-room blower, weighing about 4,000 pounds, was flung into the air high enough to knock off the radar antenna and land on the port wing of the bridge. The bursting plane scattered firebrands across the deck, and flame spurted from the wreckage.

The fires were beaten down by damage-control crews, and water-tight integrity was preserved sufficiently to keep the vessel afloat. Destroyer COLHOUN came in from a near-by picket station to offer assistance. Then, at 1700, while all hands were battling to save the BUSH, a flight of 10 to 15 Jap planes swept in. The COLHOUN was hit immediately, and the BUSH received her second smash 25 minutes later. This *Kamikaze* crash nearly cut her in two. At 1745 a third *Kamikaze* plummeted into the blazing destroyer. That was the end of BUSH. The ship broke up and sank about 1830.

Four LCS's and several other craft searched the seascape for survivors. By daybreak of the 7th some 246 of the crew were recovered. Eighty-seven officers and men were killed in the murderous action, and 42 were wounded. Among those who died in BUSH was Commander J. S. Willis, ComDesDiv 48.

Loss of U.S.S. Colhoun

About 1600 in that volcanic afternoon, while destroyer COLHOUN was steaming to the aid of stricken BUSH, the suicide onslaught crescendoed to its height. All up and down the Okinawa coast the rabid *Kamikazes* were striking. Trees of smoke grew everywhere on the seascape—smoke from burning planes—smoke from burning ships. COLHOUN maneuvered through this forest of death, all hands at hair-trigger, those topside watching the sky, those below concentrating on engines and instruments. This was it! Never before had these destroyermen seen a situation as "it."

In the C.I.C. the team sweated through a bedlam of calls, signals, orders, reports. "Sparks" could not keep up with the frantic radio. On the radar screen was a hailstorm—"bogies" and "bandits" appearing from all directions. Over TBS came a shouting babel, insanely frenzied by sporadic interjections of static. Voices from the air: "Lamppost, this is Lovebird. I see bogey one four zero. Do you concur? Over." Answer: "Hello, Lovebird. This is Lamppost. Affirmative. Raid coming in. Out."

COLHOUN was attacked as she stood by BUSH, offering what little help she could. Across the sky came the Jap planes, 13 of them. Down came the suiciders in screaming power dives.

They picked on two tough ships—BUSH, a veteran with a fine combat record; COLHOUN, skippered by Commander G. R. Wilson—that same George Rees Wilson who had captained hard-bitten CHEVALIER in the Solomons.

On board wounded BUSH the AA guns blazed with unstinted fury. COLHOUN's gunners hurled 5-inch thunderbolts, and pumped a firehose stream of 40 and 20 mm. at the diving madmen. Injured though she was, BUSH probably got several. And COLHOUN blew five *Kamikazes* to blazes. But four of the planes smashed into Wilson's ship in a mass murder-and-suicide assault that no destroyer could withstand.

One crashing plane threw a searing sheet of fire across COLHOUN's superstructure. Another struck on the bow with a dazzling burst that opened up the forecastle as a hammer-smash would open a melon. Skimming in low, *Kamikazes* three and four exploded against the ship's side, showering the vessel with fire, water, blazing gasoline, and debris.

Topside and below decks, bluejackets died in the inferno or were drowned at their posts by the inrushing flood. But for all this beating, COLHOUN's human casualties were less than those suffered by many another *Kamikaze*-assailed ship. As the vessel wallowed in flames, her skipper backed her into the wind to flag the fire toward her forecastle and clear the bridge of smoke. Damage-control crews struggled to shore up bulkheads and plug spurting leaks. As the ship gradually settled, guns, anchor, torpedoes, and other topside weights were jettisoned. By dusk the fires were confined, and the work of courageous seamen had prevented a disastrous blow-up of the forward magazines. COLHOUN was still afloat when the ship she had tried to save went under.

About five hours later COLHOUN, herself, went under. Wilson fought to save her as he had fought to save CHEVALIER. But the battle proved hopeless. After the fourth crash, Wilson had decided to abandon ship except for a skeleton crew. When CASSIN YOUNG approached, she was told that COLHOUN could hold on for a time, and she was urged to hunt for BUSH survivors. LCS-84 stood by COLHOUN to remove some of the crew. Then YOUNG tried to tow, but the line parted. Electrical fires broke out. By 2300 the sea was sizzling over the redhot griddle of the main deck, and the ship had listed heavily to starboard. Leaving the charred and mangled bodies of slain shipmates to man her to the last, the COLHOUN party finally went overside.

Rescue vessels were waiting. The darkness closed in around the abandoned destroyer. CASSIN YOUNG stood off to bury her with gunfire. About 2330 the hull broke up, and COLHOUN went down, wrapped in a shroud of steam. Down with her she took the bodies of one officer and 34 men. Some 295 of the crew, including 21 wounded, survived the sinking.

Endorsing Commander Wilson's Action Report, Captain Moosbrugger wrote: *"The entire performance of* COLHOUN *during her last action, including 'shooting,' damage control, and handling of personnel to minimize losses, is an outstanding example of fighting spirit and combat efficiency."*

Loss of U.S.S. Mannert L. Abele

Death stalked destroyer MANNERT L. ABELE in the afternoon of April 12, 1945, while the ship stood radar picket duty at her post off Okinawa.

That was the day Franklin D. Roosevelt died, and the enemy thought to make capital of the tragedy which stunned the Allied world. *Banzai!* A great blitz by the Special Attack Corps while the American nation was in mourning. A monster suicide assault to celebrate the death of the American President.

So the *Kamikazes* came, about 200 strong. With them they brought the *Oka*—the madman's idiot little brother. The noonday sky was blue, and sunshine flecked the sea with gold. Then, all in a breath, the sky was spattered with shrapnel bursts and the seascape was gouged by explosions, smudged with smoke, streaked with oil, and cluttered with debris.

Seventeen times the suiciders struck. Seventeen raids in which crazed *Kamikazes* and idiot *Okas* flung themselves upon the American ships off the Okinawa shore. In that fiery tempest battleship TENNESSEE was struck. So was battleship IDAHO. So were smaller vessels working near the beach. As usual, destroyers were in the vortex of this *Kamikaze* tornado.

Destroyer-escort WHITEHURST was hit. Destroyer STANLY was hit by a demented *"Baka."* Destroyer-escort RIDDLE was hit. Destroyer CASSIN YOUNG was hit. Destroyer-escort RALL was hit. Destroyer PURDY was hit. And one of the first to be struck was destroyer MANNERT L. ABELE.

She was hit by two suiciders. The first, a *Kamikaze*, came screaming at her about 1445. Plunging through fusillades of AA fire, the plane smashed into the destroyer's starboard side. The blast wiped out the after engine-room, hurling men and machinery skyward. Sixty seconds later, what was believed to be a *"Baka"* smashed into the ship's starboard side, forward, blowing up the forward fireroom.

The double blasting broke the ship's back, and with her starboard side smashed in, she was soon swamped. ABELE's captain, Commander A. E. Parker, had the satisfaction of knowing that the destroyer's guns had shot down two of the attacking *Kamikazes*. But that was slim recompense for the loss of a new destroyer. The vessel's main deck was awash almost immediately after the *Oka* smash. Three minutes later she went under.

In those three minutes Lieutenant George L. Way packed enough action for a lifetime. Blown overside by the *"Baka"* blast, Way caught a line and clambered back on board the sinking ship. One minute gone. He spent the next sixty seconds rounding up all able hands forward, and setting them to work cutting loose and launching life rafts. Two minutes gone. A fraction of the third minute he spent in opening the hatch above the passageway to the plotting room—an exit for the men in that cubicle. Then he flung himself at the port hatch of the forward engine-room. A dog was jammed. Somewhere Way snatched a crowbar—a hammer—something. Pounding and wrenching, he succeeded in breaking off the dog. Time was ticking; the main deck was awash. Way swung open the hatch as wavelets lapped and splashed at the combing. Out of the prisoned darkness below, and onto the current-swept deck came pale, grease-smeared men—ten who had been trapped—ten who were released from death. Time was up. But three minutes were enough for Lieutenant George L. Way.

A Jap plane dropped a bomb squarely in the center of a large group of swimming survivors, and those who lived through this blasting found themselves struggling in a sludge of oil and blood. Lieutenant (jg) John E. Hertner, ship's Medical Officer, worked valiantly over the wounded on the rafts and in the water. Seventy-three of the destroyer's crew were lost in the sinking; the fatalities would have been considerably higher but for Lieutenants Way and Hertner.

Rescue vessels were on hand. It was no easy task to get the injured and exhausted safe aboard. At the last, two swimmers were unable to make it. Shipfitter Arthur G. Ehrman, U.S.N.R., dived back into the sea from the deck of a rescue ship and gave each man a stalwart arm.

Named after a submarine captain who was lost in the Aleutians, the MANNERT L. ABELE was a new destroyer, and she had been inserted as a strong link in the Okinawa picket chain. Her destruction was indicative of destroyer vulnerability to death from the sky when it took such form as the suicide plane and the human projectile. By the time of the ABELE sinking it was apparent to the Navy that a sustained attack by such monstrosities spelled almost certain death to the unarmored destroyer.

Loss of U.S.S. Pringle

April 16 was another nightmare day for "The Fleet That Came to Stay." On that day the carrier INTREPID was damaged by a suicide plane, and destroyer McDERMUT, working in the flat-top's screen, was badly slashed by friendly AA fire. Destroyer LAFFEY was hit by a *Kamikaze*. Destroyer-escort BOWERS was hit. Destroyer BRYANT was hit. And destroyer PRINGLE was fatally struck by a suicide plane. This, in spite of reinforcements—VT ammunition; fighter cover of two CAP planes for each picket station; a companion destroyer or ship of comparable AA fire-power to support each picket destroyer.

The PRINGLE (Lieutenant Commander J. L. Kelley, Jr.) was patrolling Radar Picket Station No. 14 in company with destroyer-minelayer HOBSON and two landing craft. About 0900 her radar registered an aerial "pip," and lookouts sighted the "bandit" a moment later. This specimen was a "Zeke." As the plane roared in, making a shallow dive, PRINGLE's AA batteries paved the aircraft's road with fire and iron. The "Zeke" suddenly skidded, turned over on a broken wing, and plunged into the sea with a haystack splash. One *Kamikaze* down!

Ten minutes later, three "Vals" came winging across the seascape. Skimming the water, they began to stunt around the PRINGLE, dipping and weaving and alternately opening and closing the range at distances between 11,000 to 9,000 yards—bat-like tactics calculated to baffle the destroyer's gunners.

Although the wild maneuvering drew a steady fire that wore loaders and hot-shell men to a frazzle, PRINGLE's gunners were not entirely baffled. One of the outside "Vals"—the plane lowest to the water—flew smack into a shell-splash and crashed.

But the middle "Val" got in. Suddenly peeling off to make a shallow dive, the *Kamikaze* rushed at the ship with the velocity of a comet. At the "con" Lieutenant Commander Kelley tried to swing the ship away. The destroyer couldn't make it. There was a blinding crash as the plane struck the ship's superstructure just abaft the No. 1 stack. Either a pair of 500's or a 1,000-pound bomb ripped into the ship's interior. The resultant blast uprooted both smokestacks, wrecked the superstructure from pilot house to No. 3 gun mount, gutted the vessel amidships, and buckled her keel.

All power instantly lost, the PRINGLE drifted for a moment in paralysis. Then her contorted hull broke in two, opening her engineering spaces to the sea. Bluejackets and officers smeared with oil, grease, and blood struggled out of the sinking wreckage and dived, fell, or lowered themselves into the water. The sea swiftly closed over the fore and after sections of the ship. Within five minutes of the *Kamikaze* smash, PRINGLE was under.

Valiant rescuers, destroyer-minelayer HOBSON and the two landing craft which had been on station with PRINGLE were immediately on the job. Before noon most of the destroyer's 258 survivors were picked up. Almost half of these were suffering from burns, fractures, shock, or minor injuries. They considered themselves lucky. Sixty-two of their shipmates were gone.

BUSH, COLHOUN, MANNERT L. ABELE, and now PRINGLE—four destroyers downed by *Kamikazes* off Okinawa in a little over three weeks' time. And some 30 destroyers and destroyer-escorts damaged by the pagan "Divine Wind." VT ammunition was not enough. Fighter cover of two planes for each picket station was insufficient. The system of "double-banking" had to be reinforced.

After the fiery death of PRINGLE, Admiral Spruance reported to Admiral Nimitz:

"The skill and effectiveness of enemy suicide air attacks and the rate of loss and damage to ships are such that all available means should be employed to prevent further attacks. Recommend all available attacks with all available planes, including Twentieth Air Force, on Kyushu and Formosa fields."

Nimitz concurred in the recommendation. All available planes were mustered, and all available attacks were made on the designated airfields. But the lair of the *Kamikaze* was hard to find. The Special Attack Corps, brooding in secret nests in the home islands, the Nansei Shoto, and on Formosa, kept them flying—or kept them dying. Seven more destroyers were damaged by *Kamikazes* before April was out. And another, by way of variation, was struck by a suicide speed boat.

Hotter than a gust from hell, the "Divine Wind" kept on blowing throughout May. On the bottom off Okinawa, destroyers BUSH, COLHOUN, ABELE, and PRINGLE would have company.

Loss of U.S.S. Little

As the Battle for Okinawa raged into May, all hope of a quick wind-up of "Operation Iceberg" expired. It expired in the crash of shells and bombs ashore where the Shuri Line sprawled across the terrain like the swath of a forest fire. And it expired in the island's seething coastal waters where the transport areas were fouled with oil and debris, and where the destroyer picket line fought maniacal death from the sky.

Foul weather might ground the Special Attack Corps for a day or two—long enough to give exhausted sailors a chance for a second breath. But any rift in the storm clouds, any lift of the rain, and the "Divine Wind" came scorching down from the sky. May brought no rest to the destroyermen off Okinawa. Alert followed alert. Lookouts, radar watch, all hands waited in tension for the next hour's raid, or the surprise assault of the next moment. If an attack failed to develop, one could thank God for special favor. It was only a question of time before the *Kamikazes* would come.

They came for destroyer LITTLE (Commander Madison Hall, Jr.) early in the evening of May 3. She was on radar picket station with the new minelayer AARON WARD and four smaller ships—an LSM and three LCS's. Such a group of landing craft stationed in company with a picket destroyer was commonly referred to as "The Pall Bearers." Typical destroyerman humor—the wry humor that carried many a small "small boy" through the ordeal of Okinawa.

On the evening in question all the humor that could be mustered was needed. About 1415 the first "pips," deadly as smallpox, were on the radar screen. Over TBS went the warning. Into action went the CIC. In housings and tubs the gun crews adjusted their helmets; fingered their weapons, waited with stomach muscles taut.

"Here they come!"

A growing roar—a flock of Jap planes streaking through the sky. Death approaching the ship. Harpies flitting across the sea.

At 1843 they struck at the picket destroyer.

Excerpt from LITTLE's Action Report: *"One was vertical dive, one was low level, and one was gliding in. That such coordination could be achieved is almost unbelievable, but such was the case."*

LITTLE's gunners got two of them. But four of them got LITTLE. Like a chain of thunderbolts they smashed into the destroyer, shattering her superstructure, crushing her hull, wrecking her vital machinery. It was all over in two minutes of volcanic eruption—four shattering explosions between 1843 and 1845. Then the broken ship was reeling in a turmoil of fire and smoke. The dead were vanishing in floodwater and flame. The living were going overside.

"The Pall Bearers" closed in. At 1855 LITTLE sank into an Okinawa grave. Down with her she took 30 of her crew. Some 280 survivors, 52 of them wounded, were quickly picked up by the rescuers. Seldom had a ship been subjected to such punishment—and seldom so many survivors lived to fight again.

Loss of U.S.S. Luce

Next day, May 4, was still another bad day for the picket line. Or, to put it in proper perspective, a day worse than usual. For every Okinawa day was a 24-hour ordeal of sweat and apprehension and nerve strain.

May 4th was the last day for 149 of the crew of U.S.S. LUCE and 152 of the crew of U.S.S. MORRISON. The "Divine Wind" blew foul for the American Destroyer Force that morning!

Destroyer LUCE (Commander J. W. Waterhouse) was stationed as fighter-director ship in the radar picket line. At 0740—the tag-end of the morning watch, when haggard crews were gulping coffee before "going on," and weary hands were sighing with what little relief could be had from "going off"—at 0740 the enemy bat-men were sighted. Then nobody went off watch. *Bong! Bong! Bong!* General Quarters! A concerted dash for battle stations. Gunners scrambling to their mounts. Talkers hitching into their gear. The C.I.C. team pitching in. Babel on the radiotelephone. The CAP fighter planes vectored out to intercept. Back-talk between ship and sky.

"Bugeye One, this is Bugeye! Five bandits at Angel six! Vector six zero. Buster! Over!"

"Bugeye, this is Bugeye One! Tallyho! Splashed one Emily and one Judy! Out!

The CAP fighters intercepted, American and Jap planes tangling and weaving in furious dogfight. But two of the Japs escaped the aerial melee. Down the sky they came as though in grooves, straight for destroyer LUCE.

Her guns rattled and banged, flaying the air with flak, but the planes ripped in through the blazing curtain. One smashed into the ship's starboard side abreast of the No. 1 stack. The explosion showered the superstructure with fire, spreading flames over a mangle of men, guns, and machinery. The second plane roared in on the port quarter to crash the hull near the after engine-room. Framework gave under the blast; water plunged into the engineering spaces; LUCE was done for.

For several minutes the battered destroyer remained on even keel; then she slopped over in a starboard list and began to settle rapidly by the stern. Word was passed to abandon—to those who could hear it—and the survivors hustled to get overside.

There was little time. An inrush of water carried the ship down, stern first, and under a fog of smoke she was gone. Where LUCE had been, the sea was clotted with oil and debris and swimming men. "Pall Bearers" closed in to rescue the survivors. Of the 186 who were picked up, 57 were severely wounded, and 37 were suffering from minor injuries.

Referring to the sudden death which struck LUCE, a destroyer officer wrote grimly, *"This action shows the virtual impossibility of stopping a determined suicide-plane attack."*

Loss of U.S.S. Morrison

Destroyer MORRISON (Commander J. R. Hansen) had Radar Picket Station No. 1. She was on duty as fighter-director ship with a unit which included destroyer INGRAHAM and four landing craft. This group was representative of the "double-banking" which Spruance employed in an effort to shore up each picket station. Supporting each other, the two destroyers could raise a parasol of flak that would unnerve the average aviator. "The Pall Bearers," too, could contribute a lot of AA metal to the station's defense.

But the *Kamikaze* pilot was not an average aviator. Determined on suicide, he cared nothing for the dangers of combat and would face any fire with the indifference of madness.

A case in point was the MORRISON blasting. The carnage occurred shortly after LUCE was blown to the bottom. The "pips" snowed across her radar screen, and the Corsairs covering the station were coached in to meet the approaching Japs. The Corsairs shot down two of the enemy, but they were unable to block the onslaught. As in the assault on LUCE, the *Kamikazes* broke through the CAP defense, singled out their target, and launched a multiple, coordinated suicide attack.

MORRISON's gunners hurled a concentrated fusillade at the planes. Her consorts flung up hedges of 5-inch, 40 and 20 mm. fire. Proximity bursts and directs hits brought down a couple of the suiciders. But four *Kamikazes* roared in through the barrage, in through the snipe-shots and machine-gun volleys, straight for the target destroyer.

They struck MORRISON one at a time in something like two-minute intervals—one, two, three, four! The first smash knocked out some of her guns; the second added wrack to ruin; the third and fourth strikes were delivered upon a staggering, half-dead ship. At least two of the planes were carrying bomb-loads. The blasts ripped up the destroyer's superstructure and tore out her vitals. A mass of twisted metal, spouting smoke and flame, MORRISON started to go down.

There was no time to abandon. The wreck sank so swiftly that most of the men below decks were lost. Only those topside who were thrown from or washed off the ship were saved. By 0840 MORRISON was under the sea.

One of the landing craft—LCS 21—picked up the survivors after they had been in the water about two hours. Out of a total complement of 331 men, only 179 were recovered. And 108 of those rescued were wounded. Only 71 of MORRISON's company escaped injury in the *Kamikaze* death-battle.

Loss of U.S.S. Oberrender

When the Okinawa battle stormed into the second week of May, 1945, both Japanese and American forces were fighting with the utmost fury. "Operation Iceberg" was costing the U.S. Navy more effort, more suffering, more casualties than any previous invasion operation in its history. At Okinawa the Navy was paying the highest death-toll of all the Services. A whole flotilla of landing craft, minecraft, and other small vessels lay buried in the offshore shallows. Eight destroyers were on the bottom beneath the picket line. Although no warship larger than a destroyer had been (or would be) sunk, scores of vessels limped out of the area, mutilated and disabled by *Kamikaze* damage. Processions of the lamed and maimed were crawling to the Philippines, to Guam, and to other sanctuaries; the anchorage at Kerama Retto was crowded with cripples. And on May 9 this "Lost Harbor" received another *Kamikaze* victim, the destroyer-escort OBERRENDER.

OBERRENDER's is an unusual story. To begin with, the ship—skippered by Lieutenant Commander Samuel Spencer, U.S.N.R.—was patrolling off the western coast of Okinawa not as a radar picket, but as an anti-submarine sentinel. She was the only destroyer-escort to be done in by a *Kamikaze*. But she was not downed by the suicide plane; her gunners practically shot the plane to pieces before it struck. Finally, through the foresight of her captain, the ship had been well prepared for a suicide onslaught, and his intelligent provisions paid off in the saving of lives. Only eight men perished in the blasting which wrecked OBERRENDER. Here is the story, a condensation of her Action Report, prepared by a destroyer officer who made a study of this ship's performance.

On 9 May Oberrender *was patrolling on A/S Screening Station No. A-34-A off Okinawa. At 1840 her crew was called to GQ when enemy planes were reported over the inter-fighter director circuit to be in the vicinity. At 1844 an enemy plane was reported 34 miles away. Several more reports were received on this plane.* Oberrender *picked it up on her SA radar at 16 miles and plotted it in to 1.5 miles. At 1850 flank speed of 24 knots was rung up. At 1852 the plane was picked up visually, bearing about 260°, range about 9,000 yards, altitude 18,000 feet, position angle 35°. The sun was near the western horizon at this time, and the atmosphere was very clear, although visibility of the plane was impeded somewhat by the fact that it was approaching out of the west. At about the time* Oberrender *sighted the plane, it started a power dive for her at an angle of descent of about 35°. The ship was put in a hard left turn and fire was opened with both 5-inch guns. The 40 mm. guns opened fire at about 4,000 yards range. Almost immediately after these guns opened fire, a 40 mm. shell hit the engine of the plane at a range of about 3,000 yards and 40 mm. shells appeared to be registering hits from there in. At about 2,000 yards a 5-inch burst seemed to loosen the port wing. It was flapping from there in to about 250 yards, when it came off the plane altogether. Guns 21, 23, 25, 26, and 27 opened fire at about 1,500 yards. Guns 29 and 30 were not able to fire as the after 5-inch gun was firing right over them. As the plane closed in, the ship had swung around sufficiently far in the turn to bring it well back on the starboard quarter, almost dead aft. When the wing came off, the plane swerved somewhat to the right, but not quite enough to miss the ship altogether. It hit the gun platform of Gun 25 a glancing blow. The port wing, which was floating clear of the plane, hit the after fireroom uptake just below the stack, doing slight damage. The plane was on fire and smoking badly for the last 2,000 or 2,500 yards. Guns 25 and 27 continued firing until the plane actually hit Gun 25, and they were getting hits. The plane itself did little damage other than demolish the gun bucket of Gun 25. What is believed to have been a 500-pound delayed-action bomb apparently went through the main deck a few inches inside the starboard gunwale, and the bomb went off in the forward fireroom, causing very heavy damage in the amidships area of the ship. At 1940 a patrol craft—PCE (R) 855—came alongside and remained there until all serious personnel casualties had been transferred to her. At 2045 the tug* Tekesta *passed a line and towed* Oberrender *in to Kerama Retto.*

At Kerama Retto the DE's battle damage was carefully examined. Naval technicians shook their heads. Oberrender was beyond all hope of repair. On July 25, 1945, she was stricken from the Navy's roster.

This ship's destruction was another example of the deadliness of a *Kamikaze* suicide dive. The gunners riddled the plane, tore off one of its wings, and doubtless perforated the pilot. But with his last gasp, he steered his disintegrating bomber into the DE.

Eight of Oberrender's crew were lost in the action. Probably slain by the bomb explosion, they were the ship's only fatalities. Of the 53 in the ship's company who were wounded by the blasting, a number might have died but for the foresight of the vessel's captain.

Here is an explanatory paragraph taken verbatim from the ship's Action Report:

Where a large number of persons are injured at a single stroke, as was the case here, the normal Pharmacist's Mate complement is of course unequal to handling the situation. Moreover, on such occasions the services of repair party personnel are apt to be urgently needed to combat fires, etc., so that they are not available to assist the Pharmacist's Mates. With this possibility in mind, we had developed a group of about six men with considerable first-aid experience, had given them battle stations which were not of a vital nature for ship operation or gunnery, and had trained them to take the lead in first-aid work if needed. Also we had emphasized first-aid for all hands in our training program. Both of these policies paid dividends. The group which had been especially trained for first-aid turned to throughout the ship and were assisted by any men who could be spared from other stations, leaving the repair parties substantially intact to combat damage. . . .

If the ship was beyond salvage, the wounded were not. The crew expressed its gratitude to Lieutenant Commander Samuel Spencer, U.S.N.R.

Loss of U.S.S. Longshaw

Longshaw was one of the two American destroyers downed off Okinawa by some agent other than *Kamikaze*. (Lost in a minefield, Halligan was the first non-*Kamikaze* fatality.)

Nevertheless, the Longshaw sinking could be directly attributed to the "Divine Wind" hurricane. In Okinawa's stormy coastal waters the destroyer had been worn to the bone, her crew exhausted by non-stop duty and a continuous strain of aerial alerts. At the hour of emergency, officers and men were ready to drop from fatigue. Then it was that the LONGSHAW played target for a Japanese shore battery—one of those coast artillery units linked in a defense chain which Intelligence had grievously underestimated. Dedicated to the suicidal last-ditch stand were the forces of General Ushijima in Okinawa's Shuri Line, and no less dedicated were the gunners who manned the island's coastal batteries. LONGSHAW was killed, it might be said, by *Kamikaze* artillerymen.

On May 14, 1945, the LONGSHAW stepped into action as a fire-support ship on call to bombard designated beach-targets. For an unrelieved four days and four nights the destroyer worked along the molten coast, supporting the American forces ashore with constant shell fire.

All hands were bleary-eyed and haggard by the morning of the 18th. Pointers and trainers slumped, chin on chest, at the black-muzzled guns. Hoarse telephone talkers muttered at their instruments. Weary officers drank buckets of scalding coffee, trying to revive dulled senses. With glazed eyes the lookouts glared at the charred Okinawa coast, the sinister sky above—and shoaling water ahead.

Somebody was careless in plotting the ship's position on the chart, or gave the wrong order to the helmsman. Or someone failed to take action in time. At 0719 there was a shocking growl under her keel; the ship jolted to a halt like a locomotive which had lumbered through a broken switch. LONGSHAW was jammed hard aground.

She had ridden up on Ose Reef, right in the maw of one of those batteries she had been sent to demolish. Desperately the ship's skipper, Lieutenant Commander C. W. Becker, and all hands tried to get her off. Backing engines strained and propellers churned up a fury of froth. Weights were jettisoned—everything that could go to lighten ship. The destroyer could not be moved.

A call for help brought the tug ARIKARA racing up. The little tug worked with main and might to get the destroyer away. But her pull could not budge the destroyer.

Then, at 1100 of that morning, while ARIKARA was tugging her heart out, gruff thunder rumbled out from the beach, and deadly shell geysers spurted on the reef.

So LONGSHAW's hour came in a rush of salvos that splashed close aboard, then reached out to straddle, then fell upon the ship with homicidal violence. The destroyermen answered with four rounds of counter-battery fire, but there was no chance to make it a shooting match. From the start Jap shells were thrashing the destroyer's superstructure, pounding her decks, and uprooting her batteries. Fixed as she was, the ship could neither fight nor run away. In a matter of moments she was afire and bursting, her deck a shambles, her interior a slaughter-house.

From the bridge LONGSHAW's captain shouted orders to abandon. But abandonment under artillery fire was to leap from an exploding deck into exploding water.

In that charnel of blood, flame, and iron, Lieutenant Commander Becker disappeared. One of the LONGSHAW's surviving officers, Lieutenant R. L. Bly, U.S.N.R., gave the following testimony: "*He* (the ship's captain) *was last seen on the main deck, port side, amidst a huge fire. The fire was on all sides of him, according to Pharmacist's Mate Loyer. The captain had wounds in his head, around his abdomen, and had a .45 pistol in his hand. He ordered the Pharmacist's Mate to abandon ship. . . . Loyer didn't want to leave the captain, but he carried out the captain's orders. This is the last that was ever seen of the captain. Nothing is known of what happened to him after that.*"

Ten companion officers vanished in the inferno—half the ship's officer complement. Of the 11 officers who survived, four were wounded, and two of the wounded would subsequently die. Nine officers left out of 22.

Sixty-six bluejackets perished in the LONGSHAW massacre. Of the 225 who escaped, 95 were wounded, and seven would die of their wounds. But the wonder was that so many survived the murderous barrage.

Late in the afternoon of May 18 LONGSHAW's charred and shattered remains were sunk by friendly naval fire. She was the ninth U.S. destroyer to go down at Okinawa.

Loss of U.S.S. Drexler

On the 28th of May the suiciders delivered another all-out onslaught on the picket line. During all four weeks of the month the only let-up in the *Kamikaze* offensive had come when rain grounded the planes. Destroyers HUDSON, EVANS, HUGH W. HADLEY, BACHE, DOUGLAS H. FOX, STORMES, BRAINE, and ANTHONY, and destroyer-escorts ENGLAND and JOHN C. BUTLER had been damaged by the hell-bent suiciders during this period. It was just that the "Divine Wind" blew a little harder on the 28th. And destroyer DREXLER was lost in the tempest.

Skippered by Commander R. L. Wilson, the DREXLER was standing Okinawa radar picket duty. On station with her was destroyer LOWRY and two picket support craft. DREXLER had totaled 15 days as an Okinawa radar picket, in which time she had become only too well acquainted with the all-or-nothing *Kikusui* program.

On May 28 the *Kamikazes* flew over the picket line in swarms. And some 115 were reported "splashed" that day. Influence type ammunition, "double-banking," and CAP cover were exterminating more and more of the aerial suiciders. But not enough for the saving of U.S.S. DREXLER. During the later part of the morning watch six *Kamikazes* broke through the screen shielding the DREXLER-LOWRY group. This suicide squad made a coordinated attack on DREXLER.

Riddled by DREXLER's fire, two of the planes plunged into the sea. And two failed to strike the ship. But the remaining two, power-diving, rammed the destroyer full-gun. The blast of the second strike opened DREXLER's deck to the sky, and threw her over on her beam. She never returned to an even keel.

Tons of water sluiced into her torn hull, swamping her lower compartments. Deeper and deeper her beam went under, until she was lying on her side in the sea. Just 49 seconds after the final suicide strike the ship rolled over with a great, founting splash, and went down.

Nearly all hands below decks were imprisoned in the vessel. Those topside were either flung or managed to jump from the ship as it capsized. The "Pall Bearers" stood in to the rescue. About 170 officers and men were picked up, 51 of their number wounded. One hundred and fifty-eight men and eight officers died with the ship.

Captain C. A. Buchanan, ComDesRon 36, wrote of DREXLER:

"The Squadron Commander feels that the DREXLER's *combat record, though short, is one of which she can well be proud. As of 28 May, 1945, she had performed radar picket duty, off Okinawa, during a busy period, for a total of 15 days. During this period she shot down two suicide planes, possibly destroyed one or more during night attacks, assisted in the destruction of three more and, finally, took two down with her."*

HALLIGAN, BUSH, COLHOUN, MANNERT L. ABELE, PRINGLE, LITTLE, LUCE, MORRISON, OBERRENDER, LONGSHAW, DREXLER—the Navy's destroyermen were taking it in "Operation Iceberg." And four more DD's were to go down before the Okinawa campaign was over.

Loss of U.S.S. William D. Porter

By the first of June victory for the American forces on Okinawa was dimly in sight. Over Shuri Castle, citadel of the Japanese defense line, a tattered Stars and Stripes slatted in the wind. Some 50,000 corpses, one-time men of the 32nd Imperial Army, lay dead in the crumbled fortifications of the Shuri Line. The troops of General Simon Buckner were slugging relentlessly forward, while General Ushijima retreated to a "previously prepared position" in the south to make a suicide stand.

On May 27 Admirals Spruance and Mitscher had relinquished sea-air commands to Admirals Halsey and McCain. The Naval forces at Okinawa now were designated "Third Fleet," but they were the same battle-scorched ships and combat-weary men that had been there from the beginning of "Iceberg."

On June 4 the *Kamikazes* struck in a series of 18 raids. They were shot down in flocks; no picket line destroyers were so much as damaged.

On the 5th the man-made "Divine Wind" was reinforced by a tempest of nature that played havoc with the American fleet. Swirling out of the ocean east of Formosa, a rampaging typhoon smote the Okinawa area and caught Halsey's heavy ships steaming northward to strike at Kyushu. In this cataclysm of wind and water the bow was torn from the cruiser PITTSBURGH, carrier HORNET was damaged, and about 20 other ships suffered injury.

On June 5, battleship MISSISSIPPI and cruiser LOUISVILLE were struck by *Kamikaze* planes as the "Divine Wind" rushed into the vacuum in the typhoon wake. Attacking the mainstays of Halsey's fleet, the suiciders committed it the easy way. On the 7th the raids continued, and more suicide pilots died in flames. But the *Kamikazes* got a ship on the 10th of June. Victim was the WILLIAM D. PORTER.

Captained by Commander C. M. Keyes, the destroyer was on radar picket duty at Station No. 15. She was a veteran ship with old hands on her bridge and at her guns, and she gave a good account of herself in this, her last, battle.

The *Kamikaze* showed up early in the forenoon watch. At a distance of four miles the plane was identified as a "bandit," and as it hove into near view it turned out to be a "Val."

WILLIAM D. PORTER and the four LCS "Pall Bearers" with her splotched the air with ack-ack. Then they splotched ack-ack on the plane, but it still came on.

Diving at the destroyer, the *Kamikaze* struck the sea close aboard, and blew up with a shattering blast. The tremendous concussion had the effect of a mine explosion, crushing the underside of PORTER's hull and opening her stern to the flood. The inrush could not be stemmed, and in a short time the entire after part of the ship was swamped.

Moving up alongside, the four "Pall Bearers" joined in the destroyer's battle for buoyancy. All available pumping facilities were rushed into action. Everything that could be done to bail out the flood was tried. But the flooding could not be controlled. As the deck went sodden under foot and the ship's stern settled deeper in the sea, Commander Keyes ordered the vessel abandoned.

The men had time to go overside with care. The badly wounded were handled gently, and those suffering from minor injuries—sprains, lacerations, a few burns—were not compelled to endure long immersion in salt water. All 61 of the wounded were thus enabled to recover. And the entire crew was removed from the WILLIAM D. PORTER before she sank.

At 1119 the abandoned ship went under. Her survivors, watching from the LCS's, might well have pinched themselves to verify their salvation. WILLIAM D. PORTER was the eleventh American destroyer melted down in the crucible of Okinawa. Her crew was the only one to come through without a single fatality.

Loss of U.S.S. Twiggs

By the third week in June the battle for Okinawa was drawing to a bitter end. Implacably the forces of General Buckner were closing in on the remnant regiments of Ushijima's 32nd Army, standing in the craggy hills of southern Okinawa with their backs to the sea.

The Navy, too, closed in. Shore bombardments were called for as the cornered Japs neared land's end. These were dangerous assignments, for the enemy forces were dying hard. And the *Kamikaze* flyers were setting the pace.

During the evening of June 16 the rabid airmen struck again. One of them struck at a destroyer which was standing offshore for bombardment duty—the U.S.S. TWIGGS, captained by Commander George Philip.

Time: about 2030. The plane, a "Jill" torpedo-bomber, dropped down out of the dusk like a thunderbolt. When detected, it was less than 1,000 yards from the destroyer, and coming with the velocity of a bullet. An unleashed torpedo knifed into the water and raced at the ship. Before TWIGGS could be swung away, the torpedo ripped into the No. 2 magazine. Then the plane crashed into the ship, aft.

Torpedo explosion—magazine explosion—aircraft explosion—the triple blasting tore the destroyer's frame and sent sheets of fire flagging through her superstructure. Damage controlmen never had a chance. All in a gust the ship was a furnace, with men fighting their way topside to escape roasting heat and suffocating smoke, only to find the deck a burning griddle.

All able hands rallied to rescue the wounded, battle the fire, and save the ship, but the TWIGGS had become a death-trap. Thirty minutes after the *Kamikaze* smash, the ship's after magazine blew up with a shattering detonation. The vessel plunged immediately. Down with her she took 18 of her 22 officers. One hundred and sixty-five men were lost with the ship. Down with the destroyer went her captain, Commander Philip.

The survivors drifted in clots on the sea, and waited for help to come. Presently destroyer PUTNAM arrived to pick up these latest victims of the "Divine Wind." Many of the 131 who were recovered needed surgery and hospitalization. The three surviving officers were among the wounded; the TWIGGS disaster was one of the few in which every officer in the embattled ship was either killed or injured.

She was the twelfth destroyer downed off Okinawa, and she was downed in the twelfth week of the campaign. One destroyer a week, and a destroyer-escort in addition—"Operation Iceberg" and the *Kikusui-Kamikaze* program would never be forgotten by the Navy's destroyermen.

But the campaign was not over. Okinawa had yet to be secured.

Loss of U.S.S. Underhill

On June 21, 1945, Japanese resistance on Okinawa collapsed in a horror of *banzai* charges and *hari-kiri*. By evening the carnage was ended. Under a flutter of white flags, Japanese officers came stumbling across the fields of dead to surrender their long swords to the Americans. From foxholes and caves the remnant Japanese infantrymen emerged like corpses from catacombs. The frayed and hangdog left-overs of the 32nd Imperial, they had no stomach for *hari-kiri*.

The surrender of this riddled and skeletal garrison is generally regarded as the last act of the Okinawa campaign. Officially the island had fallen. "Operation Iceberg" was over. The Navy trained its big guns on Japan's home islands to the north, and Admiral Nimitz set the course for Tokyo.

But a mop-up of the Okinawa Area was imperative. In the neighboring Nansei Shoto backwaters there were hold-outs—nests of midget submarines; hidden torpedo-boats; concealed *Kamikazes*. Convoys to Okinawa, minesweepers working through the Nansei Shoto, and warships patrolling the chain from Formosa to Yaku never knew when a suicider might strike. Off Okinawa the line of radar pickets maintained vigilant watch. By all indications the "Divine Wind" hurricane had blown itself into history, but there remained suicidal undercurrents in the sea.

Late in July, 1945, one of those undercurrents

proved fatal for destroyer-escort UNDERHILL. Captained by Lieutenant Commander R. M. Newcomb, U.S.N.R., the DE was serving as a unit in a group escorting a convoy of seven LST's and a merchantman on the Okinawa-to-Philippines run.

In the afternoon of July 24 the ships were steaming in formation some 150 miles northeast of Luzon. UNDERHILL was marching along in the convoy's van, her engines drumming their smooth rhythm. The convoy was bound for Leyte, after eight days at Okinawa. It was always a relief to leave Okinawa astern.

Yet at sea one never could tell, one never knew. And on that afternoon Destiny placed her invisible finger on UNDERHILL, and the little destroyer-escort was a marked ship. Lieutenant E. M. Rich, U.S.N.R., described the action as he saw and heard it evolve:

We had just changed course and were all prepared to start a new patrol plan for the escorts when we got a sound contact just about 1400. We started an attack on the sound contact, were all set to drop our depth charges, but the contact did not look good. The ASW officer said it was mushy and seemed to have no doppler, no movement, and he didn't think it was a good contact. He advised the captain, since we were directly ahead of the convoy, not to drop any charges.

The captain decided it was the best plan and changed course to port to come over in front of the convoy again, which had changed course in the meantime, and as we changed course we sighted a floating mine on our port side about 25 yards away. So immediately we advised the convoy that we had a mine there, it was in their path, and advised them to change course. We told them we'd stand by the mine, and as soon as they were clear we'd try to sink it by gunfire.

We maneuvered around the mine waiting for them to clear, and then began firing on the mine. We still had the sound contact and as we lay there maneuvering around, the contact began looking better, began to have some movement, and we got a little down doppler on it and it seemed to be firmer.

We sent one of the PC's, the other escorts, over to see if he could pick up the contact. A few minutes later he reported he had contact and he was going to drop charges. We had lost contact in the meantime at a range of about 2,300 yards. We were still trying to sink the mine, hadn't been able to sink it yet, although I am sure we hit it several times. The PC went ahead and dropped charges. We saw the explosions in the water.

Just a few second afterwards, we saw a periscope come up aft of the place where the charges had exploded. As soon as the periscope was sighted, General Quarters were set, and I went to my position down in the log room as damage control officer.

We turned and headed for the periscope. I could get some account of what was going on over the sound-powered telephone. I heard the lookouts give the bearing a time or two of the periscope. The word was passed over the phones and over the Public Address system to stand by to ram. Immediately afterwards it was changed to set a shallow pattern of depth charges.

We went on for a short period of time and then we heard the depth charges explode and shortly after that I heard the message go out over the TBS. . . . I heard the captain report, "We got one Jap midget submarine. We can see oil and debris on the surface."

We evidently went out and began to turn to come back to the original position again when we sighted another periscope, and immediately started for that one. . . . A short time later I heard the range given from somewhere as 700 yards. Then the word was passed again to stand by to ram.

Shortly after that I heard the talker say, "He's looking right at us." Then I got braced ready for the collision. I felt two sharp jars so we just hit something—had gone over the top of it. Then right after that came an explosion. I lost my phones. Everything went dark in the log room, and in feeling around trying to find my phones I discovered water coming in. I thought the ship was sinking. . . . As soon as I got outside I tried to get ahold of Control. . . . I couldn't find a phone near-by so I went aft to the fantail where I found a set of phones. I tried to phone Control, and someone told me we didn't have any Control. Then I realized that the whole forward end of the ship had been blown off up to the forward fireroom bulkhead; all forward of that was gone. All the bridge area, the bridge structure and the mast . . . all had been blown off.

There was no Action Report left by UNDERHILL. The officers who could have written it were gone. No testimony was given by witnesses who had been on the ship's bow. None remained to testify.

But the ship herself bore evidence to what had happened. When the periscope was sighted, Lieutenant Commander Newcomb had conned the DE in a dash to ram the enemy. Wings of spray arched at the ship's stem; all hands hung on for the smash; a vague shadow lurked in the water ahead; and then—

A roaring cloud of fire that consumes the ship's forecastle in a gust. A dreadful rain of debris splashing near and far in the sea. When the smoke clears aside, the entire fore part of the ship, everything forward of the stack, is gone. Everything except a small chunk of the bow which bobs up and floats away and gradually sinks in an eddy off to starboard. The truncated destroyer-escort wallows in the sea with mangled machinery spilling out of her open wounds.

It would seem that UNDERHILL herself was target for the thing she struck. Most of the survivors thought it was a midget submarine. A few, who glimpsed it from a distance, described it as some kind of human torpedo. Whatever its construction, the vessel was packed with high explosive, and evidence suggests that it was dedicated to a suicide mission.

With reference to the tactics employed by the human torpedoes or midgets involved in that fatal scrimmage, Lieutenant Rich stated:

"There evidently was no attempt on the part of the submarines to take any action against us, nor did they seem to take any against the other ships. They did not fire any torpedoes that we know of or make any attempt of their own to ram. . . . They seemed to be just kind of teasing us on, trying to lure us on to ram them—which we did."

Patrol craft ran in to take off the destroyer-escort's survivors. Some 116 of the UNDERHILL crew were rescued; 112 had perished in the shattering blast. Ten of the ship's 14 officers were lost. Lost with them was UNDERHILL's captain, Lieutenant Commander Newcomb.

When the last of the survivors were on board PC 803 and PC 804, the rescue craft moved away, and PCE 872 stood in to sink the drifting hulk with gunfire. On the Okinawa road the Jap suiciders had claimed another Destroyer Force victim.

They would claim one more before their terrible cult was squelched.

Loss of U.S.S. Callaghan

During the last fortnight of July, 1945, destroyer CALLAGHAN (Commander C. M. Bertholf), flagship of Captain A. E. Jarrell, ComDesRon 55, was on radar picket station off Okinawa. With her on station were destroyers PRICHETT and CASSIN YOUNG and three LCS's.

CALLAGHAN had seen her share of the Pacific War. More than her share. The barrels of her guns were worn from hours of incessant firing. Her director system needed overhaul; her topside was weather-beaten; her engines were tired. For 18 months ship and crew had been on the go, climaxing this tour of duty on the rugged "Iceberg" front. Now she was due to go *home*—overhaul for the ship; recuperation for the crew. As the mid-watch came on and the ship's log entered the 29th, the crew could hardly bear the anticipation. Destroyer LAWS was coming to relieve the CALLAGHAN; this was to be her last hour on station at Okinawa.

It was to be her last hour—period.

At 0030 a "bogey" was reported.

At 0031 the crew was rushed to General Quarters.

An instant later the 5-inch batteries opened fire, smearing the night sky with splashes of flame.

Then the plane was seen as a *Kamikaze* heading straight for CALLAGHAN.

At 0041 the plane crashed into the ship near the No. 3 upper handling-room.

A thunderclap blast rocked the destroyer, and then, at 0045, the handling-room exploded.

The ship listed to starboard as flames gushed from the wreckage topside, and the sea rushed into her after compartments, swamping her stern.

At 0050 all hands, with the exception of a salvage party, were ordered to abandon.

The "Pall Bearers" closed in to pick up the survivors and bring medical aid to the 71 men and two officers who were wounded.

At 0143 the salvage party abandoned the fiery hulk.

Forty-six bluejackets and an officer were lost with the ship in this most unlucky sinking. CALLAGHAN had 12 Jap planes painted on her director; the *Kamikaze* that killed her would have been the 13th. (As Captain Jarrell remarked, the destroyer simply found one plane that she could not shoot down.) And, dying, she was the thirteenth and last American destroyer to go down in the battle of Okinawa.

LOSS OF THE CALLAGHAN

CHAPTER 38

THE BATTLE SCARRED

Okinawa Crash Bill

Eighty-eight destroyers and 30 destroyer-escorts were damaged in the Battle for Okinawa. Those figures sum up to nearly a third of the total for all warship types damaged in the "Iceberg" operation.

Not all of the wounded DD's and DE's were injured by *Kamikazes*. Several were struck by *"Baka"* rockets. Several were hit by suicide boats. A number were raked by friendly fire; a few were struck by the fire of enemy shore batteries. A few were storm-battered. And several were injured by collision. But *Kamikaze* wounds were by far in the majority and by far the worst; some of the DD's and DE's disabled by the suicide planes suffered worse punishment than the ships which were sunk by *Kamikaze* strikes. Destroyer WILLIAM D. PORTER, for example, went down without a single fatality, whereas destroyer HAZELWOOD, disabled by a *Kamikase* smash, reeled out of action with 46 dead, including her Captain and "Exec." Similarly disabled, destroyer BRAINE made port with 50 dead and 78 wounded. Destroyer-escort BOWERS came out of a sucide crash with half her crew lying dead or injured. In general, crew casualties were heaviest in the ships which went down, but there were excruciating losses in many of the vessels which survived *Kamikaze* onslaught.

A volume could be written about the masterful performances of the officers and men (so abjectly impersonalized by the term "personnel") who brought bruised and battered ships out of the Okinawa Avernus. Another volume might discuss the specific subject of damage control, devoting chapters to individual cases as remarkable as any in naval history.

This text can do no more than brief in a few of the episodes—casualties which were typical, and outstanding instances of ship-saving. On the following pages are presented an abbreviated list of the DD's and DE's damaged at Okinawa—a tabulation enumerating the ships that received combat injuries which were sufficient to hamper the vessel's operation if they did not completely disable the ship.

Destroyer FRANKS, the first DD to suffer serious injury after "Love Day," was one of the few badly hurt by collision. On April 2 she was serving in a Fast Carrier Task Group which was then about 100 miles to the eastward of Okinawa. Late in the evening, while maneuvering from a plane-guard station to a screening station, FRANKS sideswiped the battleship NEW JERSEY. The collision demolished the port wing of the destroyer's bridge, wiped out several 40 mm. directors and a 40 mm. gun, mangled the superstructure, and canted the No. 2 stack. Crushed on the bridge wing, the destroyer's captain, Commander D. R. Stephan, died the following day. Lieutenant G. F. Case, Executive Officer, took the mauled vessel into Ulithi.

The damaging of NEWCOMB, LEUTZE, MULLANY, HYMAN, HOWORTH, MORRIS, HAYNSWORTH, HARRISON, and FIEBERLING set the pattern for the Okinawa casualty list. Wounded in the "Divine Wind" tornado of April 6, all were *Kamikaze* victims.

Destroyers NEWCOMB and LEUTZE were at adjacent screening stations that day. Positioned off Okinawa, they were covering the heavy ships of Task Force 54. Down the afternoon sky same the suicide squadrons; the CAP fighters intercepted; the battle splintered

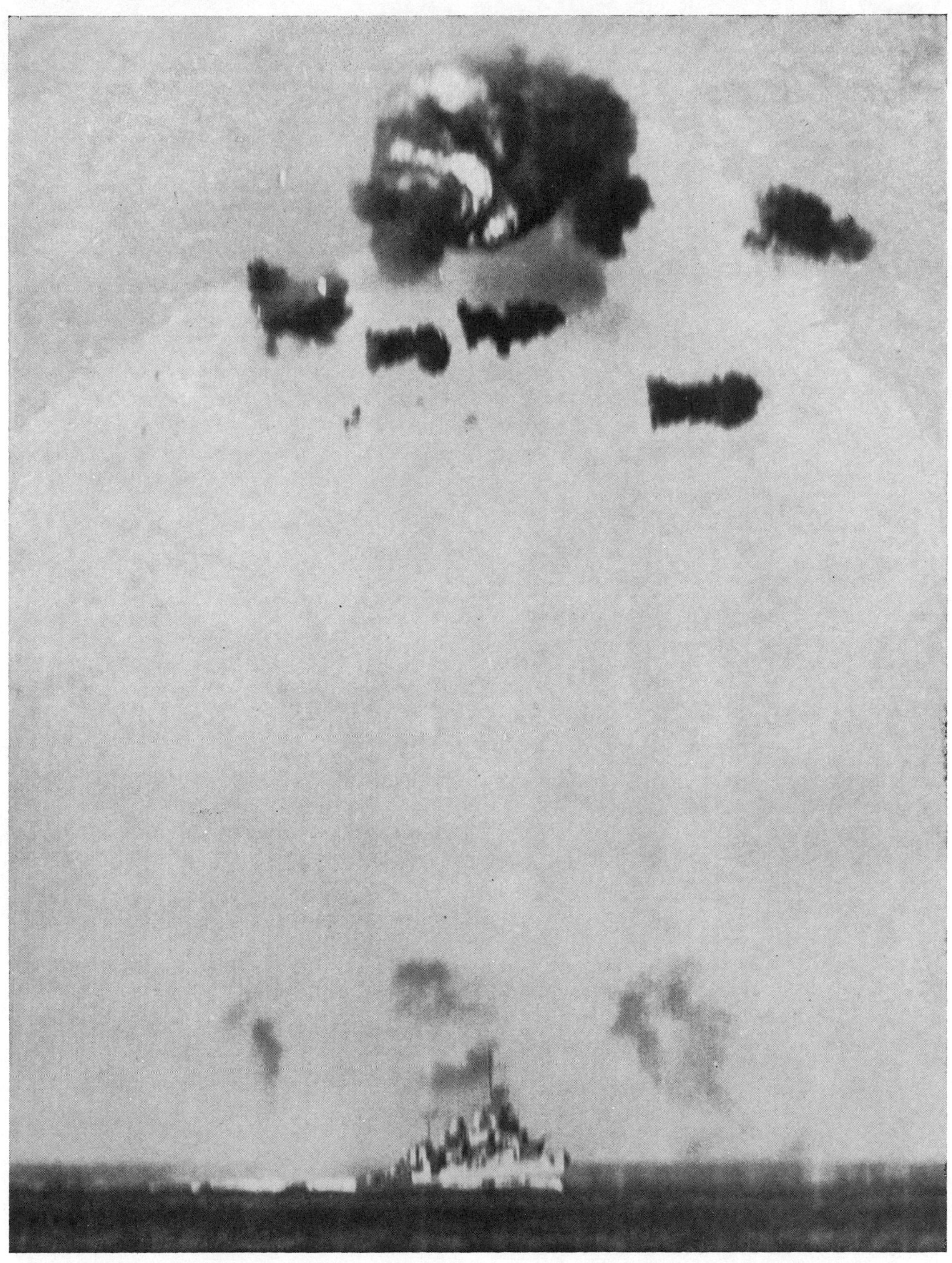

Finis for a kamikaze! Of the 88 destroyers and 30 destroyer-escorts damaged off Okinawa, most were victims of kamikaze attack. Some, like William D. Porter, sank without loss of a single man; others, like Hazelwood, survived with very heavy casualties among the crew. But the "small boys" on picket duty did their job and helped save the beaches from devastation.

It wasn't all gruesome. Pictures of battle damage can create a badly distorted impression. As a matter of cold fact, the destroyer is the most admired unit of the Fleet. Destroyer duty separates the men from the boys; a real sailor prefers it over anything else. This picture may contain a clue to the reason why. The destroyer is refueling from the battleship Wisconsin

en route to a strike on Tokyo—a routine maneuver enacted with all the drama of the eternal struggle of men against the sea. Life on a destroyer is hard and it's hilarious, too. Every simple act may be a struggle: to stand upright, to lie in your sack, to decode a message, to eat three square meals a day. The ship and the sea are equally alive with the bluejackets themselves.

What becomes of a suicide pilot? This is the wreckage created by a crash into the sick bay of Curtis (AV 4). Look hard and you can make out the fanatical messenger of the "Divine Wind."

At first, veteran Japanese pilots "volunteered" for Kamikaze duty, but toward the final days of the war any pilot and plane seemed good enough to be sacrificed in a suicide mission.

Hit by three out of four kamikazes off Kerama Retto, Newcomb (DD 586) was reduced to a wreck, but aid from destroyers Leutze (also kamikazed) and Beale helped save her.

Sigsbee, Leutze, and Laffey fought in waters where larger ships could not be risked, took the worst the foe could deal out, and returned with their dead and wounded and an indomitable will to fight again.

into a bewildering free-for-all of aerial dogfights and crash-dive attacks. At 1759 NEWCOMB's radar spotted a nearing enemy. A moment later the destroyer's lookouts saw the aircraft skimming in across the water. The AA guns roared; fragments of metal were flicked from the plane; but the aircraft came on like a streaking shadow, and smashed into the destroyer's after stack. The ship slowed rapidly as steam whistled from ruptured boilers. Fire broke out in the upper handling room of a 5-inch battery.

As NEWCOMB's crew was fighting battle damage, a second Jap plane came in on the starboard bow. This menace was shot down at a range of 6,000 yards. Then a third plane, which had followed the first one in from the west, crashed the destroyer amidships near the torpedo workshop. The explosion stopped the destroyer dead in the sea. Both engine-rooms and the after fireroom were blown into scrap. The after stack, both torpedo mounts, all of the amidship superstructure, 40 mm. mounts, and magazines disintegrated in crimson eruption. And at that critical moment a fourth *Kamikaze* slammed into the forward stack, showering the molten wreckage with gasoline.

Within 11 short minutes NEWCOMB had been reduced from a warship to a furnace, a wallowing crematorium. But her captain, Commander I. E. McMillian, and his equally stout crew hung on. With them hung Captain R. N. Smoot, ComDesRon 56, bent on saving his shattered flagship.

Destroyer LEUTZE (Lieutenant L. Grabowsky) immediately steamed to NEWCOMB's aid, boldly going alongside the burning wreck. Hoses were passed forward, and preparations were being made to pass them aft when a fifth *Kamikaze* hurtled down from the sky. An accurate VT projectile burst under the plane's left wing and tilted it just enough to send it skidding across LEUTZE's fantail, where it exploded with a huge detonation. The ship immediately lost steering control, and her torn stern settled in the water. Able to make about five knots, she succeeded in getting clear of NEWCOMB, and standing off to fight her own damage. Topside weights were hastily jettisoned, but by 1830 LEUTZE's fantail was awash. *"Am in serious danger of sinking,"* she signalled NEWCOMB, *"am pulling away."* Torpedoes went overside. Depth charges went overside. Fuel went overside. And by 1900 the crew had won the battle for buoyancy. Minesweeper DEFENSE towed Grabowsky's ship into Kerama Retto. She was not the first lifesaver to come within an inch of losing her life while playing Good Samaritan.

While LEUTZE was limping away, destroyer BEALE

DESTROYER AND DESTROYER-ESCORTS DAMAGED AT OKINAWA

Ship	*Commanding Officer*	*Date*	*Damage*	*Casualties Killed*	*Casualties Wounded*
KIMBERLY (DD)	*Comdr. J. D. Whitfield*	*March 26*	*Major*	*4*	*57*
PORTERFIELD (DD)	*Comdr. D. W. Wulzen*	*March 27*	*Minor*	–	*1*
MURRAY (DD)	*Comdr. P. L. de Vos*	*March 27*	*Major*	*1*	*4*
O'BRIEN (DD)	*Comdr. W. W. Outerbridge*	*March 27*	*Major*	*50*	*76*
FOREMAN (DE)	*Lt. Comdr. W. J. Carey, Jr.*	*March 27*	*Minor*	–	*1*
		April 3	*Major*	–	–
FRANKS (DD)	*Comdr. D. R. Stephan*	*April 2*	*Major*	–	*2*
			(Captain fatally wounded)		
PRICHETT (DD)	*Comdr. C. E. Bowley*	*April 3*	*Major*	–	–
		July 29	*Minor*	*2*	*1*
NEWCOMB (DD)	*Comdr. I. E. McMillian*	*April 6*	*Major*	*40*	*51*
LEUTZE (DD)	*Lt. L. Grabowsky*	*April 6*	*Major*	*8*	*30*
MULLANY (DD)	*Comdr. A. O. Momm*	*April 6*	*Major*	*30*	*36*
HOWORTH (DD)	*Comdr. E. S. Burns*	*April 6*	*Major*	*9*	*14*
HYMAN (DD)	*Comdr. R. N. Norgaard*	*April 6*	*Major*	*11*	*41*
MORRIS (DD)	*Lt. Comdr. R. V. Wheeler*	*April 6*	*Major*	*12*	*45*
HARRISON (DD)	*Comdr. W. V. Combs*	*April 6*	*Minor*	–	–
HAYNSWORTH (DD)	*Comdr. S. N. Tackney*	*April 6*	*Major*	*12*	*27*
FIEBERLING (DE)	*Comdr. E. E. Lull*	*April 6*	*Minor*	–	–

Ship	*Commanding Officer*	*Date*	*Damage*	*Casualties*	
				Killed	*Wounded*
WESSON (DE)	*Lt. Comdr. H. Sears,* U.S.N.R.	*April 7*	*Major*	*8*	*25*
BENNETT (DD)	*Comdr. J. N. McDonald*	*April 7*	*Major*	*3*	*18*
GREGORY (DD)	*Comdr. Bruce McCandless*	*April 8*	*Major*	–	*2*
CHARLES J. BADGER (DD)	*Comdr. J. H. Cotten*	*April 9*	*Major*	–	–
MANLOVE (DE)	*Lt. Comdr. E. P. Foster, Jr.,* U.S.N.R.	*April 11*	*Minor*	*1*	*10*
KIDD (DD)	*Comdr. H. G. Moore*	*April 11*	*Major*	*38*	*55*
HANK (DD)	*Comdr. G. M. Chambers*	*April 11*	*Minor*	*3*	*1*
HALE (DD)	*Comdr. D. W. Wilson*	*April 11*	*Minor*	–	*2*
WHITEHURST (DE)	*Lt. J. C. Horton,* U.S.N.R.	*April 12*	*Major*	*37*	*37*
BENNION (DD)	*Comdr. R. H. Holmes*	*April 12*	*Minor*	*1*	*6*
		April 30	*Minor*	–	–
STANLY (DD)	*Lt. Comdr. R. S. Harlan*	*April 12*	*Medium*	–	*3*
RIDDLE (DE)	*Lt. Comdr. F. P. Steele,* U.S.N.R.	*April 12*	*Medium*	*1*	*9*
CASSIN YOUNG (DD)	*Comdr. J. W. Ailes, III*	*April 12*	*Major*	*1*	*59*
RALL (DE)	*Lt. Comdr. C. B. Taylor,* U.S.N.R.	*April 12*	*Major*	*21*	*38*
PURDY (DD)	*Comdr. F. L. Johnson*	*April 12*	*Major*	*13*	*58*
SIGSBEE (DD)	*Comdr. G. P. Chunghoon*	*April 14*	*Major*	*3*	*75*
MCDERMUT (DD)	*Comdr. C. B. Jennings*	*April 16*	*Major*	*2*	*33*
LAFFEY (DD)	*Comdr. F. J. Becton*	*April 16*	*Major*	*32*	*71*
BOWERS (DE)	*Lt. Comdr. C. F. Highfield,* U.S.N.R.	*April 16*	*Major*	*48*	*59 (many fatally)*
BRYANT (DD)	*Comdr. G. C. Seay*	*April 16*	*Major*	*34*	*33*
WADSWORTH (DD)	*Comdr. R. D. Fusselman*	*April 22*	*Minor*	–	*1*
AMMEN (DD)	*Comdr. J. H. Brown*	*April 21*	*Minor*	–	*8*
ISHERWOOD (DD)	*Comdr. L. E. Schmidt*	*April 27*	*Major*	*42*	*41*
HUTCHINS (DD)	*Lt. Comdr. A. R. Olsen*	*April 6*	*Minor*	*1*	*3*
		April 27	*Major*	–	*18*
RALPH TALBOT (DD)	*Comdr. W. S. Brown,* U.S.N.R.	*April 27*	*Major*	*5*	*9*
DALY (DD)	*Comdr. R. R. Bradley, Jr.*	*April 28*	*Minor*	*3*	*33*
TWIGGS (DD)	*Comdr. G. Philip, Jr.*	*April 28*	*Major*	*No data*	
HAGGARD (DD)	*Lt. Comdr. V. J. Soballe*	*April 29*	*Major*	*11*	*40*
HAZLEWOOD (DD)	*Comdr. V. P. Douw*	*April 29*	*Major*	*46 (Including Captain)*	*26*
HUDSON (DD)	*Comdr. R. R. Pratt*	*April 22*	*Minor*	–	*1*
		May 4	*Major*	–	–
ENGLAND (DE)	*Lt. J. A. Williamson,* U.S.N.R.	*May 9*	*Major*	*34*	*30*
EVANS (DD)	*Comdr. R. J. Archer*	*May 11*	*Major*	*31*	*29*
HUGH W. HADLEY (DD)	*Comdr. B. J. Mullaney*	*May 11*	*Major*	*28*	*67*
BACHE (DD)	*Lt. Comdr. A. R. McFarland*	*May 13*	*Major*	*41*	*32*
JOHN C. BUTLER (DE)	*Lt. Cmdr. J. E. Pace*	*May 20*	*Medium*	–	*3*
DOUGLAS H. FOX (DD)	*Comdr. R. M. Pitts*	*May 17*	*Major*	*9*	*35*
COWELL (DD)	*Comdr. C. L. Werts*	*May 25*	*Minor*	–	*2*
STORMES (DD)	*Comdr. W. N. Wylie*	*May 25*	*Major*	*21*	*16*
ANTHONY (DD)	*Comdr. C. J. VanArsdall, Jr.*	*May 27*	*Minor*	–	–
		June 7	*Minor*	–	*5*
BRAINE (DD)	*Comdr. W. W. Fitts*	*May 27*	*Major*	*50*	*78*
SHUBRICK (DD)	*Lt. Comdr. J. C. Jolly*	*May 29*	*Major*	*32*	*28*

(Commander D. M. Coffee) moved alongside the flaming NEWCOMB. BEALE passed six hoses to the fiery vessel, and the conflagration was then brought under control in less than 30 minutes. The smolder was finally extinguished by bucket brigades, and by 1930 NEWCOMB was out of immediate danger. The tug TEKESTA chugged up through the dusk to tow the charred ship to Kerama Retto.

In his Action Report Commander McMillian paid high tribute to the members of his crew. *"Never,"* he stated, *"was there any hint that the ship would be abandoned. . . . This, although all officers and men were suffering from severe shock not lessened in any degree by the grim presence of dead and dying throughout the ship, along with the distinctly audible cries of those suffering from severe burns and shrapnel wounds."*

Both NEWCOMB and LEUTZE were to be on the binnacle list for many days, but they would sail again. So would many another DD disabled by the berserk *Kamikazes* at Okinawa.

Destroyer MULLANY (Commander A. O. Momm) was struck at almost the same moment NEWCOMB was hit. MULLANY, on that dark April afternoon, was patrolling an outer A/S screen off Cape Zampa. About 1745 a *Kamikaze* pounced. Furious anti-aircraft gunnery raked the plane as it came in, setting fire to its fuselage. Unfortunately the *Kamikaze* held together, and, veering, crashed into the port side of the destroyer's after deckhouse. Fire and explosion followed the aircraft blast. Racked depth charges glowed red hot, and could not be doused by extinguishers. At 1809 a number of the depth charges exploded, ripping great segments from the ship's superstructure. Then two more *Kamikazes* attacked the burning destroyer. Both planes were shot down by MULLANY's desperate gunners. As friendly vessels closed in to aid, the ship was convulsed by internal explosions which slung men overside and spread fire below decks. Approaching the MULLANY, destroyer-minesweeper GHERARDI and several smaller vessels were unable to maneuver alongside because the water was clotted with swimmers and boats. Advised that a magazine bulkhead was glowing like a stove lid, and that the heat threatened to set off a disastrous ammunition blast, Commander Momm ordered MULLANY abandoned.

That evening destroyer PURDY (Commander F. L. Johnson) moved up to hose the burning ship. When the fires were subdued Commander Momm led a salvage party back to the fuming destroyer. Every man who went below decks risked his life, but at 0030 in the morning of the 7th a watch was set in the forward fireroom and forward engine-room. No. 1 and No. 2 boilers were lighted off, and at 0145 the ship got under way. Operating the starboard engine, and steering by hand, the crew worked her southward down the Okinawa coast. At 0936 the MULLANY crawled into the Kerama Retto anchorage.

Flagship of Captain C. A. Buchanan, ComDesRon 63, destroyer HYMAN (Commander R. N. Norgaard) was somewhat luckier than NEWCOMB, LEUTZE, and MULLANY. Her turn came while she was steaming to a picket support station northeast of Ie Shima, where she was to conduct an anti-smallcraft patrol. Attacked by *Kamikazes,* she shot down four of the suicide crates, and destroyers STERETT and ROOKS, in her vicinity, joined the shooting to blast three more.

But a Jap plane broke through the barrage. Although a shell amputated one wing, the aircraft held together, and so did the mad pilot. Coming in on a wing and a curse, he made his unhappy landing on HYMAN's forward torpedo tubes. There was the usual smash, followed by explosions and fire as bombs and torpedoes blew their red breath through the ship's superstructure.

HYMAN came out of it with an ugly mangling. Much of her superstructure was junk; the engine of the Jap plane had plunged through the main deck; the ship's forward engine-room was wrecked. But she made port under her own power, was patched up by the tender OCEANUS, and steamed south for the repair yards of Saipan on April 14.

Destroyer HOWORTH (Commander E. S. Burns) was struck by a *Kamikaze* that same afternoon as she steamed independently toward an A/S patrol station off the Hagushi beaches. Coming in from the north and east, flocks of Japanese planes were bearing down on the beachhead. HOWORTH paused to shoot at a *Kamikaze* which was diving at the cruiser ST. LOUIS. A few minutes later the word came over TBS that HYMAN had been struck, and HOWORTH, on the injured destroyer's trail, stepped up speed to reach an adjacent station. While running at 25 knots, she shot down another "Val"—a plane that gave her a nerve-wracking shave by banking between her two stacks, slashing the radio antenna, and crashing close aboard. Reaching her picket station at 1700, HOWORTH immediately went into action to shoot down an attacking "Zeke." At 1703 she downed a second "Zeke." This suicider brushed the destroyer's fantail, carrying away several lifelines before plunging into the water.

Two minutes later the HOWORTH riddled a third "Zeke" which was diving on a nearby minesweeper. The *Kamikazes* were now coming so fast that HOWORTH's ammunition passers could hardly keep up with the guns. Then, swooping down in a long glide, another "Zeke" struck home. The plane flew squarely into the main-battery director on HOWORTH's bridge. The crash drenched the bridge with burning gasoline, and knocked out the ship's steering control. Repair parties quickly extinguished the fire; steering control was taken over aft; the ship was conned from the secondary conning station; and still another "Zeke" was killed by 40 mm. fire from the destroyer's guns. The ship, as her captain expressed it, had gone quickly "back to battery." In fact, her guns and engines never stopped working. Informed that HOWORTH was hit, the Task Group Commander dispatched a destroyer-escort to her assistance. The DE captain presently reported back that he couldn't catch the HOWORTH because she was going somewhere faster than his DE's best speed.

"Once again," HOWORTH's Commander Burns observed, *"Lady Luck was on board ship. The plane that crashed could have caused considerably more damage. The contributing factors in stopping these suiciders proved to be high speed, a large volume of accurate fire, and radical maneuvers."*

Skippered by Lieutenant Commander R. V. Wheeler, Jr., destroyer MORRIS, flagship of Captain J. B. McLean, ComDesRon 2, was patrolling Station A-11, Sector C, that same day when, at 1815, she opened fire on an attacking *Kamikaze.* As the plane approached, the destroyer sprinted at 30 knots to evade, while her gunners pumped steel into the enemy. A plume of smoke streamed from the aircraft's tail. Feathers of fire decorated the fuselage. The plane's wings were clipped, and its underbelly took a *hari-kiri* slashing from the DD's guns. The *Kamikaze* should have come apart like a dropped jig-saw puzzle, but by some weird adhesion its body remained intact. At 1817 it sloughed into MORRIS, crashing between her No. 1 and No. 2 five-inch guns.

Explosion! Fire! Damage Control! Emergency repairs! MORRIS went through the harrowing routine. At 1837 destroyer-transport GRIFFIN came alongside to starboard to pass hose lines, while destroyer R. P. LEARY edged up to port. Destroyer-transport BATES also steamed to MORRIS' aid. The ship was a furnace when the first of these assistants arrived, but by 2030 the conflagration was extinguished, the wounded had been transferred to BATES and R. P. LEARY; and MORRIS, her power plant undamaged, was on her way to Kerama Retto.

One other destroyer was maimed by a suicider on April 6—HAYNSWORTH (Commander S. N. Tackney). She got it during the noon hour while she was operating in the screen of Task Group 58.3 off Okinawa. Down the sky came a "Judy," chased by two Corsairs. The Jap plane headed away from the destroyer, then winged over in an Immelmann turn, and dived at the ship. Tackney swung his destroyer hard left while her automatic guns raked the plane. The "Judy," afire, crashed into the main radio-transmitter room. Up went an enormous gasoline fireball—an incandescent balloon that floated for a second, then splattered HAYNSWORTH's superstructure with flame. Topside, the ship became an inferno. Fighting the fire with water, fog, and CO_2, the crew quelled the conflagration in about 10 minutes. But HAYNSWORTH, her radio ruined, her C.I.C. and plotting rooms wrecked, and a number of guns junked, was another candidate for the repair yards.

The other two "small boys" which were damaged on April 6—destroyer HARRISON and destroyer-escort FIEBERLING—escaped with minor wounds which did not put them out of action. HARRISON was slightly injured by a near miss when one of three "Zekes" shot down in a suicide scrimmage exploded close aboard, and her gun-shield was pierced by a hunk of shrapnel. FIEBERLING was scathed while she was hurling an AA barrage at the *Kamikazes* which were attacking NEWCOMB and LEUTZE. Attempting to ram the DE's bridge, a Jap suicider banked in, rolled over, and, flying upside down, pancaked across the ship's SA radar antenna. The antenna cut through the plane's right wing, and sent the aircraft spinning across the sea in a crazy somersault.

As is evident from the April 6 examples, *Kamikaze* crashes caused all manner of ship-wounds. Topside damage was, of course, predominant. But the fire which inevitably followed the explosive smash usually endangered the ship more than the initial blast-damage. And casualties were often progressive, working their way below decks until, as in NEWCOMB's case, the vessel was paralyzed.

Not all of the *Kamikazes* exploded when they struck. Some piled up in trash heaps on the target ship's forecastle or fantail. Some struck and caromed off, or slithered overside in a jumble of wreckage. Occasionally a crash would produce a grisly fantasy—leave the plane jutting from a ship's funnel, or perched atop a deckhouse like some monstrous bird, or perhaps standing on its nose in a nest of wreckage, with a headless aviator clutching the controls. On several occasions a dead pilot came catapulting out of his plane in ceremonial *hari-kiri* robes.

Planes that exploded close aboard or struck a ship's hull near the waterline could deal severe damage. On April 8 destroyer GREGORY (Commander Bruce McCandless), having relieved CASSIN YOUNG at Radar Picket Station No. 3, took a hard body-blow from a *Kamikaze.* At that period the CAP fighter cover retired at sunset, and the picket destroyer mounted solitary guard. No sooner had the CAP fighters withdrawn on the evening of the 8th than a trio of "bogies" showed up on GREGORY's radar screen. McCandless braced his ship to make a battle of it. And the first plane that attacked, a "Sonia," was given a ferocious lashing.

But the "Sonia" could not be stopped. With fragments showering from her wings and with tracer eating into her fuselage, the plane advanced in a step-glide to crash the GREGORY's port side near the waterline, amidships. The gig, which was rigged out, absorbed some of the shock. But the impact was enough to start leaks which flooded the forward fireroom and the forward engine-room to a depth of three feet. While her repair parties were shoring up cracked plates and pumping brine, GREGORY's gunners knocked down two more "Sonias." One of them, skimming over the ship, carried away a radio antenna. But GREGORY needed to transmit no call for help, and the only "next of kin" to be notified were Japanese.

Early in the morning of April 9, destroyer CHARLES J. BADGER (Commander J. H. Cotten) took a bad mauling from a suicider. After delivering a harassing barrage from a fire-support station off Kezu Saki, Okinawa, the ship was lying to in the pre-dawn dark. The morning watch had just come on when a high-powered boat engine was heard to starboard, close aboard. About seven seconds later a stunning underwater blast shook the destroyer; evidently the strange craft had dropped a depth charge. The enemy escaped before BADGER's gunners could fire a shot. And the destroyer was sorely hurt. Buckled and ruptured, her leaking after fireroom let a flood into the after engine-room. Live steam spurted from broken lines, filling the after fireroom with a scalding fog. The starboard main shaft, jolted out of alignment, held the starboard main engine inoperative, and the ship was unable to get under way. Her SC radar, sonar gear, and gyro compass were scotched. All pumps in the after fireroom were damaged, and the available fire and bilge pumps, rushed into emergency service, could barely cope with the swirling flood that poured in through the ruptured plates.

Later that morning the tug TAWAKONI bustled up to moor alongside and undertake salvage operations. By 0715 the BADGER, on a tow line, was en route to Kerama Retto. One of the few destroyers disabled by a suicide boat, she was out of the war for the duration. At that she was luckier than the destroyer HUTCHINS, which was blasted by a suicide boat in the gloom before dawn of May 27. HUTCHINS managed to reach Kerama Retto under her own steam, but in addition to severe damage, she had 18 of her crew wounded.

As the casualty list indicates, April 11, April 12, and April 16 were nightmare days on the Okinawa picket line. During the afternoon of the 11th, destroyer KIDD received an atrocious blasting from a *Kamikaze* which struck her at the waterline and burst into the forward fireroom. The destroyer's captain, Commander H. G. Moore, fell wounded. Himself painfully injured, Lieutenant B. H. Brittin, U.S.N.R., assumed command and held on until he was relieved the following morning by Lieutenant R. L. Kenney, U.S.N.R. In spite of fire, flood, and heavy fatalities KIDD reached Ulithi under her own steam.

In action on the afternoon of the 12th, destroyer-escort WHITEHURST (Lieutenant J. C. Horton, U.S.N.R.) was maimed by a small but vicious bomb and a smash from a suicidal "Val." The plane plunged into the C.I.C., and the ship's entire bridge superstructure was enveloped in flames. All hands in the C.I.C. and pilot-house were killed. All in the radio room, on the deck below, and at most of the forward gun mounts were either killed or badly wounded. Although this was a baptism of fire for captain and crew, the WHITEHURST men fought conflagration, battle damage, and successive *Kamikaze* attacks with a veteran skill and discipline that saved the DE.

Here is the story of an *Oka* attack—one of the few instances wherein the idiot *"Baka"* hit the mark. Target for this weird weapon was the destroyer STANLY (Lieutenant Commander R. S. Harlan). In her company was destroyer LANG (Lieutenant Commander J. T. Bland, III), flagship of Commander W. T. McGarry, ComDesDiv 4.

During the afternoon of the 12th the two DD's were fighting off a hot *Kamikaze* attack aimed at CASSIN YOUNG, then holding the fort at Radar Picket Station No. 1. STANLY and LANG shot down a "Val," and they were training their guns on other enemy aircraft when a *"Baka"* suddenly rocketed out of the aerial melee and made a hell-bent dive at STANLY. The destroyer's gunners pumped a fusillade into the robot, but they might as well have tried to stop a meteor. Striking STANLY's starboard bow, the *"Baka"* burst like a giant grenade. Parts of the rocket went clean through the ship, as did the rocket's bomb, which was kind enough to refrain from exploding until it passed through the destroyer's port side. Afterward, the *"Baka"* pilot was found splattered against a bulkhead in the wrecked forward compartment.

Shortly after this attack, a second *"Baka"* zoomed down at the STANLY. Sharp gunnery sheared off one of the rocket's wings, and the human robot missed the ship, flitting over the superstructure just aft of the

No. 2 stack, and ripping the ensign. Then, hitting the sea about 2,500 yards to port, the *"Baka"* bounced once and exploded.

Destroyers CASSIN YOUNG (Commander J. W. Ailes, III) and PURDY (Commander F. L. Johnson), bashed by suicide planes on April 12, survived savage maulings, and were among the mutilated craft which made their way to Kerama Retto anchorage. Each ship had already acquired combat records which were recognized as outstanding, and their final anti-*Kamikaze* battles were the very antithesis of suicide. No less outstandingly anti-suicide was the fight put up by destroyer-escort RALL (Lieutenant Commander C. B. Taylor, U.S.N.R.), the sixth ship to get it that day. Three "Nates" and an "Oscar" were shot down by the DE during a cyclonic three-minute battle in which she was crashed by a "Nate." With her hull pierced by two large bomb or shell holes, riddled by over 300 shrapnel or bullet holes, and mangled by explosions, the RALL came out of it with colors flying.

April 16 was an ugly day for destroyers LAFFEY, BOWERS, and BRYANT. All three were agonizingly blistered by the "Divine Wind," and each rode out the fiery hurricane with even more fiery courage. LAFFEY's battle, fought against incredibly long odds, will be detailed as a chapter climax.

On that same April day destroyer McDERMUT was damaged by two 5-inch hits and a 40 and 20 mm. fusillade from a friendly vessel. Lucky McDERMUT! The magnitude of her fortune becomes apparent when one learns from her Action Report that her "friend" was battleship MISSOURI. The big battleship was firing at low-flying planes, and the little destroyer happened to be on the receiving end in the outfield. Perhaps she derived some consolation from the fact that she could survive a barrage from the "MIGHTY MO."

So the casualty list lengthened with the days of April and dragged on through the sulphurous weeks of May. AMMEN holed by a *Kamikaze* explosion close aboard. ISHERWOOD disabled by a smash. HUTCHINS blasted by a suicide boat. RALPH TALBOT, TWIGGS, and DALY crippled by suicide planes. HAGGARD hard hit. HAZELWOOD barbarously mutilated. HUDSON hurt by a near miss, and later injured by going alongside the burning escort-carrier SANGAMON. Destroyer-escort ENGLAND savagely mauled. EVANS battered all acockbill by four successive *Kamikaze* smashes. HUGH W. HADLEY wrecked by a bomb hit, a *"Baka,"* and two suicide crashes. Destroyer-escort JOHN C. BUTLER battered by two *Kamikazes*. BACHE and DOUGLAS H. FOX cruelly blasted. COWELL slashed by a friendly shell. STORMES maimed by a suicide plane. BRAINE mangled by a two-plane crash. ANTHONY scarred by a near miss. SHUBRICK crashed by a *Kamikaze* and disabled.

One of the DE's hard hit at Okinawa was champion sub-killer ENGLAND, now skippered by Lieutenant J. A. Williamson, U.S.N.R. On March 27 she was given an Okinawa welcome by a *Kamikaze* which struck close aboard. But ENGLAND's black-letter day was May 9. About sundown of that day, while she was on screening duty at a station midway between Kerama Retto and Tonachi Shima, she was hit by a suicide "Val." Her radar spotted this enemy at seven miles—one of three bumblebees in a melee with fighter hornets. Two of the Jap raiders were eventually shot down by the CAP fighters, but the fatal "Val" broke through to dive at ENGLAND. The DE maneuvered at flank speed to evade, while her 3-inch 50's, 20 mm.'s, and 1.10 automatic flailed at the oncoming suicider. A wheel flew from the plane; fire rushed from the cockpit; the pilot was riddled. He had been heading for ENGLAND's bridge, and for a moment it seemed as though the "Val" would miss. But the "Val's" port wing snagged in the forward boat davit, and the plane went spinning into the passageway just abaft the ship's office.

Crash! Bomb explosion! Fire! ENGLAND was blitzed. The blast cloaked her superstructure with flame and smoke. Wardroom, captain's cabin, ship's office, pilothouse and C.I.C. were turned into incinerators. Flames bushed up around the flying bridge and signal bridge. Clutching wounded shipmates, men on the signal bridge leaped overside. Hands on the main deck manned hoses to spray comrades who came fighting down out of the wreckage with their clothing afire. Within twenty seconds of the *Kamikaze* smash the ship's damage controlmen were battling the conflagration, but the vessel was an inferno for the next hour. Some of the deep-rooted fires were not extinguished until midnight.

Destroyer-minesweeper GHERARDI, minesweeper VIGILANCE, and tug GEAR steamed to ENGLAND's aid. Swimmers were soon recovered and the wounded cared for. When the flames were finally smothered, GEAR towed the fire-blackened DE to Kerama Retto. Patched up there and at Leyte, in June she set out on the long voyage home. She was decommissioned on October 15, 1945, and on November 1 of that year she was stricken from the naval registry. Her name, however, remains indelibly engraved in the annals of naval warfare.

A remarkable performance of ship-saving was staged by the destroyermen of U.S.S. HAZELWOOD. "She was one of the greats to get home from Okinawa," veteran destroyer Admiral Tisdale observed, recalling an inspection of the damaged ship at Mare Island Navy Yard. "She took one hell of a beating from the *Kamikazes.* About a quarter of her complement, including her Captain and Exec, were killed in the smash. Her bridge and much of her superstructure were reduced to scrap. A young Reserve Officer—a lieutenant (jg)—assumed immediate command, and he handled the ship like a Farragut. Then she was taken down to Ulithi and brought home by another Reserve Officer—a lieutenant. With officers like HAZELWOOD's in the line, the Navy never had to worry."

HAZELWOOD's hour came on the afternoon of April 29 while she was steaming with the 12-ship circular screen of Fast Carrier Task Group 58.4. The formation was attacked by three *Kamikazes,* and at 1710 HAZELWOOD raced to the assistance of stricken destroyer HAGGARD. Sharp gunnery and fast maneuvering saved her from a "Zeke" which tagged her from astern. Thrown off course by a bursting 5-inch salvo, the plane grazed HAZELWOOD's No. 4 gun, and hit the water with a killing belly-whacker. A few minutes later another "Zeke" plummeted out of a low cloud and came in on a shallow dive dead astern. The destroyer's skipper, Commander V. P. Douw, ordered a hard turn to port, and the ship's 40 and 20 mm.'s blazed at the plane. Although drilled from nose to tail, the "Zeke" skimmed over the superstructure; its right wing grabbed the No. 2 stack; the plane careened into the No. 1 stack, landed on the main deck level, and blew up. Flung against the base of the bridge, the "Zeke's" bombs exploded, and a gasoline fire flashed through the superstructure. The mast toppled over like a chopped pine. Showered by burning wreckage, the forward guns were put out of action. Ten officers and 36 men perished in the mangle. Commander Douw and Lieutenant J. P. Dunbar, U.S.N.R., the Executive Officer, were among the slain.

When communications with the bridge were severed, Lieutenant (jg) C. M. Locke, U.S.N.R., ship's Engineer Officer, immediately assumed command and directed the fire-fighting and damage control. Destroyers McGOWAN, MELVIN, and COLAHAN, and cruisers FLINT and SAN DIEGO quickly closed in to assist the HAZELWOOD. McGOWAN and MELVIN moved up to fight the fire while the other ships picked up survivors. Later that evening McGOWAN edged alongside to take HAZELWOOD in tow.

Around midnight, MELVIN supplied power for an electric fuel-oil service pump which enabled HAZELWOOD's engineers to light off her No. 4 boiler. At 0500 in the morning of April 30, the tow was cast off, and the damaged destroyer steamed southward in company with FLINT, McGOWAN, and MELVIN. On May 1 Lieutenant D. N. Morey, Jr., U.S.N.R., "Exec" of destroyer BUCHANAN, took over the HAZELWOOD's bridge. Actually, the ship had no bridge, and Lieutenant Morey conned her from a nest of wreckage in the superstructure. After temporary patching at Ulithi, HAZELWOOD voyaged across the Pacific to California. Those who saw her slide into Mare Island Yard knew they were witnessing a miracle of survival. But she was just another DD which lived through the death-dealing "Divine Wind."

No study of the ordeal endured by the destroyer forces at Okinawa would be complete without mention of the ships which came through unscathed, and a comparison of destroyer and *Kamikaze* casualties.

As to the first subject, not many of the 98 DD's and 50 DE's which saw duty on the "Iceberg" front escaped *Kamikaze* attack. Although the number of ship casualties constitutes an extraordinarily high percentage of the vessels engaged, and major damage was almost certain to result from a *Kamikaze* smash, a few of the DD's and DE's which fought the Battle for Okinawa were unharmed.

Some of these—vessels which were on the firing line over a long period of time—merit special mention. In "Iceberg" waters from March 21 to July 28, destroyer HEYWOOD L. EDWARDS (Commander A. L. Shepherd) came through without a scratch. Flagship of Captain A. D. Chandler, ComDesRon 58, VAN VALKENBURGH (Commander A. B. Coxe, Jr.) emerged from the carnage unscathed. After weeks on the Okinawa picket line, BROWN (Commander R. R. Craighill) and BRADFORD (Commander W. W. Armstrong) retired without a scar. WADSWORTH (Commander R. D. Fusselman), in action from April to June 24, worked like a miniature dreadnaught. Her masterful performance at Okinawa won her the coveted Presidential Unit Citation. BARTON (Commanders E. B. Dexter and H. P. McIntire), flagship of Captain B. R. Harrison, ComDesRon 60, fought through the worst of April, May, and June, and did not have an enemy hand laid on her. As flagship of Captain W. L. Freseman, ComDesRon 60, she arrived on the "Iceberg" front on March 25—an Okinawa pioneer, and one of the first on the scene. Between that date and June 30, the BARTON fired a total 26,789 rounds of 5-inch ammunition for an average of 4,465 rounds per gun. Between March 26 and June 21, she fired 22,057 rounds without accident and almost without incident. Sole personnel injury of note was a broken hand; not a single mount was out of commission more than an hour. This remarkable record speaks for itself—or for the BARTON.

BARTON's record also hints something in regard to Japanese casualties. In many instances it was impossible to discern the burst which felled the suicider.

Planes shot down by AA fire may have been previously damaged in dogfight. Firing severally as well as singly, destroyers dissected many a *Kamikaze* crate. Hundreds of suicide planes were lost through mishandling and operational breakdown. So the exact figure scored by the DD's and DE's at Okinawa remains an unknown. Of course, every *Kamikaze* ship-smash was a decided casualty—another plane lost by Japan. Altogether the Japs lost some 7,830 aircraft in the Okinawa debacle. It is estimated that over 3,000 of these were shot down by Navy and Marine planes, and that about 410 were shot down by Navy guns. Perhaps two-thirds of those guns were in the "small boys"—the destroyers and destroyer-escorts.

Another point—destroyers carrying fighter-director teams steered many a CAP squadron into battle and coached aerial duels which took the tuck out of the "Divine Wind." Such service definitely counts as an assist. Destroyer Bennion, for example. Stepping into action at Okinawa as a radar picket on March 26, she served in that capacity until the end of May. Skippered by Commander R. H. Holmes, Bennion one day received from Admiral Turner the following message:

> CONGRATULATIONS ON YOUR WORK YOU ARE KEEPING UP YOUR REPUTATION AS THE BEST OR NEARLY THE BEST FIGHTING DESTROYER OUT HERE

She was characterized by another experienced destroyer officer as *"probably the most successful radar picket and fighter-director ship at Okinawa."* Her own gunners shot down 13 Jap planes; they shared in the destruction of four more, and routed dozens of potential suicide-divers.

Probably the champion *Kamikaze*-killers in the Okinawa death struggle were destroyers Evans and Hugh W. Hadley. On May 10 this pair were teamed up at Radar Picket Station No. 15. Although Evans' Captain, Commander R. J. Archer, was senior, he turned over the duties of Officer in Tactical Command to Hadley's skipper, Commander B. J. Mullaney, as Hadley was a fighter-director ship. The two destroyers were at one of the numerous stations covering the Okinawa transport area. Their mission: to detect and report approaching enemy aircraft; to control the assigned CAP; and to prevent enemy planes from reaching the transports. The CAP group contained 12 planes.

On the morning of May 11 the *Kamikazes* came over in force. About 0740 the "bogies" were reported thick as swarming bees in the northeast mist. Five minutes later a Jap float plane zoomed out of the murk, diving at Hadley. She and Evans opened fire. End of *Kamikaze* at 1,200 yards.

That was the beginning of an action which was a miniature of the entire Okinawa sea-air battle. For the next hour and a half the Jap planes kept coming in a series of waves that rumbled across the sky much as successive combers sweep across an expanse of sea. In the first wave there were 36 Jap planes; in the second 50; in the third 20; in the fourth about 25; in the last about 20. Evans, Hadley, and the CAP planes fought it out with a total of some 150 Jap aircraft.

Excerpt from Hadley's Action Report:

> At about 0755 the entire Combat Air Patrol was ordered out in different formations to intercept and engage the horde of enemy planes closing us, and shortly we received reports from them that they had destroyed twelve planes. Then they were so busy that they could not send us reports, but we intercepted their communications to learn about 40 to 50 planes were destroyed by them. C.I.C. reported that there were no friendly planes within ten miles of this ship. . . .
>
> From this time on the Hadley and the Evans were attacked continuously by numerous enemy aircraft coming at us in groups of four to six planes on each ship. During the early period, enemy aircraft were sighted trying to pass our formation headed for Okinawa. These were flying extremely low on both bows and seemingly ignoring us. The Hadley shot down four of these. . . .
>
> The tempo of the engagement and the maneuver of the two destroyers at high speed was such as to cause the Hadley and the Evans to be separated by distances as much as two and three miles. This resulted in individual action by both ships. . . . From 0830 to 0900 the Hadley was attacked by groups of planes coming in on both bows. Twelve enemy planes were shot down by the Hadley's guns during this period, at times firing all guns in various directions. The Evans . . . to the northward, was seen fighting off a number of planes. . . . At 0900 the Evans was hit and put out of action. . . .
>
> From this time on the Hadley received the bulk of the attacks and action became furious with all guns firing at planes on all sides of the ship. . . . For 20 minutes the Hadley fought off the enemy singlehanded, being separated from the Evans (which was out of action) and the four small support ships two miles distant. Finally, at 0920, ten enemy planes which had surrounded the Hadley—four on the starboard bow . . . four on the port bow . . . and two astern—attacked the ship simultaneously. All ten planes were destroyed . . . and each plane was definitely accounted for.

This remarkable exhibition of gunnery was performed in the face of dire adversity. Early in the action Hadley was struck by a bomb. Then a low-flying "Betty" released a *"Baka"* which rocketed into the ship. Next she was struck aft by a suicide plane. And then another *Kamikaze* smashed into her rigging. Badly holed, with both engine-rooms and a fireroom flooded, the ship listed over and settled rap-

Escaping one "Zeke," Hazelwood was rammed amidships by a second which exploded and killed her skipper and 45 others. Assuming command, her engineering officer led the fight that saved her. A young Reserve officer, he "handled the ship like a Farragut," in the opinion of Admiral Tisdale, and got her to temporary safety in Ulithi, whence she made the long voyage home.

An Oscar crashed the bridge of Bowers (DE 637). That same day, April 16, 1945, Laffey and Bryant were also hit by kamikazes. Each rode out the fiery hurricane, despite heavy casualties.

One of too many: Shubrick (DD 639), disabled by a kamikaze off Kerama Retto. The "Divine Wind" put an increasing number of ships out of action, among them the famous sub-killer England.

The new minelayer Aaron Ward, after being blasted by five suicide planes while in company with Little, which was sunk at Okinawa, as were fourteen other destroyers and destroyer-escorts.

Biggest suicider of them all, the 18-inch-gun Yamato. Only seven American planes were lost in sinking this super-battleship and her escorts. Jap naval power was reduced almost to zero.

A typical group of destroyermen in their natural habitat. Shooting the breeze about their special sector of the mighty westward push across the Pacific, these men are battle-tested veterans all.

In all branches of the Service and in all the ships at sea, the morale of the destroyermen was tops. And there wasn't any tougher job in the war than their picket duty off Okinawa.

idly. Ammunition explosions raged on deck, and the vessel was engulfed in a turmoil of flame and dense black smoke. But the gun crews that were living stuck it out at guns that were undamaged, and the Jap planes fell like shot crows.

Meantime, EVANS had put up a battle-royal to carry out her end of the mission. With "bandits" swarming around her, this destroyer's marksmen staged a *Kamikaze*-shoot no less remarkable than HADLEY'S. Most of the planes in her vicinity attempted suicide dives, and EVANS' fire cut them off in mid-career. But four of them succeeded in crashing the ship. The first smashed a hole in her port bow. The second struck below the waterline, and the plane's bomb or torpedo burst in the after fireroom. Up to that time EVANS had shot down 15 *Kamikazes* and suffered no casualties, but this dual blasting left her a hobbling cripple. Less than two minutes after the second crash, a third *Kamikaze* slammed into her galley, and an instant later a fourth suicider swiped into the opposite side of the ship. A bomb penetrated the main deck, burst in the forward fireroom, and exploded both boilers. The monstrous concussion stopped EVANS dead in the water. Without light, power, steam, or water pressure, and with most of her communications apparatus ruined, the destroyer slumped bleeding in the sea.

Few ships at Okinawa were hit harder than HADLEY and EVANS. Damage control on board HADLEY appeared to be impossible, and as she seemed on the point of capsizing, her captain gave the order, "Prepare to abandon ship!" Life rafts and floats were got overside and the wounded and most of the crew quit the vessel. About 50 men and officers remained on board to fight fire, explosions, and flooding. Torpedoes were jettisoned, and weights were shifted or thrown overside to correct the starboard list. Hot munitions were wet down. Fire and flood were finally controlled, and the HUGH W. HADLEY stayed afloat. Eventually she was towed to safe anchorage at Ie Shima. EVANS' crew put up a similar battle to save their ship, fighting flood and inferno with bucket brigades and handybillies. While her desperate sailors labored in a jungle of wreckage, flame, and smoke, the ship was attacked by another *Kamikaze.* Two CAP planes pursued the suicider as it dived on EVANS' bow. With bullets nipping its tail, the Jap plane ran into a fusillade of automatic fire from the burning destroyer. Tobogganing past EVANS' port side, the riddled *Kamikaze* sloughed into the sea astern. As in HADLEY'S case, near-by ships steamed to the rescue, and that afternoon EVANS was bound for Ie Shima on a towline.

But the big feature of the HADLEY-EVANS drama was the amazing target score of this team. Including three suicide hits, the gun crews of the HUGH W. HADLEY in that hour-and-a-half battle shot down 23 Japanese planes. With four suicide hits, three assists with HADLEY, and one assist with CAP fighters, the EVANS marksmen shot down 23 planes! All told, the two destroyers accounted for 46 enemy aircraft—a massacre which must have given the Special Attack Corps a surfeit of suicide. *"Our mission,"* wrote HADLEY'S captain, *"was accomplished. The transports at the Okinawa anchorage were saved from attack. . . ."*

As a superb destroyer effort on the Okinawa picket line, the sharpshooting of EVANS and HADLEY had its match in the ship-saving endeavor which brought destroyer LAFFEY out of the Valley of the Shadow of Death. No ship at Okinawa was hit harder than this indomitable destroyer. Her survival was almost supercorporeal and superhuman. One might readily believe she was supported and sustained by the spirit of her predecessor, the LAFFEY sunk off Savo Island on November 13, 1942. Like her namesake, the LAFFEY at Okinawa attained a Presidential Unit Citation.

April 16, 1945—one of the darkest days at Okinawa, and LAFFEY (Commander F. J. Becton), with a fighter-director team on board, patrolling Radar Picket Station No. 1. At 0744 she drove off a "Val," which dropped a bomb about a mile and a half from the ship, and retired. Soon the Jap was followed by others—a few at first, and then a swarm of them flitting across the radar screen.

On station with LAFFEY were two LCS's—sturdy ships, but hardly able to cope with the coming onslaught. Converging from north, northeast, and northwest were some 50 "bandits." Under the best of circumstances the CAP fighters available would have been unable to intercept an enemy force so well dispersed. As it was, the CAP group was "changing the guard" with its relief when the assaulting planes closed in. Compelled to intercept in the vicinity of the target ship, some of the CAP fighters stormed right through LAFFEY'S AA barrage.

Two "Judy's" launched a coordinated attack on the destroyer. Both were brought down by 40 mm. and 20 mm. fire to port and starboard. The port plane exploded close aboard, and the blast put LAFFEY'S fire-control radar out of kilter. Then the ship was grazed by a "Val" which burst in the sea a few yards from the destroyer's fantail. Another "Judy" was shot down close aboard. Then LAFFEY was hit.

About 0845 a "Judy" banked in on the destroyer's port bow, lurched around her cradled motor whaleboat, and plunged into a 20 mm. mount. Blazing gasoline spurted from a crumpled cockpit and an amputated wing. Then a "Val," grasshopping across the water, crashed head on into the No. 3 mount aft, demolishing the 5-inch gun. A moment later another *Kamikaze* jumped in on the ship's starboard quarter, dropping a bomb half a second before crashing into the side of the wrecked gun mount. Fire rolled through LAFFEY's superstructure, and a pall of smoke settled over the ship. Toward this pyre jumped another helldiver, swooping down out of the sun to level off at the last moment and fling a bomb at the ship's port quarter. The blast wiped out a 20 mm. magazine, causing a shattering explosion which disabled the steering gear and jammed the rudder hard left.

Jeopardy now had LAFFEY by the throat. With her topside aflame, and all guns aft of the No. 2 stack knocked out, the ship circled drunkenly under a sky fouled with Jap aircraft.

Down came the planes like vultures trying to get their talons into a crippled wildcat. Some of the Japs were shot down by CAP fighters which trailed them until they splashed. Several were blown apart by LAFFEY's forward guns. However, two more *Kamikazes* crashed the ship. Striking in quick succession, they ploughed into the after deckhouse, feeding the flames with more firebrands and gasoline.

As LAFFEY stumbled out from under this blasting, an "Oscar" broke away from a dogfight and headed for the ship's forecastle, a Corsair in close pursuit. Machine-gunners on the bow riveted the enemy plane with bullets as it pancaked over the ship. "Oscar" and Corsair both hit the mast—a one-two that tore off the SC antenna, the port yardarm, and the SG wave guide. Raising a huge waterspout, the Jap plane plunged into the sea to starboard. The Corsair pilot was seen to bail out as his damaged plane went looping down the sky.

Meanwhile, a "Judy" struck the water close aboard to port, showering LAFFEY with burning scrap. Still another "Judy," zooming up on the starboard quarter, was shot down 800 yards from the ship. Struck by a 5-inch shell, an "Oscar" blew up about 500 yards from the ship. Another "Oscar," driving from ahead, caught a VT burst and crashed 500 yards off the bow. Then LAFFEY was struck by a bomb dropped by a "Val" which sideswiped the starboard yardarm. The bomb exploded in the ship's fiery superstructure, while the *Kamikaze* crashed in the sea. Yet another "Val" came in to drop a bomb which erased a 20 mm. battery. Riddled by 5-inch and 40 mm. fire, and scorched by the fire of a chasing CAP fighter, this plane hit the sea off LAFFEY's port quarter. The last assault was made by a "Judy" which came in from the port with a pursuing CAP fighter pouring tracer into her tail. LAFFEY's port 40's and 20's blazed at the plane, which blew up close aboard. The attack was over.

And, incredibly, the U.S.S. LAFFEY remained afloat. Her superstructure was an inferno and some of her stern compartments were swamped, but a few of her guns were still firing, and full engine power was still available. During the 80-minute action she had been attacked by 22 planes, of which nine had been shot down by the destroyermen.

But the real story of LAFFEY has to do with fortitude. Eight enemy planes struck the ship—seven with suicidal intent, and the eighth (the "Val" which slashed the mast) by accident. If one counts the Corsair which also struck the mast, the total goes to nine plane hits. Five of the Jap suiciders which crashed the ship were loaded with bombs, and the resultant explosions were devastating. In addition to this blasting, LAFFEY took four conventional bomb hits. Nine plane crashes and four bomb hits—it seems safe to say that no destroyer in World War II absorbed more punishment and still cheated the Executioner.

Progressive damage finally brought LAFFEY to a dead stop as her crew—or what was left of it—fought fire and flood. Eventually she was towed to safe anchorage off Okinawa. But—marvel no less—in six days she was steaming for Saipan under her own power. She steams on through history as one of the great DD's of the Navy's Destroyer Force—a "can" in every sense of the verb.

Out of the thunder and smoke, the searing and agony of Okinawa, came reams of wordage on the ways and means, the best methods and devices, for combating suicide air results. Various types of fire-fighting gear were recommended, and crews which had attended special classes in fire-fighting and damage control were remarked as most efficient. Special tactics were recommended—open fire at long range—maneuver at high speed as the plane dives—keep shooting until the plane is seen to crash—and so on. First-aid drills and rescue practice paid top dividends. But through all these many suggestions and advices ran the inevitable repetend—training, training, and more training. And much of it boiled down to Farragut's famous formula, *"The best defense is a well-directed fire from your own guns."*

Here is an interesting word on morale from the Action Report of the destroyer ANTHONY (Commander C. J. Van Arsdall, Jr.):

> The Commanding Officer is aware that the higher echelons of command have taken note of the performance of destroyers on radar picket stations. He doubts, however, that anyone never having been regularly assigned to such duty can fully realize the effect which this duty has upon the officers and crew, particularly of

vessels which have witnessed successful suicide crashes on other ships and have themselves been under direct attack. A tension builds up which is evident in many ways, and which is not relaxed by the periods for logistics between tours of duty on picket stations, largely because of the knowledge that coming assignments are "more of the same." Cases of active hysteria, requiring transfer, were few on this ship. How long others still on board could have held out is subject to question. After a certain time, the best efforts to boost morale are futile. The boys know what they are in for, and you can't fool them.

We found that we could take it, but we didn't like it. Everyone knew that the duty was a nasty job, but a necessary one, and was well aware that every plane which managed to get in was a separate case of "either you or us." To the great credit of the men, nobody minded admitting that he was afraid, because nobody was fool enough to pretend he wasn't and make fun of fear. And the fear was not expressed by hysteria, but by a growing tension which seemed to relax only when the guns were shooting. All hands felt much better at battle stations than at any other place. The C.O. has nothing but praise for each and every officer and crew man, for the ship has never operated more efficiently than under these conditions. . . .

Immolation of the Imperial Fleet

On the evening of April 6, 1945—the day the "Divine Wind" blew its worst—a Japanese surface force sortied from the Inland Sea and trooped southward to attack the American invaders at Okinawa. Having ordered the suicide of Kurita's Second Fleet, Ozawa's Carrier Force, and the *Kikusui* Special Attack Corps, Admiral Soemu Toyoda had now called upon the remnant Imperial Fleet to climb on the sacrificial altar.

The remnant which steamed down out of the Bungo Suido included the 63,000-ton superbattleship YAMATO, cruiser YAHAGI, and eight destroyers.

"We questioned whether there was a fifty-fifty chance," Admiral Toyoda stated in dismal post-war recollection. *"Even in assembling that squadron we had a difficult time getting the necessary 2,500 tons of fuel oil. But . . . nothing was to be gained by letting those ships lie idle in home waters, and, besides, it would have been contrary to the tradition of the Japanese Navy not to have sent them."*

This ceremonious bow to tradition sent hundreds of men in the crews of YAMATO, YAHAGI and the eight destroyers to certain death, and condemned the ten warships to destruction. And as a move in behalf of Japan's defense, this sacrifice was worse than useless.

The sortieing Jap ships were promptly spotted by American submarines and air scouts, and Admiral Mitscher raced north with Task Force 58 to intercept. About mid-morning of April 7 the Imperial remnants were caught due north of Okinawa. Descending on the pagoda-masted targets at high noon, Mitscher's bomber squadrons expected aerial opposition. But YAMATO and her company were as naked to the sky as H.M.S. REPULSE and PRINCE OF WALES had once been.

Doom closed fast on the colossal YAMATO. She dodged and roared and smoked, fighting back as best she could, but her AA weapons were unavailing, and against aircraft her 18-inch guns were as useless as blunderbusses. Plastered by bombs and holed by ten torpedoes, the giantess finally rolled over and blew up. Down with her went the cruiser YAHAGI. Down went destroyers ASASHIMO, ISOKAZE, HAMAKAZE, and KASUMI. By mid-afternoon the slaughter was over. Badly damaged, the four surviving Jap destroyers were in pellmell flight. Fought at a cost of seven American planes, the action put the final period to Japanese sea power. Out of gas and out of ships, the once great Imperial Navy was now little more than wreckage on the beach at Sasebo.

The only echoes of its former power came from the Japanese Submarine Force. Miwa's subs had been counted on to shore up the Okinawa sea defense, and a sizable midget fleet had been assembled for that purpose. This was strictly a suicide outfit, and Miwa was prepared to use it as such. Fortunately for the American invaders, most of the baby subs in the Okinawa area were snared with the capture of Kerama Retto. At this anchorage they were found lying around like seals in the Pribilof Islands. Dozens of the little boilers were taken for scrap, as were some 390 suicide boats which had been mustered for the *Kikusui* program.

Meantime, the ocean-going I-boats and RO-boats found the "Iceberg" waters too hot for their taste. As the battle for Okinawa thundered to its peak, the Jap submarines quietly withdrew. Admiral Miwa was indisposed to waste in futile sacrifice the one last Imperial naval force available for Pacific duty; the last link between Japan and remote fragments of the shattered Empire; the last sea force which could put up a defense of Tokyo Bay.

As it was, nine Japanese submarines were downed early in the Okinawa battle. Five of these were sunk by American destroyer forces holding the A/S line, part and parcel of the "Iceberg" effort.

Okinawa A/S Campaign

Haggard Kills I-371

On March 22, 1945, Task Group 58.4 (a fast carrier group under Rear Admiral A. W. Radford) finished fueling at sea from the logistics support group, and set out on a high-speed run toward Okinawa. Positioned 12 miles in advance of the formation, destroyer HAGGARD, flagship of Captain L. K. Reynolds, ComDesDiv 94, cruised ahead as radar scout.

At 2333 HAGGARD made radar contact with a foreign vessel which proved itself to be a sub by first vanishing from the radar picture and then coming in on the sonar register (about 15 minutes later).

HAGGARD's skipper, Lieutenant Commander V. J. Soballe, maneuvered the ship into attack position, and at 0019 in the morning of March 23 a pattern of 11 depth charges splashed into the sea.

Right on the stop-watch dot, the first charge exploded, generating an undersea blast of such volume and violence that it damaged the destroyer's starboard shaft. About three minutes later, destroyer UHLMANN reported a submarine broaching, a phenomenon also noted by HAGGARD's C.I.C. team.

Soballe immediately drew a bead to ram the enemy. And as HAGGARD steamed toward the moonlit target her 40 mms. opened fire on it. Shells burst on the silhouetted conning tower, then the destroyer's stem sliced into the sub's starboard side just abaft the tower. Rolling under the impact, the gashed submarine went down by the stern.

She returned to the surface presently—in a thousand pieces. Somewhere deep under, the submersible was blown apart by an enormous explosion. The moon-silvered seascape was littered with trash. HAGGARD circled about to inspect this rubbish, then in company with destroyer UHLMANN rejoined the Okinawa-bound task group.

The enemy destroyed was the I-371. She could be considered No. 1 on the Okinawa hit parade.

Morrison and Stockton Kill I-8

Eight days after the HAGGARD kill, destroyers STOCKTON and MORRISON abolished another I-boat.

STOCKTON (Lieutenant Commander W. R. Glennon) saw her first. That is, she made the radar contact which resulted in the enemy's ultimate destruction. It happened on the night of March 30-31 when STOCKTON was en route to Kerama Retto with a task unit which contained a tanker, a freighter, and another DD. At 2308, when the ships were about 90 miles southeast of their destination, STOCKTON picked up the "pip" at a range of 12,800 yards.

Because the area was teeming with friendly vessels, the commander of the task unit tried to speak the stranger by TBS. There was no answer. STOCKTON was then ordered to go after the target. As she was turning to do so, the radar contact disappeared—a diving submarine.

In his Action Report the task unit commander sharply criticized himself for delaying the investigation 20 minutes while attempting to obtain an answer over TBS. The delay, of course, gave the submarine a chance to maneuver for an attack. Fortunately the sub in question failed to seize the opportunity, and STOCKTON did the attacking after acquiring sonar contact at 1,500-yard range.

Between 2339 in the evening of March 30 and 0239 in the morning of March 31 the destroyer strove to hit the submerged target with seven depth-charge assaults. Oil spewed to the surface after the seventh attack; the sea-beast was injured and bleeding.

Meantime, an anti-sub patrol plane had arrived on the scene to drop flares. And another destroyer was approaching. This was U.S.S. MORRISON (Commander J. R. Hansen), ordered to relieve STOCKTON.

Arriving at the rendezvous point, MORRISON found the seascape brightly illuminated and STOCKTON conducting "Operation Observant." STOCKTON had lost contact with the target, but MORRISON, taking over, picked it up within two minutes. She lost it while maneuvering to attack; regained it at 0324; dropped 11 depth charges, shallow setting, at 0330.

Eruptions of water rose and fell, after which the sub was heard blowing all ballast. Up she came, spouting like a narwhal, her snout rearing from the sea only 900 yards from the destroyer. Too close to wheel and ram, MORRISON opened pointblank fire with all guns. Then, as the I-boat's superstructure bucked up, streaming foam, the destroyer let fly with three starboard K-guns.

The depth charges thudded. Shell hits slammed and banged around the exposed conning tower. For over half an hour the destroyer continued a rapid fire at the rolling, pitching submersible. She was a tough submarine. Her hull was punctured by a score of shots, her deck was all but ripped away, and her tower was shattered by an explosion before she went down, at 0412, stern first.

Daybreak revealed the usual mess of oil and debris that marked a submarine grave. In the midst of this flotsam two Jap bodies floated and a third submariner was swimming. When asked by an interpreter to name the defunct submarine, this lone survivor found the spirit to reply, "If your ship were sunk, would you release name?"

However, it was all there in Admiral Miwa's records. The sub which fell victim to STOCKTON and MORRISON was the I-8.

Hudson Sinks RO-41

On April 5, 1945—the day before the "Divine Wind" hurricane—destroyer HUDSON (Commander R.

R. Pratt) was patrolling Radar Picket Station No. 10, west of Okinawa, when she received word of a surface radar contact made by LCS-115 twelve miles distant. The landing craft had a good look at the sub before it submerged..

HUDSON raced to the scene, and established radar contact at 0345 with a target 11,000 yards distant. An anti-sub patrol plane was notified, and at 0406 the aircraft was on the spot, dropping parachute flares. A moment later the radar target vanished.

HUDSON raced toward the point of last contact, then slowed to 15 knots to conduct an "Observant" sonar search. She had the contact within two minutes, range 1,600 yards.

The contact was held almost continuously for over four hours while the destroyer made 16 approaches, concluding six of them with depth-charge runs. After the third attack a muffled explosion mumbled under the sea. Then the sub was heard blowing ballast. She failed to reach the surface, for her ballast-blowing was interrupted by a blast that unloosed a great quantity of oil.

HUDSON followed through with bombings four, five, and six, but her work was done. By daybreak the seascape was smeared with an extensive oil slick. The destroyermen noted numerous items of debris. Admiral Miwa was minus another submarine, the RO-41. This was the sub which had sunk destroyer-escort SHELTON, and indirectly caused the loss of the SEAWOLF.

Monssen and Mertz Kill RO-46

On April 9, 1945, destroyers MONSSEN (Lieutenant Commander E. G. Sanderson) and MERTZ (Commander W. S. Maddox) teamed up to down another Japanese submarine in Okinawa's bloodstained waters. The two DD's were in the screen of Rear Admiral Radford's Task Group 58.4, containing aircraft carriers YORKTOWN, INTREPID, LANGLEY, and INDEPENDENCE.

The group had just completed flight operations, and the clock was ticking to 0546, when MONSSEN's sonar watch reported a contact at 900 yards. The sub was well within the A/S screen, and MONSSEN's skipper lost no time in directing an urgent attack.

She ran in for three depth-charge assaults on the submerged target. Then MERTZ arrived on the spot to assist, as did a number of the Task Group's planes. Contact, lost for about an hour, was at length regained by MERTZ.

After three depth-charge runs, MERTZ stepped aside, and MONSSEN resumed the offensive. Two more patterns produced a series of basso underwater blasts that were the submarine's requiem.

According to Admiral Miwa's records the victim was the RO-46.

Heermann, McCord, Collett, Mertz, Uhlmann, and Aircraft Kill I-56

The RO-boat or I-boat that dabbled in Okinawa's waters during "Iceberg" was a candidate for the *Kikusui* treatment, however circumspect the approach. There was, for example, the I-56, which had the temerity to air her conning tower in the vicinity of Rear Admiral Radford's YORKTOWN group—the group which contained such sub-killers as HAGGARD, MONSSEN, and MERTZ. It also contained destroyers HEERMANN, UHLMANN, and McCORD, equally adept at sub-killing. When these last three, plus MERTZ, went after the target, and two aircraft from carrier BATAAN and destroyer COLLETT took a hand, the I-56 had about as much chance for longevity as a *Kamikaze.*

Destroyer HEERMANN (Commander A. T. Hathaway) obtained the radar contact at 2320 in the evening of April 17. So did several other ships of the YORKTOWN group. As HEERMANN closed the range, the radar "pip" flickered out, and the underwater game began. Acquiring sonar contact, the destroyer steamed down the track and at 2355 the depth-charges were thudding.

Meanwhile, the Screen Commander had ordered UHLMANN to assist. Skippered by Commander S. C. Small, this destroyer entered the contest around midnight. She delivered two depth-charge attacks within the next 45 minutes.

UHLMANN was then ordered to play the part of "linking vessel" between the task group and the subhunters. Her place on the firing-line was taken by McCORD (Commander F. D. Michael), flagship of Captain I. H. Nunn, ComDesRon 47. From 0130 until 0743 in the morning of the 18th, HEERMANN and McCORD took turns banging away at the submarine. The atmosphere in that pressure hull must have been stupefying by that time, an unmitigated Turkish bath. Both HEERMANN and McCORD had expended all their depth charges in the roundelay of attacks.

The two destroyers were directed by Squadron Commander Nunn to maintain sonar contact until other DD's could be fetched to the scene. Before the destroyer replacements arrived, a pair of torpedo bombers from the BATAAN showed up. The planes dropped bombs on the target at 0851 and 0857, but they failed to dig up the sub.

The DD replacements were there by 1030—destroyer MERTZ and destroyer COLLETT. The COLLETT was captained by Commander J. D. COLLETT; the ship had been named after his brother, Lieutenant Commander John A. Collett, who had been killed in action in 1943 while commanding an aircraft torpedo squadron in the Pacific.

The COLLETT made five attacks on the submerged submarine. MERTZ stepped in to deliver a single. After COLLETT's fifth attack, which was launched early in the afternoon, a dark current of oil gushed to the surface. Swirling up with the oil came a miscellany of submarine and submariner remains—shattered wood, cork, human fragments, and whatnot.

Again, identification was divulged after the war by the files of Admiral Miwa. The downed submersible was the I-56.

Okinawa Conclusion

At Okinawa the Rising Sun went down for the last time. History's almanac would record the date as June 21, 1945. The brief twilight that followed was no more than a crepuscular after-glow; Imperial Japan was finished on that 21st of June. On that day General Ushijima, commander of the Japanese 32nd Army, and his Chief of Staff, Lieutenant General Isamu Cho, committed *hari-kiri* rather than surrender. Some 100,000 Japanese troops had already died. The Battle of Okinawa—the "Last Battle"—was over.

For the Americans Okinawa had been a costly campaign, won at a price of over 12,000 dead. Buckner's Tenth Army paid the lion's share of this fatality toll, the General himself being among the slain, killed by an enemy shell-burst three days before the last Jap survivors surrendered. But U.S. Navy losses were well over a third of the total—about 5,000 fatalities, and a like number of wounded. In no previous campaign of a comparable time-period had ship casualties been as severe.

Although the 12 destroyers and the destroyer-escort sunk off Okinawa between late March and the end of June were the largest warships downed in "Operation Iceberg," many minecraft, patrol vessels, and landing craft were battered under. Destroyers and DE's footed most of the crash bill, but warships of all classes took savage punishment. Thirteen carriers—including BUNKER HILL, INTREPID, HANCOCK, and ENTERPRISE—were badly mauled in the Okinawa battle, as were ten battleships and five cruisers. About 80 per cent of this damage was wrought by *Kamikaze* crashes, and most of the ships struck by suicide planes were incapacitated for the war's duration.

It is not difficult to conceive of the odds accepted by destroyers when they entered combat with this enemy capable of injuring steel-coated battleships and crippling such powerful carriers as BUNKER HILL and HANCOCK. The length of those odds has its measure in the DD and DE casualty list, and in the roll call of the "Fleet that stayed permanently." HALLIGAN, BUSH, COLHOUN, MANNERT L. ABELE, PRINGLE, LITTLE, LUCE, MORRISON, OBERRENDER, LONGSHAW, DREXLER, WILLIAM D. PORTER, TWIGGS, UNDERHILL, and CALLAGHAN—twelve of these 15 ships were downed by the *Kamikazes*. In regard to their chances against this foe, the Navy's destroyermen expressed an almost undivided opinion. The consensus was that a coördinated and sustained suicide air assault spelled disastrous damage, if not doom, for the unarmored American destroyer or DE of World War II classes.

There is an old Oriental proverb which observes, "He who knows he is about to die, dies twice." Well aware of the odds they faced, the destroyermen in the Okinawa picket line endured the conviction with a stoicism that went far to invalidate the proverb.

Wrote Commodore Moosbrugger:

THE PERFORMANCE OF THE PERSONNEL OF THE SCREENING AND RADAR PICKET SHIPS, BOTH INDIVIDUALLY AND COLLECTIVELY, WAS SUPERB THROUGHOUT THE OKINAWA CAMPAIGN. ACTS OF HEROISM AND UNSELFISHNESS, FIGHTING SPIRIT, COOLNESS UNDER FIRE, UNSWERVING DETERMINATION, ENDURANCE, AND QUALITIES OF LEADERSHIP AND LOYALTY EXCEEDED ALL PREVIOUS CONCEPTIONS OF STANDARDS SET FOR THE U. S. NAVY. THE RADAR PICKET STATION GROUPS TOOK EVERY BLOW THAT THE JAPS COULD INFLICT AND ABSORBED TERRIFIC PUNISHMENT IN PERSONNEL CASUALTIES AND MATERIAL DAMAGE, BUT THE MISSION WAS SUCCESSFULLY . . . COMPLETED.

PART VII

SMALL BOYS FINISH BIG JOB

No thought of flight, none of retreat;
no unbecoming deed that argued fear;
each on himself relied as only in his arm
the moment lay of victory.

PARADISE LOST

CHAPTER 39

DESLANT SCOURS THE ATLANTIC

(SEPTEMBER '44 TO VE-DAY)

Undersea Tidal Turn

Addressing the American Society of Newspaper Editors in April, 1944, Rear Admiral Francis S. Low, Chief of Staff of the Tenth Fleet, declared, "The German U-boat today is sinking considerably less than one half of one percent of the ships being convoyed across the Atlantic." He expressed the belief that, "It takes the Germans two or three times as long to build a submarine as that vessel may expect to endure on combat patrol."

These percentage and endurance figures must have inclined Admiral Doenitz's Headquarters to pessimism. During the autumn of 1943, some 16 German shipyards had been working their arms out at the elbows constructing U-boats. Through the adoption of welding and the employment of prefabricated hull sections, the larger German yards were able to turn out a 500-ton submarine in anywhere from 36 to 40 weeks. The 740-ton class could be built in 40 to 44 weeks. This building program was speeded up in 1944 by new methods and designs which cut a day here and a process there. But the Herculean submarine construction effort was going for naught. So was the effort to equip the U-boats with *Schnorkel.*

American and Allied CVE-DD-DE teams were largely responsible for the frustration in U-boat Headquarters.

The Germans had pinned high hopes on the *Schnorkel* stack. But it became apparent that the "breather tube" would not, of itself, save the U-boat's day.

Demanded was a submarine which could not only elude radar, but could go deeper than the reach of sonar detection—a U-boat which could cruise at a depth far below the present operating level, and which could lie for many hours inert on the bottom in some deep foxhole. Such a boat—the previously mentioned Type XXI—was under construction in 1944. This long-winded, deep-going submarine was Grand Admiral Doenitz's last trump. With it the U-boat Force was to make a final try in the Battle of the Atlantic. But Type XXI's would not get to sea in any number until 1945.

In the meantime the U-boat campaign almost deadstalled in the third quarter of 1944 as Doenitz called in the submarines for *Schnorkel* refits and scraped the bottom of the Nazi barrel for personnel. In consequence American destroyermen in the Atlantic found poor hunting that fall.

But one of the DD's was engaged by an enemy tougher and more dangerous than any U-boat ever launched by Doenitz. The enemy? That "Ole Devil Sea."

Loss of U.S.S Warrington

Early in September, 1944, the destroyer WARRINGTON (Commander S. F. Quarles) was escorting the U.S.S. HYADES from Norfolk, Virginia, to the Canal Zone. Commissioned in February, 1938, WARRINGTON was a destroyer of the SOMERS class, a one-stacker of 1,850 tons. The HYADES was a refrigerated provision ship of the type known to bluejackets as "beef boats." Senior officer present was aboard HYADES.

Normally the neo-tropic seas off Florida and the

The last sinking of a Nazi U-Boat in World War II. This picture, taken from Moberly (PF 63), shows a depth-charge pattern exploding around the ill-fated U-853 on the morning of May 6, 1945, the day before the surrender instrument was signed. The sub had torpedoed a small collier off Point Judith, Rhode Island, shortly before Atherton, Ericsson, and Moberly made their kill.

A survivor of Frederick C. Davis (DE 136), the last American warship sunk in the Battle of the Atlantic, is being transferred from Flaherty to a CVE. The destroyer-escort, blasted by a stern-tube shot from U-546, suffered heavy casualties but was quickly avenged. Her hunter-killer group tracked the sub for ten hours, forced it to surface, and sank it, picking up 33 Nazis.

The destroyer-escort—a little ship that made a big difference in besting the Nazi subs in the Battle of the Atlantic. This is Martin H. Ray (DE 338).

At the end of the war, U-boats surfaced and surrendered to the Allies. Most gave themselves up to British forces in the eastern Atlantic, but U-858 (top) and U-805 popped up almost within sight of Cape May, New Jersey.

Bahamas provide some of the finest cruising weather in the world. Abnormally they kick up some of the worst. And on September 12 the bottom fell out of the glass, and the blow fell with it.

By the afternoon of that day WARRINGTON and HYADES were ploughing through high water off the northern Bahamas. Hell came with the evening—a screaming, discolored sky; blinding rain; wind-whipped, rip-roaring seas that smashed against the destroyer's port bow and buried her foredeck under avalanches of foam-laced brine. Struggling against rising winds and climbing waves, the two ships were slowed to a 4-knot pace.

WARRINGTON was an old hand at storm fighting, but she had never experienced anything like this. Striking her port side with the violence of a continual barrage, mountainous waves exploded across her deck and washed her bridge. The sky was drowned out; the heaving seascape contracted into a narrow wilderness of gray ridges and shifting canyons swept by sheets of horizontal rain, flying clouds of spray, and whistling ribbons of spume that caught and tore in the destroyer's superstructure like lengths of wool. At 1810 Commander Quarles gave the order to heave to, in deference to the mountainous seas.

Wind velocity went from 5 to 100 miles. By midnight the ships were driven off course and apart, and at about 0100 in the morning of September 13 HYADES lost radar contact with WARRINGTON. The destroyer was in trouble. The terrific beam-sea pounding had sprung her port bulwarks in two places, and her deck gear was wrenched, distorted, and bruised as though battered by gunfire. Most of the ventilating system had been closed to shut out floodwater, but it was impossible to close off everything and keep the engineering plant in operation. Water entered the ship, and her power waned.

Commander Quarles sent a message requesting HYADES to stand by in case the destroyer foundered. Fighting her own battle with the ocean, the provision ship could not promise immediate aid. Unable to cope with the main force of the hurricane, WARRINGTON reversed course. An emergency request for help was flashed on all circuits at 0417, the destroyer stating that her engineering spaces were flooded; she had lost power; she was caught in winds of hurricane force; she needed assistance. She gave her position as lat. 25-57 N., long. 73-44 W. By estimate the disabled warship was at that time only 60 miles southwest of the storm center. HYADES, some 75 miles distant, was riding out the wild night. But with house-high seas, visibility zero, and a wind that could uproot the Bahamas, there was nothing she could do to aid the imperiled destroyer.

Not long after she sent her S-O-S, WARRINGTON received a paralyzing blow. Swooping up abeam, a tremendous wave smashed the ship on the port side to flood the engine rooms and cause final loss of power.

There was no dawn for WARRINGTON that day. All morning the destroyermen fought to mend the damage below decks while giant waves swept over the ship's superstructure, inundating her bow and clawing at her bridge. Powerless and rolling, the DD had acquired a fatal list. Under one ferocious assault of wind and water her foremast carried away. Volunteers manned the deck in the teeth of blinding spray and rushing seas, and cut the wreckage loose to send it overside.

By noon of that day the helpless ship was going logy. Staggering through the hurricane like a derelict adrift, she could no longer bring her head up when battered by a collapsing hill of water.

Working in the thick, stupefying heat down below, the engineers were unable to revive the waterlogged engines. They sputtered, gasped, went silent. The life had gone out of them. The water continued to rise, coming in through the ship's sprained hull. The ocean's broadsides battered the powerless destroyer with a fury that was not to be denied.

Topside, the destroyer's bridge personnel peered desperately through the watery blindness, hoping for a glimpse of HYADES. The listed deck had a sodden feel underfoot. Down below there was a sluggish thudding, the creak and cry of straining stanchions. Commander Quarles ordered the torpedoes jettisoned. Everything that could be dispensed with was going overside. But the ship had lost that good feeling of life and buoyancy; she had swallowed too much sea water for first-aid. She could not shake off the tons of ocean that crashed across her decks and slopped her bridge. Under each fresh onslaught she settled a trifle deeper, and shuddered.

At 1345 she sent her last distress message—an S-O-S and the three words,

WE NEED ASSISTANCE

The urgent appeal brought into action all the available rescue forces of the Navy. Two sea-going tugs were ordered to the scene, and ships in near-by areas were dispatched to WARRINGTON's position, which was then about 300 miles north of Crooked Island Passage. Fighting their way across furious seas, these vessels headed for the disabled destroyer. But the tempest held aircraft grounded that afternoon of the 13th, and the rescue ships could not make it in time. Neither could HYADES, striving to locate her stricken escort.

By late afternoon WARRINGTON was beyond all mortal help. Her stack was tilted far to starboard, and solid waves were marching over her decks. A sliding hill of water swept two men overboard. One was recovered. The other caught a rescue line, then had to let go, too weak to hold on.

Commander Quarles and his "Exec," Lieutenant Wesley U. Williams, U.S.N.R., stared grimly into the bleak prospect as the seas sluiced over her.

Quarles turned to a young seaman standing by; saw the lad was without a life jacket; promptly offered the sailor his own.

"Sir," the seaman smiled, "I'd rather not, if it's all right."

And a moment later a great sea crashed over the foredeck and swept the bridge-wing. Commander Quarles and Lieutenant Williams were whirled outboard and away like chips on a millrace. The captain went deep under the foam, then fought his way to the surface, and glimpsed the destroyer's ghostly silhouette yards distant. She was over—far over. And as she slipped and slid downgrade on her starboard beam, her stern went under and her bow rose against the sky—higher—higher. The sea climbed under her, carrying her bow high in the blowing scud, and then she was gone. Some of the men who saw her go said that at the last she capsized.

They found themselves swimming in bare seas. Commander Quarles swam to a raft, and hauled bluejackets out of the swirling water. There were finally four survivors on the raft with him. The raft bounced and skipped across the wind-whipped waves. Several times during the ensuing hours of ordeal it capsized.

The ordeal became a nightmare in pitching midnight. The survivors could hear swimmers shouting somewhere off in the storming dark. Quarles and the four with him hung on. The night was endless, and then gray morning seemed without hope. Someone snatched a can of food from the crest of a wave, and Quarles distributed malt tablets. But the survivors with him had swallowed sickening quantities of sea water. That day two of the men died in convulsion.

Sharks trailed the raft, evil shadows criss-crossing through the water and occasionally showing wicked fins. The wind subsided somewhat, but the whitecaps blew like shot salt and the raft bumped along over choppy seas. And on that day (September 14) Quarles and his companions suffered that terrible disappointment known only to mariners in distress—the disappointment of seeing rescuers pass them by. They saw a PBY search plane approach and then go winging off into the distance. It had come within 3,000 yards, but had failed to sight them in the choppy seas. And some time later they saw a merchant vessel come over the horizon. The men shouted hoarsely and waved their shirts. The ship passed at about 4,000 yards—dwindled away—finally was gone.

Quarles and the survivors with him endured another endless evening and night. There were other rafts in the distance, and these survivors, too, endured. They had a two-day wait for rescue, and it came on the morning of the 15th. About 0900 HYADES steamed over the horizon, followed by a number of search planes. The CROATAN task group had been ordered to the disaster scene from a near-by area, and CROATAN's aircraft were on the hunt.

The airmen spotted the little flotsam of rafts and destroyermen. The planes dropped smoke markers, and HYADES came up at full speed through high seas to pick up the WARRINGTON survivors.

HYADES located five life rafts and floats. Altogether, she picked up 61 survivors and one who had failed to survive. Two of the men died shortly after they were rescued. The dead were buried at sea.

Other rescue forces picked up seven or eight WARRINGTON survivors. Before rescue operations were concluded, some 68 destroyermen had been saved. But the disaster exacted a most tragic toll, a loss of 251 officers and men. Aircraft flying over the area sighted at least a hundred bodies adrift on the sea's desolation.

The loss of WARRINGTON came as a decided shock to Admiral Ingersoll's flagship and to the DesLant Force. Naval officials found it difficult to believe that a modern destroyer of WARRINGTON's class could succumb to a hurricane.

But after a Court of Inquiry a subsequent Court Martial "fully acquitted" Commander Quarles. Any court could only applaud the heroic endeavors of captain and crew to save a powerless vessel from the climactic violence of a tropical hurricane.

Fessenden Kills U-1062

The U-boat Force pulled in its horns, that autumn of 1944, and American destroyermen made but one kill—a score held down by lack of game. Doenitz was rebuilding his undersea navy at this time, and only a relatively few U-boats were in the Atlantic, chiefly for their "nuisance value."

In September such a "nuisance" pack was operating in the Cape Verdes area. There it was detected by Task Group 22.1, a hunter-killer group built around the new escort-carrier MISSION BAY. Steaming southwest of the Cape Verdes, the group's scouts made contact with a submarine on the morning of September 30th. At 1120 the destroyer-escort FESSENDEN (Lieutenant Commander W. A. Dobbs, U.S.N.R.) peeled off with the DE's DOUGLAS L. HOWARD and

J. R. Y. BLAKELEY to investigate the aircraft report.

FESSENDEN picked up sonar contact at 1610. At 1628 her destroyermen fired a full pattern of Mark X projectiles. Fourteen seconds after the projectiles splashed into the sea, four explosions rumbled up from below. FESSENDEN followed through with a full pattern of depth charges. The water heaved and flattened over an outburst of deep-sea thunder. Thereafter the DE's heard nothing but the silence of extinction.

Post-war records named FESSENDEN's victim as the U-1062.

Submarine Attack on New York

Despite the slackening of the U-boat campaign, there was no relaxation for the Atlantic Fleet on Thanksgiving Day, 1944. If the populace on the eastern seaboard wondered why strict vigilance was maintained, and if disgruntled Times Square and Fifth Avenue merchants wished to know why a million dollars worth of electric lights had to remain under a blackout in New York, the answer was labeled "Top Secret" in the flagship of Admiral Jonas H. Ingram, who had succeeded Admiral Ingersoll in Command of the Atlantic Fleet.

Revealed at war's end was the news that the Navy had received intelligence reports disclosing a German plan to attack New York City with robot bombs. The bombardment was to have been unleashed by submarines.

But the robot bombardment failed to materialize. Apparently it was to have been delivered by the new deep-sea *Schnorkels*—the Type XXI's.

Admiral Ingram got the word on these ultra-modern U-boats. In a post-war report to Navy Secretary Forrestal he stated: *"We knew they had put a lot of fancy gadgets on them. Increased them in size, increased their radius, increased their effectiveness, and made it difficult to get them. But they were pressed for time. The Russian offensive drove them out of the Baltic, and the heavy bombings in their shipbuilding places put their offensive back."*

The new XXI's did not come. Not then. But something else and quite unusual did turn up—a German weather-reporting submarine.

Hayter, Otter, Varian, and Hubbard Sink U-248

When Von Rundstedt's mid-winter counterdrive developed into the "Battle of the Bulge," Allied leaders knew "this was it." If the Ardennes break-through was not contained, the war would be prolonged for many months.

And oddly enough, at the climax of the Bulge campaign, success or failure for either side hinged on the weather. Days of icy drizzle, snow, and fog had screened the German advance and kept Allied aircraft grounded. So long as this weather front persisted, Von Rundstedt's driving legions retained the advantage. Imperative, then, that his headquarters be informed by accurate forecasts. So the U-248 was dispatched to a station in the North Atlantic about midway between France and Newfoundland, where the submarine was to play weather prophet.

Early in the New Year of 1945 the U-boat was on station, serving as aerographer and transmitting the vital weather reports to the Nazi parties most interested. But the Nazis were not the only interested parties. Operating north of the Azores at this time was Escort Division 62, and the express mission of this DE division was the hunting and killing of any such weather-reporting U-boat in the vicinity.

Under Commander J. F. Bowling, with his pennant in OTTER, the division consisted of the destroyer-escorts OTTER (Lieutenant Commander J. M. Irvine, U.S.N.R.), HAYTER (Lieutenant Commander Fred Huey, U.S.N.R.), VARIAN (Lieutenant Commander L. A. Myhre, U.S.N.R.), and HUBBARD (Lieutenant Commander L. C. Mabley, U.S.N.R.). The four-ship team was working with HF/DF, and on January 16 "Huff-Duff" bearings on German sub transmissions gave them the wherewithal to plot this nervy U-boat's position—vicinity of lat. 47-00 N., long. 26-00 W.

HAYTER made the first sound contact at 0910. The DE's swung into action with the usual team work, first one, then another, running across the submerged U-boat's position and sowing lethal depth-charges. Her sonar gear out of commission, HUBBARD was unable to join in the depth-charge onslaught, but HAYTER, OTTER, and VARIAN dropped a sufficiently punishing barrage upon the target.

The ashcans and teardrops blew up tons of sea water, and finally they blew up tons of submarine. The blast came after a series of minor explosions that indicated hits. Then, at 1149, the sea echoed to a tremendous thunderclap. And up came the usual surge of debris—splintered wood, oily rubbish, and other items of flotsam.

The Nazi forces in Europe would receive no more weather reports from the aerographers of U-248.

Fowler and L'Indiscret Kill U-869

For United States and Allied A/S forces the winter of 1944-1945 meant arduous patrols and wearisome escort jobs that produced few U-boat contacts. February, 1945, was almost gone from the calendar before American destroyermen downed their second U-boat of that season.

Involved were the American destroyer-escort

FOWLER (Lieutenant Commander S. F. Morris, U.S.N.R.), and a French A/S vessel which bore the rather curious name of L'INDISCRET—*"The Indiscreet."* FOWLER was one of the units of a five-ship group escorting the slow convoy GUS 74 from Oran to the USA. "INDISCREET" just happened to be present as one of two French escorts for a half dozen merchant vessels sent from Casablanca to join GUS 74.

Slow GUS 74 steamed westward through the Pillars of Hercules late in February, and in the morning of the 28th the convoy reached a point about 100 miles due west of Port Lyautey. At that same date and time the German submarine U-869 reared its ugly head in those waters off the *"Iron Coast."* Apparently the submariners glimpsed GUS 74 and set out to make a submerged approach on the convoy, a maneuver that proved decidedly foolhardy.

KNOXVILLE (flagship, ComCortDiv 30), and DE's FOWLER and ROBINSON went into action against the sub. At 0648, FOWLER made sound contact on the stalking submarine, range 2,900 yards. Six minutes later the DE let fly with a magnetic pattern, and two explosions banged in the water at the 12th and 20th seconds after firing. These sharp bursts, indicative of hits, were echoed by three or four thunderous booms that rumbled up from the deep. The destroyermen presently sighted a litter of debris, but Lieutenant Commander Morris wanted to see more flotsam. Accordingly, FOWLER dropped another pattern of magnetics at 0718. Within 120 seconds, two voluminous but ambiguous explosions bellowed up from down under.

Enter French escorts L'INDISCRET and LE RESOLUTE. Taking a hand in the game at 0856, they joined FOWLER and KNOXVILLE in probing for the submerged target. At 0943 the two French vessels attacked a sonar contact. The American escorts terminated the search at 1104, leaving the Frenchmen to carry on until they were directed to discontinue by shore authorities.

Apparently the F. S. L'INDISCRET, teamed up with LE RESOLUTE, finally conducted a *coup de grace* attack, although the French vessel's tactics are not detailed in available reports which credit her with a share in the U-boat's kill. At any rate, the action put a period to the career of U-869. Under the circumstances it would seem it was the submarine which should have borne the name of *"Indiscreet."*

Lowe, Menges, Pride, and Mosley Kill U-866

American destroyermen scored their third U-boat kill of the year in March. The laurels in this case went to the Coast Guard's A/S warriors serving in Escort Division 46 under Commander R. H. French, U.S.C.G., who flew his pennant in PRIDE. The division consisted of the destroyer-escorts LOWE (Lieutenant Commander Herbert Feldman, U.S.C.G.R.), MENGES (Lieutenant Commander F. M. McCabe, U.S.C.G.), MOSLEY (Lieutenant Commander E. P. MacBryde, U.S.C.G.R.), and the flagship PRIDE (Lieutenant Commander W. H. Buxton, U.S.C.G.). This was the first hunter-killer group manned by Coast Guardsmen, and the hunters went all out to fulfill the high traditions of that veteran sea-going organization.

They also went all out to track down and destroy a Nazi submarine reported in Nova Scotian coastal waters about 100 miles east of Halifax. Mid-morning of March 18, 1945, LOWE picked up sound contact. Time: 1027. Commander Feldman rushed the DE through fast investigative maneuvers, and at 1105 LOWE made two depth-charge attacks. After the second attack, a volley of explosions rumbled in the sea. Oil burbled to the surface and spread across a wide area, and the Coast Guardsmen sighted splintered wood and other fragments and flotsam.

To certify the submarine's destruction, MENGES followed through with an attack. More oil and flotsam rose to the surface. Examining this submarine spoor, LOWE's Coast Guardsmen retrieved several soggy documents in German, some first-aid packets that were of German origin, and some assorted pieces of wood.

The Division leader, Commander French, remained skeptical. As Sound retained contact on the target (or what was left of it), at 1320 the group started operations to deal with a sub "playing 'possom" on the bottom.

PRIDE and MOSLEY stood ready in the backfield while LOWE and MENGES thrashed the target with a running fire of depth charges. LOWE conducted three attacks; MENGES, two. In each attack full patterns of Mark 18 depth-charges with magnetic settings were dropped. The two DE's then held sonar contact intermittently with the bottomed sub until the task group left the area late in the evening. The group returned next day to make an inquest. At 1300 of the 19th MENGES regained Sound contact and attacked with hedgehogs. Up came more oil and splintered wood. At the conclusion of this barrage it was apparent that MENGES was flogging a dead horse. The Coast Guard group retired from the area, confident of the U-boat's extermination.

Post-war records verified the kill, and the victim was identified as the U-866. The blasting served notice on Doenitz that his late-war drive was too late. *Schnorkel,* high submerged speeds, streamlined pressure hulls—these undersea devices were not going to save Nazi U-boats in American coastal waters from being blown to Halifax.

Doenitz's Last Bid (The Supersubs)

Grand Admiral Doenitz had no unrealistic illusions. He did not expect his abbreviated U-boat Force to mortally wound the United States Atlantic Fleet or seriously interfere with the convoys supplying Eisenhower's armies. A deep-sea armada, much less a small flotilla of Type XXI U-boats, could hardly have turned the war tide as of springtime 1945. The Anglo-American forces were across the Rhine. The Russians were in East Prussia. Nazi Germany was through. Nevertheless, the streamlined *Schnorkel* super-submarines might accomplish a little something. They might, for instance, inflict a last bit of reprisal on the detested Americans who were bombing Berlin into a brick heap. They might bombard the eastern seaboard of the United States, might even hurl a rocket barrage into Boston or New York.

In any event, late in March, 1945, Admiral Doenitz sent the *Schnorkel* super-submarines speeding westward across the Atlantic. Mission: to attack the United States coast in a supreme, final effort for Adolph Hitler.

This was the raid Admiral Ingram had warned of, and the Tenth Fleet had kept CinClant informed on these super U-boats. Their construction, equipment, and capabilities had been thoroughly studied, thanks to captured models and talkative prisoners. The deep-running capacities of these *Schnorkel* streamliners would have revolutionized undersea warfare, had the super-subs been in action earlier in the war.

In a report (May 16, 1945) to Naval Secretary Forrestal, Admiral Ingram wrote:

> *I know from the captive submarine crews that one ship that started out submerged on March 21 did not take air until April 9. Another captive reported that they had a submarine that could stay submerged seven weeks. In the early days of the war those fellows had to come up so many hours a day and our planes would spot them, and we'd go get them. In the last stages of this campaign, those babies spent most of their time submerged, and if we ever got them any place where the water was shallow enough—less than 600 feet—they'd just go down and stay on the bottom, and I am positive in my mind of instances where they have stayed on the bottom for two weeks. We thought they had gone, and would leave, and up they would come.*

To beat back the U-boat drive, Admiral Ingram mustered a powerhouse A/S task force which included four escort carriers and a total of 75 destroyers and destroyer-escorts. Dispatched to mid Atlantic, the CVE-DD-DE teams maintained a vigilant ocean patrol that began early in the year and went into action when the first super-sub came along. One by one the streamlined *Schnorkels* were tracked down in mid-ocean and obliterated.

"Two or three got through to the coast," Admiral Ingram wrote later. *"They torpedoed five ships and sank two, and we got them close to the coast, one right off Newport Harbor . . . the last one of the bunch."*

Gustafson Sinks U-857

Only a few informed officers on duty in the First Naval District knew, that first week in April, 1945, that a U-boat was operating within 20 miles of Cape Cod.

Of course Washington was informed, and Admiral Ingram's forces afloat knew what was up. So did most of the ships at sea in the area. Submarine warning! U-boat almost within range of Boston Light.

Also almost within range of that famous light was a fast-moving hunter-killer group composed of the frigates KNOXVILLE (flagship) and EUGENE, and DE's GUSTAFSON and MICKA, under Commander R. R. Curry, U.S.C.G., ComCortDiv 30. The vessels were undergoing refresher training at Casco Bay when ComDesLant dispatched them under Curry to hunt the sub. Early in the morning of April 7 this A/S team was sweeping the vicinity of lat. 42-15 N., long. 69-52 W. As a result GUSTAFSON (Lieutenant Commander A. E. Chambers, U.S.N.R.) swept up a Sound contact, and the hunter-killers got on the track of the deep-sea invader.

At 0226 GUSTAFSON reached attack position and opened fire with hedgehogs. The projectiles soared away and hissed down into the dark water. Silence. A miss!

Lieutenant Commander Chambers maneuvered the destroyer-escort for another attack. Again the hedgehogs soared. This time a basso explosion came rumbling up out of the sea.

GUSTAFSON circled off and waited. There was no upsurge of debris, and Chambers was dissatisfied by this lack of evidence. At 0409, 0427, 0451, and 0503 he directed successive hedgehog attacks, These failed to produce explosions.

Evidently the only hit had been echoed by that deep-bellied blast heard at 0247. The destroyermen were disappointed. They sighted a good-sized oil slick which exuded strong oil fumes. But GUSTAFSON's skipper was not convinced of a kill, and the outcome was evaluated as a "possible."

Not until after the war did investigators learn

that the U-857 had been sunk as of that date, almost within range of Boston Light.

Stanton and Frost Kill U-1235

On April 15, 1945, the destroyer-escorts FROST (Lieutenant Commander A. E. Ritchie, U.S.N.R.), STANTON (Lieutenant Commander J. C. Kiley, Jr., U.S.N.R.), and HUSE (Lieutenant Commander J. H. Batcheller) were operating in a screen for the CROATAN Killer Group (Task Group 22.5). The DE's were units of Escort Division 13 under Commander F. D. Giambattista, whose pennant was in FROST.

Task Group 22.5 was engaged in forming a mid-ocean air barrier in the vicinity of lat. 48-30 N., long. 30-00 W., almost exactly midway between Newfoundland and the British Isles. This barrier was to serve expressly as an anti-submarine net, a huge snare for the trapping of that school of *Schnorkel* subs known to be coming westward.

On the evening of April 15 the destroyer-escort STANTON was alerted. Radar contact at 2335, range 3,500 yards. The night was overcast and rainy, gray-black, with visibility about 500 yards. STANTON headed for the target. Five minutes after contact, Kiley and his Officer of the Deck thought they saw a sub "crash dive" some 300 yards off in the murk. Simultaneously the "pip" disappeared on the radar screen. But Sound picked up the undersea track immediately. Kiley opened the range to try for a hedgehog attack.

The sub, which had been on a collision course with STANTON, had promptly reversed course upon diving. STANTON had no difficulty trailing with sonar. As the range opened to 3,000 yards, Commander Giambattista ordered STANTON to attack with hedgehogs. She fired on an excellent recorder trace at 2347. The projectiles soared and plunged into the sea. Although no detonations were seen from the bridge or heard on sonar, officers and men on STANTON's fantail reported detonations as the ship passed by the splash. Then came a heavy underwater rumble.

Contact was regained at 2350. STANTON was ordered to try again. Kiley jockeyed the DE into position for another attack. Then, eight minutes after the first hedgehog salvo was fired (and as STANTON was maneuvering for a second try), the destroyermen heard a thunderous underwater blast. Other ships in the CROATAN task group felt the detonation. It sounded like a kill.

But a few minutes later STANTON's detection gear indicated the sub was still down there. And four minutes after midnight, Kiley followed through with more hedgehog. The projectiles described a nice arc, and two sharp explosions promptly answered the salvo.

At 0007 (morning of April 16) STANTON delivered a third hedgehog salvo. Two minutes later the sea roared with a blast that shook the attacking DE and sent a tremor through the escort carrier CROATAN.

By this time FROST was on hand to add her weight to the attack. Lieutenant Commander Ritchie and his crew were itching for a shot at the target, and at 0017 FROST opened fire with hedgehog. When FROST's salvo sank into silence, STANTON was ready for still another try. Then FROST stepped in again.

That the later-war *Schnorkels* could absorb punishment was evidenced by the fact that the specimen bombarded by STANTON and FROST survived at least three hedgehog hits, enough to wreck the ordinary sub. Then the damaged U-boat endured a thrashing that lasted for another hour. There was no mid-Atlantic foxhole for the submersible to crawl into. No chance for a rest on the bottom. The sub had to keep going—deep, but not too deep. Had to glide and zigzag and evade at the lowest possible level—at a depth which would not crumple her injured pressure hull. And from 0004 (the first certain hedgehog hit) until 0114 the assailed U-boat kept going.

STANTON and FROST allowed the submarine no respite. Probing, tracking, attacking in turn, they hounded the undersea enemy to the final figurative fathom.

At 0114 two tremendous explosions roared up from down under. The explosions blended into a thunder-roll that vibrated the DE's and was felt by several of the hunter-killers ten miles away. Three minutes later, more deep sea thunder. Then the echoes muttered away, and the sea in the vicinity of lat. 47-56 N., long. 30-25 W., was silent.

Stanton and Frost Down U-880

Those who fought the A/S war were instructed to take nothing for granted—not even a sea-quaking series of detonations that sounded like a bursting submarine. Early in the anti-U-boat campaign American hunter-killers had been taught to rely only on "visual remains" as proof positive of a submarine's destruction. Past masters at evasion and deception, tricky U-boats might simulate death throes, and steal away.

So FROST and STANTON went on looking, listening and probing in the immediate area for some time after the thunder died down. At 0130, HUSE joined the two in the search, and at 0141 the three ships commenced "Operation Observant." In this instance the extended search produced surprising results.

At 0155 FROST made radar contact, range 500 yards! A surfaced U-boat! FROST was immediately directed by ComCortDiv 13 to "close the target, illuminate, fire and ram."

Zigzagging, the DE headed for the target at 20 knots. The sub ran for it, zigzagging at speeds varying from 9 to 14 knots. At 0200 FROST fired starshells. The stars sprayed the seascape with eerie light, but the sub was not revealed. Then, on the target's port quarter, range 650 yards, FROST's searchlight shot a white shaft across the water, and the ghostly conning tower was silhouetted. The destroyermen opened fire with chattering automatics and a crashing 3-inch 50-caliber gun. The sea was tumbling, and the sub was running with decks awash, but the DE marksmen were right on the bull's-eye, lacing the conning tower with a deadly fusillade. At least three 3-inchers struck the mark.

With the range closed to 300 yards, Ritchie pulled out of a fast zigzag and ordered right full rudder to ram. The move was frustrated by heavy seas and low visibility. The U-boat submerged, and FROST passed ahead of the enemy's track. Boiling water and noise put the jinx on sonar, and contact with the submerged sub was lost. At 0224 Commander Giambattista directed STANTON and HUSE to form up on either side of FROST and run "Operation Observant."

The ships began an industrious sonar sweep. STANTON made contact at 0310, range 3,400 yards. Twelve minutes later FROST picked up the sub at 300 yards. Ritchie opened the range to 900, jockeyed into position, and fired hedgehog. Negative. Stepping aside, he coached HUSE and STANTON on to the target. At 0359 Lieutenant Commander Kiley started his DE's approach, and at 0406 STANTON let fly with hedgehog.

Four hits crackled and banged. The fathometer registered 110 feet. Then (time: 0410) came a ponderous explosion. This detonation was echoed by a deep-sea blast that fractured galley crockery and sent some of the sailors reeling. So violent was the thunderclap that it was felt by CROATAN, 15 miles away. Some of the hunters thought FROST had been torpedoed.

That was the climax; what followed was by way of obsequies. Far from being torpedoed, FROST fired a hedgehog salvo at 0415 at what was left of the target. STANTON regained contact at 0419 (indications pointed to a sub inanimate in the water), and at 0429 she tried again with hedgehog. The projector misfired, but no matter. The DE nosed through a thick oil slick that smelled of sunken Diesels and sudden death.

Sonar contact dwindled as the oil smell intensified. While the destroyermen were remarking this evidence, three muffled explosions boomed up from the deep—as though the submarine, a mile down, were firing a farewell salute.

Commander Giambattista was thorough. At 0445, the contact lost, he ordered his hunter-killers to run a careful "Observant" around the point of last contact. The search was conducted by FROST, STANTON, HUSE, and SWASEY (Lieutenant Commander H. A. White, U.S.N.R.)—the latter having previously arrived on the battle scene. "Observant" was followed by a box search. Planes from CROATAN joined the hunt at daylight. But the U-boat was gone for good.

Credit went to STANTON and FROST. When the war was over and the final score was in, an assessment showed that the two DE's had accounted for two U-boats in the pre-dawn hours of April 16. The first, as related, was the U-1235, sunk at lat. 47-56 N., long. 30-25 W. The second, sunk at lat. 47-54 N., long. 30-24 W., was identified by Doenitz's records as the U-880.

Going after one, STANTON and FROST had bagged a pair. That was big game hunting!

Buckley and Reuben James Kill U-879

BUCKLEY and REUBEN JAMES. Those two names meant something to veteran destroyermen who remembered BUCKLEY as the DE that won a ramming, slamming U-boat battle in the spring of 1944, and who recalled that a REUBEN JAMES was the first United States destroyer to go down from U-boat torpedoes in World War II.

In the spring of 1945 these two destroyer-escorts were operating in company with DE's SCROGGINS and JACK W. WILKE as units of hunter-killer Task Group 22.10 (Commander E. H. Headland, Jr.) which had been organized the previous November to hunt U-boats in the North Atlantic. BUCKLEY had been selected to serve as the group's flagship.

Of BUCKLEY's war duty at this time, the ship's historian wrote: *"The first months of 1945 saw . . . rigorous northern patrols continued. It is the proud record of the ship and the others associated under her command, that while sinkings occurred on several occasions from enemy submarine action, no ship was lost in the area under patrol by the* BUCKLEY *group."*

But a U-boat was lost in that area.

During the third week in April, 1945, Task Group 22.10, en route from Halifax to New York, was conducting a sweep for an enemy submarine believed to be in the immediate area. At 0348 in the morning of April 19, BUCKLEY (Lieutenant R. R. Crutchfield, U.S.N.R.) picked up a sonar contact that had all the ear-marks of a submarine. BUCKLEY left the formation to investigate. The contact was soon evaluated as "U-boat," and the DE's crew sprang into action.

Destroyer-escort REUBEN JAMES (Lieutenant Commander Grant Cowherd, U.S.N.R.) was ordered to assist. DE's SCROGGINS and JACK W. WILKE were directed to conduct a four-mile box search around the other two, and the sub hunt went into high gear.

About 0420 REUBEN JAMES also gained contact, and BUCKLEY, stepping up speed to 10 knots, opened the range to attack. The sub, which had made no evasive maneuvers, now swung to the right. At 550-yard range BUCKLEY had crossed the submarine's bow. Opening to 1,050 yards (at 0425), the DE commenced her approach.

BUCKLEY gained attack position at 0429, and Lieutenant Crutchfield gave the order for a full hedgehog salvo. The 24 projectiles described their parabolic flight. The water rustled and foamed as the barrage sank in. Ten seconds. Fifteen seconds. Twenty. Then —*Bam-bam-bam!* Strung explosions had the water boiling like seltzer.

At 0431 there was a "heavy underwater explosion." At 0434 there was an explosion described by BUCKLEY listeners as "very heavy." All ships in the group felt the detonation, and Sound lost contact with the submarine. BUCKLEY's searchlights examined the seascape. Up came a spew of oil and assorted flotsam.

In the pre-dawn gloaming a whaleboat was lowered, and the destroyermen pulled across the water to comb the debris. Pieces of wood, chunks of cork, several pillows and cushions, and some dubious anatomical items were fished from the oily sludge.

"There," said an A/S veteran, "is your evidence."

But to doubly certify this U-boat's destruction, BUCKLEY's hunter-killer team remained on the spot throughout the morning. About 1145, DE's REUBEN JAMES, SCROGGINS, and JACK W. WILKE formed a line and searched around the point of attack until evening. Forty depth charges were dropped on the "grave." If the U-boat had been playing dead, the ruse would have been discovered during this all-day inquest. By nightfall it was evident that submarine *rigor mortis* had set in.

BUCKLEY's attack was officially analyzed as excellent. The critique read: "BUCKLEY *slowed to 5 knots and waited until contact was gained also by* REUBEN JAMES *before commencing the run on the U-boat. This was a safe speed to counter the possibility of acoustic torpedoes, and at the same time the U-boat was apparently not alerted, as evidenced by lack of evasive maneuvers.*"

BUCKLEY undoubtedly made the kill in the first run over the target.

The submarine was the U-879.

Carter and Neal A. Scott Kill U-518

Two days after the BUCKLEY kill was reported, another hunter-killer group entered the Atlantic Battle. This was task Group 22.13 (Commander M. H. Harris, U.S.N.R.), on barrier patrol in mid-ocean about 550 miles northwest of the Azores.

On the night of April 21-22, this hunter-killer group was directed to leave the patrol area and proceed to Argentia, Newfoundland. The ships headed westward in the evening. Moonlight was blurred by a light overcast, but the seascape, wind-roughened, was illumined, with 5-mile visibility.

They had been steaming westward for about 40 minutes when the group's flagship, destroyer-escort CARTER (Lieutenant Commander F. J. T. Baker, U.S.N.R.), swept up a submarine contact. The team went into action. While CARTER held contact, SCOTT was coached in for an attack. Task Group Commander Harris directed the other two DE's—MUIR and SUTTON—to circle the area of contact.

The play, then, fell to NEAL A. SCOTT (Lieutenant Commander P. D. Holden). At 2156 the SCOTT had a sonar bead on the U-boat, and opened fire with hedgehog. Two muffled explosions indicated hits at a depth of some 400 feet.

At 2205 CARTER attacked with hedgehog. Again the water echoed to several deep explosions. These detonations were immediately followed by a deep-sea blast. Ten minutes later the depths emitted a volcanic thunder that was felt and heard by all hands in CARTER and SCOTT.

"That's it, boys! There goes your old U-boat!"

The DE's continued to probe and "ping." But the submarine was not there. Searching the surface, the destroyermen found the significant oil slick and floating trash. Among the residue were scraps of paper, shattered wood, and two tattered wooden boxes. The victim under this rubbish was eventually identified as the U-518.

Destroyer-escorts CARTER and NEAL A. SCOTT had sunk the fifth U-boat to be downed by American destroyermen that month.

Loss of U.S.S. Frederick C. Davis

As the plane flies from St. Johns, Newfoundland, to Fayal in the Azores, the distance is 1,180 miles. On April 23, 1945, in mid-Atlantic about halfway between St. Johns and Fayal, several escort-carriers and a parade of destroyer-escorts were strung out in a 100-mile north-south barrier patrol. This CVE-DE flotilla, one of the largest hunter-killer forces yet assembled, formed another segment of the "net" spread to catch the super-*Schnorkels* swimming across the Atlantic to invade America's Eastern Sea Frontier.

The A/S barrier was composed of two CVE task groups (TG. 22.3 and TG. 22.4) and a large detachment of DE's. The force was operating under Commander Task Group 22.3—Captain G. J. Dufek, in BOGUE. Senior DE officer was Commander F. S. Hall, ComCortDiv 4, in PILLSBURY. He was designated Commander Task Unit 22.7.1.

The DE's of Task Unit 22.7.1 included the PILLSBURY, KEITH, OTTERSTETTER, POPE, FLAHERTY, CHATELAIN, FREDERICK C. DAVIS, NEUNZER, HUBBARD, VARIAN, OTTER, HAYTER, JANSSEN, and COCKRILL.

The ships were tactically disposed so that the destroyer-escorts of the task unit formed a surface barrier between the BOGUE air group to the south and CORE air group to the north. Spaced five miles apart, the 14 DE's were ranged across the seascape like a dragnet, the carriers serving as figurative trawlers.

At 1322 in the afternoon of April 23, a search plane sighted a submarine about 70 miles from the destroyer-scort PILLSBURY. Commander Hall formed a scouting line (normal to base course, speed 16.8 knots, ships spaced 3,000 yards apart), and the DE's steamed for the spot where the enemy had been glimpsed. The sub went down and stayed down. All afternoon the hunters combed the vicinity with their detection gear. All through that evening of the 23rd. Midnight, and they were still searching. Into the early hours of April 24 the relentless hunt went on.

Destroyer escort FREDERICK C. DAVIS (Lieutenant J. R. Crosby, U.S.N.R.) worked her way across the dark water, sweeping with her acute radar, fingering the depths with her sensitive "pinging" gear. On the bridge the men standing lookout saw the night begin to pale. A tired Gunnery Officer made another check-up on the gear—hedgehogs ready, ashcans ready to roll. A mess attendant brought Lieutenant Crosby a good cup of coffee. The seascape came into view as the morning advanced. Sunrise. Another day. Routine change of watch. Routine reports. And then—

Time: 0829. Sonar contact. Range 2,000 yards. Sound man reported the echo as being "very sharp and clear with low doppler." The contact dropped rapidly aft and was lost in a muddle of other noises.

The Junior Officer of the Deck (J.O.O.D.) called the wardroom to inform the Captain of the contact. Simultaneously the Officer of the Deck ordered, "Right standard rudder!" and then informed the Task Unit Commander that DAVIS was investigating possible contact.

Sound contact was regained at about 0834. At 0839 DAVIS had reversed course. Range closed to 650 yards. And at that instant, with the ship's clock at 0840, FREDERICK C. DAVIS was struck by a torpedo, a stern-tube shot that smashed home like a thunderbolt.

A shattering blast on the DE's port side. A sheet of fire climbing the hull and tossing on its searing wings a scatter of debris. Men died instantly in the molten vortex of that eruption. A number were flung overside. Others, trapped in a mangle of bulkheads and machinery, went down with the ship.

One of the survivors, Lieutenant (jg) P. K. Lundeberg, U.S.N.R., saw the mainmast topple like a falling tree, the upper part breaking away and dangling from the lower in a tangle of shrouds. Her back broken, the FREDERICK C. DAVIS tore apart amidships. The halved vessel sank swiftly. Companion DE's of the scouting line ran in to pick up survivors.

But casualties were heavy. Although most of the men had on lifejackets and were able to reach rafts and floating nets, cold water and heavy sea took a high toll. Lieutenant Crosby and about two-thirds of the crew died in this torpedoing. Seventy-four men and three officers were rescued, and of these survivors a number were badly wounded.

Commissioned on July 14, 1943, FREDERICK C. DAVIS was the second and last American destroyer-escort to go down to enemy torpedo-fire in the Battle of the Atlantic.

So Doenitz had his "spite bite" out of the U.S. Navy's anti-submarine arm. But it was a bite that must have availed the Nazi Grand Admiral small satisfaction. One immediate result was the destruction of the U-boat responsible—the U-546.

Pillsbury, Flaherty, Neunzer, Chatelain, Varian, Hubbard, Janssen, and Keith Kill U-546

The U-boat skipper who fired at the FREDERICK C. DAVIS must have known he was courting suicide. For the DE scouting line closed around the U-boat like a noose. PILLSBURY (Lieutenant Commander G. W. Casselman, U.S.N.R.)—FLAHERTY (Lieutenant Commander H. C. Duff, U.S.N.R.)—NEUNZER (Lieutenant Commander V. E. Gex, U.S.N.R.)—CHATELAIN (Lieutenant Commander D. S. Knox, U.S.N.R.)—VARIAN (Lieutenant Commander L. A. Myhre, U.S.N.R.)—HUBBARD (Commander L. C. Mabley, U.S.N.R.)—JANSSEN (Lieutenant Commander S. G. Rubinow, Jr., U.S.N.R.)—KEITH (Lieutenant W. W. Patrick, U.S.N.R.)—these eight soon formed a "ring" around the submerged U-boat.

The submarine hunt conducted by this killer group stands as exemplary of the A/S tactics employed by hunter-killers at that stage of the war. For this reason the action is recounted in some detail.

Immediately after the FREDERICK C. DAVIS was torpedoed, Task Unit Commander Hall ordered NEUNZER and HAYTER to start "Operation Observant," PILLSBURY to circle the area, and FLAHERTY to pick up survivors. While engaged in rescue work, FLAHERTY made sonar contact on the U-boat. Time: 0917. Hall immediately directed NEUNZER and HAY-

TER to discontinue "Observant" and conduct rescue operations while PILLSBURY (his flagship) went to assist FLAHERTY.

The following, a condensation of the group's battle report, times the A/S action as it developed.

0950: FLAHERTY maneuvered into attack position and fired a hedgehog pattern.
1020: FLAHERTY made hedgehog attack, assisted by PILLSBURY.
1023: FLAHERTY fired a magnetic-set pattern of Mark 8 charges in creeping attack, directed by PILLSBURY. Depth-charge explosions were heard.
1028: PILLSBURY lost contact.
1034: PILLSBURY regained contact, range 900 yards.
1045: PILLSBURY lost contact; sub appeared to be very deep—estimated about 600 feet.

During the hour that PILLSBURY had been holding contact on the target and acting as assistant to FLAHERTY, she had found it extremely difficult to keep sonar tabs on the evading submarine. The sonar echoes were almost indiscernible, described by the Sound crew as "very weak and mushy." It was evident that the U-boat was operating at the deepest level endurable, and maneuvering radically at varying speeds from practically zero to 5 knots.

1056: PILLSBURY and FLAHERTY commenced "Operation Observant."
1059: Commander Hall ordered ComCortDiv 62 (Commander J. F. Bowling, Jr., in OTTER) to form a search line, composed of all ships not engaged in attacks or rescue operations, to ready for search sweeps.
1104: ComCortDiv 62 was ordered to remain at scene of DAVIS sinking to direct rescue operations.
1133: Task Unit Commander Hall ordered DE HUBBARD to bring search line forward through target area.
1150: PILLSBURY joined line as guide.
1152: OTTERSTETTER was ordered to join HAYTER and OTTER in rescue work.
1201: FLAHERTY obtained contact on U-boat.
1202: FLAHERTY reported her sound gear out and that contact should be ahead of DE VARIAN, range about 1,000 yards.
1205: VARIAN obtained contact.
1211: DE JANSSEN was ordered to attack, VARIAN assisting.
1228: JANSSEN delivered depth-charge attack.
1233: HUBBARD was ordered to join JANSSEN; VARIAN to assist and coach creeping attack.

With VARIAN directing maneuvers, HUBBARD and JANSSEN steamed into attack position. The U-boat was deep, but the two DE's were determined to dig it out whatever the level. Down went the depth-charges, a creeping attack that was launched at 1250.

1254: VARIAN reported a large air bubble.
1255: DE NEUNZER was ordered to the scene of contact.
1259: HUBBARD reported indications that U-boat was at depth of 600 feet.
1314: Another creeping attack delivered.
1320: JANSSEN relieved by FLAHERTY at scene of contact.
1341: Creeping attack delivered.
1346: DE CHATELAIN ordered to scene of attack.
1418: ComtCortDiv 62, in OTTER, and DE HAYTER left scene of DAVIS torpedoing to deliver survivors to escort carriers CORE and BOGUE. DE OTTERSTETTER remained on scene of torpedoing to continue search for any remaining survivors.
1515: VARIAN reported depth indication that U-boat was at depth of 580 feet.
1516: Another depth-charge attack delivered.
1545: DE COCKRILL ordered to scene of contact.
1549: Creeping attack delivered by NEUNZER, VARIAN, and HUBBARD, with CHATELAIN as directing ship.
1556: By means of depth-finding equipment, submarine located at 420-foot level. Contact lost shortly thereafter.

At 1637 CHATELAIN and NEUNZER were ordered to return to the line. During the previous attacks, Commander Hall had held the line in readiness to make a sweep forward if contact was lost. At 1649 he ordered all ships back into line, and the echo-ranging sweep was expanded.

1650: COCKRILL obtained contact.
1705: Having lost contact, COCKRILL suggested that line make sweep through area.
1723: Line started forward through area, PILLSBURY as guide.
1731: VARIAN reported contact.
1734: DE KEITH reported contact.
1737: PILLSBURY ordered to scene of contact to assist.
1743: FLAHERTY ordered to assist.
1747: By means of depth-finding equipment, KEITH reported indications that U-boat was at depth of 220 feet. Task Unit Commander Hall ordered attack to be switched to hedgehog, in view of decreased depth.
1810: FLAHERTY delivered hedgehog attack. PILLSBURY noted underwater explosion on sound gear.
1814: Small oil slick reported near scene of last attack.
1824: FLAHERTY reported bubbles coming up.
1828: FLAHERTY delivered hedgehog attack.
1838: U-boat surfaced.

From 9:50 in the morning to 6:30 in the evening —under fire for 10½ hours, the sweating Germans had had enough of it. Moreover, the U-boat had been damaged by depth charge and hedgehog. Unable to endure slow suicide, they elected to rise and get it over with. The conclusion was as swift as it was inevitable.

As the U-boat's conning tower broke water, all ships that had a clear range opened fire. Frantic submariners fought their way out of the hatches. Under a storm of hits the sub plunged and rolled. At 1844, her bridge knocked all acockbill, the U-546 went under with her *Schnorkel* throat severed.

The killer of the FREDERICK C. DAVIS had been executed. The destroyermen moved in to capture the survivors. Thirty-three U-boaters, including the submarine's Commanding Officer, *Herr Kapitan Leutnant* Paul Just, were taken prisoner.

Interrogated, *Herr Kapitan* Just said he fired at the FREDERICK C. DAVIS because it was a question of his getting the DE or the DAVIS sinking him.

Natchez, Coffman, Bostwick, and Thomas Sink U-548

Night off Cape Hatteras, with the calendar moving into the last day of April, 1945. Convoy KN-382 (Key West to New York) was steaming placidly along in the Gulf Stream about 100 miles from the entrance of Chesapeake Bay. There was nothing to disturb the routine until one of the escorts, the frigate NATCHEZ (Lieutenant J. H. Stafford, U.S.N.R.) made a sound contact.

The sub was on the frigate's starboard bow, bearing 20°. Lieutenant Stafford immediately took the conn and headed NATCHEZ for the target, intending to ram and drop an embarrassing pattern. A moment later the frigate's lookouts sighted a periscope and glimpsed a *Schnorkel* stack. The U-boat was dead ahead, trailing a broad feather, coming at high speed. Before NATCHEZ could change course to ram, the U-boat disappeared.

The frigate dropped the embarrassing pattern, then changed course to pursue. Unfortunately the convoy intervened, making an emergency turn; NATCHEZ had to turn away to avoid collision. Meanwhile her radio had enlivened the airwaves with the word, and Task Group 02.10, patrolling a nearby area, picked up the message. The group commander, Captain G. A. Parkinson, U.S.N.R., offered prompt assistance.

Holding her own astern of the convoy, frigate NATCHEZ regained contact. The target was on her starboard bow. Stafford reduced his vessel's speed to 10 knots and prepared to throw hedgehog at the *Schnorkel* submarine. The U-boat evaded, apparently releasing *Pillenwerfer* to obscure the trail. NATCHEZ regained contact at 1400 yards, and dropped a barrage of depth charges with magnetic settings. There were two detonations immediately after firing, and two explosions from great depth. Results were indeterminable. And at this point the hunt was turned over to TG 02.10.

Parkinson's task group was composed of the destroyer-escorts COFFMAN (Lieutenant Commander J. C. Crocker, U.S.N.R.), BOSTWICK (Lieutenant J. R. Davidson, U.S.N.R.), and THOMAS (Lieutenant Commander D. M. Kellogg, U.S.N.R.). COFFMAN was first to pick up the contact. At 2310, about 20 minutes after she made contact, the DE attacked with Mark X projectors. Ordered to maintain contact and prepare to direct creeping attacks after her next run, COFFMAN followed through with a second attack. At 2348 she made her third attack with hedgehog, and negative results. She then coached THOMAS into attack position.

At 0036 THOMAS stepped in to start a creeping attack. The fathometer registered 90 fathoms as the DE passed over the sub and dropped depth charges. Then BOSTWICK was coached into attack position. She laid down a barrage at 0115. Eight minutes after BOSTWICK's opening salvo, deep-sea explosions were heard over a sono buoy. Nothing definite.

Coached by COFFMAN, the frigate NATCHEZ resumed the attack and dropped a depth-charge barrage at 0207. When the pattern was completed, the frigate sighted a pond of dark oil on the ocean's surface. COFFMAN and THOMAS then ran "Operation Observant," after which COFFMAN delivered a creeping attack coached on by THOMAS. At 0447 the Sound crew in THOMAS heard a thunderous underwater explosion. Thereafter, silence under the sea.

In the dimness before dawn the hunters conducted an exhaustive search, but the sub had gone beyond the reach of detection gear. Daylight showed a seascape blotched with the dark oil stains which mark the death-bed of a hemorrhaging submarine. Somewhere deep under, a U-boat was sinking into the primal mud. Post-war inquest disclosed the submarine's identity. The frigate and the three DE's had demolished U-548.

The *Schnorkel* specimen sunk off Cape Hatteras was the seventh U-boat downed by American destroyermen in April, 1945. But the thunder of torpedoes, hedgehogs, depth charges, and bursting submarines in the Atlantic was to echo through to the war's bitter end.

Farquhar Kills U-881

On May 6, 1945, destroyer-escort FARQUHAR (Lieutenant Commander D. E. Walter, U.S.N.R.) was serving as a unit in the screen for the escort-carrier MISSION BAY, patrolling an area off the southeast reaches of the Grand Banks.

At 0313 of a morning starlit and invigorating, with the sea an expanse of indigo, FARQUHAR made Sound contact—range 1,300 yards. The Officer of the Deck sounded the appropriate alarm and gave "Right standard rudder!" With no opportunity to determine the sub's movement, he assumed from the bearing that it was headed into the screen. FARQUHAR's course had her on top of the target before the *Schnorkel* sub could draw a good breath.

At 0322 the DE delivered an urgent attack—13 depth charges, shallow setting. About 1,800 yards from the pattern, a sono buoy with night marker was dropped after the attack. Explosions thundered in the water. Then seven distinct blasts were heard over the sono buoy at 0403, and two final explosions were heard over the sono buoy at 0409. After these trailing detonations, FARQUHAR was unable to regain contact.

She ran "Operation Observant," and was presently joined by HILL and DOUGLAS L. HOWARD, under Commander E. W. Yancey, ComCortDiv 9, in HOWARD. For almost twelve and a half hours the search continued, but the sub was "sunk without trace." FARQUHAR had done her job with neatness and despatch. With a single depth-charge pattern she had obliterated another U-boat. And she had not long to wait for the victim's post-war identification. Hitler was already dead. Berlin was a heap of bricks. Within a few hours the slaughter in Europe would be over.

FARQUHAR killed U-881 on the day before VE-Day.

Atherton and Moberly Kill U-853 (Finale's End)

The waters between Point Judith, Rhode Island, and Block Island were decidedly unhealthy for German undersea boats, whether of World War I vintage or the ultra-modern *Schnorkel* variety.

The *Schnorkel* submarine that invaded that area on the evening of May 5, 1945, was a marked U-boat. Reckless to the verge of insanity, the captain of this submersible not only took her within four miles of Point Judith (near Newport Naval Base) but went so far as to strike at an American vessel. Moreover, instead of torpedoing a liner or a warship, this supersub torpedoed a little 5,300-ton coal collier, the S.S. BLACK POINT. All that naval science, marine engineering, and Prussian training to sink a small, unarmed merchantman and a load of coal hardly worth the price of a torpedo!

Certainly the torpedoing wasn't worth it to the crew of U-853. The submarine had hardly begun evasive action before the S-O-S was on the air, and all the A/S forces in the area were alerted.

Those forces were considerable. Naval craft from Providence, Newport, Mystic, New London. Coast Guardsmen from Point Jude, Block Island, Montauk. Destroyers, destroyer-escorts, corvettes, frigates, armed yachts. Land-based aircraft. Float planes. All the Army and Navy units in the region were ready to go. Among the units in the region was Task Group 60.7, which had just delivered a Gibraltar convoy to New York and was approaching the west end of the Cape Cod Canal, en route to Boston. Commander Eastern Sea Frontier dispatched three of these craft to the scene of the BLACK POINT torpedoing, to search for and destroy the vandal U-boat. The ships were under the over-all tactical command of Commander F. C. B. McCune, Commander of Task Group 60.7.

Thus the destroyer-escort ATHERTON (Lieutenant Commander L. Iselin, U.S.N.R.), the destroyer ERICSSON, and the frigate MOBERLY (Lieutenant Commander L. B. Tollaksen, U.S.C.G.) were soon combing the seascape off Point Judith. ERICSSON's hunt was fruitless. But, probing with their detection gear, both the ATHERTON and the frigate made contact with a submerged vessel lying about five miles from the scene of the torpedoing. A sunken hull? Or a U-boat down there on the bottom? Contact had been made within three hours of the attack on BLACK POINT. The target remained stationary as Lieutenant Commanders Iselin and Tollaksen maneuvered their ships into position, "pinging" carefully, listening.

Tense destroyermen waited as ATHERTON's ASW officer checked the sonar information. On the bridge, frigate MOBERLY's lookouts scanned the surface for some revelatory sign. Then Navy skipper and Coast Guard skipper jumped their crews into fast action.

"That's a pig-boat down there, all right!"

"Hold your hats, boys! We're going in!"

ATHERTON attacked. MOBERLY attacked. Down went the TNT.

Up came mounds of water and the thunder of sea-smothered explosions. The first explosions must have sent clouds of mud swirling around the conning tower of the bottomed submarine. The assailed U-boat made no move. Her machinery was not running. Either her motors were paralyzed by some casualty, or her captain had decided to sit it out. In either case, there was no escape for the U-853. At midnight the destroyermen were still pelting the target with hedgehogs and ashcans. The blasting continued through the early hours of May 6, a din that roused the fishermen on distant Block Island and rattled the windows of the island post office.

In their pressure hull the U-boaters were as confined as meats in a nut. A sledge-hammer depth-charge came down—slam!—and the nutshell cracked. *Slam! Slam! Slam!* The shell was crushed.

The men aboard ATHERTON and MOBERLY saw bubbles cluster on the surface. Up came a gurgling gush of oil. With the oil came chunks of cork. A great litter of cork that spread out across the heaving sea.

Boating through this flotsam some time later, the destroyermen picked up escape lungs, some pieces of German equipment, and other items bearing visible evidence of a kill. That afternoon divers from New London found the dead submarine. No survivors were recovered.

Downed a few hours before the Nazi surrender, the U-853 was the last German submarine demolished by American destroyermen in World War II. "X" marked the spot at lat. 41-13N., long. 71-27 W., within sight of Point Judith and Block Island, Rhode Island.

The battle of the Atlantic was finally and definitely over.

Atlantic Battle Summary

VE-Day—the radio operators of DesLant could not believe their ear-phones. Hitler cremated, Nazi Germany *Kaput,* Eisenhower at the gates of Berlin. Destroyermen, incredulous, took it at first for scuttlebutt. Then the word came over the squawk-boxes:

ATTENTION ALL HANDS AT TWO FORTY-ONE IN THE MORNING OF MAY SEVEN THE SURRENDER INSTRUMENT WAS SIGNED BY FIELD MARSHAL JODL

All hostilities ceased at midnight on May 8. Doenitz, wearing *Der Feuhrer's* tattered mantle, had capitulated.

Like woodchucks emerging en masse from their holes on some mythical Ground-Hog Day, German submarines in the Atlantic began surfacing and surrendering. Most of these popped up in the eastern Atlantic to surrender to British forces. Seven surfaced in the western Atlantic. One of these, the U-805, came up off Delaware Bay early in the morning of May 9, to haul down the flag to an A/S force which took the sub as a prize to Philadelphia. Another, the U-234, made its appearance on the Eastern Sea Frontier off the New England coast. A prize crew hauled this *Schnorkeler* into Portsmouth, N.H., where it was learned that the U-boat had been bound for Japan with a cargo of two Japanese officers—both of whom, just before the submarine's surrender, had ceremoniously committed *hari-kiri.*

With the U-boat war at an end, Navy statisticians promptly set to work on summarizations, percentages, and totals. To the American destroyermen who had fought the hot Atlantic Battle, some of these cold figures proved most interesting.

German submarines fighting in World War II to cut the Allies' trans-Atlantic lifelines, had sunk some 3,000 Allied and neutral vessels for a staggering loss of more than 14,000,000 tons of shipping.

But after the U.S. Navy entered the Atlantic Battle, the ratio of ships sunk to U-boats sunk was drastically altered in favor of the Allies. About 26 Allied vessels went down for each U-boat destroyed in 1940. By 1942 the ratio was 13 Allied vessels per U-boat. In 1943 the exchange was 2 for 1, and in the second half of that year more enemy subs were sunk than Allied vessels were torpedoed. In 1944 the Allies whittled the exchange down to .8 for 1, and in 1945 it was reduced to .4—or more than two U-boats sunk for every torpedoed Allied vessel.

Contrast the expiring U-boat effort with the increasingly successful American convoy effort, as summarized by U.S. Fleet A/S Bulletin for January, 1945.

While 5 per cent more convoys and convoyed ships were sailed in 1944 than in 1943, without increase in escorts, yet casualties to these ships from enemy action dropped from 201 to 30 ships. Of these, 136 and 16 respectively were sunk while under convoy protection. In other words, the risk of a ship which starts in convoy becoming a casualty dropped from one in 163 in 1943 to one in 1,156 in 1944.

The risk of casualty in ocean convoys dropped from one in 77 to one in 650, while the same risk in the coastals fell from one in 575 to one in 15,815.

While the number convoyed across the ocean in 1944 rose 48 per cent over 1943, ships in coastal convoys declined 21 per cent. The average size of ocean convoys increased from 43 ships in 1943 to 50 in 1944, whereas coastals declined from seven to five ships. Escorts per ocean convoy decreased slightly from 8.3 to 8.1 vessels, while average coastal escorts likewise dropped from 2.6 to 2.3 vessels.

Statistics on Allied ship-production complete the picture of Nazi Germany's defeat in the Atlantic Battle. To win that battle, the wolfpacks had to sink ships faster than Allied building yards could replace them.

Until the autumn of 1942, the U-boats consistently reduced the available total of Allied tonnage. In other words, the wolfpacks sank Allied and neutral vessels faster than those vessels could be replaced. But in 1943 American and British replacements more than quadrupled the lost shipping. The table on the next page briefs the loss and replacement picture for 1944-45.

The Nazi U-boat effort was swamped by an American shipbuilding program that produced an average of one million tons of new merchant ships per month after January 1, 1943, for a total of 24,000,000 tons by January 1, 1945.

During the war, the United States Navy, in partnership with United Nations forces, escorted some

YEAR	GERMAN SUBMARINES SUNK	ALLIED SHIPPING SUNK	NEW CONSTRUCTION UNITED STATES	BRITISH	TOTAL	NET GAINS OR LOSSES
	Number of Vessels		*(In Thousands of Tons)*			
1944	*241*	*1,422*	*11,639*	*1,710*	*13,349*	*+11,927*
1945 (4 months)	*153*	*458*	*3,551*	*283*	*3,834*	*+ 3,376*
TOTALS	*394*	*1,880*	*15,190*	*1,993*	*17,183*	*+15,303*

17,500 ships across the Atlantic Ocean. A total of 3,500,000 troops were carried overseas to North Africa and Europe. More than 150,000,000 tons of war supplies were ferried across the Atlantic to those battle fronts.

In order to achieve that tremendous transportation task the Allied navies had to conquer the German submarines. Entering the war in 1939, and bearing the brunt thereafter, British A/S forces in the Atlantic downed the most U-boats—a total of 561. American A/S forces accounted for 177. British-American A/S forces coöperatively destroyed 16. French, Dutch, Polish, Norwegian, Czech and other United Nations forces accounted for 14.

Of the 177 U-boats destroyed by American forces, Army aircraft demolished 48 in air raids on enemy-held seaports, and sank 14 at sea. The remaining 115 were downed by Navy A/S forces.

Of particular interest to destroyermen is the fact that DD's, DE's, Coast Guard cutters, and other A/S craft, operating singly and in hunter-killer teams, downed 48 U-boats—43 in the Atlantic and 5 in the Mediterranean. They also accounted for 2 Italian submarines.

All things considered, the U.S. Navy's combat losses in the Atlantic anti-submarine war were remarkably light. The American A/S forces opposed a deadly foe, superbly trained, magnificently equipped, supremely dangerous. But the U-boats were able to torpedo and sink but ten American A/S vessels—the escort-carrier BLOCK ISLAND, the destroyers JACOB JONES and LEARY, destroyer-escorts FISKE and FREDERICK C. DAVIS, and five Coast Guard cutters.

Compared with the damage dealt the undersea enemy by the sub-hunters, these losses emphasize a significant fact. Attacking slow, feebly-armed merchantmen, the U-boats were in their element. But the fast-moving warship armed with hedgehog, depth charges, and radar, and supported by aircraft, was the U-boat's Nemesis. *Schnorkel* and the capacity to dive to depths approaching 700 feet might have swung the balance in the U-boat's favor. But these submarine innovations were not developed in time. The U-boats that fought the Battle of the Atlantic were no match for the CVE-DD-DE hunter-killer teams.

In his final report to Navy Secretary Forrestal, Admiral King summarized:

"In the 12 months from 1 June, 1944, 135 convoys arrived in United Kingdom ports from overseas with a total of 7,157 merchant ships totalling more than 50,000,000 gross tonnage. The escort of this shipping and the provision of trained naval armed guard crews aboard the merchant vessels were among the primary tasks performed by the United States Navy in the prosecution of the war in Europe. The Navy's anti-submarine campaign with the British-United States integrated convoy system was in great part responsible for the vital shipping necessary for the Allied land offensive which broke into the Fortress of Europe in 1944 and overwhelmed the Germans ashore in 1945."

TORPEDOING OF THE FREDERICK C. DAVIS

CHAPTER 40

DESTROYERS TO JAPAN

Exit Last Axis Partner

On April 27, 1945, Benito Mussolini was trapped in the Alps and shot by Italian partisans. About 48 hours later Adolph Hitler, after appointing Admiral Doenitz his successor, vanished melodramatically (apparently a suicide) in the red light and smoke of a bunker deep under the Reich Chancellery. Eisenhower held his armies poised on the Elbe to allow the Russians, who had suffered the war's heaviest casualties (1,750,000 dead in the City of Leningrad alone), to storm Berlin. The Red Army swept in on May 1, and on the 7th Doenitz surrendered. The Rome-Berlin-Tokyo Axis was past history.

The Pacific War went on because the militarists on the Japanese Imperial Council refused to acknowledge defeat in a senseless effort to "save face"—and perhaps their own skins.

It was fatuous obstinacy, and Japan—which is to say the Japanese people—paid a heavy price for it. While the militarists blocked the surrender, B-29's from the Marianas, Iwo, and China flew a series of sorties which turned Japan's biggest cities into ash dumps of death and desolation. Striking Tokyo on the night of March 9-10, the Superforts set the pace by kindling a holocaust in which 97,000 people were burned to death. The fire raids were stepped up in June, as many as 500 American planes participating in a single strike. By the end of July, Japanese industry was almost burned out. Most of the inter-island shipping was on the rocks—or on the bottom. A ring of American submarines held Japan in the grip of a blockade which had all but paralyzed local commerce. Sixty-six Japanese cities had been scourged by flame-spreading bombs. Yokohama, a seaport without shipping, was a vista of wreckage and ruin. About a third of Nagoya, Japan's third largest city, was fire-ravaged. Incendiary bombings had gutted much of Osaka. Over half of Tokyo was a smoldering heap of rubble. About 300,000 Japanese had been cremated in this holocaust and the surviving populace was facing famine.

As the wrangling in Japan's Supreme War Council went on in secret, the Allied leaders were unaware of Emperor Hirohito's peace moves. Nor were they accurately informed on conditions in Japan. Accordingly plans went forward for "Operation Olympic"—the invasion of Kyushu, which was scheduled to take place five months after the securement of Okinawa.

The "Olympic" preliminaries included anti-shipping sweeps in Japan's home waters, attacks on the picket line lying off Japan, shore bombardments, and a mop-up of the enemy's transport runs to such outlying isles as the Bonins. Destroyers engaged in all these invasion overtures, conducting missions in a pattern which had long since become conventionalized.

DD's in Japan's Home Waters

On June 19 the destroyer DUNLAP (Lieutenant Commander C. R. Welte) steamed into action while patrolling off Yome Shima in the Bonin group. At 0147 in the morning of that day the ship picked up an SG radar contact, and launched a torpedo attack on what was believed to be a surfaced submarine. Two more targets were spotted within the next hour and treated to 5-inch gunnery. The torpedo spread missed, but the gunnery blasted a pair of *marus*. Fifty-two Japs were fished from the water by the DUNLAP destroyermen. The destroyer concluded the foray during the forenoon watch by sinking an oil-loaded freighter.

On June 26, destroyers BEARSS, JOHN HOOD, JARVIS (a new one named after the one that vanished off Guadalcanal), PORTER, ANDERSON, and HUGHES, under Captain R. O. Strange, ComDesDiv 114, struck farther afield. Operating with Task Force 92 (Rear Admiral J. H. Brown, Jr.), these DD's sortied from Attu in the Aleutians to visit the cold waters of northern Japan. The force left Attu on the 21st. Three days out, it split into two groups, destroyers ANDERSON and HUGHES, with cruiser TRENTON, remaining east of the Kurile Islands, while the rest of the force raced westward into the Okhotsk Sea.

United States submarines had already probed these dangerous inner waters and alarmed the defenders. A penetration by surface ships was therefore doubly hazardous. But cruisers RICHMOND (flagship) and CONCORD, and destroyers BEARSS, JOHN HOOD, JARVIS, and PORTER went boldly in. About 0540 in the morning of the 26th, the ships sighted a Japanese convoy southwest of Paramushiro. Upon discovery, the Jap convoy broke formation, scattered, and went helter-skelter across the seascape. Most of the *marus* ran northward. They could not out-run destroyer starshells and 5-inch gunnery. PORTER sank a 2,000-ton freighter. BEARSS shot at a smaller ship which disappeared from the radar screen. A large tug or a small *maru* went down under fire from JARVIS. One small unidentified vessel was damaged by 40 mm. fire from JOHN HOOD. After about an hour's shooting, the four destroyers were ordered to break off the action and rejoin the cruisers. The Task Force returned to Attu on the 27th—mission successful, and no ships damaged.

If the results of such anti-shipping sweeps as the foregoing were meager, it was not from lack of trying on the part of the sweepers. The Japanese had begun the war with a merchant marine of some 6,000,000 tons. By the summer of 1945 the figure had been reduced to about 312,000 tons, and many of the *marus* which remained afloat were tied up for lack of fuel. American naval vessels on the warpath were hunting a "ghost fleet."

Late in July, Destroyer Squadron 61, led by Captain T. H. Hederman, conducted a high-speed raid to sweep shipping from the very threshold of Honshu. Plunging through seas kicked up by the backwash of a typhoon, they shot up shipping which hugged the Honshu coast west of Nojima Saki, sinking a medium-sized and a small freighter, and damaging another medium cargoman and its escort. The gunnery was answered by AA fire, which was mistakenly directed skyward, and a few salvos rumbled out from shore batteries. No DD was hit.

The destroyers which participated in this daring sweep were DE HAVEN (flagship of Captain Hederman), MANSFIELD, LYMAN K. SWENSON, MADDOX, COLLETT, TAUSSIG, BLUE, SAMUEL N. MOORE, and BRUSH. Commander W. H. McClain, in TAUSSIG, doubled as destroyer captain and division commander. This dual responsibility invited the following comment from Squadron Commander Hederman: *"The fact that there was no regularly assigned division commander in DesDiv 122 affected my plans considerably. The Commanding Officer of a 2,200-ton destroyer has all he can do to maneuver and fight his ship without being given the added duties of division commander in a tactical set-up. Therefore, everything I did was done in an effort to keep the divisions together to be maneuvered by the Squadron Commander."*

Endorsing Captain Hederman's report, Admiral Halsey, after complimenting the squadron on its successful raid, wrote:

"Attention is particularly invited to the absence of a division commander in Destroyer Division 122. Only in cases of urgent necessity should officers in command of tactical units be detached without relief."

At this time Halsey's fleet, consisting of 105 United States warships and 28 British naval vessels, was parading up and down the Pacific coasts of Japan, bombarding shore targets almost with impunity. American carrier planes swarmed like angry bees over Japan's naval ports. Striking at the Yokosuka naval base in Tokyo Bay, they sank a Jap destroyer,wrecked the battleship NAGATO, and ruined the port facilities. During the last week of July, American and British carrier planes hammered the big naval base at Kure. Jap aircraft made a determined effort to stave off these strikes, but they were brushed aside by the Allied air armadas. Kure was battered to a pulp. Sunk were the aircraft carrier KAIYO, Japan's last CVE, and the carrier-battleship HYUGA. Cruisers KITAGAMI and OYODO were sent to the bottom. Carriers KATSURAGI and AMAGI were badly smashed, the battleship HARUNA was driven to the beach where it burned like a stove, and the carrier-battleship ISE, and cruisers TONE and AOBA, plus two destroyers, were disabled. After this massive destruction, all that was left of the once mighty Imperial Navy was a light cruiser, a training cruiser, perhaps a dozen destroyers, and some 55 ocean-going submarines. Aside from the submarines, Siam had almost as large a fleet.

Many Japanese naval units and island commands surrendered to the United States destroyer forces. Fittingly enough, one of these surrenders took place on one of the fightingest destroyers of them all, U.S.S. Nicholas (DD 449). Here we see two Japanese captains in the wardroom of Nicholas after they surrendered to Captain Harry S. Heneberger. The date is September 25, 1945.

The Allied Fleet in Tokyo Bay. On August 27, 1945, the great battleship Missouri, flying Admiral Halsey's flag and escorted by destroyers Nicholas, O'Bannon, and Taylor, steamed into the outer bay in preparation for the surrender ceremony.

Old friends in mothballs at Long Beach, California. From left to right are Charles J. Badger (DD 657), Stemble (DD 644), Wiley (DD 597), Hudson (DD 475), and Hall (DD 583). Their next active duty was to be against the Communist aggressors.

The same Pacific, but a new assignment for the "small boys." Hostilities in Korea placed a demand upon the Fleet that could be met only by putting mothballed destroyers back to work. New crew members had the old jobs to learn all over again.

Remnants of the once great Japanese fleet that was smashed in World War II. From top to bottom, the carrier Amagi; battleships Ise, Hyuga, and Haruna; the heavy cruisers Aoba and Tone; the light cruisers Oyodo **and** *Kiso, and a submarine captured in the Philippines.*

Japan's vestigial undersea arm was still capable of striking homicidal—and suicidal—blows. Preferring the former to the latter, Admiral Miwa sent his I-boats and RO-boats out to fight as well as die. On July 29 the submarine I-58 struck Halsey's Third Fleet an excruciating smash by intercepting and sinking the heavy cruiser INDIANAPOLIS off Leyte. The torpedoed cruiser sank in about 15 minutes. Down with her went 696 men and officers. Somebody failed to get the word, and the fact that the ship did not make a scheduled arrival at her port of destination went unnoticed for a number of hours. For four days the survivors were adrift. When they were finally found and picked up, only 316 remained. This was Japan's last undersea triumph. It was a Pyrrhic victory.

Meanwhile, American destroyermen were relentlessly fighting the A/S campaign. In the third week of July a DesPac DE teamed up with carrier aircraft to score the last major submarine kill, destroyer-wise, in the Pacific. The job was done by the L. C. TAYLOR and planes from the carrier ANZIO.

L. C. Taylor and Aircraft from Anzio Kill I-13

Sortieing from San Pedro Bay in the Philippines on July 6, 1945, the escort-carrier ANZIO and five DE's headed seaward for a rendezvous with a fuelling group. By July 16 the task group was cruising in an assigned area off Honshu.

At 0747 in the morning of the 16th, an ANZIO plane sighted and bombed a Jap sub which had dared daylight exposure on the surface. Trailing oil, the sub submerged. The wounded I-boat was tracked and attacked by a relief plane. At 1140 the LAWRENCE C. TAYLOR (Lieutenant Commander J. R. Grey), flagship of Commander A. Jackson, Jr., U.S.N.R., ComCortDiv 72, was guided into position by the plane. The DE let fly with a hedgehog barrage. A spatter of small explosions indicated hits. Two deep-bellied blasts echoed the rataplan.

Fifteen minutes later, destroyer-escort KELLER made a similar attack on a doubtful sonar contact, with no results. Evidently TAYLOR's hedge-hogging was sufficient. To the oil-streaked surface bobbed a miscellany of rubbish which included shattered deck planks, cork, sponge rubber, candles, Jap magazines, paper money, a snapshot (candid camera), and some soggy mail. The contents of this correspondence was not recorded; evidently it was not as interesting as some. (For instance, the postcard found on the body of a *Kamikaze* pilot, from a feminine admirer who praised him for joining the Suicide Corps and somewhat inconsistently "hoped that he would have a long and prosperous life.")

The submarine which fell afoul of the ANZIO aircraft and LAWRENCE C. TAYLOR off Honshu had a short life and an impecunious one. But it did have the distinction of being the last big Jap sub downed by destroyermen in the Pacific War. It also had a numerological distinction similar to that which haunted destroyer CALLAGHAN. Its number was I-13.

Johnnie Hutchins Versus Midgets

The war against Miwa's submarines boomed on into August, 1945. The big ones made themselves scarce. But the midgets kept appearing from time to time, suicidal to the last. During the last week of the war, destroyer-escort JOHNNIE HUTCHINS swept up a school of midget subs in the ocean below Okinawa.

On August 9, 1945, the HUTCHINS was working with a hunter-killer group, sweeping on the convoy road between Okinawa and Leyte, when her lookouts sighted what at first glance resembled a small whale breaking water about 2,000 yards on the quarter. At second glance it resembled a small submarine.

The crew scrambled to battle stations as the DE's skipper, Lieutenant Commander H. M. Godsey, U.S.N.R., headed JOHNNIE for the spot. At 1,500 yards the gunners opened fire. The DE closed the range to 300 yards. From that distance the target looked like a floating iron boiler. It was about 45 feet in length and *"similar in appearance to Jap midgets with the exception of the conning-tower structure which extended six or eight inches above the hull and appeared to be nothing more than an escape hatch."*

Reminiscent of the Confederate *Davids* of the Civil War, this weird affair undoubtedly contained munitions and a man. The DE gunners hammered the thing with shellfire while Godsey sent his ship veering away, refusing to ram. This was doubtless a discreet tactic; Godsey was taking no chances on another UNDERHILL disaster.

The DE circled off; maneuvered to bring portside guns to bear; made another approach on the target. The queer little submarine *"passed down the port side at . . . about two knots. It appeared to be trying to keep its bow pointed toward the ship."* Then a new peril was encountered. In the words of JOHNNIE HUTCHINS' Action Report:

As submarine was being closed again, torpedo noises were heard over the sound gear, and at the same time a periscope was sighted on the port bow beyond the surfaced midget. Shortly thereafter, sonar contact was obtained at 700 yards and run was begun on this contact while the first submarine was still under fire.

As the first submarine, still surfaced, passed abeam of this vessel on the port side about 100 yards away, a

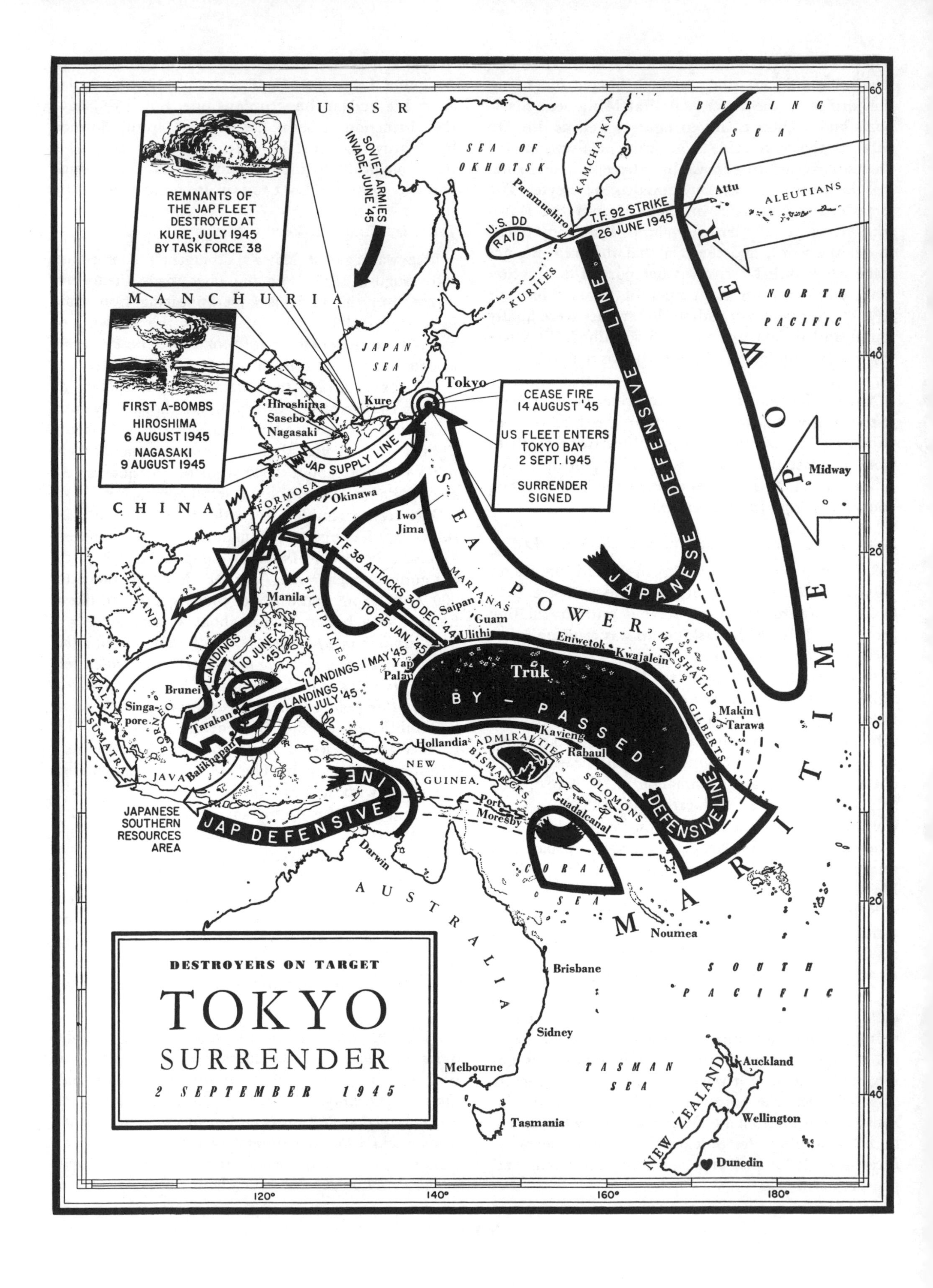
DESTROYERS ON TARGET
TOKYO
SURRENDER
2 SEPTEMBER 1945
REMNANTS OF THE JAP FLEET DESTROYED AT KURE, JULY 1945 BY TASK FORCE 38
FIRST A-BOMBS
HIROSHIMA 6 AUGUST 1945
NAGASAKI 9 AUGUST 1945
SOVIET ARMIES INVADE, JUNE '45
CEASE FIRE 14 AUGUST '45
US FLEET ENTERS TOKYO BAY 2 SEPT. 1945
SURRENDER SIGNED
U.S. DD RAID
T.F. 92 STRIKE 26 JUNE 1945
JAPANESE DEFENSIVE LINE
JAP SUPPLY LINE
TF 38 ATTACKS 30 DEC. '44 TO 25 JAN. '45
LANDINGS 10 JUNE '45
LANDINGS 1 MAY '45
LANDINGS 1 JULY '45
BY-PASSED
JAP DEFENSIVE LINE
DEFENSIVE LINE
JAPANESE SOUTHERN RESOURCES AREA
SEA POWER
MARITIME POWER
USSR
MANCHURIA
CHINA
SEA OF OKHOTSK
KAMCHATKA
Paramushiro
KURILES
Attu
ALEUTIANS
BERING SEA
NORTH PACIFIC
JAPAN SEA
Tokyo
Kure
Hiroshima
Sasebo
Nagasaki
FORMOSA
Okinawa
Iwo Jima
Midway
THAILAND
Manila
PHILIPPINES
MARIANAS
Saipan
Guam
Ulithi
Eniwetok
Kwajalein
MARSHALLS
Yap
Palau
Truk
Brunei
Singa-pore
BORNEO
Tarakan
Balikpapan
MALAYA
SUMATRA
JAVA
Hollandia
NEW GUINEA
ADMIRALTIES
Kavieng
Rabaul
BISMARCKS
SOLOMONS
Guadalcanal
Port Moresby
GILBERTS
Makin
Tarawa
Darwin
CORAL SEA
AUSTRALIA
Noumea
Brisbane
Sidney
Melbourne
Tasmania
TASMAN SEA
SOUTH PACIFIC
NEW ZEALAND
Auckland
Wellington
Dunedin
120°
140°
160°
180°
60°
40°
20°
0°
20°
40°

direct hit from the after 5-inch 38 holed it and it sank immediately.

Meanwhile the periscope of the second submarine had disappeared and a torpedo wake was seen passing down starboard side of this vessel.

A pattern of Mark 8 depth charges, set on magnetic, was dropped on the contact and three explosions were heard. Range was quickly opened and another attack made with charges. . . .

At this point destroyer-escorts CAMPBELL, MUNRO, and ROLF stepped in to join the hunt. WILLIAM SEIVERLING (flagship of ComCortDiv 70) took charge of the attack. Linking up with JOHNNIE HUTCHINS to form a scouting line, the DE's began a retiring search, as directed by Escort Division Commander R. Cullinam.

The search turned up a third midget sub. Its periscope was sighted by JOHNNIE HUTCHIN's lookouts and the busy DE laid a depth-charge pattern which produced a prodigious explosion. Water geysered 30 feet in the air, and the concussions shook the SEIVERLING a mile away.

The four DE's continued the hunt for the remaining midget. Late in the afternoon they were joined by destroyer-escorts GEORGE A. JOHNSON, CONNOLLY, METIVIER, and WITTER. The ships ran the legs of search plans until 1400 the following day. The other midget had either escaped or gone sailing to the bottom.

No debris could be found, so a positive identification of all three subs was impossible. Nor could a sinking of the trio be verified. But the strange midget plugged by shellfire from JOHNNIE HUTCHINS undoubtedly took a fatal plunge.

Concerning the novel A/S battle, JOHNNIE HUTCHINS' skipper wrote: *"The experience gained by this vessel during the past two months in training with U.S. Fleet submarines in Subic Bay proved invaluable in this engagement, particularly in regard to lookouts and other topside personnel spotting periscopes and torpedo wakes."*

Left-overs of the Imperial Navy, Miwa's midgets were dangerous. But they were as vulnerable to skillful destroyer work as any other type of submersible.

Nickel Versus Human Torpedoes

The last A/S scrimmage on the Okinawa road occurred just three days after the second atomic blast and two days before VJ-Day. The episode, featuring the Japanese version of the human torpedo, suggests that a few "Bushido" zealots were still extant. Vice Admiral Oldendorf noted that the affair was *"an excellent example of a comparatively new type of attack which threatened to become of major importance had the war continued."*

On August 12, 1945, the destroyer-escort THOMAS F. NICKEL was escorting the landing-ship dock OAK HILL from Okinawa to Leyte. Late in the afternoon the ships reached a point about 360 miles southeast of Okinawa. And sunset was enameling the seascape when, at 1829, OAK HILL's lookouts sighted a periscope feather on the port quarter.

The alarm sent the NICKEL steaming toward the periscope's reported position. At 1830 a torpedo was seen broaching in OAK HILL's wake. NICKEL's skipper, Lieutenant Commander C. S. Farmer, U.S.N.R., was maneuvering for a depth-charge attack when *"it was realized that what was first believed to be a broaching normal torpedo must be a piloted (human) torpedo. . . ."* The DE was brought about, full rudder, and headed toward this creepy menace.

OAK HILL zigzagged to evade, and the peculiar "fish" followed the ship like a trailing shark. Then, unable to overhaul, it disappeared in a ruffle of foam. A few minutes later the crew below decks in NICKEL heard something rasp along the port side of the ship, as though the DE's hull had scraped against a submerged hulk. A moment later the human torpedo broke water about 2,500 yards away from the NICKEL and proceeded to burst like an exploded mine.

While the destroyermen were thanking Providence for this upshot of a close shave, another periscope was reported skulking in OAK HILL's wake. Lieutenant Commander Farmer did some fast maneuvering to place THOMAS F. NICKEL in position ahead of the periscope's estimated track. Whereupon the DE dropped a pattern of charges set for shallow depth. There was a rumpus in the water, a heavy blast, then silence. Another human torpedo had squibbed out.

About 1918 OAK HILL sighted still another marine menace, this time dead ahead. The ship swung to evade, and destroyer-escort NICKEL steamed forward to investigate. She sighted what looked like a thin wake or oil slick, but the source could not be located by visual, radar, or sonar search. Whatever had been there was gone, and from there on out the evening seascape was serene.

A brush with human torpedoes (too much of a brush for NICKEL's comfort) was unusual so far out in the ocean. Normally these monstrosities had about the cruising range of a naphtha launch. *"It is believed,"* Lieutenant Commander Farmer reported, *"that a large submarine was controlling and observing attacks beyond sonar range, and probably to eastward of the task unit."*

This arrangement—mother submarine spawning human "fish"—was something new in the way of undersea warfare. And perhaps it was the ultimate in sea-going suicide techniques. Sealed up in something like an iron sewer pipe, the human element of the human torpedo, playing tag with a target, was compelled to sweat out a slow death. If he missed the mark, and did not bash his brains out in a contact explosion, he might be left to expire of suffocation—or quietly die of claustrophobia.

So the Japanese submarine effort foundered at the end of its sorry rope. The final kills by LAWRENCE C. TAYLOR, JOHNNIE HUTCHINS, and NICKEL nicely symbolize the downward progress of that effort—from fleet submarines to midgets to human torpedoes.

Flashback to Borneo (The last "Amphibs")

Had the war continued into the latter part of 1945, Miwa's left-over submarines would eventually have been stranded for lack of fuel. By the time of the Okinawa invasion Japanese tankers were as rare as Japanese men-of-war, oil convoys to the quondam "Southern Empire" were a thing of the past, and fuel reserves in Japan were stoking some of the more spectacular fires on the Nipponese waterfront. An occasional *maru* ran the blockade with a few barrels of petroleum—enough to keep the *Kamikazes* flying. And some of the bigger I-boats were employed as tankers to run the blockade.

The best way to stop a trickle is to shut off the water at its source, and as soon as the Okinawa campaign was well under way the Allies applied the axiom to the enemy's fuel trickle by descending upon the leaky oil ports of Borneo.

Targets were Brunei, the advanced naval base which the Japs had developed on the northwest coast of Borneo, Tarakan Island off the northwest coast, and Balikpapan, the rich oil port on Makassar Strait. Set for May 1, and June 10, 1945, the Tarakan and Brunei invasions were by way of preliminary operations for the main drive on Balikpapan, which was scheduled for the 1st of July.

The play fell to Seventh Fleet forces, which were committed to transporting, landing, and supporting Australian invasion troops. Vice Admiral D. E. ("Uncle Dan") Barbey, veteran of pioneer days on the New Guinea-Solomons front, was in charge of the amphibious effort.

The Borneo operation began with the occupation of Tarakan. For three days Allied air and surface forces blasted at the enemy installations on the island. Screening Rear Admiral F. B. Royal's Attack Group were destroyers WALLER (flagship of Captain Robert Hall Smith, ComDesRon 22), BAILEY, BANCROFT, PHILIP, DRAYTON, SMITH, and CALDWELL, DE's FORMOE and CHARLES E. BRANNON, and three Australian frigates. Operating with Rear Admiral R. S. Berkey's Cruiser Covering Group were destroyers NICHOLAS (flagship of Captain J. K. B. Ginder, ComDesRon 21), O'BANNON, FLETCHER, JENKINS, TAYLOR, and H.M.A.S. WARRAMUNGA.

The troops going ashore met no opposition, but the minesweeping work which attended the Tarakan landings was a trying chore. The enemy did not open fire until the day after the landings. Then undetected shore batteries made it hot for the minesweepers. One was sunk and two were damaged by surprise salvos.

The narrowness of the swept channels and the shallow water inshore made trouble for the fire-support ships. Only the lighter vessels could undertake the close-in missions. In the afternoon of April 30, destroyer JENKINS (Commander P. D. Gallery), while retiring from a bombardment mission and steaming in water which had previously been swept many times, was jolted by a mine blast. The explosion mashed the vessel's port side forward. Electrical power was depleted, and master gyro, sonar gear, pit log, degaussing gear, and SC-3 radar were put out of commission. One man was killed by the blast and two were badly injured. After reaching safe anchorage under her own steam, the JENKINS dropped the hook, and her damage control crew went to work on a repair job. Within 12 hours of her disablement JENKINS was again seaworthy and able to limp along at 10 knots. But she was out of the war for the duration. She was one of the two destroyers injured in the Borneo operation.

As overture to the invasion of Brunei, American and Australian planes pounded Brunei Bay and its fortifications for ten days prior to the June 10 landings. Again, extensive enemy and Allied mine plants created a difficult sweeping problem. While clearing the approaches, one minesweeper was lost with heavy casualties.

The minesweepers and Underwater Demolition teams were protected by a Cruiser Covering Group commanded by Rear Admiral Berkey. The group contained destroyers CHARRETTE (flagship of Captain J. W. Callahan, ComDesDiv 102), CONNER, BELL, BURNS, KILLEN, A.W. GRANT, and H.M.A.S. ARUNTA. On June 8 the fire-support ships entered Brunei Bay through a swept channel to plaster the beaches with shell fire. Another bombardment dose was dealt Brunei the following day. The Jap shore batteries were conspicuously silent, and the landings were virtually unopposed. Operating with the Brunei Attack Group, under Rear Admiral Royal, were ten DD's and six DE's. The destroyers were ROBINSON (flagship of Captain Robert Hall Smith, ComDesRon 22), SAUFLEY, WALLER, PHILIP, BANCROFT, BAILEY, EDWARDS, CALDWELL, FRAZIER, and MCCALLA. The DE's were

Douglas A. Munro, Charles E. Brannon, Albert T. Harris, Dufilho, Jobb, and Day.

While "Aussie" troops raced in to the beaches, cruisers and destroyers patrolled the approaches to Brunei as guards against possible attack by Jap men-of-war. But they were on the lookout for spectres. On June 8 a British submarine waylaid and torpedoed I.J.N. Ashigara. When the Japanese heavy cruiser went down, the last major combat vessel flying the Rising Sun flag south of Japan disappeared from the view of mortal man. Only a few submarines remained in Indonesian waters to contest the sea routes to Brunei.

On June 27 the destroyer Caldwell (Lieutenant Commander D. R. Robinson, U.S.N.R.) fouled a mine in the entrance of Brunei Bay. The blast damaged the destroyer's rudder and injured a screw—sole casualties. Caldwell was the last Seventh Fleet destroyer wounded in action.

At Balikpapan—fabulous fountainhead of Borneo oil—the Japs prepared to sell their possessions dearly. But with little air cover and with sea defense limited to mines, the stand was brief. Its brevity was assured by the Seventh Fleet assigned to the invasion.

Led by Rear Admiral R. S. Riggs, the Cruiser Covering Group, when fully assembled, contained an American, British, Australian, and Dutch aggregation of nine cruisers and ten destroyers. The destroyer complement consisted of: Conway (flagship of Captain S. G. Hooper, ComDesDiv 44), Eaton. Stevens, Cony, Arunta, Hart, Metcalf, Killen, A. W. Grant, Bell, Charrette, Conner, and Burns. The destroyers engaged in shore bombardments, duelling with coastal guns which had sunk three minesweepers in the inshore shallows. At first the bombardment ships were compelled to remain anywhere from 12,000 to 14,000 yards offshore. By June 24 safe passageways through the dense minefields had been cleared, and the warships of the Covering Group were able to go in for close-range shooting. Their accurate fire soon silenced most of the enemy shore batteries. When the "Aussies" hit the Balikpapan beaches on July 1, not a single soldier was felled by Jap gunnery.

Supporting the landings, a task group under Rear Admiral A. G. Noble added more shellfire to the shore bombardment. The Close Support Unit of Noble's Attack Group consisted of 24 landing craft screened by 10 destroyers, five destroyer-escorts, and a frigate. The destroyers were Flusser (flagship of Captain F. D. McCorkle, ComDesRon 5) Drayton, Conyngham, Smith, Frazier (flagship of Captain G. L. Sims, ComDesRon 14), Bailey, Robinson (flagship of Captain R. H. Smith), Saufley, Waller, and Philip. The destroyer-escorts were Chaffee, Edwin A. Howard, Key, Leland E. Thomas, and Rutherford.

On June 30 three escort-carriers joined the invasion fleet. The flat-tops were screened by destroyer Helm and destroyer-escorts Cloues, Mitchell, Kyne, Lamons and Donaldson. The ships provided CAP cover for the landing forces, and conducted anti-submarine patrols. A total of 25,304 Australian soldiers were put on the beach. Fighting inland, they ran into stubborn resistance, but this melted away with the fading days of July. No Southwest Pacific beachhead received such a lambasting as was given Balikpapan by the covering and fire-support ships which blazed the trail for the invaders. In the days immediately preceding the landings, the destroyers alone fired 18,820 rounds of 5-inch at the target beaches.

By August the Borneo oil wells were in Allied hands, and the recapture had been accomplished with a speed and economy which would have seemed unbelievable six months before, and utterly incredible in 1941. The mines, which constituted the chief menace to the Allied invasion forces, had availed the enemy little. They were pests which had to be dealt with, but they were handily swept up, a total of 462 going into the dust bin at Brunei alone. This was a record haul in the Southwest Pacific. And the last Southwest Pacific invasion operation was over.

Imperial Finish

The atom bomb fell. Hiroshima was obliterated on August 6. Nagasaki was pulverized on the 9th. Soviet Russia declared war, in accordance with Yalta agreements, and Japan was at Death's door.

The nuclear-fission blasts in Nippon and the tramp of Russian legions in Manchuria should have convinced the recalcitrant militarists in the Japanese Imperial Council that their faces and private fortunes were beyond salvage. Nevertheless, when the Council met in emergency session on August 13, a unanimous vote for surrender could not be obtained. However, the Emperor put an end to the fatuous temporizing by going over the heads of the hold-outs, and issuing an Imperial rescript which stopped the war.

On August 14, 1945, the "Cease fire" order flashed through the United States Fleet.

The Pacific War was over.

Japan Surrenders! (Destroyers in Tokyo Bay)

On August 27 Admiral Halsey led the great United States Fleet into Tokyo Bay. In attendance with battleship Missouri were destroyers Nicholas, O'Bannon, and Taylor. From the inner harbor came Japanese destroyer Hatuzakura carrying pilots to take the American ships in through the minefields. Meantime,

General MacArthur had been appointed "Supreme Commander for the Allied Powers," and Japanese emissaries had visited his Manila Headquarters to discuss the ways and means of formal surrender. Acting for Admiral Nimitz, Admiral Forrest Sherman served as representative for the United States at Manila. Nimitz was to represent the United States at the Tokyo surrender ceremonies.

On September 2, 1945, at 0855, a group of Japanese officers and statesmen boarded the "MIGHTY MO." When Japanese Foreign Minister Mamoru Shigemitsu put his signature to the surrender document, Japan was formally out of the war. Superfortresses and carrier planes roared across the bay in salute to the Allied victory, and the ceremony was at an end.

Among the ships present in Tokyo Bay during the formal surrender ceremony were the destroyers and destroyer-escorts listed on this page.

Destroyers Enter Sasebo

Rated as third most important in the Empire, the Japanese naval base at Sasebo on the west coast of Kyushu contained Japan's largest drydock and a navy yard studded with highly secret installations. For many years this vital base had been an "inner sanctum" forbidden to foreigners. Now the key was surrendered to the United States Navy, and Sasebo was opened to the forces of occupation.

The first Allied ships to enter this Imperial Navy lair were the destroyers FLUSSER (Lieutenant Commander F. de Golian, U.S.N.R.), flying the pennant of Captain F. D. McCorkle, ComDesRon 5, and RALPH TALBOT (Commander W. S. Brown, U.S.N.R.). Riding in RALPH TALBOT was Rear Admiral M. L. Deyo, ComTaskForce 55 and ComDesDiv 13. As Commander Western Japan Force, Admiral Deyo met with Japanese Navy officials to take over the Sasebo base.

Veteran Destroyer Squadron Commander, Admiral Deyo had fought the Battle of the Atlantic from the opening gun. After his promotion to Rear Admiral he had served for a cruise as ComDesLant. The Sasebo detail might have been assigned him in recognition of his devotion to those little gray ships which had shouldered so heavy a share of the combat burden. And in recognition of their heroic war service he selected the U.S.S. FLUSSER and RALPH TALBOT for the entry into Sasebo.

Destroyers FLUSSER and RALPH TALBOT, members of DesRon 5 and DesRon 4 respectively, were survivors of squadrons which had been in action since December 7, 1941. Five of the original nine ships of DesRon 5 had been lost in the Pacific War.

After leaving Captain McCorkle to act as his repre-

DESTROYERS IN TOKYO BAY

WALLACE L. LIND
DE HAVEN — *ComBatRon 2*
AULT — *ComTaskFlot 3*
CLARENCE K. BRONSON — *ComDesRon 50*
BENHAM
BENSON — *ComDesRon 7*
BLUE — *ComDesRon 61*
BUCHANAN — *ComDesDiv 38*
CAPERTON
COGSWELL — *ComDesDiv 100*
COLAHAN
COTTEN
CUSHING — *ComDesRon 53*
DORTCH
KALK
GATLING
KNAPP
HEALY
FRANK KNOX
HUGHES
LANSDOWNE
R. K. HUNTINGTON
LARDNER
INGERSOLL
MADISON
H. P. JONES
MAYO
WADLEIGH
NICHOLAS — *ComDesRon 21*
PERKINS — *ComDesDiv 21*
HALSEY POWELL
STOCKHAM
SOUTHERLAND
TAYLOR
TWINING — *ComTaskFlot 4*
UHLMANN
WREN
WEDDERBURN — *ComDesDiv 106*
YARNALL

DESTROYER-ESCORTS

WM. SEIVERLING — *ComCortDiv 70*
MAJOR
LYMAN
KENDALL C. CAMPBELL
ULVERT M. MOORE
GOSS
BARR
ROBERTS
WATERMAN
WEAVER
PIEDMONT — *Destroyer Tender*

★

sentative, Deyo departed from Sasebo to return on September 20 as Commander Task Group 55.1—the group consisting of cruiser SANTE FE (Flagship), destroyers BALDWIN, HELM, and LAMSON, and destroyer-escort STRAUS (ComCortDiv 51).

So, in September, 1945, with Allied flags flying in Tokyo Bay, Sasebo, and other Japanese harbors, the Japanese Empire of expansion and conquest came to a dead end, and the Samurai sword was sheathed for the last time.

Tell It to the Destroyermen

Fought at a cost of four trillion dollars and 40 million lives, the global war that ended in Japan in September, 1945, was without question the greatest tragedy in human history. Never in the past had civilian populaces been scourged by such cruel punishment as was inflicted upon them by invasion, starvation, and genocide. Never had armed forces waged campaigns of such scope, or fought battles as furious with weapons as devastating.

Seen in panoramic perspective, United States losses were relatively light compared with those suffered by Allied and enemy powers. With America's coasts virtually unscarred and American cities unscathed, the U.S.A. emerged from the Apocalyptic conflict as the world's leading nation, on a solid economic footing and physically secure as the foremost military power, possessed of superb ground forces, an air force equipped with the earth-shaking atom bomb, and a navy larger than all foreign navies combined.

Although United States battle deaths did not approach the millions lost by Russia, Germany, China, and Japan, the American death toll of 293,000—a toll greater than the combined total of Union and Confederate battle losses in the Civil War—was sufficiently grievous.

The Navy's fatalities were proportionately high. Ship losses (from all causes) during World War II included 2 battleships, 5 aircraft carriers, 6 escort-carriers, 7 heavy cruisers, 3 light cruisers, 71 destroyers, 11 destroyer-escorts, 52 submarines, and several hundred other vessels of various types. The great majority of these ships went down in combat.

Japanese naval losses exceeded the American figure by many tons. This, in spite of the fact that the Americans fought a two-ocean war (including the Mediterranean), whereas the Jap naval effort was almost entirely confined to the Pacific. The Pacific War cost the Japanese 11 battleships, 15 aircraft carriers, 5 escort-carriers, 36 heavy and light cruisers, 126 destroyers, approximately 130 submarines, and innumerable vessels of other types. The Japanese started the war with the world's third largest navy. When they sued for peace, the Imperial Navy was strewn across the bottom of the Pacific from the Aleutians to Australia, from Australia to the Philippines, and from the Philippines to Tokyo Bay. Most of that strewing was the work of the United States Navy.

As it would be a mistake to attribute the collapse of the Japanese Empire to any one battle or any single strategic effort, it would be a similar error to assume that any one Service arm was predominantly responsible for the victory over Japan—or the defeat of Nazi Germany and Fascist Italy. Similarly, no ship-type could be singled out as the one which carried the lion's share burden of the naval effort.

Nevertheless, a comprehensive review of the naval war effort suggests some broad generalities. The Battle of the Atlantic featured A/S warfare which was waged, by and large, by destroyer forces (and hunter-killer groups) against marauding U-boats. The Battle of the Pacific headlined the American submarine in the role of blockader and undersea raider; and there can be no gainsaying that the Navy's submariners made a most important contribution to the assault which wrought the downfall of Japan. When the defective American torpedo was finally corrected in 1943, the U.S. subs staged a ship-killing campaign which swept most of the Japanese merchant service off the sea. About 55 per cent of all Japanese shipping (merchant and naval) downed by the Allies in the Pacific War was sent to the bottom by American submarines.

Even as the American submarine effort was surprisingly effective, the Japanese submarine effort was surprisingly mediocre. As has been related, much of that mediocrity could be laid at the door of Imperial Headquarters. Japanese submarines were unable to match the U-boat wolfpacks in cunning, aggressiveness, and punch, and the Pacific convoy problem was simplified accordingly. However, the I-boats and RO-boats were never to be discounted as a threat. The anti-submarine war fought by American destroyer forces in the Pacific was as important—and as successful—as their Atlantic A/S campaign. Responsible for the sinking of 68 Japanese submarines, the Navy's DD's and DE's went far to liquidate the Imperial Navy's undersea fleet.

The 49 U-boats and 68 Japanese subs sunk by American destroyers and destroyer-escorts, operating singly and in hunter-killer teams, would have been enough to justify a Force which at war's end contained approximately 438 destroyers and 374 destroyer-escorts. Anyone who thought this fleet over-expanded and some of the squadrons superfluous could "tell it to the destroyermen." For answer, those sailors would point to the many and various missions undertaken and accomplished by DD's and DE's.

A destroyer Gunner's Mate, for example, would mention fire-support missions and shore bombardments. A Quartermaster might speak of reconnaissance, the probing of uncharted waters,the exploring of unknown beaches, or the marking of swept channels. A Torpedo Officer would talk of screening duty, of DD's leading task groups into battle and spearheading naval engagements with torpedo attacks. A DE skipper might refer to convoy duty and hunter-killer sweeps. Steward's Mates could tell of passing the ammo' to hungry AA batteries during air attacks. All hands who had participated in invasions could tell of DD operations with the Amphibs. And any Radarman who had served in a destroyer or destroyer-escort at Okinawa would certainly remind a questioner of the destroyer's heroic mission as fighter-director and radar picket.

Plane guards—scouts—vedettes—transports—weather reporters—fire-fighters—rescue vessels—the versatile "small boys" were jacks of all trades, and master operators in the bargain. Above all, they were warships. They fought the surface war, the undersea war, and the air war with weapons specifically devised for three-dimensional battle. It might be said that in destroying shore batteries, harbor and beach defenses, and such targets as highways, railroad spurs, bridges, and air strips—not to mention infantry and tank concentrations—they also fought the land war. All things were grist for the destroyer's mill—enemy warships and blockade runners, enemy aircraft and guided missiles and human projectiles, enemy submarines and motor torpedo-boats and human torpedoes. No type of ship afloat served in as many capacities as did the DD. No type fought harder or took losses more severe.

"Poor devils," a submarine admiral recalled the plight of the DD sailors in the early days of the war. "The destroyermen certainly took it on the chin. They grabbed their grub on the fly, and they picked up their repairs where they could find them. Things were tough for submarines in the early days of the Pacific War, but there was usually free beer and entertainment waiting for our boys when they came in from patrol. When the destroyers came in there was no one on hand to meet the crews with tickets for a ball game or transportation to a rest camp. Like as not, they had no time for leave and liberty, and would turn right around and go out again. They put up a rugged battle in the North Atlantic and in the South Pacific."

They put up a rugged fight everywhere. Just where they found the going toughest might be hard to say. Normandy was tough. Salerno was tough. The Aleutians were tough. The Tunisian War Channel was tough, and so was Savo Sound and the Malay Barrier and the North Atlantic haul. Destroyermen who battled in the Solomons, off Saipan, at Leyte Gulf, in Surigao Strait, and off Samar found the going tough. On reflection it might seem that Okinawa was the toughest. Yet those who were on the North Russian run in DD's and DE's would be inclined to give that front the ugly distinction.

But for all, and everywhere, combat was tough—bullets were tough; shells were tough; bombs, mines, and torpedoes were tough. *Kamikazes,* rockets, robot jets, E-boats, and human torpedoes were tough. The sea itself was on occasion a savage adversary, as the sailors who battled fog, blizzard, tempest, hurricane, and typhoon could testify. What could be said of one battle area or another, one amphibious beach or another, one action or another, one sinking or another, except that anywhere death was striking, the battle was toughest?

All who participated in the war knew the degree at its superlative when they entered combat and it could be said, as Milton said it, that *"each on himself relied, as only in his arm the moment lay of victory."* That moment came often to American destroyermen. How they acquitted themselves, and to what purpose, are questions answered by the war record.

Some called the DD's and DE's "small boys." An affectionate nickname for men-of-war. Some called them "cans"—an affectionate *nom de guerre.* Can, meaning "ready now." Can, meaning "able to."

TARE ★ VICTOR ★ GEORGE

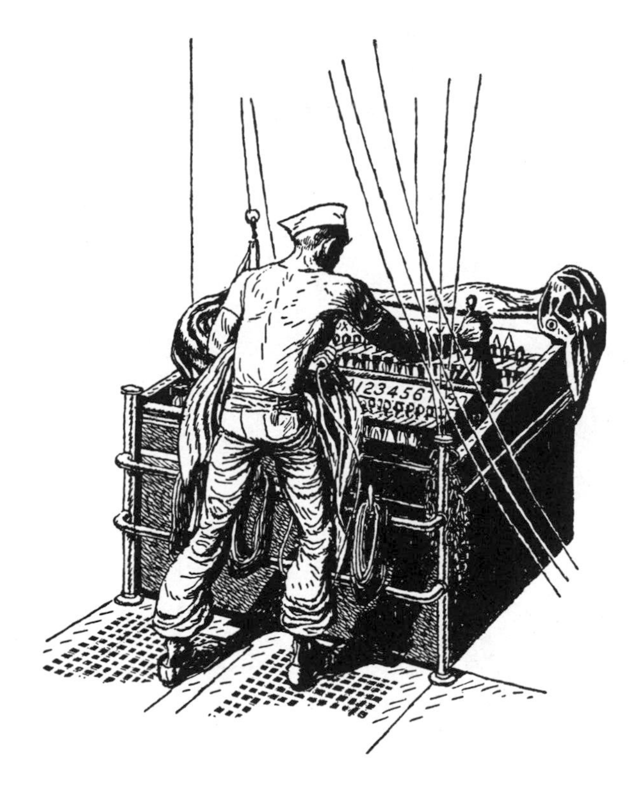

ADDENDA

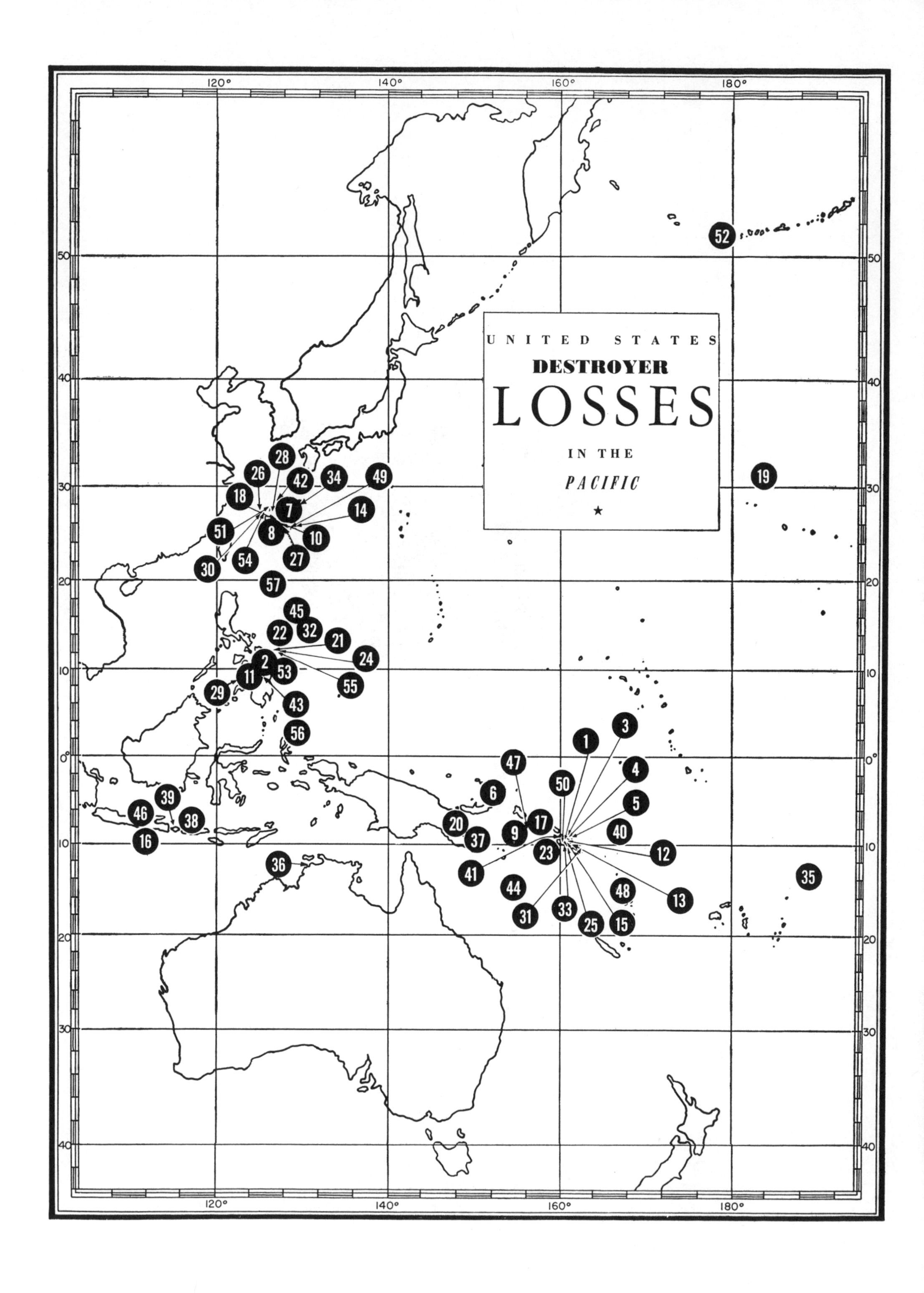

UNITED STATES
DESTROYER
LOSSES
IN THE
PACIFIC
120°
140°
160°
180°
50
40
30
20
10
0°
10
20
30
40
1
2
3
4
5
6
7
8
9
10
11
12
13
14
15
16
17
18
19
20
21
22
23
24
25
26
27
28
29
30
31
32
33
34
35
36
37
38
39
40
41
42
43
44
45
46
47
48
49
50
51
52
53
54
55
56
57

U. S. DESTROYER

LOSSES IN THE PACIFIC

★

NO.	NAME	CAUSE	DATE
1.	Aaron Ward	*Air Attack*	*7 Apr. '43*
2.	Abner Read	*Air Attack*	*1 Nov. '44*
3.	Barton	*Surface Action*	*13 Nov. '42*
4.	Benham	*Surface Action*	*15 Nov. '42*
5.	Blue	*Surface Action*	*22 Aug. '42*
6.	Brownson	*Air Attack*	*26 Dec. '43*
7.	Bush	*Air Attack*	*6 Apr. '45*
8.	Callaghan	*Air Attack*	*29 July '45*
9.	Chevalier	*Surface Action*	*7 Oct. '43*
10.	Colhoun	*Air Attack*	*6 Apr. '45*
11.	Cooper	*Submarine*	*3 Dec. '44*
12.	Cushing	*Surface Action*	*13 Nov. '42*
13.	DeHaven	*Air Attack*	*1 Feb. '43*
14.	Drexler	*Air Attack*	*28 May '45*
15.	Duncan	*Surface Action*	*12 Oct. '42*
16.	Edsall	*Surface Action*	*1 Mar. '42*
17.	Gwin	*Surface Action*	*13 July '43*
18.	Halligan	*Mine*	*26 Mar. '45*
19.	Hammann	*Submarine*	*6 June '42*
20.	Henley	*Submarine*	*3 Oct. '43*
21.	Hoel	*Surface Action*	*25 Oct. '44*
22.	Hull	*Typhoon*	*18 Dec. '44*
23.	Jarvis	*Air Attack*	*9 Aug. '42*
24.	Johnston	*Surface Action*	*25 Oct. '44*
25.	Laffey	*Surface Action*	*13 Nov. '42*
26.	Little	*Air Attack*	*3 May '45*
27.	Longshaw	*Shore Batteries*	*18 May '45*
28.	Luce	*Air Attack*	*4 May '45*
29.	Mahan	*Air Attack*	*7 Dec. '44*
30.	Mannert L. Abele	*Air Attack*	*12 Apr. '45*
31.	Meredith I.	*Air Attack*	*15 Oct. '42*
32.	Monaghan	*Typhoon*	*18 Dec. '44*
33.	Monssen	*Surface Action*	*13 Nov. '42*
34.	Morrison	*Air Attack*	*4 May '45*
35.	O'Brien	*Submarine*	*19 Oct. '42*
36.	Peary	*Air Attack*	*19 Feb. '42*
37.	Perkins	*Collision*	*29 Nov. '43*
38.	Pillsbury	*Surface Action*	*1 Mar. '42*
39.	Pope	*Surface Action*	*1 Mar. '42*
40.	Porter	*Submarine*	*26 Oct. '42*
41.	Preston	*Surface Action*	*15 Nov. '42*
42.	Pringle	*Air Attack*	*16 Apr. '45*
43.	Reid	*Air Attack*	*11 Dec. '44*
44.	Sims	*Air Attack*	*7 May '42*
45.	Spence	*Typhoon*	*18 Dec. '44*
46.	Stewart	*Captured in Drydock*	*2 Mar. '42*
47.	Strong	*Submarine*	*5 July '43*
48.	Tucker	*Mine*	*4 Aug. '42*
49.	Twiggs	*Air Attack*	*16 June '45*
50.	Walke	*Surface Action*	*15 Nov. '42*
51.	W. D. Porter	*Air Attack*	*10 June '45*
52.	Worden	*Grounding*	*12 Jan. '43*

★

U. S. DESTROYER-ESCORT

LOSSES IN THE PACIFIC

NO.	NAME	CAUSE	DATE
53.	Eversole	*Submarine*	*29 Oct. '44*
54.	Oberrender	*Air Attack*	*9 May '45*
55.	Samuel B. Roberts	*Surface Action*	*25 Oct. '44*
56.	Shelton	*Submarine*	*3 Oct. '44*
57.	Underhill	*Submarine*	*24 July '45*

★

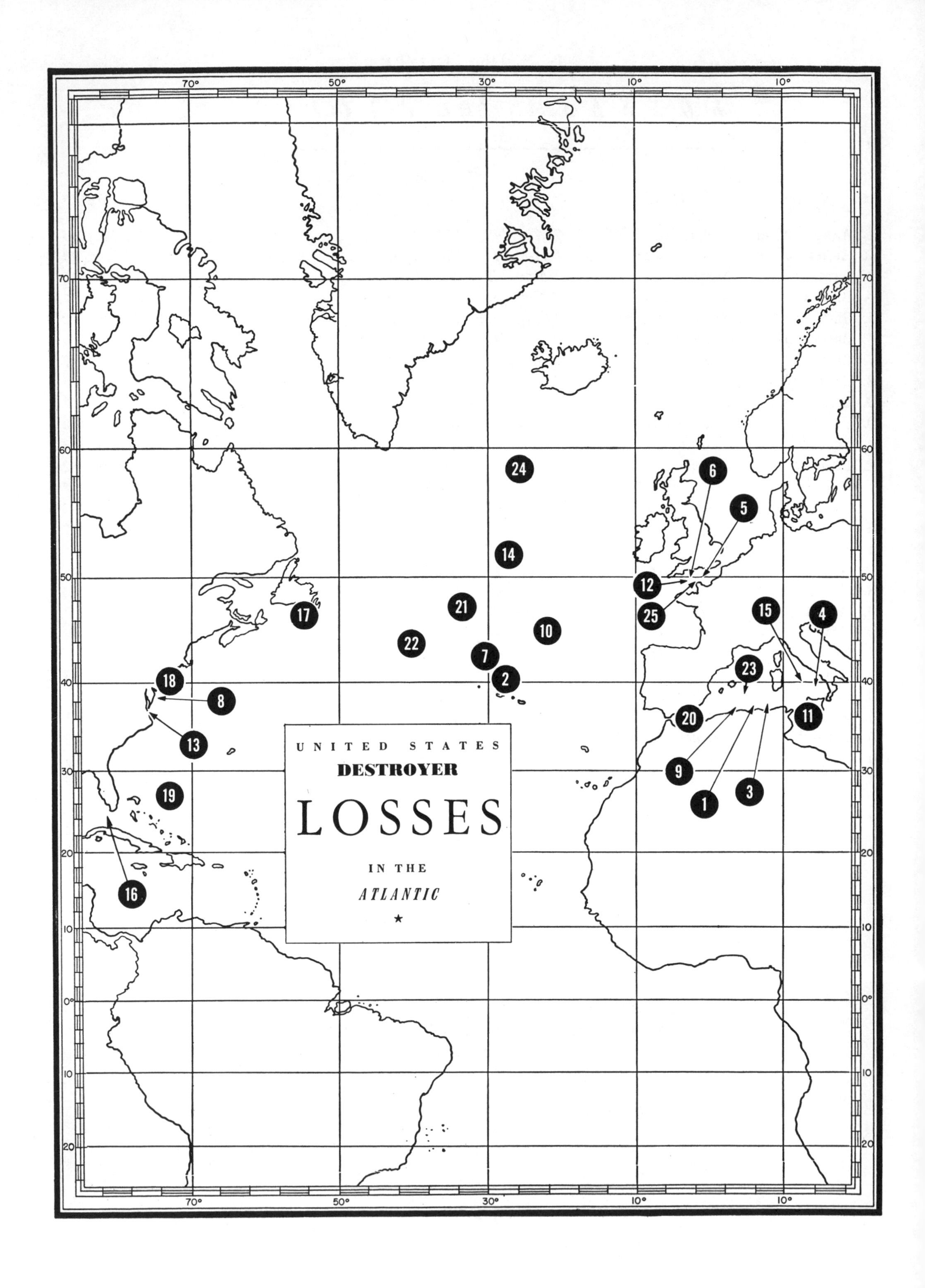
UNITED STATES
DESTROYER
LOSSES
IN THE
ATLANTIC
70°
50°
30°
10°
10°
70
60
50
40
30
20
10
0°
10
20
1
2
3
4
5
6
7
8
9
10
11
12
13
14
15
16
17
18
19
20
21
22
23
24
25

U. S. DESTROYER

LOSSES IN THE ATLANTIC

★

NO.	*NAME*	*CAUSE*	*DATE*
1.	Beatty	*Air Attack*	*6 Nov. '43*
2.	Borie	*Rammed Enemy Submarine*	*1 Nov. '43*
3.	Bristol	*Submarine*	*13 Oct. '43*
4.	Buck	*Submarine*	*9 Oct. '43*
5.	Corry	*Mine*	*6 June '44*
6.	Glennon	*Mine*	*8 June '44*
7.	Ingraham	*Collision*	*22 Aug. '42*
8.	Jacob Jones	*Submarine*	*28 Feb. '42*
9.	Lansdale	*Air Attack*	*20 Apr. '44*
10.	Leary	*Submarine*	*24 Dec. '43*
11.	Maddox	*Air Attack*	*10 July '43*
12.	Meredith (II)	*Mine*	*8 June '44*
13.	Parrott	*Collision*	*2 May '44*
14.	Reuben James	*Submarine*	*31 Oct. '41*
15.	Rowan	*Surface Action*	*11 Sept. '43*
16.	Sturtevant	*Mine*	*26 Apr. '42*
17.	Truxtun	*Grounding*	*18 Feb. '42*
18.	Turner	*Explosion*	*3 Jan. '44*
19.	Warrington	*Hurricane*	*13 Sept. '44*

★

U. S. DESTROYER-ESCORT

LOSSES IN THE ATLANTIC

NO.	*NAME*	*CAUSE*	*DATE*
20.	Fechteler	*Submarine*	*5 May '44*
21.	Fiske	*Submarine*	*2 Aug. '44*
22.	Frederick C. Davis	*Submarine*	*24 Apr. '45*
23.	Holder	*Air Attack*	*11 Apr. '44*
24.	Leopold	*Submarine*	*9 Mar. '44*
25.	Rich	*Mine*	*8 June '44*

★

DESTROYERS AND DESTROYER ESCORTS AWARDED THE

PRESIDENTIAL UNIT CITATION

SHIP	*DATE AND PLACE OF ACTION*	*COMMANDING OFFICER*
BENNION (*DD 662*)	*April 1-June 1, 1945 (Okinawa)*	*Cdr. R. H. Holmes*
BERNADOU (*DD 153*)	*Nov. 8, 1942 (Safi, French Morocco)*	*Lt. Cdr. R. E. Braddy, Jr.*
BUCHANAN (*DD 484*)	*Aug. 7, 1942-Feb. 26, 1944 (Pacific)*	*Cdr. R. E. Wilson* *Lt. Cdr. F. B. T. Myhre*
COLE (*DD 155*)	*Nov. 8, 1942 (Safi, French Morocco)*	*Lt. Cdr. G. G. Palmer*
COWELL	*April 1-June 17, 1945 (Okinawa)*	*Cdr. C. L. Werts*
DALLAS (*DD 199*)	*Nov. 10, 1942 (Port Lyautey, French Morocco)*	*Lt. Cdr. R. Brodie, Jr.*
EVANS (*DD 552*)	*May 11, 1945 (Okinawa)*	*Cdr. R. J. Archer*
FORD (*DD 228*)	*Jan. 23-Mar. 2, 1942 (Java Campaign)*	*Lt. Cdr. J. E. Cooper*
HUGH W. HADLEY (*DD 774*)	*May 11, 1945 (Okinawa)*	*Cdr. B. J. Mullaney*
LAFFEY (*DD 459*)	*Sept. 15-Nov. 13, 1942 (Southwest Pacific)*	*Lt. Cdr. W. E. Hank*
LAFFEY (*DD 724*)	*April 16, 1945 (Okinawa)*	*Cdr. F. J. Becton*
MAURY (*DD 401*)	*Feb. 1, 1942-Aug. 6, 1943 (Pacific)*	*Lt. Cdr. E. D. Snare* *Lt. Cdr. G. L. Sims*
NICHOLAS (*DD 449*)	*July 5-6, 1943 (Kolombangara Is., New Georgia, Solomon Is.)*	*Lt. Cdr. A. J. Hill*
O'BANNON (*DD 450*)	*Oct. 7, 1942-Oct. 7, 1943 (South Pacific)*	*Cdr. E. R. Wilkinson* *Lt. Cdr. D. J. MacDonald*
POPE (*DD 225*)	*Jan. 23-Mar. 1, 1942 (Southwest Pacific)*	*Lt. Cdr. W. C. Blinn*
RADFORD (*DD 446*)	*July 5-6, 1943 (Solomon Islands)*	*Cdr. W. K. Romoser*
SMITH (*DD 378*)	*Oct. 26, 1942 (Santa Cruz Islands)*	*Lt. Cdr. Hunter Wood, Jr.*
STERETT (*DD 407*)	*Nov. 12-13, 1942 (Guadalcanal, Solomon Is.)*	*Cdr. J. G. Coward*
WADSWORTH (*DD 516*)	*April 17-June 24, 1945 (Okinawa)*	*Cdr. R. D. Fusselman*
ENGLAND (*DE 635*)	*May 19-31, 1944 (Pacific)*	*Lt. Cdr. W. B. Pendleton*
BRONSTEIN (*DE 189*)	*February 29-March 1, 1944 (Atlantic)*	*Cdr. S. H. Kinney*

UNITS, COMPOSED IN WHOLE OR IN PART OF DESTROYERS AND DESTROYER ESCORTS, AWARDED THE

PRESIDENTIAL UNIT CITATION

UNIT	*DATE AND PLACE OF ACTION*	*COMMANDING OFFICER*
Destroyer Squadron Twenty-Three	*Nov. 1, 1943–Feb. 23, 1944 (Solomon Islands)*	*Capt. A. A. Burke (ComDesRon 23)*
CHARLES AUSBURNE (*DD 570*) (DesRon 23 Flagship)		*Cdr. L. K. Reynolds*
STANLY (*DD 478*)		*Cdr. R. W. Cavenagh* *Lt. Cdr. J. B. Morland*
CLAXTON (*DD 571*)		*Cdr. H. F. Stout*
DYSON (*DD 572*)		*Cdr. R. A. Gano*
CONVERSE (*DesDiv 46 Flagship*)		*Cdr. B. L. Austin, ComDesDiv 46* *Cdr. R. W. Cavenagh, ComDesDiv 46* *Cdr. D. C. E. Hamberger*
SPENCE (*DD 512*)		*Cdr. H. J. Armstrong*

UNIT	*DATE AND PLACE OF ACTION*	*COMMANDING OFFICER*
Task Group 21.14	*July 27–October 25, 1943 (Atlantic)*	*Capt. A. J. Isbell*
Card *(CVE 11)*		*Capt. A. J. Isbell*
Barry *(DD 248)*		*Lt. Cdr. J. F. Flynn* *Lt. Cdr. H. D. Hill, U.S.N.R.*
Borie *(DD 215)*		*Lt. C. H. Hutchins, U.S.N.R.*
Goff *(DD 247)*		*Lt. Cdr. H. I. Smith, U.S.N.R.*
Task Group 21.12	*April 20–June 20, 1943 (Atlantic)*	*Capt. G. E. Short*
Bogue *(CVE 9)*		*Capt. G. E. Short*
Lea *(DD 118)*		*Cdr. D. I. Thomas*
*Greene *(AVD 13) (ex-DD 266)*		*Lt. Cdr. L. J. Bellis* *Lt. Cdr. J. S. Lewis*
*Belknap *(AVD 8) (ex-DD 251)*		*Lt. Cdr. D. M. Coffee*
*Osmond Ingram *(AVD 9) (ex-DD 255)*		*Lt. Cdr. N. J. Sampson*
George E. Badger *(DD 196)*		*Lt. Cdr. W. H. Johnsen* *Lt. T. H. Byrd, U.S.N.R.*
VC Squadron Nine		*Lt. Cdr. W. M. Drane*
Task Group 21.13	*July 12–Aug. 23, 1943 (Atlantic)*	*Capt. J. B. Dunn*
Bogue *(CVE 9)*		*Capt. J. B. Dunn*
*Osmond Ingram *(AVD 9) (ex-DD 255)*		*Lt. Cdr. N. J. Sampson*
George E. Badger *(DD 196)*		*Lt. T. H. Byrd, U.S.N.R.*
Clemson *(DD 186)*		*Lt. Cdr. E. W. Yancey*
VC Squadron Nine		*Lt. Cdr. W. M. Drane*
Task Group 21.13	*Nov. 14–Dec. 29, 1943 (Atlantic)*	*Capt. J. B. Dunn*
Bogue *(CVE 9)*		*Capt. J. B. Dunn*
*Osmond Ingram *(AVD 9) (ex-DD 255)*		*Lt. Cdr. R. F. Miller*
George E. Badger *(DD 196)*		*Lt. T. H. Byrd, U.S.N.R.*
Clemson *(DD 186)*		*Lt. W. F. Moran, U.S.N.R.*
Dupont *(DD 152)*		*Cdr. J. G. Marshall*
VC Squadron Nineteen		*Lt. Cdr. C. W. Stewart*
Task Group 22.11	*Feb. 26–April 19, 1944 (Atlantic)*	*Capt. J. B. Dunn*
Bogue *(CVE 9)*		*Capt. J. B. Dunn*
Haverfield *(DE 393) (F)*		*Cdr. T. S. Lank, ComCortDiv 51* *Lt. Cdr. J. A. Mathews, U.S.N.R.*
Swenning *(DE 394)*		*Lt. R. E. Peek, U.S.N.R.*
Willis *(DE 395)*		*Lt. Cdr. G. R. Atterbury, U.S.N.R.*
Hobson *(DD 464) (until Mar. 25)*		*Lt. Cdr. K. Loveland*
Janssen *(DE 396) (until April 7)*		*Lt. Cdr. H. E. Cross, U.S.N.R.*
VC Squadron Ninety Five		*Lt. Cdr. J. F. Adams, U.S.N.R.*
Task Group 22.2	*May 4–July 3, 1944 (Atlantic)*	*Capt. A. B. Vosseller*
Bogue (CVE 9)		*Capt. A. B. Vosseller*
Haverfield *(DE 393) (F)*		*Cdr. T. S. Lant, ComCortDiv 51* *Lt. Cdr. J. A. Mathews, U.S.N.R.*
Swenning *(DE 394)*		*Lt. R. E. Peek, U.S.N.R.*
Willis *(DE 395)*		*Lt. Cdr. G. R. Atterbury, U.S.N.R.*
Janssen *(DE 396)*		*Lt. Cdr. H. E. Cross, U.S.N.R.*
F. M. Robinson *(DE 220)*		*Lt. Cdr. J. E. Johansen, U.S.N.R.*
VC Squadron Sixty Nine		*Lt. Cdr. J. D. Taylor*

* *Reconverted to a DD in 1942, but still retained the designation "AVD."*

UNIT	DATE AND PLACE OF ACTION	COMMANDING OFFICER
Task Group 22.3	*June 4, 1944 (French West Africa)*	*Capt. D. V. Gallery, Jr.*
GUADALCANAL *(CVE 60)*		*Capt. D. V. Gallery, Jr.*
PILLSBURY *(DE 133) (F)*		*Cdr. F. S. Hall, ComCortDiv 4* *Lt. Cdr. G. W. Casselman, U.S.N.R.*
POPE *(DE 134)*		*Lt. Cdr. E. H. Headland*
FLAHERTY *(DE 135)*		*Lt. Cdr. M. Johnston, Jr.*
CHATELAIN *(DE 149)*		*Lt. Cdr. D. S. Knox, U.S.N.R.*
JENKS *(DE 665)*		*Lt. Cdr. J. F. Way*
VC Squadron 8		*Lt. N. D. Hodson*
Task Unit 77.4.3	*Oct. 25, 1944 (Samar, Philippines)*	*R. Adm. C. A. F. Sprague*
FANSHAW BAY *(CVE 70) (F)*		*R. Adm. C. A. F. Sprague, ComCarDiv 25* *Capt. D. P. Johnson*
VC Squadron 68		*Lt. Cdr. R. S. Rogers*
GAMBIER BAY *(CVE 73)*		*Capt. W. V. R. Vieweg*
VC Squadron 10		*Lt. Cdr. E. J. Huxtable*
KALININ BAY *(CVE 68)*		*Capt. T. B. Williamson*
VC Squadron 3		*Lt. Cdr. W. H. Keighley, U.S.N.R.*
KITKUN BAY *(CVE 71)*		*Capt. J. P. Whitney*
VC Squadron 5		*Cdr. R. L. Fowler*
ST. LO *(CVE 63)*		*Capt. F. J. McKenna*
VC Squadron 65		*Lt. Cdr. R. M. Jones, U.S.N.R.*
WHITE PLAINS *(CVE 66)*		*Capt. D. J. Sullivan*
VC Squadron 4		*Lt. E. R. Fickenscher*
HOEL *(DD 533) (F)*		*Cdr. W. D. Thomas, Screen Cdr.* *Cdr. L. S. Kintberger*
JOHNSTON *(DD 557)*		*Cdr. E. E. Evans*
HEERMANN *(DD 532)*		*Cdr. A. T. Hathaway*
SAMUEL B. ROBERTS *(DE 413)*		*Lt. Cdr. R. W. Copeland, U.S.N.R.*
RAYMOND *(DE 341)*		*Lt. Cdr. A. F. Beyer, Jr., U.S.N.R.*
DENNIS *(DE 405)*		*Lt. Cdr. S. Hansen, U.S.N.R.*
JOHN C. BUTLER *(DE 339)*		*Lt. Cdr. J. E. Pace*

DESTROYERS AND DESTROYER ESCORTS AWARDED THE *NAVY UNIT COMMENDATION*

SHIP	DATE AND PLACE OF ACTION	COMMANDING OFFICER
AMMEN *(DD 527)*	*April 1-June 24, 1945 (Okinawa)*	*Cdr. J. H. Brown*
ANTHONY *(DD 515)*	*April 1-April 19, 1945 (Okinawa)*	*Cdr. C. J. Van Arsdall, Jr.*
BAILEY *(DD 492)*	*Mar. 26, 1943 (Komandorski Is., Bering Sea)*	*Lt. Cdr. J. C. Atkeson*
BARTON *(DD 722)*	*Mar. 21-June 30, 1945 (Okinawa)*	*Cdr. E. B. Dexter* *Cdr. H. P. McIntire*
BENNETT *(DD 473)*	*April 6-7, 1945 (Okinawa)*	*Cdr. J. N. McDonald*
BRADFORD *(DD 545)*	*May 14-June 16, 1945 (Okinawa)*	*Cdr. W. W. Armstrong*
BROWN *(DD 546)*	*April 10-May 16, 1945 June 16-20, 1945 (Okinawa)*	*Cdr. R. R. Craighill*

UNIT	DATE AND PLACE OF ACTION	COMMANDING OFFICER
BRYANT (DD 665)	June 12-Aug. 2, 1944 (Saipan-Tinian Area)	Cdr. P. L. High
	Sept. 6-29, 1944 (Palau)	Cdr. P. L. High
	Oct. 23-25, 1944 (Surigao Strait)	Cdr. P. L. High
	Feb. 14-Mar. 9, 1945 (Iwo Jima)	Cdr. G. C. Seay
	Mar 21-April 18, 1945 (Okinawa)	Cdr. G. C. Seay
HEYWOOD L. EDWARDS (DD 663)	May 29-July 29, 1944 (Saipan-Tinian Area)	Cdr. J. W. Boulware
	Sept. 5-29, 1944 (Palau)	Cdr. J. W. Boulware
	Oct. 24-25, 1944 (Surigao Strait)	Cdr. J. W. Boulware
	Feb. 10-27, 1945 (Iwo Jima)	Cdr. A. L. Shepherd
	Mar. 21-July 28, 1945 (Okinawa)	Cdr. A. L. Shepherd
GAINARD (DD 706)	April 20-June 30, 1945 (Okinawa)	Cdr. J. F. Foley
ALBERT W. GRANT (DD 649)	Oct. 24-Oct. 27, 1944 (Leyte Gulf)	Cdr. T. A. Nisewaner
HICKOX (DD 673)	Mar. 19, 1945 (Pacific)	Cdr. J. H. Wesson
HUDSON (DD 475)	April 1-May 10, 1945 (Okinawa)	Cdr. R. R. Pratt
INGRAHAM (DD 694)	May 4, 1945 (Okinawa)	Cdr. J. F. Harper, Jr.
IRWIN (DD 794)	Oct. 24, 1944 (Battle off Samar)	Cdr. D. B. Miller
HILARY P. JONES (DD 427)	Sept. 17-18, 1944 (San Remo, Italy and Port Maurizio, Italy)	Lt. Cdr. F. M. Stiesberg
LOWRY (DD 770)	April 30-June 22, 1945 (Okinawa)	Cdr. E. S. Miller
MILLER (DD 535)	Mar. 19, 1945 (Pacific)	Lt. Cdr. D. L. Johnson
MORRISON (DD 560)	May 4, 1945 (Okinawa)	Cdr. J. R. Hansen
	Oct. 24, 1944 (Battle off Samar) (Second Navy Unit Commendation)	Cdr. W. H. Price
NEWCOMB (DD 486)	May 29-Aug. 5, 1944 (Saipan-Tinian Area)	Cdr. L. B. Cook
	Sept. 6-Oct. 1, 1944 (Palau)	Cdr. L. B. Cook
	Oct. 24-25, 1944 (Surigao Strait)	Cdr. L. B. Cook
	Feb. 10-Mar. 10, 1945 (Iwo Jima)	Cdr. I. E. McMillian
	Mar. 21-April 7, 1945 (Okinawa)	Cdr. I. E. McMillian
PLUNKETT (DD 431)	Jan. 21-25, 1944 (Anzio, Italy)	Cdr. E. J. Burke
PRICHETT (DD 561)	Mar. 24-April 7, 1945 (Okinawa)	Cdr. C. M. Bowley
	May 8-Aug. 13, 1945 (Okinawa)	Lt. Cdr. J. F. Miller (From June, 1945)
PURDY (DD 734)	April 12, 1945 (Okinawa Transport Area)	Cdr. F. L. Johnson
TAYLOR (DD 468)	Mar. 15-Oct. 7, 1943 (Solomons)	Cdr. B. Katz
VAN VALKENBURGH (DD 656)	April 1-June 24, 1945 (Okinawa)	Cdr. A. B. Coxe, Jr.
WICKES (DD 578)	Mar. 27-May 15, 1945 (Okinawa)	Lt. Cdr. J. B. Cresap
WOOLSEY (DD 437)	July 9-Aug. 25, 1943 Sept. 9-13, 1943 (Licata, Gela, and Salerno)	Lt. Cdr. H. R. Wier
	Dec. 16, 1943 (Oran Area)	Cdr. H. R. Wier
	Jan. 21-Feb. 17, 1944 (Anzio, Italy)	Cdr. H. R. Wier
	Aug. 13-Sept. 23, 1944 (Southern France)	Cdr. H. R. Wier
CASSIN YOUNG (DD 793)	Mar. 25-April 12, 1945 May 30-June 15, 1945 July 18-Aug. 8, 1945 (Okinawa)	Cdr. J. W. Ailes, III
BUCKLEY (DE 51)	May 5-6, 1944 (Mediterranean)	Lt. Cdr. B. M. Abel, U.S.N.R.
JOHN C. BUTLER (DE 339)	May 20, 1945 (Okinawa)	Lt. Cdr. J. E. Pace
F. C. DAVIS (DE 136)	Jan. 22-Feb. 23, 1944 (Anzio Campaign)	Lt. Cdr. R. C. Robbins, Jr., U.S.N.R.
JOHNNIE HUTCHINS (DE 360)	Aug. 9, 1945 (Pacific)	Lt. Cdr. H. M. Godsey, U.S.N.R.
HERBERT C. JONES (DE 137)	Jan. 23-Feb. 16, 1944 (Anzio Campaign)	Lt. Cdr. R. A. Soule, III, U.S.N.R.

UNIT	DATE AND PLACE OF ACTION	COMMANDING OFFICER
RALL (DE 304)	April 12, 1945 (Okinawa)	Lt. Cdr. C. B. Taylor, U.S.N.R.
RICHARD W. SUESENS (DE 342)	Oct. 20-Nov. 29, 1944 (Leyte Operation)	Lt. Cdr. R. W. Graham, U.S.N.R.
	Jan. 9, 1945 (Lingayen Gulf Landing)	
	Jan. 31-Feb. 1, 1945 (Manila Bay-Bicol Operation)	
	Mar. 26-April 4, 1945	
	April 15-April 22, 1945 (Okinawa)	
TABBERER (DE 418)	Dec. 18, 1944 (Western Pacific)	Lt. Cdr. H. L. Plage, U.S.N.R.

ATLANTIC FLEET DESTROYERS
TYPE, SQUADRON AND DIVISION COMMANDERS

OCTOBER 1, 1941 . . . SEPTEMBER 2, 1945

ComDesLant—R. Adm. F. L. Reichmuth
R. Adm. A. S. Carpender
R. Adm. O. C. Badger
R. Adm. M. L. Deyo
R. Adm. J. C. Jones
R. Adm. O. M. Read

ComDesRon 2—Capt. W. L. Ainsworth

ComDesDiv 3—Cdr. F. G. Fahrion

ComDesDiv 4—Cdr. R. G. Tobin

ComDesRon 3—Capt. R. B. Ellis

ComDesDiv 5—Capt. R. B. Ellis

ComDesDiv 6—Cdr. G. A. Moore

ComDesRon 7—Capt. A. G. Kirk
Capt. F. D. Kirtland
Cdr. S. R. Clark
Cdr. G. L. Menocal
Capt. J. P. Clay
Capt. J. W. Adams, Jr.

DesDiv 13—Cdr. D. L. Ryan
Cdr. R. E. Webb
Cdr. P. R. Heineman
Cdr. S. R. Clark
Cdr. G. L. Menocal
Capt. J. P. Clay
Capt. J. W. Adams, Jr.

DesDiv 14—Cdr. F. D. Kirtland
Cdr. D. L. Madeira
Cdr. G. L. Menocal
Cdr. W. H. Duvall
Cdr. W. R. Headden
Cdr. V. Havard, Jr.
Cdr. W. W. Strohbehn
Cdr. K. E. Price

ComDesRon 8—Capt. T. C. Kinkaid
Capt. D. P. Moon
Capt. C. Wellborn, Jr.

ComDesDiv 15—Capt. D. P. Moon
Cdr. W. W. Warlick

ComDesDiv 16—Cdr. T. V. Cooper
Cdr. C. C. Hartman
Capt. D. P. Moon
Capt. C. Wellborn, Jr.
Cdr. R. A. Larkin
Cdr. J. W. Bays

ComDesRon 9—Capt. T. G. Peyton
Capt. J. D. H. Kane
Cdr. H. C. Robison

ComDesDiv 17—Cdr. L. K. Swenson
Cdr. L. Y. Mason, Jr.
Capt. J. D. H. Kane

ComDesDiv 18—Capt. T. G. Peyton
Cdr. R. M. Morris

ComDesRon 10—Cdr. J. L. Holloway, Jr.
Cdr. T. L. Lewis
Capt. A. F. Converse
Capt. R. A. Larkin

ComDesDiv 19—Cdr. C. Wellborn, Jr.
Cdr. T. L. Lewis
Capt. A. F. Converse
Capt. R. A. Larkin

ComDesDiv 20—Cdr. T. L. Wattles
Cdr. E. C. Burchett
Cdr. C. M. Jensen
Cdr. L. W. Nilon

NOTE: In latter part of 1944 the DD'S of this squadron were converted to DMS's.

ComDesRon 11—Capt. M. L. Deyo
Capt. J. S. Roberts
Cdr. D. L. Madeira

ComDesDiv 21—Cdr. H. B. Broadfoot
Cdr. J. C. Metzel
Cdr. D. L. Madeira
Cdr. A. H. Oswald
Cdr. G. C. Wright
Cdr. A. M. Kowalzyk, Jr.

ComDesDiv 22—Cdr. J. S. Roberts
Cdr. H. R. Holcomb

ComDesRon 13—Capt. L. H. Thebaud
Capt. J. B. Heffernan
Cdr. E. R. Durgin
Capt. H. Sanders
Capt. J. B. Rooney

ComDesDiv 25—Cdr. G. C. Hoover
Cdr. H. C. Fitz
Capt. J. B. Heffernan
Cdr. E. R. Durgin
Capt. H. Sanders
Cdr. R. B. Ellis
Cdr. A. R. Heckey
Capt. J. B. Rooney

ComDesDiv 26—Cdr. W. W. Webb
Cdr. E. R. Durgin
Cdr. V. Huber
Cdr. A. M. Kowalzyk, Jr.

ComDesRon 15—Capt. C. C. Hartman
Capt. S. W. DuBois
Capt. E. R. Durgin
Capt. H. H. Smith-Hutton

ComDesDiv 29—Capt. C. C. Hartman
Capt. S. W. DuBois
Capt. E. R. Durgin
Capt. H. H. Smith-Hutton

Com-Des-Div 30—Cdr. H. C. Robison
Cdr. R. B. Nickerson
Capt. J. M. P. Wright
Cdr. C. J. Whiting

ComDesDiv 35—Cdr. L. W. Creighton
Cdr. N. R. Curtin

ComDesRon 16—Capt. T. L. Wattles
Capt. C. J. Cater
Capt. J. W. Adams, Jr.
Capt. J. P. Clay

ComDesDiv 31—Capt. T. L. Wattles
Capt. C. J. Cater
Capt. J. W. Adams, Jr.
Capt. J. P. Clay

ComDesDiv 32—Cdr. B. R. Harrison, Jr.
Cdr. J. C. Sowell
Cdr. C. L. Melson
Cdr. B. N. Rittenhouse

ComDesRon 17—Cdr. D. L. Madeira
Capt. A. C. Murdaugh
Capt. J. S. Keating

ComDesDiv 33—Cdr. D. L. Madeira
Capt. A. C. Murdaugh
Capt. J. S. Keating

ComDesDiv 34—Cdr. J. B. Rooney
Cdr. W. L. Benson
Cdr. M. D. Matthews
Cdr. A. R. Heckey

ComDesRon 18—Cdr. W. K. Mendenhall, Jr.
Capt. H. Sanders

ComDesDiv 35—Cdr. W. K. Mendenhall, Jr.
Capt. H. Sanders

ComDesDiv 36—Cdr. W. J. Marshall
Cdr. L. W. Creighton

ComDesRon 19—Cdr. J. Connor

ComDesDiv 37—Cdr. J. Connor

ComDesDiv 38—Cdr. C. L. Winecoff
Cdr. D. M. Coffee

ComDesRon 27—Capt. L. H. Thebaud
Capt. D. P. Moon
Cdr. R. E. Webb
Capt. J. S. Roberts
Capt. G. L. Menocal

ComDesDiv 53—Cdr. W. K. Phillips
Cdr. B. S. Copping
Lt. Cdr. E. W. Logsdon
Lt. Cdr. C. H. Hutchins, U.S.N.R.

ComDesDiv 54—Cdr. S. C. Norton
Lt. Cdr. R. J. Brooke, U.S.N.R.

ComDesRon 29—Cdr. E. M. Crouch
Capt. W. H. Duvall

ComDesDiv 57—Capt. W. H. Duvall
Cdr. E. W. Yancey
Lt. Cdr. S. E. Woodard
Lt. Cdr. W. H. Stewart, U.S.N.R.

ComDesDiv 58—Cdr. R. B. Ellis
Lt. Cdr. G. P. Unmacht
Lt. Cdr. G. T. Baker
Lt. Cdr. H. M. Payne, U.S.N.R.

ComDesRon 30—Capt. M. Y. Cohen
Capt. G. W. Johnson

ComDesDiv 60—Cdr. J. B. Heffernan
Cdr. J. C. Pollock
Cdr. C. T. Singleton, Jr.
Cdr. N. C. Barker

**ComDesDiv 59—Lt. Cdr. F. D. Miller, U.S.N.R.*

ComDesDiv 61—Cdr. G. W. Johnson
Cdr. C. J. Whiting
Lt. Cdr. M. P. Huffman, U.S.N.R.

**ComDesDiv 60—Lt. Cdr. M. P. Huffman, U.S.N.R.*

ComDesRon 31—Capt. W. D. Baker
Capt. J. S. Roberts
Capt. W. K. Phillips
Cdr. S. R. Clark
Capt. G. W. Johnson

ComDesDiv 62—Cdr. W. A. S. Macklin

ComDesDiv 63—Cdr. R. W. Hungerford

ComDesDiv 66—Cdr. A. M. Kowalzyk, Jr.

** Title changed due to assignment of new number to Division.*

ATLANTIC FLEET DE'S

DIVISION COMMANDERS

JULY 15, 1943 . . . SEPTEMBER 2, 1945

**ComCortDiv 1—Lt. Cdr. E. W. Yancey*

ComCortDiv 2—Cdr. H. H. Connelley
Cdr. H. W. Howe
Cdr. R. P. Walker

ComCortDiv 3—Lt. Cdr. N. Adair, Jr.
Cdr. C. W. Musgrave

ComCortDiv 4—Cdr. F. S. Hall

ComCortDiv 5—Cdr. C. M. E. Hoffman
Cdr. R. A. Fitch, U.S.N.R.

ComCortDiv 6—Capt. H. T. Read
Cdr. H. T. Chase

ComCortDiv 7—Cdr. T. K. Dunstan, U.S.N.R.

ComCortDiv 9—Cdr. J. H. Forshew, U.S.N.R.
Cdr. E. W. Yancey

ComCortDiv 12—Cdr. H. T. Chase
Cdr. E. R. Perry
Cdr. A. B. Adams, Jr.

ComCortDiv 13—Cdr. F. D. Giambattista

**** This Cort Div was actually a group of six 4-stack DD's.***

ComCortDiv 15—Cdr. F. C. B. McCune

ComCortDiv 17—Cdr R. N. Norgaard
Cdr. A. Wildner

ComCortDiv 18—Cdr. S. C. Small

ComCortDiv 19—Cdr. H. W. Howe

ComCortDiv 20—Cdr. J. Rountree, U.S.C.G.
Cdr. P. B. Mavor, U.S.C.G.
Lt. Cdr. W. B. Ellis, U.S.C.G.

ComCortDiv 21—Cdr. L. M. Markham, Jr.
Cdr. A. B. Adams, Jr.
Cdr. E. H. Headland, Jr.

ComCortDiv 22—Cdr. W. W. Kenner, U.S.C.G.
Cdr. R. J. Roberts, U.S.C.G.

ComCortDiv 23—Cdr. E. J. Roland, U.S.C.G.
Cdr. F. P. Vetterick, U.S.C.G.
Cdr. J. H. Forney, U.S.C.G.

ComCortDiv 24—Cdr. C. T. S. Gladden, U.S.N. (Ret)
Cdr. C. G. McKinney, U.S.N.R.

ComCortDiv 35—Cdr. J. R. Litchfield, U.S.N.R.

ComCortDiv 45—Cdr. E. J. Roland, U.S.C.G.
Cdr. H. A. Loughlin, U.S.C.G.
Cdr. C. C. Knapp, U.S.C.G.

ComCortDiv 46—Capt. R. E. Wood, U.S.C.G.
Cdr. R. H. French, U.S.C.G.

ComCortDiv 48—Cdr. G. A. Parkinson, U.S.N.R.

ComCortDiv 51—Cdr. T. S. Lank

ComCortDiv 52—Cdr. C. R. Simmers

ComCortDiv 54—Cdr. M. E. Dennett

ComCortDiv 55—Cdr. R. P. Walker
Cdr. W. A. Session, U.S.N.R.

ComCortDiv 56—Cdr. W. A. P. Martin, Jr.
Cdr. W. L. Harmon

ComCortDiv 57—Cdr. W. H. Kirvan
Cdr. T. G. Murrell, U.S.N.R.

ComCortDiv 58—Cdr. E. E. Garcia

ComCortDiv 59—Cdr. A. W. Slayden
Cdr. L. S. Bailey, U.S.N.R.

ComCortDiv 60—Cdr. H. Mullins, Jr.

ComCortDiv 62—Cdr. J. F. Bowling, Jr.

ComCortDiv 66—Cdr. G. F. Adams, U.S.N.R.
Cdr. H. H. Connelley
Lt. Cdr. V. A. Isaacs, U.S.N.R.

ComCortDiv 67—Cdr. F. G. Gould

ComCortDiv 71—Cdr. E. W. Yancey

ComCortDiv 74—Cdr. C. F. Hooper, U.S.N.R.

ComCortDiv 76—Cdr. C. M. Lyons, Jr.

ComCortDiv 77—Cdr. H. G. White, U.S.N.R.

ComCortDiv 78—Lt. Cdr. D. B. Poupeney, U.S.N.R.

ComCortDiv 79—Cdr. M. H. Harris, U.S.N.R.

ComCortDiv 80—Cdr. A. L. Lind, U.S.N.R.

ComCortDiv 85—Cdr. R. B. Randolph, U.S.N.R.

PACIFIC FLEET DESTROYERS*
TYPE, FLOTILLA, SQUADRON, AND DIVISION
COMMANDERS

OCTOBER 1, 1941 . . . OCTOBER 1, 1945

ComDesPac—R. Adm. M. F. Draemel
R. Adm. R. A. Theobald
R. Adm. M. S. Tisdale
R. Adm. J. L. Kauffman
R. Adm. W. L. Ainsworth
R. Adm. W. H. P. Blandy

ComDesFlot One—R. Adm. R. A. Theobald
ComDesFlot Two—R. Adm. M. F. Draemel

ComTaskFlot One—Commo. J. T. Bottom, Jr.
ComTaskFlot Two—Commo. J. P. Womble, Jr.
ComTaskFlot Three—Commo. J. M. Higgins
ComTaskFlot Four—Commo. R. N. Smoot
ComTaskFlot Five—Commo. F. Moosbrugger
ComTaskFlot Six—Commo. R. W. Simpson

* *Includes DD's assigned to Seventh Fleet.*

ComDesRon 1—Capt. A. R. Early
Capt. S. B. Brewer
Cdr. R. E. Libby
Capt. E. R. McLean, Jr.
Capt. P. V. Mercer

ComDesDiv 1—Cdr. W. S. Popham
Cdr. W. Nyquist
Cdr. G. R. Cooper
Capt. R. E. Libby
Capt. E. R. McLean, Jr.
Capt. P. V. Mercer

ComDesDiv 2—Cdr. C. W. Flynn
Cdr. R. S. Riggs
Cdr. G. R. Cooper
Cdr. I. H. Nunn
Cdr. A. J. Greenacre
Cdr. T. H. Tonseth
Cdr. J. F. Walsh

ComDesRon 2—Capt. G. C. Hoover
Cdr. H. R. Holcomb
Capt. E. A. Solomons
Capt. J. H. Wellings
Capt. J. B. McLean
Capt. J. A. Farrell, Jr.

ComDesDiv 3—Cdr. A. E. True
Capt. H. R. Holcomb
Capt. E. A. Solomons
Capt. J. H. Wellings
Capt. J. B. McLean
Capt. J. A. Farrell, Jr.

ComDesDiv 4—Capt. R. G. Tobin
Cdr. A. E. True
Cdr. P. H. Fitzgerald
Cdr. T. H. Tonseth
Cdr. A. J. Greenacre
Cdr. J. L. Melgaard
Cdr. W. T. McGarry

ComDesRon 3—Cdr. T. J. Keliher, Jr.
Capt. I. H. Nunn

ComDesDiv 5—Cdr. L. P. Lovette
Cdr. H. F. Pullen
Capt. I. H. Nunn

ComDesDiv 6—Cdr. A. M. Bledsoe
Capt. J. V. Murphy
Cdr. W. Craig

ComDesRon 4—Capt. J. H. S. Dessez
Capt. C. W. Flynn
Cdr. F. R. Walker
Capt. R. N. Smoot
Capt. H. P. Smith

ComDesDiv 7—Cdr. L. B. Austin
Cdr. E. W. Young
Cdr. F. R. Walker
Capt. R. N. Smoot
Capt. H. P. Smith

ComDesDiv 8—Cdr. S. B. Brewer
Cdr. F. R. Walker
Cdr. J. R. Pahl
Cdr. H. O. Larson
Cdr. J. H. Ward
Cdr. E. R. Phelan
Capt. G. E. Griggs
Cdr. F. Gleim

ComDesRon 5—Capt. H. E. Overesch
Capt. C. P. Cecil
Capt. R. P. Briscoe
Capt. J. H. Carter
Capt. W. M. Cole
Capt. F. D. McCorkle

ComDesDiv 9—Cdr. G. C. Kriner
Cdr. F. X. McInerney
Cdr. L. A. Abercrombie
Cdr. G. D. Cooper
Capt. J. H. Carter
Capt. W. M. Cole
Capt. F. D. McCorkle

ComDesDiv 10—Cdr. J. V. Murphy
Cdr. G. D. Cooper
Cdr. C. D. Reynolds
Cdr. C. H. Lyman
Cdr. H. F. Stout
Capt. M. G. Johnson
Capt. W. S. Rodimon

ComDesRon 6—Capt. R. L. Conolly
Capt. E. P. Sauer
Cdr. W. Nyquist
Cdr. J. M. Higgins
Capt. E. G. Fullinwider
Capt. V. D. Long
Capt. C. E. Carroll

ComDesDiv 11—Cdr. C. P. Cecil
Cdr. F. I. Entwistle
Cdr. F. Moosbrugger
Capt. W. Nyquist
Cdr. J. M. Higgins
Capt. E. G. Fullinwider
Capt. V. D. Long
Capt. C. E. Carroll

ComDesDiv 12—Cdr. E. P. Sauer
Cdr. W. R. Cooke, Jr.
Cdr. F. Moosbrugger
Cdr. H. P. Smith
Cdr. G. R. Phelan
Cdr. J. H. Ward
Cdr. K. F. Poehlman
Cdr. B. Van Mater
Capt. F. Gleim

ComDesDiv 15—Cdr. J. C. Pollock
Cdr. R. W. Simpson
Cdr. C. J. Stuart

ComDesRon 7—Capt. J. W. Adams, Jr.

ComDesDiv 13—Capt. J. W. Adams, Jr.

ComDesDiv 14—Capt. W. S. Rodimon
Capt. R. Brodie, Jr.

ComDesRon 8—Capt. F. J. Bell

ComDesDiv 15—Capt. F. J. Bell

ComDesDiv 16—Capt. C. E. Cortner

ComDesDiv 17—Cdr. R. T. S. Keith

ComDesRon 10—Capt. H. L. Collins

ComDesDiv 19—Capt. H. L. Collins

ComDesDiv 20—Cdr. J. C. Atkeson

ComDesDiv 21—Capt. R. E. Myers

ComDesRon 12—Capt. G. C. Hoover
Capt. R. G. Tobin
Cdr. T. J. Ryan, Jr.
Cdr. A. A. Burke
Capt. R. W. Simpson
Capt. W. P. Burford
Capt. L. K. Reynolds
Capt. T. C. Ragan

ComDesDiv 22—Cdr. H. R. Holcomb

ComDesDiv 23—Cdr. J. M. Higgins
Capt. A. A. Burke
Capt. R. W. Simpson
Capt. W. P. Burford
Capt. L. K. Reynolds
Capt. T. C. Ragan

ComDesDiv 24—Cdr. T. J. Ryan, Jr.
Cdr. F. H. Ball
Cdr. J. L. Melgaard
Cdr. A. J. Greenacre
Cdr. R. Brodie, Jr.
Capt. B. N. Rittenhouse

ComDesDiv 26—Cdr. A. J. Greenacre

ComDesRon 13—Capt. J. B. Rooney
Capt. W. L. Benson

ComDesDiv 25—Capt. J. B. Rooney
Capt. W. L. Benson

ComDesDiv 26—Cdr. A. M. Kowalzyk
Capt. R. P. Davis

ComDesRon 14—Capt. R. S. Riggs
Capt. W. Craig
Capt. B. L. Austin
Capt. R. N. Smoot
Cdr. J. F. Newman, Jr.
Capt. G. L. Sims

ComDesDiv 27—Cdr. A. D. Chandler
Cdr. H. F. Pullen
Capt. W. Craig
Capt. B. L. Austin
Capt. R. N. Smoot
Capt. G. L. Sims

ComDesDiv 28—Capt. H. F. Pullen
Cdr. E. L. Beck
Cdr. J. F. Newman, Jr.
Cdr. L. W. Pancoast
Capt. B. N. Wev

ComDesRon 16—Capt. W. R. Thayer

ComDesDiv 31—Capt. W. R. Thayer

ComDesDiv 32—Capt. B. Van Mater

ComDesRon 19—Capt. R. F. Stout
Cdr. J. R. Pahl
Capt. H. D. Rozendal

ComDesDiv 37—Capt. R. F. Stout
Cdr. J. R. Pahl
Capt. H. D. Rozendal

ComDesDiv 38—Cdr. W. S. Veeder
Capt. J. B. Cochran
Cdr. B. N. Wev
Capt. L. W. Pancoast

ComDesRon 21—Cdr. F. X. McInerney
Capt. T. J. Ryan, Jr.
Cdr. A. D. Chandler
Capt. J. K. B. Ginder
Capt. H. B. Heneberger

ComDesDiv 41—Cdr. H. F. Pullen
Cdr. A. D. Chandler
Capt. F. X. McInerney
Capt. T. J. Ryan, Jr.
Cdr. A. D. Chandler
Capt. J. K. B. Ginder
Capt. H. B. Heneberger

ComDesDiv 42—Cdr. R. M. Morris
Cdr. A. D. Chandler
Cdr. H. O. Larson
Cdr. A. E. Jarrell
Cdr. L. H. Martin
Cdr. R. F. Martin

ComDesRon 22—Capt. L. B. Austin
Cdr. J. C. Pollock
Capt. W. R. Cooke, Jr.
Capt. J. E. Hurff
Capt. W. F. Petersen
Capt. R. H. Smith
Capt. R. L. Campbell, Jr.

ComDesDiv 43—Cdr. A. A. Burke
Capt. W. R. Cooke, Jr.
Capt. J. E. Hurff
Capt. W. F. Petersen
Capt. R. H. Smith
Capt. R. L. Campbell, Jr.

ComDesDiv 44—Cdr. W. M. Cole
Cdr. A. A. Burke
Cdr. J. R. Pahl
Cdr. W. L. Dyer
Cdr. S. G. Hooper

ComDesRon 23—Capt. M. J. Gillan, Jr.
Capt. A. A. Burke
Capt. T. B. Dugan

ComDesDiv 45—Capt. M. J. Gillan, Jr.
Capt. A. A. Burke
Capt. T. B. Dugan

ComDesDiv 46—Cdr. B. L. Austin
Cdr. R. W. Cavenagh
Cdr. H. H. McIlhenny

ComDesRon 24—Cdr. K. M. McManes
Capt. E. W. Young

ComDesDiv 47—Cdr. K. M. McManes
Capt. E. W. Young

ComDesDiv 48—Cdr. W. F. Petersen
Cdr. J. B. McLean
Cdr. J. S. Willis
Capt. C. M. Bowley

ComDesRon 25—Capt. E. M. Thompson
Cdr. H. Crommelin
Capt. J. W. Ludewig

ComDesDiv 49—Capt. E. M. Thompson
Capt. H. Crommelin
Capt. J. W. Ludewig

ComDesDiv 50—Cdr. H. Crommelin
Capt. H. O. Parish
Cdr. W. C. Winn

ComDesRon 29—Cdr. E. M. Crouch

ComDesRon 45—Cdr. R. Earle, Jr.
Cdr. E. B. Taylor
Capt. J. C. Daniel

ComDesDiv 89—Cdr. R. Earle, Jr.
Cdr. E. B. Taylor
Capt. J. C. Daniel

ComDesDiv 90—Cdr. E. B. Taylor
Cdr. F. L. Tedder
Cdr. J. W. Schmidt
Cdr. C. Brown

ComDesRon 46—Cdr. C. F. Espe
Capt. G. P. Hunter
Capt. C. M. Jensen

ComDesDiv 91—Cdr. C. F. Espe
Capt. G. P. Hunter
Capt. C. M. Jensen

ComDesDiv 92—Cdr. H. F. Miller
Cdr. W. M. Sweetser
Cdr. J. B. Maher

ComDesRon 47—Capt. A. G. Cook, Jr.
Capt. I. H. Nunn
Capt. J. H. Sides

ComDesDiv 93—Capt. A. G. Cook, Jr.
Capt. I. H. Nunn
Capt. J. H. Sides

ComDesDiv 94—Cdr. R. F. Stout
Cdr. J. H. Nevins, Jr.
Cdr. L. K. Reynolds
Cdr. W. M. Searles

ComDesRon 48—Capt. J. T. Bottom, Jr.
Capt. W. J. Marshall
Capt. H. H. Henderson

ComDesDiv 95—Capt. J. T. Bottom, Jr.
Capt. W. J. Marshall
Capt. H. H. Henderson

ComDesDiv 96—Cdr. C. E. Carroll
Cdr. T. H. Kobey
Cdr. L. C. Chamberlin

ComDesRon 49—Capt. H. F. Gearing
Capt. E. R. McLean, Jr.
Capt. B. F. Brown

ComDesDiv 97—Capt. H. F. Gearing
Capt. E. R. McLean, Jr.
Capt. B. F. Brown

ComDesDiv 98—Cdr. E. R. McLean, Jr.
Cdr. H. Wood, Jr.
Cdr. W. G. Cooper
Cdr. M. H. Hubbard

ComDesRon 50—Cdr. S. R. Clark
Cdr. C. F. Chillingworth, Jr.
Capt. E. R. Wilkinson
Capt. H. T. Deutermann

ComDesDiv 99—Cdr. S. R. Clark
Cdr. C. F. Chillingworth, Jr.
Capt. E. R. Wilkinson
Capt. H. T. Deutermann

ComDesDiv 100—Cdr. C. F. Chilingworth, Jr.
Cdr. W. J. Miller
Capt. E. B. Dexter

ComDesRon 51—Capt. H. F. Pullen
Capt. H. P. Smith
Capt. H. J. Martin

ComDesDiv 101—Capt. H. F. Pullen
Capt. H. P. Smith
Capt. H. J. Martin

ComDesDiv 102—Capt. H. J. Martin
Cdr. B. V. Russell
Capt. J. W. Callahan
Capt. W. H. Watson, Jr.

ComDesRon 52—Capt. G. R. Cooper
Capt. J. P. Womble, Jr.
Capt. H. C. Daniel

ComDesDiv 103—Capt. G. R. Cooper
Capt. J. P. Womble, Jr.
Capt. H. C. Daniel

ComDesDiv 104—Cdr. H. B. Bell, Jr.
Capt. W. T. Kenny
Cdr. P. L. High

ComDesRon 53—Cdr. H. B. Jarrett
Capt. W. G. Beecher, Jr.

ComDesDiv 105—Cdr. H. B. Jarrett
Capt. W. G. Beecher, Jr.

ComDesDiv 106—Cdr. T. Burrowes
Cdr. B. F. Tompkins
Cdr. J. H. Hogg
Capt. G. K. Carmichael

ComDesRon 54—Cdr. J. G. Coward
Capt. P. V. Mercer
Capt. W. H. Price

ComDesDiv 107—Cdr. J. G. Coward
Capt. P. V. Mercer
Capt. W. H. Price

ComDesDiv 108—Cdr. D. C. Varian
Cdr. R. H. Phillips
Capt. W. A. Cockell

ComDesRon 55—Capt. C. R. Todd
Capt. A. E. Jarrell

ComDesDiv 109—Capt. C. R. Todd
Capt. A. E. Jarrell

ComDesDiv 110—Cdr. M. Van Metre
Cdr. W. R. Edsall
Cdr. W. H. Price

ComDesRon 56—Capt. R. E. Libby
Capt. R. N. Smoot
Capt. H. F. Stout

ComDesDiv 111—Capt. R. E. Libby
Capt. R. N. Smoot
Capt. H. F. Stout

ComDesDiv 112—Cdr. P. H. Fitzgerald
Cdr. T. F. Conley, Jr.
Capt. B. J. Mullaney

ComDesRon 57—Capt. C. J. Stuart
Capt. J. M. Worthington

ComDesDiv 113—Capt. C. J. Stuart
Capt. J. M. Worthington

ComDesDiv 114—Cdr. H. D. Rozendal
Capt. R. O. Strange

ComDesDiv 115—Capt. P. D. Gallery

ComDesRon 58—Capt. A. D. Chandler

ComDesDiv 115—Capt. A. D. Chandler

ComDesDiv 116—Cdr. J. W. Schmidt

ComDesRon 60—Capt. W. L. Freseman
Capt. B. R. Harrison

ComDesDiv 119—Capt. W. L. Freseman
Capt. B. R. Harrison

ComDesDiv 120—Cdr. J. H. Wellings
Cdr. J. C. Zahm
Capt. P. D. Gallery

ComDesRon 61—Capt. J. M. Higgins
Capt. J. H. Carter
Capt. T. H. Hederman

ComDesDiv 121—Capt. J. M. Higgins
Capt. J. H. Carter
Capt. T. H. Hederman

ComDesDiv 122—Cdr. B. F. Brown
Cdr. C. K. Bergin
Capt. R. J. Archer

ComDesRon 62—Capt. J. M. Higgins
Capt. W. D. Brown

ComDesDiv 123—Capt. J. M. Higgins
Capt. W. D. Brown

ComDesDiv 124—Capt. G. L. Sims
Cdr. R. W. Smith

ComDesRon 63—Capt. F. Moosbrugger
Capt. C. A. Buchanan

ComDesDiv 125—Capt. F. Moosbrugger
Capt. C. A. Buchanan

ComDesDiv 126—Cdr. C. A. Buchanan
Capt. A. O. Momm

ComDesRon 64—Capt. C. C. Wood

ComDesDiv 127—Capt. C. C. Wood

ComDesDiv 128—Cdr. M. T. Dayton

ComDesDiv 130—Cdr. W. H. Price

ComDesRon 66—Capt. G. R. Hartwig

ComDesDiv 131—Capt. G. R. Hartwig

ComDesDiv 132—Cdr. H. T. Deutermann
Cdr. F. V. H. Hilles

ComDesRon 67—Capt. F. J. Bell

ComDesDiv 133—Capt. F. J. Bell

ComDesDiv 134—Cdr. C. E. Cortner
Capt. C. H. Kendall

ComDesRon 68—Capt. D. C. Varian

ComDesDiv 135—Capt. D. C. Varian

ComDesDiv 136—Cdr. W. W. Outerbridge

PACIFIC FLEET DE'S*

DIVISION COMMANDERS

JULY 20, 1943 . . . OCTOBER 1, 1945

ComCortDiv 7—Cdr. T. K. Dunstan, U.S.N.R.

ComCortDiv 8—Cdr. T. F. Fowler
Cdr. C. S. Kirkpatrick, U.S.N.R.

ComCortDiv 9—Cdr. E. W. Yancey
Cdr. E. C. Powell, U.S.N.R.

ComCortDiv 10—Cdr. J. L. Melgaard
Lt. Cdr. P. V. Walker, U.S.N.R.
Cdr. G. B. Coale, U.S.N.R.
Cdr. C. B. Henriques, U.S.N.R.
Cdr. W. H. Harrison, U.S.N.R.

ComCortDiv 11—Cdr. F. W. Schmidt
Lt. Cdr. H. E. Cross, U.S.N.R.
Cdr. H. E. Cross, U.S.N.R.

ComCortDiv 14—Cdr. L. F. Sugnet
Cdr. W. B. Pendleton
Cdr. R. McAfee, U.S.N.R.

ComCortDiv 15—Lt. Cdr. T. L. Bergen, U.S.N.R.

ComCortDiv 16—Cdr. F. L. Tedder
Cdr. J. B. Cleland, U.S.N.R.
Cdr. L. C. Mabley, U.S.N.R.

ComCortDiv 20—Lt. Cmdr. W. B. Ellis, U.S.C.G.

ComCortDiv 22—Cdr. L. M. Thayer, U.S.C.G.
Lt. Cdr. V. E. Bakanas, U.S.C.G.

ComCortDiv 23—Cdr. J. H. Forney, U.S.C.G.

ComCortDiv 24—Cdr. C. G. McKinney, U.S.N.R.

ComCortDiv 26—Cdr. T. C. Thomas
Cdr. G. F. Davis, U.S.N.R.
Cdr. G. F. Adams, U.S.N.R.

ComCortDiv 27—Cdr. W. L. David, U.S.C.G.

ComCortDiv 28—Cdr. W. S. Howard, Jr.

ComCortDiv 31—Cdr. J. D. McKinney
Lt. Cdr. J. G. Urquhart, Jr.
Cdr. C. A. Kunz, U.S.N.R.

ComCortDiv 32—Cdr. R. H. Groff, U.S.N.R.
Cdr. C. K. Hutchison

ComCortDiv 35—Capt. J. R. Litchfield, U.S.N.R.
Cdr. W. C. Hughes, U.S.N.R.

ComCortDiv 36—Cdr. R. D. Williams
Cdr. C. A. Kunz, U.S.N.R.
Cdr. R. D. Williams
Cdr. R. D. DeKay, U.S.N.R.
Cdr. R. H. Wanless, U.S.N.R.

ComCortDiv 37—Lt. Cdr. M. W. Firth
Cdr. W. H. Putnam, U.S.N.R.

ComCortDiv 39—Cdr. H. Hains
Cdr. R. R. Jackson, U.S.N.R.
Lt. Cdr. E. L. Holtz, U.S.N.R.

ComCortDiv 40—Cdr. L. M. Markham, Jr.
Cdr. C. A. Thorwall, U.S.N.R.
Cdr. F. W. Hawes

ComCortDiv 44—Cdr. E. C. Woodward
Lt. Cdr. W. B. Hinds, U.S.N.R.

ComCortDiv 47—Cdr. W. L. Harmon

ComCortDiv 49—Lt. Cdr. R. E. Lockwood
Cdr. J. G. Urquhart, Jr.
Cdr. J. W. Golinkin, U.S.N.R.

ComCortDiv 51—Cdr. T. S. Lank

ComCortDiv 53—Cdr. J. M. Fox, Jr., U.S.N.R.

ComCortDiv 55—Cdr. W. A. Sessions, U.S.N.R.

ComCortDiv 56—Cdr. W. D. Day, U.S.N.R.

ComCortDiv 57—Cdr. T. G. Murrell, U.S.N.R.
Cdr. D. H. Johnson, U.S.N.R.

ComCortDiv 58—Cdr. E. E. Garcia

ComCortDiv 60—Cdr. E. E. Lull, U.S.N.R.

ComCortDiv 61—Cdr. H. Reich, U.S.N.R.

ComCortDiv 63—Lt. Cdr. J. V. Bewick

ComCortDiv 64—Lt. Cdr. H. H. Love, U.S.N.R.
Cdr. H. H. Love, U.S.N.R.
Cdr. R. D. White, U.S.N.R.

ComCortDiv 65—Cdr. D. C. Brown, U.S.N.R.

ComCortDiv 67—Cdr. F. G. Gould

ComCortDiv 69—Cdr. T. C. Phifer
Cdr. G. R. Keating, U.S.N.R.

ComCortDiv 70—Cdr. E. E. Pare
Cdr. R. Cullinan, Jr. (Ret)

ComCortDiv 71—Cdr. W. C. F. Robards

ComCortDiv 72—Cdr. H. H. Connelley
Cdr. A. Jackson, Jr., U.S.N.R.

ComCortDiv 73—Cdr. W. N. Putnam, U.S.N.R.
Cdr. P. L. Hammond, U.S.N.R.
Cdr. R. H. Groff, U.S.N.R.

ComCortDiv 74—Cdr. C. F. Hooper, U.S.N.R.

ComCortDiv 76—Cdr. L. M. King, U.S.N.R.

ComCortDiv 77—Cdr. H. G. White, U.S.N.R.

ComCortDiv 78—Lt. Cdr. D. B. Poupeney, U.S.N.R.

ComCortDiv 82—Cdr. W. C. Jennings, U.S.N.R.

ComCortDiv 85—Cdr. R. B. Randolph, U.S.N.R.

ComCortDiv 86—Cdr. J. F. Way

ComCortDiv 87—Cdr. W. C. P. Bellinger, Jr.

ComCortDiv 89—Cdr. R. J. Toner, U.S.N.R.

* *Includes DE's assigned to 7th Fleet.*

ATLANTIC AND PACIFIC FLEET DESTROYER

TENDERS

OCTOBER 1, 1941 . . . OCTOBER 1, 1945

MELVILLE	DENEBOLA	SIERRA
DOBBIN	DIXIE	YOSEMITE
WHITNEY	PRAIRIE	HAMUL
BLACK HAWK	CASCADE	MARKAB
ALTAIR	PIEDMONT	ALCOR

DESTROYER ESCORTS TO THE

UNITED KINGDOM

DESTROYER ESCORT	DATE TRANSFERRED	DESTROYER ESCORT	DATE TRANSFERRED	DESTROYER ESCORT	DATE TRANSFERRED
BAYNTUN *(BDE 1)*	*Feb. 13, 1943*	DAKINS *(DE 85)*	*Nov. 23, 1943*	KEATS *(DE 278)*	*Oct. 28, 1943*
BAZELY *(BDE 2)*	*Feb 18, 1943*	DEANE *(DE 86)*	*Nov. 26, 1943*	KEMPTHORNE *(DE 279)*	*Oct. 31, 1943*
BERRY *(BDE 3)*	*Mar. 15, 1943*	EKINS *(DE 87)*	*Nov. 29, 1943*	KINGSMILL *(DE 280)*	*Nov. 6, 1943*
BLACKWOOD *(BDE 4)*	*Mar. 27, 1943*	FITZROY *(DE 88)*	*Oct. 16, 1943*	LAWFORD *(DE 516)*	*Nov. 3, 1943*
BURGES *(BDE 12)*	*June 2, 1943*	REDMILL *(DE 89)*	*Nov. 30, 1943*	LOUIS *(DE 517)*	*Nov. 18, 1943*
DRURY *(BDE 46)*	*April 12, 1943*	RETALICK *(DE 90)*	*Dec. 8, 1943*	LAWSON *(DE 518)*	*Nov. 25, 1943*
BENTINCK *(DE 52)*	*May 19, 1943*	HALSTEAD *(DE 91)*	*Nov. 3, 1943*	PAISLEY *(DE 519)*	*Nov. 29, 1943*
BYARD *(DE 55)*	*June 18, 1943*	RIOU *(DE 92)*	*Dec. 14, 1943*	LORING *(DE 520)*	*Dec. 5, 1943*
CALDER *(DE 58)*	*July 15, 1943*	RUTHERFORD *(DE 93)*	*Dec. 16, 1943*	HOSTE *(DE 521)*	*Dec. 14, 1943*
DUCKWORTH *(DE 61)*	*August 4, 1943*	COSBY *(DE 94)*	*Dec. 20, 1943*	MOORSOM *(DE 522)*	*Dec. 20, 1943*
DUFF *(DE 64)*	*Aug. 23, 1943*	ROWLEY *(DE 95)*	*Dec. 22, 1943*	MANNERS *(DE 523)*	*Dec. 27, 1943*
ESSINGTON *(DE 67)*	*Sept. 7, 1943*	RUPERT *(DE 96)*	*Dec. 24, 1943*	MOUNSEY *(DE 524)*	*Dec. 31, 1943*
AFFLECK *(DE 71)*	*Sept. 29, 1943*	STOCKHAM *(DE 97)*	*Dec. 28, 1943*	INGLIS *(DE 525)*	*Jan. 12, 1944*
AYLMER *(DE 72)*	*Sept. 30, 1943*	SEYMOUR *(DE 98)*	*Dec. 23, 1943*	INMAN *(DE 526)*	*Jan. 24, 1944*
BALFOUR *(DE 73)*	*Oct. 7, 1943*	CAPEL *(DE 266)*	*Aug. 24, 1943*	SPRAGGE *(DE 563)*	*Jan. 14, 1944*
BENTLEY *(DE 74)*	*Oct. 13, 1943*	COOKE *(DE 267)*	*Aug. 30, 1943*	STAYNER *(DE 564)*	*Dec. 30, 1943*
BRICKERTON *(DE 75)*	*Oct. 17, 1943*	DACRES *(DE 268)*	*Aug. 31, 1943*	THORNBOROUGH *(DE 565)*	*Dec. 31, 1943*
BLIGH *(DE 76)*	*Oct. 22, 1943*	DOMETT *(DE 269)*	*Sept. 10, 1943*	TROLLOPE *(DE 566)*	*Jan. 10, 1944*
BRAITHWAITE *(DE 77)*	*Nov. 13, 1943*	FOLEY *(DE 270)*	*Sept. 16, 1943*	TYLER *(DE 567)*	*Jan. 14, 1944*
BULLEN *(DE 78)*	*Oct. 25, 1943*	GARLIES *(DE 271)*	*Sept. 20, 1943*	TORRINGTON	*Jan. 18, 1944*
BYRON *(DE 79)*	*Oct. 30, 1943*	GOULD *(DE 272)*	*Sept. 25, 1943*	NARBROUGH *(DE 569)*	*Jan. 21, 1944*
CONN *(DE 80)*	*Oct. 31, 1943*	GRINDALL *(DE 273)*	*Sept. 30, 1943*	WALDEGRAVE *(DE 570)*	*Jan. 25, 1944*
COTTON *(DE 81)*	*Nov. 8, 1943*	GARDINER *(DE 274)*	*Sept. 30, 1943*	WHITAKER *(DE 571)*	*Jan. 28, 1944*
CRANSTOUN *(DE 82)*	*Nov. 13, 1943*	GOODALL *(DE 275)*	*Oct. 11, 1943*	HOLMES *(DE 572)*	*Jan. 31, 1944*
CUBITT *(DE 83)*	*Nov. 17, 1943*	GOODSON *(DE 276)*	*Oct. 16, 1943*	HARGOOD *(DE 573)*	*Feb. 7, 1944*
CURZON *(DE 84)*	*Nov. 20, 1943*	GORE *(DE 277)*	*Oct. 22, 1943*	HOTHAM *(DE 574)*	*Feb. 8, 1944*

DESTROYER ESCORTS TO THE

FREE FRENCH

DESTROYER ESCORT	DATE TRANSFERRED	DESTROYER ESCORT	DATE TRANSFERRED
SENEGALAIS *(DE 106)*	*Jan. 2, 1944*	MAROCAIN *(DE 109)*	*Feb. 29, 1944*
ALGERIEN *(DE 107)*	*Jan. 23, 1944*	HOVA *(DE 110)*	*Mar. 18, 1944*
TUNISIEN *(DE 108)*	*Feb. 11, 1944*	SOMALI *(DE 111)*	*April 9, 1944*

NEW DESTROYERS ADDED TO UNITED STATES FLEET DURING WORLD WAR II

DECEMBER 1941 . . . SEPTEMBER, 1945

DESTROYER	*DATE COMMISSIONED*	*FIRST COMMANDING OFFICER**	*DESTROYER*	*DATE COMMISSIONED*	*FIRST COMMANDING OFFICER**
FLETCHER	*June 30, 1942*	*Lt. Cdr. W. M. Cole*	ANTHONY	*Feb. 26, 1943*	*Lt. Cdr. B. Van Mater*
RADFORD	*July 22, 1942*	*Lt. Cdr. W. K. Romoser*	WADSWORTH	*Mar. 16, 1943*	*Cdr. J. F. Walsh*
JENKINS	*July 31, 1942*	*Lt. Cdr. H. F. Miller*	WALKER	*April 3, 1943*	*Cdr. O. F. Gregor*
LA VALLETTE	*Aug. 12, 1942*	*Lt. Cdr. H. H. Henderson*	BROWNSON	*Feb. 3, 1943*	*Lt. Cdr. J. B. Maher*
NICHOLAS	*June 4, 1942*	*Lt. Cdr. W. D. Brown*	DALY	*Mar. 10, 1943*	*Lt. Cdr. R. G. Visser*
O'BANNON	*June 26, 1942*	*Lt. Cdr. E. R. Wilkinson*	ISHERWOOD	*April 12, 1943*	*Lt. Cdr. Robert E. Gadrow*
CHEVALIER	*July 20, 1942*	*Lt. Cdr. E. R. McLean, Jr.*	KIMBERLY	*May 24, 1943*	*Lt. Cdr. Harry Smith*
HAMBLETON	*Dec. 22, 1941*	*Lt. Cdr. Forrest Close*	LUCE	*June 21, 1943*	*Cdr. D. C. Varian*
RODMAN	*Jan. 27, 1942*	*Lt. Cdr. W. G. Michelet*	ABNER READ	*Feb. 5, 1943*	*Cdr. T. Burrowes*
MACOMB	*Jan. 26, 1942*	*Lt. Cdr. W. H. Duvall*	AMMEN	*Mar. 12, 1943*	*Cdr. J. C. Daniel*
LAFFEY	*Mar. 31, 1942*	*Lt. Cdr. W. E. Hank*	MULLANY	*April 23, 1943*	*Lt. Cdr. Bacon Joseph Mullaney*
WOODWORTH	*April 30, 1942*	*Lt. Cdr. R. C. Webb, Jr.*			
FORREST	*Jan. 13, 1942*	*Lt. Cdr. Merle Van Metre*	BUSH	*May 10, 1943*	*Cdr. W. F. Petersen*
FITCH	*Feb. 3, 1942*	*Lt. Cdr. Henry Crommelin*	TRATHEN	*May 28, 1943*	*Cdr. A. J. Greenacre*
CORRY	*Dec. 18, 1941*	*Lt. Cdr. E. C. Burchett*	HAZELWOOD	*June 18, 1943*	*Cdr. Hunter Wood, Jr.*
HOBSON	*Jan. 22, 1942*	*Lt. Cdr. R. N. McFarlane*	HEERMANN	*July 6, 1943*	*Cdr. Dwight M. Agnew*
SAUFLEY	*Aug. 29, 1942*	*Lt. Cdr. B. F. Brown*	HOEL	*July 29, 1943*	*Lt. Cdr. Wm. Dow Thomas*
WALLER	*Oct. 1, 1942*	*Lt. Cdr. L. H. Frost*	McCORD	*Aug. 19, 1943*	*Cdr. Wm. T. Kenny*
STRONG	*Aug. 7, 1942*	*Lt. Cdr. J. H. Wellings*	MILLER	*Aug. 31, 1943*	*Cdr. Theodore H. Kobey*
TAYLOR	*Aug. 28, 1942*	*Lt. Cdr. Benjamin Katz*	OWEN	*Sept. 20, 1943*	*Cdr. Robert W. Wood*
DE HAVEN	*Sept. 21, 1942*	*Lt. Cdr. C. E. Tolman*	THE SULLIVANS	*Sept. 30, 1943*	*Cdr. Kenneth M. Gentry*
BACHE	*Nov. 14, 1942*	*Cdr. J. N. Opie, III*	STEPHEN POTTER	*Oct. 21, 1943*	*Cdr. Charles H. Crichton*
BEALE	*Dec. 23, 1942*	*Cdr. J. B. Cochran*	TINGEY	*Nov. 25, 1943*	*Cdr. J. O. Miner*
GUEST	*Dec. 15, 1942*	*Cdr. Henry Crommelin*	TWINING	*Dec. 1, 1943*	*Cdr. Ellis Kerr Wakefield*
BENNETT	*Feb. 9, 1943*	*Cdr. E. B. Taylor*	YARNALL	*Dec. 30, 1943*	*Cdr. B. F. Tompkins*
FULLAM	*Mar. 2, 1943*	*Cdr. Henry C. Daniel*	BOYD	*May 8, 1943*	*Lt. Cdr. U.S.G. Sharp, Jr.*
HUDSON	*Apr. 13, 1943*	*Cdr. W. R. Smedberg, III*	BRADFORD	*June 12, 1943*	*Lt. Cdr. Robert L. Morris*
HUTCHINS	*Nov. 17, 1942*	*Lt. Cdr. E. W. Herron*	BROWN	*July 10, 1943*	*Lt. Cdr. T. H. Copeman*
PRINGLE	*Sept. 15, 1942*	*Lt. Cdr. H. O. Larson*	COWELL	*Aug. 23, 1943*	*Cdr. Charles W. Parker*
STANLY	*Oct. 15, 1942*	*Cdr. R. W. Cavenagh*	CAPPS	*June 23, 1943*	*Lt. Cdr. B.E.S. Trippensee*
STEVENS	*Feb. 1, 1943*	*Cdr. F. H. Ball*	DAVID W. TAYLOR	*Sept. 18, 1943*	*Lt. Cdr. Wm. H. Johnsen*
HALFORD	*April 10, 1943*	*Lt. Cdr. G. N. Johansen*	EVANS	*Dec. 11, 1943*	*Cdr. F. C. Camp*
LEUTZE	*Mar. 4, 1944*	*Cdr. Berton A. Robbins, Jr.*	JOHN D. HENLEY	*Feb. 2, 1944*	*Cdr. C. H. Smith*
AARON WARD	*Mar. 4, 1942*	*Lt. Cdr. O. F. Gregor*	FRANKS	*July 30, 1943*	*Lt. Cdr. N. A. Lidstone*
BUCHANAN	*Mar. 21, 1942*	*Lt. Cdr. R. E. Wilson*	HAGGARD	*Aug. 31, 1943*	*Lt. Cdr. D. A. Harris*
DUNCAN	*April 16, 1942*	*Lt. Cdr. E. B. Taylor*	HAILEY	*Sept. 30, 1943*	*Cdr. Parke H. Brady*
LANSDOWNE	*April 29, 1942*	*Lt. Cdr. W. R. Smedberg, III*	JOHNSTON	*Oct. 27, 1943*	*Lt. Cdr. E. E. Evans*
LARDNER	*May 13, 1942*	*Lt. Cdr. W. M. Sweetser*	LAWS	*Nov. 18, 1943*	*Cdr. L. O. Wood*
McCALLA	*May 27, 1942*	*Lt. Cdr. W. G. Cooper*	LONGSHAW	*Dec. 4, 1943*	*Cdr. D. T. Birtwell, Jr.*
MERVINE	*June 17, 1942*	*Lt. Cdr. S. D. Willingham*	MORRISON	*Dec. 18, 1943*	*Cdr. W. H. Price*
QUICK	*July 3, 1942*	*Lt. Cdr. R. B. Nickerson*	PRICHETT	*Jan. 15, 1944*	*Cdr. Cecil T. Caufield*
FARENHOLT	*April 2, 1942*	*Lt. Cdr. E. T. Seaward*	ROBINSON	*Jan. 31, 1944*	*Cdr. E. B. Grantham, Jr.*
BAILEY	*May 11, 1942*	*Lt. Cdr. F. D. Karns, Jr.*	ROSS	*Feb. 21, 1944*	*Cdr. Benjamin Coe*
CARMICK	*Dec. 28, 1942*	*Cdr. Wm. S. Whiteside*	ROWE	*Mar. 13, 1944*	*Cdr. A. L. Young, Jr.*
DOYLE	*Jan. 27, 1943*	*Lt. Cdr. C. E. Boyd*	SMALLEY	*Mar. 31, 1944*	*Cdr. P. H. Horn*
ENDICOTT	*Feb. 25, 1943*	*Lt. Cdr. W. S. Heald*	STODDARD	*April 15, 1944*	*Cdr. H. Myers*
McCOOK	*Mar. 15, 1943*	*Lt. Cdr. S. C. Anderson*	WATTS	*April 29, 1944*	*Cdr. Joseph B. Maher*
FRANKFORD	*Mar. 31, 1943*	*Cdr. T. J. Thornhill*	WREN	*May 20, 1944*	*Cdr. E. A. McDonald*
PHILIP	*Nov. 21, 1942*	*Cdr. T. C. Ragan*	AULICK	*Oct. 27, 1942*	*Cdr. O. P. Thomas, Jr.*
RENSHAW	*Dec. 5, 1942*	*Cdr. Charles F. Chillingworth*	CHARLES AUSBURNE	*Nov. 24, 1942*	*Lt. Cdr. L. K. Reynolds*
RINGGOLD	*Dec. 24, 1942*	*Cdr. T. F. Conley, Jr.*	CLAXTON	*Dec. 8, 1942*	*Lt. Cdr. Herold F. Stout*
SCHROEDER	*Jan. 1, 1943*	*Lt. Cdr. J. T. Bowers*	DYSON	*Dec. 30, 1942*	*Cdr. Roy A. Gano*
SIGSBEE	*Jan. 23, 1943*	*Cdr. B. V. Russell*	HARRISON	*Jan. 25, 1943*	*Lt. Cdr. C. M. Dalton*
CONWAY	*Oct. 9, 1942*	*Lt. Cdr. N. S. Prime*	JOHN RODGERS	*Feb. 9, 1943*	*Cdr. H. O. Parish*
CONY	*Oct. 30, 1942*	*Lt. Cdr. H. D. Johnson*	McKEE	*Mar. 31, 1943*	*Cdr. J. J. Greytak*
CONVERSE	*Nov. 20, 1942*	*Lt. Cdr. D. C. Hamberger*	MURRAY	*April 20, 1943*	*Cdr. R. F. Stout*
EATON	*Dec. 4, 1942*	*Lt. Cdr. E. L. Beck*	SPROSTON	*May 19, 1943*	*Cdr. Fred R. Stickney*
FOOTE	*Dec. 22, 1942*	*Cdr. Bernard L. Austin*	WICKES	*June 16, 1943*	*Lt. Cdr. W. Y. Allen, Jr.*
SPENCE	*Jan. 8, 1943*	*Lt. Cdr. Henry J. Armstrong*	WILLIAM D. PORTER	*July 6, 1943*	*Lt. Cdr. W. A. Walter*
TERRY	*Jan. 26, 1943*	*Cdr. George R. Phelan*	YOUNG	*July 31, 1943*	*Lt. Cdr. G. B. Madden*
THATCHER	*Feb. 10, 1943*	*Lt. Cdr. L. R. Lampman*	CHARRETTE	*May 18, 1943*	*Cdr. E. S. Karpe*

DESTROYER	DATE COMMISSIONED	FIRST COMMANDING OFFICER
CONNER	June 8, 1943	Lt. Cdr. W. E. Kaitner
HALL	July 6, 1943	Cdr. John F. Delaney
HALLIGAN	Aug. 19, 1943	Cdr. C. E. Cortner
HARADEN	Sept.. 16, 1943	Cdr. H. C. Allan, Jr.
NEWCOMB	Nov. 10, 1943	Cdr. L. B. Cook
BELL	Mar. 4, 1943	Cdr. L. C. Petross
BURNS	April 3, 1943	Lt. Cdr. D. T. Eller
IZARD	May 15, 1943	Lt. Cdr. E. K. Van Swearingen
PAUL HAMILTON	Oct. 25, 1943	Cdr. L. G. May
TWIGGS	Nov. 4, 1943	Cdr. J. B. Fellows, Jr.
HOWORTH	April 3, 1944	Cdr. Edward S. Burns
KILLEN	May 4, 1944	Cdr. Howard G. Corey
HART	Nov. 4, 1944	Cdr. W. D. Coleman
METCALF	Nov. 18, 1944	Cdr. D. L. Martineau
SHIELDS	Feb. 8, 1945	Cdr. G. B. Madden
WILEY	Feb. 22, 1945	Cdr. B. P. Field, Jr.
BANCROFT	April 30, 1942	Lt. Cdr. J. L. Melgaard
BARTON	May 29, 1942	Lt. Cdr. D. H. Fox
BOYLE	Aug. 15, 1942	Lt. Cdr. E. S. Karpe
CHAMPLIN	Sept. 12, 1942	Lt. Cdr. C. L. Melson
MEADE	June 22, 1942	Lt. Cdr. R. S. Lamb
MURPHY	July 27, 1942	Lt. Cdr. L. W. Bailey
PARKER	Aug. 31, 1942	Lt. Cdr. J. W. Bays
CALDWELL	June 10, 1942	Lt. Cdr. J. F. Newman, Jr.
COGHLAN	July 10, 1942	Lt. Cdr. B. F. Tompkins
FRAZIER	July 30, 1942	Lt. Cdr. Frank Virden
GANSEVOORT	Aug. 25, 1942	Lt. Cdr. E. A. McFall
GILLESPIE	Sept. 18, 1942	Lt. Cdr. C. L. Clement
HOBBY	Nov. 18, 1942	Lt. Cdr. Ernest Blake
KALK	Oct. 17, 1942	Lt. Cdr. C. T. Singleton, Jr.
KENDRICK	Sept. 12, 1942	Lt. Cdr. C. T. Caufield
LAUB	Oct. 24, 1942	Lt. Cdr. J. F. Gallaher
MACKENZIE	Nov. 21, 1942	Lt. Cdr. D. B. Miller
MCLANAHAN	Dec. 19, 1942	Lt. Cdr. H. R. Hummer
NIELDS	Jan. 15, 1943	Lt. Cdr. A. R. Heckey
ORDRONAUX	Sept. 11, 1942	Lt. Cdr. R. Brodie, Jr.
EDWARDS	Sept. 18, 1942	Lt. Cdr. W. L. Messmer
GLENNON	Oct. 8, 1942	Lt. Cdr. F. C. Camp
JEFFERS	Nov. 5, 1942	Lt. Cdr. W. T. McGarry
MADDOX	Oct. 31, 1942	Lt. Cdr. E. S. Sarsfield
NELSON	Nov. 26, 1942	Lt. Cdr. M. M. Riker
BALDWIN	April 30, 1943	Lt. Cdr. G. Knuepfer
HARDING	May 25, 1943	Lt. Cdr. G. G. Palmer
SATTERLEE	July 1, 1943	Lt. Cdr. J. F. Witherow, Jr.
THOMPSON	July 10, 1943	Lt. Cdr. L. A. Ellis
WELLES	Aug. 16, 1943	Lt. Cdr. Doyle M. Coffee
ABBOT	April 23, 1943	Cdr. Chester E. Carroll
BRAINE	May 11, 1943	Cdr. J. F. Newman, Jr.
ERBEN	May 28, 1943	Cdr. J. H. Nevins, Jr.
COWIE	June 1, 1942	Cdr. C. J. Whiting
KNIGHT	June 23, 1942	Lt. Cdr. R. B. Levin
DORAN	Aug. 4, 1942	Lt. Cdr. H. W. Gordon, Jr.
EARLE	Sept. 1, 1942	Lt. Cdr. H. W. Howe
BUTLER	Aug. 15, 1942	Lt. Cdr. M. D. Matthews
GHERARDI	Sept. 15, 1942	Lt. Cdr. J. W. Schmidt
HERNDON	Dec. 20, 1942	Lt. Cdr. G. A. Moore
SHUBRICK	Feb. 7, 1943	Lt. Cdr. L. A. Bryan
BEATTY	May 7, 1942	Lt. Cdr. F. C. Stelter, Jr.
TILLMAN	June 4, 1942	Lt. Cdr. F. D. McCorkle
HALE	June 15, 1943	Cdr. K. F. Poehlmann
SIGOURNEY	June 29, 1943	Cdr. Walter L. Dyer
STEMBEL	July 16, 1943	Cdr. T. H. Tonseth
STEVENSON	Dec. 15, 1942	Lt. Cdr. Thomas C. Green
STOCKTON	Jan. 11, 1943	Lt. Cdr. R. E. Braddy
THORN	April 1, 1943	Lt. Cdr. Edward Brumby
TURNER	April 15, 1943	Lt. Cdr. H. S. Wygant, Jr.
ALBERT W. GRANT	Nov. 24, 1943	Cdr. T. A. Nisewaner
CAPERTON	July 30, 1943	Cdr. Wallace J. Miller
COGSWELL	Aug. 17, 1943	Cdr. H. T. Deutermann
INGERSOLL	Aug. 31, 1943	Lt. Cdr. A. C. Veasey
KNAPP	Sept. 16, 1943	Cdr. Frank Virden
BEARSS	April 12, 1944	Cdr. J. A. Webster
JOHN HOOD	June 7, 1944	Cdr. T. J. Thornhill, Jr.
VAN VALKENBURGH	Aug. 2, 1944	Cdr. A. B. Coxe
CHARLES J. BADGER	July 23, 1943	Cdr. W. G. Cooper
COLAHAN	Aug. 23, 1943	Lt. Cdr. Donald T. Wilber
DASHIELL	Mar. 20, 1943	Cdr. J. B. McLean
BULLARD	April 9, 1943	Cdr. G. R. Hartwig
KIDD	April 23, 1943	Lt. Cdr. Allan B. Roby
BENNION	Dec. 14, 1943	Cdr. J. W. Cooper
HEYWOOD L. EDWARDS	Jan. 26, 1944	Cdr. J. W. Boulware
RICHARD P. LEARY	Feb. 23, 1944	Cdr. F. S. Habecker
BRYANT	Dec. 4, 1943	Cdr. Paul L. High
BLACK	May 21, 1943	Lt. Cdr. Jack Maginnis
CHAUNCEY	May 31, 1943	Cdr. M. Van Metre
CLARENCE K. BRONSON	June 11, 1943	Cdr. Wm. S. Veeder
COTTEN	July 24, 1943	Lt. Cdr. Frank T. Sloat
DORTCH	Aug. 7, 1943	Lt. Cdr. R. C. Young
GATLING	Aug. 19, 1943	Lt. Cdr. A. F. Richardson
HEALY	Sept. 3, 1943	Cdr. J. C. Atkeson
HICKOX	Sept. 10, 1943	Cdr. W. M. Sweetser
HUNT	Sept. 22, 1943	Cdr. F. P. Mitchell, Jr.
LEWIS HANDOCK	Sept. 29, 1943	Cdr. Charles H. Lyman, III
MARSHALL	Oct. 16, 1943	Cdr. S. B. Wright
MCDERMUT	Nov. 19, 1943	Cdr. P. L. Wirtz
MCGOWAN	Dec. 20, 1943	Cdr. James B. Weiler
MCNAIR	Dec. 30, 1943	Cdr. M. L. McCullough, Jr.
MELVIN	Nov. 24, 1943	Cdr. W. R. Edsall
HOPEWELL	Sept. 30, 1943	Cdr. Corben C. Shute
PORTERFIELD	Oct. 30, 1943	Cdr. J. C. Woelfel
STOCKHAM	Feb. 11, 1944	Cdr. E. P. Holmes
WEDDERBURN	Mar. 9, 1944	Cdr. J. L. Wilfong
PICKING	Sept. 21, 1943	Cdr. R. S. Lamb
HALSEY POWELL	Oct. 25, 1943	Cdr. W. T. McGarry
UHLMANN	Nov. 22, 1943	Cdr. S. G. Hooper
REMEY	Sept. 30, 1943	Cdr. Reid P. Fiala
WADLEIGH	Oct. 19, 1943	Cdr. W. C. Winn
NORMAN SCOTT	Nov. 5, 1943	Cdr. S. D. Owens
MERTZ	Nov. 19, 1943	Cdr. Wm. S. Estabrook, Jr.
ALLEN M. SUMNER	Jan. 26, 1944	Cdr. Norman J. Sampson
MOALE	Feb. 28, 1944	Cdr. W. M. Foster
INGRAHAM	Mar. 10, 1944	Cdr. H. W. Gordon, Jr.
COOPER	Mar. 27, 1944	Cdr. J. W. Schmidt
ENGLISH	May 4, 1944	Cdr. J. T. Smith
CHARLES S. SPERRY	May 17, 1944	Cdr. H. H. McIlhenny
AULT	May 31, 1944	Cdr. Joseph C. Wylie
WALDRON	June 8, 1944	Cdr. G. E. Peckham
HAYNSWORTH	June 22, 1944	Cdr. Robert Brodie, Jr.
JOHN W. WEEKS	July 21, 1944	Cdr. R. A. Theobald, Jr.
HANK	Aug. 28, 1944	Cdr. G. M. Chambers
WALLACE L. LIND	Sept. 8, 1944	Cdr. G. De Metropolis
BORIE	Sept. 21, 1944	Cdr. N. Adair, Jr.
COMPTON	Nov. 4, 1944	Cdr. Robert O. Strange
GAINARD	Nov. 23, 1944	Cdr. F. J. Foley
SOLEY	Dec. 7, 1944	Cdr. J. S. Lewis
HARLAN R. DICKSON	Feb. 17, 1945	Cdr. P. G. Osler
HUGH PURVIS	Mar. 1, 1945	Cdr. B. L. Gurnette
GEARING	May 3, 1945	Cdr. T. H. Copeman
EUGENE A. GREENE	June 8, 1945	Cdr. W. V. Pratt
GYATT	July 2, 1945	Cdr. A. D. Kaplan
KENNETH D. BAILEY	July 31, 1945	Cdr. G. H. Richards, Jr.
WILLIAM R. RUSH	Sept. 21, 1945	Cdr. T. R. Vogeley
BARTON	Dec. 30, 1943	Cdr. J. W. Callahan
WALKE	Jan. 21, 1944	Cdr. J. C. Zahm
LAFFEY	Feb. 8, 1944	Cdr. F. J. Becton

DESTROYER	DATE COMMISSIONED	FIRST COMMANDING OFFICER
O'Brien	Feb. 25, 1944	Cdr. P. F. Heerbrandt
Meredith	Mar. 14, 1944	Cdr. G. Knuepfer
De Haven	Mar. 31, 1944	Cdr. J. B. Dimmick
Mansfield	April 14, 1944	Cdr. R. E. Braddy, Jr.
Lyman K. Swenson	May 2, 1944	Cdr. F. T. Williamson
Collett	May 16, 1944	Cdr. J. D. Collett
Maddox	June 2, 1944	Cdr. James S. Willis
Hyman	June 16, 1944	Cdr. Rollo Niel Norgaard
Mannert L. Abele	July 4, 1944	Cdr. A. E. Parker
Purdy	July 18, 1944	Cdr. F. L. Johnson
Drexler	Nov. 14, 1944	Cdr. R. L. Wilson
Frank Knox	Dec. 11, 1944	Cdr. J. C. Ford, Jr.
Southerland	Dec. 22, 1944	Cdr. R. C. Williams
Blue	Mar. 20, 1944	Cdr. L. Ensey
Brush	April 17, 1944	Cdr. J. E. Edwards
Taussig	May 20, 1944	Cdr. J. A. Robbins
Samuel N. Moore	June 24, 1944	Cdr. Horatio A. Lincoln
Harry E. Hubbard	July 22, 1944	Cdr. L. W. Bailey
Alfred A. Cuningham	Nov. 23, 1944	Cdr. F. B. T. Myhre
John R. Pierce	Dec. 30, 1944	Cdr. C. R. Simmers
Frank E. Evans	Feb. 3, 1945	Cdr. Harry Smith
John A. Bole	Mar. 3, 1945	Cdr. E. B. Billingsley
Beatty	Mar. 31, 1945	Cdr. M. T. Munger
Putnam	Oct. 12, 1944	Cdr. F. V. H. Hilles
Strong	Mar. 8, 1945	Cdr. C. M. Howe
Lofberg	April 26, 1945	Cdr. R. O. Beer
Lowry	July 23, 1944	Cdr. L. H. Martin
Hugh W. Hadley	Nov. 25, 1944	Cdr. L. C. Chamberlin
Willard Keith	Dec. 27, 1944	Cdr. Lewis L. Snider
James C. Owens	Feb. 17, 1945	Cdr. R. H. Blair
Zellars	Oct. 25, 1944	Cdr. B. Van Mater
Massey	Nov. 24, 1944	Cdr. C. W. Aldrich
Douglas H. Fox	Dec. 26, 1944	Cdr. R. M. Pitts
Stormes	Jan. 27, 1945	Cdr. W. N. Wylie
Robert K. Huntington	Mar. 3, 1945	Cdr. John W. Ramey
Rowan	Mar. 31, 1945	Cdr. W. A. Dunn
Gurke	May 12, 1945	Cdr. K. Loveland
McKean	June 9, 1945	Cdr. W. D. Kelly
Henderson	Aug. 4, 1945	Cdr. H. A. Knoertzer
Callaghan	Nov. 27, 1943	Cdr. F. J. Johnson
Cassin Young	Dec. 31, 1943	Cdr. E. T. Schreiber
Irwin	Feb. 14, 1944	Cdr. Daniel B. Miller
Preston	Mar. 20, 1944	Cdr. G. S. Patrick
Benham	Dec. 20, 1943	Cdr. Erle V. Dennett
Cushing	Jan. 17, 1944	Cdr. Louis F. Volk
Monssen	Feb. 12, 1944	Cdr. B. A. Fuetsch
Jarvis	June 3, 1944	Lt. Cdr. J. R. Topper
Porter	June 24, 1944	Cdr. H. R. Prince
Colhoun	July 8, 1944	Cdr. George R. Wilson
Gregory	July 29, 1944	Cdr. B. McCandless
Little	Aug. 19, 1944	Cdr. M. Hall, Jr.
Rooks	Sept. 2, 1944	Cdr. R. F. Martin
Chevalier	Jan. 9, 1945	Cdr. F. Wolsieffer
Higbee	Jan. 27, 1945	Cdr. L. Williamson
Benner	Feb. 13, 1945	Cdr. John Munholland
Dennis J. Buckley	Mar. 2, 1945	Cdr. K. C. Walpole
Myles C. Fox	Mar. 20, 1945	Cdr. J. S. Fahy
Everett F. Larson	April 6, 1945	Cdr. H. Myers
Goodrich	April 24, 1945	Cdr. D. R. Frakes
Hanson	May 11, 1945	Cdr. J. C. Parham, Jr.
Herbert J. Thomas	May 29, 1945	Cdr. R. T. S. Keith
Turner	June 12, 1945	Cdr. E. B. Rittenhouse
Charles P. Cecil	June 29, 1945	Cdr. W. Outerson
George K. MacKenzie	July 13, 1945	Cdr. Alvin Weems Slayden
Sarsfield	July 31, 1945	Cdr. H. A. Pearce
Ernest G. Small	Aug. 21, 1945	Cdr. T. D. McGrath
Power	Sept. 13, 1945	Cdr. J. M. Steinbeck
Bristol	Mar. 17, 1945	Cdr. K. P. Letts
Fred T. Berry	May 12, 1945	Cdr. N. J. F. Frank
Norris	June 9, 1945	Cdr. T. A. Nisewaner
McCaffery	July 26, 1945	Cdr. B. B. Cheatham
Harwood	Sept. 28, 1945	Cdr. Reid P. Fiala
Vogelgesang	Apr. 28, 1945	Cdr. O. W. Spahr, Jr.
Steinaker	May 26, 1945	Cdr. S. A. McCornock
Harold J. Ellison	June 23, 1945	Cdr. J. C. South
Charles R. Ware	July 21, 1945	Cdr. Henry R. Wier
Cone	Aug. 17, 1945	Lt. Cdr. K. Steen
Stribling	Sept. 29, 1945	Cdr. J. D. Bulkeley
Hawkins	Feb. 10, 1945	Cdr. Clifton Iverson
Duncan	Feb. 25, 1945	Cdr. Paul D. Williams
Henry W. Tucker	Mar. 12, 1945	Cdr. B. H. Meyer
Rogers	Mar. 26, 1945	Cdr. C. B. Smiley
Perkins	April 5, 1945	Cdr. T. M. Fleck
Vesole	April 23, 1945	Cdr. Harry E. Townsend
Leary	May 7, 1945	Cdr. E. G. Campbell
Dyess	May 21, 1945	Cdr. R. L. Fulton
Bordelon	June 5, 1945	Cdr. M. J. Luosey
Furse	July 10, 1945	Cdr. D. A. Harris
Newman K. Perry	July 26, 1945	Cdr. Norman Ernest Smith
Floyd B. Parks	July 31, 1945	Cdr. Morgan Slayton
John R. Craig	Aug. 20, 1945	Cdr. Lester C. Conwell
Orleck	Sept. 15, 1945	Cdr. John D. Andrew

• All officers named are regular U. S. Navy unless otherwise indicated

NEW DESTROYER ESCORTS ADDED TO UNITED STATES FLEET DURING WORLD WAR II

JANUARY, 1943—JULY, 1945

DESTROYER ESCORT	DATE COMMISSIONED	FIRST COMMANDING OFFICER
Evarts	April 15, 1943	Lt. Cdr. C. B. Henriques, U.S.N.R.
Wyffels	April 21, 1943	Lt. R. M. Hinckley, Jr.
Griswold	April 28, 1943	Lt. Cdr. C. M. Lyons, Jr.
Steele	May 4, 1943	Lt. Cdr. M. E. Dennett
Carlson	May 10, 1943	Lt. Cdr. James A. Stapleton, U.S.N.R.
Bebas	May 15, 1943	Lt. Cdr. G. B. Gilbertson, U.S.N.R.
Crouter	May 25, 1943	Lt. J. E. Johansen, U.S.N.R.

DESTROYER ESCORT	DATE COMMISSIONED	FIRST COMMANDING OFFICER
Brennan	Jan. 20, 1943	Lt. Cdr. M. E. Dennett
Doherty	Feb. 6, 1943	Lt. Cdr. A. Jackson, Jr. U.S.N.R.
Austin	Feb. 13, 1943	Lt. Cdr. H. G. Claudius, U.S.N.R.
Edgar G. Chase	Mar. 20, 1943	Lt. Cdr. John J. Morony, U.S.N.R.
Edward C. Daly	April 3, 1943	Lt. A. P. Chester, U.S.N.R.
Gilmore	April 17, 1943	Lt. Cdr. Selden C. Small
Burden R. Hastings	May 1, 1943	Lt. Cdr. Philip A. Walker, U.S.N.R.
LeHardy	May 15, 1943	Lt. Cdr. J. H. Prause, U.S.N.R.
Harold C. Thomas	May 31, 1943	Cdr. Herman Reich, U.S.N.R
Wileman	June 11, 1943	Lt. Aaron F. Beyer, Jr., U.S.N.R.
Charles R. Greer	June 25, 1943	Lt. N. C. Sutton, U.S.N.R.
Whitman	July 3, 1943	Lt. Cdr. C. E. Bull, U.S.N.R.
Wintle	July 10, 1943	Lt. Cdr. Leonard S. Bailey, U.S.N.R.
Dempsey	July 24, 1943	Lt. Cdr. H. A. Barnard, Jr.
Duffy	Aug. 5, 1943	Cdr. G. A. Parkinson, U.S.N.R.
Emery	Aug. 14, 1943	Lt. Cdr. R. G. Coburn, U.S.N.R.
Stadtfeld	Aug. 26, 1943	Lt. Cdr. Sigurd Hansen, U.S.N.R.
Martin	Sept. 4, 1943	Lt. P. E. Warfield, U.S.N.R.
Sederstrom	Sept. 11, 1943	Cdr. Joseph D. McKinney
Fleming	Sept. 18, 1943	Lt. Cdr. Raymond J. Toner, U.S.N.R.
Tisdale	Oct. 11, 1943	Lt. Cdr. Theodore Wolcott
Eisele	Oct. 18, 1943	Lt. Cdr. Elmer C. Long
Fair	Oct. 23, 1943	Lt. D. S. Crocker, U.S.N.R.
Manlove	Nov. 8, 1943	Lt. Cdr. J. P. Ingle, U.S.N.R.
Greiner	Aug. 18, 1943	Lt. Cdr. Frank S. Dowd, U.S.N.R.
Wyman	Sept. 1, 1943	Lt. Cdr. R. W. Copeland, U.S.N.R.
Lovering	Sept. 17, 1943	Lt. Cdr. H. Rawle, U.S.N.R.
Sanders	Oct. 1, 1943	Lt. Cdr. C. O. Ashley, U.S.C.G.
Brackett	Oct. 18, 1943	Lt. John H. Roskilly, Jr., U.S.N.R.
Reynolds	Nov. 1, 1943	Lt. Cdr. Edward P. Adams, U.S.N.R.
Mitchell	Nov. 17, 1943	Lt. Cdr. M. S. Erdahl, U.S.N.R.
Donaldson	Dec. 1, 1943	Lt. Henry L. Plage, U.S.N.R.
Andres	Mar. 15, 1943	Lt. Cdr. C. R. Simmers
Decker	May 3, 1943	Lt. Cdr. A. B. Adams, Jr.
Dobler	May 17, 1943	Lt. Cdr. A. J. Smith
Doneff	June 10, 1943	Lt. Cdr. Lewis C. Mabley, U.S.N.R.
Engstrom	June 21, 1943	Lt. Donald A. Nienstedt, U.S.N.R.
Buckley	Apr. 30, 1943	Lt. Cdr. A. W. Slayden
Charles Lawrence	May 31, 1943	Lt. Cdr. L. S. Kintberger
Daniel T. Griffin	June 9, 1943	Lt. Cdr. Perry M. Fenton, U.S.N.R.
Donnell	June 26, 1943	Lt. Cdr. F. C. Billing, U.S.N.R.
Fogg	July 7, 1943	Lt. Cdr. C. F. Adams, Jr., U.S.N.R.
Foss	July 23, 1943	Lt. Cdr. J. J. Jordy, U.S.N.R.
Gantner	July 29, 1943	Lt. Cdr. Barklie M. Henry, U.S.N.R.
George W. Ingram	Aug. 11, 1943	Lt. Cdr. Ernest R. Perry

DESTROYER ESCORT	DATE COMMISSIONED	FIRST COMMANDING OFFICER
Ira Jeffery	Aug. 15, 1943	Lt. Cdr. R. A. Fitch, U.S.N.R.
Lee Fox	Aug. 30, 1943	Lt. Cdr. W. C. Jennings, U.S.N.R.
Amesbury	Aug. 31, 1943	Lt. Cdr. A. B. Adams, Jr.
Bates	Sept. 12, 1943	Lt. Cdr. Eugene H. Maher, U.S.N.R.
Blessman	Sept. 19, 1943	Lt. Cdr. J. A. Gillis, U.S.N.R.
Joseph E. Campbell	Sept. 23, 1943	Lt. Cdr. J. F. Bowling, Jr.
*Cannon	Sept. 26, 1943	Lt. Cdr. Grinnell Morris, U.S.N.R.
*Christopher	Oct. 23, 1943	Lt. Archer W. P. Trench, U.S.N.R.
*Alger	Nov. 12, 1943	Lt. Cdr. Warren F. Porter, U.S.N.R.
Thomas	Nov. 21, 1943	Lt. Cdr. David M. Kellogg, U.S.N.R.
Bostwick	Dec. 1, 1943	Lt. Cdr. John H. Church, Jr.
Breeman	Dec. 12, 1943	Lt. Cdr. E. N. W. Hunter, U.S.N.R.
Burrows	Dec. 19, 1943	Lt. Cdr. R. W. Graham, U.S.N.R.
Carter	May 2, 1944	Lt. Cdr. F. J. T. Baker, U.S.N.R.
Clarence L. Evans	June 25, 1944	Lt. Cdr. W. C. Hughes, U.S.N.R.
Edsall	April 10, 1943	Lt. Cdr. E. C. Woodward
Jacob Jones	April 29, 1943	Lt. Cdr. W. B. Hinds, U.S.N.R.
Hammann	May 17, 1943	Lt. Cdr. R. D. DeKay, U.S.N.R.
Robert E. Peary	May 31, 1943	Lt. Cdr. Kerfoot B. Smith
Pillsbury	June 7, 1943	Lt. Cdr. Wm. H. Parker, Jr., U.S.N.R.
Pope	June 25, 1943	Lt. Cdr. F. S. Hall
Flaherty	June 26, 1943	Lt. Cdr. Maxim W. Firth
Frederick C. Davis	July 14, 1943	Lt. Cdr. O. W. Goepner, U.S.N.R.
Herbert C. Jones	July 21, 1943	Lt. Cdr. A. W. Gardes, Jr.
Douglas L. Howard	July 29, 1943	Lt. Cdr. Gordon D. Kissam, U.S.N.R.
Farquhar	Aug. 5, 1943	Lt. Cdr. L. E. Rosenberg, U.S.N.R.
J. R. Y. Blakely	Aug. 16, 1943	Lt. K. D. Talley, U.S.N.R.
Hill	Aug. 16, 1943	Lt. Cdr. G. R. Keating, U.S.N.R.
Fessenden	Aug. 25, 1943	Lt. Cdr. W. A. Dobbs, U.S.N.R.
Fiske	Aug. 25, 1943	Lt. Cdr. R. P. Walker
Frost	Aug. 30, 1943	Lt. Cdr. T. S. Lank
Huse	Aug. 30, 1943	Lt. Cdr. W. A. Sessions, U.S.N.R.
Inch	Sept. 8, 1943	Lt. Cdr. C. W. Frey, U.S.N.R.
Blair	Sept. 13, 1943	Lt. A. J. Laborde, U.S.N.R.
Brough	Sept. 18, 1943	Lt. Cdr. K. J. Hartley, U.S.N.R.
Chatelain	Sept. 22, 1943	Lt. Cdr. James L. Foley
Neunzer	Sept. 27, 1943	Lt. John E. Greenbacker
Poole	Sept. 29, 1943	Lt. Cdr. R. D. Dean, U.S.C.G.
Peterson	Sept. 29, 1943	Lt. Cdr. Richard F. Rea, U.S.C.G.
Reuben James	April 1, 1943	Lt. Cdr. F. D. Giambattista
Sims	April 24, 1943	Lt. Cdr. C. G. Raible, U.S.N.R.
Hopping	May 21, 1943	Lt. Cdr. F. D. Giambattista
Reeves	June 9, 1943	Lt. Cdr. M. S. Clark, U.S.N.R.

DESTROYER ESCORT	DATE COMMISSIONED	FIRST COMMANDING OFFICER
FECHTELER	July 1, 1943	Lt. Cdr. C. R. Simmers
CHASE	July 18, 1943	Lt. Cdr. V. B. Staadecker, U.S.N.R.
LANING	Aug. 1, 1943	Lt. Cdr. E. C. Woodward
LOY	Sept. 12, 1943	Lt. Cdr. James V. Bewick
BARBER	Oct. 10, 1943	Lt. E. T. B. Sullivan
LEVY	May 13, 1943	Cdr. Frank W. Schmidt
MCCONNELL	May 28, 1943	Cdr. Dennis D. Humphreys, U.S.N.R.
OSTERHAUS	June 12, 1943	Cdr. R. H. Groff, U.S.N.R.
PARKS	June 22, 1943	Lt. Cdr. M. McQuilkin, U.S.N.R.
BARON	July 5, 1943	Lt. Cdr. Donald McVickar, U.S.N.R.
ACREE	July 19, 1943	Lt. Cdr. W. H. Siegmund, U.S.N.R.
AMICK	July 26, 1943	Lt. Cdr. F. C. McCune
ATHERTON	Aug. 29, 1943	Lt. Paul L. Mansell, Jr., U.S.N.R.
BOOTH	Sept. 19, 1943	Lt. Cdr. Donald W. Todd
CARROLL	Oct. 24, 1943	Lt. Cdr. Frederick W. Kuhn
COONER	Aug. 21, 1943	Lt. Cdr. J. M. Stuart
ELDRIDGE	Aug. 27, 1943	Lt. Charles R. Hamilton, U.S.N.R.
*MARTS	Sept. 3, 1943	Lt. C. M. Fellows, U.S.N.R.
*PENNEWILL	Sept. 15, 1943	Lt. J. E. Allen, U.S.N.R.
MICKA	Sept. 23, 1943	Lt. John C. Spencer
*REYBOLD	Sept. 29, 1943	Lt. Cdr. A. B. Bradley, Jr., U.S.N.R.
*HERZOG	Oct. 6, 1943	Lt. Cdr. J. C. Toft, Jr., U.S.N.R.
*MCANN	Oct. 11, 1943	Cdr. C. F. Hooper, U.S.N.R.
TRUMPETER	Oct. 16, 1943	Cdr. J. R. Litchfield, U.S.N.R.
STRAUB	Oct. 25, 1943	Lt. Cdr. J. T. Kilbreth, Jr., U.S.N.R.
GUSTAFSON	Nov. 1, 1943	Cdr. Herman Reich, U.S.N.R.
SAMUEL S. MILES	Nov. 4, 1943	Lt. Cdr. G. B. Coale, U.S.N.R.
WESSON	Nov. 11, 1943	Lt. Cdr. C. F. Havermeyer, U.S.N.R.
RIDDLE	Nov. 17, 1943	Lt. Cdr. Ronald H. Cramer, U.S.N.R.
SWEARER	Nov. 24, 1943	Lt. K. N. Hannan, U.S.N.R.
STERN	Dec. 1, 1943	Lt. Cdr. J. R. Hinton, Jr., U.S.N.R.
O'NEILL	Dec. 6, 1943	Lt. D. S. Bill, Jr.
BRONSTEIN	Dec. 13, 1943	Lt. Sheldon H. Kinney
BAKER	Dec. 23, 1943	Lt. Cdr. L. B. Lockwood, U.S.N.R.
COFFMAN	Dec. 27, 1943	Lt. Cdr. W. H. Putnam, U.S.N.R.
EISNER	Jan. 1, 1944	Lt. Cdr. Donald McVickar, U.S.N.R.
GARFIELD THOMAS	Jan. 24, 1944	Lt. Cdr. R. G. Werner, U.S.N.R.
WINGFIELD	Jan. 28, 1944	Lt. Cdr. Howard E. Purdy, U.S.N.R.
THORNHILL	Feb. 1, 1944	Lt. J. B. Shumway, U.S.N.R.
RINEHART	Feb. 12, 1944	Lt. P. W. Crouch, Jr.
ROCHE	Feb. 21, 1944	Lt. R. E. Parker, U.S.N.R.
LOVELACE	Nov. 7, 1943	Cdr. R. D. DeKay, U.S.N.R.
MANNING	Oct. 1, 1943	Lt. J. I. Mingay, U.S.N.R.
NEUENDORF	Oct. 18, 1943	Lt. Cdr. J. N. McDonald
JAMES E. CRAIG	Nov. 1, 1943	Lt. Cdr. H. M. Ericsson
EICHENBERGER	Nov. 17, 1943	Lt. Cdr. N. Harrell
THOMASON	Dec. 10, 1943	Lt. Cdr. C. B. Henriques, U.S.N.R.
JORDAN	Dec. 17, 1943	Lt. Cdr. Fred C. Billing, U.S.N.R.
NEWMAN	Nov. 26, 1943	Lt. Cdr. W. C. Meyer, U.S.N.R.
LIDDLE	Dec. 6, 1943	Lt. Cdr. R. M. Hinckley, Jr.
KEPHART	Jan. 7, 1944	Lt. Cdr. I. H. Cammarn, U.S.N.R.
COFER	Jan. 19, 1944	Lt. A. P. Chester, U.S.N.R.
LLOYD	Feb. 11, 1944	Lt. Cdr. P. N. Gammelgard, U.S.N.R.
OTTER	Feb. 21, 1944	Lt. Cdr. D. M. Kerr, U.S.N.R.
HUBBARD	Mar. 6, 1944	Lt. Cdr. L. C. Mabley, U.S.N.R.
HAYTER	Mar. 16, 1944	Lt. Cdr. H. J. Theriault, U.S.N.R.
WILLIAM T. POWELL	Mar. 28, 1944	Lt. J. L. Davenport, U.S.N.R.
SCOTT	July 20, 1943	Lt. Cdr. C. S. Kirkpatrick, U.S.N.R.
BURKE	Aug. 20, 1943	Lt. Cdr. Edwin K. Winn, U.S.N.R.
ENRIGHT	Sept. 21, 1943	Lt. Cdr. A. Wildner
COOLBAUGH	Oct. 15, 1943	Lt. Cdr. L. S. Kintberger
DARBY	Nov. 15, 1943	Cdr. D. D. Humphreys, U.S.N.R.
J. DOUGLAS BLACKWOOD	Jan. 15, 1943	Cdr. R. B. Randolph, U.S.N.R.
FRANCIS M. ROBINSON	Jan. 15, 1944	Lt. J. E. Johansen, U.S.N.R.
SOLAR	Feb. 15, 1944	Lt. Cdr. H. A. Hull, U.S.N.R.
FOWLER	Mar. 15, 1944	Lt. Cdr. G. S. J. Forde, U.S.N.R.
SPANGENBERG	April 15, 1944	Lt. T. H. P. Whitney, U.S.N.R.
RUDDEROW	May 15, 1944	Lt. Cdr. M. W. Greenough, U.S.N.R.
DAY	June 10, 1944	Lt. Cdr. K. E. Read, U.S.N.R.
CHAFFEE	May 9, 1944	Lt. Cdr. A. C. Jones, U.S.N.R.
HODGES	May 27, 1944	Lt. Cdr. V. B. Staadecker, U.S.N.R.
STEWART	May 31, 1943	Lt. Cdr. B. C. Turner, U.S.N.R.
STURTEVANT	June 16, 1943	Lt. Cdr. Frederic W. Hawes
MOORE	July 1, 1943	Lt. Cdr. Henry P. Michiels, U.S.N.R.
KEITH	July 19, 1943	Lt. Drayton Cochran, U.S.N.R.
TOMICH	July 26, 1943	Lt. Hadlai A. Hull, U.S.N.R.
J. RICHARD WARD	July 5, 1943	Lt. D. A. Smith, U.S.N.R.
OTTERSTETTER	Aug. 6, 1943	Lt. Cdr. W. B. Porter
SLOAT	Aug. 16, 1943	Lt. Cdr. E. E. Garcia
SNOWDEN	Aug. 23, 1943	Lt. Cdr. A. Jackson, Jr. U.S.N.R.
STANTON	Aug. 7, 1943	Lt. Cdr. C. S. Barker, Jr.
SWASEY	Aug. 31, 1943	Lt. H. M. Godsey, U.S.N.R.
MARCHAND	Sept. 8, 1943	Lt. Cdr. G. I. Lynch, U.S.C.G.
HURST	Aug. 30, 1943	Lt. Cdr. Bret H. Brallier, U.S.C.G.
CAMP	Sept. 16, 1943	Cdr. P. B. Mavor, U.S.C.G.
HOWARD D. CROW	Sept. 27, 1943	Lt. Cdr. D. T. Adams, U.S.C.G

DESTROYER ESCORT	DATE COMMISSIONED	FIRST COMMANDING OFFICER
Pettit	Sept. 23, 1943	Lt. Cdr. Wm. B. Ellis, U.S.C.G.
Ricketts	Oct. 5, 1943	Lt. Cdr. G. L. Rollins, U.S.C.G.
Sellstrom	Oct. 12, 1943	Lt. Cdr. W. L. Maloney, U.S.C.G.
Seid	June 11, 1943	Cdr. C. A. Thorwall, U.S.N.R.
Smartt	June 18, 1943	Lt. Cdr. W. B. Pendleton
Walter S. Brown	June 25, 1943	Lt. Cdr. W. L. Harmon
William C. Miller	July 2, 1943	Lt. Cdr. Frederick G. Storey, U.S.N.R.
Cabana	July 9, 1943	Lt. Cdr. R. L. Bence, U.S.N.R.
Dionne	July 16, 1943	Lt. Cdr. Richard S. Paret, U.S.N.R.
Canfield	July 22, 1943	Cdr. J. B. Cleland, Jr., U.S.N.R.
Deede	July 29, 1943	Lt. Cdr. J. W. Whaley
Elden	Aug. 5, 1943	Lt. Cdr. George F. Adams, U.S.N.R.
Cloues	Aug. 10, 1943	Lt. Cdr. T. K. Dunstan, U.S.N.R.
Lake	Feb. 5, 1944	Lt. Cdr. A. D. Weeks, Jr., U.S.N.R.
Lyman	Feb. 19, 1944	Lt. Cdr. J. W. Wilson, U.S.N.R.
Crowley	Mar. 25, 1944	Lt. Cdr. T. J. Skewes, Jr., U.S.N.R.
Rall	April 8, 1944	Lt. Cdr. C. B. Taylor, U.S.N.R.
Halloran	May 27, 1944	Lt. Cdr. J. G. Scripps, U.S.N.R.
Connolly	July 8, 1944	Lt. W. A. Collier, U.S.N.R.
Finnegan	Aug. 19, 1944	Lt. Cdr. Huston Huffman, U.S.N.R.
Harveson	Oct. 12, 1943	Lt. Cdr. P. L. Stinson, U.S.C.G.
Joyce	Sept. 30, 1943	Lt. Cdr. Robert Wilcox, U.S.C.G.
Kirkpatrick	Oct. 23, 1943	Lt. Cdr. V. E. Bakanas, U.S.C.G.
Leopold	Oct. 18, 1943	Cdr. K. C. Phillips, U.S.C.G.
Menges	Oct. 26, 1943	Lt. Cdr. F. M. McCabe, U.S.C.G.
Mosley	Oct. 30, 1943	Lt. Cdr. James A. Alger, Jr., U.S.C.G.
Newell	Oct. 30, 1943	Cdr. R. J. Roberts, U.S.C.G.
Pride	Nov. 13, 1943	Lt. Cdr. Ralph R. Curry, U.S.C.G.
Falgout	Nov. 15, 1943	Lt. Cdr. H. A. Meyer, U.S.C.G.
Lowe	Nov. 22, 1943	Cdr. R. H. French, U.S.C.G.
Thomas J. Gary	Nov. 27, 1943	Lt. Cdr. Wm. H. Harrison, U.S.N.R.
Brister	Nov. 30, 1943	Lt. Cdr. L. H. Crosby, U.S.N.R.
Finch	Dec. 13, 1943	Lt. Cdr. A. H. Nienau, U.S.N.R.
Kretchmer	Dec. 13, 1943	Lt. R. C. Wing, U.S.N.R.
O'Reilly	Dec. 28, 1943	Lt. Cdr. W. C. F. Robards
Koiner	Dec. 27, 1943	Lt. Cdr. C. S. Judson, U.S.N.R.
Price	Jan. 12, 1944	Lt. Cdr. J. W. Higgins, Jr., U.S.N.R.
Strickland	Jan. 10, 1944	Lt. Cdr. A. J. Hopkins, U.S.N.R.

DESTROYER ESCORT	DATE COMMISSIONED	FIRST COMMANDING OFFICER
Forster	Jan. 25, 1944	Lt. Cdr. I. E. Davis, U.S.N.R.
Daniel	Jan. 24, 1944	Lt. Cdr. H. E. Waller, U.S.N.R.
Roy O. Hale	Feb. 3, 1944	Lt. Cdr. W. W. Bowie, U.S.N.R.
Dale W. Peterson	Feb. 17, 1944	Lt. Cdr. A. A. Hero, U.S.N.R.
Martin H. Ray	Feb. 28, 1944	Lt. H. V. Tucker, Jr., U.S.N.R.
John C. Butler	Mar. 31, 1944	Lt. Cdr. J. E. Pace
O'Flaherty	April 8, 1944	Lt. Cdr. D. W. Farnham, U.S.N.R.
Raymond	April 15, 1944	Lt. Cdr. Aaron F. Beyer, U.S.N.R.
Richard W. Suesens	April 26, 1944	Lt. Cdr. M. McQuilkin, U.S.N.R.
Abercrombie	May 1, 1944	Lt. Cdr. B. H. Katschinski, U.S.N.R.
Oberrender	May 11, 1944	Lt. Cdr. Samuel Spencer, U.S.N.R.
Robert Brazier	May 8, 1944	Lt. Cdr. Donald D. Snyder, U.S.N.R.
Edwin A. Howard	May 25, 1944	Lt. Cdr. Frederick Denfeld, U.S.N.R.
Jesse Rutherford	May 31, 1944	Lt. Cdr. Barklie M. Henry, U.S.N.R.
Key	June 5, 1944	Lt. Cdr. F. D. Buckley
Gentry	June 14, 1944	Lt. Cdr. D. A. Smith, U.S.N.R.
Traw	June 20, 1944	Lt. Cdr. James T. Kilbreth, U.S.N.R.
Maurice J. Manuel	June 30, 1944	Lt. Cdr. W. M. Lowry, U.S.N.R.
Naifeh	July 4, 1944	Lt. J. S. Albert, U.S.N.R.
Doyle C. Barnes	July 13, 1944	Lt. Cdr. J. P. Ingle, U.S.N.R.
Kenneth M. Willett	July 19, 1944	Lt. Cdr. J. M. Stuart
Jaccard	July 26, 1944	Lt. Cdr. C. R. Hamilton, U.S.N.R.
Lloyd E. Acree	Aug. 1, 1944	Lt. Cdr. J. E. Greenbacker
George E. Davis	Aug. 11, 1944	Lt. Frederick I. Lincoln, U.S.N.R.
Mack	Aug. 16, 1944	Lt. Cdr. J. F. Nelson, U.S.N.R.
Woodson	Aug. 24, 1944	Lt. Cdr. J. L. Foley
Johnnie Hutchins	Aug. 28, 1944	Lt. Cdr. Hugh M. Godsey, U.S.N.R.
Walton	Sept. 4, 1944	Lt. Cdr. W. S. Wills, Jr.
Rolf	Sept. 7, 1944	Lt. Cdr. Lester E. Hubbell
Pratt	Sept. 18, 1944	Lt. Cdr. R. H. Wanless, U.S.N.R.
Rombach	Sept. 20, 1944	Lt. C. B. Gill
McGinty	Sept. 25, 1944	Cdr. W. H. Harrison, U.S.N.R.
Alvin C. Cockrell	Oct. 7, 1944	Lt. Cdr. M. M. Sanford
French	Oct. 9, 1944	Lt. Cdr. T. K. Dunstan, U.S.N.R.
Cecil J. Doyle	Oct. 16, 1944	Lt. Cdr. D. S. Crocker, U.S.N.R.
Thaddeus Parker	Oct. 25, 1944	Lt. Cdr. D. R. Stoneleigh, U.S.N.R.
John L. Williamson	Oct. 31, 1944	Lt. Cdr. J. E. Allen, U.S.N.R.
Presley	Nov. 7, 1944	Lt. Cdr. R. S. Paret, U.S.N.R.
Williams	Nov. 11, 1944	Lt. Cdr. L. F. Loutrel, Jr., U.S.N.R.

DESTROYER ESCORT	DATE COMMISSIONED	FIRST COMMANDING OFFICER
RAMSDEN	Oct. 19, 1943	Lt. Cdr. Joseph E. Madacey, U.S.C.G.
MILLS	Oct. 12, 1943	Lt. Cdr. J. S. Muzzy, U.S.C.G.
RHODES	Oct. 25, 1943	Lt. Cdr. E. A. Coffin, Jr., U.S.C.G.
RICHEY	Oct. 30, 1943	Lt. Cdr. P. D. Mills, U.S.C.G.
SAVAGE	Oct. 29, 1943	Lt. Oscar C. Rohnke, U.S.C.G.
VANCE	Nov. 1, 1943	Lt. Cdr. E. A. Anderson, U.S.C.G.
LANSING	Nov. 10, 1943	Lt. Cdr. Simon R. Sands, Jr. U.S.C.G.
DURANT	Nov. 16, 1943	Lt. Cdr. C. C. Knapp, U.S.C.G.
CALCATERRA	Nov. 17, 1943	Cdr. H. J. Wuensch, U.S.C.G.
CHAMBERS	Nov. 22, 1943	Cdr. H. A. Loughlin, U.S.C.G.
MERRILL	Nov. 27, 1943	Lt. Cdr. Irvin J. Stephens, U.S.C.G.
HAVERFIELD	Nov. 29, 1943	Lt. Cdr. J. A. Mathews, U.S.N.R.
SWENNING	Dec. 1, 1943	Lt. R. E. Peek, Jr., U.S.N.R.
WILLIS	Dec. 10, 1943	Lt. Cdr. G. R. Atterbury, U.S.N.R.
JANSSEN	Dec. 18, 1943	Lt. Cdr. H. E. Cross, U.S.N.R.
WILHOITE	Dec. 16, 1943	Lt. E. B. Roth
COCKRILL	Dec. 24, 1943	Lt. Cdr. Sherman Farnham, U.S.N.R.
STOCKDALE	Dec. 31, 1943	Lt. R. W. Luther, U.S.N.R.
HISSEM	Jan. 13, 1944	Lt. Cdr. W. W. Low, U.S.N.R.
HOLDER	Jan. 18, 1944	Lt. Cdr. George Cook, U.S.N.R.
RICHARD S. BULL	Feb. 26, 1944	Lt. Cdr. A. W. Gardes, Jr.
RICHARD M. ROWELL	Mar. 9, 1944	Lt. Cdr. H. A. Barnard, Jr.
EVERSOLE	Mar. 21, 1944	Lt. Cdr. G. E. Marix
DENNIS	Mar. 20, 1944	Lt. Cdr. S. Hansen, U.S.N.R.
EDMONDS	April 3, 1944	Lt. Cdr. C. S. Barker, Jr.
SHELTON	April 4, 1944	Lt. Cdr. L. G. Salomon, U.S.N.R.
STRAUS	April 6, 1944	Lt. Cdr. D. A. Nienstedt, U.S.N.R.
LA PRADE	April 20, 1944	Lt. Cdr. C. M. Fellows, U.S.N.R.
JACK MILLER	April 13, 1944	Lt. Cdr. J. W. Whaley
STAFFORD	April 19, 1944	Lt. Cdr. V. H. Craig, Jr., U.S.N.R.
WALTER C. WANN	May 2, 1944	Lt. Cdr. J. W. Stedman, Jr., U.S.N.R.
SAMUEL B. ROBERTS	April 28, 1944	Lt. Cdr. R. W. Copeland, U.S.N.R.
LERAY WILSON	May 10, 1944	Lt. Cdr. M. V. Carson, Jr., U.S.N.R.
LAWRENCE C. TAYLOR	May 13, 1944	Lt. Cdr. R. Cullinan, Jr.
MELVIN R. NAWMAN	May 16, 1944	Lt. Cdr. Frederic W. Kinsley
OLIVER MITCHELL	June 14, 1944	Lt. Cdr. K. J. Barclay, U.S.N.R.
TABBERER	May 23, 1944	Lt. Cdr. H. L. Plage, U.S.N.R.
ROBERT F. KELLER	June 17, 1944	Lt. Cdr. Raymond J. Toner, U.S.N.R.

DESTROYER ESCORT	DATE COMMISSIONED	FIRST COMMANDING OFFICER
LELAND E. THOMAS	June 19, 1944	Lt. Cdr. L. E. Rosenberg, U.S.N.R.
CHESTER T. O'BRIEN	July 3, 1944	Lt. Cdr. Richard D. White, U.S.N.R.
DOUGLAS A. MUNRO	July 11, 1944	Lt. Cdr. G. Morris, U.S.N.R.
DUFILHO	July 21, 1944	Lt. Cdr. A. H. Nienau, U.S.N.R.
HAAS	Aug. 2, 1944	Lt. Cdr. A. M. White, U.S.N.R.
CORBESIER	Mar. 31, 1944	Lt. Cdr. Wm. B. Porter
CONKLIN	April 21, 1944	Cdr. D. C. Brown, U.S.N.R.
MCCOY REYNOLDS	May 2, 1944	Lt. Cdr. Edwin K. Winn, U.S.N.R.
WILLIAM SEIVERLING	June 1, 1944	Lt. Cdr. C. F. Adams, Jr., U.S.N.R.
ULVERT M. MOORE	July 18, 1944	Lt. Cdr. F. D. Roosevelt, Jr., U.S.N.R.
KENDALL C. CAMPBELL	July 31, 1944	Lt. Cdr. R. W. Johnson, U.S.N.R.
GOSS	Aug. 26, 1944	Lt. Cdr. C. S. Kirkpatrick, U.S.N.R.
GRADY	Sept. 11, 1944	Lt. Cdr. F. R. King, U.S.N.R.
CHARLES E. BRANNON	Nov. 1, 1944	Cdr. D. W. Todd
ALBERT T. HARRIS	Nov. 29, 1944	Lt. Cdr. Sidney King
CROSS	Jan. 8, 1945	Lt. H. L. Minshall, U.S.N.R.
HANNA	Jan. 27, 1945	Lt. Cdr. M. Johnston
JOSEPH E. CONNOLLY	Feb. 28, 1945	Lt. Cdr. M. C. Walley, U.S.N.R.
GILLIGAN	May 12, 1944	Lt. Cdr. C. E. Bull, U.S.N.R.
FORMOE	Oct. 5, 1944	Lt. Cdr. J. C. Spencer
HEYLIGER	Mar. 24, 1945	Lt. Cdr. A. F. Chace, Jr., U.S.N.R.
O'TOOLE	Jan. 22, 1944	Lt. Cdr. J. G. Enzensperger Jr., U.S.N.R
JOHN J. POWERS	Feb. 29, 1944	Lt. Cdr. E. Allan Loew U.S.N.R.
MASON	Mar. 20, 1944	Lt. Cdr. Wm. M. Blackfora, U.S.N.R.
JOHN M. BERMINGHAM	April 8, 1944	Lt. M. Beerman, U.S.N.R.
EDWARD H. ALLEN	Dec. 16, 1943	Lt. Cdr. Merrill M. Sanford
TWEEDY	Feb. 12, 1944	Lt. Cdr. T. D. Cunningham
HOWARD F. CLARK	May 25, 1944	Lt. Cdr. E. B. Hayden
SILVERSTEIN	July 14, 1944	Lt. Cdr. Franklin A. Reece, U.S.N.R.
LEWIS	Sept. 5, 1944	Lt. Cdr. R. H. Stevens, U.S.N.R.
BIVIN	Oct. 31, 1944	Lt. Cdr. M. Kelly
RIZZI	June 26, 1945	Lt. Cdr. E. K. Winn, U.S.N.R.
AHRENS	Feb. 12, 1944	Cdr. M. H. Harris, U.S.N.R.
BARR	Feb. 15, 1944	Lt. Cdr. H. H. Love, U.S.N.R.
ALEXANDER J. LUKE	Feb. 19, 1944	Lt. Cdr. H. A. Peterson, U.S.N.R.
ROBERT I. PAINE	Feb. 28, 1944	Lt. Cdr. Drayton Cochran, U.S.N.R.
RILEY	Mar. 13, 1944	Cdr. Frank Gardner Gould
LESLIE L. B. KNOX	Mar. 22, 1944	Lt. J. A. Moffett, U.S.N.R.
MCNULTY	Mar. 31, 1944	Lt. Cdr. Wm Croft Jennings, U.S.N.R.
METIVIER	April 7, 1944	Lt. Cdr. F. Kernan, U.S.N.R.
GEORGE A. JOHNSON	April 15, 1944	Lt. Cdr. Alvin Robinson, U.S.N.R.
CHARLES J. KIMMEL	April 20, 1944	Lt. Cdr. F. G. Storey, Jr., U.S.N.R.

DESTROYER ESCORT	DATE COMMISSIONED	FIRST COMMANDING OFFICER
Daniel A. Joy	April 28, 1944	Lt. Cdr. F. E. Lawton, U.S.N.R.
Lough	May 2, 1944	Lt. Cdr. B. C. Turner, U.S.N.R.
Thomas F. Nickel	June 9, 1944	Lt. Cdr. C. S. Farmer, U.S.N.R.
Peiffer	June 15, 1944	Lt. Cdr. Wesley F. Jones, U.S.N.R.
Tinsman	June 26, 1944	Lt. W. G. Grote, U.S.N.R.
Foreman	Oct. 22, 1943	Lt. Cdr. C. A Manston, U.S.N.R.
Whitehurst	Nov. 19, 1943	Lt. Cdr. James R. Grey
England	Dec. 10, 1943	Lt. Cdr. W. B. Pendleton
Witter	Dec. 29, 1943	Cdr. A. C. Davis, U.S.N.R.
Bowers	Jan. 27, 1944	Lt. Cdr. Frederic W. Hawes
Willmarth	Mar. 13, 1944	Lt. Cdr. J. G. Thorburn, Jr., U.S.N.R.
Gendreau	Mar. 7, 1944	Lt. Cdr. A. D. Kilmartin
Fieberling	April 11, 1944	Lt. Cdr. E. E. Lull, U.S.N.R.
William C. Cole	May 12, 1944	Lt Clay Harrold, U.S.N.R.
Paul G. Baker	May 25, 1944	Lt. W. G Cornell, U.S.N.R.
Damon M. Cummings	June 29, 1944	Lt. Cdr. C. R. Millett. U.S.N.R.
Vammen	July 27, 1944	Lt. Cdr. L. M. King, Jr., U.S.N.R.
Jenks	Jan. 19, 1944	Lt. Cdr. Julius F. Way
Durik	Mar. 24, 1944	Lt. Cdr. K. B. Smith
Wiseman	April 4, 1944	Lt. Cdr. W. B. McClaran, Jr., U.S.N.R.
Weber	June 30, 1943	Lt. Cdr. R. N. Norgaard
Schmitt	July 24, 1943	Lt. Cdr. T. D. Cunningham
Frament	Aug. 15, 1943	Lt. Cdr. S. T. McAdams, Jr., U.S.N.R.
Harmon	Aug. 31, 1943	Lt. Cdr. K. E. Read, U.S.N.R.
Greenwood	Sept. 25, 1943	Lt. Cdr. Alvin W. Slayden
Loeser	Oct. 10, 1943	Cdr. Chester A. Kunz, U.S.N.R.
Gillette	Oct. 27, 1943	Cdr. T. G. Murrell, U.S.N.R.
Underhill	Nov. 15, 1943	Lt. Cdr. S. R. Jackson, U.S.N.R.
Henry R. Kenyon	Nov. 30, 1943	Cdr. Charles M. Lyons
DeLong	Dec. 31, 1943	Lt. Cdr. R. C. Houston
Coates	Jan. 24, 1944	Lt. Cdr. W. S. Willis, Jr.
Eugene E. Elmore	Feb. 4, 1944	Lt. Cdr. G. L. Conkey U.S.N.R.
Bull	Aug. 12, 1943	Lt. D. W. Farnham, U.S.N.R.
Bunch	Aug. 21, 1943	Lt. Cdr. A. A. Campbell, U.S.N.R.
Rich	Oct. 1, 1943	Lt. Cdr. E. A. Michel, Jr.
Spangler	Oct. 31, 1943	Lt. Cdr. W. A. Burgett
George	Nov. 20, 1943	Lt. Cdr. J. E. Page, U.S.N.R.
Raby	Dec. 7, 1943	Lt. Cdr. James Scott, II
Marsh	Jan. 12, 1944	Lt. Cdr. Perry M. Fenton, U.S.N.R.
Currier	Feb. 1, 1944	Cdr. A. L. Lind, U.S.N.R.
Osmus	Feb. 23, 1944	Cdr. Richmond Jackson, U.S.N.R.
Earl V. Johnson	Mar. 18, 1944	Lt. Cdr. J. J. Jordy, U.S.N.R.
Holton	May 1, 1944	Lt. Cdr. J. B. Boy, U.S.N.R.
Cronin	May 5, 1944	Lt. Cdr. A. G. Cooke, U.S.N.R.

DESTROYER ESCORT	DATE COMMISSIONED	FIRST COMMANDING OFFICER
Frybarger	May 18, 1944	Lt. Cdr. G. C. Ewing, U.S.N.R.
Holt	June 9, 1944	Lt. Cdr. V. Blue, U.S.N.R.
Jobb	July 4, 1944	Lt. Cdr. Herbert M. Jones, U.S.N.R.
Parle	July 29, 1944	Lt. Cdr. J. C. Tojt, Jr., U.S.N.R.
Bray	Sept. 4, 1944	Lt. Cdr. J. A. Hetherington, II, U.S.N.R.
Bangust	Oct. 30, 1943	Lt. Cdr. C. F. MacNish, U.S.N.R.
Waterman	Nov. 30, 1943	Lt. Cdr. W. B. Hinds, U.S.N.R.
Weaver	Dec. 31, 1943	Lt. Cdr. R. S. Paret, U.S.N.R.
Hilbert	Feb. 4, 1944	Cdr. J. W. Golinkin, U.S.N.R.
Lamons	Feb. 29, 1944	Lt. Cdr. C. K. Hutchison
Kyne	April 4, 1944	Cdr. A. Jackson, Jr., U.S.N.R.
Snyder	May 5, 1944	Lt. Cdr. E. Moore, U.S.N.R.
Hemminger	May 30, 1944	Lt. Cdr. J. R. Bodler, U.S.N.R.
Bright	June 30, 1944	Lt. Cdr. W. A. McMahan, U.S.N.R.
Tills	Aug. 8, 1944	Lt. Cdr. J. L. Brooks, Jr., U.S.N.R.
Roberts	Sept. 2, 1944	Lt. R. M. Catharine, Jr., U.S.N.R.
McClelland	Sept. 19, 1944	Lt. Cdr. G. D. Williams, U.S.N.R.
Cates	Dec. 15, 1943	Lt. G. A. Prouse, U.S.N.R.
Gandy	Feb. 7, 1944	Lt. Cdr. W. A. Sessions, U.S.N.R.
Earl K. Olsen	April 10, 1944	Lt. Cdr. W. F. DeLong U.S.N.R.
Slater	May 1, 1944	Lt. Cdr. M. J. Blancq, U.S.N.R.
Oswald	June 12, 1944	Lt. E. L. Patton, U.S.N.R.
Ebert	July 12, 1944	Lt. Cdr. F. Gibbs, U.S.N.R.
Neal A. Scott	July 31, 1944	Lt. P. D. Holden, U.S.N.R.
Muir	Aug. 30, 1944	Lt. T. A. O'Gorman, U.S.N.R.
Sutton	Dec. 22, 1944	Lt. T. W. Nazro, U.S.N.R.
Tatum	Nov. 22, 1943	Lt. Cdr. W. C. P. Bellinger
Borum	Nov. 30, 1943	Lt. Cdr. J. K. Davis, U.S.N.R.
Maloy	Dec. 13, 1943	Lt. F. D. Kellogg, U.S.N.R.
Haines	Dec. 27, 1943	Lt. Cdr. Elmer C. Powell, U.S.N.R.
Runels	Jan. 3, 1944	Lt. Cdr. H. G. Claudius, U.S.N.R.
Hollis	Jan. 24, 1944	Lt. Cdr. G. D. Kissam, U.S.N.R.
Gunason	Feb. 1, 1944	Cdr. H. G. White, U.S.N.R.
Major	Feb. 12, 1944	Lt. Cdr. Augustus Knight
Weeden	Feb. 19, 1944	Lt. Cdr. C. F. Tillinghast, U.S.N.R.
Varian	Feb. 29, 1944	Lt. Cdr. C. W. Petrie, U.S.N.R.
Scroggins	Mar. 30, 1944	Lt. Herbert Kriloff
Jack W. Wilke	Mar. 7, 1944	Lt. Cdr. R. D. Lowther, U.S.N.R.

* Subsequently leased to Brazil.

DESTROYERS CONVERTED TO

MINE VESSELS

LIGHT MINELAYERS (DM)

Gamble (DD 123)
Ramsay (DD 124)
Montgomery (DD 121)
Breese (DD 122)
Tracy (DD 214)
Preble (DD 345)
Sicard (DD 346)
Pruitt (DD 347)
Robert H. Smith (DD 735)
Thomas E. Fraser (DD 736)
Shannon (DD 737)
Harry F. Bauer (DD 738)
Adams (DD 739)
Tolman (DD 740)
Henry A. Wiley (DD 749)
Shea (DD 750)
J. William Ditter (DD 751)
Lindsey (DD 771)
Gwin (DD 772)
Aaron Ward (DD 773)

HIGH-SPEED MINESWEEPERS (DMS)

Dorsey (DD 117)
Lamberton (DD 119)
Boggs (DD 136)
Elliot (DD 146)
Palmer (DD 161)
Hogan (DD 178)
Howard (DD 179)
Stansbury (DD 180)
Chandler (DD 206)
Southard (DD 207)
Hovey (DD 208)
Long (DD 209)
Hopkins (DD 249)
Zane (DD 337)
Wasmuth (DD 338)
Trever (DD 339)
Perry (DD 340)
Hamilton (DD 141)
Ellyson (DD 454)
Hambleton (DD 455)
Rodman (DD 456)
Emmons (DD 457)
Macomb (DD 458)
Forrest (DD 461)
Fitch (DD 462)
Hobson (DD 464)
Jeffers (DD 621)
Harding (DD 625)
Butler (DD 636)
Gherardi (DD 637)

DESTROYERS CONVERTED INTO

DESTROYER-TRANSPORTS

★

Manley (APD 1)
Little (APD 4)
Gregory (APD 3)
Stringham (APD 6)
Colhoun (APD 2)
McKean (APD 5)
Schley (APD 14)
Rathburne (APD 25)
Talbot (APD 7)
Waters (APD 8)
Dent (APD 9)
Tattnall (APD 19)
Kilty (APD 15)
Ward (APD 16)
Roper (APD 20)
Dickerson (APD 21)
Herbert (APD 22)
Crosby (APD 17)
Clemson (APD 31)
Goldsborough (APD 32)
George E. Badger (APD 33)
Gilmer (APD 11)
Kane (APD 18)
Humphreys (APD 12)
McFarland (APD 26)
Overton (APD 23)
Sands (APD 13)
Williamson (APD 27)
Barry (APD 29)
Belknap (APD 34)
Osmond Ingram (APD 35)
Greene (APD 36)
Hulbert (APD 28)
Noa (APD 24)

DESTROYER-ESCORTS CONVERTED INTO

DE-TRANSPORTS

Charles Lawrence (APD 37)
Daniel T. Griffin (APD 38)
Gantner (APD 42)
George W. Ingram (APD 43)
Ira Jeffery (APD 44)
Lee Fox (APD 45)
Amesbury (APD 46)
Bates (APD 47)
Blessman (APD 48)
Joseph E. Campbell (APD 49)
Sims (APD 50)
Hopping (APD 51)
Reeves (APD 52)
Chase (APD 54)
Laning (APD 55)
Loy (APD 56)
Barber (APD 57)
Newman (APD 59)
Liddle (APD 60)
Kephart (APD 61)
Cofer (APD 62)
Lloyd (APD 63)
Joseph C. Hubbard (APD 53)
Hayter (APD 80)
Scott (APD 64)
Burke (APD 65)
Enright (APD 66)
Crosley (APD 87)
Cread (APD 88)
Ruchamkin (APD 89)
Kirwin (APD 90)
Kinzer (APD 91)
Register (APD 92)
Brock (APD 93)

John Q. Roberts (APD 94)
William M. Hobby (APD 95)
Ray K. Edwards (APD 96)
Arthur J. Bristol (APD 97)
Truxtun (APD 98)
Upham (APD 99)
Barr (APD 39)
Ringness (APD 100)
Knudson (APD 101)
Rednour (APD 102)
Tollberg (APD 103)
William J. Pattison (APD 104)
Myers (APD 105)
Walter B. Cobb (APD 106)
Earle B. Hall (APD 107)
Harry L. Corl (APD 108)
Belet (APD 109)
Julius A. Raven (APD 110)
Walsh (APD 111)
Hunter Marshall (APD 112)
Earhart (APD 113)
Walter S. Gorka (APD 114)
Rogers Blood (APD 115)
Francovitch (APD 116)
England (APD 41)
Witter (APD 58)
Bowers (APD 40)
Jenks (APD 67)
Durik (APD 68)
Yokes (APD 69)
Pavlic (APD 70)
Odum (APD 71)
Jack C. Robinson (APD 72)

Bassett (APD 73)
John P. Gray (APD 74)
Joseph M. Auman (APD 117)
Weber (APD 75)
Schmitt (APD 76)
Frament (APD 77)
Kline (APD 120)
Raymon Herndon (APD 121)
Scribner (APD 122)
Diachenko (APD 123)
Horace A. Bass (APD 124)
Wantuck (APD 125)
Bull (APD 78)
Bunch (APD 79)
Bray (APD 139)
Gosselin (APD 126)
Begor (APD 127)
Cavallaro (APD 128)
Donald W. Wolf (APD 129)
Cook (APD 130)
Walter X. Young (APD 131)
Balduck (APD 132)
Burdo (APD 133)
Kleinsmith (APD 134)
Weiss (APD 135)
Carpellotti (APD 136)
Don O. Woods (APD 118)
Beverly W. Reid (APD 119)
Tatum (APD 81)
Borum (APD 82)
Maloy (APD 83)
Haines (APD 84)
Runels (APD 85)
Hollis (APD 86)

INDEX

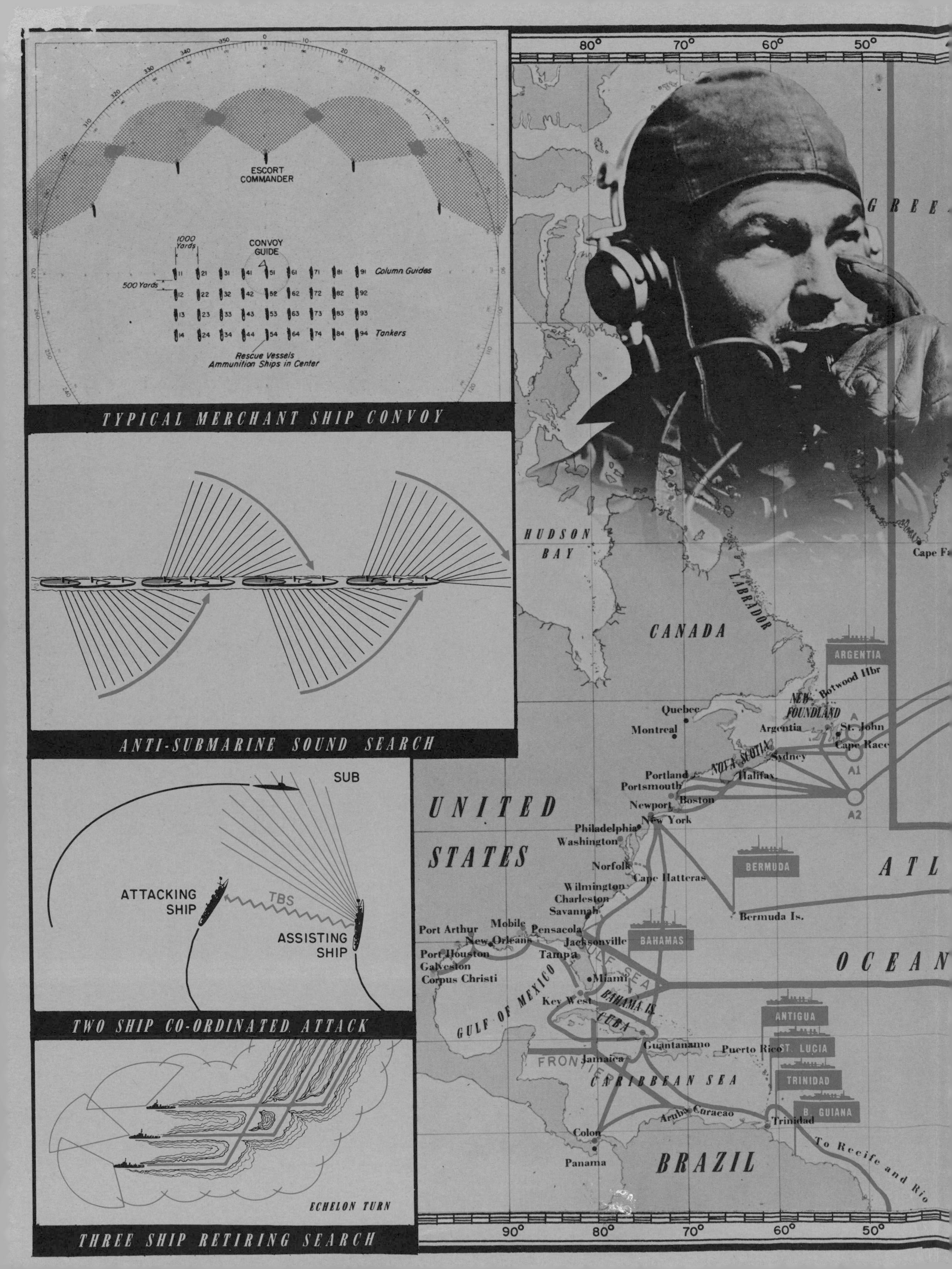
ESCORT COMMANDER
CONVOY GUIDE
1000 Yards
500 Yards
Column Guides
Tankers
Rescue Vessels
Ammunition Ships in Center
TYPICAL MERCHANT SHIP CONVOY
ANTI-SUBMARINE SOUND SEARCH
SUB
ATTACKING SHIP
TBS
ASSISTING SHIP
TWO SHIP CO-ORDINATED ATTACK
ECHELON TURN
THREE SHIP RETIRING SEARCH
HUDSON BAY
LABRADOR
CANADA
GREE
Cape Fa
ARGENTIA
Botwood Hbr
NEW FOUNDLAND
Quebec
Montreal
Argentia
St. John
Cape Race
Sydney
NOVA SCOTIA
Halifax
Portland
Portsmouth
Boston
Newport
New York
UNITED STATES
Philadelphia
Washington
Norfolk
Cape Hatteras
BERMUDA
Bermuda Is.
Wilmington
Charleston
Savannah
ATL
Port Arthur
Mobile
Pensacola
New Orleans
Jacksonville
BAHAMAS
Port Houston
Galveston
Corpus Christi
Tampa
GULF SEA
Miami
OCEAN
GULF OF MEXICO
Key West
BAHAMA IS
CUBA
ANTIGUA
Guantanamo
Puerto Rico
ST. LUCIA
Jamaica
FRONTIER
CARIBBEAN SEA
TRINIDAD
Aruba
Curacao
Trinidad
B. GUIANA
Colon
Panama
BRAZIL
To Recife and Rio